BOLLINGEN SERIES XXXVI

Ernst Robert Curtius

EUROPEAN LITERATURE

AND THE

LATIN MIDDLE AGES

Translated from the German
by WILLARD R. TRASK

BOLLINGEN SERIES XXXVI

PRINCETON UNIVERSITY PRESS

PUBLISHED BY PRINCETON UNIVERSITY PRESS, 41 WILLIAM STREET,
PRINCETON, NEW JERSEY 08540
COPYRIGHT 1953 BY BOLLINGEN FOUNDATION, INC.
COPYRIGHT RENEWED © 1983 BY PRINCETON UNIVERSITY PRESS
NEW EPILOGUE © 1990 BY PRINCETON UNIVERSITY PRESS
ALL RIGHTS RESERVED
THIS BOOK CONSTITUTES NUMBER THIRTY-SIX IN THE SERIES OF
WORKS SPONSORED BY BOLLINGEN FOUNDATION
LIBRARY OF CONGRESS CARD NO. 52-10619
ISBN 0-691-09969-3 (HARDCOVER EDN.)
ISBN 0-691-01899-5 (PAPERBACK EDN.)
PUBLISHED IN HARPER TORCHBOOK EDITION, 1973
FIRST PRINCETON/BOLLINGEN PAPERBACK PRINTING, 1973
SIXTH PAPERBACK PRINTING, 1988
SEVENTH PRINTING, WITH AFTERWORD, 1990
PRINCETON UNIVERSITY PRESS BOOKS ARE PRINTED ON ACID-FREE PAPER
AND MEET THE GUIDELINES FOR PERMANENCE AND DURABILITY OF THE
COMMITTEE ON PRODUCTION GUIDELINES FOR BOOK LONGEVITY OF THE
COUNCIL ON LIBRARY RESOURCES
15   14   13   12   11   10   9
PRINTED IN THE UNITED STATES OF AMERICA

TRANSLATOR'S NOTE

Though I set out with the intention of avoiding the ubiquitous "translator's footnote," additional notes proved, in a few instances, to be a necessary evil. They are distinguished by being excluded from the numeration and enclosed in square brackets.

Partly because, in the case of many of the passages cited in the text, previous translations either did not exist or were unsatisfactory, at least for the purposes of this book; partly for the sake of homogeneity; but chiefly because I have always regarded the rendering of poetry as the translator's greatest challenge and his greatest reward, I have, wherever my linguistic equipment permitted, made my own translations throughout. The few exceptions (preponderantly citations from Greek) are indicated, and the renderings credited, where they occur.

I welcome this opportunity to express my gratitude to my friend Dr. Alexander Gode v. Äsch, who has unreservedly put his time and his vast philological erudition at my disposal for the discussion of crucial problems.

I am also indebted to The Edward MacDowell Association for granting me residence at the MacDowell Colony during two periods when I was working on this translation.

W. R. T.

September, 1952

NOTE OF ACKNOWLEDGMENT

Grateful acknowledgment is herewith made to the following publishers for permission to quote as indicated: the University of North Carolina Press, for material from P. S. Allen and H. M. Jones, *The Romanesque Lyric*; the Harvard University Press, for several lines from two volumes of the Loeb Classical Library, *Minor Latin Poets*, translated by J. Wight Duff and Arnold M. Duff, and the *Dionysica* of Nonnos, translated by W. H. D. Rouse; and William Heinemann, Ltd., London, and Mr. Alister Kershaw for material from Richard Aldington, *Medallions in Clay*. The Henry Regnery Company, Chicago, has kindly granted permission to reprint the essay "The Medieval Bases of Western Thought," which was published in its *Goethe and the Modern Age*, edited by Arnold Bergstraesser.

For the English edition of this book a few words of explanation will perhaps be welcomed.

My central field of study is the Romance languages and literatures. After the war of 1914–18 I saw it as my task to make modern France understood in Germany through studies of Rolland, Gide, Claudel, Péguy (*Die literarischen Wegbereiter des neuen Frankreich* [1919]); of Barrès (1922) and Balzac (1923); of Proust, Valéry, Larbaud (*Französischer Geist im neuen Europa* [1925]). This cycle was closed with a study of French culture (*Einführung in die französische Kultur* [1930]). By that time I had already begun studying English and American authors. An essay on T. S. Eliot (with a translation of *The Waste Land*) appeared in 1927, a study of James Joyce in 1929. Studies published during the last twenty-five years are collected in my *Kritische Essays zur europäischen Literatur* (1950).* This contains essays on Virgil, Goethe, Friedrich Schlegel, Emerson, Stefan George, Hofmannsthal, Unamuno, Ortega y Gasset, Eliot, Toynbee.

Virgil and Dante have long had a place in the innermost circle of my admiration. What were the roads that led from the one to the other? This question increasingly preoccupied me. The answer could not but be found in the Latin continuity of the Middle Ages. And that in turn was a portion of the European tradition, which has Homer at its beginning and at its end, as we see today, Goethe.

This tradition of thought and art was severely shaken by the war of 1914–18 and its aftermath, especially in Germany. In 1932 I published my polemical pamphlet *Deutscher Geist in Gefahr*. It attacked the barbarization of education and the nationalistic frenzy which were the forerunners of the Nazi regime. In it I pleaded for a new

* Translated by Michael Kowal as *Essays on European Literature* (Princeton University Press, 1973).

Humanism, which should integrate the Middle Ages, from Augustine to Dante. I had undergone the influence of a great American book: *Founders of the Middle Ages*, by Edward Kennard Rand (1871–1945).

When the German catastrophe came, I decided to serve the idea of a medievalistic Humanism by studying the Latin literature of the Middle Ages. These studies occupied me for fifteen years. The result of them is the present book. It appeared in 1948. I put it forth with trepidation, for I did not believe that I could count upon its arousing any response. It was not in line with any of the scientific, scholarly, or philosophic trends which governed contemporary thought. That it nevertheless aroused attention and sympathy was a gratifying surprise to me.

What I have said will have made it clear that my book is not the product of purely scholarly interests, that it grew out of a concern for the preservation of Western culture. It seeks to serve an understanding of the Western cultural tradition in so far as it is manifested in literature. It attempts to illuminate the unity of that tradition in space and time by the application of new methods. In the intellectual chaos of the present it has become necessary, and happily not impossible, to demonstrate that unity. But the demonstration can only be made from a universal standpoint. Such a standpoint is afforded by Latinity. Latin was the language of the educated during the thirteen centuries which lie between Virgil and Dante. Without this Latin background, the vernacular literatures of the Middle Ages are incomprehensible. Some of my critics have objected that important phenomena of medieval literature (e.g., the *Song of Roland*, the troubadours, the drama) do not appear in my book. Perhaps these critics did not read its title. It treats of the *Latin* Middle Ages, not of the Middle Ages in general. There is no lack of good books on the vernacular literatures of France, Germany, Italy, Spain. My book does not undertake to compete with them, but to provide what they do not provide.

The Latin Middle Ages is one focus of the ellipse here under consideration. The other focus is European literature. Hence much will be said concerning Greek and Roman Antiquity, together with much concerning schools and works of the sixteenth and seventeenth centuries. I venture to hope that even specialists in these periods will find something useful in my book. My book, however, is not addressed to scholars, but to lovers of literature, that is, to those who are interested in literature as literature. In the preface to his *History of Criticism* George Saintsbury says: "A friend who is at once friendly, most competent, and of a different complexion in critical thought, objected to me that 'I treat literature as something by itself.' I hastened to admit the impeachment, and to declare that this is the very postulate of my book." Of course literature cannot be absolutely isolated, as Saintsbury well knew. In my book there will also be found things which I could not have seen without C. G. Jung; problems in the history of civilization and in the history of philosophy will also be touched upon; something is said about the seven liberal arts, the universities, and so on. But the spotlight of observation is always upon literature; its themes, its techniques, its biology, its sociology.

The reader can find information here on where the word *literature* comes from and what meaning it had originally; what a canon of writers is; how the concept of the classic author was formed and how it developed. The recurrent or constant phenomena of literary biology are investigated; the opposition between "ancients" and "moderns"; the anticlassical trends which are today called Baroque and for which I prefer the name Mannerism. Poetry is investigated in its relation to philosophy and theology. The question is raised by what means it has idealized human life (the hero, the shepherd) and nature (description of landscape), and what fixed types it has developed for the purpose. All these and other questions are prolegomena to what I should like to call a phenomenology of literature. This appears to me something different from literary history, comparative literature, and "Literaturwissenschaft" as they are practiced today.

Contemporary archaeology has made surprising discoveries by means of aerial photography at great altitudes. Through this technique it has succeeded, for example, in recognizing for the first time the late Roman system of defense works in North Africa. A person standing on the ground before a heap of ruins cannot see the whole that the aerial photograph reveals. But the next step is to enlarge the aerial photograph and compare it with a detailed map. There is a certain analogy to this procedure in the technique of literary investigation here employed. If we attempt to embrace two or two and a half millenniums of Western literature in one view, we can make discoveries which are impossible from a church steeple. Yet we can do so only when the parochialism of the specialists has provided careful detailed studies. All too often, to be sure, such studies are lacking, and from a more elevated standpoint we see tasks which would promise a rich yield to individual research. The historical disciplines will progress wherever specialization and contemplation of the whole are combined and interpenetrate. The two require each other and stand in a complementary relation. Specialization without universalism is blind. Universalism without specialization is inane.

But as far as viewing the whole in the field of literature is concerned, Saintsbury's axiom is valid: "Ancient without Modern is a stumbling block, Modern without Ancient is foolishness utter and irremediable."

My book, as I said, is not the product of purely scholarly interests. It grew out of vital urges and under the pressure of a concrete historical situation. But in order to convince, I had to use the scientific technique which is the foundation of all historical investigation: philology. For the intellectual sciences it has the same significance as mathematics has for the natural sciences. As Leibniz taught, there are two kinds of truths: on the one hand, those which are only arrived at by reason and which neither need nor are capable of empirical confirmation; on the other hand, those which are recognized through experience and which are logically indemonstrable; necessary truths and accidental truths, or, as Leibniz also puts it, *vérités éternelles et vérités de fait*. The accidental truths of fact can only be established by philology. Philology is the handmaid of the historical disciplines. I have attempted to employ it with something of the precision with which the natural sciences employ their methods. Geometry demonstrates with figures, philology with texts. But philology too ought to give results which are verifiable.

But if the subject of this book is approached through philological technique, it is nevertheless clear, I hope, that philology is not an end in itself. What we are dealing with is literature—that is, the great intellectual and spiritual tradition of Western culture as given form in language. It contains imperishable treasures of beauty, greatness, faith. It is a reservoir of spiritual energies through which we can flavor and ennoble our present-day life. I attempted some suggestions in this direction in 1949 at Aspen, Colorado, where, on the occasion of the Goethe Bicentennial Convocation, I spoke on "The Medieval Bases of Western Thought." This lecture supplements my book and hence, with the publisher's permission, is here included as an appendix.

E. R. C.

CONTENTS

GUSTAV GRÖBER
(1844–1911)

and

ABY WARBURG
(1866–1929)

IN MEMORIAM

GUIDING PRINCIPLES

1. πάλαι δὲ τὰ καλὰ ἀνθρώποισι ἐξεύρηται, ἐκ τῶν μανθάνειν δεῖ.

   HERODOTUS, I, ch. 8

2. πατέρων εὖ κείμενα ἔργα.

   POLYBIUS, XV, 4, 11

3. . . . neque concipere aut edere partum mens potest nisi ingenti flumine litterarum inundata

   PETRONIUS, ch. 118

4. Ne tu aliis faciendam trade, factam si quam rem cupis.

   Proverb

5. Guillames dist a ceus qui o lui erent:
   "Seignor," fet il, "les bones uevres perent;
   Fesom aussi con cil qui bien ovrerent."

   Les Narbonnais

6. Vielleicht überzeugt man sich bald, dass es keine patriotische Kunst und patriotische Wissenschaft gebe. Beide gehören, wie alles Gute, der ganzen Welt an und können nur durch allgemeine freie Wechselwirkung aller zugleich Lebenden, in steter Rücksicht auf das, was uns vom Vergangenen übrig und bekannt ist, gefordert werden.

   GOETHE, Flüchtige Übersicht über die Kunst in Deutschland (1801)

7. Auch die Zeiten des Verfalls und Untergangs haben ihr heiliges Recht auf unser Mitgefühl.

   JACOB BURCKHARDT, Werke, XIV, 57

8. Absichtslose Wahrnehmung, unscheinbare Anfänge gehen dem zielbewussten Suchen, dem allseitigen Erfassen des Gegenstandes voraus. Im sprungweisen Durchmessen des Raumes hascht dann der Suchende nach dem Ziel. Mit einem Schema unfertiger Ansichten über ähnliche Gegenstände scheint er das Ganze erfassen zu können, ehe Natur und Teile gekannt sind. Der vorschnellen Meinung folgt die Einsicht des Irrtums, nur langsam der Entschluss, dem Gegenstand in kleinen und kleinsten Schritten nahe zu kommen, Teil und Teilchen zu beschauen und nicht zu ruhen, bis die Überzeugung gewonnen ist, dass sie nur so und nicht anders aufgefasst werden dürfen.

   GUSTAV GRÖBER, Grundriss der romanischen Philologie, I (1888), 3

9. On aurait souhaité de n'être pas technique. À l'essai, il est apparu que, si l'on voulait épargner au lecteur les détails précis, il ne restait que des généralités vagues, et que toute démonstration manquait.

   ANTOINE MEILLET, Esquisse d'une histoire de la langue latine (1928)

10. Un libro de ciencia tiene que ser de ciencia; pero también tiene que ser un libro.

   JOSÉ ORTEGA Y GASSET, Obras (1932), 963

EUROPEAN LITERATURE
AND THE
LATIN MIDDLE AGES

1

European Literature

MAN'S KNOWLEDGE of nature has made greater advances since
the nineteenth century than in all preceding epochs. Indeed,
compared with earlier advances, they may be called incommen-
surable. They have changed the forms of existence and they open new
possibilities whose range cannot be estimated. Less well known, because
less perceptible, are the advances in historical knowledge. These alter, not
the forms of life, but the forms of thought of those who share in them.
They lead to a widening and a clarification of consciousness. In time,
the operation of this process can be of significance in the solution of
humanity's practical problems too. For the greatest enemy of moral and
social advance is dullness and narrowness of consciousness, to which anti-
social feelings of every kind contribute as powerfully as does indolence of
thought, that is, the principle of the least possible expenditure of energy
(*vis inertiae*). The advances in our knowledge of nature are verifiable.
There are no differences of opinion concerning the periodicity of the chem-
ical elements. The advance of historical knowledge, on the other hand, can
be enjoyed only through voluntary participation. It has no useful economic
effect, no calculably useful social effect. Hence it encounters indifference
or even resistance from the interested egoism embodied in powerful agen-
cies.[1] The protagonists of progress in historical understanding are always isolated individuals, who are led by such historical convulsions as
wars and revolutions to put new questions. Thucydides was induced to

[1] It is perhaps not untimely to refer to a warning which dates from 1926. "The
expansion of democracy," wrote Max Scheler, "once the ally of free scholarship and
philosophy against the supremacy of the ecclesiastically restricted mind, is slowly
becoming the greatest danger to intellectual freedom. The type of democracy which
condemned Socrates and Anaxagoras in Athens is slowly reappearing in the West
and perhaps in North America too. Only the struggling, predominantly liberal democracy of relatively 'small elites'—so the facts already teach us—is an ally of
science and philosophy. The democracy now dominant, and finally extended to
women and half-children, is not the friend but rather the enemy of reason and science." (Max Scheler, *Die Wissensformen und die Gesellschaft* [1926], 89).

undertake his history because he regarded the Peloponnesian War as the greatest war of all times. Augustine wrote his *City of God* under the impact of Alaric's conquest of Rome. Machiavelli's political and historical writings are his reaction to the French expeditions into Italy. The revolution of 1789 and the Napoleonic wars provoked Hegel's Philosophy of History. Upon the defeat of 1871 followed Taine's revision of French history, upon the establishment of the Hohenzollern empire, Nietzsche's "unseasonable" essay on the "Advantages and Disadvantages of History for Life"—a precursor of the modern discussions of "historism." The end of the first World War was responsible for the resonance Spengler's *Decline of the West* found in Germany. Deeper in intent and saturated with the entire yield of German philosophy, theology, and history was Ernst Troeltsch's unfinished work, *Der Historismus und seine Probleme* (1922). Here the evolution of the modern historical consciousness and its present problems are developed in a manner still unsurpassed. The historization of all traditional values had gone further in Germany than in other countries. In Ranke it was connected with the pleasure of aesthetic contemplation (*Mitwissenschaft des Alls*). It is also alive in Burckhardt, but corrected by an awareness of the deep shadows in the picture. The awareness inspired him with prophetic warnings of the abuses of the omnipotent state—warnings which were verified in the twentieth century.

Through publication of sources and the excavations of the nineteenth and twentieth centuries an immense amount of material accrued to history. From the caves of Périgord rose the culture of the paleolithic period, from the sands of Egypt the papyri. The Minoan and Hittite past of the Mediterranean basin, the remotest age of Egypt and Mesopotamia, together with exotic cultures such as those of the Mayas or of ancient India, became tangible. European culture stood in contrast to all these as an "intelligible unit" of unique cast, and Troeltsch's discussion of historism became a defining of the essence of "Europeanism." If in many quarters historism was deplored as an enervating relativism, or was skeptically tolerated, Troeltsch gave it the positive sign of a great task whose accomplishment will take generations: "The principle of construction is to go beyond history through history and clear the ground for new creations."

The first World War had made the crisis of European culture obvious. How do cultures, and the historical entities which are their media, arise, grow, and decay? Only a comparative morphology of cultures with exact procedures can hope to answer these questions. It was Arnold J. Toynbee who undertook the task. His historical method can signify, for all the historical sciences, a revision of bases and an expansion of horizons which has its analogy in atomic physics. It differs from all earlier philosophies of history by breadth of view and by an empiricism which is in the best English tradition. It is free from dogmatic hypotheses deduced from a principle. What are the ultimate units of the course of history, upon which the historian must train his vision in order to obtain "intelligible fields of study"? They are not states, but more comprehensive historical entities, which Toynbee calls "societies" and which we may call cultures. How many of them are there? Twenty-one—neither more nor less. A very small number, then—which, however, makes comparisons possible. Each of these historical entities, through its physical and historical environment and through its inner development, is faced with problems of which it must stand the test. They are challenges, in which it grows or fails. Whether and how it responds to them decides its destiny. In Europe, the old Greek city-states during the period from *ca.* 725 to *ca.* 325 afford examples of how different members of the same historical entity can behave in the face of the same situation. Their common problem was an increasing inadequacy of the food supply as a result of population growth. Certain states—such as Corinth and Chalcis—take the step of overseas colonization. Sparta satisfies her land hunger by conquering the neighboring state of Messene. She is thus forced into a total militarization of her forms of life, the consequence of which is cultural paralysis. Athens specializes her agriculture and her industrial products (pottery) for export and makes new political arrangements to give a share in power to the classes called into being by the new economic system. What challenges had Rome to undergo? The decisive one was the century-long struggle with Carthage. After the First Punic War Carthage conquers Spain, intending to make that country's natural resources compensate for her losses in the war. Rome opposes her here, which leads to the Second Punic War. After a hard-won victory, Rome is obliged not only to take possession of Spain but also to secure land communication thither, which finally results in Caesar's conquest of Gaul. Why do the Romans stop at the Rhine, instead of pressing on to the Vistula or the Dnieper? Because in the Augustan Age their vitality was exhausted by two centuries of wars and revolutions. The economic and social revolutions after the Second Punic War had obliged Rome to import great hordes of slaves from the East. These form an "inner proletariat," bring in Oriental religions, and provide the basis on which Christianity, in the form of a "universal church," will make its way into the organism of the Roman universal state. When after the "interregnum" of the barbarian migrations, the Greco-Roman historical entity, in which the Germanic peoples form an "outer proletariat," is replaced by the new Western historical entity, the latter crystallizes along the line Rome–northern Gaul, which had been drawn by Caesar. But the Germanic "barbarians" fall prey to the church, which had survived the universal-state end phase of antique culture. They thereby forego the possibility of bringing a positive intellectual contribution to the new historical entity. They fail in the situation which had gained the northern emigrants into the Balkan peninsula the victory over the Creto-Mycenaean culture. The "Achaeans" forced their Greek tongue upon the conquered territory, whereas the Germans learned Latin. More precisely: The Franks gave up their language on the soil of Romanized Gaul.

These indications may perhaps give an impression of the fruitfulness of

Toynbee's point of view. They contain some of its basic concepts. We shall say only what is strictly necessary for an understanding of these. According to Toynbee, the life curves of cultures do not follow a fatally predetermined course, as they do according to Spengler. Though their courses are analogous, every culture is unique because it has freedom of choice between different ways of behaving. Individual cultural movements may be independent of one another (for example, the Mayan and Minoan cultures), but they may also be connected genealogically, so that one is the daughter culture of another. Antiquity and the West stand in this relationship, as do the Old Syriac and Arabic cultures and so on. The individual cultural movements take their place in a general movement, which is not to be conceived as progress but as ascent. The cultural entities and their members are seen in the likeness of men climbing a steep cliff—some remain behind, others mount higher and higher. This ascent from the depths of subman and of stationary primitive man is a rhythm in the cosmic pulse beat of life. Within each culture there are guiding minorities who, by attraction and radiation, move the majorities to accompany them. If the creative vitality of these minorities is crippled, they lose their magic power over the uncreative masses. The creative minority then remains only a ruling minority. This condition leads to a *secessio plebis,* that is, to the rise of an inner and outer proletariat and thus to loss of social unity.

These selected and isolated details cannot give even a remote idea of the richness and illuminating power of Toynbee's work—still less of the intellectual strictness of its structure and of the precise controls to which the material presented is subjected. I feel this objection. I can only offer in reply that it is better to give even an inadequate indication of the greatest intellectual accomplishment in the field of history in our day than to pass it over in silence. Such a silence in the face of a scientific discovery represents a concession to scientific intellectual inertia—the evasion, that is, of a "challenge" which breaks unseasonably into the routine of leisurely scholastic occupations. Toynbee's work represents such a challenge to our contemporary historical methods.

But I have had another reason for referring to it: A historical concept of Europe is a presupposition for our investigation. Europe is merely a name, a "geographical term" (as Metternich said of Italy), if it is not a historical entity in our perception. But the old-fashioned history of our textbooks cannot be that. General European history does not exist for it; it sees merely a coexistence of unconnected histories of peoples and states. The history of today's or yesterday's "great powers" is taught in artificial isolation, from the standpoint of national myths and ideologies. Thus Europe is dismembered into geographical fragments. By the current division into Antiquity, the Middle Ages, and the Modern Period, it is also dismembered into chronological fragments. On pedagogical grounds, this twofold dismemberment is necessary to a certain extent (usually exceeded in practice). But it is equally necessary on pedagogical grounds to offset it by superimposing a general view upon it. To comprehend this, we need only glance at the curricula of our schools. The historical picture in the schools always faithfully mirrors academic teaching of history. But from 1864 history in Germany was under the influence of Bismarck and the Hohenzollern empire. All the electors of Brandenburg had to be learned by heart. Did the Weimar Republic drop them? I do not know. But on the basis of the Republic's curricula, I do know how medieval history (919–1517) was parceled out to the eleventh grade. First, sixteen hours of Imperial history (four for the Saxons, five for the Salians, seven for the Hohenstaufen). Then four hours for the Crusades, and the same for "inner development and intellectual life of Germany." German history of the later Middle Ages (1254–1517) got eleven hours. For the whole history of the Middle Ages outside of Germany, there remained nine hours: one for France (987–1515); one for England (871–1485); one for Spain (711–1516); two for the Discoveries; four for the Italian Renaissance. In England and France the proportions were doubtless the same. But Germany had gone through a defeat and a revolution. It could have profited by them and reformed the teaching of history. . . . Is that being done today? Europeanization of the historical picture has today become a political necessity, and not only for Germany.

The twentieth century's new knowledge of nature and new knowledge of history do not work against each other, as was the case in the era of the mechanistic view of the universe. The concept of freedom is making its way into natural science, and science is once again open to the questionings of religion (Max Planck). History, for its part, turns its attention to the problem of the rise of culture. It extends its view backwards to the prehistoric cultures. It measures the duration of the history we are able to survey by the age of humanity, and thence derives clues to the number of human cultures yet to be expected. Further, by comparing cultures, it attains to a typology of the myths which historical humanity has engendered, and interprets them as symbols of cosmic events. It opens its eyes to nature and religion.

The convergence of our knowledge of nature and our knowledge of history into a new, "open" picture of the universe is the scientific aspect of our time. At the close of his *Historismus* Troeltsch outlines the task of a concentration, simplification, and deepening of the intellectual and cultural content which the history of the West has given us and which must emerge from the crucible of historism in a new completeness and coherence: "Most effectual would be a great artistic symbol, such as the *Divina Commedia* once was, and later *Faust*. . . ." It is remarkable that in Toynbee too—even though in an entirely different sense—poetic form appears as the extreme concept of historism. His train of thought is as follows: The present state of our knowledge, which takes in barely six millenniums of historical development, is adequately served by a comparative method of investigation which attains to the establishment of laws by the road of induction. But if one imagines the stretch of history to be ten times or a hundred times as long, the employment of a scientific technique becomes impossible. It must yield to a poetic form of presentation: "It will eventually become patently impossible to employ any technique except that of 'fiction.' "

Our survey of the modern historical method has led us to the concept of poetry in the sense of a narrative produced by the imagination ("fiction"). This is an elastic formula which comprehends the antique epic, the drama, and the novel of ancient and modern times. But Greek mythology falls within it too. For, as Herodotus says, Homer and Hesiod created their gods for the Greeks. The creative imagination which makes myths, stories, poems, is a primary function of mankind. Is it a final fact, which cannot be analyzed further? Or can philosophic thought resolve it and integrate it into our comprehension of the world? Among the numerous autarchic philosophies of contemporary Germany I see none capable of doing so. They are far too occupied with themselves and with the problems of "existence," and hence have little to give to one who thinks historically. The only philosopher who attacked the problem was Henri Bergson (1859–1941). In 1907 (*L'Évolution créatrice*) he had interpreted the cosmic process under the image of an "élan vital." Nature seeks to realize in matter a life which attains to consciousness. By various roads (many of which are blind alleys) life ascends to ever higher forms. In the world of insects it drives on to social forms among the ants and bees. They work perfectly, because they are guided by instinct. But for the same reason they are unchangeable, and no development lies before them. Only in man is consciousness realized. The imaginative power which attests itself in the whole realm of life by the creation of new species has found means only in humanity to continue itself in individuals who are vouchsafed intelligence and with it initiative, self-determination, and freedom. Man creates tools with which to work matter. Hence his intellect is adapted to the world of solid bodies and is most successful in the sphere of mechanics. But just as life is safe under the guidance of instinct, so it is endangered in the sphere of the intellect.[2] If intellect encounters no resistance, it can threaten the existence both of the individual and of society. It bows only to facts, i.e., to perceptions. If "Nature" wished to take precautions against the perils of the intellect, she would have to produce fictitious perceptions and facts. They have the effect of hallucinations, i.e., they appear to the mind to be real beings and can influence conduct. This explains the simultaneous existence of intelligence and superstition. "Only intelligent beings are superstitious." The fiction-making function ("fonction fabulatrice") has become necessary to life. It is nourished by the residuum of instinct which surrounds the intellect like an aura. Instinct cannot directly intervene to protect life. Since the intellect reacts only to perceived images, instinct creates "imaginary" perceptions.[3] They may first appear as the undefined consciousness of an "operative presence" (the *numen* of the

---

[2] The following after *Les Deux Sources de la morale et de la religion* (1933).

[3] This mechanism appears from time to time today, as Bergson (p. 125) shows by an example.

Romans), then as spirits, and, not until very late, as gods. Mythology is a late product, and the road to polytheism is a cultural advance. The imagination, maker of fiction and myths, has the function of "fabricating" spirits and gods.

We shall not here trace how Bergson's metaphysics of religion culminates in its meeting with mysticism. Let it suffice to point out that Toynbee too (like Planck) confesses himself a Christian. The advance of natural and historical knowledge, like that of philosophy—upon which we have cast an all too hasty glance—also converges upon the affirmation of Christianity.

For our study, Bergson's discovery of the "fabulatory function" is of basic importance. For thereby the much-debated relations between poetry and religion are for the first time cleared up conceptually and integrated into a comprehensive scientific picture of the universe. Whoever rejects Bergson's theory must replace it by a better. It appears to me to require amplification only in one point. Bergson derives intelligence and the fabulatory function biologically. They are apparatuses brought forth by "Life" or "Nature" or the "creative drive" which underlies both. But it is a general law "that mechanisms of human nature which originally served the biological preservation of the species are in the course of evolution employed for extra-biological and superbiological ends as well" (Scheler). Eyes and ears originally served as protection in the struggle for existence. In the visual arts and music they have become organs of nonpurposeful ideal creation. The intelligence of the tool-forging *homo faber* has risen to a cognitive contemplation of the universe. The fabulatory function has risen from producing fictions for biological ends to creating gods and myths, and has finally freed itself entirely from the world of religion to become a free play. It is "the ability to create persons whose stories we tell to ourselves."

It shaped the Gilgamesh epic and the myth of the snake in Paradise, the *Iliad* and the saga of Oedipus, Dante's divine and Balzac's human comedy. It is the root and inexhaustible spring of all great literature. Great in this sense is the poetry which survives through centuries and millenniums. It is such poetry which is the farthest horizon, the background, of the complex of European literature.

Now, turning to this subject, we shall understand Europe not in the geographical but in the historical sense. The "Europeanization of the historical picture" which is to be promoted today must also be applied to literature. If Europe is an entity which participates in two cultures, the Antique-Mediterreanean and the Modern-Western, this is also true of its literature. That literature can be understood as a whole only if its two components are united in one view. But for current literary history modern Europe does not begin until about 1500. This is as intelligent as if one were to promise a description of the Rhine, but only provided the section from Mainz to Cologne. To be sure, there is a "medieval" literary history too. It begins about 1000—that is, to pursue the metaphor, as far down-stream as Strassburg. But where is the period from 400 to 1000? For that one would have to start at Basel. . . . This stretch is passed over in silence —for a very simple reason: the literature of those centuries, with infinitesimal exceptions, is in Latin. Why? Because the Germanic peoples, as we have indicated, allowed themselves to be assimilated by Rome in the form of the Roman Church. And we must go further back. The literature of "modern" Europe is as intermingled with that of the Mediterranean as if the Rhine had received the waters of the Tiber. The last great poet of Rhenish-Franconian descent, Stefan George, felt that he belonged by a secret elective affinity to Roman Germania and the Frankish intermediate kingdom of Lotharingia, from which his ancestors stemmed. In six cryptic gnomic poems on the Rhine he has as in a dream conjured the memory of that kingdom into the future. It will throw off the dominion of East and West, Germany and France:

> Ein fürstlich paar geschwister hielt in frone
> Bisher des weiten Innenreiches mitte.
> Bald wacht aus dem jahrhundertschlaf das dritte
> Auch echte Kind und hebt im Rhein die Krone.

> (In vassalage a princely pair of brothers
> Has held the center of the wide Inner Kingdom.
> Soon from centennial sleep shall wake the third
> Legitimate Child and raise the Crown in the Rhine.)

He who has ties with the Rhine may let the poet's myth sound within him. Four cities are named: the "First City" (Basel), the "Silver City" (Argentoratum, Strassburg), the "Golden City" (Mainz), and "holy" Cologne. The risen river speaks:

> Den eklen schutt von rötel kalk und teer
> Spei ich hinaus ins reinigende meer.

> (The loathsome rubble of reddle, chalk, and tar
> I spew into the purifying sea.)

A reader pointed out to the poet that "reddle, chalk, and tar" corresponded to the national colors of imperial Germany. He smilingly accepted the interpretation. The last gnome of the Rhine runs:

> Sprecht von des Festes von des Reiches nähe—
> Sprecht erst vom neuen wein in neuen schlauch:
> Wenn ganz durch eure seelen dumpf und zähe
> Mein feurig blut sich regt, mein römischer hauch.

> (Speak of the Festival's nearness, of the Kingdom's—
> Of new wine in new skin: but speak it not
> Until through all your dull and toughened souls
> Shall run my fiery blood, my Roman breath.)

The lines are from *Der siebente Ring* (1907). Beside them I set the testimony of the Rhenish-Franconian Goethe. Sulpiz Boisserée reports, under date of August 11, 1815: "The subject of Goethe's predilection for things Roman came up. He said that he certainly must once have lived under Hadrian. That everything Roman instinctively attracted him. That that great reasonableness, that order in everything, were congenial to him, whereas things Greek were not." I cite these testimonies because they document a tie between Germany, which once formed part of the Roman Empire, and Rome—a tie which is not sentimental reflection, but participation in substance. In such consciousness history enters the present. Here we become aware of Europe.

We spoke of the twofold dismemberment of Europe in our historical curriculum. If we turn to literary history, the question is no longer one of dismemberment but one of a total deficiency. In history courses the schoolboy still hears something of Marathon and Cannae, of Pericles, Caesar, and Augustus, before he is conducted from Charlemagne to the present. But what does he learn of European literature? Let us disregard the schools and ask: Is there a science of European literature, and is it cultivated at the universities? For half a century, at any rate, there has been a *Literaturwissenschaft*.[4] It undertakes to be something other and better than literary history (the relation of *Kunstwissenschaft* to art history is analogous). It is not well disposed to philology. Hence it seeks support in other disciplines: philosophy (Dilthey, Bergson), sociology, psychoanalysis, and, above all, art history (Wölfflin). Philosophizing *Literaturwissenschaft* examines literature for metaphysical and ethical problems (e.g., death and love). It wishes to be *Geistesgeschichte*. The trend which finds its support in art history operates on the extremely questionable principle of "mutual illumination of the arts" and thus begets a dilettante beclouding of facts. It then proceeds to transfer to literature the art-historical system of periodization by successive styles. Thus we get literary Romanesque, Gothic, Renaissance, Baroque, etc., down to Im- and Expressionism. Then, by the process of "essence-intuition," each stylistic period is endowed with an "essence" and peopled with a special "man." The "Gothic man" (to whom Huizinga has added a "pre-Gothic" comrade) has become the most popular, but "Baroque man" cannot be far behind him.[5] Concerning the "es-

[4] Officially introduced, as far as I know, by the *Prinzipien der Literaturwissenschaft* of the Germanist Ernst Elster (1897).—The relations between *Literaturwissenschaft* and comparative literature have not been elucidated. A *Zeitschrift für vergleichende Literaturgeschichte* was founded in 1885 by Max Koch (1855–1931). I mention also H. M. Posnett, *Comparative Literature* (New York, 1886).—W. Wetz, *Shakespeare vom Standpunkt der vergleichenden Literaturgeschichte* (1890). —L. P. Betz, *La Littérature comparée* (1900).—For criticism: Gröber, *Grundriss der romanischen Philologie*, Vol. I (2nd ed., 1904–06), 181.—F. Baldensperger, "Littérature comparée. Le mot et la chose" (*Revue de littérature comparée*, I [1921], 1–29).

[5] René Wellek, "The Concept of Baroque in Literary Scholarship," in *Journal of Aesthetics and Art Criticism*, V (1946), 77 ff.

sence" of Gothic, of Baroque, etc., there are profound views, which to be sure are partly contradictory. Is Shakespeare Renaissance or Baroque? Is Baudelaire Impressionist, George Expressionist? Much intellectual energy is expended upon such problems. In addition to stylistic periods there are Wölfflin's art-historical "basic concepts." Here we find "open" and "closed" form. Is Goethe's *Faust* in the last analysis open, Valéry's closed? An anxious question! Is there even, as Karl Joël, with much acumen and much historical knowledge, attempted to show,[6] a regular succession of "binding" and "loosing" centuries (each equipped with its own "secular spirit")? In the Modern Period the even centuries are "loosing" (the 14th, 16th, 18th; and to all appearances the 20th too), the uneven "binding" (the 13th, 15th, 17th, 19th), and so on *ad infinitum*. Joël was a philosopher. Usually, those who cultivate *Literaturwissenschaft* are Germanists. Now, of all so-called national literatures, German literature is the most unsuitable as the field of departure and field of observation for European literature, as will appear. Is this perhaps a reason for the strong need of outside support exhibited by Germanistic *Literaturwissenschaft*? But it shares with all the modern trends of *Literaturwissenschaft* the characteristic that at best it makes literature begin about 1100—because the Romanesque architectural style flowered then. But art history is as little a superdiscipline as geography or sociology. Troeltsch was already making fun of the "all-knowing art historian." [7] Modern *Literaturwissenschaft*—i.e., that of the last fifty years— is largely a phantom. It is incompetent as a discipline for the investigation of European literature for two reasons: deliberate narrowing of the field of observation and failure to recognize the autonomous structure of literature.

European literature is coextensive in time with European culture, therefore embraces a period of some twenty-six centuries (reckoning from Homer to Goethe). Anyone who knows only six or seven of these from his own observation and has to rely on manuals and reference books for the others is like a traveler who knows Italy only from the Alps to the Arno and gets the rest from Baedeker. Anyone who knows only the Middle Ages and the Modern Period does not even understand these two. For in his small field of observation he encounters phenomena such as "epic," "Classicism," "Baroque" (i.e., Mannerism), and many others, whose history and significance are to be understood only from the earlier periods of European literature. To see European literature as a whole is possible only after one has acquired citizenship in every period from Homer to Goethe. This cannot be got from a textbook, even if such a textbook existed. One acquires the rights of citizenship in the country of European literature only when one has spent many years in each of its provinces and has frequently moved about from one to another. One is a European when one has become a *civis Romanus*. The division of European literature among a number of unconnected philologies almost completely prevents this. Though "classi-

---

[6] Karl Joël, *Wandlungen der Weltanschauung. Eine Philosophiegeschichte als Geschichtsphilosophie* (1928).

[7] *Der Historismus*, p. 734.—Cf. *infra*, n. 11.

cal" philology goes beyond Augustan literature in research, it seldom does so in teaching. The "modern" philologies are oriented toward the modern "national literatures"—a concept which was first established after the awakening of nationalities under the pressure of the Napoleonic superstate, which is therefore highly time-conditioned and hence still more obstructive of any view of the whole. And yet the work of philologists in the last four or five generations has created such a quantity of aids that it is precisely their wrongly decried specialization which has made it possible for one to find one's way about each of the principal European literatures with some linguistic equipment. Specialization has thus opened the way to a new universalization. But the fact is still unknown, and little use is made of it.

As we have already indicated, no stretch of European literary history is so little known and frequented as the Latin literature of the early and high Middle Ages. And yet the historical view of Europe makes it clear that precisely this stretch occupies a key situation as the connecting link between declining Antiquity and the Western world which was so very slowly taking shape. But it is cultivated—under the name of "medieval Latin philology" —by a very small number of specialists. In Europe there might be a dozen of them. For the rest, the Middle Ages is divided between the Catholic philosophers (i.e., the representatives of the history of dogma in faculties of Catholic theology) and the representatives of medieval history at our universities. Both groups have to deal with manuscript sources and texts— hence with literature. The medieval Latinists, the historians of Scholasticism, and the political historians, however, have little contact with one another. The same is true of the modern philologists. These also work on the Middle Ages, but they usually remain as aloof from medieval Latin philology as they do from general literary, political, and cultural history. Thus the Middle Ages is dismembered into specialties which have no contact. There is no general discipline of the Middle Ages—a further impediment to the study of European literature. Troeltsch could rightly say in 1922: "The culture of the Middle Ages still awaits presentation" (*Der Historismus*, 767). That is still true today. The culture of the Middle Ages cannot yet be presented, because its Latin literature has as yet been incompletely studied. In this sense the Middle Ages is still as dark today as it—wrongly —appeared to the Italian Humanists. For that very reason a historical consideration of European literature must begin at this darkest point. The present study is therefore entitled *European Literature and the Latin Middle Ages*, and we hope that this title will justify its purport with increasing evidence from chapter to chapter.

Are we not, however, setting up an unrealizable program? The assertion will certainly be made by the "guardians of Zion"—so Aby Warburg used to call the proprietors and boundary guards of the specialties. They have inherited rights and interests to preserve—*Los Intereses creados*, as Jacinto Benavente, Nobel prize winner in 1922, entitled one of his comedies. Their objection means little. The problem of the broadening of our humanistic disciplines is real, pressing, general—and solvable. Toynbee proves it. Bergson discusses it, using metaphysics as his example: "Here is a philosophical problem. We did not choose it, we encountered it. It closes our road. Nothing remains except to remove the obstacle or else to cease philosophizing. The difficulty must be solved, the problem analyzed in its elements. Where will this lead us? No one knows. No one can even say what science is competent for the new problem. It may be a science to which one is wholly a stranger. What am I saying? It will not suffice to become acquainted with it or even to obtain a profound knowledge of it. We shall sometimes be obliged to revise certain procedures, certain habits, certain theories, to conform with precisely the facts and the grounds which raised new questions. Very good; we will study the science that we did not know, we will go into it deeply, if need be we will revise it. And if that takes months or years? Then we will spend whatever time it takes. And if one life is not long enough? Then several lives will accomplish it; no philosopher today is obliged to build up the whole of philosophy. So we shall talk to the philosopher. Such is the method we propose to him. It demands that, however old he may be, he is ready to become a student again." [8] He who would study European literature has an easier task than Bergson's philosopher. He has only to familiarize himself with the methods and subjects of classical, medieval Latin, and modern philology. He will "spend whatever time it takes." And in the process he will learn enough to make him see the modern national literatures with different eyes.

He will learn that European literature is an "intelligible unit," which disappears from view when it is cut into pieces. He will recognize that it has an autonomous structure, which is essentially different from that of the visual arts.[9] Simply because, all else aside, literature is the medium of ideas, art not. But literature also has different forms of movement, of growth, of continuity, from art. It possesses a freedom which is denied to art. For literature, all the past is present, or can become so. Homer is brought to us anew in a new translation, and Rudolf Alexander Schröder's Homer is different from Voss's. I can take up Homer or Plato at any hour, I "have" him then, and have him wholly. He exists in innumerable copies. The Parthenon and St. Peter's exist only once, I can make them visible to me by photographs only partially and shadowily. But their photographs give me no marble, I cannot touch them, cannot walk about in them, as I can in the *Odyssey* or the *Divina Commedia*. In the book, the poem is really present. I do not "have" a Titian either in a photograph or in the most nearly perfect copy, even if the latter were available for a few dollars. With the literature of all times and peoples I can have a direct, intimate, and engrossing vital relationship, with art not. Works of art I have to contemplate in museums. The book is more real by far than the picture. Here we have a truly ontological relationship and real participation in an intellectual entity. But

---

[8] Henri Bergson, *La Pensée et le mouvant* (1934), 84 f.
[9] Lessing discussed "the boundaries between painting and poetry" as early as 1766.

a book, apart from everything else, is a "text." One understands it or one does not understand it. Perhaps it contains "difficult" passages. One needs a technique to unravel them. Its name is philology. Since *Literaturwissenschaft* has to deal with texts, it is helpless without philology. No intuition and "essence-intuition" can supply the want of it. So-called *Kunstwissenschaft* [10] has an easier time. It works with pictures—and photographic slides. Here there is nothing intelligible. To understand Pindar's poems requires severe mental effort—to understand the Parthenon frieze does not. The same relation obtains between Dante and the cathedrals, and so on. Knowing pictures is easy compared with knowing books. Now, if it is possible to learn the "essence of Gothic" from the cathedrals, one need no longer read Dante. On the contrary! Literary history (and that repellent thing philology!) needs to learn from art history! In all this, one thing is forgotten—namely that, as we pointed out, there are essential differences between the book and the picture. The possibility of having Homer, Virgil, Dante, Shakespeare, Goethe at any time and "wholly" shows that literature has a different mode of existence from art. But from this it follows that literary creation is subject to other laws than artistic creation. The "timeless present" which is an essential characteristic of literature means that the literature of the past can always be active in that of the present. So Homer in Virgil, Virgil in Dante, Plutarch and Seneca in Shakespeare, Shakespeare in Goethe's *Götz von Berlichingen*, Euripides in Racine's *Iphigenia* and Goethe's. Or in our day: The *Thousand and One Nights* and Calderón in Hofmannsthal; the *Odyssey* in Joyce; Aeschylus, Petronius, Dante, Tristan Corbière, Spanish mysticism in T. S. Eliot. There is here an inexhaustible wealth of possible interrelations. Furthermore, there is the garden of literary forms—be they the genres (which Croce is forced by his philosophical system to declare unreal!) or metrical and stanzaic forms; be they set formulas or narrative motifs or linguistic devices. It is a boundless realm. Finally, there is the wealth of figures which literature has formed and which can forever pass into new bodies: Achilles, Oedipus, Semiramis, Faust, Don Juan. André Gide's last and ripest work is a *Theseus* (1946).

Just as European literature can only be seen as a whole, so the study of it can only proceed historically. Not in the form of literary history! A narrative and enumerative history never yields anything but a cataloguelike knowledge of facts. The material itself it leaves in whatever form it found it. But historical investigation has to unravel it and penetrate it. It has to develop analytical methods, that is, methods which will "decompose" the material (after the fashion of chemistry with its reagents) and make its structures visible. The necessary point of view can only be gained from a comparative perusal of literatures, that is, can only be discovered empirically. Only a literary discipline which proceeds historically and philologically can do justice to the task.

[10] I distinguish it from the historical discipline of art history.

Such a "science of European literature" has no place in the pigeonholes of our universities and can have none. Academic organization of philological and literary studies corresponds to the intellectual picture in 1850. Seen from 1950, that picture is as obsolete as the railroads of 1850. We have modernized the railroads, but not our system of transmitting tradition. How that would have to be done cannot be discussed here. But one thing may be said: Without a modernized study of European literature there can be no cultivation of the European tradition.

The founding hero (*heros ktistes*) of European literature is Homer. Its last universal author is Goethe. What Goethe means for Germany Hofmannsthal has put in two statements: "Goethe as the basis of an education can replace an entire culture." And: "We have no modern literature. We have Goethe and beginnings." A heavy judgment upon German literature since Goethe's death. But Valéry too says cuttingly: "Le moderne se contente de peu." European literature of the nineteenth and the twentieth century has not yet been sifted, what is dead has not yet been separated from what is alive. It can furnish subjects for dissertations. But the final word upon it belongs not to literary history but to literary criticism. For that in Germany we have Friedrich Schlegel—and beginnings.[11]

[11] The above chapter was published in advance of the book, in 1947, in a journal. Objection was expressed from the art-historical side. Offense was taken at the statement that literature was the medium of ideas, art not. I therefore clarify: Were Plato's writings lost, we could not reconstruct them from Greek plastic art. The Logos can express itself only in words.

2

The Latin Middle Ages

1.   *Dante and the Antique Poets*

As DANTE, following in Virgil's footsteps, begins his journey through Limbo, there looms out of the darkness a region of light, in which dwell the poets and philosophers of the antique world. Four noble shades advance to meet Virgil, with the greeting:

> Onorate l'altissimo poeta;
> L'ombra sua torna, ch' era dipartita.

> (All honor be unto the highest poet!
> His shade returns to us, that was departed.)

Virgil explains the scene to his pupil:

> Mira colui con quella spada in mano,
> Che vien dinanzi ai tre sì come sire.
> Quelli è Omero poeta sovrano;
> L'altro è Orazio satiro che viene;
> Ovidio è il terzo, e l'ultimo Lucano.

> (See him who holds that sword there in his hand,
> Walking before the rest, as he were their lord:
> Homer is he, sovereign among all poets.
> Who comes the next is Horace, satirist;
> Ovid the third; and Lucan there the last.)

Then the antique poets turn to the modern poet with gestures of greeting:

> E più d' onore ancor assai mi fenno,
> Ch' ei sì mi fecer de la loro schiera,
> Sì ch' io fui sesto tra cotanto senno.

> (And greatly more besides they honored me,
> For of their troop they made me, so that I
> Became a sixth amid such might of mind.) [1]

---

[1] *Inferno*, IV, 78 ff.

In the *Purgatorio*, Virgil and Dante are joined by the late Roman poet Statius. Dante's last guide and patron in his journey through the other world is Bernard of Clairvaux. Bernard's prayer to the Virgin Mary brings Dante the vision of God which is the final note of the *Paradiso*. For his introductory chord, however, Dante needed his meeting with the antique poets and his reception into their circle. They must legitimize his poetical mission. The six poets (including Statius in the number) are brought together into an ideal company: a "fair school" (*la bella scuola*) of timeless authority, whose members hold equal rank. Homer is only *primus inter pares*. The six writers represent a selection from the antique Parnassus. Dante's bringing them together to form a "school" epitomizes the medieval idea of Antiquity. Homer, the illustrious progenitor, was hardly more than a great name to the Middle Ages. For medieval Antiquity is Latin Antiquity. But the name had to be named. Without Homer, there would have been no *Aeneid*; without Odysseus' descent into Hades, no Virgilian journey through the other world; without the latter, no *Divina Commedia*. To the whole of late Antiquity, as to the whole of the Middle Ages, Virgil is what he is for Dante: "l'altissimo poeta." Next to him stands Horace, as the representative of Roman satire. This the Middle Ages regarded as wholesome sermonizing on manners and morals, and it found many imitators from the twelfth century onwards. Whatever else it may be, Dante's *Commedia* is also a denunciation of his times. Ovid, however, wore a different face for the Middle Ages than he does for us. In the beginning of the *Metamorphoses*, the twelfth century found a cosmogony and cosmology which were in harmony with contemporary Platonism (see *infra*, p. 106). But the *Metamorphoses* were also a repertory of mythology as exciting as a romance. Who was Phaeton? Lycaon? Procne? Arachne? Ovid was the *Who's Who* for a thousand such questions. One had to know the *Metamorphoses*; otherwise one could not understand Latin poetry. Furthermore, all these mythological stories had an allegorical meaning. So Ovid was also a treasury of morality. Dante embellishes episodes of the *Inferno* with transformations intended to outdo Ovid, as he outdoes Lucan's *terribilità*. Lucan was the virtuoso of horror and a turgid pathos, but he was also versed in the underworld and its witchcraft. In addition he was the source book for the Roman Civil War, the panegyrist of the austere Cato of Utica, whom Dante places as guardian at the foot of the Mount of Purgatory. Statius, finally, was the bard of the fratricidal Theban War, and his epic closes with homage to the divine *Aeneid*. The "Tale of Thebes" was a favorite book in the Middle Ages, as popular as the Arthurian romances. It contained dramatic episodes, arresting characters. Oedipus, Amphiaraus, Capaneus, Hypsipyle, the infant Archemorus—the dramatis personae of the *Thebais* are constantly referred to in the *Commedia*.

Dante's meeting with the *bella scuola* seals the reception of the Latin epic into the Christian cosmological poem. This embraces an ideal space, in which a niche is left free for Homer, but in which all the great figures of the West are likewise assembled: the Emperors (Augustus, Trajan, Justinian); the Church Fathers; the masters of the seven liberal arts; the luminaries of philosophy; the founders of monastic orders; the mystics. But the realm of these founders, organizers, teachers, and saints was to be found only in one historical complex of European culture: in the Latin Middle Ages. There lie the roots of the *Divine Comedy*. The Latin Middle Ages is the crumbling Roman road from the antique to the modern world.

2. *Antique and Modern Worlds*

The antique world—that is, the whole of Antiquity from Homer to the tribal migrations, not what is known as "classical" Antiquity. The latter is a creation of the eighteenth century. It is the product of a theory of art which itself has to be understood historically. Historiography has long since freed itself from the narrowness of the classicistic concept. Literary history, here as elsewhere, is still behindhand. What the later Roman period had preserved of nonclassical Antiquity, the Middle Ages took over and transformed. We have drawings by Villard de Honnecourt after antique bronzes which are preserved in the Louvre today. The drawings show a Gothic feeling for form. One does not realize that they are reproductions until one studies them side by side with photographs of their originals.[2] The artist produces "medieval Antiquity." Which means Antiquity as the Middle Ages saw it. The concept is as valid for literature as it is for the visual arts. Antiquity has a twofold life in the Middle Ages: reception and transformation. This transformation can take very various forms. It can mean impoverishment, degeneration, devitalization, misunderstanding;[3] but it can also mean critical collecting (the encyclopedias of Isidore and Raban Maur), schoolboyish copying, skillful imitation of formal patterns, assimilation of cultural values, enthusiastic empathy. All stages and forms of accomplishment are represented. Toward the end of the twelfth century they culminate in freedom to compete with respected prototypes. Maturity is reached.

Today the relation between the antique and the modern world can no longer be conceived as "survival," "continuation," or "legacy." We adopt Ernst Troeltsch's universal-historical view. According to him,[4] our European world is based "not upon a reception of Antiquity nor upon a severance from it, but upon a thorough and at the same time conscious coalescence with it. The European world is composed of the antique and the modern, of the old world which has passed through all stages from primitivism to cultural overripeness and disintegration, and of the new world which begins with the Romanic-Germanic peoples in the time of Charlemagne and which also passes through its stages." But at the same time "these two

---

[2] Jean Adhémar, *Influences antiques dans l'art du moyen âge français* (London: The Warburg Institute, 1939).

[3] For misunderstanding as a category of changes in form, see Excursus I, *infra*.

[4] *Der Historismus*, 716 f.

worlds, so widely sundered in their mentality and their historical development, are so intertwined, so coalescent in a conscious historical memory
and continuity, that the modern world, despite the fact that it has a spirit
which is wholly new and wholly its own, is intimately penetrated and conditioned at every point by antique culture, tradition, legal and political
forms, language, philosophy, and art. It is this alone which gives the European world its depth, its fullness, its complexity, and its movement, as
well as its bent toward historical thinking and historical self-analysis . . ."

Charlemagne looms from afar as the first representative of the modern
world. But his work only crowns a development which begins with the fall
of the Frankish monarchy about 650. The Austrasian mayor of the palace,
Pepin II, obtained control of the entire empire by the battle of Tertry in
687. This decided the rise of the Pepinids, or Carolingian dynasty. The
beginning of the "modern" world is to be set about 675. It is "widely sundered" from the antique world, yet at the same time "coalescent" with it
"in a conscious historical memory and continuity." A continuity, then
(that is, a homogeneous and living connection), which spans a profound
separation. How is such a relationship to be understood? Here Toynbee's
comparative historical method can help us. According to Toynbee, the
Roman Empire is the universal-state end phase of the Hellenic civilization.
This is followed, from 375 to 675, by an "interregnum," then by "the
Western civilization." The latter stands to the Hellenic civilization in the
relation of "affiliation," is its daughter civilization. In this way the facts
established by Troeltsch are defined by a more precise chronology and
terminology. The dependent relationship of "affiliation" implies the same
thing as Troeltsch's concept of "thorough coalescence" and "continuity."
Whether one is to distinguish "renaissances" within this process is a question of expedience. They must be tested individually. What is fundamental
is the concept that the substance of antique culture was never destroyed.
The fallow period of decline which extended from 425 to 775 affected only
the Frankish kingdom and was later made good. A new period of decline
begins in the nineteenth century and reaches the dimensions of catastrophe
in the twentieth. This is not the place to discuss its significance.

3. The Middle Ages

Antiquity, the Middle Ages, the Modern Period are names for three epochs
of European history—names which are scientifically "preposterous" (Alfred Dove) but indispensable for mutual comprehension on the practical
level. The most meaningless of them is the concept of the Middle Ages—a
coinage of the Italian Humanists and only comprehensible from their
point of view. Concerning the limits of these periods, and the problem of
periodization in general, there has been much controversy. The discussion
has been fruitful insofar as it has cast a clearer light on certain less well-
explored epochs.

For the beginning of the Middle Ages—and, by the same token, for the end of Antiquity—various dates have been proposed, ranging from the third to the seventh century. Michael Rostovtzeff carries his *History of the Ancient World* down to Constantine. Ernst Kornemann divides the Roman Empire into three epochs: Principate (27 B.C.–A.D. 305), period of the Renewal of the Empire by Constantine (306–337), and Dominate (337–641). But this takes us far into Byzantine history. The Western Empire had been shaken to its foundations as early as the fifth century. Though Justinian (527–565) was able to reconquer Africa, Italy, Sicily, and a part of the Spanish seaboard, the price of the accomplishment was not only complete financial exhaustion of the Empire but also neglect of the East, into which Slavs and Bulgars poured. "So the nuclear territories of the Empire were laid waste; while the Byzantine military forces celebrated victory in the distant West." [5] Justinian's work of restoration ended in a collapse. The Western Empire was finally lost, the Eastern Empire entered into serious crises, from which it did not emerge until the time of Heraclius (610–641), whose praises have been sung by Corneille and Calderón. With him begins Byzantine history proper—the history of the Medieval Greek Empire. Externally, Heraclius had to defend the Empire against the Neo-Persians (Sassanidae, 226–641). He achieved brilliant successes, but even in his lifetime the Arab incursions began. A few years after the death of Mohammed (632), the Arabs conquer Persia, Syria, Egypt (636–641), then all of Roman Africa, finally Spain (711). The Arabs are now masters of the Mediterranean. This represents an economic revolution. Maritime commerce, which supplied the West with eastern commodities, decreases steadily from 650 on. But that commerce was the Merovingians' source of wealth. All customs dues flowed into their treasury. The decline in commerce especially affected Neustria, where the commercial cities were situated. The political center of gravity shifts toward Austrasia, and from the king to the great landowning nobility. From this nobility arise the Pippinids, to establish a new political power no longer based on the Mediterranean, where Islam rules. "With the Carolingians, Europe at last sets out upon a new road. Until their time, it has still subsisted upon the life of Antiquity. But Islam has abolished this inherited state of affairs. The Carolingians see themselves facing a new situation, which they did not bring about but found already in existence and which they so employ that a new age now begins. Their role is comprehensible only in the light of the fact that Islam has shifted the center of gravity of the world." Thus Pirenne.[6] When he sees the dividing line between Antiquity and the Middle Ages in the economic and political effect of the Arab incursion, he coincides

[5] Georg Ostrogorsky, *Geschichte des byzantinischen Staates* (1940), 44.—Ostrogorsky distinguishes three periods in Byzantine history: (1) 324–610 Early Byzantine; (2) 610–1025 Middle Byzantine; (3) 1025–1453 Late Byzantine (*HZ*, CLXI [1941], 229 ff.).

[6] H. Pirenne, *Mahomet et Charlemagne* (1937).—For a criticism of Pirenne's views, see R. S. Lopez in *Speculum* (1943), pp. 14–38, and D. C. Dennett in *Speculum* (1948), pp. 165–190.

with Toynbee's date of 675 as that which marks the division between the two epochs.

Toynbee makes the breaking up of the end phase of Antiquity begin about 375. The year of the death of the Emperor Theodosius (395) has also been put forth, on good grounds, as the dividing year.[7] Under Theodosius, Britain, Gaul, and Spain still formed part of the Empire. Twenty years after his death, Germanic kingdoms had come into existence in all three of these countries. The Empire now comprised a twofold existence—Roman and Germanic. In another respect too, Theodosius' reign forms a conclusion. It consummates Constantine's religious policy by raising Christianity to the position of the state religion (381). Henceforth adherence to paganism is a political offense. In 384 the altar of Victory, the refuge of old Roman tradition, is removed from the Senate. At the same time the assault on the temples begins in the East. Hordes of monks travel through the land, laying waste sanctuaries, destroying works of art. They are followed by troops of vagabonds hungry for booty, eager to plunder villages suspected of impiety.[8] But the same period embraces the work of the greatest of the Western Church Fathers, Augustine (354–430). North Africa, Egypt, Syria, Asia Minor are bulwarks of the Church. Leo I (d. 461) represents the end of papal history within the antique *orbis Romanus*.

The period from Theodosius to Charlemagne is of the utmost importance to the European tradition. Among its writers are the great personalities whom the American scholar E. K. Rand has called the "founders of the Middle Ages."[9] Not only Jerome and Augustine, but also the first great Christian poet, Prudentius, and the first Christian general historian, Orosius, live on into the fifth century. About 400 Macrobius and Servius lay the foundations for medieval Virgilian exegesis, and Martianus Capella produces a handbook of the seven liberal arts which the Middle Ages accepts as authoritative. The years 450 to 480 see the voluminous work in prose and verse of the Gaul Sidonius, who greatly influenced the Middle Ages. Of the sixth century, W. P. Ker has said: "Almost everything that is common to the Middle Ages, and much that lasts beyond the Renaissance, is to be found in the authors of the sixth century."[10] Boethius belongs to the sixth century (d. 524). Through his translation of some of Aristotle's logical treatises he furnished the West with material for an intellectual training which was a preparation for Scholasticism. His *Consolatio philosophiae*, written in prison, is a book which has refreshed innumerable minds, even down to our own day—the only work of late Roman Antiquity which has

[7] H. St. L. B. Moss, *The Birth of the Middle Ages* (Oxford, 1935).
[8] Otto Seeck, *Geschichte des Untergangs der antiken Welt*, V, 220.—Oration of Libanius (314–ca. 393) *pro templis* (ed. Förster, III, *or.* 30; translated by R. van Looy in *Byzantion*, VIII [1933], 7 ff.).
[9] E. K. Rand, *Founders of the Middle Ages* (1928).
[10] Ker, *The Dark Ages* (1904), 101 f.—The sixth century is the subject of Eleanor Shipley Duckett's useful book, *The Gateway to the Middle Ages* (New York, 1938).

been translated into German in the twentieth century. In the sixth century too falls the foundation of Western monasticism by St. Benedict. Then comes the extensive literary activity of Cassiodorus (490–583), whose principal works are links in the medieval chain of tradition. The dividing line between the sixth and seventh centuries was reached or crossed by Venantius Fortunatus, who has been called the last Roman poet; by Pope Gregory the Great, influential through his didactic and ethical writings; by Isidore of Seville, whose encyclopedia served the entire Middle Ages as a basic book. He transmits the sum of late antique knowledge to posterity, as Fortunatus transmits models for courtly epideictic and panegyrical poetry and for the hagiographic epic. Contemporary with these three is Gregory of Tours (d. 594), the historian of the Franks. In the seventh century the intellectual life of the Continent declines. But in Ireland, which was never a part of the Empire, there arises an original monastic culture, which under Columban (d. 615) reaches out to the mainland. Bobbio and St. Gall are Irish foundations. An emissary of Gregory the Great, Augustine, lands in Kent in 597 and begins the conversion of England. From the Synod of Whitby (664) Roman Christianity wins the day over Celtic Christianity; and, in Aldhelm (d. 709) and Bede (d. 735), develops to a religious and intellectual flowering which bestows apostles (Boniface, d. 754) and a reform in education (Alcuin, d. 804) upon the mainland.

We have now named the most important men of the "Dark Ages" (they will frequently reappear in the following chapters) and, with the age of Charlemagne, have entered better-known historical territory. If we now return to the problem of delimiting historical periods, the first question that arises is: When did the Middle Ages end? When did the Modern Period actually begin? Answers differ, according to whether they are based upon power history or intellectual history. From 1492 onwards the modern national states appear in Europe as new historical entities. Italy sets the beginning of the Modern Period at the Renaissance, Germany at the Reformation. Both countries achieved national unification only in the nineteenth century. But to assume that a period begins shortly before or shortly after 1500 depends upon also admitting, at least tacitly, that the Modern Period, up to 1914, was a realization of progress—in the direction of enlightenment and democracy (England and France) and in the direction of the national state (Germany and Italy). This belief in progress, and the naive Europeanism which is concomitant with it, was refuted by the world wars of the twentieth century. But the concept "Modern Period" has become obsolete for another reason too. The decisive change that the nineteenth and twentieth centuries have brought about in the world was accomplished through industry and technique—both of which were at first hailed as "progress" but are now manifestly powers of destruction as well. Historians in times to come will presumably set our age down as the "Period of Technique." Its beginnings can be traced as far back as the eighteenth century. There, consequently, a period must be begun. This conclusion was first reached by the English historian G. M. Trevelyan. He sets forth [11] that the medieval period does not end until the eighteenth century; it was supplanted by the "Industrial Revolution," which changed human life more than did the Renaissance and the Reformation. We shall be able to show that a break with the more than millennial European literary tradition also makes its appearance in England about 1750. But does it make sense to call the period from 400 to 1750 the "Middle Ages"? Obviously not. However, this is not the place to draw terminological conclusions from the fact. If human history continues for a few more millenniums or tens of millenniums, historians will find themselves under the necessity of designating its epochs by numerals, as the archeologists now do for ancient Crete—Minoan I, II, III, each with three subdivisions. Toynbee has already drawn this conclusion. He distinguishes four epochs in the course of Western culture: 1. *ca.* 675–1075; 2. *ca.* 1075–1475; 3. *ca.* 1475–1875; 4. *ca.* 1875–x (A *Study of History*, I, 171).

4. The Latin Middle Ages

The irruptions of the Germanic peoples [12] and the Arabs into the world of late Antiquity are parallel processes—with a basic difference: the Germanic peoples assimilate, the Arabs do not. The Arab incursion had a far greater impetus than the Germanic. It is comparable only to the forward thrust of the Huns under Attila and of the Mongols under Genghis Khan and Tamerlane. But their period of dominion was as brief as Islam's was lasting. "Compared with that incursion, what are the attacks of the Germanic peoples, so long resisted and so lacking in force that for centuries they succeeded in entering only the outermost zone of Romania! . . . While the Germanic peoples had nothing to oppose to the Christianity of the Roman Empire, the Arabs burned with the fire of a new faith. That, and that alone, made them unassimilable.[13] For, in other respects, they had no more prejudices against the culture of the peoples they subdued than had the Germanic peoples. On the contrary, they adopted it with astonishing rapidity. For science they go to school to the Greeks, for art to the Greeks and the Persians. They are not even fanatical, at least not at first, and they do not seek to convert their subjects. But they seek to force them into submission to the one God Allah, to his prophet Mohammed, and, since Mohammed was an Arab, to Arabia. Their world religion is at the same time a national faith. They are servants of God. . . . The Germanic invader, entering the Roman Empire, was romanized; the Roman, on the other hand, became an Arab the moment the Arab conquest reached him." [14]

[11] In his *English Social History* (1944), 96.
[12] See Pierre Courcelle, *Histoire littéraire des grandes invasions germaniques* (1948).
[13] It is wrong, then, to reproach Pirenne with basing his views essentially upon economic and administrative history.
[14] Pirenne, *op. cit.*, 143–46.

The Germanic peoples not only brought no new ideas with them, they "also, with the exception of the Anglo-Saxons, allowed the Latin language to remain as the only means of communication wherever they settled. Here, as in all other spheres, they assimiliated . . . As soon as their kings had gained a firm footing, they surrounded themselves with rhetoricians, jurists, and poets." [15] They have their laws, their chancellery records and documents, and their letters composed in Latin. The tribal migrations did not change the essential characteristics of intellectual life in the western Mediterranean area.[16] Until the Anglo-Saxon influence became effective in the eighth century no new traits appear. The Germanic kingdoms also continue the previous state of affairs in that their rulers have only laymen as ministers and officials. This indicates the survival into the eighth century of a class of educated laymen. The Latin of daily life is corrupt, but it is Latin. "No source shows us—as is the case in the ninth century—that the people in church no longer understand the priest. The language lives on, and through it the unity of Romania is preserved into the eighth century."

The closing of the western Mediterranean by Islam threw Carolingian culture back to an agricultural level. The ability to read and write disappeared among laymen. The Carolingians can now find educated men only among the clergy, they need the collaboration of the Church. "A new characteristic of the Middle Ages appears: a priestly caste, which imposed its influence on the state." Latin now becomes a learned language, and remains so throughout the Middle Ages. The "Carolingian Renaissance" is at once a resumption of antique tradition and a break with the wreck of Roman culture. The new culture becomes Roman-Germanic, "though, to be sure, it is borne upon the shoulders of the Church." According to the current view, the Germanic contribution consists above all in feudalism—that is, in the legal and political structure of the medieval world.[17] This was the inevitable result of the centrifugal trend inherent in the system of landholding and barter. To preserve the royal or imperial power, in the face of these trends, as an "administrative state" (Alfred Weber), and to integrate the feudal system with the latter, cost struggles which every page of medieval history recounts. The stamp of feudalism was set upon all institutions and all human relations. As a further Germanic contribution the northern cities are usually cited. But let us bear in mind that "Germanic" in this sense is a difficult and not at all homogeneous concept. Charlemagne's realm included and mingled Celts, Romans, Franks, and Saxons. The strongest Germanic element is represented by the Vikings who settled in France and were civilized during the tenth century. It was their absorption which finally completed the formation of the French people. As early as the eleventh century they reach out for England and Sicily. They carry French culture over the sea. Germany was not touched by this influx. Germanic assimilation of the language and church of Rome made Antiq-

[15] *Ibid.*, 112.
[16] *Ibid.*, 116.
[17] For a contrary view, cf. J. Calmette, *Le Monde féodal* (1934), 197.

uity for the Middle Ages "an authoritative traditional stock by which it was possible to orient oneself" (A. Weber).

The flowering of the vernacular literatures from the twelfth and thirteenth centuries onward in no sense signifies a defeat or retreat of Latin literature. Indeed, the twelfth and thirteenth centuries are a culminating point of Latin poetry and learning. At that period the Latin language and Latin literature extend "from Central and Southern Europe and the North on into Iceland, Scandinavia, Finland, and, southwestward, into Palestine." [18] The common man knows as well as the educated man that there are two languages: the language of the people and the language of the learned (*clerici, litterati*). The learned language, Latin, is also called *grammatica*, and to Dante—as to the Roman Varro before him—it is an art language, devised by sages and unalterable. Vernacular compositions are even translated into Latin.[19] For centuries longer, Latin remained alive as the language of education, of science, of government, of law, of diplomacy. In France it was not abolished as the language of law until 1539, at the instigation of Francis I. But as a literary language too, Latin long survived the end of the Middle Ages. Jacob Burckhardt, in his *Kultur der Renaissance*, devotes several chapters to the general latinization of culture. Among them is one on the Latin poetry of the fifteenth and sixteenth centuries, in which he shows "how close it was to decisive victory." In France, England, Holland, and Germany it also had brilliant representatives in the sixteenth and seventeenth centuries. In 1817 Goethe, in *Kunst und Altertum*, wrote: "It would be of great advantage to a more liberal view of the world, which the German is on the way to losing, if a young and intelligent scholar should undertake to evaluate the genuinely poetical gains which German poets writing in Latin for the last three centuries have to show . . . At the same time he would note how other cultured nations too, in the period when Latin was the universal language, composed in it and were able to understand one another in a manner now lost to us." These humanistic compositions are rightly distinguished from Middle Latin as "Neo-

---

18 P. Lehmann in *Corona quernea*, 307.

19 The Italian jurist Guido delle Colonne translates a French Troy romance for those "who read Latin" (*qui grammaticam legunt*); Griffin's edition of Guido's *Historia destructionis Troiae* (1936), 4.—Other translations of vernacular works into Latin: Wolfram's *Willehalm* (fragment of a metrical translation; Lachmann, pp. cliii f.); *Herzog Ernst* (two versions; see Paul Lehmann, *Gesta ducis Ernesti* [1927]); two Latin adaptations of Hartmann's *Gregor* (Ehrismann, LG, II, 2, 1, 187). Conrad of Würzburg's *Goldene Schmiede* was rehandled in Latin by Franco of Meschede ca. 1330 (*Aurea fabrica*). The *Carmen de prodicione Guenonis* (13th cent.) is a condensed version of the *Chanson de Roland* (ZRPh [1942], 492–509); the *Historia septem sapientum* (ca. 1330) goes back to a prose redaction of the *Roman des sept sages*. Of Benedeit's *Voyage of St. Brendan*, we have two Latin versions, one in prose, the other in rhymed stanzas. Nicole Bozon's *Contes moralisés* (14th cent.) were also translated into Latin. So, even toward the middle of the sixteenth century, were Jorge Manrique's (d. 1479) celebrated stanzas on the death of his father.—Goethe enjoyed reading *Hermann und Dorothea* in Latin (to Eckermann, Jan. 18, 1825).

Latin." [20] But for the fourteenth and fifteenth centuries such a separation cannot yet be made. Petrarch and Boccaccio are still affected by the heritage of the Latin Middle Ages. As late as 1551 an Italian Humanist feels himself obliged to be on his guard against the "bad poets" of the twelfth century.[21] So they were still being read! This is to be explained by the pedagogical practice of the fifteenth and sixteenth centuries—and by the invention of printing. In those centuries the student had set before him the so-called *Auctores octo*,[22] the cloudy lees of the medieval curriculum of study and reading. But the great Latin writers of the twelfth century too still found eager readers even in the sixteenth and seventeenth centuries, as the new editions show.[23] Beside, within, and beneath the great movements of the dawning Modern Period—Humanism, the Renaissance, the Reformation, the Counter-Reformation—the influence of medieval Latin literature persisted, especially in the country which was hardly touched by the Reformation and not essentially touched by Humanism and the Renaissance: in Spain. Hofmannsthal's characterization of Baroque as the rejuvenated form "of that older world which we call the Middle Ages," is especially applicable to Spanish literature in its period of florescence.

We have rapidly traversed a long period of time. Freedom to shift from country to country and period to period is necessary to our enterprise. Strict chronology is our prop, not our guide.

Let us return to the early Middle Ages. It was through Charlemagne that the historical entity which I call "the Latin Middle Ages" was first fully constituted. This concept is not usual in historiography. For our purposes, however, it is indispensable. I use the term to designate the share of Rome, of the Roman idea of the state, of the Roman church, and of Roman culture, in the physiognomy of the Middle Ages in general—a far more inclusive phenomenon, then, than the mere survival of the Latin language and literature. In the course of many centuries Rome had learned to conceive of her political existence as a universal mission. Virgil already expresses the

[20] Georg Ellinger, *Geschichte der neulateinischen Literatur Deutschlands im 16. Jahrhundert* (1929–33). Vol. I treats of "Italy and German Humanism in the Neo-Latin Lyric."—Anthologies appeared early, for example the *Deliciae poetarum Italorum* (Frankfort, 1608, 2 vols.), which Burckhardt frequently cites. It was followed by *Deliciae poetarum Gallorum* (ibid., 1609, 3 vols.), *Germanorum* (ibid., 1612, 6 vols.), and *Belgicorum* (ibid., 1614, 4 vols.).—On Neo-Latin artistic prose, see O. Kluge in *Glotta* (1935), 18 ff.

[21] Cinthius Gregorius Gyraldus (= G. B. Giraldi Cinthio), *De poetis nostrorum temporum*, ed. K. Wotke (1894), 47.

[22] For its dissemination in print before 1500, see the *Gesamtkatalog der Wiegendrucke* (1925 ff.). The *Auctores octo* appeared in twenty-five editions between 1490 and 1500. Of these, none is German.—Ridicule of this and similar schoolbooks in Rabelais, *Gargantua*, ch. 14.

[23] The proportion of late Antique and medieval Latin literature among printed books up to 1600 is surprisingly large. Cf. Jean Seznec, *The Survival of the Pagan Gods* (Bollingen Series XXXVIII; New York, 1953), p. 225.—See also P. Goldschmidt, *Medieval Texts and Their First Appearance in Print* (London, 1943).

idea in a famous passage of the *Aeneid*. From the time of Ovid (*Ars. am.*, I, 174) the equation *orbis* (the world) and *urbs* (Rome) develops and spreads; in the time of Constantine it becomes an inscription on coins (that is, official propaganda);[24] it lives to this day in the formula of the Papal Curia, "urbi et orbi." Through the elevation of Christianity to the position of the state religion, Rome's universalism acquired a twofold aspect. To the universal claim of the state was added that of the church. The conviction of the Middle Ages that it was the continuer of Rome had yet another source—in Augustine's philosophy of history. Here three ideas are fused. The course of human history is harmonized with that of the six days of creation and that of the six periods of human life (*PL*, XXXIV, 190 ff.; XXXVII, 1182; XL, 43 ff.). To this is added a division according to the four world empires—derived from the allegorical interpretation of the prophecies of the Book of Daniel (2:31 ff. and 7:3 ff.;[25] *De civitate Dei*, XX.23 and XVIII.2). The last of these empires is the Roman. It corresponds to the period of "old age" and will continue until the end of temporal existence, which is replaced by the heavenly sabbath. That the end of the world was near at hand was assured by the words of the Apostle "nos, in quos finis saeculorum devenit" (I Cor. 10:11[26]). The early Christian expectation of the last days was thus incorporated into medieval thinking. Medieval authors quote the phrase (without mentioning its source, as is the case with almost all medieval citations), or refer to it, times without number. These references, however, are often not recognized by modern historians of culture; instead, they are understood as a self-expression of the Middle Ages. If, in a seventh-century chronicle, we find the statement, "The world is in gray old age,"[27] we must not make the psychological inference that the period "has a feeling of advancing age" but see a reference to Augustine's parallel between the (Roman) end phase of world history and human old age. Dante, in his vision of Paradise (*Par.*, XXX, 131), learns that but few places in the heavenly rose are still unoccupied. He too lives in expectation of the last days (cf. also *Conv.*, II, 14, 13).

The Bible furnished medieval historical thought with yet another theological substantiation for the replacement of one empire by another: "Regnum a gente in gentem transfertur propter injustitias et injurias et contumelias et diversos dolos" (Ecclesiasticus 10:8). "Because of unrighteous dealings, injuries, and riches got by deceit, the kingdom is transferred from one people to another." The word *transfertur* ("is trans-

---

[24] Cf. J. Vogt, *Orbis Romanus* (1929), 17.

[25] First in the Greek commentary on Daniel composed *ca.* 204 by Bishop Hippolytus of Rome; Jerome adopted it in his commentary on Daniel and gave it general currency.

[26] The wording is Augustine's (*PL*, XL, 43). The Vulgate has: ". . . ad correptionem nostram, in quos fines saeculorum devenerunt."

[27] Fredegar (ed. Krusch) in *MGH*, *Scriptores rer. Merov.*, II, 123. Fredegar's complaint "ne quisquam potest huius tempore nec presumit oratoribus precedentes esse consimilis" (*ibid.*) is to be judged in the same way as the corresponding passage in Gregory of Tours (*infra*, p. 149).

ferred") gives rise to the concept of *translatio* (transference) which is basic for medieval historical theory. The renewal of the Empire by Charlemagne could be regarded as a transferal of the Roman *imperium* to another people. This is implied in the formula *translatio imperii*, with which the *translatio studii* [28] (transferal of learning from Athens or Rome to Paris) was later co-ordinated. The medieval Empire took over from Rome the idea of world empire; thus it had a universal, not a national, character. No less universal is the claim of the Roman church. *Sacerdotium* and *imperium* are the supreme earthly administrative offices. The co-operation of the two powers remains the normal state of things into the eleventh century. It remains the ideal even in the fierce conflicts of the following period. Even at the beginning of the fourteenth century it is still the center around which Dante's thought revolves. The idea of *translatio* permeates the propaganda of Barbarossa,[29] who consciously went back to Charlemagne. From the time of Charlemagne and for centuries thereafter German history is bound up with the idea of the renewal of Rome.[30] But Germany's political and dynastic poetry too during the Hohenstaufen period is for the most part in Latin. The most brilliant stanzas on Barbarossa are written not in German but in Latin—the work of the "Archpoet" of Cologne. The acquisition of the Sicilian crown brought the Hohenstaufen court into even closer relation to Latin poetry. The works of Godfrey of Viterbo are dedicated to Henry VI. It was in Frederick II's Sicilian kingdom that the first school of Italian poets arose; but at the same time the Emperor delighted in the Latin comedies that his jurists composed, and received Latin panegyrical poems from Englishmen.[31]

Meanwhile, let us not forget that the "Latin Middle Ages" is nowise limited to the idea of Rome in the sense of a glorification of Rome or of an effort to renew it. The concept of *translatio*, indeed, implies that the transference of dominion from one empire to another is the result of a sinful misuse of that dominion. The Christian Rome of the fourth century had already seen the development of the concept of a "penitent Rome," which, "like a guilt-laden man, after remorse for the outpoured blood of the Re-

[28] The "model concept" was furnished by Horace (*Epi.*, II, 1, 156): "Graecia . . . artes / Intulit agresti Latio."—I find the concept of the *translatio studii* for the first time in Heiric's epistle to Charles the Bald (*Poetae*, III, 429, 23).—Cf. E. Gilson, *Les Idées et les lettres*, 183 ff.

[29] Thus Otto of Freising. In the contemporary historical epic *Ligurinus*, by an unknown writer, which appeared 1186–87, we are told that Charles liberated the empire and then transferred it to himself. The Rhine now rules the Tiber (I, 249 ff.; III, 543 ff. and 565 ff.).

[30] Very different ideals meet in this concept. Cf. P. E. Schramm, *Kaiser, Rom und Renovatio* (1929).—E. Kantorowicz, *Kaiser Friedrich II., Ergänzungsband* (1931), 176.—For the differing aspects of the Carolingian and Ottonian idea of empire, cf. Carl Erdmann in *Dt. Arch.*, VI (1943), 412 ff.—Fedor Schneider's fine book *Rom und Romgedanke im Mittelalter* (1926) undertakes to investigate "the intellectual foundations of the Renaissance."

[31] Ernst Kantorowicz, *op. cit.*, 132. Gives detailed references for Latin literature at the Emperor's court.

deemer, after doing penance and professing Christ, can be allowed to return to the fold of salvation." [32] Jerome, Ambrose, and Prudentius proclaim this idea. Then Augustine voices a yet more startling reversal. The widely celebrated Roman virtues are, from the Christian point of view, faults. The Christian's gaze must turn from the earthly Rome, whose history partakes of the *civitas terrena*, the Kingdom of Evil, to the *civitas Dei*, the superterrestrial Kingdom of God. Dante tacitly combated this idea of Augustine's. He connects the Rome of Virgil and Augustus with the Rome of Peter and his successors. German *Kaisertum* and Roman *imperium*, heathen and Christian, Augustinian and Dantean historical thought—these are but a few of the tensions contained in the idea of Rome. But they all originated and ran their course in the language of Rome, which was also the language of the Bible, of the Fathers, of the church, of the canonized Roman *auctores*, and, finally, of medieval learning. All these are part of the image of the "Latin Middle Ages," and they give it its exuberant fullness.

5. *Romania*

In contemporary scholarly usage "Romania" is taken to mean the sum total of the countries in which Romance languages were spoken. These languages developed on the soil of the Roman Empire—from the Black Sea to the Atlantic. If we begin in the East, they succeed one another in the following order: Romanian, Italian, French, Provençal, Catalan, Spanish, Portuguese. That there was a kinship between the languages of the Iberian Peninsula, France, and Italy was already known to the Middle Ages. Dante's treatise *De vulgari eloquentia* is the classic proof of the fact. The scholars of the sixteenth and eighteenth centuries (Pasquier, Voltaire, Marmontel) conceived Provençal—"le langage roman ou roumain corrompu" —to be the mother language of the others, and also referred to it as *roman rustique*, which goes back to the expression *lingua romana rustica* which will be discussed below. This view was adopted by François Raynouard (1761–1836). He was from Provence, and he taught that Provençal— which he called "langue romane"—had been dominant throughout the whole of France from the sixth to the ninth century, and that all the other Romance languages had developed from it. His contemporary, the French archeologist Arcisse de Caumont, transferred this idea, and with it the word *roman* (Romance, Romanesque), to the artistic style which was supposed to have been dominant from the end of Antiquity to the twelfth century. Raynouard's researches marked a considerable advance in the study of troubadour poetry. But his philological thesis was untenable. The founder of Romance philology, Friedrich Diez (1794–1876), rejected Raynouard's idea of the primacy of Provençal and taught that all the Romance languages were independent developments of Latin.

The words "Romance," "Romania," have, however, a much older and to-

[32] F. Klingner, *Römische Geisteswelt* (1943), 449.

day half-forgotten history, with which we must begin in order to obtain correct perspective. *Romania* is a derivative of *romanus,* as the latter is of *Roma;* as *latinus* ("Latin") is of *Latium.* The heritage of Rome was shared between the words *latinus* and *romanus.* Among the languages of Latium, the "Latin" dialects, the primacy necessarily went to that which was spoken in Rome. In the Roman Empire the designation "Romans," *Romani,* was long reserved only to the ruling upper stratum. The conquered peoples retained their own national names (Gauls, Iberians, Greeks, etc.). It was not until 212 that Roman citizenship was bestowed on all free inhabitants of the Empire by an edict of Caracalla's. Thenceforth all citizens of the Empire could be called *Romani.* From this extension of the Roman polity it was only a step to the coining of a new designation for the whole immense territory inhabited by "Romans." The need for such a new, brief, and expressive word for *Imperium Romanum* or *orbis Romanus* must have become even more pressing since barbarian peoples had settled within the boundaries of the Empire. In this time of crisis, the name *Romania* appears in Latin and Greek texts, for the first time under Constantine.[33] The word was used down to Merovingian times, and even later. In a poem in praise of King Charibert, Fortunatus says (ed. Leo, p. 131, 7):

> *Hinc cui Barbaries, illinc Romania plaudit:*
> *Diversis linguis laus sonat una viri.*[34]

In the Ottonian period the meaning of Romania changes. It now means the Roman portion of the empire—Italy. Finally it is restricted to the Italian province of Romagna, that is, the old Exarchate of Ravenna.

Romania in its original, late-antique sense is replaced after the seventh and eighth centuries by new historical entities; but the allied words *romanus* and *romanicus* remain alive. When the Latin of everyday intercourse (Popular Latin, Vulgar Latin) had so far diverged from literary Latin that it was necessary to find a name for the former, the old polarity Roma-Latium reappears in a new form. A distinction is drawn between *lingua latina* and *lingua romana* (also with the addition *rustica*). To these, a third term is added: *lingua barbara,* i.e., German. It is characteristic that Isidore, writing in fully Romanized Spain *ca.* 600, is not yet aware of this coexistence of three current languages.

"Romance" is the name that the early Middle Ages itself gave to the new Latin vernaculars, precisely in conscious contrast to the language of the learned, Latin. The words derived from *romanicus* and the adverb *romanice* (in French, Provençal, Spanish, Italian, Rhaeto-Romanic) are never used as national names (there were other words for the purpose), but as the

[33] Cf. Gaston Paris in *Romania,* 1 (1872), 1 ff.—More recent literature in Pirenne, *op cit.,* 289, n. 1.—Between 330 and 432 the name *Romania* appears in nine Latin texts (Zeiller in *Revue des études latines* [1929], 196). But Athanasius too (*Historia Arianorum*) designates Rome as μητρόπολις τῆς ῥωμανίας.

[34] "To the man whom both Barbariandom and Romania celebrate, there rises a single voice of praise in different tongues."

names of those languages—in the same sense, then, as the Italian *volgare*. The Old French *romanz*, the Spanish *romance*, the Italian *romanzo* are such derivatives. They were coined by the Latin-educated class and signify *all* Romance languages. These were regarded as a unity in contrast to Latin. *Enromancier, romançar, romanzare* mean: to translate or compose books in the vernacular. Such books could themselves then be called *romanz, romant, roman, romance, romanzo*—all derivatives from *romanice*. In Old French, *romant, roman* means the "courtly romance in verse," literally "popular book." In a retranslation into Latin, such a book could be called *romanticus* (supply *liber*).[35] The words *romance* and *romantic* [36] are therefore closely connected. In English and German eighteenth-century usage, "romantic" still means something "that could happen in a romance." [37] The Italian word corresponding to the Old French *roman* is *romanzo* ("the romance"). In this sense the word is already used by Dante.

Thus, in French and Italian, *romanice* gives the name of a literary genre. A similar development occurs in Spain. There too *romance* first means "vernacular," then also a composition in the same, but at first without any limitation to a single genre. The phrase *romançar libros* = "translate" is found (Garcilaso, Juan de Valdés), but also such formulas as "los romancistas o vulgares" (Marqués de Santillana). Then, toward the beginning of the fifteenth century, *romance* appears as the designation for the poetical genre which still bears that name today, and which, since the sixteenth century, has been collected in *romanceros*. The Spanish romance or novel is named from the Italian loan-word *novella* (as in English).

In the Middle Ages Romania has a community of culture which extends across language boundaries. Numerous Italians write poetry in Provençal (as, on the other hand, in the *Commedia* Dante has a great Provençal poet speak his mother tongue). Dante's master, Brunetto Latini, writes his great work in French. A poem by the troubadour Raimbaut of Vaqueiras (*ca.* 1200) is significant in this connection: its five stanzas are composed successively in Provençal, Italian, Northern French, Gascon, and Portuguese.[38] These are the languages which the Romance lyric of the period currently employed. That it was possible to alternate between them shows that there was a living consciousness of a unified Romania. In Spain such alternation is occasionally found as an artistic device in sonnets by Lope and Góngora. From about 1300 on, Romania differentiates more and more in language and culture. Yet the Romance nations remain connected through their historical development and their still living relation to Latin. In this looser

---

[35] Thus in a fifteenth-century example cited in Grimm's dictionary: "Ex lectione quorundam romanticorum, id est librorum compositorum in gallico sermone poeticorum de gestis militaribus quorum maxima pars fabulosa est."

[36] We owe the fundamental research into the word "romantic" to the Rousseau scholar Alexis François: in *Annales Jean-Jacques Rousseau*, V (1909), 237 ff. and in *Mélanges Baldensperger*, I (1930), 321.

[37] In French the corresponding word is "romanesque."

[38] Similar compositions are listed by V. Crescini, *Románica Fragmenta* (1932), 523.

sense one can continue to speak of a Romania which constitutes a unity in opposition to the Germanic peoples and literatures.

The oldest surviving specimen of a Romance language is the Strasbourg Oaths of 842, but it is a document, not a work of literature. The chain of French literature begins only with the eleventh century.[39] Spanish literature begins at the end of the twelfth century;[40] Italian not until about 1220, with St. Francis' *Hymn to the Sun* and the Sicilian art lyric. The late start of Spain and Italy is to be explained by the predominant position of France; the early appearance of Germanic literary works (in England about 700, in Germany about 750), on the other hand, by the intrinsic foreignness of "Germanic" in comparison with Romance. The Strassburg Oaths illustrate my meaning. In the Romance version they begin: "Pro deo amor et christian poblo et nostro comun salvament." That is still very close to Latin. Compare the Old High German: "In godes minna ind in thes christianes folches ind unser bedhero gehaltnissi . . ." That is an entirely different linguistic world. The Romanian could still get along for a considerable time with a more or less barbarized Latin, could start from there to acquire correct Latin. The Germanic has to learn Latin from the ground up—and he learns it very well. An amazingly pure Latin is written in England about 700, at a time when corruption is the rule in France. But even highly educated Italians could overlook grammatical blunders which set German monks laughing. The experience befell Gunzo of Novara, who came to Germany in 965 in the retinue of Otto I, and who used a wrong case in conversation with monks at St. Gall. He justified himself in a letter, in which he says that he was wrongly accused of grammatical ignorance, "although I am often handicapped by the use of our popular language, which is close to Latin."

The closeness of the vulgar languages to Latin subsists throughout the entire history of Romance. It is manifested in many different ways. All Romance languages in all periods can borrow from Latin. The old French *Song of Roland* (*ca.* 1100) begins:

Carles li reis, nostre emperere magnes.[41]

Now the word *magnus* had already been displaced in late Latin by *grandis*, and in the Romance languages only *grandis* lives on—with the single exception of *Charlemagne*.[42] Hence philologists explain that *magnes* in the line quoted is a "Latinism." They merely forget that all the great literary monuments of the Romance languages are riddled with Latinisms and indeed employ them consciously, as a rhetorical ornament. An outstanding example of this is Dante's *Commedia*. There—as one example among hundreds—we find the Latin *vir* (man) as *viro*, because Dante needed a rhyme in *-iro*. But when French in the twentieth century, need-

---

[39] The *Song of St. Eulalia* (end of 9th cent.) is without parallels and without successors.

[40] See *infra*, p. 386, n. 14a.   [41] "Charles the King, our great Emperor."

[42] The Spanish *tamaño* has no congeners.

ing a word for "flying machine," forms *avion* (from Lat. *avis* "bird"), the same process is exemplified. Borrowings from Latin in Romance languages do not give the impression of being "foreign words" as they do in German. Latin remains the common and inexhaustible reserve for all Romance languages.

The Romance literatures hold the lead in the West from the Crusades to the French Revolution, one succeeding another. Only from within Romania does one obtain a true picture of the course of modern literature. From 1100 to 1275—from the *Song of Roland* to *The Romance of the Rose* —French literature and intellectual culture are the model for the other nations. Middle High German literature takes over almost all the themes of French poetry, and even the *Nibelungenlied* turns out, according to Friedrich Panzer's researches,[43] to be partly derived from French sources. The courtly culture of France radiates to Norway and across the Pyrenees. *The Romance of the Rose* is adapted in Italy even in Dante's time, as it is later by Chaucer in England. French epic and romance literature flows in a full stream into Italy, to be reshaped by Boiardo and Ariosto in the brilliant art forms of the Renaissance. But the literary primacy had passed to Italy from 1300 onwards: Dante, Petrarch, the High Renaissance. This reacted upon France, England, Spain, as "Italianism." [44] With the beginning of the sixteenth century, Spain's "golden age" commences, in turn, to dominate European literature for more than a century. A knowledge of Spanish and of Spanish literature is as important for a "European" literary historiography as is a knowledge of Spanish painting for art history. It is not until the beginning of the seventeenth century that France finally emancipates herself from Italian and Spanish domination, whereupon she assumes a primacy which remains unshaken until about 1780. Meanwhile, since 1590 England has developed a great literature of her own, which however receives scant attention on the Continent until the eighteenth century. Germany was never able to compete with the literary world-powers of Romania. Her hour does not come until the Age of Goethe. Until then, though she receives influences from without, she radiates none.

England's relation to Romania is of a special kind. England was a part of the Empire for barely four hundred years. The Roman troops withdrew in 410, but Augustine's mission (from 597) meant a second Romanization or, as an English historian expresses it, "the return of Britain to Europe and to her past." [45] Roman monuments survived the Germanic immigrations. They stimulated the Northumbrian sculpture of the seventh century and were pointed out with pride.[46] Through the Norman conquest and her

---

[43] *Studien zum Nibelungenliede* (Frankfurt a. M., 1945).

[44] The concept that Spain, France, Germany, and so on, experienced "Renaissances" is to be rejected. It is true, however, that these countries had one or more waves of "Italianism"—which was the export form of the Italian Renaissance.

[45] C. Dawson, *The Making of Europe* (1929), 209.

[46] F. Saxl in *Journal of the Warburg and Courtauld Institutes*, VI (1943), 18 and n. 4.—For cultural relations between England and Italy in the seventh century, cf. W. Levison, *England and the Continent in the Eighth Century* (1946), 142.

Angevin kings, England was for centuries an annex to French culture. French was the language of literature and government, Latin that of higher education. Paris is the literary capital of England. Englishmen and Welshmen performed brilliantly in the Latin Renaissance of the twelfth century. It was not until 1340 that Englishmen of French and Saxon descent were put on a footing of legal equality.[47] It was only during the course of the fourteenth century that the two races and languages were fused into unity. To this century belongs Chaucer, the first representative English poet. France and Italy provide the matter of his poetry. He dies in 1400. A year earlier, English, which had been the language of school instruction from 1350, and the language of law from 1362, was for the first time used by a King in Parliament. Medieval England belongs to Romania. But "at the Reformation the English, grown to manhood, dismissed their Latin tutors, without reacting into close contact with the Scandinavian and Teuton world. Britain had become a world by itself." [48]

The English language is a Germanic dialect transformed by Romance and Latin. English national characteristics and forms of life are neither Romance nor Germanic—they are English. They represent a happy blend of social conformity and personal nonconformity, such as no other people has produced. The relation of England to Romania—which means to the European tradition—is a problem which keeps reappearing in English literature. In the eighteenth century (Pope, Gibbon) the Latin cultures exercise a strong attraction, in the nineteenth, Germany. In the twentieth century all phases of the Roman tradition are again emphasized—an interesting phenomenon, which we can here only touch upon. G. K. Chesterton and Hilaire Belloc ardently sounded the call to battle. Of greater importance is the literary criticism and literary policy that T. S. Eliot has represented since 1920: "Three or four great novelists do not make a literature, though *War and Peace* is a very great novel indeed. If everything derived from Rome were withdrawn—everything we have from Norman-French society, from the Church, from Humanism, from every channel direct and indirect, what would be left? A few Teutonic roots and husks. England is a 'Latin' country, and we ought not to have to go to France for our Latinity." [49]

Through Romania and its influences the West received its Latin schooling. The forms and the fruits of that schooling are now to be considered. That is, we must now proceed from generalities to the concrete wealth of the substance of history. We must now go into details. But, as Aby Warburg used to say to his students, "God is in detail."

[47] J. J. Jusserand, A *Literary History of the English People*, I (1895), 236.
[48] G. M. Trevelyan, *History of England* (1947), xxi.
[49] *The Criterion* (Oct., 1923), 104.

3

Literature and Education

L ITERATURE FORMS a part of "education." Why and since when? Because the Greeks found their past, their essential nature, and their
world of deities ideally reflected in a poet. They had no priestly
books and no priestly caste. Homer, for them, was the "tradition." From
the sixth century onwards he was a schoolbook. Since that time literature
has been a school subject, and the continuity of European literature is
bound up with the schools. Education becomes the medium of the literary
tradition: a fact which is characteristic of Europe, but which is not necessarily so in the nature of things. The dignity, the independence, and the
pedagogical function of poetry owe their existence to Homer and his influence. It could quite well have been otherwise. In Judaism the pupil
learns the "Law"; and the Mosaic books are not a poem. But what the
Greeks had done, the Romans imitated. Roman poetry begins with Livius
Andronicus (second half of the third century). He translates the *Odyssey*
for schools. His contemporaries, Naevius and Ennius, write national epics
which could fill the place of the *Iliad*. But Virgil was the first to compose
a universally valid Roman national epic. Its point of departure, both in
matter and form, was Homer. It became a schoolbook. The Middle Ages
took over from Antiquity the traditional connection between epic and
school. It retained the *Aeneid*, and put beside it Biblical epics which superficially imitated Virgil but which could not supplant him. To read them is
torture. Virgil remained the backbone of Latin studies. Later, the classics
of the modern nations became school reading, even though they might be
as little suitable for the purpose as Shakespeare or Goethe's *Faust*. Literary
historiography must include an elementary knowledge of European education.

1. *The Liberal Arts*

The basic characteristics of the medieval educational system go back to
ancient Greece. The sophist Hippias of Elis, a contemporary of Socrates,
was regarded by Antiquity as the originator of the pedagogical system based

upon the liberal arts. In Greek it is called ἐγκύκλιος παιδεία, which means "the customary, ordinary education." [1] Plato, we know, wanted philosophy alone to serve as the means of education. He not only fought against Homer, and drove the poets from his state, but also rejected "general education." The dictatorial claim which is inherent in every philosophy has never been so passionately and bluntly asserted as it was by the greatest of Greek thinkers. But his pedagogics suffered the same shipwreck as his politics. His contemporary, the orator Isocrates, intervened in the conflict between philosophy and general education, recognizing that both educational forces were justified. He disposed them in a hierarchy: the subjects of general education were to serve as a preparation (propaedeutics) for philosophy. Despite sporadic theoretical opposition, Isocrates' standpoint remained authoritative in practice for the whole of Antiquity. Seneca's Epistle 88 is a *locus classicus* for the system; it treats of the "artes liberales" and the "studia liberalia." These are the studies whose purpose is not to make money. They are called "liberal" because they are worthy of a free man. Hence painting, sculpture, and other manual arts ("artes mechanicae") are excluded,[2] while music, as a mathematical subject, has a stable place in the circle of the liberal arts. In late Antiquity the assumption that the liberal arts represented the propaedeutics of philosophy (an assumption which Seneca could still share) became untenable. Philosophy ceased to be a systematic discipline and an educational force. This means that at the end of Antiquity the liberal arts survived as the only fund of learning. Meanwhile their number had been fixed at seven, and they had been arranged in the sequence which they were to retain throughout the Middle Ages: grammar, rhetoric, dialectic, arithmetic, geometry, music, astronomy. The later Middle Ages put the functions of the *artes* into mnemonic verse, their sequence suffering in the process from the requirements of meter:

> *Gram. loquitur; Dia. vera docet; Rhe. verba ministrat;*
> *Mus. canit; Ar. numerat; Geo. ponderat; As. colit astra.*

The four last (mathematical) *artes* were taken collectively by Boethius as the "quadruvium" (four roads), the three first, from the ninth century onwards, as the "trivium" [3] (three roads). The concept *ars* must be rigorously distinguished from "art" in the modern sense. It means "branch of learning"—that is, "-logy," as that suffix is used in such words as "the-

---

[1] See H. I. Marrou, *Histoire de l'éducation dans l'antiquité* (1948).

[2] It was in quattrocento Florence that artists awoke to self-consciousness. They no longer wished to be confused with artisans. This gave rise to an extensive art-historical literature, which continued into the seventeenth century. Cf. Excursus XIII *infra*.—The Italian "meccanico" acquires the meaning "uneducated, crude"; "la turba meccanica" is "the common herd."

[3] Pio Rajna in *Studi medievali*, I (1928), 4–36.—For *quadruvium*, the form *quadrivium* is later more common.

ology." Antique etymology connected the word with *artus* "strait"; the *artes* enclose all things in "strait" rules.[4]

The description of the liberal arts which remained authoritative throughout the Middle Ages had been produced by Martianus Capella, who wrote between 410 and 439. Notker Labeo (d. 1022) translated it into Old High German; the young Hugo Grotius won his spurs with a new edition (1599); and Leibniz, even in his day, planned another.[5] Traces of Martianus are still to be found in the pageantry of the late sixteenth century.[6] Martianus dressed his work up as a romance, which accounts for its title, *De nuptiis Philologiae et Mercurii* ("The Wedding of Philology and Mercury"). In form it is a mixture of prose and intercalated verse, but by far the greater part of it is prose. It is a big book, filling over five hundred pages of print, and the modern reader finds it insipid. We must, however, glance at it. The first two books are devoted to the action of the romance.[7] Its figures and themes are frequently revived during the Middle Ages, especially in the twelfth-century philosophical epic. The work opens with a poem to Hymen, who is addressed not only as a conciliator of the elements and the sexes in the service of Natura but also as the matchmaker among the gods. Of these, Mercury is yet unmarried. On the advice of Virtus, he consults Apollo. Apollo proposes the learned maiden Philologia who, being well versed not only in the lore of Parnassus but also in the secrets of the starry heavens and the underworld, embraces all knowledge. Virtus, Mercury, and Apollo, escorted by the Muses, mount through the celestial spheres to Jupiter's palace. An assembly of the gods, which also includes allegorical figures, sanctions Mercury's wish and decides that Philologia shall be admitted to the ranks of the gods, as, henceforth, shall all deserving mortals (ed. Dick, 40, 20 ff.).[8] Philologia is adorned by her mother Phronesis (47, 21) and greeted by the four Cardinal Virtues and the three Graces. At the bidding of Athanasia, she is forced to vomit up a number of books (59, 5), in order to become worthy of immortality. She then ascends to heaven in a litter borne by the youths Labor and Amor and the maidens Epimelia (application) and Agrypnia (the intellectual worker's night labors and curtailed sleep). In heaven Juno, as the patroness of marriage, comes to meet her and instructs her concerning the inhabitants of Olympus, who, however, are very different from those of the Greek Olympus. Not only all sorts of demons and demigods, but also the antique poets and philosophers (78,

---

[4] Servius in Keil, IV, 405, 3 f.—Similarly Cassiodorus (ed. Mynors), 91, 12, and Isidore *Et.*, I, 1, 2.

[5] Pierre Daniel Huet (1630–1721), later bishop of Avranches, was in 1670 appointed assistant to Bossuet, who was then tutor to the Dauphin. One of his duties was supervising the edition of the Latin classics for the Dauphin's use ("ad usum Delphini"). He entrusted the edition of Martianus Capella to Leibniz, who wanted to "restore him to honor" (G. Hess, *Leibniz korrespondiert mit Paris* [1940], 22). —Martianus Capella appeared in eight editions between 1499 and 1599.

[6] A. Warburg, *Gesammelte Schriften* (1932), I, 264, n. 3.

[7] His model is Apuleius, *Met.*, VI, 23 ff. (marriage of Cupid and Psyche, sanctioned by an assembly of the gods, etc.).

[8] So Psyche too was granted immortality, Apul., *Met.* (ed. Helm), 146, 9 ff.

9 ff.), are included. As her wedding present the bride receives the seven liberal arts. To each of them Capella devotes one book of his work. In accordance with the taste of the period, they are personified as women, and distinguished by their clothing, implements, and the manner in which their hair is worn. Thus, Grammar appears as a gray-haired woman of advanced age, who boasts that she descends from the Egyptian king Osiris. Later she lived for a long time in Attica, but now she appears in Roman dress. She carries an ebony casket, containing a knife and a file with which to operate surgically on children's grammatical errors. Rhetoric is a magnificently tall and beautiful woman, wearing a dress decorated with all the figures of speech and carrying weapons with which she wounds her adversaries, and so on. These allegorical figures, with their attributes, were represented again and again in medieval art and poetry.[9] They appear on the façades of the cathedrals of Chartres and Laon, in Auxerre, in Notre-Dame de Paris; they survived even into the Renaissance to appear in the work of Botticelli.[10] What the Middle Ages enjoyed in the *Nuptiae* was not only its erudite content but also its rich use of allegorical figures, such as the contemporary Prudentius, writing from the Christian standpoint, introduced into his *Psychomachia*, and finally the theme of a journey to heaven.

2.   *The Concept of the* Artes *in the Middle Ages* [11]

In medieval pedagogy we can distinguish two theories on the subject of the *artes:* the patristic and the secular-scholastic. Naturally, they are in constant contact, but they differ in origin. Alexandrian Judaism, whose most influential representative was Philo (died probably during the reign of Claudius), had already annexed Greek learning and philosophy, though, to be sure, it transformed the Hellenic sages into pupils of Moses. The Christian apologists of the second century, especially Justin, took over this concept and bequeathed it to the great theologists of the Alexandrian school. Clement of Alexandria (*ca.* 150 to *ca.* 215) draws the conclusion that Greek learning was established by God: the Christian teacher needed it in order to understand the Scriptures. The Latin Fathers were divided on the subject. Ambrose of Milan (333–397) knows Greek philosophy but opposes it. Jerome (*ca.* 340 to *ca.* 420), on the other hand—the "Christian Aristarchus" (Ludwig Traube), of whom, in later times, Erasmus was to be a fervid admirer—was a Humanist, a philologist, and a Doctor of

---

[9] Poems on the subject of the *artes*, mostly connected with the *Nuptiae: Poetae,* I, 408–10; *ibid.,* 544 and 629 ff.; *Poetae,* III, 247, 149 ff.; IV, 399 ff.—*Carmina Cant.,* pp. 113 f.; Godfrey of Breteuil, *Fons philosophiae;* Stephen of Tournai's *rhythmus;* Walter of Châtillon (1929), 41 ff.; Neckham, *De naturis rerum* (ed. Wright), 498, etc.

[10] E. Mâle, *L'Art religieux du 13ᵉ siècle en France,* 76 ff.—Botticelli: Villa Lemmi frescoes in the Louvre.—Later representations: *Journal of the Warburg Institute,* II (1938–39), 82.

[11] Cf. also R. W. Hunt, *The Introduction of the "Artes" in the Twelfth Century* (in *Studi Mediaevalia* [Bruges, 1948], 85 f.).

the Church in one. As a boy in Rome he enjoyed the advantage of the instruction of Aelius Donatus, the grammarian and commentator on Terence. He is familiar with Plautus, Terence, Lucretius, Cicero, Sallust, Virgil, Horace, Persius, Lucan. As an old man he still remembers what pains it cost him to learn Hebrew, after he had become accustomed to "Quintilian's keenness of intellect, Cicero's flowing discourse (*Ciceronis fluvios*), Fronto's dignity, and Pliny's smoothness" (*Epistulae* [ed. Hilberg], III, 131, 13 f.). In his commentary on Jeremiah he quotes Lucretius and Persius; refers to the Sirens, Scylla, and the Lernean Hydra; compares the rhetorical figures of the prophets with Virgil's hyperboles, apostrophes, and so on. His celebrated epistle to Paulinus of Nola presents a brief but meaty discussion of the theme "Sanctity and Education." How could the Bible be understood without scholarly erudition? His 70th epistle, addressed to Magnus, is of more basic importance. Magnus had asked Jerome why he sometimes cited examples from secular literature. Jerome's answer provides an arsenal of arguments which were repeated not only throughout the Middle Ages but also in the age of Italian Humanism: Solomon (Prov. 1:1 ff.) commends the study of philosophy; Paul quotes verses by Epimenides, Menander, and Aratus. Finally, by the allegorical interpretation of a Scripture text, Jerome furnished the Middle Ages with an oft-repeated argument for utilizing antique learning in the service of Christianity. In Deuteronomy 21:12 Yahweh commands: If a Hebrew desires to marry a heathen slave, he shall cut her hair and her nails. In like manner the Christian who loves secular learning shall purify it from all errors. Then it is worthy to serve God. A philosophical theory of the *artes* is not to be sought in Jerome.

The case is different with Augustine. It is true that the relation between *scientia* and *sapientia*, to which he devoted profound research, never became clearly formulated in his writing, yet many of his trains of thought and many of his coinages became authoritative for the Middle Ages. An example is his allegorical exposition of Exodus 3:22 and 12:35. When they went out of Egypt the Israelites took gold and silver vessels with them; thus the Christian must rid pagan learning of what is superfluous and pernicious, that he may then place it in the service of truth. Of more importance for the early Middle Ages than Augustine's thought in general was his discussion of the study of the Bible in *De doctrina christiana*. A few key statements must be quoted: "Sciant autem litterati modis omnibus locutionis, quos grammatici graeco nomine tropos vocant, auctores nostros usos fuisse" [12] (III, 29). Later (IV, 6, 9–7, 21) Augustine explains that the Bible is nowise inferior to pagan writings in literary art. Its words are "divina mente fusa et sapienter et eloquenter. Quid mirum si et in istis inveniuntur, quos ille misit qui facit ingenia?" [13] (7, 21). These ideas could be inter-

[12] "Let all versed in letters know that our authors [i.e., the Biblical writers] have used all the figures of speech to which the grammarians have given the Greek name *tropi* [figurative locutions]."
[13] "brought forth by the divine mind with wisdom and eloquence. What wonder if these excellencies are found in those whom the Creator of intelligences did send?"

preted as legitimizing the antique *artes*. At the same time they contained the suggestion that the *artes* proceeded from God.

Cassiodorus was of even greater importance for the evaluation of the *artes*. In his *Institutiones divinarum et saecularium litteratum* he produced the first Christian handbook of ecclesiastical learning and the secular *artes*. The tradition of the Greek monasteries and of the Christian-Oriental universities or "catechumenical schools" (Alexandria, Edessa, Nisibis) is influential in it. This is also manifest in his concept of the *artes*, which goes back to Clement, Justin, and Alexandrian Judaism. He teaches that the seeds of the *artes* were planted from the beginning of time in the wisdom of God and in Holy Scripture; the teachers of the secular disciplines had received them thence and had reduced them to their own systems of rules, as he had shown in his explanation of the Psalms (ed. Mynors, 6, 18 ff.). And in fact Cassiodorus points out in his commentary that the Psalmist used a large number of grammatical and rhetorical figures which were current in the schools of Antiquity. He foresees the objection that "the members of syllogisms, the names of the schemata [figures of speech], the terminologies of the disciplines" are never mentioned in the sacred text. His answer runs: All these are nevertheless implicitly present in the Psalms, just as wine is implicitly present in the grape, and the tree in the seed. It is incumbent upon sacred learning to point out this circumstance through rhetorical analysis of the Biblical text. But the divine law has, we know, been spread through all the world. How do we know it? From the verse in the Psalms, "in omnem terram exivit sonus eorum" (Vulg. Ps. 18:5): "their sound went out over all the earth." In the Authorized Version this is Psalm 19, beginning: "The heavens declare the glory of God . . . There is no speech nor language, where their voice is not heard." And now verse 4: ". . . their words are gone out to the end of the world." The reference is to the speech of the heavens, which declare the glory of God throughout the world. But Cassiodorus reads the words of the Psalm allegorically as meaning that the Old Testament was known to all peoples. Thus the pagans could learn all the arts of rhetoric and reduce them to a system (*PL*, LXX, 19–21).

Beside the patristic theory of the *artes* runs a secular one; the latter, however, is not homogeneous and has many points of contact with the former. As to the origin of the *artes* opinions differ: Jupiter invented them —or perhaps Egypt, since Moses was a pupil of the Egyptians (Acts 7:22), or perhaps Chaldea.[14] But the *artes* were also frequently equated with the seven pillars of wisdom.[15] An important twelfth-century thinker sees the origin of all the *artes* in Nature.[16] The last great presentation of the *artes*

[14] Jupiter: e.g., Godfrey of Viterbo, *Speculum regum* (ed. Waitz), p. 38, 19 ff. —"Aegyptus parturit artes," Bernard Silvestris (ed. Barach), p. 16; Neckham (ed. Wright), p. 308–11; Henri d'Andeli, *La bataille des set ars*, I, 407.

[15] Seven pillars: *Poetae*, III, 439, 26 and 552, 74.—Christ as bestower of the arts: *Poetae*, III, 738, 8 f.

[16] John of Salisbury, *Metalogicon* (ed. Webb), 27, 29 ff.

before the influx of Aristotelianism is the unprinted *Heptateuchon* of
Thierry of Chartres (d. between 1148 and 1153).[17] He intended it to be
a compendium of all philosophy: "totius philosophiae unicum ac singu-
lare instrumentum."

For the Middle Ages up to the twelfth century, the *artes* are the basic
schema of the world of thought. Only the central event of the historical
process of salvation, the Incarnation, could and indeed must overthrow it
and pass beyond it. When the Creator became a creature ("factor factus
est factura"),[18] all the *artes* were invalidated: "in hac verbi copula stupet
omnis regula." [19] Mary is at once mother and virgin. "Thus in her concur
two designations which elsewhere conflict, . . . Here Nature falls silent,
Logic is conquered, Rhetoric and Reason fail. She, the daughter, has conceived the Father, has borne Him as her Son":

> *Nata patrem natumque parens concepit . . .*[20]

Dante put these paradoxes of the Incarnation into the mouth of St. Bernard
at the end of the *Paradiso* (XXXIII, 1):

> *Vergine madre, figlia del tuo figlio.*

3. *Grammar*

The first of the seven *artes* is grammar: "la prima arte" (Dante, *Par.*, 12.
138). The word comes from the Greek *gramma*, "letter." Even in the time
of Plato and Aristotle this "skill in letters" was still no more than the art
of reading and writing. In Hellenistic times exegesis of the poets was
added, so that Quintilian (I, 4, 2) divides grammar into two parts: "recte
loquendi scientiam et poetarum enarrationem" ("the science of correct
speech and the interpretation of the poets"). As a translation for *gram-
matice* the word *litteratura* was used (Quintilian, II, 1, 4), derived from
littera as grammar from *gramma*. Thus *litteratura* does not at first mean
literature in our sense; the *litteratus* is one who knows grammar and poetry
(as the *lettré* still is in France), but is not necessarily a writer. The German
word *Literat* (hack writer), now so debased, thus originally had a good
meaning. The broadening of the concept grammar made it easy to blur
or to cross the line between grammar and rhetoric, a state of affairs that
Quintilian already censures.

Of the seven *artes*, those of the *trivium* were far more thoroughly cultivated than those of the *quadrivium*, and grammar the most exhaustively

---

[17] Clerval, *L'enseignement des arts libéraux à Chartres et à Paris dans la première
moitié du 12ᵉ siècle d'après l'Heptateuchon de Thierry de Chartres (Congrès scien-
tifique international des catholiques tenu à Paris du 8 au 13 avril 1888*, Paris [1889],
II, 277 ff.).—Adolf Hofmeister, NA, XXXVII (1912), 666 ff.
[18] Walter of Châtillon (1925), p. 7, st. 4.
[19] Refrain in *A.h.*, XX, 42. The same thought, *ibid.*, 43 f. in No. 11, and p. 106,
No. 124.
[20] Alan, *Anticlaudianus*, SP, II, 362.

of all. It was, indeed, the foundation for everything else. The unequal estimation accorded to the seven *artes* is already apparent in Isidore's encyclopedia. There an entire book (58 printed pages) is devoted to grammar,
rhetoric receives 20 pages, dialectic 21, arithmetic 10, geometry 8, music 6,
astronomy 17.[21]

The medieval student of Latin was to be taught not only to read the
language of Rome but also to master speaking and writing it. Instruction
in grammar had, therefore, to be much more thorough than in a nineteenth-
century German preparatory school. The beginner had to learn Donatus'
ars minor by heart. It provides, in the form of questions and answers, a
knowledge of the eight parts of speech, and comprises ten printed pages.
From this the student proceeded to the same author's *ars maior* and to
Priscian's *Institutio grammatica*.[22] This work, composed in Byzantium at
the beginning of the sixth century (two portly volumes in the modern edition) is the most copious treatment of the subject in general. Since it cites
numerous examples from classical authors it also provides a grounding in
literature. New grammars, systematizing the material logically and specu-
latively, were not undertaken until about 1200: the *Doctrinale* of Alexander
of Villedieu (1199) and the *Grecismus* of Eberhard of Béthune (d. 1212).
This new presentation of grammar is connected with an intellectual change
which we shall touch upon later. With Donatus and Priscian the grammatical chapters in Quintilian's *Institutio oratoria* were of course read. We
are indebted to John of Salisbury for a description of the teaching of grammar at Chartres in the twelfth century (*Metalogicon* [ed. Webb], 53–59).

In medieval grammar there is a series of concepts which no longer figure
in our grammars but which originated in Antiquity. Early Roman grammar
had itself been shaped by the philology of the Greek Stoa. Not only concepts such as analogy, etymology, barbarism, solecism, metaplasm, but also
the entire method of presentation, proceeding from letters and syllables to
the parts of speech, are Greek in origin. Together with the examples, they
were retained by all Roman grammarians down to Donatus and Priscian.
I illustrate this by the summary that Isidore gives in Book I of his *Etymologiae*. He regards etymology as a part of grammar. "For if you know the
origin of a word, you more quickly understand its force. Everything can be
more clearly comprehended when its etymology is known." Since, however,

---

[21] Pages according to W. M. Lindsay's edition (Oxford, 1911).

[22] Among the blessed in the Heaven of the Sun in Dante (*Par.*, XII, 137 f.) appears "quel Donato ch' alla prim' arte degnò por la mano." Priscian, on the other
hand, is consigned to Hell for sodomy (*Inf.*, XV, 109). This goes back to a medieval
legend about Priscian which has not been thoroughly elucidated. Alan (*SP*, II, 309)
calls him an apostate; his writings contain errors, he would seem to be drunk or
mad. Hugh of Trimberg (*Registrum multorum auctorum* [ed. Langosch], l. 195)
refers to Alan, but counts Priscian among the greatest scholars (l. 244). Marie de
France invokes Priscian in the prologue to her *Lais*. Shakespeare too mentions him
(*Love's Labour's Lost*, V, 1). The report of Priscian's apostasy goes back to the
fact that he dedicated his *Institutio grammatica* to the *patricius* Julianus. Conrad
of Hirsau still understood this correctly (ed. Schepss, 48, 25). But later writers
confused the dedicatee with Julian the Apostate.

all things are not named in accordance with their "nature," and many, indeed, entirely arbitrarily, not all words can be etymologized. In etymological investigations three principles are to be observed: "ex causa" (*rex* comes from *regere* and *recte agere*); "ex origine" (man is named *homo*, because he is made of *humus*); "ex contrariis" [23]—and here we find the still familiar *lucus a non lucendo* (Isidore puts it less pointedly: "quia umbra opacus parum luceat"). Grammar also taught synonyms—in Latin, "de differentiis." Isidore devoted a separate work to this branch (*PL*, LXXXIII, 9 ff.).

Barbarisms is the name for errors in vocabulary and pronunciation brought in by barbarians. Solecism (for which the inhabitants of Soloi in Cilicia were made responsible, and which survives in English "solecism" and French "solécisme" [24]) consists in errors of construction, as for example *inter nobis* instead of *inter nos*. Metaplasm is a deviation from the grammatical norm which is permitted to poets in consideration of the demands of meter: "licentia poetarum" (Isidore, *Et.*, I, 35, 1)—it is thus a special case of the "poetic freedom" which is frequently discussed by antique authors. Finally, the so-called "figures of speech" were reckoned a part of grammar.

These were so important to the Middle Ages, and are so forgotten today, that we must discuss them more fully. Examples: "Not few" (instead of "many") is a litotes. "To win laurels" (instead of "fame") is a metonymy. If I say "Admission one dollar per head" (instead of "per person") I am using a synecdoche. In Greek such forms of expression are called *schemata*, "attitudes," in Latin *figurae*. Quintilian (II, 13, 9) elucidates this as follows: an erect human body, with hanging arms and eyes looking straight forward, has little grace. But life and art, through the most various attitudes, produce an aesthetic impression (Myron's *Discobolus*). Discourse does the same thing by means of the figures. They are conventionally divided into figures of language and figures of thought. An example of a figure of language is anaphora, that is, the repetition of the same word or words at the beginning of successive clauses. For example:

> *Sei mir gegrüsst, mein Berg mit dem rötlich strahlenden Gipfel!*
> *Sei mir, Sonne, gegrüsst, die ihn so lieblich bescheint!*
> (Schiller, *Spaziergang*)*

Another figure of language is homoioteleuton (similarity of endings, for example in Cicero's famous sentence on Catiline: "Abiit, abscessit, evasit, erupit"). Figures of thought are litotes, metonymy, allegory, and many

---

[23] This principle too goes back through Varro to the Stoa.
[24] Boileau (*Art poétique*, I, 20):

> *Mon esprit n'admet point un pompeux barbarisme,*
> *Ni d'un vers ampoulé l'orgueilleux solécisme.*

[* Or:

> *Another year! another deadly blow!*
> *Another mighty Empire overthrown!*
> (Wordsworth, "November 1806")]

others. The study of figures has never been satisfactorily systematized. Besides figures of language and thought, grammatical figures (that is, figures occurring in the exegesis of the poets) and rhetorical figures have been distinguished. Furthermore, antique and later textbooks commonly call many figures of speech *tropoi* ("turns"), *tropi*. This lack of a settled terminology, and, in short, the endless variations in enumerating and defining the figures, are to be explained historically by contacts between various schools. Grammar in the Middle Ages also included metrics—logically enough, since the exegesis of poets was in the hands of grammarians. Poetry was assigned sometimes to grammar, sometimes to rhetoric. In a poem by Stephen of Tournai (d. 1203), which describes the education of a boy, Poetry is ushered in by Grammar (ll. 113 ff.):

> *Venit ad Grammatice Poesis hortatum*
> *Ut, quem primum fecerat illa litteratum,*
> *Hec, novem Pyeridum trahens comitatum*
> *Prosa, rithmo, versibus faciat ornatum.*[25]

Walter of Châtillon likewise considers poetry a part of grammar:

> *Inter artes igitur, que dicuntur trivium,*
> *Fundatrix grammatica vendicat principium.*
> *Sub hac chorus militat metrice scribentium.*[26]

4. Anglo-Saxon and Carolingian Studies

It was not without difficulty that a knowledge of grammar was preserved through the "Dark Ages." Under the Merovingians speech and grammar degenerated increasingly after 600. Under the Carolingians their cultivation was undertaken by the Latin-Anglo-Saxon culture. This culture continued to build on the foundations laid down by Isidore and the Irish, but it also underwent influences from Italy and Gaul.[27] Its founder was Aldhelm (639–709). At the time of his middle life the English church had reached the cultural level of Celtic Christendom and had rejected the Celtic church's political claims in favor of Rome (Synod of Whitby, 664). Both in letters and in her church Ireland had gone her own way. She cultivated a fantastic and abstruse Latinity with artistic self-complacency. Aldhelm too had learned this mannered and frequently incomprehensible jargon, and used it from time to time—but only to show that England was a match for the Irish and Scottish scholars even in that which was their particular pride and boast.[28] In another letter (Ehwald, 479) he warns against the

[25] "Exhorted by Grammar, Poetry approaches, escorted by the nine Muses, in order that he whom the former had made literate, the latter may equip with poetical technique."

[26] "Among the *artes* which are called the *trivium*, grammar takes precedence as the first foundation. Under her serves the troop of those who write in verse."

[27] Wilhelm Levison's *England and the Continent in the Eighth Century* (Oxford, 1946) is an authoritative presentation. See especially ch. 6.

[28] Aldhelm (ed. Ehwald), p. 478 (Epistle to Ehfried).

studies cultivated in Ireland because they granted a place to profane Antiquity (philosophy and mythology). Aldhelm sternly forbids anything of
the sort. His position in regard to classical studies is clear-cut: They may be
cultivated only as formal disciplines (grammar, metrics); and that for but
one reason, a reason which makes their cultivation indispensable—the language of the Bible is "almost entirely" an artistic language, governed by
grammar (the term also, of course, including poetics). This, then, is the
old theory (familiar to us from Jerome, Augustine, Cassiodorus, and Isidore) of the necessity of the *artes* for a comprehension of the Bible—but
with the difference that Aldhelm forbids the *auctores*, that is, the study of
antique culture for its own sake. He encourages classical education in its
purely formal sense, and thus reveals himself as the representative of an
ecclesiastical rigorism. The feeling for classical Latin had already been lost
to the Irish, and it was lost to their pupil Aldhelm. But he found a new
authority for style and composition in the Vulgate. To be sure, Jerome,
Augustine, Cassiodorus, and Isidore had already drawn attention to literary
resemblances between the Bible and pagan writing. But these men were
still too close to antique literary culture not to be aware of the gulf between
its standards and the language of the Latin Bible.[29] In the preface to his
universal chronicle, Jerome had said: "Holy Scripture is like a beautiful
body concealed by a dirty gown. The Psalms are as well-sounding as the
songs of Pindar and Horace. The writings of Solomon have dignity ["gravitas"], the book of Job is perfect. All these books are composed in hexameters and pentameters in the Hebrew original. But we read them in prose!
Consider how much Homer would lose in prose!" (*PL*, 27, 223–24). In his
letter to Paulinus, Jerome excused the "simplicitas et quaedam vilitas verborum" ("simple and occasionally crude expressions") of the Bible. Cassiodorus (*Inst.*, I, 15) had given a list of linguistic offenses in the sacred
text. Isidore had unhesitatingly stigmatized "Vivat Ruben et non moriatur"
(Deut. 33:6) as *perissologia* (prolixity), and had praised the use of antithesis in Ecclesiasticus (33:15), but otherwise had scarcely cited Biblical
texts in discussing rhetoric. He speaks (*Sent.*, 3, 16) of the "unornamented
words" and "low style" of the Bible and thus concurs in Jerome's estimate
of Biblical Latin. This denigration of the language of the Bible, which we
still find in Visigothic-Roman Spain, could have had no force in "barbarian"
countries, which had never belonged to the Empire and had first learned
Latin from the church. This was the case with Ireland, and with the Iro-
Scottish culture which spread into Britain. And it is also true of the Anglo-
Saxon Christian culture represented by Aldhelm.

Aldhelm was the precursor and was soon forgotten. Plenitude of accomplishment was reserved for the Venerable Bede (672–735), who, as a
Northumbrian monk, devoted his entire life to learning. He gained enduring fame by his history of the Anglo-Saxon church. In connection with our
subject, however, he is of greater importance because he carried to its logi-

<hr/>

[29] W. Süss, "Das Problem der Bibelsprache" (*Historische Vierteljahrsschrift*
[1932], 1 ff.).

cal conclusion the transference of antique rhetoric to the text of the Bible, for which, as we have seen, Augustine and Cassiodorus prepared the way. He was able to do so because, for him as for Aldhelm, the grammatico-aesthetic objections to Bible Latin had lost their validity. In this sense Bede's little treatise *De schematis et tropibus* represents the end of a development which extended over many centuries. The Bible, he teaches, is superior to all other writings not only in authority, in utility, and in antiquity, but also in rhetorical art ("praeeminet positione dicendi").[30] All the figures of language and thought are already to be found in it—Bede is able to illustrate seventeen *schemata* and thirteen *tropi* from it.[31] Hebraic parallelism is nothing but ὑπόζευξις—a figure which had previously been demonstrated chiefly from Virgil. "Caro verbum factum est" ("the Word was made flesh") is—a synecdoche. Indeed, the Old Testament offers numerous cases even of ἀστεϊσμός, e.g., "egredietur virga de radice Jesse" ("a branch shall go forth from the root of Jesse"). What is ἀστεϊσμός? Bede knew from Diomedes' grammar: "Quidquid simplicitate rustica caret et faceta satis urbanitate expolitum est" (Keil, I, 463, 1, with examples from Cicero and Virgil). And Diomedes' source was doubtless Quintilian, who, following the Greek terminology, cites ἀστεϊσμός as an "urbane" form of wit. Bede's laudable zeal overshot the mark when he insisted upon finding the fine irony of the great capitals of the antique world in Isaiah. But his principle of co-ordinating the rhetorical theory of figures with the study of the Bible prevailed and was to grow like a mustard-seed.

The so-called Carolingian "Renaissance" crowns the reform of the Frankish church, which Carloman and Pepin had begun and had entrusted to the Anglo-Saxon Boniface. Charlemagne had not long been in power before he realized that much yet remained to be done. The ignorance of the Frankish clergy was then so great that it was difficult to find preachers. The Bible text swarmed with errors, which were made even worse by mistakes in pronunciation. The churches were almost all in a ruinous condition and served as barns.[32] A thorough reform of education and the scriptoria was urgently needed. But men capable of carrying out the task were not to be found in France. The young ruler first brought grammarians (Peter of Pisa, Paulinus of Aquileia, Paul the Deacon) back with him from Italy.

[30] The later influence of such views is apparent when Theodulf ascribes a "stilus arcadicus" and an "eloquium comptum" to the Apostle Paul (*Poetae*, I, 470, 10 and 42).

[31] Cassiodorus, as Garet's comparisons (*PL*, LXIX, 435 D and LXX, 1269 ff.) show, had found over 120 rhetorical figures in the Psalms. Bede undoubtedly knew Cassiodorus' commentary on the Psalms; but one cannot speak of a dependence. Bede's examples are taken from the entire Bible; but even when he cites the same passages from the Psalms as Cassiodorus he frequently uses different names for the figures. Cassiodorus' speculative theory of the sciences is entirely foreign to Bede.— Cf. also M. L. W. Laistner, "Bede as a Classical and a Patristic Scholar" in *Transactions of the Royal Historical Society*, 4th Series, XVI (1933), 69 ff., and especially 90.

[32] A. Kleinclausz, *Charlemagne* (1934), 253.

Then, in Parma, he made the acquaintance of the Anglo-Saxon scholar Alcuin, and persuaded him to come to his court in 782. Alcuin (d. 804 as abbot of St. Martin at Tours) was the organizer of the Carolingian reform of education and the not less important reform of calligraphy. From 782 onwards he directed the Palace school. It was Alcuin who transmitted Bede's heritage to Carolingian Humanism. One of our most important sources for Charlemagne's reform of studies is the edict to Abbot Baugulf of Fulda, composed between 780 and 800. A key sentence in it reads: "Cum autem in sacris paginis schemata, tropi et cetera his similia inserta inveniantur, nulli dubium est quod ea unusquisque legens tanto citius spiritualiter intellegit, quanto prius in litteratum magisterio plenius instructus fuerit" ("Since Holy Scripture is strewn with figures of speech, no one can doubt that every reader will the more quickly understand it spiritually the earlier and the more fully he has been instructed in the art of letters"). The argument according to which a knowledge of the figures is necessary for the study of the Bible is here made the cornerstone of literary education (*litterarum magisterium*). And so a great ruler includes the patristic evaluation of the *artes* in the foundation of his new political and intellectual edifice. We stand at the threshold of a new epoch. Hitherto the countries on the western rim of Europe (Spain, Ireland, England) had received the literary tradition of Rome. These streams now flow together in the Frankish state. There they unite with the active energies of the imperium renovated by the Franks and are given a new direction. The ruler's policy assigns to intellectual training great duties in the shaping of culture, and at the same time his person provides a living center for a new poetical activity.

But here an even wider prospect opens out. Charlemagne's reform of studies fertilized the whole of the Latin Middle Ages. The pedagogical precepts of the post-Carolingian period bear witness to an increasingly deeper pursuit of knowledge. One of the most accomplished scholars in the field of medieval Latin literature, J. de Ghellinck, has pointed out that the study of the figures of speech, which the Anglo-Saxons recommended and Charlemagne insisted upon in his edict to Abbot Baugulf, produced in the course of time that enrichment of poetic expression and that flowering of metaphor which we observe in Latin poetry from the latter part of the eleventh century onwards: "Ainsi s'explique la genèse des grandes oeuvres; ainsi aussi s'établit le contact avec la pensée de ces âges, et on lit le travail de l'âme humaine dans toute la série de ces efforts, qui relient au triomphe définitif de ses chefs-d'oeuvre les maladroits essais de ses premières productions." [33]

5. Curriculum Authors [34]

Instruction in grammar, as we have seen, comprised language and literature. The selection of authors studied in the medieval schools includes

---

[33] J. de Ghellinck, *Littérature latine au moyen âge* (1939), II, 186.
[34] M. L. W. Laistner publishes rectifications affecting the following in *Speculum*, XXIV (1949), 260 ff.

pagan and Christian writers. The Middle Ages makes no distinction between "gold" and "silver" Latinity. The concept "classical" is unknown to it. All authors are, as it were, authorities. Let us examine a number of medieval documents as to curriculum authors. When Walter of Speyer was in school about 975, he read Virgil, "Homer" (that is, the so-called *Ilias latina*, a crude condensation of the *Iliad* in 1070 hexameters, of the first century A.D.), Martianus Capella, Horace, Persius, Juvenal, Boethius, Statius, Terence, Lucan. This is not a casual selection, it is a normative one. It recurs as the basis of later lists. Modern evaluation would exclude "Homerus," Martianus, Boethius, Statius, Lucan, Persius, and Juvenal. The list of authors continued steadily to increase, into the thirteenth century.

Conrad of Hirsau (first half of the twelfth century) names twenty-one, in the following order: 1. the grammarian Donatus; 2. the didactic poet Cato (a collection of philosophical maxims in distichs and monostichs, dating from the Empire); 3. Aesop (a fourth- or fifth-century collection of fables in prose, which in part goes back to Aesop and which, in the introductory epistle, is also called "Romulus"); 4. Avianus (42 Aesopian fables in distichs, composed about 400); 5. Sedulius (wrote a metrical Messiad about 450); 6. Juvencus (composed a metrical harmony of the Gospels about 330); 7. Prosper of Aquitaine (versified dicta of Augustine's in the first half of the fifth century); 8. Theodulus (otherwise unknown author of a tenth-century "Eclogue" which contrasts Paganism with Christianity in a debate); 9. Arator (sixth-century Biblical epic poet); 10. Prudentius (the most important, artistic, and universal early Christian poet, *ca.* 400); 11. Cicero; 12. Sallust; 13. Boethius; 14. Lucan; 15. Horace; 16. Ovid; 17. Juvenal; 18. "Homerus"; 19. Persius; 20. Statius; 21. Virgil. This meager selection includes, as we see, both Christian and pagan (with preference for late antique) authors, with no regard for chronology; for "classics," only Cicero, Sallust, Horace, and Virgil—four authors, who, however, forfeit their privileged position as "classics" by being placed with the other fifteen and whose value was conceived to lie almost exclusively in their ethical influence. To be sure, Cicero ("Tullius") is praised as "nobilissimus auctor," but of his works only the *Laelius* (*De amicitia*) and *Cato maior* (*De senectute*) are singled out, and of Horace only the *Ars poetica* is unconditionally commended. Of Ovid, the *Fasti* and the *Ex Ponto* are "tolerated," the erotic poems and the *Metamorphoses* are rejected. Juvenal and Persius are praised for having scourged the vices of the Romans. Conrad of Hirsau represents the rigoristic standpoint. Thus it is significant that he omits Terence, who was read throughout the Middle Ages.[35] But his list of authors represents curricular material of long standing. Later scholars preserved this basic stock, but added to it considerably. Haskins has published a brief treatment of curriculum authors dating from the end of the twelfth century; he ascribes it to Alexander Neckham.[36] It recommends the whole of

[35] However on two occasions a *sententia* from him is cited.
[36] *Harvard Studies in Classical Philology*, XX (1909), 75 ff.

Horace, even the odes and epodes, which, in general, were little read [37] (even in Dante, Horace appears only as a satirist). Of Ovid, the *Metamorphoses* are omitted, the *Remedia amoris* is particularly commended (as an antidote). The selection from Cicero is increased by the *De oratore*, the "Tusculanae," the *Paradoxa stoicorum*, and the *De officiis*. We also find Symmachus, [38] Solinus' chorographical description of the world (third century; drawn from the elder Pliny's *Natural History*), Martial and Petronius ("both contain much that is useful, but likewise things unworthy the hearing"), Sidonius, Suetonius, Seneca, Livy, Quintilian, and others. The standpoint, then, is far more liberal. The early Christian poets are not represented, the emphasis is on the pagan authors of Antiquity and late Antiquity. To be sure, the discussion is very summary, and hence forbids conclusions *ex silentio*. More systematic is the list of authors which Eberhard the German gives in his didactic poem on rhetoric (written after 1212, before 1280) entitled *Laborintus*.[39] Here we find again 1. Cato (*regula morum*), 2. Theodulus, 3. Avianus, 4. Aesop. After these moralists comes (5.) the late Roman elegiac poet Maximianus (first half of the sixth century)—strangely enough from our point of view, "since the poet regards obscenity as the summit of his art." [40] But the Middle Ages—always excepting the rigorists, who were in the minority—was much less prudish than the Modern Period and zealously read Maximianus, particularly because of his rhetorical artifices. [41] Next come (6. and 7.) the comedies *Pamphilus* (end of the twelfth century; author unknown) and *Geta* (middle of the twelfth century; author Vitalis of Blois); 8. Statius; 9. Ovid; 10. Horace (the satires only); 11. Juvenal; 12. Persius; 13. the *Architrenius* of John of Hanville (end of the twelfth century); 14. Virgil; 15. Lucan; 16. the *Alexandreis* of Walter of Châtillon (*ca.* 1180); 17. Claudian; 18. Dares; [42] 19. the *Ilias latina*; 20. Sidonius; 21. the Crusades epic *Solimarius*; 22. the didactic poem on herbs ascribed to Aemilius Macer (d. 16 B.C.); 23. Marbod of Rennes' (d. 1123) poem on gems; 24. Peter

---

[37] Hugh of Trimberg in 1280 distinguishes three "libri principales" (*Ars poetica, Epistulae, Sermones*) and two "minus usuales" (the odes and epodes).

[38] On the ground that his "breve dicendi genus admiracionem parit."

[39] Faral, 358 ff.

[40] Schanz, IV, 2 (1920), 77.

[41] Cf. Baehrens, *Poetae Latini minores*, III, 313; Duckett, *op. cit.*, 271 ff.; Schanz himself (in the passage cited above) admits: "We read these productions through without being seriously disturbed."—Maximianus is considered a specialist in the description of old age: "Quae senium pulsant incommoda maxima scribit, / A se materiam Maximianus habet" (Faral, 358, 612). Survival of this topos in thirteenth- and fourteenth-century England: G. R. Coffman, *Speculum*, IX (1934), 249 ff.

[42] The *De excidio Troiae historia* of the supposititious Dares is, like the *Ephemeris belli Troiani* of the supposititious Dictys, a Latin Troy romance of the late Empire period. Both works are based on Greek models. Both lay claim to a historical truth from which Homer departed. Dares is on the Trojan side against the Greeks. Since both Franks and Britons claimed, like the Romans, to descend from Troy, Dares enjoyed great prestige in the Middle Ages.

Riga's (d. *ca.* 1209) allegorical Biblical poem *Aurora;* 25. Sedulius; 26. Arator; 27. Prudentius; 28. Alan's (*ca.* 1183) *Anticlaudianus;* 29. the *Tobias* of Matthew of Vendôme (written *ca.* 1185); 30. the *Doctrinale* of Alexander of Villedieu (1199); 31. the *Poetria nova* of Geoffrey of Vinsauf (written between 1208 and 1213); 32. the *Grecismus* of Eberhard of Béthune (d. 1212); 33. Prosper of Aquitaine; 34. the *Ars versificatoria* of Matthew of Vendôme (before 1175); 35. Martianus Capella; 36. Boethius; 37. *De universitate mundi* of Bernard Silvestris (*ca.* 1150). The old curriculum authors Cato, Aesop, Avian, Theodulus, the group of early Church poets, the masterpieces of Roman poetry (together with such a wretched piece of work as the *Ilias latina*) hold their places. Particular emphasis is placed on the Roman satirists (as admonitory poets). It is characteristic that the list includes Sidonius (as had Neckham's) and Claudian. For the new poetics of the twelfth century, both ranked as model authors. Eberhard further includes a dozen exponents of this school of erudite poetizing: the leading works of the Latin Rénaissance of the twelfth century. Especially significant is the fact that the grammarians Donatus and Priscian are supplanted by the "speculative" and versified grammars of Alexander of Villedieu (No. 30), and Eberhard of Béthune. Chronological order is disregarded, as is any arrangement by subjects.[43] All *auctores* are of the same value, all are timeless. This is and remains characteristic of the entire Middle Ages. No distinction is made between Augustan and late Antique literature, or between Theodulus and the early Christian poets. The passage of time only increases the list of *auctores*. In the *Registrum multorum auctorum* by Hugh of Trimberg (1280) there are as many as eighty. And Hugh excludes prose writers.[44] In addition to the *auctores* there were anthologies; these contained passages from authors otherwise not read: e.g., Valerius Flaccus, Tibullus, *Aetna, Laus Pisonis,* Calpurnius, Nemesianus, Macrobius, the *Controversiae* of the elder Seneca, Gellius, Caesar, etc.[45]

So much for the curriculum authors. The great scholars of the High Middle Ages, of course, know other authors too. John of Salisbury may serve as an example.[46] He holds Fronto and Apuleius in particular esteem. He knows Hyginus; the elder Seneca; Valerius Maximus; the elder Pliny; the military writer Frontinus (end of the first century); Florus; Gellius; Eutropius; Ausonius; the military writer Vegetius (fourth century); Justin's

[43] Nos. 1 to 4 are intended as elementary reading. They are easy texts. A child can enjoy the animal fables, as it can find interest in Theodulus' stories of the gods. Cato offered easy practical wisdom. In our day beginners are not given texts at all, but stupid practice sentences instead (*Filia agricolae amat columbas*). The first author read is Caesar—particularly adapted to disgust a twelve-year-old boy with Latin. Lucan, Statius, and Claudian are seldom taught today, even in universities.

[44] The limitation of the concept *auctor* to poets occurs elsewhere; cf. Thurot in *Notices et extraits*, XXII, Part 2, p. 112, n. 2.

[45] On this cf. the studies of B. L. Ullmann, listed in Paré-Brunet-Tremblay, 153, where also further literature.

[46] On this cf. Webb's introductory remarks in his edition of the *Policraticus*, pp. xxi ff.

(third century) epitome of Pompeius Trogus' history; the first Christian historian, Orosius (fifth century); Macrobius (*ca.* 400); and others. But he also uses authors who cannot be identified and whose work has not survived, for example the *De vestigiis et dogmatibus philosophorum* of Virius Nicomachus Flavianus.[47] This is his source for the story that certain seamen asked Plato a simple question which the latter could not answer. Plato took it so to heart that he died (*Policraticus* [ed. Webb], I, 141, 1 ff.). Medieval reverence for the *auctores* went so far that every source was held to be good. The historical and the critical sense were both lacking. Thus the antique authors became the subjects of legends, the best known of which is the medieval saga of Virgil. Statius frequently appears in the Middle Ages with the surname Sursulus or Surculus and is accounted a native of Toulouse; [48] this is due to confusion with a Gallic rhetor, Statius Ursulus, who is mentioned by Jerome.[49] As is well known, Dante made Statius a Christian. The Middle Ages also knew a correspondence between Seneca the philosopher and Paul—a fourth-century forgery. Through a misreading of the name A. (= Aulus) Gellius, an "Agellius" was created, and so on.[50]

We shall later have occasion to show that the Middle Ages subjected profane authors to allegorical interpretation exactly as it did the Bible, and that it regarded them as sages or "philosophers." The practice, of course, survives in Dante. But the teaching of grammar and rhetoric had already raised them to the rank of "authorities." [51] Dante (*Conv.*, IV, 6, 1 ff.) still considers it incumbent upon him to support the "authority" of the Emperor and of philosophy by an elaborate etymology of the word *auctor*. The medieval practice of invoking the *auctores* survived for centuries after Dante. A poet whom the modern reader finds so directly appealing as Villon considers it proper, in the year 1456, to begin a poem by invoking . . . Vegetius—"sage Romain, grant conseillier"—because that writer began his book by recommending "scrupulous and faithful work." [52] It is of no importance whether he read Vegetius in the original or in Jean de Meun's French version. From John of Salisbury's *Policraticus* he takes the story of

[47] For whom see Paul Lehmann, *Pseudoantike Literatur*, 25 ff.
[48] See Manitius, II, 314, 783.
[49] Forcellini, *Onomasticon*, under *Statius*, 4.
[50] How much erroneous information was carried on into the fourteenth century is shown in the *De vita et moribus philosophorum* (ed. Knust, 1886) of Walter Burleigh (Burlaeus, d. 1343).
[51] For *aucteur, auctorité, authentique* in *The Romance of the Rose* and in Scholasticism, cf. G. Paré, *Les Idées et les lettres au XIIIe siècle. Le Roman de la Rose* (Montreal, 1947), 15–18.
[52] Salimbene (ed. Holder-Egger, 389, 15 ff.) records that he read Vegetius through because he affords "multas sagacitates de arte pugnandi." He recommends the Books of Maccabees for the same reason.—Vitruvius and Vegetius were regarded as authorities on fortification in the Middle Ages (Alwin Schultz, *Das höfische Leben zur Zeit der Minnesinger* ², I [1889], 11).—The accomplished philologist David Ruhnken (1723–98) was a great hunter. With Arrian's account of the Celts for his authority, he pursued game with only a net, bow, and arrows.

the pirate Dionides (Diomedes in Villon) and Alexander. Respect for the *auctores* is still a living force in the *magister artium* François Villon.

The rule of the *auctores* was shaken in the twelfth century not only by the triumphant progress of dialectics (now called logic) but equally by the revolt of youth against the traditional school curriculum. John of Salisbury (*ca.* 1115–1180) already has to resist the new trend in his *Metalogicon* [53] and his *Entheticus*. This trend, he complains, scorns the *auctores*, grammar, and rhetoric.[54] If one shows esteem for the *auctores*, there is an outcry: "What is the old fool after? Why does he quote the sayings and doings of the ancients to us? We draw knowledge from ourselves; we, the young, do not recognize the ancients." [55] How familiar it sounds to us! We know it from the school scene in *Faust* (Part II), and from the youth movements of the twentieth century. It is refreshing to find it in the twelfth. The revival of dialectic was fruitful when, as with Abélard, it was applied to philosophy and theology. But many twelfth-century logicians contented themselves with pure dialectic, which could lead only to fruitless disputation. It was otherwise after the rise of the "new Aristotle," with the ensuing opening up of new realms of knowledge. Upon dialectic, thitherto predominantly formal, fell the task of coping with them conceptually.

We have now arrived at the period of the "twelfth-century Renaissance." [56] What was the situation in medieval education at that time? From the beginning of the century we witness a flourishing growth of the cathedral schools. They now outstrip the old monastery schools of the early Middle

[53] Ed. C. C. J. Webb (Oxford, 1929). According to Webb (Preface, xxii), the title may mean either "with the logicians" or "for the logicians." John knew no Greek, but he gave Greek titles to all his books, as did Anselm in the eleventh century (*Monologion* and *Proslogion*) and Bernard Silvestris and William of Conches in the twelfth. Cf. Webb in the Prolegomena to his edition of the *Policraticus* (which Webb interprets as "liber in usum civitates regentium"), Prolegomena, clviii. On the title of John's third great work, the *Entheticus*, Webb says (*ibid.*, xxii): "quid dicere velit, equidem nescio."—Macrobius (*Sat.*, V, 17, 19) had already pointed out that Virgil gave his works Greek titles.

[54] On this and what follows, cf. Norden, *Kunstprosa*, 713 ff. However, we cannot accept Norden's view that John, in contrast, defended "classical learning." The Platonism of Chartres, of which John is the finest flower, is humanistic, but it is a twelfth-century Humanism and in no sense Classicism. Its authorities are the *auctores* enumerated above, together with Apuleius, the Pseudo-Apuleius, and Martianus Capella—writers, in short, whom Norden banishes to the *lupanar*.

[55] These young men often appeal to the authority of the logician Adam du Petit-Pont (Parvipontanus). Cf. Gilson, *La Philosophie au moyen âge* [2] (1944), 278.

[56] C. H. Haskins, *The Renaissance of the Twelfth Century* (Cambridge [Mass.], 1928), is authoritative.—With Haskins' sketch of this Renaissance, which began in the last third of the eleventh century and ended in the first quarter of the thirteenth, we must correlate the artistic Renaissance of the Antique which Jean Adhémar has investigated (*Influences antiques dans l'art du moyen âge* [London, 1939]): "Cette renaissance, dont l'apogée est vers 1140, a été assez forte pour survivre à l'art roman et se manifeste encore dans le premier art gothique, si opposé et si hostile pourtant à la forme artistique qui l'avait précédé. Ce phénomène peut s'expliquer si on songe que les grands humanistes du 12e siecle: un Suger, un Jean de Salisbury, ont, par leur action personnelle, encouragé le mouvement antique" (p. 263).

Ages. The cathedral schools are located in towns. They are under the authority of one of the canons, who is called the *scholasticus* (*scholaster, écolâtre*). The prosperity of the school depends upon his personality. Hence now one, now another of these schools occupies the foreground. Besides the seven liberal arts, almost all of these schools teach philosophy, the revival of which dates from Anselm (d. 1109), and *doctrina sacra*, that is, what would later be known as theology. But the curriculum provides wide scope for the inclinations and free initiative of the teachers and the director of the school. At Angers, Meung, and Tours, at the beginning of the twelfth century, poetry is especially cultivated, at Orléans grammar and rhetoric in addition. But already Paris is drawing more and more students, not only the cathedral school of Notre-Dame, but also the school on Mont Ste-Geneviéve, where Abélard taught for a time, and the foundation of the Augustinian canons of St. Victor, a meeting point of theology and philosophy. Here was educated the Italian Peter Lombard (d. probably 1160, as Bishop of Paris), who, between 1150 and 1152 composed his *Libri quatuor sententiarum*, that is, a system of theology put together out of "decisions" (*sententiae*) of the Church Fathers and the moderns, which soon became a textbook (see Dante, *Par.*, X, 107) and thus contributed to making Paris the center of theological studies.

6. *The Universities*

The increasing influx to the Parisian schools created the atmosphere and the needs out of which grew the University of Paris. With the universities, a new period of medieval education begins. In no sense are they, as one reads again and again, a continuation or a renewal of the antique schools of higher learning. What are called antique universities are foundations of the late Empire period. Their primary concern was the cultivation of grammar and rhetoric. Philosophy, to say nothing of other disciplines, was obliged to accept a position far inferior to these.[57] Our universities are an original creation of the Middle Ages. Nowhere in the antique world were there any such associations, with their privileges, their established curriculum, their hierarchy of degrees (bachelor, licentiate, master, doctor). The word "university" does not, as is generally believed, mean "the sum total of disciplines" ("universitas litterarum") but the corporation of students and teachers. As early as the beginning of the thirteenth century it was explained by the circumlocution "societas magistrorum et discipulorum." As an institution of learning the university is called "studium generale." The oldest university is Bologna, to which Frederick I gave statutes in 1158. But at Bologna law predominated, a theological faculty was not established un-

[57] *Ca.* 425 there were 31 chairs at the universities in Rome and Constantinople. Of these, 20 were for grammar, 8 for rhetoric, 2 for jurisprudence—and 1 for philosophy (M. Lechner, *Erziehung und Bildung in der griechisch-römischen Antike* [1933], 222).

til 1352. The University of Paris [58] developed slowly. A keen intellectual life reigned in Paris as early as the twelfth century, kindled by such teachers as the Victorines and Abélard. From the end of the twelfth century we find various schools there. Germans too attended them, and above all, Englishmen. To all intents and purposes, the University of Paris was already in existence. But it was not designated a *universitas* until 1208 or 1209, in a brief of Pope Innocent III. However, as early as 1200 King Philip Augustus had formally recognized and bestowed privileges on the university, by removing its members from secular jurisdiction (there had been serious conflicts between the municipal authorities and the students). In 1231, on a similar occasion, Gregory IX endowed the university with the great papal privilege which completed its organization.[59] It was the same Pope who, in 1233, entrusted the office of the Inquisition to the Dominicans.[60] To the Church, which, under the great Innocent III (1198–1216), had reached the height of its power, it seemed an imperative weapon against the heretical movements of the twelfth century. But the Church also could not but see a danger in the lay culture of the closing twelfth century with its strong leaven of Antiquity, and so had felt obliged to subject education to its supervision. Thus the inauguration of the Inquisition is intimately connected with the imposition of papal superintendence on the universities. The twelfth century saw the inroads of the "new" Aristotle, that is, of the Greek thinker's natural history, metaphysics, ethics, and politics. This formidable body of treatises and ideas was given to the West through translations from the Arabic and Greek which appeared almost simultaneously in Spain and Sicily. The Arabic text was based on a Syrian translation from the Greek. Jewish and Arabic scholars and commentators were indispensable. The greatest Arabic Aristotelian was Averroes (1126–98). Averroism and the studies associated with it were irreconcilable with church dogma. At the instigation of the Pope, the public and private study of the "new" Aristotle was forbidden in 1215. The prohibition was infringed; in 1228 it was renewed—fruitlessly. But the Dominicans brought about a decisive change. Rendered invulnerable by their fight against heresies, schooled in disputation, they set themselves the task of creating a compromise between the verities of faith and a philosophy whose greatness they were obliged to recognize. So came into existence the mighty Scholastic achievement of

[58] Principal works on the medieval universities: H. Rashdall, *The Universities of Europe in the Middle Ages* (1895); to be used in the second edition, revised by F. M. Powicke and A. B. Emden (1936); St. d'Irsay, *Les Universités françaises et étrangères* (1933–36); H. Denifle, *Die Universitäten des Mittelalters* (1885; only Vol. I published); *idem, Chartularium Universitatis Parisiensis* (4 vols. 1889–97). See also Gilson, *op. cit.*, 390 ff.

[59] The name Sorbonne for the University of Paris goes back to a college founded by Robert de Sorbon in 1250. From the fourteenth century onwards it was the seat of the theological faculty. The name was not extended to the entire university until the beginning of the nineteenth century.

[60] Further details concerning its antecedents and effects in Karl Hampe, *Das Hochmittelalter* (1932), 282.

Albert the Great, to be continued by his still greater pupil Thomas Aquinas. He studied in Paris and taught there for years. By the efforts of the Dominicans at the University of Paris, the dangerous Aristotle was purified, rehabilitated, and authorized. Even more: his teaching was incorporated into Christian philosophy and theology, and in this form has remained authoritative. This process was not accomplished without friction. In 1252–57 the University of Paris had fought strenuously against the mendicant orders and papal supervision, but was defeated. Franciscans and Dominicans were at odds in their philosophical doctrines. Augustinism took up arms against Thomism and, in 1277, had it prohibited by Étienne Tempier, bishop of Paris. There finally survived a "Christian Averroism," whose most important representative was Siger of Brabant, celebrated by Dante.

Though France was already the educational center of Europe by the end of the eleventh century and all through the twelfth, this intellectual primacy reached its apogee in the thirteenth century, through the University of Paris. Papal policy had made it an instrument of the Church. The *sacerdotium* had taken possession of the *studium*. But the *studium* was concentrated upon philosophy and theology. A consequence of this was that grammatical and literary studies at the university were pushed into the background and indeed reduced to the indispensable minimum. The attempt was made to find room in the curriculum, at their expense, for philosophy and natural history, the one newly revived, the other newly opened up. Grammar became "verbal logic." [61] An adherent of the older, literary trend like the Englishman John of Garland,[62] who resided in Paris, complains in his *Morale scolarium* (1241) of the neglect of the *auctores* (Homer, Claudian, Priscian, Persius, Donatus, and many more), as does the French poet Henri d'Andeli, who in his *Bataille des set ars* brings the *auctores* into the field, under the banner of Grammar, against Logic and her champions (among them Plato and Aristotle).[63] Despite these complaints the study of the *auctores* was still alive in the thirteenth century.[64] One of the principal seats of humanistic studies in the twelfth century was the school of Chartres, where Platonism was cultivated. Englishmen were as much at home there as Frenchmen. John of Salisbury died Bishop of Chartres. In English education of the thirteenth century the tradition of Chartres was combined with Arabic natural science and a "metaphysics of light" with an Augustinian coloring. This atmosphere dominates the university at Oxford, which had begun to flourish *ca.* 1200. Here papal supervision

[61] M. Grabmann, *Mittelalterliches Geistesleben*, I (1926), 104–46. Grabmann reminds us that Husserl and Heidegger were able to take up the thread of verbal logic.—*Idem, Thomas von Erfurt und die Sprachlogik des Mittelalterlichen Aristotelismus* (SB München, 1943).

[62] L. J. Paetow, *The Morale Scolarium of John of Garlande* (Berkeley: University of California Press, 1927).

[63] L. J. Paetow, *The Battle of the Seven Arts* (Berkeley: University of California Press, 1914).—Norden, 728.

[64] E. K. Rand in *Speculum*, IV (1929), 249–69.

was only nominal. The university governed itself through its chancellors. The great Oxford thinkers of the thirteenth century, Robert Grosseteste and Roger Bacon, go their own ways and do battle with the Scholasticism of Paris. At Oxford great emphasis was placed upon philological studies.

But the *artes*, in which Thierry of Chartres still saw the sum of philosophy, had now to resign any such claim. Their framework had become too narrow for the enlarged realm of profane disciplines. Thomas Aquinas' dictum, "septem artes liberales non sufficienter dividunt philosophiam theoricam," [65] announces a new era. It indicates the conclusion of the immense philosophical transformation which had taken place in France between 1150 and 1250.

And Germany? Due to her having earlier achieved political order, her cultural and educational life had, in the tenth and the first part of the eleventh century, the start over western and southern Europe. But then she loses it. In the subsequent development of Germany we see "the consequences of the fact that that country, of all Charlemagne's domains, was the last to be Christianized, and shared in his cultural program only in isolated centers of church education." [66] In the twelfth, thirteenth, and fourteenth centuries German students had to get their education in Paris, Bologna, or Padua. The only university foundation of the Hohenstaufen period is Naples (1224), and it was for the subjects of the Sicilian crown. Teachers and pupils alike were forbidden to move to other universities. The first university within the territories of the empire was Prague (1347). There followed Vienna (1365), Heidelberg (1386), Cologne (1388), Erfurt (1389), Leipzig (1409), etc. All these foundations could not make up for the head starts of France, England, and Italy. Germany remained as good as cut off from the great intellectual movements of the twelfth and thirteenth centuries. She had little share in the Renaissance of the twelfth century and the science of the thirteenth. This had its causes—and its consequences. It was the Reformation which brought the German universities to their first flowering.[67]

7. Sententiae *and* Exempla

What does the Middle Ages seek in the *auctores*? Answering this question is a prerequisite to all that follows.

First of all, not only for the entire Middle Ages but also on into the sixteenth century, they are technical authorities. There is as yet no modern science. Medicine is learned from Galen, as universal history is learned from Orosius. Let one example serve for many. In the humanistic course of

---

[65] M. Grabmann, *Mittelalterliches Geistesleben*, II (1936), 190. "Nevertheless," Grabmann adds, " a pupil of St. Thomas', Fra Remigio de' Girolami, O. P., a teacher of Dante's, wrote a *divisio scientie* in the traditional form of the trivium and quadrivium."

[66] Gerhard Ritter, *Die Heidelberger Universität*, I (1936), 11 f.

[67] Herbert Schöffler, *Die Reformation* (1936).

study which Rabelais incorporates into his romance as a criticism of late medieval education, no hour of the day is allowed to pass without instruction. After Pantagruel eats, the properties of all manner of comestibles are discussed, with references to choice passages from Pliny, Athenaeus, Dioscorides, Julius Pollux, Porphyry, Oppian, Polybius, Heliodorus, Aristotle, "and others." When he goes walking, plants are studied after Theophrastus, Marinus, Nicander, Macer. For relaxation they sit down in a meadow and recite passages from Virgil's *Georgics*, Hesiod, and Poliziano's *Rusticus*.

But the *auctores* are not only sources of technical information, they are also a treasury of worldly wisdom and general philosophy. In the antique poets there were hundreds and thousands of lines which put a psychological experience or a rule of life in the briefest form. Aristotle discussed such apophthegms (γνῶμαι) in his *Rhetoric* (II, 21). Quintilian called them "sententiae" (literally: "judgments") because they resembled the decisions of public bodies (VIII, 5, 3). Such lines are "mnemonic verses." They are learned by heart; they are collected; they are arranged in alphabetical order that they may be ready to hand. This gives rise to philological parlor games, such as enlivened festive gatherings even in old Hellas. That amusing compilation the *Deipnosophistai* ("Scholars at a Banquet"), composed by the sophist Athenaeus *ca* A.D. 220, gives us a description (X 457): "Clearchus of Soloi, a man of the school of Aristotle, also tells us how the ancients went about this. One recited a verse, and another had to go on with the next. One quoted a sentence, and a sentence from some other poet expressing the same idea had to be produced. Verses of such and such a number of syllables were demanded, or the leaders of the Greeks and of the Trojans had to be enumerated, or cities in Asia and Europe beginning with the same letter to be named in turn. They had to remember lines of Homer which begin and end with the same letter, or the first and last syllable taken together must yield a name or an implement or a food. The winner gained a garland, but anyone who blundered had brine poured into his drink and had to drain the whole cup at a draught."

In the Middle Ages banquet, wreath, wine, and Homeric scholarship had all fallen away. There remained the Latin schoolroom and the use of the poets for edification. Ovid is prized because he is "sententiarum floribus repletus." [68] This example shows that even frivolous poets give counsel which morality must approve. He yields:

> *Intrat amor mentes usu, dediscitur usu* (*Rem.*, 503).
> (Wont lets love in, as what turns love out is wont.)

> *Lis est cum forma magna pudicitiae* (*Her.*, XVI, 290).
> (Beauty and shamefastness—great is the battle between them.)

---

[68] Hugh of Trimberg, *Registrum* (ed. Langosch), l. 125; *ibid.*, l. 612, praises Maximianus for "multi notabiles versus." "Sentences" are also called *proverbia* (ll. 17, 614, 705).

Res est solliciti plena timoris amor (Her., I, 12).
(What a thing is this love, fearful and full of disquiet.)

Nitimur in vetitum semper cupimusque negata (Am., III, 4, 87).
(What we may not, we would; what is refused, desire.)

Horace (*Epi.*, I, 16, 52):

> *Oderunt peccare boni virtutis amore.*
> (Through love of virtue, good men shrink from sinning.)

We could go on indefinitely. And the Middle Ages went on. It has left us collections of "sentences" arranged in alphabetical order, which mingle antique and medieval booty. Jakob Werner's *Lateinische Sprichwörter und Sinnsprüche des Mittelalters* [69] (over 2500 examples) makes them accessible to the modern reader. Such collections were needed as a preparation for the amusements which tested wit and mental powers. For the old Greek game enlivened the leisure of the schoolmen of the Middle Ages and the philologists of the German Reformation. Melanchthon used *versificatio secundum alphabetum* in his teaching. Each pupil had to recite a gnomic verse, the first beginning with A, the second with B. Luther and Melanchthon amused themselves with this practice during a journey to Leipzig in 1539.[70] Indeed, theology and philology were the backbone of learned Protestant Germany down to the end of the eighteenth century. In Jean Paul's novels we still find them embodied in numerous characters, for example in the headmaster Fälbel who, just before starting out on a school excursion, demonstrates, in a Latin Easter program, that "even the most ancient peoples and men of the earliest times, especially the patriarchs and classic authors, went on journeys." This German-Protestant connection between theology and philology is a preliminary stage, a preparatory school, for the modern *Geisteswissenschaften* which have flourished in Germany since 1800. Friedrich August Wolf (1759–1824) published his celebrated treatise *Darstellung der Altertumswissenschaft* in 1807 and with it triumphed over the confused concept of *humaniora* which saw them as ancillary to theological studies.

Like the *sententiae*, the examples of human excellence and weakness that the Middle Ages found in antique authors served it for edification. *Exemplum (paradeigma)* is a technical term of antique rhetoric from Aristotle onwards and means "an interpolated anecdote serving as an example." A different form of rhetorical *exemplum* was added later (*ca.* 100 B.C.), one which was of great importance for after times: the "exemplary figure"

[69] Heidelberg, 1912 = *Sammlung mittellateinischer Texte* (ed. Alfons Hilka), No. 3.
[70] O. Clemen in ZfKG (1940), 422 f.—Melanchthon's pupil Moritz Heling (ADB, XI, 690) published in 1590 a *Libellus versificatorius ex graecis et latinis scriptoribus collectus et secundum alphabeti seriem in locos communes digestus.*— In England the game is called "capping verses" (Fielding, *Joseph Andrews*, Bk. II, ch. 11).

(*eikon, imago*), i.e., "the incarnation of a quality": "Cato ille virtutum viva imago." [71] Cicero (*De or.*, I, 18) and Quintilian (XII, 4) urge the orator to have at his disposal examples not only from history but from myth and heroic legend. For schools of rhetoric Valerius Maximus, in the reign of Tiberius, produced his "Collection of memorable deeds and sayings" (*Factorum ac dictorum memorabilium libri IX*), which Radulf of La Tourte (1063–1108 +) versified. Familiarity with the most important exemplary figures remains a requisite for scholarly poetry in the Middle Ages. We shall find an established canon of such figures in the Platonizing poetry of the twelfth century. There they appear as archetypes which Divine Wisdom deliberately introduced into the course of history.

In some instances, however, persons who did not form part of the antique repertory were raised to the rank of exemplary figures. Plutarch, in his *Parallel Lives* (written between 105 and 115) tells how Caesar, threatened in Epirus by Pompey's adherents, conceived the foolhardy scheme of returning to Brundusium in a small boat to gather reinforcements. A storm comes up. The terrified steersman wants to turn back, but Caesar takes him by the hand. "Courage, my friend, fear nothing. You carry Caesar and his fortune!" The same story had previously been told by Lucan in one of the finest episodes in his epic (V, 505–677). He gives the role of the steersman to the boatman Amyclas, whose poor hut is a haven of peace of mind while the civil war rages and the ruler of Rome trembles for his victory. Lucan, the "intermediary for antique pathos," "a representative of Roman poetry much read and extremely influential until the educational breakdown of the nineteenth century, but now for several generations completely in the shade, at least in Germany," [72] had created in Amyclas an exemplary figure of contented poverty which did not belong to the classical canon. But its potentiality for pathos makes it beloved of twelfth-century poetry. [73] In Dante, Thomas Aquinas cites Amyclas as an example of virtuous poverty in his eulogy of Francis of Assisi, and Petrarch still mentions him (Eclogue 8). As the examples from twelfth-century Latin poetry demonstrate, it is not

[71] F. Dornseiff in *Vorträge der Bibliothek Warburg 1924–1925* (Leipzig, 1927), 218—Hildegard Kornhardt (*Exemplum. Eine bedeutungsgeschichtliche Studie.* Göttingen dissertation [1936], p. 14): "They are brief accounts of deeds and accomplishments, unusual sayings, in which some quality or trait of character is particularly clearly expressed . . . The word *exemplum* applies both to the act and to the account of it."—The medieval view is stated by John of Garland: "Exemplum est dictum vel factum alicuius autentice persone dignum imitatione" (*RF*, XIII [1902], 888).

[72] Eduard Fraenkel, *Lucan als Mittler des antiken Pathos* (*Vorträge der Bibliothek Warburg 1924–1925* [Leipzig, 1927], 229 ff.).

[73] Abélard: "Securus quia pauper erat vivebat Amyclas" (*Notices et Extraits* 34, II, p. 168, 5); *Architrenius* (*SP*, I, 340): "Julius orbem / Sorbuit et somnum vacui laudavit Amyclae."—Matthew of Vendôme in a dedicatory poem calls himself "vester Amyclas" (*PL*, CCV, 934 B). Many scribes failed to understand this and substituted *amiclus* or *amicus*, which has likewise crept into the text in Manitius, III, 739.—In the *Metamorphosis Goliae* 211, the reading should be Amyclae.—A. Neckham, *De laudibus divinae sapientiae* (ed. Wright), p. 360, 163.—Anonymous in *Stud. med.* (1936), 109, 15.

permissible to deduce an "early Renaissance Amyclas cult" from Dante and Petrarch, as Konrad Burdach sought to do.[74] That would be to bestow on them a trophy which belongs to the Latin Middle Ages. The state of the case is, rather, that Dante took over the twelfth-century exemplary figures and made increased use of them with systematic and deliberate art. He even put Ripheus the Trojan in the Heaven of Jupiter (*Par.*, XX, 68). This figure owes its existence to Virgil's imagination (*Aeneid*, II, 426 f.) and its inclusion in the *Paradiso* simply to Dante's reverence for Virgil. In Dante alone does Ripheus become an *imago virtutis*, and that only because Virgil testified to his uprightness.[75]

[74] *Kommentar zum Ackermann*, 274; *Der Dichter des Ackermann*, 294.

[75] In the Middle Ages *exemplum* can also mean any story "which serves to illustrate a theological doctrine" (Klapper in Merker-Stammler's *Reallexikon der deutschen Literaturgeschichte*, I, 332). Hence arose the popular and often farcical "preachers' fables" which Dante condemns (*Par.*, XXIX, 94 ff.).—J. T. Welter, *L'exemplum dans la littérature . . . du moyen âge*, Paris thesis (1927).

4

Rhetoric

1. *Position of Rhetoric*

RHETORIC is the second of the seven liberal arts. It takes us deeper into the world of medieval culture than does grammar. To us, it has become unfamiliar. As an independent subject, it has long since vanished from the curriculum. Some scanty scraps of rhetoric were still offered to the nineteenth-century German grammar-school pupil when he was taught to turn out German themes. He was expected to draw up a preliminary "outline," divided into introduction, main body, and conclusion. The introduction had to contain a generalization. One must on no account pass directly on to the theme, but must find a suitable "transition." These transitions were a torment. Even La Bruyère incurred Boileau's censure because he spared himself "le travail des transitions"—"qui sont ce qu'il y a de plus difficile dans les ouvrages d'esprit." Boileau must have known. His "transitions" are famous for their clumsiness. The grammar-school student encountered rhetoric again when he studied Latin poetry (and Schiller's too)—here metaphors, metonyms, hyperboles, and the like were to be found in abundance.

In our present culture, rhetoric has no place. Germans appear to have an innate distrust of it. Goethe characterized this attitude in Faust's words to Wagner:

> Es trägt Verstand und rechter Sinn
> Mit wenig Kunst sich selber vor;
> Und wenn's euch ernst ist, was zu sagen,
> Ist's nötig, Worten nachzujagen?
> Ja, eure Reden, die so blinkend sind,
> In denen ihr der Menschheit Schnitzel kräuselt,
> Sind unerquicklich wie der Nebelwind,
> Der herbstlich durch die dürren Blätter säuselt!

62

(With little art, clear wit and sense
Suggest their own delivery;
And if thou 'rt moved to speak in earnest,
What need, that after words thou yearnest?
Yes, your discourses, with their glittering show,
Where ye for men twist shredded thought like paper,
Are unrefreshing as the winds that blow
The rustling leaves through chill autumnal vapor!) *

The words accord with Faust's psychological state, for all the learning of the schools has but confused him and he is seeking a refuge in magic. They do not express Goethe's opinion. In his Leipzig period, Goethe found "everything to do with poetics and rhetoric pleasant and gratifying." In his Strassburg period he fills his "Ephemerides" with extracts from Quintilian. In his older years (1815) he holds rhetoric "with all its historical and dialectic demands" to be "commendable and indispensable," and reckons it among "humanity's highest needs." In him the entire European tradition was alive. Among the Romance peoples natural aptitude and the heritage of Rome have combined to make rhetoric familiar. Orators like Bossuet are among the classics of France. In England from the eighteenth century onwards, eloquence has been the expression of political forces, the concern of the nation. In Germany these preliminary conditions were lacking. Adam Müller's magnificent *Reden über die Beredsamkeit und deren Verfall in Deutschland* (Discourses on Eloquence and Its Decay in Germany) (1816) could find no echo. Until very recent times even antique rhetoric was largely regarded by the German learned world as an aberration. With this we may well contrast the opinion of a Jacob Burckhardt, words in which we catch the breadth of the universal-historical point of view: "But did not Antiquity overestimate the value of an intensive cultivation of oratory and composition? Would it not have done better to fill the heads of its boys and youths with useful and substantial facts? The answer is that we have no right to decide the question so long as we ourselves are pursued by formlessness in all our speaking and writing, so long as perhaps barely one in a hundred of our scholars knows anything about the real art of constructing periods. To the ancients, rhetoric, with its sister studies, was the most indispensable complement to their life of regulated beauty and freedom, their arts, their poetry. Our present existence has, in part, higher principles and aims, but it lacks homogeneousness and harmony; the highest beauty and the greatest tenderness exist side by side with coarseness and barbarity; our excessive business does not even leave us time to be shocked by it." [1]

[* Trans. Bayard Taylor.]
[1] Jacob Burckhardt, *Die Zeit Constantins des Grossen* (1852), Kröner ed., 304.

2. Rhetoric in Antiquity

Rhetoric [2] signifies "the craft of speech"; hence, according to its basic meaning, it teaches how to construct a discourse artistically. In the course of time this seminal idea became a science, an art, an ideal of life, and indeed a pillar of antique culture. Through nine centuries rhetoric in various forms molded the intellectual life of the Greeks and Romans. Its genesis is sufficiently clear. Place: Attica; time: after the Persian Wars.

Into the genesis of rhetoric various factors entered. Delight in discourse and in artistically elaborated discourse is a natural gift of the Greeks. The Homeric heroes already regard eloquence as one of the greatest of excellencies. It is a gift of the gods: " '. . . true it is that the gods do not give every gracious gift to all, neither shapeliness, nor wisdom, nor skilled speech. For one man is feebler than another in presence, yet the god crowns his words with beauty, and men behold him and rejoice, and his speech runs surely on his way with a sweet modesty, and he shines forth among the gathering of his people, and as he passes through the town men gaze on him as a god.' " [3] But eloquence is also a goal of education. Phoenix was sent to the young Achilles "to teach thee all these things, to be both a speaker of words and a doer of deeds." [*] Later writers frequently cited this line in proof that Homer was the father of rhetoric. Almost half of the *Iliad* and more than two thirds of the *Odyssey* are devoted to speeches by the characters, often quite long speeches. One may search the *Chanson de Roland* and the *Nibelungenlied* in vain for anything of the kind. But the domination of the Greek mind by rhetoric does not begin until much later—when Athens entered upon the inheritance of Ionia and her own period of florescence began. Oratory and the art of oratory now win a place in public life. Funeral orations over fallen soldiers appear to have come into use in Athens soon after the Persian Wars. The development of democracy under Pericles, and the "Greek Enlightenment" which began about the middle of the century, in turn afforded the widest possible field for political and legal oratory. Every citizen was drawn into public life. The ability to speak became the prerequisite for a successful career. Traveling philosophers ("sophists" [4]) gave instruction in it for money. Oratorical training, together with instruction in logic and dialectics, was supposed to enable the student to influence an audience and, on occasion, to "make the weaker cause the stronger" [5] (Aristotle, *Rhetoric*, II, 24, 11). Thus

[2] There is a survey of antique rhetoric in general down to the Christian era in Wilhelm Kroll, *Rhetorik* (1937; reprint from *RE*). Additions in *RE Suppl.*, VII, 1039 ff.

[3] *Odyssey*, VIII, 167 ff. [Butcher and Lang translation, replacing R. A. Schröder's]. Cf. Hesiod, *Theogony*, 81 ff.

[*] *Iliad*, IX. Trans. Lang, Leaf, and Myers.]

[4] The word originally means the same as σοφός and designates one "who stood out above the masses through his intellectual abilities" (Kroll).

[5] Rhetoric has often been reproached with this. Cf. the discussion in Quintilian, II, 16, 3 ff.

rhetoric could pass over into the technique of conducting pleas. But the sophist also desires to be a molder of men, an educator of the nation. He serves *paideia* through the power of the word. A momentous innovation is next introduced by the Sicilian Gorgias, who comes to Athens as ambassador in 427: the conscious employment of rhyming words to achieve a musico-poetic effect. Thus the study of rhetoric becomes the study of style, a literary technique. "Symmetry between periods of parallel construction, reinforcement of antithesis by assonance and rhyme, abundant use of metaphors, and ingratiating delivery achieved effects, such as only poetry had previously attained." Eloquence entered into conscious competition with poetry. "Hardly anyone at the period was entirely uninfluenced by the new stylistic trend, and its procedures remained in use throughout Antiquity" (Paul Wendland). Gorgias is the first master of epideictic eloquence. In the course of the centuries it developed a rich variety of styles. Without a knowledge of its history,[6] antique literature is incomprehensible.

Greek rhetoric, then, came into existence with and through Sophistic. Plato rejected both—just as he did poetry—on philosophical and pedagogical grounds. But Greece could not or would not sacrifice to philosophy the demonic power of artistic eloquence—that intoxicating discovery of the Sophists. And philosophy itself was soon able to comprehend as legitimate productions of the human spirit the artistic forms that Plato had rejected. This was the work of Aristotle. He included both poetry and rhetoric in his philosophical investigation of the arts. There is no doubt that in so doing, he wished to oppose the one-sidedness of Plato's judgment. His theory of the emotions (as in his *Poetics*), typology of characters, and detailed examination of style were a valuable contribution, an enrichment of rhetoric. His aim is to show that rhetoric is an equally legitimate counterpart to dialectics, which latter, according to Plato, was the crown of all the sciences.

For the history of rhetoric, however, Aristotle's book, which came to be little read,[7] was of much less significance than the long line of rhetorical textbooks [8] which begins about 340 with that of Anaximenes. In Attica political eloquence was even then attaining its highest dignity and power in Demosthenes (384–322), the leader of the resistance to the Macedonian menace. After the destruction of freedom, however, political eloquence could not but lose all meaning. Judicial oratory also declined, since there were no more state trials. Greek rhetoric took refuge in school exercises, among which the treatment of fictitious legal cases also figured.

Beginning with the second century, Greek rhetoricians poured into Rome to teach. Rome's intense political life could not but give the art of oratory a strong stimulus. But contrary to what had been the case in Greece, its ends were almost wholly practical. Not until the first century do the rhetorical artistic styles of the Hellenistic East reach Rome. The oldest rhe-

---

[6] Eduard Norden, *Die antike Kunstprosa* (1898).

[7] Wendland-Pohlenz, *Die griechische Prosa* (1924), 115.

[8] Greek τέχναι. Their authors are called "technographers."

torical textbook in Latin is the *Rhetorica ad Herennium* (*ca.* 85 B.C.) by an unknown author, previously ascribed to Cicero or to a certain Cornificius. This treatise and Cicero's youthful *De inventione*, which shows points of contact with it, add nothing to the teaching of the Greek handbooks of the fourth century, yet they were of the greatest importance simply because they transmitted the Greek teaching to Rome. The *ad Herennium* was accounted an authority both in the Middle Ages and the Renaissance. Cicero's rhetorical treatises were also read in the Middle Ages, but not often his orations. Cicero was not, as he came to be under Humanism, the model author. His style was not in harmony with late antique and medieval Mannerism. For his politico-legal eloquence, the Middle Ages had no use.

The fall of the Republic and its consequences affected Roman eloquence in much the same way as the Macedonian (later Roman) domination had affected the eloquence of Greece. Under the principate of Augustus and his successors political oratory could not but fall dumb. Rhetoric becomes school eloquence, it concocts exercises (*declamationes*) based on fictitious legal cases. The decay of eloquence was investigated by Tacitus in his *Dialogus de oratoribus*. But rhetoric had long since entered upon a new field of activity by its transfer to Roman poetry. This was Ovid's accomplishment.[9] He "sets himself a theme, in order that he may enlarge upon it himself or, as was the case in the declamations, may make an assumed personage enlarge upon it" (Walther Kraus). His poetry revels in antitheses and conceits, in plays on sound and sense. Here rhetoric enters the service of a charming, witty poetry and makes its themes all the more alluring by adding its own piquancy to them. But rhetoric can also give the utmost effect to tragic material by piling up horrors, by suspense, climax, exaggeration. The result is the "pathetic" style, represented under Nero by Seneca's tragedies and Lucan's epic. Later, in Statius (*ca.* 40–96), we find occasional poems which closely follow the rhetorical receipts for hymeneal and funeral orations, for descriptions of works of art and buildings. Thus, during the first century of the Empire, rhetoric gains ground everywhere. The end of this period sees the most comprehensive and most influential presentation of rhetoric, Quintilian's *Institutio oratoria* (published *ca.* 95), "one of the most excellent treatises which Roman Antiquity has left to us" (Mommsen).

Quintilian's book does not belong to the class of handbooks which had been common in Greece and Rome for centuries. It is an interestingly written treatise on education. For Quintilian the ideal man can only be the orator. For the supreme god and architect of the universe [10] (II, 16,

[9] He proclaims the relationship of his poetry to rhetoric in an epistle to the teacher of rhetoric Salanus (*Ex Ponto*, II, 5, 69 ff.).—W. Kroll (*Studien zum Verständnis der römischen Literatur* [1924], 109) rightly remarks that their training in rhetoric gave the Augustan poets their ability to coin pointed phrases. "Hence the many quotations from Roman poets which have become the common property of world literature and with which the English especially are familiar, due to their college system."

[10] Cf. Excursus XXI *infra*.

12) bestowed speech on man alone. Eloquence therefore stands far above astronomy, mathematics, and other disciplines (XII, 11, 10). But the perfect orator must also be a good man (I, *pr.* 9). Hence the orator is to be defined, as Cato defined him, as "vir bonus dicendi peritus" (XII, 1, 1). More comprehensively, he must be a wise man, "vere sapiens; nec moribus modo perfectus, sed etiam scientia et omni facultate dicendi" (I, *pr.* 18). Thus rhetoric, through Quintilian, claims to be able of itself to satisfy all the needs for which philosophy and general education were held to be competent.[11] Eloquence proceeds directly from the source of wisdom ("ex intimis sapientiae fontibus," XII, 2, 6). Quintilian takes the future orator in charge even in the cradle, and then accompanies him through childhood, school, and higher studies. All curricular subjects and curricular authors are discussed. After the entire subject of rhetoric is disposed of, there follows, in Book X, a guide to the study of literature, with characterizations of the best authors from Homer to Seneca. Here and there in Quintilian's treatise the subject of rhetoric is transformed into something wholly different—into the humanistic recognition of literary studies as the highest good in life. "The love of literature and the reading of the poets are not confined to school days, but end only with life itself" (I, 8, 12). "The enjoyment of literature does not become wholly pure until it is freed from all activity and can rejoice in the contemplation of itself" (II, 18, 4). Such statements anticipate typical cultural experiences of the Western world.

Meanwhile Greek rhetoric continued to flower, but in Asia Minor now, instead of in Attica. There it developed a style which, compared with that of the classic Attic orators (Demosthenes, Lysias), is something new and strange. Does the fault lie in the unnaturalness of the fantastic legal cases upon which these fictitious forensic speeches were based? Or is this "unctuous and luxuriant mode of expression" (Cicero, *Orator*, 25) to be explained by Oriental taste? Perhaps both explanations are only superficial, and the real reason is to be sought in an inner law analogous to that which was realized in Italian painting after Raphael and which has parallels in many periods and areas of art history. The new manner was called Asianism, its opponents were called Atticists. Following Cicero's precedent (*Brutus*, 325), it is customary to distinguish two styles in Asianism: the subtle-sententious and the grandiloquent-impetuous. There is, however, no clear division between them. Common to both is a feverish striving for astonishing effects. Their peculiarities and nuances need not concern us. But the phenomenon itself is of extreme importance for the understanding of European literature. It represents the first appearance of what we shall henceforth designate as literary Mannerism. Asianism is the first form of European Mannerism, Atticism that of European Classicism.

Atticism developed a classicistic literary aesthetics which carried the day

[11] Even as Isocrates already regarded his rhetoric as φιλοσοφία.

from the first half of the first century before Christ. It is also dominant in the renaissance of Greek ideals of art and life which begins in the second century after Christ and lasts in the West until about the middle of the fourth century. The leading role in this movement falls to rhetoric. For it is rhetoric, and not poetry or philosophy, which appears as the representative of the old Greek intellectual values. It terms itself the new or Second Sophistic. The Flavian educational reform, then Hadrian's phil-Hellenism, promote it. It goes so far that educated men, with the Emperor at their head, speak Greek, and Roman literature suddenly comes to an end. For the second time Rome makes an intellectual surrender to Greece. The universal language, the universal culture, are Greek. The cult language and the literary language of Christianity will also be Greek.[12] The great fourth-century preachers, Basil, Gregory of Nazianzus, and John Chrysostom, went to school to the Sophists. How are we to think of these Sophists? Nietzsche has given a striking characterization of them: "They are reproductive virtuosos through their hero-worship of the great ancients; their souls behold the vision of an earlier Hellenism, though it is not without rivals . . . To be sure, in all things they laid the strongest emphasis upon form, they created the most form-demanding audience that has ever existed. . . . They have in common a very early maturity, an eventful and exhausting life, service under monarchs, more than enough of admiration, adoration, and deadly enmities; usually they are rich; they were not scholars but practicing virtuosos of oratory and thus differ from the fifteenth-century Italian humanists, who, as needy scholars, lived a harder life, but in other respects are very like them." [13] The earliest, and still unsupplanted, evaluation of the Second Sophistic was produced by Erwin Rohde, the friend of Nietzsche's youth.[14]

Clearly: Antique rhetoric has a long and protean history.

3. System of Antique Rhetoric

Now that we have glanced at its development, we must make a brief summary of the system of teaching it. The schema remained unchanged for centuries. Place could be found in it for later innovations.

Rhetoric as an art (*ars*) has five divisions: *inventio* (εὕρεσις, invention), *dispositio* (τάξις, disposition), *elocutio* (λέξις, diction), *memoria* (μνήμη, memory), *actio* (ὑπόκρισις, delivery). The subject matter of the art of rhetoric (*materia artis*) comprises the three kinds of eloquence: judicial oratory (*genus iudiciale,* γένος δικανικόν), deliberative oratory (*genus*

---

[12] Theodor Klauser was recently able to show that it was not until between 360 and 382 that Greek was officially given up as the liturgical language in Rome, and Latin was made obligatory (*Miscellanea Giovanni Mercati* [1946], I, p. 3.)

[13] From Nietzsche's series of lectures, given in 1872–73, *Geschichte der griechischen Beredsamkeit* (*Werke*, XVIII [1912], 232).

[14] In his *Der griechische Roman und seine Vorläufer* (1876). Chapter 3 (288–360) treats of "Greek Sophistic of the Imperial Age."

deliberativum, γένος συμβουλευτικόν), panegyrical or epideictic oratory (*genus demonstrativum*, γένος ἐπιδεικτικόν or πανηγυρικόν).[15]

After the extinction of Greek and Roman freedom, judicial eloquence lost almost all meaning. But there was in existence a fund of procedural technique which had been highly developed and which those who possessed it were not willing to let die. Judicial oratory "always dominated theory; satisfactory and exhaustive rules had been set up for it alone" (Kroll). For this very reason it was practiced in fictitious legal cases and handed down as a formula—as, for a late example, by Alcuin in his work on rhetoric, which introduces Charlemagne as one of the speakers in the dialogue. However, judicial rhetoric could have meaning only in countries where the Roman law was known, and even there only after the revival of legal studies —for example, in Italy from the end of the eleventh century onwards.[16] Deliberative eloquence is originally political oratory in a public assembly or a senate. Under the Empire it too becomes a school exercise. It is now also called *suasoria* or *deliberativa*. The pupil puts himself in the situation of some celebrated personage of past times, and considers how he should act. For example, as Agamemnon, he deliberates whether to sacrifice Iphigenia; as Hannibal, whether, after Cannae, he shall lead his troops to Rome; as Sulla, whether he shall retire to his estates.

During the Hellenistic period, however, far greater importance came to be attached to epideictic eloquence than to either of the two preceding. Its subject matter, reduced to the most general terms, is praise,[17] "especially the praise of gods and men" (Quintilian, III, 7, 6). It became politically important under the Empire. Latin and Greek eulogies of rulers were one of the principal tasks of the Sophists. The praise of a ruler (βασιλικὸς λόγος) was now introduced as a separate genre. Other genres were: funeral orations, birthday orations, consolatory orations, orations of greeting, of congratulation, etc. Not until late Antiquity was epideictic or panegyrical rhetoric systematized and taught in the schools. Among the "preparatory exercises" (προγυμνάσματα) for rhetoric were precepts "for eulogy." We find them, for example, in Hermogenes (second century A.D.). His little treatise was translated by the celebrated grammarian Priscian (beginning of the sixth century) and thus became a part of the Latin curriculum. The influence of epideictic oratory on medieval literature was very great, as we shall see. Another of the stylistic techniques of the New Sophistic was the elaborate "delineation" (ἔκφρασις, *descriptio*, description) of people, places, buildings, works of art. Late antique and medieval poetry used it lavishly.

From the three genres of oratory we pass to the five divisions of rhetoric.

15 The term ἐπίδειξις (*ostentatio*) goes back to its aspect of display, the term πανηγυρικός to the outward occasion (festal gathering—πανήγυρις—e.g., at the Olympic or other games).
16 On the relation of Roman jurisprudence to rhetoric, cf. F. Schulz, *History of Roman Legal Science* (1946), 259 and 269.
17 "Praise and blame," even the earliest handbooks say; cf. *infra*, p. 182, n. 37.

Divisions IV and V (*memoria* and *actio*) usually receive the least space in antique theoretical treatises. They comprise the practical part of oratorical technique and hence are of value only for speeches that are actually delivered. "Invention" is the most important. It is divided according to the five parts which make up the judicial oration: 1. introduction (*exordium* or *prooemium*); 2. "narrative" (*narratio*), that is, exposition of the facts in the matter; 3. evidence (*argumentatio* or *probatio*); 4. refutation of opposing opinions (*refutatio*); 5. close (*peroratio* or *epilogus*). This division was also applied or adapted to the other oratorical genres. The purpose of the introduction was to make the hearer favorably disposed, attentive, and tractable (*benivolum, attentum, docilem*[18]). In the close, the orator addressed himself to the hearer's emotions, in an effort to turn them in the desired direction. As for the "evidence," antique theory made this division the field of supersubtle distinctions into which we may not enter. Essentially, every oration (including panegyrics) must make some proposition or thing plausible. It must adduce in its favor arguments which address themselves to the hearer's mind or heart. Now, there is a whole series of such arguments, which can be used on the most diverse occasions. They are intellectual themes, suitable for development and modification at the orator's pleasure. In Greek they are called κοινοὶ τόποι; in Latin, *loci communes*; in earlier German, *Gemeinörter*. Lessing and Kant still use the word. About 1770, *Gemeinplatz* was formed after the English "commonplace." We cannot use the word, since it has lost its original application. We shall therefore retain the Greek *topos*. To elucidate its meaning—a topos of the most general sort is "emphasis on inability to do justice to the subject"; a topos of panegyric: "praise of forebears and their deeds." In Antiquity collections of such topoi were made. The science of topoi—called "topics"—was set forth in separate treatises.

Originally, then, topoi are helps toward composing orations. They are, as Quintilian (V, 10, 20) says, "storehouses of trains of thought" ("argumentorum sedes"), and thus can serve a practical purpose. But we have seen that the two most important oratorical genres, the judicial and the political, disappeared from political reality with the extinction of the Greek city-states and the Roman Republic, and took refuge in the schools of rhetoric; that eulogy became a technique of praise which could be applied to any subject; that poetry too was rhetoricized. This means neither more nor less than that rhetoric lost its original meaning and purpose. Hence it penetrated into all literary genres. Its elaborately developed system became the common denominator of literature in general. This is the most influential development in the history of antique rhetoric. By it the topoi too acquire a new function. They become clichés, which can be used in any form of literature, they spread to all spheres of life with which literature deals and to which it gives form. In late Antiquity we see the new ethos

---

[18] Still familiar to us as "captatio benevolentiae" (Cicero, *De inventione*, I, 16, 21).

give birth to new topoi. To trace this development will be one of our tasks.

In comparison with the other divisions of rhetoric, "disposition" was given but inadequate treatment by the antique theorists. It was separated from "invention" only at a late period, and then not very clearly. For "disposition" was already anticipated in the five parts or sections of an oration, which for their part provided the clue to "invention." What we mean today by "composition" has no equivalent in antique and medieval literary theory. Antiquity knew the concept of composition in its strict sense only in epic and tragedy, for which Aristotle prescribed a limited action. Antiquity had no general theory of prose literature and its genres and could not have one, since it had rhetoric for a general theory of literature. As a result, modern critics have frequently deplored the lack of composition in antique literature. But what we perceive as elements of composition in late antique and medieval literature are for the most part taken from the traditional succession of the five sections of an oration. Instead of five sections, we sometimes find four or six—this goes back to differences in the practice of various antique schools. Sometimes glosses in the margin of a poem urge its rhetorical structure upon the reader.[19] *Narratio* could serve for every form of narrative.[20] To the "narration," a digression ($\pi\alpha\rho\acute{\epsilon}\kappa\beta\alpha\sigma\iota\varsigma$, *egressus*, *excessus*) may be attached. Of this the Middle Ages made lavish use. *Prooemium* and *peroratio* are indispensable to any piece of writing.

The third division of rhetoric, diction ($\lambda\acute{\epsilon}\xi\iota\varsigma$, *elocutio*) is the most comprehensible to modern minds. It contains exhaustive stylistic rules for every variety of literary production. Choice and collocation of words, the theory of the three genres of style, and finally figures of speech are treated. To this last subject special textbooks were often devoted. The dominating point of view in all this is that discourse must be "decorated." The "ornatus" (Quintilian, VIII, 3) is the great desideratum, and it remains so into the eighteenth century. Beatrice sends Virgil to aid Dante because he is master of the "parola ornata" (*Inf.*, II, 76). Of his canzoni Dante says: "La bellezza e nell' ornamento delle parole" (*Conv.*, II, 11, 4). Marmontel, in his *Eléments de littérature* (1787), which was widely used at the time, can still say: "Le style de l'orateur et celui du poète a besoin d'être orné."

The foregoing is an attempt to acquaint the modern reader with the principal facts and basic concepts of antique rhetoric. I have set forth only the most important aspects of this extensive and complex subject: the bare essentials required by the reader if he is to consider the problems posed in this book. The following chapters will increase and refine upon this equipment.

4. *Late Roman Antiquity*

Like grammar, rhetoric enters the Middle Ages in association with the *artes liberales*. As part of the "authoritative traditional stock," it was conserved by the schools. Thenceforth its destiny is no longer a living growth. It

[19] Cf. Dracontius (*Romulea*, 5); also Buecheler-Riese, *Anthologia latina*, I, 1, No. 2. Also in the Middle Ages.

[20] The concept *narratio* can be taken very widely. Jerome (Epistle 65) comments on Psalm 44:3 (Vulgate): "finito prooemio, hic narrationis exordium est."

exhibits symptoms of degeneration: torpor, atrophy, distortion. Hence it is impossible to present a simple picture of it in the first centuries of the Middle Ages. The stage of history in the dubious twilight of the transition centuries presents us simultaneously with a great diversity of styles and values. We will survey them briefly.

The political, social, and economic crisis of the Empire in the third century had shaken Roman culture to its foundations. What the second flowering of the fourth century was able to preserve is a greatly reduced capital. The old Roman tradition finds a refuge in the senatorial nobility of Rome. The attempts at a restoration made by Symmachus and his circle have to combat not only Christianity, now the state religion, but also Byzantium. The Romans cease to read Greek. Macrobius interprets Cicero's *Somnium Scipionis* and Virgil's *Aeneid* as infallible scientific, philosophic, theological and rhetorical authorities, in the iridescent light of allegory. Quintus Aurelius Symmachus resumes the rhetorical treatment of the prose letter begun by the younger Pliny, and finds a mannered disciple in the Gallic Sidonius Apollinaris (430–86).[20a] For the twelfth-century Renaissance, both Symmachus and Sidonius will be model authors. Here, as so often, we may observe that examples of late antique culture which have long since vanished from our own cultural stock enjoyed a recrudescence of influence in the medieval period of florescence.

5. *Jerome*

Symmachus' letters embrace the years 365 to 402. The same period saw the struggle between Antiquity and Christianity which is associated with the names of Jerome and Augustine and which was momentous for the history of the world. Two very dissimilar natures, which also exhibit a minimum of mutual comprehension. Jerome went through a course of the best Latin schooling, then fled to the Syrian desert to save himself from the temptations of the world. He remained in the desert, however, for only three years, employing his time in learning Hebrew from a Jewish scholar. He next went to Constantinople, where he made up his arrears in Greek. Pope Damasus called him back to Rome. There he frequented a circle of patrician ladies, with whom he studied the Bible. His letters of this period cast a satirical light on Roman society, including ecclesiastical circles. The learned philologist is also an eager controversialist—a similarity in temperament which made him beloved of the Renaissance Humanists. Damasus set him to revising the Latin translation of the Bible. After the Pope's death he returned to Bethlehem with some of his patronesses and pupils, and resumed his study of Hebrew, so that he could verify the Greek translation of the Old Testament (*Septuaginta*). Thus he became the pioneer of modern Biblical criticism. He next began to translate almost the whole of the Bible from the original texts. This led to his being attacked by conservative churchmen (as was Luis de León in the Spain of Philip II)—he

---

[20a] E. Faral, *Sidoine Apollinaire et la technique littéraire du moyen âge* (in *Miscellanea Giovanni Mercati* [1946], II) was inaccessible to me.

was accused of humbling the Church before Jewish learning. These attacks
provoked Jerome to polemics in which his temperament and his erudition
made a fascinating mixture. It was not until 1546 that, by a decree of the
Council of Trent dated April 8, his "old and widely circulated (*vulgata*)"
translation was accepted as the only authentic one. The revised text, which
is still the officially approved version to this day, appeared in 1592. This is
the text that every Roman Catholic bookstore supplies. But the purchaser
of the Vulgate today gets not only the Latin Bible, but also Jerome's introductions to the Bible as a whole and to separate books—twenty-five printed
pages which are a breviary of Christian Humanism as Jerome understood
it. It is based upon the idea of a correspondence between pagan and Christian tradition. Numbers contains "the mysteries of all arithmetic," the
Book of Job "all the laws of dialectics." The Psalmist is "our Simonides,
Pindar, Alcaeus, Horace, and Catullus." Thus, for Jerome, the Bible is not
only a witness of salvation, but also a literary corpus, which need not shrink
from comparison with the thesaurus of *gentilitas*. In Jerome this system of
correspondences is not carried through, but it is so clearly indicated that in
the Middle Ages it could be further developed, as we shall see (ch. 17, § 4).

   E. K. Rand has contrasted Jerome the Humanist with Ambrose the Mystic: "A humanist is one who has a love of things human . . . ; one who
cares more for art and letters, particularly the art and letters of Greece and
Rome, than for the dry light of reason or the mystic's flight into the unknown; one who distrusts allegory; one who adores critical editions with
variants and variorum notes; one who has a passion for manuscripts, which
he would like to discover, beg, borrow or steal; one who has an eloquent
tongue which he frequently exercises; one who has a sharp tongue, which
on occasion can let free a flood of good billingsgate or sting an opponent
with an epigram." [21] Almost all these traits appear in Jerome as a literary
personality—as they do in Poggio and Filelfo in the fifteenth century, and
in Budé, Casaubon, and Erasmus in the sixteenth. They are characteristic
of that role in the human comedy which we may name "the impassioned
philologist."

6. Augustine

Philology and monasticism, literary Humanism and the passion for research, were united in Jerome. We find none of these in Augustine. But
he has everything that Jerome lacks: the most delicate emotional life and
spiritual fire; that longing to know essence which soars above all factual
science. He is not a man of learning, but a thinker. He makes no attempt
to harmonize the Greek and the Hebraic traditions; he opposes the two
worlds as sharply as he does the secular state and the City of God. But he
grew up under the influence of the late antique ideal of man, he became a
teacher of rhetoric and a pupil of the Platonists. His conversion convinced
him that all educational effort must be placed at the service of the Faith.
He had seen that the Bible had a rhetoric of its own. But in his study of the

[21] E. K. Rand, *Founders of the Middle Ages* (1928), 102.

sacred text he persisted in the antiquarianizing and allegorizing method which Macrobius had applied to Cicero and Virgil.[22] The Bible was full of dark sayings, but Paul had taught that it was inspired: "omnis scriptura divinitus inspirata" (2 Tim. 3:16). Augustine concludes: Everything in the Bible which is not directly concerned with faith and morals has a hidden meaning. In this he follows the precedent not only of late antique Homeric and Virgilian allegoresis but also of the Biblical allegoresis which had been accepted since Origen. He adds support to it by the idea that an effort to unravel the hidden meaning is a wholesome and enjoyable intellectual activity. Thus unobtrusively were literary-aesthetic considerations, which could not but have been attractive to late antique literati, introduced once again into the study of the Bible. Theologians today criticize Augustine for having misused allegoresis in his exegeses.[23] But his theory became a permanent possession of the Middle Ages.

But Augustine's connection with rhetoric must also be examined from another point of view. Augustine is not only a profound thinker but also a writer of high rank. His *Confessions* is, on all counts, one of the great books of the West. Its style is—antique artistic prose. The methods of antique rhetoric are made to serve the new spiritual world of Christianity. In particular, Augustine employs three means which were recommended by Cicero (*De oratore*, III, 173–198; *Orator*, 164–236): *isokolon* (the coupling of period-members of equal length), *antitheton* (connection of two period-members which contain contrasting ideas), *homoioteleuton* (*isokolon* with rhyme at the ends of the cola). The *Confessions* end with a prayer. Its last sentences, in English, run: "Thou art ever quiet because thou thyself art thy quiet. And comprehension of this, what man shall give it to any man? what angel to any angel? what angel to any man? Of thee must it be asked, in thee sought, at thy gate knocked for; thus, thus will it be received, thus found, thus will the gate be opened." But now here it is in Latin: "Semper quietus es quoniam tua quies tu ipse es. Et hoc intellegere quis hominum dabit homini? quis angelus angelo? quis angelus homini? A te petatur, in te quaeratur, ad te pulsetur: sic, sic accipietur, sic invenietur, sic aperietur." No modern prose can reproduce these solemn parallelisms and assonances. Here rhetoric becomes poetry—as so often in the Roman liturgy.

7. Cassiodorus and Isidore

In the first half of the sixth century the connection between antique rhetoric and political life is revived once again—through Cassiodorus. His official letters, composed in the service of the Ostrogothic kings Theodoric and Athalaric, still breathe the sentiments of Antiquity. In Athalaric's service he sent a communication (*Variae*, VIII, 12; ed. Mommsen, p. 242,

---

[22] Henri Irénée Marrou, *Saint Augustin et la fin de la culture antique* (1938).
[23] "Des abus incontestables du sense mystique . . . Allégorisme exagéré" (E. Portalié in *Dictionnaire de théologie catholique*, s.v. *Augustin*, cols. 2343 f.).

in MGH, *auct. ant.*, XI) to the advocate, diplomat, and poet Arator, summoning the latter to serve the state, especially on the ground of his excellence in rhetoric ("moribus armata facundia"). As the leader of an embassy he had used "not ordinary words but the full stream of eloquence" ("non communibus verbis, sed torrenti eloquentiae flumine"). In a letter to the Roman Senate (*Variae*, IX, 21; Mommsen, p. 286) Athalaric turns his attention to education and, through Cassiodorus, argues that grammar, the study of antique authors, and eloquence are necessary to the state. "The barbarian kings make no use of the latter; it remains with lawful rulers. Other peoples have arms and the rest, but eloquence is only at the command of the ruler of the Romans." With the collapse of the Ostrogothic state, this last echo of the old Roman spirit was stilled. Cassiodorus retired to his estates in Calabria, where he founded the monastery of Vivarium. The second half of his long life was devoted to works of erudition in the service of Christian culture. "With this step he symbolically prepared the entrance of classic culture into the cramped cell of the Middle Ages" (Fedor Schneider). In his *Institutiones* Cassiodorus includes a brief discussion of rhetoric. It is significant that the antique precepts for memorizing and delivering speeches are here adapted for liturgical use by monks (II, 16).

Isidore's epitome of rhetoric (*Et.*, II, 1–21) betrays his embarrassment before the wealth of material handed down by tradition. It was impossible to take it all in ("conprehendere impossibile"). Martianus, for all the whimsicality of his presentation, was yet, as an advocate, professionally familiar with the material. The Visigothic bishop is reduced to compiling a series of extracts. He makes things easier for himself by cutting and simplifying radically. Following Cassiodorus' example, he limits rhetoric to judicial oratory: "Rhetorica est bene dicendi scientia in civilibus quaestionibus." But there follows a thorough treatment of the figures of speech, with many examples from poetry. Thus the compilation could be used as a handbook of style.

8. Ars dictaminis

We encounter no new developments until the eleventh century. The art of style is now treated in didactic poems as the theory of the *ornatus*—for example by Ekkehart IV (*De lege dictamen ornandi*, *Poetae*, V, 532) in Germany; by Marbod of Rennes (*ca.* 1035–1123) in France (*De ornamentis verborum*, PL, CLXXI, 1687, closely connected with the *Rhetorica ad Herennium*, IV, 13–30; *De apto genere scribendi*, PL, CLXXI, 1793, with a strong personal coloring). Of far greater importance, however, is the contemporaneous development of a new system of rhetoric: the *ars dictaminis* or *dictandi*. It grew up out of the needs of administrative procedure, and was primarily intended to furnish models for letters and official documents. To be sure, model letters (known as *formulae*) were already in existence in Merovingian and Carolingian times and were circulated in collections. The royal and ecclesiastical chancelleries had need of them.

But toward the end of the eleventh century the step from theory to practice was taken. The model letters were preceded by introductions and rules.

That rhetoric became an art of letter-writing is in no way surprising. The development was prepared not only by the collections of letters by Pliny, Symmachus, and Sidonius, but also by Cassiodorus' official letters. Ennodius uses "epistolaris sermo" in the sense of "artistic prose." In late Greek Antiquity too we have directions for writing letters, rhetorical letter-stereotypes, and finally collections of letters which provide models for describing various social categories (fishermen, peasants, parasites, hetairai). This is an aftereffect of Attic comedy. Latin epistolary rhetoric offers nothing so entertaining.

But what is new in the eleventh century is the attempt to subordinate *all* rhetoric to the art of epistolary style. This imports both an adaptation to contemporary needs and a conscious turning away from the traditional curriculum of rhetoric. A new name was required to show that the new art was something modern. Naturally, even the new name was taken from the old tradition. *Dictare* originally signifies "to dictate." Now, even in Antiquity it was usual to dictate, and not only letters but especially compositions in elevated style. Hence, from the time of Augustine, the word *dictare* acquires the meaning "to write, to compose," and particularly "to write works of poetry." It is to this development in the Latin language that German owes the words "dichten," "Dichter," and "Gedicht." The usage is thus the result of a historical situation of the same kind as we are able to determine for the Greek ποίησις. "Dichter" and "dictator" are made of the same linguistic material. Dante calls the troubadours "dictatores illustres" (*De vulgari eloquio*, II, 6, 5).

We shall have to deal more fully with the *ars dictandi* in another connection. And also with the Latin arts of poetry produced by Frenchmen and Englishmen from about 1170 onwards. These *poetriae* too represent a new adaptation of antique rhetoric. Dante's poetics and rhetoric are based upon them.

9. *Wibald of Corvey and John of Salisbury*

An expert opinion on the contrast between rhetorical theory and practice in the twelfth century is to be found in a letter by the celebrated statesman Wibald of Corvey (also known as "of Stavelot"), who during the course of an eventful life had come to know Italy and who died (1158) in Asia Minor on a journey to the Byzantine court. In the monasteries, he writes, it was impossible to acquire a mastery of the art of speaking, because there was no opportunity to use it for practical purposes. Oratory was a lost art. There was no place for it in the practice of either ecclesiastical or secular law. Lay advocates were often gifted by nature, but they were without literary culture, especially in Germany: "in populo Germaniae rara declamandi consuetudo" (*PL*, CLXXXIX, 1254B).

In the twelfth century there stands beside and above the *ars dictaminis* the antique ideal: rhetoric as the integrating factor of all education. The concept was common to Cicero, Quintilian, and Augustine. It survives in Martianus Capella's idea of arranging a marriage between Mercury and the maiden Philology. In the first half of the twelfth century it nourishes the Humanism of the School of Chartres. Its atmosphere pervades the writings of John of Salisbury. Both as man and writer, he is one of the most attractive figures of the twelfth century. Through him we become acquainted with the change in the educational ideal. His rejection of the fashionable influx of dialectics is directed against a certain Cornificius (not otherwise identifiable) who regards rhetoric as superfluous and undertakes to philosophize without it. John counters: Rhetoric is the beautiful and fruitful union between reason and expression. Through harmony, it holds human communities together. He who would put asunder what God has brought together for the good of men deserves the name of public enemy ("hostis publicus"). For to take Mercury from the arms of Philology, to eliminate rhetorical theory from the study of philosophy, is to destroy all higher education ("omnia liberalia studia") (*Metalogicon* [ed. Webb], p. 7, 13 ff.). John here reproduces the doctrine set forth by Cicero (*De officiis*, I, 50) and going back to Posidonius and Isocrates, according to which reason and speech (*ratio* and *oratio*) together form the basis of manners and society. John also expressed the idea in verse (*Entheticus*, p. 250, 363 ff.):

> *Eloquii si quis perfecte noverit artem,*
> *Quodlibet apponas dogma, peritus erit.*
> *Transit ab his tandem studiis operosa juventus*
> *Pergit et in varias philosophando vias,*
> *Quae tamen ad finem tendunt concorditer unum,*
> *Unum namque caput Philosophia gerit.*

The full flowering of Scholasticism in the thirteenth century made this humanistic cultural ideal unseasonable north of the Alps. But the Italian Humanism of the fourteenth century gave it a new development. Between the world of John of Salisbury and the world of Petrarch there is an intellectual kinship.

10. *Rhetoric, Painting, Music*

Rhetoric set its stamp not only on literary tradition and production. In the Florentine quattrocento L. B. Alberti advised painters to familiarize themselves "with the poets and rhetoricians," who could stimulate them to discover (*inventio!*) and give form to pictorial themes. In conformity with this is the fact that Poliziano was Botticelli's erudite counselor. As A. Warburg showed, Botticelli's *Birth of Venus* and *Primavera* can be interpreted iconographically only by reference to antique authors with which contemporary poetry and erudition had familiarized him.[24]

[24] A. Warburg, *Gesammelte Schriften*, I (1932), 27 ff.

But there are also close connections between rhetoric and music.[25] We owe our knowledge of this fact to Arnold Schering (1877–1941).[26] The system of teaching music was adapted from that of teaching rhetoric. There was a musical "art of invention" ("ars inveniendi"; cf. Bach's "Inventions"), a musical topics, and so on. "How often," says Gurlitt, "do we not see in a melody or rhythm, in a motif or a figure, in a melodic or harmonic movement, a discovery or indeed an inspiration in the modern poetic sense, whereas basically it represents nothing but one of these developments from the traditional store of topoi—that is, a resumption, a mutation, a reworking of specific typical themes, formulas, and phrases." Here we have a description of precisely the same state of affairs that we shall find in the realm of literature. The points of agreement are so striking that we are forced to say: The reception of antique rhetoric was a determining factor of artistic self-expression in the West for long after the close of the Middle Ages.

In the seventeenth and eighteenth centuries rhetoric was still a recognized and indispensable branch of learning. The Académie Française, founded in 1635, was charged with producing not only a dictionary and a grammar (which it did) but also a rhetoric and a poetics (which it did not). Private individuals undertook to supply the deficiency, for example, Charles Rollin in his *Traité des Études* (1726–31), the relevant articles in Voltaire's *Dictionnaire philosophique* (first complete publication in the so-called "edition of Kehl," 1784–90), Marmontel's *Éléments de littérature* (1787; reprinted as late as 1867). In England the *Lectures on Rhetoric and Belles Lettres* (first edition, 1783) of the Scotch clergyman and professor Hugh Blair (1718–1800) had a great success.[27] Today, all that is waste paper. But it shows that, down to the Revolution of 1830, Europe remained convinced that it could not do without a constantly renewed presentation of rhetoric which should keep pace with contemporary literary production. Out of this waste land Adam Müller's book, which we mentioned earlier, rises proud and solitary. Though still unread today,[28] it contains an intellectual history of Germany *in nuce*.[29]

[25] W. Gurlitt, in the journal *Helicon*, V (1944), 67 ff.

[26] See Gurlitt's epilogue to Schering's posthumous book *Das Symbol in der Musik* (1941).

[27] They were translated into French in 1797 by Cantwell, in 1808 by P. Prévost, in 1821 by Guénot, in 1825 by S.-P.-H. (Harlode).

[28] Despite Arthur Salz's new edition of 1920 (Munich: Drei Masken Verlag). There is a characteristic rejection of Blair on p. 71.—Müller said to his auditors: "When my words have struck home to you, a greater than I was speaking through my mouth: my greatest merit is that I understood the greatest orator of my century, that I understood Burke."

[29] Rhetoric retains a secure place in the Jesuit Order. The *Ars dicendi* of Joseph Kleutgen (1811–83) appeared in 1847 and had twenty-one editions to 1928.

5

Topics

ANTIQUE RHETORIC is a forbidding subject. Where are there still readers who, like the young Goethe, would find "everything to do with poetry and rhetoric attractive and delightful"? Where a public to be fascinated by *Curiosities of Literature* and *Amenities of Literature?* [1] And if rhetoric itself impresses modern man as a grotesque bogey—how dare one try to interest him in *topics*, a subject which even the "literary specialist" hardly knows by name because he deliberately shuns the cellars —and foundations!—of European literature? Anxiously indeed must the author ask himself:

> *Nunc quid ago et dubiam trepidus quo dirigo proram?*
> (What do I? Where fearful do I steer my doubtful boat?)

"Textbooks," says Goethe, "should be attractive; they will be so only if they present the brightest and most approachable side of learning and science." Let us try to present topics approachably if not brightly. Things human and divine lie hidden even there.

In the antique system of rhetoric topics is the stockroom. There one found ideas of the most general sort—such as could be employed in every kind of oratory and writing. Every writer, for example, must try to put the reader in a favorable frame of mind. To this end, until the literary revolution of the eighteenth century, a modest first appearance was recommended. The author had next to lead the reader to the subject. Hence for the introduction (*exordium*) there was a special topics; and likewise for the conclusion. Formulas of modesty, introductory formulas, concluding formulas, then, are required everywhere. Other topoi can be used only for some particular species of oratory—for the judicial oration or the epideictic oration. An example!

---

[1] A series of books by Isaac D'Israeli (1766–1848), the father of the statesman. *Curiosities* was published 1791–93, *Amenities* 1841.

1. *Topics of Consolatory Oratory*

A sub-species of epideictic oratory is the consolatory oration (λόγος παρα-
μυθητικός, *consolatio*), or consolatory treatise, whose abbreviated form
is the letter of condolence. This genre will serve to show us what topics is.

Achilles knows that he is destined to an early death. He accepts his lot,
finds consolation in the thought (*Iliad*, XVIII, 117 f.): "Not even the
mighty Herakles escaped death, albeit most dear to Kronian Zeus the
King." * At Archytas' grave Horace reflects upon the theme: all must die.
Even the heroes (*Odes*, I, 28, 7 ff.):

> *Occidit et Pelopis genitor, conviva deorum,*
> *Tithonusque remotus in auras,*
> *Et Jovis arcanis Minos admissus; habentque*
> *Tartara Panthoiden . . .*

> (Gone too the sire of Pelops, guest of the gods,
> Tithonus too, snatched into air,
> And Minos who Jove's secrets knew; yea, Tartarus
> Holds Panthous' son . . .)

In an elegy on the death of Tibullus, Ovid argues that the greatest poets
of the past also had to die (*Amores*, III, 9, 21 ff.). The imperial philosopher
Marcus Aurelius points out that Hippocrates, who cured many sicknesses,
himself fell sick and died. And Alexander, Pompey, Caesar, "they who so
often razed whole cities to the very ground," had to depart this life. Such
were the grounds of consolation found by the poets and sages of Antiquity.

But in the Christian era people must certainly have found other things
to say? Yes, a great Christian like Augustine found deeper consolation. He
recalls the friend of his youth, Nebridius, with the words: "Now his ear
hangs no longer on my mouth, but the mouth of his soul lies at the eternal
fount . . . and he is blessed without end. Yet I believe not that he is so
intoxicated therewith as to forget me. For thou, Lord, whom he drinks, re-
memberest us" (*Conf.*, IX, 3, 6). But the literati of the Christian era
cling to the well-tried grounds of consolation supplied by pagan rhetoric.
Only now they no longer enumerate heroes or poets who had to die, but
patriarchs. They were very long-lived, to be sure, but . . . Fortunatus (ed.
B. Leo, p. 205 f.) names Adam, Seth, Noah, Melchizedek, and many
others in proof of the statement:

> <u>Qui satus</u> ex homine est, et moriturus erit.
> (Who comes of the seed of man, for him death waits.)

Agius of Corvey heightens this biblical *consolatio* in the poem he composed
in 876 on the death of the Abbess Hathumod (d. 874). He points out that

[* Trans. Lang, Leaf, and Myers.]

not only the patriarchs but also their wives died; likewise the Apostles and others besides. It takes him over a hundred lines (*Poetae*, III, 377, 229 ff.). Laudable industry! But hardly a "touching lament," as it has been called.

Grief for one dead is greatest when he has sunk into the grave in youth, like Drusus, brother of Tiberius, son of Livia, adopted son of Augustus, who, not yet thirty, died near the Elbe in 9 B.C. as the result of a fall from a horse. The unknown author of the *Consolatio ad Liviam*, however, puts forth the consideration that a glorious life must not be judged merely by the number of its years:

Quid numeras annos? vixi maturior annis:
Acta senem faciunt: haec numerandi tibi.

(Why do you count my years? More ripely I lived than by years.
What makes the old man is deeds; count you then those.)

The same writer asked his Muse to sing the death of the sixty-year-old Maecenas. Would that he had lived to be as old as Nestor, who saw three generations of men pass him by and yet was wept by his kindred because he died too soon (*In Maecenatis obitum*, I, 138)!

Thus from the theme of the consolatory poem there branches reflection upon the ages attained by men. When Horace, in the lines quoted above, names Tithonus among the heroes, he already verges on the theme: "Even the oldest must die."—Tithonus and Nestor are pagan examples of longevity as the patriarchs are biblical ones. But who is Tithonus? He was once one of the handsomest youths of the Heroic Age (Priam's brother), wherefore Eos stole him away ("la concubina di Titone antico": *Purgatorio*, IX, 1). She prayed Zeus to grant him immortality; but since she forgot at the same time to beg eternal youth for him, he became decrepit with age. His consort shunned him and at his request transformed him into a cicada. What finally became of him? Horace (*Odes*, II, 16, 30) knew:

Longa Tithonum minuit senectus.
(Long old age Tithonus minisheth.)

But in the lines quoted earlier Horace makes him die. No matter: among the personages of Greek mythology there was no mortal more aged than Tithonus. But was there among them someone who died in earliest youth, and hence, like Tithonus, represents a maximum? Yes, the infant Archemorus (the Greek name means "dying in the beginning" [2]). His nurse Hypsipyle (put in Limbo with other heroines by Dante: *Purg.*, XXII, 112) left him behind in a forest, where he succumbed to the bite of a snake. This story is a part of the saga of Thebes, which the Middle Ages read in Statius.

Now, as the writers of *consolationes* discovered, it makes little difference

---

[2] Archemorus is a "speaking name." Cf. Statius, *Thebais*, V, 738, and Lactantius Placidus on the passage.

whether a person dies young or old, it must always be effective to confront famous examples of longevity with equally famous examples of the reverse, hence Tithonus with Archemorus. We find this device in the most famous *consolatio* of modern times. François Malherbe counsels his friend Du Périer not to grieve because his daughter sank so young into the grave:

> Non, non, mon Du Périer; aussitôt que la Parque
>   Ôte l'âme du corps,
> L'âge s'évanouit au deçà de la barque,
>   Et ne suit point les morts.

> Tithon n'a plus les ans qui le firent cigale,
>   Et Pluton aujourd'hui
> Sans égard du passé, les mérites égale
>   D'Archémore et de lui.

In the scales of the Judge of the Dead the lifetime of the oldest man weighs no more than that of the infant.

2. *Historical Topics*

Not all topoi can be derived from rhetorical genres. Many stem originally from poetry and then pass over into rhetoric. Since Antiquity there has been a perpetual exchange between poetry and prose. To poetic topics belongs the beauty of nature in the widest sense—hence the ideal landscape with its typical equipment (*infra*, ch. 10). So do dreamlands and dream ages: Elysium (with eternal spring without meteorological disturbances), the Earthly Paradise, the Golden Age. So do the active principles in life: love, friendship, transience. All these themes concern basic relations of existence and hence are timeless—some more, others less. Less: friendship, love. They reflect the sequence of psychological periods. But in all poetical topoi the style of expression is historically determined. Now there are also topoi which are wanting throughout Antiquity down to the Augustan Age. They appear at the beginning of late Antiquity and then are suddenly everywhere. To this class belong the "aged boy" and the "youthful old woman," which we shall analyze. They have a twofold interest. First, as regards literary biology, we can observe in them the *genesis of new topoi*. Thus our knowledge of the genetics of the formal elements of literature is widened. Secondly, these topoi are indications of a changed psychological state; indications which are comprehensible in no other way. Thus our understanding of the psychological history of the West is deepened, and we approach spheres that the psychology of C. G. Jung has explored. In this chapter only the outlines are drawn. We adhere to the antique concept of topics. It has stood the test for us as starting-point and heuristic principle. But whereas antique topics is part of a didascalium, and hence is systematic and normative, let us try to establish the basis for a historical topics. It is capable of many uses. It must prove itself in the analysis of texts.

We shall first treat the topoi of most general application.

3. Affected Modesty

In his exordium it behooved the orator to put his hearers in a favorable, attentive, and tractable state of mind. How do this? First, through a modest presence. But one has to draw attention to this modesty oneself. Thus it becomes affected. According to Cicero (*De inv.*, I, 16, 22), it is expedient for the orator to show submissiveness and humility ("prece et obsecratione humili ac supplici utemur"). Here, then—and this is to be noted—humility is a pre-Christian term. The orator's referring to his feebleness (*excusatio propter infirmitatem*), to his inadequate preparation ("si nos infirmos, imparatos . . . dixerimus": Quintilian, IV, 1, 8) derives from judicial oratory, it is intended to dispose the judges favorably. But it is very early transferred to other genres. A model example is the exordium of Cicero's *Orator*, addressed to Brutus. To treat the theme is beyond Cicero's powers; hence he fears the criticism of learned men; dares not hope to accomplish the thing successfully; foresees that Brutus will find him lacking in discretion, and resigns himself only because Brutus's request is justified. Such "modesty formulas" achieve an immense diffusion, first in pagan and Christian late Antiquity and then in the Latin and vernacular literature of the Middle Ages. Now the author protests his inadequacy in general, now bemoans his uneducated and rude speech (*rusticitas*). Even such a refined stylist as Tacitus would have us believe that his *Agricola* is composed "in artless and unschooled language." Gellius puts such excuses at the beginning of his *Attic Nights* (*praef.*, 10). Ennodius is "dismayed by his poverty of mind" (*Ep.*, I, 8). Fortunatus works out virtuoso variations (ed. Leo, 157, 15; 162, 58):

1. *Quae tibi sit virtus, si possem, prodere vellem;*
   Sed parvo ingenio magna referre vetor.
   (What virtues are thine, if I could, I would gladly set forth;
   But little wit cannot relate great things.)

2. *Materia vincor et quia lingua minor.*
   (The matter conquers, and my tongue threats silence.)

Walafrid writes "with slight talent" ("tenui ingenio"). There are apologies for uncultivated language, for metrical errors, for simplicity and lack of art, etc.[3]

A particular form of "affected modesty" is the author's assurance that he goes to work only "trembling," "fearfully," "with trembling and agitation." Thus Jerome writes (*PL*, XXV, 369 C): "Your prayers have overcome my

[3] *Poetae*, II, 359, No. XII, 2; *ibid.*, 627, 63; *Poetae*, III, 5, 32 ff.; *ibid.*, 305, 1.

fear and agitation" ("trepidationem meam"). Or Paulinus of Périgueux in
his life of St. Martin (II, 6):

> *Nunc quid ago et dubiam trepidus quo dirigo proram?*

I used this line at the beginning of this chapter. It expresses a difficulty
which every writer knows. In every book there are particularly "hard" passages. The author has to take breath and find new strength. Ninth- and
tenth-century poets put their embarrassment into verse, under the title:
"Trepidation before the matter which lies ahead" ("materiei futurae
trepidatio" [4]).

We had traced the modesty topos as far back as Cicero. In diplomatics it
is sometimes confused with the so-called "devotional formula" (such as
Dei gratia, servus servorum Dei).[5] The authority of the Bible brought it
about that the antique topos was often combined with formulas of self-
disparagement derived from the Old Testament. David declares that, in
comparison with Saul he is as a dead dog and as a flea (I Samuel 24:15 and
26:20). Jerome takes this over: "Ego pulex et Christianorum minimus."
We have an example of a choice variation when the writer calls himself a
louse ("pedunculus iste": *Poetae* IV, 1053, 26.) From the Old Testament
we must cite too the ninth chapter of the Wisdom of Solomon. It is a prayer
for wisdom, or as the Vulgate more expressly puts it, an "oratio sapientis
cum agnitione propriae imbecillitatis, ad impetrandam a Domino sapientiam" ("prayer of the wise man begging God for wisdom, with acknowledgment of his own infirmity of mind"). Verse 5 runs: "Quoniam servus tuus
ego, et filius ancillae tuae; homo infirmus et exigui temporis, et minor ad
intellectum judicii et legum." (A.V.: "For I thy servant and son of thine
handmaid am a feeble person, and of a short time, and too young for the
understanding of judgment and laws.") Here formulas of submission and
protestations of incapacity stand side by side.

In the Rome of the Empire formulas of submission could not but develop as courtly glorification of the person of the Emperor increased. The
title "maiestas tua" already appears in Horace (*Epi.*, II, 1, 258) in the
apostrophe to Augustus. The younger Pliny (*Ep.*, X, 1) says instead "tua
pietas." To this exaltation of the Emperor there had to correspond an
abasement of the individual. And so Valerius Maximus in the dedication to
Tiberius which occurs in the preface to his collection of *exempla* already
calls himself "mea parvitas"—which is frequently repeated in later times,
and still survives in "meine Wenigkeit." Similarly, "mediocritas mea" is
used to designate the writer's own person (thus in Velleius Paterculus, II,
111, 3; in Gellius, XIV, 2, 5). In the pagan Rome of the Empire, then,
formulas of self-disparagement were current which could be taken over by
Christians; *mediocritas*, for example, is found in this sense in Arnobius,

---

[4] Heiric (*Poetae*, III, 505, 151 ff. with the marginal gloss); Dudo of St. Quentin
(*PL*, CXLI, 613).
[5] Cf. Excursus II, *infra*.

Lactantius, Jerome, and others. Formulas such as "my littleness, pettiness, smallness" ("mea exigutas, pusillitas, parvitas") occur in Carolingian times. So here we have the transfer of a pagan formula of self-disparagement to Christian use.

The modesty formula is often connected with the statement that one dares write only because a friend or a patron or a superior has expressed such a request or wish or command. This was Cicero's procedure in the *prooemium* of the *Orator*, referred to above. Brutus had asked him to write the treatise. Virgil (*Georgics*, III, 41) complies with Maecenas' commands (*iussa*). The younger Pliny collects his letters because he was admonished to do so (I, 1). This example is followed by Sidonius (*Ep.*, I, 1) with emphatic exaggeration ("diu praecipis summa suadendi auctoritate"). Eugenius of Toledo concludes a poem to the king with the lines:

> *Haec tibi, rex summe, jussu compulsus herili*
> *Servulus Eugenius devota mente dicavi.*

> (These, highest king, by lordly will compelled,
> To thee thy less than slave devoutly dedicates.)

Innumerable medieval authors assert that they write by command. Histories of literature accept this as gospel truth. Yet it is usually a mere topos.

Among modesty topoi also belongs the assurance that the author wishes to spare his reader satiety or boredom (*fastidium, taedium*). Quintilian already (V, 14, 30) warns against *fastidium*. Medieval examples are to be found everywhere. Sometimes decidedly misplaced! The dreary compiler Raban Maur thinks that he can recommend his prose paraphrase of his poem on the cross by the fact that the "twofold style . . . will spare the reader satiety" (*Poetae*, III, 371, n. 5). Dante too uses *fastidium* at the beginning of his *Monarchia* (I, 1, 4). Concern over the reader's satiety could, however, also serve as a topos for the end of a work or a section. So we find it in Macrobius (*Sat.*, V, 22, 15), in Prudentius (*Contra Symmachum*, I), in Milton (*Hymn on the Morning of Christ's Nativity*):

> *Time is our tedious song should here have ending.*[6]

4. Topics of the Exordium

This branch of topics serves to give reasons for the composition of a piece of writing and is extensively developed. We give a few samples.

a) The topos "I bring things never said before" appears even in ancient

---

[6] Other examples: *Carm. cant.* (ed. Strecker), p. 31, st. 15; *Walter of Châtillon* 1929, p. 52, ch. 37; *Archpoet*, ed. Manitius, p. 22, st. 43; *Poetae*, IV, 171, 68.—In a celebrated hymn Ambrose appears to assume that God created the divisions of the day to spare man satiety: "Aeterne rerum conditor, / Noctem diemque qui regis / Et temporum das tempora, / Ut alleves fastidium."

Greece as "rejection of trite epic material." [7] Choerilus (end of the fifth century), who sought to rejuvenate the epic by historical material, held that the old sagas were worn out and called those happy who served the Muses when "the meadow was still untouched." Virgil observes (*Georg.*, III, 4):

> *Omnia iam vulgata: quis non Eurysthea durum*
> *Aut inlaudati nescit Busiridis aras?*

(All things are staled; who knows not cruel Eurystheus,
Who not the altars of ill-famed Busiris?)

This refers to the twelve labors of Hercules, a subject treated all too often. Horace promises "songs never heard" (*Carm.*, III, 1, 2). Manilius (II, 53) seeks pastures which have never been grazed ("integra prata") and rejects the old legendary material (III, 5 ff.). So does the poet of the *Aetna* (l. 23). Statius praises Lucan for having forsaken the well-worn wheel tracks ("trita vatibus orbita": *Silvae*, II, 7, 51). Rightly could Dante say that in his *Monarchia* he wished to present truths which others had not yet attempted ("intemptatas ab aliis ostendere veritates": I, 1, 3). And in the *Paradiso* (II, 7):

> *L'acqua ch'io prendo già mai non si corse.*

Boccaccio to his book (*Teseida*, 12, 84):

> *Seghi queste onde, non solcate mai*
> *Davanti a te da nessun altro ingegno.*

Ariosto promises (*Orlando Furioso*, I, 2):

> *Cosa non detta mai in prosa nè in rima.*

Milton takes this over (*Paradise Lost*, I, 16):

> *Things unattempted yet in Prose or Rhime.*

b) In the exordium the topos of dedication is also a favorite. Statius sends his friend Rutilius Gallicus a poem on his recovery and compares it with an offering brought to the gods (*Silvae*, I, 4, 31 ff.). The Roman poets commonly call their dedications "consecrations" (*dicare, dedicare, consecrare, vovere*). Christian authors like to present their works to God. The Bible afforded numerous justifications for this practice. The writer's assurance, so frequent in the Middle Ages, that he consecrates his work to God as an offering goes back to Jerome, who elaborated it out of Biblical elements. In his *prologus galeatus* [8] Jerome writes: "In the temple of God

---

[7] Aristophanes criticizes outworn tragic effects; cf. W. Schmid, *Geschichte der griechischen Literatur*, I, 2 (1934), 535, n. 1.

[8] Jerome is said to have called his prologue "helmeted" because it was intended to guard the authority of the Bible.

each presents what he can: one gold, silver, and precious stones; another fine linen, scarlet, and hyacinth; it must suffice for us if we offer skins and goats' hair" (after Exodus 25:3). But reference to the widow's mite ("aera minuta"; Luke 21:2) also goes back to Jerome. It became very popular.[9]

Yet another Biblical precept is used allegorically in this sense. God said to the children of Israel through Moses: "When ye be come into the land which I give unto you, and shall reap the harvest thereof, then shall ye bring a sheaf of the firstfruits of your harvest ("manipulos spicarum, primitias messis vestrae") unto the priest" (Leviticus 23:10). To this commandment of the Old Covenant Walter of Speyer went back in the prologue to his *Scolasticus* (*Poetae*, V, 11). With it he combines the Parable of the Sower and, as the firstfruits of his "harvest," presents his poem to his teacher Balderich, bishop (970–86) of Speyer.[10]

c) A favorite topos is: "The possession of knowledge makes it a duty to impart it." Earlier antique versions of this are to be found in Theognis (769 ff.) and Seneca (*Ep.*, 6, 4). The didactic poet Cato offered the following moral maxim:

> *Disce, sed a doctis, indoctos ipse doceto:*
> *Propaganda etenim est rerum doctrina bonarum.*

> (Learn from the learned; the unlearned, teach;
> For knowledge of goodly things should be spread wide.)

The Bible afforded much that could be used: "Wisdom that is hid, and treasure that is hoarded up, what profit is in them both?" (Ecclesiasticus 20:32). "Let thy fountains be dispersed abroad, and rivers of waters in the streets" (Proverbs 5:16). The parables of the talent that must not be buried and of the light that must not be put under a bushel (Matthew 25:18 and 5:15) are employed in the same sense. Only a few examples! The Archpoet (Manitius, 16, st. 3):

> *Ne sim reus et dignus odio,*
> *Si lucernam ponam sub modio,*
> *Quod de rebus humanis sentio,*
> *Pia loqui iubet intentio.*

> (Lest I do ill and gain despite,
> Under a bushel hiding my light,
> Whatever I know of the human race
> My pious intent to tell it is.)

[9] *Poetae*, I, 209, 15 and 236, No. XI, 23; III, 37, 505; IV, 172, 79 and 917, 9; V, 245, 334.—Rahewin's *Theophilus*, 1. 6.—Archpoet, ed. Manitius, p. 38, to Frederick I: "Vidua pauperior tibi do minutum."—Dante, *Par.*, X, 106 ff.

[10] On the interpretation, cf. *RF*, LIV (1940), 135.

Alan (*PL*, CCX, 586 B):

> Non minus hic peccat qui censum condit in agro
> Quam qui doctrinam claudit in ore suam.

> (Not less sins he who hides his wealth in field
> Than he who shutteth knowledge in his mouth.)

Maugis d'Aigremont (ed. Castets, 8918):

> Mes li sages le dit, sel trueve on en l'autor,
> C'on doit mostrer son sen au besoin sanz trestor.

> (But the sage saith, as doth mine author here,
> If need be, tell thy thoughts with right good cheer.)

Chrétien de Troyes, *Erec*, 6 ff.:

> Car qui son estuide entrelet,
> Tost i puet tel chose teisir,
> Qui mout vandroit puis a pleisir.

> (For he who study leaves
> Lightly may silence what
> Would soon bring pleasure great.)

Roethe, in 1899 (*Die Reimvorreden des Sachsenspiegels*, 9), noted Eike's "profound" comparison of knowledge "to a treasure which he will not . . . bury in the earth." The Old Spanish *Libro de Alixandre* begins:

> Deue de lo que sabe omne largo seer,
> Sy non podria en culpa e en yerro caher.

> (Of all that he doth know a man should generous be,
> Else he may fall in sin and error grievously.)

Dante, *Monarchia*, I, 1, 3 ". . . ne de infossi talenti culpa redarguar" ("lest I be convicted of the charge of burying my talent").

d) Another favorite exordial topos is: "Idleness is to be shunned." In Horace one could read an exhortation to write poetry on the ground (*Sat.*, II, 3, 15):

> . . . Vitanda est improba Siren
> Desidia.

> (. . . Shun the evil siren
> Idleness.)

Ovid counseled his stepdaughter (*Tr.*, III, 7, 31):

> *Ergo desidiae remove, doctissima, causas,*
> *Inque bonas artes et tua sacra redi.*

(Sloth's causes banish, then, most learned daughter;
Return to the sacred circle of noblest studies.)

Nor did Ovid (*Rem. am.*, 161) fail to recognize the harmful consequences of sloth:

> *Quaeritur Aegisthus quare sit factus adulter;*
> *Causa est in promptu: desidiosus erat.*

(Many have asked why Aegisthus became an adulterer;
The answer lies close to hand: he lived in idleness.)

Martial (VIII, 3, 12) and Seneca also warned against idleness. Much quoted was the latter's: "Otium sine litteris mors est et hominis vivi sepultura": "Leisure without studies is the death and burial of a living man." The didactic poet Cato had put the maxim into verse (III, *praef.* 6). Molière will still quote it (*Le bourgeois gentilhomme*, II, 6). In Mantegna's *Triumph of Wisdom over the Vices* (Louvre), Otium, represented as an ugly, armless woman, bears the legend (from Ovid, *Rem. am.*, 139):

> *Otia si tollas, periere Cupidinis arcus.*
> (Take leisure away, and Cupid's bow shoots awry.)

The idleness topos can be so turned as to recommend the practice of poetry as a cure for sloth and vice.[11]

5. *Topics of the Conclusion*

Whereas the exordial topics of medieval poetry could lean heavily upon rhetoric, this was hardly possible in conclusions. The conclusion of an oration was supposed to resume the principal points and then to make an appeal to the emotions of the hearer, that is, stir him to enthusiasm or to sympathy. These precepts were inapplicable to poetry as well as to all non-oratorical prose. Hence quite often we find that conclusions are lacking (as in the *Aeneid*) or abrupt. Thus Ovid, concluding the *Ars amandi* (III, 809), says: "The game is over." An abrupt conclusion is (*Poetae*, III, 25, 732):

> . . . *nunc libri terminus adsit*
> *Huius, et alterius demum repetatur origo.*

---

[11] For example, *Ecbasis captivi*, 12 ff.—Lehmann, *Pseudoantike Literatur*, 53, 74 ff. and 52, 1 ff.—*Speculum* (1931), 116.—In the vernacular in Alberic's *Alexander*, l. 6.

(. . . now be the end of this book
Here, and let the next begin at once.)[12]

In the vernacular, for example, in Wace (*Vie de sainte Marguerite*):

> *Ci faut sa vie, ce dit Wace,*
> *Qui de latin en romans mist*
> *Ce que Theodimus escrist.*

(Here ends her life, so sayeth Wace,
Who in Romance has fairly put
The Latin that Theodimus wrote).

To this "abrupt type" belongs also the closing line of the *Song of Roland*:

> *Ci falt la geste que Turoldus declinet.*
> (Here ends the tale which Turoldus sets forth.)

These concluding formulas, especially the "abrupt" ones, make sense in the Middle Ages: They inform the reader that the work is finished, that he has the whole of it. To know this was satisfying in an age which knew no method of reproduction except copying—an uncertain procedure. The scribe could be called away, go on a journey, fall ill, die—many medieval poems have reached us only as fragments, many lack their conclusion. But the brief concluding formula also allowed the author to put in his name— as did Wace, and the poet of the *Song of Roland*.

The most natural reason for ending a poem in the Middle Ages was weariness. Writing poetry was such a strenuous thing.

Often poets end "seeking rest," or rejoice that they may rest again. When the poet lays down his pen, we sense that he breathes easier. Often he alleges that the Muse has wearied, often his own feet have grown tired. It is very understandable—one poet has treated the eight parts of speech in verse after Donatus, another has versified a saint's life, yet another has even composed a history of literature in rhyme.[13]

Only one antique concluding topos passed over into the Middle Ages: "We must stop because night is coming on." This, of course, befits only an outdoor conversation. Such is the feigned situation in Cicero's *De oratore*, which hence also ends (III, §209) because the setting sun admonishes to brevity. But it is also the situation of bucolic poetry: the first, fifth, and

---

[12] Other examples: Fortunatus, *Vita s. Martini*, IV, 621; *Walter of Châtillon* 1929, p. 30, 30.—Conclusions of letters in Pliny, *Ep.*, III, 9, 37; VI, 16, 21.

[13] Examples: Smaragdus (*Poetae*, I, 615, No. XV, 17): "Carminis hic statuo finem defigere nostri / Ut teneam requiem iam tribuente deo."—Purchard (*Poetae*, V, 227, 492): "Carminis hic finem dat clausula fertque quietem / Cure scribentis, quia labilis est labor omnis, / Premia sed semper stabunt sine fine potenter."— Anonymous (*NA*, II, 396, 215): "Haec ubi complevit, iam lassa Thalia quievit." —*Passio s. Catharinae* (ed. Varnhagen), 698: "Pennam pono fruor operisque fine; quieti / Mentem reddo, manum subtraho, metra sino."—Hugh of Trimberg at the end of the *Registrum multorum auctorum*: "Nunc in hoc opusculo lassum pedem sisto / Rogans et in domino nostro Jesu Christo."

eighteenth idyls of Theocritus, the first, second, sixth, ninth, and tenth eclogues of Virgil, and the fifth of Calpurnius, end with sunset.[14] Garcilaso de la Vega in his first eclogue draws out the singing of the two shepherds through an entire day. Salicio begins at sunrise, Nemoroso ends at sunset. Herrera censured this. But the daylong shepherd's complaint met with approval. Milton ends his *Lycidas* with the lines:

> *Thus sang the uncouth Swain to th' okes and rills,*
> *While the still morn went out with Sandals gray,*
> *He touch'd the tender stops of various Quills,*
> *With eager thought warbling his Dorick lay:*
> *And now the Sun had stretch'd out all the hills,*
> *And now was dropt into the Western bay;*
> *At last he rose, and twitch'd his Mantle blew:*
> *To morrow to fresh woods, and Pastures new.*

Once become a convention, this concluding topos can be used at will, and without any pastoral accouterment. The results are variously comic. An anonymous poet writes a poem on London containing all of twenty-eight lines. It appears to have cost him an entire day (NA, I [1876], 602), at least so he gives us to believe:

> *Cetera pretereo quia preterit hora diei,*
> *Terminat hora diem, terminat auctor opus.*

(The rest I pass by, for the time of day passes by;
The hour ends the day, the poet his work.)

Sigebert of Gembloux ends the first book of his *Passio Thebeorum* because he has gone so far with his account that he must cross the Alps; but that is impossible by night. The Spaniard Berceo (13th century) has lingered over his prologue. So he will get on with his narrative. For the days are short, soon it will be night, to write in the dark is difficult. Walter of Châtillon uses the topos very ingeniously. He too must close because of falling night—and close his entire epic. But he has exhausted the subject and now thirsts for another.[15]

---

[14] Likewise the *Ecloga Theoduli* (1. 343) and Warnerius of Basel's *Synodicus*, which is dressed up as an eclogue.

[15] Berceo, *Santa Oria:*
> *Avemos en el prologo mucho detardado,*
> *Sigamos la estoria, esto es aguisado:*
> *Los dias non son grandes, anochezra privado,*
> *Escrivir en tiniebra es un mester pesado.*

Walter of Châtillon, *Alexandreis*, X, 455 ff.
> *Phoebus anhelantes convertit ad aequora currus:*
> *Iam satis est lusum, iam ludum incidere praestat,*
> *Pierides, alios deinceps modulamina vestra*
> *Alliciant animos: alium mihi postulo fontem;*
> *Qui semel exhaustus sitis est medicina secundae.*

6. *Invocation of Nature*

As an example of a poetic topos let us take the invocation of nature. Originally it had a religious significance. In the *Iliad*, besides the Olympians, earth, heaven, and streams are invoked in prayers and oaths. In Aeschylus, *Prometheus* (88 ff.) invokes the ether, winds, streams, sea, earth, and sun: they must witness what he, the god, suffers. Sophocles' *Ajax* (412 ff.) calls upon the sea, its caves, its shores, or (859 ff.) upon the light and soil of his native land, its springs and streams—not however as a suppliant but in leave-taking. Natural powers and natural objects are no longer addressed as divinities in Sophocles but are humanized. They are sympathetic beings. Thenceforth they are at the poet's service when he wishes to heighten the effect of a lament for the dead. The choir of nature, divided into many voices, fills space around the poet with the volume of its sound. The finest such treatment is Bion's *Lament for Adonis*, from the late Hellenistic period. Greek prose of the Empire introduces the topos into the romance.[16] Streams, trees, cliffs, beasts testify to Nature's sympathy. In Latin poetry Statius, the master of literary Mannerism, makes prolific use of the invocation of nature.[17] In late Latin Antiquity nature can be reduced to the four elements.[18] Indeed, late pagan piety bestowed religious veneration upon them. Paul rejects this cult (Col. 2:8). The adoption of the topos by Christian poetry was expedited by the Evangelists' account of the disturbance of nature at the time of the Redeemer's death. The earth quaked, the rocks were rent (Matt. 27:51); a darkness came over the whole land (Mark 15:33); the sun lost its light (Luke 23:45). But the Bible also told of nature sharing in joy: "Let the heavens rejoice, and let the earth be glad; let the sea roar, and the fulness thereof. Let the field be joyful, and all that is therein: then shall all the trees of the wood rejoice before the Lord." [19]

Medieval poetry was far too lacking in independence to give a living development to the topos which it had received from pagan late Antiquity. The Christian poet knows, of course, that nature was created by God. He can therefore address its component parts as creatures of God or of Christ. He can even increase their number: the Bible (Vulgate: Daniel 3:56–88 and Psalm 148) authorized him to add to the old catalogue (trees, streams, rocks, etc.) meteorological phenomena (which he does with painful accuracy): storm, clouds, rain, raindrops, frost, hoarfrost, snow, ice, etc.[20] The

[16] Erwin Rohde, *Der griechische Roman* (1876), 160, n. 1.
[17] *Silvae*, II, 7, 12; III, 4, 102; IV, 8, 1–14.
[18] Nemesianus, *Ecl.*, I, 35.
[19] A.V. Psalm 96:11 ff. = Vulgate 95:11 ff.
[20] *Omnis factura Christi: sol, sidera, luna,*
Colles et montes, valles, mare, flumina, fontes,
Tempestas, pluvie, nubes, ventique, procelle,
Cauma, pruina, gelu, glacies, nix, fulgura, rupes,
Prata, nemus, frondes, arbustum, gramina, flores,
Exclamando: vale! mecum predulce sonate.

medieval poet does not invoke nature, he enumerates its component parts, and does so according to the principle, "The more the better!" At the death of the margrave Eric of Friuli nine rivers and nine cities are made to share in the mourning (*Poetae*, I, 131). But this is far outdone by Jotsald's lament on the death of Odilo of Cluny. The entire world must mourn too. The poet will "move all things," including quadrupeds, birds, and reptiles.[21]

In the Renaissance the topos again converges with late antique bucolic (Garcilaso's first eclogue, Ronsard[22] and many others). This is continued in French Classicism. Maynard makes his "age-stricken beauty" ("la belle vieille") complain:

> *Pour adoucir l'aigreur des peines que j'endure,*
> *Je me plains aux rochers, et demande conseil*
> *À ces vieilles forêts, dont l'epaisse verdure*
> *Fait de si belles nuits en dépit du soleil.*

Racan retires happily to rural solitude, but wants witnesses:

> *Agréables deserts, séjours de l'innocence,*
> *Où, loin des vanités de la magnificence,*
> *Commence mon repos et finit mon tourment,*
> *Vallons, fleuves, rochers, plaisante solitude,*
> *Si vous fûtes témoins de mon inquiétude,*
> *Soyez-le désormais de mon contentement.*

La Fontaine, in his epistle to Huet, parodies the obligatory apostrophe to the rocks:

> *Je le dis aux rochers, on veut d'autres discours:*
> *Ne pas louer son siècle est parler à des sourds.*

In the Spanish drama the medieval style of accumulated enumeration is exploited to the utmost. Calderón commands all the stops—all nature's realms and all their inhabitants lie ready like brightly colored bits of stone.

(J. Werner, *Beiträge*, No. 120, st. 11).—Participation of nature in the joy of Easter: *Poetae*, I, 137, No. VI, st. 2, 4.—Summons to nature to share in the author's grief for his sins: *Poetae*, I, 148, st. 14–15; in Florus of Lyon's complaint on the partition of the Frankish kingdom (*Poetae*, II, 559 f.) raindrops are summoned and, with them, the elements again.—The invocation of nature early makes its way into hymn poetry. An example from the eleventh century (*A.h.*, 22, 27): "Coelum, tellus et maria / Mellita promant carmina, / His nempe dignus laudibus / Est martyr Anastasius."

21 *Plangite vos, populi, vos linguae, sidera, coeli,*
  Proruat in tenebras resplendens orbita solis,
  Deficiant plene radiantia cornua lunae,
  Lugeat et mundus, protenso corpore, totus:
  Nunc terras, pelagus, montes silvasque ciebo;
  Quadrupedes, bipedes, reptantia cuncta movebo.

Text: *Studi medievali*, N. S. I (1928), 401. Cf. P. A. Becker, *Vom Kurzlied zum Epos* (1940), 67.

22 Cf. P. Laumonier, *Ronsard poète lyrique*, 448 ff.

They can be put together into whatever patterns he pleases. New and ever new figures rise kaleidoscopically—rhetorical bravura pieces whose exuberance pours out like a cascade. But looking more closely, we see that everything is well ordered and symmetrical. The topos can be employed in any context. It serves the heroic emotion of tragic situations. When Calderón's heroes and heroines execute it with the most elaborate coloraturas, they are often interrupted by the mockery of the *gracioso* (the comic servant in the Spanish drama), but he does not throw them off. Calderón once amused himself by travestying the topos. By the dead body of his wife Céfalo complains: [23]

> *Dead is the brightest light*
> *Of day; the night has come.*
> *Republic of the sky,*
> *Birds, fish, wild beasts, and men,*
> *Sea, cliffs, crags, mountains high,*
> *Plants, flowers, grasses, fields,*
> *Together weep and cry!*
> *Saddlecloths, coaches, mules,*
> *With every beast alive,*
> *Peacocks and pheasants, hens,*
> *Black puddings, pig's-feet, tripe,*
> *Procris is dead! Then say:* .
> *In peace may her topknot lie!*

7. The World Upsidedown

One of the freshest pieces among the *Carmina Burana* begins:

> *Florebat olim studium,*
> *Nunc vertitur in tedium;*
> *Iam scire diu viguit,*
> *Sed ludere prevaluit.*
> *Iam pueris astutia*
> *Contingit ante tempora,*
> *Qui per malevolentiam*
> *Excludunt sapientiam.*
> *Sed retro actis seculis*
> *Vix licuit discipulis*
> *Tandem nonagenarium*
> *Quiescere post studium.*
> *At nunc decennes pueri*
> *Decusso iugo liberi*
> *Se nunc magistros iactitant . . .*

---

[23] Keil, IV, 671 b.—Intervention of the *gracioso*: Keil, IV, 269 b.—Natural objects designated "requisitos de solilóquio": Keil, II, 256 b.—Some outstanding loci: Keil, IV, 14 a; IV, 462 a; IV, 591 b. There are countless others, some in the *autos sacramentales*.

(Once learning flourished, but alas!
'Tis now become a weariness.
Once it was good to understand,
But play has now the upper hand.
Now boyish brains become of age
Long before time can make them sage,
In malice too of age become,
Shut wisdom out of house and home.
In days long gone and passed away
A scholar hardly dared to say
When he had reached his ninetieth year,
"My hour of rest from toil is here."
But now see little boys of ten
Lay down the yoke, strut out as men,
And boast themselves full masters too . . .)

The poem begins as a "complaint on the times": youth will no longer study! Learning is in decay! But—so the thought proceeds—the whole world is topsy-turvy! The blind lead the blind and hurl them into the abyss; birds fly before they are fledged; the ass plays the lute; [24] oxen dance; plowboys turn soldiers. The Fathers Gregory, Jerome, Augustine, and the Father of Monks, Benedict, are to be found in the alehouse, in court, or in the meat market. Mary no longer delights in the contemplative life nor Martha in the active. Leah is barren, Rachel blear-eyed. Cato haunts the stews, Lucretia has turned whore. What was once outlawed is now praised. Everything is out of joint.

The content of the poem is purely medieval. Only Cato and Lucretia as exemplary figures of virtue point to Antiquity. And yet the basic formal principle, "stringing together impossibilities" (ἀδύνατα, *impossibilia*) is of antique origin. Its first appearance seems to be in Archilochus. The eclipse of the sun on April 6, 648 b.c., would seem to have given him the idea that nothing was any longer impossible now that Zeus had darkened the sun; no one need be surprised if the beasts of the field changed their food for that of dolphins (Fragment 74). The Virgilian *adynata* were known in the Middle Ages. A shepherd forsaken by his beloved is ready to compound for the reversal of the entire order of nature. "Now may the wolf of his own free will flee the sheep, the oak bear golden apples, owls compete with swans,[25] the shepherd Tityrus be Orpheus . . ." (*Ecl.*, VIII, 53 ff.). Theodulf (*Poetae*, I, 490, No. XXVII) mocks the poetasters at the court of Charlemagne. "What shall the swans do, when crows sound forth such songs, when the parrot imitates the Muses . . . ?" Now one can be prepared

---

[24] The Greek proverb ὄνος λύρας ("the ass is deaf to the lute") was known to the Middle Ages through Boethius, *Cons.*, I, pr. 4.

[25] The swan as possessing the most beautiful voice among all birds (whence "swansong").

for anything, "the order of things is changed to its opposite. Orpheus may tend sheep, Tityrus enjoys the pleasures of the court." The motif of the exchange of roles between Tityrus and Orpheus is enough to show that Theodulf had Virgil in mind. Theodulf's *adynata* aim at a bad poet, but then mention the royal court with honor. It is otherwise with Walafrid. His *adynata* series ("similitudo impossibilium"; *Poetae*, II, 392) is the inspiration of a pedagogue. He sets out to increase Virgil's examples (piling up erudition counts as rhetorical ornament for the Middle Ages). Hence he chooses the same verbal form as Virgil's shepherd: "May such and such happen." May hens bear kids, may goats lay eggs, etc.

Virgil's *adynata*, then, act as a stimulus in Carolingian poetry. In Theodulf they are interwoven into a description of the times. But everything remains within Virgilian limits. We are in the "aetas vergiliana" (Traube). In the twelfth century Virgil is supplemented by Ovid and the Roman satirists. The richly developed cultural life of the time engenders a new self-assurance. Writers venture on large-scale contemporary criticism. The degeneration of the church (Jerome, Augustine, Gregory) and of monasticism (Benedict; Mary's contemplation in contrast to the active life symbolized by Martha), even the condition of the peasants—all are targets. The frame of the antique *adynaton* serves both censure of the times and denunciation of the times. Out of stringing together *impossibilia* grows a topos: "the world upsidedown."

It had happened once before, a millennium and a half earlier: in Aristophanes.[26] Comic motifs have more vitality than any others. The "world upsidedown" also delighted the Greeks as a parody of the Homeric journey to Hades (*Nekyia*). As such it appears in Lucian ("Menippus"), and, with Lucian as a model, in Rabelais (*Pantagruel*, ch. 30). This line runs parallel with the transformation of the *adynata* to the world upsidedown.

Florebat olim is not alone in its time. In the monastery of Grandmont near Limoges a dispute broke out between clergy and lay brothers in 1185 and, as a result of the French-English conflict, became a political affair. A poem in the *Carmina Burana* (Schumann, No. 37) treats the subject as an example of the "world upsidedown": cattle talk; the ox is harnessed behind the cart; capital and pedestal are interchanged; an ignorant fool becomes prior. In his *Mirror of Fools* (written before 1180) Nigel Wireker shows that the present has stood the entire past on its head (*SP*, I, 11). About 1183 Alan (in the *Anticlaudianus*) describes the grove of Fortune. There great trees are small, instead of the nightingale the lark sings, etc. (*SP*, II, 397). In John de Hanville's *Architrenius* the Hill of Presumption is the scene of the world upsidedown. The turtle flies, the hare threatens the lion, etc. (*SP*, I, 308 f.).

In the animal world the roles are reversed too—this is a very old *adynaton*. It often occurs in proverb form. There are the lute-playing ass, the

[26] *Ecclesiazusae* and *Plutus*. Wilhelm Schmid derives this from the topos of the *adynaton* (*Geschichte der griechischen Literatur*, I, 2 [1934], 532, n. 9).

dancing ox, the draught-animal hitched to the wrong end of the cart, the bold hare, the timorous lion, and others. Many of these phrases are documented in Antiquity. They show the gnomic stamp of the people. In Chrétien de Troyes (*Cligés*, 3849 ff.) the dog flees from the hare, the fish hunts the beaver, the lamb the wolf: "Si vont les choses a envers." In the realm of a very exclusive art *adynata* of this type and others are taken up again by Arnaut Daniel, the great and distant master of Dante.[27]

A "world upsidedown" made up of *adynata* is displayed in Breughel's painting known as "Dutch Proverbs." P. Fruytiers made an engraving after it with a legend which renders "the general idea Breughel intended to convey":

> *Par ce dessin il est montré*
> *Les abus du monde renversé.*[28]

In the twilight of a distracted mind the "world upsidedown" can express horror. It does so in a poem by Théophile de Viau (d. 1626), with which the *surréalisme* of the 1920's found connections:

> *Ce ruisseau remonte en sa source;*
> *Un boeuf gravit sur un clocher;*
> *Le sang coule de ce rocher;*
> *Un aspic s'accouple d'une ourse,*
> *Sur le haut d'une vieille tour*
> *Un serpent deschire un vautour;*

[27] In Arnaut Daniel's eighteen poems there are five *adynata*. Only one of them, however, corresponds to the classical type as found in Roman elegy and bucolic (14, 49–50). In the four other passages the *adynaton* has acquired a new function. In No. 4 the effect of false love is described. Whoever follows it must take the cuckoo for a dove and the Puy de Dôme for a plain (ll. 33–36). In No. 10 (43–45) Arnaut describes himself as one "who snatches at air, hunts the hare with the ox, and swims against the stream." Diez comments: "This proverb, whose meaning is clear, also appears in other poems"—namely in No. 14, 1 ff. where Arnaut says that love and joy had restored his understanding and healed it of the trouble he had felt "when he hunted the hare with the ox." In these three examples, then, the *adynaton* appears to indicate the havoc wrought in the poet's mind by "false love" (as in No. 4) or by love grief. But in No. 16 the topos obviously has a wholly different meaning. Obeying a command from love, the poet states his purpose. He intends to compose —chiasmus and antithesis are combined in this *propositio*—
> breu chansson de razon loigna.

"For," he continues, "Love has taught me the arts of his school: I can even bring the mountain torrent to a stand, and my ox runs faster than the hare." Arnaut Daniel is still a puzzling figure to us. This is shown too in his use of the *adynaton*, whose meaning is by no means as clear to me as Diez thought it. For in the last example the *adynaton* does not have a pejorative meaning. On the contrary, it is intended to indicate the poet's artistic mastery and is connected with his fondness for the *ornatus difficilis* of the medieval arts of poetry. It has acquired a new psychological function. Petrarch in his Sonnet 177 followed Arnaut, as Diez pointed out.—Rudolf Borchardt, whose comprehension of Arnaut was profound (*Neue Schweizer Rundschau* [July, 1928]), appraises his *adynata* as "an inspired invention of the contradictions of passion" (*Die grossen Trobadors* [1924], 50).

[28] K. Tolnai, *Jahrbuch der kunsthistorischen Sammlungen in Wien*, VIII (1934), 113.

Le feu brusle dedans la glace;
Le soleil est devenu noir;
Je voy la lune qui va cheoir;
Cet arbre est sorty de sa place.

And now to the revolt of youth against learning, which put us on the track of the "world upsidedown." The opposition of generations is one of the conflicts of all tempestuous periods, whether they are under the sign of a new spring flowering or of an autumnal decline. In the history of letters it appears as the battle of the "moderns" against the ancients—until the moderns themselves have become old classics. The Augustan poets began as moderns. Horace (*Epi.*, II, 1, 76–89) complains that the public esteems only the old writers. Old gentlemen do not care to learn anything new and cling to the favorite poets of their youth. Often it is sheer envy which makes them hate the efforts of the young! Ovid grants others the right to praise the "good old times"; he himself is glad that he is a man of today; the present is the only time in which he would like to live (*Ars am.*, III, 121 f.). The Latin florescence of the twelfth century knows similar conflicts. It was charged with explosive creative urges and delight in intellectual warfare. But, having to learn Latin as a literary language, the *moderni* of that period are so dependent upon schooling in antique models that they still imitate (and sometimes imitate Horace's protest) even when they protest. Josephus Iscanus (Joseph of Exeter), in the introduction to his Troy epic (*De bello troiano*, I, 15–23) makes youth speak forcefully against age. Likewise John of Hanville (*SP*, I, 242 f.) : he did not go through the Flood, is no contemporary of Homer's, but a *modernus*. Age had raised its reprimanding voice in Nigel Wireker's *Mirror of Fools*. The title is a program. Boys scarce born think themselves older than Nestor, more eloquent than Cicero, more learned than Cato (*SP*, I, 12). The mirror held up to them is the story of the ass Brunellus, who is dissatisfied with his short tail. We accompany him as he journeys to study at Salerno and at Paris. But donkey remains donkey. That is the moral of the story. *Florebat olim*, like the "Mirror of Fools," is age's criticism of youth. We see now how it echoes the tensions of the conflict of generations which the poetry of the period from 1180 to 1200 so variously documents for us.

8.   *Boy and Old Man*

This is a topos which grew out of the psychological situation of late Antiquity. All early and high periods of a culture extol the young man and at the same time honor age. But only late periods develop a human ideal in which the polarity youth-age works toward a balance.

Virgil (*Aeneid*, IX, 311) praises the virile mind of the lad Iulus:

Ante annos animumque gerens curamque virilem.
(Having manhood's spirit and forethought before man's years.)

Ovid explains the combination of maturity and youth as a gift from heaven granted only to emperors and demigods (*Ars*, I, 185 f.). Valerius Maximus (III, 1, 2) makes it Cato's praise that in his tender years he already had the dignified seriousness of the senator. In praise of a boy who died young Statius says (*Silvae*, II, 1, 40) that he had a moral maturity which went beyond his tender years. But then in the same period we find a rhetorical exaggeration—the boy to be praised had the maturity of an *old man*. Silius Italicus (VIII, 464) says of a boy: "In sagacity he equaled old age." The younger Pliny mourns the death of a girl of thirteen: in her, sweet maidenhood was united with the wisdom of an aged woman, the dignity of a matron ("suavitas puellaris, anilis prudentia, matronalis gravitas"; *Ep.*, V, 16, 2). Similarly, Apuleius on a youth ("senilis in iuvene prudentia"; *Florida*, IX, 38). The examples show that by the beginning of the second century the *puer senilis* had established itself as a topos. *Ca.* 400 Claudian frequently used it (e.g., in the panegyric on the consuls Probinus and Olybrius, I, 154). Julian, prefect of Egypt under Justinian, puts it into an epigram (*A.P.*, VII, 603): " 'Charon is savage.' 'Kind rather.' 'He carried off the young man so soon.' 'But in mind he was the equal of greybeards.' 'He cut him off from pleasure.' 'But he thrust him out of the way of trouble.' 'He knew not wedlock.' 'Nor the pains of wedlock.' " * The topos can also be found in the New Sophistic, sometimes in the reversed form of "old man as boy." Of Apollonius of Tyana, Philostratus (VIII, 29) relates that it was not known whether he lived to be eighty, ninety, a hundred, or even more, and indeed whether he ever died at all. As an old man he was physically "unscathed"—more charming even than he had been in youth. Eunapius (p. 474) calls the Emperor Julian before his accession "an old man in a boy." In the Latin romance of Apollonius (Ring 29) there is a physician "aspectu adolescens et . . . ingenio senex."

The *puer senilis* or *puer senex* is, we see, a coinage of late pagan Antiquity. It is all the more significant, then, that the Bible had something corresponding to show. Of Tobias we read that he was youngest of all, but never acted childishly: "Cumque esset junior omnibus . . . nihil tamen puerile gessit in opere" (1:4). The Wisdom of Solomon, 4:8 ff. declares that age is honorable but is not to be measured by years: "Wisdom is the gray hair unto men." The Vulgate has: "Cani sunt sensus hominis." The old man's gray hair, then, here serves as a figurative expression for the wisdom which old age should possess. But this widom of old age can also be the portion of youth.[29] This is the Biblical idea which cor-

[* Trans. W. R. Paton.]
[29] I find an ancient Indian parallel in Georges Dumézil, *Mitra-Varuna* (1940), 21. According to Manu (II, 150 ff.) the young Brahmin Kawi instructed his paternal uncles in sacred learning, addressing them as "Sons!" Angered, they complained to the gods. The gods answered: "The lad addressed you rightly, for the unknowing is a child; he who teaches the sacred learning is a father . . . Not because he is white-headed is a man old; he who has read the scripture, even though he be young, him the gods account old."

responds to the *puer senex*. "Gray" (*canus*), "grayhairedness" (*canities*) pass into the language of the Fathers as metaphors: "canities animae" (Ambrose); "canities morum" (Augustine); "canities sensum" (Cassianus). The corresponding Greek is πολιὸς τὸ νόημα (Gregory of Nazianzus, A.P., VIII, 152). Prudentius says of the twelve-year-old Eulalia that her childish modesty aspired to the wisdom of age:

> *Moribus et nimium teneris*
> *Canitiem meditata senum.*

Claudian follows this usage when he praises the Consul Mallius Theodorus for "canities animi" (XVII, 21). The topos *puer senex* was impressed on the memory of the West by a much-read text. Gregory the Great began his life of St. Benedict with the words: "Fuit vir vitae venerabilis . . . ab ipso suae pueritiae tempore cor gerens senile" ("he was a man of venerable life . . . even from his boyhood he had the understanding of an old man"). This becomes a hagiographic cliché, whose influence continues into the thirteenth century.[30] But the reverse formula also appears. The monasticism of the Eastern Church, inspired by Bible text (Matt. 18:3; Mark 10:15; I Peter 2:2; I Cor. 3:2), valued a spiritualized childlikeness as an ideal (cf. Pachomius, *Bibliothek der Kirchenväter*, XXXI [1917], 787). The desert father Macarius (d. 391) was called "child-old-man" (παιδαριογέρων) even as a youth (*PG*, LXVII, 1069 A). It could still be said of an eighteenth-century Russian starets that "even in his youth the Lord gave him wisdom, humility, and the old age of reason." [31]

The topos *puer senex* remains alive down to the seventeenth century as a eulogy schema for both profane and Christian use.[32] Alan of Lille makes the ideal man, Juvenis, share in the virtues of old age (*SP*, II, 385). In the Latin poetics of the twelfth and thirteenth centuries the topos degenerates into mannered trifling.[33] J. J. Scaliger uses it in praise of the fifteen-year-old Hugo Grotius,[34] Góngora in praise of the Viceroy of Naples:

> *Florido en años, en prudencia cano.*
> (Blooming in years, in prudence gray.)

---

[30] Jordanus of Saxony, *De initiis ordinis praedicatorum* (ed. Berthier, 1891), 5.

[31] J. Smolitsch, *Leben und Lehren der Starzen* (1936), 99.

[32] *Poetae*, I, 424, No. XXXI, 9; *Poetae*, II, 90, 183; 135, st. 1; 277, 17; *Poetae*, III, 430, 1 ff.—Hugh Primas (ed. W. Meyer), p. 92, 107; *Ligurinus*, I, 286.

[33] Matthew of Vendôme in *PL*, CCV, 959 C and 934 C; *SB München* (1872), 620; Faral, 130, 45 ff.—Geoffrey of Vinsauf, in the dedication of his *Poetria nova*, celebrates Innocent III as "senex iuvenis" (Faral, 198, 23). In the body of the work the motif reappears five more times (ll. 174 f.; ll. 674–86 in three variants; l. 1309 f.); in the same author's *Documentum* twice (Faral, 295, §57 and 303, §101). The motif became a cliché. It is applied to Pyramus (Lehmann, *Pseudoantike Literatur*, 31) and Hippolytus (John of Garland, *Integumenta Ovidii* [ed. Ghisalberti, 1933], II, 507 f.). It appears parodied in "elegiac comedy": Cohen, I, 140, 265 and 196, 15 and 207, 296).

[34] Jacob Bernays, *J. J. Scaliger* (1855), 176.

Let us look back. From Virgil's "puer maturior annis" there develops in Flavian times the *puer senex*, which Claudian then uses in panegyrics upon high officials. It might be possible to explain this as part of the Mannerism of a late period, which delighted in antitheses. Yet behind it there is also a new human ideal (Pliny, Apuleius). In Philostratus pagan religious motifs enter in. A vision vouchsafed to second-century African martyrs is of remarkable interest in this connection. They see God "as a hoary old man with snow-white hair and a youthful countenance." [35] This has nothing to do with literary reminiscences. But it permits us to understand the admission of the topos into the monastic ideal and into hagiography.

Digging somewhat more deeply, we find that in various religions saviors are characterized by the combination of childhood and age. The name Laotzu can be translated as "old child." [36] Concerning the birth of the Buddhist saint Tsongkapa (b. 1357), we are told: "When the woman went down to the spring one day to fetch water she saw in the mirror of the water a man's face wonderfully beautiful. While she was lost in contemplation of the image, she bore a strong boy with long hair and a full white beard." [37] Among the Etruscan gods we find Tages, "the miraculous boy with gray hair and the intelligence of old age, who was plowed up out of the ground by a plowman at Tarquinii." [38] From the nature worship of the pre-Islamic Arabs the fabulous Chydhyr passed into Islam. "Chydhyr is represented as a youth of blooming and imperishable beauty who combines the ornament of old age, a white beard, with his other charms." [39]

The coincidence of testimony of such various origins indicates that we have here an archetype, an image of the collective unconscious in the sense of C. G. Jung. We shall encounter such primordial images on one or another occasion. The centuries of late Roman Antiquity and of early Christianity are filled with visions which can often be understood only as projections of the unconscious.

9. *Old Woman and Girl*

The combination of youth and age—or alternation between them—was also employed at this period in the characterization of female ideal figures, which are often something wholly different from "personified abstrac-

[35] *Passio SS. Perpetuae et Felicitatis* (ed. van Beek, 1936), 32, 6 f. Jesus as *puer senex*: W. Bauer, *Das Leben Jesu im Zeitalter der neutestamentlichen Apokryphen* (1909), 313.

[36] Lao-tse [Lao-tzu], *Tao te King*, trans. R. Wilhelm (1911), p. vii. Cf. Dschuang Dsi [Chuang Tzu], *Das wahre Buch vom südlichen Blütenland*, trans. R. Wilhelm (1912), 49: "Kui . . . questioned the gynecologist and said: 'You are old in years, yet your appearance is that of a child . . .'—'I have learned understanding.'"

[37] Wilhelm Filchner, *Sturm über Asien* (1924), 218.

[38] Ernst Kornemann, *Römische Geschichte*, I (1938), 36.

[39] Georg Rosen in his translation of the *Mesnewi* [Mesnevi] of Jalāl-ud-dīn Rūmī (1849), p. 28 n.

tions." The striking frequency of these figures in late Antiquity (in both pagan and Christian authors) is not merely a stylistic fashion. It could become so only because to the men of those transitional centuries such ideal figures formed part of the world of experience. It could become so only after visions of such personages which had been actually experienced had become fixed in literature and thus superficially imitable. A multitude of supersensual beings fill the space between men and gods. The younger Pliny relates (*Ep.* VII, 27) that a Roman, attached to the suite of the governor of the province of Africa, was strolling one evening in a portico; there appeared to him a woman of superhuman beauty and stature. She told the terrified man that she was the tutelary spirit of the province, and prophesied his future destiny to him.[40] Pliny has previously doubted whether spirits really appeared, but now is inclined to believe it. The Emperor Severus dreams that he is looking down from a high peak upon Rome and the world, while the provinces sing to the music of lyre and flute (Aelius Spartianus, *Severus*, 3, 5). *Ca.* 300 the Christian Arnobius discusses divine and demonic intermediate beings (*Adversus nationes*, II). They peopled the psychological cosmos of late Antiquity: sibyls, tutelary spirits, demons, supernatural redeemers and noxious creatures. In art as in the coins of the Empire, in the visions of monks as in pagan poetry, such figures confront us. Often we think that we are moving through a hallucinated world, through a world of waking dreams. Visions and dreams have immense power over men in this period. The world of the antique gods is repudiated by enlightened pagans. But it rises again in dreams. In a discussion of religion which dates from the end of the second or from the third century, the representative of paganism admits to a Christian: "Even in sleep we see, hear, and know the gods whom by day we impiously repudiate, reject, and offend by our forswearing" (Minucius Felix, *Octavius*, 7, 6). This epoch finds its expression in visions and allegories.

Philosophy appears to Boethius as a dignified matron. She is full of vitality, though very old ("inexhausti vigoris . . . aevi plena"). Her stature varies. Now she is of human size, now her head seems to touch the sky. Age and youth combined, then, but here raised to the supernatural level. Despite all literary models, Boethius' youthfully vital old woman impresses us as a redemptress seen in a vision. She has a numerous progeny in medieval literature.[41]

[40] The same story in Tacitus, *Annals*, XI, 21.

[41] In Peter of Compostella the World (*Mundus*) appears as "puella aspectu pulcherrima," who though "grandaeva" and gray-haired is at the same time "iuvenilis." Alan uses this motif extensively. In *De planctu Naturae* Hymenaeus is described as old-young (*SP*, II, 502). So is Castitas (506) and Genius (517). In the *Anticlaudianus* Ratio contemplates the "formas in subiecto" in a mirror of glass, the "formas sine materia" in one of silver. These become young again (289–90). A process of rejuvenation paradoxically takes place in Senectus when she sets out to do battle with Iuvenis (*ibid.*, 417). Natura too is presented as an old-young woman in John of Hanville's *Architrenius* (*SP*, I, 369).

Boethius' old-young Philosophia alternates between human and gigantic proportions. This motif too is current in allegorical poetry.[42] Attempts have been made to trace it back to Homer. Among Homer's allegorical personifications was Strife (*Iliad*, IV, 442 f.): "Her crest is but lowly at the first, but afterward she holdeth up her head in heaven." * In Virgil Fama does the same (*Aen.*, IV, 177). Change of stature for allegorical figures, then, had classical precedents—but not the rejuvenation motif. This obviously belongs in the same psychological sphere as the polarity youth-age in the *puer senex*. We encounter it first in the apocalyptic literature of early Christianity. In Hermas's *Shepherd* (middle of the second century) visions are reported in which the "Church" appears as an old woman who grows younger.[43] The text was circulated from the second century onwards in Latin translations. It is worth noting that the "Church" is here at the same time "the pre-existent Holy Ghost" in the form of a woman, and that the state of salvation of the Church, which is identical with Him, "undergoes an evolution, this being indicated by the gradual rejuvenation of the old woman." [44] So, at least, the majority of modern scholars interpret the rejuvenation—but is not this a *post facto* rationalization? The *Shepherd of Hermas* is the most important document of early Christian vision literature. The question of how it is to be interpreted is therefore of great consequence. For the author of the work, the supernatural redemptress undoubtedly possessed reality. His style also argues against his having allowed himself to be guided by literary models, as it does against his having "clothed" in allegory so bloodless a modern abstraction as the idea of evolution. The work exhibits highly personal features. The appearance of the rejuvenated old woman is personally experienced too. What impelled the author to write was

[42] Natura in Brunetto Latini in the *Tesoretto* (*ZRPh* [1883], 338, 29) and in the *Tresor* (ed. Chabaille, p. 3).—Henry of Settimello, III, 1 ff. (*PL*, CCIV, 843 ff.).—Dialectica in Anselm of Besate (ed. Dümmler, p. 48).—The Sibyl in Bernard Silvestris' commentary on Virgil (ed. Riedel, p. 43).—But Reason in Guillaume de Lorris (2978) is "ne trop haute ne trop basse."—The *Annales Palidenses* (*MG SS*, XVI, p. 64) relate, under the year 968: Someone sees in a dream a woman of superhuman stature. She says: "My name is Dysentery and I shall live in your belly awhile, after which I shall hide in the entrails of seven great lords." A short time afterwards he falls sick himself, and the seven die within the year.
[* Trans. Lang, Leaf, and Myers.]
[43] E. Hennecke, *Neutestamentliche Apokryphen* [2] [1924], p. 336, No. 4; p. 341, No. 10, etc.
[44] Selma Hirsch, *Die Vorstellungen von einem weiblichen Pneuma Hagion im Neuen Testament* (Berlin dissertation, 1926), 40 f. Martin Dibelius (*Der Hirt des Hermas* [1923], 451 f.) holds that the model for the old woman who appears as the bearer of revelation was the Cumaean Sibyl; that the rejuvenation was added by the author, to indicate that the church was visibly improving (477). That, in other words, the author had transferred age as a predicate of dignity from the original figure of the Sibyl to the ideal church, but had then tried to interpret the image of the Sibyl Ecclesia on the basis of his reflections upon the empirical church, and had corrected his image of the woman to correspond with this newly conceived interpretation (479).

the impact upon his being of a reality which transcended consciousness.

Claudian conducts the Goddess of Rome, grown gray and decrepit, into the presence of Jupiter, who encourages her and rejuvenates her (*De bello Gildonico*, I, 17–212). He describes the goddess Natura as at once aged and youthfully beautiful (*De consulatu Stilichonis*, II, 431 ff.). He too, then, like the *Shepherd of Hermas*, has the schema of the old-young redemptress. His rejuvenation of Rome has been explained as an expression of the national recovery under Theodosius.[45] But this fails to recognize the root of the conception. We must not forget that in Claudian the goddess Natura stands beside the goddess Roma. For late pagan Antiquity both are actual divine powers, more real than the gods of Olympus.[46] The image of the aged goddess, which had risen from the depths, had become a possession of the period. Even after the conquest of Rome by Alaric, Rutilius Namatianus (I, 47–164) directs a prayer to the gray and aged Dea Roma, and his prayer culminates in the hope that she will be rejuvenated.

By the fifth century the figure of the old-young supernatural woman had degenerated into a rhetorical cliché.[47] But in Boethius it again gains religious consecration.

In messianically and apocalyptically excited periods, faded symbolic figures can be filled with new life, like shades which have drunk blood. France experienced such a period before and after the 1830 revolution. In the work of the young Balzac allegorical figures appear. They incarnate the powers which are battling one another for dominion over the newborn age . . . and over Balzac's soul. In the enthralling *Jésus-Christ en Flandre* (1831) the church appears in a dream vision in the form of a toothless, bald old woman. The dreamer asks her: "Qu'as-tu fait de beau?" Suddenly she is transformed: "À cette demande la petite vieille se redressa sur ses os, rejeta ses guenilles, grandit, s'éclaira, sourit, sortit de sa chrysalide noire. Puis, comme un papillon nouveau-né, cette création indienne sortit de ses palmes, m'apparut blanche et jeune, vêtue d'une robe de lin. Ses cheveux d'or flottèrent sur ses épaules . . ." This is the "Church" of Hermas, set in an entirely different period but still preserving the function of the late Antique superhuman redemptress, and changing from age to youth as well as from

---

[45] Prudentius also has the rejuvenated Roma (*Contra Symmachum*, II, 655 ff.); he thus supplies a Christian rejoinder to Claudian.

[46] The cult of the ancient city-goddess was still alive in Rome under Otto III (Fedor Schneider, 151 f.).

[47] Philosophia in Fulgentius' *Mitologiae* (Helm, p. 14) falls in this category. Then the Liberal Arts in Martianus Capella. Grammar is "aetate quidem longaeva, sed comitate blandissima" (ed. Dick, p. 82, 11); Dialectic, "pallidior paululum femina, sed acri admodum visu" (151, 15); Rhetoric, "quaedam sublimissimi corporis . . . vultus etiam decore luculenta femina" (211, 10); Geometry, "reverenda venerabili dignitate . . . luculenta maiestate resplendens" (291, 7 ff.); Arithmetic, "femina miri decoris, sui quaedam maiestas nobilissimae vetustatis" (365, 5); Astronomy, "femina quadam venerabilis excellentiae celsitudine reverenda" (422, 5); Harmony (482) is not described in detail. In Martianus, then, we have six variations of the same schema.

human stature to gigantic proportions. Balzac was an avid reader, with a passionate interest in theosophy, illuminism, and mysticism. But far more important than the question of his sources is the fact that Balzac could re-charge an age-old idea with the magic spell of life. Here we can observe the way in which, after a millennium and a half, a seemingly long-outworn topos can become rejuvenated.

This is only comprehensible by the fact that it is rooted in the deeper strata of the soul. It belongs to the stock of archaic proto-images in the collective unconscious. The attributes of the woman whom we found in Hermas, Claudian, Boethius, Balzac, correspond to the language of dreams. In dreams it can befall that beings of a higher order come to us to encour-age, to teach, or to threaten. In dreams such figures can be at once small and large, young and old; they can also simultaneously possess two identi-ties, can simultaneously be known and wholly unknown, so that—in our dream—we understand: This person is really someone else. But such images can also appear in the state of meditation. In this, for example, some-one sees an old woman "with wavy silvery white hair," who reappears in a later vision rejuvenated "with blonde hair." [48] The phenomenon of re-juvenation, which occurs regularly in all the texts we have discussed, sym-bolizes a regeneration wish of the personality. From the enlightened modern standpoint medieval monks' visions, accounts of miracles, and the like have been dismissed as the silly fables of credulous times. Today we can approach these things with deeper understanding. An analysis of early Christian hagiography would yield valuable results. What Athanasius, for example, in his celebrated life of St. Anthony, reports concerning the dem-ons who tormented the Egyptian monk—devils who "reach to the ceiling" (ch. 23), "to the clouds" (ch. 60), who change into women—these are negative correspondences to the positive visions of redemption. They too speak the eternal language of dreams.

The connections between the archaic psychological world and literary topics will become even clearer when we follow the goddess Natura on her journey through the ages.

[48] So Oscar A. H. Schmitz reports in his autobiography *Ergo sum* (1927), 360 and 384. In the rejuvenated woman he recognizes "the image of his own soul."

6

The Goddess Natura

1. *From Ovid to Claudian* / 2. *Bernard Silvestris*
3. *Sodomy* / 4. *Alan of Lille*
5. *Eros and Morality* / 6. *The Romance of the Rose*

1. *From Ovid to Claudian*

OVID BEGINS his cosmogony with a description of chaos (*Met.*, I, 5 ff.). Cold battles with hot, wet with dry, soft with hard, heavy with light. The conflict was composed by a god or milder Nature:

Hanc deus et melior litem natura diremit.

Ovid does not decide between Nature and the god: "whichever of the gods it was" ("quisquis fuit ille deorum"). Four centuries later Claudian takes up the theme again. The concept of the universe has changed. Not a god but Natura parted the ancient strife of the elements. For Claudian she is a powerful goddess. She appoints gods to serve the young Zeus. She is the marriage-maker ("pronuba") of the gods. She weds Proserpine to Pluto in the hope that new gods will be born. When Zeus ends the Age of Gold, because men have become enervated by their idleness, Natura lays a complaint before him, which leads to the institution of agriculture. Her seat is before the cave of gray Aevum (= Aion) as "guardian of the threshold," "age-old, but fair of face" ("vultu longaeva decoro").[1]

Natura is cosmic power. She stands between Zeus and the gods, governs marriage and generation, and through her complaint can intervene in the course of history. Claudian is here close to a late antique theology which has been best preserved for us in the Orphic hymns, a collection made in the third or fourth century by an unknown author, presumably in Egypt or Asia Minor.[2] The tenth hymn is dedicated to Physis. Over eighty predicates of the goddess are compressed into its thirty hexameters. She is the age-old

---

[1] The passages from Claudian: "veterem . . . tumultum Discrevit Natura parens" (*De raptu Proserpinae*, I, 249).—"famulosque recepit Natura tradente deos" (*De quarto consulato Honorii*, 198 f.).—"pronuba" (*Magnes*, 38).—"Jam laeta futuros Expectat Natura deos" (*De raptu Proserpinae*, II, 370 f.). Complaint of Nature: *De raptu Proserpinae*, III, 33 ff.—Seat before the cave: *De consulatu Stilichonis*, II. 424 ff.

[2] *Orphei Hymni*, ed. Guilelmus Quandt (Berlin, 1941), *Prolegomena*, p. 44.

Mother of All; father, mother, nurse, sustainer; all-wise, all-bestowing, all-ruling; regulator of the gods; creator; first-born; eternal life and immortal providence. This universal goddess is not the personification of an intellectual concept. She is one of the last religious experiences of the late-pagan world.[3] She possesses inexhaustible vitality. But what varied masks the Orphic Physis can assume! Among Goethe's writings on the natural sciences there is a celebrated "Fragment on Nature," which first appeared anonymously in 1782 or 1783 in the "Tiefurter Journal," which was circulated in manuscript. Goethe writes to Knebel (March 3, 1783), that he is not the author. A few weeks later Frau von Stein announces that the fragment is by Tobler, of Zurich, who had visited Weimar in 1781. In 1828 Goethe saw it again. On May 24 he wrote to Chancellor von Müller: "Although I cannot remember composing these observations, they are quite in accord with the conceptions to which my mind then soared." Georg Christoph Tobler (1757–1812), however, had translated the Orphic hymn into hexameters. The fragment which appeared in the "Tiefurter Journal" is an analysis and amplification of this translation—with additional matter from Shaftesbury.[4]

That the goddess Physis or Natura had power over men's souls is proved by the Christian polemic against her. It begins with Lactantius (d. after 317) and is continued by Prudentius in his poem *Against Symmachus* (written 402). Among the defeated pagan deities he places Nature. God is her master. She is not the begetter of men, but only their sustainer. Prudentius is a fourth-century *Anticlaudianus*. Echoes of this controversy are to be found throughout the Middle Ages.[5]

---

[3] On the hymn to Physis, cf. Otto Kern, *Die Religion der Griechen*, (1938), 83 f.—For the goddess Natura: Joseph Kroll, *Die Lehren des Hermes Trismegistos* (1914), 130 ff.—R. Reitzenstein, *Das iranische Erlösungsmysterium* (1921), 183 f. —Ernst Bernert, *RE Neue Bearb.*, half-vol. XXXIX (1941), 1129. H. Leisegang, *ibid.*, 1130.—In the Orphic collection the hymn to Physis is followed by a hymn to the universal god Pan.—In Lucretius Venus is the creator of universal life; she governs the "nature of things" (I, 21), which in another passage is called "natura creatrix" (II, 1116). In Apuleius (*Met.*, ed. Helm, p. 98) Venus is called "rerum naturae prisca parens, elementorum origo initialis"; in Martianus Capella (ed. Dick, p. 36, 18) she appears as "generationum omnium mater."—Together with Physis and Pan, Priapus also becomes a universal god, for example in a metrical inscription of the Antonine period: "O Priape potens amice, salve, / Seu cupis genitor vocari et auctor / Orbis aut Physis ipsa Panque, salve" (Buecheler, *Carmina epigraphica*, 1504 C).—Physis appears in Nonnus (ed. Ludwich, I, p. 59, 650) as "Creatress of the Cosmos" and p. 152, 4 as "Nurse of Becoming."—In Sidonius (*Carmina*, I, 1) Natura raises the young Jupiter to power.

[4] The fact was published almost simultaneously by Franz Schultz in *Internationale Forschungen zur Literaturgeschichte—Festschrift für Julius Petersen* (1938), 79 ff. and Franz Dornseiff in *Die Antike*, XV (1939), 274 ff.

[5] Lactantius, *Div. inst.*, II, 8, 21–25 and III, 28, 4.—Prudentius, *Contra Symmachum*, I, 12 and 327; II, 796 f.—Sedulius, I, 85.—Dracontius, *De laudibus dei*, I, 23 ff.; I, 329 ff.; III, 3 and 549.—Isidore refers to the heretical doctrine of Hermogenes (impugned by Tertullian) "qui materiam non natam introducens deo non nato eam comparavit, matremque elementorum et deam adseruit" (*Et.*, VIII,

And yet the pagan Natura never entirely vanishes from consciousness. Even in the tenth century she is occasionally referred to and called by her Greek name.[6]

2. *Bernard Silvestris*

Among the philosophical trends of the first half of the twelfth century, Abélard's dialectics arouses the greatest interest among modern scholars. As a theologian, he is "the creator of the scholastic method." The mysticism of his great antagonist, Bernard of Clairvaux, is also studied and appreciated. The doctrine of the Victorines arouses less sympathy. For Platonism, the greater part yet remains undone. Before the advent of Aristotelianism, the Platonic influence is everywhere apparent in the Middle Ages. "Platon lui-même n'est nulle part, mais le platonisme est partout," says Gilson in a happy phrase. "Disons plutôt," he continues, "qu'il y a partout des platonismes." [7] The Platonisms, however, are of very various kinds. The Platonism of the cathedral school of Chartres is distinguished from the others by a Humanism buttressed by grammar and rhetoric. Of Plato's works, the Middle Ages knows only the—incomplete—*Timaeus*, in the translation, with commentary, by Chalcidius (fourth century). But the Platonizing treatises of Apuleius (second century), *De Platone et eius dogmate*, *De mundo*, and (incorrectly ascribed to the same author) the *Asclepius*, together with Macrobius and, finally, Boethius, are made to serve as authorities. Martianus Capella too appears to be indispensable. Turbid sources! The Platonism of Chartres, then, is a rather protean phenomenon. It awaits scientific treatment. For the history of literature, it is more important than Abélard and Bernard of Clairvaux.

That singular figure, Bernard Silvestris of Tours, is closely connected with the school of Chartres. He was a poet, a philosopher, and the author of an allegorical commentary on the *Aeneid* and of a "summa" of rhetoric and poetics (no longer extant), from which the most important Latin arts-of-

---

5, 30.—*Poetae*, IV, 812, 57: "Solus naturae creator Deus et dispositor."—"Deus naturae formator": *Carm. cant.*, p. 36, No. 12, 1a.—Giraldus Cambrensis (ed-Brewer), I, 341: "Naturae genitor generum concepit ydeas."—John of Salisbury, *Entheticus*, p. 258, 625: "Unica causarum ratio divina voluntas, Quam Plato naturae nomine saepe vocat. Illius imperio servit natura creata, Ordoque causarum totus adhaeret ei."—*A.h.*, XV, 241: "Stoici munda naturam, / Formam et substantiam / Deum dicunt et figuram / Eius circumstantiam, / Facturae praestant culturam, / Factori blasfemiam."

[6] In an anonymous poetical epistle (*NA*, II [1877], 227 f.) she is called "natura creatrix, deum generatio, inclita physis."

[7] E. Gilson, *Philosophie du moyen âge* [2] (1944), 268.—A scientifically satisfactory treatment of medieval philosophy is impossible without a foundation of philology. In this respect much remains to be done. There is no presentation of the material such as Zeller's *Philosophie der Griechen*. R. Klibansky, *The Continuity of the Platonic Tradition during the Middle Ages* (London, 1939), announces a corpus of medieval Latin and Arabic Platonic texts.

poetry of the twelfth and thirteenth centuries stem.[8] For us, Bernard's most important work is the *De universitate mundi* [9] (*On the Universe*), written between 1145 and 1153. In form it is a mixture of prose and verse (*prosimetrum*), like Boethius' *Consolatio* and Martianus Capella's *Nuptiae*. It consists of two books: *Megacosmus* and *Microcosmus*. We are first given a description of the condition of matter (*silva*; hence Bernard's surname Silvestris): the formless chaos, longing for harmonious order. It is the "slumbrous vitality of the cosmic substrate, awaiting development." [10] Natura complains of this to Noys (= Greek νοῦς), a feminine emanation of the Godhead. As "Intellect of the highest God" (13, 152) and Providence (5, 17) Noys sees as in a mirror the predetermined succession of the ages, the appearance of culture heroes and of the principal exemplary figures. The selection is significant. The first lawgiver and king of Greece, Phoroneus, opens the list (he was known through Augustine, *Civ. dei*, 18, 3; through Isidore, *Et.*, VI, 1; and through the mythographers). Next come the warring Theban brothers; Phaeton who perished in flames; Deucalion, who escaped the Flood; Codrus (the poor starveling of Juvenal I, 2, where today we read *Cordus*) and Croesus; the adulterer Paris and the chaste Hippolytus; Priam and the brave warrior Turnus (from the *Aeneid*). Other complementary pairs follow: Ulysses the wily and Hercules the strong; Pollux, the first boxer, and Tiphys, the first steersman; Cicero as rhetor and Thales as geometrician; the poet Maro (Virgil) and the sculptor Myron; Plato the sage and Achilles the warrior; the splendor-loving Nero [11] and the munificent Titus; the next-to-last place is given to the Virgin Mary, the last to Pope Eugenius III, under whose pontificate Bernard wrote. All these personages are preordained by the stars ("praeiacet in stellis series").[12] The Noys and her poet appear to have attached more importance to Phoroneus, Paris, Pollux, and their colleagues than to the Christian revela-

[8] For the study of Bernard Silvestris, Faral (*Studi medievali, Nuova Serie*, IX [1936], 69–88) is fundamental. Bliemetzrieder's discussion of the *Mathematicus* (*Adelard von Bath* [1935], 213–42) appears to have escaped him.

[9] Ed. C. S. Barach and J. Wrobel (Innsbruck, 1876). The editors confuse him with Bernard of Chartres.

[10] I borrow this phrase from Pascual Jordan's essay *Die Stellung der Naturwissenschaft zur religiösen Frage*, which treats the problem of nature as creation (in the journal *Universitas* [Tübingen, Jan., 1947]). "That actually almost everything in inorganic existence proceeds according to necessity, is certain. Nevertheless, our vision, sharpened by atomic physics, sees everywhere, even in the inorganic, at least *traces* of what we have called freedom and have defined according to the criteria of the natural sciences—and concerning which, to be sure, we cannot, using the means of natural science alone, determine whether it is merely the lowest degree of that creative freedom which we see fully unfolded in man—the slumbrous vitality of the cosmic substrate, awaiting development—or whether it is a trace and sign of what in the religious sense we call creation or dispensation."

[11] The affirmative evaluation of Nero must have been drawn from pagan sources of the fourth century. Cf. A. Alföldi, *Die Kontorniaten* (1943), 59.

[12] In Chaucer (*The Man of Law's Tale*, 197 ff.) the following are enumerated as astrologically preordained: the deaths of Hector, Achilles, and Caesar; the War of Thebes; Hercules, Samson, Turnus, Socrates.

tion and its prefiguration in the Old Testament. Universal history becomes a series of rhetorical exemplary figures.

As emanations of Noys, *Endelechia* (13, 168), that is, the Aristotelian entelechy,[13] and the World-Soul appear—links in the "golden chain"[14] whence they cause the heavens to issue, as the heavens the stars and the stars the world (31, 76). Above the heavens dwells the "superessential" God. In heaven Noys is enthroned between Cherubim and Seraphim. Next come the lower ranks of angels, the fixed stars, constellations, signs of the zodiac, and planets, in over fifty distichs. The description of the earth takes the form of a poetical catalogue. Of the twenty-four mountains mentioned, over twenty are taken from antique poets (Sinai appears in the list simply in honor of Moses). The knowledge that Oeta is the grave of Hercules, Rhodope dear to the poets, and Pholoe the home of the centaurs is part and parcel of a rhetorical education. The animals are enumerated in order of size, beginning with the largest. Between the elephant and the ground squirrel there is room for the wild ass, who refuses to serve man, and for the lynx, whose urine hardens into a gem. Famous among rivers are the Euphrates (because of Semiramis); the Tigris (defeat of Crassus); the Nile (on whose bank Pompey met his death) . . . There was much in the Bible concerning these rivers, but Bernard prefers recollections of Antiquity. The only Biblical waters mentioned are the pool of Siloam and the Jordan. The trees are chosen on the same principle. Cypresses, holm oaks, the lotus, the sycamore, Venus's myrtle and Apollo's laurel mingle with the forest trees of the North. The first among mountain ranges is the Boeotian (because of Helicon)—created "for the delight of poets," as Ida to furnish wood for Paris's ship—without which there would have been no Trojan war and no Homer. The Grove of Academe had to exist, in order that Plato might frequent it. Vegetables and herbs are sanctioned not by poetry but by medicine: hyssop is good for the chest, mustard and "satyrion" are aphrodisiacs. In the catalogue of fish there is another, which makes old men fit for Venus's wars again. Thus the entire cosmos is duly organized. It is eternal, because the causes which produced it are eternal.

Natura praises her work—she has shaped matter, given the stars their courses, endowed earth with the seeds of life. Now she plans to crown her creation with man. For this she needs help. Noys counsels her to seek out Urania and Physis. Natura journeys through the several heavens. At the uppermost limit of the firmament lies the circle *aplanon* (*aplanes*[15] in

---

[13] Drawn from Martianus Capella: "Aristoteles per caeli culmina Entelechiam scrupulosius requirebat" (ed. Dick, 78, 17). All the manuscripts give *endelechia*. Old Greek –nt– becomes new Greek –nd–.

[14] The so-called "aurea catena Homeri" (from *Iliad*, VIII, 19) was frequently employed in the emanatistic systems of late Antiquity and their descendants.— Goethe, *Dichtung und Wahrheit*, II, Book 8 (Jubiläumsausgabe, 23, 153).—A. O. Lovejoy, *The Great Chain of Being* (Cambridge, Mass., 1936).—Emil Wolff, *Die goldene Kette. Die aurea catena Homeri in der englischen Literatur* (1947).

[15] ἀπλανής ("not wandering") means "fixed."

Macrobius, *Comm. in Somn. Scip.*, I, 11, 8); immutable, because it is composed of the fifth element; also called *pantomorphos*. There Nature finds an "Usiarch" (planetary ruler) and a Genius who is engaged in writing. Urania greets Nature as a sister and mounts with her to the celestial holy of holies, the seat of the highest divinity, whose name is Tugaton: in other words, the Platonic idea of the Good.[16] Macrobius had already described Tugaton as supreme ruler of all gods (*Comm. in Somn. Scip.*, I, 2, 14). The goddesses address the "triune majesty" in prayer. Then begins their descent through the heavens of the planets. To each of them one of the antique gods is appointed to "Usiarch." The travelers can hardly tear themselves away from the heaven of the Sun, which is beautified by Phaethon and Psyche. They make their way to Venus, Cupid, and the Elysian Fields, then must descend into the region of the Moon, which separates the pure ether from the troubled atmosphere of Earth. It is the midpoint of the Golden Chain, navel of the upper and lower worlds. There dwell thousands of happy spirits; some are angels, but others are antique field, forest, and ocean gods. In the pleasance named Granusion, scented with all the flowers and herbs of the East, lives Physis, with her daughters Theory and Practice. Noys now joins the travelers. She frames the idea of man. He shall be at once divine and human. The motions of the stars shall prefigure his life, he shall know the cosmos, rule the earth, and after death shall ascend to the Ether. Urania, Physis, and Natura create him together, after Noys has given them the Mirror of Providence, the Table of Fate, and the Book of Memory. The work closes with a poetic description of man, his organs and their uses. The last lines sing the praises of the male organs of generation, whose use "is pleasant and fitting when it accords, as to when, how, and how much, with what is needful." They war with death, restore Nature, and continue the species. They prevent the return of chaos. With this, Bernard's work returns to its starting point; the Macrocosm is mirrored in the Microcosm.

This singular work is worthy of thorough study. It is a link in the "golden chain" which connects late Paganism with the Renaissance of the twelfth century.[17] Alan of Lille's speculations stem from it, as do the Latin arts-of-poetry the series of which begins about 1170 with Matthew of Vendôme [18] and continues into the thirteenth century. Eberhard the German accepts it into the canon of curricular authors (Faral, 361, l. 684).

Twelfth-century Humanism is often referred to today, but its various aspects are not distinguished. John of Salisbury is rightly considered its

---

[16] *Tugaton* = τὸ ἀγαθόν.

[17] Its popularity is shown by the fact that it has come down to us in more than twenty-five manuscripts. The editors of the edition of 1876 knew only two. To Gervase of Melkley (b. *ca.* 1185, still living in 1220) Bernard is a rhetorical authority (*Studi medievali*, N. S., IX [1936] 68 f.). The *Megacosmos* is still cited by Boccaccio in his commentary on Dante (ed. Guerri, I, 233).

[18] He was a pupil of Bernard's: "Me docuit dictare decus Turonense: magister / Silvestris, studii gemma, scolaris honor" (*SB München* [1872], 581).

purest representative. He is a Christian Humanist. In contrast, Bernard represents a pagan Humanism which eliminates everything Christian except for a few ultimate essentials. Its geography, its history, its botany are determined by Roman poetry. Its Natura is Claudian's. Her complaint intervenes in the process of the universe (*Natura plangens*). She is the ruler of generation through the whole circle of life, she is the ever-fruitful womb: "mater generationis." [19] As daughter of Noys, who is "a goddess sprung from God," she shares in the being of the Godhead, but she is also linked to matter. We have here a syncretistic picture of the universe, in which there are higher and lower gods, emanations, astral spirits and nature spirits. The whole is bathed in the atmosphere of a fertility cult, in which religion and sexuality mingle. We have no other indications of this in the Middle Ages, except in certain Grail romances. The youthful hero of the Grail legend comes to a waste land where water and vegetation have failed. Its ruler is the sick fisher king, who is sustained only by the miraculous vessel of the Grail. What is his sickness? Many versions disguise it euphemistically, others speak it out: loss of virility—precisely, then, what is signified by the mutilation of the Phrygian Attis, the death wound of Adonis. The healing of the priest-king will save the dying land, for the king's sickness is the cause of the parching of the land. Ancient vegetation cults seem to have coalesced with the symbolism of the Eucharist in late Antiquity and to have survived esoterically into the Middle Ages. This complex then passed over into the legend of Arthur and the courtly romance. In most (though not in all) late versions it has wholly lost its original meaning, in some cases by being handed on by poets who did not understand it, in others by being subjected to tendentious ecclesiastical revision.[20]

A mixture of cosmological speculation with the praise of sexuality is as foreign to Platonism as it is to Christianity. But Bernard found it in the *Asclepius*, a treatise handed down among the works of Apuleius.[21] But Apuleius was accounted a Platonist. Bernard's points of contact with the *Asclepius* are numerous and, in some cases, verbal. But other late antique

[19] Matter is "Naturae vultus antiquissimus, generationis uterus indefessus" (p. 10, 48); "mater generationis Natura" (p. 53, 31).

[20] This concept of the Grail legend, into the details of which I cannot enter, was independently developed by W. A. Nitze ("The Fisher King in the Grail Romances," *PMLA*, XXIV [1909], 365) and Jessie L. Weston (*The Legend of Sir Perceval* II [1909]; *From Ritual to Romance* [1920]). Cf. also W. A. Nitze, *Perceval and the Holy Grail* (University of California Press, 1949).

[21] Ed. P. Thomas, *Apulei opera*, III (1908), 36–81.—The *Asclepius* is a translation of a Greek original; Apuleius' authorship of it was not impugned until the nineteenth century. The edition by Walter Scott, *Hermetica I* (Oxford, 1924), has been superseded by A. D. Nock and A.-J. Festugière, *Corpus Hermeticum* (Paris, 1945: *Collection des Universités de France*), 2 vols.—Cf. further Festugière, *La Révélation d'Hermès Trismégiste*, I (1944), 67–88.—From the *Asclepius* Bernard took the Usiarchs, the concepts *pantomorphos* and *imarmene* (*De univ.*, 32, 123 = *Asclepius*, ed. Thomas, p. 54, 6 ff.); the *malignitas silvestris* (p. 9, 27 = *Asclepius*, p, 50, 24); the religious consecration of propagation (*Asclepius*, p. 56, 21 ff.).—Cf. Festugière, *Les Dieux ousiarques de l'Asclépius* (*Recherches de*

texts also declare the universal sexuality of the highest God. For example, a hymn by Tiberianus, a few lines from which may be quoted here:

> *Tu genus omne deum, tu rerum causa vigorque,*
> *Tu natura omnis, deus innumerabilis unus,*
> *Tu sexu plenus toto, tibi nascitur olim*
> *Hic deus, hic mundus, domus haec hominumque deumque,*
> *Lucens, augusto stellatus flore iuventae.*

> (Thou who are every god, of all things cause and force,
> Nature and all her works, one God and numberless,
> Thou charged with generation, to Thee long since were born
> This god, this world, this home of gods and men,
> All luminously starred with the noble bloom of youth.)

Bernard's pagan Humanism was fed, as we have seen, by many springs, and it abundantly fertilized succeeding times. To suppose, however, that he reintroduced the antique divinity of nature and fertility into the Christian era would be wholly to misunderstand his historical significance. In this respect, he stands entirely alone. But in his work he raises to the level of consciousness the vital bases of that *iuventus mundi* which the twelfth century was. The "Renaissance" of that period is comprehensible only in the light of a sense of life nourished by the springs of life itself.

3. Sodomy

On her journey through the heavens, Bernard's Natura also visits the sphere of Mercury. There she finds Cyllenius (actually a surname of Mercury, but here apparently discriminated from him; the passage is difficult) engaged in forming hermaphrodites, under the influence of the fiery Mars or by "the indulgence of Jupiter" (an allusion to Ganymede? pp. 45, 166ff.). In late Antiquity the hermaphrodite was a favorite subject for sculpture as well as for minor lyric poetry: [22] one of the many evidences that the syncretism of Antiquity in its decline extended to the realm of sex. This was doubtless Bernard's reason for giving this phenomenon too a place among the stars. Only a fluid boundary separates it from male homosexuality, which was also widespread in the Middle Ages. The Church termed it sodomy (after Genesis 19:5) and found it a fruitful theme for moralizing sermons. On the other hand, it was countenanced by Greek mythology

---

science religieuse, XXVIII [1938], 175).—E. Gilson's attempt to see Bernard's work as an interpretation of Genesis is mistaken. Gilson makes Noys masculine, equates it with the Logos, emphasizes the Hermetic elements, and thus distorts the whole (*Archives d'histoire doctrinale et littéraire du moyen âge*, III [1928], 5 ff.).— There are still other sources to be taken into account: pp. 70, 158 ff., where a verbal and ideological connection is made with Maximianus, V, 110 ff.

[22] As such, it was frequently imitated in the twelfth century. Traube, *O Roma nobilis*, 317 ff.

(Jupiter, Apollo, Heracles) and by antique culture.[23] However, it is quite often candidly admitted or even celebrated in verse.

Among the pearls of medieval poetry is the song of a ninth-century Veronese *clericus* to a boy whom a rival had taken from him:

> *O admirabile Veneris ydolum,*
> *Cuius materiae nichil est frivolum:*
> *Archos te protegat, qui stellas et polum*
> *Fecit et maria condidit et solum.*
> *Furis ingenio non sentias dolum:*
> *Cloto te diligat, quae baiulat colum.*
>
> *Saluto puerum non per ypothesim,*
> *Sed firmo pectore deprecor Lachesim,*
> *Sororem Atropos, ne curet heresim.*
> *Neptunum comitem habeas et Thetim,*
> *Cum vectus fueris per fluvium Athesim.*
> *Quo fugis amabo, cum te dilexerim?*
> *Miser quid faciam, cum te non viderim?*
>
> *Dura materies ex matris ossibus*
> *Creavit homines iactis lapidibus.*
> *Ex quibus unus est iste puerulus,*
> *Qui lacrimabiles non curat gemitus.*
> *Cum tristis fuero, gaudebit emulus:*
> *Ut cerva rugio, cum fugit hinnulus.*

(O thou eidolon of Venus adorable,
Perfect thy body and nowhere deplorable!
The sun and the stars and the sea and the firmament,
These are like thee, and the Lord made them permanent.
Treacherous death shall not injure one hair of thee,
Clotho the thread-spinner, she shall take care of thee.

Heartily, lad, I implore her and prayerfully
Ask that Lachesis shall treasure thee carefully,
Sister of Atropos—let her love cover thee,
Neptune companion, and Thetis watch over thee,
When on the river thou sailest forgetting me!
How canst thou fly without ever regretting me,
Me that for sight of my lover am fretting me?

---

23 Marlowe excuses the love of Edward II for Gaveston by citing antique *exempla*: "The mightiest kings have had their minions: / Great Alexander loved Hephestion; / The conquering Hercules for Hylas wept; / And for Patroclus stern Achilles drooped / And not kings only, but the wisest men: / The Roman Tully loved Octavius; / Great Socrates wild Alcibiades. / Then let his grace, whose youth is flexible, / And promiseth as much as we can wish, / Freely enjoy that vain, light-headed earl" (*Edward the Second*, I, 4).

Stones from the substance of hard earth maternal, he
Threw o'er his shoulder who made men supernally;
One of these stones is that boy who disdainfully
Scorns the entreaties I utter, ah, painfully!
Joy that was mine is my rival's tomorrow,
While I for my fawn like a stricken deer sorrow!) [24]

The Veronese poem is overlaid with erudition, but it expresses a definite, experienced situation. Nevertheless, when poets of the twelfth century
choose male homosexuality as material, it is often difficult to decide whether
we have to do with the imitation of literary models (*imitatio*) or whether
actual feeling is speaking. Ovid had declared (*Amores*, I, 1, 20) that the
subject of his verse was

> *Aut puer aut longas compta puella comas*
> (Either a lad or else a long-tressed maid).[25]

In the Middle Ages the Ovidian "either . . . or" usually amounts to
"both . . . and." Baudri of Meung-sur-Loire (1046–1130), abbot of the
monastery of Bourgueil, later archbishop of Dol in Brittany, justifies himself:

> *Obiciunt etiam, iuvenum cur more locutus*
> *Virginibus scripsi nec minus et pueris.*
> *Nam scripsi quaedam quae complectuntur amorem;*
> *Carminibusque meis sexus uterque placet.*

> (This their reproach: that, wantoning in youth,
> I wrote to maids, and wrote to lads no less.
> Some things I wrote, 'tis true, which treat of love;
> And songs of mine have pleased both he's and she's.)

Baudri's contemporary Marbod (*ca.* 1035–1123), head of the cathedral
school at Angers, later bishop of Rennes, in his old age regrets the follies
of his youth (PL 171, 1656 AB):

> *Errabat mea mens fervore libidinis amens . . .*
> *Quid quod pupilla mihi carior ille vel illa?*
> *Ergo maneto foris, puer aliger, auctor amoris!*
> *Nullus in aede mea tibi sit locus, o Cytherea!*
> *Displicet amplexus utriusque quidem mihi sexus.*

---

[24] [Howard Mumford Jones's translation, in P. S. Allen, *The Romanesque Lyric*
(replacing Samuel Singer's versified version from Traube's prose translation, in
Germanisch-romanisches Mittelalter [1935], 124).]—The poem was first published
(1829) by G. B. Niebur, who ascribed it to late Antiquity. Gregorovius saw in it
the lament of a Roman bidding farewell to his favorite statue.—Re-edited, with
commentary, by Ludwig Traube, *O Roma nobilis* (1891), 301 ff.
[25] But cf. *Ars*, II, 683.

(My mind did stray, loving with hot desire . . .
Was not or he or she dearer to me than sight?
But now, O winged boy, love's sire, I lock thee out!
Nor in my house is room for thee, O Cytherea!
Distasteful to me now the embrace of either sex.)

A wandering scholar Hilary, who attended Abélard's lectures about 1125 (we know neither the dates of his birth or death nor of what country he was a native) has left us a small collection of poems in which piety and secular pleasures, lyrics and miracle plays of St. Nicholas, are jumbled together. He writes poetical epistles to nuns, and also to beautiful boys. One example will suffice (*Hilarii versus et ludi,* ed. L. B. Fuller [New York, 1929], p. 70):

Crinis flavus, os decorum cervixque candidula,
Sermo blandus et suavis; sed quid laudem singula?
Totus pulcher et decorus, nec est in te macula,
Sed vacare castitati talis nequit formula . . .

Crede mihi, si redirent prisca Jovis secula,
Ganimedes iam non foret ipsius vernacula,
Sed tu, raptus in supernis, grata luce pocula,
Gratiora quidem nocte Jovi dares oscula.

(Hair of gold and face all beauty, neck of slender white,
Speech to ear and mind delightful—why, though, praise for these?
For in every part's perfection, not a fault hast thou,
Save—protesting chastity jars with forms so fair! . . .

Ah, believe me, were the Golden Age to come again,
Ganymede should be no longer slave to highest Jove,
Thou, to heaven ravished, shouldst by day his cup refill,
Thou by night shouldst give him kisses, nectar far more sweet.)

The preceding texts show, for the end of the eleventh century and the beginning of the twelfth, an unprejudiced erotic candor even among the higher clergy, which, though it was not generally disseminated, was certainly to be found in humanistic circles.[26] Only this atmosphere makes

[26] To the same ambiance belongs the anonymous metrical debate between Ganymede and Helen on the question whether the love of girls or of boys is to be preferred. The question is referred to an assembly of the gods, at which Natura is also present. Walther (*Streitgedicht—vide infra*) dates it at the beginning of the twelfth century. But since Natura, Ratio, and Providencia ("quam Naturae genitor mente gerit pura," st. 14) undertake the work of creation in Jupiter's palace, it would seem that the poem must have Bernard Silvestris as its source: "Jovis in palatio genitrix Natura / De secreta cogitans rerum genitura / Hilem (hylen = silvam) multifaria vestiens figura / Certo res sub pondere creat et mensura" (st. 13). The reference to *Sap.,* 11, 21 "omnia in mensura et numero et pondere disposuisti" is the only trace of Christianity in the poem. The arguments adduced in favor of the

Bernard Silvestris comprehensible. Meanwhile, of course there was constant complaint about the prevalence of vice. In no other point was the humanist attitude so irreconcilable with Christian doctrine. Complaints had already been heard in the sixth century, they recur in the ninth.[27] From 1150 onwards they increase.

4. *Alan of Lille*

Alan (b. *ca.* 1128 at Lille, d. 1202 at Cîteaux) is one of the most significant figures of the twelfth century; a poet with a prodigious power of expression; a speculative theologian who tapped fresh springs. To the Middle Ages he was known as *doctor universalis,* as was Albertus Magnus after him.[28]

---

love of boys are: "Ludus hic quem ludimus, a dis est inventus / Et ab optimatibus adhuc est retentus" (st. 30) and "Rustici, qui pecudes possunt appellari, / Hii cum mulieribus debent inquinari" (st. 34). The erotic debate, then, expresses a class distinction between the *clerici* (or, more generally, the ruling classes) and the peasantry. For the word *optimates* (st. 30) is explained: "Approbatis opus hoc scimus approbatum, / Nam qui mundi regimen tenent et primatum, / Qui censores arguunt mores et peccatum, / Hii non spernunt pueri femur levigatum" (st. 40). This appears to refer to secular and ecclesiastical dignitaries.—Comparing the kinds of love is a Hellenistic topos (Christ-Schmid, II [6], 1 [1920], 22, n. 2), and is found later in Plutarch, the Pseudo-Lucian, Achilles Tatius, and, in thirteenth-century Byzantium, in John Katrarios. The poem is discussed in Walther, *Streitgedicht,* 141 f. He considers a "distant connection" with the Pseudo-Lucian quite probable. As a curiosity we cite Wattenbach's opinion that the author was from southern France because olive-trees and pines are mentioned (cf. p. 184 *infra*).—CB, No. 95 and No. 127 are also highly significant. Cf. Otto Schumann in *ZfdA,* LXIII, 91–99.

[27] Gildas (*ca.* 500–570), *De excidio et conquestu Britanniae,* ch. 28 and 29; ninth-century anonymous (NA, XIII [1888], 358); *ca.* 897 Abbo of St. Germain (*Poetae,* IV, 115, 603).—Further documentation in Alwin Schultz, *Das höfische Leben zur Zeit der Minnesinger,* I [2] (1889), 585.—Faral in *Romania* (1911), 213, n. 1.—John of Salisbury, *Policraticus,* ed. Webb, I, 219, 16 ff.—Cf. also J. S. P. Tatlock, *The Legendary History of Britain* (University of California Press, 1950), pp. 352 ff.

[28] For Eduard Norden, Alan was "the craziest of all stylists" (*Kunstprosa,* 638, n. 1). Karl Strecker more justly called him "a genius of language and style" (*Hist. Vierteljahrsschrift,* XXVII, 158).—Alan is the first to quote the *Liber de causis.* "This book contains verbatim extracts from Proclus's *Institutio theologica,* was composed by a Moslem who lived east of the Euphrates *ca.* 850 and who must have had access to the *Stoicheiosis theologike,* a work by a pupil of Proclus's, in an Arabic translation, so the treatise too was originally written in Arabic. As a supposed work of Aristotle it was translated into Latin at Toledo between 1167 and 1187 by Gerard of Cremona, was ascribed by Albertus Magnus to a certain David Judaeus . . . and despite Albertus's and Thomas's better judgment was long regarded by many as a work of Aristotle" (Ueberweg-Geyer, 303). Alan also knows the pseudo-Hermetic *Book of the Twenty-four Philosophers,* from which he takes the thesis: "deus est sphaera intellegibilis, cuius centrum ubique, circumferentia nusquam." Dante will put this definition into the mouth of Love. Alan calls the *Asclepius* "logos tileos" (= *teleios*). He attempts to comprehend the Trinity through Pythagorean numerical speculation. Cf. Nock-Festugière, *Corpus Hermeticum,* II, 276 f.—Alan knows the Arabic word *sifr* "cipher." Of the bat he says that in the realm of birds "ciphri locum obtinebat" (*SP,* II, 439).

Alan's principal literary works are the *De planctu Naturae* and the *Anti-claudianus*.

"Complaint of Nature"—by choosing this title, Alan indicates that he is a follower of Bernard Silvestris and Claudian. But he had to produce a fresh ground of complaint. He found it in sodomy. In form, the *De planctu Naturae* is another *prosimetrum*. When Natura appears to the poet she is described in the style of Martianus Capella, but with a greater display of rhetoric—her hair and dress alone receive ten pages of description. Natura has created man in the image of the Macrocosm. Exactly as the motions of the planets run counter to the revolution of the firmament, so in man sense and reason are in conflict. This conflict is preordained in order that man may be tried and rewarded. The cosmos is a sublime state, in which God reigns as eternal emperor, the angels work, and men obey. Natura acknowledges herself to be God's humble pupil. His work is perfect, hers imperfect. He is beyond birth ("innascibilis"), she has known birth. Man receives his birth from Natura, his rebirth from God ("homo mea actione nascitur, Dei auctoritate renascitur"). Natura is not conversant with theology: they teach not contrary but different things ("non adversa, sed diversa"). Natura "coins the pure ideas of Noys." [29] But man alone, of all beings, does not obey her. He reserves the law of sexual love. Natura had conferred the regulation of it upon Venus, her husband Hymenaeus, and her son Cupid. But Venus herself illicitly consorted with Antigamus (Enemy of Marriage) and bore him a bastard son Jocus (Sport). The betrayed Hymenaeus is accorded the seat on the right hand of Natura. Weeping Chastity follows him. Natura summons the priest Genius.[30] He paints images of all things on parchment. The antique exemplary figures are introduced as prefigured Ideas. Helen represents beauty, Turnus courage, Hercules strength, Capaneus gigantic stature, Ulysses cunning, Cato frugality, Plato intellectual brilliance, Cicero eloquence, Aristotle philosophy. As examples of perversity we have Thersites, the adulterer Paris, the lying Sinon, the early Roman poets Ennius and Pacuvius [31] (disdained by the Augustans). The work ends

[29] Named only in this passage.

[30] The origin of Genius had not hitherto been elucidated (Huizinga in *Mededeelingen der Kgl. Akad. van Weetenschappen, Afdeeling Letterkunde,* LXXIV, Ser. B [1932], p. 139). In Bernard Silvestris (*De univ.,* p. 38, 92 and p. 49, 82) Genius was already a scribe, tutelary spirit, and vegetation god (p. 53, 32). In Bernard's commentary on the *Aeneid* (VI, 119) Genius is called "humanae naturae deus" after Horace, *Epi.,* II, 2, 187: "genius, natale comes qui temperat astrum, / Naturae deus humanae." Bernard combined this with Isidore, *Et.,* VIII, 11, 88: "Genium dicunt quod quasi vim habeat omnium rerum gignendarum" (after Augustine, *Civ. dei,* VII, 13).—The priest Genius survived for a long time. In Jean Lemaire de Belges (*La Concorde des deux langages* [1512]) he is archpriest of Venus's temple, in Spenser he is porter to the Garden of Adonis (*The Faerie Queene,* III, 6, 32): "A thousand thousand naked babes attend / About him day and night, which doe require / That he with fleshly weeds would them attire."

[31] Sinon's tissue of lies brought about the fall of Troy (*Aeneid,* II, 76 ff.). Dante condemns him to hell for it (*Inf.,* XXX, 98).—Ennius and Pacuvius: Horace, *Epi.,* II, 1, 50–55.

with Genius pronouncing a solemn anathema upon all sinners. The author wakes: it was all a vision which he had beheld in a state of ecstasy.

Alan retains Bernard's concept of Natura, but gives it a Christian retouching. Natura remains the intermediate power between God and man, but she humbly subordinates herself to God. She is no longer the fruitful mother but the modest maiden. The golden chain of emanations is suppressed. Theology and natural philosophy are delimited with respect to one another. The ontological relationships are elucidated by grammatical metaphors. God's power is the superlative degree, Nature's the comparative, man's the positive. Perverted sexual love is a metaplasm "carried too far."

Of far greater importance is Alan's *Anticlaudianus de Antirufino* (written 1182 or 1183). So runs the complete title. It is not to be understood as a refutation, like the *Anti-Lucretius* of Cardinal de Polignac (1661–1742) or the *Anti-Machiavel* of Frederick the Great, but rather as a counterpart to Claudian's poem *In Rufinum*. A native of Aquitania, Rufinus had risen to be Theodosius' all-powerful minister: "an odious favourite," as Gibbon says, "who, in an age of civil and religious faction, has deserved, from every party, the imputation of every crime." To describe the hateful monster, who had been killed by Gothic soldiers and trampled by the mob at Byzantium in 395, Claudian had made full use of the mythological machinery: the fury Alecto, angry because the world is happy and at peace, summons all the Vices and Evils to a conference in the underworld, to scheme vengeance. At the recommendation of Megaera, Rufinus, the prodigy of all fiendish wickedness, is entrusted with the destruction of the earth. Over against this utterly evil Rufinus, Alan, in his *Antirufinus*, sets the ideal man.

The prose prologue is an important document. Since 1170 the field of Latin poetry had been divided between two hostile factions: the humanistically minded disciples of antique poetry, and the *moderni*. The latter also write in Latin—there is never any mention of vernacular literature in these debates—but they represent a "new" poetics. They are masters of a virtuoso style formed in the practice of dialectics, and hence consider themselves superior to the "ancients." Alan rejects the modern manner ("modernorum ruditatem"). He alludes to the saying of Bernard of Chartres (d. between 1126 and 1130): the moderns are dwarfs who stand upon the shoulders of giants. The *Anticlaudianus*, Alan says, is a scientific poem, a *summa* of the seven *artes*. But divine revelation ("theophanicae coelestis emblema") is added to their company. Readers who do not rise above sense to reason, who pursue the dreams of imagination or find their delight in poetic fables, are not wanted. Alan asks for readers who can climb the road of reason to the vision of the divine Ideas ("ad intuitum supercoelestium formarum").[32]

[32] It has not previously been remarked that the theological terminology of the *Anticlaudianus* coincides with that of Alan's *Regulae de sacra theologia*. Theology is "supercoelestis scientia" (PL, CCX, 621 B), because "supercoeleste est deus" (623 D). The axioms of theology can be called not only rules and maxims but also *emblemata* "quia puriore mentis acumine comprehenduntur" (622 A).

Here we have the program for a new poetic genre, the philosophical-theological epic. It is distinguished from the scientific or philosophical didactic poem by the fact that the ascent of reason to the "regions where the pure forms dwell" [Goethe] is accomplished under the guidance of an epic action. Hence Alan is obliged to reject the mythological and historical epic, which was being contemporaneously revived by Joseph of Exeter (*De bello Troiano*) and Walter of Châtillon (*Alexandreis*). Both poets are then scornfully dismissed.[33]

Natura plans the creation of a perfect man. She summons her divine sisters Concord, Abundance, Favor, Youth, Laughter, Modesty, Discretion, Reason, Chastity, Adornment, Prudence, Piety, Faith, Liberality, Nobility to a council in her realm: a garden of perpetual spring, walled round by a forest. In the midst of it rises Natura's house. It is decorated with paintings, in which twelve culture heroes and exemplary figures are represented: Aristotle, the "more divine" Plato, Seneca, Ptolemy, Cicero, Virgil, Hercules, Odysseus, Titus, Turnus, Hippolytus, Cytherea. Here the divine committee holds its sessions. Natura announces her program: the forming of the new man, who shall be both man and God. Prudence praises the plan but warns that the soul will have to be formed by a higher artificer; as for herself, she hesitates before the enterprise. This arouses a certain amount of discouragement. But her elder sister Reason advises that they call in Phronesis, i.e., Wisdom (later also called Sophia), who understands all the divine mysteries. Concordia agrees and harmony once again prevails. Seven beautiful maidens embody the gifts of Phronesis and assist her. She bids them construct a car for a journey to heaven: the secrets of Noys and the will of the highest Master must be penetrated. Grammar makes the shaft, Dialectic the axletree; Rhetoric gilds them. Arithmetic, Music, Geometry, and Astronomy produce the four wheels.[34] The five senses are harnessed to draw the cart. Phronesis, Ratio, and Prudentia mount through all the celestial spheres until they reach the seat of Theology, who drinks at the spring of the Holy Spirit ("haurit mente noym, divini flaminus haustu ebria"). Phronesis sets forth Natura's wish to Theology and asks to be shown the way to the citadel of "highest Jupiter" (Dante: "sommo Giove"). They are obliged to leave behind not only horses and car, but also Ratio. At this point (*SP*, II, 354)—it is the middle of the

---

[33] "Illic pannoso plebescit carmine noster / Ennius, et Priami fortunas intonat; illic / Maevius in coelos audens os ponere mutum / Gesta ducis Macedum tenebrosi carminis umbra / Pingere dum temptat . . ." (*SP*, II, 279 = PL CCX, 492 A).

[34] The allegorical car was a favorite motif in the twelfth and thirteenth centuries. The cardinal virtues are the wheels of the car in which the soul journeys to Heaven (Hildebert, PL, CLXXI 171, 163–166). Science is a car (*Walter of Châtillon* 1929, p. 68, st. 22). Ovid's car of the sun has grammar for pole, logic for axletree, etc. (John of Garland, *Integumenta Ovidii*, ed. F. Ghisalberti [1933], l. 121).—Dante describes the triumphal car of the church: beside the right wheel dance the theological, beside the left the cardinal virtues (*Purg.*, XXIX, 121 ff.).—The car has antique prototypes (Parmenides, the car of the Muses) as well as Biblical ones (Ezek. 1:1 ff.).

work—there is a digression in which the poet gathers his forces for a higher strain.

Phronesis mounts through the heaven of crystal to the Empyrean, the seat of the angelic choirs, of the blessed, and of the Virgin Mary. Among the blessed, Abraham, Peter, Paul, Lawrence, and Vincent of Lérins are conspicuous. In God's palace the eternal ideas, causes, and foundations of all things are depicted—including, for example, the beauty of Adonis, and the cultural functions of an Odysseus, Cicero, Tiphys, Pollux, Cato, Ovid, and others. A luminous spring gives rise to a brook, the brook to a river— all three of the same substance and brightness. All three are at once water and light (SP, II, 373). God in majesty grants Phronesis' prayer. He bids Noys form the Idea of a perfect soul, and stamps it with his seal. The Fates are present, as proper procedure demands. Phronesis anoints the soul with a salve, to protect it from the inauspicious influences of the planets, through whose spheres the return journey must be made.

Natura can now set to work. She seeks out the best materials to house the soul and forms a body which can rival Narcissus and Adonis. Each of her divine sisters contributes gifts. Even Fortuna, though her functions require her to be perpetually changing her moods, puts her best foot foremost. Fame spreads the sensational news. Alecto too hears it. She summons all the vices and plagues of mankind to Tartarus. As no new Rufinus is available, the whole fiendish horde marches to battle. But Natura mobilizes the Virtues. They meet the forces of Evil (as in Prudentius' *Psychomachia*). The new man, Juvenis (Youth), emerges from the struggle victorious. The forces of evil flee back to the underworld. Love and harmony reign on earth. The fields and vineyards bear fruit of themselves, the rose blooms without thorns.

In the *Anticlaudianus*, the figure of Genius and the discussion of sexual love and propagation are eliminated. The revision to accord with Christian doctrine which was already discernible in the *Planctus* is increased. Yet Bernard Silvestris' optimistic naturalism is preserved in its basic outlines. The creation of the perfect man is the work of Natura. Her function in the twelfth-century view of the universe—a Christian structure from foundations to vault, but enriched by Platonism and Humanism—must be understood as an attempt to find a place in the divine order for the forces and drives of life. We observe non-Christian elements in the *Anticlaudianus* too: Christ's act of redemption appears not to have helped; the only help lies in the creation of a new man; with him the Golden Age returns. The *doctor universalis* would not be given the church's imprimatur today.[35]

To evaluate the Platonizing cosmogony of a Bernard Silvestris and an Alan historically, we must hear it impugned by the Cistercian Ernald of Bonneval (d. after 1156) (*PL*, CLXXXIX, 1515 A): "In God was nothing confused and formless; for the matter of things was formed into its congru-

[35] Alan is still reckoned an authority by Chaucer and Spenser. Cf. *The Faerie Queene*, VII, 7, 9 (with a reference to *The Parlement of Foules*).

ent species immediately after its creation. All that the philosophers have taught concerning the eternity of the world, matter, and the world-soul (which they call Noys) is invalidated and brought to naught by the first chapter of Genesis." So orthodoxy could not but speak. But Ernald of Bonneval is usually mentioned only as the biographer of Bernard of Clairvaux. Histories of medieval philosophy have nothing to say about him. His exegetical correctness was no match for Alan's high intellectual flight.

5. Eros and Morality

About 1140 the Cluniac monk Bernard of Morlaix wrote his powerful satire *De contemptu mundi* (*On Contempt of the World*). A fervent piety, which longs ecstatically for the heavenly Jerusalem, fills his soul. His monkish mind, turned to the other world, is deeply grieved to perceive the corruption of the times. In his poem he not only inveighs against impiety, sodomy and other vices of the age, but curses love and womankind. During the same period Bernard of Clairvaux (d. 1153) brings the mystical love of the Madonna to its highest and tenderest development. From the same period (*ca.* 1150) we have a Latin poem in eighty stanzas—*The Council of Love at Remiremont*—which gives a cynical description of the erotic orgies in a convent in Lorraine: It is the revolt of the senses. The ethical norms of Christianity are trampled upon with naive shamelessness. What attitudes do the three Bernards manifest toward this "emancipation of the flesh"? Bernard of Morlaix would extirpate not only vice but also love and with it the primary energy of Nature. Bernard of Clairvaux spiritualizes love into a divine love which takes its figurative language from the Song of Songs. Woman is elevated to the status of the Mother of God, the divine dispenser of joy. Bernard Silvestris, turning to old Eastern sources, revives a religio-speculative picture of the universe in which Noys, as a feminine Pneuma Hagion, through the intervention of Physis, gives forth Bios and Eros so that propagation is consecrated as a sacred mystery. Thus about the middle of the twelfth century we find in four works four different attitudes toward Eros: the ascetic ideal curses him, profligacy debases him, mysticism spiritualizes him, and gnosticism consecrates him. *Contemptus mundi* rejects him; but the *universitas mundi* includes him. In Bernard's mysticism the Mother of God becomes "the great mediatrix of salvation, who restrains her Son from pronouncing judgment by showing him her maternal breasts." [36] Thus—like *Natura plangens*—she intervenes in the divine process of the cosmos. Here, in the setting of Christianity, something analogous to Silvestris' gnosticism occurs: a feminine power invades the concept of the Godhead. It is the archetype of the unconscious, which C. G. Jung calls the "anima." "Historically," Jung tells us, "we encounter the anima above all in the divine syzygies, the paired male-and-female gods. These syzygies reach, on the one hand, into the darkness of primitive my-

[36] F. Heiler, *Der Katholizismus* (1923), 111.

thology, on the other to the philosophical speculations of Gnosticism and of Chinese classic philosophy . . . One may safely hold that these syzygies are precisely as universal as the occurrence of man and woman. This fact leads naturally to the conclusion that the imagination is conditioned by this motif, so that at all times and in all places it is to the highest degree instigated to project this motif again and again." [37] This takes place especially in epochs of religious excitement. "That such projections are actual occurrences and not merely traditional opinions (so-called articles of faith) is proved by historical documents. These show that such syzygies are projected in complete opposition to the traditional attitudes of the faithful and moreover in a visionary and experiential form." The speculations of Bernard of Clairvaux and Bernard Silvestris may be understood in this sense too. But, in the work of the latter, the feminine component of the Godhead is at the same time *mater generationis, uterus indefessus, Natura praegnabilis.* Here, then, as through an opened sluice, the fertility cult of the earliest ages flows once again into the speculation of the Christian West.

By introducing clerical celibacy during the reign of Gregory VII (d. 1085), the Church had created an inner conflict for many priests. This conflict produced a great variety of results. An English cleric who wrote *ca.* 1100 and who is known as the "Anonymous of York" defended marriage for priests because it was in harmony with the order of Nature decreed by God (*M. G. Libelli de lite,* III [1897], 645–48). This obvious idea was frequently advanced in the twelfth and thirteenth centuries. About 1180 the Englishman Nigel Wireker writes a *Mirror of Fools* (*Speculum stultorum*) in the form of a satire on students and monks. The ass Brunellus wishes—as does Rabelais' Frère Jean des Entommeures later—to found an order which will be more agreeable than any extant. Even marriage will be permitted (*SP*, I, 96):

> *Ordine de reliquo placet ut persona secunda*
> *Foedere perpetuo sit mihi juncta comes.*
> *Hic fuit ordo prior et conditus in paradiso;*
> *Hunc deus instituit et benedixit ei.*
> *Hunc in perpetuum decrevimus esse tenendum,*
> *Cuius erat genitor cum genitrice mea.*

> (Furthermore, this Order grants me that a second person shall
> Be forever my companion, bound in links of faith.
> This the first and best of Orders, founded firm in Paradise;
> God himself did institute it, God his blessing gave.
> This the Order which we 'stablish, never any stray therefrom!
> This the Order which my father lived in with my mother!)

Criticism of celibacy and monasticism received fresh stimulus from the fact that the orders frequently attacked one another. In a letter to Abbot

[37] *Zentralblatt für Psychotherapie* (1936), 264. [Cf. Coll. Works, 9 I, 59 f.]

William of St. Thierry, (*PL*, CLXXXII, 209), Bernard of Clairvaux censures the gluttony of the Cluniacs: "Dish after dish is served. It is a fast day for meat, so there are two portions of fish . . . Everything is so artfully prepared that after four or five courses one still has an appetite . . . For (to mention nothing else) who can count in how many ways eggs alone are prepared and dressed, how diligently they are broken, beaten to froth, hard-boiled, minced; they come to the table now fried, now roasted, now stuffed, now mixed with other things, now alone . . . What shall I say of water-drinking, when not even watered wine is admitted? Being monks, we all suffer from poor digestions and are therefore justified in following the Apostle's counsel (I Tim. 5:23); only the word 'little,' which he puts first, we leave out, I know not why . . . During a meal you can see a beaker still half-full taken away three or four times; different wines are rather sniffed at than drunk, not swallowed but tasted, until, after discerning trial, the strongest is chosen." Along with St. Bernard's delicate irony, however, we also hear raucous voices. In the squabbles of the twelfth century, breeches played a painful part.[38] St. Benedict had declared this article of clothing superfluous and had permitted it only for travel. At Cluny, it appears, this rule was departed from in the second half of the tenth century. As early as the beginning of the eleventh, the fact affords material for monastery jokes. In the twelfth century the matter crops up in the polemic between the Cistercians and the Cluniacs. The latter reproach the former with wearing no breeches in order to be all the readier for lechery—for example, in a versified debate between two carousing monks, who finally come to blows.[39] The theme is frequently treated. It leads to an important and complex chapter of medieval literature, which lies outside of our theme—the criticism of curia, clergy, and monasticism which has such a large place in the poetry of the twelfth and thirteenth centuries.[40] It is revived by the English and German reformers and used as a weapon against Rome.[41] Many a text has escaped destruction for no other reason.

6.   *The Romance of the Rose*

The thirteenth century, the period of High Gothic and High Scholasticism, is considered the greatest century of the Middle Ages. But the representative poem of the period, *The Romance of the Rose*, stands in sharp contrast to the glorified picture of the epoch which is generally held. The first part of it, written *ca.* 1235 by Guillaume de Lorris, unfolds an allegory of love

[38] F. Lecoy in *Romania*, LXVII (1943), 13 f.
[39] Walther, 164.
[40] Excerpts in Olga Dobiache-Rojdestvensky, *Les poésies des Goliards* (Paris, 1931), pp. 73 ff.—On monasticism in the twelfth and thirteenth centuries, cf. Albert Hauck, *Kirchengeschichte Deutschlands*, IV, 325 ff.
[41] John Bale (1495–1563), Bishop of Ossory.—Matthias Flacius (properly Vlacich), born 1520 at Albona (Istria, whence his surname Illyricus), pupil of Luther's at Wittenberg, died 1575 at Frankfurt am Main.

in four thousand lines. The young poet dreams: It is May and he comes upon a garden surrounded by a wall. In the garden reigns Love, surrounded by Mirth, Youth, and Largesse. The youth sees a rose and wishes to pick it. But it is surrounded by a hedge of thorns and guarded by Danger, Shame, Evil Speech, and kindred powers. A long series of allegorical figures prevent approach to it. Here the first part, which was to have ended with the winning of the Rose, abruptly breaks off. Some forty years later, the translator and poet Jean de Meun continued the work and completed it in eighteen thousand lines. He takes over the fable and the cast of characters, but he makes them the vehicle of a long-winded didacticism. "The point with which Guillaume was primarily concerned is treated with unrestrained cynicism." The continuator intends, by imparting erudite matter, "to enlighten the lay mind . . . in the framework of a piquant discussion of sexual love" (Gröber). Jean de Meun borrows freely from Alan. We encounter Nature and her priest Genius again. In contrast to the spirit of *amour courtois,* whose last harvest was reaped by Guillaume de Lorris, Jean de Meun warns against love. Propagation is Nature's sole concern. Eros has yielded to Sex. The misogynistic literature of the Middle Ages is used as a stern warning against marriage; woman is displayed as corrupt and worthless. There is room for digression not only on business and trade, on friendship, justice, and the goddess Fortuna, but also on "beauty culture" and table manners. An old procuress proclaims erotic communism:

> *Toutes pour touz e touz pour toutes.*

As in Alan's *Planctus,* Nature is the mistress of Venus's forge:

> *Toujourz martele, toujourz forge,*
> *Toujourz ses pieces renouvele*
> *Par generacion nouvele.*

She presents her complaint to Genius, describes God's work of creation, discourses (following Boethius) on predestination and prophecy. Genius reads out Nature's decree, criticizes the ideal of virginity,[42] condemns sodomy, and advocates unceasing sexual activity, alleging the authority of Virgil (*Buc.,* 10, 69):

> *Omnia vincit amor; et nos cedamus amori.*
> (Love conquers all things; yield we too to love.)

Or in Old French:

> *Quant Bucoliques cherchereiz,*
> *"Amours vaint tout" i trouvereiz,*
> *"E nous la devons receveir."*

---

[42] Were it to reign for sixty years, mankind would die out (l. 19, 555); cf. Shakespeare's sonnet quoted at the end of this chapter.

The goddess Natura has become the servant of rank promiscuity, her management of the life of love is travestied into obscenity. The unaffected and playful eroticism of Latin Humanism, the stormy attacks of youthful *vagantes* against Christian morality, have sunk to the level of a sexual liberalism which concocts a spicy stew out of erudite tinsel and philistine pruriency. How was this possible? It corresponded with the libertinism of an epoch which had exchanged the heritage of antique beauty for the small coin of academic hair-splitting. For in Parisian university circles round about 1250 there was a heretical Scholasticism of love which appears to be akin to Averroism.[43] Thomas Aquinas attacked it in a passage of his *Summa contra Gentiles* (III, 136): "Certain men of distorted mind have spoken against the good of sexual moderation . . . For the union of man and woman is ordained for the good of the species. But this is more divine than the good of the individual . . . Organs of generation are given to man by divine ordinance . . . To this may be added the Lord's commandment to our first parents: Be fruitful and multiply and fill the earth." Jean de Meun is a man of letters, not a philosopher. But he shares the atmosphere of the trend against which Thomas argues; he is, then, no strange and solitary phenomenon. Together with many other heresies, that for which he speaks is aimed at in the condemnatory decree issued by Étienne Tempier, bishop of Paris (March 7, 1277).

The decree, however, did no harm to its popularity. Among the pilgrims whose journey to Canterbury Chaucer so delightfully describes is the Wife of Bath, who lets herself be heard from as follows:

> *Telle me also, to what conclusioun*
> *Were membres maad of generacioun,*
> *And for what profit was a wight y-wrought?*
> *Trusteth right wel, they wer nat maad for noght.*
> *Glose who-so wole, and seye both up and doun,*
> *That they were maked for purgacioun*
> *Of urine, and our bothe thinges smale*
> *Were eke to know a femele from a male,*
> *And for noon other cause: sey ye no?*
> *The experience woot wel it is noght so.*

The *Romance of the Rose* still found many readers in the sixteenth century, as did Alan's work, to which printing had given a new circulation. An echo of his thought is perceptible in Shakespeare's eleventh sonnet:

> *As fast as thou shalt wane, so fast thou grow'st*
> *In one of thine, from that which thou departest;*

---

[43] M. M. Gorce, *La lutte Contra gentiles à Paris au 13ᵉ siècle* (*Mélanges Mandonnet*, I [1930]). *Idem, Le Roman de la Rose. Texte essentiel de la scolastique courtoise* (1933).—G. Paré, *Les Idées et les lettres au XIIIᵉ siècle. Le Roman de la Rose* (Montreal, 1947).

And that fresh blood which youngly thou bestow'st,
Thou mayst call thine, when thou from youth convertest.
Herein lives wisdom, beauty, and increase;
Without this, folly, age, and cold decay:
If all were minded so, the times should cease,
And threescore year would make the world away.
Let those whom Nature hath not made for store,
Harsh, featureless, and rude, barrenly perish:
Look, whom she best endow'd, she gave thee more;
Which bounteous gift thou shouldst in bounty cherish.
She carv'd thee for her seal, and meant thereby,
Thou shouldst print more, not let that copy die.[44]

[44] The peregrinations of this topos since the Middle Ages remain to be investigated. It also occurs in Lorenzo Valla, *De Voluptate*; cf. E. Garin, *Der italienische Humanismus* (Bern, 1947), 53.

7

Metaphorics

*1.   Nautical Metaphors / 2.   Personal Metaphors
3.   Alimentary Metaphors / 4.   Corporal Metaphors
5.   Theatrical Metaphors*

WE HAVE oriented our investigation upon the didascalium of Greek rhetoric. From its systematic concepts we have derived historical categories. This book, then, can be called a *Nova Rhetorica*. We had outlined the program of a historical topics; the method proved to be fruitful. But the antique treatment of the "figures" also appears capable of a renewal. The most important "figure" is the metaphor (Quintilian, VIII, 2, 6). Μεταφορά, *translatio*, means "transfer." An old school example is *pratum ridet*, "the meadow laughs." Human laughter is "transferred" to nature. Beside our historical topics, let us place a historical metaphorics.

1.   Nautical Metaphors

We begin with a metaphor which appears insignificant. The Roman poets are wont to compare the composition of a work to a nautical voyage.[1] "To compose" is "to set the sails, to sail" ("vela dare": Virgil, *Georgics*, II, 41). At the end of the work the sails are furled ("vela trahere": *ibid.*, IV, 117). The epic poet voyages over the open sea in a great ship, the lyric poet on a river in a small boat. Horace makes Phoebus warn him (*Carm.*, IV, 15, 1):

> *Phoebus volentem proelia me loqui*
> *Victas et urbes increpuit lyra,*
> *Ne parva Tyrrhenum per aequor*
> *Vela darem . . .*

> (Phoebus, when I of battles thought to tell
> And conquered cities, struck his lyre, warning
> Lest on the open sea I set
> My little sails . . .)

In poems that consist of several books each book can begin with "setting" the sails and end with "furling" them. The end of the whole work is enter-

---

[1] Ovid, *Fasti*, I, 3; III, 789; IV, 18.—*Ars amandi*, I, 772; III, 748.—*Tristia*, II, 329 and 548, etc.—Propertius, III, 3, 22; III, 9, 3 and 36.—Manilius, III, 26. —Statius, *Silvae*, V, 3, 237.—This is only a small selection.

ing port, with or without casting anchor (Statius, *Silvae*, IV, 89; *Thebais*, XII, 809; *Ilias latina*, 1063). The poet becomes the sailor, his mind or his work the boat. Sailing the sea is dangerous, especially when undertaken by an "unpracticed sailor" ("rudis nauta": Fortunatus, ed. Leo, 114, 26) or in a "leaky boat" ("rimosa fragilis ingenii barca": Aldhelm [ed. Ehwald], 320, 20). Often the boat must be steered between cliffs ("sermonum cymbam inter loquelae scopulos frenare": Ennodius [ed. Hartel], I, 3). Alcuin fears sea-monsters (*Poetae*, I, 198, 1321 ff.); Smaragdus the raging tides (*Poetae*, I, 609, 55 ff.). Unfavorable winds and storms often threaten.

Nautical metaphors originally belong to poetry. Pliny writes to a poet (*Ep.*, VIII, 4, 5): "Loose the hawsers, spread the sails, and let your genius voyage freely. For why should I not discourse poetically with a poet?" But Cicero had already adopted these expressions in prose. Shall he use the "oar of dialectics" or set "the sails of eloquence" at once (*Tusc.*, IV, 5, 9). Quintilian feels like a solitary sailor on the high seas (*prooemium* to Book XII). Jerome sets "the sails of interpretation" (*PL*, XXV, 903 D). His sailing breeze is the Holy Ghost (*ibid.*, 369 D). Prudentius refers to Paul's shipwreck and Peter's wanderings over the sea (ed. Bergmann, 215 f. and 245). This class of metaphor is extraordinarily widespread throughout the Middle Ages [2] and long survives into later times.

Dante begins the second book of the *Convivio* with nautical metaphors: ". . . proemialmente ragionando . . . lo tempo chiama e domanda la mia nave uscir di porto; perchè, drizzato l' artimone de la ragione a l' òra del mio desiderio, entro in pelago." As a practiced stylist Dante freshens up the worn metaphor: instead of an ordinary sail he uses a mizzensail ("artimone"). Good! But the reader will rightly ask: What induces Dante to begin a philosophical treatise with a display of navigational technique? The reader will consult a commentary. And what does he find in the latest and most erudite one? "We also find these images in the preface to Cassian's *Collationes*, which were widely known in the Middle Ages" (ed. Busnelli and Vandelli [1934]). Cassian (*ca.* 360–*ca.* 435) must, then, have been one of Dante's favorite authors, yet he never mentions him. The reader is misled into assuming that these nautical metaphors could not be derived from any other source. Now Dante began his metaphor with the words "proemialmente ragionando." He is using the metaphor, then, because it was traditional in introductions. It is precisely this tradition which we have tried to evince. A commentator on Dante ought to be aware of it.

For the opening of the *Purgatorio* (I, 1 f.),

> *Per correr miglior acqua alza le vele*
> *Omai la navicella del mio ingegno,*

---

[2] Carolingian examples: *Poetae*, I, 613, 20 ff. (Uncommon nautical terms such as *nauclerus, carcesia, carabus, pronesia*; drawn from Isidore, *Et.*, XIX, 1–4).— *Poetae*, I, 366, No. VI, 1; *ibid.*, 517, 955.—*Poetae*, II, 5, 23; III, 66, 175; 487, 508; 611, 41; 674, 1021 ff.

Propertius has been cited ("ingenii cymba," III, 3, 22). Dante does not know him and does not need to know him. The "boat of the mind" is already a commonplace in late Antiquity and is conscientiously preserved by the Middle Ages.[3] But, not knowing this, the commentator turns to Propertius as cheerfully as he did to Cassianus. He could, with Goethe, object to me:

> Also das wäre Verbrechen, dass einst Properz mich begeistert?
> (Must I account it a crime that once Propertius could charm me?)

No, it is not a crime—unless one makes Dante a reader of Propertius. For by doing that one distorts historical perspective. One turns Dante into a humanistic lover of Roman elegy, detaches him from the poetic and rhetorical tradition of the Latin Middle Ages. At the beginning of the *Paradiso* (II, 1–15) nautical imagery appears once again, magnificently heightened:

> O voi che siete in piccioletta barca
> Desiderosi d' ascoltar, seguiti
> Dietro al mio legno che cantando varca,
> Tornate a riveder li vostri liti:
> Non vi mettete in pelago, chè, forse,
> Perdendo me rimarreste smarriti.
> L' acqua ch' io prendo già mai non si corse:
> Minerva spira, e conducemi Apollo,
> E nove Muse mi dimostran l' Orse.
> Voi altri pochi che drizzaste il collo
> Per tempo al pan de li angeli, del quale
> Vivesi qui ma non sen vien satollo,
> Metter potete ben per l' alto sale
> Vostro navigio, servando mio solco
> Dinanzi a l' acqua che ritorna equale.

Spenser too uses an elaborate nautical metaphor at the close of *The Faerie Queene* (VI, 12, 1), and with it we shall enter port:

> Like as a ship, that through the Ocean wyde
> Directs her course unto one certaine cost,
> Is met of many a counter winde and tyde,
> With which her winged speed is let and crost,
> And she her selfe in stormie surges tost;
> Yet making many a borde, and many a bay,
> Still winneth way, ne hath her compasse lost:
> Right so it fares with me in this long way,
> Whose course is often stayd, yet never is astray.

[3] Among the few examples of nautical metaphorics which we have adduced, we have already found "sermonum cymba" and "ingenii barca." There are countless others.

2. *Personal Metaphors*

For Homer, flight is the "companion" of panic (*Iliad*, IX, 2); panic the son of Ares (*Iliad*, XIII, 299); infatuation (Ate) the eldest daughter of Zeus (*Iliad*, XIX, 91). Pindar [4] calls the Muses daughters of memory; rains children of the clouds; wine son of the vine; songs daughters of the Muses; hubris the mother of satiety, etc. Pindar goes beyond these genealogical connections only rarely. Aetna is "nurse of the sharp snow," law "king over all" (cf. Herodotus, III, 38). Aeschylus calls decorum "mother of success" (*Septem*, 224), soot "brother of the flickering fire" (*ibid.*, 494), dust the "neighbor and brother of dirt" (*Ag.*, 495). Epaminondas' last words were: "I leave two immortal daughters behind, Leuctra and Mantineia."

From Homer to Aeschylus, these metaphors give the impression of the archaic poet-seer forcing his way through to the image he beholds. In Roman eloquence they are replaced by colorless reflection. According to Cicero all arts and sciences are "companions and handmaids" ("comites et ministrae") of the orator (*De or.*, I, 17, 75). Hence that rhetoric calls for censure which gives eloquence to jurisprudence only as a servant and waiting-woman ("ancillula, pedisequa": *De or.*, I, 55, 236).

Horace calls utility the mother of justice and equity (*Sat.*, I, 3, 98):

> . . . *Utilitas, iusti prope mater et aequi.*

Quintilian will grant the name of orator only to the good man and adds: Nature herself were not a mother but a stepmother ("non parens sed noverca") had she bestowed speech on man that he might use it for criminal ends (XII, 1, 2). The mothers, stepmothers, companions, handmaids, and maids of Roman rhetoric had a most extensive progeny in the Middle Ages.

There were, further, the oriental personal metaphors of the Bible. "I have said to corruption, Thou art my father: to the worm, Thou art my mother, and my sister" (Job 17:14). "And he shall rise up at the voice of the bird, and all the daughters of music shall be brought low" (Ecclesiastes 12:45 [5]). The Psalmist makes mercy and truth meet together, righteousness and peace kiss each other: "Misericordia et veritas obviaverunt sibi; justitia et pax osculatae sunt" (Ps. 84:11 [A.V. 85:10]). From this passage the Middle Ages evolved the "Strife of the Daughters of God for the Soul of Man before the Judgment Seat of God" which circulated in many versions.[6] In John 8:44 the Devil is called the father of lies (in the Vulgate: "mendax et pater eius"). Much more of this sort is to be found in the Bible. Antique and Biblical usage then meet in patristic literature. Patience, according to Tertullian (*De patientia*, 15), is "alumna Dei." He calls the Jordan the arbitrator ("arbiter") of boundaries, the letters of the alphabet "indices

---

[4] F. Dornseiff, *Pindars Stil* (1921), 51.
[5] Valery Larbaud, *Technique* (1932), 138.
[6] Walther, 87 and 221.

custodesque rerum" (*Apol.*, 19). Once again, then, we are able to observe antique-pagan and Biblical stylistic forms meeting and reinforcing one another. Personal metaphors are just as characteristic of the style of pagan late Antiquity as they are of the ecclesiastical writers. In Claudian Fides and Clementia are sisters (*De consulatu Stilichonis*, II, 30). Avarice is the mother of crime (*ibid.*, 111), Ambition the nurse of Avarice (*ibid.*, 114). Since abstract nouns are mostly of the feminine gender, personal metaphors generally deal with females. So later, in medieval didactic poems on the virtues and vices, we find the rudiments of a "genealogy of morals." These genealogical relationships are not always clear. Is desire for fame the sister, the granddaughter, or the daughter of Pride? Theodulf (*Poetae*, I, 449, 175) leaves it undecided,

> Seu soror est eius, seu neptis, filia sive.

In Hugo Sotovagina (*SP*, II, 226) Simony is the mother of whores. As the mother of Hate, who bore Envy, Ira (Wrath) is a grandmother (*SP*, I, 327). Here we are on the borderline of the burlesque. Matthew of Vendôme crosses it playfully when he calls coughing "the stepmother of the chest" (*PL*, CCV, 977 C).

Dante too was fond of using personal metaphors. Belacqua appears lazier "than if Sloth were his sister" (*Purg.*, IV, 111). The sixth hour is "the sixth handmaid of the day" (*Purg.*, XII, 81). A reflected ray is "a pilgrim who wishes to return" (*Par.*, I, 51). The tributaries of the Po are its "attendants" (*Inf.*, V, 99). Human art is "the granddaughter of God" because it is the daughter of Nature, who herself is the daughter of God (*Inf.*, XI, 105). Dante calls his philosophical commentary on his canzoni their "servant" (*Conv.*, I, 5, 6). In the *Purgatorio* (XXI, 98) Statius calls the *Aeneid* his "nurse." It is preciosity when in Dante's canzone *Tre donne* we are told that Amore has an aunt named Drittura.

Like so many other characteristics of medieval style, the personal metaphor was awakened to new life in seventeenth-century Spain. In Góngora (*Soledad segunda*, 521) Cupid is "nieto de la espuma," "nephew of the foam" (because son of Venus). This is conceptistic trifling. In Keats ("Ode on a Grecian Urn") the personal metaphor becomes formally classicistic again, but with a modern psychological content:

> Thou still unravish'd bride of quietness,
> Thou foster-child of silence and slow time . . .

Among personal metaphors we must also count the concept of the book as a child. This goes back to Plato's doctrine of Eros. In the *Symposium* Diotima sets forth that all men are governed by a strong love of fame and immortality. Many seek to immortalize themselves by begetting children, but others "beget more in the soul than in the body." Such a man goes about and "seeks beauty, in which he may beget." He finds it in beautiful bodies which are linked with noble souls. When he has found such a "beautiful person" a spiritual begetting arises out of converse with him. "And every man," Diotima continues, "would rather see such children born to him than human children, when he looks at Homer and Hesiod and the other good poets, envying them because they left behind such children as prepare everlasting fame and remembrance for them . . ." The works of the poets, then, are their children. The image does not often appear in Antiquity. Catullus calls poems "dulces Musarum fetus" (65, 3), which can mean children but can also mean fruits. Ovid is clear (*Trist.*, III, 14, 13):

> *Palladis exemplo de me sine matre creata*
> *Carmina sunt; stirps haec progeniesque mea.*

Ovid uses the comparison several times (*Trist.*, I, 7, 35 and III, 1, 65) and presumably contributed to its diffusion. Petronius (c. 118) uses a new turn of expression: "Neque concipere aut edere partum mens potest nisi . . ." This introduces *partus* into the vocabulary of Latin and the Romance languages as a designation for literary work. Synesius says that he has begotten books not only with noble philosophy and with poetry, who dwells in the same temple, but also with vulgar rhetoric (Epistle 1; cf. Epistle 141). For the Latin Middle Ages Ovid would seem to have been the intermediary. Near the beginning of his poem John of Hanville calls it a boy (241):

> *Nascitur et puero vagit nova pagina versu.*

Toward the end he addresses it as the child of his mind (*SP*, I, 392):

> *O longum studii gremio nutrita togati*
> *Ingenii proles, rudis et plebeie libelle,*
> *Incolumis vivas.*

This metaphor is a favorite in the Renaissance and Baroque periods. In his elegy to Pierre Lescot, Ronsard says:

> *Je fus souventes fois retancé de mon père*
> *Voyant que j'aimais trop les deux filles d'Homère.*

Agrippa d'Aubigné, in the prologue to the *Tragiques*, addresses his poem as "pauvre enfant" and calls his early work (*Le Printemps*) "un pire et plus heureux aîné." In the much-discussed dedication of Shakespeare's sonnets, Mr. W. H. is called "the onlie begetter of these insuing sonnets," but here "begetter" does not mean the poet but the inspirer (spiritual begetter) of the sonnets. In one sonnet (77) the friend is urged to set down his thoughts —"those children nurs'd, deliver'd from thy brain"—in a notebook. In a dedication to the Virgin Queen Elizabeth, Bacon uses the sentence: "Generare et liberi, humana; creare et opera, divina." [7] In the preface to *Don Quijote* Cervantes calls it "hijo de mi entendimiento." We are still within the same circle of concepts when we find in John Donne: "the mistress of my youth, Poetry . . . the wife of mine age, Divinity." [8] This is reminis-

---

[7] E. Wolff, *Fr. Bacon und seine Quellen*, I (1910), 35.
[8] Ed. Grierson (1912), II, 106.

cent of Synesius' expressions. The Marinistic lyric poet Tommaso Stigliani (1573–1651) writes to a friend:

> Coppini, io vo' di me novella darte.
> Talora, leggo in parte
> Ciò che del ver fu dai due greci scritto;
> Talora, mi tragitto
> Dell' alme muse all' arte,
> Ed o concepo in mente
> O partorisco in carte.

In the preface to his essays on the fable Lessing writes: "Years ago I cast a critical eye over my writings. I had forgotten them for long enough to be able to regard them as the offspring of someone else." Schlegel in *Lucinde* calls novels "sons of wit." In the preface to the *Promessi Sposi* Manzoni uses "questo mio rozzo parto" as a modesty formula, with conscious archaism. That was in 1827. In the same year the young Ranke writes from Vienna on the subject of his studies. He gets to the library every morning about nine, where he is working his way through the relations of the Venetian ambassadors. "Here with the object of my love, beautiful Italian that she is, I spend sweet and luxurious hours of happiness, and I hope that we shall bring forth a Romano-German wonder-child. I rise about twelve, wholly exhausted" (*Zur eignen Lebensgeschichte*, 175).

3.   Alimentary Metaphors

These are not unknown to Antiquity. Pindar praises his poetry as furnishing something to eat.[9] The word satire (*satura*) means "mixed dish." Quintilian, II, 4, 5 speaks of a milk diet for beginners. But the Bible is the principal source of alimentary metaphors. In the Christian story of salvation the tasting of the forbidden fruit and the institution of the Last Supper are dramatic episodes. Those who hunger and thirst are called blessed. In the Gospel of St. John (4:15 f.; 6:27) a distinction is made between earthly water and the water of eternal life, between the meat which perishes and the meat "qui permanet in vitam aeternam." Newly converted Christians are compared to babes who drink milk but do not yet eat solid food (I Cor. 3:2; I Peter 2:2; Hebrews 5:12 f.).[10] Ecclesiastical literature altered these and related images in the most various ways, a subject which cannot be followed up here. It need only be pointed out that according to Augustine alimentary metaphors are justified. The learner, he says, has something in common with the eater; the food of both must be made palatable by seasonings: "Inter se habent nonnullam similitudinem vescentes atque discentes; propter fastidia plurimorum etiam ipsa, sine quibus vivi non potest, ali-

---

[9] Dornseiff, *Pindars Stil*, 61.

[10] For milk in Christian literature, cf. F. Dornseiff, *Das Alphabet in Mystik und Magie*, 2, 18 f.—A text of Indian philosophy is entitled "The New-churned Butter of the Milk of Perfection" (*Kaivalya-navanita*). Heinrich Zimmer, *Der Weg zum Selbst* [Zurich, 1944], 56.

menta condienda sunt" (*De doct. chr.*, IV, 11, 26). For Augustine God is "interior cibus" (*Conf.*, I, 13, 21, 5), truth is nourishment (*Civ. dei*, XX, 30, 21) and food (*Conf.*, IX, 10, 24, 12). In using the concept "to spice" (to salt) Augustine is also within the Biblical tradition (e.g., Col. 4:6: "Sermo vester semper in sale sit conditus"), which we later find again in Walafrid. The latter calls his prose life of St. Gall "agreste pulmentum," which he will flavor with salt—that is, put into verse (*Poetae*, II, 428; VI, 4, n. 5). Biblical in origin too is designating Christian teaching a meal ("coena mea," Luke 14:24; "coena magna Dei," Rev. 19:17 and elsewhere). Hence are derived such expressions as "lucifer pastus" in Prudentius (*Psychom.*, 625), "cena spiritalis" in Walter of Châtillon (*Moralisch-satirische Gedichte*, ed. Strecker, p. 101, st. 7). Gregory the Great calls Augustine's writings wheaten flour, his own bran (*MGH, Epist.*, II, 251, 30 ff.). A ninth-century poet compares Christ's teaching to a life-giving meal spiced with honey, oil, and red Falernian wine (*Poetae*, III, 258, 49 ff.). But profane learning is called food too. The word *ferculum* (properly: "course" of a meal) is used for it in Walafrid (*Poetae*, II, 334, 27) and in Arnulf, the author of the *Delicie cleri* (*RF*, II, 216). Eupolemius ends the second book of his *Messiad* with the hope that his work may be milk for the tender and strong meat for the strong. The wisdom of the Greek philosophers is served in beakers in the *Architrenius* (*SP*, I, 354).

Sigebert accumulates the rarest luxuries in his *Passio Thebeorum* (p. 47). He finds himself in the Palace of Philosophy, among the Christian poets, who are offering rich gifts:

> 123 *Zinziber et peretrum dat dives, cinnama, costum,*
> *Hic piper, hic laser, largior ipse laver.*
> *Offert hic mulsum, tu condis melle Falernum,*
> *Et certant vitreo gemmea vasa mero.*
> *Ipse feram limpham ligno testave petitam,*
> *Unde manus unctas unctaque labra lavent.*

L. 123, *peretrum* = *pyrethron* "pellitory, pellitory-root" (Ovid and others; Isidore, *Et.*, XVII, 9, 74); 1, 124, *laser* = "juice of the plant *laserpicium*" (Isidore, *Et.*, XVII, 9, 24); *laver* "a plant" (Plin., *N. H.*, XXVI, 50; not in Isidore).

Here—and that is why I cite the passage—we have a sample of the not uncommon "lexical" poetry or "versified lexicography" [11] : the poet writes verses in order to bring in rare words recorded by glossographers. Similar literary games are popular in Greek literature from the end of the fourth century B.C. [12]

The evolution of this as of every group of metaphors exhibits two phases. In the first, the traditional stock is mechanically taken over or at best en-

[11] Ernst Schulz, *Corona quernea*, 223.
[12] Christ-Schmid, II, 1 (1920), 116, n. 3. Notable names are Leonidas of Tarentum and Lycophron.

riched only by accumulation. But from the twelfth century onwards it is subdivided dialectically. Let us take as an example the milk which is indispensable as intellectual food among both pagans and Christians. As Alan of Lille says (*PL*, CCX, 240 B), if one looks at it more closely three substances can be distinguished in it: watery liquid (*serum*), cheese, and butter. Now in the Bible the sacred doctrine (*sacra doctrina*) is "elegantly" compared to milk. This is naturally a reference to the threefold meaning of scripture: historical, allegorical, tropological. The watery liquid represents history; the substance of both is common, both afford little enjoyment.[13] Cheese (allegory) is solid and substantial nourishment. But the butter of tropology tastes sweetest to the palate of the mind ("palatum mentis"). The theological separation of milk reaches its conclusion in St. Francis of Sales: "Si la charité est un lait, la dévotion en est la cresme" (*Introduction à la vie dévote*, I, ch. 2).

Alimentary metaphorics was richly developed by Dante.[14] The *Convivio* is a banquet for all who hunger after knowledge, the "bread of angels." Dante does not himself sit at the "blessed table" but he picks up the crumbs that fall from it (I, 1, 6–10). He serves up canzoni, with which the commentaries are passed round as "barley loaves" (John 6:13). We shall not trace this class of images further in Dante.

4. *Corporal Metaphors*

Alan, we saw, can speak of the palate of the mind. That too is the late fruit of a long metaphorical tradition.

In a somewhat daring image, Plato says that the dialectical method gently raises "the eye of the soul, buried in barbaric mud" (*Republic*, 533 d). Thenceforth the "eye of the soul" became a favorite metaphor, which we find both in pagan [15] and Christian authors. In this usage the visual power of the physical eye is transferred to the perceptive faculty of the intellect. Inner senses are co-ordinated with the outer.[16] The mind has ears as well as eyes. Paulinus of Nola: [17]

Ergo oculos mentis Christo reseremus et aures.

[13] Such is the medieval evaluation of history.

[14] Walter Naumann has collected Dante's metaphors of hunger and thirst in *RF* (1940), 13–36.

[15] E.g., Cicero, *Orator*, 29, 101. Lucian, ed. Jacobitz, I, 239.

[16] Systematically in Origen. Cf. H. U. v. Balthasar, *Origenes. Ein Aufbau aus seinen Werken* (1938), 319–80.—Cf. also Kurt Rahner, "La Doctrine des sens spirituels au moyen âge," in *Revue d'ascétique et de mystique*, XIII (1932), 173 ff. and XIV (1933), 265 ff.

[17] *Carmina*, 31, 226.—Juvencus had already used "aures mentis" as an explanatory rendering of Matthew 13:9. Jerome uses the same expression in commenting on the Bible, and Gregory the Great follows him. Augustine too knows "the ears of the heart" (*Conf.*, I, 5 and IV, 27), as does the liturgy ("aures praecordiorum" in the prayer for catechumens on Good Friday), the "os spirituale" (*Conf.*, IX, 3, 6), and the like. We find the "ear of the heart" again in the prologue to St. Benedict's Rule.

After eyes and ears it is the turn of the other bodily organs. The Christian writers hark back to Israelitish metaphors. The Old Testament had "praeputium cordis" (Deut. 10:16; Prov. 4:4); Paul took this up in his sentences concerning "the circumcision of the heart" (Romans 2:25–29). In the same way Peter transposes the Mosaic "girths of the loins" (Exodus 12:11): "succincti lumbos mentis vestrae" (I Peter 1:13). Metaphors of this sort are frequent in late Antiquity and the Middle Ages. Characteristic of Augustine are metaphors which violate visual perception: "the hand of my tongue" (*Conf.*, V, 1), "the hand of the heart" (*ibid.*, X, 12), "the head of the soul" (*ibid.*, X, 7). The soul tosses to and fro, "on its back, on its sides, and on its belly" (*ibid.*, VI, 16, 26). Prudentius introduces "the belly of the heart;" [18] Aldhelm the "vulva of regenerating grace," the "neck of the mind," the "groins of the bowels." The "eye of the heart" and the "brow of the mind" in Guigo, "the belly of the mind" in Alan and Peter the Venerable. Godfrey of Breteuil can say: "After it has drunk all this thoughtfully and sufficiently, the belly of my mind thirsts for more." [19] Dante too uses this realm of metaphor: "the back of our judgment," "spatulae nostri iudicii" (*De vulgari eloquio*, I, 6, 3). He also has "oculi mentis" (*De mon.*, II, 1, 3); "occhi della ragione" (*Conv.*, I, 4, 3), "dell' anima" (*Conv.*, I, 11, 3), "dell' intelletto" (*Conv.*, II, 15, 7); and "l' agute luci de lo 'ntelletto" (*Purg.*, XVIII, 16).

The field is immense and unexplored. An entire volume could be filled with examples from patristic literature alone. Here as elsewhere, our task is to point out and to stimulate, not to be exhaustive. I should like to cite but one more corporal metaphor—a particularly striking one. In the apocryphal *Oratio Manassae*, which was probably written *ca.* A.D. 70 [20] and which appears in the appendix to the Vulgate, we read: "et nunc flecto genua cordis mei," "and now bow I the knees of my heart." In Clement's first epistle, ch. 57, this is taken over and the editor remarks that the expression occurs frequently in the Fathers and the Councils.[21] It also entered the liturgy [22] and thus was impressed upon the memory of the church, and then appears in medieval poetry.[23] In later times as well, like so many of the emotive formulas of Antiquity, the phrase "knees of the heart" had a very strong in-

---

[18] Prudentius, *Apoth.*, 583. But according to H. Rahner (*Biblica*, XXII [1941], 296) the "doctrine of the belly as the inmost heart, which was made current by Ambrose and had its roots in the psychology of Origen," was modeled upon John 7:38. Augustine: "Venter interioris hominis conscientia cordis est" (*PL*, XXXV, 1643 CD).

[19] Aldhelm, ed. Ehwald, 260, 19; 477, 13; 243, 19.—Carolingian: *Poetae*, I, 413, 30 and 455, 151.—Guigo (*Meditationes*, ed. Wilmart [1936]), 155.—Alan, *SP*, II, 491.—Peter the Venerable, *PL*, CLXXXIX, 1009 C.—Godfrey of Breteuil, *Fons philosophiae*, st. 195.

[20] Bousset, *Die Religion des Judentums im späthellenistischen Zeitalter* [3] (1926), 32, n. 2.

[21] F. X. Funk, *Patres apostolici*, I (1901), p. 172.

[22] *Postcommunio* of the mass *pro reddendis gratiis*.

[23] *Poetae*, IV, 765, 86 (where the editors were not aware of its origin).

fluence—even among Protestants rigorously trained in the Bible. Heinrich von Kleist uses it in his *Penthesilea* (l. 2800) and in a letter to Goethe (Jan. 24, 1808).

Modern style-psychology would perhaps call this entire class of metaphors "Baroque." In that case, literary Baroque is as old as the Bible and comes down to Heinrich von Kleist.

5. Theatrical Metaphors

In the work of Plato's old age, the *Laws*, we read: "May we not regard every living being as a puppet of the gods, which may be their plaything only, or may be created with a purpose?" (I, 644 de). And later: "Man is made to be the plaything of God, and this, truly considered, is the best of him" * (VII, 803 c). In the *Philebus* (50 b) Plato speaks of the "tragedy and comedy of life." In these profound thoughts, which in Plato still have the bloom of their first creation, lie the seeds of the idea of the world as a stage upon which men play their parts, their motions directed by God. In the popular lectures on philosophy ("diatribes") of the Cynics, the comparison of man to an actor became a much-used cliché.[24] Horace (*Sat.*, II, 7, 82) sees man as a puppet. The idea "mimus vitae" became proverbial. Thus Seneca writes (*Ep.*, 80, 7): "hic humanae vitae mimus, qui nobis partes, quas male agamus, adsignat." Similar ideas are found in primitive Christianity. Paul (I Cor. 49:9) says of the Apostles that God appointed them to death as a spectacle ($\theta \acute{\epsilon} \alpha \tau \rho o \nu$) for the world, angels, and men. Here the idea in mind is not the stage but the Roman circus. We find a related concept in Clement of Alexandria: "For from Zion will go forth the law and the word of the Lord of Jerusalem, the divine word, the true fighter for the prize, who gains the crown of victory on the theater of the whole world" (Hortatory Address to the Heathen, I, 1, 3 = *Clemens Schriften, übersetzt von Stählin*, I [1934], 73). Here the cosmos is seen as a stage. In Augustine (*Enarr. ad ps.*, 127) we read: "Here on earth it is as if children should say to their parents: Come! think of departing hence; we too would play our comedy! For nought but a comedy of the race of man is all this life, which leads from temptation to temptation." Augustine's pagan contemporary, the Egyptian Palladas, has the same thought, with a different ethical point, in a beautifully turned epigram (A.P., X, 72):

> Σκηνὴ πᾶς ὁ βίος καὶ παίγνιον. ἢ μάθε παίζειν
> Τὴν σπουδὴν μεταθείς, ἢ φέρε τὰς ὀδύνας.

("All life is a stage and a game: either learn to play it, laying by seriousness, or bear its pains." †)

As we see: the metaphor "world-stage," like so many others, reached the

Middle Ages both from pagan Antiquity and the Christian writers. Both sources mingled in late Antiquity. When Boethius says "haec vitae scena," we hear Seneca in it, and also Cicero ("cum in vita, tum in scaena"; *Cato maior*, 18, 65). The Latin poetry of the early Middle Ages echoes it in turn: "secli huius in scena" (*Carm. cant.*, p. 97, l. 15). Yet the comparison is rare in this period. But in the twelfth century it is influentially revived by one of the leading minds of the age: John of Salisbury. In his chief work, the *Policraticus*, published in 1159 (ed. Webb, I, 190), he quotes from Petronius (§ 80):

> *Grex agit in scena mimum, pater ille vocatur,*
> *Filius hic, nomen divitis ille tenet;*
> *Mox ubi ridendas inclusit pagina partes,*
> *Vera redit facies, dissimulata perit.*

(The troop is on the stage, the mime begins: One is
Called father, one his son, a third the rich man;
But soon the page is closed upon their humorous parts,
The real face reappears, the assumed has vanished.)

This text contains the useful application: "Learn from the actor that outward splendor is but empty show, and that after the end of the play the personages keep their real countenances." But what does the medieval philosopher and humanist make of the lines? He immediately appends a chapter which he entitles, "De mundana comedia vel tragedia." The old, threadbare actor simile here becomes the conceptual framework for a comprehensive critique of the age. Job, our author says, called life a "term of war service." [25] Had he foreseen the present, he would have said: "Comoedia est vita hominis super terram." For everyone forgets his part and plays another. John is willing to leave it undecided whether life is to be called a comedy or a tragedy, if the reader will merely grant him "quod fere totus mundus iuxta Petronium exerceat histrionem." [26] The stage of this immense tragedy or comedy is the world. In John's next chapter, the heroes of virtue are praised. With God and the angels, they look down from eternity upon the tragicomic business of the world-stage. John revivified the old metaphor by a detailed treatment (it extends through two chapters). In addition, he combined its separate elements, which usually occur singly, into a general view. He finds his starting point in the moralizing commonplace rehandled by Petronius. The first extension of the horizon is achieved by a comparison with the text from Job. The conception is then deepened by pondering the question: tragedy or comedy? It is again enlarged by the

---

[25] In the Vulgate Job 7:1 runs: "Militia est vita hominis super terram." Luther's translation reads otherwise [as does the A.V.].

[26] The attempt has been made to reconstruct a fragment of Petronius from this passage. But Buecheler (critical ed. of Petronius, [1862], p. 95) is undoubtedly right when he says that the passage is John's free rendering of the lines quoted.

extension of the stage to the entire world. Finally a new enlargement—and
the last: from earth to heaven. There sit the spectators of the terrestrial
play: God and the heroes of virtue. The *scena vitae* has thus become a
theatrum mundi. The idea that God assembles virtuous men about him
would seem to have stemmed from Cicero's *Somnium Scipionis*, of which
work John's expressions in Chapter 9 are also often reminiscent, except that
the concept of the world-theater is entirely lacking there. But the harmonizing of Christian doctrine and Ciceronian wisdom is a characteristic tendency of the Christian Humanism which the European North brought to
flower in the twelfth century.

The *Policraticus* was very widely circulated throughout the Middle Ages,
as library catalogues testify. But it was much read in later times too. We
know that it was printed in 1476, 1513 (once in Paris, once in Lyon), 1595,
1622, 1639, 1664, 1677. If the metaphor *theatrum mundi* frequently reappears in the sixteenth and seventeenth centuries, the popularity of the
Policraticus would seem to have had a great deal to do with it.

Let us look around Europe in the sixteenth century. We begin in Germany, and come upon—Luther. As Erich Seeberg (*Grundzüge der Theologie Luthers* [1940], 179), sets forth, Luther employs the "extraordinarily
bold" expression "God's play" for what takes place in justification. For
Luther all of profane history is a "puppet play of God's." In history we see
only God's "masks" at work—that is, heroes like Alexander or Hannibal
. . . Seeberg would derive these formulas from Master Eckhart. But they
belong to the common stock of tradition.

We proceed to France. The year is 1564. The court is celebrating the
carnival at Fontainebleau. A comedy has just been played. We hear the
epilogue, written by Ronsard. It begins:

> *Ici la Comédie apparaît un exemple*
> *Où chacun de son fait les actions contemple:*
> *Le monde est un théâtre, et les hommes acteurs.*
> *La Fortune qui est maîtresse de la scène*
> *Apprête les habits, et de la vie humaine*
> *Les cieux et les destins en sont les spectateurs.*

A *theatrum mundi*, then, with men as actors, Fortune as the stage director,
and Heaven as spectator.

We proceed to England. 1599—in London the Globe Theatre has just
been opened. The new building displays the motto, "Totus mundus agit
histrionem." One of the first plays to have its original production here is
Shakespeare's *As You Like It*. In this play (II, 7), occurs Jacques' famous
speech in which the world is equated with a stage ("All the world's a
stage") and the "seven ages" with the seven acts of a human life. A recent
editor, G. B. Harrison (in The Penguin Shakespeare [1937]) comments on
this: "This is Shakespeare's little essay on the motto of the new Globe
Theatre which the company had just occupied." And whence comes this

motto? Not from Petronius, as some writers have averred, but from the *Policraticus*, except only that the "exerceat" of the latter is changed to "agit." Whoever was responsible for the display of this motto, then, knew the *Policraticus*—which had had a new edition in 1595. The Globe Theatre, then, was under the banner of the medieval English humanist.

We pass to Spain and the seventeenth century. Don Quixote (Part II, ch. 12) explains to his squire the similarity between a play and the life of man. When the play is over and the costumes taken off, the actors are all equal. Even so men in death. "A splendid comparison," Sancho replies, "though not so new that I have not heard it many a time before." Thus does Cervantes make fun of a literary cliché. Witty—indirect—mockery of a fashionable rhetorical ornament: That is the first form in which the theatrical metaphor meets us in the Spain of the seventeenth century—in the country and the period in which Calderón's genius will run its brilliant course. Rightly has Vossler pointed out that the comparison of the life of man to a play was a commonplace in the Spain of the *siglo de oro*.

The second chapter of Baltasar Gracián's *Criticón* (1651 ff.) bears the title, *El gran teatro del universo*. Here, however, there is no question of the theater, the chapter treats of Nature as the stage of life (cosmos as pageant). But the name which, above all others, must be named, is Calderón. His too is a mind of the most subtle culture and the most comprehensive literary education. He is a virtuoso, if you like; but a virtuoso who is at the same time a child and a genius; a deeply pious artist. The *theatrum mundi* makes part of the permanent stock of his conceptual world, though with iridescent changes in meaning. In his best-known play, *La vida es sueño*, the imprisoned Prince Segismundo speaks of the theater of the world, speaks of it in dream, and, himself a prisoner, gives it the meaning of the wide world of reality (ed. Keil, I, 16 b):

> *Salga a la anchurosa plaza*
> *Del gran teatro del mundo*
> *Este valor sin segundo . . .*

> (Now let this valor unseconded
> Go forth upon the wide extent
> Of the great theater of the world.)

Taken as a whole, Calderón's work has the scope of a world-stage, since his characters act their parts before a cosmic background (Keil, I, 19 a):

> *El dosel de la jura, reducido*
> *A segunda intención, a horror segundo,*
> *Teatro funesto es, donde importuna*
> *Representa tragedias la fortuna.*

(The throneroom of the oath, reduced
To new intent, to horrow new,
A baleful theater is; molesting
Fortune there plays her tragedies.)

Here and occasionally elsewhere Fate takes over the role of stage manager. Calderón gave the traditional uses of the metaphor a new splendor by his sparkling diction.[27]

More important, however, is this: Calderón is the first poet to make the God-directed *theatrum mundi* the subject of a sacred drama. The profound thought, which Plato once threw out and which lies as if lost among the immense riches of his work, which was afterwards transferred from theology to the study of man,[28] and made an ethical commonplace, undergoes a brilliant rebirth in seventeenth-century Catholic Spain. The theatrical metaphor, nourished on the antique and the medieval tradition, reappears in a living art of the theater and becomes the form of expression of a theocentric concept of human life which neither the English nor the French drama knows.

As we trace this connection, wider European perspectives open before us.

The form of a poetry which undertakes to represent human existence in its relations to the universe can be only the drama. But certainly not the classicistic tragedy of the French or the Germans. This classical form of the drama, born of the Renaissance and Humanism, is anthropocentric. It separates man from the cosmos and from the forces of religion; it shuts him into the lofty solitude of the realm of ethics. The tragic figures of Racine and Goethe are placed before decisions. The reality with which they have to deal is the play of man's psychological powers. The greatness and the limitation of classical tragedy is its confinement to the psychological sphere, the strict circle of whose laws is never broken. The tragic hero can only shatter himself against it. He can effect no reconciliation with fate. But this tragedy is an artificial growth in the soil of the European tradition. It arose out of a misinterpretation of the teachings of the Humanists. Its impossible ambition was to span the millenniums that lay between Pericles and Louis XIV: Goethe himself had to shatter the form when he created his cosmic poem, *Faust*.

The theocentric drama of the Middle Ages and of Spain's period of florescence has been rejuvenated in our time by Hofmannsthal. A fifteenth-century English morality play [*Everyman*] is the starting-point for his

[27] Cf. also Keil, I, 124 a and 147 a; IV, 445 a.

[28] So also in La Bruyère (*De la cour*, No. 99). In the 18th century in Diderot (Excursus XXV, *infra*).—Further examples: Apuleius, *De mundo*, ch. 27, ed. Thomas, 164, 2 (marionettes); Ps.-Aristotle, περὶ κόσμου; Tertulian, *De spectaculis*, ch. 30 (Christ's Parousia and the Last Judgment as *spectaculum*); Augustine, Epistle 73 (Goldbacher, 274); Lambert of Hersfeld (ed. Holder-Egger, 240); John of Salisbury, *Entheticus* (ed. Petersen, 53); Campanella, sonnets 14 and 15 (*Poesie*, ed. Gentile [1938], 37 f.); Sir Henry Wotton's (1568–1639) poem *De Morte*; Sir Thomas Browne, *Religio Medici*, Pt. I, sec. 41.

Jedermann (1911), a "play of the death of the rich man." God, angels, and devils appear. Allegorical figures such as Death and Faith take part. And the figure around whom the whole play revolves is not a named hero, but the nameless Everyman—man, entangled in the terrestrial and now set before God's judgment seat. This mystery play was produced in Salzburg, in the cathedral square. With his *Everyman*, Hofmannsthal had conjured up a timeless Middle Ages and had set foot on the road to metaphysical drama. Following it further, he could not but encounter Calderón. From that encounter came the *Grosse Salzburger Welttheater* ("Great Salzburg Theater of the World"; 1921). Upon this, and likewise suggested by Calderón, followed *Der Turm* ("The Tower"; 1925) and *Semiramis* (published as a posthumous fragment in 1933). These works are not "adaptations" of plays by Calderón, but new creations of the "integrating imagination." The seminal force was the psychological compulsion to renew in poetry the intellectual tradition of Europe, which catastrophes had destroyed. Conception was brought about by contact with material from that tradition. This was made possible by the insight that all intellectual substance which has been given form can in turn become the material of new creations: "Actually, nothing has been done when an epoch has brought forth intellectual products; then is the time when something ought to be done." The higher always comes into existence through integration. "Every higher thing is of necessity a composite. The higher man is the union of several men, the higher work of poetry, if it is to be produced, demands several poets in one." Hofmannsthal felt himself to be the heir of the Hapsburg tradition, whose foci in the seventeenth century were Madrid and Vienna. The poetry of the Spanish period of florescence was untouched by the classicistic literary systems of France and Italy. Artistically, and for its conception of the world, it drew from the unexhausted wealth of a tradition which had never broken with the Middle Ages. It preserved the substance of the Christian West. In history it saw an "archive of the ages" in which the peoples of all times and places had entered their memories. Kings and heroes, martyrs and peasants, are actors on the great stage of the world. Immaterial powers intervene in destiny. Over everything arches the dispensation of divine mercy and wisdom.

Calderón was free to create in a world whose monarchical and Catholic structure still stood firm and indeed seemed unshakable. The beginnings of the collapse of state and nation were concealed beneath dynastic and ecclesiastical pomp and display. Hofmannsthal's historical situation is the very reverse. He found himself born into a world decomposed by materialism and relativism. As a grown man he had to live through its dissolution to its catastrophic end. His task—an almost superhuman task—was to descend again to the "persisting root of things"—to find curative virtues in the buried treasures of tradition; finally, to set up eidolons of a restored world again. It was his deepest insight "that life becomes livable only through valid ties." To cleanse and illuminate these ties once again—that was his task, his painful and laborious mission in this world: tie between man and wife in marriage; tie between people and rulers in the state; tie between man and God in time and eternity. Upon this road the wisdom of Asia [29] could be a station and a symbol—but not home and solution. These could be found only in the revelation which had gone forth to West and East—in Christianity. To this Hofmannsthal was directed by the tradition of his people and his native soil; by his Neo-Platonic cast of thought; by a secret call which he could not but follow. When Hofmannsthal wished to connect his Christian plays to a great tradition, it could only be to the tradition of Calderón.

From the Middle Ages and the Spanish drama Hofmannsthal took, not local color but that timeless European mythology which he has revealed to us: "There is a certain timeless European mythology: names, concepts, figures, with which a higher meaning is bound up, personified forces of the moral or mythical order. This mythological firmament spans all the older Europe." But reaching back to this older Europe was, in Hofmannsthal's eyes, a matter which extended far beyond poetry and the drama. It was but a symbol within an immense historical process, which Hofmannsthal saw coming: "an inner countermovement against that intellectual revolution of the sixteenth century which in its two aspects we are accustomed to call the Renaissance and the Reformation . . ."

[29] In *Semiramis.*

8

Poetry and Rhetoric

ANTE'S TREATISE on vernacular poetry bears the title *De vulgari eloquentia*. About 1300, then, it is still normal to conceive of poetry as a species of eloquence. There is no one generally available word for poetry. How is this to be understood historically?

1. *Antique Poetics*

The "Literaturwissenschaft" of our day has as yet neglected to lay the foundation upon which alone it could raise a stable structure—a history of literary terminology. What do the English "poetry," the German "Poesie" and "Dichtung" mean? The words give no indication of the essence of the thing, because they are late and derivative. In Homer the poet is the "divine singer," the Romans call him *vates*, "soothsayer." But all prophecy is linked to rhythmical speech; hence *vates* can be said of the poet. For "to compose poetry" (*dichten*) the Roman says "to sing." The *Aeneid* begins:

Arma virumque cano . . .

But Horace too can call the language of his satires, which approaches everyday speech, a "singing" (*Sat.*, II, 3, 4). Indeed there was no other word. The Greek εἶπτοι means "to make" in the sense of "to produce," "to fabricate." Herodotus uses ποίημα ("a thing made") for goldwork, ποίησις ("making") for making wine. Plato defines the usage as follows: All production of things is *poiesis*. Producing poetry stands to the general domain of production as a part to the whole. "Poets" are "those who possess this small part of *poiesis*" (*Symp.*, 205 C). The poet, then, is at the same time the "maker κατ' ἐξοχήν." But that is a late development. In the earliest times the poet himself presented his own work. Later there came a division of labor. The *aoidoi* presented poems which others had "made." These composers of texts were now called "makers" in the more restricted sense.

Ποιητής designates the "originator of the work" and thus corresponds to the concept of the "composer" in contradistinction to the "performing" musician.[1] In Isocrates πεποιημένος means "artistic"; the composer of elaborate written orations is λόγων ποιήτης. To translate ποίησις as "creation" is to inject into the Greek view of things a foreign idea—the Hebraeo-Christian cosmogony. When we call the poet a creator, we are using a theological metaphor. The Greek words for poetry and poet have a technological, not a metaphysical, still less a religious, significance. At the same time no people has had a stronger sense of the divine in poetry than the Greeks. But this divine element—precisely because it is divine—is something that exists without and above man, something which, as a muse, as a god, as a divine frenzy, bursts upon him and fills him. Poetry receives its metaphysical value not from the subjectivity of the poet but from a superhuman authority.

The concept of "making" in the sense of "producing" finally acquired pregnant meaning in Aristotle's systematization of the various branches of knowledge. He divides philosophy into "theoretical," "practical," and "poietic." In Aristotle's application of his system there are inconsistencies with which we are not here concerned. But the distinction between the "practical" and the "poietic" disciplines is important. "Praxis" has to do with human action (in Scholastic terminology *agibilia*), "poiesis" with "making" (*factibilia*), under which fall the useful arts and the fine arts: technology and what (following Aristotle) we call "poetics" in the restricted sense. Aristotle's teaching on the art of poetry must, then, be seen in connection with his entire system: as a parallel discipline to ethics, politics, rhetoric, economics. To seek out the element of reason and the element of value content in all the action and production of man—this was the goal of Aristotle's universal inquiry.

Save for a minor residuum, Plato had banished poetry from his ideal philosophical state, because in his opinion it was pedagogically harmful—and indeed the more harmful the more it was "poetic" (*Republic*, 387 B). Aristotle now restored it to the circle of the highest intellectual goods, and conceded it both an ethical and a philosophical value. He established poetics as a philosophical science of poetry. This was at once a culminating and a terminal point of Greek thought. And this also explains why, ever since the middle of the sixteenth century, Aristotle's *Poetics* has been central to all attempts to discuss the nature of poetry philosophically. However conditioned by the period in which it was written, the little book yet contains points of view which have proved stimulating again and again.

In the period which followed upon Aristotle's own, to be sure, it had little influence. This is connected with the great cultural transformation which we call Hellenism. From the unity of philosophy there emerge the separate branches of learning: grammar, rhetoric, philology, history of lit-

---

[1] H. Weil, *Etudes sur l'antiquité grecque* (1900), 237.

erature. Philosophy is transferred from philosophers to professors of philosophy and develops traditional school viewpoints. The Peripatetic school co-ordinates the *Poetics* and *Rhetoric* with the master's logical treatises (the *Organon*). But Peripateticism fell into decay soon after the death of the second head of the school, Theophrastus (d. 287), the Aristotelian texts became unprocurable, and did not reappear until the first century of our era. With Hellenism, a new period in Greek poetic theory begins. Stoics and Epicureans debate over the means, the effects, and the duty of poetry. Only scanty fragments of the original treatises remain to us. But their substance is preserved in the *Ars poetica* of Horace. Like Aristotle's *Poetics*, this too represents at once the culminating and the terminal points of a development. After Horace, there are no more Roman didactic poems on the art of poetry, just as all the "great" Roman literary genres fall silent after the end of the first century: tragedy with Seneca, epic with Statius, Valerius Flaccus, and Silius, history with Tacitus.[2] As early as the beginning of the Imperial period, the teaching of poetry passes into the curricula of grammar and metrics (the latter being usually connected with the former). The concept of a poetics as an autonomous discipline is lost in the West for a millennium and only reappears briefly *ca.* 1150 in Dominicus Gundissalinus' treatise *De divisione philosophiae*—together with the other branches of the Aristotelian system, which our author had received from Islamic tradition.[3] But since Latin poetry, because it had a firm support in the schools and the Church, survived even through the "darkest" period, this meant that instruction in the art of poetry, its metrical forms, its genres, and its rhetorical ornaments, had to be given—in short "poetics"; but the same sort of instruction had also to be given in prose—in short, an elementary "theory and technique of literature."

2.   *Poetry and Prose*

Antiquity did not conceive of poetry and prose as two forms of expression differing in essence and origin. On the contrary, both fall within the inclusive concept "discourse." Poetry is metrical discourse. But artistic prose competes with it from the time of Gorgias on. The question whether poetry or prose is "more difficult" was discussed even in the time of Isocrates. Turning poetry into prose is introduced into the schools of rhetoric as an exercise about the first century of our era. Quintilian recommends it to orators (X, 5, 4). Augustine had to paraphrase passages from the *Aeneid* in school (*Conf.*, I, 17, 27). In late Greek and Roman Antiquity, as in the Byzantine Middle Ages, paraphrase became an end in itself. Statius boasts that his father not only explained the most difficult poets but also bore

[2] The Syrian Ammianus Marcellinus and the Egyptian Claudian belong to the late flowering of the fourth century.
[3] Only the title of his "poetics" is Aristotelian, the content is medieval.

"the same yoke as Homer," turning his verses into prose "without falling a step behind."

It has heretofore remained almost unnoticed that a large part of early Christian poetry is a continuation of the antique rhetorical practice of paraphrase. We first find books of the Bible recast in hexameters. The Spaniard Juvencus (*ca.* 330) applies this procedure to the Gospels, the Egyptian Nonnus (fifth century) to the Gospel of John (in Greek), the Ligurian Arator to the Acts of the Apostles. A public recitation of his work in the church of St. Peter *ad vincula* (San Pietro in Vincoli) at Rome in 544 earned him enthusiastic applause. The procedure could also be applied to lives of the saints. The *vita* of St. Martin by the Aquitanian Sulpicius Severus (*ca.* 400) was versified in the second half of the fifth century by Paulinus of Périgueux, who calls his work a "translatio" or "transcripta oratio" (IV, 1 and V, 873); it was again versified in the sixth century by Fortunatus. But it was possible to go still further, and turn a versified version into prose afresh. So the grandiloquent and vainglorious Italian Sedulius (active between 425 and 450) followed his *Carmen paschale* with an *Opus paschale*. This practice of double versions had many disciples among the Anglo-Saxons (Aldhelm, *De virginitate;* Bede's *vita* of Cuthbert; Alcuin's *vita* of Willibrord). The fashion spread to France with English Humanism: Raban Maur (poem on the Cross); Sedulius Scottus (*De christiana vita*). In Germany, Walter of Speyer belongs to this company with his *vita* of Christopher (*ca.* 980). About 1050 Onulf of Speyer composes his *Rhetorici colores* in prose and adds a versified version with the words: "idem idem eidem de eodem." This is the last example of the stylistic transposition which the Middle Ages took over as a heritage from the antique schools of rhetoric. The practice shows us that metrical and nonmetrical discourse were felt to be interchangeable arts.

But the reciprocal relation between rhetoric and poetry is not exhibited only in this department. It had its foundation in the rhetorization of Roman poetry which began with Ovid. It was strengthened by grammatico-rhetorical exegeses of the poets. As Homer for the Greeks, so for the later Romans Virgil was the pattern of all rhetoric. The speakers in Macrobius' *Saturnalia* (V, 1, 1) agree that Virgil must be accounted an orator no less than a poet ("Virgilium non minus oratorem quam poetam habendum, in quo et tanta orandi disciplina et tam diligens observatio rhetoricae artis ostenderetur.")

The dominion of rhetoric over poetry appears in the Middle Ages in yet other forms.

3. *System of Medieval Styles*

In theory the *ars dictaminis* embraced both prose and poetry. The *artes dictandi* commonly begin with this definition, even when they treat of nothing but writing prose letters. The view that poetry and prose are two kinds of discourse was, then, adhered to. But since the Middle Ages knew two poetic systems—the syllable-measuring, or metric, and the accentual, or rhythmic—the *ars dictaminis* came to be divided into metrical, rhythmical, and prose *dictamina*. To these was later added, as a fourth recognized kind of style, rhymed prose (*mixtum sive compositum*).[4] This division too assumes that poetry and prose are regulated discourse: prose being regulated by rhythm, poetry by meter or by rhythm and rhyme.

The division of the *ars dictaminis* had as a result the replacement of the dyad poetry-prose by a triad or a tetrad. The boundaries between poetry and prose thus became more and more blurred. But the confusion was further increased by the fact that the concept "prose" itself is far from unequivocal. In the most general sense, prose is defined as free discourse (Isidore, *Et.*, I, 38, 1). But there are several levels of prose. The highest form is that which, since Norden's day, has been called *Kunstprosa* ("artistic prose"). Antiquity called it "rhetoricus sermo" (Sedulius) or "eloquentiae prosa." This is the term which Isidore applies to the style of Isaiah. Ennodius designates artistic prose by the significant expression "fabricata latinitas." Little attention, however, has hitherto been paid to the fact that, in addition to artistic prose, which required a great expenditure of time, talent, and erudition, there was also a plain prose of factual communication. Seneca already insisted (Epistle 40, 4) that the language of the philosopher should be "incomposita [5] et simplex." Pliny complains that the press of business forces him to send letters lacking in literary style ("inlitteratissimas litteras") (*Ep.*, I, 10). Plain prose was indispensable when one was in a hurry; hence Jerome calls it "subita dictandi audacia" in contradistinction to "elucubrata scribendi diligentia" (*PL*, XXVI, 200). Ennodius correspondingly distinguishes between "sermo simplex" and "sermo artifex," or, as alternative terms, "plana" and "artifex locutio." [6] Aldhelm makes the same distinction ("cursim pedetemptim, non garrulo verbositatis strepitu").[7] From the fifth century onwards the literary language became more and more artificial, until finally it was incomprehensible to all but scholars. A writer who hoped for a wider public and who had to deal with voluminous material could not employ this medium but was obliged to avail himself of a *sermo simplex* approaching ordinary speech. It is in this light that a frequently cited passage from the preface to Gregory of Tours's *History of the Franks* is to be understood. When Gregory says that there is no "grammaticus qui haec aut stilo prosaico aut metrico depingeret versu" ("no man of letters to depict these things in literary prose or metrical verse") and that he himself writes "inculto effatu" ("crudely"—affected modesty!), it means only that in composing his work he approached ordi-

---

[4] So designated by Thomas of Capua (*ca.* 1230). Rhymed prose is "ordinary prose, whose members or cola, as delimited by pauses in delivery, are rhymed at the ends of the colon" (K. Polheim, *Die lateinische Reimprosa* [1925], p. ix).

[5] Represents the Greek ἀτεχνίτευτος.

[6] Ennodius (ed. Hartel), 521, 18; 93, 26; 405, 24; 58, 18–23.

[7] Aldhelm, ed. Ehwald, 478, 3 ff. Cf. M. Roger, *L'enseignement des lettres classiques d'Ausone à Alcuin*, 295.

nary speech,[8] in contradistinction to the rhetorical artistic Latin of his
contemporary Fortunatus. No other course was open to a historian in those
days. It is not permissible to draw the conclusion that "the range of his
literary acquirements" was "rather limited."[9] Traube calls the passage
"grandiose," and adds: "Such apologies were a part of the style, such complaints and ostensible rejections and depreciations of grammar are themselves merely rhetorical artifices." Gregory had reached the pinnacle of the
culture of his time, and his oft-quoted complaint concerning the lack of
"grammarians" must not be hastily accepted as historical testimony to the
"darkness" of the Middle Ages. Fortunatus himself, in the dedication of
his writings to Pope Gregory the Great, felt it incumbent upon him to refer
to himself as "my inexperience" ("imperitia mea")—a choicer wording of
the current formulas "my littleness" or "my mediocrity."

In the early Middle Ages *prosa* was also used for "rhythmic poem." In
this genre too there are very different levels. In a poem composed in the
Lombard kingdom and which can be dated 698, the author explains that
he had not learned to write metrical verse and therefore wrote "in prose
like a discourse" ("scripsi per prosa ut oratiunculam"; *Poetae*, IV, 731,
st. 18). This is the earliest text in which *prosa* is applied to a poem. But
the poem is reducible to no rhythmical pattern, and the author uses *prosa*
to escape from his dilemma. Here the word is, as it were, half way to the
meaning "rhythmic poetry." The "transition" is accomplished in a poem
of the eighth or ninth century composed in regular fifteeners and described
as "prosa compositum" (*Poetae*, I, 79).[10]

The use of *prosa* for poetry was next extended through the invention of
the sequence in the eighth century. "Sequence" is originally a technical
term in music and means the elaborately prolonged melody by which the
final *a* in the *Alleluia* of the Mass was protracted. To the wordless series of
notes (*sequentia*) was fitted a text "which had as many syllables as the
corresponding section of the melody had notes; this text naturally had no
connection with either metrical or rhythmical verse, but was pure prose,
and in France it was, and still is, so called" (Strecker). The subsequent
development is as follows: first the entire *sequentia* is provided with a text;
finally new melodies, and texts for them, were composed simultaneously.
"Since the sequences were performed by two half-choirs, the second repeat-
ing the melody of the first, the characteristic of the new poetical form was
that every two sections of the prose text must have the same number of
syllables. The innovation was therefore of epochal significance, because
here for the first time poets learned to free themselves from the fetters of

---

[8] He writes "a realistic Latin which oscillates between the language of the
people and the language of the schools" (E. Löfstedt, *Syntactica*, II [1933], 365).
[9] Manitius, I, 217.
[10] Wilhelm Meyer says: "The lines of . . . rhythmic poetry are prose with a
terminal cadence" (III, 12). But this obliterates the striking distinction between
regular and irregular rhythm.—Cf. also W. Meyer, II, 183 n.

the small number of traditional metrical and rhythmical patterns." [11]

Sequence: origin of the modern lyric from the spirit of music.

A review of these developments shows that the tripartite division of the *ars dictaminis* gives no complete picture of the variety of linguistic art-forms in the Middle Ages. *Dictamen prosaicum* is artistic prose. But "plain" prose (*sermo simplex*) naturally remains the normal vehicle for letters and for chronicle, history, science, and hagiography. There is also rhymed prose, already mentioned; and, finally, mixed prose—that is, texts in which prose alternates with verse inserts. Such texts are called *prosimetra*.[12] In addition, there are metrical and rhythmical poetry.

But the picture becomes yet more complex through the introduction of the rhythmical cadence into artistic prose. Antique artistic prose had followed metrical laws (that is, based on syllabic quantity) in its cadences. In late Antiquity, the metrical cadence becomes a rhythmical (accentual) cadence, to which the name "cursus" was applied. From the eighth century the *cursus* degenerated. At the end of the eleventh century the Papal Curia revived it, taking as point of departure the epistolary style of Leo the Great —hence the terms "leoninus cursus" and "leonitas." These in turn furnished the name for the hexameter with internal rhyme ("versus leonini")[13] which became so popular. That starting from *cursus leoninus* it was possible to arrive at the designation of a hexameter with internal rhyme is further support for our observation that in the Middle Ages the terminologies of poetry and prose easily interchange. The testimony of John of Garland's *Poetria* is especially significant in this respect: he distinguishes three poetic styles and four "modern" prose styles.[14]

It is characteristic of the Middle Ages' unformulated but living feeling for art, that writers are fond of uniting and crossing these stylistic devices. One such cross had come down from late Antiquity (Petronius, Martianus Capella, Boethius): the *prosimetrum*, in which the verse inserts had to be in various meters (polymetric). Rhyme and prose are crossed in rhymed prose.

Especially attractive is the cross between meter and rhyme in the hexameter with internal rhyme, the *versus leoninus* referred to above. Example:

Lucifer ut stellis, sic es praelata puellis.[15]

---

[11] Karl Strecker in Merker-Stammler, *Reallexikon der deutschen Literaturgeschichte*, II [1926–28], col. 391b.

[12] Cf. F. Dornseiff in *Zeitschrift f. d. alttestamentliche Wissenschaft*, XI (1934), 74. [13] Shown by Carl Erdmann (*Corona quernea*, 16 ff.).

[14] "Stilus gregorianus, tullianus, hilarianus, ysidorianus." John makes an attempt to distinguish them by cadences, but does not carry it through: "In stilo tulliano non est observanda pedum cadentia, sed dictionum et sententiarum coloratio; quo stylo utuntur vates prosayce scribentes . . ." "poets who write in prose." A most confusing doctrine, which his pupils must have found it difficult to unravel (*RF*, XIII [1902], 928).

[15] "As the morning star among the other stars, so art thou pre-eminent among maidens."

The effect can rise to heights of impassioned greatness in hexameters rhymed in couplets and with double internal rhyme, as in Bernard of Morlaix's poem on the Last Judgment and Paradise:

> *Hora novissima, tempora pessima sunt, vigilemus.*
> *Ecce minaciter imminet arbiter ille supremus:*
> *Imminet, imminet, ut mala terminet, aequa coronet,*
> *Recta remuneret, anxia liberet, aethera donet . . .*
> *Patria splendida terraque florida, libera spinis,*
> *Danda fidelibus est ibi civibus, hic peregrinis.*[16]

Rhythm and meter are crossed in the so-called "Goliardic stanza with *auctoritas*," a name which has been applied to a stanza composed of three Goliardic lines followed by a hexameter which is usually a quotation from some classical poet and which rhymes with them. As an example, I give a stanza by Walter of Châtillon on the vices of the clergy:

> *A prelatis defluunt vitiorum rivi,*
> *Et tantum pauperibus irascuntur divi;*
> *Impletur versiculus illius lascivi:*
> *Quicquid delirant reges, plectuntur Achivi.*

Forms transitional between metrical and rhythmic verse occur.[17] Here too falls the mixture of Latin and vernacular verse popular in Germany and France from the eleventh to the thirteenth century. All these minglings and transitional forms testify to the same taste. They betray a childish delight in play and variegated color. On the side of content, this tendency to cross forms corresponds to the mingling of jest and earnest, and indeed of the sacred and the burlesque, which was so popular in the Middle Ages.[18]

From what has been said above, it will be clear that the Middle Ages had no word which embraced both metrical and rhythmical poetry. The word *poesis* could not be used. For according to antique theory, represented for us by Lucilius (fr. 339 ff.), *poesis* meant a long poem (*Iliad*, Ennius),

---

[16] The world is very evil;
    The times are waxing late;
  Be sober and keep vigil,
    The Judge is at the gate;
  The Judge Who comes in mercy,
    The Judge Who comes with might,
  To terminate the evil,
    To diadem the right . . .
  The home of fadeless splendor
    Of flowers that bear no thorn,
  Where they shall dwell as children
    Who here as exiles mourn.
              [Trans. J. M. Neale]

[17] Cf. *Poetae*, III, 674, 1032.
[18] See Excursus IV, *infra*.

poema a short one.[19] This terminology is represented in the last line of the *Waltharius*:

> Haec est Waltharii poesis. Vos salvet Jesus.

Otherwise, *poesis, poema, poetica, poeta* appear infrequently in the Middle Ages: poetry was simply not recognized as a separate art. For *dichten* ("to compose poetry") the early Middle Ages had no word at all. "Metrical poetry," "metrical poem," "to compose in meter" were paraphrased: *metrica facundia; metrica dicta; textus per dicta poetica scriptus; dictum metrico modulamine perscriptum; versibus digerere; lyrico pede boare; poetico cothurno gesta comere; metrica amussi* ("straight-edge") *depingere; metrorum versibus explanare; metricare.*[20] "To compose poetry" can also be rendered by *ponere* (*Poetae*, IV, 357, 30, the gloss on which refers to *reponere* in Horace, A.P., 120 and in Juvenal, I, 1). The metrical poet is called *versificus metricae artis peritia praeditus; dictor; positor; compositor.*[21] About 1150, in addition to *poesis*, appears the word *poetria*, which survives in English "poetry" and in Opitz's "deutscher Poeterey." Some have wished to see in this word the symptom of a new concept of poetry. The fact, however, is quite different. The Greek for "poetess" is ποιήτρια. In this sense, the word, latinized as *poetria*, appears occasionally in Cicero, Ovid, and Persius, and once in Martianus Capella (§ 809, ed. Dick, p. 427, 14). From the list of various readings for this passage, one sees that the strange word was not always understood here, and was by many readers taken to mean "poetry." Odo of Cluny (d. 942) uses it in this sense in his didactic poem *Occupatio*, 1219. The Archpoet (active *ca.* 1160–65) uses it by preference for both "poetry" and "poem." Then a third meaning was added: "art of poetry." Horace's *Ars poetica* was commonly called his *Poetria*. So Geoffrey of Vinsauf, author of the *Poetria nova* (*ca.* 1210), intends no more by his title than to say that he is putting forth a new poetics. In the same sense, it was usual to refer to Cicero's *De inventione* as *Rhetorica vetus* or *prima* or *prior*, to distinguish it from the *Rhetorica ad Herennium*, which was known as *Rhetorica nova* or *secunda* or *posterior*. Even more. In jurisprudence, we find *Digestum vetus* contrasted with *Digestum novum*; in the study of Aristotle, *Metaphysica vetus* with *Metaphysica nova, Ethica vetus* with *Ethica nova, Logica vetus* with *Logica nova.*[22] In this system of

---

[19] See Excursus V, *infra*.

[20] Aldhelm, ed. Ehwald, 232, 4; *Poetae*, IV, 964; *Poetae*, V, 263; Froumund, ed. Strecker, p. 133, 37; Fortunatus, ed. Leo, 293, 93; *Poetae*, I, 486, 132; Ermenrich to Grimald, MG., *Ep.* V, 566, 30; *Poetae*, V, 63, 267; *Poetae*, I, 95, 1. Odo of Cluny, *Occupatio*, praef. to I, l. 19.

[21] Aldhelm, 75, 21; *Poetae*, II, 464, 1421; *Poetae*, IV, 78, 1; preface to the *Heliand*.

[22] Cicero: Schanz-Hosius I ⁴, 589; *Digestum*: Paul Kretschmar in *Zeitschrift der Savigny-Stiftung, Romanistische Abteilung*, LVIII (1938), 210; *Metaphysica* and *Ethica*: Ueberweg-Geyer, 345 and 347; *Logica*: Duckett, *The Gateway to the Middle Ages*, 161.

parallels there is clearly a reference to the two Testaments of the Bible. Isidore (*Et.*, VI, 1, 1) offered the explanation "vetus testamentum ideo dicitur, quia veniente novo cessavit." And he cites II Cor. 5:17: "Vetera transierunt, ecce facta sunt omnia nova." The very same saying is adduced by the representatives of the "new poetics." [23] "Old things are passed away; behold, all things are become new"—this was the cultural consciousness of the new period which began about 1200. Contemporaneously with *poetria*, a new word for "to compose poetry" appears—*poetari* (also *poetare*). Priscian had cited the word as obsolete. It occurred once in Ausonius ("ineptia poetandi": ed. Schenkl, p. 121, No. 1, 6). In the *Ars versificatoria* of Matthew of Vendôme (written *ca.* 1170) the use of unusual words is recommended (Faral, p. 163). It is doubtless due to this fashion that *poetari*, like *poetria*, was taken up again. We find it in Walter Map (*De nugis curialium*, ed. James, 13, 1 ff.). Dante uses it frequently in the *De vulgari eloquentia*, as he once [24] uses the "precious" *poire*.

4. *Judicial, Political, and Panegyrical Oratory in Medieval Poetry*

The question now arises whether the rhetorical concept of poetry could take anything from the antique division of the *materia artis* into judicial, political, and epideictic oratory. Although the French "arts of poetry" of the twelfth and thirteenth centuries were largely emancipated from the antique system of teaching rhetoric, that system yet remained accessible in the writings of Cicero, the elder Seneca, and Quintilian. Even during the darkest centuries, interest in judicial oratory did not entirely die out in the country which, during Roman Antiquity and again during the "Renaissance of the Twelfth Century," was the chief stronghold of juristic studies: Italy. In Naples about 900 the grammarian Eugenius Vulgarius treated the subject of judicial rhetoric in twenty hexameters (*Poetae*, IV, 426, No. XXI). About 1050 Anselm of Besate in his *Retorimachia* sets forth the arguments in a fictitious dispute. At that period the study of law was connected with that of grammar and rhetoric only in Italy.[25] The academic epideictic oration of an Italian jurist (presumably delivered in 1186) has recently been made accessible to us.[26] But even in the Rome of the Empire judicial oratory had already sunk to the level of a rhetorical exercise. Fictitious matters of dispute, which no longer had any connection with reality, were invented (*controversiae*). A fictitious legal machinery and even fictitious statutes were assumed. Pirates and wizards were introduced to make these imaginary situations more exciting. In the schools subjects of this sort were also treated in verse. A few such compositions have come down to us.[27] The Middle

---

[23] Faral, 181.
[24] In the second eclogue, l. 97.
[25] Prantl, *Geschichte der Logik im Abendlande*, II, 67–71.
[26] By Hermann Kantorowicz in *Journal of the Warburg Institute*, II (1938/39), 22 ff.
[27] E.g., *Anthologia latina*, No. 21, 198. Dracontius, *Romulea*, 5.

Ages regarded these fabricated lawsuits as fiction. The elder Seneca's *Controversiae* are a principal source of the *Gesta Romanorum*, which was so popular in the Middle Ages.[28] Many of them survived even longer. A romance by Mlle de Scudéry, *Ibrahim ou l'illustre Bassa* (1641), is based on Seneca's *Controversia de archipiratae filia* (I, 6). The *Mathematicus* ("Astrologer"), a tale in verse which is to be found among the works of Hildebert,[29] goes back to a school oration (*declamatio*) of Quintilian's. From the days of Nero, political oratory undergoes a change similar to that which affected judicial oratory. It becomes a fictitious deliberative speech (*suasoria* or *deliberativa*).[30] A question of universal interest is: Ought a man to marry? [31] In the Middle Ages it was usually answered in the negative, with references to the evil nature of women. This gives rise to an eloquence of dissuasion (*dissuasio*). An example (*dissuasio Valerii ad Rufinum philosophum ne uxorem ducat*) is to be found in Walter Map's lively collection of anecdotes, "Courtly Recreations" (*De nugis curialium, ca.* 1190). It also circulated separately, however, and was extremely popular; we have five scholastic commentaries on it.

Of the oratorical genres, the epideictic oration had by far the strongest influence upon medieval poetry. Its principal subject matter is eulogy. The division of rhetoric which pertained to it was expanded and methodized by the Neo-Sophists. As subjects of eulogy this later period recognized gods, human beings, countries, cities, animals, plants (laurel, olive, rose), seasons, virtues, arts, professions. Even this list of subjects suggests how close the contact between poetry and the rhetoric of eulogy could be. One of the most important didactic writers on rhetoric, Hermogenes of Tarsus (b. A.D. 161) could even define poetry as panegyric and add that it was "the most panegyrical of all *logoi*" (ed. Rabe, 389, 7). Isidore, to be sure, had condemned the panegyric style as an invention of the frivolous and mendacious Greeks (*Et.*, VI, 8, 7). But even in his time, and throughout the entire Middle Ages, there was a strong demand for poems eulogizing or glorifying secular and spiritual magnates. In the Merovingian court circle, Fortunatus strews incense before counts, dukes, and princes in his verses. The Caro-

---

[28] Ludwig Friedlaender, *Darstellungen aus der Sittengeschichte Roms*, II [10], 205.

[29] According to Bliemetzrieder, *Adelard von Bath* (1935), 224 ff., its author is Bernard Silvestris. Faral is of the same opinion in *Studi med.* (1936), 77. Another versified judicial oration is to be found in *PL*, CLXXI, 1400 B ff. (by Serlo of Wilton, according to Hauréau).

[30] *Supra*, p. 69.

[31] The popularizers of Stoic philosophy (Hierocles, Dio Chrysostom, and others) had already treated it; their arguments are found again in Jerome's *Adversus Jovinianum*. Cf. P. de Labriolle, *Histoire de la littérature latine chrétienne* [2] (1924), 487 ff. Jerome's treatise and Walter Map's *Dissuasio Valerii* are alluded to by Chaucer (*The Wife of Bath's Prologue*, 671 ff.). The most elaborate piece of misogynistic writing in the Middle Ages is the *Lamentationes Matheoli* (thirteenth century), cf. Gröber, *Grundriss*, II, 431. The controversy on the subject of woman and marriage is a principal theme of Rabelais' *Tiers livre* (cf. Georges Lote, *La Vie et l'oeuvre de François Rabelais* [1938], 140 ff.).

lingians demanded the same tribute, and later every prince, archbishop, bishop, and abbot.

The word "panegyricus" [32] was known to the Carolingian poets (*Poetae*, III, 628, 427):

> *Materie fandi series panegyrica abundat.*

Ermenrich of Ellwangen (*MG Scriptores*, XV, 156, 39) understands pan-egyric to mean the whole body of pagan poetry. The unknown author of the *Gesta Berengarii imperatoris* (between 915 and 924) calls his work "Panegyricon" in the title (*Poetae*, IV, 357). So does the anonymous twelfth-century author of a complimentary poem (*NA*, II, 392, 37):

> *Dum tibi, dulcis homo, breviter panegerica promo,*
> *Conlige nobiscum vernos flores et hibiscum.*

Much more frequently, however, the idea is expressed in Latin: *laus, laudes, praeconia*. This is already the case in the pagan poetry of late Antiquity. In reading medieval poems, the critic must be careful to ascertain whether the word *laus* is being used in its general sense or in that of rhetorico-poetical technique. The latter is the case, for example, in the *Laus temporum quattuor* and the *Laus omnium mensuum* (Buecheler-Riese, *Anthologia latina*, Nos. 116 and 117) as well as in Smaragdus' didactic poem on grammar (*Poetae*, I, 615, XV):

> *Partibus inferior iacet interiectio cunctis,*
> *Ultima namque sedet et sine laude manet.*[33]

This passage becomes a term in a larger sequence if we realize that stylistic elements belonging to panegyric can find application in all genres and to all kinds of subjects—a matter of great importance for an understanding of medieval literature. Let us consider a few examples. One might think that the praise of God had a purely Biblical origin. In Dracontius' *De laudibus dei* (III, 735 ff.) we read:

> *Servatum reparare iube pietate sueta,*
> *Ut merear cantare tuas per carmina laudes.*
> *Quamvis nemo tua praeconia congrua dixit*
> *Aut umquam dicturus erit, nam formula laudis*
> *Temporibus tribus ire solet, tu temporis expers.*

This is to be understood as follows. For panegyrics on human beings, technique (*formula laudis*) prescribed that the subject's ancestors, youthful

[32] Also occurring as "panagericus" and "panegericus."

[33] "Sad is the lot of the interjection, for of all the parts of speech it has the lowest place. There is none to praise it." On the way from Latin to French the penultimate syllable of the proparoxytone succumbed. Mallarmé was so touched by this, that he wrote a prose-poem on the "Death of the Penultimate" (*Le Démon de l'analogie* in *Divagations*). It ends: "Je m'enfuis, bizarre, personne condamnée à porter probablement le deuil de l'inexplicable Pénultième." Grammar too has its tragedies.

deeds, and mature life be commended in emphatic terms. Three chronological periods *(temporibus tribus)*, then, were to be taken into consideration. The rhetor Emporius (fifth century) sets forth: "Laudatur aliquis ex
his quae sunt ante ipsum, quae in ipso quaeque post ipsum. Ante ipsum, ut
genus et patria . . .: in ipso, ut nomen, ut educatio, ut institutio, ut corporis species, ut ordo factorum: post eum, ut ipse exitus vitae, ut existimatio
mortuum consecuta" (Halm, 567). This was taken over by Isidore (*Et.*,
II, 4, 5). But this schema cannot be applied to God, because he is timeless
(*temporis expers*).—Crossing of panegyrical and ecclesiastical elements
frequently occurs in the metrical lives of the saints—which, however, have
their own particular topics besides.

A direct connection between antique epideixis and medieval poetry is to
be found in poems in praise of cities and countries. Roman poetry, as we
know, already showed a predilection for *laudes Italiae* and *laudes Romae*.[34]
The rules for eulogies of cities were developed in detail by late antique
theory.[35] The site had first to be treated, then the other excellencies of the
city, and not least its significance in respect to the cultivation of the arts
and sciences. In the Middle Ages this last topos is given an ecclesiastical
turn. The greatest glory of a city now lies in its martyrs (and their relics),
its saints, princes of the church, and theologians.

In a Lombard rhythm on Milan [36] the following are eulogized: 1. Its site
in a fruitful plain; 2. walls, towers, and gates; 3. forum,[37] paved streets,
baths; 4. churches; 5. the piety of the inhabitants; 6. saints' tombs; 7. Ambrose and later bishops; 8. cultivation of science, art, and liturgy; 9. wealth
and charity of the citizens; 10. the rule of King Liutprand (d. 744); 11.
Archbishop Theodore II (d. 735); 12. achievements of the citizens in the
war against infidelity. Most of these topoi correspond either directly or
mutatis mutandis to the antique rules for eulogies of cities. But the antique
epideictic oration has here become a powerful and skillfully composed profession of the Italian civic pride of the early Middle Ages. Of the same order
are the *Versus de Verona* (*Poetae*, I, 119; written *ca.* 810), in which (st. 8)
the pious author is amazed that the pagan—"mali homines"—could build
so beautifully. Properly enough, it is to Italy, where alone the Roman tradition of urban life survived all through the Middle Ages, that we owe a number of such panegyrical poems, some of which must be reckoned among the
pearls of medieval poetry.

For eulogies of countries too, antique theory and practice supplied rules.
Of continuing significance is the *laus Spaniae* with which Isidore begins

---

[34] *Laudes Neapolis* in Statius, *Silvae*, III, 5, 78–104.
[35] Further material in T. C. Burgess, in *Studies in Classical Philology*, III (Chicago, 1902), 89–248.
[36] *Poetae*, I, 24. Written soon after 738 (L. Traube, *Karolingische Dichtungen*
[1888], 114).
[37] In st. 6, 1 Traube reads *fori*.

his chronicle. By it he inaugurated a Spanish national tradition.[38] Isidore found models in antique chorographical and historical writing; then himself became a model not only for the historians but also for the epic poets of the Middle Ages. To begin a narrative poem with praise of a city or country became a usage which appears as yet to have received little notice. It represents a cross between panegyric and epic. Alcuin's *De sanctis Euboricensis ecclesiae* may serve as an early example (*Poetae*, I, 170, 16 ff.). Heiric's life of St. Germanus begins with a eulogy of Auxerre (*Poetae*, III, 438), the *Waltharius* with a eulogy of Hungary and the Huns, Abbo of St. Germain's historical poem with a eulogy of Paris (*Poetae*, IV, 19, 1 ff.), Letald of Micy's poem on Swithin the Fisherman [39] (end of the tenth century) with a eulogy of England. A eulogy of Spain occurs as a digression (st. 144 ff.) in the *Poema de Fernán González* (*ca.* 1250). Eulogy of rulers is, naturally, frequent everywhere; its topics demands separate treatment. Like the eulogy of countries, it can find a place in epic—for example in the *Karolus Magnus et Leo papa* (*Poetae*, I, 316) [40]—as well as in the eclogue [41] and the lament.[42] The Irishman Dungal sets a eulogy of poetry, full of antique sensibility, in the framework of eclogue. This is a great rarity in the Middle Ages. When things are to be praised, the virtues are chosen (Aldhelm, *De virginitate*; Milo, *De sobrietate*; and the like), not the arts.

The influence of the panegyric style extends to lyric poetry too. The majority of lyric themes, which the modern poet "creates" out of his "experience," were included in the list of epideictic topoi by late antique theory. They were material for rhetorical exercises. And as such they were used in the teaching of poetry in the Middle Ages. Occasionally we have external evidence to show this. We have, for example, two descriptions of winter composed on the same rhymes. The rhymes, therefore, were given in advance, and both versions are school exercises.[43] Merely from the rhetorical character of medieval poetry, it follows that, in interpreting a poem, we must ask, not on what "experience" it was based, but what theme the poet set himself to treat. This is especially distasteful to the modern critic when he has to criticize poems on spring or nightingales or swallows. Yet these very themes were prescribed by rhetoric. Thus, for example, in the late antique treatise by the Pseudo-Demetrius, *De elocutione* (written *ca.* A.D. 100), the section devoted to the "graceful" style (*charientismos*) names as particularly appropriate themes gardens, swallows, and love. The

---

[38] Gifford Davis in *Hispanic Review* (1935), 149 ff.—Stach (*Hist. Vjft.*, XXX [1935], 429, n. 22) doubts Isidore's authorship; on insufficient grounds, according to W. Levison (*in litt.*).

[39] Ed. by Wilmart in *Studi medievali*, IX (1936), 193 ff.

[40] The structure of the fragment is as follows: ll. 1–12 exordium; 13–94 eulogy of Charles; 95–136 his architectural activity in Aachen; 137–325 the hunt; 326 ff. Pope Leo.

[41] Modoin in *Poetae*, I, 385 f.

[42] *Poetae*, I, 430 is a good example ("formam laudis describere," 7).

[43] W. Meyer, GGN (1907), 237.

Progymnasmata (preparatory rhetorical exercises) of Hermogenes were also extremely influential. They were translated by the grammarian Priscian under the title *Praeexercitamina* and in this form descended to the Latin Middle Ages. The frequency of poems on the swallow and the nightingale [44] is explained by these recommendations of the rhetorical handbooks. In a poem on the swallow [45] by Bishop Radbod of Utrecht (d. 917) a recent English critic [46] finds "something gathered from the freshness of everyday life or, better still, from observation in the open air." He amicably describes it as "a true German product." How does the matter stand? The swallow speaks in its own person [47] and addresses the reader (l. 19). It sets forth: 1. how well its body is adapted to its mode of life; 2. its significance for agriculture; 3. its medical skill,[48] in which it is superior to Pythagoras; 4. its skill in nidification; 5. its manner of life; then follows 6. the *probatio* that the existence of the swallow can be a lesson to man. The last lines form 7. the *peroratio*: man must be obedient to his creator. In other words, a well-ordered discussion tricked out with erudition and aimed at edification!

We now pass to the topics of personal eulogy. A book could be written on it. But here as elsewhere we shall give only so much of the material as is necessary for an understanding of the subject and as shall serve to carry forward the main line of our investigation.

5. Inexpressibility Topoi

The root of the topoi to which I have given the above name is "emphasis upon inability to cope with the subject." From the time of Homer onwards, there are examples in all ages.[49] In panegyric, the orator "finds no words" which can fitly praise the person celebrated. This is a standard topos in the eulogy of rulers (βασιλικὸς λόγος).[50] From this beginning the topos

[44] E.g., *Poetae Latini minores*, ed. Baehrens, IV, p. 206; V, pp. 363 and 368.—Eugenius of Toledo in *A.h.*, L, p. 89.—Alcuin, *Poetae*, I, 274.—Fulbert of Chartres (cf. Manitius, II, 690).—Further sources in Strecker, *Carm. cant.*, p. 32.—A copious collection of passages from antique literature in Burgess, 188 f.

[45] *Poetae*, IV, 172 f.

[46] Raby, *Secular Latin Poetry* . . . I (1934), 250.

[47] The piece, then, is a *conformatio* ("quando rei alicui contra naturam datur persona loquendi," Keil, II, 437, 32).

[48] This refers to the celandine or "swallow-wort." The source is Isidore (*Et.*, XVII, 36): "Chelidonia ideo dicitur vel quod adventu hirundinum videtur erumpere, vel quod pullis hirundinum si oculi auferantur, matres eorum illis ex haec herba mederi dicantur."

[49] *Iliad*, II, 488. Cf. W. Schadewaldt, *Von Homers Welt und Werk* (1944), 312, n. 3.—*Aeneid*, VI, 625 f.—Macrobius, *Sat.*, VI, 3, 6.—Dracontius, *De laudibus dei*, III, 568 ff. (using *Aeneid*, IV, 181 ff.) specializes "inexpressibility" into "innumerability."—*Aliscans*, ed. Guessard and Montaiglon, p. 150.

[50] Burgess, 122.—Julian's panegyric on Constantius (Hertlein, p. 1, §1).—Pacatus in Baehrens, *XII panegyrici latini* [2] (1911), p. 90.—Nazarius, *ibid.*, p. 157.—Corippus, *Johannis*, I, 2.—Ennodius, ed. Hartel, 509, II, 9.—Dudo, *PL*, CXLI, 731 A.

already ramifies in Antiquity: "Homer and Orpheus and others too would fail, did they attempt to praise him." The Middle Ages, in turn, multiplies the names of famous authors who would be unequal to the subject.[51] Included among the "inexpressibility topoi" is the author's assurance that he sets down only a small part of what he has to say (*pauca e multis*).[52] This procedure is especially frequent in the *vita sancti*—a genre which first appeared in the fifth century and which had an enormous need for panegyrical phraseology, since the saint must have performed as many miracles as possible. Such lives of saints are frequently made up of traditional clichés. "Not only the themes of many narratives passed from hand to hand," says Wilhelm Levison, "but very many turns of phrase were repeated word for word again and again, and more than one *vita* is to a greater or less extent pieced together, like a mosaic, from fragments intended for the portraits of other saints." [53]

Another way of exalting the person to be praised is to say that "all" shared in the amazement or joy or grief on his account. The author's art has an opportunity to show itself in particularizing and amplifying the concept "all." One of the oddest flowers of rhetorical style appears in the assurance that every age and sex celebrates so-and-so—as if there were as many sexes as ages. "Omnis sexus et aetas" becomes a standard formula.[54] It is still to be found in Diderot and Manzoni.[55] But some go even further and dare to say: "All peoples, countries, and times sing so-and-so's praises." [56] Fortunatus asserts of King Chilperic no less than of St. Martin, that he is known in India; of St. Hilary, that he is known in India and Thule.[57] To be known in India is obviously the greatest fame. India—coupled, if need be, with

---

[51] Walafrid, *Poetae*, II, 352, 7 ff.—*Ligurinus*, II, 219.—Benzo of Alba, ed. Pertz, 598, 47 ff. provides the fullest development of the topos by accumulation of authors who would have failed in the attempt: Daniel, Tully, Demosthenes, Maro, Lucan, Statius, Pindar, Homer, Horace, Grillius, Quintilian, Terence.—Foulché-Delbosc, *Cancionero castellano del siglo XV*, vol. II, 83 n.—Further particulars Dt. Vjft., XVI (1938), 471 f.

[52] Virgil, *Georgics*, II, 42 and *Aeneid*, III, 377 provided points of departure.— Aelius Donatus in the dedicatory epistle to his commentary on Virgil: "de multis pauca decerpsi."—Prudentius, *Apotheosis praef.*, 1. In the text of the work, l. 704. —Fortunatus, ed. Leo, p. 172, XVII, 4.—Corippus, *Johannis*, VIII, 530.—The grammarian Clemens: *Poetae*, II, 670, XXIV, 1.—Prologue to the *Gesta Berengarii*: *Poetae*, IV, 357, 30.—Regino of Prüm, ed. Kurze, p. 1.—Stephen of Bec, *Draco Normannicus, Prooemium*, 56.

[53] NA, XXXV (1910), 220.—Such phrases as "de mirabilibus praetermissis et quod nullus sermo ad eius omnia opera sufficiat" (*Poetae*, IV, 960) are stereotypes.

[54] Cf. *Bulletin Du Cange* (1934), 103.—Examples: Julius Capitolinus, *M. Antoninus*, 18, 5; Dracontius, *De laudibus dei*, III, 394; Corippus, *In laudem Justini*, III, 40; *Poetae*, I, 67, 31; *ibid.*, 132, 12 ff. and 386, 41.

[55] Diderot criticizes the Jesuits for their treatment of the Indians in Paraguay: "Ils marchaient au milieu d'eux un fouet à la main, et en frappaient indistinctement tout âge et tout sexe" (*Supplément au voyage de Bougainville*).—Manzoni, *I Promessi Sposi*, ch. 4: "signori d' ogni età e d' ogni sesso."

[56] Merobaudes, ed. Vollmer, 9, 21.—Corippus, *In laudem Justini*, II, 218.— Fortunatus, ed. Leo, 219, 16; 239, 5 f.

[57] Chilperic: Fortunatus, ed. Leo, 201, 13 ff.; Martin, 296, 48; Hilary: 187, 15.

Thule—is indeed the farthest corner of the world (China was hardly known). It serves as *pars pro toto* for "the whole earth." This pre-eminence of India was attested by Virgil. Had he not made Anchises prophesy (*Aeneid*, VI, 794) that Augustus would extend his rule over the Indians? But when the ruler is incapable of ruling his own soul, what boots it "if even distant India trembles before his power, if Thule serves him"? Thus Boethius taught (*Consolatio*, III, 5), and found a crowd of imitators, among them Fortunatus.—So we can make the topos "all sing his praises" yield a subdivision: the "India topos." The Latin poetry of the Middle Ages takes it along. In the chronicle of Novalesa it is applied to Waltharius (*MG Scriptores*, VII, 85, 49). It makes its way into the late phase of the Old French epic. The Emperor Charles is urged to take such vengeance on Ganelon that men will talk of it even in India.[58]

The schema "the whole earth sings his praise"[59] becomes a standard topos. The Carolingian poets frequently apply it to Charles.[60] When the monks of St. Quentin affirm that the deeds of St. Quentin are sung among all peoples (*Poetae*, IV, 997, 11), we have only another example of the usual rhetorical exaggeration. The first historian of the Normans, Dudo of St. Quentin, who wrote *ca.* 1017, says of a Norman duke that the history of his deeds has very often been recited ("historia gestorum eius saepissime recitata"; *PL*, CXLI, 657 C). Dudo constantly indulges in the conventional topics of the praise of princes. Frequently he copies earlier writers (Fortunatus, for example) word for word. Presumably, then, we have here a variant of the familiar topos. Anyone acquainted with the avid appetite for "evidence of lost heroic poems" which possessed nineteenth-century specialists in the epic cannot but be surprised that they failed to register this piece of "evidence"—vague though it be.

Cassiodorus' account of the Goth Gensimund (*Variae*, ed. Mommsen, 239, 3 ff.) is frequently cited as evidence for early Germanic heroic poetry. Gensimund, Cassiodorus relates, was such a faithful servant of the Amal family that he deserves to be sung through all the earth ("in toto orbe"). He refused the throne and thereby gave an example of Gothic integrity. Therefore the Goths celebrate him ("ideo eum nostrorum fama concelebrat"). For "he lives forever in tales who once has scorned the perishable" ("vivit semper relationibus, qui quandoque moritura contempsit"). This statement points to the existence of a general condition, not to a single historical event. There is no justification, then, for writing—as one historian[61] does: "The statement 'ideo eum nostrorum fama concelebrat: vivit semper relationibus' shows that Gensimund too was actually celebrated as such a man." Here the quotation is misunderstood and the last part of it is

---

[58] *Aymeri de Narbonne*, 1284.
[59] There is more modesty in the phrase "dignus ubique cani," in an epitaph on a grammarian (*NA*, I (1876), 181, No. III, 17).
[60] *Poetae*, I, 91 and 483, No. XXV; *Poetae*, IV, 1007, No. II, 9 and 1008, 23.
[61] L. Schmidt, *Geschichte der deutschen Stämme bis zum Ausgang der Völkerwanderung. Die Ostgermanen*[2] (Munich, 1934), 254.

suppressed. Contempt for all that, being perishable, is impermanent, is not at all in harmony with Germanic sentiment. I do not mean to deny that Gensimund was celebrated—although forgoing the royal dignity is hardly the theme for a heroic poem. I only wish to show that one must proceed with caution in interpreting such passages. The rhetorical topos "all sing his praises," "he is worthy of song," easily becomes the statement: "There are songs about him." An example: Bishop Hildegar of Meaux (d. 875), in his life of St. Faro of Meaux (d. 672), tells of a victory over the Saxons by the Frankish king Clotaire: "ex qua victoria carmen publicum juxta rusticitatem per omnium paene volitabat ore." Nor is this all. Hildegar is able to give the beginning and the end of the Latin poem. Here was irrefutable evidence for Merovingian heroic poetry. Unfortunately, historical criticism has shown that the whole story is indubitably a forgery. Hildegar made the popular topos bear fruit. He is thus the forerunner of the eleventh-century monastic forgeries which made Count William of Toulouse (d. 812) into a miracle-working saint. The sturdy forger of Meaux has misled generations of students of the epic.[62]

6. Outdoing

If a person or thing is to be "eulogized" one points out that he or it surpasses anything of the kind and to this end employs a special form of comparison,[63] which I call "outdoing." On the basis of a comparison with famous examples provided by tradition, the superiority, even the uniqueness, of the person or thing to be praised is established. In Latin poetry Statius is the first to make this a manner. In his epithalamium for Stella and Violentilla he rejects comparisons with the "lying" tales of the gods and sets forth that the bridegroom outdoes all traditional examples of love. Manilius Vopiscus' villa "outdoes" the gardens of Alcinous. Domitian's festivals "outdo" the Golden Age.[64] Statius' favorite formula for expressing the idea of "outdoing" is "now let . . . yield" ("cedat nunc").[65]

After Statius the panegyrical topos of outdoing, together with the *cedat*-formula, becomes a permanent stylistic element. Claudian is a virtuoso of "outdoing." Stilicho outdoes Perseus and Hercules, indeed all Antiquity: "taceat superata vetustas" (*In Rufinum*, I, 280 ff.).[66] And Sidonius and Fortunatus follow him.[67] A favorite piece of flattery is to the effect that the

[62] Cf. ZRPh (1944), 248.

[63] For the connections between comparison and encomium (panegyric) see F. Focke in *Hermes*, LVIII (1923), pp. 327 ff., and especially pp. 335 ff. The Hellenistic technical term for "outdoing" is ὑπεροχή. The systematic employment of this device begins with Isocrates. Focke traces the phenomenon down to Plutarch.— Quintilian, VIII, 4, 9: "amplificatio . . . quae fit per comparationem, incrementum ex minoribus petit."

[64] *Silvae*, I, 2, 27; *ibid.*, 90 and 213 ff.; I, 3, 81 ff.; I, 6, 39 ff.

[65] *Silvae* I, 1, 84; I, 3, 83; I, 5, 22; II, 2, 61; II, 7, 75; III, 1, 142; III, 4, 84.

[66] Other examples: *De consulatu Stilichonis*, I, 97 ff. and 368 ff.; *ibid.*, III, 30 ff.; *De sexto consulatu Honorii*, 331 ff.

[67] Sidonius, c. II, 149 ff. and 288 ff.; Fortunatus, ed. Leo, p. 159, 1 f.

person celebrated surpasses the gods.[68] The beauty of landscape can also be indicated by "outdoing." Thus, according to Ausonius (*Mosella*, 287 ff.) the valley of the Moselle surpasses the Hellespont.—If men are to be praised, the "outdoing" refers to strength, courage, wisdom, and similar qualities.[69]

A special case of panegyric "outdoing," which deserves particular attention, occurs when a poet or prose writer is praised as having put all the greatest works of the past in the shade. This motif too is already to be found in Statius. He sets the short-lived Lucan above Ennius, Lucretius, and even Virgil (*Silvae*, II, 7, 75 ff.). Yet the same Statius ends his *Thebais* with expressions of the most profound respect for the "divine Aeneid," which he can but imitate from afar and whose footprints he worships. It would be mistaken to find any contradiction in these two passages. When Statius sets Lucan above Virgil, he is simply following the convention of panegyric poetry. Where he speaks in his own name, he can do homage to Virgil as the greatest of poets. Ausonius says (ed. Schenkl, p. 65, No. 14, 6) in praise of a colleague that his youthful verses surpassed the poems of Simonides. Walafrid Strabo praises a certain Probus for writing better poetry than Virgil, Horace, Naso, Lucan, Ausonius, Prudentius, Boethius, and Arator.[70] The manner recurs in every century of the Middle Ages. In the panegyric style writers permit themselves the most daring "outdoings"; elsewhere they gratefully admit the pre-eminence of the ancients. Thus John of Salisbury, for instance, does not hesitate to praise his patron Thomas Becket hyperbolically (*Policraticus*, ed. Webb, I, p. 2, 17 ff.): in intellect he far surpasses Plato, Quintilian, and others. But when in the course of his philosophical investigations John has to weigh the claims of the ancients and the moderns, his conclusion is very different (*Metalogicon*, ed. Webb, p. 136, 8 ff.).

In conclusion I should like to point out the following. At the very height of the Middle Ages, poets were entirely conscious that "outdoing," or at least the indiscriminate employment of it, could arouse demurral. An anonymous poet insists that the praise he lavishes is not intended hyperbolically but corresponds to his subject's real merits (*ZRPh*, L, p. 84, st. 10):

> *Ne quid iperbolice*
> *Dixerim, conspicere*
> *Nec dubita,*
> *Quin omnis ad merita*
> *Se velit laus aptari*
> *Quin omnis indebita*
> *Debeat retractari.*

[68] Walter Map, *De nugis curialium*, ed. James, p. 136, 31.—*Gesta Friderici metrice*, 1109 ff.

[69] Archpoet, ed. Manitius, p. 29.

[70] *Poetae*, IV, 1079, No. VIII.—Similarly Sedulius Scottus (*Poetae*, III, 200, No. XXXV, 7).—Notker Balbulus: *Poetae*, IV, 1097.

Is hyperbolical panegyric ethically permissible? About 1140 the question led to a controversy which is of interest for the history of culture. The Cluniac monk Peter of Poitiers had paid homage to the Abbot Peter the Venerable in several poems in which he made free use of "outdoing." [71] He was attacked in consequence. Peter the Venerable defended him in a poem "Against the Slanderers." He argues (*PL*, CLXXXIX, 1005 ff.): "A poet to be blamed for bestowing praise? Then the most famous poets and doctors are blameworthy. Let us leave the pagans aside. Jerome, Augustine, Ambrose, Cyprian, Sidonius, Fortunatus were masters of the panegyric style." Its chief trope is the hyperbole. The hyperbolic style is authorized not only by the pagan writers but also by the entire Bible. Thus, even so late as the age of the Crusades, the early Christian Biblical rhetoric and Biblical poetics are revived.[72]

A great deal more could be drawn from the "outdoing" topos if I were to analyze a larger number of examples, instead of referring to them in the notes, as I have done out of consideration for the reader. I should like to be permitted to point out only one thing more. Even historical events can be increased in importance by "outdoing." Lucan describes the line of fortifications which Caesar drew around Pompey's camp near Dyrrhachium. He goes on bombastically: "Now let the old legends praise the walls of Ilium and ascribe them to the gods; now let the Parthians wonder at the brick walls of Babylon . . ." Wido of Amiens (351 ff.) describes the battle of Hastings as the greatest "since Julius Caesar overcame Pompey with arms and took the walls of Rome." According to Willibald Alexis * the battle of Mollwitz (1741) was celebrated in the doggerel:

Pharsalus ist nun nichts, und Cannä gar kein Name,
Denn Mollwitz! ruft allein der Blinde wie der Lahme.

(Pharsala's nothing now, and Cannae not a name;
Mollwitz! the only cry alike from blind and lame.)

The great outdoer Lucan was himself outdone by—Dante. For him, certainly—as for us—Virgil is the greatest Roman poet. But that makes it easy to forget that in the *Inferno* Dante is competing with Lucan and Ovid in describing gruesome and fantastic scenes. One of the most famous passages in Lucan's poem was the description of the African serpents. Two soldiers of Cato's army, Sabellus and Nasidius, die a horrible death in the Libyan desert as a result of being bitten by a snake (IX, 761 ff.). Ovid

[71] Cf., e.g., *PL*, CLXXXIX, 50 D.—The end of the poem was first published in 1939 by Dom Wilmart (*Revue bénédictine*, LI, 54 ff.).
[72] The use of hyperbole was later defended by Henry of Avranches (ed. Russell and Heironimus, p. 119, 13 ff.).—In ancient India too it was discussed how far hyperbole might go. Cf. Georges Dumézil, *Servius et la fortune* (1943), 157.
[* Pseudonym of Wilhelm Häring.]

(*Met.*, IV, 562 ff.) had described the transformation of a man into a snake. Dante outdoes both (*Inferno*, XXV, 94 ff.):

> *Taccia Lucano omai là dove tocca*
>   *Del misero Sabello e di Nassidio,*
>   *E attenda a udir quel ch' or si scocca.*
> *Taccia di Cadmo e d' Aretusa Ovidio;*
>   *Chè se quello in serpente e quella in fonte*
>   *Converte poetando, io non l' invidio:*
> *Chè due nature mai a fronte a fronte*
>   *Non transmutò, sì ch' amendue le forme*
>   *A cambiar lor matera fosser pronte.*

> (Let Lucan now be mute, there where he tells
> Sabellus' and Nasidius' hapless fate,
> And let him hearken to what now comes forth;
> Mute Ovid too, of Cadmus and Arethusa;
> For though to serpent him, to fountain her,
> He turn them in his poem, I envy him not;
> For never did he so transmute two natures,
> Setting them brow to brow, that both their forms
> Were ready to exchange their very substance.)

The commentators cite the passages from Lucan and Ovid to which Dante refers. But they do not point out that the passage is based on the schema of "outdoing" and that even the formula "taccia" was to be found in the tradition, for example in Claudian (*In Rufinum*, I, 283):

> *Taceat superata vetustas.*

Only when one is aware of things of this sort can one understand—and explain—Dante from the point of view of the history of style.

7. *Eulogy of Contemporaries*

The schema of "outdoing" depreciates the past in favor of the present. The *taceat*-formula and the *cedat*-formula express this. Out of this it was possible to develop another topos: "Not only the past deserves praise; later men and the very latest should be praised too." Among the Romans [73] it first appears in the Flavian period. Tacitus (*Ann.*, II, 88) observes that Arminius is unknown to the Greeks and the Romans, "because we glorify only ancient times and take no interest in more recent history." He begins his *Agricola* with a like sentiment. Martial (V, 10) complains that fame is denied to the living.[74] Pliny admires the ancients but without, "like many

[73] In Greek it is already to be found in Isocrates, *Euagoras*, §5 ff.

[74] The passage was used as subscription to a satirical composition by Hogarth in the catalogue of the London art exhibit of 1761. Rudolf Wittkower in *Journal of the Warburg Institute*, II (1938/39), 82.

people," scorning the talents of his contemporaries. It is by no means true, he says, that exhausted Nature no longer produces anything worthy of praise (*Ep.*, VI, 21, 1). Sidonius (*Ep.*, III, 8, 1) repeats this, adapting it to his own times. Under the powerful impression made by Charlemagne's appearance on the stage of history the topos reappears (*Poetae*, I, 74). Einhard, in the preface to his life of Charlemagne, turns on those who scorn the present. Sometimes (*Poetae*, I, 400, No. V) the concept is expanded to include the idea that praise of the past is henceforth unseasonable. Among historical writers, Regino of Prüm adopts the topos in the preface to his chronicle (908), and later Guibert of Nogent (*PL*, CLVI, 183). The topos next appears in the Latin rhythm on the Cid composed *ca.* 1100 (first printed by E. Duméril, *Poésies populaires latines* [1847], p. 302; reprinted by Menéndez Pidal, *La España del Cid* [1929], p. 889 f.). It begins:

> Ella [75] gestorum possumus referre
> Paris [76] et Pyrri nec non et Eneae
> Multi poetae plurimum laude
>   Que conscripsere.
>
> Sed paganorum quid iuvabunt acta,
> Dum iam vilescant vetustate multa?
> Modo canamus Roderici nova
>   Principis bella.

It is not permissible to infer a "modernistiç" attitude on the part of the poet (Menéndez Pidal, 609) from this ancient topos. It reappears in Peter the Venerable (*PL*, CLXXXIX, 1010 C):

> Nam, si sunt digni, nec vivi laude carebunt,
> Ne dicam laudes nil nisi mortis opus.

The argument Pliny uses, that Nature's creative power is still not exhausted, reappears in Fontenelle's *Digression sur les anciens et les modernes* (1688). Thus a topos developed in the Flavian period could serve to authorize the self-assurance of French literature under Louis XIV.

We now pass to the principal theme of the panegyric style, eulogy of heroes and rulers.

[75] As can be seen from the facsimile published by Menéndez Pidal, p. 7, E is written as the initial. Presumably the text from which the scribe copied had *ella* with the initial omitted. It must be read *Bella*. The *bella* of l. 8 corresponds to it.

[76] Paris as a warrior also in the Archpoet (ed. Manitius, p. 34, st. 18). Achilles falls by the hand of Paris (*Iliad*, XXII, 359 and Dares). Cf. K. Reinhardt, *Das Parisurteil* (1938), 18.

9

Heroes and Rulers

1.   Heroism

ACHILLES, Siegfried, and Roland are presented to us in Greek, German, and French epic as "heroes." The "hero" is one of humanity's ideals, like the saint and the sage. To enumerate all these ideal types, to trace their descent, to determine their relative value, is a task for philosophy. Scheler, in his study of ethics, indicates five basic values, in descending order: the holy, the intellectual, the noble, the useful, the pleasant. To these there correspond five "personal value types" or "models for emulation": the saint, the genius, the hero, the directing minds within a civilization, the hedonist or artist.[1] The idea of the hero is connected with the basic value of nobility. The hero is the ideal personal type whose being is centered upon nobility and its realization—hence upon "pure," not technical, values—and whose basic virtue is natural nobility in body and soul. The hero is distinguished by a superabundance of intellectual will and by its concentration against the instincts. It is this which constitutes his greatness of character. The specific virtue of the hero is self-control. But the hero's will does not rest here, it presses on into power, responsibility, daring. Hence the hero can play the role of statesman or general, as in earlier times he played the role of warrior.

The ontological ranking of "personal value types" is a conceptual schema. In the historical world it encounters and is modified by the prodigious diversity of cultures differentiated by their several social, ethical, and religious systems.[2] In ancient Egypt, for example, the dominant social stratum is a bureaucratic caste of scribes which imprisons the king in a network of ceremonies and also casts its spell on priests and warriors. In ancient China the whole of public life is ordered by a body of ritual which is under the control of the hierocratic mandarinate. In India the Brahman is enthroned "on the

---

[1] Max Scheler, *Der Formalismus in der Ethik und die materiale Wartethik* [3] (1927), 609.—*Idem, Schriften aus dem Nachlass*, I (1933), 157 ff.
[2] What follows is based on Alfred Weber, *Kulturgeschichte als Kultursoziologie* (1935), and *Das Tragische und die Geschichte* (1943).

topmost storey of the pagoda of caste in a position of really extraordinary sublimity such as no other caste on earth has ever held." In ancient Israel the priesthood rules and guards the tradition. In none of these cultures is the direction of affairs in the hands of the warrior caste, with its heroic ethos. In China it is despised, in India the warriors constitute the second-highest caste, and the ancient heroic epic is revised by the Brahmans. Ancient heroic epic with a tragic view of existence is to be found only among the Greeks; in late form among the Persians, the Germans, the Celts, and among the French at the moment when the era of the Crusades awakened them to a consciousness of a national mission.

Greek and Germanic heroic poetry differ in essential points. First, in form. The Greek is epic—that is, a voluminous poetry which was probably written down from the first, and hence was literary. The recitation of an epic took several days. During the period of the tribal migrations, the Germans produced heroic lays which, according to the view current today, comprised from eighty to two hundred lines. They were not written down. Yet Germanists know thirty lays from the period between 400 and 600 (T. Frings), though it should be remarked that we are here dealing with "a poetic genre whose existence is established only deductively and intuitively" (Hermann Schneider). According to Heusler [3] the creators of the heroic lay were the Ostrogoths. He characterizes it as follows: "The Germanic heroic lay is in no sense a poem in praise of ancestors and race.[4] Its focus is neither dynastic nor patriotic nor is it tuned to eulogy. What it intensely values is man and the arts of man, and with all its enthusiasm for heroism, the tragic predominates in action and atmosphere. The spirit of the early Germanic epic is heroic: a concept which is not the same as the warrior ideal."[5] But what accounts for the transition from the short "heroic lay" (lost because not written down) to the Anglo-Saxon and Middle High German "heroic epic"? Only the example of Virgil, who for his part follows Homer. "Wherever the Middle Ages achieved a heroic literature, it was treading in Homer's footsteps" (Heusler). The medieval epic, then, is secondary, the Greek epic primary: a special case of the dependence of Modern-Western upon Antique-Mediterranean culture. What the primary Germanic heroic lay looked like, only the Germanists know. In any case—unlike the *Iliad*—it was not linked to a comprehensive historical picture. This was precluded by the very briefness of the heroic lay, but above all by the fact that the Germanic tribes did not regard themselves as constituting a unity, as did Homer's Achaeans. Yet another distinction from Homer: Germanic heroic poetry is without religion, not bound to the world of the gods.[6] The strongest social bond is the clan. The Old French epic presents

[3] *Die altgermanische Dichtung* [2] (1943), 155.

[4] The theme of the Homeric bard is, on the contrary, "the praise of men," κλέα ανδρῶν.

[5] Hermann Schneider's characterization (*Heldendichtung, Geistlichendichtung, Ritterdichtung* [2] [1943], 8 ff.) differs considerably.   [6] Schneider, p. 9.

entirely different features. It is circumscribed by the nation, the dynasty, and the church. Roland dies for "sweet France," for the Christian faith, for the Emperor Charles. The cultural leadership of France during the High Middle Ages is apparent in the fact that the Middle High German epic is dependent upon the *Song of Roland*: "From the poet of the *Song of Roland* . . . all later full-scale epic art derives, in France itself, in Germany, and in Spain" (Frings).[7]

Philologists relate the word *Held* ("hero") to Celtic words meaning "hard." Not much is to be got from this. The Germanic *Held* and the Greek *heros* are two different things. But even of the *heros* the most ancient Greek poetry gives two different pictures: the one colonial, developed by the Ionians of Asia Minor (Homer), the other that of the motherland (Hesiod). In his *Works and Days* Hesiod tells the myth of the ages of the world, ranked in accordance with the metals gold, silver, bronze, and iron. The series is broken between the Bronze and Iron Ages by the insertion—out of respect for the Homeric epic—of a "Heroic Age": "the godlike race of hero-men who are called demigods." Some of them come to their end in wars. But to the rest Zeus gives life and a dwelling place at the ends of the earth. They live without cares in the Isles of the Blessed as "happy heroes," far from the immortal gods. They enjoy honor and fame.

Here we have the earliest poetical testimony to the Greek hero cult, which developed out of the cult of the dead and goes back to the Mycenaean period.[8] But in Hesiod the hero cult is already modified by mythical concepts. The earlier religious concept is that the hero exercises an influence from his grave. His power is linked to his corpse, which was therefore sometimes transferred to another place, like the relics of martyrs in the Middle Ages. During the period of the city-states the hero cult developed into an extremely influential political mythology.[9] But the Homeric poems were composed by Ionic immigrants, "who had to give up the cult of graves, because they could not carry the graves of their fathers with them. This led to a weakening of this important aspect of religion, which was accentuated by the traditionless, extrovert life in the colonies, where each man forged his own fate; the Greek tendency to self-assertion and rationalism had free play." A concomitant of this is the dwindling of belief in the soul and immortality which appears in the Homeric *Nekyia* and in Achilles' famous

---

[7] Further particulars in my paper "Über die altfranzösische Epik" (ZRPh [1944], 233–320; especially 307 ff.).

[8] For what follows cf. Martin P. Nilsson, "Die Griechen" in Bertholet-Lehmann, *Lehrbuch der Religionsgeschichte*, II (1925), 281 ff.

[9] The Peloponnesian War led Athenian democracy *ad absurdum*. It was politically incompetent. At the same time, by indicting Socrates, it had showed itself to be the enemy of philosophy. The answer is the Platonic Utopia. It combines two motifs: the political system of Sparta as starting point, and the introduction of a caste system. The philosophers form the ruling caste, the warrior caste is relegated to second place (Toynbee, *A Study of History*, III, 92 ff.). Plato robbed both the hero and the poet of his pre-eminence.

words (*Od.*, XI, 488 ff.): "'Mock not at death, glorious Odysseus. Better to be the hireling of a stranger, and serve a man of mean estate, whose living is but small, than be the ruler over all these dead and gone.'" * Here the contrast with the Hesiodic concept is perfectly clear. But the old idea that after death pre-eminent men shared in a blessed immortality never disappeared and in the final phase of Antiquity acquired fresh life. The antique belief in immortality is "heroification." Its recession in Homer has the result that the gods interfere all the more actively in the affairs of men, since the dead no longer do so. Here lies the origin of the "divine machinery" of epic. At the same time, the earthboundness of the Homeric world is one of the roots of heroic tragedy. The Christian concept of the world knows it not.

A comparative phenomenology of heroism, heroic poetry, and the heroic ideal is yet to be given us.

2. Homeric Heroes

The epic fable of the *Iliad* is set in motion by the anger of Achilles. Without the angry hero (Achilles, Roland, the Cid) or god (Poseidon in the *Odyssey*, Juno in the *Aeneid*), there is no epic. Achilles is angry with Agamemnon because he has to surrender a captured girl to him. He retires to the ships and refuses to take part in the fighting. An embassy sent to plead with him is unable to make him change his mind. Only grief at Patroclus' death and the need for vengeance send him into battle, where he kills Hector. The fall of Troy will be the conclusion of a concatenation of events which, like the prehistory of the Trojan War, begins with the stealing of a woman. And this concatenation is motivated by the character of Achilles. Homer draws him with deliberate art. Achilles is not only hot-tempered (IX, 254 ff.) but he is thoughtless, so that Odysseus is obliged to stop him from rushing ahead with ill-considered military tactics (XIX, 155 ff.) and Patroclus, who is older than he, to guide him by wise counsel (XI, 786), even as old Phoenix has been given him as tutor. He may indeed be the mightiest warrior among the Achaeans; his fate may indeed be tragic, because an early death hangs over him, as he himself knows. Yet, to Homer, he is not an ideal figure. The poet disapproves of Achilles' dishonoring the dead Hector.[10] To be sure, he has received the divine gift of physical strength (I, 178), but the true hero must also have such wisdom as Nestor personifies. Though Nestor is weakened by age, he is indispensable to the expedition not only because he can give excellent counsel to the leaders, but also because he knows how to array his men by the tried and true methods of earlier times (IV, 294–310), so that Agamemnon does not know whether to wish that he had ten more such counselors (II, 372) or that Nestor were young again (IV, 312). In any case, it is of great value for the

[* Trans. G. H. Palmer.]
[10] W. Schadewaldt, *Von Homers Werk und Welt* (1944), 261.

conduct of the war that Nestor can still help with counsel and words (IV, 323). Wise counsel is as needful as brave deeds. But only age possesses such wisdom based on experience. Youth has little understanding (XXIII, 590 and 604). Odysseus too, the man of many wiles, is older than Achilles and can be compared with Zeus in wisdom (II, 407). He restrains Achilles from folly and shows himself superior to the imprudent Menelaus (III, 212–224). Achilles becomes an epic hero and a tragic victim not through the decree of fate alone but also through his own uncontrolled emotions. Homer holds that strength and intelligence in equipoise (VII, 288; II, 202; IX, 53) represent the optimum in warrior virtue. Even of the ordinary warrior, "battle-lore" is expected (II, 611; VI, 77 f. and *passim*). He must know the business of war. But the leaders must combine courage with wisdom on a far higher level. How seldom, however, are the two found together! Even the shepherd of the people, Agamemnon, frequently allows himself to be "blinded" by passion. Only in Odysseus do heroism, proficiency in war, and wisdom appear to be in equilibrium. Even Hector has to bear with the reproach that he is fit for battle but not for counsel (XIII, 727 ff.). Polydamas appears as the foil to Hector. Both were born on the same day, but they are of different natures: "For to one man has god given for his portion the works of war, but in the heart of yet another hath far-seeing Zeus placed an excellent understanding, whereof many men get gain." * The contrast between age, with its wisdom born of experience, and stormy youth, runs all through the *Iliad*. How are we to interpret this? Certainly not as psychological speculation on the different characteristics of various ages, such as became popular in later Attic comedy and in Hellenistic-Roman literary theory. Here in Homer we are confronted with something primal.

We are confronted with a residuum or echo of the prehistoric Indo-European religion, which Georges Dumézil has been able to reconstruct in a long series of publications. On the basis of comparative linguistics, mythology, and sociology he shows that the Indo-Iranians, the Celts, the Germanic and Italic peoples, possessed a common religious, cosmic, and social system, whose structure corresponded with three functions: sovereignty (government), war, and fertility. In India this triad hardened into the caste system: Brahmans, warriors (*Kshatriyas*), cattle-breeders and farmers (*Vaishyas*). The function of sovereignty is subdivided again in the polarity of the magical, fruitful king and the wise, lawmaking king. The former is represented by the god Varuna, the latter by the god Mitra. The pair Varuna-Mitra is also found among the Romans, but transposed from the metaphysical to the historical sphere. The earliest history of Rome, as reported by Livy, reflects upon the Rome of the kings a religion which is the annalists' interpretation of the pre-Roman religion. The polarity Varuna-Mitra is represented by the pair Romulus-Numa. This Indo-European polarity covers a large number of paired opposites, among them that

[* Trans. Lang, Leaf, and Myers.]

of stormy youth (*iuniores*) and thoughtful old age (*seniores*). There is not room for the details and the evidence here. I shall quote only Dumézil's conclusion: "L'un des deux termes (Varuna, etc.) recouvre ce qui est inspiré, imprévisible, frénétique, rapide, magique, terrible, sombre, exigeant, totalitaire (iunior) etc., tandis que l'autre (Mitra, etc.) recouvre ce qui est réglé, exact, majestueux, lent, juridique, bienveillant, clair, libéral, distributif, senior, etc. Mais il est vain de prétendre partir d'un élément de ces 'contenus' pour en déduire les autres." [11]

Among the Indo-European ethnic groups, the Indo-Iranians and the Italo-Celts are the most conservative. They have best preserved their religious heritage. To be sure, it had already undergone a great change among the pre-Romans. But among the Greeks the change was even greater. Their religion is essentially "Aegean." It preserves only slight traces of the Indo-European system. But must not the Homeric contrasting of the stormy young hero with the experienced old representative of "wisdom" be one of them?

From the antinomy between them arises the epic action of the *Iliad*. Its tragedy is wholly comprehensible only as a deviation from an ideal norm, which we may describe as a combination of courage and wisdom. Like the physician skilled in medicine, the omen-reading priest, the bard, and the craftsman who produces works of art, the hero as sage and warrior is a basic type of Homeric anthropology. The combination of courage and wisdom appears, as we see, in two basic forms: on a higher level as "heroic virtue" and on a lower level as "soldierly virtue." The latter again appears in three forms: 1. "battle-lore" ($\dot{\epsilon}\pi\iota\sigma\tau\acute{\alpha}\mu\epsilon\nu os\ \pi o\lambda\epsilon\mu\acute{\iota}\zeta\epsilon\iota\nu$); 2. manliness in the field and in the council of war; 3. proficiency in the use of a particular weapon. As for the intellectual component of "heroic virtue" it appears as 1. the wisdom of experience in the man of great age (Nestor); 2. the (wily) cleverness of the mature man (Odysseus); 3. eloquence (Nestor and Odysseus). To this we must add, as ideal program and broadest concept, 4. the ability (9, 443) "to be both a speaker of words and a doer of deeds." To educate Achilles in both is the pedagogical task laid upon Phoenix. Eloquence and wisdom are closely connected in the Homeric ideal of the hero; they are two facets of the same thing.

This is of course an abstract schema—and purposely so, for our task is to trace the survival of the polarity "courage and wisdom." We may, and indeed we must, view Homer as late Antiquity saw him when it projected the ideals of its own time back into him. To Quintilian, for example, Homer is the model and origin of all the departments of rhetoric (X, 1, 46); in the speeches of Nestor, Odysseus, and Menelaus he gave models for the three kinds of style (II, 17, 8); the schoolteacher, like Homer's Phoenix, must teach right action and right speaking, and so on. Our field of inquiry,

---

[11] Georges Dumézil, *Mitra-Varuna. Essai sur deux representations indo-européennes de la souveraineté* (= *Bibliothèque de l'Ecole des Hautes Etudes. Sciences religieuses. 56ᵉ volume* [Paris, 1940]), 144–5.

then, is not what Homeric heroism and Homeric wisdom *are*, but what later readers and writers could and did see in them.

3. *Virgil*

Virgil's reflective, highly conscious, and highly complex epic is connected with Homer in a great variety of ways. But it was meant to express, and could not but express, the ideals of an entirely different age. This inner tension is noticeable in the *Aeneid*.[12] Virgil is deeply imbued with the spirit of the Augustan Age of Peace and its ethical ideals. The termination of the century-old civil war by Augustus, and indeed the cessation of all war, is prophesied by Jupiter himself (*Aen.*, I, 291):

> *Aspera tum positis mitescent saecula bellis.*

In a culture of this temper there was no place for the heroic ideal in the old sense. In his *Aeneid* Virgil created a new ideal of the hero, based upon moral strength. To be sure, this hero too stands the test in battle (I, 544 f.):

> . . . *quo iustior alter*
> *Nec pietate fuit nec bello maior et armis.*

In Aeneas, then, moral virtue (*iustitia, pietas*) takes the place of "wisdom," and coexists, apparently without conflict, with his abilities as a fighter. He is (VI, 403)

> . . . *pietate insignis et armis,*

and in such cases his *pietas* is always mentioned first. Thanks to it, Aeneas surpasses even Hector (XI, 290). But Aeneas never *wants* war, in which the poet too sees something terrible, as does the young Menoetes (XII, 517 ff.):

> . . . *iuvenem exosum nequiquam bella Menoeten,*
> *Arcada, piscosae cui circum flumina Lernae*
> *Ars fuerat pauperque domus nec nota potentum*
> *Limina conductaque pater tellure serebat.*

Virgil first describes war from the point of view of the besieged—amid the horror of the fall of Troy. He postpones the decisive battle between the Trojans and the Latins until the tenth book. The Latins are led by Turnus. He is the only "Homeric" hero in the poem, well known as representing the old ideal face to face with the new (Aeneas). But among the Latins too there are figures who incline more toward *sapientia* than toward the military virtues. Drances (XI, 336 ff.), for example, who cries out his opposition to Turnus:

> *Nulla salus bello: pacem te poscimus omnes.*

And, above all, King Latinus, who is all *sapientia*, as Turnus is all *fortitudo* (XII, 18 ff.). Aeneas himself is far from being a faultless character through-

[12] For what follows, cf. C. M. Bowra, *From Virgil to Milton* (1945).

out. Virgil has him undergo a purification in the Stoic sense (*exercitatio*; [13] cf. III, 182 and V, 725). At the fall of Troy Aeneas acts like a man blinded by rage (II, 244), he seizes his weapons like a madman (II, 314):

> *Arma amens capio, nec sat rationis in armis.*

In Crete the Penates have to induce him to continue his journey (III, 147 ff.). He has another lapse when he "wastes his days" with Dido and has to be admonished by Mercury (IV, 267). Once again he is tempted to forget his fated mission and remain in Sicily. First his comrade Nautes, and then the ghost of Anchises, have to intervene (V, 700 ff.). It is as a changed and thoroughly matured man that he finally goes to meet the Cumaean Sibyl (VI, 105):

> *Omnia praecepi atque animo mecum ante peregi.*[14]

It is possible to find Aeneas a lifeless character. But the great theme of the *Aeneid* is not Aeneas, but the destiny of Rome. And, embedded in this richly allusive poem of history and destiny, is the journey to the otherworld (in Book VI), which raises us above everything earthly and is the greatest beauty of the poem. Its later influence too was most significant. To it we owe Dante's *Commedia*.

4. *Late Antiquity and the Middle Ages*

After Virgil the polarity *sapientia* and *fortitudo* declines to the domain of topics. Statius (*Achilleis*, I, 472) calls Odysseus "consiliis armisque vigil." The same poet provides a schema which was to become extraordinarily popular as a primitive differential characterizing of two persons. In the *Thebais* (X, 249 ff.) two warriors are distinguished by the antithesis that one has immense strength, the other can give good counsel. Statius is an important intermediary between antique and medieval epic. But medieval views of epic heroism were even more strongly determined by late redactions of the story of the Trojan War, particularly by the Troy romances of Dictys and Dares.

    With the *Ephemeris belli Troiani* of "Dictys" (fourth century) and the *De excidio Troiae historia* of "Dares" (sixth century) we reach the late antique end-form of the Homeric epic and of the "cyclic" epic which accreted around it. Dares and Dictys introduce a novelty: The epic has become a prose romance.[15] Here, then, we observe the same development which led from the French heroic epics and poems of chivalry to the prose rehandlings of the late Middle Ages. The Troy romances of Dictys and Dares are, as we know today, adaptations of Greek romances and are to

---

[13] Bowra refers to Seneca, *Dial*, I, 4.

[14] For *praecipere* as a Stoic concept Bowra refers to Cicero, *De off.*, I, 80 and Seneca, *Ep.*, 76, 33.

[15] Figures following citations refer to pages and lines in F. Meister's editions of Dictys (1872) and of Dares (1873).

be understood in the light of the nature of that literary genre. One of their chief characteristics—as perhaps it is of narrative fiction in general—is their insistence that everything is strictly true (mentioned, as "adtestatio rei visae," in Macrobius, *Sat.*, IV, 6, 13 among the means of arousing emotion) and is based upon written records by eyewitnesses. This motif already appears in Aeneas' account of the destruction of Troy ("quaeque . . . ipse vidi"). It was to achieve great importance in later times.

Dictys and Dares gave the Middle Ages hints for the topos *fortitudo et sapientia*. Dictys says of Achilles that in the aptitudes of a warrior he was superior to anyone; but that his energy was without reflection and his manners crude (10, 28 ff.). Achilles perishes through his unconsidered daring ("inconsulta temeritas"), whereas Agamemnon stands above all "through strength of body and mind" (49, 2) and a Memnon possesses experience in war (73, 23). In Dares we find a differentiating characterization of two brothers: Deiphobus is a brave warrior, Helenus a wise seer. Odysseus is "wily, eloquent, wise" (16, 19).

Late antique theory too has a share in the further development and interpretation of the ideal hero. According to the allegorical interpretation of Fulgentius, the opening words of the *Aeneid* conceal a deeper meaning. "Arma" signifies courage, "virum" wisdom: "For all perfection consists in bodily strength and wisdom." The entire development which leads from Homer to Dares and Fulgentius reaches its conclusion in what Isidore of Seville (d. 636) has to say about the epic: "It is called heroic song because it tells the deeds of brave men. For hero is the name given to men who by their wisdom and courage are worthy of heaven" (*Et.*, I, 39, 9). "Sapientia et fortitudo"—in Isidore's formula Homer's ideal of the hero combines with Hesiod's teaching. The reception of the hero into "heaven" was an idea already known to the ancient Greeks. But Isidore's formulation provides room for the Christian ideal hero of the eleventh century. The knights who, like Roland and his comrades, fell in battle against the infidels were also "worthy of heaven."

Medieval topics now took over the formula *sapientia et fortitudo* for laments for the dead and eulogies of rulers as well as for short narrative poems and the epic. A Carolingian epitaph (*Poetae*, I, 112, 9) gives us "great in counsel and in the craft of war." Homer's "battle-knowledge," Dares' "experience in war" ("bellandi peritia") are matched by other medieval expressions. In the powerful rhythm on the battle of Fontenoy (841) we twice hear the line:

> *In quo fortes ceciderunt, proelio doctissimi.*

Paul von Winterfeld [16] translates it:

> *Wo die Helden erlagen, wohlbewährt im Streit.*
> (Where the heroes succumbed, well-seasoned in the fray.)

[16] *Deutsche Dichter des lateinischen Mittelalters. Dritte und vierte Auflage* (1922), 165.

Literally it means: "The brave fell, the learned in battle." This immediately
suggests Homer's "battle-knowledge." But Germanists insist upon finding
traces of Norse skaldic poetry in the poem.[17] The poet, however, drew from
a very different source: the Old Testament. There he found not only the
phrase "ceciderunt fortes" (Vulg. 2 Reg. [A.V. II Sam.] 1:19 and 25),
but also "ad bella doctissimi" (Cant., 3, 8) and "docti ad proelium"
(I Macc. 4:7 and 6:30).[18] *Fortitudo* and *sapientia* frequently appear divided between two persons (Alcuin in *Poetae*, I, 197, 1281). But the ideal
continues to be their union in one person, for example in the *Waltharius*
(ll. 103 f.). Young Walther and young Hagen surpass the strong in strength
and the learned in understanding. The tragic tension between the warrior
temperament and prudence will emerge again in the *Song of Roland*.

5. Praise of Rulers

Given another turn, the topos leads to the praise of rulers. The Punic Wars
forced the earlier Rome to come to grips with Hellenism. The old Roman
virtus and Greek culture had been reconciled in the circle of Scipio Aeme-
lianus. After the period of civil war, the arts of peace flower in the *pax
Augusta*. The majority of the emperors of the first two centuries were
favorable to culture or wished to appear so. Many of them engaged in
literary activity of one sort or another, all of them saw to it that the art
of literature should sing their praises.[19] In the course of this cultural change,
the archaic polarity "wisdom-courage" acquires a new and much more
highly differentiated form. Wisdom is replaced by culture, poetry, eloquence: the alliance of Mars and the Muses. The younger Pliny accounts
those fortunate who accomplish deeds worthy of song or produce writings
worthy to be read ("aut facere scribenda aut scribere legenda"); and most
fortunate are those to whom both are granted (*Ep.*, VI, 13, 3). In the
topics of imperial eulogy the Caesars figure as such *beatissimi*. The imperator is general, ruler, and poet in one. Even a Domitian is praised by Quintilian (X, 1, 91) and Statius as being crowned with the laurel both of the
poet and the general (*Ach.*, I, 15). Dion of Prusa calls Homer to witness
that an interest in eloquence, philosophy, music, and poetry is an ornament to a king (περὶ βασιλείας, II). After the barbarism of the third century the "immense intellectual reaction of the fourth" asserts itself in the
fact that, from the time of Constantine on, intellectual culture is once
more considered the highest excellence of the emperors.[20] This was manifested in the *Liber de Caesaribus* of Aurelius Victor (published in 360)
as well as in the inscriptions and poetry of the times. Theodosius asks his

---

[17] Andreas Heusler, *Die altgermanische Dichtung*, 138 (2nd ed., 144).

[18] Further examples: *Poetae*, II, 502, 640 (*Gesta Apollonii*); Wido of Amiens,
De Hastingae proelio, 50 and 423.—Alan of Lille balances strength (Hercules)
against understanding (Ulysses) (*SP*, II, 278 = *PL*, CCX, 491 C).

[19] Cf. H. Bardon, *Les Empereurs et les lettres latines d'Auguste à Hadrien* (Paris,
1940).

[20] R. Laqueur in *Probleme der Spätantike* (1930), pp. 7 and 25 f.

"father" Ausonius to send him his works and cites the precedent of Octavian, to whom the foremost writers had brought their works. Ausonius himself addresses Gratian as "most learned Caesar" (ed. Schenkl, p. 23, 6) and boasts (Schenkl, p. 194, I, 5 ff.) that the monarch, because he excels in both words and war, alternates between battles and the Muses, between the Gothic war and Apollo. Claudian finds in Honorius "that together which is always sundered: wisdom and strength, prudence and courage" (*Epithalamium de nuptiis Honorii Augusti*, 314 f.).

The Germanic army commanders and kings—as, for example, the Vandals, the Ostrogoths and Visigoths, the Merovingians, and above all the Carolingians—frequently took over the succession of the emperors in this respect too.[21] We also find monarchs favorable to culture in England (Alfred the Great), and later in Norman Sicily; Roger studies geography, William brings the translators Aristippus of Catania and Eugene of Palermo to his court. With his book on falconry, Frederick II, of the house of Hohenstaufen, stands in the succession of Arabic natural science. We find Islamic scholars, courtiers, and officials in his entourage. But he also kept Arabic poets in his pay and collected Arabic books for the university of Naples. The ideal of the monarch favored by the Muses dominated Spanish-Islamic as it did Abbaside and Roman Imperial culture. The parallel extends even to the "mirrors for princes." [22] But the ideal of the *imperator literatus* also appears in the form of the learned ruler who bears the surname *el sabio, le sage*, the "wise" (that is, the learned).

Of Frederick II it is said (*Friderici gesta metrice*, 59 f.):

> *Cui geminum munus dederat Natura biformis:*
> *Ut fortis sapiensque foret, mirandus utroque.*

> (Nature, herself twofold, gave him a double gift:
> Making him wise and brave, in each a miracle.)

Dante praises Guido Guerra thus (*Inf.*, XVI, 39):

> *Fece col senno assai e con la spada.*
> (Enough he wrought, both with his mind and sword.)

Macbeth says of Banquo (III, 1):

> . . . *In his royalty of nature*
> *Reigns that which would be fear'd: 'tis much he dares,*

---

[21] S. Hellmann, *Sedulius Scottus* (1906), 2 f.

[22] In the twelfth century John of Salisbury urges upon princes the need for literary culture. He makes the Roman king (Conrad III) say: "quia rex illiteratus est quasi asinus coronatus." The adage was also attributed to other princes: see H. Brinkmann, *Entstehungsgeschichte des Minnesangs* (1926), 19, n. 1.—Praise of the "philosophizing" king in Godfrey of Viterbo (J. Röder, *Das Fürstenbild in den mittelalterlichen Fürstenspiegeln* . . . Münster dissertation [1933], 29).—Interesting points of comparison are given in Gustav Richter's *Studien zur Geschichte der älteren arabischen Fürstenspiegel* (1932).—Cf. also E. Booz, *Die Fürstenspiegel des Mittelalters*, Freiburg dissertation (1913), 28 and 35.

And, to that dauntless temper of his mind,
He hath a wisdom that doth guide his valour
To act in safety.

6. Arms and Studies

The topos *sapientia et fortitudo* entered the Renaissance in didactic writing on courtly ideals (Castiglione). One of the most brilliant passages in Boiardo's epic is the night conversation on arms and studies (*Orlando Innamorato*, I, 18, 41–45). The theme reappears in Ariosto (XX, 1-2), as it does in Rabelais (*Pantagruel*, ch. 8). Spenser brings it into the *Faerie Queene* (II, 3, 40) and the *Shepheardes Calendar* (*October*, ll. 66 ff.); Cervantes in *Don Quijote* (Part I, ch. 38). As the disciplines on the one hand and, on the other, the types and ideals characteristic of the several social ranks became increasingly differentiated, the question could not but arise which studies were suitable for the ideal type which was the model for the then ruling class. Seventeenth-century French literature touches upon this complex of questions in many ways. Molière derides not only the learned lady, but also the marquis with literary aspirations and the bourgeois who takes lessons in philosophy. Saint-Evremond gives his opinion on "les sciences où peut s'appliquer un honnête homme," and dismisses as beneath the gentleman all but ethics, politics, and belles-lettres.[23] La Bruyère regretfully observes: "Chez nous, le soldat est brave, et l'homme de robe est savant; nous n'allons pas plus loin. Chez les Romains l'homme de robe était brave, et le soldat était savant; un Romain était tout ensemble et le soldat et l'homme de robe" (*Caractères, Du mérite personnel, 29*).

Nowhere else has the combination of the life of the Muses and the life of the warrior ever been so brilliantly realized as in Spain's period of florescence in the sixteenth and seventeenth centuries—it suffices to call to mind Garcilaso, Cervantes, Lope, and Calderón. All of them were poets who also served in the wars. Neither France (excepting Agrippa d'Aubigné, who, however, wrote poetry *invita Minerva*) nor Italy can show anything of the sort. It is understandable, then, that the theme "armas y letras" was often treated in Spanish literature. Garcilaso wrote "tomando, ora la espada, ora la pluma" (Eclogue III). Though Don Quixote in his celebrated discourse (I, 37) gives the profession of arms precedence over studies, in another passage of the romance (II, 6) *armas* and *letras* are accounted two equally worthy roads to honor and wealth. After Cervantes, Calderón takes up the theme. In his plays there are many young noblemen who exchange the life of the student for the life of the soldier, the pen for the sword, Minerva for Mars, Salamanca for Flanders (Keil, I, 30 a) or who "follow arms by choice and letters as a pastime" (Keil, I, 99 a).

It is the glory of the Spanish Empire that there the ideal of *armas y letras* is most highly esteemed (Keil, IV, 294 a).

---

[23] *Oeuvres* (1739), I, 166.

O felice tu, o felice
Otra vez e otras mil sea
Imperio, en quien el primero
Triunfo son armas y letras!

For "arms and letters" the formula "pen and sword" also became current. In French Romanticism, it received a new content from the impression made by Napoleon's antique greatness. Balzac's motto was: "Ce qu'il a commencé par l'épée, je l'achèverai par la plume." Vigny, a scion of the nobility, to which the democratic century appeared to refuse political influence, adds the pen to his crest:

J'ai mis sur le cimier doré du gentilhomme
Une plume de fer qui n'est pas sans beauté.

The true nobility is nobility of soul, not nobility of blood or of arms; Vigny writes his name

Non sur l'obscur amas des vieux noms inutiles,

. . . .

Mais sur le pur tableau des livres de l'Esprit.

With this we reach the topos of "nobility of mind" and "nobility of soul." The revolutions of 1789, 1830, and 1848 had made it a contemporary reality for Vigny.

7. Nobility of Soul

Every period of enlightenment reaches the conclusion "that noble descent in itself is no guarantee of noble thought, that nobility is essentially a matter of the possession of wealth, but that there is an intellectual nobility of good men which does not depend upon birth." [24] This is known to the Sophists, Euripides, Aristotle (*Rhet.*, II, 15, 3), as to Menander (342/1 to 291/0), the chief representative of the "new comedy" (*Fragment* 533, ed. Kock). At the same time the rhetor Anaximenes recommends that, when a man cannot be praised for noble birth, one should fall back upon the thought that every man who has an excellent disposition for virtue is thereby born noble. The younger Seneca (Epistle 44, 5) teaches: "The soul ennobles" ("animus facit nobilem"). In Juvenal (VIII, 20) one could read: "nobilitas sola est atque unica virtus." Boethius had also discussed the theme (*Cons.*, III, pr. 6). In medieval Latin literature the topos occurs very frequently.[25] Matthew of Vendôme in his treatise on poetics puts it among the topoi for the prooemium (Faral, p. 116, §§ 27 and 28). It was

---

[24] W. Schmid, *Geschichte der griechischen Literatur*, III (1940), 695.
[25] References in Schumann in his commentary on *CB*, No. 4, and in *ZRPh*, LVIII (1938), 213.

discussed at the court of Frederick II,[26] and is dilated upon in Richard of Venosa's comedy *Paulinus et Polla*,[27] which was played before the Emperor. Naturally, the theme was discussed in vernacular poetry too—by the troubadours,[28] for example, and in the *Romance of the Rose* (l. 1860 ff.). The topos is a commonplace among the poets of Dante's generation and their predecessors.[29] It was given new life in Guido Guinizelli's doctrine that love dwells only in the "noble heart." Later, Dante himself treated it yet more fully (*Conv.*, IV, 14 ff.). Thus the thirteenth and fourteenth centuries gave new life to a commonplace which was more than fifteen hundred years old. But it had become contemporary when the ideal of the knightly caste was adopted by the town bourgeoisie, hence above all in thirteenth-century Florence. And in England too. William of Wykeham (1324–1404), chancellor to Edward III and Richard II, founder of New College, Oxford, had risen from a humble station and took as his motto "Manners makyth man"—a foreshadowing of the ideal of the "gentleman."

8. *Beauty*

For eulogies of rulers epideixis had developed fixed schemata in Hellenistic times. Physical and moral excellences were arranged in series—for example, beauty, nobility, manliness (*forma, genus, virtus*).[30] A more elaborate schema associates four "natural excellencies" (nobility, strength, beauty, wealth) with four virtues. Physical beauty is always a requisite, and the Middle Ages takes it over too; Biblical exemplary figures could, however, replace antique ones: David for strength, Joseph for beauty, Solomon for wisdom, and so on.[31] Hence we so often find medieval historical sources telling of the beauty of a ruler. In late Antiquity these and other excellencies are often represented as gifts of Nature. One of her functions is to create beautiful places [32] and beautiful human beings. In the case of prominent men she works with particular care.[33] A rhetorical textbook of the third century of the Empire recommends introducing the Natura-topos into panegyrics.[34] In the Latin poetry of the eleventh and twelfth centuries this topos is extraordinarily frequent. It is used to praise princes

---

[26] E. Kantorowicz, *Kaiser Friedrich II. Ergänzungsband*, 129.
[27] Ed. Duméril, p. 140.
[28] E. Wechssler, *Das Kulturproblem des Minnesangs*, I, 352 ff.
[29] A. Gaspary, *Geschichte der italienischen Literatur*, I, 518.—Wilhelm Berges (*Die Fürstenspiegel des hohen und späteren Mittelalters* [1938]) attempts to interpret the change from *nobilitas corporis* to *nobilitas mentis* as peculiar to the thirteenth century. This is to fail to recognize that he is dealing with a topos.
[30] C. Weyman in *Festgabe Alois Knöpfler* (1917).
[31] Theodulf in *Poetae*, I, 577, 13.
[32] *Aetna*, l. 601.—Statius, *Silvae*, I, 3, 17; II, 2, 15.—Claudian, *De sexto consulii Honorii*, 50.—Sidonius, c. VII, 139 f.
[33] Merobaudes, ed. Vollmer, 7, 21 f.
[34] Pseudo-Dion. Hal., *Ars rhetorica*, ed. Usener, p. 10, 11.

and princesses, as well as when the poet is courting some lass or lad. Hildebert of Lavardin flatters the queen of England (*PL*, CLXXI, 1143 AB):

> *Parcius elimans alias Natura puellas*
> *Distulit in dotes esse benigna tuas.*
> *In te fudit opes, et opus mirabile cernens*
> *Est mirata suas hoc potuisse manus.*

"Nature took less care in chiseling out other maidens, deferring her benevo-
lence until she came to endow you. On you she lavished her gifts, and,
beholding the wonderful work, was amazed that her hands could have accomplished so much." Hildebert uses the same schema in his celebrated
lines on the antique statues which he saw in Rome (*PL*, CLXXI, 1409 C):

> *Non potuit Natura deos hoc ore creare*
> *Quo miranda deum signa creavit homo.*

> (Nature could not create gods of such wondrous beauty
> As this which man did make to represent a god.) [35]

The rhetorical topos "Nature as the maker of beautiful human beings"
has nothing in common with "Natura mater generationis" except that
Nature is personified in both. The Natura of rhetoric completely lacks the
element of divine frenzy present in the goddess of fertility.

No literary genre has a greater need for beautiful heroes and heroines
than has the romance. Of Antiquity's narrative themes, the tale of King
Apollonius of Tyre was a favorite in the Middle Ages and the Renaissance.
Shakespeare took his *Pericles* from it. The earliest version of it is a third-
century Latin prose romance. There we read: "King Antiochus had a daughter as beautiful as a picture, to whom Nature had denied nothing, save that
she made her mortal." In the courtly romance which was cultivated in
France from 1150 onwards, the cliché "Nature created a being beautiful
as a picture" appears innumerable times. It is taken from the Latin poetry
of the period.[36]—Is it possible to outdo Nature in creation? Yes! Namely,
when God and Nature work together. A love poem from the *Carmina
Burana* (No. 170) describes a girl:

> . . . *in cuius figura*
> *Laboravit Deitas et mater Natura.*

Chrétien de Troyes goes even further (*Yvain*, 1492 ff.): "Nature could
not create such surpassing beauty. Or perhaps she had no share in making

[35] I have given further examples in ZRPh, LVIII (1938), 182 ff.—To these I
add Faral, p. 129, § 56, l. 1; p. 207, l. 335; p. 209, l. 397; p. 331, l. 15. Nature
shudders at the creation of a future schoolmaster: Faral, p. 338, l. 11.

[36] H. Gelzer, *Nature* (1917), provides a valuable collection of material. The
derivation from Alan of Lille is not tenable, cf. Faral in *Romania* (1923), 286.—
Alfons Hilka, *Der Perceval-Roman von Christian von Troyes* (1932), p. 761, note
on 7905.

it? . . . Surely God created it with his bare hand, to astonish Nature."
Descriptions of beautiful men and women are obligatory in courtly poetry
and were turned out in accordance with recipes which we need not discuss
here.[37]

[37] Ecphrasis of a beautiful man: *Stud. med.*, IX (1936), 38, No. 30.—Chrétien's
term for ecphrasis is *devise* (*Perceval*, 1805).—Description of human ugliness derives from the *vituperatio*. In its treatment of epideixis antique rhetoric made
"blame" the opposite of praise. This had consequences for medieval poetry, into
which it is impossible to go here. Sidonius' description of Gnatho (Epistles III, 13)
was the model for the style.—In medieval Latin: Vitalis' *Amphitruo*, ll. 235 ff.,
Geta in *Alda*, ll. 171 ff., Davus in the *Ars versificatoria* of Matthew of Vendôme,
I, §53 (Faral in *Stud. med.*, IX [1936], 55). Cf. *supra*, p. 69, n. 17.

10

The Ideal Landscape

1. *Exotic Fauna and Flora* / 2. *Greek Poetry* / 3. *Virgil*
4. *Rhetorical Occasions for the Description of Nature*
5. *The Grove* / 6. *The Pleasance* / 7. *Epic Landscape*

THE CLASS ideals and human ideals of late Antiquity, the Middle Ages, and the Renaissance were given expression in the schemata of panegyrical topics. Rhetoric conveys the picture of the ideal man. But for millenniums it also determines the ideal landscape of poetry.

1. *Exotic Fauna and Flora*

Medieval descriptions of nature are not meant to represent reality. This is generally recognized in respect to Romanesque art, but not in respect to the literature of the same period. The fabulous animals of the cathedrals stem from Sassanian textiles. Whence stems the exotic fauna and flora of medieval poetry? The first requisite would be to catalogue it. That cannot be done here. We shall take only a few random samples.

Ekkehart IV of St. Gall has left a series of versified graces on various foods and beverages (*Benedictiones ad mensas*), which have hitherto been held to possess "great value for the history of culture" since it was believed that they contained "a complete monastery menu." The order of the graces was supposed to correspond to the order in which the several courses were served. This produced the following picture of the eating habits of our forefathers: "First they filled their bellies with various kinds of bread, with salt, after which came at least one course of fish, fowl, meat, or game (all without sauces, vegetables, or other side dishes), after which came milk and then cheese. Then a dish containing the most pungent spices and sauces, together with honey, flat cakes, and eggs, after which vinegar was happily drunk (l. 154: "sumamus leti gustum mordentis aceti"), presumably as an apéritif for the following courses, which consisted of at least one dish each of legumes, native fruit, southern fruit, and fresh edible roots. Thirst was quenched first with divers wines, next with beer, and finally with water." [1] It is now proved that in general the *Benedictiones* refer to dishes which Ekkehart found in Isidore's *Etymologiae*, that, in short, they are

[1] Ernst Schulz in *Corona quernea*, 219 ff.

183

"versified lexicography." Among Ekkehart's graces there is one for figs, on which the editor, Egli, remarked: "Although the fig has been cultivated in Germany, it has never become a familiar or popular article of diet. In any case, the monastery of St. Gall obtained this fruit too from the South."

But what are we to say when a poet from Liége announces that spring has come: The olive, the vine, the palm, the cedar are in bud? [2] Olive trees were extraordinarily abundant in the medieval North. They appear not only in Latin love poems of the twelfth and thirteenth centuries [3] but also, by the hundreds, in the old French epic. Whence do they come? From the rhetorical school exercises of late Antiquity. But in medieval Europe there are also lions. A poetical epistle by Peter of Pisa describes the mood of mid-day: The weary shepherd takes refuge in the shade "and sleep enwrapped men and tawny lions" (*Poetae*, I, 53, 4):

Cingebatque sopor homines fulvosque leones.

Here a historian of the feeling for nature is bewildered by "the entirely meaningless mention of the lion." [4] But the feeling for nature—a concept which has never been clarified—has nothing to do with the case. It is a matter of literary technique. The lion, that is, figures in Roman poetry. The "fulvi leones" are taken from Ovid (*Her.*, X, 85). Writing in verse, Alcuin hopes that a traveler will not be attacked by lions and tigers on his road (*Poetae*, I, 265, 7). A Frenchman complains that the inroads of the Saracens have left the relics of the saints a prey to birds and lions. [5] English shepherds are warned to beware of lions. [6] Only exceptionally are these animals not dangerous; for example, in the district where the new Salisbury cathedral was begun in 1219: "There the fallow deer fear not the bear, nor the red deer the lion, nor the lynx the snake . . ." [7] The French epic swarms with lions. One, which a king received from Rome as a gift, is called "un lion d'antiquité" (*Aiol*, 1179). How rightly! Siegfried too, of course, kills a lion. "His delight in Siegfried's exploits leads the poet to tell tall stories," Bartsch commented. Hardly! It is a case of epic stylization, after the model of Antiquity and the Bible. All of these exotic trees and animals were in fact like Ekkehart's figs, imported from the South—not, however, from gardens and menageries, but from antique poetry and rhetoric. The descriptions of landscape in medieval Latin poetry are to be understood in the light of a continuous literary tradition.

---

[2] Sedulius Scottus, *Poetae*, III, 171, 45 ff.

[3] *Walter of Châtillon* 1925, p. 30, st. 2.—*Carmina Burana*, ed. Schumann, No. 79, st. 1.—Marc Bloch (*La société féodale*, I [1939], 155) is of the opinion that merchants and pilgrims had described "la beauté de l'olivier méditerranéen" to the minstrels. But the olive appeared in Latin poetry before it did in vernacular poetry.

[4] W. Ganzenmüller, *Das Naturgefühl im Mittelalter* (1914), 78.

[5] Adalbero of Laon, ed. Hückel, p. 142, 127.

[6] Bede, *Vita Cuthberti metrice*, l. 135.

[7] Henry of Avranches, ed. Russell and Heironimus, p. 114, 149.

How long did its influence last? In Shakespeare's Forest of Arden (*As You Like It*) there are still palms, olives, and lions.

2. *Greek Poetry*

With Homer the Western transfiguration of the universe, the earth, and man begins. Everything is pervaded by divine forces. The gods are they who "live at ease." They may quarrel among themselves, outwit one another, cover one another with ridicule (as Hephaestus does Ares and Aphrodite). But this strife among the Olympians is to the advantage of the heroes: Odysseus is persecuted by Poseidon's wrath, and protected by Athena. Only one dark shadow hangs over this happy world: the doom of death. This world does not yet know the chthonic—or does not speak of it; nor the demonic with its intricate and terrible toils, to the weaving of which "the gods themselves lend a hand, tangled skeins of horror which in turn produce fresh horrors, situations in which brother slays brother, the son his mother." [8] The tragic as the basic aspect of existence, the view which dominates Attic tragedy, is rejected by Homer.[9] He reflects the view of life of a knightly ruling class. But the heroic ideal is not conceived tragically, heroes are allowed to feel fear, like Hector, and war is an evil. This the Christian-Germanic Middle Ages will no longer allow.

Nature shares in the divine. Homer prefers the more amiable aspects of Nature: a cluster of trees, a grove with springs and lush meadows. There dwell the Nymphs (*Iliad*, XX, 8; *Odyssey* VI, 124 and XVII, 205) or Athena (*Od.*, VI, 291). A ravishing bit of scenery in this tonality is the uninhabited goat island near the land of Cyclops (*Od.*, IX, 132 ff.): "Here are meadows on the banks of the gray sea, moist, with soft soil; here vines could never die; here is smooth ploughing-land; a very heavy crop, and always well in season, might be reaped, for the under soil is rich. . . . Just at the harbor's head a spring of sparkling water flows from beneath a cave; around it poplars grow." * Here fertility is made an element of the ideal landscape. The most elaborate variant is afforded by the Gardens of Alcinous (*Od.*, VII, 112). Here there are fruits of the most various kinds: pomegranates, apples, figs, pears, olives, grapes. The trees bear all through the year, for it is always spring and the west wind always blows—the island of the Phaecians is indeed a land of faery. Two springs water the garden. Another fabulous place of heart's desire is the grotto of Calypso (*Od.*, V, 63). It is surrounded by a forest of alders, aspens, and cypresses. Four springs water the meadows, in which violets and parsley grow. The entrance to the

[8] Alfred Weber, *Das Tragische und die Geschichte* (1943), 240.

[9] *Od.*, I, 32 ff. Zeus here rejects the imputation that the gods inflicted woe upon men. He had sent Hermes to warn Aegisthus. Had Aegisthus heeded the warning a series of tragic horrors (the murders of Agamemnon and Clytemnestra, the madness of Orestes) would have been avoided. There would have been no *Oresteia*.

[* G. H. Palmer's translation (replacing R. A. Schröder's).]

grotto is overhung by a luxuriant grapevine. In Ithaca there is a wondrous grotto sacred to the Nymphs (*Od.*, XIII, 102): "Just at the harbor's head a leafy olive stands, and near it a pleasant darksome cave, sacred to nymphs, called Naiads. Within the cave are bowls and jars of stone, and here bees hive their honey. Long looms of stone are here, where nymphs weave purple robes, a marvel to behold. Here are ever-flowing springs. The cave has double doors: one to the north, accessible to men; one to the south, for gods. By this, men do not pass; it is the immortals' entrance." *

The *Odyssey* tells too of blessed shores which are free from ills and where the pains of death are unknown. On the island of Syria, rich in grapes, there is neither hunger nor sickness (XV, 403). When people grow old, "Apollo and Artemis come with silver bow and slay them with their gentle arrows."

It is promised to Menelaus that he will not die but instead be borne to "the ends of the earth" where lies Elysium: there is perpetual spring, refreshed by the blowing of the west wind (*Od.*, IV, 565); and it is the same on the heights of Olympus (*Od.*, VI, 42 ff.). And when the gods embrace in love, a magical nature takes part too. Zeus and Hera hide on the topmost crest of Ida in golden clouds (*Iliad*, XIV, 347 ff.): "And beneath them the divine earth sent forth fresh new grass, and dewy lotus, and crocus, and hyacinth, thick and soft, that raised them aloft from the ground." †

From Homer's landscapes later generations took certain motifs which became permanent elements in a long chain of tradition: the place of heart's desire, beautiful with perpetual spring, as the scene of a blessed life after death; the lovely miniature landscape which combines tree, spring, and grass; the wood with various species of trees; the carpet of flowers. In the hymns to the gods ascribed to Homer we find these motifs elaborated. The flowery mead of the Hymn to Demeter displays roses, violets, irises, crocuses, hyacinths, and narcissuses. The "Homeric" flowers are still used by Moschus in his epyllion *Europa* (*ca.* 150). Another procedure in the *Iliad* is the use of trees to identify epic scenes. In Aulis the sacrificial altar stands under a beautiful plane (II, 307). The battlefield before Troy displays a beech. Sarpedon is made to rest under it (V, 693). It stands by the Scaean gates (VI, 237), and serves as a meeting place for Apollo and Athena (VII, 22). They perch on it together in the form of vultures (VII, 60). Hector stands near it (XI, 70); and so on. There is a wild fig-tree too (VI, 432 and XI, 167). Later we shall again encounter this technical device for marking a scene.

As in Homer, so in all the poetry of Antiquity nature is always inhabited nature. It makes no difference whether the inhabitants are gods or men. Abodes of the Nymphs are also places where man delights to sit and rest. What are the requisites of such a spot? Above all, shade—of great importance to the man of the South. A tree, then, or a group of trees; a spring or

[* G. H. Palmer's translation (replacing R. A. Schröder's).]
[† Lang, Leaf, and Myers' translation (replacing R. A. Schröder's).]

brook for refreshment; a grassy bank for a seat. A grotto can serve the pur-pose too. Socrates encounters Phaedrus outside the gates of Athens. Soc-rates: "Look round for a place where we can make ourselves comfortable." Phaedrus: "Look over there behind that tall plane. There are shade and a breeze and grass to sit down on, or, when we please, to stretch ourselves out." The praise of the plane fills all Antiquity (Victor Hehn). Under planes the ancients wrote verse and prose, philosophized.[10]

To write poetry under trees (cf. p. 208, n. 14 *infra*), on the grass, by a spring—in the Hellenistic period, this came to rank as a poetical motif in itself. But it demands a sociological framework: an occupation which obliges him who follows it to live outdoors, or at least in the country, far from towns. He must have time and occasion for composing poetry, and must possess some sort of primitive musical instrument. The shepherd has all of these at his disposition. He has ample leisure. His tutelary deity is the spirit of the flocks, Pan, inventor of the shepherd's pipe of seven reeds. Beautiful shepherds (Anchises, Endymion, Ganymede) had been deemed worthy to be loved by gods. The Sicilian shepherd Daphnis, who scorned the love of a goddess for the sake of a mortal woman, had already been celebrated by Stesichorus in the seventh century. But Theocritus of Syra-cuse (first half of the third century) is the true originator of pastoral poetry. Of all the antique poetical genres, it has had, after the epic, the greatest influence. There are several reasons for this. The shepherd's life is found everywhere and at all periods. It is a basic form of human existence; and through the story of the Nativity in Luke's gospel it made its way into the Christian tradition too. It has—and this is very important—a correlative scenery: pastoral Sicily, later Arcadia.[11] But it also has a personnel of its own, which has its own social structure and thus constitutes a social mi-crocosm: neatherds (whence the name bucolic), goatherds, shepherdesses, etc. Finally, the shepherd's world is linked to nature and to love. One can say that for two millenniums it draws to itself the majority of erotic motifs. The Roman love elegy had a life span of but a few decades. It was little capable of development or renewal. But Arcadia was forever being redis-covered. This was possible because the stock of pastoral motifs was bound to no genre and to no poetic form. It found its way into the Greek romance (Longus) and from thence into the Renaissance. From the romance, pas-toral poetry could return to the eclogue or pass to the drama (Tasso's *Am-inta*; Guarini's *Pastor Fido*). The pastoral world is as extensive as the knightly world. In the medieval *pastourelle* the two worlds meet. Yes, in the pastoral world all worlds "embrace one another":

[10] Documentation in A. Nowacki, *Philitae Coi fragmenta poetica*, Münster dis-sertation (1927), 81.

[11] Bruno Snell, "Arkadien. Die Entdeckung einer geistigen Landschaft" (in *An-tike und Abendland, Beiträge zum Verständnis der Griechen und Römer, herausge-geben von B. Snell* [Hamburg, 1945], 26 ff.).

Die Quelle springt, vereinigt stürzen Bäche,
Und schon sind Schluchten, Hänge, Matten grün.
Auf hundert Hügeln unterbrochner Fläche
Siehst Wollenherden ausgebreitet ziehn.

Verteilt, vorsichtig abgemessen schreitet
Gehörntes Rind hinan zum jähen Rand;
Doch Obdach ist den sämtlichen bereitet,
Zu hundert Höhlen wölbt sich Felsenwand.

Pan schützt sie dort, und Lebensnymphen wohnen
In buschiger Klüfte feucht erfrischtem Raum,
Und sehnsuchtsvoll nach höhern Regionen
Erhebt sich zweighaft Baum gedrängt an Baum.

Alt-Wälder sind's! Die Eiche starret mächtig,
Und eigensinnig zackt sich Ast an Ast;
Der Ahorn mild, von süssem Safte trächtig,
Steigt rein empor und freut sich seiner Last.

Und mütterlich im stillen Schattenkreise
Quillt laue Milch bereit für Kind und Lamm;
Obst ist nicht weit, der Ebnen reife Speise,
Und Honig trieft vom ausgehöhlten Stamm.

Hier ist das Wohlbehagen erblich,
Die Wange heitert wie der Mund,
Ein jeder ist an seinem Platz unsterblich:
Sie sind zufrieden und gesund.

Und so entwickelt sich am reinen Tage
Zu Vaterkraft das holde Kind.
Wir staunen drob; noch immer bleibt die Frage:
Ob's Götter, ob es Menschen sind.

So war Apoll den Hirten zugestaltet,
Dass ihm der schönsten einer glich;
Denn wo Natur im reinen Kreise waltet,
Ergreifen alle Welten sich.

(Springs bubble out, brook joined with brook runs streaming,
Already gorge and slope and mead are green.
Where the plain heaves into a hundred hillocks,
The woolly sheep in scattered flocks are seen.

Beyond, with step as careful as 'tis certain,
The horn-browed herds toward the cliffside graze;
There could they shelter every one, for there
The stone is hollowed in a hundred caves.

There Pan protects, there vivifying nymphs
Dwell in the dripping, green-clad crevices—
And there aspire to higher airs forever
The intertangled ranks of branchy trees.

Ancient those woods! The oak's unyielding power
Casts each branch in a stubborn mold—its own.
The softer maple, running with sweet juices,
Shoots heavenward, rejoicing in its crown.

In that still circle of maternal shadow
The frothy milk streams warm for child and lamb;
Close by hangs fruit, ripe bounty of the lowlands,
And honey trickles from the hollow stem.

Here sweet content descends to son from sire,
And glowing cheek responds to cheerful lip,
And each who is at home here is immortal,
Where happiness and health are given to each.

So down the lighted days the child develops
Till through him too the strength of manhood floods.
And we, we wonder; still we feel the question—
These blest ones, are they men or deathless gods?

So like Apollo's self to shepherd's favor
That one most fair among them seemed his brother.
For there where Nature rules with none to stay her
All worlds do mingle and embrace each other.)

Goethe's *Faust* is a "restitution of all things" (Acts 3:21) in the continuity of the world's literature—hence a bringing back of pastoral poetry too. Theocritus decorated his poetry with the riches of a southern summer: "High above our heads waved many a poplar, many an elm tree, while close at hand the sacred water from the nymphs' own cave welled forth with murmurs musical. On shadowy boughs the burnt cicalas kept their chattering toil, far off the little owl cried in the thick thorn brake, the larks and finches were singing, the ring-dove moaned, the yellow bees were flitting about the springs. All breathed the scent of the opulent summer" *
(VII, 135 ff.). In an epic hymn, the poet conducts the Dioscuri to a wild mountain forest with trees of every kind. At the foot of a sheer cliff there is a spring of clear water. Its pebbles glitter like crystal and silver; pines, white poplars, planes, cypresses, fragrant flowers beautify the spot (XXII, 36 ff.). If there is to be a contest in song between two shepherds, each first proposes a favorite place: The shepherd Thyrsis: "Sweet, meseems, is the whispering sound of yonder pine tree, goatherd, that murmureth by the wells of

[* Andrew Lang's translation.]

water." The goatherd: "Beneath yonder elm let us sit down, in face of Priapus and the fountain nymphs, where is that resting-place of the shepherds and where oak trees are" * (I, 1 ff.). Variation on the motif: one shepherd decries the other's favorite place. Lacon: "More sweetly wilt thou sing, if thou wilt sit down beneath the wild olive tree, and the groves in this place. Chill water falls there, . . . here grows the grass, and here a leafy bed is strewn, and here the locusts prattle." Comatas: "That way I will not go! Here be oak trees, and here the galingale, and sweetly here hum the bees about the hives. There are two wells of chill water, and on the tree the birds are warbling, and the shadow is beyond compare with that where thou liest, and from on high the pine tree pelts us with her cones [12]" † (V, 31 ff.).

As the two last examples show, the motif of the bucolic contest between singers and poets ramifies organically to produce the description of a delightful spot—descriptions far more detailed than the corresponding passages in Homer, but still saturated with actual observation.

3. Virgil

Pastoral poetry could become a permanent part of the Western tradition only because Virgil took it over from Theocritus and at the same time transformed it. Sicily, long since become a Roman province, was no longer a dreamland. In most of his eclogues [13] Virgil replaces it by romantically faraway Arcadia, which he himself had never visited. Theocritus had sometimes introduced himself and his friends as shepherds (Idyl VII); Virgil brings into his pastoral world not only his own life, but also the figure of Octavian and Caesar's star—in other words, Roman history; and, beyond this, the religious ideas of the Saviour and the new era.[14] Thus in his earliest work he preludes his masterpiece. To know only the *Aeneid* is not to know Virgil. The influence of his eclogues on later times is hardly less important than that of his epic. From the first century of the Empire to the time of Goethe, all study of Latin literature began with the first eclogue. It is not too much to say that anyone unfamiliar with that short poem lacks one key to the literary tradition of Europe.

It begins:

> *Tityre, tu patulae recubans sub tegmine fagi*
> *Silvestrem tenui musam meditaris avena;*
> *Nos patriae fines et dulcia linquimus arva:*
> *Nos patriam fugimus: tu, Tityre, lentus in umbra*
> *Formosam resonare doces Amaryllida silvas.*

[* Andrew Lang's translation (slightly altered).]
[12] Pine seeds were eaten.   [† Andrew Lang's translation.]
[13] Virgil's "pastoral poems" (*Bucolica*) consist of ten "eclogues." *Ecloga* means "selected composition," but later becomes the generic term for pastoral poetry.— Fontenelle, *Poésies pastorales, avec un Traité sur la nature de l'Églogue et une Digression sur les Anciens et les Modernes* (1688).
[14] Friedrich Klingner, *Römische Geisteswelt* (1943), 154 ff.

(Thou, where this beech doth spread her close-leafed tiers,
Liest outstretched, O Tityrus, and wooest
The sylvan muse with that slim reed of thine;
We from our country's bounds, her dear, dear fields,
We from our country's self must fly; while thou
Dost idle here in shade, teaching the woods
To echo "Amaryllis beautiful.")

Here the very first line introduces the "motif of bucolic repose," which engendered an innumerable progeny; all that was needed was to substitute for the Virgilian beech a poplar, elm, willow, or merely "a certain tree" (*arbore sub quadam*[15] . . .). I give two of Virgil's own variations (*Buc.*, III, 55 ff. and V, 1 ff.):

> *Dicite, quandoquidem in molli consedimus herba.*
> *Et nunc omnis ager, nunc omnis parturit arbos;*
> *Nunc frondent silvae; nunc formosissimus annus.*

(Begin, since now we sit upon soft grass.
Yes, now each field and every tree brings forth,
Now leaf the woods, now is the year at fairest.)

> *"Cur non, Mopse, boni quoniam convenimus ambo,*
> *Tu calamos inflare levis, ego dicere versus,*
> *Hic corylis mixtas inter consedimus ulmos?"*
> *"Tu maior; tibi me est aequum parere, Menalca,*
> *Sive sub incertas Zephyris motantibus umbras,*
> *Sive antro potius succedimus. Aspice, ut antrum*
> *Silvestris raris sparsit labrusca racemis."*

("Why, Mopsus, since we both are well agreed
That thou wilt blow the pipes, I raise the song,
Sit we not here, where elm and hazel meet?"
"Thou art the elder; make then thou the choice,
Menalcas, all is one to me—whether
Beneath these shades that shift as Zephyr blows
We halt, or seek that cave. Look, the wild grape
Already hangs her first few bunches there.")

The close connection with Theocritus is obvious. But Virgil makes no attempt to match his model in visual richness, in the full scale of sounds and odors. Augustan Classicism does not tolerate Hellenistic colorfulness.

---

[15] Some examples of "arbore sub quadam": *Florilegium Gottingense*, No. 108 (RF, III, 292).—*SB München* (1873), 709.—"Arbore sub quadam protoplastus corruit Adam": NA, II, 402.—*Degering-Festschrift*, p. 313, No. 44.—"Arbore sub quadam stetit antiquissimus Adam": Baudri of Bourgueil, No. 196, 115.

Not until late Antiquity is color in demand again—and then it is the color of a kaleidoscope.

The pictures of nature in the *Georgics* would require an analysis which we cannot permit ourselves to undertake. And from the *Aeneid* we shall take but two ideal landscapes. In an "age-old," "immeasurable" forest pines, holm oaks, ashes, and elms are felled for Misenus' funeral pyre (VI, 179 ff.). The making of it is a pious duty for Aeneas and one condition of his entrance into the underworld. The other condition is that he must break the golden bough that grows on the sacred tree in the midst of a close grove set in a shadowy valley. The felling of the trees reminds him of it, and he finds his way to the miraculous branch. Thus Virgil's forest trembles with *numen*, the pervading presence of deity; it is the way to the other world, as it is in Dante; Virgil's wild forest is in a valley too (*Inf.*, I, 14). Virgil's golden bough, as we know, served Sir James George Frazer (1854–1941) as a key to the magic of primitive times.[16]

On his journey through the other world, Aeneas comes to Elysium (*Aen.*, VI, 638 ff.):

> *Devenere locos laetos et amoena virecta*
> *Fortunatorum nemorum sedesque beatas.*
> *Largior his campos aether et lumine vestit*
> *Purpureo, solemque suum, sua sidera norunt.*

> (To joyous sites they came and lovely lawns,
> Blest seats, in woods which no misfortune scathes;
> Fields clothed in ampler air, bathed in new light,
> Purple—their own sun sheds it, their own stars.)

In the first line the word *amoenus* ("pleasant, lovely") is used. It is Virgil's constant epithet for "beautiful" nature (e.g., *Aeneid*, V, 734 and VII, 30). The commentator Servius connected the word with "amor" (the same relationship, that is, as between "love" and "lovely"). "Lovely places" are such as only give pleasure, that is, are not cultivated for useful purposes ("loca solius voluptatis plena . . . unde nullus fructus exsolvitur"). As a *terminus technicus* the *locus amoenus* appears in Book XIV of Isidore's encyclopedia. This book treats of geography in accordance with the schema: earth, orb, Asia, Europe, Libya (the only part of Africa then known; Egypt was accounted part of Asia). Then follow islands, promontories, mountains, and other "names for places" ("locorum vocabula"), such as gorges, groves, deserts. Next in the list come "loca amoena," interpreted as Servius interprets the term. For Isidore, then, the *locus amoenus* is a geomorphological concept. But as early as the time of Horace (*Ars poetica*, 17) it was a technical term of rhetorical ecphrasis and was considered such by the commentators on Virgil. But this does not exhaust Virgil's contribution to the constitution of the ideal landscape. Antiquity accepted his authorship of

[16] *The Golden Bough.*

the minor works which modern criticism has, on more or less adequate grounds, stricken from the canon. In the mock epic on the death of a gnat (*Culex*), there is a mixed forest with nine kinds of trees, a stretch of grass with eighteen kinds of flowers (in *Bucolica*, II, 45 ff. Virgil had restrained himself to eight).

If now we look back at Homer, Theocritus, and Virgil and ask ourselves the question: What types of ideal landscape could late Antiquity and the Middle Ages get from these poets?—we cannot but answer: the mixed forest and the *locus amoenus* (with flowery meadows *ad libitum*). This heritage was twice subjected to conceptual schematization: in late antique rhetoric and in twelfth-century dialectics. Both processes worked in the same direction: toward technicalization and intellectualization. A series of clearly distinguished nature topoi was developed.

A complete analysis could set forth this development in detail. We can only sketch some of its principal lines.

4. *Rhetorical Occasions for the Description of Nature*

Richard Heinze in his *Virgils epische Technik* (1903) rejected any influence of rhetoric upon the *Aeneid*. Eduard Norden, on the contrary, in his commentary on Book VI, which also appeared in 1903, remarked on VI, 638 ("Devenere locos laetos . . ."), that Virgil had "described the Elysian grove with all the devices of that graceful λέξις which, in artistic prose, was customarily employed precisely in descriptions of ἄλση and παράδεισοι." The passage, then, would be a poetical description stylistically dependent upon rhetorical prose. Hence, for all that follows it is important for us to discover which of the systematized divisions of rhetoric might afford rules for describing landscape. In this search we come first upon judicial oratory. Since the time of Aristotle the doctrine of proof distinguishes between "inartificial" proof (i.e., such as the orator finds ready to hand and has only to use [17]) and "artificial" proofs. The latter the orator himself produced, he had to "discover" them. They rest upon reflection; or, in the language of Aristotle, upon "syllogisms" (trains of reasoning). The rhetorical syllogism is called an *enthymema*, in Latin *argumentum* (Quintilian, V, 10, 1). For the discovery of such proofs rhetoric provides general categories or "localities." The *loci* are divided into those of the person and those of the thing. The former ("argumenta a persona") are: birth, country, sex, age, education, etc. The topoi of the thing ("argumenta a re," also called "attributa") answer the questions: Why? where? when? how? etc. These topoi of the thing are again very elaborately subdivided. What is of interest to us is that the question Where? gives rise to an "argumentum a loco," the question When? to an "argumentum a tempore." The former (V, 10, 37) is concerned with discovering proofs in the character of the

---

[17] Laws, witnesses, contracts, confessions, oaths, etc.

place where the matter in question occurred. Was it mountainous or level? by the sea or inland? cultivated? frequented? lonely? etc. Of much the same nature is the "argumentum a tempore." When did the thing occur? In what season? and at what time of day? etc. It is true that both forensic and political eloquence were almost entirely supplanted in late Antiquity by epideictic eloquence: but their system was carried on by tradition, and from this there naturally resulted a blurring and mingling of the several oratorical genres. Accordingly, we find the *argumenta a loco* and *a tempore* recurring in medieval arts of poetry. But the description of landscape could also start from the rules of *inventio* for epideictic oratory. For the principal business of this genre is eulogy. Among things that can be praised, places form one category. They can be praised for their beauty, for their fertility, for their healthfulness (Quintilian, III, 7, 27). The New Sophistic later especially developed the description (ἔκφρασις, *descriptio*) as well as applying it to landscape.[18]

We conclude: Descriptions of nature could start from the topics of either judicial or epideictic oratory, and specifically from the topoi of place and time. In medieval theory[19] the technical terms *argumentum a loco, a tempore*, which stem from the forensic topics of proof, are transferred to the rules for nature description—certainly a historically fascinating episode in the great recasting process to which the Nordic West subjected the heritage of Antiquity.—But antique rhetoric dealt with the description of places elsewhere too. This third treatment occurs in its discussion of the figures—in the division, then, devoted to diction (*elocutio*, λέξις). Of this, more later. But first we must examine the ideal landscapes of post-Virgilian poetry.

5. *The Grove*

In Virgil the "ideal" or idealized "mixed forest" was still poetically felt and was harmonized with the composition of the epic succession of scenes. In Ovid, however, poetry is already dominated by rhetoric. In his work and in that of his successors, descriptions of nature become bravura interludes,

---

[18] A particular genre of style was enjoined for it, the ἀνθηρὸν πλάσμα, the "flowery style" (Proclus, *Chrestomathia* in R. Westphal, *Scriptores metrici graeci*, I, 229). Further particulars in Erwin Rohde, *Der griechische Roman*, p. 335 and p. 512, and in Norden, 285. Now, among things which can be praised, and hence "described" are the seasons. The ἔκφρασις χρόνων is treated, to name only one technographer, by Hermogenes (ed. Rabe, 22, 14). Applications of this schema are found in late antique poetry, for example in Nonnus (*Dionysiaca*, XI, 486) or in Corippus (*In laudem Justini*, I, 320) or in the *Anthologia latina* (Buecheler-Riese, No. 116, Nos. 567–578, No. 864). Frequently, however, spring is treated alone, for example by Meleager (A.P., IX, 363), by Ovid (*Fasti*, I, 151, and III, 325), later by Pentadius (*Anthol. latina*, No. 235), in Greek prose by the sophist Procopius of Gaza (*ca.* 500), and others. Such descriptions of spring frequently comprise but a few lines, especially as digressions in a longer poem (Ennodius, ed. Hartel, p. 512, 13; Theodulf in *Poetae*, I, 484, 51; *Carm. cant.*, No. 10, st. 3).

[19] E.g., in Matthew of Vendôme (Faral, p. 146, §106 ff.).

in which poets try to outdo one another. At the same time they are reduced
to types and schematized. Ovid presents the motif of the "ideal mixed
forest" in an elegant variation: the grove is not there from the beginning,
it comes into existence before our eyes. First we see a hill entirely without
shade. Orpheus appears and begins to play his lyre. Now the trees come
hurrying—no less than twenty-six species!—and give shade (*Met.*, X, 90–
106). The younger Seneca offers—in passing as it were—a grove with
eight species (*Oedipus*, 532). The groves and forests of Statius (*Thebais*,
VI, 98) and Claudian (*De raptu Proserpinae*, II, 107) are more plenteous-
ly supplied. The former mentions thirteen species of trees, the latter nine.
From late Greek poetry, finally, we must mention the Garden of Emathion
in Nonnus (*Dionysiaca*, III, 140). Clearly, what we are dealing with is a
standard topos. These bravura pieces have as little to do with observation
of nature as Ekkehart's graces have to do with monastery cooking. Whether
the species enumerated could all occur together in one forest, the poet does
not care, and does not need to care—despite the protests of a Julius Caesar
Scaliger in his *Hypercriticus*.[20] The ideal of this late rhetorical poetry is
richness of décor and an elaborate vocabulary. In the twelfth century Joseph
of Exeter (*De bello Troiano*, I, 507) put together another such forest, with
ten species of trees. His countrymen Chaucer, Spenser (*The Parlement of
Foules*, 176 and *The Faerie Queene*, I, 1, 8), and Keats (*The Fall of Hy-
perion*, I, 19 ff.) follow his example. The "mixed forest" can also be considered a subspecies of the "catalogue," which is a fundamental poetic
form that goes back to Homer and Hesiod.

6. *The Pleasance*

The *locus amoenus* (pleasance), to which we now pass, has not previously
been recognized as possessing an independent rhetorico-poetical existence.
Yet, from the Empire to the sixteenth century, it forms the principal motif
of all nature description. It is, as we saw, a beautiful, shaded natural site.
Its minimum ingredients comprise a tree (or several trees), a meadow, and
a spring or brook. Birdsong and flowers may be added. The most elaborate
examples also add a breeze. In Theocritus and Virgil such scenes are merely
backgrounds for the ensuing pastoral poetry. But they were soon detached
from any larger context and became subjects of bravura rhetorical description. Horace already disapproves of this tendency (*A.P.*, 17). The earliest
example I have found of this sort of ecphrasis in Latin poetry is in Petronius,
carm. 131:

> *Mobilis aestivas platanus diffuderat umbras*
> *Et bacis redemita Daphne tremulaeque cupressus*
> *Et circum tonsae trepidanti vertice pinus.*
> *Has inter ludebat quis errantibus amnis*

[20] I.e., Book VI of the *Poetices libri septem* (1561).

Spumeus, et querulo vexabat rore lapillos.
Dignus amore locus: testis silvestris aëdon
Atque urbana Procne, quae circum gramina fusae
Et molles violas cantu sua rura colebant.

(A moving plane cast summer shadows, so too the laurel crowned with berries, and the tremulous cypresses, and, all around, the shorn pines with their swaying tops. Among them, in wandering streams, played a foamy brook, fretting the pebbles with complaining waters. The place was fit for love: Witness the wood-haunting nightingale and the town-haunting swallow both, who, flitting over the grass and tender violets, beautified the place with their singing.)

The most beautiful presentation of the *locus amoenus* in late Latin poetry is found in a poem of Tiberianus, of the Constantine period:

Amnis ibat inter herbas valle fusus frigida,
Luce ridens calculorum, flore pictus herbido.
Caerulas superne laurus et virecta myrtea
Leniter motabat aura blandiente sibilo.
Subtus autem molle gramen flore pulcro creverat;
Et croco solum rubebat et lucebat liliis.
Tum nemus fragrabat omne violarum spiritu.
Inter ista dona veris gemmeasque gratias
Omnium regina odorum vel colorum lucifer
Auriflora praeminebat flamma Diones, rosa.
Roscidum nemus rigebat inter uda gramina:
Fonte crebro murmurabant hinc et inde rivuli,
Quae fluenta labibunda guttis ibant lucidis.
Antra muscus et virentes intus hederae vinxerant.
Has per umbras omnis ales plus canora quam putes
Cantibus vernis strepebat et susurris dulcibus:
His loquentis murmur amnis concinebat frondibus,
Quis melos vocalis aurae musa zephyri moverat.
Sic euntem per virecta pulchra odora et musica
Ales amnis aura lucus flos et umbra iuverat.[21]

(Through the fields there went a river; down the airy glen it wound,
Smiling mid its radiant pebbles, decked with flowery plants around.
Dark-hued laurels waved above it close by myrtle greeneries,
Gently swaying to the whispers and caresses of the breeze.

[21] Text after Buecheler-Riese, *Anthol. latina*, I, 2, No. 809.—L. 10 is corrupt. I have emended *forma dionis* following H. W. Garrod, *The Oxford Book of Latin Verse* (1912), p. 372.

Underneath grew velvet greensward with a wealth of bloom for dower,
And the ground, agleam with lilies, coloured 'neath the saffron-flower,
While the grove was full of fragrance and of breath from violets.
Mid such guerdons of the spring-time, mid its jewelled coronets,
Shone the queen of all the perfumes, Star that loveliest colours shows,
Golden flame of fair Dione, passing every flower—the rose.
Dewsprent trees rose firmly upright with the lush grass at their feet:
Here, as yonder, streamlets murmured tumbling from each well-spring fleet.
Grottoes had an inner binding made of moss and ivy green,
Where soft-flowing runlets glided with their drops of crystal sheen.
Through those shades each bird, more tuneful than belief could entertain,
Warbled loud her chant of spring-tide, warbled low her sweet refrain.
Here the prattling river's murmur to the leaves made harmony,
As the Zephyr's airy music stirred them into melody.
To a wanderer through the coppice, fair and filled with song and scent,
Bird and river, breeze and woodland, flower and shade brought ravishment.)*

In this sensuously fascinating poem, Tiberianus has painted a *locus amoenus* with all the vivid color of late Antiquity. At this day, someone is sure to come up with the word "impressionism"—but quite unjustifiably. The poem has a strict structure. The author works with six "charms of landscape." They are the same six which Libanius (314–ca. 393) enjoins: "Causes of delight are springs and plantations and gardens and soft breezes and flowers and bird-voices" (ed. Förster, I, 517, § 200). The theme and the enumerative schema are, then, ready to hand. The last line, with its résumé, emphatically indicates this. In addition, the scene is divided into "above-below." Finally, the poem has twenty lines, in other words a "round number." This points to the principle of "numerical composition" (*Excursus* XV). The surging wealth of sensual perceptions, then, is ordered by conceptual and formal means. The finest fruit ripens on espaliers.

In the Middle Ages the *locus amoenus* is listed as a poetical requisite by lexicographers and writers on style.[22] We encounter a great number of such pleasances in the Latin poetry which flourished from 1070 onwards.[23] Model examples are also to be found in the arts of poetry which began to appear in increasing numbers from 1170. We have one such example by Matthew of Vendôme (Faral, p. 148). It is a rhetorical *amplificatio*, to

[* Trans. J. W. and A. M. Duff.]

[22] In Papias' lexicon (*ca.* 1050): "amoena loca dicta: quod amorem praestant, iocunda, viridia."—Ekkehart IV enjoins: "delitiis plenus locus appelletur amenus" (*Poetae*, V, 533, 10).

[23] Wido of Ivrea, ed. Dümmler, p. 95, 43 ff.—Baudri of Bourgueil describes (Abrahams, p. 191) a garden, making much use of Virgil (*Bucolics*, II, 45; *Georgics*, IV, 30; *Culex*, 390; *Copa*, 10). In his garden there are fifteen species of flowers and many species of trees (including laurel and olive). I have discussed this and other passages in *RF*, LVI (1942), 219–56. Walter Map (*Poems*, pp. 237 ff.) should be added.

which an air of novelty is imparted by a strong dose of dialectics, expressed in the driest conceptualistic terms. The description takes sixty-two lines, each idea being subjected to several variations. The means employed is the school exercise of grammatical permutation. Thus we first have: "The bird twitters, the brook murmurs, the breeze blows warm"; next, "The birds give pleasure by their voices, the brook by its murmuring, the breeze by its warmth," and so on. By the inclusion of fruit, the total number of "charms of landscape" is raised to seven. They are distributed first among the five senses and then among the four elements. The logical jargon of dialectics has made its way into the writer's vocabulary.

The philosophical epic of the latter part of the twelfth century incorporates the *locus amoenus* into its structure and develops it into various forms of the earthly paradise. In his *Anticlaudianus* Alan of Lille describes the dwelling place of Natura: a towering castle surrounded by a grove which represents the height of natural beauty (*SP.*, II, 275). It is the "place of places" ("locus ille locorum"), hence the optimum of the *locus amoenus*. John of Hanville takes us to the fabulous island Thule, where the philosophers of Antiquity are gathered in a scene of perpetual spring (*SP*, I, 326). The pleasance has here acquired a new bit of luxury: a circular piece of smooth ground ("planities patulum lunatur in orbem"). This stems from a description of a villa by Pliny (*Ep.*, V, 6, 7); it is adopted by Geoffrey of Vinsauf (Faral, 274, 5), who, however, adds porticoes.[24] One of the last poet-rhetoricians of the twelfth-century flowering, Peter Riga (d. 1209), makes the *locus amoenus* the theme of an entire poem, *On Earth's Ornaments* (*De ornatu mundi*—printed among Hildebert's works, *PL*, CLXXI, 1235 ff.). Here dialectical analysis and symmetry (the sources of pleasure particularized according to the several senses, etc.) are again strongly apparent. The "delights" ("deliciae") of the pleasance are greatly increased in number—spices, balsam, honey, wine, cedars, and bees are added. Mythological decorations appear. The pleasure grove is the rose of the world. But it fades: Turn ye to the heavenly rose.

I believe that, in what precedes, I have established the *locus amoenus* historically as a clearly defined topos of landscape description. Certain further problems in the history of topics and of style are connected with it. In Theocritus' poem in praise of the Dioscuri (XXII, 36 ff.) we are given a description of a *locus amoenus* which—most surprisingly—lies in a "wild wood." Such a union of contrasts was offered by nature in a famous region of Greece, the Vale of Tempe. "The Vale of Tempe, an ideal example of landscape beauty as the ancients understood it, singularly combines the charm of a river valley with the wildness and grandeur of a deep rocky gorge. Here, in the course of a walk of an hour and a half, the river Peneus passes

---

[24] In l. 11 *serta* (Faral) should read *septa* (from Martial, II, 14, 5). The porticoes also passed into *CB*, 59, st. 2: "In hac valle florida / Floreus flagratus, / Inter septa lilia, / Locus purpuratus."—Gervase of Melkley's *locus amoenus* (*Studi medievali* [1936], 34) should also be mentioned here.

through a gorge formed by the steep slopes of Ossa and Olympus, which almost reach its bed. The cliffs on both sides form almost vertical fissured walls, picturesquely overgrown with greenery. The slopes of Olympus make a sheer descent almost all the way; but on the right bank there is generally a narrow fringe of fertile soil, often broadening into small plains which are refreshed by countless springs, covered with luxuriant grass, and shaded by laurels, planes, and oaks. The river flows steadily and quietly, making a small island here and there, now wider, now forced into a narrow bed by jutting cliffs, under a roof of plane leaves through which the sun cannot penetrate." [25] Antiquity has left us descriptions by Theopompus, the elder Pliny [26] (*H.N.*, IV, 8 and XV, 31), and Aelian (*Var. hist.*, III, 1). Tempe had long since become the generic name for a variety of *locus amoenus* [27] —a cool wooded valley between steep slopes.[28] In his praise of country life Virgil had said (*Georg.*, II, 467) that countrymen lacked the luxuries of the city, but:

> *At secura quies et nescia fallere vita,*
> *Dives opum variarum, at latis otia fundis,*
> *Speluncae vivique lacus, at frigida Tempe*
> *Mugitusque boum mollesque sub arbore somni*
> *Non absunt . . .*

> (But peace secure, life without disappointments,
> Manifold riches, ease amid wide domains,
> Caverns and living lakes, coolness of vales,
> Lowing of herds, soft sleep beneath the trees—
> These fail them not . . .)

Servius had commented on this passage that Tempe was properly a *locus amoenus* in Thessaly, but stood by catachresis for any charming place ("abusive cuiusvis loci amoenitas"). We must, nevertheless, assume that the specialized Tempe motif, as we found it in Theocritus (pleasance in a wild wood) also passed into the rhetorical tradition. Theon, in his *Preliminary Exercises*, refers to Theopompus' description. We shall find this motif again in Romance poetry.

As we have seen, the *locus amoenus* also formed part of the scenery of

[25] L. Friedlaender, *Darstellungen aus der Sittengeschichte Roms*, I⁹, 469.

[26] In Pliny's description the high mountains which shut in the valley are mentioned. Then: "intus sua luce viridante allabitur Peneus, viridis calculo, amoenus circa ripas gramine, canorus avium concentu." This description is already tinged with the colors of poetry. Tiberianus' "luce ridens calculorum" recalls Pliny's "viridis calculo."

[27] Cf. the examples in Pape's *Wörterbuch der griechischen Eigennamen*. Also: F. Jacoby, *Fr. Gr. H.*, 115, F 78–80. Burgess, 202, n. 1.

[28] Medieval Latin poetry takes this over. Fulco of Beauvais (d. after 1083), prologue to *vita s. Blandini* 15: "Dum fontes, saltus, dum Thessala Tempe reviso."

pastoral poetry and thus of erotic poetry. Hence it was also taken over by the so-called "Vagantes." [29] We find it in the *Carmina Burana*.[30]

Virgil's description of the Elysian Fields was employed by Christian poets for Paradise.[31] The *locus amoenus* can also enter into the poetical description of gardens.[32]

7. Epic Landscape

As we have already indicated, nature description is also discussed in the rhetorical treatment of the figures of speech. The orator, the poet, the historian might find it necessary to sketch the scene of an event—that is, to "situate" a place, be it real or fictitious. The Greek for this is τοποθεσία or τοπογραφία (the "situation" or "description" of a place). In Latin "positus locorum" (Statius, *Silvae*, V, 3, 236) or "situs terrarum" (Horace, *Epi.*, II, 1, 251) [33]—still used in the same sense by Hohenstaufen poets.[34] The medieval epic is always ready to impart topographical and geographical information. The poet of the *Waltharius* begins with disarming candor:

> *Tertia pars orbis, fratres, Europa vocatur.*
>
> (The world's third part, brothers, is known as Europe.)

[29] On the concepts *Vagant* and *Vagantendichtung* ("Goliard," "Goliardic poetry") cf. Otto Schumann, commentary on *CB*, I, 82* ff.
[30] Schumann No. 77, st. 3, 1: "in virgulto florido stabam et ameno."—No. 79, st. 1: the poet rests under an olive tree. St. 2: "Erat arbor hec in prato / Quovis flore picturato, / Herba, fonte, situ grato, / Sed et umbra, flatu dato," etc.—No. 92, st. 7 and 8.—No. 137, st. 1.—No. 58.—No. 145, etc.
[31] Sedulius, I, 53.—Prudentius, *Cath.*, III, 101, and *Genesis*, II, 8 ff.—Dracontius, *De laudibus Dei*, I, 180 to 250; I, 348; III, 752.—*Poetae*, I, 573, No. LXXIV.—Gibuin of Langres (*SB Berlin* [1891], 99).—Peter Riga (*PL*, CLXXI, 1309 D).—*Commendatio mortuorum* in the Roman Ritual: "Constituat te Christus inter paradisi sui semper amoena virentia."—Boniface calls Paradise "amoenitatis locus" (*RF*, II [1886], 276).—When Paradise was to be represented on the stage, there were stage directions such as those at the beginning of the Anglo-French play of Adam: "Sint in eo (in paradiso) diversae arbores et fructus in eis dependentes, ut amenissimus locus videatur." In Virgil's Elysium there are no fruit trees. For the Christian Paradise they were indispensable, because of the forbidden fruit.
[32] Flora's garden in Ovid (*Fasti*, V, 208).—Garden of love with eternal spring in Claudian (*Epithalamium de nuptiis honorii*, 49).—*Poetae*, III, 159, No. XI, st. 4.—Since Paradise is a garden, a garden can, by transposition, be called a paradise (*Poetae*, V, 275, 411).—Hence also the atrium before the narthex of Romanesque cathedrals (E. Schlee, *Die Ikonographie der Paradiesesflüsse* [1937], 138).—O. Schissel, "Der byzantinische Garten und seine Darstellung im gleichzeitigen Roman," *SB Wien*, CCXXI [1942], No. 2.
[33] *topothesia*: Cicero to Atticus, I, 13 and I, 16.—*topographia*: Halm, 73, 1.—Lucan, X, 177: "Phariae primordia gentis Terrarumque situs volgique edissere mores." Here topography broadens to embrace ethnography. Similarly in the elder Seneca: "Locorum habitus fluminumque decursus et urbium situs moresque populorum . . ." (*Contr.*, II, *praef.*).—The fact that the description of localities is treated in three different sections of the system is still reflected in the twelfth-century arts of poetry. Matthew of Vendôme refers to the "locus naturalis" under the "proprietates quae a Tullio attributa vocantur" (Faral, p. 119, § 41), again under the "attributa negotio" (p. 143, § 94 and p. 147, § 109), and finally (p. 148, § 111) as "topographia." [34] *Ligurinus*, II, 57.

But Walter of Châtillon, for all his artistry, uses the same schema (*Alex-andreis*, I, 396 ff.), which goes back to Isidore's chorography (*Et.*, XIV, 3, 1). But though distinguishing the world's "three parts" did not come amiss to the epic poet, he must have been more concerned with indicating the successive scenes of his action by topography. The turning points and climaxes of his epic must be made plain by summary scenic indications, just as dramatic performances demand a stage set, however primitive—let it be no more than a sign reading "This is a wood." We have already found such "epic adumbration of landscape" in the *Iliad*. In the *Song of Roland* trees and hills are used for battle scenes and death scenes. A council of war is held "under a laurel tree that stands in the midst of a field" (2651). We find the same laurel tree on a hill in a battle field in Walter of Châtillon.[35] It is marked as a *locus amoenus* by the addition of a spring, a brook, and grass, and is derived from the Spanish *Libro de Alexandre* ("un lorer anciano": ed. Willis, 169, 936). Another indispensable piece of epic stage setting is the orchard or plantation ("verger": *Song of Roland*, II, 103, 501). But with the rise of the courtly romance in verse, the primitive landscape requirements of the heroic epic are far exceeded. The new genre is a creation of France and first appears about 1150. One of its principal motifs is the wild forest—"una selva selvaggia ed aspra e forte," as Dante will later put it. Percival grows up in the forest. Arthur's knights often pass through wild forests on their journeys. But in the midst of the wilderness there is frequently a *locus amoenus* in the form of a verger. Thus in the *Romance of Thebes*:

> 2126 *Joste le pié d'une montaigne*
> *En un val entre merveillos*
> *Qui mout ert laiz e tenebros . . .*
> 2141 *Mout chevauchoent a grant peine,*
> *Quant aventure les ameine*
> *A un vergier que mout ert genz,*
> *Que onc espice ne pimenz*
> *Que hon peust trover ne dire*
> *De cel vergier ne fu a dire.*

---

[35] *Alexandreis*, II, 308:
> *Adscendit tumulum modico qui colle tumebat*
> *Castrorum medius, patulis ubi frondea ramis*
> *Laurus odoriferas celebat crinibus herbas.*

That epic prefers the laurel tree is explained by medieval rhetoric. This distinguishes three styles, to which certain occupations, trees, and animals correspond, and which were based upon Virgil's *Bucolics*, *Georgics*, and *Aeneid* respectively. The *stilus humilis* treats of shepherds and its tree is the beech. The *stilus mediocris* treats of farmers and calls for fruit trees (*Georgics*, II, 426). The *stilus gravis* treats of warriors. The trees provided for it are the laurel and the cedar (*RF*, XIII [1902], 900). —The system was worked out from Aelius Donatus' commentary on Virgil. Cf. Schanz, IV, 12, p. 165. In the Middle Ages it was known as "rota Virgilii" (*infra*, p. 232).

(Close to the foot of a mountain he entered a wondrous (wooded) valley which was very hideous and darksome. They rode long and hard, when adventure brings them to a verger most charming, and no spice sweet or sharp that men can find and name was lacking in that verger.)

We find the same thing in the epic of the Cid. One of the climaxes of the poem is the shame which the Infants of Carrión put upon the Cid's daughters in the forest of Corpes. The poet uses appropriately atmospheric scenery:

2698   *Los montes son altos, las ramas pujan con las nuoves,*
     E la bestias fieras que andan aderredor.
     Fallaron un vergel con una limpia fuont.

     (The mountains are high, the branches reach to the clouds,
     And wild beasts wander there.
     They found a verger with a clear spring.) [36]

Ariosto shows us Angelica fleeing through a wild forest (I, 33):

     Fugge tra selve spaventose e scure,
     Per lochi inabitati, ermi e selvaggi.

Lo and behold! in the midst of these terrifying woods, there is "un boschetto adorno" (I, 35), with a gentle breeze, two clear brooks, lawns, shade . . .

In these three examples from Romance poetry [37] the *locus amoenus* is embedded in the wild forest of the romance of chivalry.

This combination was foreshadowed in the ancient Tempe motif. All "harmonies of opposites" (*puer senex,* and the like) are emotive formulas and as such have especial vitality.

The ideal landscape can always flower again in a new spring.[38]

[36] In the vicinity of Corpes there was and is no mountain. According to Menéndez Pidal *monte* would here mean "wild wood," "arbolado o matorral de un terreno inculto." And the verger? Menéndez Pidal comments somewhat constrainedly: "Sin duda significa una mancha de floresta (álamos, fresnos, etc.) con pradera o verdegal; desconozco otros textos que usen la palabra en esta acepción." We avoid these difficulties when we realize that we are here dealing not with a passage of realistic description but with the same epic landscape topos as that cited from the Romance of Thebes.

[37] The ideal landscape of Romance poetry deserves to be studied. It would of course exhibit very numerous connections with Latin poetry, as well as attempts to add something new. Berceo, for example, describes a pleasance whose springs are cool in summer and hot in winter (*Milagros de Nuestra Señora, Introducción,* st. 3). But this novelty comes from Isidore (*Et.,* XIII, 13, 10) and Augustine (*PL,* XLI, 718). Guillaume de Lorris translates *locus amoenus* as "le lieu plaisant" (*Roman de la Rose,* 117). He adheres to the precepts of Matthew of Vendôme, as a medieval reader already observed (Langlois's note on l. 78). He has a mixed forest (1323–64), and so on.

[38] It would be fascinating to compare the flower flora of the ancients (*supra,* pp. 186, 193, 197, n. 23) with that of the moderns. C. Ruutz-Rees covers the ground from Sannazaro to Milton (*Mélanges Abel Lefranc* [1936], 75). Keats and Wilde continue the line.

11

Poetry and Philosophy

1. *Homer and Allegory* / 2. *Poetry and Philosophy*
3. *Philosophy in Late Pagan Antiquity*
4. *Philosophy and Christianity*

1. *Homer and Allegory*

TO THE QUESTION as to the poet's significance in the world, Goethe
has Wilhelm Meister answer: "Innate within his inmost heart, the
beautiful flower of wisdom grows, and if other men dream awake
and are terrified out of their wits by monstrous imaginings, he lives the
dream of life as one awake, and what befalls, no matter how strange, is to
him at once past and future. And so the poet is at once teacher, soothsayer,
friend of the gods and friend of men." There are echoes of antique thought
here. All Antiquity sees the poet as sage, teacher, educator. To be sure,
Homer himself does not know this concept. The Homeric bard, who recites
his poems in the princely courts of Ionia, entertains his hearers and holds
them "spellbound" (*Od.*, XVII, 518 and XI, 334). Is there an echo in
this word of the original kinship of poetry and magic? [1] But even if the
"spell" is meant metaphorically, the word designates the purest effect of
all poetry and points to a timelessly valid truth which stands above any
pedagogical concept of poetry.

But it was precisely the pedagogical concept which the ancients cherished. Should poetry only give pleasure, or should it be useful too? Horace
concentrated much previous discussion of the subject in the humdrum
dictum: It should do both. But was Homer useful? Was Homer true?
These came to be basic problems of antique literary theory. They had immense historical consequences. The first attack on Homer was made by
Hesiod. He addresses himself to the lower stratum of Boeotian society, denounces the degenerate nobility, sets himself up as the advocate of moral
and social reform. While he was keeping his father's sheep on Helicon the
muses consecrated him a poet and said to him: "We know how to tell
many lies that resemble truth; but we know how to tell truth too, when
we wish." Hesiod's "truths" are not only concerned with the creation of

---

[1] E. E. Sikes, *The Greek View of Poetry* (1931), 3.

the world and the stories of the gods, they also give ritual regulations concerning the processes of metabolism (*Works and Days,* 727 ff.): "Do not stand upright facing the sun when you make water, but remember to do this when he has set and towards his rising. And do not make water as you go . . . and do not uncover yourself. A scrupulous man who has a wise heart sits down or goes to the wall of an enclosed court." * [2] Hesiod put so much instruction into his work that, as a poet, he has had nothing to say to later times. In his own opinion, he was propounding truth. But opinions on what is true change very rapidly. Hesiod's thinking was mythical. From the sixth century, the scientific thinking of Ionian natural philosophy rose to oppose him. It is wonderful to watch philosophy invade the Greek mind and take one position after another by storm. It is the rebellion of Logos against Myth—but also against poetry. Hesiod had denounced the epic in the name of truth. Now both he and Homer are judged before the tribunal of philosophy. Heraclitus said: "Homer ought to be excluded from the contests and scourged with rods." Xenophanes: "Homer and Hesiod have attributed to the gods all the things that are shameful and scandalous among men: theft, adultery, and mutual treachery." The philosopher's criticism is here directed against religion, but that means against poetry; for the Greeks had no religious records, no priestly caste, no "sacred books." Their theology was shaped by poets. Homer's gods are moved by very human emotions, which give occasion for farcical episodes in the epics. But the overthrow of Uranus by Cronus and that of the latter by Zeus, of which Hesiod tells, also offended ethical sensibility. It was for this reason that the poet was banished from Plato's state (*Resp.,* 398 A and 606–7). Plato's criticism of Homer is the culmination of the quarrel between philosophy and poetry, which was already "ancient" in Plato's time (607 C).[3] This conflict is grounded in the structure of the intellectual world. Hence it can always flare up again (we shall see this in the Italian trecento), and philosophy will always have the last word—because poetry does not answer her. Poetry has her own wisdom.

The Greeks wished to renounce neither Homer nor science. They sought for a compromise, and found it in the allegorical interpretation of Homer. Homeric allegoresis follows close upon the Homeric criticism of the pre-Socratics. It begins in the sixth century and develops various trends and phases, into which we need not enter. In late Antiquity it acquires a new

[* Trans. H. G. Evelyn-White.]

[2] Wilamowitz (*Hesiods Erga erklärt* [1928], pp. 124 ff.) points out that sitting is the Oriental custom to this day and refers to Herodotus II, 35. This "Asiatic rule of propriety" (p. 130), he holds, had reached Hellas at the time the verse was written, but had not achieved general acceptance.—But this is hardly a matter of "propriety," here we have rather to deal with a religiously motivated precept of cleanliness. It is also to be found, together with many others, in the Pythagorean school (Diogenes Laertius, VIII, 17). Cf. T. Wächter, *Reinheitsvorschriften im griechischen Kult* (1910), 134, n. 3.

[3] Cf. Stefan Weinstock, "Die platonische Homerkritik und ihre Nachwirkung" (*Philologus,* LXXXII [1926], 121 ff.).

power over men's minds. It is transferred to the Old Testament by the
Hellenized Jew Philo. From this Jewish Biblical allegoresis stems the Christian allegoresis of the Church Fathers.[4] Declining paganism transferred
allegorical interpretation to Virgil too (Macrobius). Biblical and Virgilian
allegoresis meet and mingle in the Middle Ages. The result is that allegory
becomes the basis of all textual interpretation whatsoever. Here lie the roots
of that which may be called medieval "allegorism." It finds expression not
only in the "moralizing" of Ovid [5] and other authors through allegorical
interpretation, but also in the fact that personified beings of a supersensual
nature—the men of late Antiquity had, as we have seen (supra, p. 102),
a predisposition toward such experiences—could become the principal personages of poetic creations: from Prudentius' Psychomachia to the twelfth-
century philosophical epic; from the Romance of the Rose to Chaucer and
Spenser and Calderón's autos sacramentales. The allegorical concept of
Homer was still self-evident to Erasmus (Enchiridion, c. 7) and to Winckelmann. In the pre-Homeric poets, wisdom was still hidden in riddles:
"Finally, as Wisdom became more human among the Greeks and sought
to impart herself to many, she put away the veil under which it was hard
to recognize her; she was still disguised, but no longer concealed, so that
those who sought her and contemplated her were able to know her; and
in this guise she appears in the famous poets, and Homer was her highest
teacher—a position that Aristarchus alone among the ancients denied to
him. His Iliad was meant to be a handbook for kings and rulers, and his
Odyssey the same for domestic life; Achilles' wrath and Ulysses' adventures
are merely the material of the disguise. He transformed the observations
of Wisdom upon human passions into sensible images and thus gave his
ideas a body which he enlivened with delightful pictures." [6] Homeric allegoresis had come into existence as a defense of Homer against philosophy.
It was then taken over by the philosophical schools, and also by history and
natural science. It was in harmony with one of the basic characteristics of
Greek religious thought: the belief that the gods express themselves in
cryptic form—in oracles, in mysteries.[7] It was the duty of the discerning
man to see through these veils and coverings, which hid the secret from
the eyes of the crowd—an idea which still influences Augustine (supra, pp.
73 f.). From the first century of our era onwards, allegoresis gains ground.
All schools of philosophy find that their doctrines are in Homer, as Seneca

---

[4] Further particulars in the article "Allegorese" by J. C. Joosen and J. H. Waszink
in RAC.

[5] John of Garland, Integumenta Ovidii, ed. F. Ghisalberti (1933).—Ovide
moralisé, ed. C. de Boer.—J. Engles, Études sur l'Ovide moralisé (Groningen,
1943).—The best treatment is by E. K. Rand, Ovid and his Influence, n.d. [1925],
131 ff.

[6] Winckelmann, Versuch einer Allegorie (1766), ed. Dressel (1866).

[7] The following is indebted to Franz Cumont, Recherches sur le symbolisme
funéraire des Romains (1942), 6 f.

mockingly remarks.[8] The most important role was played by the neo-Pythagoreans. Homeric apologetics are transformed into an apotheosis of Homer. For the neo-Platonists too the poet becomes a hierophant, a guardian of esoteric secrets. One may see this as Homer's victory over Plato —or as the reconciliation between the greatest poet and the most profound thinker, with which dying Paganism composed the "ancient quarrel."

A twelfth-century Platonist, John of Salisbury, formulated the fundamental motif of antique allegoresis with clarity and elegance:

> . . . *insta,*
> *Ut sit Mercurio Philologia comes,*
> *Non quia numinibus falsis reverentia detur,*
> *Sed sub verborum tegmine vera latent.*
> *Vera latent rerum variarum tecta figuris,*
> *Nam sacra vulgari publica iura vetant.*[9]

Theoretically separable from allegorism, but generally connected with it in practice (as in the passage quoted from Winckelmann) is the concept that poetry contains and must contain not only secret wisdom but also universal practical knowledge. Homer was familiar with all arts, says Quintilian (XII, 11, 21). "Polymathia" is ascribed to him in a treatise that passes as Plutarch's. According to Melanchthon, Homer's description of Achilles' shield laid the foundation for astronomy and philosophy. As late as 1713 Anthony Collins (1676–1729) called the *Iliad* "the epitome of all arts and sciences." Homer had planned it for all eternity, "to please and instruct mankind." This called forth an answer from Bentley and stimulated him to his Homeric criticism.[10]

During the late Roman flowering of the fourth century, Virgil replaces Homer. That he was versed in all arts is one of Macrobius' most cherished opinions. Macrobius' contemporary Servius remarks on Book VI of the *Aeneid:* "Though all Virgil is full of knowledge, in this book it is predominant . . . Much is simply said, much taken from history, but much also from the deep wisdom of the philosophers, the theologians, the Egyptians." A combination of allegorism and polymathy is afforded by Alan. In the

---

8 Epistle 86, 5.
9 *Entheticus,* 183 ff. "Insist that Philology be the companion of Mercury; not in order that reverence shall be paid to false divinities; but under the veil of words truths lie hidden. Truths lie hidden veiled under the various forms of things, for common law forbids sacred things to the vulgar."—The old Greek concept of poetry as falsehood became meaningful through allegoresis: "mendacia poetarum inserviunt veritati" (John of Salisbury, *Policraticus,* ed. Webb, I, 186, 12).—The theory was set forth in detail by Alan (*SP*, II, 465 = *PL*, CCX, 451 B). It is thus that Alan's lines (*SP*, II, 278) are to be understood: "Virgilii musa mendacia multa colorat / Et facie veri contexit pallia falsi."—The same theory in the Carolingian period in Theodulf (*Poetae*, I, 543, 19 ff.).
10 Melanchthon, *Declamationes,* ed. Hartfelder (1891), 37.—For Collins, see R. C. Jebb, *Bentley* (1882), 146.

preface to his *Anticlaudianus* (*SP*, II, 269) he explains that his work has something to offer to students of every degree. The literal meaning is accessible to boys, the moral meaning to those who have made some progress. But the subtlety of the allegory will make even the thoroughly educated mind even keener. The arts of poetry of the period also demand encyclopedic knowledge of the poet.[11]

2. *Poetry and Philosophy*

Allegory and polymathy bring poetry close to philosophy. The "quarrel" between poetry and philosophy was also grounded in the fact that there were many intimate connections between them. Seneca recognizes this when he writes: "How many poets say things that philosophers too have said or ought to say!" (Epistle 8). In the Middle Ages poetry could be all the more readily equated with *sapientia* and *philosophia* since both words meant simply "learning." In Carolingian times poets were often honored with the title of *sophista* or *sophus*. By "moderni philosophi" a ninth-century writer understands recent writers on metrics. Virgil is one of the "old leaders of philosophy." Two kinds of content are discovered in the *Aeneid*: philosophical truth and poetical fabrication ("figmentum"). The twelfth-century Renaissance commonly equated poetry and philosophy (Baudri of Bourgueil, Walter of Châtillon). Natural science is accounted a part of philosophy. Lucan is praised for having dealt with "philosophical questions" such as the nature of tides.[12] It is expected that the poet will be familiar with natural science. Dante accedes to these demands when he finds a place in the *Divina Commedia* for excursuses on the spots in the moon (a theme often discussed from the twelfth century), on embryology, and on the origin of rain. He says of himself that he is "inter vere phylosophantes minimus" [13] and is praised by Giovanni Villani (d. 1348) as "sommo poeta e filosofo."

The composition of poetry requires the Muses. Nymphs, fauns, and other nature deities are often associated with them—because, according to Antiquity, the best place for composition was a grove. Pan is invoked there too, and, surprisingly enough, proves to be "a goodly part of philosophy." A Welshman calls composing poetry "philosophizing." The Englishman Alexander Neckham (*ca.* 1157–1217), grammarian, natural scientist, schoolman, and abbot, produced a series of poems inculcating the peren-

---

[11] Gervase of Melkley cites the authority of Vitruvius, who demanded the same of architects (*Studi med.*, IX [1936], 64).

[12] *sophista*: examples in *Poetae*, IV, 1170 b, under *artes*.—*Moderni philosophi: Poetae*, III, 295, No. III.—Virgil: Anselm of Besate, p. 16, 12. Bernard Silvestris' commentary on the *Aeneid*, p. 1.—Baudri of Bourgueil, Abrahams, No. 97, 1, and p. 272, 45 ff.—Walter of Châtillon, *Alexandreis*, I, 19 ff.—Lucan: Gervase of Melkley (*Studi medievali*, IX [1936], 64).

[13] *Questio de aqua et terra*, Introduction.

nially contemporary doctrine that the best philosophy is in wine: Bacchus is a second Aristotle, "dux philosophie." [14]

From the end of the twelfth century the vernacular poets of France undertake to spread a knowledge of antique philosophy. In the prologue to her fables Marie de France writes:

> Cil qui sevent de letreure
> Devreient bien metre lor cure
> Es bons livres e es escriz
> E es essamples e es diz
> Que li philosophe troverent.

(Those who know letters should apply themselves heartily to the good books and writings, the examples and maxims, which the philosophers have found.)

Guiot of Provins has much to tell about them in the satirical poem which he entitles *Bible*. He had heard their lives related in the church of St. Trophime at Arles. He mentions "Therades," Plato, Seneca, Aristotle, Virgil, "Cleo the Elder," Socrates, Lucan, Diogenes, Priscian, Aristippus, Ovid, Statius, Tully, Horace, Pythagoras, and others:

> Cil se garderent de mentir;
> Cil vivoient selonc reson;
> Hardi furent comme lyon
> De bien dire et de bien mostrer
> Et des malvais vices blasmer . . .
> Philosophes nomez estoit
> Cil qui Deu creoit et amoit . . .
> Li nons fu molt biaus et cortois;
> Por ce l'apelent li Grezois
> Les ameors de sapience,
> Que en aus ot plus de science
> Et de reson qu'en autre gent.

(These would not lie; these lived by reason; bold as lions were they in well speaking and well proving and in censuring evil and vice . . . Philosophers they were named, who believed in God and loved Him . . . A fair name and courteous; the Greeks called them lovers of wisdom because in them there was more of knowledge and of reason than in other men.)

In Jean de Meun composing poetry is called "travailler en philosophie" (*Romance of the Rose*, 18742).

[14] Composing poetry in groves: Wilhelm Kroll, *Studien zum Verständnis der römischen Literatur* (1924), 30.—"Pan, deus Arkadiae, pars est bona philosophiae": NA, II, 392, 41.—The Welshman: Walter Map, *De nugis curialium*, ed. James, p. 13, 1 ff.—Neckham's poems, ed. Esposito, in *English Historical Review*, XXX (1915), 450 ff. There 454, III, 6 and IV, 5; 455, 46 ff.

3. Philosophy in Late Pagan Antiquity

The amalgamation of poetry and philosophy was facilitated by the fact that, since late Antiquity, the word "philosophy" could mean very different things. Once again, then, we find ourselves obliged to undertake a piece of terminological research. We are wont to regard the history of philosophy from Plato to Plotinus and Augustine as a succession of great thinkers and schools, which then comes to a sudden end. At most Boethius is remembered, because his *Consolatio philosophiae* was a basic book for the entire Middle Ages. But it is not until the appearance of Anselm of Canterbury (d. 1109) that our interest in medieval philosophy reawakens. And our interest and our research are concentrated upon the Scholasticism of the thirteenth century.

The concept of what constitutes philosophy had already begun to grow vague in the third century of our era. To be sure, the philosophy of earlier times was carried on down, together with the remaining stock of knowledge. But the process was entirely traditionalistic and scholastic. Students were no longer taught to philosophize, but to interpret the classics of philosophy. This was accomplished by courses of lectures, which began by defining philosophy in a manner equally traditional. In the schools of late Antiquity six different definitions were transmitted: [15] 1. Knowledge of what exists and how it exists; 2. Knowledge of divine and human things; 3. Preparation for death; 4. Assimilation of man to God; 5. Art of arts and science of sciences; 6. Love of wisdom.

Some of these definitions reappear in patristic literature. Only the first has no later influence—it was too difficult. The sixth is so general and so widely disseminated that it is of no historical interest. The remaining four descend through patristic literature to the Middle Ages. In addition, however, we find late pagan Antiquity applying the word philosophy to every branch of learning [16] (a reappearance of the meaning already current in the time of the Attic Sophists). In the reign of Diocletian mining engineers are called *philosophi*.[17] In Martianus Capella's encyclopedia grammar is partially identified with philosophy and "criticism," poets and geometricians are called "philosophers." [18] The mosaic in the sweat room of a bath in Africa (fifth century) has the inscription FILOSOFI LOCUS over a representation of a garden.[19] Together with *philosophus* the word *sophus* is

[15] These definitions have been preserved for us by Cassiodorus (*PL*, LXX, 1167 D).

[16] In Byzantium *philosophos* is applied to the "educated man," but also to the fox in the beast epic. F. Dölger interprets this as the reaction of popular feeling in the late Byzantine period against the clique-control of the "learned" grandees (*Festschrift für Th. Voreas* [Athens, 1939], 125–136).

[17] Friedlaender, *Sittengeschichte*, III[10], 90.

[18] Dick, 85, 10; 268 f.; 362, 9.

[19] *CIL*, VIII, No. 10890.

used. For example in the beautiful epitaph on the City Prefect Vettius Agorius Praetextatus (d. 384), which is put into the mouth of his dead wife Paulina: [20]

> 8   *Tu namque quidquid lingua utraque est proditum*
>   *Cura soforum, porta quis caeli patet,*
> 10   *Vel quae periti condidere carmina*
>   *Vel quae solutis vocibus sunt edita,*
>   *Meliora reddis quam legendo sumpseras.*
>   *Sed ista parva: tu pius mystes sacris*
>   *Teletis reperta mentis arcano premis*
> 15   *Divumque numen multiplex doctus colis . . .*

The man thus praised was, then, an expert in philosophy, literature, and the mysteries, and also a philologist, one who emended corrupt texts.

As we see that engineering, military science, grammar, textual criticism, literary culture, gnosis—all these things can be called "philosophy" in late Antiquity. Any and every systematized branch of knowledge lays claim to the title. But the cultural ideal of late Antiquity was rhetoric, of which poetry was a subdivision. The assimilation of philosophy to rhetoric is a product of neo-Sophism. Rhetor, philosopher, sophist now mean the same thing to the Latin West too.[21] Sidonius calls the Greek philosophers (including Plato) "sophistae" (*Carmina*, II, 156). In his epithalamium for the philosopher Polemius he treats themes which should properly be reserved for the "philosophical lecture hall" ("schola sophisticae intromisi materiam," XIV, 4). He also recapitulates the teachings of the Seven Sages (XV, 45 f.)—or what were then held to be their teachings. The Seven Sages (they are often twelve) were very popular in late Antiquity—a symp-

---

[20] Buecheler, *Carmina latina epigraphica*, No. 111. "All that in either Greek or Latin has been brought forth by the labors of the wise, to whom the gates of heaven stand open, whether works in verse or prose, you lay down improved over what they were when you took them up. But these are small matters: a pious mystes, you store in the secrecies of your mind that which is found by holy consecration and you reverence the divine being with multifarious learning." It was the conviction of Antiquity that religious knowledge must be approached by many paths: "Non enim spero totius maiestatis effectorem omniumque rerum patrem vel dominum uno posse quamvis e multis composito nuncupari nomine" (*Asclepius* in *Apuleius de philosophia libri*, ed. Thomas, p. 56, 1 ff.).—The anonymous author of the *De rebus bellicis* (it cannot be dated with certainty; the centuries between Theodosius and Heraclius have been proposed) ends his *praefatio* with the sentence: "Si quid vero liberius oratio mea pro rerum necessitate protulerit, aestimo venia protegendum, cum mihi promissionis implendae gratia subveniendum est propter philosophiae libertatem." Here *philosophia* could mean "research," "science." But in the same period Persian theosophy is also called philosophy (Lactantius Placidus on Statius, *Thebais*, IV, 516).

[21] According to F. Henry the title σοφιστής was accorded in the fourth-century schools only to the head of the school, an appointment made either by the emperor or the city. The official title of his subordinates was ῥήτωρ (Karl Gerth in *Bursians Jahresbericht*, CCLXXII, 179).—The philosopher can now also be called *orator* (Boethius, *In Isagogen Porphyrii commenta*, ed. Schepss, p. 4, 12).

tom of the stunting of intellectual culture. Their apophthegms were put into Greek and Latin verse.[22] Gregory of Tours tells how a Parisian abbot spent a long night weeping and praying because he had heard that the king intended to make him bishop of faraway Avignon; for he feared that "there between the sophistical senators and the philosophizing governor his simplicity would be mocked." [23] These high officials flirted with rhetorical culture, as did so many Roman emperors and Germanic kings. They were dilettantes, not philosophers.

4. Philosophy and Christianity

Patristic literature took possession of the inheritance of Hellenized Judaism. Among the Hellenized Jews, as among all the other Hellenized peoples of the East, there existed tendencies toward universalism which dissevered their traditional religion from the national soil whence it had sprung.[24] Judaism now lays claim to a world mission and sets in motion a corresponding propaganda. For this the Greco-Roman cultural world was favorable soil. There were various points of contact between late Greek philosophy and Jewish teaching. The Greek-speaking Jews of the Diaspora became particularly aware of this and made it the basis of an apologetics which was frequently tendentious. If, to educated pagans, the Jews were cultureless barbarians because the Greek historians had nothing to say about them, the Alexandrian Jews undertook to refute this and other reproaches by glorifying their own tradition and, above all, by showing that it harmonized with Greek philosophy; nay more, that Greek philosophy owed its origin to the Jewish patriarchs and principally to Moses, who became, to late Judaism, "the most important figure in the entire history of religion," the "true teacher of mankind," the "superman." [25] In the process both he and Abraham became philosophers. So we read in Eupolemius (ca. 150 B.C.): "Moses was the first sage and the first to teach the Jews the alphabet, which the Phoenicians took from the Jews, and the Greeks from the Phoenicians; and Moses was the first to write laws for the Jews." [26] This is clearly tendentious, and of a tendentiousness which does not shrink from fables and forgeries. This is even more pronounced in Artapanus.[27] That author first tells how Abraham taught astrology to the Egyptians and Phoenicians. Then comes Moses: ". . . The Greeks call him . . . Musaeus. This

22 A. P., IX, 366; Ausonius (ed. Peiper, p. 537) under "sapientes;" Baehrens, *Poetae Latini minores*, IV, p. 119 f.

23 F. Kiener, *Verfassungsgeschichte der Provence* (1900), 48.

24 W. Bousset, *Die Religion des Judentums im späthellenistischen Zeitalter* [3] (1926), 53 ff. and 78.

25 Joachim Jeremias in Kittel's *Theologisches Wörterbuch zum Neuen Testament*, IV, p. 854, 6; 855, 17; 680, 15.

26 Text in P. Riessler, *Altjüdisches Schrifttum ausserhalb der Bibel* (1928), p. 328.

27 Wrote "at the latest in the first half of the first century B.C." (Bousset, p. 121). Text in Riessler, p. 187.

Moysos (*sic!*) was Orpheus' teacher. As a mature man he bestowed many things of great use upon mankind. He invented ships and machines for transporting stones, as well as the weapons of the Egyptians and machines for irrigation, implements of war, and philosophy." Two things here are worthy of remark: first, the juxtaposition of Abraham, Moses, Musaeus, and Orpheus as "sages" or "philosophers"; second, placing engineering technique (suitable for Egyptian conditions—pyramids and irrigation) on the same level as philosophy. Josephus' portrayal of Moses has points of contact with Artapanus'. The conclusion of the process is reached in Philo's life of Moses,[28] which belongs to the genre of Greek lives of prophets and philosophers, that is, the antique "romances of philosophers."

The next step is taken when second-century Christian apologetics adopts the arguments of Jewish apologetics. Indeed, the former has been called the "daughter" of the latter. After the apologists, the third stage in the process, which can only be mentioned here, is represented by the two great Alexandrians, Clement and Origen. Clement revived the old equivalence between Christianity and the "true philosophy" and gave it a new effectiveness. He taught that pagan philosophy was to be regarded as a propaedeutics bestowed on the Greeks by God. These ideas which, though (like Origen's Platonizing Christianity) they were rejected by the ecclesiastical authorities, yet retained the power of generating other ideas.[29]

In the ecclesiastical historian Eusebius (d. 339), philosophy is not only the Christian faith, it is also asceticism. He was too early to have known monasticism. But among his successors the meaning of "asceticism" could be narrowed to the point where philosophy was equated with anchoritism or monasticism. For Nilus of Ancyra, for example (d. *ca.* 430), the monastic life is the true philosophy taught by Christ.[30]

The equating of Christianity with philosophy then passes into Latin patristic literature.[31] It is also to be found in the Latin Middle Ages. Bruno

---

[28] In Philo's works (Berlin Academy edition) the principal *loci* for Moses as philosopher are III, 66, 16; III, 195, 18; IV, 13, 2; for Abraham I, 167, 8 and 171, 8.—The Jewish religion is the πάτριος φιλοσοφία of the Jews (VI, 70, 19 and IV, 250, 18).

[29] Here also belong the many attempts (differing greatly in origin, milieu, and intellectual level) to turn antique philosophers and poets into witnesses or prophets of the Christian revelation. Such claims were made not only, as we know, for Plato, Virgil, and Seneca, but also for the Seven Sages (cf. von Premerstein, *Festschrift der Nationalbibliothek Wien* [1926], 652 ff. and *Byzantinisch-neugriechische Jahrbücher*, IX [1932], 338).

[30] Viller-Rahner, *Askese und Mystik in der Väterzeit* (1939), 168 f.

[31] J. Kollwitz, who incidentally touches upon the concept of Christianity as the "true philosophy" (*Römische Quartalsschrift* [1936], p. 49), gives examples only for Eusebius, Lactantius (*Epitome*, 36; Brandt, 712), Rufinus, Socrates. But Lactantius has only: "Ad veram religionem sapientiamque veniamus." Minucius Felix, on the other hand, has the apologetic topos that much in Christianity coincides with philosophy: "aut nunc Christianos philosophos esse aut philosophos iam tunc fuisse Christianos" (20, 1). Though Tertullian calls Christianity "melior philosophia" at the end of his *De pallio*, in his *Apologeticon* (c. 46, § 2), he gives a

of Querfurt (born 973 or 974, beheaded 1009 by a pagan Prussian prince) writes in his life of St. Adalbert (c. 27): "in monasterio quo sanctus iste philosophia Benedicti patris nutritus erat." Bruno was close not only to the Emperor Otto III, but also to Romuald of Camaldoli, who wanted to renew Oriental anchoritism in the West. From here, then, threads run back to the ascetic ideal of Eastern Christendom. But the parallel between monasticism and philosophy lived on in the Latin West too, as John of Salisbury and Wibald of Corvey testify.[32] So two contemporaries of Barbarossa, an Englishman and a German, still live by concepts which go back in part to the apologists, in part to Alexandrian theology, and in part to antique ecclesiastical history—in other words, to systems of ideas which appeared between 150 and 400. Here we have a fine example of the autonomy of the individual strands in a historical development: It cuts across any periodization into epochs. I will pursue this no further, but will merely remind the reader that Erasmus of Rotterdam calls Christianity "philosophia Christi." From time to time one reads that this was a typical humanistic misapprehension, against which Luther . . . But to say this is to fail to be aware of the continuity of a mode of thought which goes back to the early Church.

Scholasticism put an end to the confusion of philosophy with poetry, rhetoric, proverbial lore, and the various learning of the schools. The old connection between *artes* and philosophy is severed at a blow. The blow lay in Thomas's dictum: "Septem artes liberales non sufficienter dividunt philosophiam theoreticam." [33] Yet Leopardi can still write: "La scienza del bello scrivere è una filosofia, e profondissima e sottilissima, e tiene a tutti i rami della sapienza." [34]

---

detailed refutation of this view. No one yet appears to have made use of a passage in Arnobius, *Adversus nationes*, I, 38 (Reifferscheid, p. 25), the substance of which is that Christ is the great teacher of all truth concerning (a) the being of God, (b) the creation of the world, (c) the nature of the heavenly bodies, (d) the creation of animals and man, (e) the being of the soul. Here the subjects of antique philosophy are named and Christ appears as the promulgator of the true philosophy; but the word itself is not used.

[32] John of Salisbury, *Policraticus*, ed. Webb, I, p. 100. Wibald in Jaffé, *Bibl. rer. germ.*, I, 278.

[33] Grabmann, *Mittelalterliches Geistesleben*, I, 190.

[34] *Zibaldone*, 2728.

12

Poetry and Theology

1. *Dante and Giovanni del Virgilio* / 2. *Albertino Mussato*
3. *Dante's Self-Exegesis* / 4. *Petrarch and Boccaccio*

1. *Dante and Giovanni del Virgilio*

IN HIS LAST YEARS Dante entered into relations with the Bolognese poet
and university professor Giovanni del Virgilio—so named because of
his admiration for Virgil. An exchange of poetical epistles in the form
of Latin eclogues between Dante and Giovanni has come down to us. After
his great friend's death Giovanni composed an epitaph in Latin. It begins:

> *Theologus Dantes, nullius dogmatis expers*
> *Quod foveat claro philosophia sinu,*
> *Gloria Musarum, vulgo gratissimus auctor,*
> *Hic iacet, et fama pulsat utrumque polum:*
> 5 *Qui loca defunctis, gladiisque regnumque gemellis*
> *Distribuit laicis rhetoricisque modis.*
> *Pascua Pieriis demum resonabat avenis.*

(The theologian Dante, stranger to no knowledge which philosophy
fosters in her noble breast, the glory of the Muses, whose works are the
delight of the people, lies here, and his fame extends to either pole: he
assigned their places to the dead and their realms to the twin swords [1]
in the language of the unlearned and the learned. Finally he celebrated
pastures on the pipes of Pieria.[2])

The epitaph is a summary of Dante's accomplishment and career from
the point of view of a scholarly Latin poet and professor. That Giovanni
del Virgilio gave scholarly poetry precedence over poetry in the vernacular,
we know from the verse correspondence which he exchanged with Dante.[3]
In the name of the guild, he there says (*Ecl.*, I, 15): "Clerus vulgaria tem-
nit," "the learned scorn poetry in the vernacular."

---

[1] In the *Monarchia*. It is composed in Latin artistic prose (*rhetoricis modis*).
[2] In the Latin eclogues.
[3] Best edition in P. H. Wicksteed and E. G. Gardner, *Dante and Giovanni del
Virgilio* (London, 1902).

We are familiar with this contempt [4] of the unlettered from the Latin poetry of the Middle Ages. That Dante still wrote Latin eclogues towards the end of his life seemed to Giovanni del Virgilio a satisfactory conclusion ("demum" in l. 7). A remarkable development indeed for a "theologian" and "philosopher"! But "theologus" means "theologian" as little as "dogma" means "dogma" and "philosophia" "philosophy"—or, we might add, as "commedia" in Dante means "comedy." We must understand Giovanni del Virgilio's verbal usages in the light of his historical situation. Giovanni was born in Bologna, of a Paduan father. He is closely connected with the group of Latin poets which is usually known as the "cenacolo padovano."

2. *Albertino Mussato*

The most important of them was Albertino Mussato (1261–1329). He made a name for himself as statesman, historian, and Latin poet. He is also of interest in the history of poetical theory. Mussato was awarded the poet's crown at Padua in 1315 for his Latin tragedy *Ecerinis*. This gave him the occasion to express himself on the origin and value of poetry in several Latin epistles. Poetry is a science sent down from heaven and "exists of divine right."

> *Haec fuit a summo demissa scientia caelo,*
> *Cum simul excelso ius habet illa Deo.*

The pagan myths tell the same things as Holy Scripture, only in a mysterious manner (*nigmate = enigmate*):

> *Quae Genesis planis memorat primordia verbis,*
> *Nigmate maiori mystica Musa docet.*

Thus, the war of the giants against Zeus corresponds to the story of the Tower of Babel, Jupiter's punishment of Lycaon to the banishment of Lucifer to Hell. The books of the Bible are in part in poetical form—for example, the Pentateuch and the Apocalypse. Poetry may therefore be accounted philosophy, and can be a substitute for Aristotle:

> *Hi ratione carent, quibus est invisa Poesis,*
> *Altera quae quondam Philosophia fuit.*
> *Forsan Aristotelis si non videre volumen*
> *Carmen cur de se iure querantur habent.*[5]

[4] Walter of Châtillon calls the unlettered "animae brutae" (*Moralisch-satirische Gedichte*, ed. Strecker, p. 63, 2, 1). We also find such expressions as "laicorum pecus bestiale."

[5] These and the previously cited lines are from Epistle 4. I use the text of the edition of 1636 (*Albertini Mussati Historia Augusta Henrici VII. Caesaris et alia quae extant opera* [Venetiis, 1636]), which is reprinted in J. G. Graevius, *Thesaurus antiquitatum Italiae*, VI, 2 (Leiden, 1722).—The last line (*Carmen . . .*) is corrupt.

But Mussato goes still further. In his seventh epistle he sets forth that the old poets were prophets of God and that poetry is a second theology:

> *Quidni? Divini per saecula prisca poetae*
> *Esse pium caelis edocuere deum . . .*
> *Hique alio dici coeperunt nomine vates.*
> *Quisquis erat vates, vas erat ille dei.*
> *Illa igitur nobis stat contemplanda Poesis,*
> *Altera quae quondam Theologia fuit.*

Moses, Job, David, Solomon were poets. Christ spoke in parables, hence in a form related to poetry.[6]

This is the Biblical poetics with which we are already familiar and which Jerome bequeathed to the Middle Ages. But here (as in Alan and, later, in seventeenth-century Spain) it is developed into a theological poetics. It is the same poetics which Giovanni del Virgilio sets forth. Philosophy, theology, and poetry are fused into one.

Mussato's theory of poetry drew an answer from the Dominican Giovannino of Mantua (of whom we have no other record). He refuted it on nine grounds in a prose letter to Mussato. Mussato replied in prose and in a poem (*Ep.*, 18). This controversy has been frequently treated in Italian literary history.[7]

All the critics agree upon this thesis: Mussato was a Humanist and thus a forerunner of the Renaissance; this is demonstrated by the fact that he opposed the enemies of poetry. But all the critics fail to go into Fra Giovannino's theses and hence into the central issue of the controversy. The monk makes his attack not on poetry but on the idea that poetry is an *ars divina* and even a theology. Certainly, he admits, Aristotle testified that the earliest poets, the greatest of whom was Orpheus, were philosophers and held water to be the supreme deity. But since they were treating of false gods, they could not have transmitted the true theology. Furthermore, poetry was not bestowed upon men by God but, like the other secular sciences, was invented by man. Moses' Song of Praise after the passage of the Red Sea was composed in verse only so that it could be performed by the prophetess Maria (Miriam) and a chorus of women (Exodus 15:20). But even if the entire Bible were in poetical form, or were put into verse, as Arator and Sedulius attempted to do, it would not follow that poetry should be called divine. For every branch of knowledge can be imparted in metrical form, but that does not make it become poetry. To be sure, Holy Scripture too uses metaphors—as poetry does—especially in the prophetic books and the

---

[6] Cf. Ps. 77:2: "Aperiam in parabolis os meum."
[7] Gustav Körting, *Geschichte der Literatur Italiens im Zeitalter der Renaissance,* vol. III, 1, 308 f. (1884); Adolf Gaspary, *Geschichte der italienischen Literatur,* I, 400 (1885); Karl Vossler, *Poetische Theorien der italienischen Frührenaissance* (1900); A. Galletti, "La ragione poetica di Albertino Mussato ed i poeti-teologi" (in *Scritti vari di erudizione e di critica in onore di Rodolfo Renier* [Turin, 1912]).

Apocalypse; but with a great difference. Poetry uses metaphors to depict and to delight; but the Bible uses them to veil divine truth so that it may be discovered by the worthy but remain hidden from the unworthy. This idea has its roots in the Bible (Isa. 6:9 f. and Matt. 13:13 ff.) and is, as we saw (p. 73), further developed by Augustine. Finally, Fra Giovannino continues, the three earliest poets—Orpheus, Musaeus, and Linus—lived long after Moses, namely in the age of the Judges. Hence theology is older than poetry, for it was imparted by God to Adam or Enoch, as Augustine (*Civ. Dei*, XVIII, 38) and Peter Comestor's *Historia scholastica* testify.

It is clear that the Dominican is not concerned with "attacking" or "belittling" poetry, but with assigning it a place in the system of the disciplines which Thomas had firmly established. The crucial point of the discussion is the question of the nature of the metaphors found in the Bible. Thomas had expressed himself on the subject in his commentary on Peter Lombard's *Sentences* (1 *Sent., prol.* 1, 5 c and *ad tertium*). The objection is raised: "The methods of sciences which are entirely different cannot be the same. But poetry is sharply distinguished from theology, the truest science, as containing the least portion of truth ("minimum continet veritatis"). Now since poetry uses metaphorical expressions, theology must not do so." Answer: "The science of poetry is concerned with things which, because of their lack of truth ("propter defectum veritatis"), cannot be comprehended by reason; reason must therefore be beguiled by certain similarities. But theology is concerned with the suprarational; hence the symbolical method is common to them both, 'modus symbolicus utrique communis est.' " In this passage, then, metaphor is still acknowledged to be common to both poetry and theology. In the *Summa theologiae*, as we shall see, Thomas abandons this position.

To understand Fra Giovannino's argument historically, we must take up the first book of Aristotle's *Metaphysics* together with Thomas's commentary upon it. Aristotle begins with a genetic theory of culture. In man, sense perception and reflection lead to experience, of which the sciences and arts are to be regarded as the result. At first the inventors of all arts were admired. Later the inventors of the useful arts were regarded less highly than the inventors of the "pleasurable" arts, among which Aristotle also places the "poietic" (productive) arts. The last stage in the development of culture gave birth to the theoretical sciences and arts. Among these in turn the highest place belongs to the science of first causes, that is, metaphysics. It alone is "divine science," and indeed in two senses, because it is most worthy of God, and because it is a science of the divine. Its sources lie in wonder at natural phenomena and finally at the origin of the universe. The first thinkers sought to explain this mythically. Hence one may say that "one who delights in myths is also in a certain sense a philosopher" (982 b 19). But is metaphysical knowledge in general attainable by man? The poet Simonides says it is reserved to God. But poets are proverbially liars (983 a 3, quotation from Solon). In this connection (983 b 29)

Aristotle uses the word "theologian." He speaks of those "who in the earliest times first reflected upon the gods" (οἱ πρῶτοι . . . θεολογήσαντες); they had regarded Oceanus and Tethys as the authors of creation and had taught that the gods swore by the Styx. Thales too had seen the primal cause in water.[8] In *Metaph.* 1000 a 9 Aristotle speaks of Hesiod "and the other theologians." In other passages no poets are named but Aristotle mentions the theologians in connection with the investigators of nature (φυσικοί ; e.g., 1071 b 27; 1075 b 26). In all these passages "theology" means speculative cosmology—or in other words, archaic natural science. This the scientific thinker Aristotle rejects. Philosophy and cosmological poetry are irreconcilable opposites. In the *Poetics* too he explains that Empedocles, despite the fact that he wrote in verse, is not a poet but a natural philosopher. Indeed, that poetry is or can be theology is in complete contradiction to Aristotle's *Poetics*. To him, of course, poetry is "the representation of life" (μίμησις). Hence its only subject is men in action (*Poetics*, 1448 a 1).

In Thomas's commentary[9] Giovannino could find, among other things, that poetry was a secular science and had been invented by men. But he also read: ". . . Ista scientia" (metaphysics, for which Thomas synonymously employs the terms "theologia" and "prima philosophia") "est maxime divina: ergo est honorabilissima" (Cathala, p. 21, No. 64). These passages alone were enough to refute Mussato's claim that poetry was an *ars divina*. But the text of Aristotle and of his Christian commentator further made it clear that the Doctor Universalis set no very high value on poetry. In one passage he called poets liars: ". . . Sed poetae non solum in hoc, sed in multis aliis mentiuntur, sicut dicitur in proverbio vulgari" (Cathala, p. 21, No. 65). Furthermore, when they have philosophized, they have taught falsely. Thomas comments on the passage concerning the first theologians, who made Oceanus and Tethys the creators of the world: "ad cuius evidentiam sciendum est, quod apud Graecos primi famosi in scientia fuerunt, sic dicti quia de divinis carmina faciebant." Then he adds a passage of explanation, which corresponds to nothing in Aristotle's text: "Fuerunt autem tres, Orpheus, Musaeus et Linus, quorum Orpheus famosior fuit. Fuerunt autem tempore, quo iudices erant in populo Judaeorum . . . Isti autem poetae quibusdam aenigmatibus fabularum aliquid de rerum natura tractaverunt. Dixerunt autem quod Oceanus . . . Ex hoc sub fabulari similitudine dantes intelligere aquam esse generationis principium" (Cathala, p. 29, No. 83). These assertions, which we have already seen in Fra Giovannino's epistle, are interesting. Aristotle does not mention the names of the three mythical poets. Obviously by way of explanation, Thomas took them and their chronology from a different tradition—

---

[8] The assertions concerning Oceanus, Tethys, and Styx refer to Homer (*Iliad*, XIV, 201 and 246; II, 755; XIV, 271; XV, 37).

[9] *S. Thomae Aquinatis in Metaphysicam Aristotelis commentaria*, ed. M. R. Cathala; 2d ed. (Turin, 1926).

from Augustine (*Civ. Dei*, XVIII, 14 and XVIII, 37: ed. Dombart, II, 274 and 312, 20 ff.).

But Mussato and his contemporaries did not need to go to Aristotle for the concept of the poet-theologian. It had been current in Latin literature since Cicero (*Nat. d.*, III, 53). According to Augustine, Varro distinguished three kinds of theology: mythical, natural, and political.

Mythical theology is that which the poets employ (*Civ. Dei*, VI, 5). Lactantius too speaks of the "earliest Greek writers, who are called theologians" (*De ira Dei*, 11, 8). But the doctrine of the poet as theologian was also to be found in some grammarians of late Antiquity, and Isidore adopted it.[10] But what Isidore accepts is copied by all the later encyclopedists (Raban Maur, Papias, Vincent of Beauvais). Derived directly or indirectly from Isidore, it becomes the common property of the entire Middle Ages.

The *poeta theologus*, then, is an old Greek creation which reached the Middle Ages by way of the Romans and the Fathers, and which was eminently adaptable to Christian reinterpretation. But not only the *poeta theologus*, but also the word "theology" itself is borrowed from Paganism. The Greek Fathers employ it for both pagan and Christian divinity; Tertullian and Augustine, however, almost exclusively for the latter. Thus, when Mussato calls poetry theology, he is in the line of established medieval tradition. It is the same, as we have seen, when poetry and philosophy are equated.

But Mussato's concept contains other elements which are also medieval in origin—especially the establishing of parallels between biblical history and Greek mythology. Judaeo-Christian apologetics and, later, the Alexandrian catechumenical schools taught that the Old Testament was earlier than the writings of the Greek poets and sages; that the latter had known the Old Testament and had learned from it. This led to the establishment of parallels between the teachings of the Bible and pagan myths. Thus, for example, Josephus had compared the fallen angels with the giants of Greek mythology, and this was taken over by Tertullian (*Apol.*, 22) and Lactantius (*Div. inst.*, X, 14).[11] This harmonizing of Judaeo-Christian revelation with Greek thought reaches its peak in the theology of Clement of Alexandria. Clement finds references to the Flood in Plato (*Strom.*, V, 9, 5), and teachings concerning God in Empedocles and Solon (*ibid.*, V, 81 1 f.). He points out (*ibid.*, V, 28, 1 ff.), "that the Greeks not only took their learning from the barbarians, but they also, in the fabulous tales of their legendary history, imitated the marvelous deeds which among us and for our salvation have been accomplished since ancient times by men of holy life supported by the power of God." This harmonistics was rejected *in toto* by later Latin theology. But the memory of it never quite died. If the theologians did not cultivate it,

---

[10] Grammarians: Marius Plotius Sacerdos (3rd cent.) in Keil, VI, 502, 15 ff.—Isidore, *Et.*, VIII, 7, 9.

[11] P. Heinisch, *Der Einfluss Philos auf die älteste christliche Exegese* (1908), 171.

the poets did. Alcimus Avitus (d. 518) in his biblical epic parallels the giants of the Bible with the Greek giants (IV, 1–132). In Aldhelm we find Hercules equated with Samson. The *ecloga Theoduli* is built up on correspondences between biblical stories and Greek myths. Thus, for example, Deucalion's flood and Noah's flood are paralleled, as are the Gigantomachia and the Tower of Babel (also by Mussato, see above, p. 215). Eupolemius (middle of the eleventh century), in his *Messiad*, follows in Theodulus' footsteps. The wooing of Europa by Jupiter as a bull goes back to the golden calf of the idolatrous Jews (I, 502); Hercules is an imitation of Samson (II, 282), as Achilles is of David (II, 409); the Gigantomachia is similarly interpreted (I, 671); Noah's flood and Deucalion's flood are paralleled (II, 65); and there is much more of the like.

Are there any examples of theologico-poetic composition in Mussato's own work? No. His poems comprise eighteen epistles, three elegies (one of them a cento from Ovid's *Tristia*), and eight poems on ecclesiastical subjects (*Soliloquia*). The most interesting and lively are the epistles. Almost without exception they are poetical letters to friends and for the most part treat of autobiographical material and contemporary political events. Another leading theme is the nature and value of poetry; it is usually introduced in connection with Mussato's personal relations, often when he is defending himself from attacks. The often-quoted lines from Epistle 7, for example, are addressed to a critic who had censured two priapic poems of Mussato's. So it was not only "monkish zealots" who provoked Mussato to defend poetry; and it makes a strange impression when a priapic poet defends poetry as theology.[12] Other epistles treat of natural curiosities: a fish with a head shaped like a sword; a bitch with six toes on each paw; the question whether lionesses can bear young in captivity; a comet. Anyone who is looking for a "universal poet-theologian" will be disappointed in Mussato. Indeed, he would have to go to France and to the twelfth century to find a poet properly entitled to any such designation: Bernard Silvestris or Alan of Lille. To be sure, that would be to leave the confines of Italian Humanism.

If Mussato is to be considered a "pre-Humanist" or a "Humanist," it must be on the basis of his historical works, for which he went to school to Livy, or of his *Ecerinis*—an attempt to renew Senecan tragedy which, however, had little influence. But his theory of poetry and his controversy with Fra Giovannino have little to do with the Humanism of the trecento. As a poet and as a theorist of poetry, Mussato follows paths which the Latin poetry of the North had long since opened. In the controversy, he represents tradition—or, if anyone prefers, reaction. The Dominican, on the other hand, represents the thinking which at that time was modern: Aquinas's theory of knowledge and of art. Behind this opposition, to be sure, there

---

12 The two Priapeia were suppressed by the editors of the edition of 1636 "in gratiam aurium honestarum." They were not printed until toward the end of the nineteenth century.

lies the eternal quarrel between the philosopher and the poet. Thomism made the quarrel flare up anew. Medieval Aristotelianism, which was un-acquainted with the *Poetics*, could find Aristotle's theory of poetry only in the *Metaphysics*; hence it could only regard poetry as a human invention and—compared with philosophy—as an *infima scientia*. Thus it necessarily came into conflict with "theological poetics." Giovannino of Mantua's pro-test against Mussato has an interesting contemporary parallel in a judgment pronounced by the Dominican Guido Vernani of Rimini (taught at Bo-logna between 1310 and 1320; died an old man after 1344). Among other things, he wrote a *Tractatus de reprobatione Monarchie composite a Dan-te*.[13] In the preface Dante is described as a poetizing visionary and verbose sophist, whose delusive pictures lead the reader away from the truths of salvation ("conducit fraudulenter ad interitum salutiferae veritatis").

3. Dante's Self-Exegesis

Servius' commentary on the *Aeneid* begins by saying that in interpreting an author the following points are to be considered: 1. author's life; 2. title of the work; 3. poetic genre; 4. author's intention; 5. number of books; 6. order of the books; 7. explanation. Donatus[14] has the same schema with inessential modifications (between "title" and "intention" he inserts "cause"). Boethius inquires into 1. intention, 2. profitableness, and 3. ar-rangement of the work; 4. is it genuine? 5. title? 6. to what division of philosophy does it belong? Later we sometimes find the author himself answering these questions and prefixing the answers to his work as an in-troduction. An example is Warnerius of Basel (eleventh century) in his *Paraclitus*, a didactic poem on theology. He explains his title and sets forth that the "efficient cause" (*causa efficiens*) of his work is himself, its "final cause" (*causa finalis*) the instruction of penitents, and its "matter" consola-tion for the repentant. Of particular interest to us, however, is his distinc-tion between "forma tractatus" and "forma tractandi." By form of the "treatise" he means literary form, in this case Leonine verse; the form of

---

[13] It appeared *ca.* 1329. New edition by Thomas Käppeli in *Quellen und For-schungen aus italienischen Archiven*, XXVIII (Rome, 1937–38). The passage quoted above occurs on p. 123.

[14] *Vitae Vergilii*, ed. Brummer, p. 11, 149 ff.—The schema is of Greek origin. Boethius, in his *In Isagogen Porphyrii commenta* (ed. Schepss, IV, 14), calls it "didascalia" and later "accessus" (Traube, II, 165; Manitius, III, 196, 314, 316). —Conrad of Hirsau adds something new: "In libris explanandis VII antiqui re-quirebant: auctorem, titulum operis, carminis qualitatem, scribentis intentionem, ordinem, numerum librorum, explanationem; sed moderni IV requirenda censue-runt: operis materiam, scribentis intentionem, finalem causam et cui parti philoso-phiae subponatur quod scribitur" (*Dialogus super auctores*, ed. Schepss, 27 f.).— Further examples: Albert of Stade, *Troilus*, ed. Merzdorf, p. 3.—Paul Meyer in *Romania*, VIII (1879), 327.—Rabe, *Prolegomenon sylloge* (Leipzig, 1931), vi-vii. —A new treatment of the subject: Edwin A. Quain, "The Medieval *accessus ad auctores*" in the journal *Traditio* (New York), II (1944), 319–407.

"treatment" he designates as "persuasion" (*persuasiva*). *Tractare* is a technical term in medieval philosophy and means "to treat philosophically." We find the word at the beginning of the *Divine Comedy*: "ma per trattar del ben ch' io vi trovai . . ." (*Inf.*, I, 8). The final result of "philosophical treatment" is the "treatise" (*tractatus*). This, for example, is what Dante calls his *Monarchia*.

Dante makes uses of this old tradition of the schools in his letter to Can Grande (written *ca.* 1319). It is a letter of dedication to accompany a present of the *Paradiso*. Here Dante speaks at the end of his life, after the completion of his greatest work, in full possession of his learning and his powers. He gives an introduction to the *Commedia*. The letter is a self-exegesis. It has not hitherto been properly valued because it has not been understood.

The letter comprises ninety paragraphs and fills eleven printed pages.[15] I cite only a few of the chief points. "At the beginning of every work of instruction (*doctrinale opus*) six things are to be asked, namely, subject, author, form, purpose, title, and philosophical genus" (§ 18). "The form is twofold: form of the treatise (*tractatus*) and form of treatment (*tractandi*) . . . The form or manner of treatment consists in poetry, fiction, description, digression, metaphor, but at the same time also in definition, division, proof, refutation, and the citing of examples" (§ 27). In the original: "Forma sive modus tractandi est poeticus, fictivus, descriptivus, digressivus, transumptivus, et cum hoc diffinitivus, divisivus, probativus, improbativus, et exemplorum positivus."

The modern reader—and Dante scholarship—does not know what to make of this exposition—"this curious list," as the admirable English Dante scholar Edward Moore put it (*Studies in Dante*, III, 288). Let us try to get to the bottom of the matter. The first thing we notice is that the *forma tractandi*, which we know from Warnerius, is replaced by *modus tractandi*. Ten such *modi* are named. They consist of two series of five, which are connected and set apart by an "et cum hoc" ("and at the same time"). Obviously they correspond to two different aspects or intentions of the *Commedia*. Both are important to Dante. Whence comes the concept *modus*? From Scholasticism.

The theological summas of the thirteenth century commonly begin by discussing the question whether theology is a science or not. Are the truths of faith in Holy Scripture set forth in accordance with the rules of art, that is, scientifically? Alexander of Hales (*S. th.*, I, 1. Quaracchi edition [1924], p. 7) asks: "An modus sacrae Scripturae sit artificialis vel scientialis?" *Ars* and *scientia* are not, as might be supposed, contraries, but extremely closely related concepts.[16] An *ars* is knowledge reduced to rule. Now, the objection

---

[15] Letter 13 in *Opere di Dante. Testo critico della Società dantesca italiana* (1921). The division into paragraphs first appears in this edition and facilitates reference. It should not, however, be overlooked that the earlier editions have only the division into 33 chapters. But 33 is a symbolic number (see Excursus XV, *infra*).

[16] Hugh of St. Victor, *PL*, CLXXVI, 751 B.

is raised: The *modus* of Holy Scripture is neither in accordance with the rules of art nor scientific, for: "omnis modus poeticus est inartificialis sive non scientialis, quia est modus historicus vel transumptus, qui quidem non competunt arti." "No poetic mode of representation is in accordance with the rules of art or scientific, because poetry is a historical mode of representation or a figurative one; neither pertains to science." Alexander answers: Certainly, the mode of representation of Holy Scripture is not scientific according to the power of conception of the human reason, but was brought into being by the command of divine wisdom, to give the soul instruction in the truths of salvation. Divine wisdom stands beyond human wisdom, and likewise above the alternative poetry or science, upon which the objection was based. In refutation Alexander sets forth the following: Certainly the Bible makes use, and indeed most skillful use, of poetical methods of representation. This is so, because our minds fail in the comprehension of divine things ("in comprehensione divinorum"), and because the dignity of truth demands that it be concealed from the wicked. But if the objector goes on to say that the *modus* of science is *definitivus, divisivus, collectivus* [17] (which is lacking in the Bible), then a distinction must be drawn between the systematics of human science and the knowledge imparted by grace. The *modus* of human science must indeed be *definitivus, divisivus, collectivus;* but that of divine wisdom is *praeceptivus, exemplificativus, exhortativus, relativus, orativus.* Thus, in Alexander of Hales, we find a large number of *modi tractandi,* among them five of the ten which make up Dante's "curious list": *poeticus, transumptus* (Dante: *transumptivus*), *definitivus, divisivus, exemplificativus* (Dante: *exemplorum positivus*). We have managed to pick up the right trail.

In Albert the Great's *Summa theologiae* (I, q. 5, *membrum* 1; Lyons ed. [1651], vol. XVII, p. 13 a) the scientific method is defined (as we found it defined in Alexander) as "modus definitivus et divisivus et collectivus"; the Bible, on the other hand, teaches by stories (*historice*), parables (*parabolice*), metaphors (*metaphorice*).[18] Albert too has to take precautions lest the Bible be classified as belonging to the *modus poeticus.* A traditional objection was that the poetic *modus* was the weakest among the philosophical *modi;* its origin was in miraculous fables, as Aristotle had said. Answer: A distinction must be made between a poetry based upon human fictions and a poetry of which divine wisdom makes use to impart absolute truth and certainty. Nevertheless they have something in common formally: the use of symbols and metaphors. This Thomas too had recognized in his commentary on the *Sententiae.* Later, in his *Summa theologiae* (I, 1, 9 ad 1), he introduces a distinction: "The poet employs figurative modes of expression for the sake of visible representation ("utitur metaphoris propter representationem"). But Holy Scripture employs images and parables because

---

[17] I.e., the scientific method employs definitions, it divides problems, and afterwards brings the results together.

[18] This is the *modus transumptus* or *transumptivus.*

it is needful and profitable." Every article of the *Summa* begins, as we know, with arguments against the expected answer (*objectiones*, objections), which are intended to lead up to the problem. In the "objection" to I, 1, 9 poetry is said to be the lowest of all sciences ("infima inter omnes doctrinas").[19] We have already met this objection in Albert ("poeticus modus infirmior est inter modos philosophiae"). It is the common property of Scholasticism. Thomas has no cause to examine it. Scholasticism is not interested in evaluating poetry. It produced no poetics and no theory of art. Hence the attempt to extract an aesthetics of literature and the fine arts from it is senseless and profitless, no matter how often it may be made by historians of art and literature.[20] Scholasticism had come out of twelfth-century dialectics. It maintains the latter's opposition to the *auctores*, rhetoric, and poetry. It eliminates the philosophical justification of poetry from Aristotelianism. Hence it necessarily arrived at the opposite pole from the poetics and the poetry of a Mussato as well as of a Dante. This is a historical phenomenon which has not hitherto been apprehended. Why not? Because literary history takes its task too lightly, and, shirking its duty to knowledge, remains *infima inter omnes doctrinas*. Students of Scholasticism, on the other hand, too often give only a hasty glance at problems in philology and literary history. Too often they also succumb to the temptation to assert a providential harmony between Dante and Thomas.[20a]

As the result of our investigation, we first note: Dante's table of *modi* is close to the pattern of Alexander of Hales and Albert. Thomas offered nothing corresponding. Dante has six *modi* which are not in Alexander: *fictivus, descriptivus, digressivus, probativus, improbativus, exemplorum positivus.* Where could he have found them? One thinks, of course, of Gentile da Cingoli, who taught philosophy as a member of the arts faculty of the university of Bologna at the end of the thirteenth century. And in fact we find in him the following: "Forma tractandi est quintuplex secundum aliquos: diffinitivus"—this is the correct reading—"divisivus, probans, improbans, et exemplorum positivus." [21] Here, then, we find three of the six *modi* which were still missing. But we must not limit our search to Scholasticism. The expressions *fictivus, descriptivus,* and

[19] The disparagement of poetry is foreshadowed in Hugh of St. Victor (see Excursus XI, *infra*).

[20] When Scholasticism speaks of beauty, the word is used to indicate an attribute of God. The metaphysics of beauty (e.g., in Plotinus) and theories of art have nothing whatever to do with each other. "Modern" man immeasurably overvalues art because he has lost the sense of intelligible beauty that Neo-Platonism and the Middle Ages possessed. "Sero te amavi, pulchritudo tam antiqua et tam nova, sero te amavi," says Augustine to God (*Conf.*, X, 27, 38). Here a beauty is meant of which aesthetics knows nothing.

[20a] Thomas Aquinas' distrust of poetry and metaphorics has now been admirably explained by Father M.-D. Chenu, *Introduction à l'étude de Saint Thomas d'Aquin* (Montreal and Paris, 1950), 93 f.

[21] M. Grabmann, *Gentile da Cingoli, SB München* (1940). The quotation *ibid.*, p. 62.

digressivus belong to rhetoric. Did Italian rhetoric about 1300 know rhetorical *modi?* Let us remember Giovanni del Virgilio: "rhetoricisque modis." Now the meaning of this expression becomes clear to us. But we have yet another witness, who has hitherto been disregarded. Cardinal Iacopo Gaetani Stefaneschi has left us an *Opus metricum* (written after 1297, final version 1319). In his preface the author proudly enumerates the following *modi*, which he has employed: "narrativus, historicus, descriptivus, demonstrativus, exclamativus, prolocutivus, suasivus, dissuasivus . . . totusque rhetoricus." [22] This indulging in the greatest possible number of *modi* is, then, characteristic of the rhetoric of the period. Scholasticism and rhetoric meet in respect to a single topic: that of the *modi tractandi*.

Dante's creative production is governed by a symmetrical tectonics. This is evidenced in his table of *modi* too. From the wealth of available *modi* he makes a carefully considered choice. It comprises ten items: a perfect number.[23] It falls into two series of five. The first, as we now see, characterizes the poetico-rhetorical aspect of the work, the second its philosophical aspect. The formula "et cum hoc" connects them programmatically. It states: "My work affords poetry, but at the same time philosophy too." With this Dante claims for his poetry the cognitional function which Scholasticism denied to poetry in general. Dante's table of *modi* contains his autonomous and sovereign stand in the dispute to which Mussato's polemic is the prelude.

4. *Petrarch and Boccaccio*

Homer is at once the ancestor and the apogee of Greek poetry. This conjunction portends both good fortune and limitation. Homer overshadows everything—one of the reasons for the opposition to him, in which not only philosophers like Heraclitus and Plato but also poets like Hesiod, Pindar, Euripides, and Callimachus are at one. This conjunction recurred only once: In Italy. Dante stands at the beginning and remains alone. Italian literature begins with him, certainly. But it would also not be wrong to say: It begins after him. He is impossible to fit into it. Naturally, the attempt was nevertheless made. It was made by "Vernacular Humanism" ("umanesimo volgare," Toffanin). This transferred to Italian literary practice the basic principle of Latin Humanism: imitation of great models (*imitatio*). Pietro Bembo put the three great Tuscans, Dante, Petrarch, and Boccaccio, together in a canonical triad (*Prose della volgar lingua* [1525]). They were meant to fulfill for Italian literature the function which Virgil had exercised for Latin poetry and Cicero for Latin prose. What came out of this theory? Petrarchism, which was soon to flood Italy and France with "sugared sonnets." Petrarch was imitable. But Dante was admitted as one of the three

[22] F. X. Seppelt, *Monumenta Coelestiniana* (1921), p. 5, 15 ff.
[23] According to Pythagoras, because $1 + 2 + 3 + 4 = 10$. Man has ten fingers, the catechism ten commandments, etc.

canonized authors only with reservations. Faults against taste were found
in him, his poetic style had not known the file. Like Homer, Dante brought
his country the greatest glory; but he dwells apart like a star. For us he
stands beside Virgil and Shakespeare, not beside Petrarch and Boccaccio.
They are both interesting, but Dante is great.

Dante had found a solution for the quarrel between poetry and philosophy which was exercising men's minds about 1300, but it was not trans-
ferable. After Dante, the old arguments were brought out again. Petrarch
knew the Church Fathers, and hence also Biblical poetics; but he knew
about poetic theology too. To his brother, the Carthusian Gherardo, he
writes (*Le Familiari*, X, 4): "Poetry is in no sense opposed to theology.
I might almost say that theology is a poetry which proceeds from God.
When Christ is called now a 'lion,' now a 'lamb,' and now a 'worm,' [24]—
what is that if not poetic? . . . What are the Saviour's parables but
allegories? . . . But the subject matter is different! Who denies it? The
Bible treats of God and divine things, poetry of gods and men, wherefore we read in Aristotle that the poets were the first to practice theology . . ." Petrarch cites the authority of Varro, Suetonius, and Isidore;
of Moses, Job, David, Solomon, and Jeremiah, who all wrote in hexameters.
Further witnesses are Ambrose, Jerome, Augustine, and the Christian writers dear to the schools, Prudentius, Prosper, Sedulius . . . The letter
ends with an allegorical interpretation of Petrarch's first eclogue. Petrarch
here repeats Mussato's doctrine.

Theological poetics reappears in Boccaccio. The key sentence of his prolix
remarks runs: "Dunque bene appare, non solamente la poesia essere teologia, ma ancora la teologia essere poesia." [25]

Petrarch and Boccaccio, then, follow the same line as Mussato. Coluccic
Salutati (d. 1406) will do likewise after them. But circumstances have
changed.[26] Thomas of Aquino was a doctrinal authority only for the Dominicans. The Franciscans adhere partly to Duns Scotus, partly to Ockham.
Thomas's work is not carried further in the fourteenth century. Petrarch
has no contact with Scholasticism, he adheres to Cicero and Augustine.
The attack on poetry in quattrocento Italy does not proceed from philosophers but from monkish rigorists. They stand on the line that leads from
Peter Damian to Savonarola. It was precisely against this trend that "poetical theology" could be brought into the field. For poetry had to receive
Christian legitimation. Did not Petrarch and Boccaccio, in their Latin

[24] Lion: Apoc. 5:5; lamb: John 1:29; worm: Ps. 21:7, etc. The enumeration
and interpretation of the *nomina Christi* forms a *locus theologicus*, which is already
treated by Isidore (*Et.*, VII, 2) and which through Luis de León (*De los nombres
de Cristo* [1583]) entered general literature. See my paper on *nomina Christi* in
Mélanges Joseph de Ghellinck (Gembloux, 1951), 1029 f.

[25] Giovanni Boccaccio, *Il Commento alla Divina Commedia e gli altri scritti
intorno a Dante*, ed. D. Guerri, I (1918), p. 43 = *La Vita di Dante*, c. 22. Somewhat altered in the shorter version, *ibid.*, pp. 87 ff.

[26] On this cf. E. Gilson, *La philosophie au moyen âge* [2] (1944), 710 ff.

eclogues, continue the medieval allegorical bucolic too? Tasso still follows Boccaccio's teaching.[27]

Even today Thomism finds itself embarrassed when it undertakes to make a place for poetry in its system. Jacques Maritain, the author of *Art et scolastique,* once criticized the concept of "pure art." Pure art, desiring to exist by itself, loses all relation to mankind and to things. But thereby art destroys itself: "L'art se détruit, car c'est de l'homme, en qui il subsiste, et des choses, dont il se nourrit, que dépend son existence . . . Rappelez-lui que 'la Poésie est ontologie.' " The last phrase is a quotation from Maurras: "Poésie est Théologie, affirme Boccace . . . Ontologie serait peut-être le vrai nom, car la Poésie porte surtout vers les racines de la connaissance de l'Être." [28] Maurras—Maritain—Boccaccio: to find them assembled together under the sign of St. Thomas is a spectacle not without attractions. But how piquant if one considers that the banner of theological poetics was fetched from the arsenal of the Middle Ages by the Italian trecento to rally the defence against Thomist intellectualism—only to be raised once again by the Neo-Thomism of the twentieth century!

[27] *Discorsi del Poema eroico* (Torquato Tasso, *Prose,* ed. Flora [1935], 355).
[28] Jacques Maritain, *Frontières de la poésie* (1935), 12 f.

13

The Muses

THE STARTING POINT of our inquiry was the historical fact that the Mediterranean-Nordic West was culturally one. Our goal was to demonstrate the same unity in its literature. We had, therefore, to make manifest certain continuities which had hitherto been overlooked. A technique of philological microscopy permitted us to find identical structural elements in texts of the most various origins—elements which we were justified in regarding as expressional constants of European literature. They indicated a general and generally disseminated theory and practice of literary expression. One of these common denominators was rhetoric. We found that poetry frequently entered into combination with rhetoric, as it also did with philosophy and theology. All these complexes had to be examined and clarified. An intricate skein had carefully to be disentangled. In each chapter a different aspect of the same historical material was investigated. In each, as it were, a new net was cast. Our hauls of fish brought to light many individual historical facts—a welcome subsidiary result. But our principal object was to obtain a more accurate knowledge of the structure of our literary material by the use of precision methods which were sound both empirically and systematically. From the most general concepts we descended, by the road of analysis, to particular concepts: from rhetoric to topics, from topics to the topics of eulogy, and so on. The further one proceeds along this line, the more one may hope to approach the historical concrete. One finds it in the "fruitful bathos of experience" . . .

Among the "concrete" formal constants of the literary tradition are the Muses. In the view of Antiquity, they belonged not only to poetry but to all higher forms of intellectual life besides. To live with the Muses means to live humanistically, as Cicero puts it ("cum Musis, id est, cum humanitate et doctrina": *Tusc.*, V, 23, 66). For us the Muses are shadowy figures of a tradition that has long since had its day. But once they were vital forces. They had their priests, their servants, their promise—and their enemies.

Every page in the history of European literature speaks of them.[1]

The history of religion considers the Muses to be deities of springs and connected with the cult of Zeus. In the Pierian sanctuary of the Muses, it is conjectured, there was cultivated a poetry dedicated to the victory of Zeus over the gods of the primal world. This would account for the connection of the Muses with poetry.[2] Homer, to be sure, gives us no hint of such an origin. His Muses are Olympians. Their function in epic is to infuse into the poet the things he is to say. At the beginning of the *Iliad* Homer asks the goddess to sing the wrath of Achilles; at the beginning of the *Odyssey* he asks the Muse to tell him of the man who . . . A more elaborate development of the invocation to the Muses is found in the *Iliad* at the beginning of the Catalogue of the Ships (II, 484 ff.). Here Homer needs the Muses not only because they bestow inspiration but also because they know all things. For our purposes it is immaterial whether the Catalogue of the Ships is an interpolation by a Homerid or not. We should read Homer only as he was read for two thousand years. The Catalogue of the Ships is the model for innumerable poetical catalogues even down to our own period. The originator of didactic poetry, Hesiod, also feels bound to the Muses. In him and in Pindar the invocation of the Muses must serve to prove the poet's pedagogical vocation.

Unlike the Olympians, the Muses had no well-marked personalities. No one knew much about them. They incarnate a purely intellectual principle, which could be dissociated from the Greco-Roman pantheon. The only figure in Homer's world of gods with whom they were regularly associated was Apollo. Their image was vague even in ancient Greece. From the earliest times there were conflicting traditions as to their number, lineage,

[1] I published a survey of the Muses from the Augustan Age to *ca.* 1100 in ZRPh, LIX (1939), 129–88. Some 25 pagan and 70 Christian authors were treated in it. I added to it in ZRPh, LXIII (1943), 256–268. The text of the present chapter is based on these two studies, but uses only a part of them. Those who may wish to familiarize themselves with the evidence or to obtain further details on the subject of the Muses in the Middle Ages are referred to these two essays. For philological readers I add the following: In Walter of Speyer's *Scolasticus* (*Poetae*, V, 19, 81) Apollo appears, then "Pales Hinnidum plebe secuta," which the editor, Karl Strecker, found incomprehensible. I conjectured (ZRPh, LVIII [1938], 139 n.) that the reading should be Hymnidum = "Muses." Later I came upon an essay by H. Chamard, "Une Divinité de la Renaissance: les Hymnides" (*Mélanges Laumonier* [1935], 163). According to this, the Hymnids are a class of nymphs who are frequently mentioned together with Dryads and Oreads in French texts of the first half of the sixteenth century. They come from Boccaccio's *De genealogia deorum*, where, in Bk. VII, c. 14, he treats "De nymphis in generali." There he says: "Aliae Hymnides appellantur, ut placet Theodontio, quas dixit pratorum atque florum Nymphas existere." Who Boccaccio's "Theodontius" is, no one knows. Cf. Jean Seznec, *The Survival of the Pagan Gods* (Bollingen Series XXXVIII; New York, 1953), pp. 221f. Boccaccio's Hymnids, then, were already known to Walter of Speyer. But even in Antiquity the Muses were occasionally equated with nymphs (Virgil, *Ecl.*, 7, 21). And later in Isidore, *Et.*, VIII, 9, 96. The Hymnids appear neither in Roscher's *Lexikon der Mythologie* nor in *RE* under *Nymphai*.

[2] Otto Kern, *Die Religion der Griechen*, I (1926), 208.

dwelling-place, and function. Hesiod's Muses are different from Homer's, those of Empedocles from those of Theocritus. But from of old the Muses had been patronesses not only of poetry but also of philosphy and music. The schools of both Pythagoras and Plato were connected with the cult of the Muses from their beginnings. But the consensus also placed all higher intellectual pursuits under the sign of the Muses. We have already seen this concept in Cicero. He is a cultured writer who feels at ease in the possession of his culture. Virgil's profound, soulful, and passionate love of the Muses is a very different thing. He has expressed it in but one passage in his works, in his poem on husbandry (*Georgics*, II, 475 ff.). He has praised the happy life of the countryman, and now he contrasts with it his own aim in life:

> *Me vero primum dulces ante omnia Musae,*
> *Quarum sacra fero ingenti percussus amore,*
> *Accipiant, caelique vias et sidera monstrent,*
> *Defectus solis varios, lunaeque labores,*
> *Unde tremor terris, qua vi maria alta tumescant*
> *Obicibus ruptis, rursusque in se ipsa residant,*
> *Quid tantum Oceano properent se tinguere soles*
> *Hiberni, vel quae tardis mora noctibus obstet.*
> *Sin, has ne possim naturae accedere partis,*
> *Frigidus obstiterit circum praecordia sanguis,*
> *Rura mihi et rigui placeant in vallibus amnes;*
> *Flumina amen silvasque inglorius . . .*
> *Felix qui potuit rerum cognoscere causas,*
> *Atque metus omnis et inexorabile fatum*
> *Subjecit pedibus strepitumque Acherontis avari!*

(Me indeed first and before all things may the sweet Muses, whose priest I am and whose great love hath smitten me, take to themselves and show me the pathways of the sky, the stars, and the diverse eclipses of the sun and the moon's travails; whence is the earthquake; by what force the seas swell high over their burst barriers and sink back into themselves again; why winter suns so hasten to dip in Ocean, or what hindrance keeps back the lingering nights. But if I may not so attain to this side of nature for the clog of chilly blood about my heart,[3] may the country and the streams that water the valleys content me, and lost to fame let me love stream and woodland . . . Happy he who hath availed to know the causes of things, and hath laid all fears and immitigable Fate and the roar of hungry Acheron under his feet!)*

It is not the gifts of poetry that Virgil begs from the Muses, but knowledge of cosmic laws. He moves in a circle of ideas in which some scholars have

---

[3] According to Empedocles the seat of the intellectual faculty is the blood. Virgil, then, is using a dignified periphrasis for "poor intellectual capacity."
[* J. W. Mackail's translation (replacing R. A. Schröder's).]

wished to see the eclectic stoicism of Posidonius. The Muses are here the patronesses of philosophy. They bestow the knowledge which conquers the fear of death and the underworld. In the *Aeneid* Virgil again brings in a poet who recites a didactic poem on natural philosophy (I, 740).

In the concluding lines of the *Georgics* (IV, 559–566) the poet turns to contemplate Augustus, contrasts his military exploits with the life of the poet, signs the work with his own name, and connects it with the bucolic poetry of his youth by quoting from himself:

> *Haec super arvorum cultu pecorumque canebam*
> *Et super arboribus, Caesar dum magnus al altum*
> *Fulminat Euphraten bello, victorque volentis*
> *Per populos dat iura, viamque adfectat Olympo.*
> *Illo Virgilium me tempore dulcis alebat*
> *Parthenope, studiis florentem ignobilis oti,*
> *Carmina qui lusi pastorum, audaxque iuventa,*
> *Tityre, te patulae cecini sub tegmine fagi.*

(Thus I sang of the tending of fields and flocks and trees, while great Caesar hurled war's lightnings by high Euphrates and gave statutes among the nations in welcome supremacy, and scaled the path to heaven. Even in that season I Virgil, nurtured in sweet Parthenope, went in the flowery way of lowly Quiet: I who once played with shepherds' songs, and in youth's hardihood sang thee, O Tityrus, under the covert of spreading beech.) *

Some introductory verses to the *Aeneid* have come down to us (their authenticity is doubted—rightly, it would seem):

> *Ille ego qui quondam gracili modulatus avena*
> *Carmen, et egressus silvis vicina coegi,*
> *Ut quamvis avido parerent arva colono,*
> *Gratum opus agricolis: at nunc horrentia Martis . . .*

(I who once piped a song on a slender reed; who, quitting the woods, then caused the nearby fields to obey the ever greedy tiller of the soil—a work pleasing to farmers; I now sing the dread weapons of Mars.)

Here Virgil's epic is linked with his bucolic and didactic poetry. This biographical sequence of Virgil's works was regarded by the Middle Ages as a hierarchy grounded in the nature of things—a hierarchy not only of three poetical genres, but also of three social ranks (shepherd, farmer, soldier) and of three kinds of style. It extended to the corresponding trees (beech—fruit-tree—laurel and cedar), locales (pasture—field—castle or town), implements (crook—plow—sword), animals (sheep—cow—horse). These

[* *Idem.*]

correspondences were reduced to a graphic schema of concentric circles, known as *rota Virgilii* (Virgil's wheel).[4] In Renaissance England bucolic is still regarded as preparatory to epic (Spenser, Milton).

The Muses could not be fitted into this schema. Pastoral poetry, however (in honor of Theocritus), kept its connection with the Sicilian Muses. In Virgil, as we have seen, the Muses of didactic poetry are the patronesses of science and philosophy. The Muses of epic, on the other hand, are close to the Homeric Muses. They impart the mythological prehistory of Aeneas' sufferings (I, 8), give information concerning ancient Latium (VII, 37) and are invoked in connection with the catalogues of troops [5] (VII, 641; X, 163). Through the *Aeneid*, the Muses were once again confirmed as stylistic elements of the Western epic. The epic invocation of the Muses, which could be repeated before particularly important or particularly "difficult" passages,[6] serves in Virgil and his followers to decorate the narrative and to emphasize its high points.

Horace devoted to the Muses a poem (*Carm.*, III, 4) by which he sought to further the ethico-religious restoration desired by Augustus. It is not among his happiest productions. More convincing is the high-pitched eloquence with which he celebrates his lyrical activity as a service of the Muses which makes him fellow of the gods (*Carm.*, I, 1, 30):

> *Me doctarum hederae praemia frontium*
> *Dis miscent superis, me gelidum nemus*
> *Nympharumque leves cum satyris chori*
> *Secernunt populo, si neque tibias*
> *Euterpe cohibet, nec Polyhymnia*
> *Lesboum refugit tendere barbiton.*

(Me the ivy, prize of learned brows, makes to mingle with the gods above; me the cool grove and the light-footed companies of nymphs and satyrs set apart from the people: if Euterpe withhold not her flute and Polyhymnia refuse not to tune the Lesbian lyre.)

Declining esteem for the invocation of the Muses is evidenced in Horace in the form of parody (*Sat.*, I, 5, 51); instead of the Muse, Tibullus invokes his friend (II, 1, 35), Propertius his beloved (II, 1, 3). Ovid treats the Muses ironically (*Ars*, II, 704). His own Muse is called "wanton" by his censors (*Rem.*, 362), "playful" by himself (*Rem.*, 387). This Ovidian *musa iocosa* is often invoked by the hedonistically-minded poets of the twelfth century.

Even during the reigns of Augustus' first successors we find a conscious

---

[4] Faral, 87.

[5] The historian Gibbon (1737–94) could still make a study of the question whether the catalogue of troops is a necessary element of an epic.

[6] Hence the "second" or even multiple *invocatio*. The *locus classicus* for it is Quintilian, IV, *prooemium*, § 4.

turning away from mythology and heroic poetry: typical examples are
Manilius and the poet of the *Aetna*. People had wearied of material which
had been thrashed over countless times. A further cause lay in the moralistic criticism of the heroic epic, developed by the Stoic-Cynic philosophy
and reproduced by Cicero (*De natura deorum*, III, 69 ff.). While the myths
of Hellas paled, the Imperial Age brought a new cult: the apotheosis
of the Caesars. Invocation of the ruler could now replace that of the Muses.
The first example of this innovation is in Virgil (*Georgics*, I, 24 ff.); and
he was followed by Manilius, Ovid, Seneca, and others. Statius clings to
the Muses in epic, but in his occasional poems he takes pains to find substitutes for the invocation of the Muses. He becomes a mannered specialist
in these substitute forms.

Persius (34–62), by rejecting the Muses, influenced later times. He
had cultivated philosophy. His first satire is an attack on the degenerate
poetry and rhetoric of his time from the standpoint of Stoic ethics. Hence,
in the brief prologue to his book, he represents himself as an "outsider" of
poetry who has never drunk at the spring of Hippocrene. He is "half a
layman"—"semipaganus": that is, he has no proper place in the village
festival ("paganalia") of the professional poets or at least he but half shares
in it:

> *Nec fonte labra prolui caballino*
> *Nec in bicipiti somniasse Parnaso*
> *Memini, ut repente sic poeta prodirem.*
> *Heliconidasque pallidamque Pirenen*
> *Illis remitto, quorum imagines lambunt*
> *Hederae sequaces: ipse semipaganus*
> *Ad sacra vatum carmen adfero nostrum.*[7]

How must a medieval clerk have read these lines? He could hardly translate *semipaganus* otherwise than as "only half a pagan." So—he must have
thought to himself—this Persius, this contemporary of Paul and the half-
Christian Seneca, must have abjured his erroneous faith in the pagan gods!
That was why he would have no more converse with the Muses!

In addition to invoking the Muses, antique poetry also invoked Zeus.[8]
Christian poetry was able to establish contact here too: Paradise was equated
with Olympus, God with Jupiter (Dante still writes: "sommo Giove").
Finally late Antiquity developed the poet's apostrophe to his own soul.
The preparatory stages are found in early Greek poetry. The Homeric

[7] "I have never wet my lips at the fountain of the horse [Hippocrene] nor do I
remember that I ever dreamed on two-peaked Parnassus in order that I should
thereby suddenly come forth a poet. The Muses of Helicon and the pale [or pallor-
inducing] fountain of the Muses Pirene [near Corinth], I leave to those whose
statues supple ivy caresses; I myself bring my verses to the sacred festival of the poets
only as an outsider."

[8] Pindar, *Nem.*, 2; Theocritus, XVII, 1; Aratus; Virgil, *Bucolica*, II, 60; Ovid,
Met., X, 148.

Ulysses speaks "with himself in his stout heart" (*Od.*, V, 298). Pindar calls upon his soul.[9] In the first line of the *Metamorphoses*, Ovid tells us that his soul ("animus") urges him to write poetry. Lucan (I, 67) borrowed this formula. In addition to *animus*, we find more emphatic expressions for the poet's creative urge.[10] Prudentius addresses his soul (ed. Bergmann, 54, 82):

> *Solve vocem, mens sonora, solve linguam nobilem*
> *Dic tropaeum passionis.*[11]

Here the poet's soul has entered the *invocatio* as a substitute for the Muse.

It is characteristic of the poetry of the Imperial Age that the Muses lose ground, are devalued or replaced. But the same period sees the accomplishment of a change in thought which takes the Roman world from scepticism to belief in the survival of the soul after death. Franz Cumont has given us an insight into this change, which he was the first to infer from the sarcophagi of the first to fourth centuries.[12] The sculptural decorations of these precious marbles represent scenes from mythology and the heroic age, but understood in accordance with the philosophical principles of Homeric and mythological allegoresis. Pythagorean speculation interpreted the Muses as divinities of the celestial sphere. Their song produced the harmony of the spheres. Thus they were included in the eschatology of late pagan Antiquity and became bestowers of immortality—not for all men but for those who had dedicated themselves to their service as poets, musicians, scholars, or thinkers. Virgil admits not only pious priests and bards into Elysium but also the introducers of higher culture (*Aen.*, VI, 663). The search for knowledge—either profane or religious—is a road to immortality and is connected with the cult of the Muses.[13] It is in this light that we are to understand the Muses of the late Roman sarcophagi. Until recently they were supposed to have been the graves of poets. Cumont refuted this view. He summarizes his conclusions as follows: "The sister goddesses, who govern the harmony of the spheres, awaken in the human heart through music a passionate longing for that divine melody and a nostalgia for heaven. At the same time the daughters of Mnemosyne cause the reason to remember the truths which it had known in a previous life. They impart to it wisdom, a pledge of immortality. By their favor thought mounts toward

9 *Nem.*, 3, 26; *Ol.*, 2, 89; *Pyth.*, 3, 61.

10 Statius: "Pierius calor," "Pierium oestrum" (*Thebais*, I, 3 and 32); Claudian: "mens congesta" (*De raptu Pros.*, I, 4).

11 "Loose thy voice, sonorous mind, loose thy noble tongue, tell the triumph of the Passion."

12 *Recherches sur le symbolisme funéraire des Romains* (Paris, 1942). In the discussion above I follow this great work of the eminent scholar.

13 Among the many examples that Cumont publishes, the following are particularly noteworthy: Themistius, 234 a; Maximum of Tyre, X; Proclus, *Hymn to the Muses* (ed. Ludwich, 143).—The funeral epigram for Vettius Agorius belongs here too (*supra*, p. 210).

the ether, is initiated into the secrets of nature, and comprehends the evo-
lutions of the choir of stars. It is delivered from the cares of this world,
transported to the world of the ideas and of beauty, and purified from
material passions. And after death the divine virgins summon to themselves in the starry spheres the soul which has sanctified itself in their service, and cause it to share in the blessed life of the Immortals." Cumont was
the first to answer the question which Bachofen raised in his *Gräbersym-
bolik* (1859) and which he confused by fantastic theories; he has made it
possible for us to see a new side of the religion of late antique paganism.

The religious significance of the Muses during the decline of paganism
is in all likelihood the fundamental reason for their express rejection by
early Christian poetry. This rejection then becomes a poetic topos itself,
the history of which can be traced from the fourth to the seventeenth century. It is an index of the rise and fall of ethical and dogmatic rigorism. It
is frequently connected with the attempt to find a Christian substitute for
the antique Muses. This opened the way to more or less intelligent innovations. The entire development is important for the history of literature
because it reveals continuities; but it also reflects the religious atmosphere
of the several periods.

The earliest Christian epic poet, Juvencus, turns for assistance to the
Holy Ghost, imploring him to sprinkle him with the water of Jordan—
which thus takes the place of the Muses' spring. Sedulius, in his verse preface to his work, explains it as a Passover meal at which nothing is served
but vegetables in vessels of red clay.[14] Toward the beginning of the poem
(I, 60 ff.) he invokes God. He says nothing about the Muses, but he inveighs against the pagan poets (I, 1 ff.). This appears to be the first seed
of the topos "Contrast between Pagan and Christian Poetry," which we
shall frequently encounter hereafter. Prudentius bids the Muse exchange
her wonted ivy crown for "mystical crowns," for the glory of God (*Cath.*,
3, 26). Paulinus of Nola (d. 431) rejects the Muses (X, 21):

> *Negant Camenis nec patent Apollini*
> *Dicata Christo pectora.*[15]

Instead of the Muses and Apollo, Christ shall be the choregus and inspirer
of his song (XV, 30). The pagan poets have set forth false fictions; this a
servant of Christ cannot do (XX, 32 ff.). In addition to his protest against
the pagan Muses, Paulinus has a christological theory of inspiration and a
concept of Christ as the cosmic musician which suggests Alexandrian speculations upon Christ as Orpheus (see *infra*, p. 244).

The hagiographic epic naturally affords particular occasion for the protest against the Muses. About 470 Bishop Paulinus of Périgueux composes
his metrical paraphrase of Sulpicius Severus' *Life of St. Martin.* In Book

---

[14] This image was a favorite in the Middle Ages, e.g., in Marbod of Rennes (*PL*,
CCXXI, 1548 C). It stems from II Cor. 4:7.
[15] "Hearts dedicated to Christ are closed to the Muses and Apollo."

IV, 245 ff., he introduces an original invocation. It is addressed to his personal Muse, to whom he ascribes the dignity of a priestess, and to his powers of mind. Then follows the rejection of the antique Muses:

> . . . *Vesana loquentes*
> *Dementes rapiant furiosa ad pectora Musas:*
> *Nos Martinus agat. Talis mutatio sensus*
> *Grata mihi est, talem sitiunt mea viscera fontem.*
> *Castalias poscant lymfatica pectora lymfas:*
> *Altera pocla decent homines Jordane* [16] *renatos.* [17]

The Italian Fortunatus also had a particular devotion to St. Martin. He, after all, had been cured of an ophthalmic disease by anointing his eyes with oil from a lamp on the altar of St. Martin in a church at Ravenna. In gratitude he visited the saint's grave at Tours; then remained in France. He too wrote a metrical life of St. Martin. But in his secular poems he has no objection to the Muses. In the preface to his collected poems he describes how, when he was on a laborious journey through the countries along the Danube, Germany, and Gaul, a Muse—albeit more frigid than intoxicated, it would seem—inspired him to sing to the woods as a new Orpheus (ed. Leo, p. 2, 8). In his case secular and Church poetry go side by side. There can be no doubt that his convictions are genuinely Christian. But he has a warm sympathy for antique poetry too. He describes for us (ed. Leo, p. 161 f.) how, in summer, a traveler finds a seat in the shade and then recites to himself: Whether he chooses Virgil and Homer or the Psalmist, each bewitches the birds by his own Muses.

Patristic allegoresis [18] makes the Muses harmless through euhemeristic explanations and reinterprets them as concepts in musical theory (this reappears later in the sequences).

In the seventh century and the Germanic North, we again find a rigoristic rejection of the pagan Muses: in Aldhelm. But it is of a very different caste from Paulinus of Nola's. It is not to Christ that the Anglo-Saxon turns in the prologue to his collection of riddles, but to the almighty Creator who formed behemoth (Job 40:10 ff.). He rejects the "Castalian Nymphs" and Apollo. Like Persius, he "has not dreamed on Parnassus." God will vouchsafe him a song—did He not inspire Moses to "metrical poems"? Aldhelm, then, combines the rejection of the Muses with patristic "Biblical poetics." Balaam's ass (Num. 22:27) is cited as proof that Jehovah can bestow eloquence—a motif which had already appeared in Sedulius (*Car-*

---

[16] Here, then, the Jordan has the same function as in Juvencus.

[17] "Let those madmen who discourse folly clasp the Muses to their raging breasts. Our guide be Martin. Such a frenzy of the mind I welcome, for such a fount my vitals thirst. Let frantic hearts demand Castalian dews; other drink is fit for men reborn in Jordan."

[18] Clement, *Protreptikos*, II, c. 31; Augustine, *De doctrina christiana*, II, c. 17 after Varro.

men paschale, I, 160 ff.) and which became very popular later.[19] It is one of the aberrations of Biblical or Jehovistic poetics.

Linking poetic theory with the Old Testament, one of the results of patristic Biblical exegesis, struck deeper roots in England than in any other country. It exhibits a continuity from which the conclusion may be drawn that England, and even Saxon England, was especially receptive to the poetry of the Old Testament. We shall still find it in Milton. John Bunyan, in his prologue ("The Author's Apology") to *Pilgrim's Progress*, takes his stand on Biblical poetics. It was also influential in English Pre-Romanticism, which was the prelude to the European literary revolution of the eighteenth century. Robert Lowth (1710–87) who held the chair of poetry at Oxford from 1741 to 1751 and died Bishop of London, caused a sensation with his treatise on Hebrew poetry.[20]

One may see an expression of Carolingian Humanism in the fact that it restored the Muses to honor. The Anglo-Saxon Alcuin felt himself out of place in a court life which found heightened expression in a secular poetry of eulogy and friendship. He granted the Muses a place in this realm, but banned them from spiritual poetry. We find the same separation in Angilbert, Theodulf, Raban Maur, and Modoin. Only a strict churchman like Florus of Lyons, known for his orthodox writings and his persecution of heretics, represents rigorism: if poets need mountains for inspiration, let them take Sinai, Carmel, Horeb, Zion. The Humanism of the period was also of advantage to the schools and to school poetry. A teacher in a monastery school like Mico of St. Riquier bids the Muse sing Christian festivals. As her reward she asks a tankard of beer, but of wine at Christmas. The Irishman Sedulius Scottus (in Liége from 848) pays homage to the Muses in a cult of hedonistic enjoyment, delight in life, and praise; he is not afraid to ask a kiss from the lips of the bucolic Muse that he may worthily celebrate a bishop. His Muse is Greek and gives him ambrosia to drink. But he too occasionally borrows something from the Old Testament. He knows a dark-skinned Muse, whom he calls "the Aethiopian woman" after Moses' wife (Num. 12:1), and who provides a charming conclusion to a request for a roast of mutton. Here Anglo-Saxon Biblical poetics is parodied by a Celt.

---

[19] Cf., e.g., Orientius, *Commonitorium* I, 29 ff.—Bede, *Vita Cuthberti metrice*, ed. Jaager, p. 63, 74.—*Poetae*, III, 308, 18; 509, 37.—In *Poetae*, III, 7, 34 ff., there are references not only to Balaam's ass but also to the verse "Dilata os tuum, et implebo illud" (Ps. 80:11) and to Christ who, since he is "verbum" (logos) can also bestow "munera linguae."—Odo of Cluny, *Occupatio*, p. 2, 25 and p. 68, 18.—Bede (*Vita Cuthberti*, 35) prays to the Holy Ghost for "munera verbi."

[20] *De Sacra Poesi Hebraeorum* (Oxford, 1753). According to Lowth the Greek view of poetry as a sacred gift from heaven is a memory of the primitive concept of poetry which was once common to all mankind. The Greeks lost it in practice, the Old Testament has preserved it to us.—The treatise produced such an effect at the time because everyone was looking for primitive poetry. Lowth stimulated Herder. See Goethe, *Dichtung und Wahrheit*, Book 2, ch. 10.—Paul Van Tieghem, *Le Préromantisme*, I (1924), 39.

Of great significance is the appearance of the Muses in the sequence
poetry which is cultivated in southern France and whose centers are St.
Martial in Limoges and Moissac. According to recent research,[21] we must
accept the view that the rise of the sequence is explained by the combined
action of two processes: the penetration of secular music into the services
of the church and the importation of Byzantine hymns into France after
800. Accordingly, it is precisely in the earliest sequence poetry that we find
secular materials too—"extravagances" which the process of development
swept into the discard "as soon as the sequence gained official recognition
and thus passed into the hands of church musicians and church poets."
Now, that the Muses were invoked in the liturgical sequences of the earliest
period is explained by the musical origin of the sequence. The Muses are
here to be regarded as representing the art of music, not the art of poetry;
and this the Fathers had sanctioned. From the sequence arose the new
lyrical poetry of the West (*supra*, p. 150). The Muses, then, stand at its
cradle too. In the Renaissance of the twelfth century, the antique concept
of the Muses lived again in a great variety of forms. We will pass this over
and come to Dante.

Carlyle said of Dante that in him "ten silent centuries found a voice."
And it is true that, in the garb of poetry, the *Commedia* provides a
"summa" of the Middle Ages. But Dante attained to a freedom and
breadth which the Middle Ages did not know. Yet his freedom is not to
be regarded as heralding the Renaissance or the Reformation. Boccaccio
and Petrarch immediately sink back into medieval bondage. Dante's freedom is the unique freedom of his great and lonely soul. It allows him to
pass judgment upon popes and emperors; to reject Augustine's interpretation of history no less than the total claims of Scholasticism; to present
his personal view of history as messianic prophecy. Dante's uniqueness lies
in the fact that he takes such freedom to himself *within* the hierarchical
Christian historical cosmos. It is the last time that the aristocratic-heroic
man who had formed the West [22] is able to do this. The "ten silent centuries" had bridged over the strained relationship between Antiquity and
Christianity partly by a cautious harmonizing, partly by a questionable
syncretism, or else had found an answer to it in rigorism and ascetic denial
of the world. The majority, to be sure, were not even capable of realizing
the acuteness of the dilemma. Dante, the greatest poet of the Christian
world, took the liberty of assigning an Elysian precinct in the other world
to the poets and heroes of Antiquity. He had them accept him into their
circle, had Virgil guide him as far as the earthly paradise. Such a minor

---

[21] I refer especially to the work of Hans Spanke. For a summary, see his
Beziehungen zwischen romainischer und mittelalterlicher Lyrik (Berlin, 1936).
Idem, "Aus der Formengeschichte des mittelalterlichen Liedes" (in the journal
Geistige Arbeit [Sept. 5, 1938]). On the question of priority (southern France or
St. Gall?), cf. *idem in HVjft*, XXVII, 381 *and ZfdA* (1934), 1.

[22] Alfred Weber, *Kulturgeschichte als Kultursoziologie* (Leiden, 1935), 389.

scruple as the question—may the Christian poet mention the Muses?—could not affect him. The *Commedia* is not an epic in the antique sense, yet it took over the epic invocation of the Muses. For Dante as for Virgil they are "our nurses" (*Purg.*, XXII, 105), the "most holy virgins" (*Purg.*, XXIX, 37), the "Castalian Sisters" of his last poetical work (*Ecl.*, I, 54). They nourish poets with their sweet milk (*Par.*, XXIII, 56). They are invoked—in strict accordance with classical practice—at every important turning-point: *Inferno*, II, 7 and XXXII, 10; *Purg.*, I, 8 ("O sante Muse poi che vostro sono") and XXIX, 37–42. Even at the beginning of the *Paradiso* (II, 8) they must impart inspiration, together with Minerva and Apollo; they reappear once more before the description of the Heaven of Jupiter (XVIII, 82). Elsewhere too they are frequently mentioned, especially Calliope, Clio, Polyhymnia, and Urania. A generic designation is (*Par.*, XVIII, 82) "diva Pegasea" (the name also appears in Walter of Châtillon). Dante calls one of his sonnets a "sermo Calliopeus" (Letter 3, § 4). Apollo is invoked alone in *Par.*, I, 13–27; the Greek God must help the Christian poet to describe the realm of the blessed. Dante himself gave a detailed explanation of this *invocatio* in his letter to Can Grande, § 86 ff. There too he discusses the prologue and its varieties (§ 45 ff.), distinguishing between the rhetorical and the poetical *exordium*. Poets need the *invocatio* because they must ask a "divine gift" from the "higher substances." Among these higher powers Dante counts not only Apollo and the Muses but also the constellations (*Par.*, XXII, 121). Dante also knows the address to his own mind (*Inf.*, II, 8). In his prose he chooses Christian forms of the *invocatio*. In the *Monarchia* (I, 1, § 6) he leans upon Augustine's preface to the *Civitas Dei*, at the same time continuing the invocation of God which was so cherished by the Middle Ages. He puts an *invocatio* at the beginning of the *De vulgari eloquentia* too: "Verbo aspirante de coelis." The invocation of Christ as the Word was already current in the early Middle Ages.[23] It was one of the most obvious Christian substitutes for the antique *invocatio*.

Boccaccio already considers it necessary to explain the invocation of the Muses in *Inf.*, II, 7 by lengthy antiquarian considerations.[24] He cites the authority of Isidore, who was a man of such sanctity ("christiano e santissimo uomo e pontefice"), of Macrobius and Fulgentius. The Muses are daughters of Zeus and Mnemosyne, that is, of God the Father and Memory; for God shows the reasonable truths of all things, and his "demonstrations," stored in the memory, bring forth knowledge in men. Boccaccio, then, has relapsed into the venerable practice of interpreting the Muses allegorically for purposes of edification. This tendency is even more obvious

---

[23] Cf. *supra*, p. 237, n. 19.—Further examples: Smaragdus (*Poetae*, I, 619) and Arnulf in his *Delicie cleri* (RF, II, 217).—What Marigo says in his commentary on the passage is misleading.

[24] *Il Commento alla Divina Commedia*, ed. D. Guerri, I (1918), 198 ff.

in four hexameters that he composed as a conclusion to the *Commedia*.[25]
God and the Virgin Mary are invoked: May they grant Paradise to suffering mortals after death. Boccaccio composed his commentary on Dante
during a painful illness, not long before his death. In a letter of the same
period he regrets having written the *Decameron*. Between his conception
of the Muses [26] and Dante's there lies an abyss. From the first, the rejection
of the Muses by Christian poets is scarcely anything but a badge of conventionally correct ecclesiastical thought. The more vehemently it is expressed, the less does it carry conviction. It is very seldom more than an
obligatory topos. But this is perfectly consistent with the general character
of medieval poetry, in so far as it is metrical literary composition. The force
of religious feeling is seldom to be found in it. Didacticism and a liturgically
objectified devotion predominate. It is not until the twelfth and thirteenth
centuries that the tone for the *mysterium fascinosum* is found. The question of the forms and degrees of religious fervor in the Latin poetry of the
Middle Ages still awaits investigation. But even the outworn topos of rejection of the Muses can become alive in the mouth of a true poet. It found
its finest expression in Jorge Manrique's (1440?–1478) stanzas on the death
of his father, the most celebrated poem in Spanish literature:

> *Dexo las invocaciones*
> *De los famosos poetas*
>   *Y oradores;*
> *No curo de sus ficciones,*
> *Que traen yervas secretas*
>   *Sus sabores.*
>
> *Aquel solo me encomiendo,*
> *Aquel solo invoco yo*
>   *De verdad,*
> *Que en este mundo biviendo,*
> *El mundo no conoscio*
>   *Su deidad.*
>
> (I will not here invoke the throng
> Of orators and sons of song,
>   The deathless few;
> Fiction entices and deceives,
> And, sprinkled o'er her fragrant leaves,
>   Lies poisonous dew.

[25] *Opere latine minori*, ed. A. F. Massèra (1928), 99.

[26] In his introduction to the 4th *Giornata* of the *Decameron* Boccaccio defensive-
ly points out that his book of tales is compatible with the service of the Muses. "The
Muses too are women," one of his arguments runs. In the vicious satire of the
Corbaccio the tables are turned: Certainly the Muses are women, "ma non pisciano"
(ed. Bruscoli [1940], 218). Here devotion to the Muses is placed at the service
of medieval misogyny (222 f.). Boccaccio's relation to the Muses is not flawless.
The medieval clerk's resentment has a place in it.

To One alone my thoughts arise,
The Eternal Truth, the Good and Wise,
To Him I cry,
Who shared on earth our common lot,
But the world comprehended not
His deity.) *

That in every century the Muses continued to trouble Christian poets may seem strange. Would it not have been more natural simply to say nothing about the Muses, instead of attacking them or finding ingenious substitutes for them (which after all was a way of recognizing their existence)? Had not Christianity conquered? Certainly it had—but the tradition of Antiquity *had conquered too*. The dominion of the Church was uncontested; with the Inquisition, by the persecution of heretics, it could stamp out all resistance—save one, the "famosos poetas y oradores," to use Jorge Manrique's phrase. The Muses alone could have been successfully dealt with. But they were not alone: since the times of Homer and Virgil they had been indissolubly connected with the epic form. The West was able to get along without the drama for over a thousand years, but before 1800 there is not a single century without epic. The Christian Biblical epic is older than the Christian hymn. It is succeeded by the metrical saint's-life; Virgil, as W. P. Ker and Heusler point out, provides the model for the heroic poetry of the Germanic-Romance Middle Ages. In the twelfth, thirteenth, and fourteenth centuries it flowers anew in Latin; in the sixteenth and seventeenth centuries, in Italy, Portugal, and England, it produces masterpieces of world literature, sanctioned as to theory by the authority of Aristotle, whose *Poetics* had begun to triumph about 1550 as his theoretical and practical philosophy had triumphed since 1200. Even in the eighteenth century, Biblical epic and historical epic produce a belated succession in Klopstock and Voltaire. But already the first waves of the literary revolution are running. Like the industrial revolution, it starts from England about 1750. It breaks the spell of the antique tradition; the "voices of the peoples" can ring out. There is no longer a problem of the Muses . . . To be sure, the Christian tradition too entered upon a crisis at the same time. The philosophical Enlightenment reaches its peak in Rationalism, the social Enlightenment in Rousseauism.

The French and the German epic of the Middle Ages produced important works. But not one of them has remained alive in our cultural heritage. Why not? Not one of them could even distantly approach the perfection and beauty of the *Aeneid*. Dante's *Commedia* first scaled those heights— but in form and content that cosmic poem has no connection with the vernacular heroic epic. Lines of Virgil and lines of Dante are of the living present to all those to whom great poetry means something great. But who —aside from specialists—quotes *Beowulf*, the *Song of Roland*, the

[* Trans. Longfellow.]

Nibelungen, or *Parzival?* This poetry has always to be artificially revived, has always to be re-created in a new medium, to produce an effect upon modern men. For some of this material Richard Wagner accomplished a re-creation in the form of the opera, though it already seems very dated today and, in any case, is more significant musically than textually. But long before that, the "matter of Arthur" and the "matter of Roland" had been given a brilliant new life in poetry: in Ariosto's *Orlando Furioso* (1516).

By its perfection of form, its variety, its music, its mood, the *Orlando Furioso* puts the epics of Petrarch and Boccaccio in the shade. It is the one work of Italian poetry which can be set beside the great painting of the cinquecento. But, aside from its beauty, it is also important historically, for it is wholly indifferent to antique epic theory—just as indifferent as it is to the intellectual problems of the age. Ariosto knows and loves Latin poetry, and borrows a great many themes from it. But he has no wish to produce a Virgilian epic with invocations of the Muses and mythological machinery. He continues Boiardo's *Orlando Innamorato*, and takes over his predecessor's form—the minstrel's romance of chivalry elevated to the tone of the court. In this form there was a mixture of contradictory tendencies: the religious earnestness of militant faith; the chivalric ideal (which, however, the noble pagan too could fulfill); love in both its higher and lower forms; delight in festive amusements. Ariosto was able to resolve these tensions in the medium which was the gift of his poetic personality: the magic of irony. But in an inharmonious personality they could be sounding boards augmenting ethical and religious conflicts—both such as resulted from the realm of problems suddenly opened up by Luther and those inherent in the antinomy between the old pagan and the old Christian traditions. This is illustrated in Ariosto's contemporary Teofilo Folengo. His inner discord is reflected in the linguistic form which he chose for his epic parody *Baldus* (first published in 1517)—macaronic Latin.[27] His Muses feed him on macaroni and polenta:

> *Non mihi Melpomene, mihi non menchiona Thalia,*
> *Non Phoebus grattans chitarrinum carmina dictent;*
> *Panzae namque meae quando ventralia penso,*
> *Non facit ad nostram Parnassi chiacchiara pivam.*
> *Pancificae tantum Musae doctaeque sorellae,*
> *Gosa, Comina, Striax, Mafelinaque, Tona, Pedrala*
> *Imboccare suum veniant macarone poetam*
> *Dentque polentarum vel quinque vel octo cadinos.*

The macaronic epic remained a thing apart, an episode. But it illuminates the intellectual crisis of the period, as the intellectual crisis of our day is

[27] On antique forerunners of macaronic poetry cf. W. Heraeus, *Kleine Schriften* (1937), 244 f.

illuminated by our contemporary macaronic prose epic, James Joyce's *Finnegans Wake*.

The elevation of the three great Tuscans to the position of models of language and Trissino's program for a "Hellenization" of Italian literature now acted in conjunction with poetic Aristotelianism. Though Aristotle saw tragedy as the highest genre of poetry, Trissino, who had produced a tragedy based on Greek models in 1515 and who in 1548, after twenty years of work, completed the first classicistic epic in unrhymed Italian verse (*L'Italia liberata dai Goti*) brought up the point that the general consensus held Virgil and Homer to be greater than any of the tragedians. He could not but disapprove of the *Orlando Furioso*; it was a romance ("romanzo"), not an epic. The answer was made that the rhymed romance of chivalry was a new genre; Aristotle could not know it, hence his rules were inapplicable to it.[28] Was it possible to reconcile the "romantic" and the Aristotelian epic? Tasso sought a solution to the problem. In subject matter and versification (the faith militant, in ottava rima) his *Gerusalemme liberata* starts from the romance of chivalry, but it obeys the schema of the classicistic epic. He begins by rejecting the antique Muse and the fading laurels of Helicon and invoking instead the heavenly Muse whose dwelling is in Paradise with the choirs of the blessed. On the other hand, he also has the *invocatio* of Memory (I, 36), and charges the Muse (who here has no Christian elements) to enumerate the embattled peoples (XVII, 3). Tasso's poetic theory corresponds to the moralizing Aristotelianism of the Counter Reformation.

In the England of Elizabeth there were neither Aristotelian nor Tridentine scruples to hamper poets. Edmund Spenser can take up the thread of Chaucer and medieval allegory and at the same time situate his *Faerie Queene* in the succession of Homer, Virgil, Ariosto, and Tasso. The artfully wrought prologue comprises four stanzas: The first states the theme in a formula which combines elements from Virgil and Ariosto, the second and third are the *invocatio*, the fourth the dedication of the poem to Queen Elizabeth. In the *invocatio* Spenser addresses a Muse whom he calls "holy virgin chief of nine" and who has been variously interpreted. He also asks the aid of Venus, Cupid, and Mars. Later he has invocations to Clio, daughter of Phoebus and Mnemosyne (III, 3, 4), to the sacred child of Zeus (hence one of the nine Muses) who knows the names of all the ocean and water deities (IV, 11, 10). Book VI opens with a "second *invocatio*" of the Muses, because the poet feels that his powers are failing.

The seventeenth century in England brings us Milton's protestant Muse. The artistic yet artificial prologue of *Paradise Lost* comprises: 1. statement of the theme; 2. invocation of the Christian (Davidian) Muse; 3. promise of a theme never yet attempted; 4. invocation of the Holy Spirit. The "heavenly Muse" is here (1, 6 ff.) derived from the Old Testament, which

---

[28] Giraldi Cintio, *Discorso intorno al comporre dei Romanzi* (1549).

was a spiritual power in Puritanism. This Hebraic Muse inspired Moses on
Horeb and Sinai. She is to raise Milton above Helicon. In the "second
invocatio" (7, 1 ff.) she is addressed as Urania. But she is not one of the
nine Muses, she does not dwell on Olympus, she is older than the earth.
Before creation she played with her sister, Wisdom, in the presence of
the Almighty (Proverbs 8). She drives off Bacchus and the Maenads. She
is a heavenly being, the antique Muse but an empty dream. Thus Milton
goes back to the rigorism of an Aldhelm. But he is as unsuccessful as Tasso
or Prudentius in filling the Christian Urania with life. She remains the
product of an embarrassing predicament. Milton and Tasso both came to
grief over the deceptive phantom of "Christian epic." The Christian cosmos could become poetry in Dante's journey to the otherworld, and after
that only in Calderón's sacred plays.

Calderón produced a Christian solution to the problem of the Muses.
An apologistic tradition of the early Church which the patristic studies of
the sixteenth century had revived taught that pagan mythology contained
a proto-revelation—in more or less distorted form—and that it told of many
things which were also related in the Bible. This harmonistics is developed
in Calderón's work. He accepts both the entire Christian tradition and the
antique tradition and reconciles them in the sense of the Christian Gnosticism of Clement of Alexandria, for whom Greek wisdom was a "second"
Old Testament. We find this view clearly expressed in Calderón (*Autos
sacramentales* [1717], II, 172):

> . . . *la voz de la Escritura*
> *Divina en los Profetas*
> *Y humana en los poetas.*

It pervades the entire system of concordances in which Calderón raises all
arts to God. In Calderón the divine Logos is musician, poet, painter, architect.[29] The "Logos as poet" inspired his sacred play *El Divino Orfeo*. There
the system of concordances is expounded more thoroughly (*Autos*, VI,
249 ♮). Holy Scripture (*divinas letras*) and the wisdom of Antiquity (*hu-
manas letras*) are related by "consonance," even though they are severed
in religion. How often prophets and poets agree when hidden truths are
touched upon! The text of the Eternal Wisdom and the harmony of the
world are linked by proportion and number. God is the musician who plays
on the "instrument of the world." Christ is the divine Orpheus.[30] His lyre
is the wood of the Cross. By his singing he draws human nature to himself.
This is the "Christus musicus" of Sedulius, and behind both stands the
Orphic Christ of Clement. In the *Sacro Parnaso* the concordance is carried

[29] Cf. Excursus XXIII, *infra*.
[30] Orpheus as witness to Christianity: Clement of Alexandria, *Ausgewählte
Schriften*, trans. O. Stählin, I (1934), 150 f.

further. Faith bids Pagandom and Jewry read something from their books. The latter finds the Psalm verse, "Praevenerunt principes conjuncti psallentibus, in medio juvencularum tympanistriarum" (Ps. 67:26). A.V. (68:25): "The singers went before, the players on instruments followed after; among them were the damsels playing with timbrels." For Calderón these timbrelplaying damsels correspond to the Muses. But the Musagetes is Christ, "el verdadero Apolo" (V, 35 a). To the earthly Parnassus, Paradise corresponds as "sacro Parnaso."

Spain needed no Counter Reformation because it had had no Reformation—even as it had had no Renaissance Paganism. It also remained almost untouched by the tyranny of Aristotelianism. Hence the Catholic poetry of Spanish "Baroque" exhibits, in form and in philosophic content, a freedom which Italy, cramped by classicistic preoccupations, and France, infected with Jansenism, could not know. The timid scrupulosity in literary theory, religion, and ethics, which darkened the mind of a Tasso, which made a Racine forsake the stage, had no place in Spain. The Spanish drama produced no classic tragedy, but it caught the color and variety of the stage of the world, as in a magic mirror.

From Ariosto's poetic *romanzo* to the modern novel runs a broad and winding road which we need not follow here. The first great modern novel which we can still read today with pleasure is Fielding's *Tom Jones* (1749). The author is writing a "history" and does not want the word "romance" applied to it (I, ch. 1). In the introductory chapters to the eighteen books there are leisurely reflections upon literary subjects. Classicistic literary theory is at once the point of reference and the object of attack throughout (a parody of a battle "in the Homeric style" appears in IV, ch. 4). One chapter (VIII, 1) is devoted to a discussion of "the Marvellous." As an enlightened man of reason Fielding must reject Homer's mythology, unless the illustrious poet intended to mock at the supersitions of his age. In any case a Christian poet makes himself ridiculous when he troubles pagan deities who have long since been dethroned. Nothing is more chilling and absurd than for a modern to invoke the Muses. Better—as Samuel Butler did in his *Hudibras* (1663)—to invoke a jug of beer, which perhaps has inspired more poetry and prose than all the waters of Hippocrene and Helicon. (We remember that even in Carolingian times the Muses had a fondness for beer.) The year Fielding died (1754) Thomas Gray (1716–71) composed a "Pindaric ode" on "the Progress of Poesy." It is a rehabilitation of the antique Muse. Her realm is far wider than had been supposed. In the icy North she cheers the shivering native. In Chile's odorous forests too she lends her ear to the young savage. These are ideas in which the spirit of English Pre-Romanticism is perceptible. But the attempt to save the Muses by transplanting them to the Arctic or the Tropics shows only that they have been retired. Their music, which once was the harmony of

the spheres, has ceased to sound. It was left for the great William Blake
to bid them farewell in a heart-rending lament:

> *Whether on Ida's shady brow*
> *Or in the chamber of the East,*
> *The chambers of the Sun, that now*
> *From ancient melody have ceased;*
>
> *Whether in heaven ye wander fair,*
> *Or the green corners of the earth,*
> *Or the blue regions of the air*
> *Where the melodious winds have birth;*
>
> *Whether on crystal rocks ye rove,*
> *Beneath the bosom of the sea,*
> *Wandering in many a coral grove,*
> *Fair Nine, forsaking Poetry:*
>
> *How have you left the ancient love*
> *That bards of old enjoy'd in you!*
> *The languid strings do scarcely move,*
> *The sound is forced, the notes are few.*

14

Classicism

O**UR DISCUSSION** of the Muses may serve as an example of the tasks which lie before a science of European literature. What that discipline is, and what it is good for, Novalis has expressed in two sentences: "Philology in general is the science of literature," and, "The art of letters, investigated by and in terms of the art of letters, yields the science of the art of letters (*scientiam artis litterariae*)." Perhaps such a point of view can also help us to understand the phenomenon which we call "Classicism."

1. *Genres, and Catalogues of Authors*

Ever since music has been taught, there has been a science of music. The child learns the rudiments of it (tonalities, rhythms, and so on) when he takes his first piano lessons. The study of musical forms is indispensable to the understanding of a sonata, a symphony. The study of music is incomplete without the study of composition, and demands practical exercises in the strict style. Whoever aspires to become a musician must learn to write a fugue. In the Middle Ages, whoever aspired to become a poet (*dictator*) had to learn poetics (the *ars dictandi*).[1] The parallel could be pursued further. We have drawn it here only to the extent required to show that: Wherever literature is a school subject, we have elements of a systematized study of literature. We have the science of literature, in a form suitable for beginners. Anyone who read Homer as a school text could not but learn that the *Iliad* is a poem in narrative verse (*epos*) and that verse is a form of discourse subject to rules. These things are part of the "rudiments," that is, of the earliest education of the yet "raw" (*rudes*). Its purpose is "to remove the rawness through knowledge" (*eruditio*). The Sophists treated literature scientifically. Aristotle contributed his *Poetics* and

[1] Anyone who aspires to become a poet today would do well to learn the craft of poetry by imitating established forms, before he meddles with "free verse."

Rhetoric. The apogee of antique literary science is third-century Alexandrian philology. Under the protection of the first Ptolemies there arose in Alexandria the greatest research center[2] of the antique world, the Museion (from which our museums have taken only the name)—in form a cult organization under a priest of the Muses, in fact an academy of scholars, together with a library of over 500,000 scrolls. The unrestricted power of princes who were patrons of learning had to meet with Greek science and poetry in order to create an institution which formed one of the pillars supporting the aqueduct of the Western tradition. Neither Augustus nor Hadrian (whose Athenaeum survives only in the "Athenaeum Club" or as a newspaper title) created anything comparable. The financial magnates of our time endow literary prizes, but no institute for literature. Such an institute has no use which can be calculated.

Having grown up under the aegis of Greek philosophy, literary science came of age in the form of Hellenistic philology. It was called upon to classify the matter of literature—"studiorum materia," as Quintilian puts it (X, 1, 128)—in accordance with two different principles: by genres and by authors.[3] The selection of authors presupposes a classification of genres. The antique system of genres does not correspond with the modern system.[4] For together with genres based on the work as a whole, such as epic, comedy, and tragedy, others, based on versification (iambus, elegy, etc.), are used as classifying principles. Once the genres are fixed, their rank yet remains to be determined. There are "major" and "minor" genres. Is epic the highest, or is tragedy? How many minor genres are there? Boileau reckons nine, but excludes the fable. Is he right? Can a writer rise to the rank of a classic if he practices only a "minor" genre? Or, indeed, if he confines himself to the fable? Boileau's theory had to answer No. Nevertheless La Fontaine was able to carry the day. There are readers who see in him the finest fruit of French Classicism. But what makes an author a classic, and since when have there been classics?

This brings us back to the selection of authors. Several catalogues of authors from the Hellenistic period have come down to us. One such list[5] names five epic poets, three iambic poets, five tragedians, seven representatives of the "old," two of the "middle," and five of the "new" comedy, nine lyric poets, ten orators, ten historians. We note a preference for certain numbers which have a "distinguished" value. We shall return to this subject (Excursus XV, *infra*).

In the course of time the number of model writers diminishes. We shall here consider neither the causes of this process nor its stages. Yet in its turn

---

[2] Not a university. Its members were not required to lecture.

[3] The formation of this twofold classification has not yet been sufficiently investigated.

[4] The division of poetry into epic, lyric, and dramatic is of modern origin. Cf. Irene Behrens, *Die Lehre von der Einteilung der Dichtkunst, vornehmlich vom 16. bis 19. Jahrhundert* (1940).

[5] *laterculus Coislinianus.*

it produced a historical effect. The number of tragedians was reduced from five to three (Aeschylus, Sophocles, Euripides). We have documentary evidence for ninety plays by Aeschylus and a hundred and twenty-three by Sophocles. Only seven by each remained extant at the end of Antiquity. Seneca and Racine wrote but nine tragedies each.[6] They conformed to the straitened tragic canon, and the small number of their tragic creations is to be explained not only in terms of the history of the stage. Numbers themselves can be exemplary. The *Iliad* and the *Odyssey* have twenty-four books each. Virgil compresses the action of both epics into the twelve books of the *Aeneid*. The epic division into twelve books is maintained by Statius and Milton, whereas Nonnus, to contain the swirling abundance of his epic on Dionysus, needs four times as many—that is, the total number of books in the two Homeric poems, which he employs in conscious emulation.

The Alexandrian philologists are the first to put together a selection of earlier literature for the use of grammarians in their schools. The terminology for the classification of literature according to forms is unsettled. Quintilian (X, 1, 45) uses the expression "genera lectionum"; for "catalogue of authors" he says "ordo a grammaticis datus" (*ibid.*, 54). No less unsettled is the term for "model authors." The Alexandrians call them "the received (into the selection)" (ἐγκρινόμενοι, ἔγκριτοι; in Pollux, IX, 15 κεκριμένοι). This term defied Latinization. It could no more pass into modern usage than Quintilian's "genera lectionum" or his prolix circumlocutions with *ordo* ("auctores in ordinem redigere," I, 4, 3) and *numerus* ("in numerum redigere," X, 1, 54). A new and convenient word had to be found. But it was not until very late, and then only in a single instance, that the name *classicus* appears: in Aulus Gellius (*Noctes Atticae*, XIX, 8, 15). This learned compiler of the Antonine period discusses a large number of grammatical problems. Are *quadriga* and *arena* to be used in the singular or the plural? The thing to do is to follow the usage of a model author: "e cohorte illa dumtaxat antiquiore vel oratorum aliquis vel poetarum, id est classicus adsiduusque aliquis scriptor, non proletarius": "some one of the orators or poets, who at least belongs to the older band, that is, a first-class and tax-paying author, not a proletarian." According to the Servian constitution, citizens were divided into five classes based on property qualifications. Citizens of the first class were soon called simply *classici*. Cicero (*Ac.*, II, 73) already uses the word metaphorically when he puts Democritus above Stoic philosophers whom he assigns to the fifth class.[7] The *proletarius*, whom Gellius mentions by way of comparison, belongs to *no* tax class. When Sainte-Beuve, in 1850, discussed the question What is a Classic?, he paraphrased this passage in Gellius: "un écrivain de valeur et de marque,

---

[6] If we disregard the two Biblical tragedies that Racine wrote to order for devotional-pedagogical purposes after his "conversion," his cycle includes only seven plays.

[7] Giving it a different turn, Arnobius (*Adv. nat.* II 29) uses the tax-class metaphor in a philosophic context.

un écrivain qui compte, qui a du bien au soleil, et qui n'est pas confondu dans la foule des prolétaires." [8] What a titbit for a Marxist sociology of literature!

The passage from Gellius is instructive. It shows that, in Antiquity, the concept of the model author was oriented upon a grammatical criterion, the criterion of correct speech. The history of modern languages should investigate when and where the absolutely isolated usage which we find in Gellius made its way into modern culture.[9] That such a basic concept of our culture as Classicism, and one which has been so debated and so misused, should go back to a late Roman writer who is known today only to specialists, is more than an interesting philological curiosity. It illustrates what we have already been able to establish more than once—the sway of chance in the history of our literary terminology. What would modern aesthetics have done for a single general concept that should embrace Raphael, Racine, Mozart, and Goethe, if Gellius had never lived? Imposing systems which have harassed centuries would never have arisen if the Servian tax classification had never been made. There could not well have been any argument over Classicism, if the word *classicus* had been understood. But because it was not understood, it was surrounded by a mysterious nimbus, which suggests the polished marble of the Apollo Belvedere. We can no longer do without the concept of the classical and we need not give it up. But neither will we renounce our right to illuminate our aesthetic categories historically. This is a widening of our horizon for which we are grateful to the "Historism" of the nineteenth and twentieth centuries.

The concept of the "classical" has, so we see, a very humble and prosaic origin. In the last two hundred years it has become unduly and immeasurably inflated. It was a step as full of consequences as it was dubious when, about 1800, Greco-Roman Antiquity *en bloc* was pronounced "classical." Any impartial estimate of Antiquity, not only historically but also aesthetically, was thereby obstructed for a century. Those who love Antiquity in all its periods and styles (a love which is certainly less common than might be supposed) are precisely those who will feel its apotheosis as the "classical" to be empty and misleading pedantry. The glorified and glorifying grammar-school Humanism, which even today still tends to scale the heights of edification, is at the opposite pole from the real and bold Humanism of liberal minds. We long for a Humanism which is purged of all

[8] *Causeries du lundi*, III, 39.

[9] In French the word first appears in 1548, in the *Art poétique* of Thomas Sebillet: "l'invention, et le jugement compris soubz elle, se conferment et enrichissent par la lecture des bons et classiques poètes françois, comme sont entre les vieux Alain Chartier et Jan de Meun." So here we have classics in the French Middle Ages. Ronsard and his school seem not to know the word *classique*. Gracián writes: "gran felicidad conocer los primeros autores en su clase" (*Agudeza, Disc.* 63). In England Pope is the first to use the word: "Who lasts a century, can have no flaw, / I hold that Wit a Classic, good in law" (*Imitations of Horace. The First Epistle of the Second Book of Horace*, 1, 55 f.). This corresponds to the Horatian "est vetus atque probus, centum qui perficit annos" (*Epi.*, II, 1. 39).

pedagogy (and politics!) and which rejoices in beauty. In such a Humanism there is also room for an aesthetic criticism which, for example, clarifies what is meant by such an expression as the Classicism of a Virgil.[10]

2. The "Ancients" and the "Moderns"

Let us return to Gellius. To introduce the classic *scriptor*, he refers to the "cohors antiquior vel oratorum vel poetarum." And with that he touches upon something of decisive importance. The classic writers are always the "ancients." They can be acknowledged as models, but they can likewise be rejected as superseded. Then we have a *querelle des anciens et des modernes*. This is a constant phenomenon of literary history and literary sociology.[11] In Alexandria Aristarchus contrasted the "moderns" (νεώτεροι) with Homer. Among them is Callimachus, who conducted a polemic against the epic. Terence often contrasts ancient and modern tendencies in his prologues (*Heautont.*, *Prol.*, 43; *Eun.*, *Prol.*, 43; *Phormio*, *Prol.*, 1). In the first century B.C. the *poetae novi* or νεώτεροι (Cicero, *Or.*, 161; *Ad Atticum*, VII, 2, 1) oppose the old Ennean trend, only to be replaced in their turn by Augustan poetry, which now felt itself to be "modern." Under the Antonines a school of modern poets appeared whom the later grammarians called *neoterici*. Thus Cicero's νεώτεροι is now latinized. The older Antiquity became, the more a word for "modern" was needed. But the word "modernus" was not yet available. The gap was filled by "neotericus." [12] Originally it had designated a stylistic manner which came out of Alexandrian poetry. From the fourth century on it means "recent writer"; for example in Jerome, Sulpicius Severus, Salvian, Claudianus Mamertus, Aurelius Victor. The glossators explain "neoterici" as "libri novi vel recentes"; also as "novicii, minores." Columban (d. 615) periodizes: "evangeliorum plenitudo, apostolica doctrina, neoterica orthodoxorum auctorum doctrina." [13] Here, then, the Fathers become neoterics. For Erasmus, Thomas Aquinas is "neotericorum omnium diligentissimus." [14] The Grecism caused many writers embarrassment. We find the form "neutericus" —which indicates both formal and semantic association with the word "*neuter*" ("neither of both").

The distinction between old and new need, however, have no polemic significance. It can indicate the succession of two styles or periods one of which replaces the other, such as the "old," "middle," and "new comedy," or the two Testaments of the Christian church. The contrast is employed in yet another sense when a leading representative of the New Sophistic,

[10] T. S. Eliot has done this in *What Is a Classic?* (1945).

[11] It is found in Arabic literature also.—A forerunner of the French *querelle* is the polemic (1401) between Salutati and Niccoli (R. Sabbadini, *Il Metodo degli umanisti* [1920], 49, n. 1).

[12] The following after J. de Ghellinck, *Neotericus, neoterici* (ALMA, XV [1940], 113–126).   [13] MGH, *Epistolae*, III, 175, 21.

[14] Quoted in E. Gilson, *Héloïse et Abélard* (1938), 215, n. 1.

Philostratus, sets forth *ca.* 230 that the "new" Sophistic should rather be called the "second" Sophistic, for it was already "old," even though it set itself other aims than the first. Here it is a matter of renovation and succession. In the Atticism of the Imperial Age, Arrian (*ca.* 95–175) can be called a "new Xenophon" because in his life and writings he copies the old. The "Ancients" are called οἱ παλαιοί. This very indefinite expression is still current in the Byzantine Middle Ages. Eustathius, archbishop of Thessalonica and interpreter of Homer (twelfth century), uses it to mean the books he has before him, which however "can also be quite recent" as research has shown.[15] Antiquity had no historic sense in our meaning of the phrase, which is determined by our consciousness of definitely distinguishable periods. And if possibly it had some trace of it, it was unable to express it for lack of crystallized historical concepts.[16] It is as if instead of our clearly outlined concepts Antiquity, the Middle Ages, the Modern Age (with their many subdivisions) we had only the expression "the past" to use.

[15] K. Lehrs, *Die Pindarscholien* (1873), 167 n.—On "antiqui" and related expressions in juristic literature, cf. Fritz Schulz, *History of Roman Legal Science* (1946), 274, n. 9–12.

[16] F. Klingner (*Römische Geisteswelt* [1943], 67) says that the Romans "had a bent for history from the first." As evidence he adduces Polybius' account (VI, 53) of the funeral ceremonies of the great families, in which the close connection of the Roman with his ancestors is shown. "The past effectively extends into the present." This is convincing. But this holding the past as present signifies a sort of timelessness, and in any case is not the same as what we call the historic sense. What do we find among the Roman historians? Livy presents "neither an overall picture of Roman history . . . nor a recognition of causes, nor any serious philosophical speculation whatsoever" (Klingner, 88), but instead "a decently pious attitude in the presence of lofty things" (89). There is no historical ideology in Tacitus either (325). A. Alföldi (*Die Kontorniaten* [1943], 58) speaks of the atrophy of the historic sense in the fourth century and shows "how even the bearers of classic culture thenceforth saw their own history only through fog and clouds." In the Dea Roma of donative coins he finds the Republican consciousness which was characteristic of late Rome. The Rome-idea lives "in an abstract and dogmatic form," dissociated from the emperors and from political realities. Symmachus' historical writing "marks no real progress. The greatness of Rome, having come into existence, is now eternal, imperturbable, and unchangeable. The course of history is nothing but an alternating defection from and return to the old greatness and the old values" (W. Hartke, *Geschichte und Politik im spätantiken Rom* [1940], 141; quoted in Alföldi, 59). Significant of the spirit of Justinian's codification of the laws is the statement: "Tanta nobis antiquitatis habita est reverentia" (Fritz Schulz, *History of Roman Legal Science* [1946], 283). Is one justified in seeing, in the beautiful strophes on transitoriness by Sulpicius Lupercus Servasius Junior and in those of Phocas to Clio, an expression of a late Roman sense of time? Is it different from the early Roman one? Is it psychologically connected with the Roman *pietas*? Does not precisely this pious treasuring of the past exclude a historical view of the world? What is the influence of ancestor worship on the historical picture (Romans, Egyptians, Chinese)? There is history among the Jews. The patriarchal age, the periods of Moses, of the Kings, of the Judges were felt as distinct, the exile as a caesura, the Messiah as promise. Among the Romans, did the Age of the Kings, the Republic, the Century of Conflicts, the Principate constitute epochs in an analogous sense? Or was Augustine the first to overthrow the static Roman picture of history?—The philosophical side of the problem has been illuminated by Schelling: "How few know a past

Even the words ἀρχαῖος and παλαιός, *antiquus*, *vetus*, and *priscus* appear to have no essential difference in meaning.[17] The relativity of the concept antiquity is discussed by Cicero; the Attic orators, from the point of view of Rome are ancient ("senes"), according to the Athenian chronology, they are late (*Brutus*, 39). He himself reckons Aristotle and Theophrastus among the *antiqui* (*Orator*, 218).

Naturally, from century to century, the line of demarcation shifts. The public will read only "ancient" poets, Horace complains. But who is "ancient"? Shall we say someone who has been dead a century (*Epi.*, II, 1, 20 ff.)? For Quintilian, Cicero is among the *antiqui*. In Tacitus' dialogue on orators (chs. 16, 17, 25) the question of historical periodization is answered by the concept *antiqui* in a different sense. But there is agreement upon the proposition that men who lived a hundred or six-score years ago must not be called *antiqui* because six-score years are "a human lifetime."[18]

---

in the full sense of the term! Without a strong present, brought into existence by separation from oneself, there is no past. The man who is incapable of confronting his past has none, or rather he never gets out of it, he lives in it permanently" (*Die Weltalter, Urfassungen*, ed. by M. Schröter [1946], 11).

[17] Cf. Tacitus, *De oratoribus*, ed. Gudeman [2] (1914), 287.—*priscus vetus antiquus* used together in Cicero, *De legibus*, II, 7, 18.—*Priscus* has the connotation "worthy of honor."

[18] In Tacitus, *Dialogus de oratoribus*, ch. 16, Aper, citing the authority of Cicero's lost *Hortensius*, assumes the Platonic year (= 12954 years) as a basis and then in ch. 17 reckons that since Cicero's death 120 years have passed, otherwise "unius hominis aetas."—Arnobius, *Adv. nat.*, II, 71 refutes the thesis that Paganism is superior to Christianity because of its greater age. "Nova res est quam gerimus, quandoque et ipsa vetus fiet: vetus quam vos agitis, sed temporibus quibus coepit nova fuit ac repentina." According to the reckoning of early Roman history, it appears that from Picus to Latinus three steps ("gradus") elapsed, "ut indicat series. Vultis Faunus, Latinus et Picus annis vixerint vicenis atque centenis? Ultra enim negatur posse hominis vita produci." In fixing a human lifetime at 120 years, does Arnobius depend on Tacitus or are they both following earlier tradition? Reckoning time by generations is of course already to be found in Homer (γενεή, φῦλον). *Saeculum* is generally the same as γενεή. According to Wissowa, it is the extreme duration of a human life calculated in such a way that the *saeculum* which begins on a certain day ends on the day of the death of the last man who was alive on the day of its beginning. Varro (*L.L.*, VI, 11) sets the *saeculum* at a hundred years. As a sacramental and political period, however, the *saeculum* was set at 110 years under Augustus. But this was not strictly applied. Domitian held the Secular Games in 88 instead of 94. The Roman Secular Games cross with the series of celebrations of the founding of the city, which we know to have been held in 47, 147, 248 (postponed for a year). Thus two irreconcilable secular reckonings are in effect at the same time.—Utter confusion reigns in Isidore (*Et.*, V, 38): "Saecula generationibus constant; et inde saecula, quod se sequantur: abeuntibus enim aliis alia succedunt. Hunc [sic Lindsay] quidam quinquagesimum annum dicunt, quem Hebraei iubileum vocant . . . Aetas plerumque dicitur et pro uno anno, ut in annalibus, et pro septem, ut hominis, et pro centum, et pro quovis tempore . . . Aevum est aetas perpetua, cuius neque initium, neque extremum noscitur, quod Graeci vocant αἰῶνας; quod aliquando apud eos pro saeculo, aliquando pro aeterno ponitur." Servius (on *Aen.*, VIII 508) reckons the *saeculum* at 30 years.— In pagan and Christian Antiquity, then, there reigns a nebulously vague sense of time. Hence no possibility of settled periodization.

The word *novi*, "the moderns," seems not to have been employable as a contrasting concept to *antiqui*. Macrobius (*ca.* 400) calls the "ancients" "bibliothecae veteris autores" (*Sat.*, VI, 1, 3), but has no designation for the "moderns." Not until the sixth century does the new and happy formation *modernus* (related to *modo*, "now," as *hodiernus* to *hodie*) appear, and now Cassiodorus can celebrate an author in rolling rhyme as "antiquorum diligentissimus imitator, modernorum nobilissimus institutor" (*Variae*, IV, 51). The word "modern" (which has nothing to do with "mode") is one of the last legacies of late Latin to the modern world. In the ninth century, then, the new age of Charlemagne can be called "seculum modernum." [19] But let there be no mistake: The dividing line between Antiquity and the Modern Age is not put back somewhere toward the beginning of the Christian Era. Rather, the Christian Revelation and the Fathers belong to Antiquity. [20] This view may seem strange to the modern reader. When we speak of the "Ancients," we mean the pagan writers. In our view Paganism and Christianity are two separate realms, for which there is no common denominator. The Middle Ages thinks differently. "Veteres" is applied to both the Christian and pagan authors of the past. [21] The con-

[19] Walafrid in *Poetae*, II, 271, XI and 318, 453.

[20] In the dedicatory poem of a certain Bruno to an emperor (*Poetae*, V, 378, 21 ff.), which Strecker attributes to the 10th–11th century, we read: "Deciderat studium veterum / Et vigilancia pene patrum / Cecaque secula barbaries / Seva premebat et error iners." In my opinion "veteres" and "patres" are the Fathers, whom Notker Balbulus calls "antiqui patres" *ca.* 890 (E. Dümmler, *Das Formelbuch des Bischofs Salomo* . . . [1857], 64, 17).

[21] In a complaint on the immorality of his times Walter of Châtillon ([1929], 97, 2) says:

> Nescimus vestigia veterum moderni,
> Regni nos eternitas non trahit superni,
> Ardentis sed nitimur per viam inferni.

I.e.: "We moderns stray from the footsteps of our ancestors; no longer are we drawn toward divine eternity, instead we strive after the fires of hell." But when the same poet wants to say, "Why should I not do as the pagan poets did and write for gold?" he uses the image of "the ancestral footsteps" over again ([1929], 83, 4):

> Cur sequi vestigia veterum refutem
> Adipisci rimulis corporis salutem,
> Impleri divitiis et curare cutem?
> Quod decuit magnos, cur mihi turpe putem?

With this Strecker compares Persius, Prologue, 10: "Magister artis ingenique largitor / Venter."—Langosch is mistaken when in his edition of Hugh of Trimberg's *Registrum* he takes "veteres" to mean "antique authors" in our sense. The consequence is that, for him, Hugh's division of the *auctores* is inconsistent. Hugh divided his work into three *distincciones* of two *particule* each. According to Langosch (p. 14), "the antique authors" should "appear in the first particle, the medieval in the second," but (p. 245, in reference to l. 643) he has to admit that, of eighteen authors who should be "antique" only "three or four" are so; but the inconsistency is the commentator's fault, not the author's.—Hugh of Trimberg sets forth: The worthy pagan authors should be held in the same regard as the Biblical authors (*hagiographi*; Is., Et., VI, 1, 7). They remained true to "their faith," and even wrote much that is "theological": "Forsan dicet aliquis, quod multi gentiles / Multos libros scripserint claros et subtiles, / Qui propter incredulos auctores non damnan-

trast between the "modern" present and Pagan-Christian Antiquity was felt by no century so strongly as by the twelfth. The concept of the twelfth-century Renaissance, which Haskins has made current, is valid.[22] But the fact becomes apparent only when one inquires into the period's own conception of its place in history; and this has not hitherto been done.

In previous chapters we have discussed the change which the disciplines underwent in the twelfth century (Ch. 3, § 6) and the parallelism of the new poetics, jurisprudence, logic, metaphysics, and ethics (Ch. 7, § 3). We can now connect these two phenomena. They are two aspects of the same cultural change. The parallelism, as we saw, was based terminologically upon the Biblical use of "old" and "new"—a use whose development we traced historically. The twelfth-century "Renaissance" could not call itself that, the term being the reflection of the Italian period of florescence in the mirror of nineteenth-century historical thought. We find in the period none of those philosophico-religious speculations upon a *vita nova* in which Burdach wished to see the seed of the Italian Renaissance. But we do find a clear consciousness of the turn of an era. More precisely: of the dawn of *the* new era, compared with which *everything* earlier is "old"—Horace's poetics, the Digests, philosophy—and old in precisely the same sense as the Old Testament. It is the first time that the Nordic West experiences and itself states the dawning of a new intellectual era. The new era is an ideological upwelling, accompanied by an upwelling of the very springs of life (*supra*, p. 113). Thus our picture of the period gains in comprehensiveness and depth.[23]

---

tur, / Verum a Christicolis adhuc usitantur. / Satis probabiliter tales excusantur, / Ut cum agiographis quodammodo ponantur: / Si fidem catholicam hi non didicerunt, / Tamen fortes in sua fide perstiterunt / Tantisque virtutibus scribendo floruerunt, / Quod et theoloyce multociens scripserunt. / Si fidem catholicam plene cognovissent, / Credo quod finetenus huic adhesissent."

[22] There are certainly convincing reasons against the multiplication of Renaissances (Theodosian, Carolingian, Ottonian, etc.). But Haskins was justified in using a current concept because he had to make apparent something that had never been seen as a unity.

[23] The twelfth-century period-consciousness serves to explain Walter Map's remarks on *modernitas* in his *De nugis curialium* (written between 1180 and 1192; ed. M. R. James [Oxford, 1914]): "Nostra dico tempora modernitatem hanc, horum scilicet centum annorum curriculum, cuius adhuc nunc ultime partes extant, cuius tocius in his que notabilia sunt satis est recens et manifesta memoria, cum adhuc aliqui supersint centennes, et infiniti filii qui ex patrum et avorum relacionibus certissime teneant que non viderunt. Centum annos qui effluxerunt dico nostram modernitatem, et non qui veniunt, cum eiusdem tamen sint racionis secundum propinquitatem; quoniam ad narracionem pertinent preterita, ad divinacionem futura. Hoc tempore huius centennii primum invaluerunt ad summum robur Templarii . . ." (p. 59, 17 ff.). Here, then, the concept *saeculum* "lifetime" (Tacitus, Arnobius) is combined with the modern reckoning by centuries. The century, however, is called *centennium*, not *saeculum*. Compare the same author's reflection that one of his writings will not be properly appreciated until after his death (158, 15 ff.): "Scio quid fiet post me. Cum enim putuerim, tum primo sal accipiet, totusque sibi supplebitur decessu meo defectus, et in remotissima posteritate mihi faciet

3. *Canon Formation in the Church*

The formation of a canon [24] serves to safeguard a tradition. There is the literary tradition of the school, the juristic tradition of the state, and the religious tradition of the Church: these are the three medieval world powers, *studium, imperium, sacerdotium*. The "classic" period of Roman jurisprudence comprises the time from Augustus to Diocletian. It is followed by the "bureaucratic" period, which ends with the completion of Justinian's codification. The canon of jurists to whom "authority" is conceded is formed by 426.[25] The Church—not without opposition from within its own ranks—received the sacred writings of the Jews into its canon as the "Old Testament." The Jewish canon consists of the "Law" (the Pentateuch), the "Prophets" (among which the older historical books were reckoned, as "earlier" prophets), and the "Writings" (*Ketubim*) which Jerome in his *Prologus galeatus* to the Vulgate calls "hagiographa" ("sacred writings"), following the precedent of the Septuagint. But in Judaism and in early Christianity there were numerous books which were excluded from being read at divine service and which were therefore known as "the hidden" (ἀπόκρυφοι). At the Council of Trent the Old Testament canon was established as dogma, but three apocryphal books of the Vulgate were added because they were cited in the writings of the Fathers. Luther says that the apocryphal books are "not held equal to Holy Scripture and yet are profitable and good to read." Even in the early Church the concept of the canonical had to be considerably expanded because the Church was a juridical institution. All legal prescriptions of the organs of the church are called "canones," in contradistinction to secular laws ("leges"). In the course of centuries the *canones* had become a mass of contradictions. In Italy, where the spirit of Roman law had never wholly failed and where Irnerius of Bologna (d. 1130) revivified it, Gratian produced the *Concordia discordantium canonum* (*ca.* 1140), which, with later sources for ecclesiastical law, served as the foundation for the *Corpus iuris canonici*, so entitled in 1580.[26] Gratian's work also bears the title *Decretum*. After Gratian "de-

---

autoritatem antiquitas, quod tunc ut nunc vetustum cuprum preferetur auro novello. Simiarum tempus erit, ut nunc, non hominum; quod presencia sibi deridebunt, non habentes ad bonos pacienciam. Omnibus seculis sua displicuit modernitas, et quevis etas a prima preteritam sibi pretulit." Worth noting here is the estimation of Antiquity as copper and of the modern age as gold; a reversal of the scale of metals which Hesiod applied to the ages of the world. On "simiarum tempore" cf. Excursus XIX, *infra*.

[24] I have avoided this word hitherto because it first appears with the meaning "catalogue of authors" in the fourth century of our era, specifically in relation to Christian literature. The great philologist David Ruhnken (1723–98; born in Pomerania, in Holland from 1744 on) introduced the concept canon into philology. Cf. H. Oppel, *Kanon* (1937), 70 f.

[25] Fritz Schulz, *History of Roman Legal Science*.

[26] The development of Church law after 1580 necessitated a new codification, which appeared in 1917 as *Codex iuris canonici*.

cretals" (*epistulae decretales*) became the generic name for collections of ecclesiastical laws. The secularization of the church is denounced by Dante in the words (*Par.*, IX, 133 ff.):

> *Per questo l' Evangelio e i dottor magni*
> *Son derelitti; e solo ai Decretali*
> *Si studia sì che pare ai lor vivagni.*

(For this the Gospels and the greatest doctors
    Are now deserted; only the Decretals
    Are studied, as their margins plainly show.)

But among the blessed in the Heaven of the Sun Gratian appears (*Par.*, X, 103 ff.) with Dominic, Albertus, Thomas, Solomon, Dionysius the Areopagite, Orosius, Boethius, Isidore, Bede, Richard of St. Victor, Siger of Brabant:

> *Quell' altro fiammegiar esce dal riso*
> *Di Grazian che l' uno e l' altro foro*
> *Aiuto sì che piacque in Paradiso.*

(That other radiance issues from the smile
    Of Gratian, who the one and the other forum
    So served that favor it wins in Paradise.)

Since the time of Gregory the Great "canon missae" has been the name for the invariable part of the Mass. Canons are originally clergy installed according to the laws of the church, later the clergy included in a cathedral chapter with choral devotions performed in common. Sanctification is preceded by a canonical suit (the only kind of suit which cannot be lost [27]). Its end is inclusion in the catalogue (canon) of the saints (canonization). Church law also fixes canonical ages for ecclesiastical offices. Only in the case of a priest's female cook is there no definite stipulation. Here "advanced age," *provectior aetas*, suffices. The whole of ecclesiastical life is pervaded by the juristic spirit: "ecclesia vivit lege romana." [28] Roman jurists took part even in the development of the liturgy. [29]

Christianity became the religion of a book but, unlike Islam, it did not

[27] It can, however, be interrupted. Philip IV brought an action for the canonization of Cardinal Jiménez [Ximenes] in 1650 and 1655, and it is not yet concluded.

[28] *Lex Ribuaria*, LVIII, 1 on ecclesiastical manumission: "Episcopus archidiacono iubeat, ut ei tabulas secundam legem Romanan, quam ecclesia vivit, scribere faciant." For legal matters involving the church—not the individual cleric—Roman law applies. Later, Roman law became the personal law for the individual cleric too (*MG Leges*, IV, p. 539: "Ut omnis ordo aecclesiarum secundum legem Romanum vivat"). H. Brunner, *Deutsche Rechtsgeschichte*, I 2 (1906), 395.— Muratori, *Scriptores*, II b 1002, of the year 1086: "Sicut in lege scriptum est, omnis ordo ecclesiarum secundum legem romanam vivant et faciant, ego . . . sic facio."

[29] Mary Gonzaga Haessly, *Rhetoric in the Sunday Collects of the Roman Missal* (Cleveland, 1938).

begin as such. The Pauline epistles are earlier than the Gospels. Still earlier
are the words of consecration of the Mass, which Paul "delivers" to the
Corinthians even as he had "received" them (I Cor. 11:23 ff.), and the
creed (I Cor. 15:3 ff.), which goes back to the original congregation at
Jerusalem. A sacramental formula and a creed formula, then, are the earliest
documents of the Christian revelation within our knowledge. Unwritten
sayings of the Lord (ἄγραφα) were passed on by word of mouth; and the
Phrygian bishop Papias, even as late as the beginning of the second century,
went about listening to presbyters in the hope of hearing sayings of the
Lord's disciples, because he believed that he received more profit from
a "living voice" than from books. The canonical books of the New Testament were surrounded by a large number of apocryphal Gospels, Acts of
the Apostles, Epistles, and Apocalypses. One of these is the *Shepherd of
Hermas*, which appeared shortly before 150 and enjoyed high esteem.[30]
Then come the so-called "Greek apologists" of the second century, the
writings of the "heretics," the gnostics, and their opponents, and much
else which belongs to the history of early Christian literature. In the system
of Catholic theology all this matter falls within the domain of the theological discipline of patrology,[31] which investigates the early Christian
writers as to their value as witnesses to the faith and is today in process of
becoming a historical discipline. It is principally interested in the "Fathers."
But since when has such a group been recognized? We saw that Columban
does not know them, but instead makes a threefold classification: the Gospels, the doctrine of the Apostles (that is, the epistles of the New Testament), and the doctrine of modern orthodox writers. Sidonius distinguishes
authentici[32] (i.e., the Biblical writers) and *disputatores* (authors of "discourses") in early Christian literature; Cassiodorus distinguishes *introductores, expositores, magistri, patres*. We need not pursue the subject here.[33]
I cite these examples only to show how the Church, after forming the Biblical canon, had to form a theological canon, and how tentative the first
steps in this direction also were. The first author of a *Patrologia* was the
Protestant Johann Gerhard.[34] Even into the nineteenth century the concept

[30] Notker Balbulus puts it among the *passiones sanctorum*—a dilemma-dodging
makeshift.

[31] B. Altaner, *Patrologie* (1938).—*Idem*, "Der Stand der patrologischen Wissenschaft und das Problem einer altchristlichen Literaturgeschichte" (*Miscellanea
Giovanni Mercati* [1946], I, 483).

[32] The term ("with one's own hand, genuine") is borrowed from jurisprudence
and, like *sententiae* ("legal decisions") later passes over into Scholasticism.

[33] Further details in Excursus VI, *infra*.

[34] Gerhard (1582–1637) was "the archtheologian, master, and model dogmati-
cian of Lutheran orthodoxy and probably the greatest among the heroes of orthodox
Lutheranism" (*ADB*, VIII, 767).—Principal works: *Loci theologici* (1610–22);
Doctrina catholica et evangelica (1633–37), in which the evangelical church is
represented as being the truly catholic church. The *Patrologia* appeared posthumously in 1653.

patrology included all ecclesiastical and theological literature down to *ca.* 1200 and sometimes down to the Reformation.

The reader of this book has so often come upon the abbreviation *PL* that we must not pass over the man to whom, among nineteenth-century patrologists, we owe the most, not as a research scholar but for his labors in diffusing the writings of the Fathers. He is the Abbé Jacques Paul Migne (1800–1875), a "writer of moderate intelligence and a publisher of astonishing activity," as an ecclesiastical reference book rather acidly calls him. Why? "As a result of uncanonical business activities [the canon again!], by which he tried to rehabilitate his enterprises which had suffered severely by fire in 1868, he underwent suspension by the archbishop of Paris in 1874." [35] The *Patrologiae cursus completus* comprises in its *Series latina* (our *PL*) 221 volumes (1844–55), and in its *Series graeca* (*PG*) 162 volumes (1857–66). It is equally indispensable to the philologist, the historian, the philosopher, and the theologian. Despite its many failings, the gigantic corpus, in which ecclesiastical learning entered into a strange alliance with the initiative of a private capitalistic entrepreneur, deserves our most sincere gratitude.

Canon formation in literature must always proceed to a selection of classics. The Fathers are the classics among ecclesiastical writers. They are at the same time *antiqui*. But among them, again, a more limited selection was made. The Eastern Church took the lead by setting Basil the Great (d. 379), Gregory of Nazianzus (d. 389–90), and John Chrysostom (d. 407) apart as the three "oecumenical great doctors." To these the West added Athanasius (d. 373). From the eighth century onwards Ambrose, Jerome, Augustine, and Gregory the Great are accounted the four great Latin Doctors of the Church.[36] The colossal structure of Bernini's "Cathedra Petri" in the apse of St. Peter's is ecstatically borne up by Ambrose and Augustine, Athanasius and Chrysostom. The four greatest Doctors of East and West are here united. But the Doctors are in turn only a selection among the Fathers. Indeed, they need not even be Fathers. The definition of a Father of the Church includes not only orthodoxy, saintliness, and recognition by the church but also the attribute of *antiquitas*. The canon of the Fathers is closed. But in the Middle Ages patristic literature found a rival in Scholasticism as a flowering of theology. With the Council of Trent a new consolidation and extension of the church's powers commences. At the same time there begins a wholesale creation of peerages, which makes the great moderns Doctors of the Church: Thomas, Anselm, Bernard of Clairvaux, Alphonsus de' Liguori and François of Sales (both under Pius IX), John of the Cross, Bellarmine, and Albertus Magnus under

---

[35] Buchberger's *Lexikon für Theologie und Kirche*.—Migne had already run into difficulties with the ecclesiastical authorities in 1833 over a brochure *De la liberté*, "par un prêtre." Further details in Pierre Larousse's *Grand Dictionnaire Universel du 19ᵉ siècle*, XI (1874).

[36] The tetrad would seem to be modeled on the Evangelists.

Pius XI. The *doctores ecclesiae* form a sacred corporation in which *antiqui*
and *moderni* are peacefully united. Presumably the ancients within it have
much to learn from the moderns. Isidore, upon whom we have so often
relied, rose to be a Doctor in 1722. The Spanish monarchy had made shift
without one until then.

The Biblical and patristic canons are far from exhausting Christian
literature. The Bible was as little accessible to the faithful as the liturgical
books, the writings of the Fathers only to the intellectual élite among the
secular and regular clergy. But the life of the Church brought forth new
literary genres. Out of the needs of religious ceremonial arose hymnography
in the fourth century. The persecutions of the Christians produced the
acta and *passiones* of the martyrs. The *vitae* of the saints followed upon
these. These new genres could be put into the system of forms of pagan
literature. Thus, Biblical poems and saints' lives appear in the form of the
Latin epic. We have already observed the phenomenon of medieval stylistic
crossing (*supra*, pp. 151 f.). But the genres too are crossed, and this at the
same time signifies: crossing of the pagan and Christian canons.

4.   *Medieval Canon*

At the beginning of our study (*supra*, pp. 48 ff.) we submitted several lists
of writers, in order to give the reader a preliminary view of the curriculum
of the medieval school. We have now reached a point from which a deeper
understanding is possible. About 890 Notker Balbulus rejects the pagan
poets and recommends the Christians Prudentius, Avitus, Juvencus, and
Sedulius. On the other hand, a century later students in the cathedral
school at Speyer were reading "Homer," Martianus Capella, Horace, Persius, Juvenal, Statius, Terence, Lucan; and of the Christian writers only
Boethius. If we go a century further we come upon Winrich, teacher in the
cathedral school at Treves (*ca.* 1075). To his sorrow he was demoted from
the school to the kitchen. He utters his complaint in a poem which also contains a catalogue of authors. Of pagans there appear Cato, Camillus (?),
Tully, Boethius, Lucan, Virgil, Statius, Sallust, and Terence. These nine
are matched by nine Christians: Augustine, Gregory, Jerome, Prosper,
Arator, Prudentius, Sedulius, Juvencus, Eusebius. So here the Christian
writers who were esteemed at St. Gall and neglected at Speyer are received
into the canon (ἐγκρινόμενοι). We find them in Conrad of Hirsau too,
but increased by Theodulus' eclogue. Reviewing Conrad's catalogue of authors we see that Nos. 1–4 constitute a class by themselves—beginners'
reading. Nos. 5–10 are the Christian poets. There follow three prose writers, one of whom is the Christian Boethius, then the pagan poets, except
that Terence is replaced by Ovid. If we subtract the four elementary authors from the list of twenty-one, there remain seventeen: six Christian
and eight pagan poets, one Christian and two pagan prose writers. The

effort to establish a balance between Christians and Pagans is evident. It is a deliberate plan of study: from the best of the pagan and Christian canons a *medieval school canon* is formed. It remains the skeleton for the very greatly enlarged catalogues of the thirteenth century.

The most notable of Conrad's new additions is Theodulus' spiritual eclogue.[37] The employment of the Virgilian eclogue form to treat Christian matters is found as early as the fourth century in a Virgilian cento by a certain Pomponius (otherwise unknown), who introduces the Virgilian shepherds Tityrus and Meliboeus as partners in a dialogue. Theodulus then had the excellent idea of replacing them by the allegorical figures of Pseustis ("Liar") and Alithia ("Truth"). The latter represents Christianity, the former Paganism. The role of judge in the poetic contest is conferred upon Phronesis ("Understanding")—a personification introduced by Martianus Capella and still found in the twelfth century. Pseustis comes from Athens and recites stories from mythology; Alithia is descended from David and replies with counter-examples from the Old Testament. The victory, naturally, goes to her. I conjecture that the poem was written by a schoolman for pedagogical purposes. It was eminently suited to teach, and at the same time to detoxicate, mythology. In the medieval canon the pagan and Christian authors were simply ranged side by side. There was a lack of any Christian corrective. Our pseudonymous poet provided it in the form of a pleasant fiction. It would have been necessary to invent such a school author if he had not appeared of himself in the nick of time. He thus became an essential ingredient of the medieval canon and survived its downfall.[38]

That downfall is the reverse side of the brilliant period of learning brought in by the Age of the Universities. As late as *ca.* 1150 dialectics is still the only enemy of the study of the *auctores*. But even before 1200 jurisprudence, medicine, and theology are added to the roster; and, after 1250, Aristotelianism in philosophy and natural science. In the first half of the thirteenth century John of Garland is still working in Paris but he seems to have found no successors there. There are still teachers of literature—they are now called "auctorists"—but they have become very unassuming. The Bamberg schoolmaster Hugh of Trimberg calls himself an

---

[37] The name Theodulus was earlier considered a translation of Godescalc (805–866 or 869). Strecker showed that this was an error and placed the poem in the tenth century.

[38] Theodulus in Old French literature: Gröber, *Grundriss*, II, 755 and 1067. G. L. Hamilton's essay on Theodulus in the Middle Ages (*Modern Philology*, VII [1909], 169) is inaccessible to me. As "Theodolet" Theodulus appears in Rabelais (*Gargantua*, ch. 14). The poem formed part of the *Auctores octo morales*, a schoolbook which was still used in the middle of the sixteenth century, and which represents the final stage of the medieval canon of authors.—The diminutive form (Theodolet) is customary in the Middle Ages for elementary authors, e.g., Catunculus for Cato.

auctorista [39] in his *Registrum multorum auctorum*. But he modestly gives his profession the lowest place:

> Qui perfectus fieri nequeat artista
> Vel propter penuriam rerum decretista,
> Saltem illud appetat ut sit auctorista!
> Sicque non inglorius erit latinista.
>
> Sibique grammatica sit nota regularis,
> In qua studens sedulo proficiat scolaris,
> Ut prodesse valeat pluribus ignaris;
> Tamen se non preferat doctoribus claris!

Literature no longer brings anything in, it is not one of the *artes lucrativae* such as theology, jurisprudence, medicine.

Dante, as we saw, selected from the list of authors the "bella scuola" of the five greatest antique poets. But they are only the élite within an élite, as the Doctors of the Church are among the Fathers of the Church. Among the dwellers in the "nobile castello" Dante further names Aristotle, Socrates, Plato, Democritus, Anaxagoras, Thales, Empedocles, Heraclitus, Zeno, Dioscorides, Orpheus, Cicero, Linus, the younger Seneca, Euclid, Ptolemy, Hippocrates, Avicenna, Galen, Averroes. Here philosophers, natural scientists, geometricians, physicians are joined with the mythical pre-Homeric poets (*Inf.*, IV, 131 f.). Later Dante uses Statius' meeting with Virgil (*Purg.*, XXII) to receive Juvenal, Terence, Caecilius, Plautus, Varro, Persius, Euripides, Antiphon, Simonides, and Agathon into the number of approved authors. In Dante, together with the Romans we find Arabs and Greeks. Of course he could no more read these than could his contemporaries. But their names were handed down by tradition.[40] Chaucer has two catalogues of authors. In the house of Fame the most famous authors stand—in true medieval fashion—each on his pillar (l. 1419 ff.). Here the poet combines two or three principles of classification but carries none of them through. Josephus, as representing the Jews, stands alone. A remarkably heterogeneous collection of authorities for the Trojan War comprises Statius (because of his *Achilleis*), Homer, Dares, Dictys, Lollius (an unsolved crux), Guido delle Colonne, Geoffrey of Monmouth. These all stand upon pillars of iron (= Mars) or of iron and lead (lead = Saturn). Virgil stands alone on bright tinned iron, Ovid on copper, Claudian on sulphur (because he tells of Pluto, Proserpine, and Hell). We have, then, a principle of classification according to historical subject-matter—which,

---

[39] On *auctorista, theologus, decretista, logicus* cf. H. Denifle, *Die Universitäten des Mittelalters*, I, 475, note.—The following quotation in Langosch's edition, ll. 43 ff. *Ibid.*, l. 822 on the "artes lucrativae" in contrast to literature. *Auctorista* appears as *autoristre* in Henri d'Andeli (13th cent.).

[40] Isidore knows Simonides and Euripides.—On knowledge of Arabic: Ugo Monneret de Villard, *Lo studio dell' Islàm in Europa nel XII e nel XIII secolo* (1944) (= *Studi e Testi*, 110).

however, is not applied to Virgil, Ovid, and Claudian; and a principle of classification according to the value scale of the metals—but with silver and gold missing;[41] and a co-ordination between metals on the one hand and planets and psychological types on the other—but only for iron and lead. The poet did an untidy job: it is "a ful confus matere" (l. 1517). Far more satisfactory is the close of the *Troilus*, in which the poet takes leave of his work (V, 1789 ff.):

> But litel book, no making thou n'envye,
> But subgit be to alle poesye;
> And kis the steppes, wher-as thou seest pace
> Virgile, Ovyde, Omer, Lucan and Stace.

Chaucer here had in mind the close of the *Thebais* (XII, 816 f.):

> Vive, precor; nec tu divinam Aeneida tempta,
> Sed longe sequere et vestigia semper adora.

From the dim and musty vault of Fame, Chaucer has stepped out under the sunny sky of Italy. The schoolmaster Francis Meres in his *Palladis Tamia* (1598), which gives us our earliest list of Shakespeare's works, names as the greatest Latin authors Virgil, Ovid, Horace, Lucan, Lucretius, Ausonius, Claudian, and—Silius Italicus![42] By no means a happy addition. But the Elizabethans appear to have had rather confused ideas about antique poetry. William Webbe tells us (*A Discourse of English Poetrie*, 1586) that Homer was later than Pindar. In a long list of authors he distinguishes Silius and Lucan as "Hystoricall Poets, no lesse profitable then delightsome to bee read," but also names Boethius, Lucretius, Statius, Valerius Flaccus, Manilius, Ausonius, Claudian, as well as Baptista Mantuanus and other Neo-Latin poets. The Middle Ages hardly knew Silius. He was discovered by Poggio in 1417 and then introduced to England by Italian Humanism. It would be a useful task for literary science to determine how the canon of antique authors has changed from 1500 to the present, i.e., how it has diminished.[43] At the height of French Classicism authors were still considered worth reading who now are known only to specialists. For the education of the then heir to the French throne (*in usum Delphini*) Pierre Daniel Huet directed the publication of a library of classics, of which twenty-two volumes appeared between 1674 and 1691. Among them are Manilius, Florus, Aurelius Victor, Eutropius, Dictys, and others. That an edition of Martianus Capella by Leibniz was also contemplated we have already seen (*supra*, p. 38, n. 5). For Huet,

---

[41] On the scale of metals, cf. Excursus VI, *infra*.

[42] Macaulay in his diary notes with relief the day on which he finished reading this tedious epic poem. René Pichon calls him "un écrivain tout à fait classique dans le mauvais sens du mot" (*Histoire de la littérature latine* [1898]).

[43] For the estimation of the *auctores ca.* 1500 cf. B. Botfield, *Praefationes et epistolae editionibus principibus auctorum veterum praepositae* (Cambridge, 1861).

all these authors ranked as examples of "pure Latinity." [44] This is but another expression of the fact that *ca.* 1680—at the height of French Classicism—the literary world still adhered to a canon of authors which on the whole coincides with that of Hugh of Trimberg (1280). The separation and proscription of "silver" Latinity appears to have been first accomplished by German Neo-Humanism about 1800. [45] Frederick the Great still favored the reading of Quintilian in school. Since when have Virgil's *Bucolics* and *Georgics*, Persius, Lucan, Statius, Martial, Juvenal, and Quintilian ceased to be read in the schools of Germany, France, and England?

5. Modern Canon Formation

Of the modern literatures, the Italian was the first to develop a canon. This is explained by the cultural position of Italy about 1500. Both the study of the ancients and Neo-Latin poetry were in such a flourishing state there, that they represented a competition which vernacular poetry might not disregard. If the latter was to thrive, it must be able to legitimize itself through model authors who could serve as a standard for Italian literary practice as Virgil did for Latin. The situation was further complicated by the fact that there was no common literary language in Italy. This problem had already occupied Dante (*De vulgari eloquentia*). It forms (as the so-called "questione della lingua") a constant of Italian intellectual history down to Manzoni and even later. None of the other great modern nations presents anything comparable. A study of the differentiating characteristics of the modern literatures would have to deal with this. It was Pietro Bembo's accomplishment to advance a theory of the Italian language which was to be accepted as the norm for vernacular poetry. The three great fourteenth-century Tuscans (Dante, however, being included only under severe restrictions) were set up as linguistic models. The classicistic tendencies of the cinquecento ran themselves into the ground in interminable discussions of Aristotle's poetic theory. No one will maintain that they were of any profit to Italian poetry. They found an echo in France in the school of Ronsard, which Sainte-Beuve described as "notre première poésie classique avortée."

For the general picture of modern European literature, the classicistic tendencies of the Italian cinquecento were of importance only indirectly —through their influence on French theory in the sixteenth and seventeenth centuries. There is no closed, "classical" system of Italian literature. Dante, Petrarch, Boccaccio, Ariosto, Tasso are great authors for whom there is no common denominator. Each of the five has a different relation to Antiquity.

[44] *Memoirs of the Life of Peter Daniel Huet, written by himself and translated by John Aikin,* M.D., II (London, 1810), p. 168.

[45] However, we find a classicistic reaction in Italy as early as the first half of the eighteenth century, e.g., in the Latin academic orations of Jacopo Facciolati (1682–1769).

Only France has a classical literary system in the full sense. The will to *systematic* regulation is in fact an earmark of the French seventeenth century. Boileau puts Malherbe far above Villon and Ronsard because Malherbe, supposedly, first wrote correct verse

Et réduisit la Muse aux règles du devoir.

Poor Muse! Boileau himself, narrow-minded and dull as he was,[46] could set himself up as the law-giver of Parnassus. As a French Horace, he turned out satires, epistles, an *ars poetica*—and odes. Common sense ("tout doit tendre au bon sens"!) and "reason" were his panacea, poetry was degraded to the level of correct rhymes, tragedy was bound to the supposed "rules" of Italian Aristotelianism. The system could not have prevailed if it had not corresponded to the tendencies of the French mind, which at precisely this juncture, under Louis XIV, had attained to a powerful self-expression supported by the nation's hegemony over Europe. French Classicism is not an artificial imitation of antique models (upon which, rather, it merely looks back to reassure itself), but the expression of a native and national content, in which the rationalism which is a basic characteristic of the French mind predominates. That then, and for generations after, France labored to promulgate the forms which correspond to her national mind as universally binding, exemplifies a trait which we find throughout the course of French history.

What various meanings have been attributed to the concept Classicism in France during the last two centuries, we cannot here trace. An epoch is marked by Fénelon's declaration in his address to the Academy in 1693: "On a enfin compris, Messieurs, qu'il faut écrire comme les Raphaël, les Carrache et les Poussin ont peint." Here for the first time the classical ideal is conceived as one common to all the arts; here, by being linked with the painting of the Renaissance, it is set in a realm beyond the wranglings of scholars and aestheticians and partisans of the Ancients or the Moderns. It is the "great" style of modern art, born in the Rome of Julius II and Leo X.

This pointed the way for the historians. In his *Siècle de Louis XIV* (1751) Voltaire treats of classical literature in the chapter *Des beaux arts*, where we read: "Le siècle de Louis XIV a donc en tout le destinée des siècles de Léon X, d'Auguste, d'Alexandre." [47] Periclean Classicism was not yet apprehended. The flowering periods of the arts were co-ordinated

[46] French criticism and literary history still maintain today that Boileau was a great critic. For the contrary view I refer the reader to George Saintsbury, who in his *History of Criticism* (II [1902], 280 ff.) carefully analyzes Boileau's work and concludes (p. 300): "I am not conscious of any unfairness or omission . . . in this survey; and after it I think we may go back to the general question, may ask, Is this a great or even a good critic? and may answer it in the negative."

[47] For Voltaire's estimate of French Classicism see Raymond Naves, *Le Goût de Voltaire* (Paris, n.d.).—Cf. also the chapter "Les Idées et les Lettres" in Paul Hazard, *La Pensée européenne au XVIIIᵉ siècle*, II, (1946), 293 ff.

with great rulers. Thus a new type of historical concept is introduced, independent of the word "classic." To an Augustus, a Louis XIV, England opposes her queens: Elizabeth, Anne, Victoria. She coins the concept of the "Augustan Age"—for so Goldsmith baptized the period of Queen Anne in his essay "The Augustan Age in England." [48] It is generally considered to have lasted from 1700 to 1740. But with Dr. Johnson (d. 1784) and Gibbon (d. 1794) classic taste dominates the following decades too. The eighteenth century is one of those periods in which England's "Latin" element (*supra*, p. 35) wells up.

Goethe had in mind the fact that French Classicism was rooted in the national state when he made his significant observations on the nature of Classicism (1795), which he regarded as impossible in Germany.[49] The classic system still represents the firmest support of France's cultural tradition today. From this point of view, it was of the greatest advantage that it was attacked by Romanticism from 1820 onwards. It was in these debates that the word *classicisme* first became current; as late as 1823 Stendhal (*Racine et Shakespeare*) still regarded it as a neologism.[50] Since then it has become the palladium not only of the French intellectual world but also of French cultural propaganda. The nature of Classicism is perpetually being defined, distilled, and modernized in new phrases. Even the France-ideology of so subtle a mind as Paul Valéry's runs at last into this conformism. How long it will continue to convince other peoples and cultures may perhaps be asked. France has gained a great deal from her Classicism, but she has paid a high price for it: that of being tied to forms of consciousness which have become too narrow for the European spirit. Gide is the sublime exception.

From the point of view of canon formation and of the naming of periods, Spain is as different from the rest of Europe as it is in many other respects. The first peculiarity of Spanish literary history is that it has a Romanticism

[48] French criticism (e.g., Hazard in his book on the eighteenth century cited in the previous note) does not think very highly of English Classicism. It is amusing to note that, on the other hand, Coleridge (*Biographia Literaria*, ch. 1) describes the school of Pope as "that school of French poetry, condensed and invigorated by English understanding."

[49] In his essay "Literarischer Sansculottismus" (Jubiläumsausgabe, XXXVI, 140 f.).

[50] "*Romantico!* A strange word to the Italians, still unknown in Naples and the happy Campagna, in Rome used at most among German artists, it has been making a great stir lately in Lombardy, especially in Milan. The public is divided into two parties: They are mutually hostile, and if we Germans quite innocently chance to use the adjective 'romantic' there, the words 'Romanticism' and 'Criticism' immediately bear witness to the existence of two irreconcilable sects . . . Among us Germans, the turn towards the Romantic from a culture acquired first from the Ancients and later from the French was prepared by specifically Christian religious sentiments and encouraged and strengthened by cloudy Nordic heroic lays": Goethe, 1820 (Jubiläumsausgabe, XXXVII, 118 f.).—Stendhal's *Racine et Shakespeare* is connected with these Italian polemics.

but no Classicism.[51] Even more noteworthy is the fact that the Iberian authors of the Imperial Age are considered to belong to Spanish national literature. The two Senecas, Lucan, Martial, Quintilian, Pomponius Mela, Juvencus, Prudentius, Merobaudes, Orosius, Isidore, and others appear in the most widely circulated modern textbooks, which herein faithfully follow the practice of the Middle Ages and the Renaissance. The Marqués de Santillana's poetics (15th century) comes from Isidore and Cassiodorus. In his epicedium on Enrique de Villena (d. 1433) he has a catalogue of authors containing the following names: Livy, Virgil, Macrobius, Valerius Flaccus, Sallust, Seneca, Tully, Cassalianus (?), Alan, Boethius, Petrarch, Fulgentius, Dante, Geoffrey of Vinsauf, Terence, Juvenal, Statius, Quintilian. What does this signify? Santillana represents the first wave of Italianism in Spain, but at the same time he preserves the medieval concept of the *auctores*: all are equally good, all belong to no period and have no history. But this is still precisely Baltasar Gracián's attitude when, at the beginning of his *Criticón* (1651), he says that in his book he imitates the excellencies of the following "autores de buen genio": Homer (allegories), Aesop (fictions), Seneca (instruction), Lucian (judgment), Apuleius (descriptions), Plutarch (moralizing), Heliodorus (complications), Ariosto (interruptions which increase suspense), Boccalini (literary criticism), Barclay[52] (mordant polemic). Gracián is writing when Spain's period of florescence is in decline. Yet he regards world literature from Homer to his own age with the same timeless universalism with which Calderón contemplates world history from Semiramis to the siege of Breda. Neither Humanism nor the Renaissance, neither Antiquity nor the Middle Ages, represent divisions of the total literary tradition to the subjects of the last Hapsburgs. Spain has its own particular sense of time, as it has its own particular national consciousness. There Visigothic kings like Wamba are as celebrated as the Roman emperors of Spanish origin: Trajan, Hadrian, Theodosius. All that ever took place on Spanish soil is accounted a part of the greatness of Spain—recently even the Islamic culture of the south. Universal and national points of view coincide. For Gracián (*El Discreto*, ch. 25) Latin and Spanish are "the two universal languages, the keys of the world," while Greek, Italian, French, English, and German rank together as "individual languages."

Spain neither refers to its period of literary florescence as "Classicism" nor connects it with the name of a monarch; instead, it calls it "the golden age" (*el siglo de oro*). Garcilaso de la Vega (d. 1536) stands at the beginning of it, Calderón (d. 1681) at the end. It embraces all contraries: the popular style of the Romancero, and the hermeticism of Góngora;

---

[51] Many histories of literature set the eighteenth century down as a "Classic" or "Neo-Classic" period. The period, however, is one of decline. Spain had no Addison, no Pope, no Dr. Johnson, no Gibbon.

[52] John Barclay's (1582–1621) Latin romance *Argenis* was one of the successful books of the seventeenth century.

the corrosive realism of the picaresque novel, and the heights of speculative mysticism; the classic symmetry of a Luis de León, and the extravagances of conceptism; the greatest, wisest, and gayest novel in modern literature, and a world theater of a thousand plays.[53] The lyric poetry of the *siglo de oro* is, in Valery Larbaud's words, "la seule, de toute la Romania, qui nous rapproche un peu du paradis perdu de la lyrique latine." Only English lyric poetry between 1590 and 1650 can stand beside it. The wealth and originality of the *siglo de oro* would be incomprehensible historically if one did not reflect that all the strength and savor of the Middle Ages, including the Latin and the Islamic Middle Ages, flowed into the period of the conquistadores and of Spain's transatlantic empire. The contradictions within her "golden" literature are usually interpreted as contradictions of the Spanish national character. But this psychological explanation is insufficient. The Spanish literary system preserves the crossing of styles, genres, and traditions which we have found to be a distinguishing characteristic of the Latin Middle Ages. Italy had no Middle Ages in the sense in which the northern nations had,[54] France broke with her Middle Ages about 1550. Spain preserved hers and incorporated it into the national tradition. The waves of Italianism which swept over to Spain in the fifteenth and sixteenth centuries exerted a formal influence, but they never touched the core of Spain. The literary theorists of the Italian cinquecento were scandalized by the lack of a "classical" Spanish literature,[55] but fortunately they were unable to change the course of things. The English continuity from Chaucer to Spenser affords the closest analogy to the uninterrupted course of Spanish literature—but with the important qualification that both of those poets were far more strongly influenced by Italianism than were the Spaniards between 1400 and 1650. Spanish literature cannot be measured by "classic" (one might say, by "European") standards. Its exuberant wealth and variety are its own and are still unexhausted. Its future rests upon the cultural development and the world-wide importance of the Spanish-speaking nations.

"Golden Age"—a Latin coinage; a concept in which the Augustan Age of Rome is reflected. It was in this sense that Friedrich Schlegel understood it: "The moderns followed the Romans in this; what happened in the times of Augustus and Maecenas was a foreshadowing of the Italians

53 Of Lope's more than 2000 plays, 468 are extant; of Tirso de Molina's 400, only some 80. The latter figures also apply to Vélez de Guevara. Of Calderón, we have 200 plays.

54 Its share in the "Latin Middle Ages" down to 1200 was very modest.

55 J. F. Montesinos in his edition of Juan de Valdés, *Diálogo de la lengua* (*Clásicos de "La Lectura"* [1928]), p. lxiv, n. 1, with a reference to Croce, *La Spagna nella vita italiana durante la Rinascenza*[2] (1922), 170 f.—In his treatise Valdés names, as authors worth reading, Juan de Mena, Jorge Manrique, Juan del Encina, Boethius and Erasmus, Catherine of Siena, John Climacus (*ca.* 579–*ca.* 649), Livy, Caesar, Valerius Maximus, Quintus Curtius, and . . . romances of chivalry (*Amadis, Palmerin, Primaleón*). This in only a selection!

of the cinquecento.[56] Louis XIV tried to force the same spring of the spirit in France; the English agreed to regard the taste of Queen Anne's day as the best; and thenceforth no nation was willing to be without its own golden age; each succeeding one was emptier and poorer than the last, and what the Germans finally considered 'golden' cannot be described in terms consonant with decency" (*Gespräch über die Poesie* [1800]). What Schlegel left unsaid in that last clause, he expressed in 1812 in his lectures at Vienna on the history of ancient and modern literature (*Geschichte der alten und neuen Literatur*): "How relative, at least in respect to our literature, the concept of a golden age is, how strong the inclination to put it farther and farther back, can be exemplified in one writer. Gottsched in one of his poems puts that happy golden age back in the days of Frederick, the first king of Prussia. The writers whom he praises as the classics of that period . . . are especially Besser, Neukirch, and Pietsch." Gottsched had the France of Boileau in mind, as Opitz had the France of Ronsard. He overhastily inaugurated a German section of Parnassus with unqualified candidates. He had to live to see his fiat overthrown by the attacks of the Zurich group * and Lessing. Schlegel's statements contain a belated echo of this polemic. They are the answer of romantic criticism to the flat reasonableness of the German Enlightenment.

Classicism and Romanticism! The controversy over these words and over the "essences" ascribed to them is one of the latest forms of the opposition between the "Ancients" and the "Moderns." To estimate it correctly, one may well bear in mind the following simple facts.

French literature has a clearly defined and codified Classicism and an equally clearly defined and codified Romanticism. French Romanticism is distinguished from all others by the fact that it is a conscious Anti-Classicism. In France Romanticism and Classicism stand in the same kind of opposition as Revolution and Ancien Régime. Spain and England have a Romanticism but no Classicism. Germany has both, but with a very significant modification: Romanticism and Classicism exist at the same time and to some extent in the same place. The Jena Romanticism of 1798 is a reflection, a clarification, and partly a criticism of the Weimar Classicism of 1795. In the older Goethe, on the other hand, there is much that is essentially Romantic. But there are also great writers of our classic period —Jean Paul, Hölderlin, Kleist—who can be put in neither camp. The German period of florescence from 1750 to 1832 is not divisible by the divisor Classicism-Romanticism. What is the case with Italy? Is it still meaningful today to oppose the "classic" Leopardi to the "romantic"

---

[56] Here the age of Leo X has become the cinquecento. The Italian system of periodizing by centuries would seem to go back to art history. It has been transferred to literature. Modern literature is called *Novecento*. The system has great advantages, e.g., it proceeds automatically and has no value connotations.

[* Bodmer and Breitinger.]

Manzoni? [57] Scholastic antitheses which meant something around 1830 have become empty echoes now, a century later. The only modern literature and literary history in which they are still rigidly preserved, as if they were metaphysical essences, is the French. This is psychologically comprehensible in the light of the stiffening and petrification of the classical system in France, at which generations of doctrinaire critics—from Laharpe by way of Nisard to Brunetière—have labored. It was strengthened by fusion with political ideologies (e.g., in the *Action française*). In this position of affairs, Romanticism had to take the form of a revolt which fought "battles" with the existing order (*la bataille d'Hernani*) as Napoleon did with reactionary Europe.

Modern French criticism introduced some degree of shading into this rudimentary palette of black and white by discovering premonitory signs of the Romantic Revolution in the great authors of the eighteenth century (Rousseau, Diderot, and others). This necessitated a slight change in the system of literary periods: between Classicism and Romanticism the period of "Pre-Romanticism" (*préromantisme*) was inserted.[58] Upon similar considerations Italian criticism recently introduced a "Pre-Humanism" (*preumanesimo*) of the thirteenth century. The epistemological value of such retouched period names is very slight. They may occasionally be of some practical use as auxiliary constructions. But their effect is harmful and misleading when they are misused as hypostatized concepts. Finally, a gross distortion of the historical picture results if the development of the several literatures of Europe since 1500 is squeezed into such an inadequate schema, and one derived wholly from the course of French literature. This error has unfortunately been raised to the status of official doctrine by the French school of comparative literature.

Paul Van Tieghem, who is entitled to much gratitude for his researches into the Pre-Romanticism of the eighteenth century, constructs his *Histoire littéraire de l'Europe et de l'Amérique de la Renaissance à nos jours* (1941) according to the following plan: Renaissance, Classicism, Romanticism, Realism, the Present. Pre-Romanticism is thus included under Classicism. This leads to all sorts of incongruities. Since the Spanish drama is non-Classic, it belongs to the Renaissance. So the latter lasts in Spain down to 1681, the year of Calderón's death. To Classicism are assigned, among others: Brockes, the Brazilian epic *Caramurú* (1781) by Santa Rita Durão, Hölderlin, and the Abbé Delille (d. 1813). Goethe and Schiller are "Pre-Romantics" as are Bilderdijk, Csokonai Vitéz, and Niemcewicz. Some 1400 authors, divided among 35 languages and 37 nations, are disposed of in this fashion. To be sure, many of these nations did not come into existence until after 1800 (Brazil and the other South American states), some of

---

[57] On this cf. the pertinent comments of Guido Mazzoni, *L'Ottocento*[3] (1934), I, 566.

[58] D. Mornet, *Le Romantisme en France au 18e siècle*, 1912.—P. Van Tieghem, *Le Préromantisme. Etudes d'histoire littéraire européenne*, 2 vols. (1924 and 1930).

them not until 1919. This approach to literary history makes the naive attempt to take a schema (the sequence: 17th century = Classicism, 18th century = Classicism and Pre-Romanticism, 19th century = Romanticism, etc.) which applies to France and France alone and force it upon European literature, and combines it with the political map of the peace settlements after the first World War. It is democratic, in that all literatures enjoy the same rights. In the League of Nations they did not. It will hardly, however, prove possible to avoid distinguishing major and minor literatures among these 35 or 37.

The French literary system was breached by the discovery of England (Voltaire, 1734), Germany (Mme de Staël, 1813), and Asia (Burnouf, Renan). In 1850 Sainte-Beuve announced that the Temple of Taste must be rebuilt as the "Panthéon de tous les nobles humains." He admitted Valmiki and Vyasa (a gesture which cost very little), "et pourquoi pas Confucius lui-même?" Shakespeare was taken in (ἐγκρινόμενος) as the "plus grand des classiques sans le savoir," Goethe not. That did not come until 1858, when Sainte-Beuve announced: "Goethe agrandit le Parnasse, il l'étage, il le peuple à chaque station, à chaque sommet (Parnassus has two peaks), à chaque angle de rocher; il le fait pareil, trop pareil peut-être, au Mont-Serrat de Catalogne (ce mont plus dentelé qu'arrondi); il ne le détruit pas." To be sure, in his posthumously published notes Sainte-Beuve says: "Je ne me figure pas qu'on dise: les classiques allemands."

The concept of a world literature could not but shatter the French canon. Sainte-Beuve sensed the dilemma. He did not solve it. From his day to Van Tieghem's, France's tie to the Classicism of the seventeenth century has proved to be a tenaciously maintained attitude of opposition to Europeanism. But today it strikes one as a pure anachronism. It has been breached by French writers of the last decades who have come to experience the breadth and variety of the European (and American) spirit. None of them has treated of literary cosmopolitanism as subtly and expertly as Valery Larbaud, whose full significance only the next generations will perceive.[59] He rejects the transfer of political concepts to literature (which we still found in Van Tieghem): "Il y a une grande différence entre la carte politique et la carte intellectuelle du monde. La première change d'aspect tous les cinquante ans; elle est couverte de divisions arbitraires et incertaines, et ses centres prépondérants sont très mobiles. Au contraire, la carte intellectuelle se modifie très lentement et ses divisions présentent une grande stabilité, car ce sont les mêmes qui figurent sur la carte que connaissent les philologues et où il n'est question ni de nations ni de puissances, mais seulement de domaines linguistiques . . . Il existe un triple domaine central: français-allemand-italien, et une ceinture de domaines extérieurs, de 'marches': scandinaves, slaves, roumain, grec, espagnol, cata-

[59] My book *Französischer Geist im neuen Europa* (1925) contains a study of him.

lan, portugais et anglais, dont les plus importants, par leur antiquité et
à cause de leurs immenses rallonges d'outre-Atlantique, sont les domaines
espagnols et anglais." [60] From this view Larbaud arrives at a program
for a politics of mind which has left behind all pretensions to hegemony,[61]
and is concerned only with facilitating and accelerating the exchange of
intellectual merchandise.

[60] Valery Larbaud, *Ce Vice impuni, la Lecture* . . . (1925), 46 f.
[61] "une politique qui, avec la fin de la domination du 'gout français,' a dépassé
la phase des accaparements, de l'impérialisme."

15

Mannerism

1. *Classicism and Mannerism*

WE FEEL the Classicism of Raphael and of Phidias as Nature raised to the Ideal. To be sure, every conceptual attempt to circumscribe the essence of great art is a makeshift. Yet the above formula would to some extent apply to what affects us as "classical" in Sophocles, Virgil, Racine, and Goethe. Classic art in this highest sense thrives only in brief periods of florescence. Even in Raphael's late period art history finds the seed of what it calls "Mannerism" and interprets as a decadent form of Classicism. An artistic "manner," which can find expression in the most various forms, overruns the classic norm. It is left to the taste of the individual to decide what place in the scale of values he will assign to this change. Anyone who prefers Tintoretto to Raphael can give good grounds for his preference. This is not the place to discuss whether the word "Mannerism" is a good choice as the designation of a period in art history and to what extent it is justified. We may borrow it because it is well adapted to fill a gap in the terminology of literary science. For that purpose, to be sure, we must free the word from all art-historical connotations and broaden its meaning until it represents simply the common denominator for all literary tendencies which are opposed to Classicism, whether they be pre-classical, post-classical, or contemporary with any Classicism. Understood in this sense, Mannerism is a constant in European literature. It is the complementary phenomenon of the Classicism of all periods. We had found that the twin concept Classicism-Romanticism was not good for much. The polarity of Classicism and Mannerism is far more useful as a conceptual instrument and can illuminate connections which it is easy to overlook. Much of what we shall call Mannerism is today set down as "Baroque." But this word has caused such confusion that it is better to eliminate it. The word Mannerism further deserves the preference because, compared with "Baroque," it has a minimum of historical associations. The concepts of intellectual history should be so constructed that they offer the least possible opportunity for misuse.

273

Within the concept "Classicism" we must introduce another distinction. What we have called classical periods of florescence are isolated peaks, which we can bring together as "Ideal Classicism" only for purposes of practical communication. They rise out of the spreading plateau of "Standard Classicism." [1] By this term I designate all authors and periods which write correctly, clearly, and in accordance with the rules, without representing the highest human and artistic values. For example: Xenophon, Cicero, Quintilian, Boileau, Pope, Wieland. Standard Classicism is imitable and teachable. It is of advantage to the economy of a literature if a large stock of such goods is available. But the situation is alarming if the literature does not maintain a consciousness of the difference in level (which is at the same time a difference in essence)—and this should be the task of criticism. French Classicism did not avoid this danger, perhaps did not see it. This is true even of the great Sainte-Beuve. In his *Temple du goût* he reserves a place after Shakespeare for the "tout dernier des classiques en diminutif." [2] His name is Andrieux.

The standard classicist says what he has to say in a form naturally suited to the subject. To be sure, he will "decorate" his discourse according to well-tried rhetorical tradition, that is, he will furnish it with *ornatus*. A danger of the system lies in the fact that, in manneristic epochs, the *ornatus* is piled on indiscriminately and meaninglessly. In rhetoric itself, then, lies concealed one of the seeds of Mannerism. It produces a luxuriant growth in Late Antiquity and the Middle Ages.

2.   Rhetoric and Mannerism

I hope to make my meaning clear by means of a minimum of examples.

1. *Hyperbaton* (*transgressio, transcensio*) signifies a freer word order in which what belongs together grammatically is separated by intervening words. A mild example: "animadverti omnem accusatoris orationem in duas divisam esse partes" (Cicero) instead of "in duas partes divisam esse." This is a short and normal hyperbaton; only two words intervene. But as soon as writers begin playing with this figure, it is natural to make it longer and longer. The younger Pliny already asks coquettishly: "Num potui longius hyperbaton facere?" (*Ep.*, VIII, 7). To be sure, Isidore (*Et.*, II, 20, 2) still warned against overlong hyperbata, because they made a period

[1] Jean Paul: "That the Classical is the height of form (or representation) can be misunderstood in two ways. The common herd of writers and readers, insensitive to poetical perfection and form, are glad—by jumping to conclusions from works in dead languages, where every word is final and authoritative, to living languages —to make grammatical perfection and form the star of the Order of Classicism. But then no one would be classical except a few grammarians and schoolmasters, and not one genius; then the majority of the French are classical, with the exception of a few men like Rousseau and Montaigne, and everybody could learn to be classical." (*Vorschule der Ästhetik*, Dritte Abteilung, *Miserikordias-Vorlesung für Stylistiker*, ch. 4; *Sämtliche Werke* [2] [1841], XIX, 28 f.)

[2] *Causeries du Lundi*, III, 50.

harder to understand. But Bede (Halm, 614, 29 f.) could praise the hyperbaton "ex omni parte confusum" in a verse of the Psalms (68:14). Hyperbaton appears as a stylistic Latinism in the classicist Garcilaso (Sonnet 16, 8):

> *Por manos de Vulcano artificiosas.*

In Góngora, as is well known, it became a manner.

2. *Circumlocution* (*periphrasis*) has been a current figure since Antiquity. Goethe has a periphrase for Venice in the words:

> *Jene neptunische Stadt, allwo man geflügelte Löwen*
> *Göttlich verehrt . . .*

> (That city of Neptune where to winged lions
> Honors divine are paid . . .)

The earliest examples are in Hesiod, in the language of oracles, and later in Pindar. The latter says "the bored work of bees" for "honey." The solemn and poetic language of Attic tragedy also runs to rare formations, to veiled and periphrastic expressions. In all these earliest forms we should perhaps see reminiscences of cult language. Periphrase, later so hackneyed, was most probably sacerdotal in origin. Quintilian (VIII, 6, 59) distinguishes two uses of circumlocution ("circuitus eloquendi"): the euphemistic (to preserve decorum) and the decorative. He adds that this embellishment can easily degenerate into a blemish. Virgil is fond of using periphrastic indications of time. For "night will fall" he says (*Aen.*, I, 374):

> *Ante diem clauso componet Vesper Olympo.*

"The next day broke" (IV, 6 f.):

> *Postera Phoebea lustrabat lampade terras*
> *Umentemque Aurora polo dimoverat umbram.*

"At dawn" (IV, 118 f.):

> *. . . ubi primos crastinus ortus*
> *Extulerit Titan*[3] *radiisque retexerit orbem.*

Such circumlocutions remain within the bounds of good taste. To indicate time they were even required. Quintilian (I, 4, 4) observes that an acquaintance with astronomy is necessary to an understanding of the poets, since they "totiens ortu occasuque signorum in declarandis temporibus utantur." Seneca makes fun of this mannerism (*Ep.*, 122, 11 ff.) and parodies it in the form of "double indications of time," a literary joke which has enjoyed an extraordinary vogue since Antiquity.[4] The astronomical periphrase was also current in medieval Latin poetry (*Gesta Friderici me-*

---

[3] The phonetic succession *rit ti* is an offense against euphony.
[4] Otto Weinreich, *Phöbus, Aurora, Kalender und Uhr* (1937), in which the subject is followed from A.D. 54 (Seneca) to 1931 (Robert Musil).

trice, 1797 f.), and its use is inculcated in Gervase of Melkley's treatise on poetics (*ca.* 1210; *Stud. med.*, IX [1936], 64): "Perfecto versificatori non hyemet, non estuet, non noctescat, non diescat sine astronomia." Dante makes abundant use of it.[5] Shakespeare parodies it in the play in *Hamlet*:

> *Full thirty times hath Phoebus' cart gone round*
> *Neptune's salt wash and Tellus' orbed ground,*
> *And thirty dozen moons with borrow'd sheen*
> *About the world have times twelve thirties been.*

The abuse of periphrase begins with Statius. If someone has to climb a ladder, we find (*Thebais*, I, 841 f.):

> *Innumerosque gradus, gemina latus arbore clusos,*
> *Aerium sibi portat iter*[6] . . .

Ausonius self-complacently says (*Epist.*, XVI, 2, 7 ff.; ed. Schenkl, p. 175):

> *Possem absolute dicere,*
> *Sed dulcius circumloquar*
> *Diuque fando perfruar.*[7]

Claudian (*Carmina min.*, XXX, 147 ff.) finds a periphrase for "reading Homer and Virgil":

> . . . *quos Smyrna dedit, quos Mantua libros*
> *Percurrens*[8] . . .

Sidonius (*Carm.*, II, 184 ff.) imitates this and adds Cicero and Demosthenes:

> *Mantua quas acies pelagique pericula lusit*
> *Zmyrnaeas imitata tubas, quacumque loquendi*
> *Arpinas dat consul opem, sine fine secutus*
> *Fabro progenitum*[9] . . .

[5] He uses periphrases for: the time of the Trojan War (*Inf.*, XXI, 108); "in childhood" (*Purg.*, XI, 105); "before the expiration of some fifteen years" (*Purg.*, XXIII, 110 f.); "before the expiration of fifteen months" (*Inf.*, X, 79 f.); "before the arrival of some very distant time" (*Par.*, XXVII, 142 f.); "at the last full moon" (*Purg.*, XXIII, 119 f.); "in winter" (*Inf.*, XV, 9); "in summer" (*Inf.*, XXVI, 26 f. and XXXII, 32 f.); "at the beginning of the year" (*Inf.*, XXIV, 1 ff.); "transition from the ruddiness of dawn to sunrise" (*Purg.*, II, 7 ff.); "the coldest hour of the night" (*Purg.*, XIX, 1 ff.); "before sunrise" (*Purg.*, XXVII, 94 f.); "early in the morning" (*Purg.*, IX, 13 ff.); "eleven in the morning" (*Purg.*, XXII, 118); "twelve noon" (*Purg.*, XII, 80 f.); "one p.m." (*Par.*, XXVI, 141 f.); "two p.m." (*Purg.*, XXV, 2 f.); "three p.m." (*Purg.*, XV, 1 ff.); "sunset" (*Purg.*, XXVII, 1 ff.); "at dusk" (*Inf.*, XXVI, 28).

[6] "innumerable steps, enclosed between twin trees, an airy road."

[7] "I could speak directly but I prefer circumlocution and relish long-drawn-out discourse."   [8] "reading the books which Smyrna and Mantua bestowed."

[9] "What battles and sea dangers Mantua's poetry played with, imitating the Smyrnean trumpets; whatever aid to oratory the Arpinian consul brings—he who followed the offspring of the smith" (Demosthenes' father owned a manufactory of swords).

The medieval Latin arts of poetry make periphrase a division of the theory of *amplificatio* (artistic inflation of diction). Geoffrey of Vinsauf (Faral, 204, 229 ff.):

> *Longius ut sit opus ne ponas nomina rerum.*
> *Pone notas alias: nec plane detege, sed rem*
> *Innue per notulas, nec sermo perambulet in re,*
> *Sed rem circuiens longis ambagibus ambi*
> *Quod breviter dicturus eras* [10] . . .

Dante consciously adopted this stylistic prescription. In his letter to Can Grande (§ 66) he glosses *Par.*, I, 4—

> *Nel ciel che più della sua luce prende*

—by "prosequitur . . . circumloquens paradisum." There are more than a hundred and fifty periphrases in the *Divina Commedia*.[11] Dante is especially fond of using geographical[12] and astronomical[13] periphrases. To

[10] "To prolong the work you must avoid naming things by their names. Use other designations; reveal not a thing entirely but suggest it by hints [*innue*—cf. "innuendo"]; nor let your words course through your subject but rather take a long and circuitous route around what you were going to say briefly."

[11] Antique personages: Apollo (*Par.*, I, 31 f.); Apollo and Diana as sun and moon (*Purg.*, XX, 132); Aurora (*Purg.*, IX, 11); Circe (*Par.*, XXVIII, 137 f.); Lachesis (*Purg.*, XXI, 25); the centaurs (*Purg.*, XXIV, 121 ff.); Iris (*Purg.*, XXI, 50); Minotaur (*Inf.*, XII, 12); Procne (*Purg.*, XVII, 19 f.); Daedalus (*Par.*, VIII, 125 f.); the Seven against Thebes (*Purg.*, XXII, 55 f.); Hypsipyle (*Purg.*, XXII, 112); Amphiaraus (*Inf.*, XX, 31 f.); Phaethon (*Par.*, XVII, 3); Aeneas (*Inf.*, I, 73 f. and II, 13; *Par.*, VI, 3); Dido (*Inf.*, V, 61 and *Par.*, IX, 97); Homer (*Purg.*, XXII, 101 f.); Aristotle (*Inf.*, IV, 131 and *Par.*, XXVI, 38 f.); Virgil (*Par.*, XV, 26; *Inf.*, VIII, 7; *Purg.*, XVIII, 82 f. and XXII, 57); Trajan (*Purg.*, X, 73 ff.).— Bible: Gabriel (*Purg.*, X, 34 f.); Raphael (*Par.*, IV, 48); Lucifer (*Inf.*, XXXIV, 18; *Purg.*, XII, 25 f.); Adam (*Par.*, VII, 26; XIII, 37 ff.; XXXII, 136); Eve (*Purg.*, XI, 63 and XXXII, 32; *Par.*, XXXII, 4 ff.); Potiphar's wife (*Inf.*, XXX, 9); David (*Purg.*, X, 65); Elisha (*Inf.*, XXVI, 34); Mary (*Purg.*, XX, 97 f.); Paul (*Inf.*, II, 28 and *Par.*, XXI, 127 f.).—Modern personages: Bertran de Born (*Inf.*, XXIX, 29); Giraut de Bornelh (*Purg.*, XXVI, 120); Celestine V (*Inf.*, III, 59 f.); Henry VI (*Par.*, III, 125); Philip the Fair (*Purg.*, VII, 109 and XX, 91; *Par.*, XIX, 120); Prince Henry (*Inf.*, XII, 120).—*Nomina sacra.* God: *Purg.*, XXV, 70; *Par.*, I, 1; *Inf.*, II, 16 and VII, 73; *Purg.*, III, 36 and 120; *Purg.*, VIII, 68; X, 94; XIII, 108; XV, 67; XXVIII, 91; XXXI, 23 f. Christ: *Inf.*, XII, 38 f.; *Purg.*, XXXII, 73 f.; *Par.*, II, 41 f.; XXII, 41 f.; XXV, 113; XXVII, 36. Heaven: *Inf.*, III, 95 f.; V, 23 f.; *Purg.*, VIII, 72; XXXII, 102.

[12] *Inf.*, XXXIV, 45; *Purg.*, XXXI, 72; *Par.*, VIII, 58 and 65 f.; *Purg.*, VII, 98; XVI, 115; *Par.*, XIX, 131 f.; *Purg.*, IX, 21 f. and XIV, 32; *Inf.*, XXXIII, 30 and XXVIII, 74 f.; *Purg.*, V, 97 and XIV, 17; *Inf.*, XIII, 9 and XIII, 143; *Purg.*, XII, 102; XIII, 151 f.; XV, 97 f.; *Par.*, XXXI, 31.

[13] *Inf.*, I, 17; *Par.*, X, 28; *Purg.*, XV, 2 f.; *Par.*, I, 38; *Par.*, XXII, 142; *Purg.*, XXIX, 78; *Inf.*, XX, 126; *Purg.*, VIII, 86; *Par.*, VIII, 11 f.; X, 14; *Purg.*, XXXII, 53 f.; *Purg.*, IX, 5 f.; *Inf.*, II, 78; *Par.*, XXI, 25 ff.; *Purg.*, XI, 108; XXVIII, 104; XXXIII, 90; *Par.*, XXIII, 112 f.; I, 4; II, 112; *Purg.*, VIII, 114; XXX, 52; XXIV, 15.—I add periphrases for the human body and its separate members: *Purg.*, IX, 11; XI, 44; XVI, 37; *Inf.*, XXXI, 66; XXXII, 34 and 139; XXV, 85 and 110; *Purg.*, VII, 13; XXV, 43 f.; *Inf.*, XXVIII, 24.

him, periphrase was an obligatory ornament of poetic diction. It is sometimes exaggerated to the point of becoming a tasteless mannerism. To
express the idea: "If your idle imagining has not hardened and darkened
your mind," Dante says (*Purg.*, XXXIII, 67 f.):

> . . . *se stati non fossero acqua d'Elsa*
> *Li pensier tuoi intorno alla tua mente,*
> *E il piacer loro un Piramo alla gelsa* . . .

A torture for the translators! One * has:

> . . . *and were not vainer thoughts,*
> *As Elsa's numbing waters to thy soul,*
> *And their fond pleasures had not dyed it dark*
> *As Pyramus the mulberry* . . .

Another † :

> *And if thy vain imaginings had not been*
> *Water of Elsa round about thy mind,*
> *And Pyramus to the mulberry, their pleasure* . . .

To understand this we must know: 1. That the mineral content of the
river Elsa in Tuscany deposits a crust on objects placed in its water; 2. that
the mulberry was dyed dark by Pyramus' blood.[14] Here as in many cases
(as in early Greek poetry and the Old Norse kennings) periphrase passes
over into "riddling" (γρῖφος). Dante often has the feeling that it is too
hard to understand (*Par.*, XI, 73):

> *Ma perch' io non proceda troppo chiuso.*[15]

3. By *annominatio* (παρήχησις or παρονομασία or παρωνυμία) the rhetoric of Antiquity understands the bringing together not only of various
inflectional forms of the same word and of its derivatives but also of words
perfectly or approximately homophonous. The *Rhetorica ad Herennium*
(IV, ch. 21, §§ 29 ff.) gives the following examples: 1. *ăvium dulcedo
ducit ad āvium:*[16] the two *aviums* are homonyms except for the quantity
of the *a.* 2. *hic sibi posset temperare, nisi amore mallet obtemperare:* use
of a word and of one of its compounds in the same clause. 3. *dilegere
oportet quem velis diligere.* The *ad Herennium* advises a sparing use of
annominatio. Virgil amused himself by using the first example in a poem
(*Georgics*, III, 328):

> *Avia tum resonant avibus virgulta canoris.*

[* Cary (in substitution for Bassermann).]
[† Longfellow (in substitution for Borchardt).]
[14] Conscious playing with difficult rhymes is also an element.
[15] A reference to the Provençal *trobar clus.*—A particularly elaborate periphrase
for Marseille is put into the mouth of the troubadour Folquet (*Par.*, IX, 82–93).
[16] Censured by Quintilian, IX, 3, 66.

From the *Aeneid* I cite:

    a) *Discolor unde auri per ramos aura refulsit* (VI, 204).
    b) *Nunc etiam manis—haec intemptata manebat*
       Sors rerum—movet . . . (X, 39).
    c) *Murmura venturos nautis prodentia ventos* (X, 99).
    d) *Nec Turnum segnis retinet mora, sed rapit acer*
       Totam aciem in Teucros . . . (X, 308 f.).

Late Antique and medieval Latin Mannerism loves accumulated *annominatio*:

    a) Sidonius (*Carmina*, II, 3 f.):

> *Annum pande novum consul vetus, ac sine fastu*
> *Scribere bis fastis; quamquam diademate crinem*
> *Fastigatus eas* . . .

    b) Alan (*SP*, II, 278 and 279):

> *More suo Seneca mores ratione monetat,*
> *Optimus exculptor morum* . . .
> *Militis excedit legem, plus milite miles*
> *Aiax, militiaeque modus decurrit in iram.*

    c) Walter of Châtillon:

> *Tanto viro locuturi*
> *Studeamus esse puri,*
> *Set et loqui sobrie,*
> *Carum care venerari,*
> *Et ut simus caro cari,*
> *Careamus carie* . . .

In the medieval Latin arts of poetry *annominatio* is commended. Marbod gives as an example (*PL*, CLXXI, 1687 B):

> *Cur illum curas qui multum dat tibi curas?*

Matthew of Vendôme (Faral, 169, § 9):

> *Fama famem pretii parit amentis nec amantis;*
> *Est pretium vitae depretiare decus.*

In this distich two pairs of homophonous words and three inflections of the same stem are introduced in true virtuoso fashion. Geoffrey of Vinsauf (Faral, 323) also gives "forma deformis" as an example; a type, then, which is reduced to but two members. *Annominatio* early makes its way into vernacular poetry. It occurs in Chrétien de Troyes, in Rutebeuf, in the later troubadours, and elsewhere.[17] Dante uses it in his *Rime*, but above

---

[17] References in *RF*, LX (1947), 275.

all in the *Commedia*. Right at the beginning of it (*Inf.*, I, 5 and 36), the modern reader is curiously surprised by "selva selvaggia" and "più volte volto." Epideictic (many-membered) *annominatio* is used by Dante at rhetorical climaxes, e.g., in the meeting with the antique poets (*Inf.*, IV, 72–80): *orrevol—onori—onranza—onrata—onorate*. Or in homage to Pier della Vigna's Latinity (*Inf.*, XIII, 67 ff.): *infiammò—infiammati—infiammar*. *Annominatio* with two members is especially frequent. I have noted 56 examples in the *Inferno*, 65 in the *Purgatorio*, and 78 in the *Paradiso*—that is, some 200 in the 100 cantos.[18] Its use increases from *cantica* to *cantica*. A comparison of Dante's practice with that of the Medieval Latin, Old French, and Provençal poets leads to the following conclusion: Dante uses the device so discreetly that the commentators have noticed it only in a few places. But not one of them has recognized it as *annominatio*. They are content to explain it wrongly ("alliteration") or vaguely (*artifizi, bisticci*). As a result Dante's stylistic connection with the Middle Ages is misapprehended. As might be expected, *annominatio* also occurs with extreme frequency in Spanish Mannerism. Calderón (Keil, IV, 202 b):

> *Granjas tengo en Balafor;*
> *Cajas fueron de placer,*
> *Y son casas de dolor.*[19]

Gracián's prose is full of such figures of sound. The effect is happily reproduced in Hofmannsthal's *Turm*. Anton to Julian: "This means neither more nor less than that you are being recalled to court, that honors (*Ehren*) or rather annoyances (*Beschwerden*), dignities (*Würden*) or rather burdens (*Bürden*), will be thrust upon you—positions of trust, sinecures (*Sinekuren*), and importunities (*Sekkaturen*) . . ."

4. *Mannered Metaphor*. I limit myself to two extremely curious metaphors.

The word *hydrops* ("dropsy") and its derivative *hydropicus* were used in fourth and fifth century Latin in the sense of "spiritual tumidity." The *Thesaurus Linguae Latinae* lists examples from Augustine, Peter Chrysologus (whom we shall encounter again in Gracián as a model of style), and Sidonius. It becomes fashionable again in the twelfth century; *hydrops* now means "morbid thirst":

a) Abélard (*Ad Astralabium filium*, p. 168, 21):

> *Hydropico similis nemo est ut dives avarus,*
> *Ex lucro lucri multiplicando sitim.*

b) Alan (*SP*, II, 491):

> *Dum stomachum mentis hydropicat ardor habendi,*
> *Mens potando sitit . . .*

---

[18] *Loc. cit.*, pp. 277 ff.
[19] The containers (*cajas*) of pleasure are become houses (*casas*) of grief.

c) Walter of Châtillon ([1929], 67, 18):

> *Nam sicut ydropicus, qui semper arescit,*
> *Crescit amor nummi, quantum ipsa pecunia crescit.*

In seventeenth-century Spanish poetry (Góngora, Calderón) and prose (Gracián) the metaphor is a familiar one.[20]

Góngora (*Soledad*, I, 108 f.):

> *No en ti la ambición mora*
> *Hidrópica de viento.*

Calderón (*La Vida es sueño*, Act I, scene 4 [Keil, I, 2 ᵇ]):

> *Con cada vez que te veo*
> *Nueva admiración me das,*
> *Y cuando te miro más,*
> *Aun más mirarte deseo:*
> *Ojos hidrópicos creo*
> *Que mis ojos deben ser . . .*

"Hydroptic" is also a favorite word of Donne's, who could get it from medieval Latin and from Spanish sources.[21]

Another twelfth-century mannerism is the metaphor "cither-playing" for "bird song."

a) Alan (*SP*, II, 276): the birds are "cytharistae veris."

b) *Idem* (*SP*, II, 438): the swan sings his death song "with the organum of honey-sweet cither-playing" ("mellitae citharizationis organo").

c) Again in Walter Map (*Poems*, 238, 39): "cignus citharizat."

d) Peter Riga (wrongly ascribed to Hildebert [*PL*, CLXXI, 1236 B and 1289 C]):

> *Rivus garrit, olor citharizat, pavo superbit*

and:

> *Vernat humus, garrit fons, citharizat avis.*

e) John of Garland (*RF*, XIII [1902], 894:

> *Cum citharizat avis . . .*

We find this again in Góngora (*Soledad*, I, 556):

> *Pintadas aves, cítaras de pluma.*[22]

---

[20] Cf. Gracián, *El Criticón*, ed. Romera-Navarro, I, 136, n. 36.

[21] And who bequeathed it to Browning. Cf. H. Heuer in *Englische Studien*, LXXII (1938), 227–244.

[22] Variations: "aladas musas, que de pluma leve / engañada su oculta lira corva . . ."; "aquel violín que vuela," etc. Cf. Eunice Joiner Gates, *The Metaphors of Luis de Góngora* (Philadelphia, 1933), 95 f.—Sonnet 337 (*Obras*, ed. Millé y Giménez, p. 521).

From Calderón one example may serve for many (*El Magico prodigioso*, II, scene 19):

> *El ave, que liberal*
> *Vestir matices presuma,*
> *Veloz cítara de pluma* . . .

If the Spanish writers of the seventeenth century use such studied and far-fetched metaphors as "dropsy" and "bird-cither," and if the Latin poets of the twelfth century do the same, that fact alone suffices to show that Spanish "Baroque" is descended from medieval Latin theory and practice. I advanced this thesis in 1941.[23] The investigations to follow will confirm it. A satisfactory historical and stylistic understanding of Spanish cultism and conceptism will be attained by listing all the artifices and metaphors of Latin poetry between 1100 and 1230 and then making a corresponding list for Spanish poetry from 1580 to 1680. A comparison of the two lists will show what use Spanish Mannerism makes of medieval Latin, and wherein it goes beyond it. In that transcendence, finally, it will be permissible to see what is idiosyncratic in Spanish "Baroque." Similar studies should compare the metaphors of the English "metaphysical poets" with those of the Spanish conceptists. Here there are offered to philology tasks whose accomplishment would have consequences for literary history.

3.   *Formal Mannerisms*

The mannerist wants to say things not normally but abnormally. He prefers the artificial and affected to the natural. He wants to surprise, to astonish, to dazzle. While there is only one way of saying things naturally, there are a thousand forms of unnaturalness. Hence it is short-sighted and useless to reduce Mannerism to a system, as has been done again and again. The result is only to bring into existence competing and contradictory systems, which dispute fruitlessly among themselves. Such disputes rather confuse than promote an understanding of the facts. In view of the present state of literary science, so little disciplined and so little secure methodologically, I consider it expedient to leave any such search for systems severely alone and instead to provide new concrete material for the history of Mannerism. This procedure is further recommended by the fact that the splitting up of European literature into national linguistic domains and into too many and too brief periods has had an unhealthy influence in this department too.

Mannerism can begin with linguistic form or with intellectual content. In its periods of florescence it combines both. We shall first trace certain formal mannerisms.

1. The oldest example of systematic affectation of which I am aware is reported in connection with the poet and musician Lasus (middle of the

[23] *Modern Philology*, XXXVIII (1941), 333.

sixth century), who was Pindar's teacher. He wrote poems in which no σ
appeared. The historical background of this trifling is unknown to us. But
it was revived in Late Antiquity. Nestor of Laranda in Lycia wrote an
Iliad in each book of which one letter of the alphabet did not appear.
The Egyptian Tryphiodorus (fifth century) added an Odyssey constructed
on the same principle. It was of significance for later times that Fabius
Planciades Fulgentius (fifth century) used this "lipogrammatic" (λειπο-
γράμματος) game in his epitome of world history.[24] For it was thus introduced into the tradition of the Latin West, where it reappears—for a
survey of history, as with Fulgentius—in Peter Riga (*ca.* 1200) and then
again in the seventeenth century in Spain.[25] Here it is naturally considered
to be a symptom of the Baroque style. Are we to place its beginnings in
sixth-century Greece? That would be as absurd as the lipogrammatic game
itself. No—we rather have to do with a manneristic artifice whose genealogy we can trace for over two thousand years. We should find examples of
it more frequently if it were not quite so difficult.

2. The reverse of this is the "pangrammatic" affectation, which consists
in having as many successive words as possible begin with the same letter.
It is easier and hence more widely disseminated. A famous example and
one cited again and again by the grammarians and rhetoricians of the
Middle Ages is Ennius' ingenious achievement:

> *O Tite, tute, Tati, tibi tanta, tyranne, tulisti.*

Here we have to do not with alliteration in the sense in which we know it
from Germanic poetry, but with a barbaric and naïve form of ornamenta-
tion which was prohibited in Cicero's day. In late Antiquity the thing was
again found enjoyable. Geta, Caracalla's brother, arranged banquets at
which all the courses began with the same letter (according to Aelius Spartianus). The late Roman grammarians invented the name παρόμοιον for
pangrammatic writing.[26] In the Middle Ages it became an extremely popular piece of virtuosity.[27] Hucbald took the cake with his eclogue on bald-
ness addressed to Charles the Bald.[28] It consists of one hundred and forty-

---

[24] *De aetatibus mundi et hominis.* Cf. the prolix explanation in Fulgentius, ed.
Helm, p. 130, 20 ff.

[25] Peter Riga: Gröber, *Grundriss*, II, 1, 394.—F. J. E. Raby, *A History of Christian-Latin Poetry* . . . (1927), 303.—*Idem*, *A History of Secular Latin Poetry*
. . . (1934), II, 36.—Spain: a *romance* without an o terminates the anonymous
picaresque novel *Estebanillo González.* Other examples from the same period:
Pfandl, *Geschichte der spanischen Nationalliteratur in ihrer Blütezeit* (1929), 363.
—On the whole subject cf. J.-F. Boissonade (1774–1857), *Critique littéraire
sous le premier Empire* (1863), I, 370 ff. and 388.

[26] Further details in Eduard Wölfflin, *Ausgewählte Schriften* (1933), 239.—W.
Heraeus, *Kleine Schriften* (1937), 251.

[27] Aldhelm, ed. Ehwald, 488, 4.—*Poetae*, III, 644, 977; IV, 610 and 787, 12.

[28] *Poetae*, IV, 267 f. Hucbald deforms the word παρόμοιον into *parano-
moeon.*—I do not consider it my duty to produce as many examples as possible
of the thing in medieval Latin, but I add a reference to *Carm. cant.*, p. 78,

six lines, every word of which—in honor of the King—begins with *c*. The game early passed over into vernacular poetry, e.g., into Provençal. The *grands rhétoriqueurs* cultivated it in the fifteenth century, and from them it descended to the poets of the sixteenth.[29] In Spain it is still alive in the seventeenth.[30]

3. Manneristic virtuosity celebrates its greatest triumphs when it combines grammatical with metrical trifling. The so-called "figure poems" (τεχνοπαίγνια)—that is, poems whose outline in manuscript or print represents that of some object: a wing, egg, axe, altar, bagpipe—can look back upon a respectable antiquity. They have come down to us in the corpus of the Greek bucolic poets and in the Greek Anthology.[31] In the reign of Constantine, Porfyrius Optatianus revived the game in Latin. He was followed by Alcuin and Raban Maur.[32] The Hellenism of the sixteenth century brought the artifice into credit again. Mellin de Saint-Gellais (1481–1558) composed a poem in the shape of a pair of wings.[33] In Persian literature there are figure poems whose lines imitate trees with trunk and branches or parasols with handles.[34] A Hellenistic legacy?

4. A rich mine of late Latin verbal artifice is Ausonius. He designates it by a term which Plato once passingly applied to the mannered rhetoric of the Sophists: *logodaedalia* (Ausonius, ed. Schenkl, p. 139, 1 and p. 173, 26). The concept passed into the vocabulary of medieval Latin rhetoric.[35] One section of Ausonius' works is entitled "Technopaegnion." It comprises poems in which various ingenious methods of using monosyllables in verse are displayed.[36] One poem is so constructed that each line begins and ends with a monosyllable while at the same time the last word of each line reappears as the first word of the next. Another enumerates monosyllabic

---

No. 30. Strecker (like Manitius, I, 590 and *passim*) here cites "alliteration." Thus he conceals the subsequent influence of the late antique (Donatus, Charisius) grammatical term παρόμοιον. For the Middle Ages it also had the authority of Isidore (*Et.*, I, 36, 14).—Cf. further Wilmart, *Rev. bén.*, XLIX (1937), 342 n.

[29] Provençal: Bartsch, *Chrestomathie*, 192, 31 f.—H. Guy, *Histoire de la poésie française au 16e siècle*. I, *L'Ecole des rhétoriqueurs* (1910), 92.—The French term for pangrammatic verses is "vers lettrisés."

Marot: *Triste, transi, tout terni, tout tremblant,*
              Sombre, songeant, sans sûre soutenance . . .

Baïf against du Bellay:

              Beau Belier bien beslant, bellieur, voir bellime
              Des beliers les belieurs qui beslent en la France . . .

[30] Cf. Gracián, *El Criticón*, ed. Romera-Navarro, I, 322, n. 28 and n. 30.

[31] Further details in Christ-Schmid [6], II, 1, 124.—Kluge in *Münchener Museum*, IV (1924), 323 ff.

[32] Ebert, II, 32 and 142 f. traces the connection.

[33] T. Heinermann, *Lesebuch der französischen Literatur des 16. Jahrhunderts* (1942), 11.

[34] Paul Horn, *Geschichte der persischen Literatur* (1901), 54.

[35] In *Poetae*, IV, 369, 246 "doctiloquus" is glossed by "dedalogus."

[36] This too was imitated in the Middle Ages, e.g., by Reginald of Canterbury (*ca.* 1100); cf. Manitius, III, 843.—Another example in Werner, No. 216.

parts of the body, a third monosyllabic deities, a fourth monosyllabic foods. A fifth summarizes mythological stories in lines which end monosyllabically. In a sixth each line puts a question which is answered by a monosyllabic word which ends the line. In the last poem (*Grammaticomastix*) Ausonius borrows from Ennius and Virgil (*Catalepton* 2, 4). The examples which he takes from them (*gau* for *gaudium*, *tau* for *taurus*, *min* for *minimum*, etc.) are, however, not originally monosyllables but artificially detached [37] initial syllables of polysyllabic words (as, in contemporary newspaper German, *Lok* for *Lokomotive*). We find this again in the so-called "versos de cabo roto" ("nipped-off verses"—which become rhymed only if the last syllable of each line is cut off). An example is the poem ascribed to the enchantress Urganda which Cervantes put after the prologue to *Don Quixote*.[38]

5. Another manneristic deformation of the line consists in getting as many words into it as possible. To attain this end the superfluous "and" must be omitted. Hence this piling up of words was also called "verse-filling asyndeton." [39] Examples from Lucretius (I, 685 and 744):

> *Concursus motus ordo positura figurae.*
> *Aëra solem ignem terras animalia fruges.*

Horace uses this type of asyndeton when he wants to dispose scornfully of an entire class of things—objects of value, for example (*Epi.*, II, 2, 180 f.):

> *Gemmas, marmor, ebur, Tyrrhena sigilla, tabellas,*
> *Argentum, vestis Gaetulo murice tinctas . . .*

or forms of superstition (*Epi.*, II, 2, 208 f.):

> *Somnia, terrores magicos, miracula, sagas,*
> *Nocturnos lemures portentaque Thessala . . .*

[37] Another method of splitting up words may be included here. Quintilian, X, 1, 29 had remarked that metrical considerations sometimes forced poets to alter certain words either by lengthening them, contracting them, or dividing them. In VIII, 6, 66 he had cited Virgil's line "Hyperboreo septem subiecta trioni" (*Georg.*, III, 381) as a classic example. But medieval Mannerism took delight in outdoing this. Eugenius of Toledo (*MG Scr. ant.*, XIV, 262, No. 70) writes ten lines all of which have tmesis and cites the authority of Lucilius for it. They begin:

> O JO—*versiculos nexos quia despicis*—ANNES,
> *Excipe* DI—*sollers si nosti iungere*—VISIS;
> *Cerne* CA—*pascentes dumoso in litore*—MELOS.

The last line is: "Instar Lucili cogor d'srumpere versus."
Further discussion in Strecker, *Einführung* [3], 29. Here—as above in Ausonius' appeal to Ennius—we can see how late and medieval Latin Mannerism attempted to legitimize itself by establishing a connection with the Mannerism of early Latin. The role of intermediary would seem to have been played by grammar.

[38] More detailed discussion of such "cropped verses" in Otto Jörder, *Die Formen des Sonetts bei Lope de Vega* (1936), 136 f.—In his brilliant book on Cervantes (Oxford, 1940, pp. 36 and 45) W. J. Entwistle tries to trace the practice back to Sevillan thieves' cant. But is he right?

[39] Carl Weyman, *Beiträge zur Geschichte der christlichlateinischen Poesie* (1926), 126; *ibid.*, 51 f. and 154, n. 1.

The practice becomes more frequent in Statius, and in Dracontius is carried to excess.[40] In the Middle Ages it is a well-known stylistic device, recommended by the rhetoricians.[41] I give but one medieval Latin example, from Alan (*SP*, II, 473):

> *Furta doli metus ira furor fraus impetus error*
> *Tristities hujus hospita regna tenent.*

The seventeenth-century German poets are fond of using the device, especially Gryphius. It still occurs in Brockes:

> *Blitz, Donner, Krachen, Prasseln, Knallen,*
> *Erschüttern, stossweis abwerts fallen,*
> *Gepresst, betäubt von Schlag zu Strahl,*
> *Kam, ward, war alles auf einmal*
> *Gesehn, gehört, gefühlt, geschehn.*

> (Flash, thunder, crashing, rustling, booming,
> Shudd'ring, a sudden falling back,
> Oppressed, benumbed from stroke to streak,
> Came, was, then suddenly had been
> Seen, heard, felt, done.)

I take this example from a dissertation on "The Accumulation of Words in Baroque." The author comments: "Such an exhaustion of all the possibilities of accumulation in a single sentence belongs only to Baroque." [42] So people say, but I am on another track . . .

6. The lines quoted from Brockes exhibit not only word accumulation but also a metrical schema which the interpreter of German Baroque has not noticed. They are "versus rapportati," to use the medieval Latin technical term. A late Latin specimen, which served as a model, is the so-called "Epitaph on Virgil" (*Anthologia latina* [ed. Riese [2]], No. 800):

> *Pastor arator eques pavi colui superavi*
> *Capras rus hostes fronde ligone manu.*[43]

The sequence *Bucolics, Georgics, Aeneid* is here indicated by symmetrical grammatical dovetailing. The normal sentence structure would be: *Pastor pavi capras fronde, arator colui rus ligone, eques superavi hostes manu.* Three similarly constructed grammatical clauses of four members are, then, broken up and put together anew.

This ingenious device would seem to go back to late Greek Antiquity.

---

[40] Statius, *Thebais*, I, 341; VI, 116; X, 768.—Dracontius, *De laudibus Dei*, I, 5 ff.; I, 13 ff., etc.

[41] Bede in Keil, *Grammatici latini*, VII, 244.—Albericus Casinensis, *Flores rhetorici*, ed. Inguanez and Willard (1938), p. 44, § 4.

[42] Hans Pliester, *Die Worthäufung im Barock* (Bonn, 1930), 3.

[43] Literally: "As shepherd, farmer, knight, I pastured, tilled, conquered goats, the soil, foes, with leafage, mattock, hand."

An ἀδέσποτον in the Anthology (IX, 48) connects Zeus's transformations with his erotic adventures. He became swan, bull, satyr, and gold for Leda, Europa, Antiope, and Danae:

Ζεὺς κύκνος, ταῦρος, σάτυρος, χρυσὸς δι' ἔρωτα
Λήδης, Εὐρώπης, 'Αντιόπης, Δανάης.[44]

From the Latin Middle Ages the schema passes into the French, Spanish, English, and German poetry of the sixteenth and seventeenth centuries, as may be seen from the examples given in the note.

7. Every reader of Calderón remembers the spectacular monologue at the beginning of *La vida es sueño* in which Segismundo complains of his imprisonment. The piece is built up of seven ingeniously rhymed ten-line stanzas (*decimas*). The train of thought is as follows: (1) What kind of crime have I committed by being born? (2) Why are not other creatures punished for the crime of birth? (3) The bird is born and enjoys freedom. (4) The beast of prey likewise. (5) The fish likewise. (6) The brook likewise. (7) What justice robs man of the gift which God bestowed upon these creatures—brook, fish, beast of prey, bird: freedom?

> *Heavens, I ask you, answer me:*
> *Since ye treat me as ye do,*
> *How have I offended you*
> *By my birth so outrageously?*
> *Though, by being born, I agree*

[44] Paul Dimoff printed this piece among Chénier's works, apparently without being aware of its origin (*Oeuvres complètes de André Chénier, publiées d'après les manuscrits*, Vol. I. Bucoliques [1931], 35).—Agathias' pretty epigram (A.P., VI, 59) is constructed after the same pattern.—In medieval Latin, *versus rapportati* (also called "applicati" or "singula singulis") are extraordinarily frequent: Faral 123, 39 ff.; 125, 59 ff.; 127, 89 ff.; 361, 699 ff.; Marbod in PL, CLXXI 1689 D, etc. Cf. Schumann, *Kommentar* I p. 8.—The device passes from medieval Latin to the French Renaissance: Bruno Berger, *Vers rapportés*, Freiburg-im-Breisgau dissertation (1930).—
Shakespeare has (*Lucrece*, 615 f.):
> For princes are the glass, the school, the book
> Where subjects' eyes do learn, do read, do look
and (*Hamlet* III, 1, 159):
> The courtier's, soldier's, scholar's eye, tongue, sword.
Milton (*Paradise Lost*, VII, 502 f.):
> . . . Aire, Water, Earth
> By Fowl, Fish, Beast, was flown, was swum, was walkt.
A Spanish example (Lope de Vega in Menéndez y Pelayo, *Las cien mejores poesías*, p. 106):
> Cuando a las manos vengo
> Con el muchacho ciego,
> Haciendo rostro embisto,
> Venzo, triunfo y resisto
> La flecha, el arco, la ponzoña, el fuego . . .
The device also occurs in German "Baroque"; see the example from Brockes above. —According to J. Bolte, *versus rapportati* also occur in ancient India (*Herrigs Archiv*, CXII [1904], 265 ff. and CLIX [1931], 11 ff.).

That I did commit a sin
Your justice well may discipline,
Your justice and your rigor too,
Since, whatever wrong he do,
Birth's a sin man cannot twin.

Therefore, leaving that aside,—
That my sin of being born,—
Heavens, from my thoughts forlorn
One thing only do not hide:
What greater sins in me abide
That ye give me greater woe?
Born were not all things? Then why
Me the privileges deny
Granted to all else below?

Born the bird was, yet with gay
Gala vesture, beauty's dower,
Scarce it is a wingèd flower,
Or a richly-plumaged spray,
Ere the aërial halls of day
It divideth rapidly,
And no more will debtor be
To the nest it hates to quit,
But with more of soul than it,
I am grudged its liberty.

And the beast was born, whose skin
Scarce those beauteous spots and bars,
Like to constellated stars,
Doth from its great Painter win,
Ere the instinct doth begin
Of its fierceness and its pride,
And its lair on every side
It has measured far and nigh,
While with better instinct I
Am its liberty denied.

Born the mute fish was also,
Child of ooze and ocean's weed;
Scarce a finny bark of speed
To the surface brought, and lo!
In vast circuits to and fro
Measures it on every side
All the waste of ocean wide,
Its illimitable home;
While with greater will to roam
I that freedom am denied.

Born the streamlet was, a snake,
Which unwinds the flowers among,
Silver serpent, that not long
May to them sweet music make,
Ere it quits the flow'ry brake,
Onward hastening to the sea
With majestic course and free,
Which the open plains supply;
While with more life gifted, I
Am denied its liberty.

At this height of all my grief,
An Etna I, a volcano,
Bid my boiling heart o'erflow
But to give my breast relief:
What law, what justice, like a thief
Takes from man a privilege conferred
By the Creator of the world
Without exception, it would seem,
On other earthly things—a stream,
*A fish, a wild beast, and a bird? ***

In the original the last lines run:

¿Qué ley, justicia ó razón
Negar á los hombres sabe
Privilegio tan suave,
Excepción tan principal,
Que Dios le ha dado á un cristal,
Á un pez, á un bruto y á un ave?

These lines present a brief recapitulation which sums up the parallel examples of the preceding stanzas—bird, beast of prey, fish, brook. This compositional schema is very frequent in Calderón. I call it the "summation schema." It is common property during Spain's period of florescence.[45] It is also to be found in the Italian cinquecento, for example in Panfilo Sasso (d. 1527):

Col tempo el villanel al giogo mena
El tòr sí fiero e sí crudo animale;
Col tempo el falcon si usa a menar l' ale
E ritornar a te chiamato a pena.

[* Stanzas 3–6 are given in R. C. Trench's charming version; unfortunately he did not translate the entire poem; I have attempted to supply the deficiency. Dr. Curtius uses a translation by Max Kommerell which he describes as "masterly."—TRANS.]

45 Cf., for example, Antonio Mira de Amescua in Menéndez y Pelayo, *Las cien mejores poesías*, 150.

> *Col tempo si domestica in catena*
> *El bizzarro orso, e 'l feroce cinghiale;*
> *Col tempo l' acqua, che è sí molle e frale,*
> *Rompe el dur sasso, come el fosse arena.*
>
> *Col tempo ogni robusto arbor cade;*
> *Col tempo ogni alto monte si fa basso,*
> *Ed io col tempo non posso a pietade*
>
> *Mover un cor d' ogni dolcezza casso;*
> *Onde avanza di orgoglio e crudeltade*
> *Orso, toro, leon, falcone e sasso.*

Lope imitated this sonnet.[46] The summation schema is not far removed from the technique of the series of examples (*Priamel*),[47] but differs from it in that the latter has no concluding summary. If we go in search of the origin of the summation schema, we come upon Tiberianus' poem which has already received our attention in another connection (*supra*, p. 196). The similarity of structure is striking. But classical philology unfortunately gives us no information.[48] Was the summation schema known in the twelve hundred years between Tiberianus and Panfilo Sasso? I can give but one example. Walafrid Strabo in his poem *De carnis petulantia* (*Poetae*, II, 360) cites as exemplifying the propensity to sin:

> Stanza 1: *a ball on a steep incline.*
> Stanza 2: *a feather in the wind.*
> Stanza 3: *a ship on the waves.*
> Stanza 4: *a fire in the fields.*
> Stanza 5: *a wild beast, a bird.*
> Stanza 6: *a foal.*
> Stanza 7: *a rushing stream.*

Then Stanza 8 sums up:

> *Haec carnem, stolidissime,*
> *Nostram respiciunt, homo,*
> *Consuetam male vivere:*
> *Puppis, pluma, focus, sphera,*
> *Pullus, flumen, avis, fera,*
> *Haec attende sagaciter.*

We have already encountered Walafrid Strabo as an erudite imitator of Virgilian *adynata* (*supra*, p. 96). That he should himself have invented

---

[46] Ernst Brockhaus in *Herrigs Archiv*, CLXXI (1937), 200. *Ibid.*, 197 ff. there are other *Priamel* poems on the same topos, which goes back to Ovid. Maximianus (I, 269 ff.) should be compared.

[47] Walter Kröhling, *Die Priamel (Beispielreihung) als Stilmittel in der griechisch-römischen Dichtung* (Greifswald, 1935).

[48] Cf. the article "Tiberianus" by F. Lenz in *RE*, 2nd. series half-vol. XI (1936), 766 ff.

the summation schema is unthinkable, because it is irreconcilable with the imitative style of Carolingian Humanism. He must, then, have had late Antique forerunners. Presumably there were others beside Tiberianus. Perhaps they are lost. Did he have imitators in medieval Latin? Are there connecting links between Walafrid and Panfilo Sasso? In the present state of our knowledge it is impossible to determine.

4. *Recapitulation*

How have we proceeded? What results can we set down?

We have traced seven leading varieties of formal Mannerism, taking them in chronological order: the lipogrammatic manner pointed back to the sixth century B.C., the pangrammatic to the third B.C. The first figure poems appear to belong to the same period (beginning of the Alexandrian Age). With Ausonius' *logodaedalia* we reach the fourth century of the Empire. Next, under the Vandal rule in Africa at the beginning of the fifth century, comes the systematic employment of "verse-filling asyndeton" by Dracontius. To the late Empire belong the *versus rapportati*, whose first appearance cannot be accurately dated (Agathias is of the sixth century). Tiberianus, the late Antique representative of the summation schema, was a contemporary of Constantine.

Lasus's isolated experiment deserves attention as a symptom of a preclassic, archaic Mannerism. Leaving it aside, the other phenomena fall in one or the other of two epochs: the Alexandrian period and the period of the Late Empire. Between the two lies Roman Classicism. All the phenomena discussed are continued in the Latin Middle Ages. There is a medieval Latin Mannerism. Karl Strecker has this to say on the subject: "The fact that the language was learned in school led in itself to a particularly strong emphasis on the formal. This predilection for form, or one may often say for trifling, is characteristic and must be studied by anyone who would understand the Middle Ages." [49] Medieval Latin Mannerism then finds its way into vernacular literature, and there, unaffected by the Renaissance and Classicism, it can be traced through the centuries. It flares up for the last time in the seventeenth. It takes deepest root in Spanish soil, a fact that is explained by the characterization of the *siglo de oro* given above (p. 267). To separate seventeenth-century Mannerism from its two thousand years of prehistory and, contrary to all historical testimony, to call it a spontaneous product of (Spanish or German) Baroque is possible only as a result of ignorance and of the demands of pseudo-art-historical systems. The two usually reinforce each other.

I have made my characterization of the formal elements of Mannerism as brief as possible—partly from choice, partly from necessity. From choice: to avoid an undue quantity of trifling details and to present a general view which can be taken in at a glance. From necessity: because earlier

[49] *Einführung* [3], 27.

works and monographs either do not exist or are unusable. As yet, indeed, literary science has not acquired the European perspective—either chronologically or geographically. Hence I have purposely selected phenomena so concrete in themselves and so clear genealogically that they resist any attempt at wire-drawn interpretation on the part of *Geistesgeschichte*. They make up a homogeneous strand, which will become more and more apparent as we proceed with our investigations.

5. *Epigram and the Style of* pointes

Mannerism in form usually goes hand in hand with mannerism in thought, and to this we now turn. No poetic form is so favorable to playing with pointed and surprising ideas as epigram—for which reason seventeenth- and eighteenth-century Germany called it "Sinngedicht." This development of the epigram [50] necessarily resulted after the genre ceased to be bound by its original definition (an inscription for the dead, for sacrificial offerings, etc.). The epigram became the vessel of a judicious or ingenious idea. In itself this is not incompatible with a true poetic content. A very charming example is the epigram to Agathon (*A.P.*, V, 78) ascribed to Plato:

> Τὴν ψυχὴν, Ἀγάθωνα φιλῶν, ἐπὶ χείλεσιν ἔσχον.
> Ἦλθε γὰρ ἡ τλήμων ὡς διαβησομένη.

(Kissing Agathon, I stayed my soul at my lips, while it rose, poor wretch, as fain to cross over.) *

An English Humanist of our day, Sir Stephen Gaselee,[51] for many years librarian of the Foreign Office, has traced the influence and the imitations of this idea through world literature.[52] He found it in Bion's *Lament for Adonis* (l. 45 f.), in Meleager (*A.P.*, V, 171), in Favorinus of Arles (first half of the second century A.D.), in Achilles Tatius' erotic romance (fourth century A.D.), in Aristaenetus. Among the Romans he names Petronius (c. 79 and c. 132) and Gellius (XIX, 11). Then come Politian and Pontano in Italy, with Latin verses, and, in England, Marlowe (*Dr. Faustus*, sc. 14), Herrick (the epigram "Love Palpable"), and Donne (ed. Grierson [1912], I, 180, 1).

This charming play of thought, which tradition ascribes, whether rightly or wrongly, to Plato, may serve as our example of an ingenious idea not yet affected in the slightest degree by Mannerism. It is not necessary to our purpose to trace when and how the epigrammatic play of thought degener-

[50] On its origins cf. Paul Friedländer, *Epigrammata. Greek Inscriptions in Verse from the Beginnings to the Persian Wars* (University of California Press, 1948).
[* J. W. Mackail's translation (replacing Thudichum's).]
[51] Died 1943. Obituary notice in Harold Nicolson, *Friday Mornings 1941–1944* (London, 1944), 172 ff.—We are indebted to Gaselee for two medieval Latin anthologies: *An Anthology of Medieval Latin* (London, 1925), and *The Oxford Book of Medieval Latin Verse* (Oxford, 1928).
[52] "The Soul in the Kiss" in *The Criterion*, II, 349 ff. (April, 1924).

ated into a manneristic passion for *pointes*. Let a particularly crass example serve to mark the final phase. I chose it deliberately, because it played a role in seventeenth-century manneristic theory.

In the *Anthologia Latina* (Riese², No. 709) there is a poem under the title *De puero glacie perempto*:

> *Thrax puer adstricto glacie cum luderet Hebro,*
> *   Frigore frenatas pondere rupit aquas,*
> *Cumque imae partes fundo raperentur ab imo,*
> *   Abscidit a iugulo lubrica testa caput.*
> *Quod mox inventum mater dum conderet igni,*
> *   "Hoc peperi flammis, cetera" dixit "aquis.*
> *Me miseram! plus amnis habet solumque reliquit,*
> *   Quo nati mater nosceret interitum."*

(While a Thracian lad was playing on the frozen Hebrus, his weight broke through the cold-bound water, and as his lower parts were swept along its bed, a smooth fragment of ice severed his head from his neck. His mother soon found the head and, as she consigned it to the fire, "This," she said, "I bore for the flames, the rest for the water. Woe is me! The river has the greater part, leaving me enough to tell me that my son has perished!")

A truly pathetic tale and an unnaturally witty mother! In the MSS the epigram is ascribed to Julius Caesar or Augustus or Germanicus. It is, however, Carolingian, and is to be found in Paulus Diaconus (*Poetae*, I, 50) at the end of a poem in which he says that he had forgotten his Greek and remembered only this one short piece, which he had learned by heart in school. The Greek original has come down to us in two versions (A.P., VII, 542 and IX, 56). In its unnaturalness it is reminiscent of the fictitious legal cases of the rhetorical schools under the Empire. We shall return to this strange production.

6. *Baltasar Gracián*

In referring to Mannerism as the style of *pointes* we have adopted a terminology which accords with Boileau's (*Art poétique*, II, 105 ff.):

> *Jadis de nos auteurs les pointes ignorées*
> *Furent de l'Italie en nos vers attirées.*
> *Le vulgaire, ébloui de leur faux agrément,*
> *À ce nouvel appas courut avidement.*
> *La faveur du public excitant leur audace,*
> *Leur nombre impétueux inonda le Parnasse.*
> *Le madrigal d'abord en fut enveloppé;*
> *Le sonnet orgueilleux lui-même en fut frappé;*
> *La tragédie en fit ses plus chères délices;*
> *L'élégie en orna ses douloureux caprices;*
> *Un héros sur la scène eut soin de s'en parer,*

Et sans pointe un amant n'osa plus soupirer . . .
La prose la reçut aussi bien que les vers;
L'avocat au Palais en hérissa son style,
Et le docteur en chaire en sema l'Évangile.

The word *pointe* ("point") is the French equivalent for the "pointed" diction or thought which the Romans designated by *acutus* and *acumen*.[53] Neither Latin nor French was able to derive an abstract noun from *acutus*, though Italian and Spanish did. In 1639 there appeared at Genoa Matteo Peregrini's *Delle acutezze, che altrimenti spiriti, vivezze, e concetti volgarmente si appellano . . . trattato*; in 1642 at Huesca Baltasar Gracián's *Arte de Ingenio, tratado de la Agudeza*.[54] The second edition (1649) is entitled: *Agudeza y arte de Ingenio en que se explican todos los modos y diferencias de Conceptos*. In Matteo Peregrini as in Gracián we find the "acute" or "subtle" mode of expression interpreted by the term *concetto* (Spanish *concepto* and *conceto*, English "conceit").[55] We have, then, three related concepts (*agudeza, ingenio, concepto*) to illuminate. The matter is further complicated by the fact that, contemporaneously with Conceptism, there flourished in Spain the stylistic manner know as Cultism and represented by Góngora.[56] There have been frequent attempts to separate Cultism and Conceptism, but they cannot be separated.[57] Care-

[53] Cicero (*Brutus*, 27, 104): "orationes nondum satis splendidas verbis, sed acutas, prudentiaeque plenissimas."—*Acumen* and *prudentia* are often employed in Cicero as closely allied concepts. Both belong in the realm of *inventio* (*Brutus*, 62, 221).

[54] It has sometimes been supposed that Gracián was dependent upon Peregrini. This view has been convincingly controverted by E. Sarmiento (*Hispanic Review*, III [1935], 23 ff.).

[55] L.-P. Thomas, *Le lyrisme et la préciosité cultistes en Espagne* (1909), 32, appears to regard Camillo Peregrino's *Del Concetto poetico* (written 1598, printed 1898) as the first Italian conceptistic treatise. But as early as 1562 there appeared in Venice a new and corrected edition of the *Concetti divinissimi di Girolamo Garimberto*. In the preface *concetto* is defined as "l'acutezza d' un bel detto." The collection contains only prose.

[56] It appears hitherto to have been overlooked that *culto* is a Latinism. Quintilian (VIII, 3, 61) says concerning *ornatus* (ornaments of eloquence): "Eius primi gradus sunt in eo quod velis concipiendo et exprimendo, tertius, qui haec nitidiora faciat, quod proprie dixeris cultum." The word means "elegantly expressed." Ovid (*Ars*, III, 341) calls his poems "culta carmina." He twice (*Am.*, I, 15, 28 and III, 9, 66) calls Tibullus "cultus." Martial (I, 25, 1 f.) tells an author that he should now finally publish his productions "et cultum docto pectore profer opus," etc. "Modern" philology cannot do justice to its task if it thinks it can ignore the literature a knowledge of which was taken for granted by modern writers down to the end of the eighteenth century. This still applies to Montesquieu and Diderot, see Excursuses XXIV and XXV, *infra*.

[57] The attempt to represent Cultism and Conceptism as opposites and to impute this view to Gracián goes back to Menéndez y Pelayo (*Historia de las ideas estéticas en España* [2], III, 526).—Mérimée-Morley, *A History of Spanish Literature* (New York, 1930), says (p. 233): "Conceptism is to thought what cultism is to word. But one of these defects does not necessarily exclude the other. On the contrary, they are mutually attractive and are often found together." *Ibid.*, the admission that "Góngora was already a conceptist."

ful expression is a preliminary condition for the penetrative power of ingenious ideas. In this sense Gracián (*Agudeza*, Preface to the Reader [58]) commended acuteness of intellect "para exprimir cultamente sus conceptos." [59]

Conceptism, Cultism, and related matters have been the subject of valuable and erudite studies. But these studies are all unsatisfactory in so far as they fail to investigate the relations between Spanish Mannerism and the Latin tradition. Its various forms are commonly interpreted as products of the Renaissance or of Italianism or of Baroque—that is, they are pulled out of pigeonholes in which they have previously been put. This process explains nothing. Those who look at the matter from the French point of view see in Cultism and Conceptism two "dangerous" diseases of the Spanish mentality and explain them by the fact that Spain, to her misfortune, never "had such severe schoolmasters as Malherbe, Vaugelas, and the Academy." [60] Quite clearly such pedantic judgments fail to further either historical comprehension or aesthetic appreciation. Here again we observe that French standard Classicism, with its insistence upon applying its particular system everywhere, still causes trouble in the realm of learning three hundred years after Vaugelas (his *Remarques sur la langue française* appeared in 1647). Gracián's reputation too has suffered under it down to today.[61] Is there no guide to Spanish literature whose erudition is as unassailable as his love of Spain and whose vision is not impeded by French blinders? Yes, there is Ludwig Pfandl.[62] He shows a sympathetic understanding for Spanish "Baroque temperament," but he too does nothing to improve our historical understanding, for he explains "Spanish Baroque" . . . by the nature of Spanish Baroque.[63]

[58] I cite Gracián (except for the *Criticón*, which I use in H. Romera-Navarro's critical edition with commentary, Philadelphia and London [1938 f.]) from the only complete modern edition: Baltasar Gracián, *Obras completas. Introducción, recopilación y notas de E. Correa Calderón* (Madrid, 1944). The 1942 reprint of the *Agudeza* in the Colección Austral (Espasa-Calpe) omits the foreword *Al lector*. In both editions, unfortunately, the Latin quotations are frequently much mutilated.

[59] For Gracián *agudeza* and *cultura* are two sides of the stylistic optimum (*Agudeza, Disc.* 61, *Obras*, p. 282 a).

[60] Mérimée-Morley, 232. Conceptism is "the deep constitutional vice of Spain," 233.—Pfandl, to be sure, censures Gracián because he exhibits an "eclectic combination" of *cultismo* and *conceptismo* "instead of a clear-cut distinction as understood by modern literary-historical research" (552). Unfortunately—we add—its "clear-cut" results could not be known to Góngora.

[61] Cf. Sarmiento's criticism of Croce and Coster in the essay cited *supra*, p. 294, n. 54.   [62] *Supra*, p. 283, n. 25.

[63] Spanish Baroque is "the period in which the Spanish psyche reached a certain heightening of its native contradictions, because . . ." (p. 215). What is the source of Pfandl's knowledge of the Spanish psyche and its contradictions? Spanish literature . . . Though explaining the essence of a national literature by a hypostatized national psychology is very much in favor in France, Germany, and Spain, it has a minimum of scientific value.—For Pfandl the "Symbolisierungsidee" (?) ["idea of symbolization"; the parenthetical question mark is Dr. Curtius's] is the "soil in which *cultismo* thrives" (231); *conceptismo* corresponds to the "Baroque exaltation of the individual" (240); and so on.

Gracián's term "arte de ingenio" gives the clue for historical comprehension. We must go back to classical rhetoric. Quintilian (X, 1, 88) censures Ovid's rhetorical Mannerism in the words: "nimium amator ingenii sui, laudandus tamen in partibus." As the gifts which are most valuable to an orator, and which, moreover, are not imitable, Quintilian names genius, invention, power, and facility: *ingenium, inventio, vis, facilitas* (X, 2, 12). *Ingenium*, then, belongs in the realm of *inventio*. But a genius for clever invention degenerates into a fault if it is not coupled with judgment. *Ingenium* and *iudicium* can, then, be in opposition.[64]

Quintilian undertook to systematize and promulgate the criteria of Ciceronian standard Classicism in the Flavian period—that is, in an epoch which had already produced not only the manneristic poetry of a Lucan, a Statius, and a Martial, but also such unclassic prose as that of Petronius, Seneca, and Tacitus. Quintilian's taste, regulated as it was by the exemplary, the typical, the pedagogically valuable, was divorced from the literary currents of his time. He was no more able to influence production than Horace's poetics had been. The Latin Mannerism of late Antiquity and the Middle Ages could not but decrease his influence even further, especially in such a country as Spain, which had preserved the medieval tradition uninterruptedly and in all its strength.[65] Here it must be borne in mind that, with Quintilian, Martianus Capella was also the teacher of the Latin West. He summons up his highest eloquence in the passage where he introduces Dame Rhetoric into the assembly of the gods and describes the effect of her discourse: "Hac vero loquente qui vultus vocisve sonus quantaque excellentia celsitudoque sermonis! audire operae pretium etiam superis fuit tantae inventionis ingenium, tam facundae ubertatis eloquium, tam capacis memoriae recordationisque thesaurum. Qualis disponendi ordo, quam pronuntiandi congruens modulatio, qui gestus in motu, quae profunditas in conceptu!" (Dick 212, 8 ff.). In this passage Martianus sought to bring together the most brilliant aspects of Rhetoric, and we may be sure that later generations so understood it.[66] The essence of *inventio* is here seen in *ingenium*. Of *iudicium* we now hear nothing. Instead, as the concluding and crowning concept, there is the "depth of conception" which has no place in Quintilian's system. It appears to be only another way of expressing *inventionis ingenium;* and so it would seem that here we have discovered two basic concepts of

---

[64] VIII, 3, 56: "κακόζηλον, id est mala adfectatio, per omne dicendi genus peccat. Nam et tumida et pusilla et praedulcia et abundantia et arcessita [the far-fetched] et exsultantia [the extravagant] sub idem nomen cadunt. Denique κακόζηλον vocatur, quidquid est ultra virtutem, quotiens ingenium iudicio caret et specie boni fallitur, omnium in eloquentia vitiorum pessimum."

[65] Even Góngora continued the vernacular poetry of the Spanish Middle Ages; cf. Dámaso Alonso, *La lengua poética de Góngora,* I (1935), 69 ff.

[66] Gracián uses the expression "profundidad de concepto" in his *Agudeza* (*Disc.* 45, *Obras,* 228 b.).

Spanish Mannerism.[67] The word *conceptus* in this sense is unknown to classical Latinity (which uses *conceptio* instead), but it was adopted by medieval philosophy in the sense of "concept."

How is the relation between *ingenium* and *iudicium* to be defined? This question was discussed by Spanish theorists in the sixteenth century. Juan de Valdés sets forth that it lies with the judgment to choose the best from among the stock of the *ingenium* and to put it in its proper place; "invention" and "disposition" *(disposición, ordenación)* are the two principal parts of rhetoric; the former corresponds to the *ingenio*, the latter to the *juicio*.[68] This is the linguistic usage from which Gracián also sets out. Astonishing that the fact has been overlooked hitherto! For Gracián's foreword to the reader of his *Agudeza* begins: "Some of my works—among them, and quite recently, my *Arte de Prudencia* [69]—I have allotted to the judgment; this one I dedicate to the *ingenio*." For anyone acquainted with Roman rhetoric this sentence was perfectly clear.[70] For our contemporary Hispanists, it appears not to be so.[71]

But Gracián's originality consists precisely in the fact that he, first and alone, declares the system of antique rhetoric to be insufficient and supplements it by a new discipline, for which he claims systematic validity.[72] At the beginning of the *Agudeza* (*Disc.* 1, *Obras*, p. 60) he argues: The ancients, it is true, established the rules of the syllogism and made an art

[67] Cf. Dante, *De vulgari eloquentia*, II, 1, 8: "Optime conceptiones non possunt esse nisi ubi scientia et ingenium est."—"conceptus": VE I 2, 3.

[68] Juan de Valdés, *Diálogo de la lengua*, ed. Montesinos, p. 165.

[69] Subtitle of the *Oráculo manual.—El discreto* also belongs among his works on the judgment. "Various attempts have been made to interpret the word *discreto*," says Pfandl (549), who translates it correctly by "gescheit" ("discreet") (from *scheiden*, as *discretus* from *discerenere*). The concept of the *vir discretus* is medieval Latin. Metrical characterizations of the *vir prudens* and the *vir discretus* are found in Werner, Nos. 235 and 236.

[70] Elsewhere Gracián defines the difference between the two concepts as follows: "No se contenta el ingenio con sola la verdad, como el juicio, sino que aspira a la hermosura" (*Agudeza, Disc.* 2; *Obras*, 63 b).—The proportion between *ingenium* and *iudicium* determines Gracián's value-judgments. Cicero: "Tiene también eminente lugar entre los ingeniosos y agudos, aunque como orador se templaba y como filosofo ejercitaba más el juicio que el ingenio" (*ibid., Disc.* 61, *Obras*, 281 a).—Lucian: "varón de sublime ingenio, pero acre, y con demasía juicioso" (*ibid., Disc.* 23, *Obras*, 146 a).—Traiano Boccalini (1556–1613) was able to unite "lo juicioso y lo ingenioso" (*Disc.* 16, *Obras*, 121 a).

[71] Pfandl, 236 f.: "In Antiquity the sage is the collective ideal, in the Middle Ages the saint, in the early Renaissance the scholar, in the later Renaissance the perfect courtier, but from Spain proceeds the Baroque ideal of *ingenio* . . . The inclusive term for this peculiarity of Spanish Baroque man is the word *ingenio*, and indeed it expresses not only an intellectual situation but also a definite species of individual . . ." This too is nothing but a Latinism! Seneca speaks of "Romana ingenia." Suetonius says in praise of Augustus: "Ingenia saeculi sui omnibus modis fovit." The younger Pliny: "Sum ex iis, qui mirer antiquos: non tamen, ut quidam, temporum nostrorum ingenia despicio." And so on.

[72] Hence it is unintelligible and misleading to say that *agudeza* is "nothing but a theory of tropes and figures spun out into the finest possible ramifications" (Pfandl, 551).

of the figures of speech.[73] But they did nothing corresponding for the "faculty of acuteness" (*agudeza*). They left it to the strength of the *ingenium* and were content to marvel at it. We have an outstanding example of this in the "imperial epigram of the prince of all heroes, Julius Caesar, who desired to win every kind of fame." [74] Then follows the medieval Latin epigram discussed above, p. 293. If a syllogism is constructed according to rules, it must also be possible to subject the conceit (*concepto*) to rules.[75] The rhetorical figures are merely the material and the basis for the system of *agudeza* (*Disc.* 20, *Obras*, 133 b). Hence the ancients have left an essential task of literary theory to be performed by the moderns. "An erudite knowledge of modern things is usually more piquant and finds more auditors than the old learning. The sayings and deeds of the ancients are very well-worn; modern ones win favor by their novelty; their curiousness doubles their brilliance" (*Disc.* 58, *Obras*, 269). "It is a great happiness to know the first authors of every class and especially the moderns who have not yet been scoured by time nor have undergone the rigorous verdict of a judging (*juicioso*) Quintilian. He does not even spare a Seneca, who moreover was his countryman." [76] Gracián's historical and aesthetic position in respect to the ancients and the moderns bears no relation to the French *Querelle des Anciens et des Modernes*. It has but one valid analogy: the position of the "Moderns" of 1170. That period produced the *poetria nova*. Gracián too constructs a new theory out of his period's sense of style. But it is not a poetics, as is sometimes said.[77] The conceit (*concepto*) "is a mental act which expresses the correspondence between two things" (*Disc.* 2, *Obras*, 64). It is valid for poetry and for prose,[78] and can be employed in every genre and style of the two mediums. "What is fit for an epigram is not suitable for a sermon." History requires other ideas than poetry, the letter other ideas than the oration. (*Disc.* 60, *Obras*, 275 f.). But every literary form and every realm of subject matter can support the ornament of conceit. "The preacher will esteem the substantial conceit of Ambrose; the humanist the biting conceit of Martial. Here the philosopher will find the judicious style of Seneca, the historian the malicious style of Tacitus, the orator the subtle style of Pliny, and the poet the brilliant style of Ausonius . . . I took my examples from the language in which I found them; for if Latin praises the great Florus, Italian boasts of the admirable Tasso, Spanish of the cultivated Góngora, and Portuguese of the tender Camões . . . If I prefer the Spanish, it is because they have the

---

73 "Hallaron los antiguos método al silogismo, arte al tropo." Syllogisms and *tropi* are put in parallel by Cassiodorus too (*supra*, p. 41).

74 I.e., that of the *héroe*, that of the *discreto*, and that of *agudeza*.

75 *Disc.* 1, *Obras*, 61 a.

76 *Disc.* 63, *Obras*, 290 a. The typographical errors make nonsense of this sentence. Read: "Quintiliano en el . . ."—Quintilian, X, I, 125 on Seneca.

77 Pfandl, 551.

78 "Esta urgencia de lo conceptuoso es igual a la prosa y al verso" (*Disc.* 1, *Obras*, 62 a).

most wit, as the French have the most learning, the Italians the most eloquence, and the Greeks the most invention" (Foreword to the Reader,
Obras, 59 f.).

Anyone introducing a new central concept into aesthetic theory must
make it intelligible by typical examples. Gracián circles around an ideal
canon of the masters of the *concepto*. He gives different versions of it. The
one in his Foreword (Ambrose, Martial, Seneca, Tacitus, Pliny,[79] Ausonius, Florus, Tasso, Góngora, Camões) we must regard as a carefully considered selection. Another comprises Augustine, Ambrose, Martial, and
Horace (*Disc.* 1, *Obras*, 62 a). These two groups are put at the beginning
of his book, like two preliminary suggestions. There is a corresponding
résumé at the end of the book: Tacitus, Velleius Paterculus, Florus, Valerius Maximus, Pliny, Apuleius, Martial (*Disc.* 60, *Obras*, 274 b). As we
see, ancient authors preponderate in the canon (otherwise it would not be
one). But if we ask ourselves what literary "experiences" and preferences
formed the basis for Gracián's canon, the answer is plain: Martial and
Góngora. Martial was not only a Spaniard, but also an Aragonese—that is,
he was a fellow countryman of Gracián's in both the wide and the narrow
sense. He is the author whom Gracián most frequently quotes, the "first-
born of *agudeza*" (*Disc.* 5, *Obras*, 78 b). But Góngora is "the swan, the
eagle, the phoenix of euphony, wit, and utmost perfection" (*Disc.* 3,
Obras, 67 a). He represents the pinnacle of the florid style, "above all in
his *Polifemo* and his *Soledades*" (*Disc.* 62, *Obras*, 287 b). The "Góngora of Italy" is Marino (*Disc.* 16, *Obras*, 120 a).

The Mannerism of late Latin poetry was naturally also included,[80] and
with it a certain amount of medieval Latin crept in—for example the
epigram on the Thracian lad, or an even more artificial "famous antique
epigram" which Ludwig Traube restored to its rightful author, Matthew
of Vendôme [81] (*Disc.* 39, *Obras*, 212 a). That the "Silver" Latinity of the
later Empire is classed with the Mannerism of the Latin Middle Ages will
no longer surprise anyone who has understood the *siglo de oro* in its continuity with the Middle Ages, i.e., with the "reception of the whole of
Antiquity." The same basis makes comprehensible another characteristic
element of *agudeza*, to which I find no reference anywhere, though it
should not have been easy to overlook it: profane and sacred literature are
reduced to the same common denominator of Conceptism. We have
already seen that Ambrose and Augustine belong to the conceptist canon.[82]

---

[79] His panegyric on Trajan is of everlasting value ("se mide con la eternidad":
Disc. 1, *Obras*, 61 b).

[80] Pentadius (*Disc.* 2, *Obras*, 63 a), Claudian (*Disc.* 8, *Obras*, 89 a).

[81] Ludwig Traube, *O Roma nobilis* (1891), 319.—Text in Riese, *Anthol. lat.* 2,
No. 786.

[82] In Ambrose, Gracián particularly esteems the highly rhetorical panegyric of
St. Agnes (in *De virginibus*; PL, XVI 200 ff.). From Augustine he quotes a *pointe*
whose original source I cannot give: Mary was betrothed to a carpenter and then
married the architect of the heavens (*Disc.* 4, *Obras*, 69 b).

Peter Chrysologus appears with them (*Disc.* 31, *Obras*, 182 b). But Greek Fathers, such as Clement of Alexandria,[83] Basil (*Disc.* 10, *Obras*, 98 a), Gregory of Nazianzus (*ibid.*), are also taken in. This may surprise modern readers, but it is fully justified. We have seen elsewhere that Augustine absorbed the Mannerism of late Roman Antiquity and that the Greek Fathers continued the Second Sophistic.[84] An important link in the manneristic tradition which leads from late Roman Antiquity and the writings of the Fathers to Gracián is the "Biblical rhetoric" which we traced from Augustine and Cassiodorus to Bede. When the latter recognizes the figure of ἀστεῖσμός in the Old Testament, when Alan praises Paul's metaphor of milk as "elegant," [85] the line which Gracián will follow to its end is traced out. He dares go so far as to call Christ's words to Peter: "Tu es Petrus, et super hanc petram aedificabo ecclesiam meam" a "divine subtlety" ("delicadeza sacra"; *Disc.* 31, *Obras*, 183 b).

This occurs in the chapter devoted to "playing on proper names" ("agudeza nominal")—the only play on words and ideas which can be traced back to Homer.[86] Gracián contributes some things of his own—for example, when he finds Augustine's rank as "king of the *Ingenios*" foretold in the similarity between the sound of his name and that of Augustus (*Disc.* 3, *Obras*, 67 b), or when he distinguishes an "Apollonian" and a "Martial" element in Martial (*Disc.* 26, *Obras*, 156 a). Nor are even the most sacred things forbidden ground to this form of *agudeza*: "The holy and adored name of God (*Dios*) says, divided: DI OS ("I gave ye"); I gave ye earth and heaven and being; I gave ye my grace, gave ye myself, gave ye all: so that in our Spanish language the Lord took his most holy and august name from giving" (*Disc.* 32, *Obras*, 189 b).

Acoustic conceits, that is, plays on words in the stricter sense ("figures of sound"), especially *annominatio* or paronomasia,[87] for which the entire Middle Ages and Dante too showed such a great liking, are also intellectual products and hence can find a place in conceptistic theory.

Is *agudeza* limited to epigrammatic *pointes* or is it capable of supporting an entire work of art? Does "free" wit or wit adjusted to the schema of a discourse deserve the preference? Can *ingenium* produce a work of art on a large scale ("un todo artificioso mental")? Gracián raises these questions at the beginning of the second part of his treatise (*Disc.* 51, *Obras*, 242 a). "Our Bilbilis [Martial's birthplace] sent as tribute to the great Empress of the world no monsters, like Africa, but him who was a monster in *ingenio*. Martial went to Rome destined for oratory, but his extreme intellectual agility would not suffer the fetters of concatenated eloquence but instead rose to the heights of every species and kind of *agudeza*, which are immortalized in his epigrams. This taste remained a possession of this ingenious province, the fair face of the world, and was

<hr />

[83] *Disc.* 6, *Obras*, 81 a; *Disc.* 52, *Obras*, 248 a; *Disc.* 59, *Obras*, 271 a (Christ as Orpheus).   [84] *Supra*, p. 68.   [85] *Supra*, p. 136.   [86] Excursus XIV.
[87] *Disc.* 32, *Obras*, 186 b.

never stronger than in this fruitful century, in which wits have blossomed with its expanded monarchy, all using the free form in sacred as well as profane literature" (*Disc.* 51, *Obras,* 243 a). Gracián, then, prefers the free forms of *agudeza,* which shoot up like the rockets of a fireworks display. Yet he is able to find examples of the use of *agudeza* in epic and the romance (Homer, Virgil, Heliodorus, Mateo Alemán; *Disc.* 56, *Obras,* 258 f.) and in the complications of dramatic intrigue (Lope de Vega, Calderón; *Disc.* 45, *Obras,* 228). Gracián's Conceptism is not doctrinaire. He is able to appreciate opposed virtues and styles: Asianism and "Laconism" [88] (*Disc.* 61, *Obras,* 278 a); the "natural" and the "ornamented" styles (*Disc.* 62, *Obras,* 282 ff.).

For the last two decades there have been signs of a revaluation of Góngora and Gracián. The *Agudeza* (which Menéndez y Pelayo called his worst book) has hardly figured in it. Yet the book is unique in its kind. It was a fruitful and timely idea to submit the widely ramified tradition of Mannerism to systematic consideration, to obtain an intellectual apprehension of its central source, to sort its forms, while guarding the dignity of their spirit. Gracián's book is an intellectual achievement of high rank. The intellectualism of the *siglo de oro,* which also pervades the drama of Calderón, may confidently face to the rationalism of a Boileau. Certainly, it is closer to the taste of the twentieth century. What else is the life work of a James Joyce but a gigantic manneristic experiment? The pun is one of its pillars. How much Mannerism there is in Mallarmé, and how closely connected he is with hermetism of contemporary poetry!

Gracián produced a "Summa" of *agudeza.* It was a national achievement. The Spanish tradition from Martial to Góngora was brought into a universal context. Thus, to use a striking phrase from Gracián's *Discreto* (c. 25, *Obras,* 350 a), there came into existence "un capacísimo teatro de la antigüedad presente." Whoever loves the overflowing originality of Spain will admire it in Gracián too.[89]

[88] He appears not to know Atticism.

[89] The Mannerism of the English "metaphysical poets," of Marino and the Marinists, and of the second Silesian school should be restudied against the background of Spanish Mannerism. The French variants (the *précieux,* etc.) are less interesting.

16

The Book as Symbol

PROGRESSING spirally, our course has led us to a height which permits a retrospect and a new prospect. From thence let us turn once again to metaphorics, and let us consider one of its most illuminating domains (though literary science has given it hardly any consideration): writing (the use of letters) and the book.

1. *Goethe on Tropes*

The subject, so far as I am aware, has hitherto been touched upon by no one but Goethe. In his universal thinking, reflection upon literature occupies an important place. Sainte-Beuve could rightly call him "the greatest of all critics." Goethe as critic—what a wonderful theme! But it has as yet found no one to treat it.[1] There is an extensive literature on Goethe as a natural scientist. But his writings on literature are passed over in silence. Lessing, Goethe, the Schlegels, Adam Müller had brought literary criticism in Germany to highest flowering. But they were not able to assure it a permanent place in the nation's intellectual life. And so matters have remained down to today.

One of the subjects to which the thinking of the older Goethe returned again and again is figurative expression. In the language of textbooks of rhetoric, a language with which Goethe was still familiar, such a mode of speech is called a "trope" (Greek τρόπος , "turn"). Goethe too used the word, normally in the form *Tropus*, sometimes in the form *Trope*. The idiosyncratic nature of poetic figurative language was forced upon Goethe's attention in his study of Oriental poetry. In his "Notes and Essays" attached to his *West-östlicher Divan* we read, under the heading "Primordial Elements of Oriental Poetry": "In the Arabic language there are to be

[1] Since the above was written, I have published a chapter on the subject in my *Kritische Essays zur europäischen Literatur* (1950).

found few stem-words and root-words which are not related to camel, horse, and sheep, if not immediately at least through the medium of certain slight modifications. These primary expressions of nature and life cannot rightly be called tropes. All the things which man expresses freely and naturally are life relations; now, the Arab is as intimately connected with camel and horse as is body with soul; nothing can happen to him which does not at the same time affect these creatures and vitally connect their existence and their activity with his own. If we also consider the other wild and domestic animals which the wandering Bedouin frequently sees, we shall find these too in all the relations of his life. If we proceed to consider everything else visible: mountain and desert, cliff and plain, trees, herbs, flowers, river and sea and the starry heavens, we find that, to the Oriental, all things suggest all things, so that, accustomed to connecting the most remote things together, he does not hesitate to derive contrary things from one another by very slight changes in letters or syllables. Here we see that language is already productive in and of itself, and indeed, in so far as it comes to meet thought, is eloquent and, in so far as it coincides with the imagination, is poetic. If, then, we should begin with the first, necessary, primary tropes and then mark the freer and bolder, until we finally reached the most daring and arbitrary, and even the inept, the conventional, and the hackneyed, we should have obtained a general view of Oriental poetry." In this passage, then, Goethe outlines the program for an investigation of figurative language in poetry. It would have to extend to all literatures, ascertain their peculiarities, and present the facts in orderly fashion. Thus it would have to be at once general and comparative.

Modern literary science has not followed up Goethe's sketch of a program for a "tropics" or metaphorics of world literature. It has also passed over an observation which is buried in the Maxims and Reflections: "Shakespeare is rich in wonderful tropes which stem from personified concepts and which would not suit us at all, but which in him are perfectly in place because in his time all art was dominated by allegory. Furthermore, he finds images where we would not go for them, for example in the book. Printing had been invented more than a century earlier; nevertheless, a book was still regarded as something sacred, as we know from the bindings of the times, and hence to the noble poet it was a thing to love and to honor; whereas we put everything between covers and are hard put to it to respect either the binding or the contents."

The use of writing and the book in figurative language occurs in all periods of world literature, but with characteristic differences which are determined by the course of the culture in general. Not every subject matter, that is, can be employed by figurative language, but only such as are value-charged; which, as Goethe puts it, are "life relations" or through which the "interdependent life of earthly things" is discernible. Hence Goethe emphasizes the fact that to Shakespeare the book was "still something sacred." The question therefore arises: Where and when has the book been accounted a sacred thing? We should have to go back through the sacred books of Christianity, of Islam, of Judaism to the ancient Orient —the Near East and Egypt. Here, thousands of years before our era, writing and the book have a sacred character, are in the hands of a priestly caste, and become the medium of religious ideas. Here we encounter "divine," "holy," and "cult" books. Writing itself is felt to be a mystery and the scribe is accorded particular dignity.[1a] Egypt had a god of scribes and writing in Thoth, whom the later Greeks associated with Hermes. To the Babylonians the stars were "the writing of the sky."

2. Greece

The Greeks regarded the Phoenician Cadmus as the bestower of writing. And in fact they adopted writing and the names of the letters from the ancient East. *Alpha, beta, gamma, delta* are Semitic words (cf. Hebrew *aleph, beth, gimel, daleth*). But in ancient Greece there is hardly any idea of the sacredness of the book, as there is no privileged priestly caste of scribes. The figurative use of writing and the book is therefore foreign to Greek poetry from the beginning. It is unknown to Homer and Hesiod. Pindar and the tragedians are the first to conceive of memory as a written record.[2]

Typically Greek is the disparagement of writing and books at the end of Plato's *Phaedrus* (274 C–276 A). Socrates relates that the Egyptian god Theuth (i.e., Thoth), the inventor of writing, commended his discovery to King Thamus: it would make the Egyptians wiser and increase their capacity to remember. But the king would have none of it: "For this will create forgetfulness in the souls of those who learn it because they will neglect to use their memories . . . You offer but the semblance of wisdom to your pupils, not its true self." Written records are, according to Socrates, only a mnemonic aid for him who already knows that with which the writing is concerned. They can never impart wisdom. That can be done only by speech "written in the pupil's soul with knowledge." Writing here becomes a metaphor for oral philosophical instruction. From this image others immediately grow. Wisdom is a seed which the intelligent husbandman will not "sow with the reed pen" and "write in black water." At most he will "sow and write in the garden of letters as an amusement, storing up memories for himself against the time when he shall reach forgetful old age" (276 CD). To "write in water" became

---

[1a] Franz Dornseiff, *Das Alphabet in Mystik und Magie* [2] (1925), 1 ff.

[2] Pindar, *Ol.*, 10, 1.—Aeschylus, *Suppliants*, 179; *Prometheus*, 789; *Choephori*, 450.—Sophocles, *Trach.*, 683; *Philoctetes*, 1325.—Hades records men's deeds (*Eumenides*, 275), moral laws are written in the book of Dike (*Suppliants*, 707). —Euripides compares the human heart to a written scroll rolled up (*Trojan Women*, 662).

proverbial as an image of instability and transience.[3] Related to the metaphor of writing is Plato's comparison of the soul to a wax tablet, upon which things imprint themselves as with a seal ring (*Theatetus* 191 C). Aristotle (*De anima*, III, 4, 430 a 1) says that the state of the mind before it applies itself to an object of cognition is "like that of a tablet upon which nothing has yet been written." The commentator Alexander of Aphrodisias paraphrases the passage by: "reason, resembling an unwritten tablet." Albertus Magnus and Thomas Aquinas substitute "tabula rasa."

Greek intellectual culture takes a new form in the Hellenistic period. Its characteristic is cosmopolitan education. Hellenistic poetry is a luxury import, a superficial acquisition of foreign peoples. With no political or ethnic roots, it seeks, under the protection of the Diadochi, to safeguard its own heritage by industrious compilation. It lives at courts, in libraries and schools. It establishes connections with the sciences (philology, natural history, astronomy, etc.). The "erudite poet" ("doctus poeta" among the Romans) is the ideal type. Culture becomes a culture of books. It lives in and by tradition. Hence in the Hellenistic period the book attains a new and higher position. This remains true in Imperial and Byzantine times. In Rome too the pacification of the Empire by Augustus had opened the way to such a development. "Arms lay idle," writes Eduard Norden, "the storms of war were stilled. Hermes and the Muses, fostered by the Emperor and his eminent men, could make their entrance into the city. Now learning was no longer cultivated out of resignation, with the feeling that something better was being sacrificed for it; it became an end in itself, which it had never been in the free commonwealths, either Greek or Roman. Cicero's friends had even considered it a reproach to him that he, a man who had so well served the state, should waste his powers teaching young men rhetoric: henceforth no such reproaches were heard, on the contrary literary activity bestowed distinction and—at least during the later Imperial period—carried a claim to promotion in the government service. The situation was, then, completely reversed . . . How strongly this was the consensus is shown by the following fact. In 269 Dexippus, with great personal courage and strategic genius, had saved his native city, Athens, from the Germanic hordes; his children set up a statue in his honor with an inscription which has come down to us and in which he is praised simply as a *rhetor* and *syngrapheus*, while his heroic deeds, from which he had promised himself 'eternal fame,' . . . receive no mention whatever." This is precisely the reverse of the epitaph which Aeschylus composed for himself; and in which he sought to immortalize only his share in the Battle of Marathon, not his work as a poet.

[3] A. Otto, *Die Sprichwörter der Römer* (1890), p. 31 under 5, gives examples from Sophocles (fr. 742, ed. Nauck), Catullus (70, 3), Augustine (*Civ. Dei*, XIX, 23, 1).—Shakespeare: "Men's evil manners live in brass; their virtues/We write in water (*K. Hen. VIII*, IV 2).—The inscription which marks Keats's grave beside the pyramid of Cestius and which he chose himself runs: "Here lies one whose name was writ in water."

The collection of minor lyrics known as the *Greek Anthology*, which for the most part contains poems from the times of the first Ptolemies to the sixth century A.D., may well serve to illustrate the newly attained position of the book. Poetical composition itself has become laborious nocturnal desk work, the poet a "maker of pages"; the work of an inferior poet is a "scrap" he has "torn" from the book of a greater (13, 21). Epigrams on libraries and their treasures become poetical exercises. But the finest epigram on a library has come down to us not in a book but on stone —the inscription on a herma from Herculaneum (*CIG*, 6186), found in Rome in 1878. The Muses address the herma:

῎Αλσος μέν Μούσαις ἱερόν λέγε τοῦτ' ἀναχεῖσϑαι

τὰς βίβλους δείξας τὰς παρὰ ταῖς πλατάνοις.

'Ημᾶς δὲ φρουρεῖν χῆν γνήσιος ἐνϑάδ' ἐραστὴς

ἔλϑη, τῷ χισσῷ τοῦτον ἀναστέφομεν.

(Say that this grove is dedicated to us, the Muses, and point to the books over there by the plane-tree grove. We guard them here; but let him who truly loves us come to us: We will crown him with ivy.)

This epigram was apparently intended for a library which stood in a place planted with planes and adorned with statues of the Muses. The epigrams on individual classic writers would also seem to have been intended for libraries. Thus we have epigrams on the works of Aristophanes, Menander, Plato ("the greatest voice in the entire page [4] of Greek literature," πανελλήνων σελίs); their charm can lie in subtle literary characterization (*A.P.*, IX, 186–188), or else in the description of a historical or genre situation, be the subject a textbook on tactics or the Homeric epics (IX, 210 and 192). The materials and implements necessary for writing now also become worthy of the poet's art. We have epigrams on the writing tablet (XIV, 60); on the wax with which it is covered (XIV, 45); on the calamus (IX, 162); as well as a threat to the boring beetle, "enemy of the Muses" (IX, 251). A poet expresses his gratitude for a present of fine papyrus sheets and pens, only ink being lacking (IX, 350); another praises Nature, who invented writing materials to unite parted friends (IX, 401). Professional copyists beg kindly acceptance of their work and, at its end, complain that their eyes and limbs ache. The learned philologist who has produced an emended edition of Homer introduces himself too (XV, 36–38). A particular class of epigram is the inscription for a votive offering. An offering is made to a deity not only after an illness or after an escape from some peril, but also when a man takes leave of his life's work.

---

[4] σελίs means the written page of a book, later the book itself; for example, in the *Vita Homeri* of the Pseudo-Plutarch the *Iliad* and *Odyssey* are called δισσαὶ σελίδες; finally the word comes to be used for literature in general. The Latin *pagina* shows a corresponding development in meaning. In Jerome (*Ep.*, 22, 17) and frequently later *pagina sancta* means "Holy Scripture." Further discussion by de Ghellinck in *Mélanges A. Pelzer* (Louvain, 1947), 23 ff.

The craftsman dedicates his tools. The poets are fond of putting on this mask. An entire book of the *Anthology* is filled with dedicatory epigrams. Among them some are put in the mouths of scribes. An old scribe, for example, dedicates his pencil, rule, inkwell, reed pens, and pen-knife to Hermes (VI, 63–68 and 295). Variations on this motif are especially popular. This is perhaps explained by the fact that the art of calligraphy was particularly esteemed and cultivated in Byzantium from the fifth century onward. Such an Emperor as Theodosius II (d. 450) distinguished himself in it. Furthermore, the subject afforded an opportunity for the poet's virtuosity to shine: To describe the implements of writing (generally five or six were listed) "poetically" demanded no little skill. If the examples cited bear witness to a new "life relation" to the book, the old writing-metaphors for "memory" naturally also reappear in late Greek poetry. A dead man remains engraved on the "memorial-stone" of the human heart (VIII, 147). Finally, life itself is compared to a book which is unrolled until the curved stroke or flourish with the pen—the koronis—is put under the text (XI, 41). This image was also used by Meleager of Gadara (XII, 257) in the epigram with which he concluded his "Garland," a collection of epigrams by himself and other poets, which he dedicated to his friend Diocles:

"I, the koronis [colophon], the faithful guardian of the written pages, announce the final boundary stone and I say that Meleager has completed in one work the songs which he gathered from all the poets and from those flowers he wove for Diocles this garland of the Muses which shall endure for ever.

"And I, curved round like a snake's back, am placed at the end of this pleasant work." *

In secular poetry, the Christian Greeks of the Eastern Empire preserved the forms and images which had served the old pagan world. As late as the fifth century the East still has such eminent poets as Synesius and Nonnus, producing both pagan and Christian works. There are analogies for this in the Latin West, to be sure; but the authors who might be cited—Sidonius Apollinaris, for example—are of far lower rank. Since the poets of the *Anthology* are active exclusively within the narrow limits of the occasional lyric or of poetry-to-order, their "life relation" to the book is exhausted in the realms of philology and the library, of calligraphy, bibliophilia, and bibliomania. Beside this, however, we have the philosophical speculation of a Plotinus. Writing affords him comparisons intended to serve cognition, not literary effect. Thus, the stars for him are "like letters forever being written in the sky, or like letters written once and for all and forever moving" (II, 3, 7; Müller, I, 93, 8). The motion of the stars serves to maintain the universe but it also has another use: "If they are regarded as letters (γράμματα), he who knows that alphabet (γραμματική) reads the

[* Richard Aldington's translation (replacing August Öhler's).]

future according to the figures they form." Concerning the seer, Plotinus says that his art is "to read the written characters of Nature, which reveal order and law" (III, 1, 6; ed. Müller, I, 167, 30; III, 3, 6; ed. Müller, I, 199, 12). These are ideas which we shall meet again in connection with the "Book of Nature."

In its religious end phase, pagan Antiquity also had the concept of the evangelical significance and sacredness of the book. The Homeric poems had become "the sacred books of Paganism." The Neo-Platonists cited lines from Homer in support of their speculations, as the Fathers cited verses from the Bible.[5] Proclus invokes the Muses who purify earth-bound souls by blessed influences from "spirit-awakening books" (Hymn III, 2 ff.). In a hymn to all gods (IV, 5 ff.) he prays to the "powerful redeemers" for enlightenment from "divinest books." Nonnus uses the conventional writing metaphors with great frequency. For example: The stars "write on the air with flame" (*Dion.*, II, 192). He found room in his gigantic *Dionysiaca* for the introduction of writing by Cadmus (IV, 259 ff.): ". . . Cadmos brought gifts of voice and thought for all Hellas; he fashioned tools to echo the sounds of the tongue, he mingled sonant and consonant in one order of connected harmony. So he rounded off a graven model of speaking silence [6]; for he had learnt the secrets of his country's sublime art, an outside intruder into the wisdom of Egypt, while Agenor dwelt nine years in Memphis and founded hundred-gated Thebes. There he pressed out the milk [7] of the holy books ineffable, scratched their scratches across with backfaring hand and traced their rounded circles." * Nonnus also has a variation of the "Book of Fate": The primordial spirit (ἀρχέγονος φρήν) inscribed the future history of the world on tablets in vermilion letters (XII, 29-113, especially 67 f.). Thus the last centuries of Greek poetry exhibit an increasing linking of the mind with the book and the world of books.

3. Rome

Roman literature in its period of florescence made very little use of book metaphors. To be sure, the general upswing under Sulla at first produced a new fertility under the influence of Alexandrian-Hellenistic literature and culture. With pleasure in deliberately cultivated form, there also awoke pleasure in beautiful books. Significant in this respect is the celebrated poem in which Catullus dedicates his collected verse to his friend and fellow Veronan Cornelius Nepos; it begins:

> *Quoi dono lepidum novum libellum*
> *Arida modo pumice expolitum?*

[5] Cumont, *Recherches sur le symbolisme funéraire des Romains*, p. 8.
[6] This oxymoron occurs with great frequency in Calderón (*retórico silencio*).
[7] Cf. Dornseiff, *Alphabet* . . . , 18 f.
[* W. H. D. Rouse's translation (replacing T. v. Scheffer's).]

Nepos had written a universal chronicle:

> . . . *ausus es unus Italorum*
> *Omne aevum tribus explicare cartis* [8]
> *Doctis, Jupiter, et laboriosis.*

The Alexandrianism of this poem lies not only in its connecting the idea of poetry with the art of the scribe and bookcraft but also in its display of admiration for scholarly work. But through Cicero, Virgil, and Horace, Rome's cultural aspirations were guided back to the flowering time of ancient Greece. A classicistic ideal of art arose. And with it the imagery of the book suffered recession. It is barely represented in the stock of images of Augustan poetry. Thus, for example, Horace's metaphor "mors ultima linea rerum est" (*Epi.*, I, 16, 79) means not a line of writing but the starting line in the stadium, where the race began and ended. Writing and the book do not play a role again until we reach Martial. The fourteenth and last book of his epigrams bears the title *Apophoreta*: that is, gifts which guests are given at table to take home.[9] To each gift Martial devotes a distich. The list includes books (183-196), as well as writing tablets simple or elaborate, writing paper, stylus boxes, etc. In the twelfth century, which had a liking for Martial, we shall encounter these themes again. In the second and third centuries Roman poetry practically dries up. Then the late flowering of the fourth century produces the two very different poetical personalities of Ausonius and Claudian. Ausonius, despite his charming *Mosella* and his carefully turned and prettily introduced lines on the Swabian girl Bissula, is a humdrum schoolmaster. Reading him, we breathe the dusty air of a library. He takes pride in calling the letters of the alphabet "little black daughters of Cadmus" (*Ep.*, 14, 74 and *Ep.*, 15, 52). In a poem (19, 1) *in chartam* he addresses his writing paper. Claudian is very different: a poet with a magnificent gift of language, infusing both late Greek and Egyptian culture into the powerful flood of his political poems, the best of which were written to praise the German-Roman Stilicho. Here the imagery of the book is not put at the service of empty grammatical trifling as it is in Ausonius but of panegyric homage: On the occasion of his consulship the stars write Stilicho's name in the annals of the sky ("Scribunt aetheriis Stilichonem sidera fastis": *De cons. Stilichonis* II, 476). This and similar expressions of Claudian's become current again or are exaggerated in later periods, especially in the sixteenth and seventeenth centuries. In late Roman prose we find a new book metaphor: *album*. Originally this is the white tablet for official notices, then a register of officeholders (e.g., senators). In

---

[8] *Carta* "means papyrus prepared for writing and hence the roll which normally constitutes a book" (W. Kroll).—Later the word is also used for parchment (*membrana*), e.g., by Ausonius.
[9] The model, as is well known, for Schiller's and Goethe's "Xenien."

Apuleius (*Metamorphoses*, ed. Helm, p. 145, 25), Jupiter opens an assembly of the gods [10] with the words: "Dei conscripti Musarum albo."

The concept of the "Book of History," in which someone enters his name—sometimes "in golden letters"—must also have been rooted in Antiquity. But I have hitherto been unable to elucidate the origin of this metaphor completely. A first step is to be seen in Herodotus' account (I, 82) of the Spartan Othryades, who in the battle between the three hundred Spartans and the three hundred Argives in Thyrea remained victorious, but then took his own life because he was ashamed to return to Sparta when all his comrades had fallen. To Herodotus' account late Antiquity added the detail that Othryades inscribed his victory on the spoils with his own blood (*A.P.*, VII, 526 and elsewhere; Lucian [ed. Jacobitz, I, 222]). Othryades also became a favorite theme for rhetorical declamations.[11] The Victory of Brescia is writing the history of a victorious war on a shield.[12] A transposition of this idea to monumental proportions is Trajan's Column. Of the basilica Ulpia, Carcopino says: ". . . elle était subordonnée de trois degrés aux bibliothèques voisines; et la colonne historiée qui s'interposait entre elles . . . à qui personne n'a pu, jusqu'ici, découvrir de modèle, doit sans doute être comprise . . . comme la réalisation originale, par l'architecte Apollodore de Damas, d'une conception propre à l'empereur; en l'érigeant au milieu de la cité des livres, Trajan aurait voulu dérouler, dans les spirales qui la revêtent les deux volumina qui retraçaient sur le marbre ses exploits guerriers et exaltaient vers le ciel sa force et sa prudence."

4. The Bible

It was through Christianity that the book received its highest consecration. Christianity was a religion of the Holy Book. Christ is the only god whom antique art represents with a book-scroll.[13] Not only at its first appearance but also throughout its entire early period, Christianity kept producing new sacred writings—documents of the faith such as gospels, letters of apostles, apocalypses; acts of martyrs; lives of saints; liturgical books. The Old Testament itself contained a large stock of metaphors from the book. The tables of the law are "written with the finger of God" (Exod. 31:18). In an eschatological vision "the heavens shall be rolled together as a scroll" ("complicabuntur sicut liber caeli"; Isa. 34:4). Revelation 6:14 is modeled on this: "Caelum recessit sicut liber involutus." The Psalmist begins

[10] On this motif, cf. O. Weinreich, *Senecas Apocolocyntosis* (1928), 84 ff.

[11] F. J. Brecht, *Motiv- und Typengeschichte des griechischen Spottepigramms* (1930), 16.

[12] This motif is also common on coins; see M. Bernhard, *Handbuch zur Münzkunde der römischen Kaiserzeit*, I, 102; II, 2 and 6.

[13] T. Birt, *Die Buchrolle in der Kunst* (1907) and T. Michels in *Oriens christianus* (1932), 138 f.—Writing deities are found in Etruscan art, see F. Messerschmidt in *Archiv für Religionswissenschaft* (1931), 60 ff.

a festal song with the words: "Lingua mea calamus scribae velociter scribentis" (44:2 = A.V. 45:2): "My tongue is the pen of a ready writer." The Old Testament also has the "Book of Life," written by God (Exod. 32:22; Ps. 68:29; 138:16; whence Rev. 3:5 etc.). The prophet receives divine instruction: "Scribe hoc ob monimentum in libro" (Exod. 17:14) or: "Sume tibi librum grandem, et scribe in eo stylo hominis" (Isa. 8:1). Job wishes that his declaration of his innocence might be written and graven forever: "Quis mihi tribuat ut scribantur sermones mei? Quis mihi det ut exarentur in libro stylo ferreo et plumbi lamina [14] vel celte [15] sculpantur in silice" (19:23 f.). The sin of Judah "is written with a pen of iron and with the point of a diamond" (A.V.), "stylo ferreo in ungue adamantino, exaratum super latitudinem cordis eorum" (Jer. 17:1). Roman and Jewish state documents on bronze tablets are found in I Macc. 8:22; 14:18; 14:26; 14:48.—In the New Testament Luke shows us the twelve-year-old Jesus among the scribes in the Temple, and the Risen Lord who "expounded the scriptures" to the disciples at Emmaus. John (8, 6) shows Jesus writing on the ground with his finger. Paul likens the congregation to a letter: "Epistola estis Christi . . . scripta non atramento, sed spiritu Dei vivi; non in tabulis lapideis, sed in tabulis cordis carnalibus" (II Cor. 3:3). Finally, books decide the fate of the soul in eternity [16] (Rev. 20:12 f.).

These selected passages show how magnificent the religious metaphorics of the book can be, in contrast to the purely literary form of it with which we had previously become familiar (on the borderline between the two is Ecclesiastes 12:9–12). It is characteristic of the Middle Ages in the West that the two so different worlds not only come into contact but also intersect and interpenetrate one another—as do Church and school, piety and learning, symbolism and grammar.

5. Early Middle Ages

On the threshold of the transition centuries stands the Spanish poet Prudentius (ca. 400). In his lyrical legends of martyrs (Peristephanon) we find many images from the book and a constant "life relation" to it. St.

[14] From this passage the Middle Ages derived the popular lead-tablet metaphor. In a satirical rhythmus written in 996 Adalbero of Laon says ironically:

Plumbi scribatur lamina,
Ne transeat memoria.

Cf. P. A. Becker, Vom Kurzlied zum Epos (1940), 50 ff. In the Apocalypsis Goliae (st. 9) we read:

Vidi quorumlibet inscripta nomina
Tanquam in silice vel plumbi lamina.

Both lead and bronze tablets were used in Rome, see Dessau, Römische Epigraphik. Calderón (ed. Keil, II, 23 b) plays conceptistically with lead and bronze tablets.

[15] Celtis = stonecutter's chisel. The real name of the German Humanist "Conrad Celtis" was Pickel.

[16] The idea of God's book in heaven in which our sins are written was already known to the Greeks of the fifth century (A. Dieterich, Nekyia [1893], 126 n.).

Eulalia likens the wounds which the torturers inflict on her to purple writing [17] in praise of Christ (III, 136 ff.). An angel who measures each individual wound writes down the passion of the martyr Romanus while it is in progress (X, 1121 ff.). The martyr himself is an "inscripta Christo pagina" (*ibid.*, 1119). The martyr Vincent, deacon of Saragossa, refuses to give the "secret books of his sect" to the judge with the words (V, 186): "Thou thyself wilt be burnt by the fire, because thou threatenest the sacred writings (*mysticis litteris*)".[18] In the martyrdom of the sainted schoolmaster Cassian, writing plays not a metaphorical but an intensely real part. He is delivered over to his pupils, who break writing tablets on his head and pierce him with styluses. He became the victim of his profession (IX). In his other works too, Prudentius is accustomed to emphasize everything connected with the sacred books and collections of books (*Perist.*, XIII, 7; *Apoth.*, 376 and 594 ff.).

Christian Antiquity is also the Church of the Martyrs. Prudentius' *Peristephanon* represents the close of that epoch in literary terms. Viewed from this aspect Prudentius' metaphorics of the book gain a deeper meaning. The antique Church of the Martyrs is succeeded by the Church of the Monks. Monasticism, taking root in the West from 350, and after 500 given a form and a norm for millenniums by St. Benedict, signifies the turn from Christian Antiquity to the Christian Middle Ages. One of the tasks which monasticism took over was that of transmission—not only of the truths of the faith and of Christian history, but also of both profane and sacred learning. It became one of the chief supports—and from the eighth century onwards the only support—of writing and the book. In the sixth and seventh centuries the lay culture of Antiquity was still alive in the kingdoms of the Visigoths and the Merovingians. But this is especially true of the Ostrogoths. In the collection of official letters and decrees which Cassiodorus wrote for the Ostrogothic kings, there is a letter to a scribe (*Variae*, XII, 21; Mommsen, pp. 377 f.), which impressively sets forth the value of that profession and its significance for the state, for administration, and for justice.

Oriental monasticism penetrates Gaul in the fourth century. Of St. Martin, his biographers report (Sulpicius Severus, 13, 3–9, and thence Paulinus of Périgueux, II, 119 ff.), that the only art which he permitted to his monks was writing, because it occupied mind, eye, and hand together and thus helped concentration. But the disorders of Merovingian France are no favorable climate for the pursuit of intellectual culture. It thrives better in the Atlantic borderlands of the West—Spain, Ireland, Britain.

---

17 In Byzantium purple ink, *sacrum incaustum*, was reserved to the Emperor and had a special chamberlain to guard it. It is to be distinguished from the red color which was used in medieval calligraphy and illumination (*minium*): Wattenbach, *Das Schriftwesen im Mittelalter* [3] (1896), 248.

18 It was the deacon's duty to take care of the books used in services. According to T. Klauser, this is the explanation for the Gospel shrine in the St. Lawrence mosaic in the mausoleum of Galla Placidia at Ravenna.

The first book of Isidore's *Etymologiae* treats of the first of the seven arts: Grammar. There (c. 3) we are also told everything of importance on the subject of the letters of the alphabet. They are "signs" of things and "have such power that they bring the speech of one absent to our ears without voice." Some of them have a mystical meaning.[19] Thus Isidore accepts and passes on a magico-mystical concept of the very elements of writing. This was of great moment for succeeding times. The same may be said of the considerations upon writing and the book to which Isidore devotes Book VI of his work. It begins with a discussion of the Bible, its books, their authors, and then treats of libraries among the Jews, the Greeks, the Romans, and the Christians; polygraphs;[20] literary genres; subjects for descriptions; books; writing implements. To conclude there are several chapters on liturgical and chronological matters and church history. As writing implements Isidore names the reed (*calamus*) and the quill (*pinna*, a variant of *penna*, whence Ger. *Pennal*, "pencil case, pencil box"). By the incision in its point, the quill represents a unity which diverges into a duality: symbol[21] of the divine Word, the Logos, which is revealed in the duality of the Old and the New Testament and whose sacrament flows forth in the blood of the Passion (*Et.*, VI, 14, 3). Isidore further says that the Romans first used an iron stylus for writing on wax tablets and later one of bone. In proof he quotes from a lost comedy by the poet Atta, whose name alone is known to us (*Et.*, VI, 9, 2):

> . . . *Vertamus vomerem*
> *In cera mucroneque aremus osseo.*

That is: "Turn we the ploughshare upon the wax and plow we with a point of bone." Isidore knows too that the "Ancients" made their lines as the ploughman his furrows (*Et.*, VI, 14, 71), that they wrote "furrow-wise."[22] The metaphor "ploughshare" for "stylus" (*vomer* for *stilus*) occurs, so far as I am aware, nowhere else in Roman literature, but is found in medieval poets. Wherever we encounter it, then, it must stem from Isidore. The basic comparison is of course older. So early as Plato, we find the comparison between the dressing of a field and writing. The Romans seldom used *arare* as a metaphor for writing. The compound *exarare* ("plough up") is much more frequent, but seems no longer to be felt as a figurative expression but simply means "to write," "to compose." I do

---

[19] In southern France a different mysticism of the alphabet was represented by the abstruse grammarian Virgilius Maro, who was influenced by the Kabbala. Cf. his *Epitomae*, ed. Tardi, p. 41.

[20] VI 6: "Qui multa scripserunt." Admiration for polygraphy is typically Spanish. *Poligrafo* is still an honorable designation in Spain today and means something like "universal scholar"; whereas in France *polygraphe* expresses derogation.

[21] According to Cassiodorus (PL, LXX, 1145 A) the fact that men write with three fingers indicates the Trinity.

[22] In Greek βουστροφηδόν: turning like oxen in ploughing, writing from left to right and from right to left alternately.

not find the line of writing referred to as a "furrow" before Prudentius
(*Perist.*, IX, 52 and IV, 119; *Apoth.*, 596). The two passages quoted from
Isidore would seem to have been decisive in inculcating the comparison
into the minds of medieval writers and maintaining it as a standard mode
of expression. The parchment is the field, the writer knows the art of
"cleaving the book-fields" ("bibliales . . . proscindere campos"; *Poetae*,
I, 93, 5). He knows that the Emperor Charles tolerates no "thorn bushes,"
that is, no scribal errors, as a note in an eighth-century codex informs us
(*Poetae*, I, 89 f.). The metaphor "plough" for "write" passes from medieval Latin literature into the vernacular literatures. In a manuscript of the
eighth or ninth century, preserved at Verona (a Mozarabic prayer book),
the following notation was discovered in 1924: "Se pareva boves alba pra-
talia araba et albo versorio teneba et negro semen seminaba"; [23] that is,
"He urged on the oxen, ploughed white fields, held a white plough, and
sowed black seed." By altering the forms and order of the words, an attempt was made to turn this into a rhymed quatrain in early Italian and it
was given out to be a precious relic of popular pastoral poetry. As a matter
of fact it is a scribal adage of erudite origin. The white fields are the pages,
the white plough the pen, the black seeds the ink. Our examples from
Plato, Isidore, Prudentius, and Carolingian poetry clarify this imagery.
Once again the phantom of "popular poetry" has misled scholars. That
solitary masterpiece of the declining Middle Ages in Germany, the *Ackermann aus Böhmen*, which occupied Konrad Burdach for decades, also employs the image of writing as ploughing. Chapter 3 begins: "Ich bins
genannt ein ackerman, von vogelwat ist mein pflug." In *vogelwat* (*Vogel-
kleid*, "bird dress") Burdach rightly recognized a "riddling description of
the writing quill." But in the word *ackerman* he insisted upon seeing a
reference to a mysticism of the ploughman, and attempted to demonstrate
it with a lavish display of erudition. It was Arthur Hübner who found the
correct interpretation (*Kleine Schriften zur deutschen Philologie* [1940],
205 f.): "The quill is my plough—this is a well-known scribal adage." It
goes back, I might add, to the Latin Middle Ages.

Carolingian poetry provides frequent testimony to the renewed cultivation of writing. Alcuin has left us metrical inscriptions for various monastery rooms. The monastic scriptorium is the subject of one poem (*Poetae*,
I, 320), in which a dignified gravity in speech and demeanor is enjoined
upon the scribe. This is demanded by the holiness of the books he is to
copy, as well as by accurate reproduction of the text in word and punctua-
tion. Not only is writing more genteel work than tilling the soil, it also
serves the soul's welfare. Here we have *in nuce* the essential definition of
the medieval *clericus*. Writing also includes dictation. This activity too is
utilized for figurative language. God is the *dictator*, under whom holy men
write (Alcuin in *Poetae*, I, 285, LXVI, 4 and 288, 15). In accord with an
Old Testament concept, Raban Maur (*Poetae*, II, 186, XXI, 11) sets

[23] G. Lazzeri, *Antologia dei primi secoli della letteratura italiana* (1942), 1 ff.

forth that writing is already sacred by virtue of the fact that God used it when he wrote the tables of the law. In a poem to Abbot Hatto of Fulda, Raban justifies the philosophical and ethical superiority of writing over painting. He put forth a combination of the two arts in his *Liber de laudibus sanctae crucis*. It consists of twenty-eight figure poems (*technopaignia*), that is, metrical compositions which, through the arrangement of the characters and the use of different colors, present pictures to the eye, for example, a cross. The book was also adorned with illustrations: two dedication scenes, a portrait of Louis the Pious, and a picture of the author under a cross which results from the disposition of the characters on the page.[24] Raban's models were the figure poems of Optatianus Porfyrius (under Constantine), which, in turn, stem from *technopaignia* of Alexandrian poetry. Thus Carolingian artistic practice remains within the orbit of that of late Antiquity. At Aix-la-Chapelle, Fulda, Ingelheim the life relation to writing is the same as at Byzantium. Hence in France too we find poetical eulogies of calligraphy and calligraphers (*Poetae*, I, 92 f. and 589, 5 f.): riddles the answers to which are "pen," "ink," "letter," "paper" (*Poetae*, I, 22, IX and 23, XII; IV, 746; cf. Aldhelm, ed. Ehwald, 124, LIX, 3 ff.)—in other words, a dilettante genre poetry which takes its subjects from the craft of the scribe. We also find verses by scribes (for example *Poetae*, IV, 402 f. and IV, 1056–1072). A metaphor to be noted is the line of writing, which must be kept straight: "linea vitae sacrae" (*Poetae*, I, 42, st. 15; after St. Benedict's Rule); "linea karitatis" (*Poetae*, I, 80, 10). Thus the Carolingian period shows us many things, but few new things. It is a purely receptive era, with little intellectual independence— the strict, monastic school years of the Western mind.

6. High Middle Ages

The Humanism of the twelfth century, like every true humanism, delights simultaneously in the world and in the book. The richness of the world and of life is reflected for it in the treasures and springs of power of the literary tradition, its assimilation, continuation, and transformation. This is the source of a new imagery of the book. Metaphors from books and writings are now more numerous and bolder.

I shall give a few examples, first from twelfth and thirteenth century Latin poetry, then from theological and philosophical literature.

We saw that Prudentius likened the wounds of martyrs to purple writing. This comparison now recurs, in manneristic conceits. In the handwritten books of the Middle Ages red was frequently employed, partly for ornament, partly to make the text more perspicuous. Usually the title of the book and the headings of the principal divisions were executed in red. What was written in red was called *rubrica* (our "rubric"), the red color

[24] Reproductions in J. Prochno, *Das Schreiber- und das Dedikationsbild in der deutschen Buchmalerei* (1929), 11 ff.

was red oxide of lead (*minium*). As a rule a special scribe (*rubricator, miniator*) was entrusted with producing the rubrication.[25] His craft—*rubricare*—serves as a metaphor for the spilled blood of martyrs. Thus Peter the Venerable apostrophizes the doctor and martyr Cyprian of Carthage (d. 258) in the words (*PL*, CLXXXIX, 1009 D):

> *Jungeris his verbo, praecellis sanguine sacro,*
> *Quo melius solito Punica terra rubet,*
> *Quam tua multorum rubricavit lingua cruore,*
> *Quos monuit vitam perdere morte pia.*

We shall find the same metaphor again in Calderón. Like many others, it was transmitted to the *siglo de oro* through the Mannerism of medieval Latin literature.

Writing imagery is richly developed in Alan. Natura sets forth the theory of sexual love ("cupidinariae artis theorica") and adds: "You can learn its practice from the book of experience ("per librum experientiae")." [26]

The comparison, already found in Alan, of a man's face to a book, from which his thoughts can be read, was adopted by Henry of Settimello in his widely read elegy (ed. Marigo, l. 73 ff.):

> *Nam facies habitum mentis studiumque fatetur,*
> *Mensque quod intus agit, nuntiat illa foris;*
> *Internique status liber est et pagina vultus.*

The same poet uses writing imagery in bewailing his grief (ed. Marigo, 235 f.):

> *Pagina sit caelum, sint frondes scriba, sit unda*
> *Incaustrum: mala non nostra referre queant.*[27]

An epitaph (by Peter Riga?) of the same period begins (*PL*, CLXXI, 1394 C):

> *Quem studio morum Naturae pinxerat unguis,*
> *Incausto tinguit Mors inimico suo.*

---

[25] "These red letters, or letters distinguished by the use of red, produced a whole rich branch of art which was therefore called *miniare* . . . *Minium* was frequently used for decorated initials . . . The idea of redness was forgotten." Wattenbach, *Das Schriftwesen im Mittelalter* [3], 346 f.—Joinville in his life of St. Louis draws a beautiful simile from illumination: "Et ainsi comme l'écrivain qui a fait son livre, qui l'enlumine d'or et d'azur, enlumina ledit roy son royaume."

[26] *SP*, II, 474.—Natura writes on the paper of Alan's mind: "chartulae tuae mentis" (*ibid.*, 481).—Procreation as *scriptura* (*ibid.*, 475).—The robe of Rhetoric is a book ("hic velut in libro legitur"; *ibid.*, 315).—Likewise the human face (*ibid.*, 319).—This becomes a manner in John of Hanville. A pretty girl has lips which Natura painted with *minium* (*SP*, I, 255) and calves that remind one of the smooth page of a book (*ibid.*, 259).—Gervase of Melkley transfers this to the face (Faral, 332, 35 ff.). He turns book imagery into obscenity (*Studi med.*, IX [1936], 106). Cf. *litteras discere* = *voluptate frui* (Plautus, *Truc.*, IV, 2, 26) and *The Thousand and One Nights* (tr. E. Littmann, VI, 488).

[27] On the formula "And if the sky were paper" cf. Reinhold Köhler, *Kleinere Schriften*, ed. Bolte, III (1900), 296.

That is: Nature made a splendid man and painted him with moral excellences—but Death dyes him with his ink. For persons or personified beings to appear displaying words or letters was common in the Middle Ages.
When Philosophy came to comfort Boethius in prison, had she not appeared with a Greek Π (= Praxis) and Θ (= Theoria) on her robe? Alan,
as we saw, compares the robe of Rhetorica to a book. Pythagoras, finally,
as the representative of all scholastic learning, appears to an unknown poet
in a vision as a man transformed into a book (*Apocalypsis Goliae*). On
his brow shines astrology, grammar governs his teeth, rhetoric brightens
on his tongue, from his lips spouts logic, etc.; the mechanical arts are
drawn on his back, on his right hand is written: "Dux ego previus, et tu
me sequere."

In the same twelfth century we find a pleasant poet who had a particular
fondness for the scribal art: Baudri of Bourgueil. Ausonius had written a
poem to his writing paper, but Baudri outdoes him, for he dedicates numerous poems to his tablets, or to put it more exactly, to his wax-tablet
notebooks. He owns several such. A particularly fine one is described in
No. 47. It has eight wooden tablets, and thus provides fourteen writing
surfaces, for the outsides of the two outer tablets are not written on. They
are of an unusually small but highly practical format. Each surface will
hold six hexameters written the wide way of the tablet. To save the eyes,
they are coated with green wax. The craftsman (*tabularius*) who made them
was an artist. If only a needlewoman would make a bag to keep the little
wooden book in! In another poem (No. 234) Baudri tells his *tabulae* that
he is going to have them coated with fresh wax and fitted with new thongs.
Or he offers thanks for a gift of *tabulae* (No. 206), gives some himself
(No. 210), complains in verse over breaking a stylus (No. 154). In poems
to his scribe he gives instructions for the execution of initials in color (No.
146) or asks that the copying be done more speedily (No. 44). He addresses his book and discusses its format (No. 36, 95 ff.). His "life relation" to calligraphy [28] finally gives him a new metaphor. In an epistle to a
friend, he puts the request for correction, which is so frequent in the Middle Ages, in the following form (No. 2, 47):

> Tu quoque sis titulus, tu littera sis capitalis,
> Tu castigator codicis esto mei.

That his poetry has many themes in common with the Greek Anthology
and Martial is obvious. It is the poetry of a library Humanism; meant to
be read, not sung. Beside it there exists the rhymed and sung "Goliardic
lyric." Satire, mockery, and invective, together with the appetites, revelry,
and love longing, are the material of this poetry, of which the collection
known as the *Carmina Burana* gives us the most comprehensive idea. In
this province the erudite book metaphors lose prominence or are com-

[28] Cf. also Propertius, III, 23.—On book decoration cf. also Sidonius, *Ep.*, III,
8, 5.

pletely lacking.[29] The poems are for the most part the work of students, in other words of nurslings of Minerva who also worship Venus. If love brought them unhappiness, they took it as a reading ("a lesson") in the book of grief:

> Si de more
> Cum honore
>   Lete viverem,
> Nec meroris
> Nec doloris
>   Librum legerem.

Secular Latin poetry passed its apogee about 1220, but religious poetry puts forth some of its most wonderful blossoms in the thirteenth century. Among them is Thomas of Celano's *Dies irae*. In his hymn we meet the book once again, and in the terrible description of the Last Judgment:

> Liber scriptus proferetur,
> In quo totum continetur
> Unde mundus iudicetur.

This is the book of doom of the Apocalypse. But behind it there would also seem to be Malachi 3, 16: "Attendit Dominus, et audivit, et scriptus liber monumenti coram eo timentibus Dominum . . ." These concepts dominate medieval religion and also find embodiment in the fine arts. Often an angel writes down a man's good deeds, a devil his evil ones. "So they both appear in stone," wrote Wilhelm Wackernagel almost a century ago, "to right and left of the Romanesque portal of Bonn cathedral, each seated and writing on a sheet held on his knees." [30]

We have arrived at a Romanesque church. What might be heard there in the course of a Sunday sermon? We are well informed by the numerous *artes praedicandi* and collections of sermons. In his little treatise on the construction of a sermon Guibert of Nogent (d. 1121) sets forth that, after the Bible, one should use one's own psychological and moral experience as the best source of material; that will be understood by everyone, because each can read something corresponding to it in himself, as in a book: "intra se ipsum quasi in libro scriptum attendat." [31] Thirdly, however, he continues, one can find indications of the truths of religion in all natural things. But the preacher found them in the book too. A sermon ascribed to Hildebert of Lavardin treats the text: "Audi, Israel, praecepta vitae, et scribe ea in corde tuo" (Deut. 4:1). The preacher explains to his hearers how a book is made (*PL*, CLXXI, 815 ff.): "First the scribe cleanses the parchment of fat and coarse dirt with a knife. Then he removes the hairs and fibers with a pumice stone. If he did not do this, the

---

[29] Cf. Schmeller's edition, p. 76, No. CXCVII, st. 4, and p. 251.
[30] ZfdA, VI, 149 ff.—P. Clemen, *Die Kunstdenkmäler der Stadt und des Landkreises Bonn* (1905), 78.   [31] *PL*, CLVI, 26 C.

written letters be worthless and impermanent. Then he rules the parchment, so that the writing will be regular. All this you too must do with your hearts . . ." Hildebert—or the author of the sermons ascribed to him—has a predilection for this imagery. We see how the book-metaphors of the Bible develop and multiply under his hands. Job's "librum scribat" (31:35) Hildebert interprets to mean that the Bible comprises four Books *(liber praedestinationis, liber doctrinae, liber scripturae corporalis, liber conscientiae)*; in this connection he discusses other "book passages" from the old Testament.

Hildebert's comparison of the heart to a book was foreshadowed in Paul's phrase "tabulae carnales cordis," which was adopted by early Christian poetry (Paulinus of Nola, ed. Hartel, I, 266). Later it was shortened to "book of the heart." Thus in a late *florilegium (RF*, III [1886], 297, No. 164):

> *In libro cordis lege quicquid habes ibi sordis;*
> *Non legis hoc alibi tam bene sicut ibi.*

The medieval sermon sometimes refers to the teaching of writing. From the twelfth century at the latest it was the practice in schools to teach the alphabet from a large sheet of parchment "which was stretched over a wooden frame and perhaps also fastened directly to the wall." This practice is the basis of a simile which we find in the Cistercian Odo of Cheriton (d. 1247): "Sicut enim carta, in qua scribitur doctrina parvulorum, quatuor clavis affigitur in postem, sic caro Christi extensa est in cruce . . . cuius quinque vulnera quasi quinque vocales pro nobis ad Patrem per se sonant" (B. Bischoff in *Classical and Mediaeval Studies in Honor of E. K. Rand* [1938], 9 f.).

Even the Christ-centered mysticism of a Francis of Assisi does not disdain to find in writing a relation to holy things. Thomas of Celano tells us that the saint picked up every written piece of parchment which he found on the ground, even if it were from a pagan book. Asked by a disciple why he did so, Francis answered: "Fili mi, litterae sunt ex quibus componitur gloriosissimum Dei nomen."

7. The Book of Nature

It is a favorite cliché of the popular view of history that the Renaissance shook off the dust of yellowed parchments and began instead to read in the book of nature or the world. But this metaphor itself derives from the Latin Middle Ages. We saw that Alan speaks of the "book of experience." For him, every creature is a book (*PL*, CCX, 579 A):

> *Omnis mundi creatura*
> *Quasi liber et pictura*
> *Nobis est et speculum.*

In later authors, especially the homilists, "scientia creaturarum" and "liber naturae" appear as synonyms. For the preacher the book of nature must figure with the Bible as a source of material. This idea still appears in so late a writer as Raymond of Sabunde (d. 1436), who however overshot the mark (and hence was condemned by the Council of Trent) when he wrote: "Scripturas sacras facile quis impia interpretatione subruere potest, sed nemo est tam execrandi dogmatis hereticus, qui naturae librum falsificare possit." The "book of the creature" remained a favorite concept of orthodox asceticism and mysticism. Thus in the *Imitatio Christi* (II, 4): "Si rectum cor tuum esset, tunc omnis creatura speculum vitae et liber sanctae doctrinae esset." And later in Spain, in the preacher and mystic Luis de Granada (1504–1588). In his *Simbolo de la fé* he uses the expression "filosofar en este gran libro de las criaturas" and varies it: "Qué seran luego todas las criaturas deste mundo, tan hermosas y tan acabadas, sino unas como letras quebradas y iluminadas que declaran bien el primor y la sabiduría de su autor? . . . Así nosotros . . . habiendonos puesto vos delante este tan maravilloso libro de todo el universo, para que por las criaturas del, como por unas letras vivas, leyesemos la excelencia del Criador . . ."

From the twelfth century, philosophy too takes up book metaphors. Hugh of St. Victor gives the book and writing a function in his system. He divides universal history into three epochs, those of the *lex naturalis*, of the *lex scripta*, and of the *tempus gratiae* (PL, CLXXVI, 32 B; *ibid.*, 343, 347, 371). Both the creation and the God-Man are "books" of God (*ibid.*, 644 D ff.). Hugh of Folieto (earlier often confused with Hugh of St. Victor) makes the metaphor of the book a minor system of theology. According to him there are four books of life. The first was written in Paradise, the second in the desert, the third in the Temple, the fourth has been written from all eternity. God wrote the first in the human heart, Moses the second on tablets, Christ the third on earth, and Divine Providence the fourth. He develops this further, in the course of which the stock phrase "book of reason" appears.[32] Book imagery is also to be found in contemporary schools of philosophy of wholly different orientation. The hermetic-Neo-Platonic speculation of Bernard Silvestris teaches that in the Deity's spirit conceived as a feminine power (Noys), the entire course of history is written (as in our example from Nonnus): "Illic exarata supremi digito dispunctoris textus temporis, fatalis series, dispositio seculorum" (*De universitate mundi*, p. 13, 160). Heaven is opened like a book covered with pictures (*ibid.*, 33 f.). Thus all earthly things are prefigured as in a transcendent book. But man's faculty of cognition is also likened to a book. Thus in John of Salisbury (*Policraticus*, ed. Webb, 1, 173). In the book of our reason are inscribed not only pictures of things but also the divine ideas. In the thirteenth century Bonaventura uses the simile, though in

---

[32] "Cum aliquis cogitat quid agere debeat, et hoc rationaliter disponit, quasi in libro rationis legit" (*PL*, CLXXVI, 1170 C).

cautious language, to illustrate his "exemplarism": "Creatura mundi est quasi quidam liber in quo relucet . . . Trinitas fabricatrix" (*Breviloquium*, II, c. 12). But, together with the book of the creature, Bonaventura also recognizes the *liber scripturae*: It is God's will that he be known through both books (*ibid.*, II, c. 5). In another passage the book of the world itself reappears as twofold: "Duplex ist liber, unus scilicet scriptus intus, qui est Dei aeterna ars et sapientia, et alius scriptus foris, scilicet mundus sensibilis" (*ibid.*, II, c. 11). Here Bonaventura alludes to the Biblical phrase (Ezek. 2:9 and Rev. 5:1) "liber scriptus intus et foris." The simile of the book is not logically confined to a single function and a single significance but rather serves to illustrate very various facts. Thus the fall of Eve is explained by the fact that she followed, not the "inner book" of reason, but the outer book of appetite (*ibid.*, III, 3).

The concept of the world as a book was secularized in Germany in the fourteenth century by Conrad of Megenberg (1309–1374), who in 1350 translated into German the encyclopedia of the Dominican Thomas of Cantimpré *De naturis rerum* (written between 1228 and 1244) and did so under the title *Buch der Natur* (*Book of Nature*).[33] Nicholas of Cusa adopted the metaphorics of medieval philosophy. He remarks that there had been saints who regarded the world as a written book.[34] For him, however, the world is the "showing forth of the inner word" ("interni verbi ostensio").[35] Hence the things of sense are also to be regarded as "books" through which God as our teacher declares the truth to us.[36] In a disputation the layman proves superior to the scholar, because he had acquired his knowledge not from the books of the schools but "from God's books," which He "has written with His own finger." They are "to be found everywhere," hence "here in this market-place too." [37] The human mind too is called a book: "Mens vero est ut liber intellectualis, in se ipso et omnibus intentionem scribentis videns." [38]

Summing up, we find that the concept of the world or nature as a "book" originated in pulpit eloquence, was then adopted by medieval mystico-philosophical speculation, and finally passed into common usage. In the course of this development the "book of the world" was frequently secularized, i.e., was alienated from its theological origin, but this was by no means always the case. I should like to show this by a few more examples.

In the thought of Paracelsus book metaphors have a basic function. To

[33] Edited by Franz Pfeiffer (Stuttgart, 1861).—Cf. H. Ibach, *Leben und Schriften des Konrad von Megenberg*, Berlin dissertation (1938).—Conrad's *Buch der Natur* was printed six times before 1499.

[34] Basle edition (1565), 133.

[35] *Ibid.*, 244 (*Compendium*, c. VII).

[36] *Drei Schriften vom verborgenen Gott*, German version by E. Bohnenstädt (1942), 84.—Cf. Romans 1: 20.

[37] *Der Laie über die Weisheit*, German version by E. Bohnenstädt (1936), 43.

[38] *De apice theoriae*, theorem 6 (Basle ed. [1565], p. 336).

written books—"codices scribentium"—he opposes the book "which God himself promulgated, wrote, set forth, and composed." The physician's book must be the sick. Nature too seems to be conceived as a collection of books which are entire and perfect "because God himself wrote, made, and bound them and has hung them from the chains of his library." "From the light of Nature must enlightenment come, that the text *libri naturae* be understood, without which enlightenment no philosopher nor natural scientist may be." The firmament is "another book of physic" from which a "firmamental meaning" is to be spelled out. Finally, the whole earth is a book or a library "in which the pages are turned with our feet," which must be used "pilgrimly." [39]

These book metaphors were taken over by the thinkers of the Renaissance. For Montaigne the book of the world is an epitome of the discernible truths of history and life: "Ce grand monde . . . c'est le miroir où il nous faut regarder pour nous connaître de bon biais. Somme, je veux que ce soit le livre de mon écolier" (*Essais*, I, 36). Still more significantly in Descartes (*Discours de la Méthode*, Part I, toward the end): "Sitôt que l'âge me permit de sortir de la sujétion de mes précepteurs, je quittai entièrement l'étude des lettres; et me résolvant de ne chercher plus d'autre science que celle qui se pourrait trouver en moi-même, ou bien dans le grand livre du monde, j'employai le reste de ma jeunesse à voyager, à voir des cours et des armées . . ." The theological concept is preserved by Francis Bacon: "Nam salvator noster inquit: Erratis, nescientes scripturas et potentiam Dei (Matt. 22, 29), ubi duos libros, ne in errores incidamus, proponit nobis evolvendos" (*De augmentis scientiarum*, Bk. I: *Opera*, Frankfurt [1655], 26). Campanella too knows the "two books": the *codex scriptus* of the Bible and the *codex vivus* of Nature. Book metaphors serve him in his protest against Scholasticism. [40]

An elegant inversion of the topos "book of the world" was made by the celebrated epigrammatist John Owen (1563?–1622). He called (I, 3) his book a world:

> *Hic liber est mundus; homines sunt, Hoskine, versus:*
> *Invenies paucos hic, ut in orbe, bonos.*

The book of nature has many pages. One of the most curious of them treats of insects. In Proverbs 6:6 we read: "Vade ad formicam, o piger, et considera vias ejus, et disce sapientiam." And *ibid.* 30:24, in the A.V., "There be four things which are little upon the earth, but they are exceeding wise: the ants are a people not strong, yet they prepare their meat in the summer; the conies are but a feeble folk, yet they make their houses

---

[39] The references in W. E. Peuckert, *Paracelsus, Die Geheimnisse. Ein Lesebuch aus seinen Schriften* (1941), 172–78.—Eichendorff, in his *Taugenichts*, ch. 9, makes a student talk in Paracelsus's vein: "Let the others read their compendiums, while we study in the great picture book which God has opened for us outdoors."

[40] For references, see F. Schalk in *RF*, LVII (1943), 139.

in the rocks; the locusts have no king, yet go they forth all of them by bands; the spider taketh hold with her hands, and is in kings' palaces." The wisdom of God, then, is displayed particularly in the smallest creatures (the opposite idea, of course, occurs in the Book of Job in the discussion of the two beasts behemoth [41] and leviathan). That original English philosopher Sir Thomas Browne takes up the thought of these Biblical passages in his *Religio Medici* [1643], Pt. I, ch. 15): "Indeed, what Reason may not go to School to the wisdom of Bees, Ants, and Spiders? what wise hand teacheth them to do what Reason cannot teach us? Ruder heads stand amazed at those prodigious pieces of Nature, Whales, Elephants, Dromidaries and Camels; these, I confess, are the Colossus and majestick pieces of her hand: but in these narrow Engines there is more curious Mathematicks; and the civility [42] of these little Citizens more neatly sets forth the Wisdom of their Maker [43] . . . I could never content my contemplation with those general pieces of wonder, the Flux and Reflux of the Sea, the increase of Nile, the conversion of the Needle to the North; and have studied to match and parallel those in the more obvious and neglected pieces of Nature, which without further travel I can do in the Cosmography of myself. We carry with us the wonders we seek without us: there is all Africa and her prodigies in us; we are that bold and adventurous piece of Nature, which he that studies wisely learns in a compendium what others labour at in a divided piece and endless volume.

"Thus there are *two Books* from whence I collect my Divinity; besides that written one of God, another of His servant Nature, that universal and publick Manuscript, that lies expans'd unto the Eyes of all: those that never saw him in the one, have discover'd Him in the other . . . Surely the Heathens knew better how to joyn and read these mystical Letters than we Christians, who cast a more careless Eye on these common Hieroglyphicks, and disdain to suck Divinity from the flowers of Nature."

A contemporary of Sir Thomas Browne's, Francis Quarles (1592–1644), has the following lines in his pious *Emblems* (1635):

> *The world's a book in folio, printed all*
> *With God's great works in letters capital:*
> *Each creature is a page; and each effect*
> *A fair character, void of all defect.*

The metaphor also occurs in Donne,[44] Milton (*Paradise Lost*, III, 47 and VIII, 67), Vaughan, Herbert, Crashaw. It became the common property

[41] The name means "great beast."

[42] "Civility" refers to the societies of the bees and ants, but in the broad sense in which Goethe spoke of a "civische" (civic) epoch of social structure (Jubiläumsausgabe, XXXVIII, 232).

[43] One of the recurring themes of Pascal's thought is the correspondence between the infinitely little and the infinitely great.

[44] He uses similes from the book to express love, in panegyric, etc. (Cf. Grierson's edition, I, 30, 19 f.; I, 238, 227; I, 235, 147).

of poetry. The founder of exact natural science gives the book metaphor a significant new turn. Galileo speaks of the great book of the universe, which lies forever before our eyes but which we cannot read if we have not learned the script in which it is written. "It is written in a mathematical language, and the characters are triangles, circles, and other geometrical figures." [45] The book of nature no longer legible?—a revolutionary change had occurred, which penetrated the consciousness of the humblest. Now too the plant and animal kingdoms are newly studied by the aid of optical instruments. Jan Swammerdam (1637–1680) investigated the anatomy of insects with the microscope. The celebrated Boerhaave published these studies in 1737 under the edifying title *Biblia Naturae*. He had in mind the verses from Proverbs quoted above, which also stimulated Sir Thomas Browne. On the other hand Montaigne's usage lives again in Diderot, among whose aphorisms is the following fragment: "Les grandes connaissances, les vraiment importantes, nous ne savons où nous les avons prises. Ce n'est pas dans le livre imprimé chez Marc-Michel Rey ou ailleurs, c'est dans le livre du monde. Nous lisons ce livre sans cesse, sans dessein, sans application, sans nous en douter. Les choses que nous y lisons, pour la plupart ne peuvent s'écrire, tant elles sont fines, subtiles, compliquées; du moins, celles qui donnent à un homme le caractère de pénétration singulière qui le distingue des autres . . . Oh! les ineptes, les plates créatures que nous serions, si nous ne savions que ce que nous avons lu. Les pauvres choses que tous ces principes écrits même dans les ouvrages les plus profonds, en comparaison des besoins et des circonstances de la vie. Ecoutez un blasphème: La Bruyère, La Rochefoucauld sont des livres bien communs, bien plats, en comparaison de ce qui se pratique de ruses, de finesses, de politique, de raisonnements profonds, un jour de marché à la halle."

In the guise of the Oriental sage Voltaire says almost contemporaneously: "Rien n'est plus heureux qu'un philosophe qui lit dans ce grand livre que Dieu a mis sous nos yeux . . ." (*Zadig*, ch. 3). Rousseau gives the commonplace—for such the image had certainly now become—precisely the turn required for his world-reforming rhetoric, when he makes Lord Edward write: "Vous recevrez aussi quelques livres pour l'augmentation de votre bibliothèque; mais que trouverez-vous de nouveau dans les livres? O Wolmar! il ne vous manque que d'apprendre à lire dans celui de la nature pour être le plus sage des mortels" (*La Nouvelle Héloïse*, VI, Letter 3).

The catchy dictum that Nature is a book superior to all books found its way during the age of Rousseau into the theory of poetry too. The English Pre-Romantics, who so strongly stimulated Herder and Goethe, brought about this eventful change. Edward Young (1683–1765) published his

[45] *Opere, ed. nazionale*, VI, 232.—Further passages on the book of nature are to be found in A. Favaro, *Galileo Galilei: Pensieri, motti e sentenze* (Florence, 1935), p. 27 ff.

Conjectures on Original Composition in 1759; in this essay he sets forth that Shakespeare was not a scholar but that he had mastered "the book of nature and that of mankind." Robert Wood interpreted Homer as an original genius (*Essay on the Original Genius and Writings of Homer* [1769]). A German translation of Wood's book appeared at Frankfurt in 1773 and made a strong impression on the young Goethe. In Wood we read that Homer could study only the great book of nature. The new poetics of English Pre-Romanticism and of the *Sturm-und-Drang* thus makes use of the same book metaphor which we have found exercising an influence at so many other junctures of intellectual history. The "book of Nature" appears in Goethe's *Sendschreiben* (1774):

> *Sieh, so ist Natur ein Buch lebendig,*
> *Unverstanden, doch nicht unverstandlich;*
> *Denn dein Herz hat viel und gross Begehr,*
> *Was wohl in der Welt fur Freude wär,*
> *Allen Sonnenschein und alle Bäume,*
> *Alles Meergestad und alle Träume*
> *In dein Herz zu sammeln miteinander . . .*

> (See, thus is Nature a living book
> Whose sense may be taken, though oft mistook;
> For in thy heart is the wish, strong and deep,
> That all the joys that the world may keep,
> All the sunshine, and every tree,
> Each dream and every coast of the sea,
> In thy heart to gather them one and one . . .)

From the poetics of the *Sturm-und-Drang*, the concept of "natural poetry" passed into Jacob Grimm's Romantic theory of literature: "One may call natural poetry life itself in pure action, *a living book*, full of true history, which one may begin to read and understand at any page, but which one has never done reading or understanding. Art poetry is an effort of life, and is philosophical in its very beginnings." [46] In Grimm the Biblical "book of life," the "living book" of Victorine mysticism, is secularized and combined with the poetic theory of English Pre-Romanticism. On this shaky foundation was built the concept of medieval poetry entertained by nineteenth-century Germanists. In Germany medieval studies sprang from the soil of Romanticism. But they drew from thence only the element of emotional enthusiasm—not the sublimation of historical understanding, not the illumination of consciousness, which constitute the high and enduring value of German Romanticism. Novalis, the Schlegels, Schleiermacher, and Adam Müller, though they traveled different roads, were united through a new spirit, and hence also through a new concept of his-

[46] Quoted in A. E. Schönbach, *Gesammelte Aufsätze zur neueren Literatur* (1900), 100.

tory. The Grimms, the Uhlands, and their associates had no part in either. From the threadbare metaphorics of the book, which in Jacob Grimm led to a depreciation of the book, we rise into a higher dimension when we find in Novalis the statement: "Books are a modern species of historical entities, but a most significant one. They have perhaps taken the place of tradition."

But we must now once more turn our steps to the Middle Ages.

8. Dante

In Dante's youthful lyrics we already find the book of memory (*E' m' incresce da me*, l. 59). It appears too in the first lines of the *Vita nuova*. It has been sought to derive the expression from a passage in Pier della Vigna: "In tenaci memoriae libro perlegimus." [47] But to accept such a derivation is to misunderstand the historical situation in which Dante's artistic style developed. We have already encountered the concepts of the book of the heart, of the mind, of memory, of reason, of experience, in medieval Latin authors. And the fact is that the entire book imagery of the Middle Ages is brought together, intensified, broadened, and renewed by the boldest imagination in Dante's work—from the first paragraph of the *Vita nuova* to the last canto of the *Divina Commedia*. A novelty, as compared with twelfth-century practice, is the abundance of similes taken from academic life, which had meanwhile attained to a flourishing existence in Bologna, Naples, Paris, and elsewhere. For the Middle Ages, all discovery of truth was first reception of traditional authorities, then later—in the thirteenth century—rational reconciliation of authoritative texts. A comprehension of the world was not regarded as a creative function but as an assimilation and retracing of given facts; the symbolic expression of this being reading. The goal and the accomplishment of the thinker is to connect all these facts together in the form of the "summa." Dante's cosmic poem is such a summa too. At least that is one of its aspects. The "hero" of the *Divina Commedia* is a student. His teachers are Virgil and Beatrice: Reason and Grace, Knowledge and Love, Imperial Rome and Christian Rome. The highest activities and experiences of the mind are for Dante connected with learning, with reading, with assimilating through books a preexistent truth. Hence, for him, writing and the book can be the media of expression for the "highest moments" of poetry and human life. Dante expressly recommends that the *Divina Commedia* be read and studied. It is to be studied by the reader "on his bench" (*Par.*, X, 22) as a *lezione* (*Inf.*, XX, 20), as a lesson, it will afford him spiritual fruit (*Inf.*, XX, 19) and food (*Par.*, X, 25). Dante frequently addresses the reader, and always the individual reader (*Inf.*, XXII, 118; *Inf.*, XXIV, 23; *Purg.*, XXIII, 136; *Par.*, V, 109; *Par.*, X, 7; *Par.*, XXII, 26), whom he urges to think too ("or

[47] N. Zingarelli in *Bullettino della Società Dantesca N. S.*, I (1894), 99. All the later commentators follow him even when they do not mention him.

pensa per te stesso," *Inf.*, XX, 20). Access to the Comedy can be gained—could and should be gained, the poet would have it—only by study. For Dante and for the Middle Ages, the basic plan for any education of the intellect is, in general, the reading of books, the "lungo studio" *(Inf.*, I, 83)—in contradistinction to the conversational method (διαλέγεσθασ) of the Greeks, to the "spoken word" of the East as Goethe conceived it. The desire for learning, the ardent love, which had brought Dante to Virgil's *Aeneid* ("m' han fatto cercar lo tuo volume," *Inf.*, I, 84), which had made him study it until he knew it through and through ("tutta quanta," *Inf.*, XX, 114), which means by heart (*Par.*, V, 41 f.), were such a passion in him that he could address the poet of that "high tragedy" as "lo mio maestro e il mio autore" *(Inf.*, I, 85). The "vital relations" between teacher and pupil serve Dante as similes in which he illustrates his spiritual mission. To his great teacher Brunetto Latini he pays—in Hell—the most beautiful homage which gratitude ever inspired in a pupil *(Inf.*, XV, 85). Brunetto then prophesies to Dante that his native city's hate will be turned against him, and Dante promises to write down (in his memory) what Brunetto has told him and so keep it *(Inf.*, XV, 89 f.):

> E serbolo a chiosar con altro testo
> A donna che 'l saprà, s' a lei arrivo.

Beatrice, he knows, will show him the future course of his life yet more clearly, and he will compare her rede with Brunetto's, interpret and "gloss" one text by the other. Glosses are explanatory comments, such as were part of the apparatus of erudition first in Antiquity and later in the Middle Ages. Dante was the first to use this concept from the sphere of the book metaphorically. When, in the Antepurgatory, the subject of the efficacy of prayer arises, Dante refers to a text ("alcun testo") of the *Aeneid* —it is the verse: "Desine fata deum fiecti sperare precando" (VI, 376)— and Virgil settles his pupil's doubt: "La mia scrittura è piana . . ." Had Dante remembered the episode of Polydorus in the *Aeneid* (III, 22 ff.) in time, he would have been saved from hurting the soul of Pier della Vigna in its tree prison. But Dante would seem not to have believed that passage in the "alta tragedia." So at least Virgil says (*Inf.*, XIII, 46 ff.):

> S' egli avesse potuto creder prima,
>   —Rispose il savio mio—anima lesa,
>   Ciò c' ha veduto pur con la mia rima,
> Non averebbe in te la man distesa.

Ignorance of a text and faulty reading can, then, be the causes of evil deeds. After the battle of Benevento (1266) the bones of the Hohenstaufen Manfred would not have been scattered on unconsecrated ground if the Bishop of Cosenza had rightly read that page of the Gospel according to St. John—"avesse in Dio ben letto questa faccia" *(Purg.*, III, 126)—in which it is written: "Et eum, qui venit ad me, non eiiciam foras" (John

6:37). To be sure, pride of reason and idle striving after novelty lead many to philosophical eccentricities. But heaven is less provoked to wrath by this than it is when God's word is slighted or twisted (*Par.*, XXIX, 85 ff.):

> Voi non andate già per un sentiero
> Filosofando, tanto vi trasporta
> L' amor dell' apparenza e il suo pensiero.
> Ed ancor questo quassù si comporta
> Con men disdegno che quando è posposta
> La divina scrittura o quando è torta.

The word is set aside (*posposta*) by the degenerate avaricious clerks who read nothing but the Decretals until their margins are used up (*Par.*, IX, 133 ff.). It is twisted (*torta*) by the theologians who interpret it as they please.

Now, to reading conceived as the form of reception and study, corresponds writing conceived as the form of production and creation. The two concepts belong together. In the intellectual world of the Middle Ages they represent as it were the two halves of a sphere. The unity of this world was shattered by the invention of printing. The immense and revolutionary change which it brought about can be summarized in one statement: Until that time, every book was a manuscript. Merely materially, then, as well as artistically, the written book had a value which we can no longer feel. Every book produced by copying represented diligence and skilled craftsmanship, long hours of intellectual concentration, loving and sedulous work. Every such book was a personal achievement—we find this expressed in the colophon, in which the scribe often tells us his name and unburdens his heart: "Sicut aegrotus desiderat sanitatem, item desiderat scriptor finem libri."

"Tell me, O Muse, of the man," "Sing, goddess, the wrath," "Arms and the man I sing"—so the epics of Antiquity begin. In Dante the Muses are invoked too, but immediately afterward the poet also invokes his own mind, and, instead of telling and singing, we find writing (*Inf.*, II, 7 ff.):

> O Muse, o alto ingegno, or m' aiutate.
> O mente che scrivesti ciò ch' io vidi,
> Qui si parrà la tua nobilitate.

"Alto ingegno" designates the poet's intellectual powers (as *Inf.*, X, 59 with "altezza d' ingegno"); "mente," as often, his memory. To compose poetry, then, is to copy the original text recorded in the book of memory ("libro della mia memoria" of the *Vita nuova*, and compare "il libro che il preterito rassegna," *Par.*, XXIII, 54). The poet is both scribe and copyist ("quella materia ond' io son fatto scriba," *Par.*, X, 27). He "notes" what Love "dictates" to him (*Purg.*, XXIV, 52–59).

The scaffolding for the *Commedia* was supplied by numerical composition.[48] To each *cantica* the same extent was apportioned, and hence the

48 Cf. Excursus XV, *infra*.

same quantity of writing material. This determines the extent of what can be said (*Purg.*, XXXIII, 139):

> Ma perchè piene son tutte le carte
> Ordite a questa cantica seconda
> Non mi lascia più ir lo fren dell' arte.

In the *Paradiso* Dante touches upon much that is essentially inexpressible (*Par.*, I, 70). He is therefore obliged to "skip over" much (*Par.*, XXIII, 61):

> E così figurando il Paradiso
> Convien saltar lo sacrato poema.

This "skipping" is originally derived from the manipulation of the pen (*Par.*, XXIV, 22 ff.):

> E tre fiate intorno di Beatrice
> Si volse con un canto tanto divo
> Che la mia fantasia nol mi ridice.
> Però salta la penna, e non lo scrivo.

The pen's place can be taken by the ink (*Par.*, XIX, 7):

> E quel che mi convien ritrar testeso
> Non portò voce mai, nè scrisse inchiostro.

When the medieval scribe's goose quill became blunt, he sharpened it with a knife (*pennam temperare*). Dante uses this metaphorically at the beginning of *Inf.*, XXIV. It is a description of early spring. The ground is covered with frost. It tries to assume the image of its white sister the snow, but it soon melts away, and its quill loses its sharpness (*Inf.*, XXIV, 4 ff.):

> Quando la brina in su la terra assempra
> L' imagine di sua sorella bianca,
> Ma poco dura alla sua penna tempra.

Paper ("papiro") appears once in the *Comedy* as a writing material, but this is in a simile. The subject is a strange and terrible metamorphosis: a man and a six-footed dragon twine around each other and merge into one being. Their two colors combine into one, in which both can still be glimpsed: like that brown color which burning paper takes on before it turns black (*Inf.*, XXV, 64 ff.):

> Come procede innanzi dall' ardore
> Per lo papiro suso un color bruno
> Che non e nero ancora, el' bianco muore.

The usual word for any material used for writing upon, and for the un-written or written sheet, is "carta." [49] To write on such a sheet is expressed

---

[49] *Carte* means "book" in *Purg.*, XXIX, 104.

by the word "vergare" (literally "to stripe" or "to line"). On the seventh terrace of the Mount of Purgatory Dante questions the souls of the lustful (*Purg.*, XXVI, 64 f.):

> Ditemi, acciò ch' ancor carte ne verghi
> Chi siete voi . . .

The costliness of such material is used figuratively by St. Benedict in his account of the decline of his Order. His Rule is still copied out, but unavailingly, since it is no longer obeyed. It is a pure waste of parchment (*Par.*, XXII, 74 f.):

> . . . e la regola mia
> Rimasa è giù per danno delle carte.

Turning the pages of a book is alluded to in the passage where Virgil refers Dante to Aristotle's *Physics*, II (*Inf.*, XI, 101 ff.):

> E se tu ben la tua Fisica note,
> Tu troverai, non dopo molte carte,
> Che l' arte vostra quella, quanto puote,
> Segue, come 'l maestro fa il discente;
> Sì che vostr' arte a Dio quasi è nipote.

A measure of speed is provided by the time which suffices to write an O or an I (*Inf.*, XXIV, 100 ff.):

> Nè O si tosto mai, nè I si scrisse
> Com' ei s' accese, e arse, e cener tutto
> Convenne che cascando divenisse.

On the other hand, it is not original with Dante, but a reference to a medieval idea [50] found elsewhere, when he reads the letters OMO (*homo*) in the human countenance (*Purg.*, XXIII, 31 ff.):

> Parean l' occhiaie anella senza gemme;
> Chi nel viso degli uomini legge OMO,
> Bene avria quivi conosciuto l' emme.

With this passage we enter the domain of alphabetical symbolism. This is again exemplified in the *Commedia* in the soteriological, numerical, and alphabetical enigma DXV in *Purg.*, XXXIII, 43 and Canto XVIII of the *Paradiso*, where the round dance of the souls of the just judges writes in flaming letters the sentence "Diligite justitiam, qui judicatis terram" and then from the final letter M forms the image of the imperial eagle.

The written sheets ("carta") become a book only when they have been arranged in quires (fascicles, gatherings, *quaderni* [51]) and bound in a vol-

---

[50] R. Köhler (*Jahrbuch der deutschen Dante-Gesellschaft*, II, 237) points it out in Berthold of Regensburg.
[51] Latin *quaterni, quaterniones* = four double sheets or sixteen pages.

ume (*volume*). This realm of craftsmanship also affords Dante figurative expressions. In the *Convivio* he had attributed the spots on the moon to variations in the thickness of the moon's crust. When, on his journey through the heavens, he travels through the sphere of the moon himself, Beatrice refutes his earlier theory. If it were correct, she says, one would have to assume that behind the thin layers of the moon lay thicker layers, "as fat and lean alternate in an animal body, or the pages of a book with one another" (*Par.*, II, 76 ff.):

> . . . sì come si diparte
> Lo grasso e il magro un corpo, così questo
> Nel suo volume cangerebbe carte.

Paralleling St. Benedict's complaint, Bonaventura denounces the decay of the Franciscan Order in a metaphor drawn from the book. He calls the order a volume, whose leaves are the brothers. Leafing through it, one would still find the uninjured tradition on a page here and there (*Par.*, XII, 121 ff.):

> Ben dico, chi cercasse a foglio a foglio
> Nostro volume, ancor troveria carta
> U' leggerebbe: "Io mi son quel ch' io soglio."

The higher Dante ascends on his journey through the spheres, the more extensive the prospect becomes. From the heaven of the fixed stars he looks out upon the planets and, lowest of all, the earth. The tellurian and sublunary shrink to an insignificant part of the universe, to a quire in the volume of the cosmos. Only in this material quire does contingency hold sway; so Cacciaguida instructs the poet (*Par.*, XVII, 37 ff.):

> La contingenza che fuor del quaderno
> Della vostra materia non si stende,
> Tutta è dipinta nel cospetto eterno.

In comparison with this "quire" the several celestial spheres are "volumes." The ninth—the *Primum Mobile*—wraps them all round like a royal mantle (*Par.*, XXIII, 112 f.):

> Lo real manto di tutti i volumi
> Del mondo . . .

The commentators here rightly refer to Revelations 6:14: "et caelum recessit sicut liber involutus." Of course, to a man of the Middle Ages the image was no longer evident, since his gathered and bound book was no longer the written scroll (*volumen*) of Antiquity. But Dante retains the image (*Par.*, XXVIII, 13 f.):

> E com' io me rivolsi, e furon tocchi
> Li miei da ciò che pare in quel volume . . .

What the appearance of the *Mater gloriosa*, that darkly mysterious homage to the Eternal Feminine, signifies to Goethe—the climax and conclusion of the cosmic poem—resides for Dante in the inexpressible experience of the vision of God, of which all Christian mystical theology tells.
A series of spiritual illuminations—the river of light, the sea of light, the
heavenly rose, the Virgin Mary—leads upward to the beholding of the
Eternal Light. Here Dante's mystical vision is consummated. It shows him
a spiritual cosmos held together by the bond of love. What he sees is at
once a simple light and the wealth of all ideas, forms, and beings. How is
he to describe it? Once again and for the last time, in the highest and
most sacred ecstasy, Dante employs the symbolism of the book. All that
has been scattered throughout the entire universe, that has been separated
and dissevered, like loose *quaderni*, is now "bound in one volume"—by
love (*Par.*, XXXIII, 82 ff.):

> *O abbondante grazia ond' io presunsi*
> *Ficcar lo viso per la Luce Eterna,*
> *Tanto che la veduta vi consunsi.*
> *Nel suo profondo vidi che s' interna,*
> *Legato con amore in un volume,*
> *Ciò che per l'universo si squaderna;*
> *Sustanzia ed accidente, e lor costume,*
> *Quasi conflati insieme per tal modo*
> *Che ciò ch' io dice è un semplice lume.*

The book—*in quo totum continetur*—is the Godhead. The book is the
symbol of the highest salvation and the highest value.

In Dante the imagery of the book is no longer an ingenious game; it
can assume a central intellectual function.

9. Shakespeare

The prodigal array of Shakespeare's plays on words and conceits is led up
to by rhetoric, which in the Age of Elizabeth overflowed the lyric and the
drama. But this rhetorization of English poetry has its preparatory stages
in the first half of the sixteenth century, and takes us back to the Middle
Ages. The imagery of the book affords an illustration of this. The Latin
poets of the twelfth century had already employed it to describe the beauty
of a woman's face (*supra*, p. 316, n. 26). This occurs again in John Hey-
wood (1497–1580). He pays homage to the youthful Mary Tudor (b.
1516; reigned 1553–58) in the lines:

> *The virtue of her lively looks*
> *Excels the precious stone;*
> *I wish to have non other books*
> *To read or look upon.*

Sir Philip Sidney (1554–86) refuses to compete with contemporary poets who parade the newly fashionable rhetorical figures ("new-found tropes"; "strange similes"; "you that do dictionary's methods bring into your rhymes"); it is enough for him to read in his Stella's face what love and beauty are; thus he has only to copy "what Nature in her writes." Samuel Daniel (1563–1619) in his sonnets to Delia (1592) opens the account book of his soul, in which he has entered all his cares and sighs.

Shakespeare draws every stop. To discuss Shakespeare is, of course, to enter a territory which bristles with unsolved enigmas. An authoritative trend in today's Shakespeare criticism insists that everything in Shakespeare must be seen as depending upon plot and characterization; he must be judged as a dramatist, not as a poet. How much in harmony is this with the rhetorical splendor of his poetry? The opposition is artificial, and breaks down with Shakespeare as it does with Calderón. Do the imagery of the book and the technique of writing perform a dramatic function anywhere in Shakespeare? Yes, but only in two plays. One is *Titus Andronicus* (written 1589–90 according to some, 1593–4 according to others) —if this gory thriller is by Shakespeare.[52] The unfortunate protagonist employs writing in the most various ways. He flings himself on the ground before his sons' judges and thus "writes" his grief "in the dust" (III, 1). His daughter Lavinia is ravished by two monsters. To keep her from denouncing them, they cut off her tongue and her hands. Now let her disclose the crime! She can play the scribe with her stumps (II, 4). The situation, then, is not dramatic but melodramatic. But Lavinia is well-read. She used to read "sweet poetry and Tully's *Orator*" with her young nephew Lucius. She rummages through her books with her stumps, then turns the leaves of Ovid's *Metamorphoses* until she comes to the tale of Tereus (VI, 424 ff.). Tereus had ravished his sister-in-law Philomela and cut out her tongue. But he left her her hands. And so she was able to weave her story into a piece of tapestry and send it to her sister Procne, Tereus' wife. Procne plans revenge, strangles her son, cooks his flesh, and gives it to his father to eat. Andronicus rightly surmises that by her reference to this passage in Ovid, Lavinia wishes to indicate something. He shows her how it is possible to write without hands by taking a stick in his mouth, guiding it with his feet and drawing it over the ground. Lavinia imitates him and reveals the gruesome deed (IV, 1). The monsters are thus "decipher'd." Andronicus sends them weapons wrapped in a scroll on which he has inscribed a moral maxim from Horace (IV, 2). He then uses this method a second and a third time: he has arrows shot off to which are fastened letters to Jove, Apollo, and other gods, and later sends his enemy

---

[52] Its authenticity was contested by J. M. Robertson (*Did Shakespeare Write Titus Andronicus?* [1905]) on cogent grounds, which however have made no impression upon the scholars (see W. Keller in *Shakespeare-Jahrbuch*, LXXIV [1938], 137 ff.).—T. S. Eliot calls the piece "one of the stupidest and most uninspired plays ever written" (*Selected Essays*, p. 82).

Saturninus a petition wrapped around a knife (IV, 3). The principal villain of the piece, the Moor Aaron, also displays a fondness for expressing himself in writing. He often digs up dead men from their graves, carves provocative words in their backs "as on the bark of trees," and sets them up at their friends' doors (V, 1). Andronicus' vengeance upon the villains who had dishonored Lavinia is to cut off their heads, bake them in a pasty (after the example of Procne!), and, dressed as a cook, serve the dish to their mother. Then he strangles her and Lavinia, and is killed by Saturninus, as the latter is by Lucius. Aaron is buried breast-deep in the ground and left to die of starvation. Now a bright future can begin in an ordered state. If the play, as I believe, is not by Shakespeare, it is nevertheless of interest as showing us how writing and the book could be turned to poetical account in the hands of an Elizabethan writer of horror plays.

The university too is a part of Shakespeare's world: Wittenberg in *Hamlet*. In *The Taming of the Shrew* we are introduced to Lucentio at the beginning of his first semester at Padua. "Here let us breathe," he says to his servant Tranio (I, 1):

> *Here let us breathe and haply institute*
> *A course of learning and ingenious studies . . .*

Lucentio naturally wants to study philosophy (in the sixteenth century Padua was a stronghold of Aristotelianism). But—the shrewd Tranio advises—neither should the *auctores* be neglected:

> *Only, good master, while we do admire*
> *This virtue and this moral discipline,*
> *Let's be no stoics nor no stocks, I pray;*
> *Or so devote to Aristotle's ethics,*
> *As Ovid be an outcast quite abjured:*
> *Balk logic with acquaintance which you have,*
> *And practise rhetoric in your common talk;*
> *Music and poesy to quicken you . . .*

As in the twelfth century, Ovid is the king of rhetoric. A command of it, if only for conversational purposes, is demanded of an educated man. Study requires books. Lucentio has bought some and is carrying them under his arm; whereupon Gremio (I, 2):

> *O, very well; I have perused the note.*
> *Hark you, sir; I'll have them very fairly bound:*
> *All books of love, see that at any hand;*
> *And see you read no other lectures to her.*

With this we may consider *Much Ado About Nothing*, I, 2: "I can tell you strange news . . .—Are they good?—As the event stamps them; but they have a good cover; they show well outward."

Both passages show Shakespeare as a lover of fine bindings—evidence of a "life relation" which can be felt in other "book passages." We had encountered but one earlier instance of the binding performing a metaphorical function: in Dante. There it was a simile for the summation of the universe within God; a symbol of the all-comprehending vision. In Shakespeare it is far otherwise: the binding (often provided with gold clasps) is an aesthetic delight for the booklover. This adds visual content to the comparison of a beautiful face with a book.

Thus in *Romeo and Juliet* (I, 3):

> *Read o'er the volume of young Paris' face*
> *And find delight writ there with beauty's pen . . .*
> *And what obscured in this fair volume lies,*
> *Find written in the margent* [53] *of his eyes.*
> *This precious book of love, this unbound lover,*
> *To beautify him, only lacks a cover:*
> *The fish lives in the sea, and 'tis much pride*
> *For fair without the fair within to hide:*
> *That book in many's eyes doth share the glory,*
> *That in gold clasps locks in the golden story.*[54]

From *A Midsummer Night's Dream* (II, 2):

> *Reason becomes the marshal to my will*
> *And leads me to your eyes; where I o'erlook*
> *Love's stories, written in love's richest book.*

From *King John* (II, 1):

> *If that the Dauphin there, thy princely son,*
> *Can in this book of beauty read 'I love,'*
> *Her dowry shall weigh equal with a queen.*

From *Love's Labour's Lost* (IV, 3):

> *From women's eyes this doctrine I derive:*
> *They sparkle still the right Promethean fire;*
> *They are the books, the arts, the academes,*
> *That show, contain and nourish all the world.*

From *Othello* (IV, 2):

> *Was this fair paper, this most goodly book,*
> *Made to write 'whore' upon?*

[53] Where the book's text is obscure, the explanatory notes printed in the margin explain the meaning. "Margent" in the same sense, *Lucrece*, st. 15.
[54] Gerard Manley Hopkins wrote to Coventry Patmore in 1887: "Is there anything in *Endymion* worse than the passage in *Romeo and Juliet* about Count Paris as a book of love that must be bound and I can't tell what? It has some kind of fantastic beauty, like an arabesque, but in the main it is nonsense" (G. F. Lahey, *Gerard Manley Hopkins* [1930], 73).

Grief and sin disfigure the book of the human countenance.
From *The Comedy of Errors* (V, 1):

> *O, grief hath changed me since you saw me last,*
> *And careful hours with time's deformed hand*
> *Have written strange defeatures in my face.*[55]

From *Richard II* (IV, 1):

> *. . . I'll read enough*
> *When I do see the very book indeed*
> *Where all my sins are writ, and that's myself.*
> *Give me the glass, and therein will I read.*

In this scene a mirror is brought onto the stage, so that the king can read the book of his face. The mirror is a favorite metaphor of the Latin Middle Ages, often used as a book title. It is of antique origin.[56] As in *Macbeth*, book and mirror are combined in Lady Percy's lament for her husband (2 *Henry IV*, II, 3):

> *. . . he was, indeed, the glass*
> *Wherein the noble youth did dress themselves.*
> *He had no legs that practised not his gait;*
> *And speaking thick, which nature made his blemish,*
> *Became the accents of the valiant;*
> *For those that could speak low, and tardily,*
> *Would turn their own perfection to abuse,*
> *To seem like him: so that in speech, in gait,*

[55] "When forty winters shall besiege thy brow / And dig deep trenches in thy beauty's field . . ." (Sonnet 1).

[56] Plato compares the activity of an artist to a reflecting of things (*Resp.*, 596 DE) and seeks thereby to belittle art. The Sophist Alcidamas had used the image positively and called the *Odyssey* "a beautiful mirror of human life." Aristotle (*Rhet.*, III, 3, 4) censures this metaphor as "frigid." But it became extremely popular. Terence (*Adelphoe*, 415 f.) has:

> *Inspicere tamquam in speculum in vitas omnium*
> *Jubeo atque ex aliis sumere exemplum sibi.*

Cicero called comedy "imitatio vitae, speculum consuetudinis, imago veritatis" (Donatus, ed. Wessner, 1, 22). But the mirror is biblical too. Wisdom is "speculum sine macula Dei majestatis, et imago bonitatis illius." With this, I Cor. 13: 12: "Videmus nunc per speculum in aenigmate." The human mind is compared to a mirror ("speculum mentis") in Cassiodorus (*PL*, LIX, 502 C). Notker Balbulus (E. Dümmler, *Das Formelbuch des Bischofs Salomo*, 71) affirms that Gregory's *Regula pastoralis* were better named *speculum* because every priest would find himself "portrayed" in it. In the twelfth and thirteenth centuries *speculum*, as is well known, became very popular as a book title. To his *Speculum stultorum* Nigel Wireker prefixes the remark: "Qui [liber] ideo sic appellatus est, ut insipientes aliena inspecta stultitia tamquam speculum eam habeant, quo inspecto propriam corrigant . . ." Here the mirror is an instrument of improvement, later it is one of instruction. Thus in the most voluminous of medieval encyclopedias, the *Speculum naturale, historiale, doctrinale* of Vincent of Beauvais (*ca.* 1250). Cf. the rhymed preface to the *Sachsenspiegel*, ll. 97 and 175–82.

> *In diet, in affections of delight,*
> *In military rules, humours of blood,*
> *He was the mark and glass, copy and book*
> *That fashion'd others.*[57]

As the metaphor "face as book" points back to the Middle Ages, so does that of "the book of nature." It is to be found everywhere in the sixteenth century. But in Shakespeare the conceit is imbued with freshness and color.

In the Forest of Arden (*As You Like It*, II, 1) the banished Duke finds the voices of nature:

> *And this our life exempt from public haunt,*
> *Finds tongues in trees, books in the running brooks,*
> *Sermons in stones, and good in every thing.*[58]

In this fairy forest lovers can use the bark of trees—that means of transmitting information from which Ariosto gained such charming effects and which was already known to Callimachus [59] and Propertius (III, 2):

> *O Rosalind, these trees shall be my books,*
> *And in their barks my thoughts I'll character,*
> *That every eye which in this forest looks,*
> *Shall see thy virtues witness'd everywhere.*

Friends too are books to one another. Thus in *Richard III* (III, 5):

> *So dear I loved the man, that I must weep.*
> *I took him for the plainest harmless creature*
> *That breathed upon the earth a Christian;*
> *Made him my book, wherein my soul recorded*
> *The history of all her secret thoughts.*

From *The Two Gentlemen of Verona* (II, 7):

> *Counsel, Lucetta; gentle girl, assist me;*
> *And, even in kind love, I do conjure thee,*
> *Who art the table wherein all my thoughts*
> *Are visibly character'd and engrav'd,*
> *To lesson me . . .*

---

[57] "Copy" is here the text to be copied.—Cf. in *Lucrece*: "For princes are the glass, the school, the book / Where subjects' eyes do learn, do read, do look."

[58] It is wrong to derive these lines from any particular "locus." A sentence from Sidney's *Arcadia* has been proposed as their "source": "Thus both trees and each thing else be the bookes of a fancy." Or a sentence from Bernard of Clairvaux: "Aliquid amplius invenies in silvis quam in libris" (*Shakespeare-Jahrbuch*, LXIX [1933], 189). The same objections apply to such assumptions as to deriving Dante's "book of memory" from Pier della Vigna.—Socrates wished to learn not from trees but from men (Plato, *Phaedrus*, 230 D). The medieval Goliard says: "Schola sit umbra nemoris, liber puellae facies" (P. Lehmann, *Parodistische Texte* [1923], 49).

[59] *Kydippe*, fr. 9 g (ed. Pfeiffer).

From *Twelfth-Night* (I, 4):

> . . . I have unclasped
> To thee the book even of my secret soul.

To the guard who will not let him in to see Coriolanus, Menenius says (*Coriolanus* V, 2, 13 ff.):

> . . . I tell thee, fellow,
> Thy general is my lover; I have been
> The book of his good acts, whence men have read
> His fame unparallel'd, haply amplified.

In the Sonnets the poet's heart is a table on which his eye portrays the beauty of his friend (No. 24). He writes with "my pupil pen" (No. 16), Time with "antique pen" (No. 19).

In some of the plays book metaphors are frequent. *Macbeth* and *Troilus* are examples.

From *Macbeth* (I, 5):

> Your face, my thane, is as a book where men
> May read strange matters.

Macbeth to his wife (III, 2):

> . . . Come, seeling night,
> Scarf up the tender eye of pitiful day,
> And with thy bloody invisible hand
> Cancel and tear to pieces that great bond
> Which keeps me pale!

Macbeth has hired men to murder Banquo. He tries to find out if they are ready for the deed. Answer (III, 1): "We are men!" Macbeth replies:

> Ay, in the catalogue ye go for men,
> As hounds and greyhounds, mongrels, spaniels, curs,
> Shoughs, water-rugs and demi-wolves, are clept
> All by the name of dogs: the valued file
> Distinguishes the swift, the slow, the subtle,
> The housekeeper, the hunter, every one
> According to the gift which bounteous nature
> Hath in him closed, whereby he does receive
> Particular ambition, from the bill
> That writes them all alike: and so of men.[60]

Here the book appears in the sense of an inventory ("catalogue," "file," "bill"). The metaphor has been transferred to the economic-administrative realm.

[60] Shakespeare scholarship pretends to have ascertained that Shakespeare "rejects housedogs, perhaps because of their uncleanliness" (*Shakespeare-Jahrbuch*, LXXII [1936], 141)!

In *Troilus and Cressida* (I, 3) Nestor calls the duel between Hector and Achilles an index to the volume of events to come. Hector addresses Nestor as "good old chronicle" (IV, 5, 202), and says that Achilles will read him over like a jestbook (IV, 5, 239). Troilus wants to proclaim his passion to the world in red letters: "In characters as red as Mars his heart, inflamed with Venus" (V, 2).

Shakespeare, of course, also knows the book of memory (elaborately worked out in Hamlet's words to his father's ghost; I, 5), which also appears as "Jove's book" (book of the heavens; *Coriolanus*, III, 1).

Metaphors from writing can express the deepest grief. Thus in *Richard II* (III, 2):

> . . . of comfort no man speak:
> Let's talk of graves, of worms, of epitaphs;
> Make dust our paper, and with rainy eyes
> Write sorrow on the bosom of the earth.

But they can also be used humorously. Thus in *Comedy of Errors* (III, 1):

> Say what you will, sir, but I know what I know;
> That you beat me at the mart, I have your hand to show:
> If the skin were parchment, and the blows you gave were ink,
> Your own handwriting would tell what I think.

Gallows humor in the most literal sense breathes from the words of the jailer in *Cymbeline* (V, 4), who sees life as an account book: "O the charity of a penny cord! it sums up thousands in a trice: you have no true debitor and creditor but it; but of what's past, is and to come, the discharge. Your neck, sir, is pen, book and counters."

What kinds of books occur in Shakespeare? We have found love books, jest books, inventories, chronicles, account books. But there are also conjuring books. They stem from folk tales, but Ariosto introduced them into higher literature (XV, 13 ff. and XXII, 16 ff.). In Shakespeare's latest and most beautiful work, *The Tempest*, the conjuring book plays an important dramatic role. Prospero was duke of Milan, but he left the business of government to his brother,[61] being himself immersed in study, a master of the "liberal arts" and "secret studies." His library "was dukedom large enough." His false brother attempts to destroy him, he is forced into a ship to sail for foreign shores, but the noble Gonzalo manages to convey a few books to him (I, 2). Thus the exposition. In the course of the action, however, Prospero mentions only a single book: "I'll to my book" (II, 1); he will drown it (V, 1), to renounce all his magic art. Here—and here only in Shakespeare's work—has the book become a poetic symbol. And, that parody too should not be wanting, the drunken sailor Stephano calls the bottle "the book" (II, 2).

---

[61] Voluntary or involuntary abdication is one of Shakespeare's favorite themes—perhaps a psychological cipher that we cannot solve.

Shakespeare's imagery of the book—of which only especially characteristic examples have been quoted—is the emanation of a prodigal vitality
which fertilizes the brain no less than the heart. His relation to the world
of the book is wholly different from that of the Middle Ages as well as from
Dante's. The sphere of writing and the book as a vital concern, as atmosphere, as the symbolic medium of science and philosophy is foreign to him.
From the rhetorical poetic style of his period he takes the imagery of the
book and raises it to the level of the many-faceted play of ideas with which
he brilliantly outshines his contemporaries. His "life-relation" to the book
is that of aesthetic enjoyment.[62] Richly bound books are a feast for his
eyes.[63] But *one* book is more precious to him than all else: his verses to his
friend (Sonnet 23):

> O, *let my books be then the eloquence*
> *And dumb presagers of my speaking breast;*
> *Who plead for love, and look for recompense,*
> *More than that tongue that more hath more express'd.*

To modern taste, formed by Romanticism, Shakespeare's book metaphors may seem like bits of applied decoration. But if this is an objection,
it must also be raised against the Latin Middle Ages and against Oriental
poetry. Yet poetry is as rich in forms as is nature, and we feel neither entitled nor inclined to decide what is poetry and what is not. Let us rejoice
in all the flowers and fruits of the Gardens of the Hesperides—as well as of
the "hanging gardens" of the East.

10.   *West and East*

For now we must also glance at Oriental poetry. That it displays a wealth
of extravagant and strange imagery is well known. Goethe's "Notes and
Essays" on his *West-östlicher Divan*, which provided our starting point,
brought this Eastern province within the realm of German culture. But history had spun threads between the Islamic East and the Christian West a
thousand years earlier. Islamic poetry is paralleled by a very extensive and
hitherto little studied literature on rhetoric, style, and poetics. Both—the
poetry as well as the poetics of the Arabs and Persians—were certainly influenced by Hellenistic models, especially in regard to figures of speech,

[62] Two recent studies of Shakespeare's imagery (see *Shakespeare-Jahrbuch*,
LXXII [1936], 141 f.) together fill some 750 pages. Book imagery *is not mentioned
in them.*

[63] A critic writing in 1917 held that one would conjecture the author of Shakespeare's plays to be a nobleman, "né pour l'opulence et une haute position sociale
. . ., un amoureux de l'équitation et des sports de chasse, un ami plus ardent
encore des livres" (according to Abel Lefranc, *Sous le masque de William Shakespeare* [1919], I, 24). What we know about the life of the actor Shakespeare and
especially about his latter years reveals painful and petty characteristics and is in
complete contrast with this picture. Here too are riddles.

panegyric, and the use of conceits.[64] This Oriental poetry was then transplanted to Andalusia. There it flourished from the tenth to the thirteenth
century. Oriental and Spanish sensibility unite in it.[65] The treasures of this
art still lie largely unrevealed. However, we owe a few precious examples to
the erudition and taste of Emilio García Gómez.[66] This delicate poetry,
which is reminiscent of the Moorish gardens of the Generalife, is one of the
channels through which the spirit of Islamic art could find its way into the
Spanish poetry of the *siglo de oro*. The critic who has earned our highest
gratitude for his evaluation of Góngora—Dámaso Alonso—says: "As we
read García Gómez's translations we discovered a new, untouched world:
it became apparent that all that the genius of Góngora had accomplished
for the technique of metaphor . . . had already been done by poets of
southern Spain from the tenth to the thirteenth century."

We cannot here enter into the fascinating historical problem of these
connections. Let us restrict our survey again to the imagery of the book. We
know that in the Islamic culture script and calligraphy were especially cultivated. Arabic script can give the connoisseur aesthetic pleasures to which
nothing in the realm of our scripts corresponds. Thus the German Orientalist Julius Euting (1839–1913) used to say that a beautifully curved *alif*
could delight him more than a Madonna of Raphael's, though, to be sure,
one must often have tried to copy examples by famous masters, in order to
feel the nobility of form of Arabic script.[67] A glance into *The Thousand and
One Nights* [68] suffices to illustrate Islam's relation to script.[69] Says a king's
son: "I read the Koran according to seven traditions . . . I studied astronomy and the works of the poets . . . The beauty of my script surpassed
that of all scribes, and my fame spread into all countries" (1, 138). A trained
ape (according to Littmann, a reminiscence of the old Egyptian god of
writing Thoth, who was often represented as an ape) writes successive

[64] Helmut Ritter, *Über die Bildersprache Nizamis* (1927), 19 f.—H. H. Schae-
der, *Goethes Erlebnis des Ostens* (1938), 112. Readers should now (1952) refer
to the excellent studies of G. von Grunebaum, author of *Medieval Islam* (Chicago,
1947).

[65] C. Brockelmann, *Geschichte der islamischen Völker und Staaten* (1939), 173
and 180 f.

[66] His *Poemas arábigoandaluces* appeared in 1930 (Madrid: Editorial Plutarco).
I quote from this edition. New enlarged edition (1940). Cf. Dámaso Alonso in the
journal *Escorial*, No. 3 (Madrid, Jan., 1941), 139 ff.

[67] Georg Jacob, *Der Einfluss des Morgenlandes auf das Abendland* (1924), 13.—
Cf. Ernst Kühnel, *Islamische Schriftkunst* (1942), and the review by Enno Littmann, *Deutsche Literaturzeitung* (1943), 127.

[68] Used in Enno Littmann's translation (Inselverlag).

[69] The high esteem which Islam accords to calligraphy is connected with the fact
that it possesses a "sacred book." But the sacredness of the Koran is taken far more
literally than is that of the Bible amongst us. It irradiates all writing. In Islam there
is a "philosophical" interpretation of the alphabet (Louis Massignon, *Essai sur les
Origines du lexique technique de la mystique musulmane* [1922], 80). The Sufistic
mystic philosophy of script teaches "l'extinction de la totalité des lettres dans l'iden-
tité du point" (Sheik A. Allawi, *Nouvelle Revue Française* [May, 1939], p. 897).

quatrains in cursive hand, slim hand, steep hand, round monumental hand, large document hand, and large decorated hand (1, 157 f.). This appreciation of script is reflected in numerous metaphors, of which I will give but a few examples. To impress something upon the mind is "to engrave it in the corner of the eye with a graver." Expression of astonishment: "The death of this hunchback should be written in letters of molten gold" (1, 436). The book of fate: "The reed entered in the book of time what Allah had determined from eternity" (1, 528). Beauty as calligraphy (5, 107): "The down of his cheeks wrote with amber in pearl script / Two lines painted finely with jet on apples." From Nizami (1141–1202) H. Ritter cites the following examples: "The scribe of the revelation of the law, the rose, has written the doom of blood for the anemones with the water of life," that is, "when the rose begins to bloom, the time of the red anemones is over." Or: "When Schirin moves her beautiful hands, she as it were signs death-sentences for her unhappy lovers. To sign the order which will take their lives she has ten writing-reeds on her hands," that is, ten fingers. Nizami's *Iskandarnāma* (*Book of Alexander*) begins with an invocation to God, in which there occurs the line:

*Thy quill is wisdom, Thy writing-book the world.**

In the same century in Seville, Abenhayyun celebrates the beauty of his beloved with metaphors from writing: "Does all this white signify all thy marks of favor, and are these black dots [70] signs of thy unyieldingness?— She answered me: My father is scribe to kings, and when I approached him to show him my filial love, he feared that I might learn the secret of what he had written, he shook his pen, and the ink spotted my face" (*Poemas arábigoandaluces*, 47 f.). Or a beauty's blond hair drew an *l* on the white page of her cheek, like gold flowing over silver (p. 64). But calligraphy serves also to praise the warrior: "The lances put the points upon the script of the swords; the dust of battle was the strewing-sand which dried what was written, and the blood perfumed it" (p. 92). These images and comparisons are not to be regarded as products of spontaneous fancy. Arabic poetics and rhetoric had carefully defined and classified them. Even those who know no Arabic can obtain some knowledge of the subject from such a book as A. F. Mehren's *Rhetorik der Araber* (Copenhagen, 1853). There, for example, one learns that the simile is "either easily comprehensible and obvious or strange and recondite" and that the latter is "considered unbeautiful" (p. 28 f.). Or one learns that "beauty of thought in the adducing of grounds" is a rhetorical figure (p. 117). It consists in attempting to establish a statement "by adducing not a real but a merely apparent ground, which contains a beautiful or a witty thought." Would not the ground upon which the beautiful daughter of the scribe of Seville explains her moles accord with this formula? Such studied subtleties are characteristic of Spanish poetry

[* After Platen's translation.]
[70] Moles.

too. Goethe felt the connection. He wrote in 1816 to the translator of Calderón, Gries, "that my stay in the Orient only makes me more highly esteem the excellent Calderón, who does not deny his familiarity with things Arabic." The thought passed into the *West-östlicher Divan*:

> *Herrlich ist der Orient*
> *Übers Mittelmeer gedrungen;*
> *Nur wer Hafis liebt und kennt,*
> *Weiss, was Calderón gesungen.*

> (Across the Middle Sea
> The splendid East has pressed;
> Love and study Hafiz, else
> You shall not know Calderón.)

In the history of the modern literatures, the Spanish *siglo de oro* stands alone by the abundance and the preciosity of its imagery, including that derived from writing and the book. If we attempt to explain this fact, two reasons, I think, suggest themselves: first, the influence of medieval Latin poetry (far stronger in Spain than elsewhere); second, the community of culture which existed for centuries between Christian and Moorish Spain.[71] The medieval Latin and the Eastern ornamental styles could meet and mingle only in Spain. They helped to form that playful Spanish Mannerism which is known as Gongorism and Conceptism. Let me cite but a few examples from Góngora. Cranes form winged letters [72] on the transparent paper of the sky (*Soledades*, 1, 609 f.). The swallow writes the shameful deed of her brother-in-law Tereus on the leaves of a tree; songs in praise of the beloved are written with a feather torn from one of Cupid's arrows. The author of a history of the Popes eternizes the keepers of the heavenly keys on the bronze tablets of history with his pen. Not perishable bronze but two oceans are the tablets upon which the victories of a naval hero are written for aftertimes, etc.[73]

Lope, who is often considered a "popular" author, swarms with metaphors from writing—frequently of the utmost preciosity. The whole creation writes. The sea writes letters with foam, dawn writes with dew on

[71] It should be remembered that in Spain calligraphy continued to flourish long after the discovery of printing. Pedro de Madariaga wrote his *Honra de Escribanos* in 1565, Calderón composed a sonnet on calligraphy for his friend the calligrapher José de Casanova (printed in E. Cotarelo y Mori, *Ensayo sobre la vida . . . de D. Pedro Calderón*, p. 59 n.). It does not appear to have been noticed that Calderón paraphrases Isidore's statements concerning the alphabet cited on p. 313 *supra*—another proof of the survival of the Latin Middle Ages in the *siglo de oro*.

[72] Góngora has here refurbished an antique *concepto*: cranes in flight form the Greek Λ (*lambda*). Claudian (*De bello Gildonico* I [= XV], 477) had been the last author to state this. The Middle Ages did not let it escape: Arnulf, *Delicie cleri* (RF, II, 242, 780 f.). But Claudian had only letters; Góngora adds paper. Cf. also Gates, *The Metaphors of Góngora* (1933), 47.

[73] These and other examples are to be found under the catchword "Schriftwesen" in Ernst Brockhaus, *Góngoras Sonettendichtung*, Bonn dissertation (1935), p. 212.

flowers. With his plough the ploughman draws lines "which April looks upon and May reads." Gloves are writing to the lover who receives them. Night is "the secretary of love's secret writing," and a cavalier whose honor has been offended "answers with but one leaf to a whole book of insults." Lope here plays on the double meaning of *hoja* (Lat. *folia*, Fr. *feuille*): "leaf" and "blade." Baltasar Gracián uses the same word in another verbal and semantic pun. The travelers of his allegorical romance mount painfully from the summer of youth to the autumn of "manhood." Sweating, they climb a steep hill. Here there are no more flowers, but there are fruits. The trees bear more fruits than leaves, "including those of books." [74] They are the fruits of experience, which are superior to the "leaves" of books. Here even the "book of nature" is belittled, because it has only "leaves." Gracián has improved on a time-worn topos.

Calderón's figurative language employs some forty concepts from writing and the book.[75] Here too everything writes: the sun on cosmic space, the ship on the waves, the birds on the tablets of the winds, a shipwrecked man alternately on the blue paper of the sky and the sand of the sea. The rainbow is a stroke of the quill, sleep a written sketch, death the signature of life. The martyrs execute that signature in red with their blood (as in the Latin Middle Ages).[76] Heroic deeds are written in golden letters on the diamond tablets of fame, or engraved with the "graver of time." From the realm of official documents Calderón takes such expressions as "authenticated copy" or "translation" and "register." They can also be applied to men. Finally, the book is the symbol of wisdom, and in this sense Christ may be called

> . . . *el libro soberano*
> *De la ciencia de las ciencias,*

which is then expounded.[77] The cosmos too appears in Calderón as a book. The vault of heaven is a bound book with eleven sapphire leaves (the spheres). These examples may serve to illustrate Calderón's poetic style. Goethe characterized it: "The poet stands on the threshold of hyperculture; he offers a quintessence of mankind. Shakespeare, on the contrary, hands us a full ripe bunch from the vine; we may enjoy it grape by grape if we choose, squeeze it, press it; taste it or swallow it as grape-juice or as fermented wine—whichever we choose, we are refreshed. In Calderón, on the other hand, nothing of this is left to the reader's choice or will; we receive decanted and highly rectified spirits of wine, pungent with many spices and mellowly sweetened; we must drink it as it is, as a tasty and

---

[74] *El Criticón*, ed. Romera-Navarro, II, 19 (1939).

[75] Irmhild Schulte, *Buch- und Schriftwesen in Calderóns weltlichem Theater*, Bonn dissertation (1938).

[76] Writing in blood passed from Spanish Mannerism to French Classicism. In Corneille's *Cid* Chimène says: "Son sang sur la poussière écrivait mon devoir" after Guillén de Castro's "Escribió en este papel con sangre mi obligación."

[77] We found Christ as a book in Hugh of St. Victor, *supra*.

precious stimulant, or leave it alone." In conjunction with this we should consider Goethe's significant observation that the student of the poetic imagery of the East "would soon be convinced that there can be no question in that literature of what we call taste, of the separation, that is, of the seemly from the unseemly. Its virtues cannot be severed from its faults, they are dependent upon one another, spring from one another, and we must let them be what they are without cavilling or carping. Nothing is more unendurable than when Reiske and Michaelis now praise these poets to the skies, now treat them as if they were silly schoolboys." Now, the very same thing applies to the Mannerism of Góngora, Lope, and Calderón—if only our contemporary cavillers would reflect upon the fact. Only in antique Athens and in the London of Queen Elizabeth has there ever existed a drama as national and as popular as that of the Spanish period of florescence. The mannered ornamental style of a Calderón was understood and enjoyed by the Madrid public, always eager for a good show. His recondite images and comparisons were borne on the stream of a ringing rhetoric which delighted the ears even of the common man. To the *conceptos*, with their plays on words and ideas, the common man was receptive too. The imagery of writing and the book was for the most part, we have seen, a private domain for educated, if not for erudite, circles. Calderón makes it popular once again; at the same time he represents its final apogee in Western poetry.

To Islamic-Spanish culture we owe yet another metaphor which I should like to include here: the cipher. This is the Arabic word *sifr*. It means "empty" and in the Arabic system of numerals represents the zero.[78] From the middle of the twelfth century it appears as *cifra* and *cifrus* in Latin, and thereafter in the Romance languages. Now the intellectual history of Germany shows that from Hamann and Winckelmann to Novalis and the young Ranke [79] the metaphor of the "cipher writing" of nature, of the world, of history, of the human figure, etc., is extremely prevalent, together with "hieroglyphics" in the same sense. Eduard Spranger, Franz Schultz, and Oskar Walzel have treated the subject.[80] Only Spranger discusses the origin of the two metaphors. He derives them from Shaftesbury, but is unable to give any example from his writings.[81] It seems quite to have escaped these scholars that both metaphors stem from Italian and Spanish Renaissance culture. On this subject we shall make only the following brief observations. In the "autumn of the Middle Ages" mottos

[78] Examples in Du Cange and in Leo Jordan, *Archiv für Kulturgeschichte*, III, 158, where its semantic development in the Romance languages to 1500 is discussed.
[79] *Zur eigenen Lebensgeschichte*, 89 f.
[80] Spranger, *W. v. Humboldt und die Humanitätsidee* (1909), 153–182; Schultz, *Klassik und Romantik der Deutschen*, I (1935), 43–45; Walzel, *Poesie und Nichtpoesie* (1937), 70 f.
[81] Spranger's example is Shaftesbury's remark that we read in the world of the deity as "in characters." But "characters" here means "letters." So this is only a variant of the "book of the world."

(devices), which were often interpreted by "emblems," were popular in France.[82] Through the expeditions of Charles VIII and Louis XII the fashion spread to Italy, a fact which determined its future development. Since the beginning of the fifteenth century Italian Humanists had been occupied with Egyptian hieroglyphics and with inventing new hieroglyphics: pictures without words (principal example, the *Hypnerotomachia Poliphili*). The fashion for mottos and the study of hieroglyphics met in Italy and produced a luxuriant crop of emblems and *impresas*. Among the prominent men who turned their attention to hieroglyphics and emblems we find L. B. Alberti, Mantegna, Poliziano, Marsilio Ficino, Erasmus, Reuchlin, Pirkheimer, Dürer, Tasso, Rabelais, Fischart. The emblem is a "symbolic picture," usually with a text. The *Emblemata* of the jurist Andrea Alciati (1531) became classical and were published in more than 150 editions. The *impresa* (the thing that one "undertakes," one's personal maxim in life) also consists of a picture and a motto. Hence emblem and *impresa* cannot be separated. Most important treatise: Paolo Giovio, *Dialogo delle Imprese militari e amorose* (1555). Emblem and *impresa* were also eagerly taken up in Spain,[83] especially in the seventeenth century. Significant for us is the fact that in Spain the pictorial part of the *impresa* or emblem is called *cifra*, the explanatory motto *mote* or *letra*. For *emblema* in Spanish the word *jeroglífico* is also used. The juxtaposition of "cipher writing" and "hieroglyphic" can be found dozens of times in Calderón, but is also current in theological literature. It can have reached Germany only from Spanish baroque.

Let us leave the East and turn to Goethe once again. In the *Denkwürdigkeiten von Asien* (1811–15) of Heinrich Friedrich von Diez he found the following mystical poem by Nischani, a high official at the court of the Suleiman who besieged Vienna in 1529: "Regarding the art of love I read with great attention many chapters of a book filled with texts of grief and paragraphs of separation. It had abbreviated the chapter of union but it had varied the explanations of sorrow endlessly. O Nischani! in the end the Master of Love led thee to the right way. Answering insoluble questions is the privilege of the Beloved only." Ernst Beutler [84] comments that we have here the typical experience of which every mystic tells: the happi-

[82] Literature: Karl Giehlow, *Die Hieroglyphenkunde des Humanismus in der Allegorie der Renaissance* (*Jahrbuch der Kunsthistorischen Sammlungen des Allerhöchsten Kaiserhauses*, XXXII [1915]).—Ludwig Volkmann, *Bilderschriften der Renaissance* (1923).—Mario Praz, *Studi sul Concettismo* (1934).—Idem (1937) in English under the title *Studies in 17th century Imagery.*—Also Praz's articles "Emblema" and "Impresa" in the *Enciclopedia Italiana* (Treccani).—J. Huizinga, *The Waning of the Middle Ages.*

[83] Spain is not given its just due in the studies of Volkmann and Praz. The first Spanish translation of Alciati's *Emblemata* appeared in 1549. Further discussion in V. García de Diego in his introduction to Saavedra Fajardo, *Idea de un principe . . . en cien empresas* (Madrid: La Lectura, 1927), Vol. I, p. 23.—In Gracián (*El Criticón*, ed. Romera-Navarro, I, 143) the sage studies divine perfection in the book of the world "en cifras de criaturas."

[84] *Goethes Westöstlicher Divan herausgegeben und erklärt* (1943), 421.

ness he feels when he is filled with God and his grief when God withdraws himself. "Nischani—Goethe confuses the name with that of the Persian poet Nizāmī—in pious resignation puts it into the hands of God himself ('Master of Love,' 'Beloved') to save him from this grief of soul." But Goethe himself turned the mystical poem back to earthly love and made it the vessel of his feeling for Marianne von Willemer ("Lesebuch" in the "Buch der Liebe" of the *Divan*). Goethe also played wittily and musically with Oriental "ciphers" in the *Divan*. Goethe's relation to writing, to script, to calligraphy, to the book in general—this is a theme which deserves separate treatment. Here, in the age of Goethe, we bring our journey to an end. To be sure, many examples of writing imagery could be found in the succeeding centuries. But it no longer possesses a unique, a felt, a conscious "life-relationship," could no longer possess it after the Enlightenment shattered the authority of the book and the Technological Age changed all the relations of life. Yet Gottfried Keller's apophthegm remains timelessly true:

> *Es ist ein weisses Pergament*
> *Die Zeit, und jeder schreibt*
> *Mit seinem roten Blut darauf,*
> *Bis ihn der Strom vertreibt.*

> (Time is a parchment white
> And thereon each doth write
> With his red blood, until the day
> The stream sweeps him away.)

17

Dante

1. *Dante as a Classic*

W E ARE ACCUSTOMED to regarding Dante, Shakespeare, and Goethe as the three peaks of modern poetry. But this evaluation first imposed itself only in the century after Goethe's death. In Germany it has become canonical through Stefan George and his school. For England, T. S. Eliot sets forth: "We feel that if the classic is really a worthy ideal, it must be capable of exhibiting an amplitude, a catholicity . . . which are fully present in the medieval mind of Dante. For in the Divine Comedy, if anywhere, we find the classic in a modern European language." [1] Goethe's relation to Dante was ambivalent. At Rome in July, 1787, he is displeased by the empty argument whether Ariosto or Tasso is the greater. "But it was much worse when Dante was brought up. A young man of station and intelligence, with a true sympathy for that extraordinary man, took my praise and approval somewhat amiss, for he asserted outright that any foreigner must renounce the attempt to understand such an extraordinary mind, even the Italians themselves being unable to follow it at all points. After some arguing back and forth I finally became annoyed and said that I must admit that I was inclined to agree with him, for I had never been able to understand how anyone could spend time over these poems; that, as for me, I found the *Inferno* monstrous, the *Purgatorio* ambiguous, and the *Paradiso* boring." We do not find an "outright" approbation until 1805: "The few tercets into which Dante puts the death by starvation of Ugolino and his children belong among the supreme productions of poetry." [2] In the twenties distaste has the upper hand:

---

[1] T. S. Eliot, *What Is a Classic? An address delivered before the Virgil Society on the 16th of October 1944* (London, 1945), 18.
[2] Jubiläumsausgabe, XXXVI, 267.

Modergrün aus Dantes Hölle
Bannet fern von eurem Kreis,
Ladet zu der klaren Quelle
Glücklich Naturell und Fleiss!

(Banish far from your circle mouldy green from Dante's hell, Invite to the clear spring a happy disposition and industry!)

"Dante's repulsive and often monstrous greatness" [3] is censured. An essay on Dante (1826; Jubiläumsausgabe, XXXVIII, 60 f.) recognizes the poet's "great intellectual and emotional qualities," compares him with Giotto, but then qualifies the praise as follows: "The whole plan of Dante's infernal region has something reminiscent of *Micromégas*, and hence highly confusing, about it. One is asked to imagine circle within circle, from above down into the deepest abyss; but this immediately evokes the idea of an amphitheater, which, however vast it may be, yet presents itself to our imagination as something artificially limited, since from above the eye takes in everything down to the arena and the arena itself . . . The invention is more rhetorical than poetic; the imagination is stimulated but not satisfied." In the *Maximen und Reflexionen* we find: "Dante has excellently described metamorphosis in the higher sense through giving and taking, gaining and losing." This tells more about Goethe's concept of metamorphosis than it does about Dante.[4] Weimar Classicism could not appreciate Dante unreservedly. That was reserved for Romanticism.

In France resistance was even stronger. Rivarol's translation of the *Inferno* (1784) and his evaluation of Dante were premonitory, the daring sally of a man of genius.[5] The history of the comprehension of Dante in France can be traced in Sainte-Beuve. In 1854 he devoted one of his *Causeries du lundi* (XI, 198 ff.) to the translation of Dante by a certain Monsieur Mesnard, "premier vice-président du Sénat et président à la Cour de Cassation." In the France of old, prominent legal lights would translate Horace—but Dante? Here was something unusual. "Ma première pensée," Sainte-Beuve says, "en recevant le livre de M. Mesnard et en voyant un magistrat éminent et un homme politique aussi distingué profiter de quelques moments de loisir pour traduire Dante . . . a été de me dire qu'il avait dû se passer en France toute une révolution littéraire . . .'" But Sainte-Beuve is as little inclined as Goethe to renounce the classicistic position: "S'il nous est donné aujourd'hui, grâce à tant de travaux dont il a été l'objet, de le mieux comprendre dans son esprit, et de le révérer inviolablement dans son ensemble, nous ne saurions abjurer (je parle au moins

---

[3] *Ibid.*, XXX, 360.

[4] G. v. Loeper commented: "See *Inferno*, XXV. Here *allungare* and *accorciare* (see especially ll. 113, 114, and 125–28) are described in a manner which perfectly corresponds with Goethe's metamorphosis of animals."

[5] See the fine study by Karl-Eugen Gass, *Antoine de Rivarol under der Ausgang der französischen Aufklärung*, Bonn dissertation (1938), 178 ff.

avec la confiance de sentir comme une certaine classe d'esprits) notre goût intime, nos habitudes naturelles et primitives de raisonnement, de logique, et nos formes plus sobres et plus simples d'imagination; plus il est de son siècle, moins il est du nôtre." Not until very recent times has academic criticism in France broadened its horizon sufficiently for Louis Gillet (1876–1943; made a member of the Academy in 1936) to say: "Je voudrais parler de Dante comme d'un grand poète, la plus haute figure poétique qui s'élève en Europe entre Virgile et Shakespeare." [6]

In Italy Dante was long forgotten. Alfieri judged that not thirty men could be found there who had read the *Commedia*. According to Stendhal, Dante was disdained in Italy about 1800. He was "awakened" [7] there by the Risorgimento, as in Germany by Romanticism and in England by the Pre-Raphaelites. The rediscovery of the Middle Ages was the common background. The Italian Dante celebrations of 1865—like the German Schiller celebrations of 1859—preluded national unification. Both as the greatest intellectual representative of his nation and as the greatest poet of the Christian Middle Ages, Dante entered the pantheon of world Classicism in the nineteenth century—a Classicism freed from all classicistic theory.

If a new classic is received into the canon (ἐγκρινόμενος), this signifies a revision of the norms previously obtaining as classical. They are seen to be something historically determined and limited by doctrinaire preconceptions; they become relative, and their power is taken from them. To illustrate this by the influence of Dante would be a task for literary criticism. Eliot's considerations upon the nature of the classic should be regarded in this sense. In this sense Hofmannsthal could say of Molière in 1922: "There is something bourgeois about his work. True, the *Misanthrope* is an imperishable serious comedy, and the *École des Femmes* perhaps even surpasses it, the latter has been called his *Hamlet*. Nevertheless, there is nothing here which, as regards intellectual content, can be placed beside the great works of Goethe, to say nothing of beside Calderón, beside Shakespeare, beside Dante." [8]

2. *Dante and Latinity*

How was the *Commedia* possible? This question need not trouble the appreciative reader. But the historian of literature cannot avoid it. It has not yet been satisfactorily answered—despite the immense increase in Dante research, which contains a great deal of chaff. [9] Francesco De Sanctis in his philosophical and systematizing history of Italian literature maintains the thesis "that the *Commedia* expresses the view of life common to all, the common stock of knowledge, and embodies the same idea which had pre-

[6] Louis Gillet, *Dante* (1941), 8.
[7] Albert Counson, *Le réveil de Dante*, in *Revue de Littérature comparée*, I (1921), 362 ff.
[8] Hofmannsthal, *Die Berührung der Sphären* (1931), 282.
[9] Cf. my critique in *RF*, LX (1947), 237 ff.

viously formed the basis of all literary forms, of plays as well as visions, of treatises as well as 'treasures,' 'gardens,' sonnets, and canzoni." According to this, Dante's poem would be the synthesis of Italian literature before Dante. This thesis is as unsatisfactory philosophically as it is historically, and hence is of no value to knowledge. Adolf Gaspary tried to explain the *Commedia* by the fact that Dante "united in himself the two different streams which until then had remained separate in Italian literature—the popular, in religious poetry, and the literary, in the art lyric." [10] It is one of this excellent scholar's merits that he saw the problem. His solution was brilliant, but impossible to substantiate. It had no influence but, so far as I am aware, was replaced by nothing more conclusive. The generally prevailing opinion maintains that Dante's study of Antiquity, and especially of Virgil, acted to purify his taste, to turn him toward the classical.[11] We must reject this thesis. Time and again the course of our study has obliged us to exemplify the forms and traditions of the Latin Middle Ages by Dante. The conclusion is inescapable: With the Provençal and the Italian lyric, the Latin Middle Ages is the principal element which must be adduced to explain the genesis of the *Commedia*. The fertilizing of the Romance languages and literatures through Latinity is, as we pointed out, an essential characteristic of Romania. But in France, Italy, and Spain it takes different forms. In Italy the process is made easier by the greater closeness of the language to Latin in pronunciation and vocabulary. Take the first two lines of the *Commedia*:

> *Nel mezzo del cammin di nostra vita*
> *Mi ritrovai per una selva oscura.*

"Nostra vita" is both Italian and Latin. "Una selva oscura" is very close to the Latin "una silva obscura." Spanish "nuestra vida" and "bosque oscuro," Old French "nostre vie" and "forest oscure" are different phonetically and lexically. At the same time, however, the closeness of Italian to Latin is a difficulty for the Italian poet. It can induce him to measure the Volgare by Latin and extensively to assimilate the former to the latter—especially when rhyme is thereby facilitated. From this a tension between Volgare and Latin may arise. The tension becomes the more perceptible the more the poet is imbued with Latin culture and the more he is inclined to technical experiments. Both are true of Dante.[12]

10 Gaspary, *Geschichte der italienischen Literatur*, I (1885), 305.

11 Vossler too appears to incline toward this view (*Die Göttliche Komödie*[2], II, 598).

12 There is as yet no "History of the Italian Language" nor any study of Dante's language nor, finally, any collection of his Latinisms. Merely as a sample I give a few lexical Latinisms from the *Paradiso*. They occur only partly in rhyme. *Sempiterni* (I, 76); *repe* (II, 37); *cerne* (III, 75); *labi* (VI, 51); *atra* (VI, 78); *cive* (VIII, 116); *urge/turge* (X, 142 ff.); *pusillo* (XI, 111); *iube* (XII, 12); *numi* (XIII, 31); *turpa* (XV, 145); *iattura* (XVI, 96); *carmi* (XVII, 11); *opima* (XVIII, 33); *beatitudo* (XVIII, 112), etc. Cf. RF (1947), 250 ff.

From the Provençal poets, especially from Arnaut Daniel, he adopted the stylistic ideal of difficult technique. In his work technical reflections constantly occur during the process of creation.[13] He would like to summon up "rough and hoarse rhymes" for his Hell (*Inf.*, XXXII, 1), he wrestles with his "arduous material" (*Par.*, XXX, 36) and strives for perfection (*Par.*, XXX, 33)

> Come all' ultimo suo ciascuno artista.

He is a technician and artist of discourse. Hence, if for no other reason, antique and medieval Latin literary theory is something with which he has perpetually to come to terms. For no other Romance poet—not even for Góngora—is the relation between the vernacular and Latin so fraught with problems as it is for Dante. This tension can be traced through all his work. It is expressed in his vacillation between Latin and Italian, as well as in his extensive Latinization of Italian. It explains technical mannerisms like his use of periphrase and *annominatio*, as well as much in the realm of the topoi and themes of the *Commedia*.

Dante studied at Paris.[14] He stood upon the summit of the Latin culture of his time. Stylistic Latinisms [15] are already to be found in the *Rime*.[16] The first of the "stone" canzoni ("Io son venuto al punta della rota") begins with an astronomical indication of time which can only be referred to December, 1296. This is the first time that Dante uses this periphrase, enjoined by rhetoric. The old theory (purification of his taste by the Antique) is thereby refuted. By *ca.* 1295 Dante was already thoroughly familiar with Latin rhetoric and poetics. Dante's Latinism is common to all phases of his production. It is a medieval, not a humanistic, Latinism. We saw that in his letter to Can Grande Dante adheres to the medieval schema of the *accessus* (*supra*, p. 221, n. 14). The letter belongs to Dante's latest years, as do his two Latin eclogues and the *Questio de aqua et terra*. The final phase of his production is Latin.

What of its beginning? In the *Convivio*, II, 12, 4 Dante says that after Beatrice's death he began to read Boethius and Cicero, so far as his knowledge of Latin and his gifts of mind permitted; though through the latter he had understood many things earlier "as in a dream," as could be read in the *Vita nuova*. Like all of Dante's autobiographical revelations, this is to be regarded as self-stylization. This is evident from its inner contradiction (which is concealed by a deliberate obscurity), as well as from its purpose: setting the *donna gentile* (VN, 35 ff.) on a level with philosophy. What does the *Vita nuova* tell us of Dante's Latin education? It reveals

---

[13] G. Contini speaks of the "perpetuo sopraggiungere della riflessione tecnica accanto alla poesia" (Introduction to his edition of the *Rime*).

[14] Giovanni Villani states this. Robert Davidsohn refers to the fact as "unnecessarily contested" (*Geschichte von Florenz*, IV, Pt. 3 [1927], 140. In the note which attacks Rajna and Farinelli).

[15] Cf. RF, LX (1947), 251.

[16] Ed. Gianfranco Contini (1939, ²1946). Cf. RF, LX (1947), 245 ff.

a knowledge of the *ars dictaminis*.[17] Chapter 25 is an excursus, which does not fit into the framework and is not very convincingly motivated; the only explanation for it is that Dante considered it important to show that he had been educated in rhetoric. He says that he has represented Love as a living person, which in truth it is not; but he was justified in this, for "anciently there were among us no singers of love in the vernacular, but instead the singers of love were certain poets in the Latin tongue." Dante calls them "litterati poete." To these "some rhetorical figurativeness or color[18]" is permitted, and hence also to vernacular poets. Even in this first sketch of his vernacular poetics, then, Dante feels obliged to borrow from Latin theory and practice. In addition, he makes Love and the spirits of life speak Latin. A philosophical showpiece is Love's self-definition: "I am like the center of a circle to which the parts of the circumference stand in equal relation" (c. 12, p. 12). This is a modification of Alan's seventh "theological rule" (*PL*, CCX, 627 A): "God is an intelligible sphere whose center is everywhere and whose circumference is nowhere." This speculative formula obtained wide currency in the thirteenth century. Dante need not have taken it directly from Alan.[19] But it shows that even as a youth he was interested in philosophy and theology. That in the *Vita nuova* he applies this theological formula to Love, and yet in another passage (c. 25, 1; p. 34) again sophistically states that Love is not a substance but pure accident, is a flaw of youthful work. Did Dante really acquire "as in a dream" the knowledge of Latin which he exhibits in the *Vita nuova*?

The treatise *De vulgari eloquentia* * undertakes to set up rules for ver-

---

[17] In c. 28 (*Testo critico*, p. 38) and in c. 31, 3 (p. 40) Dante uses "proemio" in the technical sense. He twice alludes to the stylistic ideal of brevity (*infra*, Excursus XIII): c. 10, 1 (p. 11) and c. 17, 1 (p. 20). The etymologizing of proper names (*infra*, Excursus XIV), which Gracián will later call "agudeza nominal," is also common property of medieval style. Whether Dante knew the passages from poets quoted in c. 25 (p. 35) from the originals or from anthologies is of no concern to us.

[18] "Color" is the general character of the discourse. Cicero, *De or.*, III, 52, 199. —Quintilian, VIII, 4, 28; IV, 2, 88, etc.—Norden, 871, n. 2.—The concept was modified in the Middle Ages. "Colores" are the individual forms of the "ornatus verborum," as in the *Colores rhetorici* of Onulf of Speyer.

[19] On the origin of the definition: Beck in ZRPh, XLI (1921), 21 ff. and 473; Huizinga (*Mededeelingen van de Kgl. Akademie van Wetenschappen, Afdeeling Letterkunde*, LXXIV, Series B, [1932], 100). Dietrich Mahnke has devoted a book to "Infinite Spheres and the Universal Center" (*Unendliche Sphäre und Allmittelpunkt* [1937]; cf. especially p. 177), but he ignores both the passage from Dante and Huizinga. Alan's definition is to be found in Alexander of Hales, Vincent of Beauvais, Bonaventura, Thomas, Jean de Meun. In Italy, according to Salimbene (ed. Holder-Egger, 182, 23 ff.) a hymn by Philippe de Grève was known beginning "Centrum capit circulus" (printed A.h., XX, 88, No. 89). Another hymn begins: "Tu es circumferentia, / Centrum, tui positio / Loci negat obsequia" (A.h., XXI, 12, st. 11). May an Oriental origin be conjectured? In Hafiz I find: "Around the point of union vainly runs the course of the circle forever: shalt thou ever approach the goal of thy striving, its center?" (Georg Jacob, *Unio mystica. Hafisische Lieder in Nachbildungen*, [1922], 21).

[* Dr. Curtius here cites this in the translation by F. Dornseiff and J. Balogh, 1925, to which the reference figures apply.]

nacular poetry. But this is done in Latin. Poetical use of the Volgare is permitted only subject to many precautions. It is suitable only for a certain cycle of themes, welfare, love, virtue (*salus, venus, virtus:* II, 2, 8) and only for the canzone (II, 3, 11). But these restrictions do not yet suffice. Even the poets who obey them "are different from the great poets, that is from the regular poets; for the great poets wrote their poems in regulated language, but the others at random . . . Therefore: the more closely we imitate the former, the better we write. Hence we who have undertaken the enterprise of a theory must emulate their theoretically thought-out poetics" (II, 4, 2 f.). Here, then, Dante reformulates the distinction already made in the *Vita nuova* (c. 25, § 3) between "litterati poete" and "poete volgari." But who, then, are the "magni poetae," the "regulares"? They are the Latin poets. Dante prefers not to say this expressly—understandably enough. He wishes to glorify the vernacular, he chooses examples from Italian and Provençal poetry; hence it might seem strange that the Volgare was to model itself upon Latin; that *imitatio* of the Ancients and adherence to the "doctrinatae poetriae" were enjoined. Of these poetics, Dante names only Horace's. But since he uses the plural, he has others in mind too— namely, the Latin poetics of the twelfth and thirteenth centuries. That he knew them and guided himself by them, we have already learned from his use of periphrase and *annominatio.* Now, before the poet, paying due heed to the precepts set forth by Dante, goes to work, he must "drink from Helicon." First, however, he is given yet more counsel: "But to have caution and discretion, as is fitting—here lies the difficulty, for that can never be attained without strenuous effort of mind and assiduous practice of the art and familiarity with the sciences. And such men it is whom the poet in the sixth book of the *Aeneid* calls the beloved of God and says that they are exalted to the heavens by their ardent virtue and are sons of the gods; although he speaks figuratively. And hence are they guilty of folly who, innocent of art and science, trusting but in their genius, rush forward upon the highest subjects, which must be sung in the highest style (*ad summa summe canenda prorumpunt*). Let them refrain from such presumption and, if they are geese by nature or indolence, let them not imitate the sky-seeking eagle." [20]

[20] What does this appeal to Virgil's authority imply? In *Aeneid*, VI, 126 ff. Aeneas is warned by the Sibyl: it is easy to descend into the underworld, but to return from it had hitherto been possible only to the sons of gods:

> . . . *facilis descensus Averno,*
> *Noctes atque dies patet atri ianua Ditis;*
> *Sed revocare gradum superasque evadere ad auras,*
> *Hoc opus, hic labor est. Pauci, quos aequus amavit*
> *Juppiter aut ardens evexit ad aethera virtus,*
> *Dis geniti potuere.*

Marigo (commentary on the *Vita nuova*) holds that the allegorical interpretation of these verses from Virgil is Dante's own idea. He has overlooked the fact that Dante took it from Bernard Silvestris' commentary. This gives the following inter-

But Dante's demands go even further. He distinguishes (II, 6) four kinds of sentence-structure ("constructio"). The highest is that which is "both flavorful and charming and at the same time elevated" ("sapidus et venustus etiam et excelsus"). It is used by the "famous stylists" ("dictatores illustres"). Provençal, French, and Italian examples are quoted. But . . . "perhaps the most useful thing would be . . . if we should read the regular poets, namely Virgil, Ovid in his Metamorphoses, Statius, and Lucan; as well as other writers who have employed the highest prose, such as Titus Livius, Pliny, Frontinus, Paulus Orosius, and many more."

From Dante's poetics I have selected only his statements concerning the relation which the artistic diction and artistic poetry which he enjoins bear to Latin. It is really remarkable to see how he keeps piling up new difficulties before the poetic fledgling and making more and more severe demands upon him. They come close to being unrealizable. Must one really have read Orosius [21] before one can write a canzone in the lofty style? Is the vernacular emancipated and urged to full development by Dante's treatise? Is it not rather intolerably shackled? And for what reason? The reason is the tension between Romania and Rome. Dante was unable to resolve it theoretically. This is presumably one of the reasons the treatise was never finished. It is noticeable how, as the demonstration proceeds, Latin assumes greater and greater prominence. Nothing is more significant than the "perhaps" at the beginning of our last quotation, that tentative, questioning "perhaps" introducing a sentence which goes so far beyond the obedience to Latin poetics previously enjoined, that it ends with Frontinus, Orosius, "and many more." Each of the successive limitations to which Dante subjects poetry in his mother-tongue is like another turn of a screw. The *De vulgari eloquentia* is a conglomerate of very different elements: a general theory of language, the linguistic organization of Romania, the demand for a common Italian artistic language, the technical theory of the canzone —all this has always received due attention. But little attention has been paid to an element which for Dante is a matter of the utmost importance: the tying of vernacular poetry to a schooling in Latin poetry and prose, to Latin rhetoric and Latin poetics of antique and medieval origin. The treatise is impressive testimony to what, for brevity's sake, I call Dante's Latinism.

The *Convivio* is written in Italian, though Dante apologizes for this as a "substantial blemish" (I, 5, 1). Latin is superior to the vernacular in nobility (it is incorruptible), in expressiveness, in beauty (I, 5, 8–15). For

---

pretations: "Noctes" and "dies" (l. 127) are ignorance and the sciences. "Dis geniti" (l. 131) are (a) "filii Apollinis: sapientes," (b) "filii Calliopes: eloquentes," (c) "filii Jovis: rationabiles" (*Commentum Bernardi Silvestris super sex libros Eneidos Vergilii*, ed. G. Riedel [Gryphisvaldae (Greifswald), 1924], 57). This is the forbidding material which Dante transformed into his enthusiastic praise of scholarly vernacular poetry formed after Latin models.

[21] He appears in the Heaven of the Sun (*Par.*, X, 118).

that very reason Dante cannot use it for his commentary on his canzoni, since that would be to make the master the servant. A tortuous explanation! But the Italian of the *Convivio* is full of reminiscences of Latin rhetoric.[22]

The beginning of the *Commedia* also acknowledges Dante's faith in rhetoric. His first words to Virgil are (*Inf.*, I, 79 ff.):

> Or se' tu quel Virgilio e quella fonte
> Che spandi di parlar si largo fiume?

(Art thou that Virgil then, that fount from which
There floweth forth so broad a river of speech?)

Then his homage (85 ff.):

> Tu se' lo mio maestro e 'l mio autore,
> Tu se' solo colui da cu' io tolsi
> Lo bello stilo che m' ha fatto onore.

(Thou art my master and my author thou,
And thou alone art he from whom I culled
The fair style which has brought me into honor.)

What do these verses tell us of Dante's view of Virgil? "Fiume" ("river") is a stylistic Latinism and corresponds to the Latin "flumen orationis" and related expressions used to praise an author's eloquence and copiousness.[23]

---

[22] The commentary of Busnelli and Vandelli (1934) leaves us in the lurch here. —On "canzoni sì d'amor come di virtù materiate" (I, 1, 14) we may remark that Matthew of Vendôme commends "materiatus" as an "elegant" word (Faral, 157, § 21).—On I, 2, 3 cf. *ZRPh*, LXII (1942), 465.—In IV, 15, 11 we have "dico intelletto per la nobile parte dell' anima nostra, che con uno vocabolo 'mente' si può chiamare." Busnelli-Vandelli here refer to III, 2, 10: There they give a quotation from Thomas Aquinas which has nothing to do with the case but is merely misleading. The right explanation was naturally to be looked for in Isidore, from whom scores of medieval Latin encyclopedias and dictionaries copied: "Mens vocata quod emineat in anima . . . Quapropter non anima, sed quod excellit in anima mens vocatur" (*Et.*, XI, 1, 12).—In *Conv.*, I, 8, 5 Galen's treatise on the art of medicine is referred to as "li Tegni di Galieno." Note: "Tegni è materiale ed errata riduzione in lettere italine del greco τέχνη." But "tegni" is neither an Italian nor an "erroneous" but a medieval Latin form. John of Garland (first half of the 13th cent.) calls one variety of prose "tegnigrapha: a 'tegni' quod est 'ars' et 'graphos' 'scriptum' " (*RF*, XIII [1902], 886). In England "tegna" first appears in 1040, "tegni" in 1345 (Baxter-Johnson, *Medieval Latin Word-List* [1934]).—In *Conv.*, IV, 16, 6 Dante waxes indignant over deriving the word "nobile" from "nosco"; on the contrary it comes from "non vile." This is to be found in Isidore, *Et.*, X, 184: "nobilis, non vilis." Instead of this the commentators offer an absurd reference to Ambrose, *De Noe et arca*. Etc.

[23] "Flumen orationis," "flumen verborum" frequently in Cicero and Quintilian. —Petronius, c. 5: "sic flumine largo / Plenus Pierio defundes pectore verba."— Examples from late Antiquity of "flumen" and the like in the sense of eloquence are to be found in Hans Bruhn, *Specimen vocabularii rhetorici ad inferioris aetatis latinitatem pertinens*, Marburg dissertation (1911), p. 57. Dante's contemporary, Cardinal Iacopo Gaietani Stefaneschi, praises Virgil in his *Opus metricum* as "rhetoricae suavitatis profluus" (F. X. Seppelt, *Monumenta Coelestiniana* [1921], p. 5, 24 ff.; on this publication cf. F. Baethgen, *Beiträge zur Geschichte Coelestins V* [1934], p. 286, 3).

For Dante, then, Virgil is the master of rhetoric in the late antique and medieval sense. Beatrice sends him to Dante that he may assist him with his "ornate word" (*Inf.*, II, 67 ff.):

> Or movi, e con la tua parola ornata
> E con ciò ch' ha mestieri al suo campare
> L' aiuta sì ch' i' ne sia consolata.

(Betake thee now, and with thine ornate word
And that whereof for safety he hath need,
Aid him in such wise that I be consoled.)

Virgil's rhetoric is prized in Paradise (*Inf.*, II, 112 ff.):

> Venni quaggiù del mio beato scanno,
> Fidandomi nel tuo parlare onesto
> Ch' onora te e quei ch' udito l' hanno.

(I came down hither from my blessed seat,
Myself entrusting to thy noble speech
Which honors thee and those who ere have heard it.)

Dante learned his rhetorical art from Virgil ("lo mio maestro"). Among the *auctores* of the medieval schools, Virgil is the closest to him ("lo mio autore"). The *auctores* are, as we know, at the same time authorities: sages. So for Dante, as for Macrobius (*Sat.*, I, 16, 12) Virgil knows all sciences. He represents the encyclopedic sum of human knowledge (*Inf.*, IV, 73; VII, 3; VIII, 7, etc.)

3. The Commedia *and the Literary Genres*

In his poetics (*VE*, II, 4, 5) Dante distinguishes the tragic, the comic, and the elegiac as three literary styles between which the poet must choose. The tragic is the "high" style, the comic the "low," the elegiac the "style of the unhappy." But there is no strict parallel here, for tragedy and comedy are defined in respect to diction, elegy in respect to subject matter. Somewhat different is the theory of genres in the letter to Can Grande (§§ 28 ff.). Here comedy and tragedy are genres of poetic narrative ("poetice narrationis"), which are distinguished both thematically ("in materia") and stylistically ("in modo loquendi"); thus tragedy at the beginning is "admirable and tranquil" and at the end "fetid and terrible," as its etymology [24] "goat-song" would lead one to expect and as may be seen in Seneca's

---

[24] The derivation of *tragedia* from τράγος and of *comedia* from κώμη (also in Isidore *Et.*, VIII, 7, 6), Dante found in the *Derivationes* of Uguccione of Pisa, whom he cites in *Conv.*, IV, 6, 5. Cf. P. Toynbee, *Dante Studies and Researches* (1902), 103. But Uguccione must not be regarded as the sole source of Dante's medieval Latin knowledge. The word "polisemos," for example (Epistle 13, § 20),

tragedies. Comedy, on the contrary, begins "harshly" and ends happily—see Terence. As further genres of poetic narrative he then—without further explanation—names pastoral, elegy, satire, and the "votive sentence" (*sententia votiva*); this last rests upon a misunderstood passage in Horace.[25] Dante is not consistent in his use of designations for the genres. When he calls the *Aeneid* "high tragedy" (*Inf.*, XX, 113), this can only refer to its style. If its action is taken into account, it would have to be called a comedy.[26] The antique system of poetic genres had, in the millennium before Dante, disintegrated until it was unrecognizable and incomprehensible. Dante's title was a makeshift. Our current title *Divina Commedia* (first appearance in the Venice edition of 1555) was a happy supplement. Dante himself referred to the Comedy as "the sacred poem" (*Par.*, XXIII, 62 and XXV, 1). May one see in this the title which he would have chosen if a scholarly rhetorical designation had not seemed to him more suitable? Late Antiquity had bestowed this title of honor on the *Aeneid*.[27]

The conception of the *Commedia* is based upon a spiritual meeting with Virgil. In the realm of European literature there is little which may be compared with this phenomenon.[28] The "awakening" of Aristotle in the thirteenth century was the work of generations and took place in the cool light of intellectual research. The awakening of Virgil by Dante is an arc of flame which leaps from one great soul to another. The tradition of the European spirit knows no situation of such affecting loftiness, tenderness, fruitfulness. It is the meeting of the two greatest Latins. Historically, it is the sealing of the bond which the Latin Middle Ages made between the antique and the modern world. Only when we are once again able to comprehend Virgil in all his poetic greatness, of which we Germans have lost sight since 1770, shall we wholly appreciate Dante.[29]

Dante's Virgil is a medieval, hence unclassical, Virgil, in contrast to Tasso's or Milton's. He is the mouthpiece of the temporal and the eternal

---

which, according to Toynbee, Dante got from Uguccione, is in Servius in his commentary on line 1 of the *Aeneid*; later in Lactantius Placidus on *Thebais*, I, 104; in *Poetae*, IV, 363 gloss and 373, 26 gloss; in a ninth-century glossary (*Bulletin of the John Rylands Library*, VII, 432); in John of Salisbury, *Policraticus*, ed. Webb, I, 94, 10, etc. The word was a current technical term.

[25] Horace (A.P., 75 f.) says that the elegiac measure was the medium first of complaint, later (in the epigram) of gratitude for granted prayers ("voti sententia compos").

[26] The best discussion of the title of Dante's poem is Pio Rajna's (*Studi danteschi*, IV [1921], 5–37).—For the use of "comicus," "comedus," "comedia," cf. further John of Salisbury, *Policraticus*, ed. Webb, I, 405 b and 489 d.—A narrative of the life and death of Thomas Becket in 129 stanzas is entitled "comedia" (Duméril, *Poésies populaires latines du moyen âge*, II [1847], 70 ff.). St. 8: "Sequor morem comici, scio vos hunc scire, / Primum vae! et tristia, post Evax! et lyrae." St. 115: "Morem sequor comici; malis finem pono, / Flebile principium fine mutans bono."

[27] Macrobius *Sat.*, I, 24, 13.—Cf. Martial, VII, 63, 5 and VIII, 56, 2.

[28] Goethe's meeting with Hafiz, Hofmannsthal's with Calderón.

[29] Cf. Rudolf Alexander Schröder, *Die Aufsätze und Reden* (1939), I, 79 ff. (*Marginalien eines Vergil-Lesers*).

Rome whose name can be symbolically applied to Paradise (*Purg.*, XXXII, 102). At the same time he is adept and mouthpiece of the otherworld. The sixth book of the *Aeneid*, the poem's solemn center, is the august model for the *Commedia*. Aeneas and Paul (II Cor. 12:2) are the only two mortals whose journeys into the beyond Dante considers authenticated (*Inf.*, II, 13–33). Both are figures of world history: the Father of Rome and the Apostle to the Gentiles. If Dante makes himself a third in their company, it implies a claim to an analogous historical mission—only comprehensible from the fact that Dante felt himself to be a reformer and a prophet.

To cite Dante's hundreds of imitations of the *Aeneid*, and especially of Book VI; to point out his taking over of Virgilian persons and otherworld localities; to pursue the transposition of Virgil's verses into Dante's lines (*Aen.*, IV, 23 = *Purg.*, XXX, 48; *Aen.*, VI, 883 = *Purg.*, XXX, 21)—these tasks cannot be attempted here. Whoever undertakes them will need the most delicate tact, together with intensive scholarship. He would have to raise the question of which elements of the *Commedia* were borrowed from the *Aeneid* or based upon it, and how they were modified. How was Virgil's vision of the beyond divided among Dante's three realms? Ripheus, we saw (*supra*, p. 61), could be placed in the heavenly eagle—a touching tribute to Virgil. For his Elysium, to be sure, there was no place to be found either in the Mount of Purgatory or in Heaven—but neither could it be sacrificed. By a bold stroke Dante transformed it into the "nobile castello" of Limbo. It is from Virgil's consigning the "pious poets" ("pii vates et Phoebo digna locuti") to his Elysium, and singling out Orpheus and Musaeus among them, that Dante drew the suggestion for the "fair school" of the antique poets, and he saves their patron Phoebus and two-peaked Parnassus for the *invocatio* of the *Paradiso*. So the entire *Commedia* bears witness to the spiritual presence of the *Aeneid*.

Virgil, however, is not the only antique model for Dante's otherworld. The structural framework of the *Paradiso* is formed by the ascent through the nine celestial spheres, which the tenth, the infinite Empyrean, encloses. This journey through the spheres is not in Virgil. But even in pre-Christian times it has passed from the East into the late antique religious concept of the universe.[30] It is in the background of Cicero's greatest work, the "Dream of Scipio," which was preserved by Macrobius and was read in the Middle Ages with his commentary. The younger Scipio is transported in a dream to the Milky Way and there receives philosophical instruction and the prophecy of his own fate from his father and grandfather. "As I viewed everything from thence, all else seemed to me beautiful and admirable. There were stars which we never glimpse from the earth, and they were all larger than we ever supposed . . . The starry spheres were much larger than the earth; yes, the earth itself seemed to me so small that I despised our empire which covers but a point upon it. As I continued gazing at it, Africanus said: 'How much longer will thy mind be fixed upon the earth?

[30] Paul Wendland, *Die hellenistisch-römische Kultur*[2·3·] (1912), 170 ff.

Seest thou not into what temple thou art come? Those are the nine circles, or rather spheres, by which the universe is joined. One of them, the outermost, is the celestial. It contains all the others and is itself the highest God, who embraces all the other spheres within himself' . . ." (*De re publica*, VI, 16 f.). The meeting, in the highest heaven, of the younger Scipio with his grandfather, who prophesies his future life to his descendant, gave Dante the suggestion for his Cacciaguida episode.[31] Dante's journey through the spheres was also foreshadowed in Cicero's work. But such a journey had become the common property of the Middle Ages through Martianus Capella and the twelfth-century philosophical epic which took its rise from him (Bernard Silvestris and Alan).

Despite the opposition of official Dante scholarship, which seeks to explain Dante only from Romance sources or at best from the unimpressive [32] Latin production of the Italian Middle Ages, and would like to transfer the principle of national autarchy to the age whose label is the three universal powers *Imperium, Sacerdotium, Studium*, it is beyond all doubt that Dante was at home in the intellectual world of the Latin Middle Ages. Here only a few indications can be given. We may regard it as established that Dante knew Alan. We saw (*supra*, pp. 117 ff.) that Alan, in conscious opposition to the Antiquity-aping Latin epic of his period, drew up the program for a new poetic genre which should treat the ascent of reason into the realm of transcendental truth. This conception could mature only in the mind of a remarkable man who, like Alan, was poet, philosopher, and thinker in one. His contemporaries and followers—John of Hanville, for example—did not comprehend it but merely imitated it superficially. Dante, first and alone, seized upon it once again and recast it in new experiential material.

Dante mentions Alan no more than he does the "Dream of Scipio" or the medieval Latin arts of poetry which he followed. He conceals his sources as he does his education and the story of his youthful years. He feels the need to stylize his personal portrait. The *Vita nuova* is a highly conscious, occult, and reinterpretative self-analysis.[33] It also contains a literary-historical schematization invented by Dante himself, which until now has frequently been taken as an historical account, and which also extends into the *Commedia*.[34] The effect of Dante's deliberate obscurity is sometimes esoteric (*Inf.*, IX, 61 ff.), sometimes mystical, sometimes sibylline or prophetic, but not infrequently it also verges upon mystification. This is to be accepted as an element of Dante's personality. But scholarship must not allow itself to be led astray by it.

The subject of Alan's *Anticlaudianus* was the creation of a new man. The ascent through the spheres to the Empyrean forms but a part of the

[31] A reminiscence of the Anchises episode is interwoven with it (*Par.*, XV, 25).

[32] In support of this judgment I refer to Novati-Monteverdi, *Le Origini* (1926), especially p. 646.

[33] "Sistemazione leggendaria," Contini.

[34] RF (1947), 216.

general plan. Nevertheless there are obvious points of contact between Alan and Dante. When Phronesis (the human soul) meets Theology on her journey through the heavens, she has to leave Reason (*Ratio*) behind (*SP*, II, 354 = *PL*, CCX, 534 B). She enters a region where the wisdom of Tully, Virgil, Aristotle, and Ptolemy fails (*SP*, II, 358 = *PL*, CCX, 536 B). So Virgil must remain behind when Beatrice takes over Dante's guidance. In Alan's Empyrean the Trinity is symbolized by a spring, a brook, and a river, which are at once water and light (*SP*, II, 373 = *PL*, CCX, 544 C):

> *Cum sint distincti fons, rivus, flumen, in unum*
> *Conveniunt, eademque trium substantia, simplex*
> *Esse, sapor similis, color unus, splendor in illis*
> *Unicus, et vultus horum conformis, et idem*
> *Ad speciem fontis sol vincens lumine solem.*[35]

To this corresponds Dante's river of light (*Par.* XXX, 60):

> *E vidi lume in forma di riviera,*[36]

which subsequently changes into the sea of light and the heavenly rose. Two central motifs, then, are common to both works.[37] There are other coincidences as well.[38]

If our observations are correct, Virgil's epic which brought together history and the transcendent, and the philosophico-theological epic of the Latin Middle Ages originated by Alan, were both factors in the literary form which Dante created in his *Commedia*. That form itself can be assigned to no genre. If it is commonly classed as "epic," that can be ascribed

[35] "Whilst they are different, spring, brook, and river come together as one; the three have the same substance, a simple being, a like taste, one color, a single brightness; their appearance is uniform: the same sun, which in the form of a spring exceeds the sun in light."—Spring, river, ocean symbolize the Trinity in the Franciscan mystics Francisco de Osuna and Bernardino de Laredo: Dámaso Alonso, *La Poesía de San Juan de la Cruz*, 1942, 61.—This confrontation of Alan with Franciscan mysticism may be taken as an indication of a *modus dicendi* of mystical experience which cannot be pursued here. The identity of light and stream occurs in Mechthild of Magdeburg ("The Flowing Light of the Godhead").

[36] "And I saw light in the form of a river."

[37] An attempt to show that Dante knew Alan was made by E. Bossard, *Alani ab Insulis Anticlaudianus* (Angers, 1885).—F. Torraca contested it in 1905, with an unfortunate choice of arguments (*I precursori della Divina Commedia* in *Lectura Dantis*, Florence).—Salvadori stated that it was beyond doubt (*Sulla vita giovanile di Dante* [1906], 16). F. Beck agreed with him (*ZRPh*, XLI [1921], 47 and XLVII [1927], 23).—The possibility was cautiously considered in 1926 by A. Monteverdi (in Novati-Monteverdi, *Le Origini*, 522) and in 1934 by Busnelli-Vandelli (*Convivio*, I, 188, note on the comparison of heaven to the sciences in *Convivio*, II, 13, 2).—See also my paper "Dante and Alan" in *RF*, LXII (1950), 28-31.

[38] God is "incircumscriptus" (*SP*, II, 350 = *PL*, CCX, 531 C) as in *Purg.*, XI, 3 and *Par.*, XIV, 32. He is called "supremus Jupiter" (*SP*, II, 354 = *PL*, CCX, 533 D) and in Dante "sommo Giove." The problem of the spots on the moon is discussed in Alan (*SP*, II, 341 = *PL*, CCX, 526 D) as it is in *Paradiso*, II.—Alan's doctrine of the happiness of the blessed (*SP*, II, 361 = *PL*, CCX, 538 A) corresponds to Dante's.

only to the inanity which thinks that the *Iliad* and *The Forsyte Saga* are to be spoken of in the same breath.

Other genres also contributed formal elements to the *Commedia*. It begins with straying in a wood, a motif of the French romance of chivalry. But the motif also occurs (as a variant of the bucolic "al fresco" motif) in medieval Latin vision poems.[39] Such poems sometimes employ motifs from Revelations, and in such cases the guide into the higher world may be an antique sage, as in the *Commedia*.[40] Common to several genres of medieval literature are the comic topoi which Dante employed in the episode of the devils (*Inferno*, XXI to XXIII).[41] The smallest contribution—if indeed there was any at all—came from the legendary otherworld—visions of popular religious stamp which circulated so widely in Latin and the vernaculars during the Middle Ages. Dante stands within the learned tradition of the Middle Ages, and at the beginning of the *Paradiso* (II, 1–6) he advises the ignorant to cease reading. He shares in the contempt for the laity which is to be found everywhere in medieval Latin literature.[42]

4. *Exemplary Figures in the* Commedia

We have become acquainted with the importance of exemplary figures (*exempla*) in late antique and medieval literature (*supra*, p. 59). Parallelism of biblical and antique exemplary figures has its roots in Jerome's system of correspondences (*supra*, pp. 46 f.). It was first systematically carried out in the *Ecloga Theoduli* and first given a systematic basis by Baudri of Bourgueil. We have to deal, then, with a stylistic tradition which, like many others we have considered, has not hitherto been recognized. So perhaps I may be permitted to quote the passage from Baudri (ed. Abrahams No. 238) here.

105   *Ut sunt in veterum libris exempla malorum,*
          Sic bona quae facias sunt in eis posita.
        Laudatur propria pro virginitate Diana,
          Portenti victor Perseüs exprimitur.

[39] With falling asleep as prelude to the vision in the *Metamorphosis Goliae* (Thomas Wright, *The Latin Poems . . . attributed to Walter Mapes* [1841], 21 ff.):

> *Pirru sub florigera nuper pullulante*
> *Membra sompno foveram, paulo fessus ante.*
> *Nemus quoddam videor mihi subintrare . . .*

[40] In the *Apocalypse of Golias* (ed. Strecker, 1928) Pythagoras is the guide (st. 7: "Dux ego previus, et tu me sequere"). Bucolic opening with straying in a wood: "A tauro torrida lampade Cinthii / Fundente iacula ferventis radii / Umbrosas nemoris latebras adii, / Explorans graciam lenis Favonii. / Estive medio diei tempore / Frondosa recubans sub Jovis arbore / Astantis video formam Pithagore: / Deus scit, nescio, utrum in corpore."

[41] Cf. Excursus IV.

[42] "Moderni bruti" (*Epist.*, XI, 18). Cf. ZRPh, LX (1940), 2, n. 3 and Excursus XII.—*Supra*, p. 214.

> *Alcidis virtus per multos panditur actus.*
> *Omnia, si nosti, talia mystica sunt . . .*
> 117 *Quod si de libris nostris exempla requiris,*
> *Ipsa tot invenies quot videas apices . . .*
> 121 *Sed volui Grecas ideo praetendere nugas,*
> *Ut quaevis mundi littera nos doceat,*
> *Ut totus mundus velut unica lingua loquatur*
> *Et nos erudiat omnis et omnis homo.*
> *Captivos ideo gentiles adveho nugas,*
> *Laetor captivis victor ego spoliis . . .*
> 131 *Hostili praeda ditetur lingua latina,*
> *Grecus et Hebreus serviat edomitus.*
> *In nullis nobis desit doctrina legendi,*
> *Lectio sit nobis et liber omne quod est.*

That is: "The books of the pagans contain not only examples of immorality but also of virtue: Diana's chastity, Perseus' victory over the sea-monster, the labors of Hercules. All these stories have allegorical meanings. This is especially true of the Bible. But I have wished to cite Greek feignings, so that the entire literary tradition shall serve for our instruction. All the world speaks a single language, and all mankind shall teach us. I bring forth the fables of the pagans as prisoners, and rejoice in the spoil," etc. There is here an allusion to the allegorical interpretation of Deuteronomy 21:12 (*supra*, p. 40).

The theory of the parallelism of exemplary figures, here documented from Baudri (but traceable elsewhere [43]), must have been known to Dante. For he made it the skeleton of the *Purgatorio*. In twelve of its cantos there are series of exempla. Antique and Christian exempla are systematically co-ordinated. David and Mary figure with Trajan (X); Lucifer, Nimrod, Saul, Rehoboam, Sennacherib, and Holofernes with the Titans; Niobe, Arachne, Alcmaeon, and Tomyris, with the Trojans (XII); Mary with Orestes (XIII); Cain with Aglauros (XIV); Mary and Pisistratus with the protomartyr Stephen (XV); Procne with Haman (XVII); Mary with Caesar (XVIII); and with Fabricius (XX); Pygmalion, Midas, Polymnestor, and Crassus with Achan, Sapphira, and Heliodorus (*ibid.*); Mary with the women of ancient Rome, Daniel, and John the Baptist (XXII); the Centaurs with Gideon's warriors (XXIV); Mary with Diana (XXV); the inhabitants of Sodom with Pasiphaë (XXVI).

Here, with great art, Dante has developed a stylistic schema which is a part of the medieval Latin tradition. The form of presentation varies. The exempla of X and XII are reliefs in stone, those of XIII and XIV spirit voices which pass by. The exempla of XV are seen in an "ecstatic vision"

---

[43] After an enumeration of pagan exempla Walter Map says: "Gentilium novi supersticionem sed omnis creatura Dei aliquod habet exemplar honesti . . ." (*De nugis curialium*, ed. M. R. James, 155, 17 ff.).

(l. 85), as are those of XVII. Those of XVIII and XX sound mournfully from the lips of unknown sinners by day, from Hugh Capet's by night.[44] In Canto XXII they sound from the leaves of a tree (l. 140 ff.), as they do again in XXIV (l. 121 ff.). The exempla of XXV are interpolated into a hymn (l. 121 ff.). Those of XXVI are divided between a twofold choir (l. 40 ff.). We have, then, six ingenious variations of the schema. Its systematic use contributes not a little to the highly manneristic character which the *Commedia* exhibits in some passages. Such confrontations as those of Cain and Aglauros, of Mary, Pisistratus, and St. Stephen, must appear strange if not offensive to classicistic taste.

The use of exempla is not confined to the *Purgatorio*. We have already mentioned that Dante cites Amyclas, one of the favorites of the Latin school poetry of the twelfth century, as an example of virtuous poverty (*supra*, p. 60). Thomas Aquinas in his eulogy of St. Francis (*Par.*, XI, 58 ff.) explains that Lady Poverty was first betrothed to Christ; Caesar's finding her hidden in Amyclas' cottage availed nothing; Francis was the first to wed her again. These names too form a strange group, which St. Thomas himself would hardly have brought together. But we are to find more of the like.

Among exemplary figures in the wider sense we must also count Trajan (humility towards the widow; *Purg.*, X, 73 ff.); the Jewess Mary who during Titus's siege of Jerusalem "bit into" [45] her son and hence is referred to in the circle of the gluttonous (*Purg.*, XXIII, 30); and finally the courtesan Thais (*Inf.*, XVIII, 133). The origin of this legend of Trajan has not yet been discovered.[46] The story of the cannibal Mary comes from Flavius Josephus; that of Thais from Terence. Dante probably knew Terence only by name, but he could find this passage from him quoted in Cicero's *Laelius*. Are we to assume three separate sources for the three exempla? It would seem to me more satisfactory methodologically if we can derive them all from a single source. Dante could find them all in the *Policraticus* of John of Salisbury, one of the most prominent and widely read of twelfth-century authors.[47]

[44] The suggestion came to Dante from Virgil. Among the sinners in Tartarus is Phlegyas, who is referred to as follows (619 f.):

> *Admonet et magna testatur voce per umbras:*
> *"Discite iustitiam moniti et non temnere divos."*

[45] According to the source she tore her nursing babe from her breast, strangled, broiled, and half devoured him. She was almost insane from hunger. Dante—illogically—sets this down to her as "gluttony."

[46] It would seem to have arisen from a misinterpretation of an antique relief representing a female figure (a province?) doing homage to an emperor.—Cf. R. Eisler, "Die Hochzeitstruhen der letzten Gräfin von Görz," in *Jahrbuch der K. K. Zentralkommission*, N. S. III, Pt. 2 (1905), p. 79.

[47] *Policraticus*, ed. Webb, I, 317, 6 ff. The dialogue between Trajan and the widow as there given is very close to Dante's wording. The Jewess Mary is the subject of a chapter of the *Policraticus*, ed. Webb, I, 79, 23 ff.—Thais: Webb, I, 179, 22 ff. —In *Inf.*, XXIII, 121 ff. Dante sets forth that souls are to be found in hell whose

5. *The Personnel of the* Commedia

If we go through the names of these exemplary figures, we shall find many which the modern reader has never encountered: to know Aglauros, Tomyris, and Polymnestor, one must have read the writers of Antiquity with a studiousness and respect which no one today possesses or need possess. Such studiousness and respect were a matter of course for the Middle Ages, because all authors were authorities. The antique tradition was a treasury of names, deeds, sayings, teachings—the obligatory orientation for an understanding of the world and history. Orosius and Ripheus were for Dante points of reference in his historico-metaphysical picture of the world. But we no longer know even the Bible. Hezekiah, Haman, Achitophel [48]—who is familiar with them? Dante counted upon an erudite culture among his readers. That is one reason he is hard to understand. But the exemplary figures make up only a very small part of the proper names which occur in the *Commedia*. The personnel of the poem has never to my knowledge been investigated. Yet the introduction, grouping, and classification of persons is the first factor which analysis of the poem encounters. There are over five hundred of them. No medieval work has an even remotely comparable number. Of antique poems, only Ovid's *Metamorphoses* can be named with it—understandably so, for, aside from everything else, the *Metamorphoses* is a historical poem which begins with the birth of the universe and comes down to its author's own times. As a guiding thread through this chronological succession, of which he boasts as his own invention (*Met.*, I, 3; *Trist.*, II, 559), Ovid employed the transformation of human beings into plants, animals, stones, streams, etc. He has brought together some 250 such stories. In each there are naturally several persons. If they were counted up, Ovid's personnel would doubtless be even larger than Dante's. The *Metamorphoses* has 12,086 lines, the *Commedia* 14,230.

The great number and variety of persons in the *Commedia* is explained by the most impressive and most fertile innovation which Dante's genius incorporated into the antique and medieval heritage: his drawing upon contemporary history. Dante summons popes and emperors [49] of his own times to judgment; kings and prelates; statesmen, tyrants, generals; men and women from the nobility and the bourgeoisie, from guild and school. An obscure artisan like Belacqua has his place in the otherworld just as

---

bodies, possessed by a devil, still wander on earth. This too he could find in the *Policraticus*, ed. Webb, I, 190, 20 ff.: "Nam qui captivi vitiorum impulsu trahuntur ad penam . . . , abeuntes post concupiscentias suas, etsi corpore videantur inhabitare superficiem terrae, vivi tamen absorti sunt et descendunt in infernum viventes." —Yet other points of contact could probably be found.

[48] In 1681 Dryden could still put Achitophel in the title of a popular satire and count upon being understood.

[49] Such a precedent as Walafrid's putting Charlemagne in Hell (*Poetae*, II, 318, 446 ff.) stands quite alone.

do thieves, murderers, saints. Artists and poets, philosophers and hermits, all sorts and conditions of men are represented. The *Divina Commedia* is at the same time a *Comédie Humaine*, for which nothing human is too high or too low. Dante's poem moves wholly in the transcendent. But it is everywhere penetrated by the breath of history, by the passion of the present. Timelessness and temporality are not only confronted and related, they are also merged and so interwoven that the threads are no longer distinguishable. The explosive irruption of subjectively experienced history into the culture world of the Latin Middle Ages with its epic, mythological, philosophical, and rhetorical stamp, created the constellation which determined the birth of the *Commedia;* was the answer of Dante's spirit to Dante's fate of exile. For him, his exile was but the personal corroboration of a disorder in the life of the world. *Imperium* and *Sacerdotium* were turned from their proper course, the church was debased, Italy dishonored (*Purg.,* VI, 76 ff.):

> *Ahi, serva Italia, di dolore ostello,*
> *Nave senza nocchier in gran tempesta,*
> *Non donna di provincie, ma bordello!*

> (Woe, servile Italy! abode of grief,
> Ship without steersman in a mighty storm,
> Not lady of provinces but house of whores!)

The world was out of joint. Upon Dante fell the immense task of setting it right. In the *Monarchia* he undertook to define the relationship between Empire and Papacy. In the *Commedia* the entire cosmos of history is unfolded, to be apportioned anew in the astrophysical cosmos of the structure of the world and in the metaphysical cosmos of the transcendent. Physical cosmology and the metaphysical realm of values are interconnected in the strictest correlation.

The historian of Florence, Robert Davidsohn, writes: "Of the 79 persons whom, either naming them or otherwise revealing their identity, he condemns to his Hell, 32 are Florentines, 11 former Tuscans . . . In Purgatory he saw but 4 of his fellow-citizens and 11 persons from his native region, in Paradise but 2 Florentines . . . " [50] This is an important division of the personnel summoned up by Dante but it is a small one. In that personnel I find some 180 Italians and some 90 foreigners: over 250 historical personages, preponderantly from the period which Dante's memory could compass.[51] Another 250 names come from Antiquity (including poetical figures like Ripheus as well as all the mythological personnel). There remain some 80 Biblical personages. Dante scholarship would be performing a useful task if it would re-examine this summary classification of Dante's personnel and work it out in detail. This preliminary work once

[50] Robert Davidsohn, *Geschichte von Florence*, IV, pt. 3 (1927), 190.
[51] In which connection I remind the reader of the establishment of the equivalence between 120 years and "unius hominis aetas" (*supra,* p. 253).

done, artistic and technical analysis could begin, and give us answers to the questions: How did Dante control and classify this extensive personnel? Can various stylistic phases be distinguished in this respect?

Here as elsewhere we must satisfy ourselves with merely indicating a few points of view. Dante's personality, while it towers above the centuries, adapts itself to the corporatism of the Middle Ages—though only to an extent which we shall define. The antique poets in Limbo at the beginning of the *Commedia* form a consecrated corporation (*la bella scuola* [52]). The poem ends with a corporation of the blessed—eight of the Old Covenant and seven of the New (*Par.*, XXXII). Both groups form an "elite within the elite." The canon of Old Testament worthies (Adam, Moses, Eve, Rachel, Sarah, Rebecca, Judith, Ruth, Anna) surprises us because women preponderate and the prophets are not represented. The elite of the Christian blessed may be even more surprising. Of the evangelists only John, of the apostles only Peter appear, of the fathers only Augustine, who, however, has to share a single line with the founders of orders Francis and Benedict (*Par.*, XXXII, 35). The only women in the Christian elite are Lucia and Beatrice, but Rachel sits close to them (the Virgin Mary seems to have a place outside of either group). The insertion of Lucia and Beatrice breaks the hierarchy of Christian tradition.

The division of the personnel of the *Commedia* into groups can suggest the corporative social forms of the Middle Ages only in those categories which correspond to the natural order of souls according to their value and quality. Where that order is perverted, as in Hell, another principle of grouping and arrangement must enter in: the (Aristotelian) classification of sins and sinners, which can be combined with the enumeration of exempla of some vice. But to this Dante also adds something of his own: As far as possible he assigns to each class a symbolically significant number of sinners. We pay no attention to such things, because numerical symbolism is something of which we no longer know more than the most rudimentary details.[53] Even the commentators on the *Commedia* seldom analyze its structural principles (they have enough to do with explaining facts and giving "aesthetic" appreciations). But it is clear that precisely this kind of analysis permits us a glimpse into Dante's conception of art.

The first circle of upper Hell (*Inf.*, V) contains the carnal sinners.

> 40   *E come li stornei ne portan l'ali,*
>   *Nel freddo tempo, a schiera larga e piena,*
>   *Così quel fiato li spiriti mali . . .*

[52] The "school" as a way of life is something more real, more valid, and more definite to the Middle Ages than it is to us. Aristotle heads the school of the philosophers ("il maestro di color che sanno"). In Raphael's *School of Athens* he is made to share this primacy with Plato.

[53] On numerical symbolism, see Excursus XV, *infra*.—Popular German piety preserves the "fourteen holy deliverers."—"The seven holy planets which comfort us in every need" (Hofmannsthal, *Der Turm*).

46   *E come i gru van cantando lor lai,*
        Facendo in aere di sè lunga riga,
        Così vidi venir, traendo guai,
49   *Ombre portate dalla detta briga* . . .

(And as their wings do bear the starlings on
        In the cold season, in wide and serried troop,
        Thus did that breath bear on the evil spirits . . .
And as the cranes come on singing their lays,
        In that long line they draw across the sky,
        So saw I coming on and uttering wails
Shades borne upon the storm of which I spake . . .)

A great multitude, an indeterminate number of spirits, comparable to a dense flock of birds. But from among these, seven are singled out and named:

52   *'La prima di color, di cui novelle*
        Tu vuo' saper,' mi disse quelli allotta,
        'Fu imperadrice di molte favelle.
55   *A vizio di lussuria fu si rotta,*
        Che libito fe' licito in sua legge,
        Per tòrre il biasmo in che era condotta.
58   *Ell' è Semiramis, di cui si legge*
        Che succedette a Nino e fu sua sposa;
        Tenne la terra che 'l Soldan corregge.
61   *L' altra è colei che s' ancise amorosa,*
        E ruppe la fede al cener di Sicheo:
        Poi è Cleopatràs lussuriosa.
64   *Elena vedi, per cui tanto reo*
        Tempo si volse; e vedi 'l grande Achille,
        Che per amore al fine combatteo.
67   *Vedi Paris, Tristano.' E più di mille*
        Ombre mostrommi, e nominommi, a dito
        Ch' amor di nostra vita dipartille.
70   *Poscia ch' io ebbi il mio dottore udito*
        Nomar le donne antiche e' cavalieri,
        Pietà mi giunse, e fui quasi smarrito.
73   *I' cominiciai: 'Poeta, volentieri*
        Parlerei a quei due, che 'nsieme vanno . . .'

("The first woman of those, tidings of whom
        Thou ask'st to know," he answered me in turn,
        "Empress was once of many languages.
So to the vice of luxury was she broken
        That in her law she made 'lust' read as 'must'
        To take away the blame she had incurred.

Semiramis is she, of whom we read
  That to Ninus she succeeded and was his wife.
  She held the land which now the Soldan rules.
The next is she who killed herself for love
  And broke her faith unto Sichaeus' ashes;
  After her comes luxurious Cleopatra.
See Helen there, for whom so long a time
  Of ill came round, and see the great Achilles,
  Who fought at last and to the end for love.
See Paris, Tristan." More than a thousand shades
  He showed to me and named with pointing finger,
  All shades whom love had parted from our life.
And when thus I had heard my learned teacher
  Naming the dames and knights of antique times,
  Pity came on me, and I was as lost.
And I began: "Poet, most willingly
  Would I to those two speak who go together . . .")

The transition from the indeterminately large number to the seven souls
concerning whom Dante wants to "know tidings" is not clear. Clear, however, even though surprising to the modern reader, is the choice of the
seven. Semiramis comes first because the Assyrian Empire belongs to an
age which preceded even the Trojan War (Isidore, *Et.*, V, 39, 7) and because Orosius, whose account Dante follows verbatim, had handed down
the tradition of her lustfulness. We have seen how highly Dante regards
Orosius. Dido, as a Virgilian heroine, could not be omitted. Cleopatra was
memorable because of her connection with Caesar; Helen, Achilles, and
Paris because of Homer in his medieval dress.[54] Tristan follows upon the
antique exemplary figures in the most natural manner possible, for to Dante
as to the entire Middle Ages the antique heroes were knights. All seven
could therefore be classed together as "le antiche donne e i cavalieri." They
are exemplary representatives of lust. Virgil then points out and names over
a thousand more, but Dante gives us a carefully considered[55] series of
seven. Then he asks and receives tidings of two others—which brings the
total to the highly symbolic number nine; they are Paolo and Francesca.
Contemporary Dante scholarship usually displays interest in them alone.
But they do not acquire their full significance until they are seen in conjunction with the exemplary figures. They contrast with the latter by their
modernity. More clearly than many scenes in the *Commedia*, their appearance illustrates what I have called the explosive irruption of subjectively
experienced history into the culture world of the Middle Ages with its epic,
mythological, philosophical, and rhetorical stamp.

[54] *Ilias latina* (71 ff.) is the source for the medieval conception of Achilles.
[55] This is missed in Rossi's commentary: "Sono nomi vuoto d' ogni intimità, come
suole accadere in queste enumerazioni, di cui Dante tolse la consuetudine dalla tradi-
zione letteraria del tempo." Exemplary figures cannot have the charm of "intimacy."

We find another example of the use of a "perfect" number as a principle of composition in *Inferno*, XII, 107 ff. Here there is a decad of "the violent against their neighbors," made up of Alexander, the Sicilian tyrant Dionysius, Ezzelino da Romano, Obizzo of Este, Guy of Montfort, Attila, Pyrrhus, Sextus Pompeius, Rinier of Corneto, and Rinier Pazzo. A heptad of sodomites consists of Brunetto (XV, 30), Priscian (XV, 109), Accursius (XV, 110), the bishop of Vicenza Andrea de' Mozzi (XV, 112), Guido Guerra (XVI, 38), Tegghiaio Aldobrandi (XVI, 41), and Jacopo Rusticucci (XVI, 44). To go through all the circles of hell in this fashion is superfluous.

In the *Purgatorio*, as we saw, the predominant principle of composition is the parallelism of exemplary figures. In the *Paradiso* the corporative principle preponderates again, in connection with numerical composition. In the Heaven of the Sun we have two groups of twelve, usually regarded as representatives of wisdom. The first (*Par.*, X) consists of Albertus Magnus, Thomas Aquinas, Gratian, Peter Lombard, Solomon, Dionysius the Areopagite, Orosius, Boethius, Isidore, Bede, Richard of St. Victor, Siger of Brabant. The commentators generally discuss only Solomon and Siger. Why in this group of twelve, who are enumerated by Thomas himself, did Dante include Siger, who, for Thomism, is a heretical teacher? This difficulty has frequently been discussed. In *Paradiso* XII we see a second group of twelve, in a concentric circle around the first. Its leader, spokesman, and nomenclator is St. Bonaventura, the great thinker of the Franciscans as Thomas of the Dominicans. With him appear Illuminatus and Augustine (two companions of St. Francis), Hugh of St. Victor, Peter Comestor (author of an encyclopedia of biblical history, d. 1179), Petrus Hispanus (celebrated logician, d. 1277), the prophet Nathan, the Doctor of the Church Chrysostom (d. 407), the philosopher Anselm of Canterbury (d. 1109), the grammarian Donatus (4th cent.), the encyclopedist Raban Maur (d. 856), and finally Abbot Joachim of Floris (Cistercian monastery in Calabria), the prophet of the "Eternal Gospel" (d. 1202). Joachim raises the same difficulties as Siger. His teaching was condemned by the Church and expressly disapproved by both Thomas and Bonaventura.[56] The inclusion of Siger and Joachim, then, in the groups of twelve blessed spirits raises a problem. But we must not isolate it, as is usually done. Did not the inclusion of Solomon raise a problem too? We must go still further. Have the groups of twelve, gloriously introduced as they are, anything in common, except that they are blessed spirits? Chrysostom, Boethius, Anselm, Hugh and Richard of St. Victor, Peter Lombard, Siger, Petrus Hispanus, Bonaventura, and Thomas are philosophers and theologians of high rank; independent thinkers. The unknown author of the group of writings which appeared toward the end of the fifth century and which go under the name

---

[56] E. Gilson, *Dante et la philosophie* (1939), 261. There are ingenious attempts in this book to remove the difficulties by the thesis that Dante's Thomas and Bonaventura are to be taken not as "historic" but as "poetic" figures.

of Dionysius the Areopagite (Acts 17:34) is one of the principal sources
of medieval philosophy and mysticism and thus is closely connected with
the thinkers last named. But what has the grammarian Donatus, what have
the compilers Isidore, Raban, Peter Comestor, what has the historian Orosius to do here? What the polyhistor Bede, the jurist Gratian? These names
have but one thing in common: they are representatives of the *artes* (Donatus, Isidore, Raban, Bede), of history (Orosius and Peter Comestor), and
of jurisprudence. The ten theologians and philosophers represent *sapientia,*
the seven scholars *scientia.* Dante prizes the learning of the schools as highly as he does metaphysics and theology. He enforces this in the most impressive manner when he vouches for the beatitude of late antique (Donatus, Orosius) and medieval scholars, or rather has it vouched for by such
great authorities as Thomas and Bonaventura. If either of them had been
asked whom among the blessed they would choose to make up a list of
twenty-four names of the elite, their selection would certainly have been
different, provided that they considered any such constitution of an elite
theologically permissible. But a modern student of the ecclesiastical and
philosophical history of the Middle Ages would certainly make a different
choice too. He would above all object to the exclusion of Augustine.[57] He
might also think of Ambrose and Gregory the Great, with neglect of whom
Dante reproaches the cardinals (Epistle XI, 16). But what is one to think
of the eminence accorded to the prophet Nathan, who belongs neither to
the "majors" nor the "minors"? [58] Here we must acknowledge our ignorance. Gilson, to be sure, writes: "Dante n'écrit pas d'ordinaire un nom
propre sans avoir quelque raison de le faire," [59] but in his study of Dante
and philosophy he did not have to concern himself with Nathan. From the
standpoint of literary history, however, the naming of a Nathan among the
blessed twelve is no less a difficulty than the naming of Siger and Joachim.
Perhaps a greater, because it offers nothing which might make it comprehensible.

A third group distinguished among the blessed comprises the cross of
shining spirits in the Heaven of Mars (Par., XIV, 97 ff.). The first to stand
out from this group is Dante's ancestor Cacciaguida (Par., XV, 20), who
then dominates the scene for some time (to Par., XVIII, 49). As nomenclator, he introduces (Par., XVIII, 37 ff.) the other warriors of God: Joshua,
Judas Maccabaeus, Charlemagne, Roland, William of Orange, Rinoardo,

---

[57] Augustine, as has always been observed, is systematically passed over by Dante.
The brief mention of him among the dwellers in the heavenly rose does not alter the
fact. On Dante's doctrine on the subject of the Empire, Gilson says (Dante et la
philosophie, 219, n. 2): "C'est une thèse que saint Augustin eût repoussé avec
horreur . . ."

[58] According to Robert L. John's esoteric interpretation of Dante (Dante [Vienna,
1946]) Dante was a partisan of the Order of the Temple, his message is "Temple
Gnosticism." Solomon appears among the blessed because he built the Temple.
In the biblical account Nathan is connected with Solomon, etc.

[59] Dante et la philosophie, 261.

Godfrey of Bouillon, Robert Guiscard. With Cacciaguida they make up an ennead.[60]

In the *Paradiso* Dante has connected the groups of related spirits not only by symbolic numbers but also by forms depicted in light. After the concentric circles he has a cross, and after that the eagle of the six just rulers in the Heaven of Jupiter (XX, 37 ff.): David, Trajan, Hezekiah, Constantine, William II of Sicily, Ripheus. Here there was no settled tradition to be followed. Dante could make up the elect corporations as he pleased.

If one reviews the persons of the *Paradiso*, they present themselves as constituting a personal canon. We are expected to see the learning and philosophy of the Christian tradition embodied in the two groups of twelve, the heroic warriors of God in the cross, the model monarchs in the eagle. But still more is demanded of us.

6. *Myth and Prophecy*

We have seen (p. 224) that Dante claims an epistemological function for his poetry and thus places himself in opposition to Scholastic philosophy. We reached this conclusion simply by analyzing a passage in the epistle to Can Grande. Our conclusion is confirmed by Gilson's study of Dante's relation to philosophy. That study finally rid us of the mistaken idea that Dante was a Thomist. In the canon of the blessed intellectuals in the Heaven of the Sun we found an independent and autocratic treatment of the tradition. But even this is far outdone by the singular "apparatus of salvation" of the *Commedia*. Dante's guides on his journey through the otherworld are successively Virgil, Beatrice, and St. Bernard. On this Gilson well says: "L'ordonnance générale du poème requiert que la charité s'ajoute à la foi, et la couronne, come la foi s'ajoute à la raison et l'illumine." [61] He appears, then, to agree with the currently accepted view which sees reason incarnated in Virgil, faith in Beatrice, and love in Bernard. For Gilson these are "des faits massivement évidents."

The most "massive" of these facts is certainly the function of Beatrice— if Beatrice was a Florentine woman who died in 1290 at the age of twenty-five. That a poet should have a religious awakening and be purified through his beloved is a psychological experience which can occur in a thousand gradations. It is reflected in Goethe's *Marienbader Elegie* and in the conclusion of *Faust*. Guido Guinizelli (d. 1276) had made the exaltation of the beloved to an angel of paradise a topos of Italian lyric. To choose as guide in a poetic vision of the otherworld a loved woman who has been thus exalted is still within the bounds of Christian philosophy and faith. But Dante goes much further than this. He gives Beatrice a place in the objec-

---

[60] The basis of this is the schema of the "Neuf preux" (three pagans, three Jews, three Christians) who in England are called "The Nine Worthies" (Caxton, preface to *Morte d'Arthur*; Shakespeare, *Love's Labour's Lost*, V, 2).

[61] *Dante et la philosophie*, 238.

tive process of salvation. Her function is thought of as not only for himself but also for all believers. Thus, on his own authority, he introduces into the Christian revelation an element which disrupts the doctrine of the church. This is either heresy—or myth.

The most eminent Dante scholars and specialists in Florentine history are agreed that Dante's Beatrice was the daughter of the banker Folco Portinari. But the earliest commentaries [62] know nothing of this. Graziuolo de' Bambaglioli, state secretary of Bologna, in his commentary (1324) on *Inferno*, II, 70:

I' son Beatrice che ti faccio andare

says only "ipsa domina erat anima generose domine Beatrice condam domini . . ." ("this lady was the soul of the noble lady Beatrice, daughter of the late . . ."). Then a blank. The author, then, could learn nothing of Beatrice's father. Iacopo della Lana (1328) has nothing to say about Beatrice. The author of the *Ottimo Commento* (*ca.* 1334) asked Dante about Beatrice on several occasions, but learned nothing. The anonymous author of the glosses (before 1337) knows no more. Boccaccio is the first to make the identification, and this was in the commentary which he wrote in 1373–74: In October 1373 he had been called to Florence to lecture publicly on the *Commedia*.[63] The information, then, appears for the first time more than eighty years after the hypothetical death of Beatrice. Boccaccio claims to have learned it from a "trustworthy person" who was closely related to Beatrice. Searching for this trustworthy lady, Zingarelli came upon Boccaccio's stepmother, Margherita dei Mardoli. Her mother, Monna Lippa (d. 1340), was the daughter of a cousin of Folco Portinari's and hence second cousin to Beatrice. Did Boccaccio know the old lady? It could only have been in the year before her death; Boccaccio *is supposed* to have lived in his father's house during 1339. On that occasion he *could*—Zingarelli surmises [64]—have secured the information. How remarkable that he kept this interesting piece of biography to himself for thirty-five years thereafter! How remarkable that the commentators mentioned above could learn nothing! To be sure, Pietro di Dante also gives the information, but not until the third redaction of his commentary, which is contemporary with Boccaccio's *Vita* and can have been derived from it. The identification of Dante's Beatrice with the daughter of Folco Portinari, who died in 1289, is,

[62] On these cf. N. Sapegno, *Il Trecento* (1934), 115 ff.

[63] Boccaccio's novelistic *Vita di Dante* would also seem to go back to this period of teaching (*Il Trecento*, 386), at least in the version before us.

[64] Michele Barbi (*Problemi di Critica dantesca*, II, 419 [1941]) speaks of a "probability."—But this probability is exceedingly small, for the chronology of Boccaccio's life between 1330 and 1340 is much debated and depends upon deciphering an astronomical indication of time in the *Filocolo*. The majority of critics hold that Boccaccio did not return to Florence before the beginning or the end of 1340, (*Il Trecento*, 280). So also Enrico Burich in his valuable study "Boccaccio und Dante" (*Deutsches Dante-Jahrbuch*, XXIII [1941], 36).

then, first maintained fifty years after Dante's death and is unknown to Dante's contemporaries, as well as to the four commentators who wrote between 1324 and 1337. This is very remarkable and justifies us in doubting Boccaccio's information. But above all—if Boccaccio's step-grandmother had been able to identify Dante's Beatrice with the daughter of Folco Portinari in 1339, she would have talked about it to other people too in the course of her long life. It would have been known in Florence. Dante's contemporaries recognized that he was a great poet. The *Commedia* was circulated in numerous copies, versified abridgments were made of it, several commentaries were written on it in the first two decades after Dante's death. Interest in Dante, then, was widespread—and yet no one was able to produce any information about Beatrice.

But Boccaccio's testimony is also suspect for another reason. His exposition of Dante involved him in a polemic. An opponent whose name has not survived reproached him with having bared the mysteries of poetry to the uninitiate. Boccaccio justified himself in four sonnets [65] (Nos. 122–125 in A. F. Massèra's critical edition [Bologna, 1914]). In the last sonnet he boasts that he has merely led the ungrateful vulgar astray (p. 174):

> *Io ò messo in galea senza biscotto*
> *L' ingrato vulgo, et senza alcun piloto*
> *Lasciato l' ò in mar a lui non noto,*
> *Benchè sen creda esser maestro et dotto . . .*[66]

Are Boccaccio's allegations supported by documents? Zingarelli[67] remarks on Boccaccio's testimony that the documents confirm it to the extent that documents can do so. They frequently mention Folco Portinari. In his will, drawn up in 1288, six daughters are remembered; among them Madonna Bice appears as the wife of Simone de' Bardi. That is all. We know the date neither of the birth nor death of Beatrice Portinari. What current Dante literature is able to say on the subject is drawn entirely from the *Vita nuova*, hence from a conscious mystification. If one attempts to grasp its intellectual content, one feels that one has been transported into a maze. The entire little book is devoted to demonstrating a set of theses. The most important of these, strange as it may seem to us, is the following (§ 29): "The number three is the root of the number nine, because it gives nine of itself without any other number, as we manifestly see that three times three makes nine. Consequently, if the three is by itself the maker of the nine, and likewise the maker of miracles is by Himself three, namely Father, Son, and Holy Ghost, which are three and one, so was this lady

[65] According to D. Guerri, *Il Commento del Boccaccio* (1926), 21, the sonnets are not genuine. The contrary is maintained by Branca in his edition of the *Rime* (Bari, 1929), 374.

[66] "I put the ungrateful vulgar in a ship without biscuit, and left them without any pilot on a sea that they know not, although they think themselves masters and men of learning."

[67] N. Zingarelli, *La vita, i tempi e le opere di Dante* [2] (1931), 298.

accompanied by the number nine, to make it understood that she was a nine, that is, a miracle, whose root is solely the wondrous Trinity. Perhaps some more subtle person would see a more subtle reason for this; but this is the reason which I see for it and the one which pleases me best." And how is it proven that Beatrice was a nine? First proof (§ 6): Dante wrote a poem on the sixty most beautiful ladies in Florence [68] (which unfortunately he does not give us). And "it befell in wondrous wise that my lady's name would not suffer itself to stand in any place but in the ninth." The second proof is more complicated. It requires the assistance of the Arabic and Syrian eras and of astrology (§ 29): "I say that according to the use of Arabia her most noble soul departed hence in the first hour of the ninth day of the month; and according to the use of Syria she departed in the ninth month of the year, because the first month there is Tismin, which for us is October. And according to our use she departed in that year of our era (that is, in the year of the Lord) in which the perfect number was nine times made full in that century in which she was placed in this world; and she was of the Christians of the thirteenth century. Why this number was so nearly allied to her, this might be the reason thereof: Since according to Ptolemy and according to Christian truth, the heavens which move are nine, and according to the common astrological opinion the said heavens work here below according to their position in respect to one another, therefore that number was allied to her, to make it understood that at her conception all the nine moving heavens stood in the most perfect relation to one another." Beatrice must, then, have died in 1290 if the contention that she was a nine is true. Dante scholars regard this date as a historical fact—which is questionable. The only thing of which we can be sure is that the nine is a "soteriological numerical riddle." Here Dante is within a widespread antique and medieval tradition.[69] The nine of the *Vita nuova* is to be regarded in the same way as the 515 of the *Commedia* (*Purg.*, XXXIII, 43). Dante scholarship appears to pay no attention to this. Barbi falls back upon the position that certain questions are not of importance for an understanding of what "counts most" in Dante's work (which is "the miracle of poetry and ideality");[70] hence it is better not to discuss them at all. There is a great deal to be said for such restraint. It is indicated as a means of self-defence against the dilettante solvers of riddles. And the deciphering of these hieroglyphics is irrelevant to an appreciation and comprehension of Dante's poetry. But the fact that, beginning with the *Vita nuova*, Dante interspersed his works with references to an esoteric meaning, is to be accepted. The numerical and alphabetical mysticism remains. This is philologically established—not least for Beatrice, who was a nine. To overlook it

[68] A reference to it in the sonnet *Guido i' vorrei*, l. 10. According to Contini (p. 42), however, this line cannot be applied to Beatrice.
[69] Franz Dornseiff, *Das Alphabet in Mystik und Magie* [2] (1925). On numerical mysticism (gematria), 91 ff.; on numerical riddles, 106 ff.
[70] Michele Barbi, *Con Dante e i suoi interpreti* (1941), 52.

is impossible. This must be objected to all those who insist upon the insufficiently attested historical Beatrice—including Robert Davidsohn who, for his part, holds it "inadmissible to doubt that she lived and no less so to doubt that she was the daughter of the banker Folco Portinari." He did not succeed in entirely convincing Barbi, who in 1931 stated that, though he inclined toward the identification, he regarded the problem as a matter of mere curiosity; for the study of Dante it was enough to know that Beatrice was a real person.[71] We must, then, distinguish two theses which affirm the historical Beatrice: identification (a) with Beatrice Portinari; (b) with an unknown Florentine woman. On the basis of the tradition I believe that the first thesis must be eliminated.

There is no doubt that some of the *Rime* are dedicated to a real Beatrice, for example *Lo doloroso amor* (Contini, No. 21), where Beatrice is named in line 14. Presumably also the canzone *E' m' incresce di me* (Contini, No. 20). But here Beatrice has characteristics which do not accord with the legendary style of the *Vita nuova*, for which reason the poem is not included in it. The exclusion of this canzone from the *Vita nuova*, then, together with *Lo doloroso amor*, demonstrates two things: Dante paid homage to a Florentine woman, whom he called Beatrice; later he stylized her into the myth of the Lady Nine. We know that Dante performed this process of stylizing a "real" woman into a myth, symbol, or allegory once again when he transformed the *donna gentile* of the *Vita nuova* into the Lady Philosophy of the *Convivio*. Furthermore there are a number of women in the *Commedia* who are obviously to be taken allegorically—for example Lucia, Lia (*Purg.*, XXVII, 101), Matelda (*Purg.*, XXVIII, 37 ff.).

At the beginning of the *Commedia* Beatrice is addressed by Virgil: "O lady of virtue, through whom alone the race of man excels all that is within the heaven which has the smallest circles" (*Inf.*, II, 76 ff.)—namely, the heaven of the Moon. Through Beatrice alone, mankind surpasses everything earthly. Whatever this may mean: Beatrice has a metaphysical dignity for all men—Beatrice alone. She is addressed by Lucia as "true praise of God" (*Inf.*, II, 103). Neither of these things can be said of the soul of a dead Florentine woman. Beatrice is sent by Lucia, Lucia by a *donna gentile* of heaven whose throne is yet higher (usually identified with Mary, but not named). Why the Syracusan martyr Lucia? She is supposed to be of special efficacy against eye trouble, and Dante had sometimes strained his eyes by overstudy (*Conv.*, III, 9, 15), "presumably he therefore had a special devotion to St. Lucia"—thus Rossi, after many others. But Dante says: "Lucia, nimica di ciascun crudele" (*Inf.*, II, 100). Now this obviously has nothing to do with eye trouble. So Lucia is interpreted as "illuminating grace" (first by Buti at the end of the fourteenth century) or as the personification of hope, etc. But if Beatrice is more than and different from the immortalized woman of Florence, if Lucia is more than and different from an almost unknown saint of the Breviary, if both intervene in the action

[71] *Studi danteschi,* XV, 116 n.

at the bidding of a higher who remains unnamed—then the three heavenly ladies must be understood as parts of a supernatural dispensation. Pietrobono attempts this: The liberation of mankind from the she-wolf requires a process of redemption in which the *tre donne benedette* act together as did the three persons of the Trinity in the "first" redemption. The explanation is unsatisfactory in this form. But it is in the right direction: Beatrice can be understood only as a function within a theological system. To this system belong the three beasts which block Dante's road and which have always been interpreted as three vices. These beasts draw the Veltro after them, and later the *Cinquecento cinque e dieci*. With this the theological system becomes a prophetic system. No amount of ingenuity has yet succeeded in unraveling it. But it is there. No one should deny it. It was Dante's central message. It concerns a prophecy whose fulfilment he expected in the immediate future. When he died at fifty-six, his certainty was presumably still unshaken. Had he reached the "perfect" age of eighty-one (*Conv.*, IV, 24, 6), he would perhaps have been obliged to admit the collapse of his historical construction. But he could not retract his work. His imperious spirit believed that it could command even the future. A future, however, which could envisage only fourteenth-century Italy.

Even if we could interpret his prophecy, that would give it no meaning for us. What Dante hid, Dante scholarship need not now unriddle. But it must take seriously the fact that Dante believed that he had an apocalyptic mission. This must be taken into consideration in interpreting him. Hence the question of Beatrice is not mere idle curiosity. Dante's system is built up in the first two cantos of the *Inferno*, it supports the entire *Commedia*. Beatrice can be seen only within it. The Lady Nine has become a cosmic power which emanates from two superior powers. A hierarchy of celestial powers which intervene in the process of history—this concept is manifestly related to Gnosticism: as an intellectual construction, a schema of intellectual contemplation, if perhaps not in origin.[72] Such constructions can and must be pointed out. We do not know what Dante meant by Lucia. The only proper procedure for the commentator, then, is to admit that we do not know and to say that neither the ophthalmological explanation nor the allegorical interpretations are satisfactory. Exegesis is also bound to leave their full weight to all the passages at the end of the *Purgatorio* and in the *Paradiso* which are opposed to the identification of Beatrice with the daughter of the banker Portinari. Beatrice is a myth created by Dante.

The transformation of experience into myth was Dante's basic attitude in the *Rime* and in the *Vita nuova*; an attitude given as an elemental phenomenon of his personality; materialized in creations which are consummated in a series of discrete experiments. They burst out from Dante— "prorumpunt ad summa summe canenda." These outbursts often have

---

[72] I may nevertheless be allowed to remind the reader that twelfth-century Platonism contains emanatistic concepts. The *Noys* of Bernard Silvestris is an emanation of God and from it further powers emanate.

something ruthless about them. Ruthlessness is itself the theme in the "stone" canzoni. In the *Vita nuova* it assumes the character of mystification. In *De vulgari eloquentia* it narrows a spiral of demands on language and poetry to the limit of the possible. In the *Commedia* it challenges—and conquers!—the universe: the entire historical cosmos (foreshadowed in the catchword Orosius), the entire astral cosmos, the entire cosmos of salvation. The mediatrix of this "metacosmos" is the beatifying female power—"luce e gloria della gente umana" (*Purg.*, XXXIII, 115). This Beatrice is not the recovered love of youth. She is the highest salvation in the form of a woman—an emanation of God. For no other reason can she appear without blasphemy in a triumph in which Christ himself has a place.

7. Dante and the Middle Ages

Those who wish to see Dante's place in the transition from the Middle Ages to the Renaissance from the point of view of universal history may be referred to the medallion, cast as it were in bronze, which we owe to Alfred Weber.[73] Our considerations must remain within the more modest framework of literary history.

On October 20, 1828, Goethe said to Eckermann: "Dante appears great to us, but he had a culture of centuries behind him." Carlyle heard in Dante the voice of "ten silent centuries." What Goethe and Carlyle saw, we can designate precisely in historical terms: It is the cultural cosmos of the Latin Middle Ages, and of Antiquity seen through the eyes of the Middle Ages. The clash between Dante's philosophically transformed imperial idea, which rises high above any Ghibellinism, and the new, capitalistic, highly organized city-state of Florence, is the fountainhead of Dante's political passion. From this conflict springs his consciousness of a world-historical mission, which he clothed in the form of a prophecy concealed in symbols. The prophecy could not but apply to both Church and state: To Dante as to the entire Middle Ages both universal powers were ordained by God. But they were corrupt and required reform. The Church must renounce power and the thirst for power. It must become a church of the spirit. The thirteenth-century mendicant orders had failed in their work of reform, were themselves degenerate. Another, one more powerful, would and must come: the hound (*veltro*[74]). He would drive the she-wolf back into hell. Dante puts this prophecy into Virgil's mouth at the beginning of the *Inferno* (1, 101). At the end of the *Purgatorio* (33, 37 ff.) it is resumed by Beatrice. Theologico-political prophecy is a feature which constantly recurs in the twelfth- and thirteenth-century picture.[75] But in Dante it is given an intellectual substructure, and the power of his poetic vision, the

---

[73] Alfred Weber, *Das Tragische und die Geschichte* (1942), 26 f. Idem, *Kulturgeschichte als Kultursoziologie* (1935), 273.

[74] Whether the *Veltro* and the DXV are the same is a matter of argument.

[75] Zingarelli (864 ff.) gives references.

passion of his denunciation, the unbroken articulation and concatenation of the one hundred cantos raise it to a fortissimo. It is a leaven which Dante casts into the tradition of the medieval West. The leaven penetrates the coagulated mass to its most remote regions and organizes it into a realm of new forms. It is the projection of Dante's personality on "the book and school of the ages" (George)—on the total literary tradition. Dante's mind and soul, his architectonic thinking and his glowing heart, the tension of his will, which demanded stupendous efforts of itself, which stubbornly forced itself to express the inexpressible—these are the powers which conjured "ten silent centuries" into form. A single man, a solitary man, sets himself face to face with an entire millennium and transforms that historical world. Love, order, salvation are the foci of his inner vision—spheres of light in which immense tensions are collected. They dart together, circle one another, become constellations, figures. They must be expanded into shapes, choirs, chains of spirits, laws, prophecies. The whole plenitude of his inner vision must be applied to the whole extent of the world, to all the depths and heights of the world above. The most immense frame of references is required. From every point of his mythically and prophetically amplified experience connections run to every point of the given matter. They are forged and riveted in material as hard as diamonds. A structure of language and thought is created—comprehensive, with many layers of meaning, and as inalterable as the cosmos. Its medium is terza rima: a metrical form which combines the principle of continuous progressive concatenation with ineluctable discipline. Goal and accomplishment of the whole: perfect superposition of Dante's within upon the cosmic without, and mutual interpenetration of the two; congruence of soul and world.

The world drama of the Latin Middle Ages is played for the last time in the *Commedia*—but transposed into a modern language, reflected in a soul which ranks with Michelangelo's and Shakespeare's. The Middle Ages is thereby transcended—but also, of course, the periodization of a short-sighted science of history. Its periods will be long forgotten when Dante is still admired.

Before Dante scholarship lies the great task of methodically studying Dante's relation to the Latin Middle Ages, which has here been made apparent.

18

Epilogue

1. *Retrospect*

W E HAVE an arduous journey behind us and now we may relax. Looking back, we can see the stages of our road. How have we proceeded? "The strict method," says Novalis, "is merely for study, and should not be printed; one should write for the public only in a free, unconstrained style, and only have the strict demonstrations, the systematic working out, at hand. One must not write uncertainly, etc., fearfully, etc., or confusedly or roundabout the subject, but decisively, clearly, firmly, with apodictic, tacit hypothesis. A man who knows his own mind also makes a wholesome and decisive and lasting impression." Novalis knows that this demand can be realized only in an ideal world: "Those will be wonderful days when no one will read anything but beautiful compositions, literary works of art. All other books are means and are forgotten when they cease to be serviceable means, a thing which such books cannot remain for long."

A scientific presentation cannot avoid "strict demonstration." Hence, regarded as literary composition, it is a problem which has only an approximate solution (Principle 10).* In the historical sciences demonstration must rest upon witnesses, in philology upon texts. Fresh dilemma! If the writer gives too many examples, his book becomes unreadable; if he gives too few, he weakens its demonstrative force. As Louis Havet puts it: "On trouvera l'ouvrage un peu gros; j'estime qu'il gagnerait à être grossi encore. La certitude de la doctrine, en effet, dépend de la constance des phénomènes; sa justesse et sa précision, de leur variété." [1] In practice, the dilemma reduces itself to a question of proportion, hence to an aesthetic norm. I have therefore tried to give in the text only as many examples as were necessary to confirm the argument. Anything further I have relegated to the footnotes below the text [2] or to the Excursuses.

[* See "Guiding Principles," at the beginning of this book.]
[1] L. Havet, *Manuel de Critique verbale* (1911), § 2.
[2] The modern habit of relegating them to the end of the book is a bad one. In a book review by Bonamy Dobrée I read: "One is thankful to say that the notes, conveniently full, but never distended, are in the right place, that is at the bottom of the page" (*The Spectator* [Jan. 11, 1935]).

The arrangement of the presentation and the succession of the chapters are such as to result in a step-by-step progress and a spiral ascent. The first chapters present facts whose significance is illuminated later. A first acquaintance with the medieval school *auctores* (pp. 48 ff.) prepares for an understanding of the medieval canon (pp. 260 ff.); the section on sentences and exempla (pp. 57 ff.) is a presupposition for the discussions of exemplary figures in Bernard Silvestris (pp. 108 ff.), Alan (pp. 117 ff.), Dante (pp. 362 ff.), etc. The structure is determined not by logical order but by thematic continuity. The interweaving of threads, the reappearance of persons and motifs in different designs, reflects their concatenated historical relations.

This concatenation first emerged dimly—a possibility intimated but not demonstrable. In the course of years and decades its outlines became clear, its content articulated. It was now possible to expose it in a test case (Chapter 13). It became palpable. But I wished it to be palpably evident. There is evidence in the historical sciences too. It is the evidence of intellectual perception. What is manifested in perception can no longer be overlooked. What we have gained is a new perception of the inner connections of European literature.

The studies out of which this book grew began with definitely circumscribed individual problems which I picked up in the course of my reading. The topos "aged youth," for example, I found in Gregory, applied to St. Benedict.[3] It was striking, but it had struck no one.[4] It could be traced back to Silius Italicus and the younger Pliny and forward to Góngora. Was it unique? Or might other topoi of like durability be tracked down? The task of a historical topics (p. 82) was thus prescribed. This led to antique rhetoric (Chapter 4). It was necessary to analyze it. For the possibility had to be taken into account that it might open up yet other regions of medieval literature. Its relation to poetry had to be cleared up (Chapter 8). Could a continuity from the Empire to the seventeenth century be demonstrated here too? The histories of literature had nothing to say on the subject; they did not ask themselves such questions. No preliminary studies had been made. I had to undertake them myself (Principle 4). I soon became convinced that the current dicta on the literatures of the Middle Ages needed to be revised from the ground up. There was a Latin tradition which was ignored by "modern philology." That discipline had remained at a standstill. Its self-complacent autarchy was obsolete. It did not suffice for Dante, for Gracián, for Diderot . . . "Literaturwissenschaft" was equally a failure—in both its variants, the "art-historical" and the "geistesgeschichtliche." The irresponsibly interpretative "Geistesgeschichte" which took the place of philology in Germany after the first World War was a symptom

---

[3] ZRPh, LVIII (1938), 143.

[4] In the Benedict Festschrift issued by the Abbey of St. Ottilien ([1947], 149) Gregory's phrase "cor gerens senile" is referred to as "not particularly appealing."

of decadence in scholarship,[5] a fact which I sadly corroborated in an excursion into a favorite field of Germanistics, the "chivalric system of the virtues" (Excursus XVIII, *infra*).

Perhaps this decadence cannot be halted. Since the sixteenth century classical philology has stood on firm ground. It exhibits many stars of the first magnitude; and even the lesser stars have their function in a constellation. In this discipline the emendation, restoration, and interpretation of texts are rigorous skills. Without sound grammatical training and extensive reading nothing can be accomplished. Germanic studies, Romance studies, English studies are without an old tradition. Hence they are easy prey for the fashions and aberrations of the "Zeitgeist." They could improve this situation only if they would resolve to go to school to the older philology. But to do that, one must learn Greek and Latin—a demand which no sensible man would even dare to express. The founders of modern philology had, to be sure, been schooled in the ancient languages. They created a tradition of rigorous scholarship. It may be useless, but it is a duty, to plead for this legacy of the great teachers. For me, it goes back to Gustav Gröber, whose pupil I was forty years ago. One of the "guiding principles" of this book is drawn from him.

One of the tasks of the philologist is observation (*observatio* in the methodologic vocabulary of classical philology). To that end one must, of course, read a great deal (Principle 3) and sharpen one's eye for "significant facts" (Bergson). One encounters a phenomenon which appears to mean little or nothing. If it recurs constantly, it has a definite function. One pins it down terminologically—and perhaps finds that one has discovered a "pleasance" (pp. 195 ff.), which reveals an "ideal landscape." There are phenomena which appear to occur but once. It is a great temptation to leave them alone. It would cost an expenditure of energy to hit upon something comparable. Perhaps one would have to read through the Latin poets of the Carolingian period for the fifth or sixth time. Here the Sibyl's saying (*Aeneid*, VI, 129) applies: "Hoc opus, hic labor est." If one does not lose courage, perhaps years later[6] one finds the "missing link," for example a poem by Walafrid (p. 290).

When we have isolated and named a literary phenomenon, we have established one fact. At that one point we have penetrated the concrete structure of the matter of literature. We have performed an analysis. If we get at a few dozen or a few hundred such facts, a system of points is established. They can be connected by lines; and this produces figures. If we study and associate these, we arrive at a comprehensive picture. That is what Aby Warburg meant by the sentence quoted earlier: "God is in detail." We can put it: analysis leads to synthesis. Or: the synthesis issues from the analysis; and only a synthesis thus brought into existence is legiti-

---

[5] I refer to my criticism of "Literarästhetik des europäischen Mittelalters" by H. H. Glunz (ZRPh, LVIII [1938], 1–50).

[6] Cf. *Modern Philology*, XXXVIII (1941), 331.

mate. Bergson defines analysis as "la capacité de pénétrer à l'intérieur d'un fait qu'on devine significatif." "Penetration" is also a basic concept in Ranke's historical method. But what facts are "significant"? That one must "divine," says Bergson. He does not elucidate this point further. Let us employ a comparison. The dowser discovers the veins of gold with his rod. The "significant facts" are the lodes in the rock. They lie hidden in the object and are "divined"—more properly, "tracked down"—by the seeker's dowsing-rod. This consists in a psychological function: a highly differentiated faculty of receptivity which "responds" to the significant. If the faculty is present potentially, it can be made actual. It can be awakened, used, guided. But it can neither be taught nor transferred. Analysis employs various methods according to the matter to be dealt with. If it is directed upon literature it is called philology. It alone penetrates into the heart of this matter. There is no other method of exploring literature. The controversies over methods in the last decades and the windmill battle against so-called "Positivism" are liquidated by this fact. They merely show that there was a wish to evade philology—on grounds which we will not discuss. To be sure, there are good and bad musicians—and philologists. But it is generally possible to learn something even from the bad ones.

Through our analysis of texts we were led to understand that the Middle Ages must be seen in its continuity not only with Antiquity but also with the Modern period. Only thus did we gain an "intelligible field of study" (Toynbee). But that field was—European literature.

2. The Beginnings of the Vernacular Literatures

French literature begins in the eleventh century with religious narrative poems. The pearl among them, the *Song of St. Alexis* (*ca.* 1050), is the well-considered composition of a scholarly poet who knew the devices of rhetoric and had read Virgil.[7] A new genre, the national heroic epic,[8] next appeared, with its splendid beginning in the *Song of Roland* (*ca.* 1100). Roland and Oliver are the names of two pairs of brothers, who appear in documents between 1090 and 1100. A Song of Roland must, then, have been in existence when they were born (between 1050 and 1070?). It cannot have been the one that has come down to us, because the latter is much later linguistically than the *Alexis*. Our *Roland* exhibits stylistic elements which show a knowledge of Virgil, of late antique Virgilian interpretation, and of medieval clerical education. Numerous Guillaume epics appear after 1150. About the same time, a new genre appears: the courtly romance in verse. Its subjects are antique (after Virgil, Statius, Dictys, Dares) and Celtic. Its subtle rhetorical technique and sophisticated casuistry of love have gone to school to Ovid. The courtly romance shows the

---

[7] ZRPh, LVI (1936), 113 ff.

[8] Further discussion in my essays "Über die altfranzösische Epik" (ZRPh, LXIV [1944], 233–320; RF, LXI [1948], 4; *ibid.*, LXII [1950]).

influx of the Latin Renaissance of the twelfth century into French poetry. Allegorico-didactic poetry also draws upon Latin learning. One of the principal sources of the second part of the *Romance of the Rose* (*ca.* 1275) is Alan's *Planctus Naturae.*

The rich development of French poetry in the eleventh, twelfth, and thirteenth centuries, then, stands in close relationship to the contemporary Latin poetry and poetics which flourished in France and in French England. Latin culture and poetry precede, French follows. Latin loosed the tongue of French. Because France was the pillar of *studium*; because the *artes*, with grammar and rhetoric in the lead, had their headquarters there —that is why the flower of vernacular poetry blooms first in France.

It is the merit of Edmond Faral that he was the first to recognize the influence of medieval poetics and rhetoric upon Old French poetry.[9] Most of the vernacular poets were people of education. They had learned the *artes* and the *auctores* at the twelfth-century cathedral schools. The attendance was so great that there were not enough ecclesiastical positions for the clerks who had taken their degrees. Thus an oversupply of intellectuals developed. It was for the most part absorbed by the feudal courts of France and England.[10] The feudal lords had long since replaced owner-management economy by a system of imposts. "From the knight upwards," says Alfred Weber, "to the highest feudal lords, the feudal pyramid . . . is dis-economized. The feudal structure changes into a system of social strata which become available for noneconomic, for intellectual interests. The knights especially become an extensive class which, during the periods when it is not occupied with war and feuds, is obliged to look for some intellectual activity." [11] The courtly society of France wants to be entertained, just as the Ionians did in the days of Homer. The heroic epics and romances of chivalry satisfy this demand.[12] Their authors are unbeneficed clerics. They bring their hearers the tales of Troy, Thebes, and Rome, as well as works of Ovid; [13] these they furnish with all the ornamental devices of rhetoric, to which they also cling for modern material, such as the Celtic. These poets know of the "transference of learning" (*translatio studii*) from Athens to Rome, from Rome to France. At the beginning of his *Cligés*—in the sixties of the twelfth century—Chrétien de Troyes writes (ll. 27 ff.):

> *Par les livres que nous avons*
> *Les fez des anciiens savons*
> *Et del siecle qui fu jadis.*
> *Ce nos ont nostre livre apris,*

[9] Edmond Faral, *Les Jongleurs en France au moyen âge* (1910).
[10] Faral in Bédier-Hazard, *Histoire de la littérature française illustrée,* I (1923), 3 f. and 15 f.
[11] Alfred Weber, *Kulturgeschichte als Kultursoziologie* (1935), 259.
[12] Excursus X, *infra.*
[13] Chrétien de Troyes did so in his lost early poems.

Que Grece ot de chevalerie
Le premier los et de clergie.
Puis vint chevalerie a Rome
Et de la clergie la some,
Qui or est en France venue.
Deus doint qu'ele i soit retenue
Et que li leus li abelisse
Tant que ja mes de France n'isse.

That is: "Through the books which we have, we know the deeds of the ancients and of times long passed. Our books have taught us that Greece had the first fame of chivalry and learning. Then came chivalry to Rome, and the sum of learning, which now is come to France. God grant that it remain there, and that it find the place so pleasant that it will never depart from France." Gilson wished to see an expression of "medieval Humanism" in these lines.[14] But he did not consider how they go on:

L'enor qui s'i est arestee,
Deus l'avoit as autres prestee:
Car de Grejois ne de Romains
Ne dit an mes ne plus ne mains;
D'aus est la parole remese
Et estainte la vive brese.

"The honor which has taken up its abode here [in France], God had but lent to the others: for of the Greeks and the Romans no one any longer says either much or little; their word has ceased, their bright flame is put out." This is the reverse of a humanistic creed. But it perfectly fits the period of change around 1170. If even the Latin *moderni* of the time consciously matched themselves with the ancients—how much more might a vernacular poet do so! There is a Latin Humanism in twelfth-century France, and we have come to know it. But the threads become tangled again when one reads it into Chrétien.

Spain had hardly any share in the Latin Renaissance of the twelfth century. The Islamic culture of her south was far superior to that of her Christian north. Only in the northeast, in Navarre and above all in Catalonia, do we find, from the eleventh century, nurseries of a Latin culture which radiates from France. The most important of them is the monastery of Santa Maria de Ripoll, stronghold of Cluniac reform. There a school of Latin poets flourishes, to whom we owe love songs and panegyric laments for the dead. Among these is a poem on the Cid, of which unfortunately only the first stanzas are extant, so that it is impossible to determine whether it was written before or after his death. In any case it is the earliest poem on the Cid. The earliest prose record of him is the *Historia Roderici* (*ca.* 1110). The Spanish epic of the Cid, then, takes up material which

[14] E. Gilson, *Les Idées et les Lettres* (1932), 184.

had already been treated in Latin. It fashions it after the model of the French epic, and employs stylistic clichés which first appear in France between 1150 and 1170. Hence it can hardly have been composed before 1180. Spanish literature, then, begins more than a century later than French.[14a] The reason is obvious: In Spain the stimulus of a Latin intellectual flowering was lacking. Not until the thirteenth century does scholarly culture push its way across the Pyrenees. The poets of the period contrast Latin rhythms and Latin rhetoric as "learned technique" ("mester de clerecía") or "new skill" ("nueva maestría") with "minstrel technique" ("mester de joglaría"). Berceo boasts: "We write only what we have read" ("al non escribamos sin non lo que leemos"). The subjects are preponderantly of ecclesiastical or antique origin (the saga of Alexander, the romance of Apollonius). Then about 1330 Juan Ruiz makes a bold innovation with his *Libro de buen amor*. He imports Ovid's eroticism and its medieval derivatives. To a free rendition of the *Ars amandi* (which he read in the original) he added a recasting of the extremely popular medieval comedy *Pamphilus de amore*, which in turn goes back to an elegy of Ovid's (*Amores*, I, 8). In his elegy Ovid describes a bawd in talkative pursuit of her trade. Juan Ruiz followed the *Pamphilus* almost word for word, only introducing Spanish names of persons and places. This gave local color and contemporaneity. Through him, the bawd Trotaconventos ("convent trotter"—but we hear nothing of convents) became a typical figure of Spanish poetry. She appears as Celestina in F. de Rojas' masterpiece of the same name (1499), as Gerarda in Lope de Vega's *Dorotea* (1632). There are critics who rank the *Libro de buen amor*, the *Celestina*, and *Don Quixote* together as the three peaks of Spanish literature.[15] It is usually cited as one of the principal testimonies to the "realism" which is supposed to be characteristic of Spanish literature. Dámaso Alonso has trenchantly criticized this view.[16] His new interpretation of the spirit of Spanish poetry gains fresh support, I think, from the connections here discussed.[17]

[14a] Spanish refrains have recently been discovered in Arabic and Hebrew poems of the eleventh century and have given rise in some quarters to the conclusion that Spanish lyric poetry is about a century older than has hitherto been believed. Concerning the historical evaluation of this find, the last word has not yet been said. E. García Gómez provides a summary of the research in the journal *Clavileño* (May, 1950).

[15] Cejador in his edition of the *Libro de buen amor*.

[16] In *Cruz y Raya*, Oct. 15, 1933.—As early as 1927 Ortega said that Menéndez Pidal's view of history had two weak points: "The first is the wholly arbitrary belief that the essential artistic characteristic of Spain is realism. With this is bound up the equally arbitrary conviction that realism is the highest form of art. The second unsubstantiated proposition is overvaluation of the 'popular' " (*Obras* [1932], 966).

[17] Ovid's bawd stems from the repertoire of antique comedy from the time of Menander. This "new" comedy eliminates political invective, mythology, and hero tales. It limits its range of themes to everyday bourgeois life. The dramatic complications result from love. For antique literary theory love is set aside for comedy (cf. Excursus IV). The *dramatis personae* of the new comedy consists of "characters," who are typified in the Theophrastean sense: avaricious old men, parasites, whores,

The Latin poetry of the Middle Ages reached Spain only gradually. One impulse arrived *ca.* 1230, with Berceo; a second *ca.* 1330, with Juan Ruiz; a third with Alfonso de la Torre. As late as *ca.* 1440 the latter could produce an allegorized encyclopedia of the seven liberal arts, which draws from Martianus Capella.

Since the Spanish count the Iberian authors of the Imperial age as belonging to their national literature, the late rise of their vernacular literature does not cause them any embarrassment.[18] The epic of the Cid provides a magnificent opening for it. Italy cannot show anything comparable. There, before 1200, there is practically nothing.[19] Italian poetry does not begin until *ca.* 1220. Why so late? The question has been discussed for decades.[20] To answer it is surprisingly easy if one looks at Romania as a whole. In twelfth-century Italy jurisprudence, medicine, and the epistolary style flourish. But the study of the *auctores* languishes, and with it Latin poetry and poetics. There is no Humanism and no philosophy. The vernacular lyric of the thirteenth century derives from the art poetry of Provence. Dante is the first to set off on a different course and nourish his poetry on the thesaurus of the Latin Middle Ages. The question "Why does Italian literature begin so late?" is wrongly put. The question to ask is, "Why does French literature begin so early?" We believe that we have given the answer. But there is another question which needs to be asked: "Why did the Latin Renaissance (1066–1230) occur only in France and Gallicized England?" Because Charlemagne's reform of education laid a foundation which was able to survive the convulsions of the ninth and tenth centuries.[21] The in-

---

slaves, brothel-keepers, etc. The bawd belongs to this circle. We find her in one of Herondas' mimiambi. Ovid transposed the motif from comedy to erotic elegy. In the *Pamphilus* it returns to comedy—or rather to what was understood by "comedy" in the twelfth century: funny stories put into dialogue in elegiac verse. Collection of texts in G. Cohen, *La "Comédie" latine en France au 12e siècle*, 2 vols. (1931). Dante (Epistle to Can Grande) still regards comedy as a narrative poetic genre in the low style ("remissus est modus et humilis, quia locutio vulgaris"). In VE, II, 4, 5 he uses the expression "stilus inferior" instead. This goes back to the antique doctrine of the three kinds of style. Where we think we see "realism," we are dealing with a literary convention: the "low" style.

[18] Menéndez Pidal, to be sure, wished to infer from the chronicles a lost tenth- and eleventh-century epic which would have Visigothic connections. But this thesis is hardly tenable. S. Griswold Morley concludes: "The existence of epics in the vernacular before the 12th century must be regarded as purely conjectural" (Mérimée-Morley, A *History of Spanish Literature* [1930], 28 n. 3).

[19] "Non c' è in Italia prima del Duecento poesia di nessun genere," Monteverdi in Novati-Monteverdi, *Le Origini* (1926), 647.

[20] A. Monteverdi gives references in *Un cinquantennio di studi sulla letteratura italiana* (1886–1936). *Saggi . . . dedicati a Vittorio Rossi* (1937), I, 74 f.

[21] Crisis of the Empire under Louis the Pious; the Normans before Paris, 885–87; the Saracens in the south; fall of the West Frankish Carolingians, etc. Halphen (*Les Barbares*, 269) says of the political disorders of the ninth century: "Il s'en est fallu de peu que la civilisation renaissante ne sombrât une seconde fois." A religious and intellectual revival takes place about the middle of the tenth century (*ibid.*, 351).

tellectual leadership which Germany held under the Ottos could not be maintained. The history of Western culture from Charlemagne to Dante has not yet been comprehended and presented as a coherent whole.[22]

3. Mind and Form

In our analyses the formal element of literature has been strongly in the foreground. But rhetoric was a power. Civic and judicial oratory could not but have a political function of the first rank in the antique city-state. But that Athens during the vital crisis of the Peloponnesian War enthusiastically took up Gorgias's ornamental forms, that Thucydides wrote the history of that war in the new florid prose, is an aesthetic and not a political phenomenon. This Greek delight in the sound of words is of the same sort as the Italian delight in arias and coloratura. Epideictic oratory could of course be connected with public occasions, but only because it was a virtuoso technique which had acquired independence and was conscious of it. For the same reason, with all its artistic devices, it could also make its way into poetry. Among the northern peoples, the Gauls, we know, attracted the attention of the ancients by their taste for pointed speech. Are we here confronted with something common to the Celts? The abstruse and self-complacent idiosyncrasy of Irish Latinity might suggest it. When the Gauls were Romanized, the toying with form which was characteristic of late Roman Antiquity could find a favorable soil in what is now France. Ausonius came from the neighborhood of Bordeaux, Sidonius from the Auvergne. The Carolingian reform of education, however, was based on eighth-century English Humanism. The latter was closely allied to the church, the school, and grammar, and as little understood toying with form as did the Cluniac reform later. The thing was unsuited to the Germanic character. It is the greatest paradox of the Latin Middle Ages that the educated stratum of the northern peoples adopted the foreign language of the south, and learned to master its forms and finally its affectations. What an alienation from what was their own! But how richly it was to be rewarded when the vernacular languages came of age! It was political forces, it was the will of a great ruler, which transplanted the *studium* to France. But perhaps it could develop so brilliantly there only because Gallo-Roman taste for elaborate discourse met with the solid discipline of English schooling. The school was first and foremost a school of language. But, following an inner law, it had to seize upon even the most difficult and most remote elements of its material. This can already be seen in the generation which fol-

[22] Carl Erdmann (1898–1945) planned a "history of Franco-German culture in the eleventh century, during which French cultural primacy arose in a highly original development and twelfth-century Humanism was prepared to a far greater extent than has been recognized in previous presentations" (*in litt.*, Jan. 23, 1938). He did not live to carry out this plan.

lowed Alcuin. Through the Iro-Scots, who emigrated under the pressure of the Danish invasion, fresh stores of antique culture poured into France [23] under Charles the Bald, and with them fresh artifices. Between art and artifice the borderline is fluid. The genetic relation between the two is not at all clear. Artifice is usually regarded as a late product and a symptom of decadence: the degeneration of art. But the reverse can occur. The stylistic history of the Latin Middle Ages demonstrates it a hundred times over. Late antique literary artifice became a technical stimulus and awoke artistic ambition. The possibilities of language were probed to the utmost, and new effects were produced from it. This can be observed in the development of Latin rhyme, which took many centuries. The first phase is the Ambrosian hymn stanza without rhyme. In Fortunatus' hymns, two centuries later, there are assonances, for example two on *u* and two on *o* in the stanza:

> *Vexilla regis prodeunt,*
> *Fulget crucis mysterium,*
> *Quo carne carnis conditor*
> *Suspensus est patibulo.*

In the next stanza all four lines are connected by the final *a* of the last syllable:

> *Confixa clavis viscera*
> *Tendens manus, vestigia*
> *Redemptionis gratia*
> *Hic immolata est hostia.*

No strict schema is followed. At the beginning of the eleventh century we find a tendency to rhyme the lines of a stanza in pairs. This may predominate in a given poem, but need not be carried through.[24] But it is also possible to rhyme a poem of 48 lines entirely on *a*.[25] This is called "tirade rhyme." We cannot here pursue the matter in detail. But what an advance from these awkward experiments to the glory of the *Stabat mater* or the

[23] Above all, the knowledge of Greek, in which Johannes Scotus (Eriugena) was far superior to all his contemporaries. Cf. the chapter "The Study of Greek" in M. L. W. Laistner, *Thought and Letters in Western Europe A.D. 500–900* (1931), 191 ff. P. Courcelle, *Les Lettres grecques en Occident de Macrobe à Cassiodore* (1943) should be added. Heiric of Auxerre obtained a knowledge of Greek from the Irish monks at Laon. His pupil was Hucbald of St. Amand. I believe I have shown that the latter knew Synesius' φαλάκρας ἐγκώμιον (ZRPh, LIX [1939], 156 f.). Johannes Scotus' commentary on the *Nuptiae* was printed for the first time in the United States in 1942. *Iohannis Scotti annotationes in Marcianum*, ed. Cora E. Lutz (= *Publications of the Mediaeval Academy of America*, No. 34 [1942]; inaccessible to me). The last treatment of the subject is by B. Bischoff in *Byzantinische Zeitschrift*, XLIV (1951), 27 ff.

[24] An example is *Carm. Cant.*, ed. Strecker, No. 42.

[25] *Ibid.*, No. 10. One line has impure rhyme.

Dies irae! [26] We should have to go through the two hymns—which are entirely different in structure—stanza by stanza to show the wealth of means and their variations. Before Dante there is nothing comparable to them in art.[27]

Rhyme—as foreign to the Romans as to the Germanic peoples, hesitantly taken up, not bound by rule and consistency, finally developing into an ordered and miraculous splendor—is the great new creation of the Middle Ages, as, in Goethe, the astonished Helen learns from Faust. The manifold possibilities of the rhymed stanza represent a whole new system of forms. But the innumerable less pretentious formal devices which we have encountered are for language what the stops are for the organ. We were able to observe how Dante can use them. In the hands of a master techniques become heightened means of expression. Artifice passes over into art and is absorbed in it.

Literary history usually devotes but little attention to the system of forms. Today it usually prefers *Geistesgeschichte,* whose guiding viewpoints are likely to be borrowed from other disciplines. This is to overlook the fact that analysis of literary forms can itself lead to such insights in the realm of culture as are the aim of *Geistesgeschichte.* If one traces such a personification as the goddess Natura, one discovers connections which escape the history of problems (*Problemgeschichte*) or the history of concepts (*Begriffsgeschichte*). There are formulas like *sapientia et fortitudo,* metaphors like the theater of the world, which open up wide vistas. The figurative use of expressions from the world of the book was for us a lens in which rays from millenniums were concentrated. Mind became living in and through a form.

Forms are configurations and systems of configurations in which the incorporeal things of the mind can manifest themselves and become apprehensible. Dante orders the blessed in circles of light and crosses of light. A crystal consists in a space lattice of electrons and molecules. Mathematics and optics employ the concept of the lattice (Concept? metaphor? Does natural science use metaphors?). Literary forms perform the function of such lattices. As diffused light is concentrated in the lens, as crystals form, so the matter of poetry is crystallized into a configurational schema. In English criticism the concept "pattern" has become familiar. If I am not mistaken, William James used the word to designate structures in the "stream" of consciousness. The *locus classicus,* however, is a passage from one of Gerard Manley Hopkins' letters: "As air, melody, is what strikes me

26 "Fortunately there is not likely ever to be a lack of those who in youth and in age, after much reading or without much, in all time of their tribulation and in all time of their wealth, will hold these wonderful triplets, be they Thomas of Celano's or another's, as nearly or quite the most perfect wedding of sound to sense that they know." George Saintsbury, *The Flourishing of Romance and the Rise of Allegory* (1897), 9.

27 The Provençal poets overdid rhyme, especially Arnaut Daniel. In the forced virtuosity of an exhibition of rare rhymes music vanishes and meaning is lost.

most of all in music and design in painting, so design, pattern or what I am in the habit of calling inscape is what I above all aim at in poetry" (1879). Hopkins did not find even "pattern" close enough, he coined a new word. The meaning remains the same: a structure-determining form. German can use neither "pattern" nor "inscape." But the image of the lattice seems to me at once precise and visual.

The invention of new metrical schemas from the twelfth century onwards marks the course of the new poetry: the Provençal canzone, the rondeau, the sonnet, terza rima, ottava rima and Spenser's magical development of it, are a few examples. Rhyme can be eliminated again, as in blank verse. But when poets give up rhythm too, as Whitman did and then (from 1890) the vers-librists, they are in danger of giving up the spirit with it. Valéry's significance does not lie in his thought but in his example: The material of poetry, which Symbolism had refined, he again subjected to the law of strict form. T. S. Eliot can alternate between free and formal verse.

Bergson repeatedly insists that our thinking has a tendency to reduce the creatively new to something already existing, something finished ("un réarrangement du préexistant"). He illustrates his meaning by a comparison. A musician composes a symphony. Was his work "possible" before it became a reality? Answer: "Yes, if by that one means that there was no insuperable obstacle to its realization. But from this negative meaning of the word we pass, without being aware of it, to a positive: we imagine that everything that occurs could have been perceived beforehand by a sufficiently informed mind; and that thus it existed, in the form of an idea, before it was realized —an absurd assumption in the case of a work of art, for as soon as the musician has a distinct and complete idea of the symphony he is going to compose, his symphony is composed." [28] Naturally, the composer has no "distinct and complete" idea of his work, but he has an indistinct one. Presumably it includes themes, but in any case it includes the schema of the musical form named the symphony. Without that, the composer cannot write. In the world of the mind, the creatively new is much less frequent than Bergson appears to suppose. Without a configurational schema (Platonically: εἶδος) hovering before him, the poet cannot compose. The literary genres, the metrical and stanzaic forms, are such schemata. They are an element of endurance, but they come under the law of "diminishing returns." Epic, tragedy, the ode, etc., could be studied from this point of view.

4. Continuity

We have frequently had to discuss literary constants. We have traced and collected them—some respectable and long known (yet not wholly known), like the Muses; others misunderstood, reviled, like the long-lived topoi, the threadbare metaphors, the played-out mannerisms. These are particularly

---

[28] H. Bergson, *La Pensée et le Mouvant* (1934), 20.

odious to the correct pedagogues of standard Classicism. And for centuries literature has been under a censorship which is often not perceived. Attached to education, handed down in the schools, literature is judged by pedagogical authorities—in the name of a "good taste" which easily acquires a certain flavor of morality. For the pedagogues also grade behavior, tidiness, and diligence, as everyone knows. For our investigation there is no distinction between respectable and reviled elements of tradition. The whole stock must be taken together. Only then do we grasp the continuity of European literature. Only then can we see Antiquity without bias, and re-evaluate the Middle Ages. Only then can we gauge how the modern literatures continue the tradition and how they differ from it, and how in the three centuries between Ariosto (d. 1533) and Goethe they shared the work of transmission among themselves.

Continuity! We have met it in a hundred forms, which we shall not recapitulate. It occurs on all levels, from learning the rudiments to conscious and successful taking over a heritage; from piecing together a cento to a mastery of Latin verse which equals antique models—there are medieval poems which even nineteenth-century philologists differed by a thousand years in dating. A morphology of the literary tradition might be outlined. But here too the *scientia infima* of literary history lacks the tools of differentiated concepts worked into shape by itself. It has a half dozen concepts. They are blocks—massive and unshaped. Humanism, Renaissance, Classicism, Romanticism, Pre-Romanticism, Pre-Classicism—nothing more can be accomplished with this miserable equipment. Tradition can be systematically and literally transmitted, as in the medieval schools. Reception can be imitative, as in the eighth and ninth centuries; productive as in the eleventh and twelfth. It can encounter indignant resistance (*Florebat olim* . . .) or open revolt or apathy. But there is also conscious reaching back for remote reserves, by which centuries are bridged. As we have mentioned the music of Latin hymn poetry, we may call to mind the fact that it could still tempt Baudelaire to imitation (*Franciscae meae laudes*), just as the iridescence of late antique and medieval Latinity fascinated a Huysmans and a Remy de Gourmont, and the delirious splendor of a Nonnus the young Stefan George. "We still remember," he wrote in his eulogy of Mallarmé, "what a strong impression was left in us by the writings of the Byzantines and the late Latin authors, as by those of the Fathers, who could not refrain from portraying their repented sins in iridescent colors; how, in their tormented and subjugated style we pleasurably felt the beat and throb of our own souls, and how the hard-born verses of the hot-blooded Egyptian, which hum and hurry along like Maenads, filled us with more delight than those of old Homer." The *décadence* of 1890 was the discovery of new aesthetic excitements and a form of separation from the "barbarians" as in Verlaine's sonnet

Je suis l'Empire à la fin de la décadence.

The modernism of the Symbolists relished late antique elements as a stimulant. Bilingual editions of the classics brought out by the publisher Ambroise-Firmin Didot (1790–1876) were to be found in the libraries of Paris. Nowhere in the world had the atmosphere of the *studium* been so well preserved as on the hill of St. Geneviève, where Abélard taught. It was part of the vital atmosphere of the *quartier latin.*

Continuity of the literary tradition—a simplified expression for a very complicated state of things. Like all life, tradition is a vast passing away and renewal. Ilion's sea of flame blazes at the beginning of our tradition. What we possess of the literature of ancient Greece are but fragments. Where are the epics of Thebes and the Argonauts? We have lost almost all of ancient Greek lyric poetry, the greater part of Attic tragedy and comedy. Augustan Classicism supplanted Hellenistic poetry and let it perish. The canon became smaller and smaller. The crisis of the Empire in the third century not only means a crippling of production but also produces an indifference to the older literature which was fatal to its preservation. What was no longer read was no longer copied—or rather, rewritten, for from the fourth century the papyrus scroll was replaced by the parchment codex. A technical innovation and a change in taste combined to result in a diminution of Latin literature. The beginning Middle Ages found Roman literature only a heap of fragments, "which compared with its original stock was as insignificant as, say, the ruins of the Forum compared with the Forum of the Imperial age" (Eduard Norden). The assets which were saved by the Carolingian reform of education and calligraphy hardly diminished down to the end of the Middle Ages. Printing seemed at last to safeguard literature. But the second World War destroyed millions of books. The transmission of intellectual values is tied to material bases; and these are subject to destruction.

But continuity of transmission can also be endangered by the general course of culture. In the twelfth century the passion for disputation which characterized dialectics begins to attack the authorities. In the thirteenth century the new university disciplines displace literary studies. These studies themselves degenerate as soon as they cease to be inspired by enthusiasm. "Is there not a breath of death and decay," asks Hofmannsthal, "about all the institutions in which life loses priority to the machinery of life, to government offices, public schools, the assured functioning of the clergy, and so forth?" And Goethe in 1820: "He who is occupied only with the past finally runs the risk of clasping to his heart what is defunct, what to us is as dry as mummy. But precisely this clinging to what has departed always engenders a revolutionary transition, in which the forward-striving new can no longer be held back, can no longer be fettered, so that it tears itself free from the old, and will no longer recognize its superiorities, no longer make use of its advantages." Fifty years earlier Goethe had learned from Herder "that poetry is a universal gift of all peoples, not the private heritage of a refined and educated few." The Pre-Romanticism of the middle eighteenth-century (*supra*, pp. 324 f.) taught that true poetry was incompatible with literary culture; it flowered only among barbarians and savages. No one has expressed this with such beautiful finality as Simon Pelloutier (1694–1757), pastor of the French church in Berlin: "L'ignorance et le mépris des lettres sont la véritable origine de la poésie." The statement lay concealed in a history of the Celts (1740) and was only disinterred by modern research after the first World War.[29] If Pelloutier's inflammatory formula were true, we ought to look forward to a new blossoming of poetry. Relationship to the literary tradition is bounded by two ideal concepts: the treasury (*thesaurus*) and the *tabula rasa*. To collect, preserve, and enjoy the transmitted store is a cultural function. In the Alexandrian world it could still release creative forces; in the Byzantine world it could barely conserve them. Turning away from the tradition begins with indifference (as in the third century of the Empire). It can become hostility when new disciplines enter education. This takes place under the banner of the ever-effective slogan "Things, not Words" (*res, non verba*[30]). Natural science and technology could not but drive back the humanistic tradition from about 1875. In 1926 Hofmannsthal saw in the "wide horizon of the Catholic church the only great Antiquity which remains to us in the West—nothing else is great enough, almost nothing remains to us; I see the moment, indeed it is actually here, when all this Humanism of the eighteenth and early nineteenth centuries in Germany will seem to us a paradisiacal episode, but absolutely an episode." [31] But in the harsh chronicle of history everything great and beautiful is only an episode. Continuity is under the law of the Brazen Age. If, nevertheless, we trace its course, we become aware that we cannot reckon by generations, and hardly by centuries. Very long periods of time are necessary to overcome epochs of enervation and barbarization. That is the teaching of history, but also its consolation and its promise. Even in times of educational atrophy and of anarchy the heritage of the European mind, which is bound up with language and literature, can be fostered, as was the case in the monasteries of the early Middle Ages under the assaults of barbarians and Saracens. Nothing can replace that heritage. Not philosophies, techniques, political or economic systems. All these can produce what is good—not what is beautiful. The Lacedemonians were pleasing to the gods because they prayed to be given the beautiful with the good: τὰ καλὰ ἐπὶ τοῖς ἀγαθοῖς (Plato, *Alcibiades*, II, 148 C).

Only in words does mind speak its own language. Only in the creative word is it in its perfect freedom: above concept, above doctrine, above precept. It is safeguarded, but it is also emptied and externalized by the trans-

---

[29] This and other examples are given in P. Van Tieghem, *Le Préromantisme*, I (1924), 38 in his instructive "La notion de vraie poésie dans le préromantisme européen." Pelloutier considered the Germanic tribes to be Celts.

[30] On *res* and *verba* cf. Cicero, *De or.*, II, 63.

[31] Carl Burckhardt, *Erinnerungen an Hofmannsthal* (1943), 79.

missional techniques of grammar, rhetoric, the "liberal arts," the schools. These techniques are not an end in themselves, nor is continuity. They are aids to memory. Upon memory rests the individual's consciousness of his identity above all change. The literary tradition is the medium by which the European mind preserves its identity through the millenniums. Memory (Mnemosyne), according to the Greek myth, is the Mother of the Muses. Culture, says Vyacheslav Ivanov, is memory of ancestral initiations: "In this sense, culture is not only monumental, but is also initiatory in the mind. For memory, its supreme mistress, permits its true servants to share in the ancestral initiations and, by renewing these within them, gives them the strength for new beginnings, new departures. Memory is a dynamic principle; forgetting is weariness and interruption of movement, descent and return to the condition of a relative inertness." Memory can be understood according to the letter—and according to the pneuma.

Here, certainly, we have arrived at a critical point, where a dialectic reversal occurs. We already sensed it when we spoke of form and mind. Mind needs forms in order to crystallize. But the crystalline is incorruptible. Mind-pervaded form, on the contrary, can become empty, an untenanted room. "Jerome in his study" was a favorite theme of Renaissance painting: symbol of the Humanist at work among his books. But what remains when Jerome leaves his study? In what condition does Mephistopheles find the high-vaulted, narrow Gothic room in which Faust once studied?

> Blick ich hinauf, hierher, hinüber,
> Allunverändert ist es, unversehrt:
> Die bunten Scheiben sind, so dünkt mich, trüber,
> Die Spinneweben haben sich vermehrt;
> Die Tinte starrt, vergilbt ist das Papier . . .
> Auch hängt der alte Pelz am alten Haken.

> (Look where I will, or here, or there, or yond,
> Nothing has changed, nothing is much the worse.
> The painted panes, I think, a little duller,
> The cobwebs certainly have multiplied;
> The ink is dry, the paper turning yellow . . .
> The old fur cloak still hangs on the old hook.)

Various and sundry creatures have moved in:

> Dort, wo die alten Schachteln stehn,
> Hier in bebräunten Pergamen,
> In staubigen Scherben alter Töpfe,
> Dem Hohlaug jener Totenköpfe,
> In solchem Wust und Moderleben
> Muss es für ewig Grillen geben.

> (There, where the ancient boxes stand,
> Here, in the parchment turned to brown,
> In the dusty shards of those old pots,
> And in this death's-head's hollow eye,
> In all this rubbish and springing mould,
> Crickets must live eternally.)

The empty forms of mind are like such a room. The sonnet was an invention of genius. To modulate an erotic theme through hundreds of sonnets was an only too attractive invention of Petrarch's, which spread almost like an epidemic disease and made the sixteenth century sonnet-mad. Shakespeare was able to refill the outworn form with his soul's tensions. But by 1666 Molière was mocking at the degenerate sonnet of the Précieux in his *Misanthrope*. In 1827 Wordsworth warned the critics: "Scorn not the sonnet . . ." Hérédia regarded the sonnets at which he had labored with the file for decades as so precious that he collected them under the title *Les Trophées* (1893). Hardly any form has so depreciated today. It has become the emaciated circus horse of the dilettantes. But the tragedy in alexandrines or iambics, the epic, the didactic poem, are also forms on which the dust lies thick. And the case is the same with many classic writers. They are artificially preserved by modern canon formation. But though they are still carried on the inventory, they already show worm-eaten spots. Corneille is threatened, and in 1936 Jean Schlumberger had to give instructions on how to get pleasure from him.[32] It would not be an easy thing to do for Boileau.

Culture as initiatory memory . . . Ivanov recorded his thoughts in 1920 in the Moscow convalescent home "for workers in science and literature." [33] Since then, cultural collapses have ensued whose effects cannot yet be measured. In the present situation of the mind, there is nothing more pressing than to restore "memory." Educational and re-educational programs of all sorts are perhaps less important than the task of seeing the function of continuity in culture and impressing it. But, for us, this can be but a glance aside. If we resume our historical consideration, we find that forgetting is just as necessary as remembering. Much must be forgotten if the essential is to be preserved. That is the relative truth of the *tabula rasa*. Its opposite concept, the "treasury" (*thesaurus*) has likewise altered. Sainte-Beuve's *Temple du goût* was carried away by a century of iconoclasm. There is no longer a place for "diminutive" classics like Andrieux. We have no use for a warehouse of tradition, we want a house, in which we can breathe—that "House Beautiful," as Walter Pater put it, "which the creative minds of all generations are always building together" (*Appreciations* [1889], Postscript).

These words contain a truth to which Sainte-Beuve had yet no access. They are a landmark in the history of literary criticism and they signify the

[32] Jean Schlumberger, *Plaisir à Corneille*.
[33] Cf. my *Deutscher Geist in Gefahr* (1932), 116.

break-through into a new freedom. The tyranny of Standard Classicism is surmounted. Obedience to the rules and imitation of model authors no longer bestows any right to a good grade. Only the creative minds count. The concept of tradition is not abandoned in consequence, it is transformed. A community of the great authors throughout the centuries must be maintained if a kingdom of the mind is to exist at all. But it can only be the community of creative minds. This is a new kind of selection—a canon if you like, but bound only by the idea of beauty, concerning which we know that its forms change and are renewed. That is why the House Beautiful is never finished and closed. It continues to be built, it remains open.

5. Imitation and Creation

As we recognize from the point of view we have gained, it is this transformation of the canon which is outstanding in Walter Pater's concept of the House Beautiful, not the evaluation of the poet as a creator. The latter idea has become self-evident to us, but it first appears sporadically in the eighteenth century. It comes to flower in Goethe. In July, 1775, on his return from Switzerland, he stopped in Strassburg. He pays homage to Strassburg Cathedral with the "Prayer": "Thou art one and living, procreated and unfolded, not pieced and patched together. Before thee, as before the foaming rush of the mighty Rhine, as before the bright crown of the eternal snow peaks, as before the view of the serenely spreading lake and of thy cloudy cliffs and wild valleys, gray Gotthard! as before every great thought of the Creation, there wakens in the soul that which is creative power in her too. Her stammering overflows in poetry, she daubs on paper her adoration of the Creator . . ." The poet's creativity is here experienced as the same force which operates in external nature. Goethe then turns to the "creation-filled artists." With his friend Lenz he climbs to the platform: "With every step, conviction increased: creative power in the artist is a mounting awareness of relationships, proportions, and seemliness, and only by these can an autonomous work be produced, as other creatures are produced by the individual seminal power." English Pre-Romanticism had already called the poetic imagination "creative," [34] but its guiding ideas are feeling, enthusiasm, originality, genius. Goethe, still fresh from the impression of the Alps, to which Erwin's cathedral by the Rhine responded, was the first to find in creativity the redeeming word which stood above nature and art and allied the poet with cosmogonic powers. Seldom can the road from experience to aesthetic theory be so clearly traced.

Antiquity lacked this concept. Ancient Greece put the poet in the category of "godlike men," beside heroes, kings, heralds, priests, seers. They are called godlike because they surpass human standards. They are favorites of the gods, intermediaries between them and men. The concept represents a Greek form of the higher ideal of man, from Homer and Plato to Philo and

[34] Thomas Warton (1756): Van Tieghem, *Le Préromantisme*, I, 57.

Plutarch.[35] The Augustan poets incorporate Homer's godlike singer into the Latin tradition as *divinus poeta*.[36] Statius reveres the "divine Aeneid" as an unattainable model (*Thebais*, XII, 816). In like manner Boccaccio first calls Dante's *Commedia* "divine." [37] But the Greeks did not know the concept of the creative imagination. They had no word for it. What the poet produced was a fabrication. Aristotle praises Homer for having taught poets "to lie properly" (*Poetics*, 1460 a, 19). For him, as we know, poetry was mimesis, "imitation," and indeed "imitation of men doing something" (1448 a, 1). Imitation can present things as they are or as they appear or as they ought to be (1460 b, 10–11), hence is not to be understood as a copy of nature but as a rendering which can be a refashioning or a new-fashioning. By much interpretation, it has been thought possible to make the tortured text yield the meaning of "creative vision." [38] But does this square with Aristotle's intention? We shall leave the question unsettled. But it is certain that no critic of Antiquity so understood him. Cinquecento Aristotelianism too could turn and twist the basic concepts of the *Poetics*, but imitation remained imitation. Aristotle remained Aristotle.

But is Aristotle really the last word of antique literary criticism? Fortunately we have the treatise περὶ ὕψους. It goes under the title *On the Sublime*, and its author under the name of Longinus. Both are wrong. We do not know its author, and the word ὕψος means "height," not sublimity.[39] High literature, great poetry and prose—that is the subject. The author does not treat it with Aristotle's cool yet inadequate abstraction, but with enraptured and clear-sighted love. He cuts the tie between rhetoric and literature. "For the extraordinary arouses not persuasion but transport (ἔκστασις) in the hearer; what inspires wonder in us is in every way superior to what is only convincing and pleasing." How can one attain these heights? Not by following rules (τεχνικὰ παραγγέλματα). "Greatness is innate and not teachable, and only one art leads it: Nature." "Literary judgment is the last fruit of long experience" (ἡ γὰρ τῶν λόγων κρίσις πολλῆς ἐστι πείρας τελευταῖον ἐπιγέννημα). The natural predisposition is a gift, not acquired. "Hence we must raise our souls to high things, that they may become pregnant with the impulse toward what is noble." "High literature is the reverberation of a noble mind." The examples "Longinus" cites are taken from Greek literature from Homer to Thucydides and Plato. But he once quotes "the legislator of the Jews," who was "no ordinary man"; he had formed a worthy conception of the power of the deity and hence could write: "God

---

[35] L. Bieler, θεῖος ἀνήρ (Vienna, 1935–36).

[36] Virgil, *Bucolics*, 5, 45 and 10, 17.—Horace, AP, 400.

[37] *Vita di Dante*, ch. 26.

[38] J. W. H. Atkins, *Literary Criticism in Antiquity* (1934), I, 79.

[39] E. E. Sikes, *The Greek View of Poetry* (1931), 209 translates the title as "On great writing."—I refer further to George Saintsbury, *A History of Criticism and Literary Taste in Europe*, I (1900), 152 ff.—Aulitzky (*RE, Neue Bearbeitung*, XIII 1415 ff.) places the work in the second quarter of the first century A.D.—Edition with translation by H. Lebègue (Paris, 1939).

said, Let there be light: and there was light." [40] Our author also recommends that the great historians and poets of earlier times be emulated
(μίμησις τε καὶ ζῆλωσις)—but not in order to learn literary devices from
them but to allow the soul to be inspired by the breath of their spirit, as the
Pythian priestess on her tripod inhales the divine vapor that pours from
the riven earth. "So from the greatness of the ancients there flows into the
souls of their emulators emanations from sacred mouths."

These indications must suffice. Across two millenniums we breathe the
breath of life, not the mold of schools and libraries. The appearance of this
unknown Greek in the first century of our era has something miraculous
about it. "All ages are alike," says Blake; "but the genius always stands
above his time." "Longinus" stood so high above it that he was not read.
No ancient writer quotes him. Our text goes back to a tenth-century manuscript, which has regrettable lacunae. But that it was preserved at all is
another miracle. How precariously has the past come down to us! The
treatise was first printed in 1554. It was . . . hardly noticed. "Longinus"
has been pursued by misfortune. It seems grotesque that a schoolmaster
like Boileau made his name known. For Boileau's *Réflexions sur Longin*
(1693) belie their title. They are a pamphlet, equally devoid of wit and
ideas, against Perrault—a pedantic catalogue of his philological, stylistic,
and orthographical errors. And this in the name of "Longinus," who so
deliberately rejects the confusion between "faultlessness" and "perfection."
Greatness is never "correct." Boileau appears not to have read Chapter 33
of περὶ ὕψους or not to have understood it. As little did his contemporaries,
if we will believe Swift, who counsels poets (1733):

> *Get Scraps of Horace from your Friends,*
> *And have them at your Fingers Ends.*
> *Learn Aristotle's Rules by Rote,*
> *And at all Hazards boldly quote:*
> *Judicious Rymer oft review:*
> *Wise Dennis and profound Bossu.*
> *Read all the Prefaces of Dryden,*
> *For these our Criticks much confide in,*
> *(Tho' meerly writ at first for filling*
> *To raise the Volume's Price a Shilling).*
> *A forward Critick often dupes us*
> *With sham Quotations Peri Hupsous:*
> *And if we have not read Longinus,*
> *Will magisterially outshine us.*
> *Then, lest with Greek he overrun ye,*
> *Procure the book for Love or Money,*
> *Translated from Boileau's translation,*
> *And quote Quotation on Quotation.*

[40] An anticipation of patristic Biblical poetics.

We shall not trace the subsequent career of "Longinus" in the eighteenth century. He has been much discussed and much misunderstood. He has never found a congenial spirit. His case is instructive as exemplifying a continuity which has been denied its due influence. A spark which has never set fire. Great criticism is something extremely rare. Hence it is rarely recognized. If the whole of late Antiquity has not a single word to say about "Longinus," that is one of the clearest symptoms of its debilitated intellectual energy. "Longinus" was strangled by that unbreakable chain, the tradition of mediocrity. Is that tradition perhaps the strongest support of literary continuity?

Declining Antiquity was yet able to produce magical creations, such as that beautiful episode in Apuleius' romance—the story of Cupid and Psyche, which Walter Pater incorporated into his *Marius the Epicurean*; such as the *Pervigilium Veneris* by an unknown Roman poet. It rises out of the rubble of the centuries as the three slender columns of the Temple of the Dioscuri rise above the *Campo vaccino* in Piranesi's views. Works of such budding beauty could flower in the most decried times of decadence— and our thoughtless concept of history is again revealed in all its dubiousness. The "House Beautiful" assimilates all the spoils of the centuries, as the cathedral of St. Mark unites them in the opal light of Venice.

We had asked ourselves when the assimilation of the poet to the creator of the universe first appeared, and we must take up this thread again in order to bring our investigation to a meaningful end, if not to a conclusion. "Longinus" had rejected the criticism of blemishes as ancillary. The great authors are not free from blemishes, but they are all above mortality (ἐπάνωτοῦθνητοῦ). Their "height" raises them close to the mighty mind of God (ἐγγὺς αἴρει μεγαλοφροσύνης θεοῦ). Attempts have been made to find related ideas in the Neo-Pythagorean Numenius, in Philostratus, in Plotinus, that is, in writers of the second and third centuries. But it is always a case of incidental and barely comprehensible expressions, which have to be strained to give the result sought.[41] None of the authors named advances the proposition that poetic production can be compared with that of the creator of the universe. Yet one writer of declining Antiquity drew this comparison in respect to Virgil, and developed it. But even historians of criticism no longer read him, or read him only hastily, because he passes as dreary compiler and antiquarian: he is Macrobius.[42] He finds connections between the structure of the *Aeneid* and that of the cosmos. He concludes his considerations by indicating an analogy between Virgil's production on the one hand and that of "Mother Nature" ("Natura parens") and the divine maker of the universe on the other. Macrobius' erudite compiling cannot be compared with the lofty flight of the Greek Neo-Platonists. But

---

[41] Sikes, 238 ff.—Atkins, II, 344 f.—Zeus as creator of the universe: Julius Ammann, *Die Zeusrede des Ailios Aristeides* (1931), pp. 15, 19, 46.

[42] Further discussion *infra*, p. 443.—New evaluation of Macrobius in Pierre Courcelle, *Les Lettres Grecques en Occident* [2] (1948).

his erudition is a form of piety. Grammar, rhetoric, antiquarianism guide
him in his study of Virgil. It is based upon a religious veneration for the
poet. Hence there is a deep historical meaning in the simple fact that the
Virgil cult of late paganism first expressed the idea of the poet as creator,
if only gropingly. It gleams like a mystic lamp in the evening of the aging
world. For almost a millennium and a half it was extinguished. It shines
once again in the dawning radiance of Goethe's youth.

We call a halt. The investigations into the Middle Ages here presented
form an organic sequence which can stand by itself. But both methodologically and thematically, our viewpoint reaches beyond the Middle Ages.
This I hope to show in future studies "in questa tanto picciola vigilia de'
nostri sensi ch' è del rimanente."

EXCURSUSES

I

MISUNDERSTANDINGS OF ANTIQUITY
IN THE MIDDLE AGES

Anyone who has visited Rome knows the antique *Horsetamers* (Dioscuri) on the Quirinal, which to this day bears the name Monte Cavallo after them. Adolph Goldschmidt reports what the *Mirabilia Romae*, a twelfth-century guide to Rome, has to say about them: "The marble horses—hearken to why they are naked [i.e., unbridled], and the men too naked, and what they signify.—In the days of the Emperor Tiberius there came to Rome two young philosophers named Praxiteles and Fidias,[1] whom the Emperor, because he was well versed in such arts, gladly received into his palace. He asked them: Why come ye naked? To which they answered: Because all things are naked and unconcealed to us and we hold the world as naught, therefore we go naked and possess nothing; for example, we can tell you to the letter, Lord Emperor, everything that you do in your chamber, by day or night, in our absence. Whereto the Emperor answered: If you indeed do as you have said, I will give you whatever you wish. They answered: We ask no gold, Lord Emperor, but a monument to ourselves. The next day they told the Emperor, one after the other, all the things that he had done during the past night; wherefore he had made for them the monument he had promised them, in such manner as they wished it, namely, naked horses stamping on the ground, and half-naked men standing by the horses, and with raised arms and clenched fingers they prophesy the future, for just as they are themselves unconcealed so is all the wisdom of the world unconcealed to their minds" (*Vorträge der Bibl. Warburg* 1921–22 [1923], p. 43). Another example of medieval originality in interpreting antique documents is to be found in the equestrian statue of Marcus Aurelius on the Capitol. "The statue was saved from destruction; by being rechristened under the name of Constantine, the first Christian emperor, it not only lost its objectionable character but was actually given a place of honor in front of the Lateran Palace, which Constantine was supposed to have presented to the Popes. There it kept the imaginations of the Romans awake and weaving the most various legends about the horseman. Gradually belief in his princely rank disappeared, for every medieval ruler legitimized himself by wearing a crown. Reasons were sought for the absence of the saddle (it has been recovered since); the decoration between the horse's ears was thought to be a pigeon and as such required interpretation. Indeed, the very existence of the equestrian figure had to be explained. But the strangest thing of all was the conquered barbarian who once crouched, arms bound, under the steed's fore hoofs. This favorite motif of classical art had become completely incomprehensible. But the story of the brave Marcus had answers for all these questions. Marcus, the story went, had been promised a monument if he should succeed in freeing sorely threatened Rome. So he rode out at night on an unsaddled

[1] In the fourth and fifth centuries the inscriptions *opus Fidiae, opus Praxitelis* were placed on the statues by pagan art lovers to prevent their destruction by the Christians (J. Geffcken, *Der Ausgang des griechisch-römischen Heidentums* [1920], 181 and 306, n. 34).

405

horse and, through the crying of a bird, discovered the enemy's king, who was as small as a dwarf, captured him, and brought him to the Romans with his arms bound. The Romans then drove away the remaining besiegers and raised a monument to their savior which should perpetuate all the details of his bold exploit for posterity" (Percy Ernst Schramm in *Vorträge der Bibl. Warburg* 1922–23, Pt. 1 [1924], 152 f.).

Jean Adhémar (*Influences antiques dans l'art du moyen âge français* [1939], 208 ff.) gives examples of the medieval cult of Constantine from Honorius of Autun (*PL*, CLXXII, 710 f.) and Adam Scotus of Prémontré, who recommends giving Constantine a place on the walls of churches (*PL*, CXCVIII, 713). Such representations are very frequent in France and go back to the Lateran statue. Indeed, the Bamberg *Knight* would also appear to be a Constantine.—The "romances of Antiquity" which were the fashion in France from 1150 onward contain descriptions of sculptures which are significant for Antiquity *alla francese*. Cf. Otto Söhring, *Werke bildender Kunst in altfranzösischen Epen*, Erlangen dissertation [1900], and Adhémar, 231.

In the Carolingian period the Verona amphitheater was supposed to be a labyrinth (*Poetae*, I, 119, 3).

But there are also misunderstandings which arise from sheer ignorance. An eighth-century Anglo-Saxon makes Venus a man.[2] There are also examples of the reverse process. Boethius (*Consolatio philosophiae*, III, pr. 8) tells us that Aristotle, in a treatise now lost, says: If men had Lynceus' eyes and could see through walls, they would perceive the hideous entrails within Alcibiades' most beautiful body. "Alcibiadis pulcherrimum corpus"—that could only refer to some woman of Antiquity famous for her beauty. She appears in Villon's *Ballade des dames du temps jadis*:

> Dictes moy ou, n'en quel pays,
> Est Flora la belle Romaine,
> Archipiada, ne Thais . . .

Misunderstandings occur in Dante too.[3]

[2] Wilhelm Levison, *England and the Continent in the Eighth Century* (1946), p. 302.
[3] I have collected a number in *ZRPh*, LXIII (1943), 228 ff.—For medieval misunderstandings of a passage in Horace, cf. Excursus XIX, *infra*.

DEVOTIONAL FORMULA AND HUMILITY

"Devotional formula" is a technical term of medieval diplomatics, the study of written instruments. Part of the "protocol" of an instrument is the statement of the drawer's name and title (*intitulatio*). But this is "frequently connected with the devotional formula, which expresses the idea that the drawer owes his earthly mission to the grace of God" (H. Bresslau, *Handbuch der Urkundenlehre*, I [2] [1912], 47). The "origin and history of the devotional formula" were investigated by Karl Schmitz in a work which appeared in 1913.[1] By devotional formula he understands those formulas "by which the drawer gives expression to his feeling of his own lowliness or of his dependence upon a higher, namely God, usually in a humble addition to his title." Schmitz, then, has enlarged Bresslau's definition, but has thereby decidedly obscured it. Bresslau's version makes it clear that he has in mind expressions like *Dei gratia* or *servus servorum Dei*: these are formulas in which a superior (e.g., king or pope) proclaims his God-given authority to those beneath him. But the case is quite different when a subject calls himself the thrall, slave, or servant of the king. Here the formula is not one of authority but one of submission, similar to the English "your obedient servant," the German "Ihr ergebenster Diener," the Spanish "su seguro servidor" (or "el último de sus servidores"). An "earthly mission" (Bresslau) is never expressed in the submission formula but only in the authority formula. That Schmitz lumped them together led to increased confusion. He found his earliest examples of the devotional formula in the Ancient East (Babylon, Old Testament, Persia), and from these he at once proceeded to the linguistic usage of the Apostle Paul. In the preambles of his letters Paul refers to himself as servant (slave) of Jesus Christ, servant of God, and appointed apostle. Schmitz, however, did not—as consistency with the beginning of his book would have demanded—relate these self-designations of Paul's with older devotional formulas. Rather, he undertook to explain them psychologically, and specifically upon the ground of the apostle's Christian humility. But, remarkably enough, as Schmitz is forced to note, devotional formulas disappear almost completely after Paul and do not reappear until the middle of the fourth century. Are we to assume a temporary suspension of Christian humility? Schmitz tried to explain this striking state of affairs by saying that from the middle of the fourth century the influence of monasticism and of the "ascetic movement" which was also alive in the lay world had brought about the resumption of devotional formulas. He believed, then, that he could explain the Western devotional formula solely from the psychology of Christian piety—either Paul's or that of monasticism—and for him the devotional formula turned into an expression of humility. J. Schwietering accepted Schmitz's view in his "Die Demutsformel mittelhochdeutscher Dichter" ("The humility formula in Middle High German poets" [Berlin, 1921]=*Göttinger Abhandlungen* [1921], No. 3), which furnishes valuable material for the study of medieval poetic style. Yet Schwietering still further exaggerated

---

[1] More recent literature on devotional formulas can be found in *Neues Archiv*, XLIX (1932), 718 and in G. Tellenbach, *Libertas* (1936), p. 199 f.

the one-sidedness of Schmitz's view by referring all of the phenomena which he studies ("1. The veiling of the author's name; 2. the formula of poetic incompetence and intellectual inadequacy; 3. the formula of spiritual infirmity and sinfulness") back to Paul. His study begins: "When the Apostle Paul, in the salutations of his letters, added to his name the devotional formula of oriental origin in the forms "servus Jesu Christi" (Rom. 1:1; Phil. 1:1), "servus Dei" (Tit. 1:1), when he, the least of the apostles ("minimus apostolorum," I Cor. 15:9) boasted of his weakness ("infirmitas," II Cor. 11:30; 12:5, 10) in Christian humility, and exaggerated his acknowledgment of his oratorical incapacity ("imperitus sermone," II Cor. 11:6), even to the admission "non ego autem, sed gratia Dei mecum" (I Cor. 11:6), he gave to all practitioners of prose or poetry in the Christian East and West an ever-living, if not always equally influential, pattern of Christian *humilitas.*" Although in the course of his study Schwietering occasionally speaks of the "formulistic apparatus of courtly servility," of the "empty formula of courtly devotion," and thus touches upon a state of affairs which is certainly to be distinguished from Christian humility, he nevertheless considers it incumbent upon him to derive all his Middle High German examples from Christian humility. The possibility of antique models, he has not considered.

The first thing to be noted is that *humilis* (from *humus,* corresponding to Greek ταπεινός) originally means lowness in the concrete and spatial sense, then by extension the ordinary and common (*sordida et humilia*), what is "infra dignitatem" (Quintilian, VIII, 2, 2 f.); also social inferiority, as in "humilibus parentibus natus" or in French:

L'humble condition d'un gardeur de moutons.

The word *humilitas* first acquires the commendatory meaning "humility" in Church Latin, at the same time keeping the old meaning "low, mean."

The question now arises whether we are justified in tracing all of Schwietering's "humility formulas" back to Paul. But what of Paul himself and humility? Was it to humility that he wished to give expression in the *intitulatio* of his letters? A truly humble Christian is not wont to vouch for his humility himself. The Rhenish prelate to whom is ascribed the saying, "Humility is the rarest of all virtues; God be praised, I have it!"—this eminent ecclesiastic can hardly serve as a model of humility. As recent research shows, the formulas "servus Dei," "servus Jesu Christi" in Paul and other New Testament writers are not the spontaneous expression of personal humility but modeled after the Old Testament δοῦλος θεοῦ, which in turn is a rendering of the secular submission formula of officials and subjects in the old Oriental despotisms.[2] It must not, however, be overlooked that these δοῦλος formulas in Paul are only elements of a more or less richly developed manner of self-designation in which Paul's apostolic and hierarchic consciousness of authority finds expression[3] (as, for example, Rom. 1:1; Gal. 1:1; I Cor. 1:1). In other words: the "humility formulas" in the preambles to Paul's letters are formal phrases intended to reinforce the apostle's appointment as a teacher; they are, to put it pointedly, to be taken from the point of view of ecclesiastical law, not of psychology. Paul calls himself "servant of Christ" (as the Pope will later call himself *servus servorum Dei*) to reinforce his spiritual mission and

---

[2] Cf. Kittel's *Theologisches Wörterbuch zum N.T.* under δοῦλος; Lietzmann, *Kommentar zu Röm.,* I, 1.

[3] Cf. Otto Roller, *Das Formular der paulinischen Briefe* (1933), pp. 99 ff.

appointment—in accordance with the Lord's saying (Matt. 20:26 f.): "Quicumque voluerit inter vos maior fieri, sit vester minister: et qui voluerit inter vos primus esse, erit vester servus."

The attestations of humility which occur in the body of Paul's letters must be judged entirely differently from the "devotional formulas" of the *intitulatio*. In the body of the letter the writer can express himself freely; in the *intitulatio* he is confined to a schema, even though an elastic one. Schwietering lays particular emphasis upon Paul's testimony in regard to his vocation (I Cor. 15:9-11). But if we compare Schwietering's wording with the original, we find that out of the whole context he first takes "minimus apostolorum" (v. 9) and then—after interpolating three passages from another letter—extracts "non ego autem sed gratia Dei mecum." But the complete text runs: "Ego enim sum minimus Apostolorum, qui non sum dignus vocari Apostolus, quoniam persecutus sum Ecclesiam Dei. Gratia autem Dei sum id quod sum, et gratia eius in me vacua non fuit, sed abundantius illis omnibus laboravi: non ego autem, sed gratia Dei mecum. Sive enim ego, sive illi: sic praedicamus, et sic credidistis." This complete text shows: 1. "minimus Apostolorum" is in no way a humility-"formula," in no way an *intitulatio*, and hence must not be equated with a "servus Jesu Christi." The words are, rather, an essential part of a sentence which states the highly cogent reason why Paul, in view of his life before his conversion, must have appeared to himself the least among the apostles. 2. But upon this profession of his own unworthiness follows the proud announcement of his own accomplishment ("abundantius illis omnibus laboravi"). Paul knows that he has accomplished more than the other apostles: because God's grace was in him. In the final sentence Paul dismisses the comparison between himself and the others: his preaching is the same as theirs.

The whole passage testifies to Paul's proud consciousness of his apostleship, not to his humility. Finally, we have still to examine the expressions of "humility" in II Corinthians. Schwietering lays stress upon the "admission of oratorical incapacity" ("imperitus sermone," II Cor. 11:6) as typical. But this phrase must not be isolated. It is only intelligible in the light of the preceding 10:10: "Quoniam quidem epistolae, inquiunt, graves sunt et fortes: praesentia autem corporis infirma, et sermo contemptibilis." In these words, Paul repeats the criticisms of his Corinthian opponents. They admit that his letters are weighty and powerful but they consider his personal appearance weak and censure his oratory. To this Paul answers in 11:6: "Though I be unschooled in oratory, I am not so in knowledge . . ." ("etsi imperitus sermone, sed non scientia"). Knowledge (*scientia*), however, the apostle obviously regards as far above skill in discourse (similarly I Cor. 2:4). He is in possession, then, of the higher, the better. He is superior to his opponents. As protestations of Paul's incapacity, the passages considered are not particularly apt. They can, however, be employed to good account in the *captatio benevolentiae* and are extraordinarily popular among ecclesiastical writers. But Paul's phrase is also to be found used in a different sense. The author of the *Visio Anselli* writes, in a prologue only recently discovered by Dom Wilmart: "Nempe apostolus gloriatur et dicit: etsi imperitus sermone, sed non scientia. Sed ego misellus utroque careo." [4] In Paul's phrase, then, the author has seen no humility formula but the

---

[4] A. Wilmart, *Analecta Reginensia* (= *Studi e Testi*, LIX) (1933), p. 285.

expression of a self-satisfaction compared with which he seems to himself poor and miserable.

What has been said should suffice to restrict the "Paul theory" considerably and at the same time to eliminate the term "humility formula." We find ourselves obliged once more to separate the facts which Schmitz and Schwietering lumped together. We use "devotional formula" only in the narrower sense defined by Bresslau. "Submission formula" and "protestation of incapacity" represent two further, clearly delimited series of facts. An example: Schmitz states (pp. 103 f.) that Eugenius of Toledo frequently uses a devotional formula in his poetic work. One of his poems ends with the lines that I quoted above, p. 85. Yet these lines represent a dedication [5] to the king and use a submission formula, not a devotional formula. Finally, under "protestations of incapacity" we comprehend everything that appears in Schwietering as "formula of poetic incapacity and intellectual inadequacy." The protestation of incapacity is distinguished from the devotional formula and the submission formula, first by the fact that it represents a topos of the *prooemium;* second by the fact that it is addressed to the reader but not, or at least not necessarily, to a person of different social rank from the writer. What is common to the three types which we have distinguished is the element of self-belittlement. But this is a social convention, which arises spontaneously in all cultures. It is to be distinguished from the phenomenon of humility, which with the advent of Christianity entered history as something entirely new.[6] It existed both before humility and contemporaneously with it, as a social convention, and it still does so today. In China "I" can be replaced by "the little younger brother," "the mean one," "the blockhead"; in Japan by "my selfishness," "the irrational offspring." Wundt refers this phenomenon back to the patriarchal despotism of Chinese culture [7] (*Völkerpsychologie*, II, Pt. 23, [1912], pp. 45 f.).

Schmitz's derivation of devotional formulas from the spread of monasticism from *ca.* 350 was unsatisfactory even on internal grounds. It overlooks the fact that the development which led from Constantine's Edict of Toleration to the religious edicts of the Emperors Theodosius and Gratian (elevation of the Catholic Church to the position of the recognized state church with exclusive rights [8] and interdiction of the pagan cult), though it resulted in the Christianization of the empire, also brought about a far-reaching secularization of the Church. There can, then, be no question of the progress of an "ascetic movement." The increasing use of

[5] On dedications cf. Gräfenhain, *De more libros dedicandi* (Marburg, 1892), and J. Ruppert, *Quaestiones ad historiam dedicationis librorum pertinentes* (Leipzig dissertation, 1911).

[6] Cf. the phenomenological analysis of humility in Max Scheler's essay *Die Rehabilitierung der Tugend.*

[7] Cf. also Cassirer, *Philosophie der symbolischen Formen,* I, 211 f.

[8] This action is, quite comprehensibly, hailed by ecclesiastical history and viewed as the beginning of a "period of florescence." Jerome thought otherwise. He planned a history of the Church which should reach to the "dregs" of the present and, among other things, show that, though the Church had gained power and wealth, it had declined morally. This is set forth in his *Vita Malchi* (PL, XXIII, 55), written *ca.* 390. The passage runs: "Scribere enim disposui ab adventu Salvatoris usque ad nostram aetatem, id est ab apostolis usque ad nostri temporis faecem, quomodo et per quos Christi Ecclesia nata sit, et adulta, persecutionibus creverit et martyriis coronata sit; et postquam ad Christianos principes venerit, potentia quidem et divitiis major, sed virtutibus minor facta sit."

"humility" formulas should rather be explained by the fact that from the time of Diocletian imperial ceremonial was more and more elaborately developed. We are dealing with conventions of courtly submission, which were observed by pagans and Christians alike. This also permits us to understand the great frequency with which ceremonious forms of address appear in Symmachus.[9]

If, then, the medieval formula of submission is dependent upon pagan Roman prototypes, this is even more so of the protestation of inadequacy. We were able (*supra*, p. 84) to find only two Biblical models for this, Paul's "imperitus sermone" and the "agnitio propriae imbecillitatis" in the Wisdom of Solomon. Compared with these two "Christian" prototypes, the antique examples must have weighed much more heavily. With a thousand other topoi and conventions of antique rhetoric, affected modesty also passed into the literature of the Christian Middle Ages. One of the principal intermediaries must have been St. Jerome. He knows the *parvitas* formula and unhesitatingly employs it in a sentence in which—with little modesty—he calls his opponents "filthy swine": "Non mirum . . . si contra me parvum homunculum immundae sues grunniunt" (*PL*, XXIII, 935 A). Other variants of the *captatio* with the *parvitas* formula in Jerome are: 1. "Tuae benevolentiae erit non eruditionem nostram, quae vel nulla vel parva est, sed pronam in te suscipere voluntatem"; 2. "Cudimus non ignari imbecillitatis nostrae et exilis ingenii rivulum vix parvo strepentem murmure sentientes" (both cited in W. Stade, *Hieronymus in prooemiis quid tractaverit* . . . [Rostock, 1925], p. 78). These expressions of Jerome's are typical—not, however, of Christian sentiment but of the affected late Roman literary Mannerism which is common to pagans and Christians. In Jerome and the other great churchmen it naturally only appears sporadically. But beside them, from the fourth century, there was also a Christian literature which took the greatest conceivable pains to compete with the pagan authors in rhetorical affectations: for example, Ausonius, Sedulius, Fulgentius, Sidonius, Ennodius, Fortunatus, to name only a few. Like their pagan contemporaries—a Symmachus for example—what they value most in literature is rhetorical virtuosity. For the purposes of the *captatio benevolentiae* they are accordingly wont to protest that they are utterly without any kind of eloquence. For these protestations there is a large number of stereotyped phrases, which Hans Bruhn has collected.[10] The author apologizes for his style (*sermo*) or his talent (*ingenium*) or both; they are dry, hard, thin (*ariditas, siccitas, ieiunae macies orationis*; the last already Tacitean); artless (*rudis, simplex, communis, incompositus, incomptus, incultus*); crude (*impolitus, scabies*); rusty (*rubigo*); unclean (*sordidus*); paltry (*egestas, inopia, paupertas, exilitas, sterilitas*). These writers are also especially fond of accusing themselves of *rusticitas*, i.e., of a rustically crude and faulty style. The excessive use of such clichés does not become general until the fifth and sixth centuries. But it is precisely the rhetoricians of this period (especially Sidonius and Fortunatus) who were regarded as models of style throughout the Middle Ages and

---

[9] On Symmachus cf. Norden, *Kunstprosa*, 643 f., but especially August Engelbrecht, *Das Titelwesen bei den spätlateinischen Epistolographen* (= *Jahresbericht des Gymnasiums der K.K. Theresianischen Akademie in Wien*, Pt. I [1893]). According to Engelbrecht, ceremonius titles and forms of address first became fashionable in the fourth century.

[10] Hans Bruhn, *Specimen vocabularii rhetorici ad inferioris aetatis latinitatem pertinens* (Marburg dissertation, 1911).

were sedulously imitated. The medieval "protestations of incapacity," then, have their origin for the most part in the stylistic Mannerism of late Antiquity, not in the Bible. Among the *termini technici* of the *excusatio* listed above, none is of Biblical origin. Occasionally, to be sure, some connection with the Bible is sought (on the whole very rarely). This cannot but lead to amusing results. In the dedicatory letter to his life of Amandus, Mico, for example, writes: "Rusticitati autem meae veniam date; necesse est, quia rusticatio, ut quidam ait, ab altissimo creata est." This is a reference to Ecclesiasticus 6:16: "Non oderis laboriosa opera, et rusticationem (husbandry) creatam ab altissimo." Our good Mico has permitted himself a theological joke. From a later period I may be permitted to quote, as an ingenious example of a protestation of incapacity pieced together from Bible texts and late antique formulas, Walter of Châtillon's *prooemium* (*Moralisch-satirische Gedichte*, ed. Strecker, p. 38): "In domino confido. Quomodo dicitis anime mee: 'Transmigra in montem sicut passer,' quoniam ecce peccatores intenderunt arcum [11]? in consilio iustorum et congregatione dicturus, cum verbis elegantibus non floream, quibus erubescentis imperitie mee verecundiam valeam redimere— non enim labra prolui [12] decretorum fonte nectareo nec Justiniani thoris accubitans [13] legum pabulo sum refectus—de proprii viribus ingenii diffidens in domino confido."

A collection and stylistic analysis of submission formulas and protestations of incapacity would be rewarding. The foregoing remarks can supply a few guiding principles and furnish a warning against making the Middle Ages more Christian or more pious than it was. A constant literary formula must not be regarded as the expression of spontaneous sentiment. One final example of this, one related to the matters here treated: S. Singer (*Germanisch-romanisches Mittelalter* [1935], p. 98) has attempted to show that the antique ideal of kalokagathia was continued in the Middle Ages and, specifically, "first in the *dulcedo* of the Merovingian period." How, we may ask, did the Merovingians happen to have the *dulcedo* ideal? Quite simply: through R. Koebner's book on Venantius Fortunatus, which appeared in 1915. The virtuoso of panegyric who is the subject of Koebner's study sometimes emphasizes the *dulcedo* in the persons he celebrates; hence it must "have appeared to his friends themselves to be the highest value of noble sentiment" (p. 32), indeed it must have been considered "the highest proof of personal nobility at the Austrasian court" (*ibid.*). Here a historian of culture [14] has inferred fictitious facts from misunderstood [15] texts. We must begin with the fact that the characterization *dulcis, suavis, dulcissimus, suavissimus* is, in Latin, perfectly usual for one's acquaintances (as well as relatives and friends). Horace (*Sat.*, I, 9, 4) is addressed as *dulcissime rerum* by an importunate chatterbox. Then *dulcis* gives *dulcedo* in

[11] To this point quotation from Ps. 10:2 f.

[12] Persius, *Prol.*, 1.

[13] Sedulius, *Carmen paschale praef.*, 2: "nostris accubitare toris" (reference from Strecker).

[14] Koebner's book appeared in the series edited by W. Goetz, "Beiträge zur Kulturgeschichte des Mittelalters und der Renaissance."

[15] In one of the poems which Koebner quotes for his theory, *dulcedo* means simply "eloquence":

> Admiranda etiam quid de dulcedine dicam,
> Nectare qui plenus construis ore favos?
>
> (ed. Leo, p. 160, 73 f.)

appellation, as *parvus* gives *parvitas mea,* etc. According to the *Thesaurus, dulcedo* as a personal designation appears for the first time in 360 in a Christian epitaph. Macrobius writes: "Eustachi fili, vitae mihi dulcedo pariter et gloria." As a ceremonious epistolary appellative, Theodosius uses "dulcedo tua," corresponding to the Greek ἡ σὴ γλυκύτης. "Dulcissima gratia vestra" and the like appear in Merovingian documents (Zeumer, *Formulae* . . ., p. 24, 23). *Dulcedo,* then, is not "kalokagathia among the Merovingians" but a term which appears in Italy from 350, first as an expression of affection, then as part of the ceremonial style.[16]

[16] Engelbrecht in his *Titelwesen* cites only two examples of *dulcedo* (one from Avitus and one from Ruricius).

GRAMMATICAL AND RHETORICAL
TECHNICAL TERMS AS METAPHORS

It is to the schools of late Antiquity and the Middle Ages that we owe the metaphorical use of grammatical and rhetorical terms. The symbiosis of the pursuits of grammar and poetry begins to define itself under Nero. From the Neronian period comes Lucilius' epigram (*AP*, XI, 139) in which, for the first time, we find grammatical and rhetorical terms used figuratively—and in an obscene sense (*casus, coniunctio, figurae, coniugatio*). Such examples of school wit were also dear to the Latin Middle Ages. Paul Lehmann (*Die Parodie im Mittelalter* [1922], 75 ff. and 152 ff.) and Otto Schumann (Commentary on *CB*, 16, 7 and 9) have collected examples. The names of the cases in particular were often used as "cryptic language" in a suggestive sense. Two leading themes of medieval satire were varied by this device: the avarice of the Curia (in Rome only *accusativus* and *dativus* pass current) and the corruption of morals (*genetivus*). From this we should distinguish the grammatically disguised praise of the pleasures of love.[1] Such poems may be lusty, but they need not be obscene. The Latin scholar poetizes most gracefully:

> *Schola sit umbra nemoris*
> *Liber puelle facies.*[2]

He is able to make not only declension and conjugation but also conjunction and interjection fit his sense. This erotic reinterpretation of grammatical terms once entered the realm of "higher literature" in the twelfth century, namely in Alan of Lille's *Planctus Naturae*. There Dame Nature complains (*SP*, II, 436 f.): Humanity commits "barbarisms" in the relations between the sexes; "metaplasms" which infringe the law of Venus. Men pay no heed to Venus's "orthography," they have degenerated to erroneous "anastrophe."[3] In their madness they even proceed to "tmesis."[4] Of those who follow Venus's "grammar," some choose only the masculine gender, others only the feminine, yet others both. Here the grammatical metaphors serve neither parody nor eroticism. Rather, they are put at the service of a philosophical criticism of contemporary culture which seeks to make its serious demands acceptable through studied elegance of form. In the last quarter of the twelfth century such forms of expression were the height of fashion. To grammatical metaphors we must add those from the figures of speech. One of the masters of the new poetics, Matthew of Vendôme, referring to a hardhearted father who lets

---

[1] Also Oriental: "plying the particle of copulation in concert and joining the conjunctive with the conjoined, while her husband was a cast-out nunnation of construction," *The Thousand Nights and a Night*, trans. Richard F. Burton, IX, 272 [replacing reference to E. Littmann's translation].

[2] P. Lehmann, *Parodistische Texte* (1923), p. 49, ll. 37 f.

[3] Inversion of the normal word order: *litora circum* instead of *circum litora* (Isidor, *Et.*, I, 37, 16).

[4] "Cutting apart" a word: "circum dea fudit amictum" (*Aen.*, I, 412) instead of *circumfudit* (Isidor, *Et.*, I, 37, 19).

his son starve, says that he could be called a father only "per antiphrasin" [5] (*SB München* [1872], 618).[6]

Like many similar things, this stylistic curiosity too was taken up again by seventeenth-century Spanish Mannerism. Góngora makes a river a rhetorical period in which the islands represent "wooded parentheses." [7] Gracián calls an earthquake "eclipse del alma, paréntesis de mi vida." [8] Lope too employs this mannerism. *Prólogo* and *epílogo* are words which are constantly on the lips of his characters (New edition of the Spanish Academy, XI, 455 b and 467 a). A village mayor expresses himself most learnedly (*ibid.*, XII, 91 a):

> Pues como de esa suerte vives,
> Sirves, pides por Dios, y, sin paráfrasis,
> Andas hecho bribón por las tabernas?

A lover too shows that he has been well educated (*ibid.*, XII, 645 b):

> Tirano amor, cuya opinión temática
> Nos muestra bien la librería histórica;
> Escura ciencia en lengua metafórica
> De la esfinge de Tebas enigmática.
>   Dichoso el que se queda en tu grammática
> Y no llega a tu lógica y retórica;
> Pues el que sabe mas de tu teórica
> Menos lo muestra en tu experiencia prática.
>   Pues igualas amor en tu matrícula
> Los sabios y los bárbaros salvájicos,
> El mar y el fuego, el hielo y la canícula,
>   Yo seré Ulises a tus cantos mágicos,
> Pues solo vemos en tu acción ridícula
> Principios dulces para fines trágicos.

Calderón is fond of such expressions. A lady tells her cavalier that she was observed as she set out to see him. So love has made a passive out of an active and thus committed a crime against grammar (Keil, I, 308 a):

> Barbarismo de amor grande,
> Salir a ver, y ser vista;
> Pues, mal gramático, sabe
> Persona hacer que padece
> De la persona que hace.

[5] As the classic example of this figure, which exaggerates euphemism to the point of reversing the original meaning, the rhetoricians give the name Eumenides ("the gracious ones") for the Furies.

[6] Further examples: *epenthesis* and *syncope* in a pretty girl (*SP*, I, 256 f.); *prolembsis* (Walter of Châtillon; *Revue bénédictine*, XLIX [1937], 144, 54); *parenthesis* (id., *Alexandreis*, I, 65); *hendiadyoin* (Anon. in *Zs. f. rom. Phil.*, L, 80); *apostrophe* (Henry of Avranches, in *Forschungen z. dt. Geschichte*, XVIII [1878], 73).

[7] E. Joiner Gates, *The Metaphors of Góngora* (1933), 92.

[8] *El Criticón*, ed. Romera-Navarro, I, 118.

Other rhetorical terms are similarly used by Calderón in dialogue; for example, *metáfora, hipérbole, prólogo, epílogo, énfasis*, etc. I will give but one more example, involving prosopopoeia. A court festival at Madrid is to be described. But the narrator hesitates before the task (IV, 352 a):

> . . . *aunque mas lo pretenda,*
> *No es posible, sino es*
> *Que la retórica quiera*
> *En sus figuras prestarme*
> *El uso de sus licencias,*
> *Cometiendo una que llaman*
> *Tropo de prosopopeya*
> *Que es . . .*

The word *prosopopeya*, originally the name for a rhetorical figure, underwent an interesting change of meaning in Spanish: it also signifies "afectación de gravedad y pompa" (Dictionary of the Academy). Cervantes uses it in this sense (*Don Quixote*, II, ch. 36) and soon thereafter introduces us to a Princess Antonomasía [9] (ch. 38). In such passages we should perhaps see a protest against contemporary Mannerism.

[9] We have antonomasia when a rich man is called "a Croesus" or a patron of the arts "a Maecenas."

JEST AND EARNEST IN MEDIEVAL
LITERATURE

1. Late Antiquity

In the Homeric epic the base and the heroic (Thersites and Achilles) stand side by side. Nestor is treated with delicate humor. Hephaestus' surprising Ares and Aphrodite is a farce in which gods take part. The comic and the tragic enter the epic style. "It was tragedy which first attempted to carry out the idea of σπουδαῖον, of perfect and uninterrupted seriousness such as was consonant with the Apollonian religion, to the exclusion of the 'petty' (φαῦλον), with complete consistency, and thus consciously turned away from βίος and from primitive mixed forms" (Wilhelm Schmid, *Geschichte der griechischen Literatur*, I, 2 [1934], 85). It is not until Euripides that tragedy occasionally approaches the comic. Plato and Aristotle cling to the distinction between serious and light poetry (Schmid, I, 1 [1929], 12, n. 2). But from the third century B.C. there evolves from the popular lecture of the Cynics and Stoics (diatribe) the mixed style of the σπουδογέλοιν (serious-humorous) which Horace imitated in his satires (cf. *Sat.*, I, 10, 11 ff. and *Epi.*, II, 2, 60). Jesting here, as in the Christian preaching of the late Middle Ages, serves the purpose of *ridendo dicere verum*. The entrance of comic elements into prose and poetry is also furthered by the fact that the Greek and Roman comedy had died out at the beginning of the Imperial age. Only the mime and the pantomime still remain really alive under the Empire. The pantomime, i.e., the mimic dance with musical accompaniment, usually without words, was already popular among the Greeks even in the classic period. The mime—first a realistic representation of a single scene from popular life, later also developed to a dramatically constructed farce—had its florescence in the Hellenistic Age and could be either in monologue or dialogue. In Rome both genres were popular from the time of Augustus. Despite numerous attacks on the part of philosophers, and later of the Church, they held their own until the end of Antiquity, and indeed longer. For the mimes for which we have such manifold evidence in the Middle Ages are, as Hermann Reich was the first to see,[1] the successors of the antique mimes. In late Roman Antiquity mime and pantomime become species of entertainment which belong on the same program with musical and acrobatic performances. A few examples may serve to illustrate this. The hero of the *Historia Apollonii* (3rd century) shows himself skilled in all arts. He is an excellent ball-player, but also a lute-player. "Post hoc deponens lyram ingreditur in comico habitu et mirabili manu et saltu inauditas actiones expressit. Post hoc induit tragicum et nihilominus admirabiliter complacuit ita" (Ring, p. 18). He appears, then, as a pantomimist: in the dress first of the comic

---

[1] H. Reich, *Der Mimus* (1903).—According to Christ-Schmid, *Geschichte der griechischen Literatur* II [6], 1, 25 n., the *ioculatores* of the Middle Ages sprang from the latest form of the antique associations of technitai.

and then of the tragic actor, he acts by gestures and leaps—that is, without verbal expression. Pantomime is described in No. 111 of the *Anthologia latina* (Buecheler-Riese). In the same collection there follow uniformly constructed poems on the art of the rope-dancer, of the citharoedus, of the weapon-dance—obviously a brief survey of the late antique variety repertoire. Clown, mime, comic and tragic actor, musician, acrobat appear—also ranked together—in Claudian's panegyric on Mallius Theodorus (311 ff.).

The influence of rhetoric also contributed toward obliterating the boundaries between jest and earnest.[2] Rhetorical theory had already acquainted the Greeks with discussions "on the risible."[3] In the *Rhetorica ad Herennium* (3, 13) *iocatio* is defined as "oratio quae ex aliqua re risum pudentem et liberalem potest comparare." Cicero discusses it in *De oratore* (2, 58–71). Quintilian's treatment is very thorough. In ordinary life ("in convictibus et cottidiano sermone") he permits "lasciva humilibus, hilaria omnibus." But the *vir bonus* must never allow his dignity to suffer thereby.[4] Since dignity is a panegyrical topos, controlling laughter is often eulogistically emphasized in connection with it.[5] The younger Pliny's remarks on the subject also became authoritative, and remained so for the Middle Ages too. He advises the orator to relax occasionally by composing short witty poems: "hi lusus non minus interdum gloriam quam seria consequuntur" (VII, 9, 10). He followed this counsel himself. He sends a friend such productions of his Muse, some of which are "petulantiora paulo." However, he adds by way of apology, even the most serious and dignified men have on such an occasion refrained "non modo lascivia rerum, sed ne verbis quidem nudis" (IV, 14, 4). And he cites a number of such "exempla maiorum"[6] (V, 3, 5) to justify his practice: "facio nonnumquam versiculos severos parvum, facio tamen, et comoedias audio, et specto mimos et lyricos lego et Sotadicos intellego; aliquando praeterea rideo, iocor, ludo, utque omnia innoxiae remissionis genera breviter amplectar, 'homo sum'" (V, 3, 2). In Pliny this attitude is both a literary program and an ideal of life: "Ut in vita sic in studiis pulcherrimum et humanissimum aestimo severitatem comitatemque miscere, ne illa in tristitiam, haec in petulantiam excedat. Qua ratione ductus graviora opera lusibus iocisque distinguo" (VIII, 21, 1).

In Roman poetry the theme "jest and earnest" is treated from the Augustan period onward. The contrast between the serious and the frivolous Muse is already a favorite theme in Ovid. Wanton Cupid calls him away from lofty heroic poetry (*Am.*, I, 1). Roguishly laughing Elegy estranges him from Tragedy (*Am.*, III, 1). In the Muses' choir the comic Thalia exercises her influence beside the tragic Melpomene. In the age of Nero the author of the *Laus Pisonis* expatiates on the fact (l. 139 ff.) that the subject of his praises was a master both of jest and earnest as

---

[2] "Jest and earnest" as a collocation of contraries like "word and deed," "old and young," etc. is treated by E. Kemmer, *Die polare Ausdrucksweise in der griechischen Literatur* (Würzburg, 1903), 185 ff.

[3] Quintilian, VI, 3, 22.—On the theory of wit according to Aristotle, Cicero, Quintilian, cf. Ernst Walser, *Die Theorie des Witzes und der Novelle nach Jovianus Pontanus* (Strassburg, 1908), p. 1–63.—E. Arndt, *De ridiculi doctrina rhetorica* (Bonn dissertation, 1904).

[4] VI 3, 28 and 35.

[5] Volkmann, *Die Rhetorik der Griechen und Römer*[2] (1885), 348.

[6] This technical term is here used parodistically.

an orator, and Tacitus (*Annals*, 15, 48) stresses the same point in regard to Calpurnius Piso. To justify their preference for comic material, poets could point out that Virgil (*Culex*) and Homer (*Battle of Frogs and Mice, Margites*) had written comic epics. Statius (preface to *Silvae*, IV) answers the question whether jesting poems are permissible by pointing out that after all people watch ball-games and swordsmen. Elsewhere he cites the example of Virgil and Homer: "sed et Culicem legimus et Batrachomachiam etiam agnoscimus, nec quisquam est inlustrium poetarum qui non aliquid operibus suis stilo remissiore praeluserit" (Epistle to Stella, preface to *Silvae*, I). In a much later period Fulgentius (ed. Helm 7, 25 ff.) mentions in one breath

> Quod cecinit pastorali
> Maro silva Mantuae,
> Quod Maeonius ranarum
> Cachinnavit proelio.

The collocation of jest and earnest is, however, not merely a piece of rhetorical elegance and a poetic conceit but, as we have already seen in Pliny, an ideal of life and accordingly a panegyrical topos. Aelius Spartianus (*Vita Hadriani*, 14, 11) can say of Hadrian: "Idem severus comis, gravis lascivus, cunctator festinans, tenax liberalis, simulator simplex, saevus clemens, et semper in omnibus varius." The philosopher, and later bishop, Synesius of Cyrene (*ca.* 400) divides his life between the serious and the pleasurable σπουδή and ἡδονή) and is glad to be able to tell of an incident of travel "which the deity harmoniously composed of the comic and the tragic" (Epistles 1 and 4). In late Latin Antiquity the scholastic practice of rhetoric and poetry was a perpetual temptation to linguistic, metrical, and poetical trifling which sometimes far oversteps the bounds of decency. An Ausonius, teacher of rhetoric, tutor to a prince, Christian only in name, outdoes himself in such things and hence takes particular pains to justify them. "Laetis seria miscere," but within the limits of the "regula morum," is his program (*Commendatio codicis*, ed. Peiper, 320). In another version it runs (Peiper, 261, 1):

> Sunt etiam musis sua ludicra: mixta camenis
> Otia sunt . . .

He designates this manner "mysteria frivola" (Peiper, 247, 67); "satirica et ridicula concinnatio" (*ibid.*, 250, 8); "venustula magis quam forticula" (260, 13); "frivola gerris Siculis vaniora" (197, 12). He uses for it the term "ridicula" (159, 5), which in the Middle Ages will mean "funny story." In the macaronic form which Horace had censured in his time [7] (*Sat.*, I, 10, 20 ff.), his program reads (233, 21 ff.):

> κεῖνος ἐμοὶ πάντων μέτοχος qui seria nostra,
> Qui ioca παντοδαπῆ novit tractare παλαίστρῃ.

His friend Symmachus praises Ausonius' "oblita Tulliano melle festivitas" (220, 3).

But the mixture of jest and earnest, which reappears in certain late antique portrait busts, is not only a stylistic ideal in Ausonius but also a schema of eulogy:

> Ambo pii, vultu similes, ioca seria mixti (34, VIII, 11).

[7] W. Heraeus, *Kleine Schriften*, 1937, 244 ff.

Sometimes the *seria* are omitted:

> *Qui ioca laetitiamque colis, qui tristia damnas* (41, XVIII, 1).
>
> *Facete, comis, animo iuvenali senex* (63, XV, 1).

Ausonius' *ioci* include not only verbal artifices but also ingenious devices for the treatment of content. For example, he starts to rouse his servant in sapphics and then, when the latter does not wake, changes to iambics (6, 21 ff.). The *Ludus septem sapientum* is a diverting mime—a school farce of late Antiquity. But the crown of his comedy is the *Cento nuptialis*—a philological entertainment, with the obscenity which is characteristic of the genre, such as we shall find again in Italian Humanism. By order of the Emperor Valentinian, Ausonius has put together an epithalamium out of verses from Virgil: an "opusculum de inconexis continuum, de diversis unum, de seriis ludicrum, de alieno nostrum" (207, 27 ff.). With feigned modesty he says: "ut bis erubescamus, qui et Virgilium faciamus impudentem" (215, 6 f.). It is understandable that, for all his respect for his teacher Ausonius, Paulinus of Nola, who took Christianity seriously, drew away from Ausonius' conception of the comic (304, 260):

> *Multa iocis pateant; liceat quoque ludere fictis.*
> *Sed . . .*

But for late pagan Antiquity the program *ioca seriis miscere* remained a valid convention. There is a specifically late-antique mixture of the serious and comic styles which can be exaggerated to the point of burlesque. Rutilius Namatianus (1, 28 ff.) has a comic interlude. Martianus Capella's *Nuptiae* is in this mixed style, as is the fictional background of Fulgentius' allegorical interpretation of Virgil. Sidonius has much of the same sort.

2. The Church and Laughter

What position did the church take regarding laughter and humor? The answer is not simple. The testimony accessible to me exhibits a diversity of views which affords fascinating pictures of cultural history. A dictum of Paul's forbade *stultiloquium* and *scurrilitas* to Christians (Eph. 5:4). As early as Clement of Alexandria (*Paidagogos*, II, 45 ff.) we find lengthy discussions of laughter. John Chrysostom (d. 407) taught (PG, LVII, 69) that Christ had never laughed (cf. Egbert's *Fecunda ratis* (ed. Voigt), p. 155). The antique ideal of dignity was taken over by early Christian monasticism. Athanasius can say of Anthony that he was neither morose nor unrestrained in his joy nor did he have to struggle against laughter (ch. 14). Sulpicius Severus (ed. Halm, 136, 22) says of St. Martin: "Nemo unquam vidit iratum, nemo commotum, nemo maerentem, nemo ridentem." The saintly Syrian Ephraim (d. 373; *doctor ecclesiae* since 1920) composed a parenesis against laughter in monks.[8] Similar utterances are to be found in Basil and Cassianus.[9] Finally, St. Benedict bade his monks "verba vana aut risu apta non loqui;

---

[8] See Heffening in *Oriens christianus* (1927), 94 f.
[9] Referred to in Butler's edition of Benedict's Rule.

risum multum aut excussum non amare." [10] He could find support for this in the Biblical text: "Stultus [Vulg. *fatuus*] in risu exaltat vocem suam" (Ecclus. 21:23). However he left out the rest of the sentence: "vir autem sapiens vix tacite ridebit." But the formula "risum multum et excussum" tacitly permitted moderated laughter. So even St. Anthony's discourse was, according to Athanasius (ch. 37) "spiced with godly wit," even as Paul had advised the Colossians (4, 6): "Sermo vester semper in gratia sale sit conditus." Sulpicius Severus (Halm, 191, 28 ff.) relates a few of St. Martin's devout jests ("spiritualiter salsa").

Benedict's precepts remained the authoritative norm. We find them again in the (Merovingian or Carolingian?) rhythmus *De habitu et conversatione monachorum* (*Poetae*, IV, 483):

> 14 *Obscena verba, turpia*
> *Et risum que moventia*
> *Tantum vitemus plurimun,*
> *Velut venenum aspidum.*

A poet writes in praise of a bishop (*Poetae*, II, 629, 37):

> *Non umquam gaudens vacuum crispare cachinnum*
> *Effugiebat ovans semper ubique leves.*

The intensive intellectual movement of the twelfth century led to renewed discussions of the admissibility of laughter. Hugh of St. Victor teaches "quia aliquando plus delectare solent seriis admixta ludicra." [11] May a Christian and a man of honor delight in jests? Hildebert discusses the theme in twelve distichs, of which I quote one (*PL*, CLXXI, 1060 C):

> *Admittenda tibi ioca sunt post seria quaedam.*
> *Sed tamen et dignis ipsa gerenda modis.*

Radulfus Tortarius [12] (322, 70 ff.) expatiates on the theme in detail. John of Salisbury permits a "modesta hilaritas" now and then; so long as everything is done decently, the man of wisdom too may attend entertaining performances: "nec apologos refugit aut narrationes aut quaecumque spectacula." But a more fundamental question is raised too. Is laughter a part of human nature? [13] But the God-Man shared in human nature. Are we to believe that he ever laughed? [14] Is there a specifically holy gaiety? The very dry compiler Petrus Cantor raises such questions in his *Verbum abbreviatum* (Paris after 1178): "Sectemur ergo mentis hilaritatem, sic ut non comitetur lascivia: 'Jucundemur secundum faciem sanctorum, habentes faciem euntium' (Judith: 16) in Jerusalem. Sed numquid potuit Deus bene risisse? Videtur quidem quod habita causa interiore laetitia bona, quod eam exterius in opere ridendi monstrare possit, maxime cum omnes defectus nostros praeterquam culpae assumpserit; etiam cum risibile, vel risibilitas, proprium sit hominis a natura datum. Quomodo ergo eo uti non potuit? Forte potuit, sed non legitur eo usus fuisse" (*PL*, CCV,

---

[10] Ch. 4 of the Rule. Cf. ch. 6.
[11] Brinkmann, *Zu Wesen und Form mittelalterlicher Dichtung*, p. 27.
[12] Ed. Schullian-Ogle.
[13] According to Aristotle laughter distinguishes man from the animals.
[14] Cf. John of Salisbury, *Policraticus* (ed. Webb), I, 305, 8 ff., where the apocryphal Lentulus epistle is referred to. The matter must, then, be earlier than is commonly assumed.

203). The question to what extent clerics might jest occupied one of the most important thinkers and scholars of the twelfth century, Walter of Châtillon (*Moralisch-satirische Gedichte*, ed. Strecker, p. 14):

> *Nostri moris esse solet*
> *Quando festum turbas olet,*
> *Loqui lingua clerici,*
> *Ne, si forte quid dicamus,*
> *Unde risum moveamus,*
> *Cachinnentur laici.*
>
> *In conventu laicorum*
> *Reor esse non decorum*
> *Proferre ridicula,*
> *Ne sermone retundamus*
> *Aut exemplo pervertamus*
> *Mentes sine macula.*
>
> *Pauca tamen plena iocis*
> *Ordinata suis locis*
> *Placet interserere,*
> *Ne, dum semper latinamur,*
> *Ab indoctis videamur*
> *Arroganter agere.*

During the Counter-Reformation the question whether the pious Christian might laugh still played a part in the intellectual battles of the time. Jansenism and Rancé's "Malheur à vous qui riez!" are characteristic of an ethical rigorism which in the present-day judgment of Catholic historians represents a blameworthy extreme. In contrast, Henri Bremond [15] has celebrated San Filippo Neri, whose favorite reading was a book of *facetiae*, as "le saint patron des humoristes." [16] The saint's maxim was: "Lo spirito allegro acquista più facilmente la perfezione cristiana che non lo spirito malinconico" (M. Praz, *Il Secentismo*, 63).

3. Jest and Earnest in the Eulogy of Rulers

As we see, the theoretical position of the church left all possibilities open—from rigoristic rejection to benevolent toleration of laughter. Lay morality would seem to have corresponded to the command of the *Dicta Catonis* (3, 6):

> *Interpone tuis interdum gaudia curis,*

[15] *Divertissements devant l'arche* (1930) 85 ff.
[16] On laughter in early monasticism cf. also Steidle in *Benediktinische Monatsschrift*, 20 (1938).—Unseemly monkish jesting: Reitzenstein, *Hellenistische Wundererzählungen* (1906), 66; H. Lietzmann, *Byzantinische Legenden* (1911), 61; Wendland in *Neue Jahrbücher* (1916), 234.—St. Bernard's rigoristic view is referred to by Giraldus Cambrensis (ed. Brewer), II, 176.—Conciliatory view in Peter of Poitiers and Peter the Venerable (PL, CLXXXIX, 51 B and 354 C).— Lenient judgment upon *mendacium iocosum* in early Scholasticism: *Theologisch-praktische Quartalsschrift*, 93 (1940), 128.

to the authority of which, in much later times, wags like the Archpriest of Hita and Rabelais appealed. Of the *vir discretus* it was commonly said: "Urbanus iocos miscet seriis." [17] This is the continuation of that antique personal ideal which we encountered, for example, in the characterization of Hadrian. As a panegyrical topos it reappears in Carolingian court poetry. For example, when Theodulf, at the beginning of his poem to Charlemagne, in which the latter's milieu is humorously characterized, writes the following lines (*Poetae*, I, 483, 9 ff.):

> *Ludicris haec [laus] mixta iocis per ludicra currat,*
>   *Saepeque tangatur qualibet illa manu,*
> *Laude iocoque simul hunc illita carta revisat,*
>   *Quem tribuente celer ipse videbo deo.*

Similarly the Poeta Saxo says of Charlemagne (*Poetae*, IV, 61):

> 261 *Non umquam nimium laetus, non valde remissus,*
>   *Non multum tristis atque severus erat.*

This topos is then also used for princes of the church. When the poet of the elegy on the death of Archbishop Heribert of Cologne (d. 1021) formulates as his *propositio*:

> *Fibris cordis*
> *Caute tentis*
> *Melos concinamus,*
> *Partim tristes,*
> *Partim letas*
> *Causas proclamantes*
> *De pastore pio*
> *Ac patrono Heriberto,*

we would seem to have a case of thoughtless repetition of the fixed school-formula— very inappropriate in this instance, for later (st. 4 a) we are told concerning Heribert:

> *Severitatem*
> *Facie tristem*
> *Monstrans*
> *Letum toto*
> *Corde sprevit*
> *Mundum.*[18]

The late antique pair of concepts *ludicra-seria* was preserved in literary theory. It appears in this application in the passage from Theodulf quoted above.

The usage could be abundantly illustrated from twelfth-century Latin poetry. I confine myself here to two examples. The first is from a eulogistic poem on a bishop of Regensburg by an unknown poet (published by Wattenbach in *Neues Archiv*, II, 387). It is interesting because the poet has obviously taken over the antithesis between *seria* and *ludicra* as a fixed formula but has used it very unskilfully. The

[17] J. Werner, *Beiträge zur Kunde der lateinischen Literatur des Mittelalters* 2 (1905), No. 236, l. 7.
[18] *Carm. Cant.* (ed. Strecker), p. 23.

seria, namely, include all the gifts of grace which God granted to the bishop. Then we read:

> 28 *Attamen ut quedam paulisper ludicra dedam,*
> *Preter dona dei sunt hic lucra materiei.*
> *Vomere vel cultro non illa quis eruet ultro,*
> *Sed studio mentis, quod non est insipientis,*
> *Tantum quero viam causasque per astronomiam;*
> *Sed vereor multum, ne trufas sit dare stultum*
> *Istius artis opus Chaldea sacerque Canopus*
> *Et primum Siria dedit . . .* (a horoscope follows).

A very penetrating ethico-aesthetic discussion is found in Marbod's poem, filled with the ripe wisdom of old age, *De apto genere scribendi*, which for both form and content would deserve inclusion in an anthology. I select but a few lines from it (PL, CLXXI, 1693 B):

> *Ergo propositum mihi sit, neque ludicra quaedam*
> *Scribere, nec verbis aures mulcere canoris;*
> *Non quod inornate describere seria laudem;*
> *Sed ne, quod prius est, neglecto pondere rerum,*
> *Dulcisonos numeros concinnaque verba sequamur.*
>
> . . . .
>
> *Nec tantum omnino me poenitet illa secutum,*
> *In quibus, exercens animum, sudare solebam,*
> *Nam gravior iuveni labor aptior esse videtur,*
> *Et citus a gravibus fit transitus ad leviora.*
> *Praeterea iuvenem cantare iocosa decebat;*
> *Quod manifesta seni ratio docet esse negatum,*
> *Cuius morali condiri verba sapore*
> *Convenit, et vitiis obsistere fronte severa.*

From what has so far been set forth, it follows that the polarity "jest and earnest" is, from the late antique period onward, a conceptual and formal schema which appears not only in rhetorical theory, in poetry, and in poetics, but also in the circle of the ideal of life established by the panegyric style (in this respect it is comparable to the topos *puer senex*). But, having determined this, we can take a further step. The testimony already discussed itself permits the assumption that the mixture of jest and earnest was among the stylistic norms which were known and practiced by the medieval poet, even if he perhaps nowhere found them expressly formulated. We may, then, view the phenomenon as a fresh substantiation of the view that the Middle Ages loved all kinds of crossings and mixtures of stylistic genres. And in fact we find in the Middle Ages *ludicra* within domains and genres which, to our modern taste, schooled by classicistic aesthetics, absolutely exclude any such mixtures. This is true also of the literature of the church. We must now place this in a rather broader context.

4. Jest in Hagiography [19]

The ecclesiastical poetry of the Middle Ages is a continuation of early Christian poetry. But the latter is itself in no way homogeneous but rather exhibits various streams which flow side by side in separate beds. To understand it historically, it is not enough to treat the Christian poets in chronological order; they must rather be divided among the different genres which develop from the fourth century onward in the literary system of the Christian Empire. First we have the hymn poetry which grew out of the ritual and is bound up with it. Beside it there develops the early Christian Biblical epic. This is an artificial product of *literati* and owes its rise to an attempt to take over the form of the pagan epic and fill it with the matter of the story of salvation. It has nothing to do with the ritual, and stands closer to the school than either to the church or to the trends and forces of popular piety. These latter are fed by two springs, the cult of martyrs and the cult of saints. The former finds its literary precipitate in the *passio*, the latter in the *vita sancti*. There are crosses between the two, e.g., when the *passio* is later supplemented by an account of the martyr's earlier life (βίος καὶ μαρτύριον). *Passio* and *vita* can also take the form of panegyric. The researches of the erudite Bollandist Hippolyte Delehaye have cast light upon these literary forms.[20] The genus of the *passio* comprises two entirely different species: on the one hand, the authentic acts of the martyrs from the period of the persecution of Christians ("passions historiques"), on the other hand the artificial literary products of the late period—namely, of the state church which came into existence in the fourth century. In this period martyrdom is no longer a contemporary reality. For the contemporaries of Theodosius, the Diocletian persecution is already a thing of the distant past. But the martyr cult now reaches its full flower and produces a huge mass of accounts of passions which have a thoroughly conventional and legendary character; these are what Delehaye calls "passions artificielles" or "passions épiques." For the history of literature it is now important that the Spanish poet Prudentius (*ca.* 400) in his *Peristephanon* put such epic passions into the form of Latin literary poetry: "qu'avant la fin du 4e siècle, il existât bon nombre de passions du modèle épique, on peut l'affirmer avec assurance après la lecture de Prudence, des pères Cappadociens, de St. Jean Chrysostome et d'autres auteurs. Quelques hymnes du Peristephanon sont la traduction poétique de textes de cet ordre. Le poème de S. Vincent, de sainte Eulalie, de S. Laurent ne laissent aucun doute à cet égard." [21] Prudentius' poems of martyrs, then, deserve a closer scrutiny in our context. For they offer an example of grotesque humor within a sacred poetic genre. The poet makes Lawrence, suffering martyrdom on a red-hot grid, say to the executioner:

---

[19] Cf. Weinreich, *Antike Heilungswunder* (*Byzantinisch-neugriechische Jahrbücher,* XIV [1937–38], 157); H. Günter, *Legendenstudien* (1906); L. Zoepf, *Das Heiligenleben im 10. Jahrhundert* (1908), 236.—"Confession-box comedy" too is already to be found in saints' lives: Marie de France, *Espurgatoire* (ed. Warnke), 18 b.

[20] Cf. especially *Les Passions des martyrs et les genres littéraires* (1921).

[21] Delehaye, *op. cit.*, 312.

Converte partem corporis
Satis crematum iugiter
Et fac periclum, quid tuus
Vulcanus ardens egerit.
Praefectus inverti iubet.
Tunc ille: coctum est, devora:
Et experimentum cape,
Sit crudum an assum suavius.

One is surprised to find this sort of thing in a poet who is so serious and so affected by his subject. Ramón Menéndez Pidal, to be sure, adduces precisely these two stanzas as testimony to Prudentius' basic Spanishness, thus supporting his "teoría del provincialismo," i.e., the thesis of the continuity of the Spanish character for two millenniums (Introducción a la Historia de la España Romana [1935], p. XXIX): "poesía que acierta a no exluir las complejas discordancias vitales, acogidas también siglos después por nuestro teatro: el humorismo atroz de Lorenzo en el suplicio, junto a la plegaria de histórica sublimidad; el infantil descomedimiento de Eulalia, mezclado al fuerte y magnífico heroismo, como la restallante llama concurre con la lenta nieve para velar los miembros de la atormentada virgen emeritense; en todo muestra Prudencio una fantasía vigorosa, pero sobria, que no quiere dejar demasiado atrás la realidad de las cosas: muy respetuosa idealizadora de la verdad histórica, como después será el arte del juglar del Cid, el del cantor de San Millán y el de sus continuadores. Asi colocó Prudencio en los cimientos de la nueva poesía cristiana, como piedra fundamental, características muy peculiares hispanas, disonantes a veces para la psicología de otros pueblos y a veces embarazo de timoratos comentadores." So far as Prudentius' hymn of St. Laurence is concerned, the stanzas quoted above, to which Menéndez Pidal's characterization refers, are not at all, as might be thought, a free invention of the Spanish poet's. The celebrated scholar of course knows this, even though the reader is not told of it. Prudentius has simply put into verse an expression of the martyr's ("assum est, versa et manduca") which Ambrose, De officiis, I, 41, transmits and which also occurs in a sermon ascribed to Augustine, in Maximus of Turin, in Peter Chrysologus, in the passio s. Laurentii, in an Ambrosian hymn, and in the Roman Breviary. In the Pseudo-Augustine the words run: "Versate me; rex, manduca, iam coctum est." From the researches of P. Franchi de' Cavalieri,[22] which I here follow, it appears that Ambrose's account is the source for all the authors mentioned, and that early Greek martyrologists give accounts of analogous sarcasms from other martyrs. Prudentius' "humorismo atroz" is taken verbatim from the Roman tradition. It is a part of the ecumenical stock of motifs of the early Christian passio. The passio of St. Maura, analyzed by Delehaye, affords a striking analogy: "Plongée dans une chaudière d'eau bouillante, elle plaisante le gouverneur, qui lui fait prendre, dit-elle, un bain malheureusement un peu froid. Le gouverneur veut s'assurer par lui-même de la température de l'eau, et apprend à ses dépens que les ordres ont été bien exécutés." [23] And what of Prudentius' poem on Eulalia? It belongs to the mixed genre mentioned above, which combines vita and passio. In this genre the βίος πρὸ μαρτυρίου represents a later supplement, com-

[22] In Studi e Testi pubblicati per cura degli scrittori della Biblioteca Vaticana, XXVII (1915), 63 ff.
[23] Delehaye, op. cit., 289.

parable to the genre of *chansons de geste* which depict the childhood of famous epic heroes (*Enfances Guillaume*, etc.). "Tout ce qui s'est produit dans ce genre," says Delehaye, "est nécessairement de la fantaisie." [24] For the childhood of Eulalia, who suffered martyrdom at thirteen, Prudentius obviously had no historical testimony, for in describing it he uses hagiographic topoi which can be documented a hundred times over. When he says of Eulalia (ll. 23 ff.):

> Ore severa, modesta gradu,
> Moribus et nimium teneris
> Canitiem meditata senum,

we have the topos *puer senex*. The judge's exhortation (101 ff.) corresponds to the topos, "Ayez pitié de votre jeunesse" (Delehaye, 254). More of the same sort of thing could be enumerated. When Menéndez Pidal regards "el infantil descomedimiento de Eulalia" as particularly characteristic of Prudentius' Spanishness, he doubtless has in mind ll, 126 ff.:

> Martyr ad ista nihil, sed enim
> Infremit inique tyranni oculos
> Sputa iacit . . .

I do not know, and it should not much matter, if spitting at someone as a sign of provocative contempt can be documented elsewhere. But it is perfectly in place in a typical situation of "artificial" passion literature: "On prête au martyr un langage qui convient bien mal au rôle de victime résignée. Il traite le juge de fou et d'insensé, de buveur de sang, plus cruel que toutes les bêtes sauvages." When a Greek martyr addresses his judge as "dog," this can also be described as "descomedimiento," and Eulalia's *sputa* would seem to belong to what Delehaye calls "ce genre d'aménités" (*op. cit.*, 265 f.). Of the fourteen poems of the *Peristephanon* we have considered only two, but even this partial analysis could not but convince us that Prudentius' martyriological poetry, precisely in the passages in which Menéndez Pidal would like to see typically Spanish characteristics, holds fast to ecclesiastical traditions which have no Spanish roots: the tradition represented by Ambrose and that represented by the anonymous "passions artificielles." Now whence do these latter stem? Not from Rome but from Asia Minor and Egypt (Delehaye, *op. cit.*, 313 f.). In the *Peristephanon*, then, we have an Ibero-Latin reflection of the *Oriens christianus*, even as the later hagiographic literature of the West in general continually received streams from the Greek East—one has but to call to mind Walafrid Strabo's life of St. Mammes, the legend of St. Alexius, the cult of St. Nicholas. But the Christian East, we know, also played a great part in the dramatic poetry of the *siglo de oro*, and in this sense it is certainly possible to speak of a Spanish continuity.[25]

[24] *Ibid.*, 321.

[25] Menéndez Pidal was so good as to explain his conception to me as follows: "Lo que doy como característico de Prudencio es el haber dado cabida a ese humorismo atroz en la poesía de un himno. De igual modo, que las truculencias de otros martirios estaban en las Actas conocidas por todos los pintores hagiográficos, pero el haberlas llevado con especial acritud al lienzo es típico de ciertos pintores españoles. Lo mismo digo del descomedimiento de Eulalia. El introducir las estridencias de las passiones martiriales prosísticas en la poesía latina es la que yo doy como característico de Prudencio." The revered scholar will, however, permit me to believe that, for a historical comprehension of Prudentius, it is not wholly a matter of indifference that his "most Spanish" poems stand in an ecumenical literary tradition.

As in the *passio*, comedy is also to be found in the *vita sancti*. One of the earliest and most influential *vitae* of the Latin West, Sulpicius Severus' prose life of St. Martin (written *ca.* 400) and the same author's additional writings on the same subject, exhibit touches of comedy. The saint sees a train of pagans approaching and commands them to halt. They become paralyzed. As they strain their strength to the utmost to advance, they are forced to turn in a circle—"ridiculam in vertiginem rotabantur" (Halm, 112, 8). A similar miracle occurs when a pagan wants to kill the saint and draws his sword. Martin stretches out his neck, but the sword arm remains immovably raised. Sulpicius Severus does not emphasize the comedy of this situation (Halm, 125, 1 ff.), but Paulinus of Périgueux does so in his metrical paraphrase of the *vita s. Martini* (2, 451). St. Martin was much tormented by the Devil, who appeared now as Mercury, now as Jupiter: "Mercurium maxime patie- batur infestum, Jovem brutum atque hebetem dicebat" (Sulpicius Severus, ed. Halm, 196, 17). Paulinus of Périgueux (3, 204 ff.) expunges this comic note, where- as Fortunatus, who rehandled the *vita* later, keeps it. These examples are typical. The pagans, the devils, the men of evil may behave as savagely as they will—they are the fools, and the saint reduces them *ad absurdum*, unmasks them, dupes them. I will cite a few more examples, taking them only from metrical *vitae* of the Carolin- gian period. Einhard tells us how the exorcist Peter laughingly proposes a divine test of strength to his jailor (*Poetae*, II, 128, 21) and how the latter comes off worst. The unmasking of a horse-thief brings a merry note into Heiric's life of St. Germanus (*Poetae*, III, 481, 229 ff.). Here too there is comedy in the complaints of the Devil, whose sphere of action the saint steadily reduces (*Poetae*, III, 496, 291 ff.). Some- times it is the poet himself who laughs at the Devil and—spits at him (following Eulalia's example?). Milo of St. Amand, for example (*Poetae*, III, 583, 191):

> *Hactenus ergo, pater, communi ingessimus hosti*
> *Probra alapas risus iras maledicta cachinnos*
> *Ac sputa, non versus dedimus . . .*

With complacent humor (*ludibunde, satis ludicre*), the rhythmical life of St. Christopher describes how two maids, who had been sent to tempt the saint but whom he had converted, convince the pagan ruler of the powerlessness of his idols (*Poetae*, IV, 822, 152 ff.). Occasionally, however, the comedy is on the other side —in refractory mockers, who are then drastically punished. In the life of St. Amandus by Milo of St. Amand we are shown a mime as opponent of the mission (*Poetae*, III, 600):

> 70   *Unus, iners, facilis, male lubricus atque superbus,*
> *Turpis et impurus scurrilia probra susurrans,*
> *Quem merito vulgus vocitat cognomine Mimmum,*
> *Obstitit infelix stolido bachante cachinno,*
> *Sed mox arreptus miser atro daemone . . .*

Humoristic elements, then, are a part of the style of the medieval *vita sancti*. They were present in the material itself, but we may be sure that the public expected them as well. Now exactly the same thing is true of secular narrative poetry.

5. *Comic Elements in the Epic*

Even in the medieval "epic," comic interpolations are popular. This may at first appear strange, since the medieval epic uses the *Aeneid* as its formal model, and we find nothing comic in the *Aeneid*. But late antique literary theory taught otherwise. Servius says of Book IV: "Est autem paene totus in affectione, licet in fine pathos habeat, ubi abscessus Aeneae gignit dolorem. Sane totus in consiliis et subtilitatibus est; nam paene comicus stilus est: nec mirum ubi de amore tractatur." [26] The intermixture of comic strokes in the serious epic was, then, justified by theory. They are, furthermore, to be found in another antique model epic: the *Achilleis* of Statius. Even in the same poet's *Thebais* (on II, 353) the commentator Lactantius Placidus (6th cent.) found an invitation to laughter. In Ermoldus Nigellus' poem on Louis the Pious comic matter is deliberately introduced. We hear the people of Orléans mocking at hasty travelers who swim the Loire (*Poetae*, II, 28, 133). We see the Breton chieftain Murman who can hardly get his eyes open after overindulging in drink (47, 207). The poet himself good-heartedly allows himself to be teased (62, 135 ff.), because, though a monk, he performs a soldier's duty:

> *Huc egomet scutum humeris ensemque revinctum*
> *Gessi, sed nemo me feriente dolet.*
> *Pippin hoc aspiciens risit, miratur et infit:*
> *"Cede armis, frater; litteram amato magis."*

Finally Ermoldus, in an apostrophe to the converted king of the Danes, Herold, advises him to make some use of his now superfluous idols: he should have Jupiter turned into a cooking pot and Neptune into a water-ewer, so that each will remain in his element (70, 453 ff.). In the *Waltharius* we have the delicious episode of Attila's hangover. The *Gesta Berengarii* also contains a humorous scene (*Poetae*, IV, 380, 200 ff.). Eupolemius' (11th cent.) "Messiad" also has humorous interludes.[27] Even in the *Ligurinus*, whose unknown author sings Frederick I's warlike deeds in Italy, humor breaks out in one passage. We are told that, driven by hunger, the Slavs become cannibals (6, 48):

> *Nec genitor nato, nec fratri parcere frater*
> *Novit, et elixa recreatur filia mater.*

This touches upon the realm of kitchen humor, with which we shall presently have to deal.

These examples show that the Latin epic of the ninth-twelfth centuries took the principle *ludicra seriis miscere* to heart. But let us go further. If the epic demands comic interludes, this clearly means that it was regarded as "entertaining literature." This certainly is at variance with the views of classicistic periods and aestheticians. The classicistic epic is emotional and elevated throughout: for example the *Aeneid*, Lucan, Silius, the *Gerusalemme liberata*. The Middle Ages does not know norms of

---

[26] Servius in Thilo-Hagen, 1, 459. Cf. also A. Philip McMahon, "Aristotelian Definitions of Tragedy and Comedy," in *Harvard Studies in Classical Philology*, XL (1929), 126.
[27] *RF*, VI, p. 523, 335 ff. and p. 540, 223 ff.

this sort. Hence we must not presuppose any unity of the elevated style in the medieval epic. In general we must consider that, within the medieval scale of values, secular poetry could not have the place of honor and the dignity which other epochs bestowed upon it. What did the Middle Ages itself think of its epic? Understandably enough, there is not much testimony on the subject. But we can cite a few witnesses. In the prologue in which Geraldus dedicated the *Waltharius* to Bishop Erchanbald we read:

> Ludendum magis est Dominum quam sit rogitandum.

The epic of *Waltharius*, then, was considered *lusus*, like all poetry without a Christian-ethical trend. In the prologue to the *Gesta Berengarii* we have (Poetae, IV, 356, 21):

> Seria cuncta cadant, opto, et labor omnis abesto,
> Dum capiti summo [28] xenia parva dabo.

We find the same conception a century later in Bishop Wido of Amiens. In the proem to his historical epic *De Hastingae proelio* he says:

> 18   Elegi potius levibus cantare camenis
> Ingenium nostrae mentis quam subdere curis.

This, if one sets aside the scholastic formulas, means simply: I have written a secular poem. The sacred and the profane—that is the fundamental division in the medieval intellectual world. Within the realm of the profane the *ludicra* have their place.[29] So too the poet of the *Ligurinus* says that previous historians of Frederick I had scorned to employ poetic form, because they considered it too frivolous (1, 147)

> . . . puduitque, reor, puerilibus illos
> Lascivire iocis et inanes texere nugas.

Geoffrey of Monmouth begins his *Vita Merlini*:

> Fatidici vatis rabiem musamque iocosam
> Merlini cantare paro.

Among the pleasures of life Guido of Bazoches enumerates "societas convivarum, elegancia ministrorum, poculorum et ciborum exquisita varietas atque suavitas, blanda garrulitas diversos rhidmice casus narrancium, gesta canencium virorum forcium, fidicinum atque mimorum" (*Neues Archiv* [1891], 98 f.). The *chansons de geste*, then, are set on a level with the pleasures of the table and the performances of mimes.

The medieval vernacular epic now carries on the stylistic tradition of the Latin epic. Even in the *Song of Roland*, which contrasts so markedly with the other early French epics by its elevation of thought and its tragic grandeur, we find scenes which are not at all adapted to the "elevated style" but invade the territory of *ludicra*—

---

[28] Glossed: "imperatori."

[29] Hence *ludicra* can also acquire the general meaning "verses." Peter of Blois in a letter expatiates on the vanity of everything earthly, esteems a dead man happy because he is now safe from the wicked world, and ends abruptly: "Mitte mihi versus et ludicra quae feci Turonis." He wants to have them copied (*PL*, CCVII, 39 B). —Perhaps an echo of Horace *Epi*. l. 1, 10: "Nunc itaque et versus et cetera ludicra pono."

for example when Charles rudely dresses down the venerable Naimes (251), when Roland permits himself to joke with Charles (386 ff.), when Ganelon is subjected to the cook's practical jokes (1816 ff.). There is comedy in the *Gormont* too (239 ff., 581 f.).[30] It flourishes luxuriantly in the *Pélerinage de Charlemagne* and in the *Chanson de Guillaume*. There are comic episodes in the epic of the Cid, too, for example the account of the cowardice of the Infants of Carrión. There is a humorous overtone to the duping of the two Jews, as well as to such lines as

> 2382   *Nos d'aquent veremos commo lidia el abbat*

or

> 3373   *Vermejo viene, ca era almorzado.*

When the medieval Latin, the earliest French, and the earliest Spanish epic conform in this, we may conclude that a comic element had always been part of the stock of medieval epic and was not first introduced by corrupt minstrels.

If we now consider the motifs of epic humor, they prove to be typical. The joke "veremos commo lidia el abbat" reminds us of the passage quoted from Ermoldus Nigellus. We find the humor of the hangover not only in Ermoldus and the *Waltharius* but also in Milo of St. Amand. There a man with a hangover says:

> 336   *Verbere non dolui necque tractus somnia rupi;*
> *Nunc vigilans ubi vinam petam? capitisque dolorem*
> *Unguine quo pellam? quibus escis ora resolvam?*

The poet adds a long reflection, of which the end reads (*Poetae*, III, 655):

> 356   *Horreo, sordidus quod multis contigit unum:*
> *Multiplicata prius non Bachica pocula cessant,*
> *Quam nimis impletus revomat, quas hauserat, offas*
> *Venter et immixto fundantur stercora vino,*
> *Quo malus ingressus, gravior sit ut exitus illi*
> *(Perifrasin vito, quia multis cognita dico).*

6. *Kitchen Humor and Other* Ridicula

But the favorite source of humor is "kitchen humor," which in the wider sense includes everything that has to do with food. Like most comic motifs it must have been universally human. For the Middle Ages, however, we must also bear in mind that cooks· are not uncommon among the slaves of Roman comedy and that the cook was regarded as "vilissimum mancipium" (Livy, XXXIX, 6).[31] We find

[30] In 239 ff. there is implicit a fabliau motif, which it is no longer possible to recognize clearly from the text itself. Perhaps the comparative study of motifs could clarify it. Huelin has slipped unrecognized into his enemy's camp, served him "come pucele," brought him roast peacock to eat. Why was that so funny? In any case there is certainly a connection with kitchen humor.

[31] References in R. Pfeiffer in *Philologus*, LXXXVI (1936), 459. Pfeiffer shows that the expression "kitchen Latin" was first used by Lorenzo Valla in a polemic against Poggio. Cf. P. Lehmann in *Historische Zeitschrift*, CXXXVII, 210 f.— Kitchen humor in Terence: *Eunuchus*, 814 ff.

kitchen humor again in late Antiquity. In his *Metamorphoses* (X, 14) Apuleius has a comic interlude of the quarrel between two brothers, one of whom is a cook, the other a confectioner. A contention between a cook and a baker under the presidency of Vulcan was written in the second or third century by a poet named Vespa (Buecheler-Riese, *Anthologia latina*, No. 199). The cook is made fun of for his smoke-blackened face. Fortunatus employs this motif in a complaint on the subject of the royal court cook in Metz, who had taken his boat from him (Leo, p. 148):

> 11   *Corde niger, fumo pastus, fuligine tinctus,*
> > *Et cuius facies caccabus alter adest,*
> > *Cui sua sordentem pinxerunt arma colorem,*
> > *Frixuriae cocumae scafa patella tripes,*
> > *Indignus versu potius carbone notetur,*
> > *Et piceum referat turpis imago virum.*
> > *Res indigna nimis, gravis est inuria facti:*
> > *Plus iuscella coci quam mea iura valent.*

The same Fortunatus, in ten lines which parody the epic style, describes a stomach-ache caused by an immoderate consumption of peaches (Leo, p. 170). We find kitchen humor in Carolingian poetry too. Charlemagne's high steward appears in Theodulf and Alcuin under the bucolic name of Menalcas (*Poetae*, I, 488):

> 181   *Pomiflua sollers veniat de sede Menalcas,*
> > *Sudorem abstergens frontis ab arce manu.*
> > *Quam saepe ingrediens, pistorum sive coquorum*
> > *Vallatus cuneis, ius synodale gerit.*

Menalcas is to have porridge cooked for Alcuin (*Poetae*, I, 246):

> 48   *Ipse Menalca coquos nigra castiget in aula,*
> > *Ut calidos habeat Flaccus per fercula pultes.*

Did the erudite Biblical scholar remember "pone ollam grandem et coque pulmentum filiis prophetarum" (II Kings 4: 38)?

Kitchen humor in the epic is echoed in Ermoldus' advice to King Harold. We next find it in the historical epic of Abbo of St. Germain des Prés (*Bella Parisiacae urbis*, written 897). There the powerful Abbot Ebolus (a fighting cleric!) spits seven Normans at once and laughingly hands them over to the cook (*Poetae*, IV, 83, 108 ff.). Wounded Normans who retire from the fray are berated by their wives: "You devil's son! Haven't I set enough bread and roast boar and wine before you? Do you want more, you glutton?" To the same period belongs the ethical didactic poem of Milo of St. Amand, *De sobrietate*. The principal theme is resistance to gluttony. The poet gives us a glimpse into the medieval kitchen (*Poetae*, III, 654):

> 303   *Perspice fumantes iam nocte dieque culinas*
> > *Sudantesque coquos tetra fuligine nigros,*
> > *Fercula portantes, pallentes fasce ministros.*
> > *Stat pincerna potens iam lassus in aede reclinis,*
> > *Alternis vicibus varians vestigia stertit*
> > *Et tacita ventri maledicit fauce capaci.*

But Milo's comedy is involuntary. He is a zealous and pious man. His first *exemplum* for the doctrine that gluttony is the ruination of man, he takes from the Old Testament. The captain of the guard, Nebuzar-adan, who conquered and plundered Jerusalem for King Nebuchadnezzar, was a cook! Allegorically interpreted, the king signifies the Devil, his cook the *gastrimargia* which ravages the church's flock (Jerusalem) (*Poetae*, III, 617 f.). In the Vulgate, to be sure (II Kings 24: 11 ff. and Jerem. 52:12), there is nothing about Nebuzar-adan's being a cook, but there is in the earlier translations (see Traube on the passage), which were also known to Augustine, Fulgentius (Helm 160, 22) and Isidore. We find Nebuzar-adan used allegorically again in the *Fecunda ratis* (ca. 1000) of Egbert of Liége (ed. Voigt, p. 208):

> *Succendit Nabugodonosor cocus ardua templi*
> *In Solimis, regi dum prandia lauta pararet:*
> *Nos templum domini violamus et igne cremamus,*
> *Copia dum mentem suffocat larga cyborum.*

We next find kitchen humor in the *Ecbasis captivi*, where the eagle, for his pride, is degraded to the position of kitchenboy (l. 695 f.); in Hroswitha's *Dulcitius*; in a droll tale among the Cambridge songs (Strecker, p. 65), in which St. Peter is made the *magister cocorum*; in Walter of Châtillon [32]:

> *Templum dei violat ordo praelatorum,*
> *Jam furantur fuscinis carnes caccaborum.*

Here there is a reference to I Sam. 2:12 ff.

Kitchen humor, as we saw, also occurs in the *Roland*. Then in the *Chanson de Guillaume* (1056 ff., 1312, 1427 ff.). In the epic of Rainouart the coarsely comic kitchenboy finally becomes an epic hero. The connection between the kitchen and military life appears, furthermore, to have existed in reality. Ordericus Vitalis names a "Harcherius regis Franciae coquus et miles insignis" (A. Schultz, *Das höfische Leben* [2], 1, 55). Medieval kitchen humor is once more complacently displayed in Rabelais. Among many other episodes, we have the theme of the warlike cook too (Bk. IV, ch. 39). Frère Jean traces it back to the Old Testament. He makes Potiphar "maistre queux des cuisines de Pharaon" and continues: "Pourquoi Nabuzardan, maistre cuisinier du roy Nabugodonosor, feut entre tous aultres capitaines esleu pour assiéger et ruiner Hierusalem?" One source of medieval kitchen humor was undoubtedly the monastery kitchen, which is also occasionally deemed worthy of poetical mention (*Poetae*, I, 521, 59 and *Poetae*, I, 332, II). Kitchen duty was certainly not always a pleasure. We have a moving complaint by the poet Winrich, teacher in a monastery at Treves (ca. 1070) who was detailed to the kitchen.[33]

Together with kitchen humor, another *ridiculum* [34] is very popular. Medieval man finds nothing so comic as involuntary nudity. The motif occurs with great frequency. It belongs to the timeless stock of folklore. But it had literary authority as well. It could be found in Latin poetry, in Ausonius for example (Peiper, 246, 33); certain passages in the Bible too could be misapplied in this sense: Genesis 9:22 [35];

---

[32] *Moralisch-satirische Gedichte*, p. 65.
[33] See H. Walther, *Das Streitgedicht* . . . (1920), 56.
[34] *Ridiculum* as a genre-concept: *Carm. Cant.*, No. 35 and 42.
[35] Versified and amplified in Claudius Marius Victor's *Alethia*, 3, 76.

Nahum 3:5; Jeremiah 13:26. The last passage is contained in a reprimand by God to Jerusalem and runs: "Nudavi femora tua contra faciem tuam, et apparuit ignominia tua." The passage is interesting, because we have Jerome's [36] allegorical interpretation of it: " 'Nudavi'—sive nudabo et revelabo—'femora'—et posteriora—'tua' . . ." The moral application runs: "Rogemus, ut nec in praesenti nec in futuro saeculo revelet femina et posteriora nostra." The church naturally disapproved most sharply of profanations of such Biblical passages. But monastery humor was permissible even in earlier times. Mico of St. Riquier sketches a scene of nudification (*Poetae*, III, 363, 19 ff.). Egbert, teacher at the cathedral school at Liége, included in his *Fecunda ratis*, written for schoolboys, a droll story *De Waltero monacho bracas defendente* (Voigt, p. 203). From the time of the founding of Cîteaux (end of the eleventh century), which was a reaction against the moral decline of Cluny, a voluminous controversial literature between the two orders grows up. An argument against the Cistercians consists in the reproach that "they wore no breeches, that they might be more ready for unchastity." [37] The ass Brunellus in Nigel Wireker's *Speculum stultorum* weighs the pros and cons of this costume (*SP*, I, 95):

> Taedia de nocte femoralia nulla iacenti
>   In lecto facient; sit procul iste timor.
> Nescia braccarum, genitalia membra deorsum
>   Nocte dieque simul libera semper erunt.
> Ergo quid facerem, veniens si ventus ab Austro
>   Nudaret subito posteriora mea?
> Qua facie tantum quis sustinuisse pudorem
>   Possit, et ad claustrum postea ferre pedem?
> Quod si contingat mea nuda pudenda videri
>   Numquam de reliquo monachus albus ero.

We find the same topos in the complaint of a poor scholar in Matthew of Vendôme (*SB München* [1872], 588):

> Insultat misero mihi barbara turba, negatur
> Hospicium, careo paene, pudenda patent.

The droll tale *de monacho bracas defendente*, which we found in Egbert of Liége, serves in the *Moniage Guillaume* as a motif which carries forward the epic action. For the first version of this "heroic epic," which like so many other *chansons de geste* has a strong admixture of coarse comedy, the date *ca.* 1160 has been proposed; for the second, *ca.* 1180. William, who has become a monk, is ordered by the abbot to offer no resistance to the robbers unless they try to take off his breeches (*Moniage*, I, 361). In the corresponding passage of *Moniage* II an explanation is added which is lacking in I:

> 688   S'il les me tolent, chou sera grans contraire
>   Car on porra veir tot mon afaire.

[36] In his commentary on Jeremiah (ed. Reiter), p. 71.
[37] H. Walther, *op. cit.*, 164.—The "breeches problem" plays a part in the anecdote which Walter Map tells in *De Nugis curialium* (ed. James), p. 49.—J. Greven, *Die Exempla des J. v. Vitry* (1914), 47, No. 77.

In the Italian Franciscan preacher Bernardino de' Busti we still find the motif in an edifying application.[38] It adds piquancy to the *sel franciscain* as to the *sel rabelaisien* and later to the humor of Cervantes.

The "motif of πρωκτὸς λαλῶν, which is to be found everywhere in coarse folk humor" (Otto Weinreich [39]) is also very popular in the Middle Ages. It appears as early as in the hagiographic comedy of the Merovingian period. The body of St. Gangolf works miracles. A woman who is told of this cries: "Sic operatur virtutes Gangulfus, quomodo anus meus." This was avenged: the designated organ immediately emitted an "obscenus sonus." This happened on a Friday. During all the rest of her life the woman could not speak a word on a Friday but that it was followed by a detonation (*MGH, SS. rer. mer.*, VII, 166 f.). In the Carolingian period we find (*Poetae*, III, 362, No. 161):

> 14   *Tum podex carmen extulit horridulum,*

as well as the droll tale of the musical donkey (*Poetae*, IV, 1080).

Matthew of Vendôme has (Faral, 126, 71):

> *In pateris patinisque studet, ructante tumultu*
> *Et stridente tuba ventris utrimque conat.*

This drastic humor still has its place in the diabolic comedy of Dante's *Inferno* (XX, 139).

We have touched upon but a few sides of medieval humor.[40] Here too a rich booty awaits the investigator.

[38] Gilson, *Les idées et les lettres* (1932), 227.

[39] Weinreich, *Senecas Apocolocyntosis* (1923), 55 with n. 3.

[40] On ecclesiastical humor cf. also H. Fluck, "Der risus paschalis" (*Archiv für Religionswissenschaft* [1934], 188 ff.). On the *ioca monachorum* and the *Cena Cypriani*: Paul Lehmann, *Die Parodie im Mittelalter* (1922). On the Feast of the Staff (*Bakelfest*): H. Spanke in *Volkstum und Kultur der Romanen* (1931), 204; K. Young, *The Drama of the Medieval Church* (1933), I, 106 and 501 ff.; Wilmart in *Revue bénédictine*, XLIX, 139 and especially 338 ff.—On dance music and ball-playing in church: Spanke in *Neuphilologische Mitteilungen*, XXXI, 149 and *Hist. Vjft.*, XXVI, 384.—Among *ridicula* Walter of Châtillon also includes "Veneris copula" (1925, p. 59, st. 4). This is reminiscent of the antique conception (cf. *supra*, p. 429, n. 26), according to which the domain of the erotic was reserved for comedy. The classification of the erotic under comedy could be copiously documented from medieval texts.

LATE ANTIQUE LITERARY STUDIES

1. *Quintilian*

Quintilian's influence during the Middle Ages is far greater than the notices make it appear.[1] Inasmuch as the *Institutio oratoria* is a draft for the education of an ideal man, it can be compared with Castiglione's *Cortegiano* (1528). The "harmonious rounding-out of the intellectual life" which Burckhardt found characteristic of the Renaissance ideal of the *uomo universale* is also alive in Quintilian. The art of speaking is "the most precious gift of the gods," and for that very reason it is the perfection of the human mind. "Ipsam igitur orandi maiestatem, qua nihil dii immortales melius homini dederunt et qua remota muta sunt omnia et luce praesenti ac memoria posteritatis carent, toto animo petamus" (XII, 11, 30). Certainly the goal is high and hard to reach. But has not man learned to cross seas, to understand the courses of the stars, to measure the universe? These arts are even harder, yet in value they are far inferior to eloquence ("minores sed difficiliores artes": XII, 11, 10): I know few utterances which so sharply illuminate the contrast between the antique and the modern hierarchy of goods as these sentences. Without them we should not understand why for Quintilian the ideal orator is also the ideal man. Cicero, to be sure, had preceded him: he had undertaken to sketch the perfect orator in his *Orator*.[2] But his picture was too obviously accommodated to his own personality and was also too specialized, too dependent, that is, on the *ars dicendi*. When, then, in the twelfth book of his work, Quintilian approaches the same task —"ad partem operis destinati longe gravissimam"—he can say that he feels like a solitary sailor driven out into the main sea—"caelum undique et undique pontus."[3] To be sure, he sees Cicero in the vast immensity—and Cicero alone. But even Cicero now takes in his sails, rows more slowly, and contents himself with discussing the kind of eloquence suitable for the perfect orator. So he, Quintilian, has no predecessor whose course he can follow. He must find his own way and pursue it as far as the subject demands.

From Quintilian's book I select some passages which are of importance for later literary theory. If at first Quintilian (I, 4, 2) distinguishes only two parts of grammar, the art of correct speech and the interpretation of the poets, he nevertheless adds (I, 4, 3) that grammar also includes the art of writing—in other words what we call composition. This system of instruction, which Quintilian found in existence and which he learnedly elucidates, is the historical ground for the fact that from the Roman Empire to the French Revolution all literary art rests upon school rhetoric. In a subsequent passage (I, 9, 1) the two parts of grammar are distinguished, with a new terminology, as *methodice* and *historice*. The interpretation of

---

[1] Paul Lehmann in *Philologus*, LXXXIX (1934), 349–83.—A. Mollard believes that he can prove a "conspiration du silence" against Quintilian in the twelfth century (*Le Moyen Age* [1935], 9).

[2] "summum oratorem fingere" (*Or.*, 7). Castiglione uses the same expression: "formar can parole un perfetto cortegiano."

[3] *Aeneid*, III, 190.

the poets, then, is equated with "historics," and so we have literary history *in nuce*—not only as a term but as a thing. An entire chapter (I, 8) is devoted to the reading of the poets, "lectio." Only those poets are to be read who have moral value (§ 4). Accordingly, as Quintilian notes with satisfaction, it has recently become the practice to teach Virgil in school. The lyric poets too must be read, though with exceptions. Even Horace has passages which Quintilian would be loath to interpret in class. The erotic elegy is altogether rejected. Comedy, on the other hand, is recommended. It is important for students of oratory because it presents the various characters and passions, which Aristotle too had treated in his *Rhetoric*. This remark on comedy can explain the fact—at first sight so surprising—that Terence was one of the favorite school authors of the entire Middle Ages. For the rest, we see that Quintilian was stricter than the monks and priests of the Christian Middle Ages, who, as we know, made extensive use of Ovid in teaching, at least from the eleventh century on.—With this chapter on the interpretation of the poets, we must take Book X, 1. The whole subject-matter of rhetoric as a communicable science has been treated in the preceding books. But even the student who has assimilated all this does not yet possess that facility of speech which has become habit (ἕξις). This requires an extensive and always available reserve of words and matter—"copia rerum ac verborum" (X, 1, 5). Neither can be acquired except by reading. Thus Quintilian is led to treat of literature a second time, but now on a higher plane. What is the right way to read? The answer to this question (X, 1, 19) runs: "Let us review and reconsider what we have read, and as we swallow our food well-masticated and almost dissolved, in order that it may be more easily digested, so too what we read must not be committed to the memory and reserved for imitation in a crude state but must first be softened and as it were reduced to a pulp." Quintilian now adds a distribution of authors by classes: poets, historians, philosophers. The reading of the poets recommends itself not only through the delight and refreshment which accompany it; it inspires the mind, gives sublimity to expression, and teaches the orator to influence the emotions of his audience. To be sure, it must not be forgotten that poetry [4] is close to epideictic (not to forensic) oratory; that, further, its aim is solely pleasure, that, finally, it realizes this end by inventing not only things that are untrue but things that are incredible: "genus ostentationi comparatum et praeter id quod solam petit voluptatem eamque etiam fingendo non falsa modo, sed etiam quaedam incredibilia" (X, 1, 28). As for history, it is closely related to poetry: a sort of prose poem ("proxima poetis et quodammodo carmen solutum": X, 1, 31). It contains a wealth of facts which the orator can use as examples. Finally, the philosophers too must be read.[5]

How must this concept of eloquence have been understood in a medieval monastery school? Rhetoric was one of the three lower *artes*. Quintilian taught that it must be connected with the study of poetry and philosophy. From this the Middle Ages drew the conclusion that *eloquentia, poesis, philosophia, sapientia* were only

[4] Quintilian uses the neutral expression "hoc genus" (X, 1, 28), which is presumably to be completed by "eloquentiae." Or is it used absolutely? Ordinarily he says "poetae." Only once (XII, 11, 26) does the word "poesis" appear, and it is extremely rare elsewhere in Latin. Horace has it once (*Ars poetica*, 361), but in the meaning "poem." *Poetica* or *poetice* is also rarely "poetry." Neither Roman Antiquity nor the Latin Middle Ages had a current word for poetry.

[5] Quintilian's relation to philosophy is exhaustively discussed by B. Appel, *Das Bildungs- und Erziehungsideal Quintilians* (Munich dissertation [1914]).

different names for the same thing. But let us hear Quintilian further. Within phi-losophy, the emphasis is upon morality: "Mores ante omnia oratori studiis erunt excolendi" (XII, 2, 1). And still more imperatively: "Evolvendi penitus auctores, qui de virtute praecipiunt, ut oratoris vita cum scientia divinarum rerum sit humanarumque coniuncta" (XII, 2, 8). With this, finally, let us take: "iam quidem pars illa moralis, quae dicitur Ethice, certe tota oratori est accommodata" (XII, 2, 15). Now let us remind ourselves that the poets too were recommended as school reading on account of their influence in forming morals. If we take all this together, it becomes comprehensible that grammatical and literary instruction in the medieval school is considered as at the same time a course in morals. When this view put its stamp upon terminology, the curricular authors could be called *ethici*. That in fact is the usual, but to my knowledge so far unexplained, term. It becomes, I believe, comprehensible through Quintilian.[6]

We see what a large place purely literary studies take in Quintilian's textbook. It contains passages where, through the oratorical ideal of life, a wholly different one is perceptible: that of a Humanist living only in his studies, a lover of literature and devotee of the Muses. How is rhetoric to be fitted into the Aristotelian schema of the arts as theoretical, practical, and poetic? It is usually assigned to the realm of practice. But certainly it is also present in the orator who does not use it, as is the art of medicine in a doctor who has given up his "practice." "For there is some gain, and I know not but it be the greatest, in solitary study; and delight in literature is then wholly pure when it is dissevered from all activity and can enjoy the contemplation of itself"—"nam est aliquis, ac nescio an maximus, etiam ex secretis [7] studiis fructus ac tum pura voluptas litterarum, cum ab actu, id est opera, recesserunt et contemplatione sui fruuntur" (II, 18, 4). The mood of Late Antiquity—but one which could be revived and has been felt again in each of the centuries that have followed. In such a statement, the stuff of antique rhetoric is transformed into something wholly different; into what the French call "la religion des lettres"; what Erasmus incarnated in the sixteenth century. Quintilian could be the guide of such a Humanism too. But of greater importance and influence historically is his significance for the pedagogical treatment of the antique authors and the basic concepts of literary criticism current in the Middle Ages.

2. *Late Roman Grammar*

Of the surviving Roman grammars,[8] none is earlier than the third century, the majority of them, and the most important, fall in the fourth. The writers of this late and unproductive period are content to copy from earlier sources and to compile

[6] This may serve to supplement and correct K. Langosch's statements in his edition of Hugh of Trimberg's *Registrum* (1942), 30 f.

[7] Quintilian was fond of connecting "secretus" with literary studies. In such a usage we hear something like a longing for private life—understandable in a man who was for decades a practicing forensic orator and in his old age became tutor to a prince. Of the study of literature he says finely: "necessaria pueris, iucunda senibus, dulcis secretorum comes" (I, 4, 5). Tacitus too speaks of "litteratum secreta," which are unknown to the Germans (*Germania*, 19).

[8] Fundamental: K. Barwick, *Remmius Palaemon und die römische Ars grammatica* (Leipzig, 1922).

in various ways. The subject matter is now increased by the inclusion of metrics, which is reckoned a part of the grammatical *ars*.[9] With very few exceptions [10] the early Middle Ages changed nothing in the late Roman grammatical stock, but for the most part reproduced the precepts of the third and fourth centuries almost verbatim. Thus for example the Irishman Clemens, who taught at the palace school under Charlemagne and Louis the Pious, defines the four tasks of grammar (*lectio, enarratio, emendatio, iudicium*) in close correspondence with Marius Victorinus' *ars* (4th century).[11] The *grammaticus* (*litterator*) of the imperial age left the legacy of his *ars* to his medieval successors: the stock of Roman literature which declining paganism still possessed was preserved as indispensable scholastic material. The method of transfer was unintelligent, uninspired, and mechanical—and for that very reason it was durable. This becomes especially clear when the grammarians impart elements of poetics, as Diomedes (4th century) did. To his *ars grammatica* he added a third book, devoted to metrics. Thus something which we should account a part of poetics is missing. But here by *poetica* is meant neither the theory nor the technique of poetry, but the art of poetry in general [12] in contradistinction from the individual poem: "poetica est fictae veraeve narrationis congruenti rhythmo ac pede metrica structura, ad utilitatem voluptatemque accommodata" (Keil, I, 473). A purely formal definition, which succeeds in uniting contrary views. The essence of poetry lies in its metrical structure.[13] Its content is a narrative (*narratio*). The end of poetry is, according to Diomedes (and his model, Horace), to afford profit and pleasure. But let us read on: "distat autem poetica a poemate et poesi, quod poetica ars ipsa intelligitur, poema autem pars operis, ut tragoedia, poesis contextus et corpus totius operis effecti, ut Ilias Odyssia Aeneis." This we cannot understand—because the author himself did not understand what he was copying from. But we can reconstruct the meaning.[14] In Hellenistic poetics it had become customary to organize the didactic subject-matter according to three points of view: ποίησις, ποίημα, ποιητής. This schema is also followed by Horace, "who divides his *Ars poetica* into three sections of equal extent, the first concerned with the composition of poetry (1–152), the second with the individual poem (153–295), and the third with the poet." [15] In addition, Hellenistic theory propounds two contrary doctrines. The one considers ποίησις to mean the matter of

---

[9] In Martianus Capella, Minerva decides that metrics belongs not to grammar but to music (150, 5).

[10] Above all the still enigmatic Virgilius Maro (7th cent.) must be named, though Clemens Scottus integrated him into the main tradition.—According to D. Tardi (*Les Epitomae de Virgile de Toulouse* [1928], 23), Virgilius Maro was an adept of the cabbala (as transmitted by Aquitanian Jewish congregations), whose principles of interpretation (gematria among others) he transferred to Latin grammar.

[11] *Clementis ars grammatica* (ed. J. Tolkiehn [1928]), pp. 11, 22 ff.

[12] As already in Cicero, and in Aristotle in the first sentence of the *Poetics*.

[13] This is the prevailing concept (Plato, *Phaedrus*, 258 d), from which only Aristotle diverged.

[14] Following C. Jensen's fundamental studies on Hellenistic and Horatian poetics. The latest is *Herakleides vom Pontos bei Philodem und Horaz* (*Berl. SB. Phil. hist. Kl.* [1936]).

[15] Jensen, *Herakleides*, p. 3.—Cf. also Hermogenes (ed. Rabe), p. 4, 9 ff. Also G. Röttger, *Studien zur platonischen Substantivbildung* (Kiel dissertation [1937], p. 30.

the poem, ποίημα its verbal formulation. The other, already known to Lucilius (*frs.* 33 ff.), considers *poesis* to mean a long poem (*Iliad*, Ennius), *poema* a short one (Lucilius gives the epistle as an example [16]). This second doctrine is reproduced by Diomedes when he designates tragedy as *poema*, epic as *poesis*. For the Middle Ages, the division of poetic genres (*poematos genera*) transmitted by Diomedes was of particular importance. He distinguishes (p. 482) three major genres, each with several subordinate genres. This may be schematically reproduced as follows:

1. *genus activum vel imitativum* (*dramaticon vel mimeticon*). Characteristic: the poem contains no interlocutions by the poet (*sine poetae interlocutione*); only the dramatic personages speak. To this genre belong not only tragedies and comedies but also pastorals such as Virgil's first and ninth Eclogues.—Four subordinate genres: *tragica, comica, satyrica, mimica*.

2. *genus enarrativum* (*exegeticon vel apangelticon*). Characteristic: here the poet alone speaks. Example: Virgil's *Georgics*, Books I–III, together with the first part of Book IV. (This means that the story of Aristaeus [IV, 314–558] falls outside of the *genus enarrativum*.) Further example: Lucretius.
   Three subordinate genres:
   a) *angeltice*: contains "sentences" (Theognis and chrias).
   b) *historice*: contains narratives and genealogies. Example: Hesiod's catalogue of women.
   c) *didascalice*: the didactic poem (Empedocles, Lucretius, Aratus, Virgil).

3. *genus commune* (*koinon vel mikton*). Characteristic: both the poet and the characters speak. Examples: *Iliad, Odyssey, Aeneid*.
   Two subordinate genres:
   a) *heroica species*: *Iliad* and *Aeneid*.
   b) *lyrica species*: Archilochus and Horace.

This system, which at first glance appears very strange, needs to be understood.[17] Classifying the genres according to the person speaking (the poet alone; the personages alone; poet and personages alternately) goes back to Plato (*Republic*, 392–394). It is contained in his great attack on poetry. Plato wants to show that all "mimetic" poetry (tragedy, comedy, epic) must be banished from the ideal state. Mimesis includes reproduction of the emotions, hence also of the evil and base (395–396). In the republic no poetry is permitted except hymns to the gods and songs in praise of good men (607 a)—hence only a recital by the poet in his own person (δι᾽ ἀπαγγελίας αὐτοῦ τοῦ ποιητοῦ. 394 c). To reach this conclusion, Plato set up or took over the tripartition of poetry by its most external formal characteristics, according to which only the "mixed genre" (δι᾽ ἀμφοτέρων) remains for epic.[18] That this classification is unsatisfactory [19] is obvious. But it was preserved by Plato's authority and later taken over by Aristotle [20] as one of the three possible methods of

[16] Jensen, *Philodemos über die Gedichte*, p. 103.
[17] Cf. Usener, *Kleine Schriften*, II, 290 f. and Georg Kaibel, *Die Prolegomena περὶ κωμῳδίας* (= *Gött. Abh.*, Vol. II, No. 4 [1898]), 28 ff.
[18] According to J. Stroux (*Das Problem des Klassischen und die Antike, acht Vorträge*, ed. W. Jaeger [1931], 2 ff.), Plato advanced the doctrine of the "legitimacy of the genres" in the *Laws*. But there is nothing of this in Plato's text.
[19] But cf. Kroll, *Studien zum Verständnis der römischen Literatur* (1924), 45.
[20] Only Gudeman (*Aristoteles Poetik* [1934], 104) appears to dispute this.

classification for the arts of rhythm, language, and tune (*Poetics*, ch. 1-3). In Aristotle, however, it has a place only among the preliminaries and performs no systematic function in the remainder of his investigations. Aristotle's interest is not centered upon the external classification but upon the inner essence of the poetic genres. In tragedy, he observes the development of its "nature," he "defines its essence" (τὸν ὅρον τῆς οὐσίας). Plato's schematism, however, by ways which we can no longer follow precisely, entered fourth-century grammatical teaching, as we find it in Diomedes. By then the great genres of antique Classicism had long since died out. What examples of them had survived were used as teaching material in the schools. The doctrine of the genres was put on the same plane as that of the parts of speech. It became a crude system of pigeonholes into which disparate things were forced. In the process, genres which Plato and Aristotle never knew, had to be provided for—above all pastoral poetry, which Virgil had made classical. Quintilian (X, 1, 55), after naming Homer, Hesiod, Antimachus, Panyassis Apollonius, and Aratus among the *epici* had added Theocritus—in other words, he conceived of the epic purely formally, as a poem in hexameters. But Diomedes goes further. His schematism forces him to divide Virgil's eclogues between two genres.[21] Numbers 1 and 9, which consist purely of dialogue, without interpolations by the poet, belong to the "dramatic" genre, like tragedy and comedy. It follows logically (even though Diomedes does not expressly say so) that the remaining eight eclogues (and with them the greater part of bucolic poetry) belong to the *genus commune*—and that means to the epic. The Latin Middle Ages maintained this concept. Diomedes further provides a special definition of the epic: "epos dicitur graece carmine hexametro divinarum rerum et heroicarum humanarumque comprehensio[22] . . . latine paulo communius carmen auditum" (483 f.). Here we obviously have the reflection of a note by Diogenes Laertius (VII, 60), who claims to have taken it from Poseidonius. This is not in accordance with Diomedes' tripartite classification. But Diomedes simply compiles excerpts from various sources. In poetry he distinguishes, besides the three genres, four kinds of style[23] and six *qualitates carminum: heroica, comica, tragica, melica, satyrica, dithyrambica* (502, 13). Diomedes' influence is documented partly by mentions of his name, partly by adoption of his doctrines.[24]

Another fourth-century grammarian, the Neoplatonist Marius Victorinus, of Africa, concludes his *ars* with a philosophical contribution to poetics, which he takes from his Greek sources. After discussing meters, he passes to the question of the origin of music and poetry and traces them back to a native predisposition which *Natura parens* bestowed upon man together with life and consciousness. This natural predisposition was gradually developed into a teachable art by observation and practice. A further factor—according to Theophrastus—was the stimulus proceeding from the three chief emotions, pleasure, anger, and enthusiasm (= *sacri furoris*

21 Servius (Thilo-Hagen, III, 1, 29) classifies the eclogues according to Diomedes' three genres.

22 This formula is connected with the definition of philosophy as the "knowledge of divine and human things"; on which cf. Karl Reinhardt, *Poseidonios* (1921), 58.

23 μακρός: *Aen.*, XI, 539; βραχύς: *Aen.*, V, 250; μέσος: *Aen.*, I, 343; ἀνθηρός: *Aen.*, VII, 30, "ubi amoenitatem luci ac fluminis describendo facit narrationem" (p. 483).

24 Diomedes in the Middle Ages: Manitius, Index.—Diomedes' *Ars grammatica* was printed at Paris in 1498, and there again, with Donatus, in 1527. It is still influential during the French Renaissance; see W. F. Patterson, *Three Centuries of French Poetical Theory* (Ann Arbor, 1935), I, 620 and 626.

instinctus). Following Plato, Victorinus advances the doctrine of the poet's divine frenzy, and following Horace (*Carm.*, III, 21, 11), that of the inspiring effect of wine. But love too can make a man a poet.[25] Victorinus, then, represents a source from which the Middle Ages could take the Platonic theory of poetic madness. It is characteristic of the cultural situation of late Rome that the doctrine was set forth as a supplement to a grammatical textbook. Victorinus was much used in the Middle Ages.

As we know, the most widely circulated textbooks of Latin grammar in the Middle Ages were those of Aelius Donatus (4th century) and Priscian. In Donatus there is nothing on poetics. Priscian occupies a unique position.[26] A native of Mauretania, he became a teacher of Latin in Byzantium under the Emperor Anastasius (491–518). His grammar is not only more comprehensive but of more intrinsic value than the fourth-century Roman *artes*, because, in the Eastern Empire, he was able to find access to higher Greek theory. We find nothing on poetics in it. But the omission is supplied by a briefer treatise of Priscian's, the so-called *Praeexercitamina*. This is a translation of Hermogenes' προγυμνάσματα (written under Marcus Aurelius). These "preliminary exercises" had a regular place in the teaching of rhetoric. They are exercises in style, comparable to our school themes, and proceeding from easier to more difficult.[27] They included fable, chria, narrative, sentence, commonplaces, exercises in panegyric, similes, prosopopoeias, description, treatment of a thesis (e.g., *an navigandum, an ducendum uxorem, an philosophandum*). Whether these progymnasmata, which were already common in Cicero's time and later were reduced to systematic form, should be assigned to the grammatical or the rhetorical curriculum was debated even in Antiquity.[28] It was no less difficult to apportion the study of the figures between the two subjects. Such jurisdictional quarrels were a matter of indifference to practical teaching. The significance of Priscian's *Praeexercitamina* lies in the fact that, as a supplement to his grammar, they brought the Latin Middle Ages the elements of Greek rhetorical theory, and did so with the omission of everything which was pertinent only to political and judicial oratory. From Priscian's treatise the medieval grammar-school student could, among other things, learn the difference between *narratio fictilis* (*ad tragoedias sive comoedias ficta*) and *narratio historica* (*ad res gestas exponendas*); the nature and use of the sentence (*oratio generalem pronuntiationem habens*); the kinds of the simile. The section *De laude* (Keil, 435 ff.) must have been especially influential. For it contains the principal panegyrical topoi of Greek Antiquity. Here one thing is of interest from the point of view of the history of culture. In Priscian's time, the struggle between paganism and Christianity had been decided for a century: the Parthenon had been transformed into a Christian church and only scanty remains of pagan culture were still tolerated.[29] Yet Priscian could calmly take over the mythological decoration of his pagan original. This appears especially in the discussion of the schemata of panegyric. Thus, for example, in praise of hunting, it must be mentioned that it was

---

[25] Marius Victorinus in Keil, VI, 158–160.

[26] On Priscian, cf. R. W. Hunt in *Mediaeval and Renaissance Studies* (London), I, 1943, pp. 194 ff.

[27] W. Kroll, *Rhetorik* (1937), 79 ff.—G. Lehnert in *Bursians Jahresbericht*, CCXLVIII (1935), 100 ff.

[28] Cf. also Barwick, 260.—Isidore, *Et.*, II, 1, 2.—Quintilian, II 4.

[29] Christ-Schmid, *Geschichte der griechischen Literatur*, II⁶, 954.

invented by Diana; in praise of the horse, that it is sacred to Neptune; of the dove, that it is sacred to Venus. On analogous grounds, in panegyrics on trees the laurel (Apollo) and the olive (Minerva) are to be preferred. That Priscian could recommend such exercises was possible only in the Byzantine culture of *ca.* 500. As a man and a citizen, one is a Christian; as a rhetor, a pagan: through Priscian, this tensionless coexistence was shown to the western Middle Ages as a possibility.[30] Anything really analogous to it will not be found until Italian Humanism. An Augustine would have considered the *Praeexercitamina* scandalous.

3. *Macrobius*

As we know, this pagan Neoplatonist [31] (documented as a high official from 399 to 422) became a philosophic and scientific authority for the entire Middle Ages; [32] Chrétien himself mentions him in *Erec* (6738). For this esteem his commentary on Cicero's *Somnium Scipionis* was responsible. In this work Homer and Virgil already appear beside Cicero and Plato as doctrinal authorities. The four corypheuses are infallible; any contradiction between them is wholly out of the question. Homer is "divinarum omnium inventionum fons et origo," Plato "ipsius veritatis arcanum," Cicero "nullius sectae inscius veteribus approbatae," Virgil "disciplinarum omnium peritissimus" and "erroris ignarus." [33] But in our connection the interesting work of Macrobius is his *Saturnalia*. A great part of it is devoted to interpretation of Virgil. The *Saturnalia*, then, is implicitly a compendium of late antique poetics. From it we can reconstruct the concept of poetry which a highly educated pagan contemporary of Augustine and Jerome possessed. Let me set it forth as briefly as possible. For Macrobius, Virgil is a sage, expert in all branches of knowledge (I, 16, 12). Often in a single word he betrays "profundam scientiam" (III, 2, 7). His work conceals esoteric secrets (I, 24, 13). When he says "quo numine laeso" (*Aen.*, I, 8), referring to Juno, he means to indicate that the various *numina* are the effects of a single godhead (I, 17, 4), who is of two sexes (III, 8, 1), as Virgil indicates when he says of Venus "ducente deo" (*Aen.*, II, 632). Antique polytheism is merely allegorical disguising of philosophical postulates: the myth of Saturn, who devours his children and then vomits them up, is an allegory of time, which devours all things and makes them arise again (I, 8, 10). For Macrobius, then, Virgil is a theologian. He is also the model of all rhetoric (V, 1, 1). He commands and employs all methods of arousing emotion. Among others: 1. apostrophizing lifeless or speechless things, as a weapon or a horse (IV, 6, 9); 2. *addubitatio* or ἀπόρησις, i.e., rhetorical questions beginning with *quid faciat* and the like (IV, 6, 11 f.); 3. eyewitness evidence or *adtestatio rei visae* (IV, 6, 137); 4. hyperbole (IV, 6, 15); 5. *exclamatio* (ἐκφώνησις), both "ex persona poetae" and "ex ipsius quem inducit loquentem" (IV, 6, 17); 6. address of the epic narrator to the reader, as in Homer's

---

[30] Ennodius affords an analogy in the West, but in his case the situation is different.

[31] Subtly characterized by Alföldi, *Die Kontorniaten* (1943), 56.

[32] M. Schedler, *Die Philosophie des Macrobius und ihr Einfluss auf die Wissenschaft des christlichen Mittelalters* (1916).

[33] K. Mras in *Berl. SB* (1933), 234.

ἴδοις ἄν, Virgil's *cernas*, etc. (V, 14, 9); 7. employment of sentences (V, 16, 6). These seven points represent only a selection from the rhetorical excellencies which Macrobius emphasizes in Virgil. They are such as we find constantly used in medieval poetry, including the *Chanson de Roland*. The reader will permit a few references: 1. apostrophizing of weapons: *Roland*, 2316; 2. *addubitatio*: *Roland*, 1185; 3. *adtestatio rei visae*: *Roland*, 2095; 4. hyperbole: *Roland*, *passim*; 5. *exclamatio ex persona poetae*: *Roland*, 9, 179, 716, etc.; 6. address of narrator by the *cernas*-formula: *Roland*, 349, 1655, 1680, 3387, etc.; 7. employment of sentences: *Roland*, 315. Of course I do not mean to say that Turold got these devices from Macrobius, but merely that they belong to the stock of a tradition of literary technique, i.e., of a scholastic analysis of the poets and teaching of poetry, which was already fully developed in Macrobius and which persisted throughout the Middle Ages. Macrobius is convinced that Virgil, in composing, guided himself by the rules of rhetoric. The medieval poets themselves generally proceeded in the same manner. It is clear that Macrobius already sees in poetry everything that the Middle Ages saw in it: [34] theology, allegory, universal knowledge, rhetoric. Accordingly, he also has a conception of the poet which was foreign to classical Antiquity: The poem is comparable to the cosmos. Virgil is a master in all the genres of style. His eloquence is "nunc brevis, nunc copiosa, nunc florida, nunc simul omnia, interdum lenis aut torrens: sic terra ipsa hic laeta segetibus et pratis, ibi silvis et rupibus hispida, hic sicca harenis, hic irrigua fontibus, pars vasto aperitur mari." Hence there is a great similarity between the "divinum opus mundi" and the "poeticum opus"; between the "deus opifex" and the "poeta" (V, 1, 19 f. and V, 2, 1). In the mouth of a pagan Neoplatonist of late Antiquity, then, we first find the "cosmic" conception of the poet which compares him to the architect of the universe. Virgil's poetry was produced by divine inspiration. And Virgil, in some mysterious way, foreknew that he would have to be profitable to all readers. Hence he mingled in his work all the kinds of eloquence, and indeed "non mortali, sed divino ingenio." In doing this he followed the universal mother, Nature: "non alium secutus ducem quam ipsam rerum omnium matrem naturam hanc praetexuit, velut in musicam concordiam dissonorum" (V, 1, 18). In this interesting passage, various motifs are mingled: the poet's divine prescience; Nature as the model of technique (Pseudo-Aristotle, περὶ κόσμου, 396 b 7); weaving as symbol and metaphor; poetry as music. In our connection, the decisive element is the idea of an analogy between poetic creation and the process of the birth of the universe. In this sense, for Macrobius and his authorities, the poet is a higher màn, related in essence to the divine nature. Within a century or thereabouts the concept had degenerated into a cliché. Ennodius pays the poet Faustus the compliment: "Est vobis quoddam cum hominum factore collegium: ille finxit ex nihilo, vos reparatis in melius" (Hartel, 524, 7 ff.) and:

Quod Natura Deo, hoc tibi dant studia (525, 20).

But let us return to Macrobius. His conception of Virgil is surprisingly similar in approach to the medieval conception of poetry. He feels that he is no longer sharing in a living literature but that he is the conserver and interpreter of a consummated tradition. For him the classics are already "the Ancients." The canon of them has

[34] Macrobius also discussed the question which came first, the hen or the egg (VII, 16, 1 ff.).

dwindled to a few names: Homer, Plato, Cicero, Virgil. This reduction is the result
of a changed psychological attitude toward literature. The canon includes only those
authors who can be regarded as religious, philosophical, scientific authorities. Accordingly, the works of the canonized authors are read and interpreted for their didactic
content. Allegory thus becomes the standard method of exegesis. All these characteristics of a changed mentality and the view of literature which followed from it, we
find again in Dante, still exercising all their influence. Only one thing has changed;
in Dante, Virgil has been drawn into the universal system of Christianity; in Macrobius, he is the sanctified authority for the piety of pagan late Antiquity. To be sure,
we find earlier attempts toward a philosophico-religious evaluation of Virgil,[35] but
in the fourth century this too accrues to the benefit of Christianity. This is shown
by Constantine's application of the Fourth Eclogue to Christ. It is all the more
significant that, two generations later, this interpretation was sharply rejected by
Jerome. From the end of the fourth century, the opposing points of view begin to
crystallize. Jerome's position produces the effect of a conscious reaction to the pagan
cult of Virgil which culminated in Macrobius. It is also characteristic that a dogmatic Christian like Prudentius, who disparages everything pagan, never mentions
Virgil. Augustine too objects to the reading of Virgil. The religious edicts of 380–81,
by which the Catholic church was raised to the status of state church, naturally led
to Christian intolerance toward paganism. Virgil too, it appears, was affected by
this. But on the other hand the infant literature of Christianity could not give up
the literary forms of antique culture. It was from this discordant situation that
Christian poetry arose.

[35] Alexander Severus called him "the Plato among the poets" and put his portrait
in his private chapel.

EARLY CHRISTIAN AND MEDIEVAL
LITERARY STUDIES

1. Jerome

The vast realm of patristics has not yet been explored in respect to the problems posed by European literary history and literary theory. Here, naturally enough, text-books of patrology leave us in the lurch. For they treat the material from the points of view of theology and ecclesiastical history. In this state of the matter, what follows can offer only indications and suggestions. It will be the task of an early Christian philology to rectify and complete them.

We must ask: How did preoccupation with the Bible and the rise of Christian writing influence literary theory? Between the antique-pagan and the patristic poetics, the Hellenized Judaism of the two last pre-Christian and the first Christian centuries represents an intermediary which came to exercise a far-reaching historical influence. The Judaeo-Hellenic culture developed a highly conscious propaganda which did not stop at literary forgeries (Sibylline oracles, verses attributed to Orpheus). "One of the chief tools of this propaganda was the attempt to show the correspondences between the Jewish law and religion and the teachings of Greek philosophy." [1] To this end, the system of allegorical exegesis developed by the Stoa was taken over. In connection with it appears the so-called "authority of antiquity": the sacred writings of the Jews are far older than those of the Greek poets and sages, who had known them and learned from them. Thus Josephus, in his treatise against Apion, proved that the Greek philosophers were dependent upon Moses. All these ideas were taken over by the early Christian apologists. According to Justin, Plato's cosmogony is derived from Genesis (*First Apology*, chs. 59 and 60). The Syrian Tatian (end of 2nd century), in his *Oration to the Greeks*,[2] makes synchronistic calculations which also serve apologetics. Similar things are found in the pseudo-Justinian *Cohortatio ad gentiles* and in Theophilus of Antioch. From the early Christian apologists these speculations pass to Alexandrian theology, a process which cannot be traced here. They finally flow into the work of the great doctors of the church. For us, Jerome is of primary importance.[3] In his epistle to Paulinus of Nola he sets forth, among other things: Neither Peter nor John were uneducated fisher-

---

[1] Otto Stählin in Christ-Schmid, *Geschichte der griechischen Literatur* [6], II, 1, 540.

[2] Translated by R. C. Kukula, 1913. *Ibid.*, p. 69 n. literature on the "authority of antiquity."

[3] The literature on Jerome leaves us in the lurch here. J.'s literary opinions are but briefly touched upon by P. de Labriolle (*Histoire de la littérature latine*). Part I of F. Cavallera's monograph (*S. Jérôme* [Louvain, 1922], 2 vols.; all that has yet appeared) gives only the biography.—A. Ficarra, *La posizione di S. Girolamo nella storia della cultura* (Palermo, 1916) was inaccessible to me.—Useful: E. Lübeck, *Hieronymus quot noverit scriptores* (Leipzig, 1872). But cf. Traube, *Vorlesungen und Abhandlungen*, II, 66.

men; otherwise, how could the latter have grasped the meaning of the logos-concept, which remained hidden from a Plato, a Demosthenes? How could the Bible be understood without learning and study? To be sure, there are male and female dilettantes who consider themselves capable of practicing allegorical interpretation. Here the letter-writer's tone is satirical (*garrula anus, delirus senex, sophista verbosus*) and a line of Horace (*Sat.*, II, 1, 116) flows from his pen:

> *Scribimus indocti doctique poemata passim.*

As we see, the antique classics are his familiar acquaintances; he sometimes puts them in their place, but he uses them for his purposes: they are always at hand. Even when he has to characterize the Biblical writers, the comparison with antique culture forces itself upon him. In the Book of Numbers he finds all the secrets of arithmetic, in Job "all the laws of dialectics." Finally, there is great significance in his: "David Simonides noster, Pindarus, et Alcaeus, Flaccus quoque, Catullus atque Serenus." This statement is the expression of a literary system of concordances or correspondences which, though Jerome does not formulate it coherently, nevertheless pervades all his writing and survived the occasional changes induced by pious scruples. Epistle 57, "On the Best Manner of Translating," imitates the title of Cicero's *De optimo genere oratorum*, as the title of Jerome's history of Christian literature imitates Suetonius' *De viris illustribus*.[4] In his epistle to Magnus he sets forth: The greatest apologists and fathers, in both the Greek and Latin tongues, show thorough knowledge of pagan literature, and that very thing made it possible for them to defend the Gospel victoriously. Juvencus too is eulogistically mentioned in this connection. For literary culture is by no means permissible only as a means of combating pagan attacks. With this important thesis, which unfortunately is left undemonstrated, the letter breaks off.

Jerome was not the first to recommend the study of antique profane literature. Origen and Basil, Lactantius and Ambrose had preceded him. But for the beginning Middle Ages and later times, Jerome was the great representative of the Humanism of the Church. By his adaptation of Eusebius' universal chronicle, which contains numerous literary-historical notices, he also became the originator of "chronicler's historiography,"[5] to which we shall return in connection with Isidore. This concept of history coincides with the system of "correspondences" insofar as, like the latter, it posited a common denominator between Scripture and the writings of the pagans: and that denominator was the literary one. Hence the books of the Bible must be interpreted as literary monuments. The study of "grammar," and that means of the antique poets, was thereby legitimized, but at the same time the road to grammatico-rhetorical analysis of the Biblical text was pointed out.

But Jerome also substantially enlarged the concept of poetry by teaching that certain books of the Bible were written partly or wholly in verse: for example, the Psalms, Job, Jeremiah. This provided a new basis for Christian poetry. It appears in Arator (6th cent.) in his *Epistula ad Vigilium*:

[4] On this literary genre, cf. Traube, *Vorlesungen und Abhandlungen*, II, 162.
[5] P. Lehmann in *Germ.-Rom. Monatsschrift*, IV (1912), 578. Reprinted in Lehmann's *Erforschung des Mittelalters* (1941).—R. Helm, *Hieronymus' Zusätze in Eusebius' Chronik* . . . (Leipzig, 1929).

23   *Metrica vis sacris non est incognita libris;*
Psalterium lyrici composuere pedes.
Hexametris cantare sonis in origine linguae
Cantica Hieremiae, Iob quoque dicta ferunt.[6]

2. Cassiodorus

Handbooks of philosophy and literary history usually cite the *Institutiones* and *De Anima*, as Cassiodorus' most important works. But his *Expositio in Psalterium*,[7] which fills over 2000 columns in Migne, is undoubtedly the richest of them. It seems to be neglected today; presumably because it is regarded as a technical philological work which has no significance for Cassiodorus' "philosophy." To be sure, that would be to measure the work by an unhistorical (modern) standard and to misunderstand Cassiodorus' intention. We have become acquainted with Cassiodorus' concept of the *artes* (ch. 3, sec. 2). While Jerome and Isidore systematically teach the correspondence between Biblical and profane literature, and at most the chronological priority of the former, Cassiodorus carefully explores the dependence of profane upon sacred learning. The former is nothing but a development of what is contained in principle in the latter. This concept, then, substitutes a monism at once speculative and historical, for the harmonistics which, developing from the fourth century from the confluence of pagan and Christian culture, was able to effect a compromise between the dualism of the two forces but not to end it. This monistic concept is evinced in rhetorical analysis. And the result of it is a reversal of the usual literary evaluation. Now the Bible no longer needs to be justified before profane literature by a demonstration that the former too employs the recognized figures of speech—no, the figures stem from the Bible, and the Bible alone gives them their "dignity." How much of this theory is Cassiodorus' own must remain undecided, as the subject has not been studied.[8] But, in my opinion, it first explains his tolerance in respect to antique culture. He is able to praise Jerome especially because "ubicumque se locus attulit, gentilium exempla dulcissima varietate permiscuit." The *saeculares litterae* are indispensable to the study of the Bible (*Inst.* I, c. 28). Grammar for him is "peritia pulchre loquendi ex poetis illustribus auctoribusque collecta: officium eius est sine vitio dictionem prosalem metricamque componere" (II, c. 1). To go into the content of the disciplines did not lie within Cassiodorus' plan. But the *litterae saeculares* were safeguarded by his guiding ideas.

The "sanctification" of the *artes* is usually credited to Alcuin: "Alcuin insiste avec une force singulière sur la nécessité des arts libéraux: il sanctifie ces arts, en montrant leurs relations avec la création divine: 'Les philosophes n' ont pas créé, mais ont seulement découvert ces arts; c'est Dieu qui les a créés dans les choses naturelles (in

---

[6] Cf. Theodulf in *Poetae*, I, 534, 58.

[7] The title *Complexiones in Psalmos* (Labriolle 675 and Ueberweg-Geyer 138) rests upon an error.

[8] A. Franz, *M. Aurelius Cassiodorus Senator* (Breslau, 1872) deals with the treatise on the Psalms most superficially (pp. 93 ff.).—A. Schneider ("Die Erkenntnislehre bei Beginn der Scholastik," in *Philos. Jahrbuch der Görres-Gesellschaft* [1921]) makes a well-grounded study of Cassiodorus (pp. 227–252), but does not touch upon the treatise on the Psalms.

naturis); et les hommes les plus sages les y ont trouvés.' " So Emile Bréhier [9] recently propounded. But these ideas of Alcuin's go back to Cassiodorus' teaching.

Because of their significance for medieval writing on literature, Cassiodorus' *Institutiones divinarum ac saecularium litterarum* must be examined. In his preface (*PL*, LXX, 1105) Cassiodorus says that, for secular literature (*mundani auctores, mundi prudentia, saeculares litterae*) a lively interest existed, but there was a lack of such professors of Biblical studies as had once flourished in Alexandria and now flourished in Nisibis. Further, the founding of such a school of higher studies in Rome, which Cassiodorus had planned with the blessed Agapetus, "Pope of the City of Rome," had come to nothing on account of Justinian's military campaigns: "non habet locum res pacis temporibus inquietis." Therefore Cassiodorus has decided to write an introduction for his monks ("introductorios [10] vobis libros istos"), which should serve both the health of their souls and their secular education. In matter, he will present nothing new but rather adhere to the fathers' interpretation of Scripture (*priscorum dicta—expositiones probabiles patrum*). Book I begins with an enumeration of the best commentaries on the individual books of the Bible. An understanding of the Bible can be attained in six ways. First the "introductores scripturae divinae" (Ticonius, Augustine's *Doctrina christiana*, etc.), should be consulted, then the *librorum expositores*, thirdly the *catholici magistri*; fourthly the fathers of the Church; fifthly counsel should be sought in conversation with experienced elder persons. Adding the study of the *Institutiones* themselves, we have six *modi intelligentiae*. A peculiarity is the specialized use of *catholicus* in the sense of "orthodox" as a criterion for authors; it has an influence upon later terminology: "studiosissime legamus catholicos magistros, qui propositionibus factis solvunt obscurissimas quaestiones" (1123 A). Unfortunately Cassiodorus cites no names. After mentioning the fathers, he goes on: "Ita fit ut diversorum catholicorum libri commodissime perlegantur . . .," so that the previously distinguished categories (*introductores, expositores, magistri, patres*) now appear to be only subdivisions of the *catholici*. Some other points in Book I are also of interest for medieval philology. First the discussion of the various ways of subdividing the Bible. Jerome gave the Old Testament 22 books, the New Testament 27, which added together makes 49. If to this number the Holy Trinity, which created the whole, is added, the sum is the number of the jubilee year: 50. Augustine reckons 71 books in the Bible: "Quibus cum sanctae Trinitatis addideris unitatem, fit totius librae competens et gloriosa perfectio" (1125 A). There follow discussions of biblical Latin, whose lapses from good Latinity are not to be emended (1128 B). Under *studia Christiana* the Christian historians are also mentioned (1133): Josephus (almost a second Livy), Eusebius and his continuers, Orosius, Marcellinus, Prosper. At the end of the chapter we read: "sequuntur multarum lectionum venerabilium conditores." The reference is to the fathers (1134 C). Some of them are then characterized, Jerome most fully and subtly. Thus Cassiodorus too supplies literary characterizations, as Quintilian had done in his spare Classicism. The "literary histories" of the Middle Ages partly repeated this in very much cruder form. Cassiodorus' second book deals with gram-

---

[9] *La philosophie du moyen âge*, 1937, 47.

[10] Translation of the Greek εἰσαγωγή. According to Altaner, *Patrologie* (1950), 290, the Greek Hadrianos wrote, "presumably in the first half of the fifth century, a biblical hermeneutics, for which he chose the title *Introduction to Holy Scripture*, used for the first time on this occasion." He is also mentioned by Cassiodorus.

mar and rhetoric. The latter is "bene dicendi scientia in civilibus quaestionibus" (1160 B). Interesting is the carefully balanced comparison between Cicero and Quintilian (1164 C: better text in Mynors [11] pp. 103 f.), to whom Fortunatianus is now added as "doctor novellus." Cassiodorus employs his chapter De Dialectica to set forth all that he knows about philosophy in general; so that "ars artium et disciplina disciplinarum" [12] (1167 D) is here squeezed into one of the seven artes and subordinated to it—in complete contradiction to the awakening consciousness of the Middle Ages, as we find it in Hugh of St. Victor. Following Varro, the relation of dialectics to rhetoric is compared to that of the fist to the open hand. Next come the subdivisions of philosophy, then discussions of the categories, of the syllogism, of definition (15 kinds!), then topics (chs. 15 ff.), which serves orators, dialecticians, poets, and jurists, and which Cassiodorus praises in words which Isidore later borrowed from him. It is unnecessary for us to follow the discussion of the remaining artes liberales. An impressive feature is the tone of deep religious emotion which keeps breaking out in Cassiodorus—quite in contrast to Isidore—particularly at the end of the treatise. There we read (Mynors, p. 162, 1 ff.): "O felicitas magna fidelium, quibus promittitur sicuti est Dominum videre, cui devotissime credentes iam beatitudinis spe magna repleti sunt! quid, rogo, praestabit aspectus, quando talia iam largitus est creditus? inaestimabile quippe donum est conspicere Creatorem, unde vivunt quaecumque vitalia sunt, unde sapiunt quaecumque subsistunt, unde amministrantur quaecumque creata sunt, unde reparantur quaecumque in melius instaurata consurgunt, unde veniunt quaecumque salutariter appetuntur, unde virtutes manant per quas ipse vincitur mundus. Sed licet omnia sustentet, omnia inenarrabiliter pius arbiter amministret, illa tamen nimis suavissima dona sunt, quando nostro conspectui clementissimus Redemptor apparere dignabitur." Here the stylistic art of the Variae has entered into the service of a genuine faith.

Cassiodorus' work soon passed beyond the boundaries of the limited audience for whose use it was written. It became a basic book of medieval culture.

3. Isidore

Of great importance to literary theory after Cassiodorus were the writings of Isidore of Seville, especially his Etymologiae. Into this handbook of knowledge he put not only the seven artes but an epitome of universal history as well. But with the latter he also continues Jerome's "chronicler's literary historiography." The Etymologiae, then, contains a compendium of universal literary history. This characterization may seem pretentious for Isidore's scanty chronographic notices. But when they are taken together with the related material treated in various sections of the Etymologiae, the result is a stock of information concerning the theory and history of literature, which the Middle Ages could find in no other writer. Not even in Jerome.

---

[11] Cassiodori Senatoris Institutiones. Edited from the Manuscripts by R. A. B. Mynors (Oxford, 1937).—Cf. E. K. Rand, "The New Cassiodorus" (Speculum [1938], 433).
[12] This definition is taken from Macrobius (Sat., VII, 15, 14).

Jerome's adaptation of Eusebius' universal chronicle is in tabular form [13]—suitable for reference, but not for reading. Nor does Jerome have the systematic use of chronology for a Christian theory of literature, which we find in Isidore. At most he has rudiments of it, as for example his statement that Moses wrote before Homer and Hesiod. But these rudiments were not developed. For pre-medieval poetics, Isidore is epoch-making.

Isidore's literary history [14] and poetics may be summarized as follows.

The course of universal history comprises six (Augustinian) ages: 1. From Adam to Noah; 2. from Noah to Abraham; 3. from Abraham to David; 4. from David to the Babylonian Exile; 5. from then to the Incarnation; 6. from then to the End of the World. Greece did not appear until the third age, when it received laws (from Phoroneus) and agriculture. Writing was first invented by the Hebrews, later transmitted to the Greeks by Cadmus, then to the peoples of Italy by Carmentis. Homer was presumably contemporary with Saul. The only fact of literary history to fall within the fourth age is the philosophy of Thales. Within the fifth fall the composition of the Book of Judith; the tragedies of Sophocles and Euripides; the Book of Esther; Plato, Demosthenes, and Aristotle; the Books of Maccabees; the Septuagint; Ecclesiasticus; the beginning of rhetoric in Rome. Even this sampling permits us to apprehend the view of history which Isidore transmitted to the Middle Ages: the history, culture, and literature of the ancient East and the classic peoples are presented in a synchronistic survey. Isidore's further notices of literary history are set in this framework. The oldest and noblest meter is the hexameter (*metrum heroicum*). Moses was the first to use it (Deut. 32), "long before Pherecydes and Homer." Hymns in praise of God were first composed by David; "long after him" came Timothoe.[15] The first epithalamium was composed by Solomon; the pagans took over the genre from him. Solomon's songs are made up—according to Jerome—of hexameters and pentameters. Isaiah writes rhetorical prose. The inventor of the threnody is Jeremiah; later, among the Greeks, Simonides. The cithara was invented by Tubal, astrology by Abraham; the Greeks attribute the former to Apollo and the latter to Atlas. The Greeks divided philosophy into physics, ethics, and logic. But Holy Scripture already falls into these disciplines: Genesis and Ecclesiastes, for example, present physics; [16] ethics is to be found in the Proverbs of Solomon; logic ("pro qua nostri Theoreticam sibi vindicant") in the Song of

[13] *Eusebii Pamphili Chronici Canones latine vertit S. Eusebius Hieronymus.* Edidit J. K. Fotheringham (Londinii, 1923).—The chronographic portions of the *Etymologiae* coincide only in part with Jerome's chronicle. The question of sources may remain uninvestigated here.

[14] Not previously studied. G. v. Dzialowski, *Isidor und Ildefons als Literarhistoriker* (Münster i. W., 1898), makes a critical study of the sources of Isidore's *De viris illustribus* but does not discuss the *Etymologiae*. P. Lehmann, "Literaturgeschichte im MA." (GRM [1912], 569 ff. and 617 ff.) does not mention Isidore.— Menéndez y Pelayo attempted an appraisal of Isidore's poetics (*Historia de las ideas estéticas*, II).

[15] Isidore means Phemonoe, a priestess of Apollo, who first used the hexameter for oracles: Proclus, *Chrestomathia* (Westphal, *Scriptores metrici graeci*, I, 230). Cf. Lucan, V, 126.

[16] This idea too has been attributed to Alcuin, see Bréhier, p. 47. Erroneously, as we see.—Cf. also *Poetae*, I, 524, 62 ff. and 608, 23 ff.

Songs [17] and in the Gospels. The Hebrew language is the mother of all others.

Here, we see, the "system of correspondence" has become a doctrine of the primacy and prerogative of Israel in philosophy, science, and poetry.[18] To the patriarchs and the Biblical writers goes the praise of having invented the poetic genres, which the Greeks later took over from them. Isidore applies this concept rigorously. But we also find in him elements of a systematic poetics. The terminological distinction between *poesis* and *poema* is simplified to the extreme: "poesis dicitur graeco nomine opus multorum librorum, poema unius." Isidore's definition of *fabula* is confused. He includes under it not only beast fables but also myths and comedies. Mythical fables "ad naturam rerum" are, for example, the story of the limping Vulcan ("quia per naturam numquam rectus est ignis") or that of the Chimaera (Lucretius, V, 903), who was a lion before, a goat in the middle, and a snake behind: in youth man is as wild as a lion, in middle life he has the goat's sharpness of sight (i.e., intellectual clarity), at its end he coils up like a snake. But the works of Plautus and Terence are entertaining fables too. Under *fabula* Isidore appears to include everything that is "mere invention." *Historia*, on the contrary, is "narratio rei gestae," report of facts. It belongs to grammar "quia quidquid dignum memoria est litteris mandatur." [19] The first historian was Moses, then, among the pagans, Dares, and after him Herodotus. *Historia* has three subdivisions: *ephemeris* (daily report), *kalendaria* (monthly report), and annals. "History" in the narrow sense is an account of the writer's own time: Sallust, Livy, Eusebius, Jerome "are made up of annals and history." History relates real events; fable tells of things which never happened and never could happen because they are contrary to nature. Between the two there is an intermediate genre: a report of things which are possible even if they did not happen. Isidore calls this genre *argumenta*. With this we pass from the domain of grammar to that of rhetoric.

The concept *argumentum* stems from the rhetorical doctrine of proof (*probatio*). With Aristotle, Isidore distinguishes two kinds of proofs, "inartificial" proofs (e.g., legal precedents, testimony of witnesses, etc.), which "fall outside of the art of oratory" and "artificial" proofs, which the orator himself derives from the matter in dispute and as it were "engenders." Artificial proof is an operation of the reason, seeking to produce credibility. It rests either upon indicia (circumstances) or upon arguments or upon examples. The *argumentum*, then, is a "ratio probationem praestans." To find such arguments (*loci argumentorum*) the orator avails himself

[17] "Pour tirer la logique du Cantique des Cantiques, il fallait vraiment une imagination intrépide," Valery Larbaud says charmingly (*Sous l'invocation de Saint Jérôme* [1946], 198).

[18] According to Acts 7: 22, Moses studied the wisdom of the Egyptians; hence later authors derive the seven *artes* from Egypt. Isidore ascribes the invention of geometry to the Egyptians. They received writing from the Greek princess Isis, astrology from Abraham. The Egyptians invented painting independently. Isidore appears purposely to disregard Moses' Egyptian education. It would contradict his system.—Cassiodorus (*Inst.*, I, c. 28) mentions it, in connection, moreover, with Augustine, *De doctrina christiana*, II, 50.

[19] Cf. Augustine: "Poterat iam perfecta esse grammatica, sed quia ipso nomine profitetur se litteras clamat, unde etiam latine litteratura dicitur, factum est, ut quidquid dignum memoria litteris mandaretur, ad eam necessario pertineret. Itaque . . . huic disciplinae accessit historia" (*De ordine*, II, c. 12; *PL*, XXXII, 1012).—Grammar as a "medicine" for poor memory: Sextus Empiricus, *Adv. mathematicos*, I, 1, §52.

of topics. Now many arguments employ fiction (ὑπόθεσις).[20] Hence Cicero gives the definition (of which a trace can be found in Isidore): "argumentum est ficta res, quae tamen fieri potuit." And this would seem to explain the extension of meaning of *argumentum*. In classical Latin, that is, it means not only "rhetorical argument" but also "narrative, matter, content, substance, subject-matter of a poem," and finally the poem itself, so that Quintilian (V, 10, 9) can say, *argumentum* means "omnis ad scribendam destinata materia." Here we see again how closely the terminologies of rhetoric and poetics are connected. This is confirmed when we return to Isidore's poetics. After defining topics as "disciplina inveniendorum argumentorum," he sets forth that a knowledge of it is indispensable to poets, who, according to both Isidore's and the general opinion, are called upon to "prove" something, just as are orators, jurists, and philosophers. For Isidore as for the entire Middle Ages, topics is a wonderful invention of the human mind: "mirabile plane genus operis, in unum potuisse colligi, quidquid mobilitas ac varietas humanae mentis in sensibus exquirendis per diversas causas poterat invenire, conclusum liberum ac voluntarium intellectum. Nam quocumque se verterit, quascumque cogitationes intraverit, in aliquid eorum quae praedicta sunt, necesse est cadat ingenium."

The schema of the seven humanities, together with the plan of the *Etymologiae*, brings it about that Isidore's book contains no comprehensive chapter on poetry, though there is one *De poetis* (VIII, 7). The first half of Book VIII consists of five chapters devoted to theology and the church. These are symmetrically followed by six chapters dealing with the heathen world, specifically with the heathen philosophers, the Sibyls, the images, the pagans in general, and their gods. Between the philosophers and the Sibyls come the poets. It follows that Isidore regards them essentially as representatives of *gentilitas*. He sets forth: When men, from their original wild state, had attained to a knowledge of themselves and of the gods, culture received a new stimulus.[21] In honor of the gods, men invented beautiful houses (temples), as well as a sublime form of discourse: poetry. Poetry, then, is originally praise of the gods, "verbis inlustrioribus et iucundioribus numeris." Then follows the etymology: "id genus quia forma quadam efficitur, quae ποιότης dicitur, poema vocitatum est, eiusque fictores poetae." The statement in this form is incomprehensible, but it becomes clear when we read in Fortunatianus (Halm, 125 f.) that there are three *genera orationis: posotetos* (how great?), *poiotetos* (how constructed?), *pelikotetos* (how long?). Based on *posotes* there are three subordinate genres: *amplum sive sublime; tenue sive subtile; mediocre sive moderatum* (theory of the "three kinds of style," *genera dicendi*.) Based on construction, there are the three Diomedean genres; based on length: μακρόν, βραχύ, μέσον (= three of Diomedes' four kinds of style). Of the theory represented by Fortunatianus, then, Isidore has taken only the middle section. He next discusses the Roman designation *vates*, adding a remark on the poet's divine *furor*; the tragedians ("excellentes in argumentis fabularum ad veritatis imaginem fictis"), who treat unhappy affairs of

[20] Hence the tenth-century Veronese cleric who composed the rhythm O *admirabile Veneris ydolum*, published by Traube, affirms the genuineness of his feeling in the line (*supra*, p. 114):

Saluto puerum non per ypothesim.

[21] Isidore here cites Suetonius' *Prata*, which we do not possess. P. Wessner (*Hermes*, LII, 200 ff.) points out that Isidore's quotations from Suetonius are at second or third hand.—Isidore and Diomedes: J. Kayser, De *veterum arte poetica quaestiones selectae* (Leipzig dissertation, 1906), 44 f.

state and stories of kings; the writers of comedy, who take amusing events of private life as their subject-matter. But the "old" comic writers (Plautus, Terence) must be distinguished from the "new" (Flaccus, Persius, Juvenal) who are also called satirists [22] and are represented naked (*nudi pinguntur;* misunderstanding of *Ars poetica* 221) because they lay bare the vices. We next learn that certain poets were called *theologici* because they composed songs of the gods.[23] The three poetic genres are enumerated (in abbreviated form) after Diomedes. Of importance is the summarizing statement: "Officium autem poetae in eo est ut ea, quae vere gesta sunt, in alias species obliquis figurationibus cum decore aliquo conversa transducat.[24] Unde et Lucanus ideo in numero poetarum non ponitur, quia videtur historias composuisse, non poema." A source of these sentences would seem to have been Servius (on *Aen.*, I, 382): "hoc loco per transitum tangit historiam, quam per legem artis poeticae aperte non potest ponere . . . Quod autem diximus eum poetica arte prohiberi, ne aperte ponat historiam, certum est. Lucanus namque ideo in numero poetarum esse non meruit, quia videtur historiam composuisse, non poema." [25] But Isidore was also copying Lactantius. In the first decade of the fourth century Lactantius produced seven books of *Divinae Institutiones.* In his polemic against antique religion he has occasion to speak of the poets. By poetical presentation they transformed real events into fantasy, for which they gained belief. This is the explanation of the Greek myths. An example: Zeus was said to have had Ganymede carried off by an eagle: "Poeticus color est. Sed aut per legionem rapuit cuius insigne aquila est, aut navis in qua est impositus tutelam habuit in aquila figuratam, sicut taurum, cum rapuit et transvexit Europam."

And now Lactantius explains how poets commonly proceed: "Non ergo res ipsas gestas finxerunt poetae, quod si facerent, essent vanissimi, sed rebus gestis addiderunt quendam colorem. Non enim obtrectantes illa dicebant, sed ornare cupientes. Hinc homines decipiuntur . . . Nesciunt enim qui sit poeticae licentiae modus, quousque progredi fingendo liceat, cum officium poetae in eo sit, ut ea quae vere gesta sunt in alias species obliquis figurationibus cum decore aliquo conversa traducat" (*Div. Inst.*, I, 11, 19, 24). Isidore, as we see, took this doctrine of Lactantius' over word for word, but at the same time combined it with the antique criticism of Lucan, and thus gave it a meaning which it did not have in the context of Lactantius' rationalistic mythological interpretation.[26] What authority Lactantius fol-

---

[22] This is fabricated out of Horace, *Sat.*, I, 4, 1–6. Cf. F. Leo in *Hermes*, XXIV, 67 ff.

[23] Kayser, p. 50, comments on this: "Paragraphus . . . Isidoro ipsi ut homini Christiano esse attribuenda videtur." The Greek concept of the "theological" poet is here, as usual, overlooked.

[24] Lindsay reads *transducant.* To me this is incomprehensible, besides being hardly tolerable as *constructio ad sensum. Traducat* in Lactantius, *Inst.*, I, 11, 24 and in some MSS.

[25] Quintilian concluded: "Lucanus . . . magis oratoribus quam poetis imitandus est" (X, 1, 9).

[26] Lactantius also expressly rejects equating poetry with lying: "totum autem quod referas fingere, id est ineptum esse et mendacem potius quam poetam." Cf. also § 30 of the same chapter.—The definition of the *officium poetae* was taken over word for word by later writers, e.g., Cruindmelus (ed. Huemer, p. 50).— *Officium* (ἔργον) is a technical term. Quintilian defines the *officia* of the orator (Preface to Book XII, § 4). On the *officia* of the historian, cf. the anonymous writer in Halm 588.

lowed in his distinction between poetry and history, I cannot say. But we are dealing with an old tradition. The author of the *ad Herennium* (I, 8, 13) distinguishes: "Fabula est, quae neque veras, neque veri similes continet res, ut hae, quae in tragoediis traditae sunt. Historia est res gesta, sed ab aetatis nostrae memoria remota. Argumentum est ficta res quae tamen fieri potuit." Cicero (*De legibus*, I, 5) teaches that history is subject to other laws than poetry; the former is concerned with real events, the latter with entertainment (*delectatio*). Ovid has (*Am.*, III, 12, 41):

> *Exit in inmensum fecunda licentia vatum,*
> *Obligat historica nec sua verba fide.*

Similar judgments were expressed by the younger Pliny (*Ep.*, IX, 33, 1) and Quintilian (II, 4, 2). But Petronius' statement is the most interesting (c. 118): "Non enim res gestae versibus comprehendendae sunt—quod longe melius historici faciunt —sed per ambages deorumque ministeria et fabulosum sententiarum commentum praecipitandus est liber spiritus, ut potius furentis animi vaticinatio appareat quam religiosae orationis sub testibus fides." Here history and poetry are distinguished in accordance with their fundamental intellectual attitude. Macrobius returns to the subject, but once again with a new base: Homer makes the epic narrative begin in the middle (*ordo artificialis* of the medieval arts of poetry [Faral, 55 f.]), to set himself apart from the historical method of narration ("vitans in poemate historicorum similitudinem": *Sat.*, V, 2, 9 and V, 14, 11).

Isidore's "poetics" integrates the doctrines of pagan late Antiquity into the systematized didascalium of the western church. His writings thereby acquired an importance which can hardly be overestimated. He is usually regarded as a compiler, his work as a mosaic. If one's concern with him is that of a student of sources, no other conclusion can be reached. But even in his day Ludwig Traube wrote: "We ought to make up our minds to read Isidore, whom we merely consult; we ought, even if we are dealing with the stones of a mosaic, to try for a moment to see the mosaic as a whole." [27] Above all, we must read the *Etymologiae* as the medieval reader did—as a book which is all of a piece and of binding authority. Even at the end of the Middle Ages, an English reader could still write on a codex of the *Etymologiae*:

> *This booke is a scoolemaster to those that are wise,*
> > *But not to fond fooles that learning despise,*
> *A Juwell it is, who liste it to reede,*
> > *Within it are Pearells precious in deede.*[28]

So men thought from Merovingian to Tudor times. So Isidore presents himself to the medieval philologist. If we call his work a compilation, we must further reflect that the derogatory designation does not quite do justice to the facts in the case. The compilation is a literary genre which was highly popular and highly respected in late Antiquity, and whose nature and designations were discussed at length by Gellius, for example, in the preface to his *Noctes Atticae*. He divided his work into twenty books, in which Nonius Marcellus (4th cent.) and Isidore follow him.

---

[27] *Vorlesungen und Abhandlungen*, II, 160.
[28] W. M. Lindsay gives the lines at the beginning of his edition of the *Etymologiae*. Cf. "Isidorus, li parfonz puis / La grant fontaine de clergie" (Barbazan-Méon, *Fabliaux*, I, 292 f.).

Macrobius' *Saturnalia* is also a compilation. That very author, who was so much read in the Middle Ages, emphasized, at the beginning of his work (I, 1, 6), that even a collection of the fruits of one's reading can become something new and individual by its arrangement and form of presentation. We may presume that Isidore had the same concept: to impart knowledge was his aim. But in his period the only possible literary form for such an aim was to collect and arrange excerpted matter. The mere fact that he regarded pagan learning as worth knowing, and integrated it with ecclesiastical learning to form his encyclopedia, is a program. The theory of the primacy of Israel in the development of culture, and of Greece as the pupil of Biblical wisdom—which, though he did not originate it, was safeguarded by his authority—represents a harmonistics which, if primitive, was nevertheless extremely influential. If the poetic genres of Antiquity stemmed from Israel, that very fact also legitimized them from the Christian standpoint. The contrast in philosophical viewpoint between Christian and antique poetry, which, as we shall see, was to lead in later centuries to the most various tensions and attempted solutions— accurately registered by the fluctuations in the evaluation of the antique Muses— was not touched upon by Isidore in the *Etymologiae*. If we wish to know Isidore's opinion on the subject, we must turn to the lines which he wrote for his library,[29] and which were painted "on the bookcases or walls" of the library in the Bishop's Palace in Seville. Here Isidore was following an antique usage which was never intermitted; "but his model and chief source is the great master of the epigram, his fellow countryman Martial." [30] The first poem is a general *titulus* in four verses:

> Sunt hic plura sacra, sunt mundialia plura;
> Ex his si qua placent carmina, tolle, lege.
> Prata vides plena spinis et copia floris;
> Si non vis spinas sumere, sume rosas.

Sacred and secular books, then, are set side by side without any value judgment. Now lines 2–4 could be understood to refer to the poets contained in the library, some of whom (the pagans?) would be full of thorns, the others (the Christians?) of flowers. But according to Beeson *carmina* refers to Isidore's own *tituli*: "If any of these *tituli* please you, take out the works to which they refer." Further, the distinction between thorns and roses in this context is borrowed from Antiquity and refers to differences in literary quality or in readers' tastes, not in philosophical point of view. *Tituli* 2–9 are devoted to the Bible and the fathers, *titulus* 10 to the poets. It says: "If Virgil, Horace, Ovid, Persius, Lucan, Statius do not please you, read Juvencus, Sedulius, Prudentius, Avitus, and turn from the pagan poets":

> Desine gentilibus ergo inservire poetis:
> Dum bona tanta potes, quid tibi Calliroen? [31]

Neither a condemnation of the antique poets nor a rigoristic attitude can be read from this *titulus*. Isidore's counsel is given only in case the user of the library finds no pleasure in profane poetry. Isidore's attitude is that of a somewhat impersonal tolerance, here as in the *Etymologiae*.

In his principal theological work, the *Sententiae*, Isidore appears to take a dif-

[29] Edited by Beeson (*Isidorstudien* [1913], 135 ff.).
[30] Beeson, 150.
[31] The spring Callirrhoe near Athens?

ferent stand. There we read (III, 13): "Ideo prohibetur Christianus figmenta legere poetarum, quia per oblectamenta inanium fabularum mentem excitant ad incentiva libidinum." But this sentence is connected with the decisions of the fourth Council of Carthage (398), which were only locally and temporarily valid.[32] Isidore's personal opinion is not to be found in the words quoted. He concludes the chapter with the conciliatory sentences: "Meliores esse grammaticos quam haereticos. Haeretici enim haustum letiferi succi hominibus persuadendo propinant, grammaticorum autem doctrina potest etiam proficere ad vitam, dum fuerit in meliores usus assumpta." This sounds like an answer to Augustine's famous dictum: "Melius est reprehendant nos grammatici quam non intellegant populi" (*In Psalmos*, 138, 20). So we may say that Isidore's *Sententiae* give as large a place to antique culture as his *Etymologiae*.

4. Aldhelm

Upon the foundation laid by Isidore and the Irish, Latin-Anglo-Saxon culture continues to build. Its first representative is Aldhelm. As a literary personality he has generally been judged unfavorably. Traube (*Vorlesungen und Abhandlungen*, II, 175) calls his Latin "wholly artificial and completely without style" and seems to concede him no merit. For Roger he is a "témoin parfois naïf, superficiel, peu mesuré" (290) of his period. Laistner finds his work "utterly unpalatable." [33] Such judgments are comprehensible. They do not affect Aldhelm's historical significance nor do they comprehend it. It lies in his concept of a culture at once ecclesiastical and literary. The concept may be called narrow and primitive, nevertheless it is, in itself, clear and logical. It is the first expression of the new Christian culture of England, which arose between 650 and 680 after the conversion of the Anglo-Saxons (begun 596, completed 634), and in which not only Irish and Roman but also Graeco-Oriental (Theodore of Tarsus and the African Hadrian) influences mingled with British and Anglo-Saxon native culture.[34] Aldhelm (b. 639) first studied under the Irish Abbot Mailduib, founder of Malmesbury. Later he benefited by the teaching of Theodore and Hadrian at Canterbury. Aldhelm's theory of literature is to be found in his letter to Prince Aethilwald: "Si quid . . . saecularium litterarum nosse laboras, ea tantummodo causa id facias, ut, quoniam in lege divina vel omnis vel paene omnis verborum textus artis omnino grammaticae ratione consistit, tanto eiusdem eloquii divini profundissimos atque sacratissimos sensus facilius legendo intelligas, quanto illius rationis, qua contexitur, diversissimas regulas plenius ante didiceris" (Ed. Ehwald, 500, 9 ff.). This, then is the old theory, known to us from Jerome, Cassiodorus, and Isidore, of the indispensability of the *artes* for an understanding of the Bible. Aldhelm does not wish to exclude poetry; but it must sing Christian subjects. Aldhelm himself, in his voluminous poem *De virginitate*, produced a sample of this kind of poetry and thereby continued the line of Sedulius and Prudentius. Thus he assimilates several streams of pre-medieval literary theory. Aldhelm wanted to have Latin become the literary language of the Anglo-Saxons.

---

[32] P. de Labriolle, *Histoire de la littérature latine chrétienne* [2] (1924), 29.

[33] M. L. W. Laistner, *Thought and Letters in Western Europe: A.D. 500 to 900* (London, 1931), 120.

[34] C. Dawson, *The Making of Europe* (London, 1932), 206 f.

To this end, they had to be instructed in the system of Latin metrics. Aldhelm set it forth in his letter to Acircius (King Aelfrid of Northumbria). In his view, this was to perform an act of historical importance. He points with pride to the fact that he is the first of Germanic stock to treat the subject and that he may compare himself to Virgil, who boasts (*Georg.*, III, 11–13 and 292 ff.) to have introduced pastoral poetry into Roman literature (ed. Ehwald, 202, 4–24). This appears to be one of the first direct testimonies in medieval literature to the Germanic will to culture. Most of the lines given as examples in Aldhelm's letter on metrics come from Virgil and Sedulius; there are none from Horace and Statius, and very few from Ovid. Does the explanation for this lie in the material which Aldhelm had before him in composing his treatise, or from a conscious desire to take from secular poetry no more than was absolutely necessary? His own poetic creation, Aldhelm seeks to justify from the Bible. To be sure, when, in his metrical riddles, he makes animals, plants, and inanimate objects speak, he cites Isidore's remarks on the four kinds of metaphor (*Et.*, I, 37, 3 ff.). But while Isidore justifies himself by examples from secular poetry, Aldhelm chooses Biblical ones. He points out that in ancient times there were talking trees (Judges 9:8) and the like, and continues didactically: "Haec idcirco diximus, ne quis forte novo nos et inusitato dicendi argumento et quasi nullis priorum vestigiis triti praedicta enigmata cecinisse arbitretur" (77, 16 ff.). Another example: One of the regular practices of medieval literature is to put a concluding formula at the end of a work. This goes back to antique models. But for this too Aldhelm finds a Biblical authority: "Igitur digesto . . . libello . . . stilus iam finem quaerit et dictandi tenor terminandus est, quia illustris contionator 'Tempus,' inquit, 'loquendi et tempus tacendi' " (Eccles. 3:7).

5. *Early Christian Poetry*

The beginnings of Christian-Latin poetry [35] fall in the Constantine period. Its flowering time lies between 400 and 600. It is of importance for the development of literary theory. I shall illustrate this by at least a few examples. In this connection we may omit the hymn poetry composed for the services of the church, because it stands outside of the antique genres and represents a new beginning. From this cult poetry we distinguish the antique Christian poetry which was conceived as literature. Within this last, there are again two directions. On the one hand, the Christian poet could treat the matter of Christian piety (sanctification of daily work, cult of martyrs) and of Christian dogma and ethics (doctrine of the Trinity, the origin of sin, apologetics, battle of the vices and virtues). It was Prudentius' great accomplishment that he followed this path. With full command of classical literary style he opened up great new realms to poetry. High gifts and intense experience were the

---

[35] No existing history of Christian poetry between 300 and 800 meets today's standards. Manitius' book (1891) is inadequate, cf. Traube's devastating review, *AfdA*, XVIII (1892), 203 ff. Labriolle treats poetry only cursorily. Otto J. Kuhnmuench's *Early Christian Latin Poets* (Chicago, Loyola University Press, 1929) is a useful anthology with a 12-page introduction. The best treatment is F. J. E. Raby's in the first chapters of his *History of Christian-Latin Poetry from the beginnings to the close of the Middle Ages* (Oxford, 1927).

springs of his creation. The rich flood of his poetry is independent of the system of the antique genres and hence is not forced to come to terms with antique literary theory.[36] He is the most important and most original of the early Christian poets. But he is also a solitary phenomenon. The majority of early Christian poets followed another path: that of keeping to the antique genres and filling them with Christian matter. Only Virgil was regarded as a model. Accordingly we find Christian eclogues and Christian epics. How greatly these genres are dependent upon their Virgilian models is shown by the fact that they begin with Virgilian centos. The poetess Proba (ca. 350), who before her conversion had dealt with contemporary matter in epic form, put forth her Christian cento as a "Maro mutatus in melius" (Schenkl, 568, 3). Pomponius' *Tityrus*, of the same period, is also a cento: the earliest example of the "spiritual eclogue" which was to be so popular in the Carolingian period and yet later. A monograph on this genre is one of the desiderata of medieval literary history. The Christian epic begins as Bible epic. The first important work in the genre is the harmony of the Gospels by the Spanish priest Juvencus (ca. 330). It begins a long series of Latin biblical poems which is later continued in the vernaculars: from Caedmon, Cynewulf, Otfrid, the *Heliand*, the Clermont Passion,[37] to Milton and Klopstock. In our connection this series is more important than the work of Prudentius. For it was precisely the fact that they were continuing an antique genre which made it possible for the Christian epic poets to sense a gulf between their pagan form and their Christian matter. Hence they could not but feel obliged to study pagan literary practice. Here lies one of the starting points of premedieval thinking about literary theory. It can be demonstrated in Juvencus and Sedulius.

Juvencus preceded his Gospel poem by a metrical foreword in 27 verses in which he justifies his undertaking.: "By God's will all earthly things are subject to mortality. Yet countless men, because of their deeds and their virtues, live on in the praise of poets, as in the noble songs of Homer, in the sweet art (*dulcedo*) of Virgil. And these poets themselves are also sure of eternal fame, although they weave lies [i.e., mythology] into the deeds of past times. How much more will my poem outlive ages, for it sings the deeds of Christ and perhaps will yet save me at the Last Judgment. May the Holy Ghost assist me and lave my mind in the water of Jordan." At the end of his work Juvencus describes his accomplishment by saying that through his verses the Christian religion (*divinae gloria legis*) has put on the ornament of earthly rhetoric (IV, 804 f.). The poet's attitude toward antique poetry, then, is one of admiration, he rejects only its philosophical basis and wishes to furnish a Christian counterpart to the pagan epic. Accordingly, his work springs from a conscious program, which was to be of importance for medieval literary theory: the building up of a literature of Christian content in antique form. In Juvencus the transition is made without friction. Polemic against antique poetry is reduced to a

---

[36] This point is not made clear in I. Rodriguez Herrera's useful *Poeta Christianus. Prudentius' Auffassung vom Wesen und von der Aufgabe des christlichen Dichters* (Munich dissertation, 1936).

[37] To be accurate, we must point out that the Passion goes back to the model of rhythmical, not of metrical, Bible poems. We have such rhythms on the resurrection of Lazarus (by Paulinus of Aquileia: *Poetae*, I, 133), on the Passion (*Poetae*, IV, 501), etc. (cf. Strecker, NA 47, 143). Their effect is more popular and more powerful than that of the metrical literary productions.

minimum. We encounter a very different situation in the second Christian poet: Sedulius, the poet of the *Carmen Paschale* (middle of the 5th cent.). In contrast to Juvencus' smooth, clear poetic language, elevated by Virgilian echoes, to Prudentius' ringing Christian Classicism, Sedulius gives us our first example of magniloquent rhetoric in Christian guise. We frequently encounter the concept that pagan poetry dried up because of lack of essential content and degenerated into a toying with forms; that Christianity, on the other hand, breathed the breath of a new spiritual experience into Roman literature.[38] But this is true only with reservations. Among the Christian poets of the fourth to sixth centuries there are not only deep thinkers, fiery zealots, earnest scholars, and pious singers, but also inflated, vain, soulless, and unintelligent rhetors. To this category belongs Fulgentius, and with him Ennodius. Sidonius is not far removed from them. Sedulius represents this class among the Christian poets. He demonstrates that even a recent convert could take over the frippery of the pagan school rhetor into his Christian life, could indeed make it over into Christian clothing and strut about in it. If Juvencus had treated the life of the Saviour (*Christi vitalia gesta*) epically, Sedulius chose Christ's miracles as his epic subject. He calls his poem *Paschale carmen* in allusion to Paul's "Pascha nostrum immolatus est Christus" (I Cor. 5:7). The prose letter of dedication to the presbyter Macedonius sets forth the writer's views and intentions. Sedulius fears that he will be censured for having dared, without learning (*nulla veteris scientiae praerogativa suffultus*) "to travel, a novice in a little boat, over the boundless ocean of the Paschal majesty, which terrifies even the most learned of men." At first he had pursued secular learning and turned the "energy of his active mind," a gift of divine providence, to literary trifling, until grace touched him. Now however he would consider it a guilty failure if he had not put his literary activity in the service of truth. "Further, my bewildered heart was again troubled by another storm, and I had often to sigh wretchedly in my consciousness of the profit I had drawn from your teaching and that of others equally illuminated by divine grace. Though you all believe and tell me that a little fire could brighten in me too, yet the numbness of my callous heart, like a veined flint, will hardly give forth a tiny spark (*scintillula*) . . . Tossed about in the mazes of fear and hesitation (*anxiae trepidationis ambages*), I have nevertheless decided to write this work." Why did Sedulius choose to write in metrical form? Because many readers prefer the charms of poetry to those of prose (*rhetorica facundia*) and because the former better impresses itself upon the memory. Further, it really makes no difference in what form anyone is won for the Faith. There follows a list of the excellent friends, both men and women, to whom Sedulius might have dedicated his work. But he offers it to Macedonius because in him he "sees them all." "So, I implore you, may the use of many words come to an end, to an end the circumstantial length of this apology. May it not vex you to bestow the anchor of your authority upon my work, tossed as it has been upon the waves in its course through the perils of so wild a whirlpool." What an assumption of importance for himself and his accomplishment! What affected modesty! Certainly we are here dealing with a stylistic convention. But it is employed with such self-satisfaction that we cannot but doubt the seriousness of the poet's religion. His dedicatory letter is nevertheless of interest for medieval poetics. Not only do many of Sedulius' expressions (such as *scintilla, trepidatio*)

[38] Cf. e.g., Labriolle, p. 14.

reappear in later authors, but his attitude toward literature established a tradition. As, for instance, when a writer believes that he must furnish a justification for his work (an edifying aim) and for his choice of an artificial form (poetry).[39] An antique poet can at most motivate the publication of his collection of poems (as Statius in the preface to his *Silvae*), but never his poetical activity itself. To do the latter does not make sense until the post-Constantinian epoch. Since the artistic epic represented a major item in pagan culture, [40] it was necessary to give one's reasons for taking it over for Christian ends. But Sedulius' literary practice attained importance in another respect too. He followed his *Carmen Paschale* by a prose version, which he entitled *Opus Paschale*. This striking juxtaposition of versions in poetry and prose, historians of early Christian literature usually explain by saying that Macedonius was shocked by the "free handling of the sacred text" in the *Carmen Paschale*.[41] But this is extremely improbable. In the first place the alleged "shocks" cannot be documented. In the second place no one had objected to Juvencus' metrical harmony of the Gospels. In the third place the rhetorical magniloquence of the *Opus Paschale* is at least as far from the "sacred text" as the verse of the *Carmen*. To explain the matter, we must carefully read the letter of dedication to the *Opus Paschale*, in which Sedulius presents this second work too to Macedonius. He says: "You bade me translate my poem into artistic prose (*in rhetoricam sermonem transferre*). Did you like it so much that you wanted to read it again in a different form (*geminari volueris*)? Or did you dislike it, and therefore wished it put into freer form (*stilo censueris liberiore describi*)? I hesitate to judge (*sub dubio videor fluctuare iudicio*), but follow your sacred command . . . I add some things which the bonds of meter made it impossible for me to put into the poem. To be sure the fault-finders will complain that the translation is not truly made. But I can answer such critics with Terence [*Andria*, Prologue 17]:

Faciuntne intellegendo ut nil intellegant?

That is, 'By this use of their critical faculty, do not the censurers show that they understand nothing?' They ought to be aware that in my rehandling I followed classical models: the famous jurist Hermogenianus and the celebrated theologian Origen published their works in three editions and revisions. Further, my new version is not pure repetition, but supplementing and recasting." If we now examine the manner of rehandling, we discover that it affects neither ideas nor subject-matter (as Macedonius' alleged "shock" would lead one to expect), but exclusively form. In the artistic prose of the *Opus Paschale* 3349 *clausulae* have been counted in 2414 lines! [42] From a classicistic standpoint such a linguistic procedure may be viewed as "depravity"—that is no concern of ours. What is essential is that, for

---

[39] T. Mayr, *Studien zu dem Paschale Carmen des Sedulius* (Munich dissertation, 1916, 6 f.), refers to Statius' and Martial's prose prefaces, but they provide no more than a formal model.

[40] Isidore treats *de poetis* in his section on the pagan world (*supra*, p. 453).

[41] G. Krüger in Schanz, IV, 2 (1920), 370. To the same effect, O. Bardenhewer, *Geschichte der altchristlichen Literatur*, IV (1924), 644 and E. S. Duckett, *Latin Writers of the Fifth Century* (New York, 1930), 80. A. G. Amatucci, *Storia della letteratura latina cristiana* (1929), 342 f., passes over the point. So does U. Moricca in his *Storia della letteratura latina cristiana*, III, 1 (1932), 56.—What an imposing consensus of specialists who do not trouble to acquire special competence!

[42] J. Candel, *De clausulis a Sedulio . . . adhibitis* (Tolosae, 1904).

Sedulius, literary form, whether in poetry or prose, is mere playing with forms. The composition of the *Opus Paschale* is not to be explained on theological grounds,[43] but from the virtuoso's need to show off. Sedulius had a large measure of literary ambition, but he had nothing to say. So he hit upon the device of saying something over again in a different form—a thing, as he impressively points out, which others had done before him. He always needs the legitimation of literary predecessors and models. Like Juvencus, Sedulius is active within the techniques of pagan poetry, but he zealously rejects its matter. Juvencus had found words of ingenuous admiration for Homer and Virgil. Sedulius does not mention their names. At the beginning of both his works he puts an invective against antique poetry, whose matter is "priscorum temporum gesta, nonnulla etiam probrae narrationis arte composita" (176, 10 f.). He, on the contrary, will sing his matter in the manner of David: "Daviticae modulationis cantus exercens" (176, 14; cf. 17, 23). These statements are significant. They contain the germ of a Christian theory of literature (sacred subjects should be treated after the model of the Biblical bard). But they also announce a rigoristic rejection of antique poetry and the antique pantheon.[44] This is the sign of a new period. The religious sentiment of late Antiquity—as we saw in the case of Macrobius —had been able, by spiritualizing interpretations, to harmonize the cults of the gods with its own particular consciousness. But it was swept away by the increasing power of the church. After 415, pagans were excluded from all state offices. The iconoclastic assault was to a great extent carried through. The shadowy world of the Olympians became either a necessity of a mythology serving purely literary ends— or an invention of the Devil. It became both at once. For the wedding of the Frankish king Sigebert and the Visigothic princess Brunhild (566) Fortunatus composed an epithalamium (VI, 1), in which Venus and Cupid bless the marriage. But in his metrical *Vita s. Martini* (written 573–4) the same writer reports that the saint threatened the demons by calling them by their names; he said that Mercury was an especially evil enemy but that Jupiter was a stupid lout. Christianity did not allow the antique gods to die in peace. It had to degrade them into demons—because they lived on in the subconscious. But in the antique poetry which was a part of schooling—especially in Virgil—the reader was constantly encountering the Olympians. Poetry and fables of the gods could hardly be separated. Metrical literary poetry, then, always had something suspect about it. Its suspiciousness could only be lessened by using poetry for ecclesiastical ends and explaining why this was done.

Throughout its existence—from Juvencus to Klopstock—the Biblical epic was a hybrid with an inner lack of truth, a *genre faux*. The Christian story of salvation, as the Bible presents it, admits no transformation into pseudo-antique form. Not only does it thereby lose its powerful, unique, authoritative expression, but it is falsified by the genre borrowed from antique Classicism and by the concomitant linguistic and metrical conventions. That the Biblical epic could nevertheless enjoy such great popularity is explained only by the need for an ecclesiastical literature which could be matched with and opposed to antique literature. So a compromise solution was reached.

[43] Macedonius' "sacred command" must have been feigned—or bespoken—by Sedulius. Lactantius used the same device in the preface to his *Epitome*; cf. P. Monceaux, *Histoire littéraire de l'Afrique chrétienne*, III, 312.

[44] Hence the esteem which Luther still accorded Sedulius as "Christianissimus poeta" (Schanz, IV, 2, 373).

6. Notker Balbulus

About 890 Notker Balbulus wrote two didactic letters [45] on the study of the Bible and of literature to his pupil Solomon, later bishop of Constance (*ca.* 855–920). He first names and characterizes commentaries on separate books of the Bible. For the Psalms alone he recommends the exegetical writings of Origen, Augustine, Arnobius, Hilary, Cassiodorus. Among modern interpreters of the Bible Bede is praised above all others; though he is a barbarian whose writings are despised by the snobs of Roman culture, God, who made the sun to rise in the east on the fourth day of creation, now in the sixth and last age of mankind made Bede to rise in the west as a new sun—to illuminate the whole earth (p. 67).[46] But if Solomon still hungers for "Roman delicacies," he may read—Gregory the Great. With the commentators Notker puts the ecclesiastical writers "qui ex occasione disputationis propriae quasdam sententias divinae auctoritatis explanaverunt." This circumstantial designation corresponds to what Isidore called "maiores disputationes." As an expression it is a way out of a dilemma, a periphrase for "theological tractate." The latter expression could not be chosen because the word *theologia* usually meant "Bible." [47] Cassiodorus' term "catholici magistri" would have been a better choice. In this category Notker names various works of Augustine and Isidore, then Gregory's *Cura pastoralis*, Eucherius, Alcuin (with special praise). Next, as the third kind of book, Notker discusses poems, which he terms "metra" (p. 73). He rejects the "gentilium fabulae" since "in Christianitate" there are Prudentius, Alcimus Avitus, Juvencus, Sedulius, and the Ambrosian hymns. A new division is formed by the "ecclesiastici scriptores," [48] for whom Notker refers to the relevant works of Jerome and Gennadius. Notker's second letter adds to the first: "passiones sanctorum" (among them, surprisingly enough, Hermas' *Shepherd*), ecclesiastical history, the Greek fathers (who, after the providential removal of Julian the Apostate, "quasi post rigidissimam hiemem verni flores in terra nostra apparere coeperunt, qui prius quasi in theca vel cortice clausi tenebantur"). The letter concludes with an enumeration of ecclesiastical personages of the West.

Notker remains within the beaten path of the tradition; but, since Isidore, it has

---

[45] E. Dümmler, *Das Formelbuch des Bischofs Salomo III. von Konstanz* (1857), p. 64–78.

[46] Ulrich Zeller, in his *Bischof Salomo III. von Konstanz* (1910), p. 36, comes to the conclusion: "It appears that Notker was not very well versed in modern literature. Thus he obviously knew little of Raban's writings." He apparently knew more of them than his critic, who overlooks the fact that though Raban was a very learned man, he was not a man of any intellectual independence. His Biblical commentaries are excerpts from the fathers, but it seems that Notker preferred to read these in the original. "Sa prose," says J. de Ghellinck of Raban, "pratique le plagiat sans vergogne, mais en général il choisit bien les passages qui lui servent d'extraits" (*Littérature latine au moyen âge* [1931], I, 103).

[47] This does not change until the twelfth century: J. de Ghellinck, *Le mouvement théologique du 12e siècle* [2] (1948), 91 f.

[48] The term comes from Jerome and in him first means the apocrypha in contrast to the canonical books of the Bible, then ecclesiastical writers in general (*PL*, XXII, 606, § 2).—In Cassiodorus' *Institutiones* and Isidore's *Etymologiae, ecclesiasticus* does not appear in this sense.

received the addition of an important link: Anglo-Saxon and Carolingian Humanism. Notker appreciates it in the figures of Bede and Alcuin. Nevertheless he exhibits a greater monastic narrowness, as his rejection of the pagan poets shows. A new and German note enters his thinking in the contrast between Rome and the barbarians, which he feels as a profound dichotomy.

7. Aimeric

Cassiodorus and Notker were monks, Isidore a bishop: around their literary studies hangs the atmosphere of cloister and church. The Frenchman Aimeric's *Ars lectoria* (written 1086), on the other hand, is the work of a grammarian, who speaks of himself with great self-confidence:

Ecce novus toti codex hic cuditur orbi.

This eulogy refers to a didactic poem on the quantity and accent of Latin words, which makes use of many poets. The author then refers to himself too as "metricus metricorum amicus." Of interest is a prose excursus with a classification of authors which gives entirely different evaluations from those previously known to us.

Christian literature is ranked in four classes:

1. *aurum=autentica*	3. *stagnum=communia*
2. *argentum=hagiographa*	4. *plumbum=apocrifa.*

Authenticus ("original, authoritative") is originally a legal term, which Jerome transferred to the Bible. As *autentica* Aimeric names only the canonical books of the Bible (though Daniel is excluded) and the *Canon missae.* This putting the liturgy and the Bible in the same literary rank is one of his peculiarities.—The *hagiographi*, forming part of the Old Testament canon, have here become *hagiographa*, which include such different things as the Books of Maccabees, the Epistle to the Hebrews, the great doctors Ambrose, Jerome, Augustine, Gregory, and the *benedictio conjugum*.[49] But what is meant by *communia*? Perhaps "common" in the pejorative sense? And yet it includes Bede, Sedulius, Prudentius, Arator—and the *benedictio cerei* (blessing of the Easter candle). The lowest class, the *apocrifa*, includes passions of martyrs, lives of saints—and Origen.

Now follow 23 pagan authors. All are *autentici*, but ranked once again according to the scale of metals gold, silver, tin—the lead classification is missing. Golden are the seven *artes* and nine *auctores*: Terence, Virgil, Horace, Ovid, Sallust, Lucan, Statius, Juvenal, Persius. Silver: Plautus, Ennius, Tully, Varro, Boethius, Donatus, Priscian, Sergius, *Plato translatus* (in the original *aureus*). Tin: Catunculus (i.e., the gnomic poet Cato), Homerulus (the *Ilias latina*)—both as diminutives presumably because intended for abecedarians; Maximianus, Avianus, and Aesop—all three, as we know, likewise popular in schools.

As we see, an entirely new system. But perhaps only because we do not know the tradition of the secular grammarians and teachers of literature—on good grounds: if they praise the antique poets too loudly, they are condemned as heretics

---

49 I.e., the blessing at the ecclesiastical wedding (now *benedictio nuptialis*).

and executed, as we know from Radulfus Glaber (d. 1044).[50] Hence I am inclined to suppose that Aimeric reflects a concept which existed long before him but which was unable to get a hearing. This only became possible in the last third of the eleventh century, when a freer trend in study begins. When Aimeric writes "item apud gentiles sunt libri autentici," a spell is broken which had weighed upon the West for half a millennium if not longer.[51]

The metals as symbols of value—this finally leads back to the Hesiodic doctrine of the ages of the world, which, however, "corresponds to a widely diffused oriental doctrine" which we find "in Indian and Persian texts." [52] There is a Biblical correspondence in Daniel 2:32 ff. *Aureus* in the sense of *optimus* was already used by classical Roman writers. There are an *aurea mediocritas* and *aurei libelli*. But the continuation of the comparison through silver, copper, iron, tin, down to lead, appears not to be antique (except in connection with the ages of the world).

8. *Literary Studies in the Twelfth and Thirteenth Centuries*

If we continue to look for systems of classifying authors, we make a modest but not valueless discovery in the eleventh or the beginning of the twelfth century. In a poem on Embricho of Mainz (printed by Wattenbach in *SB Berlin* [1891], I, 113) we read:

> 9   *Noverat auctores maiores atque minores . . .*
> 11 *Philosophos legit, anima sacra scripta subegit . . .*
>   *Quem si vidisset, quondam Naso coluisset*
>   *Prosa Sidonium, carmine Virgilium . . .*
>   *Ethicus et logicus extitit et phisicus.*

He was, then, a sage, for, as was often said both before and after Isidore, philosophy is divided into ethics, logic, and physics. Isidore was enlightened enough actually to find these disciplines in the Bible. But this only in passing. What is of interest to us is the distinguishing of *auctores maiores et minores*. That obviously takes us into a world much more primitive than Aimeric's world: into the jargon of the school, of an average school, which must have been quite satisfied when its pupils got it into their heads that there were "lesser" and "greater" authors. But whence came this convenient school tradition? I conjecture: from Quintilian. In discussing school education he arrives at the question what beginners shall read ("qui legendi sint incipientibus"; II, 5, 18). This provokes him to the following statements: "Quidam illos minores,[53] quia facilior intellectus videbatur, probaverunt . . . Ego optimos quidem et statim et semper, sed tamen eorum candidissimum quemque et maxime expositum velim, ut Livium a pueris magis quam Sallustium, etsi hic historiae maior est auctor, ad quem tamen intelligendum iam profectu opus sit."

---

[50] Cf. E. Gebhart's masterly analysis in *Revue des Deux Mondes*, CVII (1891), 600 ff.
[51] Depending upon whether one makes Theodosius the Great or Justinian responsible for the official extirpation of pagan-antique culture.
[52] Reitzenstein in *Vorträge der Bibliothek Warburg 1924/5* (1927), p. 3.
[53] I.e., authors of less value.

To the first half of the twelfth century belongs the *Dialogus super auctores* of Conrad of Hirsau. Hirsau was a celebrated Benedictine monastery in the Württembergian Black Forest near Calw. In 1079, under Abbot William, it adopted the Cluniac reform. Conrad, a pupil of William's, was later teacher in the monastery and composed his *Dialogus* for pedagogical purposes. The rigoristic standpoint of the monks of Hirsau is seen in it throughout. Secular learning is to be used only like a cooking herb (64, 1 ff.), which is thrown away when the food has been flavored. So too the study of literature is to be given up when it has accomplished its purpose, that is, has schooled the mind. The speakers of the *Dialogus* are a teacher and his pupil. The latter has advanced from the *auctores minores* to the *maiores* (20, 14) and now asks for instruction concerning the school authors, books, and the basic concepts of literature. The following kinds of *auctores* are distinguished: *historiographi, poetae, vates, commentatores, expositores, sermonarii*. As *minores*, that is *rudimentis parvulorum apti*, we find Donatus, Cato, Aesop, Avianus. Now the study of literature has to answer four questions concerning each author: 1. What is the material of his work? 2. The author's purpose? 3. The final cause? 4. To what division of philosophy does the work belong? (27 f.). The last question is not to be asked with respect to Donatus. As grammarian he represents the foundation for everything else. He is the *abecedarium*, Cato the *sillabarium*. But for this gnomic poet the philosophical question is easy to answer: "ethicae, quae moralis dicitur, subponitur." Next come the Christian poets Sedulius, Juvencus, Prosper, Theodulus. For almost all of the authors hitherto mentioned, their place of origin has been given: Donatus was an African (confusion with the heretic), Aesop a Phrygian, Sedulius lived first in Italy then in Achaea, Juvencus was Spanish, Prosper an Aquitanian, Theodulus Italian. Then we read (46, 21): "Veniamus nunc ad Romanos auctores Aratorem, Prudentium, Tullium, Salustium, Boetium, Lucanum, Virgilium et Oratium." Here Conrad has obviously attempted to imitate Quintilian, who first discussed the Greeks and then wrote: "Idem nobis per Romanos quoque auctores ordo ducendus est" (X, 1, 85). "Roman" here, as also in Conrad, means, not Roman origin, but incorporation into Roman literature—which, however, must also be granted to Donatus, Sedulius, Juvencus. In Conrad, then, there remained a contradiction which he was not able to resolve. In his discussion of *auctores* much is striking. Thus, concerning Aeneas we are told that after conquering Turnus he made himself hated in Italy by his cruelty and was killed by lightning. The concluding portion of the work is devoted to a discussion of the seven *artes* Toward the end (83, 8) there are allusions to two famous passages in the Old Testament. They refer to the departure of the Israelites from Egypt. Moses' directions were: ". . . cum egrediemini, non exhibitis vacui; sed postulabit mulier a vicina sua . . . vasa argentea et aurea, ac vestes; ponetisque eas super filios et filias vestras, et spoliabitis Aegyptum" (Exodus 3:21–22). And so it was: "Petierunt ab Aegyptiis vasa argentea et aurea, vestemque plurimam" (*ibid.* 12:35). This passage and Deuteronomy 20:12 were interpreted by the fathers as referring to the taking over of the seven antique *artes* into the church's educational system.[54] According to Conrad of Hirsau (27, 24; 83, 22; cf.

---

[54] Augustine *De doctrina christiana*, II, 40 (*PL*, XXXIV, 63); Jerome (Epistle 21, 13 and Epistle 70; *PL*, XXII, 385 and 667). Further passages from Cassiodorus, Alcuin, Walafrid Strabo, Prudentius of Troyes, Raban, Rather of Verona, Peter Damian, Rupert of Deutz, etc., in J. de Ghellinck, *Le Mouvement théologique du 12e siècle* (1948), 94.

the note 66, 5), by the gold and silver of Egypt is meant *litteratura saecularis*. Perhaps we should see in this widely circulated schema the point of departure for the metal scale of authors.

Yet another item in Conrad's teaching deserves consideration: ". . . plurimi poetarum poetas praecedentes in carmine suo secuti sunt ut Terentius Menandrum, Oratius Lucilium, Salustius Livium, Statius Virgilium in Eneide, Theodulus eundem in Bucolicis; sic et in ecclesiasticis auctoribus multi alios secuti sunt" (27, 12 ff.). The concept of "following" (*sequi*) is a looser version of the *imitatio* theory. In Seneca (*Ep.*, 80, 1) one could read: "Non ego sequor priores? Facio, sed permitto mihi et invenire aliquid et mutare et relinquere. Non servio illis, sed assentior." Statius said, addressing his *Thebais* (XII, 816):

> . . . nec tu divinam Aeneida tempta,
> Sed longe sequere et vestigia semper adora.

According to Quintilian, Terence "followed" Menander (X, 1, 6). Quintilian also has the combination "imitari et sequi" (X, I, 122). Jerome in his *De viris illustribus* "followed" Suetonius ("Tranquillum sequens," Herding, p. 1, 1 ff.). In addition, of course, the Middle Ages knew the concept of *imitatio* from Seneca (*Ep.*, 84, 5 ff.), Quintilian, Pliny—see, for example, Geoffrey of Vinsauf (Faral, p. 249, 1706). But this must not be pursued further here.

The *Dialogus* of the monk of Hirsau is a principal source of the *Registrum multorum auctorum* of Hugh of Trimberg (written 1280). It is not my intention to discuss this historically important work here. Yet I believe that the preceding terminological investigations can clear up many difficulties in Hugh's systematics.

The literary studies of the Latin Middle Ages are completed and crowned in Dante's Epistle 13. In it Dante gives Can Grande della Scala a brief introduction (*introductionem*, §17) to the Divine Comedy. With this literary treatise too Dante stands in the scholarly tradition of the Latin Middle Ages.

VII

THE MODE OF EXISTENCE OF
THE MEDIEVAL POET

Excursuses VII through XII are fragments toward a "History of the Theory of Poetry." By "theory of poetry" I mean the concept of the nature and function of the poet and of poetry, in distinction from poetics, which has to do with the technique of poetical composition. This distinction between the concepts "theory of poetry" and "poetics" is a fruitful one for knowledge. That *de facto* the two have contacts and often pass into each other is no objection. The history of the theory of poetry coincides neither with the history of poetics nor with the history of literary criticism. The poet's conception of himself, for example, which is touched upon in Excursus XII, or the tension between poetry and science (Excursus XI) are major themes of a history of the theory of poetry, not of a history of poetics.

We still know too little today to give a comprehensive historical presentation of the theory of poetry. The problem has hardly been seen. The following Excursuses (with which Excursus XXI should be included) are, then, merely specimens of a branch of study which has yet to be established. I offer them as semi-manufactured articles, to stimulate further study.

In taking up the mode of existence of the medieval poet, I do not mean existence in the sense of contemporary "existentialisms" but in the old-fashioned (but always up-to-date) one of "living conditions and making ends meet."

Why did one write poetry? One was taught to in school. A great many medieval authors wrote poetry because one had to be able to do so in order to prove oneself a *clericus* and *litteratus;* in order to turn out compliments, epitaphs, petitions, dedications, and thus gain favor with the powerful or correspond with equals; as also for the sake of vile Mammon. The writing of poetry can be taught and learned; it is schoolwork and a school subject. This is true at least of the average writer, but also for famous scholars who wrote poetry *invita Minerva* (for example, Raban in the Carolingian period). Many a man wrote poetry groaning and sweating and could say of himself, like the author of the second Book of Maccabees (2, 27) "Nobis quidem ipsis, qui hoc opus suscepimus, non facilem laborem, immo vero negotium plenum vigilarium et sudoris [1] multi assumpsimus." That composing poetry, especially Latin poetry, which was still regarded by many of Dante's contemporaries as the only genteel variety, was to many a matter of great labor can be seen from the highly popular phrase, the poet will now end the poem or a section of it because the Muse has grown weary. What torture writing poetry could be is shown by the epistle of an unknown poet to a young man who is extolled for his cleverness and advised to submit to "the whip of poetry" if he wishes to develop his gifts to the utmost (NA [1877], 228, 24 ff.):

[1] Sweat as a metaphor. Cicero, *Or.,* I, 60: "Stilus ille multi sudoris est."—Quintilian, VI, 4, 6: "ambitiosus declamandi sudor."—Jerome, *PL,* XXIII, 772.—Ennodius (ed. Hartel), 125, 2.—Einhard, preface to the *Vita Karoli.—Poetae,* IV, 266, 25 and 1095, 22.—Alan's address to his book: "O mihi continuo multo sudata labore / Pagina" (*SP,* II, 426).—An anonymous poet commends to his patron "quae sudore meo de fonte bibi pegaseo" (*NA,* II, 392, 12).

> *Ante pilos tibi quae venit, tecum quoque gliscit;*
> *Te puerum fovit iuvenemque virumque docebit,*
> *Si maneas te intra nec te quesiveris extra,*
> *Si ceptis posthac studiis sudando fruaris,*
> *Si dorsum scuticis submiseris ipse poesis,*
> *Sique manum ferule subduxeris inde sophie.*

The author of the *Ecbasis captivi* admits at the beginning of his work that he had unfortunately spent his youth thoughtlessly, but now, even though it be late, he wishes to improve himself by assiduous work. Hence he writes verses. This banishes sleep and constrains him to a scanty diet. Very often he finds himself scratching his head and biting his nails over composition;[2] he upon whom lies such a task has renounced sloth. Underlying this is the concept that metrical composition is a very difficult, or rather the most difficult, kind of literary work. This was generally held. To be sure, Horace[3] and Quintilian (X, 1, 89) had distinguished between *versificator* and *poeta*, Petronius (ch. 118) had censured that nuisance the versifier, but this had not penetrated. Only occasionally do we find a protest against purely scholastic poetry. Thus an anonymous poet makes Apollo say to him in a dream (Jakob Werner, *Beiträge zur Kunde der lateinischen Literatur des Mittelalters*[2] [1905], p. 52):

> 33 *Miror ego nimium, miratur et ista sororum*
> *Turba sonora, meo que favet imperio,*
> *Quod nimis audacter, audacter et absque pudore*
> *Iura poetarum quilibet aggreditur.*
> *Quivis nempe rudis, expers cuiuslibet artis,*
> *Si potuit metro iungere verba duo,*
> *Protinus usurpat nomen vultumque poete,*
> *Se iam Nasonem Virgiliumque putat.*

The mechanical practice of poetry is here rejected. At the same time, however, the poem shows that the poet's problem of existence was also felt in the Middle Ages. How can the poet fit into society? What is his function in the nation, the state, the school, the church? In the Middle Ages there was yet no concept of an autonomous "culture." But since it has come into existence, the "poet's problem of existence" has not become any the easier.[4] To explain what I mean by this, I remind the reader of Wilhelm Meister's conversation with Werner (Jubiläums-Ausgabe, XVII, 89 ff.). Hermann Hesse[5] has put it even more urgently: "One could become a teacher, a clergyman, a doctor, an artisan . . . There was a road to every occupation in the world . . . a school . . . Only for the poet there was none! It was permis-

---

[2] After Horace, *Sat.*, I, 10, 71. But what is a humorous touch in Horace is taken in deadly earnest by the monkish poet.

[3] *Sat.*, I, 1, 40 and II, 1, 28.

[4] The ultimate basis of the problem and of all its manifestations is a metaphysical one: the incessant question of what the poet is to do in the world? Schiller found a quite comfortable solution for it in *Die Teilung der Erde*—idealism has its comfortable sides too. Baudelaire conceived of it as a Passion (*Les Fleurs du mal*, Nos. 1 and 2). A "metaphysics of poetry" would have to continue the search for a solution.

[5] *Kurzgefasster Lebenslauf* (1925).

sible, it was even considered an honor, to be a poet. But to become a poet was impossible; to want to become one was absurd and shameful." In the Middle Ages, to be sure, there was a school for poets—or rather, poetry itself was a school subject. To that extent the poet's "vocational problem" was simpler. But finding economic security could be a tormenting preoccupation to the poet in those days too. He was thrown back on gifts from his patrons, and he often begs in moving tones for the necessities of life. As is generally known, we have but one official document for the life of Walther von der Vogelweide: in the travel accounts of Bishop Wolfger of Passau there is an entry showing that the poet was given five *solidi* to obtain a fur coat.[6] In medieval Latin poetry there is no end to the discussion of such matters. How much better off the old Roman poets were! sighs Serlo of Bayeux (*SP*, II, 249). Imperial bounties made them rich:

> *Ut locuples fiam, non exercebo sophyam:*
> *Hic mercede labor caret, hac nil arte lucrabor.*
> *Plato subtilis foret hoc in tempore vilis;*
> *De nullis donis gauderet Musa Maronis;*
> *Sors tenuis rerum graviter cruciaret Homerum;*
> *De nulla certus mercede, poeta disertus*
> *In nostris oris est expers omnis honoris*
>
> .   .   .   .
>
> *Carminis ignari proceres, hebetes et avaris*
> *Dissimiles plane tibi sunt, pater Octaviane.*[7]

Walter of Châtillon (*Moralisch-satirische Gedichte* [ed. Strecker], p. 8) asks the Pope for a benefice and reminds him that Virgil and Lucan were wealthy:

> *Quid dant artes nisi luctum*
> *Et laborem? vel quem fructum*
> *Fert genus et species?*
> *Olim plures, nec est mirum,*
> *Provehebant "Arma virum"*
> *Et "Fraternas acies."*
> *Antiquitus et studere*
> *Fructus erat et habere*
> *Declamantes socios;*
> *Nunc in arca sepelire*
> *Nummos maius est quam scire*
> *"Bella per Emathios."*

Shall one write poetry for money? Walter refuses to do so himself in two stanzas which Strecker (p. 62) paraphrases as follows: "Many fools want to play the Juvenal; shall I, who have Pallas for my patroness, be silent? They make begging poems ("mugiendo postulant cibum"), which can be likened to the lowing of hungry cattle, while I command the delicate tones of a various art." But in another poem Walter turns the motif around and asks: "Why shall I not do as the ancients

---

[6] Edward Schröder, *Walthers Pelzrock* (*Göttinger Nachrichten* [1932]).

[7] That Augustus provided poets with clothing, food, drink, bounties, Hugh of Trimberg avers in *Registrum* (ed. Langosch), p. 162.

did, *adipisci rimulis corporis salutem?* . . . To strive after wisdom and virtue is a very fine thing, but the man who does it ends up in the gutter. Ours be the words of Horace in *Epi.*, I, 1, 53: Earn money! . . . What help is all learning if, having it, one goes hungry? . . . Great men like Diogenes and Socrates were poor starved wretches, it is true; but the lot of Juvenal and Lucan is not to be despised either" (Strecker, 81).

Study, learning, and poetry bring nothing in. Then is it not better to renounce academic education and throw oneself into practical life? This is a favorite theme for discussion among the school poets. Matthew of Vendôme (*SB München* [1872], 593):

> *Hinc studium placet, inde lucrum; cum dogmate pugnat*
> *Census, cum studio disputat aeris amor.*
>
> .   .   .   .
>
> *Me licet invito metrum suppullulat, exit*
> *Et volat in vetitum, me prohibente, foras.*
> *Metra placent, contempno lucrum, quia malo monere*
> *Quam fieri metricae gratuitatis inops.*
> *Consulo non loculis, sed famae; scribere praestat*
> *Quam fragilis census emolumenta sequi.*
> *Sum natus servire metris . . .*

Robert Partes (*Speculum* [1937], 222):

> *Unus ad obsequium desudat in arte potentum,*
> *Ille placere pari per sua scripta studet.*
> *Hic famam, sed et alter opes, hic quaerit honores,*
> *Predia nonnulli carmina ferre putant.*

When things go hard with the poet he can be very pressing in his requests: "Carmina composui: da mihi quod merui" (W. Meyer, *Arundelsammlung*, II, p. 123). Often he begs for and receives a fur coat or a horse. If the fur is a little worn, Hugh Primas avenges himself in biting epigrams. The Archpoet complains to his patron Reinald of Dassel that his wine has been watered.

A standing complaint is that mimes and buffoons are better rewarded and cared for by the powerful than are poets.

> *Tota strepit curia lusibus obscenis*
> *Et mimorum ferculis et scutellis plenis*
> *Nihil foris flentibus mittitur egenis.*[8]

Eberhard the German (Faral 341, 113):

> *Florent faex hominum scurrae, quos curia lactat,*
> *Qui dominis linguae garrulitate placent.*

The antique "warning example" against a preference for actors and mimes is Nero. John of Salisbury complains that this vice is prevalent in his day. Yet the ancient actors were something better than the present mimes. These beguile the idleness (already an evil in itself) of listeners and spectators with things yet worse:

---

[8] *Gilleberti carmina* (ed. Tross [1849]), p. 19.—Cf. also Arnulf (*RF*, II, 238, 643 ff.).

dancing, wrestling, sleight-of-hand, shameless performances ("illi qui obscenis partibus corporis oculis omnium ingerunt turpitudinem"). He who rewards such mimes
encourages an infamous trade and puts himself in moral peril (*Policraticus*, 404d–
406d).

How and to whom are bounties to be given? This question is repeatedly treated
in the literature of the twelfth century. Theological writers like Petrus Cantor
(*Contra dantes histrionibus, PL*, 205, 153) take part in it. The poets are of course
particularly interested. The author of the *Architrenius* complains of the unjust distribution of money and possessions by the powerful. Among those unjustifiably preferred is the "histrio suspectus." The passage ends (*SP*, I, 290 f.):

> . . . *infima laus est*
> *Cuncta dari, cum nulla bonis quas sorbet in hora*
> *Histrio dantis opes, logicus delibet in anno.*

A *Commendatio nobilium datorum et de causis dandi* is to be found in John of
Garland (*Morale scolarium*, 195). Petrus Cantor writes *Contra acceptores munerum*
(*PL*, CCV, 78). Nigel Wireker expatiates upon the dangers of giving (*SP*, I, 101).
Alan has something to say on the question (*SP*, II, 395). John of Hanville makes
Democritus and Cicero discuss it (*SP*, I, 335 f.). It is treated very broadly and dully,
but with great volubility, in Matthew of Vendôme's poem on Tobias (in the speech
of the elder Tobias). Finally in the *Romance of the Rose*, 5120–5250. For this
passage, as Langlois points out, Jean de Meun used Alan, Horace, and Seneca.[9]

These economic notes also sound, among others, in the complaint of a poet who
is presumably identical with Petrus Pictor of St. Omer (*ca.* 1100; in Werner, p. 139,
No. 361): "Why should I continue to strive after wisdom and virtue? Fortuna
favors only the bad. I have had enough of laboring at poetry":

> 11   *Penitet esse probum me, penitet esse poetam,*
> *Qui nunquam duco noctemve diemve quietam.*
> *Nocte vigil tota non cesso versificari,*
> *Pingo die tota cupioque deos operari.*
> 15   *Sed pereant versus! pereant simulacra deorum!*
> *Nil mihi quippe boni confert ornatus eorum.*
> *Nam mihi quid prosunt versusque stilusque tabella?*
> *Pro quibus in studiis sum passus dura flagella.*

"How many poems have I written for prelates, and received empty words as my
only reward! A buffoon is prized more highly than such as we. If anyone wants to be
miserable, let him only study diligently and write poetry! Today art and learning are
down in the market":

> *Temporibus nostris mutari secula cerno:*
> *Omne vetus studium perit accedente moderno.*

Here the poet's problem of existence is combined with the complaint over the decay
of studies which is a very frequent motif.[10]

[9] Cf. also *Carmina Burana*, 19, and Schumann's commentary, 31.
[10] Cf. Schumann in the commentary to *CB*, 6, I.—The themes of such poems
provided the suggestion for Conrad of Würzburg's *Klage der Kunst*. The historical
perspectives in Walther Rehm's valuable study *Kulturverfall und spätmittelhoch-
deutsche Didaktik* (*ZfdPh*, LII [1927], especially 304 ff.) should be corrected
accordingly.

If anyone should be shocked by this amalgamation of poetry and Mammon, he may console himself with the fact that it was even so in the noblest period of Greece —that is, as we judge today, the "high archaic" period. No less a poet than Pindar complains that poets turn out eulogies for money (*Isthm.*, 2, 6). But he himself knows how to give a broad hint. Thus he admonishes the tyrant Hiero of Syracuse to be liberal with his wealth so that he shall not fail of the lasting fame which the poet can give (*Pyth.*, 3, 107 ff.). The medieval poets too had every reason to emphasize the value and dignity of their art and to defend it from reproaches.

THE POET'S DIVINE FRENZY

The theory of the poet's divine frenzy [1] is, of course, set forth in Plato's *Phaedrus* (which the Middle Ages did not know), but in diluted form it was to be found throughout late Antiquity and it passed to the Middle Ages as a commonplace, like other elements of antique mythology. Horace (*Carm.*, III, 4, 5) once regards himself as the victim of "amabilis insania," on another occasion is carried away by Bacchus (*Carm.*, III, 25). In the *Ars poetica* (455) he had referred to the "vesanus poeta." Ovid frequently testifies that the poet is inspired by the deity (*Fasti*, VI, 5; *Ex Pont.*, III, 4, 93 and IV, 2, 25). Statius expresses this by the word "entheus" (*Silvae*, I, 4, 25 and I, 5, 1). Pliny (*Ep.*, VII, 4, 10) propounded: "Poetis furere concessum est." Finally the Middle Ages could find the "furor divinus sive poeticus," produced by Phoebus, in Claudian. He begins his epic of Proserpine (I, 4):

> . . . *Gressus removete profani*
> *Jam furor humanos nostro de pectore sensus*
> *Expulit et totum spirant praecordia Phoebum.*

The Middle Ages, then, knew the poet's divine frenzy, without knowing Plato. The frenzy of the Muses is known to Statius ("Pierium oestrum," *Theb.*, I, 32) and Nemesianus ("Aonium oestrum," *Cyn.*, 3). Fulgentius further offered (Helm, p. 13, 18): "ut insanus vates delirabam" and "poeta furens" (Helm, 3). The vulgar conception of ἐνθουσιασμός consisted in regarding the poet as insane. Isidore—or rather his source—derives *carmen* from *carere mente* (I, 39, 4). This is echoed in the Carolingian period by Modoin (*Poetae*, I, 570, 23):

> *Nonnulli adfirmant etiam insanire poetas,*
> *Carmina dum statuunt mente carere sua.*

In the Hohenstaufen period the author of the *Ligurinus* adopts the topos in his prooemium (I, 34 ff.):

> *Certa quidem vatis dementia, carmen agreste*
> *De tanto cecinisse viro: sed parce furori,*
> *Princeps magne, pio; ne te praesumptio nostra*
> *Exagitet: solis licet insanire poetis.*

And the Archpoet writes (ed. Manitius, p. 27, 19):

> *Michi numquam spiritus poetrie datur*
> *Nisi prius fuerit venter bene satur;*
> *Dum in arce cerebri Bachus dominatur,*
> *In me Phebus irruit et miranda fatur.*

The theory of "poetic madness" is based on the profound idea of numinous inspiration—a concept which reappears from time to time, and is, as it were, an esoteric knowledge of the divine origin of poetry. For example in the Florentine Pla-

[1] For its early history: A. Delatte, *Les conceptions de l'enthousiasme chez les philosophes présocratiques* (1934), pp. 28-79.

tonism of the late Quattrocento. From thence it doubtless passed into the great system of figural harmony that Raphael left to posterity in the frescoes on the walls of the Vatican *stanze*. A medallion in the vault of the Camera della Segnatura represents Poetry, with the inscription: "Numine afflatur." But the vulgar form of the concept too—to write poetry means to be mad—is preserved for us in one of Italy's classics. Manzoni says, with subtle humor: "Presso il volgo di Milano, e del contado ancora più, poeta non significa già, come per tutti i galantuomini, un sacro ingegno, un abitator di Pindo, un allievo delle Muse; vuol dire un cervello bizzarro e un po' balzano, che, ne' discorsi e ne' fatti, abbia piu dell' arguto e del singolare che del ragionevole." * If we now look back at the Middle Ages, we can see that the theory of "poetic madness"—the Platonic interpretation of the doctrine of inspiration and enthusiasm—lived on through the entire millennium which extends from the conquest of Rome by the Goths to the conquest of Constantinople by the Turks. "Lived on" is perhaps too pretentious an expression. As it did with so many other coinages of the Greek spirit, the Middle Ages took this one from late Rome, preserved it, and copied it to the letter, until the creative Eros of the Italian Renaissance reawakened the spirit in the letter. That the poetic μανία found a refuge in the medieval *scriptoria* with the rest of the authoritative stock of antique learning is a paradox when one considers that it was precisely in the Middle Ages that writing poetry was considered to be sweat-producing labor and was recommended as such. But the juxtaposition of these unconcealed contradictions gives medieval culture its attraction.

* [Manzoni, *I Promessi Sposi* (The Betrothed).]

POETRY AS PERPETUATION

Homer's heroes already know that poetry bestows eternal fame upon those whom it sings (*Iliad*, VI, 359). Poetry perpetuates. The poets like to impress this—Theognis (237 ff.) upon his Cyrnus, for example; Theocritus (XVI) upon Hiero; Propertius upon his Cynthia (III, 2, 17); likewise Horace (*Carm.*, IV, 8, 28), though in his case it is upon no one in particular. Ovid too uses the same motif of enticement (*Am.*, I, 10, 62). To be distinguished from this, is the assurance that the poet himself gains undying fame by his singing—the Horatian

> *Exegi monumentum aere perennius.*

Ovid has devoted a delightful poem to this theme. Lucan conducts Caesar to Hector's grave and adds the lines (IX, 980):

> *O sacer et magnus vatum labor! omnia fato*
> *Eripis et populis donas mortalibus aevum.*
> *Invidia sacrae, Caesar, ne tangere famae;*
> *Nam, si quid Latiis fas est promittere Musis,*
> *Quantum Zmyrnaei durabunt vatis honores,*
> *Venturi me teque legent; Pharsalia nostra*
> *Vivet, et a nullo tenebris damnabimur aevo.*

About 550 Corippus amplified the topos in the *praefatio* to his *Johannis*:

> 5   *Omnia nota facit longaevo littera mundo*
>   *Dum memorat veterum proelia cuncta ducum.*
> *Quis magnum Aeneam, saevum quis nosset Achillem,*
>   *Hectora quis fortem, quis Diomedis equos,*
> *Quis Palamedeas acies, quis nosset Ulixem,*
>   *Littera ni priscum commemoraret opus?*
> *Smyrnaeus vates fortem descripsit Achillem,*
>   *Aeneam doctus carmine Vergilius:*
> *Meque Johannis opus aocuit describere pugnas*
>   *Cunctaque venturis acta referre viris.*

A biblical parallel may be seen in Reginald of Canterbury's lines (NA, XIII [1888], 835, X):

> 5   *Flos, decor omnis abit—docti sapientia stabit;*
>   *Ut firmamentum stabilis vigor est sapientum:*
>   *Testis scriptura, quia permanet immoritura*
>   *Fama viri clari nec morte potest violari;*
>   *Id quoque testatur Daniel, quia perpetuatur*
> 10 *Gloria doctorum, laus et doctrina bonorum,*
>   *Qui nos iustitie conformant arte sophie,*
>   *Componunt mores nostros minuuntque labores:*
>   *Quomodo vivendum, quid agendum, quid fugiendum*
>   *Sit, descripserunt, idiotas edocuerunt.*

This is based upon Daniel 12:3: "Qui autem docti fuerint, fulgebunt quasi splendor firmamenti; et qui ad iustitiam erudiunt multos quasi stellae in perpetuas aeternitates."

Aeternitas—the Latin language had formed the corresponding verb *aeternare*. But the word is very rare. The *Thesaurus* gives only two examples from authors, one from Varro and one from Horace (*Carm.*, IV, 14, 3). But it was carried along in glosses and is not uncommonly found in the poets of the twelfth century. Of the Old Testament heroes Hildebert says (*PL*, CLXXI, 1231 C):

> *Tales athletas olim vetus attulit aetas,*
> *Per quos evulsi sunt hostes atque repulsi,*
> *Quos laus aeternat, quos mundi gloria vernat.*

Baudri of Bourgueil (ed. Abrahams, 154, 111 ff.) eternized his bishop and his city:

> *Ipsum carminibus, ipsam quoque perpetuasti,*
> *Et quicquid captas carmine perpetuas.*
> *Te quoque quandoquidem potes aeternare tuosque,*
> *Aeterna, quaeso, nomen in astra meum.*

Abélard writes to his son Astralabius:

> *Qui pereunt in se, vivunt per scripta poetae;*
> *Quam natura negat, vita per ista manet.*
> *Per famam vivit defuncto corpore doctus,*
> *Et plus natura philosophia potest.*

Benzo of Alba (Pertz, 597, 43 ff.):

> *Fortium quidem virorum nulla foret notio,*
> *Si periti literarum torpuissent otio;*
> *Defuisset exemplorum aurea memoria,*
> *Nisi eos propalaret aliqua hystoria.*
> *Moyses iubente Deo scripsit mundi fabricam,*
> *Alii scribae dixerunt heroum prosapiam . . .*
> *Nam si litterae celassent res aevi praeteritas,*
> *Quem, rogo, deberet sequi succedens posteritas?*

About 1184 Walter of Châtillon ends his *Alexandreis* with lines addressed to Archbishop William of Reims:

> *Vivemus pariter: vivet cum vate superstes*
> *Gloria Guillermi nullum moritura per aevum.*

Jacob Burckhardt, in his chapter "Fame in Literature" remarks: "The poet-philologist in Italy already has . . . the most intense consciousness that he is a distributor of fame and indeed of immortality; and likewise of oblivion." Our examples show that the Latin poets of France possessed this consciousness as early as 1100. In them Dante could find the word *aeternare*, which, to be sure, he fills with new meaning when he says to Brunetto Latini (*Inf.*, XV, 85):

> *M' insegnavate come l' uom s' eterna.*

Ariosto has the immortality-topos in the *Orlando Furioso*, XXXV, 22 ff.

POETRY AS ENTERTAINMENT

In ancient Greece poets and poetry were above all prized for their value as educators of the people. Even Plato, who thought quite otherwise, nevertheless reproduces the general view when he calls poets "fathers of wisdom and guides" (*Lysis*, 214 a). The Alexandrians, however, maintain an aesthetic-hedonistic view of poetry. Eratosthenes (275–195) set forth that the aim of every true poet is to entertain [1] his readers, not to teach geography or history or anything else. In a far more cautious manner the question whether poetry should only teach (be useful) or should also give pleasure was discussed as early as the fourth century and was answered by Heracleides Ponticus with a feeble "both." This was afterward taken over by Horace (*Ars poetica*, 333–44), who in his dicta on poetry (*Epi.*, II, 1, 118 ff.) of course had to take into account Augustus's reform movement. A similar plurality of aims (*docere, movere, delectare*) had been ascribed to oratory by Quintilian, but to poetry only one, "solam voluptatem." Eratosthenes' purely hedonistic view found little following elsewhere.[2] But the court poets are fond of commending themselves for having tried to provide pleasure and relaxation for the Emperor—Oppian especially (*Halieutica*, III, 1–8); likewise Philostratus at the end of the preface to his *Lives of the Sophists*. Oppian wrote under Caracalla; Philostratus between 229 and 238. A little over a century later (362–372) the African Zeno ruled Verona as bishop. In an Easter sermon (*Lib.* I, *tract.* 38; printed in *Poetae*, IV, 861) he had admonished the neophytes "not to celebrate" the customary baptismal feast "in worldly wantonness, but instead to satisfy their hunger from the Bible" (Lehmann): There three youths brought pulse (Daniel 1:12), Christ gave oil, Abraham a calf (Gen. 18:7), Peter fish, David cheeses (I Samuel 17:18) . . . This edifying *jeu d'esprit* could be extended at will. And this some wit unknown to us did. Thus there came into existence, under the title *Cena Cypriani*, a Biblical parody, which was taken up again by Carolingian scholars and was recast in the second half of the ninth century by a Roman deacon named John.[3] He sends his little work to Pope John VIII, with a dedication in which, like Oppian and Philostratus, he recommends himself as a cheerful and diverting artist (*Poetae*, IV, 900). Another court poet who wants

[1] Eratosthenes uses the word ψυχαγωγαί, which however does not mean "psychological guidance" in the modern sense of those words but the art of forcing the reader into varying moods.

[2] Strabo opposed him not only as a Stoic but also as a specialist in geography. On the other hand the philosopher and physician Galen (A.D. 129–99) supported Eratosthenes. In *De usu partium* (III, 1) Galen has occasion to speak of the myth of Ixion (told by Pindar, *Pyth.*, 11, 21-48), whose son, begotten upon a cloud, "mated with horses" and thus became the ancestor of the Centaurs. As a physician Galen points out the physiological impossibility of this *commercium* between man and beast, but as a votary of poetry he nevertheless adds: "But to thee, O Pindar, we leave it to sing and to tell myths, for we know that her own ornaments and the marvelous are not the least of the poetic Muse's needs; for, as I believe, she would agitate and enchant and enrapture her hearers, but not teach them" (ed. Helmreich, I, p. 125, 1 ff.).

[3] P. Lehmann, *Die Parodie im Mittelalter* (1922), 25 ff.

above all to "please" is Ermoldus Nigellus. In a poem to Louis the Pious' son
Pepin, who was king of Aquitaine (817–838), he argues (*Poetae*, II, 85, 3 ff.):

> *Carminibus prisci quondam placuere poetae,*
> *Carmine Naso placet atque poeta Maro.*

The mighty of this world, he goes on, had often delighted in little things—lapdogs,
pottery, and the like; so may the king give a friendly reception to the toying of the
musa iocosa. Heiric of Auxerre sends Bishop Hildebold of Soissons (871–84) the
verse prologue to a lost work which was to cheer him when cares lay heavy on his
heart (*Poetae*, II, 427, 19 ff.). The author of the *Ligurinus* says of the historians
from whom he took his material that they had chosen to write in prose because
poetry is only an entertaining game (I, 147 f.):

> *. . . puduitque reor, puerilibus illos*
> *Lascivire jocis, et inanes texere nugas.*

And the judge Richard of Venosa says in the prologue to his comedy *De Paulino et
Polla*, dedicated to Frederick II:

> *Tempus adest aptum quo ludere nostra Camoena*
> *Debeat et curis se leviare suis.*
> *Nam cum saepe jocis sapientum cura levetur,*
> *Saepius et sapiens corda iocosa domat.*

POETRY AND SCHOLASTICISM

One of the chief themes of this book is the position of poetry in the intellectual cosmos of the Middle Ages. We have investigated its relation to grammar, rhetoric, philosophy, and theology. With the scholastic disciplines (*artes*) of grammar and rhetoric poetry was connected by long usage. If it regarded itself as theology and philosophy, that was an imaginative playing with hoary traditions which the Platonism of the twelfth century revived. But it was just then that philosophy and theology began to be consolidated conceptually and established as branches of learning which shattered the system of the *artes*. Even the early Scholasticism of the twelfth century dissolves connection with the *artes*. Hugh of St. Victor (1097–1141) is the first to examine them critically. His *Didascalion* (PL, CLXXVI, 741 ff.) is an introduction to study and at the same time a general theory of science and philosophy.

Hugh explains the origin and systematic connection of the various branches of knowledge and sees in their exploration the perfection of the soul: "Summum igitur in vita solamen est studium sapientiae, quam qui invenit, felix est, et qui possidet beatus" (742 D). Knowledge and virtue united yield the fullness of human life: "Integritas vitae humanae duobus perficitur, scientia et virtute, quae nobis cum supernis et divinis substantiis similitudo sola est" (745 C). Hugh attempts to fit the traditional arts and sciences into a quadripartite schema of "philosophy" (*theorica, practica, mechanica, logica*), but this is not accomplished without difficulties. In particular, the relation of grammar to logic is not entirely clear: "Quidam dicunt grammaticam non esse partem philosophiae, sed quasi quoddam appendicium et instrumentum ad philosophiam" (763 B). Hugh has but little to say about grammar. He refers to Donatus, Servius, Priscian,[1] Isidore. It is noticeable that the *enarratio poetarum* which belongs to grammar is passed over in silence. Hugh next treats (765 C) "de auctoribus artium," i.e., the most important textbooks. Here appear Linus, Varro, Scotus Eriugena as representatives of theology; Hesiod, Cato, Virgil, Columella, etc., as teachers of agriculture and the like. This is traditional material. But the chapter *de duobus generibus scriptuarum* (768 D) introduces something substantially new. There are two classes of literature: first, textbooks (*artes*); second, everything else: these are the "appendentia artium" (the same makeshift expression was earlier employed for grammar[2]). The *artes* are subdivisions of philosophy, but the *appendentia* or *appendicia* are only indirectly related to it ("tantum ad philosophiam spectant"); they are concerned in the main with matter outside philosophy ("in aliqua extra philosophiam materia versantur"). And what sort of matter is that? It is poetry and literature: "Hujusmodi sunt omnia

---

[1] By *Priscianus de duodecim versibus* Virgilii we are to understand the *Partitiones duodecim versuum Aeneidos principalium*, also known as *Priscianellus* (Manitius, I, 508, 5). For the diminutive cf. Catunculus (*supra*, p. 464).

[2] Isidore says in his chapter *De regnis* that there were only two great kingdoms, the Assyrian and the Roman. "Regna cetera ceterique reges velut appendices istorum habentur" (*Et.*, IX, 3, 3)—which is, furthermore, very peculiar if we may regard the passage as documenting Visigothic consciousness of history.

poetarum carmina . . . illorum etiam scripta quos nunc philosophos appellare solemus, qui et brevem materiam longis verborum ambagibus extendere consueverunt, et facilem sensum perplexis sermonibus obscurare, vel etiam diversa simul compilantes, quasi de multis coloribus et formis unam picturam facere" (*sic*). [3] The *artes* stand high above the *appendentia*. "Artes sine appendentiis perfectum lectorem facere possunt; illa sine artibus nihil perfectionis conferre valent" (769 B). Such things may at most be read—but only occasionally—for recreation, "quia aliquando plus delectare solent seriis admista ludicra, et raritas pretiosum facit bonum." This is the only concession which Hugh makes to literature; his chief interest is in philosophy, mysticism, and dogma. He is anti-Humanist, like Bernard of Clairvaux and like Parisian Scholasticism later.[4]

Bernard Silvestris stands upon entirely different ground. In his commentary on the *Aeneid* (ed. Riedel [1924]) he gives his theory of learning. At the beginning of Book VI Virgil tells how Aeneas lands near Cumae and immediately sets out with his companions in search of the temple of Apollo and the cave of the Sibyl which is situated near by. Before they reach it they have to pass through a grove sacred to Trivia (Hecate):

13   *Jam subeunt Triviae lucos atque aurea tecta.*

The name Trivia naturally reminds the medieval interpreter of the three lowest school disciplines, the *trivium*. So we get the interpretation: "Appellit classem nemori Triviae i.e. applicat voluntatem studiis eloquentiae" (31, 2). These studies are divided among three disciplines ("tribus viis"): grammar, dialectic, rhetoric. The "golden roofs" of Virgil's lines, however, mean "quatuor artes matheseos in quibus philosophia que per aurum intelligitur continetur." Aeneas' faithful companion Achates has meanwhile fetched the Sibyl. This means: "Studium in artibus exercitatum adducit intelligentiam" (32, 1). Achates, namely, from *a-chere-ethis*, means "joyless habit" (*tristis consuetudo*), and that is obviously study. Now Bernard gives his theory of learning. "Est autem scientia scibilium comprehensio. Huius sunt quatuor partes: sapientia, eloquentia, mechania, poesis" (32, 18). A quaternary, then, as in Hugh of St. Victor. But only the *mechanica* or *mechania* is common to both classifications. Hugh's three remaining disciplines (*theorica, practica, logica*) must find a place in Bernard's *sapientia*. In exchange, *eloquentia* and *poesis*, which in Hugh have to play the role of Cinderella, are both given places of honor in Bernard. He then defines: "Poesis est poetarum scientia habens partes duas, metricum poema et prosaicum." As for the hierarchy of the four disciplines: the lowest is *mechania*, above it comes *poesis*, above that *eloquentia*, and highest of all *philosophia* (33, 31 ff.). The latter includes theology (35, 29). Let us return to the starting point, to the *studia eloquentiae*. Access to it is "per instructionem in auc-

---

[3] The meaning intended is: "What is called philosophy today is pure literature; a kind of writing which consists in rhetorical amplification, mannered obscurity, and random eclecticism."

[4] As is generally known, E. Norden (*Kunstprosa*, 712 ff.) attempted to cover the relation of the later Middle Ages to Antiquity by the formula "*artes* and *auctores.*" That—in 1898—was a great step forward. Today we see the matter somewhat differently. What Norden says of Hugh of St. Victor, pp. 689 ff. and p. 717, is untenable. In Norden's system Hugh would have to be reckoned an opponent of the *auctores*.

toribus" (36, 27). Thence follows a more precise identification of the place of poetry in the schema of the sciences: "Sunt namque poetae ad philosophiam intro-ductorii, unde volumina eorum cunas nutricum vocat Macrobius" (36, 28 ff.). This is the Humanism of Chartres.

The system of the *artes* was at the same time broken down by the New Aristotle. Representative of this is the treatise of the Spaniard Dominicus Gundisalvi (Gun-dissalinus) written *ca.* 1150. Of the *artes* he allows only grammar and rhetoric to remain as propaedeutic disciplines (*scientiae eloquentiae*). Above these stands logic, above logic the philosophic disciplines (*scientiae sapientiae*). They comprise phys-ics, mathematics, theology, politics, economics, ethics—an entirely new schema which will not be filled in until the thirteenth century. Though poetics is allowed a place, as is rhetoric (both are "scientiae civiles"), they are relegated to the lowest rank.

Wholly different is the thought of the Humanist John of Salisbury. In his *Meta-logicon* (written 1159), a treatise "on the value and use of logic" (Ueberweg-Geyer, 242), he has occasion to discuss the *artes liberales*. He emphasizes the fact that they originate in Nature ("ab optima parente Natura originem ducunt": *Metal.*, [ed. Webb], 27, 29) and proceeds to show this in detail. Grammar appears to offer diffi-culties: "Non a natura videtur esse profecta . . . immo ex maxima parte ab hominum institutione" (*ibid.*, 32, 18 ff.). Yet it imitates Nature (32, 25). This is shown not only by its system of inflections but also by poetics, which is also a part of grammar and which demands that the poet imitate nature (42, 32 ff.). John cites the authority of Horace and his precepts for the proper description of men of different characters and ages (*Ars*, 153–178), to which John adds that of places and periods ("locorum temporum aliorumque"). John concludes: "Adeo quidem assidet poetica rebus naturalibus, ut eam plerique negaverint gramatice speciem esse, asserentes eam esse artem per se, nec magis ad gramaticam quam ad rhetoricam pertinere, affinem tamen utrique, eo quod cum his habeat precepta communia. Rixentur super hoc qui voluerint (non enim hanc protendo litem), sed omnium pace opinor ut sit hec ad gramaticam referenda, sicut ad matrem et altricem studii sui. . . . Profecto aut poeticam gramatica obtinebit, aut poetica a numero liberal-ium disciplinarum eliminabitur[5] " (43, 17 ff.). John is imbued with the spirit of Quintilian, whom he often mentions. In his discussion of reading he puts the *auc-tores*—Hugh's *appendicia*—in the central position: "Quantum pluribus disciplinis et habundantius quisque imbutus fuerit, tanto elegantiam auctorum plenius intue-bitur planiusque docebit. Illi enim per diacrisim, quam nos illustrationem sive pic-turationem possumus appellare, cum rudem materiam historie aut argumenti aut fabule aliamve quamlibet suscepissent, eam tanta disciplinarum copia et tanta com-positionis et condimenti gratia excolebant, ut opus consummatum omnium artium quodammodo videretur imago. Siquidem gramatica poeticaque se totas infundunt, et eius quod exponitur totam superficiem occupant" (54, 17 ff.). Were we to cite his other works, his high esteem for poetry would appear from many other pages.

To understand the succeeding development we must clearly comprehend that the antique connection between the *artes* and the *auctores*, to which John of Salisbury still adheres, is undetermined from the end of the twelfth century by the rush to the new disciplines, and then is finally broken by the system of university subjects.

---

[5] This sounds as if it were said in opposition to Hugh of St. Victor.

Norden (*Kunstprosa*, 712 ff.) was the first to describe the process. But he did not see the connection with the universities. The situation is this: The *artes* are put together in one faculty. In the process the reading of the *auctores* is dropped entirely and grammar is reduced to Priscian. But the most important university subject is logic. We know this from the Paris curriculum of 1215 (Rashdall-Powicke and Emden, I, 440). There is a connection—be it said in passing—between this and the fact that the flowering of Latin literature begins to fail from *ca.* 1225 (de Ghellinck, *L'Essor*). Between men of letters and scholars a gulf opens. The poets react by an exaggerated self-assertion—as for example Jean de Meun (*infra*, p. 486). The "genus irritabile vatum" could not fail to become involved in feuds with philosophy. The conflict between Mussato and Fra Giovannino is famous. A counterpart to it which has hitherto received little attention is Michael of Cornwall's poem [6] against Henry of Avranches (*ca.* 1250). Michael showers his opponent with a hail of blunt invective, with the motives for which we need not concern ourselves. But one argument is interesting, because symptomatic of the estrangement between scholarship and poetry. The quarrelsome Michael admits that Henry knows more about poetry and grammar than he does himself. But Henry has no understanding of Aristotle and the methods of the *artes*:

> 37   *Si maior me sis, quia sit magis ipsa poesis*
>   *Nota tibi, non es adeo tamen ad raciones*
>   *Promptus Aristotilis ut ego . . .*
> 66   *Nam quamvis te sim minor et non forte poesim*
>   *Noscam, quam noscis, tamen artis non methodos scis . . .*

Michael has learned something worthwhile, Henry only how to file words and forge verses. Who takes such childish nonsense seriously! Michael aspires to higher things; he wants to become a philosopher:

> 73   *. . . Melius didici, si debent talia dici.*
>   *Sed non talia vis, immo puerilia mavis,*
>   *Utputa sunt prose vel ridmi vel metra; pro se*
>   *Talia quid prosunt? Quasi prorsus pro nichilo sunt*
>   *Hec reputanda, nisi plus noveris. Unde tibi si*
>   *Sufficit ars metrica, proponis te fieri qua*
>   *Mundi maiorem, meliorem fassus ego rem*
>   *Philosophus fiam . . .*
> 145   *Grammaticalia scis, sed naturalia nescis,*
>   *Nec logicalia scis. Tu nescius unde tumescis?*

Grammar here, as frequently elsewhere, is called *partes* (i.e., the doctrine of the eight parts of speech)—and this is sharpened into an antithesis:

> 114   *Ars mihi, pars tibi se subiecit,*

Michael's watchword and his consciousness of his place in society speak out:

> 173   *Nos sumus artistae, tu preco vocaberis artis . . .*

[6] Ed. Hilka in *Degering-Festschrift* (1926), 123. On the author, *Dictionary of National Biography* (original edition), XXXVII, 326.—Cf. also J. C. Russell and J. P. Heironimus, *The Shorter Latin Poems of Master Henry of Avranches* (Cambridge, Mass., 1935), p. 149.

It is the battle of the *artes* against the *auctores*. At the same period (*ca.* 1250) Henri d'Andeli took the field for the *auctores* in his *Bataille des set ars*. Eight years had passed since the proclamations of the *poetria nova*. 1170 was an epochal year in the history of medieval culture. But only two generations later the *moderni* of 1170 are forced into the defensive.

The educational system of High Scholasticism gave no place to philological and historical studies. Comprehension not only of Aristotle but also of the Bible could not but suffer from this. Hence the sharp criticism of the entire system in Roger Bacon (d. 1294), from which I extract a few sentences: "For the past forty years certain men have risen up in the disciplines and have made themselves masters and doctors of theology and philosophy, although they had learned nothing worth knowing . . . They are boys who know nothing of themselves or of the world or of the learned tongues—Greek and Hebrew . . . These are the boys of the two university orders, such as Albert and Thomas and others, who in many cases enter orders at twenty or even younger . . . Thousands enter who can read neither the Psalms nor Donatus, yet who as soon as they have taken their vows are set to study theology . . . Hence endless error rules amongst them. God permits it and the Devil sees to it" (ed. Brewer, I, 425).

THE POET'S PRIDE

Hennig Brinkmann (*Zu Wesen und Form mittelalterlicher Dichtung*, 46 n. 1) pointed out in 1928 "that from the eleventh century onward an increasing self-assertion among writers is characteristic of the period." The concept of poetry as a "perpetuation" already shows this. We may also draw conclusions from the suppression or statement of the author's name (*infra*, Excursus XVII). But we have in addition express testimony to the medieval poet's pride in his office and his art. Some examples may be cited. In the erotic idyl which is ascribed to a certain Wido of Ivrea and which is of the eleventh century, the author, in concluding (1. 285 ff.) his courtship, lays down as his strongest trump the fact that he is a poet:

> 285   *Sum sum sum vates, Musarum servo penates,*
>   *Subpeditante Clio queque futura scio.*
>   *Me minus extollo, quamvis mihi cedit Apollo,*
>   *Invidet et cedit, scire Minerva dedit.*
>   *Laude mea vivit mihi se dare queque cupivit,*
> 290   *Immortalis erit, ni mea Musa perit.*
>   *Musa mori nescit nec in annis mille senescit,*
>   *Durans durabit nec quod amavit abit.*

The outspoken conclusion follows:

> 299   *Ut semper dures, mihi te subponere cures,*
>   *Quodsi parueris carmine perpes eris.*

But the same pride of the poet is also to be found in the cloister. Abbot Lambert of St. Bertin thanks (*ca.* 1100) the monk Reginald of Canterbury for the latter's metrical life of the hermit Malchus. As famous authors he names Statius, Virgil, Naso, Cato, Plato. They live on. Then (NA, XIII [1888], 523):

> 18   *Non moritur, vivit, loquitur bona lingua bonorum;*
>   *Ergo deos dicamus eos vitaque fruentes*
>   *Qui scribunt artesque bibunt ratione vigentes.*
>   *Propterea te laude mea commendo probatum;*
>   *Ulterius sis egregius vir de grege vatum.*

Strong self-assertion is evident in Walter of Châtillon too, who in the preface to his *Alexandreis* says that, though he does not consider himself better than Virgil, he must point out that no poet of Antiquity dared to compose an epic on Alexander. But all this is nothing in comparison with the self-complacency of Henry of Avranches in a not easily accessible [1] poem to Frederick II, whose service he wishes to enter. Its contents are as follows: request for a favorable hearing (1–2); distinction between prose and poetry (3–6); the latter came from the Hebrews to the Greeks, and from them to the Romans (7–14); he who ranks prose with poetry may as well rank caves with houses (15–18); I am the best poet of our day and I leave

---

[1] Printed in *Forschungen zur deutschen Geschichte*, XVIII (1878), 487.

the desert of prose to others (19–21); I address myself to you at the instigation of the Bishop of Winchester (22–27a); you gather around you the best masters of all arts (27b–44); . . . the world of values is divided into intellect, things, words (*voces*); the sphere of intellect is ruled by God, that of things by you, that of words by me (55–66); hence in my realm I too am king (66–69); . . . you surpass all rulers as the sun the stars (90–101). And now the inference:

> 102 *Cum tua sic alios premat excellencia reges*
> *Simque poesis ego supremus in orbe professor,*
> *Dicendi, licet equivoce, sumus ambo monarchi,*
> 105 *Et summum reputo, quod in hoc communico tecum.*

In short: a rather tactless chumminess, which is more a testimony to the writer's vanity than to his understanding of Hohenstaufen-Sicilian culture.

During the height of Scholasticism Jean de Meun puts a sweeping eulogy of literature into the *Romance of the Rose* (18607 ff.). The train of thought is: Nobility of birth means nothing, intellectual nobility all (to 18634). This the man of letters (*clers*) can more easily attain to than can princes and kings "qui ne sevent de letreüre" (to 18676). Ethics of *gentillece*, i.e., of nobility to be proved in studies (18683) or in arms (to 18710). Honor the man of letters! In ancient times emperors and kings honored philosophers. To poets they gave towns and gardens (to 18739). Today men of intellect suffer in need (to 18754).

It has been sought to make Jean de Meun a representative of Parisian university philosophy. To be sure, he calls "clerks" those "qui toute leur vie / Travaillent en philosophie" (18742). But by this he means poets. He adheres, then, to the twelfth-century view with which we are already acquainted and to which poetry, philosophy, and scholarship are synonymous. It is precisely this view which scholastic scholarship opposed. Jean de Meun is a man of letters, not a university philosopher.

XIII

BREVITY AS AN IDEAL OF STYLE

The Archpoet says of Pavia (Manitius, p. 42, st. 18):

> Digna foret laudibus et topographia,
> Nisi quod nunc utimur brevitatis via.

What is behind this brevity-formula? This leads us back to the beginnings of Greek rhetoric. Isocrates demanded brevity for the *narratio* in judicial oratory (M. Sheehan, *De fide artis rhetoricae Isocrati tributae* [Bonn, 1901], p. 37). It was counted among the *virtutes narrationis* (ἀρεταὶ τῆς διηγήσεως; to be distinguished from the *virtutes dicendi* = ἀρεταὶ τῆς λέξεως) (J. Stroux, *De Theophrasti virtutibus dicendi* [1912], 43). Brevity in the *narratio* was recommended by the *Rhetorica ad Herennium* (I, §15), which was so popular in the Middle Ages. Cicero (*De or.*, II, §326; *Part. or.*, §19; *Brutus*, §50) and Quintilian (IV, 2, 32 and 40 ff.) and—in connection with the other *virtutes narrationis*—treated of *brevitas*.[1] Horace's "brevis esse laboro" (*Ars poetica*, 25) impressed the pursuit of brevity as a merit. Later (*Ars*, 335) comes the forceful dictum:

> Quidquid praecipies, esto brevis.

Of satiric poetry he had said (*Sat.*, I, 10, 9 ff.):

> Est brevitate opus, ut currat sententia neu se
> Impediat verbis lassas onerantibus auris.

The "brevitas Sallustiana" (Quintilian, IV, 2, 45) was celebrated: "Crispus brevitate placet" (Sidonius, *Carm.*, II, 190). Diomedes interpreted as a profession of brevity Virgil's phrase (*Aen.*, I, 342):

> ... summa sequar fastigia rerum,

which was also used by medieval poets in the same sense (*Poetae*, IV, 192, 392 f.):

> Altius eloquerer, verum sententia longa
> Sermonis; sed summa sequar fastigia tantum.

Brevitas-formulas are popular in prose and poetry alike. Jerome is fond of using them, "ne librorum innumerabilium magnitudo lectori fastidium faciat" (W. Stade, *Hieronymus in prooemiis quid tractaverit . . .* [Rostock, 1925], 69). Jerome was still within the antique tradition and had the knowledge to use rhetorical topoi intelligently. In the Middle Ages, on the contrary, *brevitas*-formulas were often used only to show that the author was familiar with the precepts of rhetoric—or else as a pretext for ending a poem. The *brevitas*-formula is out of place, for example, in Paul the Deacon's poetical obituary (*Poetae*, I, 46, 25):

> Plura loqui invitam brevitas vetat improba linguam.

---

[1] The late Roman rhetoricians handed on the corresponding rules (see Halm, *Rhetores latini minores*, Index, s.v. brevitas).

487

In a saint's life comprising 1800 lines the assurance (*Poetae*, II, 465, 1740 ff.)

> *Contigit interea clarum et memorabile signum,*
> *Quod nunc summatim contexere mentibus instat,*
> *Est quoniam multis brevitas sermonis amica*

produces the effect of an empty cliché.

That is typical of this literary genre. The authors who practiced it are fond of assuring us that the saint worked more miracles than they can enumerate. Here the *brevitas*-formula enters the service of panegyric. Thus Alcuin writes (*Poetae*, I, 196, 1204):

> *Multa alia, ut referunt, hic fecit signa Johannes,*
> *Quae modo non libuit brevitatis jure referre.*

Or Heiric (*Poetae*, III, 464, 127):

> *. . . calamum brevitas a talibus arcet.*

Or Milo (*Poetae*, III, 575, 281):

> *Plurima praeteriens studio brevitatis omitto*
> *Atque ea quae restant veloci famine curro.*

Sometimes writers go completely off the track. A certain anonymous poet writes *De translatione sancti Vincenti* in two books of three chapters each, each chapter containing ten lines. With great self-satisfaction he calls this work "rem novam et pro sui brevitate mirandam" (*Poetae*, IV, 137, 5).

The following *brevitas*-formula in Arnulf's *Deliciae cleri* (469 f.) is pure padding:

> *Ne mihi succense quod scriptito sub brevitate:*
> *Instigat residem brevior sententia mentem.*

The meaning of *brevis* can become exceedingly dim. Thus, in the preface to his *Synodicus*, Warnerius of Basel calls himself

> *Rerum priscarum brevis editor atque novarum.*

The good poet expresses himself briefly, so *brevis* and *bonus* approach one another in meaning. Thus in Peter of Poitiers (*PL, CLXXXIX*, 48 C):

> *Non opus est multis implere volumina verbis:*
> *Qui brevis et bonus est, ille poeta placet.*

Brevitas-formulas make their way even into lyric poetry (*ZRPh, L*, 79):

> *Quia parit tedium*
> *Copia similium,*
> > *Recreant diversa,*
> *Ne vertar in tedia*
> *Convertor ad alia*
> *Metri lege versa.*

We find the *brevitas*-formula in Walter of Châtillon too (*Moralisch-satirische Gedichte*, ed. Strecker, p. 40, 1): "Huius thematis compendiosa superficies quanto breviorem concipit in narratione tractatum, tanto faciliorem deo propitiante pariet intellectum."

Presumably we should know more of Charlemagne had not Einhard felt himself constrained to *brevitas*. He plumes himself on it in the beginning of his biography: ". . . quanta potui brevitate complexus sum, ut . . . nihil omitterem neque prolixitate narrandi nova quaeque fastidientium animos offenderem."

Here and in other examples which we have examined, the resolve to be brief is based upon fear of arousing the reader's distaste (*taedium, fastidium*) by immoderate length. We have already found this in Horace. The *fastidium*-formula, then, is closely connected with the *brevitas*-formula, but it can also stand alone. In the *Hisperica famina* we read:

> Caetera non explico famine stemata
> Ne doctoreis suscitavero fastidium castris.

In a *vita sancti* (*Poetae*, IV, 135, 56 ff.):

> Multa eius ad sepulchrum inde mirabilia
> Sunt ostensa, saepe fiunt largita debilius.
> Quae non parvum, si narrentur, aestimo fastidium
> Me lectorum induxisse; quod horrendum fugio.

A *précieux* variation on the *fastidium*-formula occurs in Matthew of Vendôme (Faral, 151, §118). We shall not pursue this further.[2]

The extensive and partially inappropriate use of the *brevitas*-formula in the Middle Ages has various causes. The original sense of the *brevitas*-injunctions was lost early, as was the original concept of the *narratio*. Brevity in the presentation of a state of facts which was to be judged by the law was absurdly enlarged into a *virtus dicendi* in general. The concept of the *narratio*, on the other hand, was transferred to the entire field of literature, including poetry and hence the epic. Now brevity being an "excellence" and, on the other hand, Homer and Virgil being obliged, as model authors, to exhibit all the rhetorical "excellences," the delicate question arose whether the method of presentation of these two classic authors was not often long-winded. This question must have occupied theoreticians of style as early as the first century of the Empire. We may draw this conclusion from the following statements by the younger Pliny (*Ep.*, V, 6): "primum ego officium scriptoris existimo, ut titulum suum legat atque identidem interroget se, quid coeperit scribere, sciatque, si materiae immoratur, non esse longum, longissimum si aliquid arcessit atque attrahit"·(examples from Homer, Virgil, and Aratus follow).[3] Though this solution of the dilemma had a certain neatness, it amounted in the end to confusing the concepts. Homer could describe the shield of Achilles in detail without running into prolixity because the description pertained to the subject of his work. But the briefest digression was reprehensible prolixity. One could thus be "short" and "long" at once. With this makeshift solution the attempt to transfer *brevitas* to the epic was obliged to rest. *Brevitas* was recommended for the epistolary style with better reason. The ancients already teach that brevity is the law of the letter. The medieval *ars dictaminis* took over the injunction: "Post salutationem exordium

---

[2] Cf. *supra*, p. 85.

[3] Lucian (*Hist. conscrib.*, 56 f.) should be compared. The passage would seem to allude to opposition to Callimachus' criticism of Homer; cf. Herter in *Gnomon* (1936), 452; *Bursian*, CCLV, 98 ff. and 111 f.

inibis, post exordium narrationem promovebis, que sic erit honesta, si brevis fuerit et clara." [4] For the Middle Ages, finally, we must bear in mind that *brevitas, brevis sermo, breviare*, and the like are also Biblical formulas (II Macc. 2:24–32; Daniel 7:1; Eph. 3:3). All this worked together to give *brevitas*, in the eyes of the medieval teacher of rhetoric, a significance which it had not possessed in Antiquity.

This is particularly striking in the twelfth- and thirteenth-century Latin arts of poetry published by Faral. A major portion of these didactic treatises is, indeed, devoted to the stylistic procedures of *dilatatio* (also called *amplificatio*) and *abbreviatio*. "La théorie de cette double tâche, amplifier et abréger, dont Matthieu de Vendôme ne parle pas, est exposée par Geoffroi de Vinsauf, Évrard l'Allemand et Jean de Garlande." Thus Faral (*Les Arts poétiques . . .* p. 60). But though Matthew of Vendôme in his *Ars versificatoria* (*ca.* 1175) does not yet have the antithesis between *dilatatio* and *abbreviatio*, it is all the more interesting that he lays stress upon brevity as characteristic of the modern stylistic ideal, in contrast to the ancients (Faral, 180–184). He is the first theoretician who consciously wants to be "modern." His personality has not yet been sufficiently investigated for us to be able to say what motives led this decidedly prosy schoolman to adopt such a position. In any case, he no longer shares in the enthusiastic veneration for Antiquity which we find in his contemporary Alan. He is a *modernus* and considers that the ancients had loaded down their poetic narratives with a superfluity of similes, rhetorical figures, and digressions. "Hoc autem modernis non licet." In Virgil, Statius, Lucan, Terence, Ovid, there are faulty constructions and other wrong usages. "In hoc autem articulo modernis incumbit potius antiquorum apologia quam imitatio" (Faral, 181, §8). These *moderni* of 1175, then, either consciously break with the theory of *imitatio* or restrict it very considerably. They are intellectual kindred of the French moderns of 1715, who undertook to improve Homer . . . and that meant to shorten him. Matthew, as we see from his writings, was himself a master of *amplificatio*. The systematic co-ordination of *amplificatio* with *abbreviatio* was, however, not undertaken until the next generation. In Geoffrey of Vinsauf's *Poetria nova* (written *ca.* 1200) lines 203-218 contain a comparison of the two stylistic principles, lines 219–689 deal with *amplificatio*, lines 690–736 with *abbreviatio* (Faral, pp. 203–220); to this we may add, in the same author's *Documentum*, II, 2, sections 1–70 (Faral, 271–280), and in Eberhard the German's *Laborintus* (written after 1213), ll. 299–342 (Faral, 347 f.). For Latin poetic theory *ca.* 1200, then, the situation is as follows: The art of the poet has first and foremost to prove itself in the rhetorical treatment of his material; for this he can choose between two procedures—either he ingeniously draws out his subject, or he dispatches it as briefly as possible. The absurdity of these excessively generalized precepts seems not to have entered the minds of the theoreticians. But, understandably enough, they devote more space to *amplificatio* than to *abbreviatio;* there was more to say about the former.

Geoffrey of Vinsauf compares the two methods to a fork in a road. One must make up one's mind to take one or the other (whence "brevitatis via" in the Archpoet):

[4] Albericus Casinensis, *Flores rhetorici* (ed. Inguanez and Willard [1938]), p. 36, §6, and p. 53.

Curritur in bivio: via namque vel ampla vel arta,
Vel fluvius vel rivus erit; vel tractius ibis,
Vel cursim salies; vel rem brevitate notabis
Vel longo sermone trahes. Non absque labore
Sunt passus utriusque viae . . .
Formula materiae, quasi quaedam formula cerae,
Primitus est tactus duri: si sedula cura
Igniat ingenium, subito mollescit ad ignem
Ingenii sequiturque manum quocumque vocarit. (Faral, 203)

To exemplify "abbreviation" Geoffrey gives three condensed versions of the story of the snow-child; one contains five hexameters, the others two each (Faral, 219 f.). He repeats his teaching in the *Documentum de arte versificandi*. There we read: "Sunt enim artificia duo, quorum alterum est dilatandi et reliquum abbreviandi materiam" (Faral, 271 §1). For *amplificatio* he recommends "descriptiones, circumlocutiones, digressiones, prosopopeiae, apostrophationes" (§2). In *abbreviatio*, on the contrary, only the "purum corpus materiae" (Faral, 277, §30) is to be presented. *Materia* is not "material" in our sense, but simply what has to be said. This "thing to be said" can under certain circumstances be contained in a single word, e.g., in *lego*. That is a "materia qua nulla potest inveniri minor." From this, by abstract analysis, one arrives at the bare schema: "Ego in tali loco lego." By application of the directions for amplification this can give rise to the stately product: "Locus iste in se duplicem opportunitatem studii continet, tum sua jocundus pulchritudine, tum a strepitu semotus populari. Cuius opportunitatis occasio, cum studentium concordet otio, me totum invitat ad studium et lectionibus fructuosis invenit studiosum."

In Eberhard the German's *Laborintus* we are told:

Rem dilato brevem, brevio longam. Decet ambos
Me servare modos: aptus uterque mihi.

But he hurries over this lesson. His principal interest is in the *ornatus verborum*; this is treated in great detail.

Finally we have John of Garland's precepts in his *Poetria*. They run (RF [1901], 913 f.): "De arte abbreviandi orationem. Sequitur de abbreviatione et ampliatione materie. Quae abbreviant materiam sunt quinque, scilicet: emphasis, disiunctum, verbum conversum in participium, ablativus absolute positus, dictionum materiam exprimentium electio." This is illustrated by examples. Example of emphasis: "Virginum est proprium castitas." *Disiunctum* (= asyndeton) is explained as "color rhetoricus quo copulative coniunctiones subtrahuntur, ut in Eneide verba Dydonis ad servos suos" (*Aen.*, IV, 593 f.):

Ite,
Ferte citi flammis, date tela, impellite remos.

The "verbum conversum in participium" helps brevity, inasmuch as instead of "Veni ut legerem et proficerem" we can put: "Veni ut legens proficerem." Brevity through the *ablativus absolutus* is exemplified when we write "me surgente mane" instead of "ego surrexi hodie mane." The examples show that the original meaning of *brevitas* as *virtus narrationis* had long since been obscured. The essence of brevity as of prolixity was seen in the use of particular artifices.

All the arts of poetry quoted are of the thirteenth century. Matthew of Vendôme's

Ars versificatoria is yet unaware of the alternative between amplificatio and abbreviatio. This appears to have been an "achievement" of the later period—the period, that is, in which the powerful stream of medieval Latin poetry began to silt up. But how, then, did the thirteenth-century theoreticians arrive at ·it? Could they find it in antique rhetoric? Faral (p. 61) and—with slight modifications—Brinkmann (Wesen und Form, p. 47) answer this question in the affirmative and refer to Quintilian. In the De oratore (VIII, 4, 1) the process of "amplificare vel minuere" is explained. But by this Quintilian obviously means the same thing that he had just previously (VIII, 3, 89 f.) called "augere et minuere" or "attollere et deprimere." Amplificare, attollere, augere on the one hand, and minuere and deprimere on the other, are here synonyms. By these formulas is meant the demand made by Gorgias, and after him by Isocrates and Aristotle, that the orator must know how to present great things as small, and small as great (τάτε μεγάλα ταπεινά ποιῆσαι αἰκ τοῖς μικροῖς μέγεθος περιθεῖναι).[5] The "enlargement" of small things, or more precisely, the art, equally important for judicial and epideictic oratory, "of raising acts and personal traits above their real dimensions," is called in Greek αὔξησις.[6] It corresponds to Quintilian's augere, attollere, amplificare. This artifice was known in the Middle Ages too: Alberic of Monte Cassino gives instructions, among other things, concerning "augmentum et diminutio dictaminum."[7] He uses, then, Quintilian's technical terms, and it is improbable that the thirteenth-century rhetoricians replaced them by amplificare—abbreviare, which furthermore mean something quite different. Amplificare or dilatare, namely, does not equal αὔξησις, but simply indicates, as Faral himself knows, the purely linear extension, expansion, unrolling of a theme. Amplificatio as αὔξησις is elevation, and belongs to the vertical dimension, amplificatio as dilatatio to the horizontal. Now it is true that in Quintilian (III, 7, 6) we find amplificare used in a somewhat different sense in connection with panegyrical eloquence, namely, synonymously with "to ornament": "Proprium autem laudis est res amplificare et ornare." But the distinction between augere (to increase) and ornare is fluid. Quintilian uses breviare only once (I, 8, 2), when he is discussing the school exercise of paraphrasing Aesop's fables: "versus primus solvere, mox mutatis verbis interpretari, tum paraphrasi audacius vertere, qua et breviare quaedam et exornare salvo modo poetae sensu permittitur." The alternative breviare—amplificare is not to be got from this passage. For the same reason, it cannot, in my opinion, be derived from Quintilian. So far as I know there is but one antique point of departure for the medieval doctrine, namely Plato's critique of Sophistic. In the Phaedrus (267 B) Socrates says of Tisias and Gorgias that they had invented the art of expressing themselves either briefly or at endless length upon any subject (συντομίαν τε λόγων καὶ ἄπειρα μήκη περὶ πάντων ἀνηῦρον=cf. Plato, Gorgias, 449 C). So we are led to a virtuoso display of the earlier Sophistic which was not preserved in the main tradition of antique rhetoric: Aristotle's mockery (Rhet., III, 16, 4) of the precept of "rapid" narration perhaps contains a criticism of this. I cannot say if Gorgias' "invention" was perhaps taken up again by later Sophistic and by it transmitted to the medieval tradition. But naturally there is and was at all times a need—without sophistic artifice—to present a subject more compactly or more

---

[5] Isocrates, Panegyricus, 1.

[6] W. Plöbst, Die Auxesis (Munich, 1911), p. 3.

[7] In the second part (as yet unprinted) of his Rationes dictandi. Cf. L. Rockinger, Briefsteller und Formelbücher . . . , p. 4.

extensively. For this Latin had the words *dilatare* and *coartare* (also *abbreviare* or *premere*). The *Thesaurus* supplies satisfactory information on the use of these words. *Dilatare* and *premere* occur as an antithetical pair in Cicero. *Coartare* and *dilatare* in the same sense in Julius Victor and Servius. In Jerome we find "longum sermonem brevi spatio coartavi," and in Cassiodorus "brevitatem illam . . . eloquentiae decore dilatavit." I conjecture that Geoffrey of Vinsauf's "alternative" was subtilized out of such expressions—on the basis of a pedantic Mannerism which is as characteristic of the medieval grammar-school as it was of early and late antique Sophistic.

Brevity as a *virtus narrationis* is, as we have seen from our passage from Pliny, a difficult concept and hence occurs with many different meanings. It can represent the opposite of a faulty copiousness in expression (pleonasm, perissology, macrology, parisology, etc.; Isidore, *Et.*, I, 34, 6 ff. and Faral, 182). This fault had already been condemned by antique grammar and rhetoric and brought pedantic censure even upon Virgil because he had written "sic ore locuta est," or "sidera coeli"—*ore* and *coeli* were obviously "superfluous." [8] Such stylistic criticism later found witty expression in Marbod's poem *Reprehensio superfluorum in epitaphio Johannis abbatis* (PL, CLXXI, 1675).[9] The same Marbod, giving instructions for the composition of saints' lives, says: "breviter et dilucide nec inornate omnino" (PL, CLXXI, 1566).

In the twelfth century we find a strikingly large number of condensations of antique material.[10] Some of these are school exercises, but others are on a higher level. There are examples both in the *Carmina Burana* (Schumann, Nos. 97–102) and in Primas' poems (No. 9). Is it permissible to connect them with the *via brevitatis* and with Matthew of Vendôme's criticism of the classics? In any case, noted poets of the period considered that they had deserved well by producing abbreviated versions of antique authors and they boast of it. Thus Vitalis of Blois in the prologue to his *Aulularia* (Cohen, I, 75);

> Hec mea vel Plauti comedia nomen ab olla
> Traxit, sed Plauti quae fuit illa mea est.
> Curtavi Plautum: Plautum haec iactura beavit;
> Ut placeat Plautus, scripta Vitalis emunt.
> Amphitrion nuper, nunc Aulularia tandem
> Senserunt senio pressa Vitalis opem.

That Simon Capra Aurea rehandled the *Aeneid* and then boasts:

> Plurima Virgilii corripienda premo

can be understood in the same way.[11]

---

[8] The line "Ibant qua poterant, qua non poterant non ibant" (Faral, 182) was also used as a deterrent from pleonasm. The line, though Faral appears to have overlooked this, would seem to be a parody of Ennius by Lucilius (W. Morel, *Fragmenta poetarum latinorum*, V, 172 and Charisius in Keil, I, 271).

[9] Here we have a topos of wit upon which ingenious variations were made in later times, especially by Rivarol, when, for example, he says of a distich that it had been found long-winded in places or praises an elegy which consisted of but one line (Rivarol, *Les plus belles pages* [Mercure de France], p. 61 and p. 65).

[10] Among these are *Pergama flere volo*; distichs 99 a and b in CB, etc.

[11] Cf. A. Monteverdi in *Virgilio nel medio Evo* (= *Studi medievali*, n.s. [1932]), 266 f.

Had people wearied of epic breadth? I believe that this factor must be taken into account. When Albert of Stade, a thirteenth-century epigone, has, in his *Troilus*, to describe a twelve-day battle before Troy, he gets through the business in fourteen lines and sighs (3, 345 ff.):

> *Quid juvat assidue clavas, quid tela, quid enses,*
> *Quid mortes, mortis quid numerare modos?*
> *Aut seriem scindet stilus aut fastidia gignet,*
> *Si necis omne genus enumerare volet.*

In the *chansons de geste* too, from the end of the twelfth century onward, there is a noticeable tendency to get through the obligatory androktasia briefly.

ETYMOLOGY AS A CATEGORY OF THOUGHT

When Odysseus, after twenty years of separation, sees his old father again, he does not at once reveal himself but thinks it better to try him first by "sharp-cutting" words. He comes from "Sorrowfield" (*Alybas*), his name is "Strife" (*Eperitos*), and he is the son of "Hardlife Vexation" [1] (*Apheidas Polypemonides*). The cowardly beggar Irus is threatened with being sent to the wicked king ῍Εχε τόν (Take him), who is wont to cut off strangers' noses, ears, and other things. Odysseus himself is he with whom "Zeus is wroth" (ὠδύσαο Ζεῦ). Elsewhere Homer tells us that Odysseus had received his name from his grandfather Autolycus. Because the latter was angry at many men (ὀδυσσόμενος) he named his grandson "Wrathful One" (XIX, 497). In the *Iliad* "speaking names" [2] are borne by Hector ("Holder," "Shielder"), Thersites ("Impudent"), Thoas ("Stormy"), the carpenter Harmonides ("Joiner"), and others. A girl is named Alcyone because her mother suffered the pitiable fate of the halcyon (*Iliad*, IX, 562). Etymological playing with names is also indulged in by Pindar, who interprets Themistios as "Sailspreader" (θεμόω ἱστία; *Nem.*, 5, 50), and Aeschylus, who reads Helen's historic role in her name (*Ag.*, 687).[3] In Plato's *Cratylus*, as we know, the problem of the origin of language is treated. Did the names of things originate in "Nature" or in "convention"? Can one read the essence from the name? "Yes"—says antique rhetoric. Among Aristotle's twenty-eight topoi of proof the last is the topos ἀπὸ τοῦ ὀνόματος: when one says of Draco's laws that they are those not of a man but of a dragon. For "etymology" Cicero uses "notatio" and defines: "cum ex vi nominis argumentum elicitur" (*Topica*, 35). In this he has particularly in mind the exact determination of the meaning of a word; this is useful to the orator. Quintilian (I, 6, 28) is in agreement with him. But Cicero had also mentioned the etymology of proper names among the "attributes" of the person (*De inv.*, I, 34). Quintilian also cites this *argumentum*, but with the wise restriction that it can only be employed when the name in question has been bestowed as an honorific—as Sapiens, Magnus, Pius—or when there is some other special reason (V, 10, 30). Quintilian's contemporary Theon expresses himself in similar terms: χάριεν δέ ἐστιν ἐνίοτε ἀπὸ τῦν ὀνομάτων καὶ τῆς ὁμωνυμίας ἡ τῦν ἐπωνυμῦν ἐγκωμιάζειν (Spengel, II, 111)—but here, significantly enough, there is no thought of any but epideictic use. We find the interpretation of names in Roman poetry too. It is frequent, but always sensible and dignified, in Virgil [4] (*Aen.*, I, 267; I, 277; I, 367 . . .). But in Ovid we already see the beginning of the foolish type of it which was later so popular in the Middle Ages. The festival of the Agonalia gets its name from the fact that before killing the sacrificial animal the priest asks

---

[1] The interpretations are from Pape's onomasticon, which is as useful as it is amusing.

[2] Cf. Franz Dornseiff, *Zeitschrift für Namenforschung* (1940), 24. *Idem, Das Alphabet . . .* 169.

[3] There are dozens of other examples from Aeschylus. Cf. Wilhelm Schmid, I, 2, 297, n. 3.

[4] On Virgil's philological interests cf. Marouzeau in *Mélanges Ernout* (1940), 259 ff.

"Agone?" ("Shall I perform it?"); or perhaps from the fact that the sheep do not come of their own free will but are driven (*agantur*). But in earlier times the festival was generally called *Agnalia* (sheep-festival), and an o had simply been inserted. Or is there a reference to the agony of the sacrificial animal, or to the Greek *agon*? So we have five etymologies to choose from (*Fasti*, I, 317 ff.; cf. also the beginnings of Books V and VI).

Ausonius sends Probus a flattering eulogy and charges it to submit a question to the recipient:

> *Age, vera proles Romuli,*
> *Effare causam nominis.*
> *Utrumne mores hoc tui*
> *Nomen dedere, an nomen hoc*
> *Secuta morum regula?*
> *An ille venturi sciens*
> *Mundi supremus arbiter,*
> *Qualem creavit moribus,*
> *Jussit vocari nomine?*

The same alternative also troubled Rutilius Namatianus. He speculates on the family of the Lepidi. Four members of it have brought misfortune upon Rome. And at the same time *lepidus* means "amiable, charming." What remains save the question (309 f.):

> *Nominibus certos credam decurrere mores?*
> *Moribus an potius nomina certa dedi?*

For Christians the interpretation of names was authorized by Matthew 16:18 as well as by the innumerable explanations of names in the Old Testament. Jerome had devoted his *Liber de nominibus hebraicis* to these. Another authority for medieval interpretation of names was Augustine.[5] He plays with the names Vincentius, Felicitas, Perpetua, Primus. Why is the Apostle of the Gentiles named Paulus? Because he is *minimus apostolorum*. The same sort of thing is frequent later in the acts of the martyrs.[6] But Augustine also explains *fides* by "fit quod dicitur"; *nequitia* by "ne quidquam," etc.[7]

All that I have presented so far can be taken as more or less insipid trifling. But it acquires fundamental significance for the Middle Ages by the performance of the great Isidore of Seville, who in his compilation of all human knowledge chose the road from designation to essence, from *verba* to *res*, and accordingly named his work *Etymologiarum libri*.[8] I have elsewhere discussed the importance of this work, which can hardly be overestimated; it may be called the basic book of the entire Middle Ages. It not only established the canonical stock of knowledge for eight centuries but

[5] I take the following examples from Christine Mohrmann's essay in *Mnemosyne*, III (1935-6), 33.

[6] G. Koffmane, *Entstehung und Entwicklung des Kirchenlateins* (1876), 150.

[7] J. Finaert, *Saint Augustin rhéteur* (1939), 91.—Gilson's remarks on the interpretation of Hebrew names, in his book *Les Idées et les Lettres* (1932), 159 ff., are important.—Cassiodorus: "Etymologia est oratio brevis, per certas associationes ostendens ex quo nomine id quod quaeritur venerit nomen" (*PL*, LXX, 28 A).

[8] Also entitled *Origines*. Both titles are well documented; cf. Manitius, I, 61. *Origo* is the translated equivalent of *etymologia*.

also molded their thought categories. It led to the *origo* ("origin") and *vis* ("force") of things. In Book I, 29, etymology is dealt with as a part of grammar. "Vis verbi vel nominis per interpretationem colligitur . . . Nam dum videris unde ortum est nomen, citius vim eius intellegis." For his period, Isidore's philological standpoint can be called reasonable: "Non omnia nomina a veteribus secundum naturam imposita sunt, sed quaedam et secundum placitum." Hence not all words can be etymologized. The chief classes are: "ex causa" (*reges a regendo et recte agendo*); "ex origine" (man is named *homo* because he is made of *humus*); "ex contrariis"— and here we find the still familiar *lucus*, with the explanation "quia umbra opacus parum luceat." In a later passage (VII, 6) Isidore gives the interpretation of the most important Old Testament names [9] after Jerome. Quantities of other etymologies are scattered through the 800-odd pages of the book.

Since the composition of poetry was a part of rhetoric, and since etymology was among the fundamentals of grammar and rhetoric, it was and remained an obligatory "ornament" of poetry. This is the practice in the West as early as the Merovingian period. I give some examples from the Carolingian period. Walafrid Strabo plays prolifically with the name of the erudite Florus of Lyon (*Poetae*, II, 357, 21 ff.). Milo on the Apostle Andrew (*Poetae*, III, 570, 56):

> *Ac nomen patrium patrando viriliter implet.*

St. Amandus' parents were named Serenus and Amantia—how beautiful and fraught with meaning (*Poetae*, III, 572, 131 ff.)! Britain is so named because of its "bruti mores" (*ibid.*, 467, 246). It is not always so easy. The elegant stylist Heiric has to begin his life of St. Germanus of Auxerre with an interpretation of the name of that town. In hoary antiquity it was named simply Autricus. But then it was fortified with walls and towers, hence underwent augmentation. The name had to be correspondingly "augmented" (*Poetae*, III, 438, 10):

> *Ex augmentatis verso cognomine muris*
> *Sive sequax usus dicas Autissiodorum*
> *Seu mutilare velis et dixeris Altiodorum:*
> *Nomine diverso res est cumulatior una.*

In the early Middle Ages such etymologies were often treated in accordance with the prescription "Rhyme me or I eat thee." The worthy Abbo—servant of the other Germanus, monk of Saint-Germain-des-Prés—expends much erudition on explaining the name Paris. It comes from the Greek town—unfortunately known only to Abbo—of Isia, to which Paris is equal: "Isie quasi par." [10] One poet employs much art to get a "valet fons" out of the name Atenolfus and interpret it (*Poetae*, IV,

---

[9] This theme was also handled "poetically" (*Poetae*, IV, 630).

[10] *Poetae*, IV, 79, 9. Winterfeld comments on the passage: "De Isia urbe nihil constat." I conjecture that Abbo had in mind something on the order of *par* $= \iota\sigma os'$. —On the whole subject cf. also Winterfeld, *Poetae*, IV, 264, n. 4.—Without further particulars—unfortunately—Joseph Vendryès states: "Il s'est trouvé des gens pour expliquer le nom de Paris comme issu de Par-Is, 'égal à la ville d'Is.' Cette fantaisie est parfois encore tirée de l'oubli, òu elle devrait rester pour toujours" (*Revue des Cours et Conférences*, 15. 12. [1939], p. 27).—Cf. A. Tobler, *Vermischte Beiträge*, II [2], 246.

427). A Guinemarus is "nulli dulcis, sed amarus" (*ibid.*, 175, 15). On the line (*ibid.*, 200, 33):

> *Valeriusque vigens vasti valitudine verbi,*

the glossator (presumably identical with the poet) remarks proudly: "Nota nominis veriloquium." Another poet is able to interpret the names of the planets (*ibid.* 143, 3 ff.). But a climax is the humiliation of etymology by a saint (*Poetae*, III, 596, 337): an Austrasian infant over whom the man of God prays, answers with a clear and unmistakable "Amen!"

> *Hic, aethimologia, tuus confunditur ordo:*
> *Infans dum fatur, nomen tibi tollitur istud.*

The etymological evaluation of proper names passed from the eulogies of pagan late Antiquity to Christian poetry, including hymns (e.g., *A.h.*, XXII, 28, 17).[11] In the twelfth century the procedure was taken into the arts of poetry as "argumentum sive locus a nomine" (Faral, 136, § 78) and illustrated from Ovid (*Pont.*, I, 2, 2). Marbod maintains the epistemological import of etymology (*PL*, CLXXI, 1671 C). He finds *mors* an "asper sonus" because death itself is harsh. *Vita*, on the other hand, is pleasant-sounding. He concludes:

> *Nomen commendat res nomine significata.*
> *Ergo debemus naturam quaerere rerum,*
> *Ex quo possimus de nomine cernere verum.*

Hildebert (*PL*, CLXXI, 1274 A) shares this conviction:

> *Nomen enim verum dat definitio rerum.*

Bernard Silvestris teaches: "Ethimologia divina aperit et practica humana regit" (Commentary on the *Aeneid*, ed. Riedel, p. 19, 29). Those who took this seriously had no easy time of it.[12] The touching Sigebert (*Passio Thebeorum*, ed. Dümmler, p. 49) has this to say about the insurrection of the Bagaudae:

> 59 *Cogito sollicite vim nominis, unde Bagaude*
> *Tale trahant nomen vel quod sit nominis omen,*
> *Hos seu Bachaudas dicamus sive Bagaudas,*
> *Namque in codicibus nostris utrumque videmus.*
> *Si vis Bachaudas, dic a bachando Bagaudas,*
> *Mutans cognatis cognata elementa elementis.*
> 65 *Dic ita, si censes audacter ubique vagantes.*
> *Aut dic Bacaudas bellis audendo vacantes.*

John of Salisbury (ed. Giles, II, 154) writes humorously of an unfaithful monk Manerius, "cui forte inde congruum nomen, quod mane ruens in praecipitium tendit . . ." Acerbus Morena pays courtly homage to the empress Beatrix with

---

[11] Carl Weyman, *Festschrift Knöpfler* (1917), 389.
[12] Medieval attempts to find profound meanings in the name Publius Virgilius Maro are recorded by Funaioli in *Virgilio nel Medio Evo* (= the Virgil volume of *Studi Medievali*).

obvious playing on her name.[13] A virtuoso of the interpretation of names was Henry of Avranches:

> Hinc vocor Henris: 'Hen'-in; 'ris'-risus; dicitur Henris
> 'In risu';—non in risu, quo rideo, sed quo
> Rideor . . .[14]

In Richard of Venosa's comedy *Paulinus et Polla*, the heroine Polla says sententiously:

> Nomine Polla vocor quia polleo moribus altis:
> Conveniunt rebus nomina saepe suis.

We find etymological jesting in Goliardic satire too:

> Papa, si rem tangimus, nomen habet a re:
> Quicquid habent alii, solus vult papare,
> Vel si verbum gallicum vis apocopare,
> "Paies! paies!" dist le mot, si vis impetrare.[15]

Thus from the dignified Isidore and the poets of edifying passions and lives of saints we have drifted on to carefree verse. But etymology has yet another surprise in store for us: Dante takes up the game and transforms it in the mysterious mysticism of the *Vita nuova*, purifies it in the high art of the *Commedia*.

The young Dante's "glorious lady" is called Beatrice by many "li quali non sapeano che si chiamare." According to Zingarelli, this means: They did not know what name they should give her, and called her Beatrice because they had an inkling of the truth. In § 13 of the treatise Dante cites the dictum: "Nomina sunt consequentia rerum." Italian Dante scholarship claims to have found this principle almost verbatim in Justinian's *Institutiones*. This is an interesting fact. But it is more important to know that this theory, and the corresponding practice, were familiar to the entire Latin Middle Ages, so that Dante must have known of it— even without Justinian. He used it frequently elsewhere: in the canzone *Doglia mi reca* (l. 152): above all in the lives of St. Francis and St. Dominic in the *Paradiso*. Of St. Francis' birthplace Dante says (XI, 52):

> Però chi d' esso loco fa parole
> Non dica Ascesi, chè direbbe corto,
> Ma Oriente, se proprio dir vuole.

This means: Let him who would interpret the etymology of Assisi not regard *Assisi* as derived from *ascendere* (i.e., as "ascent")—that were too little: It was the rising of a sun. In the following canto Dominic and his parents make up a sacred

---

[13] Monaci's note on *Gesta Friderici metrice*, 1114.

[14] *Forschungen zur deutschen Geschichte*, XVIII (1878), 489, 70.

[15] *Carmina Burana* (edd. Hilka and Schumann), text vol. I, p. 77, st. 13. Also Schumann's valuable references in the commentary, p. 85.—On etymology in Wace's *Roman de Rou*, cf. Antoine Thomas (*Nouveaux Essais de Philologie française* [1904], 4 f.). When he says "on n'apprendra peut-être pas sans un certain étonnement que le mot 'etymologie' est familier à nos trouvères du douzième siecle," he overlooks the fact that the French poets had studied Latin and rhetoric and also knew something of Isidore. Further material in M. H. Stansbury, *Foreign Languages in the Chansons de Geste* (Philadelphia, 1926), 37 ff.

trio of names as did Amandus, Serenus, and Amantia in Milo's life of St. Amandus. Dante says:

> E perchè fosse qual era in costrutto,
> Quinci si mosse spirito a nomarlo
> Dal possessivo di cui era tutto:
> Domenico fu detto . . .
> O padre sua veramente Felice!
> O madre sua veramenta Giovanna,
> Se interpretata val come si dice.

This detail shows yet again that Dante's poetic style came into the inheritance of the Latin Middle Ages and purified it by genius.

The thing was later taken over by Humanism,[16] the Renaissance, and Baroque. Speaking names (Critilo, Andrenio) are borne by the principal figures in Gracián's *Criticon*. Of Eugenio he says: "Este era su nombre, ya definición" (ed. Romera-Navarro, I, 366). The last catch-basin is, as usual, Calderón. He was not only a fellow countryman but a reader of Isidore. In his *Comedias* he gives us many etymologies: Toledo equals Hebr. *Toletot* and means "fundación de muchos"; *Mozárabes* is properly *Mistiarabes* ("mezclados con los Arabes"); Semiramis in Syrian means "bird"; from Syrian too—which obviously had an especial appeal for Calderón—comes the name Phaethon ("lightning"). Let us end with classical mythology. What is the meaning of Marianne?

> . . . tomando a Marte el Mar
> Y a Diana el Ana, encierra
> El nombre de Mar-y-Ana
> Imperiosas excelencias.

[16] Martin Honecker, *Der Name des Nicolaus von Cues in zeitgenössischer Etymologie* (Heidelberg, 1940).—In satiric parody Rabelais explains the name *la Beauce* from "je trouve beau ce" (I, 16).—The chapter *De los nombres en general* at the beginning of Luis de León's *Nombres de Cristo* falls here too.

NUMERICAL COMPOSITION

Concerning composition, rhetorical theory (Quintilian, III, 3, 9; VII *praef.*, 4; VII, 1, 1 f.) had little to say, and that little was misunderstood (e.g., *Poetae*, IV, 369, gloss on 229). Servius comments on *Aeneid*, I, 8: "In tres partes dividunt poetae carmen suum: proponunt, invocant, narrant. Plerumque tamen duas res faciunt et ipsam propositionem miscent invocationi, quod in utroque opere Homerus fecit, namque hoc melius est. Lucanus tamen ipsum ordinem invertit; primo enim proposuit, inde narravit, postea invocavit . . ." Basically these instructions meant nothing more than that a poem must consist of introduction (*invocatio* and *propositio*) and *narratio*. With the exception of the *Thebais* the antique model epics had no epilogue. We have a number of medieval Latin poems to which the author has added the schema of the *dispositio*. Thus in the introduction to Arnulf's *Deliciae cleri* we have, designated by headings: 1. *Salutatio ad regem*, 2. *Salutatio ad reginam*, 3. *Propositio*, 4. *Invocatio*. The conclusion is composed of: 1. *Epilogus*, 2. *Dialogica poete tetrastica* (dialogue between the poet and his book), 3. *Commendatio operis*, 4. *Confessio*. Such a wire-drawn disposition is, however, rare. Even *propositio* and *invocatio* were not taken into consideration in all genres of poetry. That there must be an organization at least into introduction and main body became, however, the prevailing view. Thus for example Sedulius Scottus divides a poem of only 44 lines, on the return of a bishop, into 8 lines of *praefatio* and 36 lines of *collatio sive narratio* (*Poetae*, III, 326). But we find the division *praefatio* and *narratio* in long narrative poems too (*Poetae*, IV, 997). The concept *narratio* had already become so extended in Quintilian (II, 4, 2) that it included "all fields of literature" (Barwick in *Hermes*, LXIII, 265 ff.). Only seldom is the disposition taken from the content presented. In saints' lives the death of the saint does occasionally mark a section. The *Vita Leudegarii* (*Poetae*, III, 5 ff.) has a prologue and two books, the first of which ends with the death of the saint. The second begins (p. 25):

> Continet ille prior sacrati gesta libellus
> Martyris, in carnis placidus quae tegmine gessit.
> Exutus spoliis carnalibus, ecce secundus,
> Miris quae gessit virtutibus, implicat acta.

The first book has 733 lines, the second 513. The author, then, has attempted approximate symmetry. The procedure of the author of the Old French life of St. Alexis is similar (cf. ZRPh, LVI, 124). The saint's death also marks a section in the *Carmen de sancto Landberto* (*Poetae*, IV, 154, 442 ff.). There are attempts towards the art of composition elsewhere in hagiographic poetry too. In the *Passio sancti Quintini* (ca. 900) the marginal notes indicate this. The judgment scene, for example, is made up of three "aggrestiones (sic) praefecti" and three "responsiones beati Quintini" (*Poetae*, IV, 983 ff.).

The Middle Ages was far from demanding unity of subject and inner coherence of structure in a work of literature. Indeed, digression (*egressio, excessus*) was regarded as a special elegance. Martianus Capella had recommended it (ed. Dick, 275, 8), and Cassiodorus had a special predilection for using it.[1] Accordingly, the medieval conception of art does not attempt to conceal digressions by transitions—on the contrary, poets often point them out with a certain satisfaction.[2]

Nor did anyone have any qualms about treating completely different subjects in a single work. Aldhelm's *De virginitate* is followed by a poem *De octo principalibus vitiis* which, as has only recently been recognized, is merely a continuation of the preceding work, whereas it has appeared in previous printings as an independent work. Ermoldus Nigellus sings the deeds of Louis the Pious in four books, but at the end (*Poetae*, II, 76, 649 ff.) appends an account of St. Mary's in Strasbourg. Walafrid's *De imagine Tetrici* deals successively with the themes poet and muse (1–27), Theodoric (to 88), the Emperor Louis and his house. Abbo of St. Germain writes two books of *Bella Parisiacae urbis* and adds as the third book an ethical admonition to the clergy. Ermenrich of Ellwangen really permitted himself to go the limit in his letter to his patron Grimald—it is a collection of the fruits of chaotic reading in which he treats of the love of God and one's neighbor, of irregular verbs, and many other things. Equally chaotic is the *Liber de fonte vitae* by Audradus Modicus (*Poetae*, III, 73 ff.). Very significant for the medieval view is John of Salisbury's testimony concerning himself in his *Metalogicon* (ed. Webb, p. 3, 19 ff.): "More scribentium res varias complexus sum, quas quisque suo probabit aut reprobabit arbitrio.

> Sunt bona, sunt quedam mediocria, sunt mala plura
> Que legis hic; aliter non fit, Avite, liber.

Sic Marcialis (I, 16); sic et ego." There is a great lack of composition in Eupolemius and Amarcius. Even in such a skillful writer as Hugh Primas there is frequently no unity of theme.

The Middle Ages, however, possessed a substitute for the modern technique of composition in an entirely different principle, which I designate "numerical composition." The germs of this are to be found in Antiquity itself. The *Iliad* and the *Odyssey* were divided, perhaps originally by the Alexandrian philologers, into 24 books each, because that was the number of letters contained in the Greek alphabet. But 24 also happens to be in some sort a "beautiful" number, as is 12. Virgil and Statius divided their epics into 12 books. The numbers 10 and 100 and their multiples are also esthetically satisfying. In the *Appendix Virgiliana*, the *Culex* has a prooemium of 10 lines, the *Ciris* one of 100. In the *Ciris* we also find numerical symmetry: a speech and the rejoinder to it have 26 lines each, as Buecheler was the first to point out. The first of the two elegies on Maecenas has 144 = 12 times

---

[1] H. Nickstadt, *De digressionibus quibus in Variis usus est Cassiodorus* (Marburg dissertation, 1921).

[2] Cf. *Poetae*, I, 501, 291; *Poetae*, III, 643, 954; *Poetae*, IV, 298, 22 (*paranthesis*); *Poetae*, IV, 798, 303. The technique of digression can be well observed in Rahewin's *Theophilus*. Lines 93–110 are an excursus on *livor*. The "long excursus" (W. Meyer, p. 107 n.) must have been of the same nature. On line 203: *eius* is not the snake (W. Meyer) but the devil (verbatim from John 8:44). Numerous digressions in Fulco's poem on the Crusade (e.g., in Duchesne, IV, 896 b and beginning of Book III).—*Ecstasis* (= *ectasis?*) used for *excessus*, Fridegod (ed. Raine, I, 159).

12 lines; the first 12 fall to the proem. Calpurnius Siculus' second eclogue has 100 lines, as has Claudian's description of Aponus (Abano Bagni near Padua). Other poems of his have 20 lines.

Richard M. Meyer (*Die altgermanische Poesie nach ihren formelhaften Elementen beschrieben* [1889], 73 ff.) originated the concept of "typical" numbers which differ with different cultures: 3, 5, and 10 among the Indians; 7, 12, 40 in the Old Testament; 17 and 50 among the Irish. There are, then, preferred arithmetical systems which are rooted in archaic thought-forms. Further research would markedly enrich and deepen these suggestions. But we cannot enter into this here.

Antiquity came into possession of a number-mysticism and a number-symbolism through Pythagoras and his school. Cicero in the *Somnium Scipionis* (*De re publica*, VI, 12) teaches that 7 and 8 are perfect numbers ("plenus numerus"). Antique number-symbolism coalesced with Christian number-symbolism.[3] The years of Jesus' life gave the number 33 a mystical meaning. Biblical allegoresis explored the "mystical" numbers in the Bible. Augustine speculated a great deal on the subject. Peter caught 153 fish (John 21:11). What is the meaning of this number? It is produced by the addition of the numbers from 1 to 17. The number 17 = 10 (the ten commandments) + 7 (the Holy Ghost). Hence the 153 fishes are the believers who fulfill the law from love, not from fear. But 53 can also be understood as 3 times 50, if 3 is taken as multiplicator. And what is 50? Answer: 40 + 10. 10 is "plenitudo sapientiae," since 7 means the creation and 3 the Trinity. 4 is the number of temporal things (seasons, winds, parts of the earth). So 40 is the temporal church. But 10 is the number of reward. So 50 signifies the future church, etc. (References in P. Charles, "L'élément populaire dans les sermons de saint Augustin" in *Nouvelle Revue théologique*, LXXIX [Louvain, 1947], 619 ff.).

All numbers which were mentioned in the Bible must needs have a secret meaning.[4] We must also bear in mind that two of the seven *artes liberales*—arithmetic and music—dealt with numerical and proportional relations, and this in accordance with the antique tradition as it was presented by Martianus Capella, Boethius, and Isidore. Raban Maur recommends arithmetic on the ground that it teaches one to understand the mystical numbers in the Bible. An anonymous poem of the Carolingian period, *De arithmetica* (*Poetae*, IV, 249 f.), offers the following interpretations: The number 1 = God; but it also = *seminarium*, since it brings forth the number 2 (*dyas, prima procreatio*). This symbolizes both the antithesis of good and evil and its conquest by the two natures of Christ. With the number 3 are coordinated both the Trinity and also the threefold sound of music, the dimensions of time, the "motus ternarius" of the soul. The number 4 is also a perfect number, which, with the three preceding, produces the number 10, and, through further progressions, rises to the combinations 40, 100, 1000, etc.[5] To it correspond the four seasons, the four faces of the Cherubim, the four Evangelists. 5 is the symbolic number of the world, made up of the masculine triad and feminine dyad, reflected in the five zones of the earth, the five senses, the five species of

3 V. H. Hopper, *Medieval Number Symbolism* (New York, Columbia University Press, 1938), was not accessible to me.

4 They are discussed in Isidore's treatise *De numeris* (PL, LXXXIII, 179 ff.), partly in connection with Martianus Capella, §§ 731 ff.

5 Radulfus Glaber exhaustively treats *De divina quaternitate* at the beginning of his history (ed. Prou, pp. 2 ff.).

living creatures (man, quadrupeds, fish, reptiles, birds).[6] And so it goes on, through 6 (*sex officia naturalia*), 7 (*pervirgo septenarius*) with the seven ages [7] of men, 8 (*perfectus octonarius* = the cube), 9 (with Muses, spheres, angelic choirs), to 10. This sample can supply an idea of the system of knowledge of the early Middle Ages—before the birth of Scholasticism. Profane school learning and *doctrina sacra* are not separated. Learning consists of traditional and memorized masses of material. The energy and the impulse to search it through are yet lacking. From the symmetries and correspondences of the basic numbers there arises a seeming order which is believed to be sacred. All *artes*, to be sure, stem from God and are therefore good. Yet the science of numbers is superior to them all. For the creation, the rhythm of time, the calendar, the celestial bodies, are based upon number. So Agius of Corvey teaches in a computistic poem (*Poetae*, IV, 937 f.; cf. *Poetae*, IV, 1076, 9).[8]

What I have here brought together to give the reader an idea of medieval number symbolism may produce the effect of an omnium-gatherum of curiosities. But something very different lies behind it. Every reader of medieval Latin texts knows that few Bible verses are so often quoted and alluded to as the phrase from the Wisdom of Solomon, 11:21: "omnia in mensura et numero et pondere disposuisti." I give but one example, from the *Praedicatio Goliae*: [9]

> *Creatori serviunt omnia subjecta,*
> *Sub mensura, numero, pondere perfecta.*
> *Ad invisibilia, per haec intellecta,*
> *Sursum trahit hominem ratio directa.*

The Book of Wisdom was probably produced at Alexandria in the first century after Christ. "The thoroughly Jewish core is embellished with all manner of traits derived from Greece, or rather from Hellenistic-Egyptian syncretism; sometimes they have not left the core itself wholly untouched" (Otto Eissfeldt, *Einleitung in das Alte Testament* [1934], 656). Is the idea expressed in chap. 11, 21 to be regarded as Greek or as syncretistic? We may leave this out of consideration. But of the very greatest importance is Hermann Krings's demonstration that the *ordo*-idea of the medieval world-picture developed from this one Bible verse.[10]

Through this verse, number was sanctified as a form-bestowing factor in the divine work of creation. It acquired metaphysical dignity. This is the imposing background of numerical composition in literature.

[6] If stones are included, there are six grades of being; as in *Fecunda ratis* (Voigt, p. 231, with references from Augustine and Gregory.)

[7] Seven degrees of sanctity were distinguished (*Poetae*, IV, 282, 132 ff.). On the number 7 cf. also Aldhelm's epistle to Acircius.

[8] References to number symbolism are to be found in *Poetae*, III, 799 under the catchword "allegorica de numeris."

[9] T. Wright, *The Latin Poems commonly attributed to Walter Mapes* (1841), 32, st. 8.—Strecker attributes the text to the school of Walter of Châtillon (*ZfdA*, LXIV [1927], 183). According to Wilmart its author is Walter himself (*Revue bénédictine* [1937], 128).

[10] Krings in DVjft, XVIII (1940), 238.—Elaborated in the same author's *Ordo. Philosophisch-historische Grundlegung einer abendländischen Idee* (Halle, 1941— not now accessible to me).—Cf. Gilson, *Introduction à l'étude de saint Augustin*, 157 f.—Dürer wished "to begin my project from measure, number, and weight" (Panofsky-Saxl, *Dürers Melencolia I* [1923], 67).

"Numero disposuisti." God's disposition was arithmetical! Must not the writer likewise allow himself to be guided by numbers in his disposition? The following preliminary remarks will clarify the concepts to be used: (1) Otto Schumann was the first to establish a "predilection for round numbers" such as 50, 100, 200, etc., in medieval poetry (commentary on the *Carmina Burana*, p. 76 * n.). We retain his terminology in calling all numbers divisible by 5 or 10 "round numbers." These round numbers can have symbolic value, but do not necessarily have it. For the most part they have only an aesthetic significance. (2) Hence "symbolic numbers" in the narrower sense is our designation for those numbers which—like 3, 7, 9, and many others—have a philosophical or theological significance. (3) Finally, it must be borne in mind that both the number of lines and the number of stanzas in a poem, as well as the number of chapters in a book or of books in a work, can be determined by number symbolism. (4) Alongside of serious number symbolism there was a literary trifling with numbers. This already exists in Ausonius ("griphus ternarii numeri" = Book 16; Book 18, No. 13 and No. 15). In these poems the characteristics of the numbers 3, 6, 30 (the latter in thanks for a gift of 30 oysters) are celebrated. In the Middle Ages too, as we shall see, literary trifling with numbers has a place beside intellectual number symbolism.

The number 33 was sanctified by the years of Christ's life. Augustine's treatise *Contra Faustum manichaeum* has 33 books, Cassiodorus' *Institutiones* 33 chapters. Godfrey of Viterbo's *Pantheon* has 33 *particulae*. The Pseudo-Turpin (Castets' text) has 33 chapters, the *Ackermann aus Böhmen* the same number plus a concluding prayer (cf. Arthur Hübner, *Kleine Schriften zur deutschen Philologie* [1940], 206), Dante's epistle to Can Grande 33 sections. Villon names the name of Christ in stanzas 3 and 33 of his *Testament*. Nicholas of Cusa provided in his will that 33 old men should be maintained in a hospital established by himself. 33 stanzas: Endelechius' eclogue (written 386) on the cattle-plague; the eulogy of Verona written *ca.* 810 (*Poetae*, I, 119); a poem of Walafrid's (*Poetae*, II, 367); a satire on the clergy published by H. Walther (*Hist. Vjs.*, XXVIII, 529); a poem of the Archpoet's (Manitius, No. 6). A pious Russian toper is advised to "recite 33 prayers to Jesus when he longs for drink" (R. v. Walter, *Ein russisches Pilgerleben* [1925], 42). This comes under religious "folk-usage." But the compositional number 33 originally stems from related thought modes.

Another sacred symbolic number is 22. Raban Maur divided his compilation *De rerum naturis* into 22 books, although his source, Isidore's *Etymologiae*, has only 20 books (like Gellius and Nonius Marcellus). The reason for the change was the doctrine put forth by Jerome (*Praefatio in libros Samuel et Malachim*; printed in F. Stummer, *Einführung in die lateinische Bibel* [1928], p. 237) that the Old Testament, in conformity with the 22 letters of the Hebrew alphabet, had 22 books, "quibus quasi litteris et exordiis, in Dei doctrina, tenera adhuc et lactens viri iusti eruditur infantia." 22 is a good example of a number which has no symbolic value in itself. It first acquires it from the circumstance that the Hebrew alphabet has 22 letters [11] and from Jerome's subsequent observation, then keeps it and comes to be used as a compositional number. Augustine's *De civitate dei* has 22 books; 22 stanzas each, the rhythms in *Poetae*, IV, p. 484 and p. 504. Merely in *Poetae* I, I find poems with 22 lines on pages 70, 76, 78, 103, 109, 251, 253, 273, 285, 320,

---

[11] Cf. F. Dornseiff, *Das Alphabet in Mystik und Magie* (1925), 73.

337, 338, 350, 522, 532, 583. The prologue to the *Waltharius* has the same number of lines, as have Williram of Ebersberg's dedicatory poem to Henry IV (*ZfdA*, LXXVI, 63), the prologue to Anselm of Besate's *Retorimachia*, etc. "Biblical" numerical composition is also exemplified when an author justifies his division of his work into two books by a reference to the widow's two mites, or when Milo divides his life of St. Amandus into four books because of the four Evangelists (*Poetae*, III, 599, 25). Thus Ermenrich of Ellwangen writes the life of a saint in ten chapters because the saint obeyed the ten commandments (*MG Scriptores*, XV, 163, 4). Abbo of St. Germain adds to the two books of his *Bella Parisiacae urbis* a third, entirely different in content, because the number 3 symbolizes the Trinity. The number 6 could also be given a place in Biblico-theological speculation. It was an original thought of Heiric of Auxerre to base the elaborate structure of his life of St. Germanus on this number. The work is prefaced by a metrical prayer of 19 6-line stanzas. An *Allocutio ad librum* in 72 (= 6 times 12) lines follows. The work itself is divided into six books. The verse *praefationes* of Books II–VI have 48, 32, 84, 48, 70 lines. The *praefatio* to Book VI begins with a eulogy of the number 6, then discusses other theological symbolic numbers (*Poetae*, III, 499 ff.). Few medieval works can compare with this rich and manifold numerical composition. Almost contemporaneously Otfrid completed his Gospel poem. He divided it into five books because it was intended to purify the five senses: thus, even in the Old High German period, we see numerical composition extending from Latin to vernacular literature.

Round numbers are also often chosen for the number of stanzas. Nos. 14, 63, and 72 in Walafrid's poems have ten stanzas each. A rhythm by Raban Maur (*Poetae*, II, 197 ff.) has one hundred 6-line stanzas, as has the Theophilus rhythm (W. Meyer, *Ges. Abh.*, I, 123 f.). There are also poems consisting of three parts of 50 Goliardic stanzas each (= 600 lines in all) or of 25 Goliardic stanzas (= 100 lines) (Otto Schumann, *loc. cit.*). The *Love Council of Remiremont* has 80 stanzas. In Strecker's edition of Walter of Châtillon's poems (*Moralisch-satirische Gedichte* [1929]) we find pieces with 20 (No. 8), 25 (No. 18), and 30 stanzas (Nos. 2, 4, 16). Among the Archpoet's poems No. 9 (Manitius' numbering) has 25 stanzas.

Finally, the number of lines in a non-stanzaic poem can also be determined by numerical symbolism. In the Carolingian period Walafrid Strabo has a particular liking for this form of numerical composition (*Poetae*, II, 275 ff.). His life of St. Mammes begins with a *praefatio* of 24 and an *oratio* of 20 lines. It ends with a section 60 lines long. His other poems present the following picture:

10 lines: No. 59	30 lines: No. 30; 56
15 lines: No. 60	40 lines: No. 6; 50, 1 [12]
20 lines: No. 28; 45; 51	50 lines: No. 24
25 lines: No. 50, 2 [12]	100 lines: No. 38

At the end of No. 38 we read (*Poetae*, II, 390, 97): "Dat decies denos vilis tibi denique versus Strabo . . .," and similarly in No. 5 (p. 355). A poem of Walafrid's which I have not yet mentioned and which contains 84 lines, seems to stand outside

[12] Nos. 50, 1 and 2 are, according to B. Bischoff, not by Walafrid (*ZRPh*, LIV, 21).

of this. We should regard this as a matter of chance—had not Walafrid explained at the end of the poem that he has devoted as many lines to its imperial recipient (*Poetae*, II, 415, 83 f.) as the prophetess Anna had lived years at the time of Christ's birth (Luke 2:37). In a system of six, such as Heiric applies, 84 can appear as an ordinary symbolic number (6 times 14). But in Walafrid's poem 84 occurs as a number sanctified by being mentioned in the Bible, and if Anna had been 83 the Emperor would have received a poem of 83 lines. In this connection it should be noted that no symbolic religious meaning is inherent in Anna's age in itself. We may, however, assume that patristic Biblical allegoresis gave a moral interpretation to this number too,[13] but there is no inner relation between such an interpretation and the content of the poem. Walafrid has here used the "Biblical number" merely as an outer framework and stopping-point, just as elsewhere he uses round numbers. Playing with round numbers is a favorite device of Sedulius Scottus. In an epistle of 22 lines (*Poetae*, III, 183 f., No. XVI) he wishes Vulfengus, to whom it is addressed, "twelvefold hail," because twelve suggests the Apostles. The names Sedulius and Vulfengus both end in *us* because both are loved by Jesus. Vulfengus has three syllables: God loves him threefold. Sedulius has four syllables: this indicates the Gospels. Sometimes round-number compositions are justified Biblically. To a poem of 100 lines (50 distichs) to the Virgin Mary, Hincmar of Reims adds the explanation: "Hanc autem suprascripti libelli subnexionem centum versibus constare disposui, quoniam decalogi denarius per se multiplicatus in centenarium surgit" (*Poetae*, III, 412). Eugenius Vulgarius similarly justifies the composition of a poem of 12 lines (*Poetae*, IV, 412, No. II).[14] In the Ottonian period an unknown poet bewails the death of a peacock in 33 lines (*Poetae*, V, 2, 382). In 1033 Wipo wrote 100 lines on the excessively cold winter. An anonymous poet from St. Omer ends (l. 99 f.): "Implevi numerum; Christo servite, valete; / Hoc iterans iterum verbum precor, opto, valete" (*Notices et Extraits*, XXXI, 1, 135).—The poet of the *Gesta Berengarii* wished to use an even thousand lines for his work (*Poetae*, IV, 401, 206).—Stephen of Bec has a prologue of 100 lines to his *Draco normannicus*. To the eleventh century also belongs Wido of Ivrea's elegy, with 300 lines. Peter of Eboli dedicated to Henry VI a poem on the baths of Puteoli in 36 sections of 6 distichs. This playing with the number 6 is a compliment to the sixth Henry, as can also be seen from the same poet's *Liber ad honorem Augusti* (l. 1572 ff.). Henry of Settimello's elegy (probably written *ca.* 1194) consists of 4 sections of 250 lines each and thus has 1000 lines. In the new edition by Marigo (Padua, Draghi, 1926) there are 1004 lines. But this edition, which Strecker called "peculiar," takes into account only Italian MSS. The apparatus criticus shows that lines 1003–4 were added later. Even then there are two lines too many. This is absolutely clear from line 995 (Marigo's numbering):

Suscipe millenis citharam quam dirigo nervis.

The new editor overlooked this indication.

In Italy round-number composition remained popular. Albertino Mussato gives

---

[13] The text makes this likely, for in the life of the prophetess Anna two septenary periods are distinguished: "annis septem" (l. 36), "annos octoginta quatuor" (l. 37) = 12 times 7.

[14] Cf. also Giraldus Cambrensis (ed. Brewer), I, 362 and 363.

his twelfth epistle 100 hexameters, his poem on his 55th birthday 50 distichs. When Dante received a Latin eclogue in 97 lines from Giovanni del Virgilio he answered in the same number of lines, but significantly regretted that Giovanni had not written three lines more, to make up a full hundred (*Egloghe*, IV, 42 f.):

> Et tria si flasset ultra spiramina flata,
> Centum carminibus tacitos mulcebat agrestes.

Cardinal Gaietani Stefaneschi wishes to treat the history of the Popes in 300 lines, that of Celestine and Boniface VIII in "*ca.* 3000" (Seppelt, p. 4, 30 and p. 5, 9). This round-number composition, to which the *Decameron* also belongs, was done to death in the Latin poems of Francesco Filelfo (1398–1481). We "owe" him 10 books of satires, each book containing 10 satires, each satire 100 lines ("Hecatosticha"), as well as 10,000 lines of epigrams, divided into 10 books; he had also planned 10 books of 100 100-line odes each—but only finished half of them. Juan de Mena, one of the Spanish Italianists, brought his *Laberinto de Fortuna* (1444?) to 297 stanzas. After his death three more were added. Hence the work also goes under the title *Las trescientas*. In the Renaissance 100 is popular as a compositional number: Pacifico Massimi, *Hecatelegium* (1489); Thomas Watson, *The Hekatompathia or Passionate Centurie of Love* (1582); Spenser, *The Tears of the Muses* (1590), with 600 lines. A Pythagorean belief in numbers still inspired the master printer Giambattista Bodoni. In the preface to his edition of Tasso's *Gerusalemme liberata* (1794) we read: "Se fra noi ritornasse Pittagora o vivesse alcuno di sue misteriose dottrine veneratore e seguace, esulterebbe senza fallo nella santità de' numeri che fu da quel magno filosofo altamente predicata. Imperocchè, per tacer degli altri, chi non ammira la costante parsimonia del tre, cui si riducono nelle scienze e nelle arti, dopo lunghissimi esami e ben sostenuti paralleli, l'opere piu maravigliose ed i nomi eziandio de' piu sublimi pensatori, artefici e poeti? Platone, Archimede, e Neutono; Rafaello, Correggio, e Tiziano; Omero, Virgilio, e Tasso." The Classicism of 1800 could believe in such a preestablished harmony. But at the same time the words reveal something of the unswerving sense of proportion which make Bodoni's printed books works of art.

We saw that Roman poetry could offer the Middle Ages some models of numerical composition. Perhaps the Psalms are also to be taken into consideration. In the Vulgate there are 9 Psalms of 10 verses, 4 of 20 verses, and one each of 25 (Ps. 30) and 40 (Ps. 40). This fact, as well as composition in harmony with Biblical symbolic numbers, discussed above, justifies us in seeing a stimulus to medieval numerical composition in "Biblical poetics." I should, however, prefer to see the final causes for the spread of this technique of composition first in the concept of number as sacred and secondly in the lack of other precepts for the *dispositio*. By the use of numerical composition the medieval author attained a twofold end: a formal scaffolding to build upon, and a symbolic profundity.

The range of numerical composition extends from the simplest sort of forms (50 hexameters, 10 stanzas, 4 books, etc.) to the most elaborate structures. An example of the latter is the life of St. Germanus by Heiric of Auxerre, mentioned above; another is Hucbald's *Ecloga de calvis*. Here various numbers are combined. The dedicatory poem (*Poetae*, IV, 265 f.) has $54 = 9$ times 6 lines, the eclogue itself 146. $146 + 54 = 200$. But this is not all! The 146 lines of the eclogue contain an *exordium* and a *conclusio*, each of 3 lines. There remain 140 lines $= 14$

sections of 10 lines. But since the first line of each of the 14 sections is the same and hence represents a sort of burden, performing the function of a sign of division between sections, there remain 9 lines for each section. Thus we find in the eclogue the same number 9 which also predominates in the dedicatory poem. Concerning the 14, finally, be it said that 14 = 2 times 7. Thus we can see in Hucbald's composition not only round numbers (10, 200) but also combinations of 3, 3 times 3, 2 and 7. No one will wish to deny the deliberate artifice of such a construction. Equally elaborate is the construction of Arnulf's *Deliciae cleri*. The main body of the poem consists of 12 groups of 24 maxims each. But at the same time we can establish the number 25 as compositional principle (Manitius, II, 588). Thus here too various basic numbers are combined. The author, probably a French monk, is not a little proud of the system he contrived ("quedam lege sub poetica non absurde a nobis enucleata" [*RF* (1886), p. 216, 11]).

The cases of numerical composition treated in the preceding pages were collected in casual reading. A systematic inventory would doubtless produce a wealth of further examples. Yet our material permits the establishment of certain basic facts: 1. Numerical composition occurs even in Roman poetry from the *Appendix Virgiliana* to Claudian and Ausonius. 2. Numerical composition can determine (a) the number of lines, (b) the number of stanzas, (c) the subordinate units (*particulae, libri*, etc.). 3. From Cassiodorus to Filelfo numerical composition repeatedly recurs in medieval Latin literature. 4. Where it appears in the vernacular literature of the Middle Ages, we have transfer of the medieval Latin practice. So in Otfrid—but also, for example, in Jorge Manrique, whose famous poem on the death of his father comprises 40 stanzas, with breaks after the 3rd and 33rd stanzas. Studies of the subject are so far non-existent or are misleading because of inadequate information.[15] But even from the material we have just surveyed it plainly appears that the wonderful harmony of Dante's numerical composition is the end and the acme of a long development. From the enneads of the *Vita nuova* Dante proceeded to the elaborate numerical structure of the *Commedia*: 1 + 33 + 33 + 33 = 100 cantos conduct the reader through 3 realms, the last of which contains 10 heavens. Triads and decads intertwine into unity. Here number is no longer an outer framework, but a symbol of the cosmic *ordo*.

[15] For example, that of Max Ittenbach (*Deutsche Dichtungen der salischen Kaiserzeit* [1937]), who, in dealing with certain German poems of *ca.* 1100, the number of whose stanzas is determined by numerical symbolism, wishes to explain these numbers as a characteristic of German aesthetic feeling in the time of the Salian emperors.

NUMERICAL APOTHEGMS

Popular in the wisdom literature of the Old Testament is the "numerical apothegm," [1] which, for example, begins: "There are three things that are never satisfied, yea four things say not, It is enough" (Prov. 30:15). This form of statement
was elaborately developed in the East. E. W. Lane [2] gives an Arabic description of
feminine beauty, which is arranged in nine tetrads: "Four things in a woman should
be black,—the hair of the head, the eyebrows, the eyelashes, and the dark part of
the eyes: four white,—the complexion of the skin, the white of the eyes, the teeth,
and the legs; four red,—the tongue, the lips, the middle of the cheeks, and the
gums; four round:—the head, the neck, the forearms, and the ankles; four long,—
the back, the fingers, the arms, and the legs; four wide,—the forehead, the eyes,
the bosom, and the hips; four fine,—the eyebrows, the nose, the lips, and the
fingers; four thick,—the lower part of the back, the thighs, the calves of the legs,
and the knees; four small,—the ears, the breasts, the hands, and the feet." *The
Arabian Nights* says with a brevity which racks our curiosity: "Always use the
toothpick, for two and seventy virtues lie therein" (Enno Littmann's translation,
I, 656). The Arabian poet Chalef finds in the horse 9 long parts, 9 short, 9 bare,
9 covered, 9 thick, 9 thin, 9 contiguous, 9 separated; 8 broad, 8 pointed; 5 dry,
5 damp, 5 birdlike (Georg Jacob, *Schanfaras Lamijat al-Arab* [1915], p. 7).

Numerical apothegms made their way from the East into Goethe's Divan ("Fünf
Dinge" and "Fünf andere" in the *Buch der Betrachtungen*).

The native soil of this form of expression would seem to have been folk poetry
and folk wisdom. Numbering, counting, enumerating are means of intellectual
orientation. Usener says of Sophistic (*Kleine Schriften*, II, 272): "Early systematics
would naturally compensate for inexperience in thinking by strict regularity of
structure. For this purpose the triad could not but especially recommend itself."
"Inexperience in thinking" was to return in far more primitive form. The entire
Middle Ages, from the tribal migrations to the rise of Scholasticism, was a great
schooling period for the West. The pedagogical technique of classifying and memorizing made the numerical apothegm and, more generally, enumerational technique
extremely popular. Paulinus of Pella in his *Eucharisticon* set forth the "ten sins of
ignorance," Sedulius Scottus "the seven most beautiful things" (*Poetae*, III, 159,
XI). Petrus Alfunsi's *Disciplina clericalis* teaches: "7 artes, 7 probitates, 7 indus-
triae" make up "perfecta nobilitas" (Hilka-Söderhjelm, abridged ed., 10 f.). The
author of a codex on deportment knew that the wise Thales himself had written
the seven "curialitates" and seven "rusticitates" in golden letters on the "colossus"
in Rome.[3] Seven evils and seven goods of love were also known.[4] Salimbene has a
predilection for numerical apothegms and the like. He gives (ed. Holder-Egger,
219) a French saying according to which a good wine must have 3 b's and 7 f's (see

---

[1] O. Eissfeldt, *Einleitung in das Alte Testament* (1934), 92.
[2] *Arabian Society in the Middle Ages* (1883), 215 f.
[3] John of Garland, *Morale scolarium*, 231.
[4] P. Lehmann, *Pseudoantike Literatur*, p. 62, 434.

Novati in *Giornale storico della letteratura italiana*, II [1883], 344). A prelate must have 3 positive and 3 negative excellences (Holder-Egger, 121, 9). Salimbene enumerates ten "infortunia" which befell Frederick II and continues: "istis possumus addere duo, ut duodenarium numerum habeamus" (344, 17).

Triads are the most frequent (Faral, 153, § 9):

> Sunt tria quae redolent in carmine: verba polita,
> Dicendique color, interiorque favus.

The apple of Paradise (*PL*, CCV, 946 B):

> In pomo tria sunt: odor et sapor et color, immo
> His tribus allicitur ambitiosa caro.

Domestic evils (*ibid.*, 946–7):

> Asserit ut Salomon: tria sunt, confusio quorum
> Excludit fragiles commodiore domo.
> Haec tria sunt: fumus, aqua stillans, noxia coniux.
> Sub palea granum spirituale latet.

Stages of love:

> Sunt in amore gradus tres, triplex gratia; fundat
> Prima, secunda fovet, tertia firmat opus.

Nigel Wireker on the English (*SP*, I, 63):

> Wessail et dringail, necnon persona secunda,
> Haec tria sunt vitia quae comitantur eos.

Idem (*ibid.*, 54):

> . . . tria sunt communia nobis:
> Votum, causa, solum; sit via quarta, peto.

Calderón distinguishes four sounds in a wilderness (Keil, IV, 587 a): the roar of the sea, the soughing of the wind, the croaking of birds, the howling of wild beasts:

> Cuatro ruidos uniendo a solo un ruido
> El mar, el aire, el canto y el bramido.

Hildebert links two tetrads (*PL*, CLXXI, 1437 A):

> Spernere mundum, spernere sese, spernere nullum,
> Spernere se sperni, quatuor hec bona sunt.
> Quaerere fraudem, quaerere pompam, quaerere laudem,
> Quaerere se quaeri, quatuor hec mala sunt.

The first of these two distichs also appears, with slight variants, in Hugh Sotovagina (*SP*, II, 222). Hildebert also treated the "seven activities of the soul" and the like in verse (*PL*, CLXXI, 1437 B ff.). Fives are also popular (cf. Nigel, *SP*, I, 133). Matthew of Vendôme on the parts of a letter: [5]

[5] Jakob Werner, *Beiträge zur Kunde der lateinischen Literatur des Mittelalters* [2] (1905), No. 28.—Another version in Egbert of Liége, *Fecunda ratis*, p. 229.

> *Dictantis partes sunt quinque: salutat, amicat,*
> *Auditum narrat, postulat arte, tacet.*

Students and professors are admonished:

> *Quinque sacre claves dicuntur stare sophie;*
> *Prima frequens studium, finem nescitque legendi.*
> *Altera: que relegis memori committere menti.*
> *Tertia: que nescis percrebra rogatio rerum.*
> *Quarta est verus honor sincero corde magistri.*
> *Quinta iubet vanas mundi contempnere gazas.*

A six: [6]

> *Si sapiens fore vis, sex serva que tibi mando:*
> *Quid loqueris, et ubi, de quo, cur, quomodo, quando.*

Enumeration is especially popular in collections of maxims, as for example in the *Florilegium Gottingense* (*RF*, III, 281 ff.) and in Egbert of Liége's *Fecunda ratis*. Egbert put into hexameters the sixfold hierarchy of existence set forth by Augustine and Gregory (p. 231), as he did the seven ways of propitiating for sin, as well as the ten kinds of bodily excretions (p. 186) and (p. 187) the five "points" of love:

> *Compages flagrantis quinque feruntur amoris:*
> *Visus et alloquium, contactus et oscula amantum:*
> *Postremus coitus, luctati clausula belli:*
> *His in honore suo poterit desistere spado,*
> *Ni temptare suum mavult post cepta pudorem.*

This numerical apothegm demands separate treatment. Its source is Aelius Donatus' widely-read commentary on Terence, in which, on *Eunuchus*, IV, 2, 10, we read: "Quinque lineae sunt amoris, scilicet visus, allocutio, tactus, osculum sive suavium, coitus." [7] Porphyry, on Horace, *Carm.*, I, 13, 15, has the same enumeration (but with *partes* for *lineae*). It reappears as a gnome in J. Werner, *Sprichwörter und Sinnsprüche des Mittelalters*, No. 60:

> *Colloquium, visus, contactus, basia, risus:*
> *Hec faciunt sepe te ludere cum muliere.*

This scholastic lore then becomes poetry. In the Latin love poetry of the Middle Ages this pentad is frequently employed. It answered to the taste for enumerations of all kinds, as well as to that for erotic intellectual trifling. I should like to trace the theme through the Middle Ages and the Renaissance, and I shall begin with the much-discussed [8] "Manerius poem," which must have been written before 1168:

> *Surgens Manerius summo diluculo*
> *Assumsit pharetram cum arcu aureo,*
> *Canesque copulans nexu binario*
> *Silvas aggreditur venandi studio.*
> *Transcurrit nemora saltusque peragrat,*
> *Ramorum sexdecim gaudens cervum levat,*

---

[6] Wright, *Latin Poems . . . attributed to Walter Mapes*, p. 46, n.
[7] Treated from the Germanist standpoint by Karl Helm, *GRM* (1941), 236 ff.
[8] Raby in *Speculum* (1933), 204 ff.

Quem cum persequitur, dies transierat,
Nec sevam bestiam consequi poterat.
Fessis consociis lassisque canibus
Dispersos revocat illos clamoribus,
Sumensque buccinam resumtis viribus
Tonos emiserat totis nemoribus.
Ad cuius sonitum erilis filia
Tota contremuit itura patria,
Quam cernens iuvenis adiit properans:
Vidit et loquitur, sensit os osculans:
Et sibi consulens et regis filie
Extremum Veneris concessit linee.

The last line presupposes a knowledge of the "quinque lineae." Of the love songs in the *Carmina Burana* the following are relevant:

1. *Visu, colloquio*
   Contactu, basio
      Frui virgo dederat;
      Sed aberat
   Linea posterior
   Et melior
      Amori.   (CB, 72, 2 a).

2. *Volo tantum ludere,*
      Id est: contemplari
   Presens loqui, tangere,
      Tandem osculari;
   Quintum, quod est agere,
      Noli suspicari.   (CB, 88, 8.)

3. From a description of Love (CB, 154, 6 ff.):

   Mittit pentagonas nervo stridente sagittas,
   Quod sunt quinque modi, quibus associamur amori:
   Visus; colloquium; tactus; compar labiorum
   Nectaris alterni permixtio, commoda fini;
   In lecto quintum tacite Venus exprimit actum.

From Latin poetry the theme makes its way into the vernacular poetry of the romances. In an allegorical canzone by the troubadour Guiraut de Calanso five gates to the palace of love are referred to: "To her palace, where she abides, there are five gates, and he who can open two of them easily passes through the three (others), but hard is it for him to come out again; and in joy lives he who can remain therein; and the way up thither is by four most slippery steps; but no common and uneducated (man) enters therein, for (such men) are slain in the outskirts of the city by the faithless, which are more than one half of mankind" ([after] W. Ernst's translation, *RF*, 44, 340). This pentad can hardly be supposed to refer to eyes, ears, and mouth [9] (2 + 2 + 1), but is rather a reference to the *lineae*. From this we must

---

[9] So Otto Dammann, *Die allegorische Canzone des Guiraut de Calanso* (Breslau, 1891), 69.

distinguish *Romance of the Rose*, 907 ff.: *Dous Regarz* carries two bows and ten arrows, of which five are fair (*Biautez, Simplece, Franchise, Compaignie, Biaus Semblanz*) and five foul. Jean Lemaire de Belges says in his *Illustrations de Gaule*, I, 25 (1510): "Les nobles poetes [10] disent que cinq lignes y a en amours, c'est à dire cinq poinctz ou cinq degrez especiaux, c'est asavoir le regard, le parler, l'attouchement, le baiser et le dernier qui est plus desiré, et auquel tous les autres tendent pour finale resolution, c'est celui qu' on nomme par honnesteté le don de mercy." Clément Marot put the "five points" into a dizain.[11] Ronsard refers [12] to them as "les cinq pas" in *Amours*, Book I, Sonnet 165 (*Ha! Bel-Acueil . . .*). After Marot and Ronsard the theme was treated by many *poetae minores* of the French Renaissance; these we need not discuss.

[10] Does this mean Terence? G. Doutrepont, *Jean Lemaire de Belges et la Renaissance* (1934), 404, names as source of the chapter only "Annius, XV, 116, 11, 40," i.e., Giovanni Nanni (1432–1502), *Antiquitatum variarum volumina XVII cum commentariis Fr. Joannis Annii Viterbensis*. Doutrepont used the Paris edition of 1512.

[11] P. A. Becker, *Clément Marot* (1926), 278.

[12] Only in the first version in Blanchemain's edition, I, 95. Cf. Laumonier, *Ronsard poète lyrique* (1909), 514.

MENTION OF THE AUTHOR'S NAME
IN MEDIEVAL LITERATURE

Julius Schwietering began his study of "The Humility Formula in Middle High German Poets" (*Die Demutsformel mittelhochdeutscher Dichter* [1921]) with a section on "Veiled Expression of the Author's Name." Complete suppression of the author's name, which frequently occurs, he refers to the precepts of Salvian, Sulpicius Severus, and others, who warn the writer against the sin of *vanitas terrestris*. If the author nevertheless gives his name, he does so, as Schwietering shows, "to gain forgiveness for his sins through the intercession of his hearers and readers," occasionally also because he at the same time gives the name of the person who commissioned the work. Mention of the name without a prayer or a veiling modesty formula appears to be very rare in Middle High German literature. The twelfth and thirteenth centuries still lacked "any terminology for immortality of the writer's name and imperishability of poetic fame" (p. 16). This observation, which is true of Middle High German poetry, must not, however, be generalized. Nor can I agree with H. Walther, when he says: "In the Middle Ages the individual personality was almost completely overshadowed by social rank . . .; pride of authorship, which indissolubly connected the author's name with his poem, did not begin to flourish until the beginning of the Renaissance; before then it occurs only sporadically" (GGA [1932], 52). Clearing this matter up is not as superfluous as it might seem. It contributes to our knowledge of medieval man's conception of himself.

What had been the practice of the antique poets? In Greek epic the poet's name is not mentioned, "because the poet merely reproduces what the Muses have told him concerning ancient things" (W. Kroll, *Studien zum Verständnis der römischen Literatur* [1924], p. 27). In didactic poetry the procedure was different: Hesiod states his name (*Theog.*, 22) and gives information concerning his family affairs (*Erga*). Theognis stamps his name on his verses as a "seal" (19 ff.) to prevent them from being stolen; this was imitated later. Virgil names himself and makes statements about his life at the end of the *Georgics* (IV, 559 ff.), but says nothing about himself in the *Aeneid*. Epic anonymity was violated by Statius at the end of the *Thebais*. Though he does not mention his name, he speaks of his work, which will win the favor of Caesar and be read in schools. Horace ends his first book of epistles with an address to his work; a finely wrought self-portrait is included. The model poets of Antiquity, then, appear to authorize both suppression and mention of the poet's name. As the texts cited by Schwietering show, giving the author's name is first prohibited in Christian times. But certainly not always and everywhere. Much that we call Christian is only monastic. Juvencus expected that his poem would outlast time, and would even survive unscathed through the conflagration of the world. The vain Sedulius speaks archly of the "force of his agile mind." He was much read throughout the Middle Ages and was still highly regarded *ca.* 1500 as "poeta Christianissimus." That he and Juvencus had given their names at least balanced the prohibition of Salvian and others.

Giving the name for the purpose of intercession I find first in Orientius (*Com-*

monitorium, 416), later in Milo (*Poetae*, III, 675, 1085). An unusual reason for suppressing the writer's name is given in an epistle to a friend (*Poetae*, III, 340, 17):

> *Ad finem nimias dicit tibi nostra salutes*
> *Fistula, quas supra conticuit capite.*
> *Mos manet in scriptis erga vitare priores*
> *Has a subiectis, nomina ceu propria.*
> *Blandiloquas ideo minime fuit ausa salutes*
> *Offerre in prima fronte salutifera.*

Here the anonymity is based not upon religious and ethical authority but upon that of the rules of good manners. But these, of course, differ greatly with the milieu. Another poet of the same period begins with greetings—which the previous author considered ill-mannered—and only declines to mention his name because he does not consider his lines good enough (*Poetae*, III, 366, No. 168). Theodoric of Saint-Trond thinks likewise. At the request of a friend he had put Solinus' *Collectanea* into verse, but upon the condition that his name should not be mentioned (*NA*, XXXIX, 161):

> 9 *"Parebo," dixi, "plus iussio posset amici.*
> *Tantum, quod scribo, penitus proferre caveto*
> *Deque meo titulis semper sit nomine mutus,*
> *Ne me verbosum, ne me testetur ineptum*
> *Et dignum poena, quod feci vile poema."*

Here too, then, the poet does not wish to see his name suppressed out of humility but because he considers his production too poor (protestation of incapacity).

Another poet gives no reason at all (*ZRPh*, L, 89):

> *O mea carta, modo si quis de nomine querat,*
> *Dic: meus innoti nominis auctor erat.*

Different again is Heiric of Auxerre's opinion upon the suppression of his name in the pompous *Allocutio ad librum* with which he prefaced his life of St. Germanus (*Poetae*, III, 437, 57 ff.):

> *Qua frontem titulus praeordinabit,*
> *Nemo ONOMA praefixerit auctor:*
> *Germanus subeat prioris arcem*
> *Auspicii, is primordia signet.*
> *Hoc forsan poteris inerme vulgus*
> *Tempnere seu discrimina mille.*
> *Tanti nominis obicem proterve*
> *Vix ausint sprevisse phalanges.*

The author, then, where he would normally give his name, accords, so to speak, the precedence to his hero, St. Germanus—out of modesty, but also because he considers that the name of the saint will protect his work from the envious.

Yet giving the name is much more frequent. Josephus Scottus (*Poetae*, I, 156, 43) names himself in the last line of a poem addressed to Charlemagne. This manner of mentioning the name (signature in the concluding line) we also find in Theodulf (*Poetae*, I, 538, 250) and in Walafrid (*Poetae*, II, 296, 60), both times connected with requests for intercession. It is not found in Vulfinus of Die (*Poetae*, IV, 976, 395), in Gislemarus (*Poetae*, IV, 1060), in Walter of Speyer (*Poetae*, V, 63, 266), in Carus (*Poetae*, V, 141, 960). Bernard Silvestris' statement in the dedicatory epistle to his *De mundi universitate* is original. He regards the work as imperfect and hence would rather suppress his name, but he leaves the decision to the dedicatee, Thierry of Chartres. In the twelfth century I find no examples of suppression of the name. On the contrary! It is actually censured by a monk. The Cluniac Peter of Poitiers writes *ca.* 1140 in a dedicatory epistle to Abbot Peter the Venerable, of Cluny (*PL*, CLXXXIX, 47): "Si quis autem adversum me indignatur quod nomine meo aliquid intitulare et libris vestris apponere ausus fuerim, sciat hoc non mea praesumptione, sed vestra, cui nefas duco contradicere, iussione factum esse. Ego vero cum in omnibus, tum etiam in hoc vobis obtemperare non dubito, non arrogantiae studio (quam semper a me longe faciat Dominus!), sed obedientiae devotione, praesertim cum sciam multos probatae religionis et humilitatis viros hoc idem de quibuslibet scriptis suis olim studiose fecisse. Quos certe magis in hoc quantulocunque opusculo nostro imitari affecto, quam quosdam nostri temporis scriptores, qui nescio qua vel cautela, vel imperitia ubique nomina sua supprimunt, incurrentes apocryphorum scriptorum vecordiam, qui sive de falsitate, sive de haeresi redargui fugientes, nusquam propria vocabula praetulerunt. Non ergo me hinc aliquis ante tempus judicare, sed Deo et conscientiae meae me dimittat, et ipse, si voluerit, Ovidium sine titulo scribat."—In this period we find unadulterated pride of authorship. A German who achieved prosperity and reputation under Frederick I and Henry VI in Italy, Godfrey of Viterbo, writes (Waitz, p. 133, 7): "Nomen autem libri est panteon Gotifredi, sicut a Lucano Lucanus et ab Oratio Oratius . . ." Godfrey, then, complacently sets himself beside a Horace and a Lucan. Boastful too is his justification of the title "Pantheon": "Ideoque hoc nomen huic operi satis convenire videtur, cum in hoc libro vetus testamentum cum novo et istorie latine cum barbaris et prose cum versibus sub uno volumine tamquam invicem pacificatae concordent." *Ca.* 1196 an Italian signs: "Ego magister Petrus de Ebulo, servus imperatoris et fidelis, hunc librum ad honorem Augusti composui. Fac mecum, domine, signum in bonum ut videant me Tancredini et confundantur." On the other hand, among Italian jurists of the same period it is considered proper to suppress the name.[1] But this applied only to legal writing. As a rule, the poets of the Sicilian school, many of whom were jurists, name themselves.[2]—Ludwig Storbeck [3] was able to cite 128 historical works of the German medieval period (from 600 to 1400) whose authors name themselves. Eleven of these fall in the Frankish period, fifteen in the Saxon, seventeen in that of the Salian kings, thirty-seven in the Hohenstaufen period, etc. His study shows the untenability of the opinion "that the Middle Ages was the period of the typical and the conventional" (p. 71).—Let us end with Dante. A celebrated passage in the *Convivio* (I, 2, 3) runs: "Non si concede per li retorici alcuno di sè medesimo sanza necessaria cagione parlare . . ." In the erudite commentary of Busnelli and Vandelli (1934), nothing is produced on this passage except two—inapplicable—passages from Thomas Aquinas, because the commentators know that writer especially well

---

[1] E. Kantorowicz, *Kaiser Friedrich II*, Supplementary volume, 131 f.
[2] In accordance with French and Provençal precedent.
[3] *Die Nennung des eigenen Namens bei den deutschen Geschichtschreibern des Mittelalters* (Halle dissertation, 1910).

and are inclined to suppose him Dante's principal source for anything and everything. But this is a preconception. When Dante referred to "li retorici," he certainly
did not mean Aquinas by it, but an *ars dictaminis* that we cannot yet identify. In
§13 f. of the same chapter Dante admits exceptions: Augustine and Boethius might
name themselves—as Dante himself was to do in *Purg.*, XXX, 33.

THE "CHIVALRIC SYSTEM OF THE VIRTUES"

Under date of November 13, 1874, Wilhelm Scherer wrote (ZfdA, XVIII [1875], 461): "I would rather read amusing things than boring ones, and I assume the same taste in my readers. So when I have succeeded in relieving serious and weighty discussions by a little unsought merriment, I have always thought that I should not deny myself so innocent a means of enlivening argument." Yet he was forced to learn that "the deplorable sensitivity of hurt self-love or the damnable desire to be right at all costs" took offence at his amusing polemics. But his final word is: "There are no party matters in science." I was motivated by similar ideas when I published the following essay in 1943.

The publication of the first volume of the *Real-Encyclopädie der classischen Altertumswissenschaft*, inaugurated by August Friedrich Pauly—a monumental work which has been frequently revised since—took place over a century ago (1837). Even then the idea was common property that Greek and Latin philology, epigraphy, ancient history, archaeology, and related disciplines were parts of a comprehensive "classical" discipline of Antiquity (*Altertumswissenschaft*)—a view which had triumphed as a result of the influence first of C. G. Heyne and Winckelmann, later of Friedrich August Wolf and August Böckh. These in turn looked back with reverence upon the men "who had established philology as a historical discipline in the grand manner of the other historical disciplines, above all to Joseph Justus Scaliger" (Ernst Curtius, *Unter drei Kaisern*, 151). In the twentieth century this comprehensive discipline has frequently been deprived of the adjective "classical," [1] with its value implications, but the thing itself has remained faithful to the legacy of its founders. This universal concept of Antiquity, which unites philology and history, has remained an admirable prerogative of German antique scholarship and has borne rich fruit.

Of medieval scholarship the same, unfortunately, cannot be said. Medieval research began under the star of Romanticism and has never lost the imprint of that origin. Old German champions, *Minnesang*, and knightly days—around these, Romanticism wove dreamy pictures. The German uprising of 1813 merged them with the national will of a new youth. Scholars, many of whom were also poets, restored the texts and added to the picture of the German past. Modern historical specialties and methods were still hardly cultivated. [2] There was no medieval Latin philology. Only classical philology could lend assistance—for example in dealing with the heroic epic. Lachmann took care of that. Under these circumstances, a universal, historically documented view of the Middle Ages could not arise. What did arise was Germanic and Romance philology. Though in the beginning, and for long afterward, they were variously allied, in the course of the last two generations they have become completely independent and at the same time have cut their ties with medieval Latin (and vice versa).

To command the numerous idioms of medieval vernacular poetry—Old Norse

[1] Gercke and Norden, *Einleitung in die Altertumswissenschaft*.
[2] The foundation for the *Monumenta Germaniae historica* was laid in 1819. The first volume appeared in 1826.

and Provençal, Celtic and Tuscan, Middle High German and Spanish, with medieval Latin to boot—was possible only to the smallest minority. Wide reading in many languages—such as W. P. Ker [3] about 1900, and in our day Samuel Singer, were able to make so fruitful—will always be attainable only by a few especially gifted men. But that is not the crux of the matter. What is crucial is that dissociation from the basic foundation of history which is observable in all the medieval philologies, is the tendency to replace unknown concretes [4] by non-existent abstractions. Dissociation from history in the widest sense: national, political, social, economic, legal history; history of philosophy and science; ecclesiastical history. Cordial relations are maintained only with art history—but it is precisely this discipline which, through a stylistic analysis which has become chronic, has repeatedly lost the historical ground from under its feet. To my knowledge there is in Germany no journal devoted to the Middle Ages as a whole and in all its phenomenal forms—like *Le Moyen Age*, *Studi Medievali*, *Medium Aevum* (England), *Speculum* (U.S.A.), the last of which bears the subtitle: *A Journal of Medieval Studies*.[5] Neither in the form of a periodical organ nor in that of a bibliography or a handbook is there a common forum for scholars whose work concerns the Middle Ages. Perhaps even the demand for it does not exist.

Let no one bring forward the excuse of specialization. This, as should finally be realized, is a pure bogeyman. Around 1900 it did perhaps cause trouble. But since then the technique and organization of scholarly work have made such immense progress that every scholar can orient himself in unfamiliar departments without difficulty. We have bibliographies, lexicons, indexes, epitomes of research, textbooks of all kinds. This whole great organizational accomplishment—which naturally is still capable of incalculable improvement—has done away with the much deplored disadvantages of division of labor—a fact which appears to have been little noticed. It is precisely the fruits of the most extensive specialization (such, for example, as the *Thesaurus Linguae Latinae*) which have cleared the road for a new universalization. And this road should be resolutely taken.

The lack of a medieval discipline whose view is not bounded by professional barriers has been prejudicial to our studies, has hampered the progress and the deepening of our insight. I should like to tell a story about this.

Once long, long ago, in the Hohenstaufen period, there lived a man. His name was Wernher of Elmendorf, he was a chaplain, and at the bidding of a certain Provost Dietrich he wrote a didactic poem on morals. It has no title. But titles were not customary in those days.[6] What did it contain? We will let Wilhelm Scherer [7] tell us: "To teach man what he owes to his honor, he puts together a series of moral precepts, which he drew not from the Bible but from a number of classical writers who must have been included in Provost Dietrich's library—from Sallust, from Boethius, Seneca, Juvenal, Horace, Ovid, Lucan, Terence, even from Xenophon.

---

[3] Cf. his little masterpiece *The Dark Ages* (1904).

[4] More accurately: the scholar's own ignorance.

[5] But even these journals—except *Speculum*—do not altogether realize the universality implied in their titles.

[6] Edward Schröder investigated the causes of this phenomenon in his study *Aus den Anfängen des deutschen Buchtitels* (Göttingen, 1937).

[7] *Geschichte der deutschen Dichtung im 11. und 12. Jahrhundert* (1875), 124 ff. Cf. Scherer's *Geschichte der deutschen Literatur*, 222.

Solomon, on the other hand, is seldom cited. Wernher expressly gives his motives for using these pagans: Solomon sets up the ant as a model to us; but if I should learn virtue from a tiny insect, I can even more easily get it from a pagan . . . Of specifically Christian sentiment there is not much trace in him: no scorn of the world, no ascetic impulses, no insistence upon humility and self-abasement; everywhere there is a healthy worldliness and humanity . . . The predominant viewpoint is always honor, public respect . . . The spirit of moderation pervades the whole . . . The poet everywhere has in view the knightly circle, he already even to some extent prefers French culture. He argues against the foolishness of 'Minne,' but it is not as an enemy of earthly pleasure but as an enemy of irrationality and extravagance that he does so."

So the passage stood to be read in 1875 and again, condensed, in 1883, in Scherer's big *Literaturgeschichte*, which was a household book among the educated *bourgeoisie*. Those were the decades villas were built in German Renaissance, and decorated with Makart bouquets, the while the *Kulturkampf* raged. No, that free-thinking chaplain, who taught a healthy worldliness, had been no hypocrite. But soon after Scherer's premature death Wernher's prestige suffered a blow from which it was long unable to recover. From 1873 the Germanist Anton E. Schönbach (1848–1911) had been living and teaching at Graz. As a student he had sat under the great Müllenhoff at Berlin, but as a convinced Catholic he had been shocked by the "almost religious veneration" with which Müllenhoff "looked up to Teutonic paganism." [8] He planned a great work which should show the significance of Christianity in the formation of the German national character. Physically handicapped, he could all the better surrender himself to his unquenchable thirst for reading. His biographer asserts that he not only looked through "the 222 volumes" [9] of Migne's *Patrologia Latina* but studied them carefully (which anyone who has worked with that monster of a collection will find it hard to believe). In any case, he turned up some valuable references, particularly for Old German sermon literature, and for the minnesingers, though he probably overrated their degree of education. In Migne (CLXXI, 1003–56) he found, among other works by the eminent Latin poet and preacher Hildebert of Lavardin, a treatise entitled *Moralis philosophia* [10]—the source of Wernher's poem (*ZfdA*, XXXIV [1890], 55 ff.). In Wernher's statement, then, that Master Dietrich

> *liz mich in sinen buchen*
> *di selbe rede suchen*
>
> (did let me search his books
> to find the selfsame rede)

[8] This and what follows, from E. von Steinmeyer's obituary notice in Bettelheim's *Biographisches Jahrbuch*, XVI (1914).—But cf. the fine memorial discourse on Müllenhoff in Schönbach, *Gesammelte Aufsätze* (1900), 82.

[9] There are 222 volumes, but the four volumes of indices may be deducted. And a good deal else besides! For the Germanistic student of sources is very unlikely to find much profit in such writers as Marius Mercator, Fulgentius of Ruspe, Dionysius Exiguus, Arator, or in the Mozarabic liturgy. Thus more volumes may be deducted. And so it could go on . . .

[10] More fully: *Moralis philosophia de honesto et utili*. The use of the shortened title has, as we shall see, caused much confusion.

"rede" was to be understood as "treatise, essay, presentation." Such statements as

alsus sagit daz buch
(thus saith the book)

were to be taken literally.[11] Wernher's performance was something half way between a translation and an adaptation. "In any event," Schönbach concluded, "his unique position in our early literature is irrevocably gone." For long after that nothing was said about Wernher. But in 1919 Gustav Ehrismann published his celebrated study "Die Grundlagen des ritterlichen Tugendsystems" * (*ZfdA*, LVI, 137–216). It begins with a rapid sketch of the history of ethics from Plato to the twelfth century —a sketch which, after the lapse of thirty years and with our increased knowledge, is completely outdated. Ehrismann lays particular emphasis upon Cicero, maintaining that in the *De officiis* the latter adhered to Aristotle (this is fatal—what he did was to copy the Stoic Panaetius and Posidonius). What follows, I must quote textually, since it is the evil spring of error from which thousands of rills have flowed into modern scholarship for a quarter of a century. It begins quite harmlessly:

Thesis 1.[12]

"Like Aristotle he (Cicero) distinguishes three values: the highest good, *summum bonum*, the theoretical category of duties which pertain to the perfect and wise man (like Aristotle, he does not go into this); moral good, *honestum* (the virtues), the practical obedience to duty of the ordinary and simply honest man; finally the useful, *utile*, external goods" (p. 139).

Unfortunately this is wholly false! Let us leave Aristotle in peace. But that Cicero teaches a triad of values (lately leading a specious and shadowy existence as "the three value realms" in numerous Germanistic studies) is simply not true. Let us take the latest edition of *De officiis* by Atzert (Teubner, 1923), with a careful index. In the 172 pages of the treatise the concept *summum bonum* appears only once (p. 3, 14 ff.). There, in translation, we read: "Who would presume to call himself a philosopher, if he did not inculcate any lessons of duty? But there are some schools that distort all notions of duty by the theories they propose touching the supreme good and the supreme evil. For he who posits the supreme good as having no connection with virtue and measures it not by a moral standard but by his own interests—if he should be consistent and not rather at times over-ruled by his better nature, he could value neither friendship nor justice nor generosity; and brave he surely cannot possibly be that counts pain the supreme evil, nor temperate he that holds pleasure to be the supreme good. Although these truths are so self-evident that the subject does not call for discussion, still I have discussed it in another connection. If, therefore, these schools should claim to be consistent, they could not say anything about duty; and no fixed, invariable, natural rules of duty can be posited except by those who say that moral goodness is worth seeking solely or chiefly for its own sake. Accordingly, the teaching of ethics is the peculiar right of the Stoics, the Academicians, and the Peripatetics." †

For Cicero, then, virtue (*honestas*) is the only good, or at least the only good to

---

[11] Such references to written sources were, of course, generally dismissed as "fictitious."   * ["The foundations of the chivalric system of the virtues."]

[12] I number such of Ehrismann's theses as I deny, so that the reader may more easily find his way.

[† Trans. Walter Miller, Loeb Classical Library (1913), pp. 7–8.]

be sought for its own sake. There is not and must not be a *summum bonum* outside of, still less above, the *honestum*. There are, then, not three but two "value realms," if anyone insists upon clinging to this misleading Neo-Kantian term:[13] virtue, and, below it, external goods (birth, beauty, health, wealth, etc.). Now according to Ehrismann the four cardinal virtues were degraded by Augustine to "merely secular values," whereas the "three theological virtues, faith, hope, charity" were "basic ingredients of the worship of God." False again, unfortunately! As a historian of ethics tells us, according to Augustine the four cardinal virtues are rooted "in the good will which is bestowed upon us by God." [14] But E. Gilson takes us far more deeply into Augustine's thought: [15] the highest virtue is the highest love (*summus amor*). The four cardinal virtues can be understood only as special forms of love.

This can be called reception of the antique system of virtues through the Church, but it is something more and something different: it is transforming absorption and re-creation. Having gone thus far, we shall refuse to credit the three following assertions of Ehrismann, which appear on p. 140:

Thesis 2.

"It was through Peter Lombard's *Sentences* that the septenary system first definitely became a matter of dogma."

Thesis 3.

"The significance thus attributed to the four cardinal virtues in the ethical system of the Church has its origin in Cicero and is connected with the recrudescence of esteem which his writings began to acquire during the eleventh century." [16]

Thesis 4.

"The separation between moral theology and moral philosophy is now also clearly carried through. It is determined by the concept of the three value-realms, which Aristotle advanced, Cicero transmitted to the Middle Ages, and Augustine implied in his separation of the divine and the terrestrial cities: knowledge of the highest good, *summum bonum*, of God, belongs only to theology; knowledge of the virtues, the *honestum*, comes under both theology and philosophy; external goods, the *utile*, are the concern of philosophy alone."

[13] Actually we are dealing with a doctrine of goods such as Antiquity delighted in because the dominant ethics was eudemonistic. For goods to be rightly assessed they had to be classified and arranged in a hierarchy. From this hierarchy, arose the concept of the highest good. It is not until the day of the Neo-Kantians that there are no longer any "goods" which can be "striven after," but only "values" which must be realized. But these values have no being; they do not exist, they merely function as standards. The *utilia*, on the contrary, are to the highest degree real, but are not highly regarded as standards by moralists.

[14] Ottmar Dittrich, *Die Systeme der Moral* (*Geschichte der Ethik*), II (1923), 224. References, p. 263.

[15] *Introduction à l'étude de saint Augustin*, especially p. 168.

[16] Cicero in the Middle Ages. In Schanz-Hosius, *Römische Literaturgeschichte* I [4] (1927), 546, we read: "In the Middle Ages Cicero was more praised than read. The reading of his works fell into abeyance; many of them came to be forgotten, many existed in incomplete form . . . The revival of Ciceronianism is connected with the name of Petrarch."—I know of no testimony to a Cicero renaissance in the eleventh century.—Ehrismann has overlooked something else too. The great transmitter of the antique heritage to the Middle Ages is, as we know, Isidore of Seville. In his chief work, the *Etymologiae*, he discusses the four cardinal virtues (II, 24, 5). The Middle Ages already knew them from there.

I merely present these untenable assertions of a man who, for all his high deserts, was unfamiliar with the history of philosophy; to refute them is superfluous. But now he goes further and subjects the great Alanus ab Insulis to the strait-jacket of his fictitious system of virtues. Again I must quote textually, to expose the evil:

Thesis 5.

"*Moralis theologia* is a part of Christian doctrine, of dogma, of the *summa theologiae* ('*Fides*,' Alanus, Migne, CCX, 112 f.); *moralis philosophia* ('*Mores*,' Alanus) constitutes the secular science of ethics, *ethica*" (p. 141).

Unfortunately this is another piece of misinformation. Let us turn to the passage cited. It is in chapter I of Alan's *Summa de arte praedicatoria* (he was a famous preacher himself). He defines *praedicatio* as "morum et fidei instructio," and from this definition he deduces two parts of theology (*PL*, CCX, 112 AB): "rationalis, quae de divinis scientiam prosequitur; et moralis, quae morum instructionem pollicetur." There is, then, a rational theology, which supplies knowledge of the truths of salvation, and a moral theology, which deals with ethical questions. Out of the first, Ehrismann, ever on the search for the chivalric system of the virtues, makes a *moralis theologia*, out of the second a *moralis philosophia*; then throws *ethica* in with the latter. All this certainly in the best possible faith, but at the same time flagrantly falsifying the text. And with what lack of knowledge of the Latin Middle Ages! For Ehrismann believes in all seriousness: "*Ethica* was also studied in the medieval schools, but it had no place in the *trivium* and *quadrivium*." [17] Ehrismann also seems not to know that ethics forms a part of the theological *summa*, e.g., in Thomas.

After this welter of misunderstandings, errors, and confusions we are ready to understand . . . Walther.

Thesis 6.

"The secular system of the virtues, then, with which we shall here be concerned, is based upon the four cardinal virtues, the *honestum*, and on goods, the *utile* (which is divided into *bona fortunae*, goods of fortune, and *bona corporis*, corporeal goods). The whole of ethical life moves in the three value-realms of the *summum bonum*, *honestum, utile*. But as the most fitting epigraph to a study of the chivalric system of the virtues we may prefix the translation which Walther von der Vogelweide made of the three concepts: 'diu zwei sint ére und varnde guot, daz dritte ist gotes hulde' [two are honor and chattels, the third is God's grace] (8, 14, 16), and in what follows there will be frequent occasion to point out this tripartite division in courtly poetry" (p. 141).

We shall come back to Walther. But first let us turn once more to our Thuringian chaplain, Wernher of Elmendorf. We had lost sight of him far too long. Ehrismann is preparing a resurrection for him. The chaplain who, in 1875, was regarded sympathetically as a "progressive," though at the same time some held that he was suspiciously communistic,[18] all unexpectedly becomes a significant figure: for it was he who put the foundation of the chivalric system of the virtues into German.

[17] The Middle Ages knew from Isidore (*Et.*, II, 24, 3) that the Greeks divided philosophy into physics, ethics, and logic. *Trivium* plus *quadrivium* was the ideal program of the medieval school, but it was seldom realized. Instruction in philosophy above and beyond that? Pure imagination.

[18] Scherer thought it possible to attribute "communistic ideals" to him (*op. cit.*, 125). Similarly Steinmeyer in *ADB*, VI, 59.

Schönbach's dragon-seed had sprung up, but it now turned against the sower. Wernher's position was by no means "irrevocably gone." For now his name remained connected with the *Moralis philosophia*. Listen:

Thesis 7.

"The point of entry for Cicero's doctrine of duties into German chivalric ethical doctrine is the well-known *Moralis philosophia de honesto et utili* . . . This *moralis philosophia* is a secular ethics, in contradistinction from *theologia* or *theologia moralis*, and contains no expressly Christian ideas" (p. 142).

That was in 1919. But the essay from which our quotations are taken was only a preliminary study for the imposing edifice of Ehrismann's *Geschichte der deutschen Literatur bus zum Ausgang des Mittelalters* ("History of German Literature to the End of the Middle Ages")—a work whose merit will not be diminished by a criticism of its "Geistesgeschichte" presuppositions, or of only one of them. In the section on "courtly ethics" (II, 2, first half, pp. 19 ff.) Ehrismann first discusses the concepts *zuht, hövescheit, tugent, mâze*, heroism, honor, courtly love (*minne*). Then (p. 23):

Thesis 8.

"The courtly moral theology laid down in the doctrine of *minne* is based upon knightly and social relations. It took something from ecclesiastical moral philosophy too. But we also encounter another system, which is far superior in moral seriousness to this courtly doctrine of *minne* and which classifies ethical values as *gotes hulde, êre und guot* (Walther von der Vogelweide, 8, 14). This ethics springs from a different order of moral concepts from that of courtly society, it is a combination of religious and secular values, or moral theology and moral philosophy."

In these statements we find, in a loose series, the concepts 1. theory of *minne*, 2. courtly moral theory, 3. ecclesiastical moral philosophy, 4. Walther's ethics. This unites in itself 5. moral theology and moral philosophy, which last, however, presumably means the "ecclesiastical" (No. 3.). But unfortunately Ehrismann does not clearly define and differentiate these five concepts. Then we have a commentary:

Thesis 9.

"The knowledge of God as the *summum bonum* belongs to moral theology. *Êre*, in medieval secular ethics, corresponds to moral philosophy, *moralis philosophia*, the *honestum*. Moral philosophy is derived from the Latin writers, especially from Cicero's *De officiis*. It was taught in the schools in the Middle Ages. *Honestum* is probity . . . these are the four cardinal virtues."

This commentary makes Ehrismann's systematization even more confused. For we now learn that there is—No. 6—a secular moral philosophy. But what its relation to No. 3 may be we are not informed. If the reader tries to clear matters up by comparing all the relevant passages,[19] he finds himself only the more bewildered. *Mora-*

---

[19] In the same volume I find: "the worldly moral system, the *moralis philosophia*" (p. 12); Hildebert of Tours and "his worldly moral doctrine" (p. 13, with a note referring to Schönbach and Wernher's source, discovered by Schönbach). On p. 157 we find: all "chivalric systems of the virtues" had "the same common basis in the *Honestum* of *Moralis philosophia*." p. 308, n. 1: "The *Moralis philosophia* of the Middle Ages took over *nobilitas animi* from antique moral philosophy (Hildebert . . .)." "*Moraliteit*" (in Gottfried's *Tristan*) teaches the "content of *Moralis philosophia*; together with pleasing God: this is the task of moral theology; and, finally, courtly *zuht* as well" (p. 311, n. 1). Then, astonishingly enough, also

lis philosophia appears now as religious, now as secular, now it seems to be a discipline in the scholastic curriculum, now it becomes nothing more than a Latin tract which Wernher translated. In the final volume of the *LG* [20] it appears only casually as "the basis of Walther's ethics"—yet with an essential modification, a fact of which the author himself seems not to have been conscious. To our astonishment, namely, we read:

Thesis 10.

"The basis of Walther's ethics is constituted by the three separate values of *moralis philosophia: gotes hulde, êre und irdisch guot* . . . The milieu for which his moral reflections are intended is courtly society. The central position is occupied by *êre;* the lesser value is *irdisch guot.* . . . Religious poems are rare (the *Mariensprüche* can hardly be attributed to Walther)" (p. 250).

One cannot believe one's eyes. Has the writer forgotten his own theory? In theses 8 and 9 it was said that the "first value realm" (*gotes hulde*) belonged to moral theology, the other two to moral philosophy. Now it is said that all three value realms belonged to *moralis philosophia.* The chivalric system of the virtues seems to consist in the systematic misuse of a terminology invented solely for the purpose. —In Ehrismann's concluding volume it appears once again, and in connection with our Wernher of Elmendorf, who however is now reproached with "not having quite understood the real meaning of the Latin scholastic [21] work" (p. 307). At any rate he did not see in the book what Ehrismann believed he had found in it—which may explain the censure.

So far as I can see, Ehrismann's theory of the chivalric system of the virtues with its three value realms found general acceptance among Germanists even in its author's lifetime. It was developed and schematized. I need not pursue this here. But one thing must be said: The theory, which reaches down into the latest dissertations, was accepted without any examination of its foundations. And its foundations are shaky.

In 1890 Schönbach accepted the *Moralis philosophia de honesto et utili* as the work of Hildebert, but he did not fail to state, in *AfdA,* XVII (1891), that B. Hauréau, in his *Notices et Extraits* (I [1890], 100 ff.), had pointed out that William of Conches was "the actual author of this cento," which had been "a much-used schoolbook in the Middle Ages" and had fifteen printings before 1513.[22] Ehrismann took cognizance of this, although in his *LG* he ascribes the work now to Hildebert,

---

on the subject of *Tristan:* "The religious element of the poem is the *religio* of moral philosophy" (315–16). Finally (p. 312, n. 2), "ecclesiastical moral doctrine" appears again.

[20] Ehrismann himself uses this abbreviation.

[21] Scholasticism! Here nonsense is pushed to extremes: the selection, from antique authors, in which neither the Church nor Christianity appears at all, is to be understood in the light of "twelfth-century Humanism," and has nothing whatever to do with Scholasticism.

[22] Did Ehrismann look into Hauréau's work? I doubt it. Various MS titles of the Latin anthology are given in it—first of all *Moralium dogma philosophorum,* as the treatise has been officially called since 1929. Hauréau casually drops the remark: "Ce centon [Schönbach's "cento"] de maximes morales qui, devenu livre scolaire, a tant de fois été copié . . . et qui devait être, ayant eu tant de succès, imprimé dès le 15e siècle." This idea is the slight foundation for Ehrismann's stubbornly repeated assertion that the *Moralium dogma* was used as a schoolbook. This statement is an unsupported conjecture of Hauréau's.

now to William. But both he and his followers overlooked the fact that medieval Latin philology had in the meanwhile accomplished something itself. In 1929 the Swedish scholar John Holmberg published "Das *Moralium dogma philosophorum* des Guillaume de Conches, lateinisch, altfranzösisch und mittelniederfränkisch" (Leipzig, Otto Harrassowitz). This publication, to which we shall return later, furnished so much new material that research into the chivalric system of the virtues could not possibly pass it by—could it? Unfortunately, we are forced to observe, it could. But perhaps this neglect may be excused by the fact that the text was a medieval Latin one (though to be sure there was a Middle Low Frankish version too) and that it was no longer entitled *Moralis philosophia*? Besides, the work came out of Sweden. Perhaps it had not been officially brought to the attention of Germanists in the course of their routine activities? But that is not the explanation either. In the *Jahresbericht für germanische Philologie*, LI (1931), 282, it was briefly noticed by H. Walther as "highly meritorious." Of course a notice of this sort can easily be overlooked. But the *Literaturblatt für germanische und romanische Philologie*, LI (1930), 332 ff., also had a notice, and a very thorough and substantial one, by Otto Schumann. It ended: "The dependable text and apparatus, the fullness of the references to sources, and the other editorial matter . . . at last furnish a solid basis for further studies, both of the Latin original and of the relation in which the other vernacular versions, especially that of Wernher of Elmendorf, stand to it." Germanists (including H. Teske, *Thomasin von Zerclaere* [1933]) have not yet followed up this lead.

But Ehrismann and his followers also unfortunately failed to inform themselves concerning the "moral theology" and "moral philosophy" of the twelfth century—although the third volume of O. Dittrich's *Geschichte der Ethik*, which appeared in 1926, provided dependable information and exhaustive *loci*. To be sure, not much of a show could be made with Dittrich's verdict on William of Conches' *Moralis philosophia*. He described it (p. 82) as a completely derivative collection of moral precepts from Seneca and Cicero. From his presentation of the scholastic systems, it further appeared that Early Scholasticism (before 1200) produced no ethical trains of thought, far less systems, which offered any point of departure for the "three value realms." Earlier authors like Alcuin, Raban Maur, etc., offered nothing but tradition and excerpts. They confined themselves, I should like to put it, to a more or less intelligent extracting and copying, a "transcribing," of Antiquity. Anything original or new is to be found only in Anselm, Abélard, Hugh of St. Victor. But the first was essentially concerned with the freedom of the will and the *rectitudo* of the volition, the second with sin and conscience (principal *loci*, II, 694 and 710 in Cousin's edition), the third (who was a confirmed anti-Humanist) with an intensification of mysticism. Peter Lombard, the Master of the Sentences, who followed them, can hardly be credited with a halfway independent train of thought, at least in ethics.[23] Not until the age of High Scholasticism (after 1250)—in the period, that is, when chivalry had degenerated and was a thing of the past—do we find searching ethical discussions, which took their start from the "new Aristotle." Thus Dittrich.[24] And what does the history of medieval philosophy tell us? Ueberweg-Geyer (1927, p. 237) disposes of the *Moralis philosophia* as of secondary impor-

[23] J. N. Espenberger, *Die Philosophie des Petrus Lombardus* (1901), 1.

[24] A. Hauck provides an important supplement (*Kirchengeschichte Deutschlands*, IV, 520).

tance. Maurice de Wulf (*Histoire de la Philosophie médiévale* I[6] [1934], 192) does likewise, only more circumstantially: "Le Moralium dogma philosophorum, attribué à G. de Conches par Hauréau, et qui pour d'autres est une oeuvre dont l'auteur reste incertain, est un des rares traités de morale du haut moyen âge. C'est un ensemble de préceptes sans originalité, empruntés surtout à Sénèque (*De beneficiis*) et à Cicéron (*De officiis*). A leur exemple, l'auteur s'attache à des questions de détail, telles que la distinction de l'utile et de l'honnête, la description détaillée des vertus: il n'y faut pas chercher l'économie de la morale scolastique, et notamment rien n'y est dit de la fin dernière et de la moralité."

A barren conclusion, indeed—but for that very reason a wholesome one. For it proves that the medieval moral philosophy and moral theology hypostatized by Ehrismann is a chimera. Present-day Catholic thinking distinguishes a discipline of moral philosophy and a discipline of moral theology, "the systematic presentation of Christian ethics according to the doctrine and practice of the Catholic church." So reads the definition in Buchberger's *Lexikon für Theologie und Kirche* (VII [1935], 319). The same work informs us that Scholasticism "from Anselm to Duns Scotus" first developed a "theology of faith and acting" (col. 320). Now in regard to the period from Anselm to Peter Lombard (roughly 1060 to 1160) we have already been oriented by Dittrich. A moral theology as a separate discipline, however, first developed later. "Nevertheless"—nevertheless!—so K. Hilgenreiner continues, in the article in Buchberger from which we have already quoted—"the great theological summas [of the thirteenth century!] already offer wholly moral-theological sections." But moral theology first really flourishes in the sixteenth and seventeenth centuries. In the twelfth century, then, and on down to Walther's time, there was neither a "moral theology" nor a "moral philosophy." But the height of absurdity is the notion that the chivalric system of the virtues borrowed one "value realm" from one, and two more from the other, of two disciplines utterly unknown to the men of the period.

From the title of a single medieval Latin text, whose author is unknown, Ehrismann concluded that in the twelfth century there must have been a separate discipline, and indeed a curricular subject (this from Hauréau), called "moral philosophy."

But to get to the bottom of the moral philosophy assumed by Ehrismann, we must now more closely examine the treatise which was the point of departure for these constructions.

Holmberg was able to base his edition of the Latin text on fifty MSS, of which four are of the twelfth century, fourteen of the thirteenth, fourteen of the fourteenth, and eighteen of the fifteenth. This distribution favors the assumption that the text first achieved popularity in the thirteenth century. The earliest MSS of the French version also date from the last third of the thirteenth century (Holmberg p. 31). The text is a material improvement over Migne's (which was based on a very inferior and frequently amplified MS). Holmberg's choice for the title was the opening words, *Moralium dogma philosophorum*; this title already appears in numerous MSS. Other titles, which appear in one MS or another, are: *Compendium morale, De moralitate, Moralis philosophia, Liber moralis philosophie, Liber philosophie de honesto et utili, Elegantiora verba moralium doctorum*, etc. These various titles and the preponderance in the MSS of the title chosen by Holmberg are enough in themselves to show that *Moralis philosophia* is to be taken not as the name of a discipline, but as a quite loose indication of the contents of the work. In the Middle Ages the word *philosophia* has the widest meaning (cf. Wolfram's *Parzifal*, 643, 14). It embraces all knowledge, all education, even rhetoric and poetry. *Moralis philosophia* would best be translated by "ethical wisdom."

Holmberg has prefixed to his work a table of contents which makes it possible to take in the structure and matter of the treatise at a glance. He has also traced and counted the quotations. Of these, 165 are from Cicero's *De officiis*, sixteen from other works of Cicero; ninety-two from Seneca; twelve from Sallust, five from Boethius, 104 from Horace, forty from Juvenal, eighteen from Terence, twenty-three from Lucan. The popularity of the anthology is shown by its having been repeatedly translated or adapted not only into Old French but also into Middle Low Frankish and Icelandic. A considerable part of it also passed into Brunetto Latini's *Trésor.* The *Moralium dogma* consists, as Holmberg says, p. 14, "almost exclusively of series of classical *loci communes,* part of which frequently reappear in the eclectic ethical literature of the Middle Ages." What its readers found in the book was best expressed by the editor of the Paris edition of 1511, Jodocus Clichtoveus: "Iste (liber) nequaquam aspernandus est, de quatuor officiorum fontibus, secundum Stoicorum partitionem quas virtutes cardinales appellant, abunde disserens et preclaras probatissimorum auctorum . . . sententias . . . colligens" (Holmberg, p. 82). The combination of ethical doctrine and classical quotations made the little book attractive.

Holmberg's edition was the occasion for an essay by John R. Williams ("The Authorship of the Moralium dogma philosophorum," in *Speculum*, VI [1931], 392–411). He offers further information concerning the diffusion and use of the book, shows that the author cannot be identified,[24a] and makes it highly probable that the book was not intended for schools but was composed to order as a summary of the ethical teachings of certain antique authors. This would explain the narrow range of sources employed, the close correspondence with antique terminology, and the complete ignoring of church and Christianity. Williams further points out that the book contains precepts for old and young, as well as for all classes of society, free or bond. Nothing about it, I might add, makes it appear suitable for a "mirror of knighthood." We hear, for example, that medicine and architecture are honorable callings; that retail trade dishonors, but that wholesale trade is not to be despised. Best of all, however, is agriculture, for which Horace's "beatus ille" is cited (Holmberg, p. 48). The servant is advised to carry out all orders and not complain (p. 59). And what of the *religio* of moral philosophy, which Ehrismann found again in the "religious element of Gottfried's *Tristan*"? I let Otto Schumann (*op. cit.,* 333) speak: "This non-Christian, purely classical character is particularly distinctive for the entire work. It finds its strongest expression in the section on *religio.* Here—and elsewhere too—the compiler has not even thought it necessary, where, in his antique originals, there was mention of the gods, to substitute the Christian 'God'—and this not merely in quotations from the poets, where a change would have spoiled the verse." Finally, the "three value realms." Here our moral philosopher fails us entirely. He puts us off with the amazing explanation—after Cicero—that the

---

[24a] According to P. Delhaye (*Recherches de théologie ancienne et médiévale,* XVI [1949], 237), the author is William of Conches.

honestum is at once *an* or *the utile* (Holmberg, p. 69). That is what the "foundation of the chivalric system of the virtues" really looks like.

Our critical re-examination of Ehrismann's system has led us from one doubt to
another. We have conscientiously examined all his theses, but in the end have
always found ourselves the more deeply perplexed, misled, and befooled. What does
Ehrismann want of us? Are we to believe that our Hohenstaufen poets studied the
Moralium dogma which was composed in France *ca.* 1150? That they attended
schools in which *moralis philosophia* was an obligatory subject of instruction?
Have Ehrismann and his followers consulted the history of the medieval school
curriculum, on which subject there are dependable works by which to orient
oneself? Or did those poets read Wernher of Elmendorf privately? But was not he
himself so far from grasping the essence of the matter—that he mocked at *Minne*,
which, after all, is one of the foundations of the system of the virtues? As soon as we
put such direct and indiscreet questions, Ehrismann's theses break down, his authorities break down. Our scepticism steadily increases. The fearful suspicion dawns:
perhaps we should never have heard anything about the chivalric system of the
virtues if the chaplain Wernher had not chanced to put together a humanistic
anthology. Could this sort of thing happen in a discipline which envisaged the
Middle Ages as a whole and which had preserved its critical sense?

If we are to believe Ehrismann, a passage from Walther's well-known political
poem *Ich saz ûf eime steine* would provide the proof. There the triad is presented:
êre, varnde guot, gotes hulde. In other words, the oft-cited "three value realms"! The
earlier Germanistics (which comes down to Wilmanns-Michels [1924]), to be sure,
found nothing particular in this triad, did not trace it back to an imaginary moral
theology or moral philosophy, but instead showed from parallel passages that we
are here dealing with courtly commonplaces.[25] But in this it seems to me that one
thing is overlooked—Walther's predilection for "numerical apothegms" (*supra*, p.
510), that is, for enumerations of 2, 3, 4 or more things which belong together in
some meaningful way. Such enumerations belong to the gnomic style of all times
and peoples, are a spontaneous and primitive product of reflective folk wisdom, but
at the same time they appeal to didactic minds everywhere, whether in the Greece
of the Sophists or the scholastic North Europe of the Middle Ages. They are primordial forms of memorizing and teaching. The 150 printed pages of Lachmann's
edition of Walther's poems as revised by C. von Kraus offer such frequent examples
of this form of expression that one cannot help being surprised that the commentators say nothing about it.[26]

Walther likes to put ideas together in pairs and to refer to them in the same
fashion:

47, 36   *Zwô fuoge hân ich doch, swie ungefüege ich sî:*
          der hân ich mich von kinde her vereinet.
          ich bin den frôn bescheidenlîcher fröide bî,
          und lache ungerne sô man bî mir weinet.

[25] Wilmanns, II⁴, 72.
[26] In the authoritative works on Walther, I have come upon no comprehensive
characterization and analysis of this artistic device. Only in Wilmanns do I find,
together with much else, much that belongs here—under the unfortunate heading
"Parallelism."

On this Wilmanns II⁴ 205: "However little I may know of right living, two social virtues have been mine from childhood." Here related concepts are paired. More often the paired concepts form a contrast:

> 63, 36 *genâde und ungenâde, dise zwêne namen*
> *hât min frowe beide. die sint ungelîch:*
> *der ein ist arm, der ander rîch.*

So also in:

> 93, 29 *Mîn frowe ist zwir beslozzen,*
> *der ich liebe trage,*
> *dort verklûset, hie verhêret dâ ich bin.*
> *des einen hât verdrozzen*
> *mich nû manege tage:*
> *sô gît mir daz ander senelîchen sin.*
> *solt ich pflegen der zweier slüzzel huote,*
> *dort ir lîbes, hie ir tugent,*
> *disiu wirtschaft næme mich ûz sendem muote,*
> *und næm iemer von ir schœne niuwe jugent.*

An enhancement of this artistic device consists in connecting two pairs:

> 63, 24 *friundinne ist ein süezez wort:*
> *doch sô tiuret frowe unz an daz ort.*
>   *Frowe, ich wil mit hôhen liuten schallen,*
> *werdent diu zwei wort mit willen mir:*
> *sô lâz ouch dir zwei von mir gevallen,*
> *dazs ein keiser kûme gæbe dir.*
> *friunt und geselle diu sint dîn:*
> *sô sî friundîn unde frowe mîn.*

or

> 13, 5 *Owê waz êren sich ellendet tiuschen landen!*
> *witze unde manheit, dar zuo silber und daz golt,*
> *swer diu beidiu hât, belîbet der mit schanden,*
> *wê wie den vergât des himeleschen keisers solt!*
> *dem sint die engel noch die frowen holt.*
> *armman zuo der werlte und wider got,*
> *wie der fürhten mac ir beider spot!* [27]

The same poem also has a third pair:

> 13, 19 *Owê wir müezegen liute, wie sîn wir versezzen*
> *zwischen (zwein) fröiden nider an die jâmerlîchen stat!*

The same procedure in:

> 22, 18 *Swer houbetsünde unt schande tuot*
> *mit sîner wizzende umbe guot,*
> *sol man den für einen wîsen nennen?*

[27] The commentators are not agreed whether the third pair is identical with the second or with 1 and 2 or introduces something new.

> Swer guot von disen beiden hât,
> swerz an im weiz unt sichs verstât,
> der sol in zeinem tôren baz erkennen . . .

22, 31   er gouch, swer für diu zwei (gotes hulde unt êre) ein
>   anderz kiese!
> der ist an rehten witzen blint.

The double pairing is emphasized by "ouch zwô" in:

59, 14   zwô tugende hân ich, der si wîlent nâmen war,
> scham unde triuwe:
> die schadent nû beide sêre. schaden nû alsô dar!
> ich bin niht niuwe:
> dem ich dâ gan, dem gan ich gar.

59, 28   Ich hân iu gar gesaget daz ir missestât:
> zwei wandel hân ich iu genennet.
> nu sult ir ouch vernemen waz si tugende hât
> (der sint ouch zwô), daz irs erkennet.
> ich seit iu gerne tûsent: irn ist niht mê dâ,
> wan schœne und êre.
> die hât sie beide vollecliche. hât si? jâ.
> waz wil si mêre?
> hiest wol gelobt: lobe anderswâ.

Series of three are naturally the most preferred. This has its basis in the age-old idea, still current in our time, that three is a pre-eminent number. Good things especially are frequently arranged in series of three—for example "wine, women, and song." Even in Antiquity, "ternaries of goods," as Carl Weyman has called them (*Beiträge zur Geschichte der christlich-lateinischen Poesie* [1926]), were very popular, and so they were in the Old Testament, and in medieval Latin poetry. Walther did not need to learn this gnomic arrangement from anyone. We have the simple seed of an undeveloped triad in:

76, 4   *der wintersorge hân ich drî:*

Example of the triad:

84, 1   Drî sorge habe ich mir genomen:
> möht ich der einer zende komen,
> sô wære wol getân ze mînen dingen.
> iedoch swaz mir dâ von geschiht,
> in scheid ir von ein ander niht:
> mir mag an allen drin noch wol gelingen.
> gotes hulde und mîner frowen minne,
> dar umbe sorge ich, wie ich die gewinne:
> daz dritte hât sich mîn erwert unrehte manegen tac.
> daz ist der wünnecliche hof ze Wiene.

Here disparate things appear to be enumerated. How can *gotes hulde* be put on a par with the court at Vienna? Or is the triad arranged "stepwise"? C. von Kraus would seem to have felt this difficulty, for he writes: "When Walther says that he is endeavoring to gain *gotes hulde*, his *frowen minne*, and the *hof ze* Wiene, he means, of course, through his entire output of song, that is through religious poetry (*gotes hulde*), through love songs (*mîner frowen minne*), and through Sprüche on Leopold; by the last he seeks to deserve the court at Vienna" (p. 328).

Now a passage invoked in season and out of season:

> 84, 22   *Ich traf dâ her vil rehte drîer slahte sanc,*
>   *den hôhen und den nidern und den mittelswanc,*
>   *daz mir die rederîchen iegeslîches sagten danc.*
>   *wie könd ich der drîer einen nû ze danke singen?*

We find a ternary of goods which has little to do with the "three value realms" in:

> 102, 25   *ez hât der tumbe rîche nû ir drîer stuol, ir drîer gruoz.*
>   [*scil.* "wîsheit adel und alter"]
>   *owê daz man dem einen an ir drîer stat nû nîgen muoz!*
>   *des hinket reht und trûret zuht und siechet schame.*
>   *diz ist mîn klage: noch klagte ich gerne mê.*

Three masculine virtues, composed of 2 + 1 (cf. Wilmanns I², 360):

> 35, 27   *An wîbe lobe stêt wol daz man si heize schœne:*
>   *manne stêt ez übel, ez ist ze wîch und ofte hœne.*
>   *küene und milte, und daz er dâ zuo stœte sî,*
>   *so ist er vil gar gelobt: den zwein stêt wol daz dritte bî.*

Three possibilities of sin:

> 87, 33   *Hüetent wol der drîer*
>   *leider alze frîer.*
>   *zungen ougen ôren sint*
>   *dicke schalchaft, zêren blint.*

Here it is interesting that the triad has its origin in the practice of confessors and preachers (Wilmanns, II⁴, 320).[28] The formula 2 + 1 = 3, which Walther is fond of bringing in, he used jestingly too. The ternary becomes a mere addition:

> 95, 11   *nû hât si mir bescheiden*
>   *waz der troum bediute.*
>   *daz merket, lieben liute.*
>   *zwên und einer daz sint drî:*
>   *dannoch seit si mir dâ bî*
>   *daz mîn dûme ein vinger sî.*

Even as the triad can be reduced to a mere series of three, it can be elevated to tri-unity, in the cryptic mode in which Walther is not always quite successful:

> 19, 8   *dâ gienc eins keisers bruoder und eins keisers kint*
>   *in einer wât, swie doch die namen drîge sint:*

[28] In sermon style the division of the matter into three or more principal points is current in all periods. Schwietering characterizes Walther the didactic poet as a "lay preacher" (*Die deutsche Dichtung des Mittelalters*, 247). Did he adopt the numerical schema of church preaching?

Here too belongs the celebrated:

> 8, 11　*deheinen råt kond ich gegeben,*
> *wie man driu dinc erwurbe,*
> *der keines niht verdurbe.*
> *diu zwei sint êre und varnde guot,*
> *daz dicke ein ander schaden tuot:*
> *daz dritte ist gotes hulde,*
> *der zweier übergulde.*
> *die wolte ich gerne in einen schrîn.*

(Here again the idea that "value realms" are to be kept locked up, as in 93, 29 *Mîn frowe ist zwir beslozzen;* the *arken* in 26, 8 belong here too.)

It is worthy of note that with the positive triad, we have an adverse dyad—certainly a conscious artistic arrangement:

> 8, 19　*jâ leider desn mac niht gesîn,*
> *daz guot und werltlich êre*
> *und gotes hulde mêre*
> *zesamene in ein herze komen.*
> *stîg und wege sint in benomen:*
> *untriuwe ist in der sâze,*
> *gewalt vert ûf der strâze:*
> *fride unde reht sint sêre wunt.*
> *diu driu enhabent geleites niht, diu zwei enwerden ê gesunt.*

Triads can be doubled too, [29] like dyads: the effect is richer and more emphatic. Thus:

> 83, 30　*der guoten ræte der sint drî:*
> *drî ander bœse stênt dâ bî*
> *zer linggen hant. lât iu diu sehse nennen.*
> *frum unde gotes hulde und werltlich êre,*
> *daz sint die guoten: wol im der si lêre!*
> *den möht ein keiser nemen gerne an sînen hôhsten råt.*
> *die andern heizent schade sünde und schande.*

But there is much more that can be done with numerical series. The dyad can pass over into a triad (formula $2 + 1 = 3$), and the triad into a tetrad. As for example:

> 85, 20　*mîn junger hêrre ist milt erkant, man seit mir er si stæte,*
> *dar zuo wol gezogen: daz sint gelobter tugende drî:*
> *ob er die vierden tugent willeclîchen tæte,*
> *sô gienge er ebne . . .*

or:

> 98, 26　*Vil meneger fråget*
> *mich der lieben, wer si sî,*
> *der ich diene und allez her gedienet hån.*

[29] Cf. a Latin example (*NA*, XXVII, 199 f., No. 4):
Sunt tria gaudia: pax, sapientia, copia rerum.
Sunt tria tedia: lis et inedia, ars mulierum.

> *sô des betraget*
> *mich, sô spriche ich "ir sint drî,*
> *den ich diene: sô hab ich zer vierden wân."*

According to the same schema a 6 can want to become a 7:

> 80, 3   *Sich wolte ein ses gesibent hân*
> *ûf einen hôhvertigen wân:*

Example of hybris (as perhaps also the preceding)? [30]

That makes twenty "numerical apothegms." There are many more of them in Walther. I have only selected those which seemed to me especially striking and have attempted to arrange them systematically. It has been my intention to show: 1. how profoundly thinking in numerical series was rooted in Walther's intellectual nature; 2. how artistically he was able to employ it and vary it; 3. how the individual examples mutually illuminate one another; 4. that for Walther, and also for a comprehension of Walther, this numerical schema is at least as important as the content of the enumerated series of goods or evils. On this last point I lay particular stress. When one compares Walther's ternaries of goods, one finds that almost every one of them contains a different triad of chivalric virtues or life-ideals (the court at Vienna.) The much-labored lines 8, 14 ff. contain only one of these triads. Hence it appears to me inadmissible to call it the foundation of Walther's system of the virtues. The practice, indeed, developed only from the fact that people believed in the phantom of a moral philosophy evoked by Ehrismann, with its three "value realms." It was satisfying to find the three "value realms" again in one of Walther's most characteristic Sprüche. But now that Ehrismann's system has turned out to be a close texture of error interwoven with error, which we have had some difficulty in disentangling, we may be permitted to suppose that the passage will no longer be regarded as the summary of Walther's system of the virtues, as his "shorter catechism."

The so-called "system of the virtues" of the knight was, then, hardly a system. It comprises ethico-aesthetic categories of a secular nature, which had in part developed long before the rise of chivalry—for example, the fealty of the vassal, or the "joy" or other stereotyped expressions of courtly love, which existed in Southern France as early as *ca.* 1100. To this we may add the praise of *liberalitas* (*milte*), which we find in countless Latin poems before 1150, as we do in the early medieval "mirrors of princes," in the Latin Alexander romances, etc. This is a ruler's virtue of antique origin, which, upon economic grounds which it is easy to perceive, remained a constant reality. Perhaps the related virtue of *clementia* fused with it. That didactic elements of ecclesiastical origin should be added to these was only natural. That Walther several times refers to *gotes hulde* is no more remarkable than that he twice refers to the Trinity. To reduce this entire circle of virtues and ideals to a barren schema and derive it from a Latin anthology seems to me no gain. The peculiar charm of the chivalric ethos consists precisely in fluctuation between many ideals, some of them closely related, some diametrically opposed. The possibility of this free interplay, of freedom to move within a rich and manifold world of values, must have been an inner stimulus to the courtly poets.

---

[30] Wilmanns has nothing to say on this; von Kraus (p. 366) considers the possibility of "a joke on the audience, as in the case of the 'three winter cares' 76, 4."

Only co-operation between the various medieval specialties can solve the problem of the courtly and knightly ethos, if it is solvable. Medieval philology must ask medieval historiography what it has to tell concerning medieval class-ideals, and the concrete political, military, and economic factors which conditioned them.

Important conclusions on this subject appear in Carl Erdmann's book *Die Entstehung des Kreuzzugsgedankens* ("The Rise of the Crusade Idea"), which appeared in 1935 (noticed by me in *Herrigs Archiv*, CLIX [1936], 48 ff.). Erdmann's thesis is roughly as follows: The early church rejected war and the military profession. Here yawned a contradiction between Germanic standards of life and Christian ethics. Not until the ninth century do we find sporadic testimonies to an attempt at a compromise between *militia Dei* and *militia saecularis*. Cluniac monasticism then brought about a decided change. Especially in Normandy it exercised a strong influence upon the chivalric nobility. The Church reform of the eleventh century, together with monasticism and the papal Church, also affected the lay knighthood. From the first half of the eleventh century the leadership in this department lies with France, "which gives decisive further development to the idea of the defence of the church, to the religious symbolism of the military life, and to the important connection with the cult of saints" (p. 84). Yet the idea of Christian knighthood and the corresponding ethics of the holy war is not fully developed before the middle of the eleventh century. From the time of Leo IX (1049–54) the reformed papacy adopts the new ideal. The idea is materially consolidated by the alliance between the Normans and the Church. The Norman wars in the papal service first have the character of a crusade. The same phenomenon appears simultaneously in the Norman expedition against England (1066) and, even more markedly, in the Spanish crusade of 1064, which led to the temporary conquest of Barbastro. Among the pertinent propaganda Bonizo of Sutri's book *De vita christiana* (written between 1090 and 1095), which has not hitherto received due attention, is especially important. It contains a collection of prayers for the Christian knight, in which early Christian ethics, ancient Roman military discipline, and the Germanic *Gefolgschaft* idea are combined. Erdmann carries his presentation down to the first crusade. Its knightly ethos is mirrored in the earliest French epics. These knights of *ca.* 1100 have nothing to do with courtly love or courtly culture. The three phenomena are essentially and radically different. *Ca.* 1100 we have, in northern France, a knightly caste which has grown up out of the Germanic *Gefolgschaft* and has received the ethical stamp of the Church, but which is without courtly love and courtly coloring; in southern France, the first exemplars of courtly love poetry and courtly, non-knightly culture.[31] As late as 1159, John of Salisbury, in his *Policraticus*, gives a sharp criticism of the *curiales* and at the same time a "Christian mirror of knighthood." [32]

---

[31] Norway occupies an exceptional position. There the old Germanic *Gefolgschaft* —without horsemen and hence without knighthood—survived and received the gift of courtly culture in the thirteenth century through the instrumentality of King Haakon Haakonsson. To this end the king had Old French verse romances translated. We have the precipitate of these efforts in the so-called *Hirdskra*, a combination of *Gefolgschaft* law and the courtly code of manners (*Das norwegische Gefolgschaftsrecht*, translated by Rudolf Meissner [1938] = *Germanenrechte*, Vol. V).

[32] Cf. W. Berges, *Die Fürstenspiegel des hohen und späteren Mittelalters* (1938), 141.

The medieval Latin "court satire" [33] of the twelfth century deserves a separate study. Finally, it must also be borne in mind that Islam too developed an ideal of knighthood, which exhibits "striking coincidences" with that of the Christian West.[34] But Islam also produced a theory of courtly love.[35] The Spanish-Arabic culture, its ideals and poetic forms, extended its influence into southern France.[36] These indications perhaps suffice to show that we need a new discipline of medieval studies, upon the broadest foundation.

[33] After the *Policraticus*, there should be named, among others: Nigel Wireker with his *Tractatus contra curiales et officiales clericos*; Walter Map, *De nugis curialium*; Giraldus Cambrensis, *De principis instructione*, etc.

[34] For a preliminary orientation I recommend Franz Taeschner's article in *Forschungen und Fortschritte* (1943), 28 f.—Cf. also Georg Jacob, *Der Einfluss des Morgenlandes auf das Abendland* (1924); W. B. Ghali, *La tradition chevaleresque des Arabes* (Paris, 1919); S. Singer, *Germanisch-romanisches Mittelalter* (1935), 151 ff.

[35] One of the principal works is ibn-Hazm al Andalusi's (d. 1064) *Necklace of the Dove* (*Das Halsband der Taube* [Leiden, 1941], translated by Max Weisweiler).

[36] Cf. Ramón Menéndez Pidal, *Poesía árabe y poesía europea* (Madrid, 1941).

THE APE AS METAPHOR

The metaphorical use of *simia* is frequent in the twelfth and thirteenth centuries.[1]

1. John of Salisbury, *Metalogicon* (ed. Webb, 130, 11): *Mathematicus ab antiquis dictus est simia naturalium philosophorum.*

2. Josephus-Iscanus, *De bello Troiano*, II, 546 ff.:

> ... *fallenda senectus,*
> *Non fingenda fuit: o si ad certamina formae*
> *Illa potens Beroe staret socianda Dionae,*
> *Incuteret celebrem simulatrix simia risum?*

3. Alanus ab Insulis, *Sententiae* (PL, CCX, 249 D): *Quid mundanae potestates, nisi potestatum histriones? Quid saeculares dignitates, nisi dignitatum larvae et simiae?*

4. Alanus (*SP*, II, 494): *famae simulatio falsa simia laudis.*

5. John of Hanville (*SP*, I, 295): *simia morum hypocrisis.*

6. *Ibid.*, 332: *Sidonis acus, naturae simia.*

7. *Ibid.*, 308: *simius humanae naturae simia.*

8. Peter of Blois (*PL*, CCVII, 115 D) calls beer *simia vini.*

9. Geoffrey of Vinsauf (Faral, 210, 446): *simia doctorum.*

10. Anonymus (Faral, 334, 125):

> *Garrulitas capitis, verbosae simia linguae.*

11. Eberhard the German (Faral, 341, 111):

> *Florent hypocritae, sapientum simia ...*

12. *Idem* (Faral, 370, 984): *simia doctoris.*

13. Jean de Meun says of art (*Roman de la Rose*, 16029 ff.):

> *Si garde coment Nature euvre,*
> *Car mout voudrait faire autel euvre,*
> *E la contrefait come singes.*

14. Dante, V.E., I, 11, 7 on the Sardinians: *grammaticam tanquam simie homines imitantes.*

15. Dante, *Inf.*, XXIX, 139:

> *Com' io fui di natura buona scimia.*

Simia, then, is a fashionable word in Latin school poetry. It appears to have been introduced by Alan, who in the thirteenth century was also a model "for vernacular

---

[1] In his *Literaturästhetik des europäischen Mittelalters* (1937), H. H. Glunz had used the concept "ars simia veri" in support of his erroneous constructions. A philological rectification seemed necessary. I published a critical discussion of Glunz's book in ZRPh, LVIII (1938), 1–50.

European poetry."[2] *Simia* can be applied not only to persons but also to abstractions and artifacts which assume the appearance of being something they are not. The real ape (*simius*) becomes the *simia*[3] when he imitates man (Example 7), as an example of which the elder Pliny (*HN*, VIII, 54, 80) had adduced the fondness of apes for playing draughts. An unintelligent imitator could thus be called *simia*. However, this use of the word is very rare in Antiquity.[4] According to the dictionaries (to which even the material for the *Thesaurus*, as the editors kindly inform me, adds nothing), there are only three examples of it: 1. in the younger Pliny: "stoicorum simia" (*Ep.*, I, 5, 2); 2. in Julius Capitolinus: "Titianus orator dictus est simia temporis su, qua cuncta imitatus esset" (*Script. hist. Aug.*, *Maximinus iunior*, 33, 5); 3. in Sidonius: "oratorum simia" (*Ep.* I, 1, 2) with reference to 2.

Now Sidonius became a model of style again in the twelfth century. The ape metaphor belongs to the *mos sidonianus*.

For the twelfth century Sidonius and Horace had equal weight as teachers of rhetoric. When Sidonius taught: "Natura comparatum est ut ni omnibus artibus hoc sit scientiae pretiosior pompa quo rarior"[5] (*Ep.*, II, 10, 6), this could not but have the force of a binding legacy of antique aesthetics, could not but strengthen the modern poet's pride in his hard-won skill in an ornate Latin. Even where—or indeed precisely where—Sidonius misunderstood Horace, he exercised an authoritative influence. Thus Sidonius (*Carmina*, 22, 5) praises Statius (he calls him "Papinius noster") because he "ut lyricus Flaccus in artis poeticae volumine praecipit, multis isdemque purpureis locorum communium pannis semel inchoatas materias decenter extendit." Horace's well-known warning against sewing on "purple patches," Sidonius not only fails to understand but changes into its opposite. This is repeated by Sigebert of Gembloux, an admirer of Sidonius:

> Scis quoque materiam quod viribus equiperandam
> Edicit Flaccus, ne grave vincat onus.
> Idem purpuream iubet intertexere tramam,
> Ut placeat melius si varietur opus.

In his *Passio ss. Thebeorum* Sigebert accordingly makes many digressions and boasts of it (cf. for example l. 664): He believes that he is obeying a Horatian precept.

The metaphor also passed into Italian Renaissance biographies of artists. Filippo Villani calls Giotto's pupil Stefano "simia naturae," obviously in reference to our example 15 (cf. Julius von Schlosser, "Lorenzo Ghibertis Denkwürdigkeiten" in *Kunstgeschichtliche Jahrbücher der K.K. Zentralkommission*, IV [1910], 132). Gelli in his dialogues (1564) calls art itself "scimia della natura" (*ibid.*, 133), as

---

[2] K. Burdach, *Berl. SB.* (1933), 612.—I should now (1952) like to add the following from the *Praeexercitamina* of Priscian: "Imitatores aliquos hominum volumus ostendere, hic simiis est locus" (Keil, III, 430, 13).

[3] On this cf. Merchie, *Musée Belge*, XXV (1921), 148.

[4] Claudian, *In Eutropium*, I, 302 f. has *simius* in a simile.

[5] A guiding principle of literary Mannerism! Does the French *précieux* stem from it? Editions of Sidonius appeared at Paris in 1598 (by Wowerius), 1599 and 1609 (by Savaron), 1614 and 1652 (by Sirmond).

Jean de Meun had done (our example 13). Shakespeare applies the topos to Giulio Romano (*Winter's Tale*, V, 2, 108).

Boileau calls himself

Écolier ou plutôt singe de Bourdaloue

(*Sat.*, 10, 346). Here we hear the echo of "oratorum simia" once again. The expression then passed into the dictionary of the French Academy: "Cet écrivain affecte le style sentencieux et concis: c'est un singe de Sénèque, de Tacite."

SPAIN'S CULTURAL "BELATEDNESS"

Vernacular literature begins in Spain considerably later than in France. The Latin culture of the twelfth century reaches there quite belatedly too. Hence Spanish literature, down to the end of the seventeenth century, preserves medieval characteristics which give it a physiognomy of its own. There are yet other symptoms of cultural "belatedness" in Spain. Are they perhaps to be understood in the light of Spain's national and economic development? Is there "belatedness" here too? Claudio Sánchez-Albornoz answered this question affirmatively in the *Revista de Occidente*, II (December, 1923), 294 ff. I give a résumé of his interpretation. It is a matter of indifference to us whether the specialists agree with it or not. If they do not, they must replace it by another. We may make use of his theory in the same sense, with the same benefit, and also with the same suspension of judgment, as we did the theories of Toynbee, Bergson, and Pirenne.

Sánchez-Albornoz' essay is entitled "España y Francia en la edad media" and it develops the following ideas: "The Franks and the Goths were on different cultural levels when they invaded the Empire. The Goths came to Spain after they had lived with Rome for a century. The Franks were still wholly untouched by Roman influence. They had no idea what to do with the Roman administrative system in Gaul, it was too complicated for them. They had to create a new system of legal relations, and they did so through institutions of Germanic origin, which finally led to feudalism. The Visigoths, who had made their way from the Danube to Spain centuries earlier, allowed the Roman administrative forms to remain. Hence in Visigothic Spain there did not occur the anarchy which very early gained a footing in the Merovingian kingdom and from which new forms then developed. But the Roman machinery of government degenerated in the hands of the Goths, and the state founded by Alaric was in crisis when the Arabs broke in.—In Spain the Gothic forms of life at first remained in existence under the Arab superstructure. In Andalusia in the tenth century there were still Spaniards who knew no Arabic. In the north of Spain in the eighth and tenth centuries there were in the main only mountaineer-horsemen on the heights of the Cantabrian range, who descended upon the Arabic divisions and then retired to their mountains. The territory between the Douro and the mountains was gradually depopulated. All fled from the accursed land which was ravaged by Saracens and Christians. It was not until the second half of the ninth century that the Christian reconquest began in the highlands north of the Douro. There towns, strongholds, and monasteries were established. In the newly conquered country there was no working population. Hence there could develop no military caste who had the soil tilled by a resident peasantry. The freemen whom the king allowed to establish themselves as landholders formed a class of small and middling proprietors. Both the great landowner and the landless man were lacking. Instead, land syndicates, collectivistic in constitution, arose. A group of families joined together and formed an autarchic community which was also legally independent and which cultivated the land in common. Perhaps this proprietorial system was the foundation for the historical fact that in Spain the people have always played a decisive role. In these conditions a feudal state could not arise. In this way Spain dropped into the rear-guard. Its development into a feudal state was delayed for some three centuries; and when it came, it was too late to be fully worked out. Herein are rooted the differences which set Spain apart from the Middle Ages in the North. In the tenth and eleventh centuries, to be sure, the landlord system arose in León and Castille. But in Spain it never attained to the same importance as in France. The people never vanished from the scene as a decisive factor. As a result of the belated establishment of the landlord system, towns grew up very early in the valley of the Douro. On the other hand the monarchy in León and Castille was never so weakened as in tenth-century France. The continuous state of war strengthened the authority of the crown, and the freemen formed a counterpoise to the nobility. Every new thrust toward the south brought the monarchy new land and with it new power. These are the grounds of Spain's difference from Europe."

Spain's cultural "belatedness" of course in no sense signifies a "backwardness," in the sense either of the old or the new progressivism. Rather, it brought to the Spanish period of florescence the rich content of the Middle Ages, and insofar was productive. But if one wishes to understand the autonomy of Spanish development, one must take into account the various forms of Spain's "belatedness." This may be made clear by an example.

In his *Historia de las ideas estéticas* Menéndez y Pelayo referred to the *Visión delectable* of Alfonso de la Torre and printed two chapters from it (Vol. II, 280 and 330 ff.). The book (accessible in *BAE*, XXXVI, 338 ff.) is an encyclopedia in the form of an allegorical novel. It treats of the seven liberal arts, then of logic, natural history, ethics, politics, economics. It was written between 1430 and 1440 and printed *ca.* 1480. Spanish critics rate it highly because of its style: "Es sin duda la obra maestra de nuestra prosa didactica del siglo XV" (Menéndez y Pelayo, *op. cit.*, p. 280, n.; *cf. idem, Orígenes de la Novela*, I, 123 f.). J. P. Wickersham Crawford published a thorough study of the book and analysis of its sources in *Publications of the Modern Language Association* (1913), 188 ff. and *Romanic Review* (1913), 58 ff. Fitzmaurice Kelly (*A New History of Spanish Literature* [1926], 108 f.) knew Wickersham Crawford's studies but gives an incomplete and to some degree inaccurate account of them. The *Visión delectable* was much read. A Catalan translation appeared in 1484 (cf. A. Morel-Fatio in Gröber's *Grundriss*, II, 2, 110), new editions of the original in 1489, 1496, 1526, 1538, 1554. Domenico Delphini produced an Italian translation in 1556, with the author's name omitted. This was translated back into Spanish by the Spanish Jew Francisco de Cáceres and published in 1623 at Frankfurt. In this form the book appeared again at Amsterdam in 1663. In 1750 it was put on the *Index*. Now this book, which maintained itself for so long and had such a remarkable career, is nothing but a skillful compilation. Wickersham Crawford's exhaustive references show that the author took everything from earlier sources: from Martianus Capella, Isidore, Alan, al-Ghazālī. Finally, the philosophical and theological portions are taken from the "Guide of the Perplexed," the principal work of the Jewish philosopher Moses Maimonides of Córdoba (1135–1204). Wickersham Crawford has made it seem probable that the author of the *Visión delectable* was a Jew converted to Christianity, but that he was considered a *judaizante* and was executed in 1485 at the instigation of the Inquisition (*PMLA* [1913], 211 f.). Although he wrote in the fifteenth century, Alfonso de la Torre is almost untouched both by the Latin Scholasticism of the thirteenth century and by genuine Aristotelianism. What he gives to the Spain of the fifteenth to the seventeenth century is an eclectic rehandling of learning which goes back partly to late Antiquity and the Pre-Middle Ages (Martianus Capella and Isidore), partly to the Latin Renaissance of twelfth-century France (Alan), partly to the heretical Aristotelianism of the Jewish and Arabic thinkers of twelfth-century Spain. In other words: An author who writes in 1440 and is published in 1480 can find readers in Spain (indeed on down into the seventeenth century), although he practically ignores all that European literature, science, and philosophy have produced since 1200—not only Thomism, that is, but also Humanism and the Early Italian Renaissance.[1] Lope, in his description of the palace of the liberal arts in the fifth book of his *Arcadia* (1598) still follows the *Visión delectable* almost word for word (cf. Wickersham Crawford in *Modern Language Notes* [1915], 13) and thus indirectly follows Alan's *Anticlaudianus*. The *Visión delectable* also contains a chapter on rhetoric (I, 3; BAE, XXXVI, 346 ff.). As masters of the art there appear in it, among others, "los elegidos profetas y sabios," together with "Cidonio" (= Apollinaris Sidonius) and Virgil.

[1] In Part II, ch. 16 (*BAE*, XXXVI, 397 f.) he names as representatives of true wisdom "en los gentiles: Anaxágoras, Platon y Aristóteles; en los judíos: rabi Aquiba et rabi Abrahan et Benazra [Abraham ben Meir ibn Ezra, d. 1167] et maestre Moisen de Egipto [Maimonides, who died in Cairo]; en los moros ha sido opinión de Alfarrabio, Avicena et Algacel; y de los cristianos han sido, segun pienso, Alberto Magno et Gil ermitano [= Aegidius of Rome, 1247–1316] et otros muchos."

GOD AS MAKER

In the Platonic mythopoeia of the *Timaeus*, God appears as demiurge, that is, as architect and maker of the cosmos. The *Timaeus* is, as we know, the only work of Plato's that the Middle Ages possessed. It exercised the strongest possible influence —by way of Cicero, of African Platonism, of Chalcidius, and of Boethius (*Cons.*, III, *Metrum* 9). Cicero translates the Greek δημιουργός by *fabricator* and *aedificator* (*Ciceronis paradoxa* . . . ed. Plasberg, 159 f.). Chalcidius uses *opifex, genitor, fabricator* in the same sense (ed. Wrobel, p. 24). For *artifex* in the sense "de deo sive natura fabricantibus" the *Thesaurus* gives examples from Cicero, Seneca, Apuleius, and the fathers. In the same sense *architectus* occurs in Cicero, Apuleius, Irenaeus. Later, Gnosticism distinguished the demiurge from the highest and only perfect God. Origen, on the other hand, revives in the Christian sense the Platonic idea of the divine demiurge, whose creation is a perfectly beautiful work of art. But in the acceptance, transformation, and development of the Greek idea by Christianity, the decisive factor was the influx of analogous concepts from the Bible. Various components must here be distinguished. God created heaven and earth "et omnis ornatus eorum" (Gen. 2:1). He made man "ad imaginem suam" (Gen. 1:27). He ordered all things "in mensura et numero et pondere" (Sap. 11:21). From his works he may be known as "artifex" (Sap. 13:1). Abraham "expectabat . . . civitatem, cuius artifex et conditor (τεχνίτης καὶ δημιουργός) Deus" (Hebr. 11:10). New, and significant for aftertimes, was the idea of man as the image of God, which in Augustine's psychology led to the concept of the soul as imaging the threefold God. The moulding of the human body from clay next suggested the comparison of God to a potter, which is already implicit in Isaiah 29:16, so that *figulus* is frequently used throughout patristic literature as = *Deus creator*,[1] to which Greek mythology afforded parallels (Prometheus as "figulus saeculi novi" in Phaedrus, *Fabularum appendix*, 4, 1). The measure-and-proportion aesthetics of Sap. 11:21 was also in harmony with the Platonic tradition. Occasionally (e.g., in Alan, *PL*, CCX, 711 C) the verse "Juncturae femorum tuorum sicut monilia quae fabricata sunt manu artificis" (Cant. 7:1) is allegorically applied to the *Deus artifex*. Finally Genesis 3:21, in which God appears as a tailor ("fecit . . . Adae et uxori tunicas pelliceas"), must also be adduced. All these ideas of Biblical origin can enter into the most various relations with the antique tradition. From the wealth of examples I give only three.

Marbod of Rennes (*PL*, 171, 1697):

> *Si genus humanum sumus hac sub lege creati,*
> *Ut quidquid gerimus fugitivae tempore vitae*
> *Transeat, et nosmet tandem simul intereamus,*

[1] *Figulus* applied to Christ in Alan (*PL*, CCX, 793 B) and in the *Arundel Sammlung*, p. 529: "Vase prodit figulus." Cf. also *Thesaurus*, *s.v. figmen*. Point of departure presumably Romans 9:21.—The Stoics also know the comparison to a potter: A. Brinkmann, *Quaestiones de dialogis Platoni falso addictis* (Bonn dissertation, 1891, 20 ff.).—Lactantius, *De opif. Dei*, I, 2, 11 (*CSEL*, XXVII, pp. 5 f.).

Insipiens opifex reprehendendusque videtur,
Cuius opus vanum veluti vas fictile transit.
Sic faber ignavus per opus culpatur ineptum,
Artificemque suum reprehendit fabrica nutans.

. . . .

Sed cum sit sapiens, immo sapientia, qui nos
Condidit atque sua signavit imagine mentem,
Cui formata luto commisit membra regenda,
Non est credendum nos funditus interituros . . .

. . . .

Sed neque justitiae dabitur locus Omnipotentis,
Per quam pro meritis referantur praemia cuique.

Ergo necesse fuit varios effingere motus
Et de diversis unum compingere mundum,
Quo velut in stadio longo certetur agone,
Dum genus humanum per tempore tendit ad aevum.

Alan (*SP*, II, 468 f.): "Deus . . . tanquam mundi elegans architectus tanquam aureae fabricae faber aurarius, velut stupendi artificii artificiosus artifex, tanquam admirandi operis operarius opifex . . . mundialis regiae admirabilem speciem fabricavit."

Matthew of Vendôme (Faral, 192, 9 f.):

Do grates figulo vas, fabro fabrica, regi
Servus, plasmanti plasma, propago patri.

For an understanding of the entire development the following remains to be considered. Together with the *Deus artifex* Antiquity already knows the parallel theme *Natura artifex*. The *artificium* of the two is the same. Production of the world and mankind, architecture, pottery, the art of the goldsmith, occasionally also painting,[2] theater direction,[3] weaving,[4] are the forms of this *artificium*. The only other art which appears with a similar function is music. The world as song—this is a thought of Augustine's. "Carmen universitatis" (*De musica*, 6, 29) is a concept from Augustine's musico-mathematical speculations and should not be translated by "poem." [5]—This image of Augustine's was then taken over by Bonaventura: "Divinae autem dispositioni placuit, mundum quasi carmen pulcherrimum quodam discursu temporum venustare" (ed. Quaracchi, Vol. II, *dist.* 13, 316 a).

Thus far the literary tradition brings us. But to elucidate the topos *Deus artifex* completely we must go behind it to the myths of the ancient world. There, in both East and West, we find numerous concurring accounts according to which the creation of the world and man goes back to the handiwork of a God—a god who appears now as weaver, now as needleworker, now as potter, and now as smith: "almost everywhere the primordial creation is burdened with the earthly weight

---

[2] Hildebert in Hauréau, *Mélanges poétiques de Hildebert*, p. 9.
[3] Borinski, *Die Antike in Poetik und Kunsttheorie*, I, 23.
[4] Alan, *Anticlaudianus* (*SP*, II, 362).
[5] Cf. W. Hoffmann, *Philosophische Interpretation der Augustinusschrift de arte musica* (Marburg dissertation, 1931).—Gilson, *La Philosophie de saint Bonaventure* (1924), 172, 206, 210.

of a lowly handicraft, with the toil of physical demiurgy" (Robert Eisler, *Weltan-mantel und Himmelszelt* [1910], 235). "It cannot be denied," Eisler con-tinues, "that the legend of creation thereby suffered a loss of sublimity in the eyes of later generations—indeed, that their mythical handiwork actually operated to diminish the prestige of individual gods. A figure like the ugly, sooty, limping devil whom his wife betrayed with a great Olympian, like that poor butt of a Hephaestus in Demodocus' song, sufficiently explains why later supernaturalism felt obliged to distinguish the creator of the universe from the Logos, the *ideator mundi*, as a sort of subordinate handyman." The sociological explanation for the divine handiwork may be referred to in Eisler. In our connection, what is of importance is to see that the world-creator of the *Timaeus* is a sublimation of the mythical artisan-god. Both elements then fuse with the potter, weaver, and smith god of the Old Testament in the medieval topos of the *Deus artifex*.[6] In seventeenth-century Spain these semi-nal ideas undergo a magnificent development as a theocentric theory of art.

[6] The following are additional references: Praechter, *Hierokles* (1901), 21 f. and 153.—Seneca, *Nat. quaest.*, II, 45, 1; *Ep.*, 65, 19 and 71, 14.—Himerius Düb-ner, p. 88, § 6 (God as the great sophist in heaven).—Hugh of St. Victor (*PL*, CLXXVI, 745 D).

THEOLOGICAL ART-THEORY IN THE SPANISH LITERATURE OF THE SEVENTEENTH CENTURY [1]

In the year 1627 there appeared at Seville an anonymous *Panegyrico por la poesia;* a facsimile edition of 200 copies was published at Seville by E. Rasco in 1886. It seems hitherto to have aroused little interest. Menéndez y Pelayo mentions it in a note among seventeenth-century works of literary theory which deserved mention "but not analysis." Though the unknown author, he says, propounds some absurd ideas, such as that the devil writes poetry, he is a well-read man.

The *Panegyrico* is in the tradition of eulogies of arts and sciences. In Antiquity these commonly appeared as a topos in a didactic work on the subject concerned—usually in the prooemium to the entire work or to one of its books. Cicero has a eulogy of eloquence in *De inventione,* Varro (*Res rusticae,* III, 1, 1–8) one of agriculture. Vitruvius opens Book IX of his work on architecture with observations on the subject of how remarkable it is that state honors are bestowed on athletes, but not on writers, whose value to the community is, nevertheless, incomparably greater.[2] This provides the occasion for a "eulogy of literature." The poet of the *Aetna* has a eulogy of natural science (ll. 274 ff.). For the historian the *commendatio historiae* had become obligatory (Polybius, I, 1 and 5, 7–8; Diodorus, I, 1–5; Halm, *Rhetores latini minores,* 588). Of especial interest to us from the point of view of form is Plutarch's treatise "On Music." The bulk of the work is given over to the lectures of two musicologists. But among its structural elements we find familiar topoi. The first speaker gives a catalog of mythical discoverers, then enumerates the later improvements in the art (ch. 13). The second speaker says that though his predecessor can cite written records for his list of discoverers, oral tradition says that not a man but a god, "Apollo decked with all virtues," was the discoverer (ch. 14). Music inspires to virtuous actions and stands the test of the perils of war (ch. 26). He who would learn it must also know all other sciences and choose Philosophy as his teacher (ch. 32). Homer illustrates the use of music by the example of Achilles. He, like Heracles and many others, was a pupil of the wise Charon, who instructed them in music, righteousness, and medicine. He who in youth has attained to the "educational style" of music will never act ignobly, for he is harmonious in thought and deed (ch. 41). Music can quiet rebellion in the *polis* and heal the plague. It is man's thanks to God, and the means whereby the soul is purified and ordered (ch. 42). Here we have a model example of *laudatio* of an art. Its topics comprises the following points: 1. human and divine discoverers of the art; 2. its moral and political use; 3. encyclopedic knowledge and philosophy as preliminaries to the art; 4. catalog of heroes. The prooemium to Xenophon's *Cynegeticus* exhibits the same structure. It has a eulogy of hunting according to the

---

[1] The following is a partly abridged, partly revised version of an article which I published in 1939 in *RF*, LIII, 145–184. Readers interested in philology are referred there.

[2] Cf. Seneca, *Ep.*, 80, 2.—The modern enthusiasm for sports, "gymnastics," Olympic games, etc., is open to the same criticism.

following schema: 1. Hunting is a discovery of the gods Apollo and Artemis; 2. these bestowed it upon Chiron because of his uprightness; 3. the heroes Nestor, Peleus, Theseus, Odysseus, and others learned hunting from him; 4. hence hunting is to be highly prized; it makes youths eager for war, at the same time that it teaches them to think, speak, and act rightly. Oppian (or the Pseudo-Oppian) in his *Cynegetica* (II, 1–35) gave a catalog of heroes who favored hunting, in the form of an invocation to Artemis.

We found in Plutarch and Xenophon, along with the catalogue of heroes, the "discoverer topos." "Who discovered it?" is, as we know, a question which was dear to the hearts of the Greeks [3] and which may well be called a characteristic of their thinking.[4] In early Greece gods and heroes were named as discoverers; with Sophistic, human discoverers took their place. The contradiction between the two views—the "theological" and the "cultural-historical"—we found expressed in Plutarch, resolved in Xenophon. It reappeared in the controversy between the Aristotelian-Thomistic and the "theological" theory of art in trecento Italy. We shall find it in our *Panegyrico* too. The "discoverer topos" led, from the fourth century B.C., to catalogs of discoverers (*heuremata*-literature), which became longer and longer in late Antiquity. A well-known example occurs in the elder Pliny's *Natural History* (VII, ch. 56). The later Sophistic,[5] as well as Alexandrian theology (Clement of Alexandria, *Stromateis*, I, 74 f.), carried along this mass of material. We find traces of it in the Middle Ages, for example in Hugh of St. Victor (*PL*, CLXXVI, 765) and Godfrey of Viterbo (*Pantheon*, ed. Waitz, p. 137). The Renaissance compilers did not allow the theme to escape them: Polydore Virgil of Urbino (1470–1555) wrote *De inventoribus rerum* (and also *De prodigiis*). A versification of this book was supplied by Juan de la Cueva (printed in Sedano, *Parnaso español*, Vol. IX [1778]). In the drama of Calderón too (e.g., *Los tres mayores prodigios del mundo*), as is well known, "first discoveries" play a considerable role, as do *prodigios*.

But among the antique formal elements which the author of the *Panegyrico* employs—panegyric style, *commendatio*, catalog of notable persons (as substitute for the catalog of heroes), "discoverer topos"—there is yet another which is borrowed from a particular antique oratorical genre: the *protreptikos* (hortatory oration, *adhortatio*, *cohortatio*, *exhortatio*). This genre—introduced into literature by Antisthenes, Aristippus, Aristotle—usually pursues the end of exhorting the reader to the practice of philosophy. From the time of Philo of Larissa, Cicero's teacher, two parts of *protreptikos* were distinguished—the "endeictic" and the "apelenctic"; in the former the advantages of philosophy were demonstrated, in the latter its "opponents" or "detractors" ("vituperatores," still used by Schleiermacher [6]) were exposed. Concerning his unfortunately lost *Hortensius* Cicero says: "Nos universae philosophiae vituperatoribus respondimus in Hortensio" (*Tusc.*, III, 4). As the one or the other element predominated, the *protreptikos* more nearly approached the epideictic or defensive oration, the panegyric or apologetic genre. In late Antiquity

[3] Raised to the plane of philosophy by Peripateticism. Cf. Friedrich Leo, *Die griechisch-römische Biographie nach ihrer literarischen Form* (1901), 100.
[4] A. Kleingünther, *Protos heuretes* (1933).—M. Kremmer, *De catalogis heurematum* (Leipzig, 1890).
[5] Christ-Schmid, 825, n. 6.
[6] *Über die Religion. Reden an die Gebildeten unter ihren Verächtern* (1799).

the *protreptikos* dissolves its connection with philosophy, or, to put it more accurately, it can be put at the service of all *artes*. We have an "adhortatio ad artes addiscendas" (such is the usual title given to this Greek treatise) by Galen. The representatives of athletics appear in it as the "detractors" of the sciences and arts. All treatises whose title begins with "Defence . . ."—especially if they defend arts or sciences [7]—may be regarded as the "apelenctic" part of a *protreptikos*.

The ancient Roman mentality was interested in the practical. Hence Cicero [8] and Horace emphasized the use of poetry, the former allowing no doubt to remain that oratory stood above poetry. Tacitus reversed the relation in his *Dialogus de oratoribus*. He deplored the decay of Roman oratory and called poetry a "more sublime" eloquence. The chapters of the *Dialogus* in which the poet Maternus praises his art are the most significant thing Antiquity has left on the theme. In the Middle Ages poetry was so closely connected with the grammatical and rhetorical curriculum on the one hand and with music, ethics, and theology on the other, that the praise of poetry was not a recognized theme. Many medieval poets, to be sure, spoke of their art with enthusiasm and exaltation, but always only incidentally. It was not until the beginning of the fourteenth century that the Paduan Albertino Mussato wrote some epistles whose theme was the defence of poetry. We find another in the diploma of Petrarch's coronation as a poet (Burdach, *Rienzo und die geistige Wandlung seiner Zeit*, p. 509). Next comes Boccaccio (Book XV of his *Genealogiae deorum gentilium*), who also remains within the circle of medieval thought. The author of the *Panegyrico* names as predecessors, among others, the Humanists Guillaume Budé,[9] Petrus Crinitus,[10] Giraldi Cintio,[11] Patrizzi.[12]

In Spain we first find a "eulogy of poetry" in the Marqués de Santillana (*Prohemio e carta al condestable de Portugal*, c. 2; written *ca.* 1448). Next comes the poetics of Juan del Encina (1468?–1529?), printed in 1496. In the dedicatory epistle he shows the "dignity and antiquity" of poetry. Even the "vain heathen" honored the poet as *vates*, i.e., as singer of divine things. But many books of the Old Testament, too, are, as Jerome testifies, written in verse, and they are older than the poetry of the pagans. For the praise of poetry Juan del Encina then refers to Justin Martyr. As *exempla* of its effects he uses Tyrtaeus, Orpheus, Stesichorus. The climax comes with a reference to the hymns of the Church. The names of Hilary, Ambrose, and Augustine (because of his treatise on music) conclude the train of argument.

Let us listen to another eulogy of poetry, from a later period. Vicente Espinel prefaced his *Diversas rimas* (Madrid, 1591; not reprinted since) with a eulogy of poetry from the pen of Alonso de Valdés. The eulogy sets forth that there are two reasons for writing poetry: honor and reward. Both are bestowed by kings. Hence

---

[7] E.g., *Defence of Poetry* (Sidney and Shelley).—A title like *Défense et illustration de la langue française* (Du Bellay) brings out both elements of the *protreptikos*.

[8] In the *Pro Archia poeta*.

[9] Budaeus, *Annotationes in pandectarum libros* (1508). In this edition the *Poeticae laudes* appear f. CXXIX.

[10] Petrus Crinitus (= Pietro Ricci, 1465–1505), *De poetis latinis*. Cf. Saintsbury, *History of Criticism*, II, 27, and C. Trabalza, *La Critica letteraria nel Rinascimento* (1915), 53 f.

[11] Lilius Gregorius Gyraldus, *De poetis nostrorum temporum* (1551); reprinted by K. Wotke (Berlin, 1894).

[12] Francesco Patrizzi (1529–1597), *Trattato della poetica* (1582).

studies always flourish when rulers patronize them. Shining examples of this are Augustus and Philip II; Ninus and Sardanapalus warn us against the contrary. The dignity of poetry is shown, first, by the fact that it contains all other arts within itself: not only the "congruence" of grammar, the "subtlety" of philosophy, the "elegance" of rhetoric, but also the occult qualities of astrology and the marvels of theology. Second, by the esteem which it enjoys in the eyes of rulers, heroes, and philosophers. Alexander wept at the grave of Achilles. Scipio Africanus had Ennius buried in his own tomb. Plato deemed the poet Agathon worthy of his friendship. Eleanor of Aquitaine patronized Bernard of Ventadorn, the son of a baker, etc. Poetry is the mistress of all disciplines, for the subjects of all of them make up her material: the glory of God and of the heavenly kingdom; astrology, cosmogony; the "natures of things" (plants, herbs, animals, humors, etc.); fiction, history, fable; morals, customs, law; war and peace; the miracles of the Old and the New Testaments; the prophecies. Modern detractors of poetry are wrong, for Cicero quotes lines from Ennius, Aristotle from Homer, the jurists "have put their laws and rules into verse." The Holy Ghost spoke in verse through the mouth of David. Solomon, Jeremiah (Lamentations), and the Virgin Mary (*Magnificat*) wrote verse. Christ himself was a poet: for in Matthew 26:30 it is written: "et hymno dicto." Poetry, then, is sacred. The nine Muses correspond to the nine angelic choirs.

Among the defenders of poetry Lope de Vega is not to be sought in vain. To the Maecenas and poet Juan de Arguijo (d. 1623) he dedicated a short essay *Question sobre el honor debido a la poesia* (Sancha edition, IV, 513–522). Among the arguments are: Plato called poetry "sacred," as Ovid did poets, "with which both Cicero and Aristotle agree." Among barbarians, pagans, and Christians there has always been ritual poetry; "como se ve en nuestros hymnos santissimos, y yo tengo referido en mi Isidro." The attacks upon poetry are explained partly by the Christian rejection of pagan mythology, partly by offences against morals and decency of which many poets have been guilty, but which are now prevented by censorship. But chaste and innocent poetry—including the erotic—is irreproachable. Next comes a retrospect of earlier, and a brief consideration of contemporary Spanish poetry, in which the emphasis is laid upon poets of noble birth. Lope sets down his thoughts in careless succession. He always does so when he theorizes.

In Juan del Encina and Alonso de Valdés, one of the principal arguments is the view that many parts of the Bible are written in verse, a fact which bestows a divine dignity upon poetry. This doctrine, as we know, goes back to Jerome. It was the result of his study of the Bible and of his ecclesiastical Humanism. But Jerome was not interested in the origin of poetry. Theological speculation on poetry belongs to an earlier period of primitive Christian literature—the period during which Christianity began to emerge from the isolation of communal life and to make literary propaganda for itself. This took place about the middle of the second century. Writers appear who set themselves the task of defending the new faith and making it acceptable to educated pagans. These "apologists"—with certain exceptions, such as the Syrian Tatian, for example—are sympathetic to antique culture, especially the most important among them, Justin Martyr. They use trains of reasoning current among the Hellenized Jews (Philo, Josephus), which sought to demonstrate the conformity of the Jewish law with Greek philosophy, especially by taking over the system of allegorical exegesis developed in the Stoa, and by the so-called "authority of antiquity": the Jewish scriptures are older than the Greek. The latter knew and used the former. "The concepts run through a whole gamut of nuances, from the assumption of a revelation of the divine Logos in pagan philosophy to the idea of plagiarism of Holy Scripture or of a distortion of the truth by demons." [13] It is this last motif which appears in Justin, in whom "the beliefs, myths, and cults of the pagans appear as a deceitful invention of demons." [14] We saw above that, among the "absurd ideas" of the *Panegyrico*, Menéndez y Pelayo reckoned the notion that Lucifer wrote poetry; we shall see below how our anonymous author justifies his statement. But—and this has escaped the great Spanish critic—the absurdity stems from the apologist Justin, who shares a belief in demons with the pagan philosophers of his time.

The harmonistics of the apologists encountered resistance. About 200 Tertullian maintains that Christ can have had no literary education. Clement of Alexandria had to combat this view. But it is precisely his influence in the Alexandrian catechumenical schools which introduces the period of early Christian literature in which Christianity made peace with Greek philosophy and science; the period, that is, from the end of the second century to Constantine. Clement drew the ideal portrait of the "Christian gnostic." He develops an Orphic Christology, which is used again and again—as in the *Panegyrico*—as an argument of theological poetics. For Origen, later, the alliance between Greek philosophy and the Christian life, prepared by Clement, has "become a perfect amalgam which he defended no less against the enemies of speculation among orthodox believers than against the Gnostics . . . It was through this alliance that Christianity became a world religion." [15] Origen had taken over the antique plan of education which included the study of the poets and philosophers and had "merely supplemented it by a Christian superstructure." [16] This Hellenized Christianity, which has its last expression in Eusebius (263–339), is closely linked with Greek thought (Plato [17]), the Stoa, Posidonius. It is musal and speculative. But it was forced to leave the stage when, after Constantine's edict of toleration (313), Christianity set out on the road which was to make it the state religion. The Church is no longer dependent upon apologetics, it takes the offensive. It consolidates itself legally and dogmatically. The ecclesiastical writers of the fourth to sixth centuries are at the same time fighting churchmen. In embittered battle against the heretics, they establish a concept of orthodoxy which restricts speculation—above all in the Latin West—to an ever narrower domain. *Ca.* 400 there begins the dispute over the orthodoxy of Origen which ended in the sixth century with his condemnation. Christian speculation among the Greeks in the period from *ca.* 150 to *ca.* 300 on the one hand, and Latin theology from Augustine to Boethius on the other, exhibit characteristic differences, which the concept "patristics" easily cloaks but whose influence is still clearly to be detected on into the sixteenth and seventeenth centuries (and even today in the opposition between

---

[13] P. Wendland, *Die hellenistisch-römische Kultur* (1912), 397.
[14] H. Lietzmann, *Geschichte der alten Kirche*, II (1936), 178.
[15] Stählin in Christ-Schmid, 1329 f.
[16] H. Lietzmann, *Christliche Literatur* (1923), 9 f.
[17] Cf. R. Arnou's article "Platonisme des Pères" in the *Dictionnaire de Théologie catholique*, XII, 2 (1935), 2258: ". . . Aristote, pour eux, est le 'physicien,' quand il n'est pas l'athée. Platon est le 'philosophe,' un voyant supérieur chez qui on se plaît à retrouver l'écho des croyances chrétiennes."

western and eastern Christendom). A speculative, Platonizing theology will incline to draw its arguments from the Greek apologists and the fathers of the third century. And the same is true of "theological poetics" which, though it uses Jerome's "Biblical poetics" and his chronological reckoning which serves the "authority of antiquity," places them in a higher speculative context. Biblical poetics and the "authority of antiquity" were handed on to the entire Middle Ages in authoritative form by Isidore of Seville. With the characteristic national pride of the Spaniard, the Marqués de Santillana reproduces them in his poetics, in which he cites the authority of Isidore. Theological poetics was always welcomed by poets, because it permitted them to assign the highest rank among the arts and sciences to poetry. In Spain, Italian Aristotelianism could nowise affect it. It was briefly touched upon by Luis de Léon in the dedication of his collected poems. But we find it in him in the *Nombres de Cristo* (*Monte*; ed. de Onís, I, 175 f.) too. During the discussion of the name of Christ "monte," Marcelo quotes a stanza from a poem. His partner in the conversation, Juliano, finds the lines very good: No doubt, he says, this is due to the subject: it is the only subject fit for poetry. Marcelo agrees: poets who sing other subjects corrupt poetry; God has put poetry into the heart of man to draw it to heaven, whence poetry comes. Poetry is a "communication of the divine breath." The spirit of God gave the prophets not only visions of the invisible but also metrical form so that they might speak "in a higher manner" than other men, etc.

To understand the passage from "Biblical" to "theological" poetics, let us cast a glance at Spanish theology. It was revivified by Melchior Cano [18] (1509–1560). In him a trend which had been adumbrated since the beginning of the century reached its peak. Under the influence of Humanism, theology strives for a new basis and method. From arguments addressed to reason it turns to the arguments of authority and tradition; from scholastic dialectics to study of the original sources; from the speculative to the "positive" [19] method; from the barbaric language of the schools to Ciceronian Latin. Philosophical systematics is replaced by theological "topics," that is, the science—not of general forms of argument employable in syllogistic reasoning, but—of the sources of faith furnished by revelation and tradition. Melchior Cano's principal work *De locis theologicis* (Salamanca, 1563) gives a classification of these *loci*, which are characterized as "domicilia omnium argumentorum theologicorum." [20] Among Cano's ten *loci* the first place is given to proofs from Scripture, tradition, and the official teaching of the church; then come, in descending order of rank, patristics, scholastic theology, philosophy; finally—a substantial novelty—the "auctoritas historiae humanae," that is, history with its ancillary disciplines. In the opinion of Catholic historians Cano's work represents

---

[18] The most important recent studies are: M. Jacquin, "Melchior Cano et la théologie moderne" *Revue des sciences philosophiques et théologiques* [1920], 121 ff.); Albert Lang, *Die loci theologici des M. Cano* (1925); Gardeil, "Lieux théologiques" in *Dictionnaire de théologie catholique*, IV (1926), 712 ff.—On the rise of the concept of "positive" theology, cf. A. Stolz in *Divus Thomas* (1934), 327.—Cf. also Menéndez y Pelayo, *Ideas estéticas*, III[4], 153 ff.

[19] The concept of "positive" theology is still the subject of argument among Catholic thinkers. A Thomist like Gardeil finds in the Jesuit François Annat (1590–1670), Louis XIV's confessor from 1654, to whom Pascal addressed his two last *Provinciales*, "un glissement des lieux théologiques vers la théologie positive."

[20] The phrase is modeled upon Quintilian's definition of forensic *loci*. Theological topics leans upon rhetoric and dialectics.

"a real revolution in theological method" (Jacquin) and has for theology "the same classical significance" as has Thomas' *Summa* for philosophy (Gardeil).[21] What is its significance for the Spanish mentality of the sixteenth and seventeenth centuries? We are accustomed to separating Spanish philosophy of that period into Humanism and Neo-Scholasticism. Yet Cano's "positive" theology combines humanistic views with a respectful recognition of Thomism which yet reserves the right to criticize both Thomas and Aristotle.[22] Cano is a Humanist in the elegance of his style; in his aversion to the "frivolous arguments" and "sophisms" of late Scholasticism; in his return to a study of the sources. With the Humanism of the Germans (Rudolf Agricola was his model) and the French he shares the trend toward philological and historical studies which also include the language of the Old Testament. On the one hand, a turning away from Scholasticism; a conjunction of Hebrew, Greek, and Latin philology on the other—that is the position of Christian Humanism in the first third of the sixteenth century. It also influences Cano's theological reform. To his pupil Luis de Léon, who simultaneously imitates the Augustan poets and studies the Hebrew text of the Bible,[23] Cano imparted this form of Humanism, which finally goes back to Jerome. But together with this Humanism we find in Cano an appeal to the fathers, especially the Greek fathers. His reading of reformist literature, together with the discussions at the Council of Trent, to which Cano was sent in 1551 by Charles V, had led him to the conviction that the scholastic method was no longer suitable for the defence of the truths of the Catholic faith, that it was necessary, instead, to go back to the earliest church writers. More patristics, less Scholasticism—to many, in that age as in later periods of the church's history, that seemed the order of the day. When we come upon references to Justin Martyr, to Origen, to John of Damascus in our *Panegyrico*, or find Philo, Clement, Origen, Basil, and others cited in the seventeenth-century debates on painting,[24] these are reflections of the ideological trend indicated by Cano and his school. Finally, the value placed upon the "auctoritas historiae humanae." Translated into our terms, this means: the whole of profane history and literature is to be searched for what testimony it may afford to reinforce the doctrine of the church. This had already been the method of the apologists and of the Pre-Nicene Fathers. But through Cano it was incorporated into the theological system. It is the distinguishing mark of a universal, harmonizing attitude of mind which seeks to exploit the intellectual stock of pagan Antiquity too for a Christian philosophy of culture. It is intolerant of heretics and unbelievers, but not of the "studia humanitatis." This attitude sets its mark on the literature of the Spanish period of florescence too, and sharply distinguishes it from French and English thought in the seventeenth century. Spain had her Inquisition and her persecution of the Moors. But she had no Puritanism and no Jansenism. The boy Racine's teachers

---

[21] Naturally, the Thomists cannot admit this. On Thomas *S. th.*, I 8 ad 2, the editors of the "German Thomas" (Salzburg, n.d., Vol. I, p. 326) comment that the doctrine of the *loci theologici* was contained in this passage and that Cano only "expanded" it.

[22] The Spanish Jesuits did likewise. Cf. Menéndez y Pelayo, *op. cit.*, p. 178.

[23] Here we may also mention Benito Arias Montano (1527–98), who devoted six days of the week to Oriental and Biblical studies, and the seventh to writing Latin verse (Menéndez y Pelayo, *op. cit.*, 226 f.).

[24] Cf. the enumeration of Greek fathers in Menéndez y Pelayo's remarks (*op. cit.*, 226) on García Matamoros' rhetoric.

tore Heliodorus' *Aethiopica* out of his hands as sinful reading. The same romance could stimulate a Cervantes to emulation (*Los Trabajos de Persiles y Sigismunda*), could be rehandled for the stage by a Calderón (*Los Hijos de la fortuna, Teagenes y Cariclea*).[25] From the Thomist side the theology of Cano and his school was re-proached with not having avoided the danger of historicism, that is, of erudition run wild. This is of importance in our connection inasmuch as the Spanish treatises on the theory of art are in fact burdened with a plethora of quotations of the most heterogeneous kind. This is evident both in Calderón's essay on painting and in our *Panegyrico*. Nevertheless, Cano's school, we may say in sum, created an at-mosphere which was particularly favorable to the development of "Biblical" and "theological" poetics.

I will now give a brief summary of the *Panegyrico*. Poetry is august because it was instilled into man by God ("concedida infusamente del origen de los versos, que fue Dios"). But it enjoys little esteem, a fact of which Ovid already complained (Ovid's "Hei mihi! non multum carmen honoris habet" had already been quoted by Lope in the *Question* referred to above). According to Homer, it is "honorable" to listen to a poet when he is "like to the gods in voice" (*Odyssey*, IX, 3). Poetry was originally instituted to praise God. Its aim is not mere enjoyment. This the author will show. For he will thereby do a service to poets. Plato teaches that its friendship should be courted (?). Seven cities claimed to have been Homer's birth-place. Alexander honored Homer. Plato imitated the poets so far as he was able, and excluded them from his state because he imitated them: "por no tener a los ojos el testimonio de su hurto, ni el autor de lo que se abrogaua . . ." Petrarch was crowned on the Capitol. Ptolemy paid the Athenians a high price for the works of Euripides and raised a temple to the memory of Homer. Other honors were bestowed upon the Sicilian poet Geronimo Perdilebro (?); the Athenian poet Archimelos[26]; Claudian; Ennius; Statius; Silius Italicus; Martial, and so on.

The value of poetry is thus proved "inductively." Now begins a line of theologi-cal proof. According to the rabbinical interpretation the "springs of Jerusalem" in the last verse of Psalm 86 [A.V. 87] mean the poets. Vatable reads: "In thy springs, O Zion, are all water-wheels, studies, and conceits (*concetos*) of my mind."[27] The next authorities cited are Ambrose and Plato. The latter was the greatest enemy of poetry, but knew it best, as the third book of the *Laws*[28] shows. Praise from the lips of an enemy is the weightiest. As authorities for "poetic frenzy as a gift of heaven," Marsilio Ficino, Lucan, Ovid, Calpurnius Siculus, Cicero, Origen, Boc-caccio, and many others are summoned. From the testimony cited the "divinity" of poetry appears. And this in turn makes it impossible to see the end of poetry in mere enjoyment. Rather, it combines a pleasurable and a useful effect, as Plutarch, Justin Martyr (*liber quaestionum ad orthodoxos*[29]), and others confirm. Strange

[25] On the popularity of the *Aethiopica* among the Spanish Erasmists, cf. Bataillon, *Érasme et l'Espagne*, p. 663.

[26] Court poet of Hiero II (Athenaeus, V, 209 b).

[27] In the passage from the Psalms cited the "fontes Jerusalem" do not appear. They occur in the Psalms only once: "In ecclesiis benedicite Deo Domino de fonti-bus Jerusalem" (Ps. 67:27 [A.V. 68:26]). Presumably this is the passage meant.

[28] The reference is obviously to *Laws*, III, 700–701, though the passage accuses poets of having destroyed the old order of music and poetry.

[29] The *Quaestiones et responsiones ad orthodoxos* is a work of the Pseudo-Justin; see Stählin, *op. cit.*, 1287.

witnesses! The author too is of the opinion that the argument is more convenient than conclusive ("mas de conueniencia que de fuerza"). Moreover, Aristotle valued poetry very highly and called it the rudder of human life (?). The principal witnesses, then, are Plutarch and a Christian apologist. Aristotle is named last and incidentally, on very surprising grounds. Nothing more clearly shows the distance of the *siglo de oro* from Aristotelianism.

The author now passes to "infallible reasonings" ("infalibles") "though with scholastic arguments." All reality is divided into the speculative and the practical. Practice is divided into *agibilia* (jurisprudence) and *factibilia* (mechanical arts, grammar, poetry, rhetoric, dialectics, logic). But poetry comprises all sciences and arts, hence both practice and speculation, and is therefore nobler than philosophy.[30] It can therefore be called a science. In any case it is the highest and eldest of the arts, as Patrizzi and Strabo bear witness. Finally comes the definition of poetry: it imitates human actions, habits, and emotions, consists in fabulatory discourse, is useful while it pleases, keeps men from vice and wins them to virtue (the author is here apparently studying Horace so closely that he forgets the theological derivation and justification of poetry). Now a brief consideration of the four genres of poetry: the epic poet ("poeta heroyco") inflames the mind to lofty deeds; the tragic poet arouses sympathy with the unfortunate; the comic poet teaches the ignorant populace; the lyric poet raises the soul from the love of creatures to the love of the creator.[31] But poetry can also proffer scientic teaching in artistic form. Like philosophy, it contains all arts and sciences, as Strabo testifies. According to the view of the ancients, it is a "Filosofia principal." [32] It can treat theological problems, can put logic as well as other sciences into verse. Vitruvius regretted that he could not put his "divine Architecture" into a poem. Poetry is better able to convince than logic. It inflames the warrior's courage (Tyrtaeus), makes the sun stand still (Joshua), is superior to artillery [33] (2. *Paral.* 20, 20 ff.), and in addition has a healing effect upon soul and body.[34] "En fin la Poesia es la sal que nos preserua de la corrucion deste siglo, es el primor con que se realzan y esmaltan los concetos, y el engaste perfectamente labrado a la piedra, que sin el no descubriera valor, ni hermosura." The dignity of poetry is exemplified by Marino's obsequies, which took place in Rome in 1626.

Most authors who have treated of the origin of poetry rely upon Augustine's account of the theological poets. As discoverers, he names Hermes Trismegistus, Orpheus, Musaeus, Linus, Hesiod. Others go farther back—to Moses and even to the days of Nimrod. "Pero tuuo mas noble origen, que fue en Dios: el qual lo dispuso y ordeno todo con tal medida,[35] que no es otra cosa (como dize Pitagoras)

[30] This is in contradiction to Aristotle (for whom poetry belongs to the *factibilia*), and to Scholasticism.

[31] The reference is doubtless to hymns.

[32] This had already been asserted by Alonso López (El Pinciano) in his *Filosofia antigua poetica* (1596), following the Platonist Maximus of Tyre. The late antique and medieval equating of philosophy and poetry is, then, still in force.

[33] ". . . esta fuerza de los versos, superior a la artilleria, esperimentaron tambien los Amonitas, Moabitas e Idumeos, quando el capitan Josafa los vencio, poniendo en la vanguardia un esquadron de Leuitas, que fueron diziendo el Salmo 135 con que començo la batalla, y apellido la vitoria."

[34] We saw that, according to Plutarch, music is a specific against the plague.

[35] Wisdom of Solomon 11:21.

sino vna cierta manera de verso limado, o vna musica peregrina (como dize Platon) de muchas naturalezas, y una correspondencia."

Augustine compared the creation to an epigram or sonnet.[36] According to Basil and Ambrose, the world is a work of art which extols its creator. The Bible contains perfect poetry ("lo mas culto de la Poesia"). God himself makes use of poetic fictions, for example, when he causes the prophet Hosea (11:4) to allude to the Incarnation. Even more: all poetic style (meters, figures, tropes) stems from the Bible. This is taught by Cyril of Alexandria, Tertullian, Jerome, Augustine, Cassiodorus. The first poets after the creation of the world were Lucifer and the angels, who praised God in hymns (Job 38:4 and 7). According to Cardinal Ximenez, the Archangel Michael instructed Adam in poetry. After Adam, Cain, Abel, and David were poets. In the Psalms there occur such rhetorical figures as anadiplosis, epanaphora, aposiopesis, epistrophe, which we also find in Ovid, Virgil, Terence, and Martial.

We may regard it as certain that Christ too was a poet since, by divine inspiration, he was master of all sciences and arts. This sounds strange to a modern reader. But it is in harmony both with the church's general dogma and with the particular dogma of the *sapientia Christi*. It is part of the permanent stock of Catholic theology. The first manual of that theology is the *Quattuor libri sententiarum* of Peter Lombard (*ca.* 1150), a "synthèse à peu près complète de la doctrine, dont les grandes lignes se retrouvent encore dans le programme actuel . . . Essentiellement impersonelle, l'oeuvre se présente, du point de vue littéraire, comme un résumé sans vie ni chaleur, sans guère de vue philosophique non plus, mais bien ordonné . . ." (de Ghellinck, *L'Essor*, I, 71 f.). There we read (III, *dist.* 14): "dicimus animam Christi per sapientiam sibi gratis datam in Verbo Dei, cui unita est, unde etiam perfecte intelligit, omnia scire quae Deus scit, sed non omnia posse quae potest Deus" (*PL*, CXCII, 783). This doctrine, which is also to be found in Albert, Thomas, Bonaventura, had penetrated into vernacular literature through Luis de León: "In the Knowledge of God are the ideas and grounds of all things, and in that soul (Christ's) is knowledge of all arts and sciences" (*Nombres de Cristo*, ed. de Onís, I, p. 99, 18 ff.).

Our anonymous author uses this dogma and gives it a fanciful interpretation. Christ employed logic when he refuted the scribes; rhetoric in his parables and in his letter to Abgar of Edessa, to whom he also sent his portrait executed by his own hand. There are various reasons for supposing that he himself composed poems, as did his glorious mother (in the *Magnificat*). We men ourselves are, according to Paul (Eph. 2:10) poetry [37] of Christ (αὐτοῦ γάρ ἐσμεν ποίημα, *ipsius sumus factura*). Clement of Alexandria calls man "un hermoso Hymno de Dios, compuesto en justicia." [38] But the Devil too was a poet: he composed the oracles, which as every-

---

[36] The allusion is to the "carmen universitatis" (*supra*, p. 545).

[37] "Poesia de Cristo." The author here takes advantage of the double meaning of ποίημα.

[38] In Clement's *Protreptikos* (Hortatory Address to the Pagans) I do not find this phrase verbatim. But Christ appears in it as the new Orpheus who is, however, at the same time the "new song," the "harmony of the world," and the divine Logos. He "despised lyre and harp, lifeless instruments; through the Holy Spirit he filled this world, and also that world in little, man . . . with harmony and praises God with that many-voiced instrument man . . . The Lord made man a beautiful

one knows were in verse.[39] For though through his fall he lost "the works of the will," yet "the works of the mind remained to him, as to the other angels."[40] Though once, when he was present in the body of a man possessed, he was ordered by the exorcist to recite some verses and made a mistake in one stanza, as is well attested, "it was only because he wished to do so, not from ignorance." Paul quoted lines from Aratus, Menander, and Epimenides. John of Damascus,[41] Juvencus, Fortunatus, Licentius,[42] Sedulius, Prudentius, Tertullian, Gregory, Cyprian, Thomas Aquinas, Orientius, and many others were Christian poets. There follows a list of popes, emperors, and kings who composed poetry. In Spain poetry had been cultivated from time immemorial, especially in Andalusia, where, according to Strabo, there were poets before the Flood. "Donde se conocera bien quan capaz es nuestro idioma de auentajarse en este Arte a algunas naciones que nos tienen por barbaros, y somoslo cierto, an el descuydo que ay del pulimento con el Arte, que como mina de oro finissimo, se ha descubierto en tantas partes: pero es el daño, que con preceto y medio, algunos nos arrojamos a hombrear con los Virgilios y Horacios de la poesia; y (mayor mal) a censurarles lo que no entendemos. Cierto, que quando veo algunos concetos de coplas antiguas, dispuestos con la poca noticia que deste Arte auia en el tiempo que se escriuieron, me parecen riquissimos diamantes por labrar, sin que me satisfaga mas lo muy culto y aliñado de otra lengua." These sentences are a pretty piece of evidence for the typically Spanish symbiosis (characteristic of Góngora too) of erudite art-poetry and the "popular" tradition of the *romanceros*. The *Panegyrico* ends with a copious list of Spanish poets, followed by a catalog of women who have written poetry (Deborah, Judith, the Sibyls, Proba, St. Teresa—and the Virgin Mary).

The little treatise contains no original thought, but for that very reason it is significant for the poetic theory and philosophical position of the Spanish period of florescence. As our analysis has shown, it is closely dependent upon the antique eulogies of arts and adopts their epideictic topoi: encyclopedic character of the art to be treated—its uses—its divine origin—"catalog of heroes." With these humanistic elements is fused the "Biblical poetics" which we know from early Christian and medieval Latin literature. In Spain alone was it able to develop fruitfully, and it did so in the soil of Spain's sixteenth-century revival of theology. Thus from Biblical poetics there could grow a theological poetics, and indeed a theocentric metaphysics of the arts, irreconcilable with Thomism. In the realm of theory it is the counterpart—seldom made philosophically explicit—to a view of the world and man which, within the rich unfolding of the *siglo de oro*, can claim a special signifi-

---

instrument, filled with the Spirit . . ." (Clement of Alexandria, *Schriften*, trans. O. Stählin, Vol. 1 [1934], pp. 75 f.). Cf. Lietzmann, *Geschichte der alten Kirche*, II, 288.

[39] The idea is already to be found in Justin's first Apology, ch. 54: "We may also say that they (the myths imagined by man) were imagined at the instigation of the evil spirits for the delusion and corruption of the race of man" (and what follows).

[40] For this the author cites Suárez, *De Angelis* and many other authorities. The doctrine is orthodox. In Calderón too (*El Mágico prodigioso*, III, 548) the Devil says: "La gracia sola perdí, la ciencia no."

[41] Ca. 675–749, "the last great universally minded theologian of the early Greek church" (Altaner).

[42] Schanz, IV, 2, p. 462.

cance and dignity. In the poetry of a Luis de León, as in the Spanish drama, as in the painting of a Zurbarán, a Valdés Leal, a Greco, the human is always shown to us in its relation to God, and above all the confusions of this earth we are given a glimpse into heaven. The deepest content of both Lope's and Calderón's poetry first becomes apprehensible from this point of view.

Man's connection with the supraterrestrial is especially characteristically displayed in the view taken of death. In the view of the world held by the great Spanish poets, death is not a pulverizing catastrophe, not a brutal finis, but a calm farewell and transition. Thus in Lope, for example, the noble robber-chieftain Pedro Carbonero speaks to his friend:

> Despidamonos los dos:
> Morir quiero, morir quiero.
>   O mundo, no mas con vos!
> Muera Pedro Carbonero,
> Y muera en la fé de Dios.

We find this reconciliation to dying, this easy and pious withdrawing from this world, in Cervantes too, although his position is farther from the view of the world engendered by the theological conception of art. The end of *Don Quixote* is characteristic. During his brief last illness, the ingenious knight falls into a deep sleep, from which he awakens changed. He has not only recovered his reason, but also his real name, Alonso Quijano *el bueno*. His physical dissolution is at the same time a spiritual restitution, in which the dying man, "with a loud cry," recognizes a proof of the divine mercy. Don Quijote gives up his soul a healed man. And his creator, "the noble Cervantes, still full of friendliness and delicate wit even as an old man in his last agony" (Friedrich Schlegel)—even on his deathbed, after receiving extreme unction, he composes the dedication of his last romance to the count of Lemos, "with his foot already in the stirrup," as he writes, referring to certain "coplas antiguas." Here too, as in the plays of Lope and Calderón, the terrestrial is reconciled with the supraterrestrial. This great Spanish art scorned not only nothing of the natural, but also nothing of the supra-natural. When French Classicism, through the lips of Boileau, decrees:

> De la foi des chrétiens les mystères terribles
> D'ornemens égayés ne sont point susceptibles,

it confines to separate compartments not only poetry and faith but also Christianity and culture. This represents a fissure in the spiritual and intellectual world which is later repeated in individuals—a Pascal, a Racine. Calderón's sacramental plays, in which so many "bright flourishes" hover around the seriousness of the Christian mystery, seem to us at once more human and more divine than the art codified by Boileau. Classicism of the Aristotelian persuasion narrows not only the world, but art itself. If all arts, in the final analysis, have their origin in God, then art itself gains a new freedom and innocence. It is a play performed in the presence of God, and thereby a symbol of life itself as the *gran teatro del mundo*, whose roles God distributes.

CALDERÓN'S THEORY OF ART AND THE *ARTES LIBERALES*

The anonymous *Panegyrico* of 1627 was an exhumation. It permitted the reconstruction of a theory of poetry which, to my knowledge, has hitherto remained unknown. In what follows, I present another exhumation. The text is not by an anonymous writer but by "none less" than Calderón. Calderón bibliographies list a "Tractate in Defence of the Nobility of Painting," which was printed but once—1781—and then obscurely, and which has been disregarded. I published a new edition with translation and commentary in 1936 (*RF*, L, 89 ff.). For all further details, I refer the reader to that publication. Here I shall present only what may contribute to a knowledge of Spanish art-theory in general and Calderón's in particular. Some of the basic themes of this book will reappear in these connections.

Calderón's "Tractate" (as it is called, but erroneously) is an expert opinion in favor of the Madrid painters, who were engaged in a suit with the tax office. It was rendered in 1677—half a century after the appearance of the *Panegyrico*. The taxing of painters was an old subject of controversy in Spain and is touched upon by Justi in his *Velázquez* (Phaidonverlag ed. [1933], p. 233): "To the painters, the distastefulness of this tax lay even more in its setting their, as they believed, liberal art on a level with a mercenary trade." But behind this, though Justi could not see it, the question of the system of the *artes liberales* and their relation to man's artistic activity arises once again—and for the last time.

The first offensive by the tax office was launched in 1600 and was directed against El Greco. The last occurred in 1676. It was the occasion for Calderón's expertise—the only theoretical statement on art by him which we possess. In order to understand the entire matter, we must go back to Italian artistic theory. It has been made accessible by Julius von Schlosser's *Kunstliteratur* (1924), by Erwin Panofsky's *Idea* (1924), and by Fritz Saxl's *Antike Götter in der Spätrenaissance* (1927).

In the Florence of the quattrocento the Renaissance becomes aware of its affinity for the thought and work of Antiquity. The fine arts develop with unprecedented creative power and win from prince and burgess such consideration as they had not enjoyed since the Roman Imperial age. The social position of artists rose, their professional pride increased. They are no longer willing to be nameless workmen, to be confused with artisans. Does not their profession require profound learning? Must they not be familiar with geometry and perspective? Do not the antique authors bear witness that painters are to be reckoned among the representatives of the so-called "liberal" arts—that is, the arts worthy of a freeborn man? Beginning with the fifteenth century all these questions were discussed and pursued in a literature which (though it has numerous connections with Antiquity) assumes the character of a new discipline.

Now what was it that distinguished the new art of Italy from the medieval painting which it conquered, a Giotto from a Cimabue? For fourteenth- and fifteenth-century feeling, it was first of all the "naturalness" of Giotto's figures. "Nature," lost since Antiquity, had been rediscovered. Painting, then, was to be conceived as an "imitation" of nature. The very definition was to be found in the Hellenistic anecdotes of artists. But nature's forms themselves—with the human body as the highest of them—were defined by the canon of proportions. These the artist must know. If he had them at command, he could compete with nature; indeed, by proceeding selectively, he could transform and elevate nature. Hence painting presupposed a thorough study of proportion. Like nature, it must be able to effect the "harmony of all proportionally connected parts in a whole" (Schlosser). It must, like one of the "sciences" (e.g. rhetoric and music), have access to a store of rules and laws. Indeed it must itself become a science enabling its practitioners to produce "correct" and "beautiful" works.

It is obvious that this "theory of imitation," like the Aristotelian poetics which only became generally known later, ca. 1550, contains an inner ambivalence: between "object-faithful representation of reality" (Panofsky) and an eclectically idealizing approach. But the early and high Renaissance were not yet conscious of this. The art theory of that period is not speculative but practical in aim—for the science of proportion, and so on, are to serve the artist as foundation and means. Together with its practical purpose, early art-theory also pursues an apologetic one. It set out to "legitimize contemporary art as the true heir of Greco-Roman Antiquity, and, by enumerating its nobilities and virtues, to win it a place among the *artes liberales*" (Panofsky, p. 26). Art theory in this phase is as yet wholly untouched by Florentine Neo-Platonism. It is not until the middle of the sixteenth century that the concept of the "idea" in art becomes more and more prominent, until it finally occupies the place of prime principle. In casual and uncogitated form the "idea" appears in the second edition of Vasari's *Lives*. Then, set forth systematically, it dominates the art theory of so-called "Mannerism," which is laid down in Lomazzo's *Trattato dell' arte della pittura* (1584) and in Federigo Zuccaro's *Idea de' scultori, pittori e architetti* (1607). The manneristic doctrine of art, then, introduces into theory the complete novelty of philosophic speculation, because (according to Panofsky), to the contemporary generation of artists "the relation of the mind to the data of sensory reality" had become a problem. From about 1600 "idea" is threatened by the new "Naturalism" (Caravaggio). Finally—from the middle of the seventeenth century—a new idealism in art theory takes up the fight against Mannerism and Naturalism at once. It conquers in 1664 with Bellori's *Idea del pittore, dello scultore e dell' architetto*, and in this form was adopted by French Classicism.

Such, in simplified outline, is the history of Italian art theory according to Panofsky and Schlosser. A corresponding study for Spain has not yet been made. Schlosser's evaluation of Spanish art theory, compressed into two pages (p. 557–8) does not fill the gap.

That Spanish art theory went to school to Italian art theory is obvious. Vasari, Lomazzo, Zuccari are frequently mentioned. Whole trains of thought are taken over from earlier writers. Spanish art theory begins as part of the history of Italianism in Spain. But then it goes its own way. (There is already an essential difference between the Italian and the Spanish development in the fact that Spanish painting assimilated the Naturalism of a Caravaggio and did not take the road to Classicism.) It does not tend toward a normative aesthetics but—like the *Panegyrico*—to a glorification of painting. To this end, Greek and Latin ecclesiastical writers of the fourth to tenth centuries are invoked. Together with them appear such antique authors as Xenophon, Pliny, Quintilian, and such Italians as Patrizzi, Possevino, Polydore Virgil, Celio Rodighino, and others.

Spanish art theory begins in 1526 with Diego de Sagredo. In the sixteenth century it confines itself to putting painting on a level with the seven *artes* or connecting it with geometry. Then, in the seventeenth century, Valdivielso points out that painting is not only one of the liberal arts but the first of them. It was left for Calderón to develop this thesis methodically.

Calderón's expertise has the form of a legal deposition made, recorded, and signed by the poet, on July 8, 1677. In opening, Calderón mentions that he has always felt a "natural inclination" toward painting. He defines it as an imitation of the work of God and an emulation of Nature. He finds its origin "in the principle, established by recognized authorities, that even as the eternal wisdom, to prove itself as creator, caused the fabric of the universe to arise from nothing," it also willed that painting should arise from a second nothing: from the play of bathing boys. One of them began tracing with his finger the outline of the shadow of another, cast on the sand. Thus "painting's first workshop was light, its first sketch shadow, its first surface sand, its first brush the boy's finger, and its first artist the youthful exuberance of chance." Painting is not counted among the seven arts only because it is the art of arts: it commands them all, in that it makes use of them all. Grammar contributes its "concordances" (agreement between variable parts of speech). So painting must give white to the rose, red to the carnation, etc., otherwise it would be guilty of "solecisms." In like manner painting is served by dialectic —here the proof becomes somewhat labored—and by rhetoric. For painting is able to move the emotions, as words can. Arithmetic and geometry contribute the science of proportion and perspective. And what of music? "If the task of music is to attach the mind to phrases in sound, painting attaches it to no less harmonious rhythms, with the advantages which the sense of sight possesses over the sense of hearing; and especially, when the distant horizon is crowned with clouds and skies, whereby it draws the imagination after it to the contemplation of the celestial signs and the planets. Thus grammar contributes its concordances to painting, dialectics its consequences, rhetoric its persuasion, poetry [1] its arts of invention, oratory its energies, arithmetic its numbers, music its harmonies, symmetry its measures, architecture its planes, sculpture its forms, perspective and optics their magnifications and reductions, and finally astronomy and astrology their symbols for the knowledge of the constellations; who then doubts that painting, as the sum of all arts, is the principal art, which contains them all?" [2]

Among patrons—and, in some cases, practitioners—of painting were the young Nero, Hadrian, Marcus Aurelius, Alexander Severus, Constantine VIII,[3] Alexander the Great, Julius Caesar, etc. In modern times Leo X, who made Raphael a cardinal, Julius II, Philip II, and others. As last and highest proof of the dignity of painting, Calderón adduces: "God as God portrayed himself in man, for He created him after the original of his Idea, as image and likeness of himself. When

[1] As part of rhetoric.

[2] "¿Quién duda que número transcendente de todas las Artes sea la principal que comprehende á todas?"

[3] Source: Sigebert of Gembloux in *MGH Scriptores*, VI, 346.—Cf. Gibbon, *Decline and Fall*, ch. 48.

God became man, he did not permit a mortal brush to portray him, but with his brightness blinded all those who attempted it. But that the world should not remain without so glorious a pledge, he portrayed himself upon the pious Veronica's white cloth," as can be seen in Rome, Savoy, Jaén, and Oviedo. "With this, the witness has completed a perfect circle in his testimony"; he ends where he began. Painting is an imitation of the work of God, "since God, in a certain measure a painter, portrayed himself in his greatest works."

The required demonstration, that painting is a "liberal art," is thus included in the much more far-reaching context of theocentric art-theory. The "natural" explanation (origin in children's play) indicates a situation which was willed by divine Wisdom itself. God the Father is the painter of the universe and the creator of man "in his own image." God's activity as painter is repeated in Veronica's napkin. The act of creation is conceived—platonistically—as a copying of a preexistent idea; as also in the *auto sacramental* (*Autos* [1717], II, 394 f.):

> *Este campo que poblado*
> *Hoy de fabricas se ve,*
> *Nada pulido era entonces*
> *Antes de labrarse en el,*
> *Una confusión, un caos,*
> *Tan informe al parecer,*
> *Que no le hiciera tratable*
> *Sino el supremo pincel,*
> *Que corrió desde la idea*
> *Del primero ser sin ser*
> *Rasgos de su omnipotencia*
> *Y líneas de su poder.*

"God as painter" is an old topos, which first appears in Empedocles and Pindar and which is transmitted to the Middle Ages through Clement (*Schriften*, German version by Stählin, I [1934], 174). Lope too has it, with a reference to the hymn, formerly ascribed to Ambrose, *Caeli deus* (*A.h.*, LI, 36), the third verse of which runs:

> *Candore pingis igneo.*

The twofold function, confirmed by tradition, of the *deus pictor* as the painter of the universe and the molder of man in his own image must have been especially important to Calderón, since it deepens the correspondence between macrocosm and microcosm, which is basic to Calderón's picture of the universe. Calderón's deposition shows, in structure, reasoning, and style, that personal refashioning of traditional ideological material with which we are also familiar from his *Comedias* and above all from his *Autos sacramentales*. Encyclopedic reading, which however is held under control by the energy and meaningfulness of his intellectual combinations; the most subtle conceptual development and harmonious intertwining of all themes; scrupulous analysis, which proceeds with strict symmetry and from which there is finally built up a manifest whole, conceived according to the laws of proportion—these stylistic characteristics of Calderón's art are also recognizably apparent in the deposition.

Analysis of the tractate confirms Lucien-Paul Thomas' valuable demonstration that Calderón had an independent and reasoned view of art.[4]

An *index pictorius* to Calderón's dramatic poetry would have to comprehend all the numerous metaphors and *conceptos* which Calderón borrowed from painting. Even the descriptions in which he is visibly competing with the art of the painter—*sit ut pictura poesis!*—cannot here be examined in detail: for example, the descriptions of Spanish court festivals and processions (e.g., in *La Banda y la flor* or in *Guárdate del agua mansa*). Only the three works in which painting is a supporting element of the dramatic structure can be briefly considered. They are the dramas *Darlo todo y no dar nada* and *El Pintor de su deshonra*, together with the *auto sacramental* of the same title.

Darlo todo y no dar nada deals, after Pliny and Aelian, with the love of Alexander the Great for Campaspe, whom he orders Apelles to paint. Apelles falls in love with his beautiful model, but believes that, out of consideration for his royal master, he must deny himself his passion. This drives him insane—until Alexander resigns the beloved Campaspe to him, thus at the same time showing Diogenes that he can conquer not only the world but himself as well. The antique accounts upon which this plot is based are among the Renaissance's favorite anecdotes of painters.[5] Calderón took his principal subject from them and drew a comic subplot from the character of Diogenes. The following passages from the play are significant for Calderón's conception of painting.

Three painters—Timanthes, Zeuxis, and Apelles—have completed portraits of Alexander. They are received by the monarch as representatives of the highest of all arts:

> *Ejerceis el mejor arte,*
> *Más noble y de más ingenio.*

Alexander then judges the three pictures. As he has a cast in one eye, which Timanthes has not represented, the latter is dismissed as a liar and a flatterer. Zeuxis is also dismissed, because he has represented the defect only too faithfully, and so has infringed due respect. Only Apelles has hit the mark (Keil, IV, 5 a):

> *Que solo vos sabeis, como*
> *Se ha de hablar á su Rey, puesto*
> *Que á medio perfil está*
> *Parecido con extremo;*
> *Con que la falta ni dicha*
> *Ni callada queda, haciendo*
> *Que el medio rostro haga sombra*
> *Al perfil del otro medio.*

Whereupon Apelles is appointed "pintor de cámara."

[4] "François Bertaut et les conceptions dramatiques de Calderon," in *Revue de Littérature comparée* (1924), 199 ff.

[5] Cf. E. Kris and O. Kurz, *Die Legende vom Künstler* (Vienna, 1934), especially pp. 49 ff.—Lope's play *Las Grandezas de Alexandro*—in Menéndez y Pelayo's judgment "una de las pocas obras enteramente malas que nos ha dejado Lope"— has hardly any points of contact with *Darlo todo y no dar nada*. The painting competition is absent. There are a few things about painting in the first act (Academy edition, V, 327–29).

Kings, then—we learn from this passage—are to be portrayed in half-profile. There is a parallel passage in the Corpus Christi play *El Lirio y la azucena*. At the end of it a painting is exhibited: "Aqui se descubre un lienzo grande pintado en el Retablo y Altar de la Iglesia de San Sebastian; encima del Ara el Copón del Santisimo Sacramento, un Sacerdote en pié, haciendo cara hácia el altar; y el pueblo, que se pinte numeroso y vario, y el Rey de rodillas en la ultima grada, procurando que se vea el rostro, aun mas que medio perfil."

The play of Alexander has yet another connection with art-theory. Campaspe is one of those characters, so frequent in Calderón's plays, who has been brought up in solitude and then, by a turn of fate, is suddenly flung into the unknown world. Campaspe grew up in the wilderness and knew only an ideal state of nature. Now her portrait is to be painted. This gives rise to a delightful dialogue between her and the Princesses Estatira and Siroes.

> CAMPASPE: *Quisiera*
> *Saber qué cosa es retrato.*
> SIROES: *¿Nunca ha visto tu rudeza*
> *El primor de la pintura?*
> CAMPASPE: *Pintura ya sé qué sea;*
> *Que en el templo he visto tablas,*
> *Que, de colores compuestas,*
> *Ya representan paises,*
> *Ya batallas representan,*
> *Siendo una noble mentira*
> *De la gran naturaleza;*
> *Pero retrato no sé*
> *Qué es.*
> ESTATIRA: *Pues que es lo mismo, piensa,*
> *Con la circunstancia más*
> *De que la copia parezca*
> *Al original de quien*
> *Se saca.*
> CAMPASPE: *¿Y de que manera*
> *Se saca?*
> ESTATIRA: *Veráslo, cuando*
> *A hacer el retrato vengan.*

Landscape and battle paintings, then, are known even to children of nature—from rural temples. But the portrait belongs to the realm of urban culture. Hence it has a bewildering effect upon Campaspe. Before her own portrait she falls into ontological doubt (Keil, IV, 21 f.).

Thus the art of portraiture is here put among the "prodigios del mundo" (such as the first ship, the first drum, etc.), that is, in the realm of cultural goods invented by man, upon the origin of which Calderón, following antique tradition, is so fond of reflecting—even as he does at the beginning of his tractate on painting.

The comedy *El Pintor de su deshonra* is among Calderón's better known works. I select only what is significant for Calderón's art-theory. Don Juan Roca remained long unmarried, spending his days and nights over books and studies. When melancholy overcame him, he sought relief in painting (Keil, IV, 62 a):

> *Y si, para entretener*
> *Tal vez fatigas de leer,*
> *Con vuestras melancolías*
> *Treguas tratábades, era*
> *Lo prolijo del pincel*
> *Su alivio, porque aun en él*
> *Parte el ingenio tuviera.*

Even after his marriage, Don Juan continues to paint. He paints a portrait of his wife Serafina, and during a sitting explains to her the difficulty of reproducing her consummate beauty (IV, 71 a).

Serafina is abducted against her will. In vain Don Juan seeks her. He turns to painting again and paints for the Prince of Urbino a picture representing the jealous Hercules, robbed of Dejanira by the Centaur Nessus. The prince then orders a portrait of a beautiful woman: it is Serafina. Don Juan shoots her: as "painter of his shame" he has "painted a picture in blood."

In this play, then, we find the concept of painting as an intellectual art, an art which distinguishes even persons of rank. But more important is the "dilemma of the portrait," if I may so express it.[6] A model of ideal beauty cannot be faithfully reproduced by the painter. Rather, the more the model departs from the canon of beauty, the greater the likeness of the portrait. Even the most beautiful portrait of a woman—we are forced to conclude—presupposes that the subject violates ideal proportion in one feature or another. The proof of this is furnished by the celebrated description of Semiramis in *La Hija del aire*, which Grillparzer—in advance of his time—admired. Semiramis' forehead is too small (II, 73 a):

> *No de espacioso te alabo*
> *La frente, que antes en esta*
> *Parte solo anduvo avara*
> *La sempre liberal maestra, etc.*

Here, then, we have a defect, even as in the face of Alexander. But this negative becomes a positive for the art of the portrait painter, indeed it becomes a condition of success. To be sure, there then arises a second dilemma—that of *Darlo todo y no dar nada*: how is the painter to proceed who has a king to portray? How does he combine conventional respect with truth to life? Behind this question there lies, as historical reality, first the court culture of Hapsburg Spain, but, secondly, the deeper problem of compromise between the naturalistic and the idealizing concept of art—or, better put, between *imitatio* on the one hand and *decorum* on the other. The norm of *decorum* is, for example, discussed in detail by Pacheco.[7] It is worth mentioning in this connection that in his so-called *romance autobiográfico* (dated *ca.* 1636 by Cotarelo y Mori, *Ensayo sobre la vida y las obras de Calderón*, p. 70), Calderón has left us a literary self-portrait which cannot be surpassed in naturalism.

There is a parallel to Calderón's considerations on portrait-painting in Pacheco: "Las faltas no se han de disimular en los retratos, aunque es alabado Apéles en

---

[6] Tirso de Molina also expatiates upon portrait-painting (*El Vergonzoso en palacio*, II, 673 ff.).

[7] *Arte de la pintura*, ed. Villaamil, I, 238 ff.—Pacheco treats *decorum* following Cicero and Horace. Here again we see the tendency, observable from the fifteenth century, to systematize art-theory after the pattern of rhetoric and poetics.

haber retratado de medio rostro al Rey Antígono, que era ciego de un ojo, poniéndole de la parte del sano . . . Esta es prudencia que se puede usar con personas graves, sin detrimento de la verdad . . ." And in the same connection: ". . . los rostros hermosos son más dificultuosos de retratar, como enseña la experiencia." [8]

Finally, we shall consider the *auto sacramental, El Pintor de su deshonra.*

Lucifer reveals to Sin (*Culpa*) his deep resentment against the Son of the Almighty. The Son is master of all sciences: theology, jurisprudence, philosophy, medicine. He also commands the liberal arts: dialectics, astrology, arithmetic, architecture, geometry, rhetoric, music, poetry.[9] But Lucifer's greatest cause for discontent is that the Son is also a painter. In the last six days he has finished the painting of creation. Now he is engaged in producing the image of man, as incarnate form of his idea. Lucifer fears that the Son will animate this image too. He turns to Sin and asks her to join him in preventing this, so that the Son of God shall become the painter of his own dishonor. Though he paints with the oil of Grace, "we will bring it about that she—Human Nature—shall bow to the temper of her desires, and thus we shall make her tempera-painting, though he is painting her with oil" (*Autos* [1717], I, 378 a):

> Que aunque al oleo de la Gracia
> La pinte, tambien nosotros
> Haciendola que se incline
> Al temple de sus antojos,
> La haremos pintura al temple,
> Aunque el la matice al oleo.

Culpa hides in a tree. The divine Painter appears. Innocence carries his palette, Wisdom his maulstick, Grace his brush. When the picture is finished, its material is given form by a breath from the painter. The picture vanishes, and in its place stands Human Nature. She begins speaking and asks about her existence. The painter answers that he has given her being so that he may one day make her his bride. But Human Nature allows the Snake to seduce her. Now God will destroy his painting, the world, and use his coarse paintbrush for the purpose:

> El Mundo, talamo injusto
> De sus adulteras bodas,
> Tengo de borrar, haciendo
> Que por todo el pais corra
> En vez de sutil pincel
> La bronquedad de la brocha.

Floods shall aid in the destruction, since water washes out tempera colors (into which Free Will, *Albedrío*, has changed the oil paints).

> Que si al temple me la ha vuelto
> Su Albedrío, quien ignora
> Que las pinturas al temple
> Con agua, no mas, se borran.

---

[8] *Arte de la pintura*, ed. Villaamil, II, 141 and 143.
[9] The system of the liberal arts is here somewhat different from that of the "Tractate."

The World and Nature begin to wail. The painter flings a board into the flood as a sign of forgiveness. The World and Human Nature save themselves first on the board, then on the mountain summits of Armenia.

Lucifer is disappointed that Human Nature was not destroyed in the Flood. He resolves to ruin her beauty, and to this end employs Sin. Sin drives a nail into Human Nature's forehead, with the words:

> Pincel será de mis obras,
> Pues que por la oposición
> Sus atributos nos tocan,
> Este clavo que en su frente
> Servirá de negra sombra,
> Porque vean que la Culpa
> Su imagen a Dios le borra.

Branded Human Nature flees. The World is thus robbed of its crown, and complains. The Painter reappears, and the World asks for a portrait of the fugitive:

> Viendo pues
> Que ausentarmela porfía,
> Para engañar mi amor, trato,
> Ya que dices ser Pintor,
> Que a los ruegos de mi amor
> De ella me hagas un retrato
> Porque le traiga en el pecho.

The Painter now receives from Divine Love, who accompanies him, the paintbox (which contains only carmine); as brush, three nails; as painting-surface, a heart-shaped bronze plate; as maulstick, a lance: Christ's passion restores the destroyed picture of Human Nature.

Between the comedy El Pintor de su deshonra and the Corpus Christi play of the same name, the attentive reader will discover numerous meaningful correspondences. In both plays we see a painter at work on a painting which is painted first with colors, then with blood. But the Divine Painter does not portray a living model, but "from the original of his idea, he brings to light a mysterious copy":

> LUCIFER: Mas nada desto me da
> Tanto sobresalto, como
> Ver que de aquel exemplar
> De su idea, en quien yo absorto
> Miré mi primera ruina,
> Quiera sacar mysterioso
> A luz el retrato . . .

The portrait—retrato—appears here too, then, as in the play of Campaspe, as a new—the final and highest—accomplishment of painting. Human nature is a portrait created by the divine Logos. He himself, prime origin and final sum of all sciences and arts, is a painter. Calderón's auto illustrates, in a poetic creation of the imagination, the art-theory which the "Tractate" sets forth in didactic form. It reveals itself to us as the magnificent and consummate conclusion of speculation which was rooted in Antiquity and patristics and which lived on through the Middle

Ages and the Renaissance. A traditional idea which had survived for more than a millennium, which had been reshaped by every historical period of the West, is for the first and perhaps for the last time brought to perfect flower, in a work of poetic art, by Calderón. Nourished by and steeped in the most ancient tradition, Calderón was not overwhelmed by its ideological weight; he controlled it with the power of a master, related it to himself, recreated it. Living in and by the tradition, he yet was able to reshape it with the utmost originality—in this he is comparable only to Dante.

Like Dante, Calderón is a Christian poet, in the highest and most definite sense of the term. This means: his picture of man and the world has as its center belief in God as postulated by the Church. But Lope too is to the highest degree a "religious poet" and "believing priest." [10] The dogma, the ceremonial, and the mysticism of Catholicism are so essentially and intimately connected with the culture of the Spanish *siglo de oro* that they are everywhere perceptible as the vital basis of the age. This historical fact—whose establishment has nothing to do with a romanticizing apotheosis of Spain—allows us to understand the necessity for also fitting into the theocentric world picture of Christianity the secular cultural forces of the period: monarchy, national consciousness, politics, together with the theater, the arts, the sciences. An art-theory founded in Christian speculation was not only preserved as part of the patristic and scholastic stock of ideas; in great poets it could also become living again as a creative and organizing principle. This is the final basis of Calderón's concept of painting too. Painting received its highest nobility from the fact that God used it in his work of creation. But in Calderón, as we saw, the divine Logos is not only a painter, but also architect, musician, poet. In him all arts have their common origin and their primal idea. In the *Gran teatro del mundo*, the world becomes a stage, on which God allots the roles. In *El sagrado Parnaso* Christ is the divine poet or the God of Poetry. He appears as Apollo:

Lope too has related ideas. In *Lo fingido verdadero* the actor Ginés returns to the stage. Formerly he had belonged to the devil's company of actors; now through martyrdom he will enter the divine *Comedia*, that is, Jesus' company:

> *Ahora mi compañía*
> *Es de Jesús, donde hay Padre*
> *Del santo Verbo, y hay Madre,*
> *La siempre Virgen María.*

In this divine troupe John the Baptist plays shepherd's roles, Gabriel messengers' roles, and so on. At the end of the play Ginés once more declares from the cross of martyrdom:

> *Pueblo romano, escuchadme:*
> *Yo representé en el mundo*
> *Sus fábulas miserables,*
> *Todo el tiempo de mi vida,*
> *Sus vicios y sus maldades;*
> *Yo fui figura gentil*
> *Adorando dioses tales;*
> *Recibióme Dios; ya soy*

[10] Vossler, *DVjft*, XIV, 168.

> Cristiano representante;
> Cesó la humana comedia,
> Que era toda disparates;
> Hice la que veis, divina . . .

So Lope shows us the passage from the earthly to the heavenly world-theater
and thereby confirms the theological dignity of the arts. I will give two further examples of this. Saint Teresa finds her soul portrayed in the breast of Divine Love
(variation on the *Deus pictor*):

> De tal suerte, pudo amor
> Alma en mí te retratar,
> Que ningun sabio pintor
> Supiera con tal primor
> Tal imágen estampar.
>
> Fuiste por amor criada,
> Hermosa bella, y así
> En mis entrañas pintada,
> Si te perdieres, mi amada
> Alma, buscarte has en Mí.
>
> Que yo sé que te hallarás
> En mi pecho retratada,
> Y tan al vivo sacada
> Que si te ves te holgarás
> Viéndote tan bien pintada.[11]

Finally, we find God as musician of the universe in Luis de León's ode to Francisco de Salinas:

> Ve como el gran maestro,
> A aquesta inmensa cítara aplicado,
> Con movimiento diestro
> Produce el son sagrado,
> Con que este eterno templo es sustentado.

Thus in the classic poetry of Spain the several arts are found in a sisterly union
and at the same time related to that which is above nature. The close companion-
ship of the arts, especially of dramatic poetry and painting, is of course not based
only upon the Christian world picture of the Spanish period of florescence but also
upon the pomp and display of the monarchy. Charles V and Philip II were art lovers
and collectors of pictures. The imperial splendor of these rulers, whose taste remained authoritative both for the nobility and for their feeble successors, gave painting, and particularly the art of portraiture, that rank in practice which the theoretical
deductions of scholars contemporaneously attested—with the success which even
the tax office unwillingly admitted. These are conditions which we do not find in
Italy, nor yet in France nor England. They constitute the cultural basis of Calderón's
"Tractate" too.

This connection between painting and poetry materially enriched the Spanish

[11] *BAE*, LIII, 510 b.

culture of the *siglo de oro*. Only in Spain could it come about that a military victory —the surrender of Breda—could contemporaneously be put on canvas by Velázquez and on the stage by Calderón. In Shakespeare painting plays a quite insignificant role. The same is true of the classic drama of the French. Only the Spanish theater has a vital relationship to the great painting of the nation.

The similarity in structure between the "Tractate" and the *Panegyrico* is striking. Calderón's production could bear the latter title too. It fits into the humanistic schema of the panegyrics on arts and shows the validity of that schema in the *siglo de oro*. But the author of the *Panegyrico* is, if we are to believe him, a lad of seventeen. Calderón made his statement at the age of seventy-seven. The former produces a talented school exercise, Calderón is able to handle the subject with the winning charm and the intellectual depth which are his own. Both pieces revolve around the system of the *artes liberales*.

The function of that system has appeared again and again in our investigations. It transmits to the West the late antique educational tradition. To the Christian Middle Ages it signifies the timelessly valid systematization of all knowledge: the totality of the *artes* can be equated with philosophy. Only the Incarnation had the power to revoke the *artes* (*supra*, p. 42). Thomas Aquinas robs the *artes* of their primacy in the system of learning (p. 56). But Dante gives them back their dignity (*supra*, pp. 370 f.). They appear upon the Gothic cathedrals—but also in the painting of Botticelli. In Calderón's speculative aesthetics, they are finally subordinated to an *ars mechanica*. But this is only possible because the latter was seen as a reflection of God's activity as Creator. It is the last time that the European mind reflects upon the rank and function of the *artes liberales*.

Today American college education is attempting to save Humanism by reestablishing contact with the seven *artes liberales*.

MONTESQUIEU, OVID, AND VIRGIL

To his chief work Montesquieu prefixed the motto from Ovid:

> . . . *prolem sine matre creatam.*

He calls his work, then, a child brought forth without a mother. Ovid's line complete (*Met.*, II, 553) runs:

> *Pallas Erichthonium, prolem sine matre creatam.*

The hero Erichthonius was supposed to have sprung from Hephaestos' unassuaged love of Pallas. The god followed the fleeing goddess, but could not overtake her. His seed fell on the ground, which bore Erichthonius; but Pallas concealed him in a reed basket and brought him up. Ariosto alludes to the myth in *Orlando Furioso*, XXXVII, 27. In 1896 Camille Jullian [1] had referred to Ovid, *Tristia*, III, 14, 13:

> *Palladis exemplo de me sine matre creata*
> *Carmina sunt; stirps haec progeniesque mea.*

Jullian comments: "Montesquieu veut dire par là qu'il a fourni à l'Esprit des Lois et la forme et le fonds, qu'il n'a dû à aucun ouvrage antérieur le cadre, le plan ou l' idée de son livre" (p. 41). Whether Ovid, in these lines, is alluding to the birth of Pallas from the head of Zeus or to the story of Erichthonius does not matter— his meaning is clear: my poems are my children.[2] Montesquieu's educated contemporaries still read the Roman poets, and must have understood the motto as it was meant: "This book was born of my brain." Montesquieu had in mind the lines quoted from the *Tristia*. But he could not take them for a motto. It was not possible to refer to the *Esprit des lois* as *carmina*. Instead a word must be found which would express the idea *stirps haec progeniesque mea* and which could be connected with the thought *sine matre creata*. These requirements were best fulfilled by the concise and weighty hemistich

> . . . *prolem sine matre creatam.*

But with Erichthonius the motto has nothing whatever to do, and any attempt to refer to the myth in explanation leads to offensive inelegancies.

The motto voices not only Montesquieu's justified self-satisfaction but also his love of antique literature and his theory of style. A good many things have been written about Montesquieu's style. The latest critic to express himself on the subject is Joseph Dedieu.[3] But a decisive point has always been overlooked. In the composition of his masterpiece, Montesquieu sought to approach the antique authors. Actually he intended the opening of the second volume of the *Esprit des lois* as an invocation to the Muses. Its concluding sentence epitomizes all that is noble in the enthusiasm of a rationalist: "Divines muses, je sens que vous m'inspirez, non pas ce qu'on chante à Tempé sur les chalumeaux, ou ce qu'on répète à Délos sur la lyre:

[1] In his selection from Montesquieu (*Montesquieu. Extraits* [Hachette]).
[2] Cf. *supra*, pp. 131 ff.
[3] *Montesquieu, l'homme et l'œuvre* (Paris, 1943), pp. 166 ff.

vous voulez que je parle à la raison; elle est le plus parfait, le plus noble et le plus exquis de nos sens." It is also in accordance with the antique concept of literary art that
the prologue of a work should be especially elaborately composed. Montesquieu does
this in his preface to the *Esprit des lois*: The following passage from it is celebrated:
"J'ai bien des fois commencé et bien des fois abandonné aux vents les feuilles que
j'avais écrites; je sentais tous les jours les mains paternelles tomber, je suivais mon
objet sans former de dessein; je ne connaissais ni les règles ni les exceptions; je ne
trouvais la vérité que pour la perdre; mais quand j'ai découvert mes principes, tout
ce que je cherchais est venu à moi, et, dans le cours de vingt années, j'ai vu mon
ouvrage commencer, croître, s'avancer et finir." In this passage Dedieu, like Chérel
before him, wishes to see testimony to the "lyricism" of Montesquieu's prose. He
remarks: "La phrase musicale atteint ici sa perfection, non seulement parce que
les thèmes mélodiques s'y poursuivent à la même cadence, mais parce que chacun
d'eux, après avoir suscité une grande image, s'achève dans l'apaisement du rhythme
et la simplicité des mots" (p. 170). But are we to believe that Montesquieu abandoned his manuscript pages to the winds a thousand times, or shall we consider this
an exaggeration and, to that extent, lyrical? Further: What is the meaning of the
sentence: "Every day I felt the paternal hands sink"? It is obscure and can perhaps
to that extent be called lyrical. But both passages become clear when the text is
printed in full, namely with Montesquieu's own notes. For the first passage he gives
the reference, "ludibria ventis"; for the second, "bis patriae cecidere manus." Latin
poetry once again, then. Whose? Montesquieu would have thought it discourteous
to name the author. For every educated reader could not but know the lines. They
come, in fact, from the beginning of Book VI of Virgil's *Aeneid*. There Aeneas
implores the Sibyl not to entrust her prophecies to loose leaves, that they may not
become the plaything of the winds; and there the doors of the temple of Apollo at
Cumae are described with elaborate ecphrasis. They are covered with scenes from
the hand of Daedalus. The artist wished also to depict the fate of his son Icarus.
But twice his hands sank. Thus Montesquieu put two subtle examples of Virgil
imitatio into a few clauses. He wanted to give the preface of his life's work something of the dignity and elevation of the antique epic style. And he achieved his
object—to such an extent that sentences of this sort have been referred to an alleged
new eighteenth-century lyrical prose. But to whom, in the last analysis, does this
poetical effect go back? To Virgil. I conclude with an observation which takes us
back to the realm of ideas represented by the motto with which we began. The
reference to Daedalus makes us see very clearly that Montesquieu regarded his work
as an artistic creation, but at the same time with the eyes of a father for his son.

DIDEROT AND HORACE

Goethe's observation on Diderot is well known: "Diderot is Diderot, a unique individual; whoever carps at him or his output is a Philistine, and they are legion" (to Zelter, March 9, 1831). What is the basis of the fascination that Diderot's writings exercise? He rises above his contemporaries not only in scope but also in vital tension and in polyphony of consciousness. I do not refer to the many-sidedness of his interests; I would indicate that, in Diderot, all particulars stand in direct relation to the universal. Or better: in the particular, and indeed in each separate particular, and in each equally, the universal shines through and is manifest. Diderot's consciousness contains a multiplicity of individual centers, each of which is connected with the others and reflects the whole. To understand Diderot, we must sense the same undivided cycle of life in each of his statements. From such a viewpoint it ought also to be possible to find a new form of presentation. We can at least prepare such a renewal of the traditional picture of Diderot by pointing out neglected connections and relations in his intellectual world.

Hitherto, we may say without unfairness, Diderot scholarship has not done justice to its great subject. Instead of seizing Diderot's intellectual world as an ἓν καὶ πᾶν[1], it has prepared it anatomically in the form of cross-sections. Diderot's most recent portrayer, Daniel Mornet, the outstanding eighteenth-century scholar, still does the same thing. In his *Diderot* (Paris, 1941) the philosopher, the story-teller, the dramatist, the letter-writer, the art critic are treated one after the other. There is no comprehensive general view.

Diderot the story-teller! The cliché has become current. In 1924, in the chapter on Diderot in Bédier and Hazard's history of French literature (II, 100), Mornet had already grouped *La Religieuse, Jacques le fataliste,* and *Le Neveu de Rameau* together as "ses romans" and passed a summary judgment upon them: "Les romans de Diderot ont un peu les qualités de ses lettres et les défauts du reste de ses oeuvres . . . Ils ne sont pas composés, parce qu'il ne voulait pas composer." May *Le Neveu de Rameau* really be put in the same category as *Jacques le fataliste* and *La Religieuse*? Has not *Le Neveu* a different law of form from that of the novel? If we pursue this question, we find that thorough confusion concerning the structure and meaning of the work is prevalent.

Though Herbert Dieckmann has stated that Goethe was the first to recognize the artistic unity of the structure of *Le Neveu de Rameau*,[2] I cannot agree. Goethe says (Jubiläumsausgabe, XXXIV, 189): "By choosing, then, the form of a dialogue for this work, he put himself at an advantage, produced a masterpiece, which one admires the more, the more one knows it. Its rhetorical and moral intention is manifold. First the author uses all the powers of his mind to depict flatterers and

---

[1] This sort of comprehension shines out only occasionally, for example in Jean Thomas: "Tout est dans cette pensée universelle, où tout est fondé sur l'homme, destiné à l'homme, ajusté aux mesures de l'homme" (*L'Humanisme de Diderot,* p. 148). To be sure, even this formulation is vitiated by the thesis of Diderot's "Humanism" (which will be discussed later).

[2] *RF* (1939), 74 and *DVjft.* (1932), 491 and 493, n. 1.

parasites in the whole extent of their depravity, not sparing their patrons in the process. At the same time he is concerned to classify his literary enemies as precisely the same kind of hypocrites and flatterers, and further takes occasion to set forth his ideas and sentiments concerning French music. Heterogeneous as this last ingredient may appear in respect to the preceding ones, it is nevertheless the part which gives consistency and dignity to the whole; for while in the person of Rameau's nephew a decidedly dependent nature, capable, under outside stimulus, of anything bad, is expressed, and hence arouses our scorn and even our hate, yet these feelings are softened by the fact that he shows himself to be a musician, at once fantastical and practical, who is not wholly without talent. From the point of view of poetic composition too, this native talent gives the protagonist a great advantage, in that the man who is depicted as the representative of all flatterers and toadies, as standing for an entire species, still lives and acts as an individually characterized being, as a Rameau, as a nephew of the great Rameau. How admirably these threads, which are introduced from the very beginning, are woven together, what a delightful variety of entertainment proceeds from this intricacy, how the whole, despite the generalization of confronting a scoundrel with an honorable man, nevertheless turns out to be made up of real Parisian element, the comprehending reader and re-reader may discover for himself." Justified and fascinating as Goethe's observations are, they yet say nothing unequivocal about the basic idea and the structure of the work. Sainte-Beuve presumably felt this too when he wrote in 1851: "On a fort vanté le Neveu de Rameau. Goethe, toujours plein d'une conception et d'une ordonnance supérieures, a essayé d'y trouver un dessin, une composition, une moralité: j'avoue qu'il m'est difficile d'y saisir cette élévation de but et ce lien. J'y trouve mille idées hardies, profondes, vraies peut-être, folles et libertines souvent, une contradiction si faible qu'elle semble une complicité entre les deux personnages, un hasard perpétuel, et nulle conclusion, ou, qui pis est, une impression finale équivoque. C'est le cas, ou jamais, je le crois, d'appliquer ce mot que le chevalier de Chastellux disait à propos d'une autre production de Diderot, et qui peut se redire plus ou moins de presque tous ses ouvrages: 'Ce sont des idées qui se sont enivrées, et qui se sont mises à courir les unes après les autres'" (Lundis, III, 311).

I pass over what Diderot scholarship in the nineteenth century had to say about the Neveu de Rameau. A decisive step toward understanding was made in Mornet's study, "La véritable signification du Neveu de Rameau," of 1927 (in the Revue des Deux Mondes for Aug. 15). Diderot's work, Mornet says, has now been known for a century.[3] "Mais il y a un siècle aussi qu'on le comprend mal ou qu'on ne le comprend pas du tout. On tient le Neveu de Rameau pour un roman, conte ou 'satire' (selon le titre même de Diderot), et pour un roman, conte ou satire réaliste." Certainly the work reveals realistic observation, but that is not the decisive factor. "Diderot a voulu composer non pas un conte historique, mais ce qu'il appelle un conte philosophique. Et ce qu'il a voulu faire vivre, ce n'est pas du tout le vrai bohème de chez Procope; c'est un personnage fictif, propre à porter ou justifier ses thèses; c'est même un confident, si semblable à celui qui se confie qu'on ne les distingue plus. Le Neveu, c'est de temps à autre un plastron; et presque toujours, c'est exactement Diderot lui-même. Lui et Moi, les deux personnages du dialogue, c'est en

---

[3] The original French text was published from a copy in 1823 by Brière, from Diderot's own MS in 1891 by Monval.

réalité Moi et Moi, c'est un Diderot qui bataille, âprement, contre un autre Diderot." The "nephew" of the dialogue undoubtedly exhibits features of the real Jean-François Rameau, but the latter was neither as corrupt or as witty as the parasite depicted by Diderot. Diderot used the real Rameau as a screen in order to pillory the toadyism in the lives of so many contemporary literati. "C'est une antithèse entre le neveu, c'est-à-dire des hommes de lettres par douzaines, et le seul être 'dispensé de la pantomime,' 'le philosophe qui n'a rien et qui ne demande rien,' c'est-à-dire Diderot." In concluding, Mornet distinguishes three elements in *Le Neveu de Rameau:* 1. Realistic observation; 2. polemic against parasites and literati; 3. refutation of a materialistic philosophy—which was Diderot's own!—by its consequences. The dialogue, then, is "une adjuration de Diderot à Diderot: 'Voilà, ô Diderot le fataliste, ce que l'on devient avec tes doctrines; voilà ce qu'elles peuvent justifier. Voilà ce que tu aurais pu, ce que tu pourrais devenir toi-même, toi qui a parfois vécu comme le Neveu, toi qui lui ressembles par quelques instincts de bohème et par les appétits de volupté.' "

Now this conclusion of the study is certainly in contradiction to the view which Mornet himself suggested in the course of his exposition: that the dialogue is an antithesis between the toadying scribbler and the self-sufficient philosopher. This last view I believe to be the right one. We set this positive contribution down to the credit of Mornet's study, but we cannot convince ourselves that in his dialogue Diderot intended to refute his own philosophy. This thesis of Mornet's has, furthermore, found no favor with more recent scholarship. The next scholar to be named is Pierre Trahard. Volume II (1932) of his *Les Maîtres de la sensibilité française au 18e siècle* is for the most part devoted to Diderot. One division (p. 254 ff.) bears the promising title "Le sens profond du Neveu de Rameau." But we are disappointed: the dialogue, we read, is principally a didactic treatise on music (p. 257). Naturally it is more too: "C'est un livre où souffle l'esprit divin (p. 263) . . . Sa grandeur lui vient de la part prépondérante que l'art y occupe, ou, plus exactement, de l'influence que l'art exerce sur l'âme humaine" (p. 263–4). This is obviously a misinterpretation. Yet another opinion is to be found in Jean Thomas' stimulating essay, *L'Humanisme de Diderot* (1933), of which we shall have to say more later. He writes: "Quand, où et pourquoi a-t-il écrit le Neveu de Rameau? Nous sommes réduits à former des hypothèses. Deux lignes d'une lettre à Mme d'Epinay, écrite de La Haye en 1773, semblent se rapporter à ce chef-d'oeuvre qu'il appelle négligemment 'une petite satire.' [4] Mais le mystère n'en est guère éclairci" (*L'Humanisme de Diderot*, p. 40). Yet in other passages Thomas seems to approach Mornet's conception. Diderot, we are told, wrote the dialogue to clarify his own ideas: "Telles idées qui, au premier examen, l'ont séduit et qui s'accordent à ses principes, à les considérer de plus près, elles l'épouvantent: s'il les poussait jusqu' à leurs légitimes conséquences, s'il les appliquait a l'ensemble de l'humanité, ne ruineraient-elles pas l'ordre moral et social tout à la fois? Son jugement s'embarrasse, et pourtant il faut sortir de l'impasse. Instituons une expérience. Supposons qu'un homme intelligent, audacieux,

---

[4] *Correspondance inédite* (1931), I, 217. In full: "Je me suis amusé à écrire une petite satyre dont j'avois le projet quand je quittai Paris." From this one would have to assume that the work was not written until 1773. Mornet (1941) differs: "Les allusions à des événements . . . semblent prouver que l'ouvrage a dû être ébauché entre 1760 et 1764 et remanié une ou deux fois entre 1772 et 1779" (*Diderot, l'homme et l'oeuvre*, p. 203).

logique, s'approprie ces théories suspectes, et modèle sa conduite à leur ressemblance. Jusqu'à quelles extravagances serait-il entraîné? En regard de ce personnage fictif, imaginons les réactions d'un interlocuteur de sens rassis, vertueux, sans pruderie, clairvoyant sans préjugé. Ecoutons leur dialogue: c'est le Neveu de Rameau. Voilà de la morale expérimentale, voilà ce que deviennent, selon le tempérament de Diderot, les Essais de Montaigne" (p. 71). Finally Thomas correctly rejects the "naturalistic" conception, according to which the work was simply the reproduction of a conversation which actually took place. This is in contradiction, first, to what we know of the historical Rameau, and further to the numerous revisions the work underwent and the great distance in time between the finished work and the event from which it grew. But above all "cet étrange ambigu de réalisme et de rêverie" is a creation which has its unity in the cosmos of Diderot's mind: "les détails sont vrais, les gestes, les paroles, les silences même sont vrais. Mais entre la réalité justement observée et la transposition artistique, la personnalité de l'auteur est intervenue souverainement. Diderot a éclairé son personnage et les objets qui l'entourent à son propre soleil, 'qui n'est pas celui de la nature'. C'est ce même soleil qui brille à travers toute son oeuvre, si diverse, si chaotique qu'elle paraisse. Il y a un univers propre à Diderot, à l'intérieur duquel tout s'ajuste, tout s'organise en une harmonie de tons, de lignes, de rythmes et de couleurs. Parce que les créations romanesques y sont peu nombreuses, l'univers de Diderot n'est pas également achevé; certaines zones n'y sont qu'esquissées; mais ces ébauches, dont Diderot préférait parfois le feu et la verve à la perfection des ouvrages minutieusement polis, suggèrent ce qu' elles ne disent pas" (p. 146–7).—Hubert Gillot, in his important work *Denis Diderot. L'homme. Ses idées philosophiques, esthétiques, littéraires* (1937) touches upon Diderot's dialogue only passingly and adopts Mornet's interpretation (p. 14, n.). Mornet himself, in his latest work on Diderot, which we have mentioned several times earlier (*Diderot, l'homme et l'oeuvre* [1941]) has softened the sharpness of statement of his theses of 1927. The *Neveu de Rameau* is characterized as "un dialogue moral et philosophique à travers lequel s'ébauche une sorte de conte réaliste sur une vie de bohème" (p. 120). In the *Neveu* and *Jacques le fataliste* Diderot "made a system out of disorder": "il avait intitulé le Neveu 'satire'; il donnait évidemment au mot le sens latin autant que le sens français, un ragoût où se mêlent, pour former un plat savoureux, les aliments les plus divers. Qu'y a-t-il dans le Neveu? une étude de caractère, le portrait physique et moral d'un bohème étrange et pittoresque et dans son allure et dans sa pensée. Mais ce neveu, mi-réel, mi-imaginaire n'est, nous l'avons dit, qu'une sorte de double de Diderot avec lequel il se lance dans une discussion éperdue. La discussion nous entraîne bien à travers l'étude d'un problème qui domine tous les autres; la morale et la vertu peuvent-elles être fondées sur des raisons solides ou ne sont-elles que des conventions et des illusions dont l'homme intelligent et sans scrupules a le droit de s'affranchir? Mais ce problème en suggère plusieurs autres autour desquels l'entretien tourne si bien que nous perdons de vue le problème central: le problème de la dignité de l'écrivain et du parasitisme, le problème des passions fortes et des caractères d'exception, des problèmes de musique qui, eux, n'ont rien à voir avec le sujet. Ces problèmes eux-mêmes ne sont pas toujours abordés successivement. Le courant de la discussion est comme celui d'un flot rapide, mais incertain de sa direction, et qui tournerait confusément autour de quelques flots ou rochers avant de retrouver sa pente définitive. Il y a maintes parenthèses,

quelques redites; les transitions ne sont, à l'ordinaire, que des transitions de conversation, sans aucune valeur logique" (pp. 125–6). In a later passage of the same
book (p. 203 f.) Mornet again expresses himself somewhat differently: "Le thème
général est l'exposé par le Neveu d'une morale cynique qui est le droit de se donner
le plus de plaisirs en se donnant le moins de peine; il s'y joint des discussions sur le
parasitisme et la bassesse d' âme des écrivains qui sont les ennemis de l' Encyclo-
pédie, sur la musique, écho de la querelle des Bouffons, entre les partisans de la
musique française et ceux de la musique italienne, Diderot prenant vivement parti
contre Rameau. Une partie du conte est d'ailleurs le portrait du Neveu et le récit
d' épisodes pittoresques et imaginaires de sa vie de bohème sans scrupules." These
analyses do justice to the philosophic richness of the *Neveu* but they leave the basic
theme—the contrast between the parasite and the philosopher—out of account and
distract attention from it.

We come, as I hope to show, perceptibly nearer to an understanding of the work
if we heed the indications which Diderot gave in his title and his motto—if, in
other words, we proceed philologically. Various writers, to be sure, passingly mention the fact that Diderot entitled his work not *Le Neveu de Rameau* but *Satire
seconde* and that a "first satire" by Diderot exists: *Satire I sur les caractères et les
mots de caractère, de profession, etc.* (printed in Diderot's *Oeuvres*, ed. Assézat and
Tourneux, Vol. VI, 303 ff.). But no one notices that both "satires" bear mottos
from Horace's *Satires*, and no one follows up Diderot's connections with Horace.
Yet to do so would easily have suggested itself ever since Jean Thomas, in the work
cited above, made Diderot into a "Humanist." To be sure, Thomas gives the much-
tortured word Humanism an unusual meaning: that of ethical individualism, empiricism, and naturalism. The secret of "Humanism" lies "dans l'effort personnel,
dans l'aventure individuelle, unique, jamais renouvelable, de chacun de ceux qui
tentent de se donner à eux-mêmes, par leurs propres moyens, suivant leurs expé-
riences privées, une règle de vie, de pensée et d'action" (p. 151). According to
Thomas, France has had only two "Humanists"—Montaigne and Diderot. With
this thesis, to be sure, we do not get very far. What Thomas calls Humanism no
longer has anything to do with the great historical manifestations of Humanism,
nor with a spiritual and intellectual connection with Antiquity. Aside from this,
Thomas' study is rich in fruitful ideas. Especially noteworthy are his remarks on
Diderot's determinism and his progressive emancipation from it after 1773 (pp.
104 f., 112, 114, 157). But it is clear that Thomas' approach to the problem could
bring out little on the subject of Diderot's real Humanism, i.e., on his relation to
antique literature. Here Gillot's book takes us much farther, especially in the chapter *Anciens et Modernes* (pp. 232 ff.). Yet the line of connection to the *Neveu de
Rameau* is not drawn. That we shall now do.

Diderot's *Satire seconde* has as its motto a line from one of Horace's *Satires* (II,
7, 14):

> *Vertumnis, quotquot sunt, natus iniquis.*

We shall return to it later. Let us first look at Diderot's *Satire première*. It too has a
motto from Horace (*Sat.*, II, 1, 27 f.):

> *Quot capitum vivunt, tot idem studiorum
> Milia . . .*

The short work is dedicated to Naigeon and bears the subtitle *Sur un passage de la première satire du second livre d'Horace*. The theme of Horace's satire from which Diderot took his motto is this: Horace justifies his continuing to write satiric poetry and the publication of a second book in the "amusing form of consulting the lawyer Trebatius as to how he shall conduct himself toward critics" (Kiessling-Heinze). With this theme Diderot's satire has nothing to do. In the course of his justification, however, Horace had pointed out that writing satires was a natural urge in him and that every man has his passion. It is in this context that the words which Diderot took for his motto occur. For Diderot it is as it were a cue: it incites him to a train of thought in which four chief elements can be distinguished. First: every man has something in common with an animal. "Il y a l'homme loup, l'homme tigre, l'homme renard, l'homme taupe," etc.[5] Second: So many kinds of men, so many natural cries. "Autant d'hommes, autant de cris divers . . . Il y a le cri de la nature [6] . . . Comment se fait-il que, dans les arts d'imitation, ce cri de nature qui nous est propre soit si difficile à trouver? Comment se fait-il que le poète qui l'a saisi, nous étonne et nous transporte? . . . Combien de cris discordants dans la seule forêt qu'on appelle société." Third: "Le cri de l'homme prend encore une infinité de formes diverses de la profession qu'il exerce. Souvent elles déguisent l'accent du caractère." Fourth: "A cette variété du cri de la nature, de la passion, du caractère, de la profession, joignez le diapason des moeurs nationales . . ." But this is only the skeleton of the piece. The logical structure is surrounded and concealed by a wealth of anecdotes about Parisian society, which Diderot tells to their best advantage in a stream of witty gossip. Significant of his literary manner is the playful self-reproach: "et voilà, me dîtes-vous, qu'au lieu de vous avoir éclairci un passage d'Horace, je vous ai presque fait une satire a la manière de Perse." If Diderot compares himself to Persius, whom philologists today reject, [7] he doubtless felt that, in his criticism of manners, a criticism based on the Stoic philosophy, the satirist was akin to him. Diderot's hobby—as he himself well knew—was moral preaching: "le tic d'Horace est de faire

[5] We find these ideas once again in the *Neveu de Rameau*: "Nous dévorons comme des loups . . . nous déchirons comme des tigres . . . il se fait un beau bruit dans la ménagerie. Jamais on ne vit tant de bêtes tristes, acariâtres, malfaisantes et courroucées" (*Oeuvres*, V, 439 f.).

[6] This theme too reappears in the *Neveu* and becomes of primary importance for Diderot's aesthetics: "Le chant est une imitation, par les sons, d'une échelle inventée par l'art ou inspirée par la nature, comme il vous plaira, ou par la voix ou par l'instrument, des bruits physiques ou des accents de la passion, et vous voyez qu'en changeant là-dedans les choses à changer, la définition conviendrait exactement à la peinture, à l'éloquence, à la sculpture et à la poésie" (V, 458 f.). A briefer formula is his: "Le modèle du musicien, c'est le cri de l'homme passionné" (V, 459 n.). Or again in the *Neveu* the characterization of the "new style" in music: "c'est au cri animal de la passion à dicter la ligne qui nous convient" (V, 466).

[7] Schanz-Hosius, *Geschichte der römischen Literatur*, pt. II (1935), p. 481: "The reader lays down the poet's volume with a feeling of relief." Mommsen had called Persius "a proud and faint-hearted youth devoted to poetry." Goethe could still prize the poet "who, concealing the bitterest discontent in sibylline gnomes, expresses his despair in somber hexameters" (*Jub.-Ausg.*, XXXVII, 217).—A phrase from Persius' Prologue—"ingenii largitor venter"—is quoted in *Le Neveu de Rameau*.—A prose *Satire contre le luxe dans le goût de Perse* is included in the *Salon* of 1767 (*Oeuvres*, XI, 89 ff.). The *Salons* are full of quotations from Latin poets.

des vers; le tic de Trebatius et de Burigny de parler antiquité, le mien de moraliser …" [8]

If we put this "First Satire" with the work known as *Le Neveu de Rameau*, we are led to conjecture that Diderot planned a series of satires in prose, in which the dialogue with Rameau was included as Number 2. Though Diderot opened the way for many modern and ultramodern aesthetic theories, he all his life remained an enthusiastic reverer of the ancients. Horace was one of his favorite poets. Gillot says on the subject (pp. 245–6): "Le poète de Tibur est, pour lui, le familier dont l'intimité le suit à travers la vie, tantôt conseiller, tantôt confident, le sage qui, entre tous les plaisirs qu'il demande à la vie, ne prise, lui aussi, rien tant que le repos et l'innocence de la campagne et, recherché des grands, plus qu'aucun autre 'corrompu' par leur faveur, mais, par ailleurs, 'le plus adroit corrupteur des puissants', maudit Mécène qui le rappelle à la cour, s'indigne, lui aussi, qu'on puisse croire l'avoir acheté par des richesses et offre de les restituer si on les met à si haut prix. 'Précepteur de tous les hommes dans la morale, de tous les littérateurs dans l'art d'écrire', son art des contrastes, son 'élévation' dans les Odes, sa 'raison' dans les Épîtres, sa 'finesse' dans la satire, 'son goût exquis dans tous les ouvrages', semblent à Diderot lui assurer la primauté sur tous les poètes de Rome." But we know still more concerning Diderot's relation to Horace.[9]

When Diderot says: "Le tic d'Horace est de faire des vers . . . ; le mien de moraliser"—this already implies that to him the most important thing in Horace's satires is their criticism of manners, while their poetic form means little to him. Diderot has neither inclination nor talent for writing verse.[10] Hence he will write his satires in prose. Yet now and again he tried to turn one of Horace's poems into French verse. In this manner he produced the—unfortunately undated—*Traduction libre du commencement de la première satire d'Horace* (*Oeuvres*, IX, 42 ff.). It begins with an imitation of the first 22 lines of the original. Then Diderot goes on:

> *Je voulais jusqu'au bout suivre les pas d'Horace;*
> *Mais le dirai-je! ici mon guide s'embarrasse.*
> *Son écrit décousu n'offre à mon jugement*
> *Que deux lambeaux exquis rapprochés sottement.*

A modern commentator on Horace also says: "From here (v. 22) there is no bridge to the following considerations, carefully as Horace tries to conceal the break . . ." (Kiessling-Heinze). Diderot's attempt at a translation is of importance to us only as a symptom of his interest in Horace. The same is true of his imitation of an ode of Horace's and of a very free treatment of a theme from one of Horace's satires (*Oeuvres*, IX, 45 and 47; undated). In addition we have the *Chant lyrique* (*Oeuvres*, IX, 35 ff.) with the Horatian motto "Nil sine divite vena." The short work is preceded by the following argument: "L'auteur s'adresse aux jeunes poètes de son temps et leur dit 'Vous qui vous proposez de chanter le beauté, laissez à Anacréon ses roses et à l'Arioste ses perles. Ces deux poètes ainsi qu' Homère, Virgile, Tibulle et

---

[8] "Moralizing" is also a weakness of the "fatalist" Jacques (*Oeuvres*, VI, 82).

[9] Cf. also the description of Horace's life in the country in *Oeuvres*, II, 434.— Diderot applies to the painter what Horace (*Epi.*, II, ll. 211 ff.) says of the dramatic poet (*Oeuvres*), XI, 79).—Other references: *Corr. inédite*, I, 99; I, 199; etc.

[10] The poems of his which have come down to us are almost all light *vers de société*.

le Tasse, ont eu leur veine. Ayez la vôtre. Voulez-vous savoir ce que c'est qu'un poète? Interrogez les mânes d'Horace, et continuez d'écrire ou n'écrivez plus.' " This program is then carried out in a series of stanzas. Finally, Horace appears in a sort of vision to the poet, who characterizes him as

> . . . sectateur de la simple nature
> Et jusque chez les morts disciple d'Épicure

and receives instruction from him concerning the nature and end of poetry. On another occasion Diderot defends Horace's *Ars poetica* against a pedantic editor (VI, 384). Or, in 1773, he writes a rather long treatise in which he proposes to the Abbé Galiani—who had composed a commentary on Horace, not published until 1821—an interpretation of a line of Horace (*Carmina*, III, 6, 1) differing from the one usually accepted (VI, 289–302). In an undated letter to Naigeon he takes Horace as compurgator for his own aesthetics: "Oui, mon ami. Horace s'est récrié sur l'anticomanie, [11] et Horace avoit raison. Je ne scaurois faire un certain cas de celui qui cherche au frontispice le nom de l'auteur, pour scavoir s'il doit approuver ou blâmer . . . Si je dis que l'Art poétique d'Horace est l'ouvrage d' un homme de génie et l'Art poétique de Boileau l'ouvrage d' un homme de sens qui a du goût et qui scait très bien faire un vers, M. de Laharpe se récriera . . ." (*Correspondance inédite* [1931], Vol. I, 304 f.). Finally, let us recall that the *Supplément au voyage de Bougainville* (1772) also has a motto from Horace (*Sat.*, I, 2, 73 ff.): [12]

> At quanto meliora monet pugnantiaque istis
> Dives opis natura suae, tu si modo recte
> Dispensare velis, ac non fugienda petendis
> Immiscere. Tuo vitio rerumne labores,
> Nil referre putas?

What does this mean? And with what is this satire of Horace's concerned? Let us follow Kiessling-Heinze again. "The satire is chiefly directed against the increasing trend toward adulterous relations in the high society of Horace's day, but not censoriously, from the standpoint of the moralist, but rather mocking at it as folly, in the frivolous tone then current, by singling out the *moechus* as a type of human folly." Horace sets forth that adultery can sometimes have very painful consequences, "whereas relations with manumitted girls are much safer." A man should obey the bidding of nature, but not indulge in the pursuit of matrons, "which produces more satiety than pleasure." Now come the lines which Diderot uses as a motto. They mean, roughly: "How much better—and how contrary to your (the adulterer's) doings—are the means which mother nature, in her bounty, offers to satisfy the urge, if you will only use them rightly and remain within the limits of pleasures worth pursuing. Do you think it makes no difference whether you are guilty of your own vexation or whether it is grounded in the nature of things?" Into this satire Diderot could read a recommendation of a purely natural sexual morality which made pleasure legitimate—an antique counterpart, as it were, to his considerations "sur l'inconvénient d'attacher des idées morales à certaines actions physiques qui

---

[11] Allusion to Horace, *Epi.*, II, 1.
[12] So do *Le Père de famille* (*Ars poetica*, 156 f.), *Le Fils naturel* (*ibid.*, 363 ff.), *De la poésie dramatique* (*ibid.*, 348 f.).—There is an allusion to Horace in Vol. VI, 44.

n'en comportent pas"—so runs the subtitle of the *Supplément*. We see, then, that
Diderot likes, by giving his works mottos, to connect them with trains of thought in
his favorite poet Horace. He, the modern, treats human problems which had already
occupied his master Horace. But he treats them in prose—which form he also used
for his plays.

Now the same applies to the *Neveu de Rameau*. This "Second Satire" of Diderot's
is connected by its motto with the seventh satire of Horace's second book. Horace's
theme here is the Stoic paradox: "Only the wise man is free, and every fool is a
slave." Now this thesis—and herein lies the charm of the piece—is maintained by
a slave, and against his own master. Davus, the slave, sets forth that most men perpetually oscillate between right and wrong. What makes them fools is this *inaequalitas*.[13] Here is a rich man who now parades in luxury, now plays the poor man; now
wants to whore in Rome, now to philosophize in Athens,

> *Vertumnis, quotquot sunt, natus iniquis.*

This is the motto of the *Neveu*. *Vertumnus* (connected with *verto*) is the change-
able god of the seasons, "an Italian Proteus" (Kiessling-Heinze), later the designation of instability itself. The fool whose defect is *inaequalitas* owes that frailty, as
it were, to the unpropitious Vertumnus-deities under whose sign he was born.[14]
Davus brazenly reckons even his master Horace among the fools: "Do you not
praise the frugal manners of olden times, and yet would not be put back in those
days for anything? You yourself do not take your conviction seriously. In Rome you
long for country life, but in the country you are mad about the city. When you are
not invited out, you praise your poor repast of greens. But you only too gladly stuff
yourself in the house of your rich patrons. You love another man's wife and are her
slave; I am contented with a wench. What is the difference between us? You pretend to be my master and yet are the slave of so many things and people whereon
the satisfaction of your desires depends. You are jerked back and forth by them like
the puppet on its string:

> 81   *Tu, mihi qui imperitas, aliis servis miser atque*
> *Duceris ut nervis alienis mobile lignum.*

Who is free? Only the wise man!"

Such is the structure of Horace's satire. If we call to mind the content of the
Neveu de Rameau, the inner connection is apparent at once. We see the resemblance between the slave Davus, who takes advantage of the fool's license granted
during the Saturnalia, and the parasite Rameau, whose *inaequalitas* is emphasized
as the chief trait of his character at the very beginning: "c'est un composé de hauteur
et de bassesse, de bon sens et de déraison . . . Quelquefois il est maigre et hâve . . .
Le mois suivant, il est gras et replet . . . Aujourd'hui en linge sale . . . Demain poudré,

[13] In the same sense Horace says (*Sat.*, I, 3, 9) "nil aequale homini fuit ille" of
the eccentric singer Tigellius.

[14] *Vertumnus* is put in the plural "as if the different manifestations of the deity
were independent divine persons" (Kiessling-Heinze). *Vertumnis iniquis nasci* is
equivalent to being born under an "unlucky star." To Diderot's question why, with
such a great musical gift, he had made nothing of it, Rameau points to the sky with
the words: "Et l'astre! l'astre!" When Nature formed him, she grimaced (*Oeuvres*,
V, 475).

chaussé, frisé . . ." (*Oeuvres*, V, 388). Compare with this Horace's characterization of the singer Tigellius (*Sat.*, I, 3). Of him we read l. 17 f. "nil fuit unquam sic impar sibi"; of Rameau's nephew: "rien ne dissemble plus de lui que lui-même" (V, 388). Perhaps Diderot also had in mind the idea of *inaequalitas* in composing the following remark addressed to Rameau: "Je rêve à l'inégalité de votre ton tantôt haut, tantôt bas" (V, 455). But this resemblance between Davus and Rameau is not all. More important, I think, is the fact that the basic theme—contrast between the fool, enslaved by want, necessities, lusts, and passions, and the self-sufficient and therefore only free man, the sage—is identical in the two works. To man's enslavement by his wants there corresponds in Diderot the theme: "l'homme nécessiteux . . . passe sa vie à prendre et à exécuter des positions." And to Horace's marionette simile there corresponds the theme of pantomime, with its conclusion: "il y a pourtant un être dispensé de la pantomime, c'est le philosophe qui n'a rien et ne demande rien." Marionette and pantomime—both derive from the realm of theatrical metaphors (*supra*, p. 138). We were able to trace the marionette simile back to Plato, the whole complex of metaphors then became the common property of the cynical diatribe, from which it presumably made its way into Horace. That Diderot substituted for it the related image of the great pantomime of life is connected with the fact that pantomime—by which, however, in contrast to German and English usage, he understands the gestures and the music which accompany an actor's performance—was a lively concern of Diderot's in connection with his theory of the drama: a chapter of his treatise *De la poésie dramatique* is devoted to it (*Oeuvres*, VII, 377 ff.) as well as a separate essay (VIII, 458 ff.). Rameau's nephew himself is not only, and perhaps, in Diderot's view, not primarily, a musician: he is at least as much a virtuoso of—here, however, mute—pantomime. He is the born, the inspired imitator: and, according to Diderot's conviction, all art is *imitatio naturae*. To that extent the nephew is not only a venal parasite, but in addition a highly gifted artistic temperament which was destroyed by its own faults, to be sure, but also by social injustice. But the "I" of the dialogue is *Denis le philosophe*,[15] who enjoyed being called Diogenes and who here mentions him by name: "Diogène se moquait des besoins" (484). The cynic sage needs nothing but nature. And which way does the savage turn? "A la terre, aux animaux, aux poissons, aux arbres, aux herbes, aux racines, aux ruisseaux" (484). The model savage from Tahiti, whom we encounter in the *Supplément au voyage de Bougainville*, and Diogenes are two incarnations of the ideal of life which appeared the worthiest to the philosopher Denis and which alone leads to inward and outward freedom. So Horace had thought and written, and the structural plan—no more!—of Horace's satire gave Denis Diderot the suggestion for his masterpiece.

The Excursuses upon Montesquieu and Diderot go beyond the legitimate concerns of this book, inasmuch as they have no relation to the Latin Middle Ages. But

---

[15] So Diderot calls himself in *Regrets sur ma vieille robe de chambre*, in which short work the self-sufficient sage is again praised.—Another significant passage occurs in *Jacques le fataliste*: "Jacques, vous êtes une espèce de philosophe, convenez-en. Je sais bien que c'est une race d'hommes odieuse aux grands, devant lesquels ils ne fléchissent pas le genou; aux magistrats . . . ; aux prêtres . . . ; aux poètes, gens sans principes et qui regardent sottement la philosophie comme la cognée des beaux-arts, sans compter que ceux même d'entre eux qui se sont exercés dans le genre odieux de la satire, n'ont été que des flatteurs . . ." (VI, 78).

the theme of the book leads naturally to a wider problem: that of the relation of European literature to the Latinity of all epochs. I have included these studies of Montesquieu and Diderot among the Excursuses because they show that modern literary historiography risks falling into error if it loses the ground of Humanistic education from under its feet.

APPENDIX
and
BIBLIOGRAPHICAL NOTE

APPENDIX

The Medieval Bases
of Western Thought*

A European scholar who has dipped into medieval lore cannot but feel deeply grateful for the contributions to our knowledge which have been made in recent times by American scholarship. You have a great institution called the Medieval Academy of America. We have nothing of the kind in Europe. Historians such as Charles Homer Haskins, philologists such as Charles H. Beeson and Edward Kennard Rand, have shed much light on the Middle Ages. The phenomenon which I might call American medievalism is highly interesting, and one which I should like to study some time. I believe that it has a deep spiritual meaning.

This was borne in on my mind when I studied those admirable works of Henry Adams, *The Education of Henry Adams* and *Mont-Saint-Michel and Chartres*. It is obvious that Henry Adams was led to northern France by the instinct of his race. He was trying to get at the roots of the civilization to which he belonged. It was an offshoot, as Toynbee would say, of that Western society which developed in Romanized Europe. From the close of the eleventh century to the first third of the thirteenth, northern France and England were more or less united politically. From the point of view of cultural history they formed a unity during those one hundred and fifty years. You find prominent Frenchmen in Britain as you find English scholars occupying French episcopal sees. Students and teachers at the great episcopal schools of that glorious twelfth century spoke Latin and French, irrespective of their origin. That is what Henry Adams realized; that is why he undertook his pilgrimage. He went in search of his origins. But there were others who followed the same track.

When America became conscious of herself she strove to acquire the cultural inheritance of Europe. American literature and scholarship can boast of a number of pioneers who, as it were, conquered the European past. Some went to Spain, like Washington Irving or Ticknor, some to Italy, others to France and Germany. But what strikes me most is this: The American mind might go back to Puritanism or to William Penn, but it lacked that which preceded them; it lacked the Middle Ages. It was in the position of a man who has never known his mother. The American conquest of the Middle Ages has something of that romantic glamor and of that deep sentimental urge which we might expect in a man who should set out to find his lost mother.

If the story of the American conquest of the Middle Ages were told, it would have to dwell on the study and the cult of Dante which flowered in New England

* A lecture delivered July 3, 1949, at the Goethe Bicentennial Convocation, at Aspen, Colorado, and added by the author to the English translation of this book.

and which is again flourishing in T. S. Eliot. To the mind of the Bostonians in the 1880's, Dante was not merely one of the world's greatest poets. They were of the opinion, as Van Wyck Brooks has it, that the world had been going to the dogs ever since the time of Dante. Dante, to them, appeared as the perfect expression of a perfect state of society. It was a romantic vision of the same kind as that which set the German romantic poets of 1800 dreaming about the ideal Middle Ages. Of late such visions seem to crystallize around St. Thomas Aquinas, in Europe as well as in America. But we may venture to believe that the poet will outshine the philosopher. The poet carries a splendor and an imaginative power with which the thinker can hardly ever vie. Plato soars to the highest flights when he abandons conceptual thought for poetical myth. But you will not be able to transpose Aristotle's or St. Thomas' severe disquisitions into poetry; they belong to another order.

When Haskins tried to interest a wider public in "the Renaissance of the twelfth century," he found it necessary to consider the question whether the Middle Ages had been "progressive," and he ventured to answer in the affirmative. I do not feel certain that this attempt can be successful, nor do I believe that it is necessary. We have learned (have we not?) to criticize the notion of linear progress in history. And we no longer feel it incumbent on us to justify the ways of God to man. A Gothic cathedral is not superseded by the magnificent dome of St. Peter's, nor is Dante's poem by Shakespeare's plays. The spiritual gems of every age are to be found in its art and poetry rather than in its philosophy and science. Scholasticism is certainly a great achievement of the human mind. It is the medieval basis of Roman Catholic thought; but that is only a part of Western thought. My experience in studying the Middle Ages has been that the orthodox view of medieval thought, such as presented for instance by a historian as eminent as Étienne Gilson, tends to be one-sided. If you view the development of medieval thinking mainly as a preparatory stage for the flowering of Thomistic philosophy, you will be likely to overlook much that is interesting in the twelfth century—even passionately interesting for a twentieth-century mind.

It would be tedious to go into details. But I could show you that such surprisingly modern problems as the value of sexual love and its place in a preordained divine world order were discussed about the time of the Second Crusade. Nor is this to be wondered at if we remember that the passion and sorrow of love were an emotional discovery of the French troubadours and their successors. The poetry of modern love is as great an achievement of the Middle Ages as the cycle of the seven liberal arts or the rise of the universities. This love enters the structure of Dante's universe. It pervades the Latin lyric of the twelfth century as it does the long-winded French tales of chivalry and romance. Some of us may find it more easily accessible than the syllogisms of the Schoolmen. It could be exalted to the ideals of courtly love, which were revived for the last time by Edmund Spenser. But it could also, of course, be debased so as to flatter the grosser instincts of man. This happened in the *Roman de la Rose*. In Chaucer you get a glimpse of both these views.

I am transgressing, you observe, the strict temporal limits of the so-called Middle Ages. But I believe it is necessary to do so. When I tried to grasp the beginnings of the medieval world, I was led back to imperial Rome and to late antiquity in general. Some features of the medieval mind would emerge in the first century of our era, some would point back to the Hellenistic epoch. On the other hand, most of them survived the so-called Renaissance and were well alive until the end of the seventeenth century, partly in Spain, partly in England or elsewhere. If you will allow me a paradox, I seemed to discover that there was no such thing as the Middle Ages which I had been looking for. I had been taught about them, but I had been taught wrongly. I felt like the schoolboy who wrote in his copybook: "The Middle Ages is what comes between antiquity and posterity." There is too much loose thinking, I believe, about the traditional period-divisions. They will have to be revised.

A great English historian, G. M. Trevelyan, is of the opinion that the real break in modern history is not the sixteenth century, but the eighteenth. The Industrial Revolution has meant a much more radical change than the Renaissance or the Reformation. Medieval forms of life subsist until about 1750, to put it roughly. When we consider on the other hand that medieval thought and expression become creative only around 1050, we get a period of about seven hundred years which manifests a unity of structure. We need not bother to find a name for this period. But if we try to consider it as a cultural unit, we may get a better understanding of our past.

The middle of the eighteenth century witnessed not only the beginnings of that great economic change which is termed the Industrial Revolution. It saw also the first powerful revolt against cultural tradition, which is marked by Rousseau. This tradition was restated by the universal genius of Goethe. But it was restated for the last time. Goethe has not been succeeded by another universal genius. He had a very clear consciousness of belonging to this tradition. He pointed to Homer, to Plato, to Aristotle, and to the Bible as its foundations. He was stepping into the shoes of the Elders, many of whom he thought greater than himself. History was to him a sequence of great minds which commanded respect and loyalty. Viewed in the light of the present, he seems to be nearer to Dante and to Shakespeare than to us. He is the last link of that golden chain. Yet he is not too remote from us. We can still grasp that link.

The medium of this tradition is literature, that is, imaginative writing. This is a trite statement, but there are reasons to remind ourselves of it. Some eminent philosophers of our time are raising the question whether Goethe's thought is adequate to the needs of the present. This question will be amply discussed in our conferences. But we may generalize the problem and ask: What is the relation between poetry and philosophy? Have they anything in common? Is there a borderland in which they meet? Or are they mutually exclusive? And does history show us a rivalry between these two forms of spiritual creation?

Goethe was still living when Auguste Comte began to publish the unwieldy volumes of his *System of Positive Philosophy*. In it he expounded a law of history according to which humanity has to pass through three stages: the theological, the metaphysical, and the positive. We are now in this third stage; therefore we have to discard theology and metaphysics. Poetry, of course, goes back to the theological stage: witness Homer. Some decades later, the German philosopher Dilthey explained that the sixteenth century had produced magnificent poetry such as that of Shakespeare and Cervantes. The poets had had their day. But in the seventeenth century they were succeeded by the great philosophical system-builders. What has philosophy to say today? Does it pretend to being a substitute for literature altogether? Does it pretend to invalidate it? Does it consider poetry as an obsolete form of spiritual utterance? Let us face these questions and consider them in the light of history.

Homer is the great ancestor of European poetry. He was the teacher of Greece. Yet when philosophy was born there, it opposed him violently. Heraclitus said: "He ought to be chastised by rods." Plato disapproved of him. These attacks proved ineffectual. In the latest phase of Greek thought the poetry of Homer was considered as Holy Writ. The Neo-Platonists interpreted it and revealed its hidden meaning.

Philosophy then disappeared from the European stage for many centuries. It was too high a form of intellectual activity for the Dark Ages. The rising northern nations had to devote their mental energy to learning the rudiments. They conned Latin grammar and scanned Latin verse. St. Anselm, who died in 1109, is the first original thinker of the Middle Ages. During the twelfth century a wonderful climate of spring spreads over Europe. Bold philosophical and theological questions are asked and beautiful blossoms of song crop up. Thought and poetry are wedded harmoniously. Yet, towards the close of the century, we witness a change. The students have come under the spell of a kind of hairsplitting which goes by the name of dialectics. The main effort of education had been the study of the *auctores*, that is to say, of a cycle of Latin writers who enjoyed a canonical authority.

Allow me to dwell a little on this point. It has not received sufficient attention, I believe. It concerns a problem which is crucial not only for the understanding but for the transmission of the humanities. The problem can be stated thus: What is a classic? T. S. Eliot, as you remember, raised this question in 1944. Sainte-Beuve had done so in 1850. Every age is confronted with this question. I am told that some American universities have listed the hundred or even the hundred and ten best books of the world. Now let us go back some seven hundred years. Which selection of the best books was proposed to students at that time?

I will not trouble you with a list of some twenty or thirty names which were considered indispensable. Most of them would be unfamiliar. Greek authors, of course, are absent. The tale of Troy was accessible only in the form of a few bungling and raw abridgments. Tedious Latin versifications of the Bible were prescribed and enjoyed the same authority as the epic and satirical poets of pagan Rome. These satirists won special favor because they were considered teachers of virtue. When Horace is mentioned by Dante, he appears as *Orazio satiro*; his odes were almost unknown. Rhetoric, history, geography were studied in textbooks dating from the late imperial era. There was a curious bias for authors who exhibit the most affected mannerisms of decadent antiquity. A pompous and sophisticated style was valued as the highest achievement of literary composition. But what may seem most surprising is that all the authors of the program are considered as of the same rank. All the authors were authorities. They form the imposing block of tradition. There is no historical sense, and we may be thankful for it. For only those massive battalions of Latinity were powerful enough to give the schooling which our barbarian forefathers needed.

And it did work. The Middle Ages had their own view of antiquity. There is such a thing as what I have called elsewhere medieval antiquity. To the refined taste of the moderns it may seem distorted, mutilated, or quaint. Yet it was a force that shaped the minds of that twelfth century, which was essentially an epoch of youth pushing to the front. To witness the contact of this youth with hoary age is a delightful spectacle. We can follow it from decade to decade. It culminates, as far as I am able to see, about the year 1170. At that date we find poetical and rhetorical manifestoes which amount to a sort of Declaration of Rights. They emanate from a group of writers who term themselves "the Moderns." They proclaim new standards in poetry, in the art of prose, in philosophy, and in all the other branches of knowledge. They believe that a new age is dawning and they quote with approval the words of St. Paul: "The old things are passed away; behold, they are become new." You may take that as a sample of the delectable naïveté of that epoch which knew a minimum of ecclesiastical censure. There was no Inquisition yet; there was no papal supervision of studies; theology and the finer elaboration of dogma were still floating. The twelfth century enjoyed an intellectual freedom which its successor was to abolish. It is a fallacy to talk of the Middle Ages as if they were a uniform age. We might just as well talk of, say, the last four centuries as if they were made of the same stuff. We must try to picture every century as something unique, differing profoundly from the others. It will mark a progress of historical comprehension if we avoid talking of the "medieval mind."

But let me turn back to the "Moderns" of 1170. About fifty years earlier the "Ancients" had been described as giants and the "Moderns" as dwarfs who could enjoy a wider perspective merely because they stood on the shoulders of those giants. But towards the close of the century we find the full-fledged Moderns boasting that they are the equals of their elders. They even profess a certain fastidiousness concerning the style of the classics. They feel that they can do things better. They coin many new words.

They are rebels—but only to a certain extent. For they go on writing Latin. But while they were polishing elaborate verses, another group rose which carried rebellion further. The greatest humanist of the twelfth century, John of Salisbury, complained about the growing contempt for grammar, rhetoric, and letters. The classical authors are despised! Those who remain loyal to them are met with the sneering response: "What does this old ass think? Why does he harp upon the sayings and the deeds of the Ancients? We find the fountainhead of knowledge in ourselves."

These wonderful young people have discovered the power of reasoning and the irresistible attraction of logical argument soaring high above facts and knowledge of any kind. It appears to them as a sublime gift which they possess by right of birth. These raving dialecticians will prove and refute, affirm and deny whatever you like. They bear a remote resemblance to the Greek Sophists. Their interest for us is that they represent a tendency to break away from the system of education based on letters. Their attempt was not successful because they had nothing to replace it.

But about 1200 we already find new domains of learning: law and medicine. A new system of education develops. The universities supplant the episcopal schools. The works of Aristotle are spread in Latin translations. They supply an immense body of doctrine on the universe, on natural history, and on metaphysics. It will be adapted and transformed in the great scholastic systems. The thirteenth century means the triumph of philosophy. Philosophy pervades everything and usurps every-thing. The splendid flowering of Latin poetry and literature comes to a sudden standstill about 1225. The reason can be found in an educational reform. The course of studies prescribed for the University of Paris was fundamentally altered in 1215. The study of the classics is abolished, and that of formal logic is put in its place.

Literature and rhetoric continued to be taught by some stray individuals and in some backward schools. But life was made miserable for its teachers. They were reviled by the lieutenants of philosophy. A formidable Battle of the Books was waged. In a poem about that subject the philosopher is made to say to the poet: "I have pursued the course of learning; but you prefer childish things such as prose and verse. What is their use? They must be reckoned for nothing. . . . You know grammar, but you have no inkling of science nor of logic. Why then do you brag? You are an ignoramus." That is the state of things about the year 1250. Some years later Roger Bacon launches his violent attacks against Albert the Great and St. Thomas. He scolds them for having shelved the study of Latin, Greek, and Hebrew. The thirteenth century is to him a falling back into barbarism. It is perhaps not beside the point to observe that Goethe praises him highly. Goethe varied in his judgment concerning the Middle Ages. On the whole he considered them a period of darkness. But the fact that a mind like Roger Bacon's was possible in that age confirmed Goethe in his belief that excellent people are to be found in all epochs and that their succession constitutes a sort of galaxy which stretches over the wide expanse of night.

What have I been driving at? I have tried to show that humanistic tradition is from time to time attacked by philosophy. It may suffer a serious setback from these aggressions. Many signs seem to point to the fact that we are faced once more with an incursion of philosophers, existentialists or others. It would be a very good thing, I think, if the issues at stake were made quite clear. The cause that I am pleading —that is, the place of letters in education—might be clarified and invigorated by such a debate.

It remains to be seen whether our age will produce a philosophy capable of uni-fying thought and of ennobling human life. It seems doubtful, because during the last twenty-five hundred years philosophy has always been split into contending schools. Even the great age of scholasticism had room for widely different systems, such as those of St. Bonaventure and St. Thomas. Surely, philosophy never before or after had such a commanding power as then. It had the support of the mightiest spiritual body that has ever existed: the Catholic Church, as yet undivided. Its au-thority was to suffer in the fourteenth century by the Babylonian Exile of Avignon and was to undergo a further diminution by the conciliar movement of the fif-teenth century.

If ever a philosophical school could boast of presenting in a luminous way the sum total of things human and divine, it was the school of St. Thomas. How is it possible then that such a magnificent and ordered system gave way so soon. How can its supporters account for that? This may well be one of the most interesting problems in the history of Western thought. A system of philosophy which even today is considered the only safe guidance for Catholic education lost its hold on men's minds after two or three generations. We look in vain for explanations of that fact. Étienne Gilson states it in the following terms: "If the fourteenth century shows thinkers who adhered to Thomism, yet nobody has really continued the work of the master. The newest and profoundest aspects of this thought only just survived, encased so to speak in the mass of his work and being transmitted with it without being creative." That is the statement of a historian. What the philosophers and theologians would have to say about it, is not for me to decide. But we may well ask ourselves whether this system of Christian philosophy does not look like a magnificent failure. Has any succeeding system been more fortunate? Evidently not. European philosophies are doomed, so it seems, to be short-lived—just as European empires have been. Is philosophy an attitude of the mind which is destined to disappear in the long run? This seems to be the outlook of Toynbee.

If philosophy is able to explain history, it ought also to explain poetry. For poetry is one of the most powerful manifestations of mankind. It is present in all ages and civilizations. It has a far wider appeal than science. One of the great features of Aristotle is that he found room for poetry in his philosophical survey. We are bound to acknowledge that, even if we feel that his account of poetry is limited by the fact that he knew nothing but Greek poetry. But has any other leading philosopher handled that problem? I am not aware of it. The rebirth of Aristotelianism which led to scholasticism neglected the Poetics. Poetry remains outside the thought of St. Thomas. It is only accidentally that he discourses on it. It is interesting to follow his argument. He quotes with approval the old Greek saying that the poets are liars; if poetry is a science, it contains a minimum of truth and it is the lowest imaginable science. It is below reason just as theology is above reason. Poets make use of the symbolical or metaphorical mode of speech in order to recommend their fables. They do so *propter defectum veritatis*. St. Albert the Great had already said: "The poetical mode is the weakest among the modes of philosophy." The great scholastics of the thirteenth century are not interested in poetry. You will look in vain for a scholastic vindication of it.

And yet St. Thomas is the author of some of the most splendid hymns of the Roman Breviary and Missal. He was entrusted by the pope with the task of composing the office for the new festival of Corpus Christi, and he produced admirable liturgical verse. "Severity of form," says a critic, "economy of expression, scholastic exactness of doctrinal statement are joined to a metrical skill which owes as much to the genius of the poet as to a study of predecessors." [1] St. Thomas then was able to write marvelous poetry, but he did not conceive of it as poetry. It was sacred song, couched in the traditional forms of the Church. Its medium was meter and rhyme, but its substance was one of the central mysteries of faith. It was a composition which embodied theological truth. That might have led him to reconsider his views on poetry. But it did not. He had more urgent business.

The case of St. Thomas is a typical instance of what we may call the medieval view of poetry. Poetry was viewed as part and parcel of the inheritance of paganism. It ranked with grammar, rhetoric, mythology, and the rest. These branches of knowledge were contained in the books of the pagans. The Fathers of the Church had proved from Scripture that it was lawful for Christians to make use of these

[1] F. J. E. Raby, A *History of Christian-Latin Poetry* (1927), p. 405.

arts. They pointed out that St. Paul had quoted verses of Greek poets. They further drew attention to the fact that the Jews, when leaving Egypt, took with them vessels of silver and gold. The allegorical meaning of that fact is, according to St. Augustine, that Christians are justified in appropriating pagan arts for their use. There have been other analogous attempts to justify the same thing. But neither the patristic nor the scholastic thinkers found it necessary to go deeply into the matter. It was a domain which was left in a certain twilight.

Poetry was Latin poetry, and it was taken over from the great storehouse of antiquity. Ought it to have been discredited because the Ancients did not know the true faith? Very few disciplinarians held so austere a view. They could always be silenced by the argument that pagan mythology was a veiled presentment of moral truth. A great amount of sagacity and ingenuity was spent on the demonstration of that proposition. A German poet who wrote in Latin in the year 1280 is less sophisticated. He says: "If these authors have not learned the Catholic Faith, yet they have been staunch supporters of their own religion. I firmly believe that they would have adhered to Catholicism, had they known it. It is far better to ignore the faith than to lapse into heresy." This solution seems admirable common sense though it may not be sound theology.

If, as I contend, Thomism thought little of poetry, then we should of course like to know what its followers had to say about a man like Dante. What strikes us is that they hardly noticed him. When Dante published his poem, about 1320, there were no literary reviews, no critics, and no highbrows. There was no lying in wait for rising geniuses and new masterpieces. People did not get excited about the fact that somebody had turned out a poem which was in keeping with Christian thought and feeling. Neither did they worry if another person wrote licentious verse. It was not yet the fashion for writers to proclaim from the housetops that they assented to the creed or dissented from it. Poetry and theology were kept apart. Religion was administered by priests, monks, and friars. They were supremely indifferent to the attitude of scribblers of verse and prose.

This was a healthy state of things. There was only one militant body in the Church: the order of St. Dominic. Its task was to fight heresy. And to this charge Dante was open, strange as it may seem to us. He was an independent thinker, and his reflections had led him to work out a system of political and ecclesiastical reform which he laid down in his treatise on monarchy, which was also a treatise on papacy. According to him, things had gone wrong for the last thousand years. The emperor Constantine was wrong when he alienated part of his privilege and endowed the successor of St. Peter with worldly dominion. The pope had been wrong to accept it. Dante advocated the return of the papacy to the poverty of St. Peter, the fisherman. He confidently expected a universal monarch who would restore the Empire to its former dignity. Indeed he went so far as to maintain that only by such a double reform could humanity be saved.

Now this was blatant heresy. Only a few years after Dante's death—in 1329—a Dominican friar published a severe censure of Dante's treatise. He does not, of course, refer expressly to the *Divine Comedy*, but in passing he abuses Dante as a self-deluded dabbler in verse and a loquacious sophist whose phantasms will divert the reader from the path of truth. Don't think that this friar was a troublesome meddler or a fanatic without authority. In 1329 Dante's treatise was publicly burnt in Rome. Even Cardinal Newman mildly censures him, saying: "Dante certainly does not scruple to place in his Inferno a Pope, whom the Church has since canonized, and his work on *Monarchia* is on the *Index*."

Today, Catholic critics as a rule assume a quite different position. They try to show that Dante was a correct Thomist and that his great poem is in strict accordance with the philosophy of the Church. But this attitude has been shown to be incorrect by the great historian of medieval philosophy whom I have already quoted: Étienne Gilson. According to him, Dante of course was well conversant with St. Thomas Aquinas, but in several important points he disagreed with him. The Thomism of Dante is an exploded myth. This becomes even more evident if one studies the famous Latin letter which Dante addressed to Can Grande when he presented to him the completed "Paradiso." This letter is a priceless document, for it reveals to us how Dante wished his poem to be considered. It has not yet received full attention because it bristles with allusions to the philosophical and rhetorical modes of expression which have baffled the commentators. Yet they can be deciphered and elucidated if placed in the context of the Latin terminology of the day. If we decode them, we get at Dante's clear meaning. It can be summed up in the statement: "My work offers poetry as well as philosophy." Dante, then, maintains that poetry has a cognitive function. That is exactly what scholasticism denied. Dante's utterance concludes and resolves the conflict between poetry and philosophy which had lasted for more than a hundred years.

It is the victorious answer of the poet who is the first among the Moderns to rank with the great classics of antiquity. This indeed is one of Dante's stupendous achievements. He proclaims it himself in the most unmistakable manner. When he is introduced into Limbo by his great guide Virgil, he is presented by him to four other masters who together with Virgil form a sort of *santa conversazione*: Homer, Ovid, Lucan, Horace. They are set apart among the choice spirits to whom a noble castle is allotted in the Elysian fields. They greet the Florentine with friendly mien and they do him even a greater honor: they formally admit him to their company as an equal. He is received as the sixth member into that Academy of Immortals. He is promoted to the peerage. Posterity has fully, if tardily, legalized and homologated this parity.

The posthumous fame of Dante is a story full of instruction. Fame was indeed meted out to him in no grudging measure by his Italian contemporaries. Commentaries began to crop up around his work very soon. The city of Florence, so much maligned by its greatest son, founded a chair for the exposition of his work and entrusted it to Boccaccio. But his fellow countrymen viewed him only as one who had ennobled their speech. In the sixteenth century he was made a canonical author together with Petrarch and Boccaccio. They were considered the triumvirate of Tuscan poetry. The unique position and grandeur of Dante were obscured by such a view. Petrarch and Boccaccio are not on a par with him, they are on a far lower plane. Yet the Italian critics opined that Dante's poetical language was rather rugged and did not compare favorably with the tasteful smoothness of his successors. That was of course a fundamental error of judgment. As time went on, Dante lost more ground. By 1800, he was nearly forgotten in Italy and hardly appreciated outside it. The Risorgimento rediscovered him. He was saluted as the herald of unified Italy. That was a second misinterpretation. It is only during the last fifty years that he has come to be recognized in his true greatness and in his full significance, which far transcends the horizon of one nation and one literature.

This tardy recognition of Dante can teach us how difficult it is to form a true estimate of a poet of the first magnitude while he is yet our neighbor in time and space. It is one of the laws which determine the literary tradition of Europe. We can observe the working of the same law in the case of Shakespeare. Do we hear that anybody in Europe lamented in 1616 the death of one of the greatest poets? Not even his name was known outside England. Britain played a considerable part in politics, but its poetry was undiscovered and remained so for more than a century. Italy enjoyed the undisputed literary leadership of Europe until about 1530. It was then supplanted by Spain until about 1650. Then came the turn of France. The predominance of French culture was undisputed for another century. Even England had to submit to it. It produced its Augustan Age. It was only in 1762 that an English critic stated:

> The French criticism has carried it before the Italian, with the rest of Europe. This dextrous people have found means to lead the taste as well as set the fashions of their neighbours. . . . They aspired to a sort of supremacy in letters. . . . Whatever their inducements were, they succeeded but too well in their attempt. Our obsequious and overmodest critics were run down by their authority. Their taste of Letters, with some worse things, was brought amongst us at the Restoration. Their language, their manners, nay their very prejudices were adopted by our Frenchified king and his Royalists.

These are the words of Richard Hurd, bishop of Worcester. They voice the rebellion against French taste which Lessing led in Germany about the same time. But it took many decades more for the European continent to free itself from French literary standards so effectively as to appreciate the full greatness of Shakespeare. Even today there are some European countries where Shakespeare has not received the undivided homage that is due him.

If Dante had to undergo a probation period of six hundred and Shakespeare one of three hundred years before being recognized as European classics, what can we say about Goethe, barely a century after his death? The Italian language as well as the English language gained world currency long ago. The German language has not been so fortunate, as you well know. Yet a classical poet must be read in his own language. Nobody is able to feel the greatness of Virgil unless he is able to enjoy him in Latin. You may read Dante in translations, but you will miss the heart and the voice of Dante. The desire to enjoy Dante is a sufficient reason for learning Italian. And the same holds good for Shakespeare and for Goethe. Spiritual treasures cannot be converted to the standard of a common currency. The best that the great classics hold in store for you will not pass into translations. You can use a common language for the purpose of bartering information, as we are doing here. But the message of the poet must be heard in his own tongue. If people are not prepared to do so, then they must do without the pearl of great price.

But to turn back to my subject. What about the medieval bases of Western thought? The bases of Western thought are classical antiquity and Christianity. The function of the Middle Ages was to receive that deposit, to transmit it, and to adapt it. Its most precious legacy, to my mind, is the spirit which it created while performing this task. Edward Kennard Rand has left us a beautiful book entitled *The Founders of the Middle Ages*. These founders were St. Jerome, St. Ambrose, St. Augustine, and a few others. They belong to the fourth and the fifth century of our era. They represent the last stage of Greco-Roman antiquity. And this last stage coincides with the first stage of Christianity. The lesson of the Middle Ages is reverent reception and faithful transmission of a precious deposit. This is also the lesson which we may draw from Dante. And it is also the lesson of Goethe, which he taught in his poetry, in his historical and philosophical writings, in his letters and his talks. The nineteenth century produced a type of writer who championed revolutionary ideas and revolutionary poetry. That is a feature which betrays an age of disintegration, to use the formula of Toynbee. It may amount to what he called "a refusal of mimesis." But the equilibrium of culture will be preserved only if those disrupting forces are balanced by new ways of stating and adapting the legacy which has been entrusted to us by the past.

To transmit tradition is not to solidify it into an immovable body of doctrine or into a fixed choice of canonical books. For the letter killeth, but the spirit giveth life. The study of literature ought to be conducted in such a way as to give the student joy and to make him marvel at beauties which he did not even suspect. Devotion and enthusiasm are the keys which will open these hidden treasures. I believe that wide stretches of medieval literature are still waiting for the divining rod which will point to sources of beauty and truth. The books of Miss Helen Waddell have performed such services for a great number of readers. Thanks to her, the songs of the wandering scholars have found new, delighted audiences. Indeed, the studious cloisters pale were also the haunts of high-spirited youth, able to voice in verse its zest for life. One of the most striking things in Dante is his delight in the beautiful structure of the universe, in the glorious spectacles of nature, in the splendor of human life. When he meets acquaintances in Hell or Purgatory, they talk with longing and love of the sphere of earthly existence to which he is to return and where they wish to be remembered. His poetry teaches a joyful acceptance of our sojourn here. And yet nobody will dare to accuse him of being blind to the dark sides of humanity. He does not shun pictures of its most terrible degradation. But that does not change his outlook. We might apply to the Middle Ages the words of Miranda in *The Tempest*:

> O wonder,
> How many goodly creatures are there here!
> How beauteous mankind is! O brave new world,
> That has such people in't!

But the whole domain of the world's poetry is an enchanted island like Prospero's. It is enlarged by every great poet. Goethe's notion of world literature has this meaning, among others. He discovered the beauty of Arab and Persian poetry and proclaimed: "East and West are no more severed, they both belong to God." He paid homage to Kalidasa as well as to Hafiz. And he set to posterity the task of expanding European tradition.

We are perhaps only in the first stage of that process. I am convinced that America will play an important part in this development. T. S. Eliot is, I believe, the first poet to have drawn inspiration from Indian thought. It was in Boston, I think, that he studied Sanskrit. But he is rooted also in the Middle Ages, and I believe that he considers Dante his greatest master. Eliot is a sad poet. He has more to say about hell and purgatory than about paradise. We live in an age of disorder and despondency. Some thinkers will tell us that we ought to feel despondent. But if anything is flatly contradicted by the medieval mind, it is certainly this. Remember the seventh canto of Dante's "Inferno." He meets there a particular class of sinners—the people suffering from depression. "We have been sad," they confess, "in the sweet air that is gladdened by the sun"—

Tristi fummo
Nel aer dolce che del sol s'allegra.

Today these people would be treated in hospitals. But Dante considered them sinners.

If I were to sum up in two words what I believe is the essential message of medieval thought, I would say: It is the spirit in which it restated tradition; and this spirit is Faith and Joy.

EPILOGUE

The Ideas of Ernst Robert Curtius
and the Genesis of ELLMA

. . . thank you for your magnificent book. I do not
know when I shall ever find time to read the whole
of it. . . .

—T. S. Eliot[1]

Who has read and understood the whole of *ELLMA*?[2] Curtius's magnificent book, widely diffused and discussed, has become an international monument that towers above the landscape of provincial literary studies. No one can afford to ignore it. But, like many monuments, its parts have proved easier to appreciate than the foundations and structure of the whole.

This has not been for want of attention. The German original, issued in 1948,[3] was one of the first works of postwar continental scholarship considered sufficiently seminal by the Bollingen Foundation to be translated into English.[4] Translations into Spanish, French, and Portuguese soon followed.[5] In 1983 there appeared a research bibliography of the re-

[1] Unpublished letter to E.R.C[urtius] dated 14 February 1949, Bonn University Library, call mark *Curtius, E. R. II.*

[2] The familiar abbreviation of the English translation, *European Literature and the Latin Middle Ages,* is used in the pages below. Curtius's name is abbreviated, in the footnotes, to E.R.C. This epilogue is designed for the English-speaking audience to which the translation of *ELLMA* is addressed. Some details which may be self-evident to a German readership are therefore glossed in the following pages. It is hoped, however, that the research into primary and unpublished sources of Curtius's life and work on which this epilogue is based may also be of use to European readers.

[3] *Europäische Literatur und lateinisches Mittelalter* (Berne, 1948).

[4] Published in 1953 for Bollingen by Pantheon in the U.S., distributed by Routledge and Kegan Paul in the U.K. A paperback edition was licensed to the Harper Torch book series in 1963. Since 1967, when rights were acquired by Princeton, more than 13,000 copies of the translation have been sold. (Information courtesy of D. Tegarden, Reprints Editor, Princeton University Press.) On Curtius and the Bollingen Foundation see W. McGuire, *Bollingen: An Adventure in Collecting the Past* (Princeton, 1982), 193–94, 224.

[5] Spanish: *Literaturea europea y Edad Media latina,* trans. M. F. and A. Alatorre (Buenos Aires, 1955). French: *La littérature européenne et le Moyen Age latin,* trans. J. Bréjoux (Paris, 1956). Portuguese: *Literatura europeia e idade média latina,* trans. P. Cabral (Rio de Janeiro, 1957). Translations into other European languages have been made.

ception of Curtius's works that describes and analyzes more than four hundred articles or reviews, many of them devoted to *ELLMA*.[6] Nor is there any sign of interest abating. No fewer than three books, wholly or substantially concerned with the author of *ELLMA*, have been published by 1990, preceded by two substantial anthologies of Curtius's journalism;[7] and a scholarly edition, in seven volumes, of his unpublished correspondence from or to his family, colleagues, and friends is projected.[8]

Yet the rise of a "Curtius-industry" has not created a consensus about the significance of his work. There is a hagiography of Curtius, and there is a demonology. For some, his writing is an unsavory anachronism, the product of a bourgeois conservative—authoritarian, elitist, and reactionary—whose outmoded ideology proved compatible with the fascism it ineptly sought to withstand.[9] For others, Curtius is a venerable figure, and *ELLMA* a proto-encyclopedia of European culture, a stride forward in Europe's quest for intellectual unity.[10] By emphasizing the typical, the recurrent, and the commonplace, Curtius is taxed with having neglected literary individuality.[11] In his use of the term *topos*, he is alleged to have been both innovative and perceptive, both inconsistent and confused.[12] "A great humanist," assert some. "An idol with feet of clay," declare others. Nonetheless, amid all these conflicting opinions, a common factor emerges. No one among the multitude who has written about Curtius has

[6] E. J. Richards, *Modernism, Medievalism, and Humanism: A Research Bibliography on the Reception of the Works of E.R.C.* (Tübingen, 1983).

[7] Journalism: R. Kirt, ed., *E.R.C. Büchertagebuch, mit einem Nachwort von Max Rychner* (Berne and Munich, 1960); id., *E.R.C., Goethe, Thomas Mann und Italien. Beiträge in der "Luxembourger Zeitung" (1922–1925)* (Bonn, 1988); W-D. Lange, ed., *"In Ihnen begegnet sich das Abendland." Bonner Voträge zum 100 Geburstag von E.R.C.* (Bonn, 1990); W. Berschin et al., eds., *E.R.C. Werk, Wirkung, Zukunftsperspektiven* (Heidelberg, 1989); D. Wuttke, *Kosmopolis der Wissenschaft. E.R.C. und das Warburg Institut. Briefe und andere Dokumente*, Saecula Spiritalia, no. 20 (Baden-Baden, 1989). I thank Professors W-D. Lange and W. Berschin for a preview of the books they have edited.

[8] See W-D. Lange, *EG Magazin* (April, 1986).

[9] See P. Jehn, *Toposforschung. Eine Dokumentation*, ed. Jehn, Respublica Literaria, no. 10 (Frankfurt, 1972), 7ff., esp. 29, 44–46. Cf. M. Nerlich, "Romanistik und Anti-Kommunismus," *Das Argument* 72 (1972):276–313. Cf. H. Westra's judgment on Curtius as a member of "a superficially apolitical but increasingly reactionary Bildungsélite" in *Festschrift für Paul Klopsch*, ed. U. Kindermann, W. Maaz, F. Wagner (Göppingen, 1988), 571.

[10] Cf. C. Dröge's introduction to the catalog of the Bonn exhibition commemorating the centennial of Curtius's birth, *E.R.C., Europäer und Romanist* (Bonn University Library, 15 April–31 July 1986). For a shrewd account of Curtius's changing image, see L. Forster, "E.R.C. Commemorated," *New Comparisons* 4 (1987):164–72.

[11] Peter Dronke, *Poetic Individuality in the Middle Ages: New Departures in Poetry, 1000–1150*, 2d ed. (London, 1986). Perceptive discussion in F. Rico, *Romance Philology* 26 (1972–1973):673–85 [id., "Estudio preliminar," *La individualidad poética en la Edad Media*, 2d ed. (Madrid, 1981.)]

[12] Cf. Jehn, *Toposforschung. Eine Dokumentation*, and the essays in his collection. See too M. L. Baeumer, ed., *Toposforschung* (Darmstadt, 1973).

failed to take him seriously or to attach to ELLMA an almost symbolic significance.

This reflects not only the reputation of Curtius's best-known book, but also the acute self-consciousness with which he himself viewed it. Equipped with ten "guiding principles," in five different languages, ranging from Herodotus to Ortega; dedicated to the memory of Gustav Gröber and Aby Warburg; and preceded (in its English translation) by an autobiographical foreword written with engagement and authority, Curtius's imposing volume was conceived and presented as the monument that posterity has both revered and reviled. What were the materials, intellectual and personal, that contributed to the building of that monument, and what does it represent now?

The Making of the Mandarin

In the evening I read for my own purposes some more of grandfather's letters from his period in Bonn, in order to be transported into an atmosphere of beautiful purity. . . . There is, in his life, a perfect harmony and simplicity that is denied to us. We are too diverse, have read and become familiar with too much—English, French, modern, even Slavonic and Oriental wisdom. How does that help us to achieve an integration of the personality such as his?[13]

The integration of Curtius's personality and work owed much to family tradition. Nostalgia for the imagined simplicity of an earlier age, recurrent at critical stages of his intellectual development and career, did not inhibit his inherited assurance in dealing with the complexity of the present. For Curtius, by birth and by accomplishment, was a German mandarin.[14] His family was well known for public service in his native Alsace.[15] Like

[13] E.R.C., unpublished letter to his mother, dated from Bonn, 28 January 1917, Bonn University Library, call mark Curtius E. R. II: "Ich las an dem Abend für mich noch in Grosspapas Briefen aus seiner Bonner Zeit, um mich in eine schöne reine Atmosphäre zu versetzen. . . . Es ist in seinem Leben eine geschlossene Harmonie und Einfachheit, die uns versagt ist. Wir sind zu vielfältig, haben zu viel gelesen und kennengelernt, Frankreich, England, die moderne, gar noch slawische und orientalische Weisheit. Wie soll man dabei zu solcher Einheit der Persönlichkeit kommen[?]" Curtius's paternal grandfather, Ernst Curtius (1814–1896), who led the excavations at Olympia, discovered the Hermes of Praxiteles, and composed a popular three-volume Geschichte Griechenlands (1857–1867); was briefly (1844–1850) tutor to the future Kaiser Friedrich III, whom he accompanied to the University of Bonn. On Ernst Curtius, see T. Hodgkin in Proceedings of the British Academy 2 (1905), 31ff. and W. Jaeger, Five Essays (Montreal, 1966), 52ff. His letters were edited by E.R.C.'s father Friedrich, Ernst Curtius. Ein Lebensbild in Briefen (Berlin, 1903). The reference here is probably to the letters from Ernst Curtius's student years in Bonn, 1833–1834.

[14] The term is used in the historical sense defined by Fritz Ringer in his The Decline of the German Mandarins: The German Academic Community, 1890–1933 (Cambridge, Mass., 1969).

[15] See J. Baumann, "L'esprit public à Thann vers la fin du 19 siècle," Annuaire de la Société des Régions de Thann—Guebwiller (1975–76), 87–98.

Curtius's grandfather Ernst, his great-uncle Georg (1820–1985) was a noted classical scholar. His father Friedrich (1851–1931), a civil servant in Alsace-Lorraine and director of the Lutheran Church, married a member of a Swiss patrician family. To his mother and grandmother, throughout his youth, Curtius was to write in excellent French and English (as well as German); and the bilingualism of the cultured household, together with Alsace's intermediary position between French and German culture, contributed to form an outlook that was cosmopolitan in its confidence.[16]

Born in 1886 at Thann, widely traveled in Germany, Switzerland, and England, Curtius began, in 1904, to study Sanskrit and comparative philology at Berlin. It was, however, through the teaching of Gustav Gröber (1844–1911), the Strasbourg Romance philologist and co-dedicatee of ELLMA, that Curtius found his métier.[17] After a first dissertation on an Old French paraphrase of the Book of Kings (1911); a formative journey to Rome in 1912, where he met Romain Rolland; and a Habilitationsschrift on the nineteenth-century French critic Ferdinand Brunetière (1913), Curtius became first Privatdozent, then (with an interruption for war service) Associate Professor (Extraordinarius), at Bonn (1914). In 1920 he was appointed to a chair in Marburg; in 1924 to one at Heidelberg; and five years later he returned to Bonn as the successor of the celebrated linguistic historian, Meyer-Lübke, in the chair of Romance Philology. Curtius remained in that post until his retirement, and died at Rome in 1956.

A thinker who emphasized continuity, Curtius himself displayed a number of striking continuities of intellectual outlook, character, and belief. The first, perhaps the most fundamental, was a profound Christian faith. Protestant by upbringing, Catholic by (mis-)repute, he found in contemporary Anglicanism much that was congenial to his tastes. Some of Curtius's reading, in his early years, was in English dogmatic theology;[18] a significant part of his correspondence was with the Anglican priest Albert Way.[19] A spiritual bond united Curtius with the Benedictine scholar Jean de Menasce and with the phenomologist Max Scheler, whose influence on ELLMA will be outlined below; and religious sympathies contributed to his relationships with writers such as T. S. Eliot, Romain Rolland, and André Gide. When, in 1923, Curtius wrote to Max Rychner (a

[16] The two best accounts of Curtius's family and biography are by Arthur J. Evans, Jr., *On Four Modern Humanists: Hofmannsthal, Gundolf, Curtius, Kantorowicz*, ed. Evans (Princeton, 1970), 85–145 and H. Lausberg, "Ernst Robert Curtius 1886–1956," in *Bonner Gelehrte. Beiträge zur Geschichte der Wissenschaft in Bonn. 150 Jahre Rheinische Friedrich-Wilhelms-Universität zu Bonn 1818–1968* 7 (Bonn, 1970), 214ff.

[17] On Gröber see Curtius, *Gesammelte Aufsätze zur romanischen Philologie* (Berne and Munich, 1960), 428ff.

[18] E.R.C., letter to his father from Bonn dated 18 May 1917 (Bonn University Library, call mark *Curtius, E. R. II*): "Wenn ich ein bischen Zeit für mich habe, lese ich englische dogmatische Theologie. Das ist ein wundervoller Schatz der ganzen christlichen Erfahrung."

[19] An edition of this correspondence, in the series described in n. 8, is projected.

gifted journalist and editor and one of his closest friends): "I am an extremely orthodox person, and feel comfortable only with what is definite. For me it is enough to recognize—to recognize again—with unconditional love, predetermined archetypes of the intellect that I was born to be."[20] He was describing, in partly religious terms, a cast of mind that influenced the conception of ELLMA and remained constant throughout his life. This spiritual element in Curtius's thought is not adequately characterized by the political shorthand "conservative" that has been applied to it so often and so unreflectively.

For politics, in the ordinary sense of the word, Curtius had little enthusiasm. That did not mean that he refrained from political comment—both ELLMA and the polemical pamphlet, Deutscher Geist in Gefahr (1932) that foreshadowed it contain, in different but related forms, political statements of deep commitment. What Curtius did not care for was parties; and this is worth emphasizing in refutation of the reactionary sentiments that have been imputed to him.[21] On 30 December 1918, for example, he wrote to his mother from Bonn: "Here everyone is now setting up political parties. . . . Naturally I have no taste for any party. They all say more or less the same thing with the same worn-out slogans. The Conservatives lack appeal and have no freedom of spirit, the Democrats are aesthetically impossible. The Center has a good deal to be said for it, but is basically antiprotestant, intolerant . . . etc. Of course one must, and I shall, vote for the Democrats. But I shall never be able to achieve a heartfelt participation in politics."[22] These were the opinions of large and vocal sections of the mandarin class to which Curtius belonged. It links him, for example, with Karl Jaspers (his future antagonist in a bitter debate about Goethe) and with Aloys Fischer who, in 1931 and 1932 respectively, issued "apolitical" defences of tradition comparable to Deutscher Geist in Gefahr, in order to reaffirm the values of a civilization they perceived as being under attack.[23] The Nazis, however, who paid Curtius the compliment of publicly condemning Deutscher Geist in Gefahr on the grounds that its author, because of his contact with Jews and "confused Jewish-minded

[20] From Heidelberg, dated 11 June 1923, ed. C. Mertz-Rychner, "E.R.C. . . . Max Rychner . . . Ein Briefwechsel," Merkur 23 (1969):372: "Ich bin ein radikal gläubiger Mensch und fühle mich wohl nur im Definitiven. Mir genügt es, bestimmte geistige Urformen, denen ich zugeboren bin, zu erkennen—wiederzuerkennen—in Liebe, aus Liebe."

[21] See above, n. 9.

[22] Bonn University Library, call mark Curtius, E. R. II: "Hier gründen nun alle Leute Parteien. . . . Ich habe natürlich zu keiner Partei Lust. Alle sagen ungefähr dasselbe mit denselben abgebrauchten Schlagwörtern. Die Konservativen sind ohne Zugkraft und ohne Freiheit des Geistes, die Demokraten ästhetisch unmöglich. Das Zentrum hat viel für sich, ist aber doch im Grunde antiprotestantisch, intolerant . . . usw. Natürlich muss man, und werde ich, demokratisch wählen. Aber eine innere Beiteiligung an der Politik werde ich nie gewinnen können."

[23] The comparison, and the term "apolitical," are Ringer's, The Decline of the German Mandarins, 432.

thinkers," failed to understand "the biological foundations of German culture,"[24] did not regard it as an "apolitical" work; and in 1942 the Bonn Orientalist, P. E. Kahle (an exile not uncritical of the political conduct of many of his former colleagues), reported the existence, in the University, of "a Democratic group . . . to which belonged Ernst Robert Curtius."[25] To note the reluctance of this member of "the community of reason" under the Weimar Republic[26] wholeheartedly to subscribe to the political programme of any of its many divided parties, is merely to associate him with a dilemma of the beleaguered mandarin class.[27] To describe Curtius as "apolitical" or as reactionary, in the sense that word acquired in the 1930s and 1940s, is a travesty of the truth.

Antipathy to party politics, and dislike of mass movements, were the natural complements of a lifelong elitism. In a euphoric account of Arnold Toynbee's theory of history, published in 1948, Curtius repeats a view often expressed in his earlier works, which also finds an echo on the first page of *ELLMA*: "The growth of scholarship . . . proceeds only through creative individuals."[28] Unconscious irony, perhaps, from one accused of emphasizing tradition to the detriment of individuality; but the irony is superficial. For Curtius, in true mandarin fashion, never doubted the importance of an elite, an aristocracy, of the intellect. In his own time, it was conceived supranationally, and enabled him to consort on equal and sometimes intimate terms with Ortega and Jung, Joyce and Mann, and the many other celebrities with whom Curtius exchanged letters and ideas. This reinforced his belief in the actuality of a European *res publica litterarum* of which *ELLMA* is an expression and a defense. And Curtius's elitism was also suprahistorical, linking him not only to poets such as Stefan George and T. S. Eliot, whom he knew personally, but also bringing him into communion with Goethe, Dante, and Virgil. Small wonder, then, that Curtius felt different from the narrow specialists among his professional colleagues[29] and wrote to Rychner with ambiguous humor: "For me personally, even scholarship does not occupy the high position in the order of values that my colleagues claim for it. The older I become, the

---

[24] H. Sauter, *Völkischer Beobachter* 83 (Beiblatt, 1933). Quoted in extract by Richards, *Modernism, Medievalism, and Humanism*, 70–71.

[25] *Bonn University in Pre-Nazi and Nazi Times, 1923–1939: Experiences of a German Professor* (London, 1942), 9.

[26] The expression is Peter Gay's in his vivid sketch, *Weimar Culture: The Outsider as Insider* (London, 1969), chapter 2.

[27] Excellently analyzed by Ringer, *The Decline of the German Mandarins*, esp. 367–449.

[28] *Essays [on European Literature]. Kritische Essays zur europäischen Literatur.* By E.R.C., trans. Michael Kowal (Princeton, 1973), 427. Cf. *ELLMA*, 3: "The protagonists of progress in historical understanding are always isolated individuals . . ."

[29] Curtius's professional relations and reception are exhaustively studied by H. H. Christmann, "E.R.C.—philologisch. Auch ein Beitrag zu seinem 100 Geburtstag," *Romanistisches Jahrbuch* 37 (1986):137–147 and "E.R.C. und die deutschen Romanisten," *Abhandlungen der Mainzer Akademie der Wissenschaften. Geistes- und Sozialwissenschaftliche Klasse*, no. 3 (1987), 3–27.

stronger is my sense that I don't 'belong' . . . I want to be free on bright summer nights to bathe in the Neckar or see friends even if a thousand gatherings or conferences are meeting that evening. . . . To me the cosmos of the mind is not a museum but a garden in which I wander and pluck fruit."[30] These are not the sentiments commonly attributed to the solemn object of an academic cult, nor should they be dismissed as frivolous. For Curtius, to the chagrin of his detractors, was a scholar by profession, but an intellectual by vocation.

That is why his journalism and correspondence are so valuable in understanding the evolution of Curtius's oeuvre and the genesis of *ELLMA*. In essays, reviews, and letters, Curtius formulated positions on a wide diversity of cultural and literary questions that were brought together in his celebrated book and in the work that is its complement, *Essays on European Literature*. Moreover, this diversity of intellectual interests was reflected in his academic teaching from the outset. In 1914, as Privatdozent in Bonn, Curtius began to lecture on Chrétien de Troyes, Old Provençal, and the then unusual subject of contemporary French literature[31]—lectures that formed the basis of his first critical book, *Die literarischen Wegbereiter des neuen Frankreich* (1919). Again at Bonn, as professor between 1929 and 1951, he taught, at one time or another, all periods of French literature, Old Provençal, medieval and renaissance Italian, medieval and modern Spanish, Vulgar and Medieval Latin, Romance philology, and renaissance literary history.[32] This list is not complete. Nonetheless it enables one to appreciate the reasonance of Leonard Forster's witty report: "Students at the University of Bonn in the 1930s used to say that Hans Naumann was the professor of German and Ernst Robert Curtius the professor of everything else. There was some truth in this."[33]

It is also true that there was (and still is) a tradition of breadth in the academic study of the Romance languages and literatures in Germany that has seldom been matched in the English-speaking world; but even among German specialists of his generation in that subject, Curtius stood out for the range of his academic expertise and critical accomplishments. Unwavering in his belief that the literary critic, in his role as cultural interpreter, had not been justly esteemed in Germany, Curtius detected in the work of Friedrich Schlegel a model for the essayistic form that attracted him.[34]

---

[30] Mertz-Rychner, "E.R.C. . . . Max Rychner . . . Ein Briefwechel," 372: "Für mich persönlich besitzt eben die Wissenschaft nicht die Rangstellung in der Wertordnung, die meine Collegen ihr einräumen. Je älter ich werde, je stärker wird das Bewusstsein, das ich nicht 'dazu gehöre'. . . . Ich will frei sein, in hellen Sommernächten im Neckar zu baden oder Freunde zu sehen, auch wenn tausend Kränzschen oder Congresse an dem Abend tagen. . . . Der Kosmos des Geistes ist für mich kein Museum, sondern ein Garten, in dem ich wandere and Früchte breche."

[31] Listed by Lausberg, "Ernst Robert Curtius 1886–1956," 220.

[32] Ibid., 230–31.

[33] Forster, "E.R.C. Commemorated," 166.

[34] The theme, which recurs in his earlier journalism (e.g. "Zur Psychologie des deutschen

It does not, therefore, diminish the stature of ELLMA if we begin by regarding it less as an encyclopedia than as the ultimate expression of many-sided interests—both medieval and modern, both philological and critical—that were present in Curtius's temperament, teaching, and writings from the beginning of his career.

Hindsight, however, should not make us inattentive to all that was unpredictable about his achievement. The personality that produced ELLMA was not that of a serene academic positivist, dispassionately drawing on stores of accumulated learning. Curtius was fiery yet introspective, hypersensitive but actively involved in the issues of his day. If we look back at the large continuities of his work and character, ELLMA may seem the book he was destined to write. Nothing could be more misleading. ELLMA was, in Curtius's own words, the product of an "isolated individual . . . led by such historical convulsions as wars and revolutions to pose new questions."[35] How this happened will affect our understanding of the nature and purpose of his great work.

The Conquest of Charlemagne's Empire

For us, people of German stock, the intellectual history of the world is not bounded by the Tiber and the Seine. The Rhine and the Danube, the Main and the Neckar are no less Roman in character. . . . The West is more than the border states of Western and Southern Europe. The West is the empire of Charlemagne.[36]

Stirring but defensive words, written only seven years after a world war in which Curtius had fought. Characteristic is the use of a medieval exemplum to affirm Germany's historical role in the culture of modern Europe. These two sides of Curtius's interest are reflected not only in his journalism and teaching, but also in his earliest academic publications. The dissertation of 1911 on the Old French translation of the Book of Kings[37] and the 1913 Habilitationsschrift on a French critic who had died but recently[38] may seem—in subject, period, and scholarly method—to stand

---

Geistes," *Luxemburger Zeitung* 7 October 1992 [Kirt, ed., *E.R.C. Goethe, Thomas Mann und Italien*, 25] is most fully treated in his lecture of 1950, *Literarische Kritik in Deutschland*, delivered on his receiving at Hamburg the Lessing prize for "Essayistik." For Curtius's view of Schlegel see *Essays*, 92ff. Cf. too his essay on "Goethe as Critic," *Essays*, 27ff. On the problematic history of the early German essay, see J. A. McCarthy, *Crossing Boundaries: A Theory and History of Essay Writing in German, 1680–1715* (Philadelphia, 1989).

[35] *ELLMA*, 3. Cf. above, n. 28.

[36] E.R.C., review of Paul Valéry's *Rhumbs*, *Europäische Revue* 2 (1926):404–5.

[37] *Li Quatre Livre deis Reis* (Dresden, 1911). An inaugural Dissertation, submitted at Strasbourg in 1910, was published under the title *Einleitung zu einer neuen Ausgabe der "Quatre livre des Reis"* (Halle, 1911).

[38] *Ferdinand Brunetière. Beitrag zur Geschichte der französischen Kritik* (Strasbourg, 1914). Brunetière died in 1906.

at opposite extremes; but they are in fact products of a single, unified vision. That vision, as Curtius generously and accurately acknowledged, both at the beginning and the end of his career, derived in large measure from the work of his mentor, Gustav Gröber.

Gröber was an empiricist, but not in any simple sense a positivist.[39] He had a critical attachment to facts. Knowledge (*Erkenntnis*) was his ideal;[40] subjective judgments of praise or blame contributed nothing to its advancement. Gröber's style was deliberately unemotional, although not devoid of a certain moral tone; his range, in the Romance languages and literatures, was encyclopedic and is reflected in the three large volumes of his *Grundriss der romanischen Philologie* (1886–1902).

That vast work offered, among many other riches, a comprehensive account of Old French literature, both (at the time) published and unpublished. It paid particular attention to linguistic history, and rested on a close philological investigation of small but significant phenomena. It is not difficult to see how a meticulous edition of a little-known Old French text fitted into this method of research, or how Gröber's interest in the analysis of style[41] stimulated Curtius's fine appraisal of the stylistic qualities of *Li Quatre Livre deis Reis*. It is a perceptive suggestion that writing that dissertation furnished Curtius with "a certain mental paradigm for the way vernacular authors are influenced by Latin materials—a paradigm that he was to apply less happily at times later on, in other contexts";[42] but even more important, perhaps, for his later development and for the genesis of ELLMA, was the appreciation, which Gröber had given him, and the understanding, which Curtius came to feel he had earned in this period of his academic apprenticeship,[43] of exact scholarship as an epistemological instrument for creating "a structure of knowledge as hard as steel."

That resounding phrase is taken from the penultimate sentence of Curtius's essay "Preface to a Book on the Latin Middle Ages and European Literature."[44] The essay begins with praise of Gröber. It is customary, and right, in this context to follow Curtius's lead and stress his debt to Gröber's insistence on the significance of Medieval Latin in the development of medieval vernacular literature—an insistence grounded in what is still the only survey of the subject that extends as far as 1350[45]—and to note Gröber's own debt to his teacher Adolf Ebert, whose unfinished general history remains one of the most intelligent treatments of this huge theme ever

---

[39] His philosophical background and scholarly methods are sketched by Curtius in *Gesammelte Aufsätze zur romanischen Philologie*, esp. 448. Gröber is described as "positivist" by Peter Dronke, *Times Literary Supplement* 79, (13 October 1980):1106.

[40] Curtius, *Gesammelte Aufsätze* zur 455.

[41] *Ibid.*, 451–52.

[42] Dronke, *Times Literary Supplement* 79, 1103.

[43] Curtius, *Romanische Philologie*, 446.

[44] Published in 1949 in *Die Wandlung*. Translated in *Critical Essays* 497–502.

[45] Gröber, *Grundriss* 2, 1, 97–432.

written.[46] But no less formative than Gröber's role in exciting Curtius's interest in Medieval Latin was the inexplicit yet clear philosophy that lay behind his comprehensive approach. Gröber, was, above all, a systematizer: "his thinking addressed itself to the entire range of the new discipline,"[47] he wished to see Romania—its languages, literatures, and culture—in the round. Just as Curtius, at the end of his preface, rejected what he had come to see as the aberrant subjectivism evinced, during the 1930s, in the "new science" fostered by the George circle with which he had once been associated; so at the conclusion of chapter 1 of ELLMA he wrote with scorn that "academic organization of philological and literary studies corresponds to the intellectual picture in 1850. Seen from 1950, that picture is as obsolete as the railroads of 1850. We have modernized the railroads, but not our system of transmitting tradition." These two positions were cognate and interdependent. They appealed to a unified, systematic view of European literature, rigorously grounded in philology and affirming the centrality of the Middle Ages, which Curtius had developed from the legacy of his academic parent Gröber and his academic grandfather Ebert. Neither the admixture of other intellectual ingredients during the course of Curtius's career, nor the fact that Gröber was a less original and less confident thinker than his pupil, should obscure the origin of this recipe. Gröber taught Curtius more than facts. He instilled in him a yearning for a system—a "structure of knowledge as hard as steel"—an implicitly philosophical approach to literature that never left Curtius, although it underwent a number of metamorphoses before reverting to something similar to the form that Gröber had adumbrated and that his pupil embodied in ELLMA.

If the 1911 dissertation reflected an influence that produced richer results than its first, austerely philological manifestation, what of the Habilitationsschrift of 1914? Here too, Gröber's impact is evident, again in a manner that is not immediately obvious from his own writings. Modern French literature and criticism attracted Gröber; he discussed them enthusiastically with his students; and from him Curtius learned of the all too eminent literary critic Ferdinand Brunetière.

Brunetière was a nationalistic writer, unencumbered by knowledge of Germany and unsympathetic to the Middle Ages. Gröber had devoted a sarcastic sentence to him in his Grundriss.[48] Nor was Curtius's dissertation on Brunetière exactly a labor of love—a Darwinian, a positivist, and a philistine, Brunetière seemed to him (not altogether justly[49]) crude and moralistic in contrast to the subtle and erudite Sainte-Beuve.[50] Yet the

---

[46] Allgemeine Geschichte der Literatur des Mittelalters im Abendlande, 3 vols. (Leipzig 1874–1889, reprint, Graz, 1971).

[47] Essays, 497.

[48] Gröber, Grundriss 1, 149.

[49] See D. Hoeges, Literatur und Evolution. Studien zur französischen Literaturkritik im 19. Jahrhundert: Taine—Brunetière—Hennequin—Guyan (Heidelberg, 1980), 78–81.

[50] Ferdinand Brunetière, 54.

study of Brunetière posed Curtius two problems that were to be raised again in his later work.

The first of these was the role of the *lieu commun*—a concept akin to Curtius's term "topos."[51] The commonplace, according to Brunetière, contains the "shared spiritual possessions of each individual"; it expresses his sense of community. The desire for originality is blameworthy: writers should renew and appropriate to themselves *le lieu commun*, that "daily bread of the mind." Boileau is therefore admirable; Baudelaire reprehensible. Perhaps Brunetière then declined into a jejunely rhetorical and narrowly nationalistic exposition of the allied notion of *idées générales*.[52] Perhaps his view of literature's function was morbidly moralistic. But when he wrote; "the role of literature . . . is to give us the entrée into the shared patrimony of the human mind,"[53] he was expressing, albeit in cruder form, a line of thought that Curtius was later to develop.

Of Brunetière's powers of reasoning, Curtius held a low opinion. The critic's limited culture and limitless desire to moralize were compounded by the inadequacy of his method. Objective criteria for literary evaluation are impossible to formulate; the validity of a judgment on a work of art does not depend on ethical, religious, or intellectual, but on aesthetic standards.[54] And Brunetière's failed defense of rationality is not redeemed by subjective insight. His mentality was simplistic, his temperament antipathetic to art.[55] "Truth consists of nuances," declares Curtius;[56] all Brunetière could see were a few idées fixes. A damning portrait, then, for all the appearance of charity and balance paraded in the conclusion. But reverse the picture, consider the qualities praised in Sainte-Beuve and found wanting in Brunetière—wide literary culture, strong aesthetic sympathies, a delight in philosophical reflection on the independence of the world of art—and you have the critical personae that Curtius was to cultivate in the 1920s. Person*ae*, rather than person*a*, for the name of the complex, changing figure who "the true critic must be" was not Brunetière but Proteus.[57]

"My first works were concerned with French literature. What poetry is can be learned from antiquity, from Spain, England, Germany. But what literature is can be learned only from France" begins the preface to Curtius's *Essays on European Literature*.[58] It ends "Without critical training I should not have been able to write my book on the Middle Ages; and my training in history has, I hope, stood my criticism in good stead."[59]

---

[51] Ibid., 21.
[52] Ibid., 22–23.
[53] Quoted by Curtius, ibid., 24.
[54] *Ferdinand Brunetière*, 124–25.
[55] Ibid., 126–27.
[56] Ibid., 127.
[57] Ibid., 126.
[58] *Essays*, xxv.
[59] Ibid., xxix. The reference is to ELLMA.

Another of the seamless continuities that Curtius was anxious to detect, in later life,[60] between his "modernist" and "medievalist" periods. How real was this continuity, and what did France teach him about the nature of literature? "My concern has always been the same: the consciousness of Europe and the tradition of the West." That assertion, in general terms, is true; but it shrouds in the expansive rhetoric of self-justification much that was distinctive about Curtius's early criticism. All his major works on modern French literature were written between 1919 and 1930.[61] Their origins have been ascribed to Curtius's Alsatian background and to filial piety. Curtius's father Friedrich had expressed in his memoirs the hope that Alsace might serve as an intermediary for peace between Germany and France; this eirenic spirit is said to animate his son's criticism;[62] and Curtius made much, in his later years, of the feeling for the exciting but problematic proximity of France that a boyhood spent in Alsace had given him.[63] Nevertheless, these factors in Curtius's development do not fully explain why this sophisticated and precocious academic chose, in his early thirties, to begin his career with a series of books and essays that cast himself in the role of a cultural and political mediator between modern France and Germany.

Curtius was to write about the *puer-senex-topos* with understanding.[64] Since his school days, he had wished to be a "German scholar" (the words had, in their German context, a resonance richer than that of their English synonyms).[65] Curtius's reason for abandoning Sanskrit, in his first year as a university student, was the slim chance of future professional advancement in that subject.[66] Nor did filial piety prevent him from rejecting his father's advice to study classical philology, on the grounds that it was boring.[67] Idealism and the linguistic skills acquired in his family doubtless directed his preference to French and English, but ambition and opportunism also contributed to this choice. Only a naive romanticism, which Curtius did nothing to discourage in the autobiographical writings

---

[60] The preface is dated "Easter 1950."

[61] Several are reprinted in his *Französischer Geist im zwanzigsten Jahrhundert* (Berne, 1952). A useful, if less than positive, account of Curtius's criticism is provided by R. Wellek, "The Literary Criticism of E.R.C." *PTL* 3 (1978):25–44 and in E. Leube, "Curtius und die französische Moderne," in *"In Ihnen begegnet sich das Abendland,"* ed. Lange, 229–44. The following paragraphs consider Curtius's French criticism chiefly in its relation to ELLMA.

[62] F. Curtius, *Deutsche Briefe und Elsässische Erinnerungen* (Frauenfeld, 1920), 241. The reference, and the point, are A. J. Evans's *On Four Modern Humanists*, 90.

[63] *Essays*, xxv; *Französischer Geist* 520ff. Cf. the early essay "Elsass!" published in *Der elsässische Garten, ein Buch von unsres Landes Art und Kunst*, ed. F. Lienhardt et al. (Strasbourg, 1912), 4ff.

[64] ELLMA, 98ff.

[65] *Literarische Kritik in Deutschland*, 17.

[66] See the letters to his father edited and discussed by H. J. Wolf, "E.R.C. und 'Li Quatre Livre des Reis' " in *"In Ihnen begegnet sich das Abendland,"* ed. Lange, 169–80.

[67] Ibid., 171–72.

of his old age, allows one to view these motives as mutually exclusive. Curtius knew from adolescence what he wanted to be, and planned his career accordingly. What he wanted was the elevated role of a cultural interpreter traditionally claimed by the German mandarins.

That is why, in order to understand the continuity that Curtius asserted between his French criticism and ELLMA, it is necessary to look beyond the illustrious cluster of professors in his own family, beyond his direct obligations to Gröber and his indirect debts to Ebert, to a wider historical setting. It does not detract from the standing of this celebrated critic of academic historicism to recognize that, for all his indisputable learning and individuality, he worked in a particular time and place, and shared with a definable body of his professional colleagues a particular view of his task.

In the mandarin ideology of late nineteenth- and early twentieth-century Germany, the origins and crisis of which have been admirably traced by Ringer,[68] the views of professors on contemporary cultural and political questions were held in a respect they have seldom commanded in the Anglo-Saxon world. Academic opinion was attended to; and academic values, especially in the humanities, attached particular importance to the comprehensive ideal of ethical and aesthetic cultivation known as *Bildung*.[69] Closely allied to this concept was the personal idea of *Kultur*, a notion increasingly appropriated by Germany throughout the late eighteenth and nineteenth centuries, in antithesis to *Zivilisation*, the term applied to the allegedly less spiritual ethos of France. The philosophical vocabulary of the mandarins was originally idealistic, and in it the word *Geist*, with its multiple meanings of 'spirit', 'soul', and 'mind', occupied pride of place. The moral impact of learning, dispensed from the national sanctuaries of the German universities, was guaranteed by its purity, its impracticality. From the most important and creative individuals the nation's *Geist* emanated. And them or their works the mandarins were uniquely equipped to interpret, because they were the guardians of tradition, the elite of the intellect.

Beside these flattering assumptions there coexisted, by 1919, a mounting anxiety and a growing wish for reform. Carl Heinrich Becker, first secretary for higher education (1919–21) and later minister at the Prussian Ministry of Culture (1921, 1925–30), sought to draw the universities into closer contact with national life; to encourage the professoriate to mediate its scholarship to a broader public; and, while widening entry to institutions of higher learning, to resist pressures for a narrowly utilitarian training.[70] Curtius enthusiastically associated himself with these aspects of Becker's reforms. But Becker's practical ideas for change also reflected a

---

[68] *The Decline of the German Mandarins*, esp. (for what follows) 81ff.

[69] The lineage of this concept is traced by W. Bruford, *The German Tradition of Self-Cultivation from Humboldt to Thomas Mann* (Cambridge, 1975).

[70] See Becker's *Gedanken zur Hochschulreform*, 2d ed. (Leipzig, 1920); E. Wende, *C. H. Becker: Mensch und Politiker* (Stuttgart, 1959), and Ringer 69–70, 72, 75, 104, 186.

larger cultural crisis that had developed during the early years of the Weimar Republic. A fresh desire for synthesis accompanied Becker's wish to
make scholarship more responsive to contemporary concerns;[71] and thinkers who influenced Curtius, such as Ernst Troeltsch, began to consider,
in the years before and after the First World War, how the fact of distinct
and irreducible nationalities could be reconciled with the ideal of an international community, symphonically conceived. "Cultural synthesis"
(Troeltsch's term) was his solution to this problem that was often posed in
terms of the ancient antithesis between French *Zivilisation*—rational, ex-
troverted, and superficial—and the profounder, more spiritual character
of German *Kultur*.[72]

Into this debate stepped Curtius, buoyed up with optimism at the blossoming "of a springtime of the mind." Looking back to November 1918
he described, in an essay on Hermann Hesse,[73] the sense of liberation,
"the wonderful cosmopolitan openness, an awakening to a new day" of the
younger generation, with whose aspirations he identified and that he
aimed to direct. In the following year, 1919, Curtius brought out his critical study on the "literary pioneers of the new France,"[74] offering it to "the
new youth of our people," which was to lead "the intellectual renaissance
of Germany in which we fervently believe."[75]

These sentences are taken from a preface dated 22 November 1918—
thirteen days after the abdication of the Kaiser and the proclamation of
the Weimar Republic, and eleven days after the Armistice. Their public
overtones were acknowledged by Curtius himself: "A political claim . . .
can be read between the lines of the *Wegbereiter*"; he observes, a belief in
a "new France" (which "was disintegrating at the moment when my book
appeared"), a faith in "the possibility and necessity of a new Europe,"
which could occur only through "a creative refashioning of Franco-German relations."[76]

Here Curtius's personal as well as professional background can be seen
as closely related. In Alsace, during his youth, he had received from Albert Schweitzer the gift of Romain Rolland's *Jean-Christophe*, a novel set
on a small town on the Rhine, whose final volume, inscribed to "the free
spirits . . . of all nations," acquired an emblematic prominence in Curtius's criticism.[77] In Alsace he had read the *Nouvelle Revue Française*, and

[71] Ringer, *The Decline of the German Mandarins*, 228.

[72] Ibid., 397ff.

[73] *Essays*, 169.

[74] *Die literarischen Wegbereiter des neuen Frankreich* is reprinted in the collection *Französischer Geist im zwanzigsten Jahrhundert*.

[75] "Der neuen Jugend unseres Volkes möchte es sich darbieten. Sie wird die geistige Wiedergeburt Deutschlands mit heraufführen, an die wir glühend glauben."

[76] *Französischer Geist*, 520.

[77] The novel, which appeared between 1904 and 1910, is discussed by Curtius, *Wegbereiter*, 84ff. For his account of the inscription see ibid., 99. For the gift and its context see
Französischer Geist, 520.

studied in Strasbourg, "a seismograph more sensitive to Franco-German tensions than Paris or Berlin."[78] When, in 1919, Curtius entered the debate about Germany and France, it was, therefore, as a politically conscious adult with a mission that sprang both from his personal history and from the assumptions of his profession.

Those assumptions were not shared by one of his chosen heroes. The poet Stefan George, to whom and to whose protégé Friedrich Gundolf Curtius had ardently sought to attach himself,[79] refused to give his *imprimatur* to *Die literarischen Wegbereiter* on the grounds, expressed to Gundolf, that "C[urtius]'s mind is as opposed to ours as it's possible to be," and "what do those Frogs understand about poetry?"[80] On these delicate pronouncements of The Master Curtius was to take subtle revenge. In a retrospective essay entitled "Stefan George in Conversation,"[81] which ends with the quotation "everyone gets a piece of my mind,"[82] Curtius dwells on the French connections of George's family, its assimilation to French culture, and on The Master's links with such unpoetical Frenchmen as Verlaine and Mallarmé. From the "great distance—a blessed distance"[83] of the Germany of 1950, Curtius pointedly recalled George's debts to a culture he had subsequently repudiated; just as, in 1934, Curtius contrasted the humane cosmopolitanism of Hofmannsthal, responsive to a Romance world that he skillfully accommodated, with George's dictatorial contempt for the same world that he had failed to master and reshape.[84] What remained, in later life, of Curtius's once positive feelings for his erstwhile hero, was the poetic symbolism of the Rhine, a living link between Germany and its Roman heritage, as expressed in George's works "Der siebente Ring"[85] and "Franken,"[86] together with a "magical" sense of the "timeless reality" of the Roman Empire "that Stefan George has incarnated in his . . . 'Porta Nigra.' "[87] The ultimate irony, then, of the troubled relations between George and Curtius, was this appropriation of his works to a serene cosmopolitanism that the poet himself had rejected.

Cosmopolitanism and criticism: the two are inseparable in Curtius's thought between 1919 and 1930. In an essay on T. S. Eliot, in 1927, he

---

[78] *Französischer Geist*, 522.

[79] On Curtius's relations with George and Gundolf see Wellek, "The Literary Criticism of E.R.C.," 26–29; Evans, *On Four Modern Humanists*, 94–97; and the edition of Gundolf's *Briefwechsel mit Herbert Steiner und E.R.C.*, ed. L. Helbing and C. V. Bock (Amsterdam, 1963).

[80] *Stefan George-Friedrich Gundolf. Briefwechsel* (Munich and Düsseldorf, 1962), 286, 288. The second (but not the first) of these judgments is quoted by Curtius, *Essays*, 124.

[81] *Essays*, 107–28.

[82] Ibid., 128.

[83] Ibid., 119.

[84] *Essays*, 142–68. The contrast is given more piquancy in the light of George's fierce antipathy to Hofmannsthal.

[85] *ELLMA*, 10–11.

[86] *Essays*, 499.

[87] Ibid., 498–99.

writes yearningly of the growing connection between them: "It is not merely a western European; it is, we may hope, also a German phenomenon that criticism is assuming a new and productive function within the economy of the intellectual energies of our age. It cannot be otherwise if we wish to accept this age, with its exploration of consciousness, its syncretism, its emerging ecumenical, cosmopolitan culture."[88] Yet in his first approach, via France, to the new Europe in which Germany was to be reintegrated, Curtius continued to betray George's influence. Curtius's critical vocabulary shows traces of the arcane diction, abstract and lofty, of the George circle; and the very notion of leading individuals reflecting and forming the intellectual life of the "new" French nation has a pronounced Georgean flavor. Equally evident are categories of analysis traditionally favored in the mandarin ideology outlined above. The first sentence of *Die literarischen Wegbereiter* is: "The life of the *Geist* develops in the tension between periods of creativity and laxness."[89] But no less salient in this book, as in the others that were to follow it, is a stereotyped view of "the French character" and "the French mind," which Curtius's criticism of the literature of modern France was never to shake off.[90]

Yet it is less than charitable to claim that his "main inspiration is a high-minded nationalism" or that "he operates with the most worn-out clichés."[91] Curtius's subject is the refashioning of an inherited image of France by its most creative writers, and its implications for their understanding of Germany. His argument is perhaps clearest in his treatment of André Suarès: "The great Germanic art of the mind was passed over by all previous generations of French intellectuals, with no understanding, or with an uncertain half-understanding, a respect that always remained very remote. The generation of Rolland, Gide, Suarès was the first to have a sensitive appreciation of the value of that art that shares common standards with ours in Germany."[92] This entailed a break with the oppressive weight of the ancien régime and with French classicism, the aesthetic weapon of the Action Française. It entailed a rejection of pragmatism,

---

[88] Ibid., 358. The relationship between E.R.C. and Eliot is outlined in my article "T. S. Eliot and E.R.C.: A European Dialogue," *Times Literary Supplement* (October, 1989):5–7. On cosmopolitanism as a concept, cf. T. J. Reed, *Thomas Mann: The Uses of Tradition* (Oxford, 1974), 298.

[89] "Das Leben des Geistes verläuft in der Spannung zwischen schöpferischen und verarbeitenden Epochen," *Französischer Geist*, 7.

[90] This aspect of his criticism has been studied by S. Gross, *E.R.C. und die deutsche Romanistik der zwanziger Jahre. Zum Problem nationaler Images in der Literaturwissenschaft* (Bonn, 1980).

[91] Wellek, "The Literary Criticism of E.R.C.," 29.

[92] "An der grossen germanischen Seelenkunst sind alle früheren Geistesgenerationen Frankreichs verständnislos oder doch mit halbem, unsicherem Verständnis, mit einer immer sehr fern bleibenden Hochachtung vorübergegangen. Erst die Generation der Rolland, Gide, Suarès hat für jede Kunst eine Empfindung und ein Wertgefühl bekommen, das mit unserm deutschen ein gemeinsames Mass hat," *Französischer Geist*, 181.

positivism, and rationalism—in short, of all the fossilized values of the nineteenth century with which Curtius had become all too familiar, through his work on the critic manqué, Ferdinand Brunetière. A new kind of criticism was now needed, a literary criticism "of a higher grade"— *Lebenskritik*, the criticism of life.[93] The target of this freer, more flexible style of interpretation was *Erstarrung*, fossilization (the word occurs time and again in Curtius's book). Fossilization meant adherence to orthodox and unvarying rules of taste, a rejection of the life-enhancing forces that Curtius's "pioneers" had espoused.[94] Curtius's critical vocabulary cannot be said to be precise; but its tone and its values are evident. They are the elated tone and the emotive values of expressionism.[95]

Curtius therefore attached cardinal importance to intuition which he justified by appeal to Bergson. A philosophy of becoming, a philosophy of life was what he found in Bergson's writings and what he sought from the literary pioneers of the new France. Gide's antipathy to romanticism and to nationalism, and his sympathy for tradition, combined with the fresh impulse he had given to French literature, were what commended him to Curtius. Gide had risen above mere aestheticism to become a moral philosopher.[96] So too had Romain Rolland, especially in *Jean-Christophe*, whose hero "functions as an ethical educator."[97] In Protestantism and music, Rolland displayed his deepest affinities with Germany.[98] The Catholicism of Claudel and Péguy endeared them to Curtius; for religion is a mark of the "heightened humanity, the heroic, and the holy" to which the "flat rationality" of the modern world of progress and materialism is inimical.[99] The university is the place where the humanistic heritage should be developed, but a new kind of university is needed; and in Péguy's attack on the conservative authorities of the Sorbonne is detected a parallel to the reform movements in German higher education.[100] Suarès had admirable thoughts on an ideal of European culture; but he too fell victim to a naive cultural nationalism.[101] *Geist* and *Glaube*, intellect and faith, in the France of 1919 have a vital contribution to make to the restoration of Europe, is Curtius' conclusion.[102]

Final admonition is perhaps a more fitting term, for *Die literarischen Wegbereiter* is less an argument than an exhortation. Passionate, discursive and ill-organized, it nonetheless contains the germs of Curtius's later method. Chronological exposition is abandoned. Rejected and ridiculed

---

[93] Ibid., 166.

[94] Eg., ibid., 168.

[95] Signaled by Forster, "E.R.C. Commemorated," 171–72.

[96] *Französischer Geist*, 52.

[97] Ibid., 93.

[98] Ibid., 99.

[99] Ibid., 216.

[100] Ibid., 216–18.

[101] Ibid., 236-38.

[102] Ibid., 242.

is an inflexible hierarchy of values. In their place are set those qualities—ethical, religious, and aesthetic—that facilitate an intellectual rapprochement between France and Germany and point to a less rigid style of philosophy. Few of the authors to whom this treatment is meted out can plausibly be viewed as cultural theorists or systematic thinkers; but that, fundamentally, is how Curtius approached them. "It is not enough to be a man," was an aphorism of Balzac's that he was to cite with approval, "it is essential to be a system."[103]

"The best minds of both nations will find one another on the basis that you indicate and which occurs to me too," wrote Curtius to Gide on 12 July 1921, "a cosmopolitan (not international) European way of thinking founded on a national (not nationalistic) sentiment that is free from partiality and distortion."[104] By "the best minds" Curtius clearly meant those of such sages as Gide and himself. The threat posed to their socioeconomic position by the inflation of the early 1920s was discussed, the same year, by Curtius in a little-known, but not insignificant, tract.[105] Its modest dimensions were, however, insufficient to deal with a greater menace, the nemesis of nationalism, as personified by a French writer who, in Curtius's view, was emphatically not one of the "best minds" of the age: Maurice Barrès.

In a full and masterly indictment of the literary and ethical foundations of French nationalism, Curtius condemns Barrès for his failure to understand the aspirations of the prewar youth of Alsace-Lorraine, their common patrimony.[106] Nihilistic, solipsistic, and decadent,[107] Barrès could feel but not understand the magical symbolism of the Rhine—the "Georgean test"—that ought to have made him see "that he could not live without German spiritual powers."[108] Barrès was incapable of comprehending tradition in its fruitful tension with new creative forces; for him, it was "something paralyzing . . . that clapped him in chains."[109] To the spontaneity of expressionism, Barrès was insensible.[110] Small wonder, then, that his later works are "childish twaddle . . . a sign of the intellectual and moral decline of a mind perverted by the poison of nationalism."[111] Those who have portrayed as sudden Curtius's emergence as a polemicist in

---

[103] *Essays*, 194.

[104] *Deutsch-französische Gespräche 1920–1950. La correspondance de E.R.C. avec André Gide, Charles du Bos et Valéry Larbaud*, ed. H. and J. Dieckmann (Frankfurt, 1980), 30. Discussed by H. Hinterhauser, "Bild eines grossen Gelehrten in seinen Briefen," *Archiv für das Studium der neuren Sprachen* 219 (1962), 146–51.

[105] *Der Syndikalismus der Geistesarbeiter in Frankreich* (Bonn, 1921); discussed by Ringer, *The Decline of the German Mandarins*, 245–46.

[106] *Maurice Barrès und die geistigen Grundlagen des französischen Nationalismus* (Bonn, 1921), 177. Barrès was born in Lorraine, ibid., 1.

[107] Ibid., 214, 222.

[108] Ibid., 235–36.

[109] Ibid., 220–21.

[110] Ibid., 99.

[111] "ein kindisches Geschwätz . . . ein Zeichen des intellektuellen und moralischen Niedergangs eines Geistes, den das Gift des Nationalismus zersetzt hat," ibid., 184.

1932, with *Deutscher Geist in Gefahr*, have forgotten his book on Barrès. And in doing so, they have omitted a significant step in Curtius's development; for that work is not only a broadside against nationalism, but also an affirmation of the standards by which the "modernist" Curtius judged the vitality of tradition.

The kind of criticism that Curtius was attempting in his book on Barrès was one that he felt was lacking in Germany. In France, Barrès and others abundantly represented the genre of sociological-intellectual analysis that Curtius believed was supplied, in German culture, solely by his friend Max Scheler.

> In general this Romance form of creative criticism occurs infrequently with us. It is kept down by our ideal of specialization and objectivity. . . . We allot our intellectual problems to specialists whom reverence for scholarship becomes a reluctance to overstep boundaries and a hindrance to synthetic conclusions. That is why all our political parties lack suggestive formulas, persuasive programs, convincing ideas. That is why our democrats are shamefaced and our nationalists rough and crude. No one has an engaging system to put forth. It is incredible but true that Germany today, while facing its gravest historical crisis, has no national ideology capable of uniting the leading elite.[112]

The cry for synthesis was, as indicated earlier, not peculiar to Curtius, nor was the lament for the absence of a cohesive ideology. What was distinctive about these sentences, when they were written in 1924, was their context: a paean of praise for the philosophical syncretism and the ecumenical culture of Ortega y Gasset. Equally at home in German and French literature yet revealing about the national identity of Spain, Ortega offered Curtius an insight into a society, the disintegration of which furnished a parallel to the parlous state of modern Germany. "Neither in affairs of state, nor of the mind, does anyone [in Spain] acknowledge a hierarchy. The worst are rebelling everywhere against the best."[113]

The final two words of this sentence recall the first two words of the letter to Gide cited above. The thought is developed in a long and not altogether exhilarating mediation on the course of history and the nature of life. "Relativism is scepticism, and scepticism as a definitive attitude is the suicide of the mind."[114] "Life possesses a transcendent dimension in which it goes beyond itself in order to participate in something that is no longer life."[115] And, Curtius's least felicitious statement in 1924, "People no longer die for political ideas."[116]

---

[112] *Essays*, 291–92.

[113] Ibid., 286–87. On this aspect of Ortega's thought, see A. Dobson, *An Introduction to the Politics and Philosophy of José Ortega y Gasset* (Cambridge, 1989), 72–85.

[114] *Essays*, 293.

[115] Ibid.

[116] Ibid., 296.

Not all of this is Curtius's—some is a summary of Ortega's writing—but the sympathy with which it is expressed reveals, despite the frequent peremptoriness of the style and the occasional muddle in the argument, a longing for change, and an enthusiasm for "the transformation in the European sense of life [that] can best be learned from the new art of our day."[117] What Curtius called Ortega's 'perspectivism' provided the key to understanding the artistic syncretism of the age—a common orientation detectable in the work of a Proust, a Keyserling, and a Scheler.[118] The terms in which Curtius discusses perspectivism are rather lyrical than lucid, but the manner in which he employs and exalts it is intelligible. Perspectivism was the transcendent mode of mutual understanding that was to be practiced by Europe's advanced cultural elite.

This is the spirit in which Curtius, with an intuition which he regarded as a defining property of good criticism,[119] hailed the innovations of T. S. Eliot and applauded the experimentation of James Joyce. *Ulysses* is "a new *Inferno* and a new *Comédie Humaine*." It "corresponds to the *Odyssey*, but at the same time recalls Rabelais and the Elizabethans. Symbolism and scholasticism bring it into proximity with the Middle Ages. It is . . . all-inclusive."[120] *The Waste Land*, which Curtius first translated into German,[121] is the work of "an Alexandrian poet. . . . His poetry draws its sustenance from the Late Latins, the *Trecentisti*, the Elizabethans, and the French symbolists."[122]

Behind this view of Eliot as a modern master, achieving classic status through Alexandrian techniques, lies the influence of Warburg's celebrated insight that "Athens must always be conquered afresh from Alexandria."[123] Applied to Eliot's poetry, that insight provided Curtius with a more flexible "paradigm of literary influence" than the one he had acquired in his dissertation of 1911. Formative for the thesis of the imaginative presence of the past, which Curtius was to advance in ELLMA, was the lesson in the creative use of the European tradition that he learned, with Warburg's aid, from *The Waste Land*.

Its author, who was delighted by Curtius's translation and who often urged him to write a book, similar to *Die literarischen Wegbereiter*, on modern English fiction, shared Curtius's sense of excitement at having "experienced firsthand one of the great eras of European literature" during the 1920s, "that period in which we both, I may say, formed no small part," as Eliot reminded him on 14 August 1947. This feeling of participation

[117] Ibid., 295.

[118] Ibid., 298. See also Dobson, *José Ortega y Gasset*, 114–62.

[119] *Essays*, 357.

[120] Ibid., 354. (An essay written in 1929.)

[121] Curtius's *Das wüste Land* appeared in 1927 in the *Neuer Schweizer Rundschau*, following Jean de Menasce's French translation of 1926.

[122] *Essays*, 359 (written in 1927).

[123] Aby Warburg, *Gesammelte Schriften* 2 (Leipzig and Berlin, 1932), 534; discussed by E. Gombrich, *Aby Warburg: An Intellectual Biography* (London, 1970), 214–15.

in a small community of gifted writers, whose friendships were fostered in private correspondence and whose intellectual exchanges were channeled through literary reviews, never left Curtius, despite the vicissitudes of the 1930s and the Second World War. It enabled him to extol Eliot as a leader of "conservative cultural politics" in 1928; it moved him to confide to Eliot, in a letter written twenty years later, his dream of "a secret director-ate for Western cultural politics"; and it added force and fervor to the argument for the importance of leading elites that Curtius advanced in ELLMA. For if that book is a defense of the aristocracy of what he called "the Europe of the mind," it is also the product of a particular generation: the generation that reached maturity during the 1920s, among whom Curtius counted as his peers and his partners Gide, Ortega, and Eliot.

To convey, in this exhilarating atmosphere, the complex stance that Curtius wished to develop the historical, biographical methods of conven-tional literary criticism were inadequate. A more flexible, more open-ended, more philosophical style of exposition had to be generated for this "act of creative intellectual freedom."[124] "Criticism," wrote Curtius in his essay on Eliot (returning to a conclusion of his study of Brunetière), ". . . always remains a risk. Evaluation cannot be grounded. . . . The funda-mental act of criticism consists in irrational contact. True criticism never seeks to prove, it only seeks to show. Its metaphysical background is the conviction that the world of the mind is organized around systems of af-finities."[125]

That conviction is reflected in Curtius's well-known critical studies of Proust and Balzac. Balzac attracted Curtius for many reasons, not the least of which was his incompatibility with traditional literary history. "Balzac cannot be fitted into any of the literary movements and revolu-tions of the nineteenth century," declared Curtius in an article of 1950, reaffirming the contentions of his book a quarter of a century earlier. "The roots of Balzac's spiritual world are embedded in the venerable traditions of the French mind."[126] All this is an implicit response to the leveling treatment of Balzac by Brunetière.[127] Balzac was not a realist but a magi-cian. His work was a world of mystery. The system it represented could not be seen against the impoverished perspective of a single national lit-erature, arbitrarily subdivided into separate periods. The essence of Bal-zac's writing is neither French nor German: it is a harmonious totality, mystically conceived.[128] What Curtius seeks to distinguish in Balzac's oeu-vre, therefore, are what Scheler called the "constituent elements of the

[124] *Essays*, 357.

[125] Ibid.

[126] *Essays*, 201. Because the book on Balzac and the study of Proust have received full treatment elsewhere, my discussion of them is kept to a minimum. See Wellek, "The Lit-erary Criticism of E.R.C.," 33ff., and the Ph.D. dissertation of I. F. Bartenbach, *The Balzac Book of E.R.C.* (University of Southern California, 1963).

[127] The criticism is made explicit in *Balzac* (Bonn, 1923), 397.

[128] Ibid., 323–15.

soul" (*seelische Formelemente*). Thus we are led through chapters entitled "Secrecy" and "Magic," "Energy" and "Passion," "Love" and "Power," in an effort to encompass, by means of a kind of literary phenomenology, the seer's unity of vision.[129] Balzac was justly appreciated, concludes Curtius in a final chapter on the novelist's influence, only by poets such as Browning, Baudelaire, and Hofmannsthal. Academic critics could not understand Balzac's imaginative universe because their methods were bankrupt.

The affinity between art and philosophy that stands at the center of Curtius's Balzac book is further developed in what is perhaps Curtius's finest work of criticism—a long essay on Proust, published even before the final volumes of *A la recherche du temps perdu* had appeared.[130] It contains one of Curtius's fullest and most considered statements on the task of criticism, and it takes as one of its premises Proust's belief that the critic should attempt to reconstruct a writer's "unique spiritual life." "The critical gift," claims Curtius, "cannot be learned." It consists in nothing but the capacity to be struck by individual features that reveal the "constituent elements of the soul." Receptivity is the precondition for perception, and this leads to conception. All art is knowledge and discovery, communicated by those precise vehicles of thought that are Proust's metaphors and style. A concern with music mediates this vision, and literary creativity is a combination of intuition and expression that represents and orders the artist's view of the world. Time is a spiritual reality, not a chronometric calculation. Proust's work embodies a true French classicism that springs from a feeling for life rather than from rules of artistic form. It unites the past with the present; it is revealed by a myriad of delicate details: his perception of lilacs, his use of the names of towns, his rhythmical sentences. Psychology and social characterization, sensibility, relativism, and love are issues that Proust treats with unparelleled insight and depth. He is a Platonist with a subtlety comparable only to that of Baudelaire.

The central motifs seen in *A la recherche du temps perdu*, like those distinguished by Curtius in Balzac, are thus patterns of thought that blend into a integrated worldview. Curtius was neither a philosopher nor a psychologist, but the rapprochement between their activities, in the context of the phenomenological movement,[131] and his conception of the task of the literary critic are directly related. On 12 April 1922 Curtius had written to Proust; "Reading your book is, for me, one of the purest and greatest

---

[129] Ibid., 317.

[130] First published in his book *Französischer Geist im neuen Europa* (Stuttgart, 1925) and reprinted in *Französischer Geist im zwanzigsten Jahrhundert*, 274–355, this essay is linked to a series of newspaper articles that Curtius wrote between 1922 and 1928 (bibliography in Richards, *Modernism, Medievalism, and Humanism*, 174–79).

[131] See H. Spielberg, *The Phenomenological Movement*, 3rd ed. (London, 1982), esp. 268ff. (on Scheler). Helpful too are Spielberg's *The Context of the Phenomenological Movement* (The Hague, 1981), and D. R. Lachtermann's introduction to his translation of Max Scheler, *Selected Philosophical Essays* (Evanston, Ill., 1973).

intellectual joys that recent years have brought me."[132] That spirit of discovery is reflected in the phenomenological criticism of his essay; for Curtius's attempt to penetrate to the essence of Proust's art, to uncover the foundations of its system, by an intuitive understanding of salient motifs, exuberantly foreshadows the methods that were to be soberly employed in *ELLMA*.

In the book in which this essay on Proust appeared, Curtius also offered a diagnosis of the cultural crisis in France that seemed to him similar to the one besetting Germany. The French *Geist* is not subordinate to Latin civilization; like the German, it is a synthesis; and its synthetic character should enable it to overcome hostile preconceptions of Germany.[133] This resistance to a narrowly conceived Latin heritage was what Curtius had admired in his earlier writings on André Gide,[134] because it indicated a European awareness, a refusal to acquiesce in the outmoded but dangerous idea of the hegemony of any one national culture. Yet it was exactly this Latin element that Curtius stressed when advancing the same thesis about Germany. In an article published in the *Luxemburger Zeitung* for 7 October 1922, entitled "On the Psychology of the German Mind," Curtius presented "the Roman provinces on the Rhine" as integrated into European history, by Christianity and ancient culture, far earlier than the rest of Germany.[135] That factor, and the urge, exemplified by Goethe and Nietzsche, to "the unlimited" lent the German way of thought its universal, cosmopolitan character and prevented the German *Geist* from being cramped by nationalism.[136] And Curtius was to write in a textbook on France intended for German university students, that although Charlemagne had been appropriated to nationalistic purposes by the historiography and literature of Germany and France, he was not a national hero of either country. Charlemagne was, as Curtius had declared so eloquently in his review of Valéry's *Rhumbs*, emperor of the West, in which Germany played an integral part.

It cannot be said that Curtius succeeded in freeing himself from the traditional stereotypes that he sought to resist in his earliest comparisons of France and Germany; the first chapter of his final book on France is devoted to the tired antithesis between German *Kultur* and French *Zivilisation*,[137] and other generalizations that he essays on time, biology, and language lend themselves to caricature.[138] Yet these tensions, even contradictions, between Curtius's adherence to national differences and his

---

[132] Unpublished letter, Bonn University Library, call mark *Curtius, E. R. I*: "Die Lektüre Ihres Buches gehört für mich zu den reinsten und grössten geistigen Freuden, die mir die letzten Jahre gebracht haben."

[133] *Französischer Geist im neuen Europa*, 268–91.

[134] *Die literarischen Wegbereiter* (in *Französischer Geist im zwanzigsten Jahrhundert*), 42.

[135] Ed. Kirt, *E.R.C.*, *Goethe, Thomas Mann und Italien*, 20.

[136] Ibid., 24.

[137] Gross, *E.R.C. und die deutsche Romanistik*, 54ff., 84–85.

[138] Wellek, "The Literary Criticism of E.R.C.," 29–30.

attachment to a syncretic European ideal were, paradoxically, the very forces that were to lend his later writing its singular power and urgency. Throughout the 1920s—against the background of the occupation of the Ruhr, of inflation, and of Hitler's November-putsch—Curtius continued to write about the best in modern French and in modern European literature.[139] He regularly attended the meetings between French and German intellectuals arranged by the industrialist, Emile Mayrisch, and his wife, Aline, at Colpach in Luxembourg, and took part in the *décades* of Pontigny.[140] "At that time" wrote Curtius in an essay on Charles Du Bos, participant in these meetings, "I was still in quest of a France founded upon the assumptions of a general European mind."[141] How was he to pursue that quest? A document that survives in the archives of the Warburg Institute in London offers a glimpse of the route Curtius might have taken. In a confidential "memorandum for my friends" (among them Aby Warburg), dated 20 July 1929, when Curtius had received the call to his chair at Bonn, he requests financial support for the foundation of an institute "for the systematic study of French culture." Practical necessity requires cooperation between the activities of politics, diplomacy and economics, and intellectual analysis. "This is the larger political perspective in which I view my task in Bonn."

Warburg replied that having set up such an institute, he would not advise anyone else to take the same risk, but the advice was not to be needed. The institutional framework that Curtius had aspired to lend to his cultural and political ambitions was never erected. Not for him the commanding role of an institute director, nor even an assured future as a cosmopolitan critic of European literature. Germany, never absent from his thinking about a new intellectual order, was to face in the 1930s a crisis about which he could not remain silent. The protean personae of the previous decade were cast off in this hour of need; and Curtius emerged, an angry prophet, to do battle for the German mind in danger.

Deutscher Geist in Gefahr

In 1932 I published my polemical pamphlet *Deutscher Geist in Gefahr*. It attacked the barbarization of education and the nationalistic frenzy which were the forerunners of the Nazi regime. In it I pleaded for a new humanism, which should integrate the Middle Ages, from Augustine to Dante.[142]

---

[139] Cf. *Französischer Geist*, 525ff.

[140] See C. Dröge, "E.R.C. und Colpach," *Galerie* 6 (1988):26–36, and id., "Das Exil und das Reich—E.R.C., Aline Mayrisch de Saint Hubert und die Emigration in den dreissigen Jahre," in *Le Luxembourg et l'Etranger. Pour les 75 ans du professeur Tony Bourg*, ed. J. C. Muller and F. Wilhelm (Luxembourg, 1987), 171–86.

[141] *Essays*, 253–54.

[142] ELLMA, vii–viii.

Hindsight suggests a natural connection, a historical inevitability, about these statements. But for Curtius, in 1932, it was not so. An attack on the precursors of Nazism did not necessarily entail a plea for a new humanism, integrating the Middle Ages. During the fruitful decade of the 1920s, Curtius had been a critic of modern European literature, and an outspoken intermediary between France and Germany. No official prohibition prevented him, yet, from continuing in that role. By 1932, however, it was evident to him that the refashioning of Franco-German relations, to which he had sought to contribute in the interests of a European cosmopolitanism, was overtaken by more urgent issues: the present dilemma of Germany, the threat posed to its intellectual traditions by the philistine nationalism of the day, and the consequent need to redefine its cultural and historical position.

Recognition of that need was always implicit, and often explicit, in Curtius's criticism of the 1920s. When he wrote about France, Spain, or England, comparisons with Germany never failed to appear. Their tone, as the pages above have indicated, is eager and anxious by turns: "The intellectual renaissance of Germany *in which we fervently believe*"; "It is not merely a Western European, *it is, we may hope, also a German phenomenon* that criticism is assuming a new and productive function."; "This Romance form of creative criticism occurs infrequently *with us*. It is kept down by our ideal of specialization. . . . That is why . . *Germany today, while facing its gravest historical crisis,* has no national ideology capable of uniting the leading elite." The last of these sentences was written in 1924. While it is accurate to stress Curtius's belief (shared by several of his contemporaries and expressed at the beginning of *Deutscher Geist in Gefahr*)[143] that 1932 represented a turning point in German history, it would be a mistake not to constate that his sense of crisis, both political and intellectual, dates from the period of undoubted productivity and apparent optimism that Curtius enjoyed in the 1920s.

Throughout that period, as we have seen, Curtius recurred to the historical example of Charlemagne's empire. It was a medieval exemplum which, for him and others, was charged with a particular relevance to modern German politics. What that relevance was, and the target at which Curtius aimed when he wrote *Deutscher Geist in Gefahr,* are vividly highlighted by a comparison between his views on Charlemagne's empire with those of another German who attached equal if disparate importance to it—the wife of Hitler's alter ego, Martin Bormann.

---

[143] For an excellent discussion of this work, to which the following is indebted and from which it partly differs, see Dirk Hoeges, "Emphatischer Humanismus. E.R.C., Ernst Troeltsch und Karl Mannheim. Von "Deutscher Geist in Gefahr" zu "Europäische Literatur und lateinisches Mittelalter," in Lange, *"In Ihnen begegnet sich das Abendland,"* 31–52. See too K. Sontheimer, "E.R.C.'s unpolitische Verteidigung des deutschen Geistes," in 53ff. and H. Weinrich, "Deutscher Geist, europäische literatur und lateinisches Mittelalter," *Merkur* 32, 12 (1978):1217–29.

A passionate Nazi, of sound Nazi stock, Gerda Bormann clung to borrowed opinions that may have shifted their crude configuration with the passage of years, but which cannot be claimed to have evolved.[144] In a letter addressed to her husband, signed "Your Mummy," and dated 9 December 1944, she gave trenchant expression to her thoughts on the teaching of history:

> Today I did homework with Eike, history—Charlemagne. . . . Her history lessons are quite impossible. That moron of a teacher told the children that the slaughter of the Saxons in Verden-on-the-Aller was not at all historically certain, that there was only one document to prove it, while all other evidence was against it. It is obvious that the Carolingians destroyed all documents proving their ignominy, as far as they could get hold of them. There are a lot of things to be learned form the era of Charlemagne. After all, even now we partly feel the after effects of his policy. Through him, Christianity and with it Jewry got a foothold in our regions.[145]

This remarkable historical analysis was, needless to say, not Gerda Bormann's own. She was merely voicing, in her strident style, a prominent theme of Nazi historiography.[146] By a fatal error, the Franks had attached themselves to the Roman heritage and to Catholicism. Charlemagne was not a hero but "the slaughterer of the Saxons," those "true Germans" whose idealized champion was Widukind. In the atavistic racism of the "*völkisch*" ideology,[147] espoused by Gerda Bormann, there was no place for the suspect figure of Charlemagne. He had betrayed the national cause; his empire was polluted by its unsavory associations with Rome.

This is the theme on which Curtius seized near the beginning of *Deutscher Geist in Gefahr* (24), describing the repudiation of Charlemagne as a destructive manifestation of *völkisch* hatred of culture. Germany had entered history as a Roman province (22); between southwest Germany and Rome there existed an "uninterrupted unity of life"; strengthened by the Greco-Roman heritage that was transmitted through the monasteries in late antiquity; deepened in the Renaissance; and lent final literary form in the eighteenth century. All this was but an expansion of points that Curtius had made in earlier essays such as "The Psychology of the German Mind" in 1922, but their application was now different. In the "intellectual emergency" of 1932, writing with "faith in Germany and faith in the universal *Geist*" (10), Curtius opened his tract by

---

[144] On the background and opinions of Gerda Bormann, see H. R. Trevor-Roper, ed., *The Bormann Letters: The Private Correspondence between Martin Bormann and His Wife from January 1943 to April 1945* (London, 1954), xviiiff.

[145] Ibid., 110–11.

[146] See K. F. Werner, *Das NS-Geschichtsbild und die deutsche Geschichtswissenschaft* (Stuttgart, Berlin, Cologne, and Mainz, 1967), 39ff.

[147] Cf. G. L. Mosse, *The Crisis of German Ideology: Intellectual Origins of the Third Reich* (London, 1965), 13ff.

denouncing the perverse appropriation of the German past by the exponents of cultural despair.[148]

Culture, in its once cherished form as *Bildung*, had lost its meaning and its content in the grip of their nihilistic doctrines. The true representatives of the *Volk* were Goethe and Schiller (17), not the likes of George and his circle, whose "bombastic dogmatism" is deplored. And as Curtius severs the final links between himself and his erstwhile mentor, he also laments the inability of the political parties to formulate a coherent cultural policy. That did not make his tract "apolitical"; it merely required Curtius to continue an already lengthy search, outside politics, for weapons with which to oppose the growing cult of irrationality, and to defend the values of a supranational humanism. Some of these weapons were supplied by familiar figures in Curtius's intellectual pantheon—Max Scheler, for example, the metaphysical philosopher and educational theorist, whose writings and friendship meant much to Curtius.[149] But new authorities, too, made an appearance—the ambiguous figure of Martin Heidegger (28),[150] C. G. Jung (24), and Aby Warburg (29).

These last two men had a significant influence not only on *Deutscher Geist in Gefahr* but also on the genesis of *ELLMA*. Jung, whom Curtius had consulted before he wrote his polemical pamphlet, is presented as "the wisest interpreter of the psyche in our times"; and in the preface of *ELLMA* (ix) Curtius declares, "In my book there will . . . be found things that I could not have seen without C. G. Jung." Warburg, co-dedicatee of *ELLMA*, whom Curtius had heard lecturing at Rome in the winter of 1928–1929, offered insights into "the great struggle between the magical-demonic and the rational views of the world" (29).

These were the models that Curtius invoked to voice his opposition to the perverted patriotism of the *völkisch* ideology. True patriotism, he declared, is supranational, just as German culture, by its historical nature, is syncretic. Hence the point and force of Curtius's many appeals to Goethe. The supreme German artist represented, in his person and work, "a living preservation of timeless values" (33). Those values were founded on a religion that German nationalism, in its current degenerate and violent form, repudiated. It fomented revolution and denied the past, with tragic consequences that Jung's psychology enabled one to foresee (41). Antiquity and Christianity, humanism and the enlightenment were "the common heritage of the European experience" (42). Yet the defense of that patrimony could no longer be grounded in a simple or exclusive reconciliation with France. "France today has no fruitful movement that can stimulate us. . . . Young Germans are not responsive to what it can offer"

[148] See F. Stern, *The Politics of Cultural Despair: A Study in the Rise of the Germanic Ideology* (Berkeley and Los Angeles, 1963), esp. 267ff.

[149] See the attractive sketch of W-D. Lange, "E.R.C. und Max Scheler. Eine Skizze" in *Wege zur Kunst und zum Menschen. Festschrift für Heinrich Lützeler zum 85. Geburtstag*, ed. F. L. Kroll (Bonn, 1987), 265–73.

[150] See P. Bourdieu, *L'ontologie politique de Martin Heidegger* (Paris, 1988), esp. 54ff.

(47). "He who cuts off the road to Paris must open it to Rome" (48). This epigram had a personal resonance: Curtius was not only describing the limitations of Franco-German interchange in 1932; he was also acknowledging the setback to his former role as a cultural intermediary between France and Germany, and the need to look for a new one.

Linked with this acknowledgment, and reflecting Curtius's earlier educational concerns, was a call for a reform of the universities, and a rejection of "academic historicism" and of arid specialization. Hatvany's splendid satire, *Die Wissenschaft des Nichtwissenswerten*,[151] expressed and justified this demand, as did Gundolf's book on Shakespeare. Curtius's basic authority, in his analysis of the need for university reform, was the pedagogical writing of Scheler, but the conclusion that he drew from it was his own: "the more the nation becomes a mass, the more indispensable elites are to it" (76).

In this context, the "sociologism" of Karl Mannheim is singled out (75ff.) for special attack.[152] To its universal pretensions, recently proclaimed, the millenial force that Curtius extols is alien and opposed (103). External, transcending each of its historical manifestations, and superior to the products of its various schools, humanism is different from scholarship in the desiccated German style. Reanimate the cultural life of the leading elites through humanism, and the classroom will follow, proclaims Curtius. Between humanism and *Wissenschaft* there is no necessary connection. In a lyrical manner that some have found embarrassing,[153] Curtius attributes to humanism the redemptive properties of an intellectual faith:

> Humanism is nothing, if it is not enthusiasm that springs from love. It can only be formative for periods, peoples, men, when it comes from a superabundance of fullness and joy. It is the intoxicating discovery of a beloved archetype. (107)[154]

Accessible only to initiates whose numbers, Curtius claims (108), are always small, humanism is a weapon against the relativistic muddle of academic historicism, against "sociologism," against the chaos threatened by the many spurious -isms spawned in 1932. Such was the faith that Curtius was preaching in *Deutscher Geist in Gefahr*. What were the articles of its credo; what was the origin of its dogma?

Much of it derived from the writings of Ernst Troeltsch. His critique of historicism stressed the inseparability of ancient and modern culture, and

[151] Republished (Oxford, 1986) with prefaces by N. Kurti and H. Lloyd-Jones; introduction and notes by A. Grafton.

[152] The controversy between Mannheim and Curtius is the subject of a forthcoming book by Dirk Hoeges, *Kontroverse vor dem Abgrund. E.R.C.-Karl Mannheim 1919–1932*.

[153] H. Sontheimer in Lange, *"In Ihnen begegnet sich das Abendland,"* 57.

[154] "Humanismus ist nichts, wenn er nicht Enthusiasmus der Liebe ist. Er kann Zeiten, Völker, Menschen nur prägen, wenn er aus dem Überschwang der Fülle and Freude kommt. Er ist rauschhafte Entdeckung eines geliebten Urbildes."

made a special place for the European Middle Ages.[155] The distinguishing feature of Europe in world history, declared Curtius, citing Troeltsch and invoking the symbolism of Rome (113), was this intermingling of ancient and modern. With a spiritual fervor Curtius pleaded "for a return to origins, a healing and strengthening bath in the sources from which our life sprang forth" (113). This almost mystical conception of humanism—bolstered by copious references to Goethe, to patristic and medieval tradition, and to Scheler—nonetheless had practical consequences. It entailed a rejection of classicism and of enthusiasm for the Renaissance, in favor of medievalism and "the principle of restoration" (126). Greek offered no hope for such a humanism, for "the study of Greek is dead." Latin persisted, however, albeit in dwindling form, and the founders of the West,[156] from Augustine to Dante, offered the forces needed to revivify it in 1932. Yet it is neither Augustine nor Dante whose memory presides over the conclusion of *Deutscher Geist in Gafahr*. It is Cassiodorus, guardian of ancient learning, who "from the burdens of state office fled into the monastery, from high politics to contemplation" (125). The autobiographical note of longing for an escape from painful actuality is evident, even as Curtius prescribes his solution to the cultural crisis of the present.

Yet Curtius's debt to Troeltsch's book on historicism in 1922 does not fully account for his advocacy of a medieval European humanism a decade later. With Troeltsch's disavowal of relativism, his fidelity to Christianity, and his attachment to the ideas of liberal progress and humane civilization, Curtius had deep sympathy. Moreover, Troeltsch's belief that the need for reform of scholarship was "a practical problem of life"[157] that could be solved by a new synthesis, capable of distinguishing the very essence of European culture[158] and reestablishing its proper values, was one that Curtius shared. Nonetheless, equally evident in *Deutscher Geist in Gefahr* is a metaphysical longing for the recurrent and the constant, which is not dissimilar to Jacob Burckhardt's;[159] an assumption—implicit in Curtius's appeals to such diverse figures as Goethe and Jung—that there are forms of thought and expression that are common not only to Western Europe but to all mankind. This profoundly anti-historicist assumption lies behind his prefatory declaration of faith in "the universal *Geist*," and

[155] Curtius cites (110ff.) Troeltsch's *Der Historismus und seine Probleme. Erstes Buch: Das logische Problem der Geschichtsphilosophie* 2 (Tübingen, 1922), 716ff. His debt to Troeltsch is valuably discussed by Hoeges, "Ernst Troeltsh and Karl Mannheim," 44ff.

[156] Curtius's notion of the "founders of the West" (*Deutscher Geist*, 126) is linked with E. K. Rand's preface to vol. 1 of *Speculum*. The debt to his "great American book," *Founders of the Middle Ages* (1929), is acknowledged in ELLMA, viii.

[157] "Die Krisis des Historismus," discussed by Ringer, *The Decline of the German Mandarins*, 344 ff.; *Historismus*, 694–730.

[158] See G. G. Iggers, *The German Conception of History: The National Tradition of Historical Thought form Herder to the Present* (Middletown, Conn., 1969), 194.

[159] See Iggers, 129ff. Burkhardt is invoked by Curtius, *Deutscher Geist in Gefahr*, 27 and in the seventh epigraph to ELLMA.

was to be one of the central themes of ELLMA. In *Deutscher Geist in Gefahr* it is combined with a fervent attachment to Rome—no less the Rome of Christianity than the ancient capital of European culture. "Scheler believes," Curtius had written to his mother as long ago as 27 February 1918 "in a renaissance of European, primarily Catholic, Christianity."[160] Catholic Curtius never became,[161] but his sympathies with Scheler's religious writings were readily compatible with the historical philosophy of Troeltsch, which itself both complements and continues Troeltsch's philosophy of religion.[162]

With these ecumenical strains in Curtius's thought, the present state of Germany was not easily reconcilable. The political significance of the date of the preface to *Deutscher Geist in Gefahr*—18 January, the day of the foundation of the German Reich in 1871, the day on which the Versailles Peace Conference, from which Germany was excluded, opened—is now unmistakable.[163] The intellectual and personal conclusions that Curtius was to draw from this situation were less obvious. One of them, however, can be defined with clarity. Less than a month before he dated the preface to *Deutscher Geist in Gefahr*, on 24 December 1932, Curtius wrote to Gertrud Bing at the Warburg Institute: "This term, for the first time, I have held a course of lectures on the interpretation of Medieval Latin literature, and will continue them next term. I am of course a total newcomer in this field."[164] Simultaneously with the composition of his polemical pamphlet that argued for a new medieval humanism, Curtius began to teach the subject that would preoccupy him throughout the thirties and the Second World War.

In a letter to Eliot, of 16 April 1937, he applied to himself the pregnant motto: "*Bene vixit qui bene latuit*," and sympathizing with his friend for the closure of *The Criterion* Curtius recalled, on 14 January 1939, their years of collaboration, detecting in his refusal to review Herbert Read's *The Sense of Glory* in 1930, a sign that the living unity of the "European" mind was already beginning to disintegrate. "The great changes for the worse over the last few years have entirely alienated me from criticism and from contemporary literature," Curtius explained. "I have traveled further and further backwards in literature and have settled in the Latin literature that stretches from Prudentius to Dante."[165] Yet this concentration on

---

[160] "Scheler glaubt an eine Wiedergeburt des europäischen in erster Linie des katholischen Christentums," cited by Lange, "E.R.C. and Max Scheler," 267.

[161] See *Deutsch-französische Gespräche*, 86, and Lange, "E.R.C. and Max Scheler," 267.

[162] See A. O. Dyson, *History in the Philosophy and Theology of Ernst Troeltsch* (unpublished Oxford Ph.D. dissertation, 1968).

[163] Thanks to Dirk Hoeges, "Ernst Troeltsh and Karl Mannheim," 51–100.

[164] "Ich selbst habe in diesem Semester zum erstem Mal ein Interpretationskolleg über mittellateinische Literatur gehalten und werde das im nächsten Semester fortsetzen. Ich bin auf diesem Gebiet natürlich ganz Neuling," omitted by Wuttke, *Kosmopolis der Wissenschaft*.

[165] "Vielleicht war das auch schon ein Anzeichen dafür, dass die Lebenseinheit des "europäischen" Geistes anfing sich aufzulösen? . . . Die grossen Veränderungen der letzten

Medieval Latin did not represent a mere tactical retreat into the past. It was central to the strategy, adumbrated in *Deutscher Geist in Gefahr*, of recovering from contemporary barbarians the European legacy of Charlemagne's empire. And it provided Curtius with what he was later to call "a welcome intellectual alibi."[166]

The Alibi

A compelling psychological necessity drove me to seek a change in my field of research. I felt the need to return to older periods—metaphorically speaking, I would say today, to the more archaic strata of consciousness: in the first instance the Romance Middle Ages. Beyond that I was seeking, without being precisely aware of it, the road to Rome.[167]

Echoes have a special resonance in Curtius's thought. They lend it the unity for which he ceaselessly strove. The final phrase of this passage from his "Preface to a Book on the Latin Middle Ages and European Literature" recalls an epigram from *Deutscher Geist in Gefahr*: "He who cuts off the road to Paris must open it to Rome." Formulation and context are similar, but their tone is different. The polemicist of 1932 here describes an "inner emigration" that was not simply political. "Psychological necessity" bound him to *Roma aeterna*; "this bond contained a secret with many layers of symbolic meaning."[168] Nonetheless, in the twenty-two studies preparatory to *ELLMA* that furnished Curtius with his "welcome intellectual alibi during the war," no theory of symbolic meaning is explicitly advanced. It lies beneath the surface of these studies, written at a time of mounting public turmoil and increasing personal insecurity. It is worked out unsystematically, by a thinker who prized instinct and "an emotional apprehension of intellectual values."[169] And yet it formed the foundation of a monument of scholarship that was to embody Curtius's personal philosophy.

That philosophy had begun to take firmer shape by 1932. Curtius was never to abandon his conviction that "beyond the pupillary stage, there is no method in the humanistic disciplines. Or there is only one that cannot be taught: the cooperation of instinct and intelligence."[170] He had come to mistrust "the 'new scholarship,' basing itself upon 'insight' or 'intuition' and proclaiming its hostility to a much cited positivism."[171] Curtius's

---

Jahre haben mich der Kritik, aber auch der actuellen Literatur ganz entfremdet. Ich bin in der Literatur immer weiter rückwärts gewandert und habe mich jetzt in der lateinischen Literatur angesiedelt, die von Prudentius zu Dante reicht."

[166] *Essays*, 500.
[167] Ibid., 498.
[168] *Essays*, 498.
[169] Ibid., 501.
[170] Ibid., 501–2.
[171] Ibid., 502.

mistrust sprang from the political and cultural crisis analyzed in *Deutscher Geist in Gefahr*, and from his recoil before the excesses of an intellectual movement of which he had once been a member. "There were those who sought to remold the great personalities of history in accordance with the dogmas of the George circle,"[172] he wrote in 1945. "History was turned now into fiction, now into 'myth.' These were for the most part aberrations, the full extent of which can be measured only today, for they paved the way for the falsification of history on a grand scale, which had been fatally at work since 1933. 'There is no objective scholarship,' was taught at the time. Scholarship had to be affiliated with race, nation, and politics. This falsehood must disappear." The perversions of scholarship in the Nazi era had discredited one method of approach, and demanded the creation of another. "Experience must be transmuted in the fire of creation into a structure of knowledge as hard as steel. . . . Scholarship must always remain objective."[173] A far cry from the expressionist critic of 1919, with his optimistic belief in spiritual renewal and his antipathy to "fossilization." The distance that Curtius traversed between 1932 and the publication of *ELLMA* in 1948 can be measured in his preparatory studies.

Several of the lines of thought that they were to develop were already anticipated, in embryo, by three articles that appeared in 1929 and 1932. The first two were devoted to Hofmannsthal, on the occasion of the writer's death.[174] In Hofmannsthal, Curtius found an intellectual and moral authority, an exponent of "the Restoration principle,"[175] who had appealed to a "new", ecumenical "German reality in which the entire nation can participate."[176] The Germany whose values the Austrian Hofmannsthal represented was one that integrated the whole of European culture, especially that of "the Romance world." It was but a step from the qualities that Curtius discerned and celebrated in Hofmannsthal, to the revived humanism of *Deutscher Geist in Gefahr*, and the studies that implemented the program it adumbrated.

The symbolic importance of Rome, which looms so large in that tract, is one of the central themes of an essay on a Spanish poem of the fifteenth century that appeared in 1932.[177] Curtius takes as its epigraph a spirited

[172] *Essays*, 502. Possibly an allusion to such works as E. Kantorowicz's *Kaiser Friedrich der Zweite* (Berlin, 1927), on which, see E. Grünewald, *Ernst Kantorowicz und Stefan George. Beiträge zur Biographie des Historikers bis zum Jahre 1938 und seinem Jugendwerk "Kaiser Friedrich der Zweite"* (Wiesbaden, 1982), and D. Abulafià, "Kantorowicz and Frederick II," *History* 62 (1977):193–210.

[173] *Essays*, 502.

[174] "Hofmannsthal's deutsche Sendung," *Neue Schweizer Rundschau* (August, 1929), 583ff. and "Hofmannsthal und die Romanität," *Die Neue Rundschau* (November, 1929), 3ff. Translated in *Essays*, 129ff.

[175] *Essays*, 134.

[176] Ibid., 135.

[177] "Jorge Manrique und der Kaisergedanke," *Zeitschrift für romanische Philologie* (hereafter *ZfrPh*) 52 (1932):129ff. Reprinted in E.R.C. *Gesammelte Aufsätze zur romanischen Philologie* (Berne and Munich, 1960), 352. Discussed by Curtius, *Essays*, 499.

statement of Américo Castro's: "The progress of philology depends on the refinement and on the precision of ideas, on how we understand human values." Through a precise philological analysis of Jorge Manrique's lament on his father's death, Curtius paints a subtle picture of "the first classic of Spanish poetry," a writer who combined in his work "the idea of the Spanish nation, *pietas* toward Rome, and the intellectual heritage of the Middle Ages and humanism."[178] The theme of the imperial virtues in literature and music is traced down to the eighteenth century in a continuous progression that culminates in Goethe's *Faust*. "Germans should remember" Curtius pointedly concludes, "that their nation bore the imperial idea of Rome throughout a millenium, that the fatherlands of Jorge Manrique, of Dante, and of Goethe were comprised in it."[179] Germany, Italy, and Spain were thus linked by an indissoluble bond forged by the classical tradition, whose ancient ideas and enduring human values provided the guiding principles of Curtius's "inner emigration."

Curtius described the unsystematic character of his publications during that period with a quotation from Gustav Gröber, the systematizer who had introduced him to Medieval Latin.[180] Gröber's *magnum nomen* is invoked in the first of the cycle of studies that Curtius published chiefly in the *Zeitschrift für romanische Philologie* and *Romanische Forschungen*. That cycle began with a long and devastating critique of "the book by the professor of English, Glunz,"[181] the title of which inspired the corrective title of Curtius's review.[182]

Gröber's exactitude is marshaled against the imprecision of Glunz. His book—singled out in ELLMA as "a symptom of decadence in scholarship," an example of "the irresponsibility interpretative 'Geistesgeschichte' that took the place of philology in Germany after the First World War"[183]—is dissected in detail, and with a thoroughness that amounts to an alternative method. It is not merely that Glunz's hypothesis of the prevailing influence of theology on twelfth- and thirteenth-century poetry is exposed as threadbare. What Curtius attacks in Glunz's work is a grandiose structure of borrowed ideas superimposed on a fragile foundation of knowledge. "Philology!" is Curtius's rallying cry,[184] the weapon with which he cuts through the tissue of Glunz's errors. And by this Curtius means not only the exact application of linguistic and literary skills; he also refers specifically to one kind of philology: the neglected philology of the Latin Middle

---

[178] *Gesammelte Aufsätze*, 370.

[179] Ibid., 372.

[180] *Essays*, 500, n. 2. The quotation is from Curtius's essay on Gröber, *Gesammelte Aufsätze*, 448 and serves as the eighth of the "guiding principles" of ELLMA.

[181] *Essays*, 500. The reference is to H. H. Glunz's *Die Literarästhetik der europäischen Mittelalters. Wolfram, Rosenroman, Chaucer, Dante* (Bochum-Langendreer, 1937).

[182] "Zur Literarästhetik des Mittelalters I," *ZfrPh* 58 (1938):1–50.

[183] ELLMA, 381–82. Cf. ibid., 538, n. 1.

[184] "Gerne lasse ich die Möglichkeit offen, dass der eine oder andere Gedanke des Buches einen richtigen Kern enthalten mag. Aber glauben werde ich das erst, wenn es mir einwandfrei-philologisch bewiesen wird!" cited in "Zur Literarästhetik des Mittelalters I," 43.

Ages.[185] That is why Gröber, who perceived its central importance in the development of vernacular literature, is cited at the opening of Curtius's article. What Gröber possessed, Curtius believed that Glunz lacked; and in his attempt to erect in its stead a chimera of generalities, he ignored detailed lines of development that were already evident to Curtius in "the sequence of *loci communes* that medieval rhetoric had borrowed from antiquity and bequeathed to modern literature."[186] They offered insight not only into the literary aesthetics of the Middle Ages, but also into "the organic context of a tradition of European culture preserved over three thousand years." Convinced, as he later declared,[187] "that the current dicta on the literatures of the Middle Ages needed to be revised from the ground up," Curtius had begun by implementing a scorched earth policy. Yet above the rubble he had made of Glunz's theories, there had already, in 1938, begun to grow a theory of Curtius's own: the survival into and beyond the Middle Ages of the rhetorical topos.

About the importance of that theory Curtius was, from the outset, in no doubt. Unlike the groundless abstractions of *Geistesgeschichte*, here was a comprehensive cultural explanation founded on fact. Between Late Antique and Medieval Latin, and vernacular poetry, continued Curtius in the same year,[188] there stretched the uninterrupted continuity preserved by the schools. "All medieval poetry is primarily school poetry";[189] ancient rhetoric exerted an influence that enables one to discern continuities of style that stretch from Statius to Calderón.[190] To study the tradition of topos is empirically to acquire the schemata by which the vast indigest mass of medieval literature can be organized. Tracing their anonymous

---

[185] Ibid., 42.

[186] Ibid., 50. But see the valid criticisms of W. Haug, "Transzendenz und Utopie. Vorüberlegungen zu einer Literarästhetik des Mittelalters" in *Literaturwissenschaft und Geistesgeschichte. Festschrift für Richard Brinkmann*, ed. J. Brummack et al. (Tübingen, 1981), 1–22.

[187] ELLMA, 381.

[188] "Zur Literarästhetik des Mittelalters II," *ZfrPh* 58 (1938):129–232.

[189] Ibid., 133. Curtius's use of the term "topos" has itself been much discussed. See Jehn, *Toposforschung. Eine Dokumentation*; Baeumer, *Toposforschung*; Dronke, *Poetic Individuality in the Middle Ages*; D. Breuer and H. Schanze, *Topik. Beiträge zur interdisciplinären Diskussion* (Munich, 1981), and the important revaluation of Peter von Moos, *Geschichte als Topik. Das rhetorische Exemplum von der Antike zur Neuzeit und die "historia" im "Policraticus" Johannes von Salisbury* (Hildesheim, Zürich, and New York, 1988), esp. 425ff. A wide-ranging analysis of the present state and future tasks of "Topos-Forschung" is provided by L. Bornscheuer, "Neue Dimensionen und Desiderata der Topik-Forschung," *Mittellateinisches Jahrbuch* 22 (1987):2ff. (with the bibliographical note 1 of his previous publications). Because the origin and application of the term in Curtius's work has received such extensive and valuable attention, to the neglect of other aspects of ELLMA, which seem to me equally important, my focus in the following pages is on them.

[190] ELLMA, 282ff. An allusion, perhaps, to his 1934 essay on George, Hofmannsthal, and Calderón (*Essays*, 142ff.), or his 'Hofmannsthal und Calderón' in *Corolla, Festschrift Ludwig Curtius* (Stuttgart, 1937), 20ff.; but cf. too the discussion of Hofmannsthal's debt to the "*Alexiuslied*" in the 1936 essay reprinted in *Gesammelte Aufsätze*, 58ff.

recurrence is like writing art history without names, rather than a conventional chronology of individual masters. In this ardent empiricist searching for a system, it is not difficult to discern the pupil of Gustav Gröber.

Yet it is misleading to see in Curtius's disavowal of the romantic preoccupation with individuality a rejection of the view that "individuality lies precisely in the way the typical is used."[191] In emphasizing the flexibility of the topos, its changes with time, and its adaptability to new cultural contexts, Curtius was attempting to annex attributes of romantic individuality to a disfavored classicism that he wished to revive. Perhaps, in his eagerness to resuscitate that unfashionable aesthetic, Curtius attached too much weight to the alleged antithesis between romanticism and classicism; but in 1938, fresh from a dispiriting encounter with the style of *Geistesgeschichte* represented by Glunz, at a time when the dangers of a subjective individualism were all too publicly evident, it is not surprising that Curtius ascribed to the topos every bit of the importance that he had once attributed to the "constituent elements of the soul." That apparently objective means of encompassing tradition held out the promise of exactitude, the reassurance of rationality.

Because many of Curtius's studies were incorporated into ELLMA, the structure and purpose of which will be analyzed below, it is less useful here to summarize his results than to indicate which of them he was to amplify and which to excise, and to consider what these expansions and omissions indicate about Curtius's view of a subject that he mastered with astonishing rapidity.

Within six years of publishing *Deutscher Geist in Gefahr* and his essay on Manrique, Curtius had written four major articles, of some 240 pages, that represented a radically new approach to Medieval Latin literature.[192] Others had written informatively about the connections between the learned language and the vernaculars; others had produced literary histories that were valuable in their time; and the leading practitioners of the subject in the previous generation—above all, Ludwig Traube—displayed, in their distinguished combination of textual criticism and paleography, a sympathy equal to Curtius's for the classical tradition of the Middle Ages. What set him apart from his precursors was the distinctiveness of his method and the breadth of his range. To Medieval Latin Curtius brought a knowledge of the full sweep of European literature that none of the specialists who had worked in this field had evinced, and which few would claim to have acquired since. In a further eighteen articles, published between 1938 and 1944, Curtius established himself as the preeminent exponent of a distinctively literary approach in a subject to which literary methods had rarely been applied with much subtlety.

[191] *ZfrPh* 58 (1938):139ff. Summarized and translated by Dronke, *Poetic Individuality in the Middle Ages*, 18–19.

[192] To the articles cited at nn. 182 and 188 add "Zur Literaturästhetik des Mittelalters III," *ZfrPh* 58 (1938):433–79, and "Dichtung und Rhetorik im Mittelalters," *Deutsche Vierteljahrsschrift für Literaturwissenschaft* 16 (1938):435–75.

And this was accomplished by a man who worked, during the later years of the Second World War, from a modest private library, in a flat whose windows had been smashed by the nearby explosion of bombs. It is not necessary to subscribe to a cult of Curtius in order to see something of the stature, human as well as intellectual, of his achievement.

Diversity, as well as rapidity, is characteristic of Curtius's earliest attempts to define a medieval literary aesthetic. Topics that were to form part of chapter 5 of ELLMA—"boy and old man" and "the world upside down"—coexist, in the second of these studies, with a treatment of the theme of "the ancients and the moderns," viewed not (as in ELLMA, chapter 14) as an aspect of classicism, but an instance of the contrasts between generations and periods. Nor is it always clear how and why Curtius shifts from a historical to what he terms a "heuristic" account of the material he marshals. Into an analysis of personified Natura, as she appears in the work of Bernardus Silvestris and Bernard of Clairvaux, is introduced "the archetype of the unconscious," the anima of C. G. Jung.[193] At one level, Curtius asserts that he is unraveling the archaic figurative language of the psyche. At another, he declares, he is investigating the relations between Medieval Latin and vernacular poetry. His approach is flexible, empirical, independent of older theories. It combines the rigor of exact philology with the intuitive insight of Curtius's modern criticism, to which he explicitly links it.[194] These are bold claims, unequally fulfilled. For Curtius's methods are implemented most successfully not on the psychological, but on the metahistorical level.

From "periodization," in the sense of units of history or literature arbitrarily subdivided by parochial specialists, Curtius had long felt alienated, as his book on Balzac reveals. This was reinforced by his hostility to the empty relativism of contemporary historicists, and by a concomitant longing for timeless and transcendent patterns of thought and expression. They are intermittently characterized, in Curtius's early studies, in terms of Jungian psychology; but perhaps more impressive and certainly more consistent is Curtius's ability to illuminate neglected areas in the sovereign sweep of his chronological range. Late antiquity provides one example; the early Middle Ages another. Curtius not only asserted the existence of stylistic continuities between Sidonius and Calderón; he also attempted to set writers such as Sidonius in their context. To describe that context as "a period of transition," in the manner of so many literary histories, seemed to Curtius a mere evasion; and in a bold attempt to trace the development of ancient and medieval poetics, he mapped out a territory that has never looked the same since he entered it. The significance of the late antique biblical epic in the evolution of Christian literary theory, or the analysis of techniques of vernacular heroic poetry, in terms of ancient grammar, are two subjects among many that Curtius made his own—

---

[193] "Zur Literaturästhetik des Mittelalters II," 196.

[194] Ibid., 197, and see above, n. 4.

subjects that are still debated with an interest that his work did much to stimulate. And it is this equal attentiveness to all periods—the "Dark Ages" and the "End of Antiquity" as well as the "High Middle Ages" and the "flowering of the vernacular"—that lends substance to his theme of continuity, and distinguishes Curtius from the chroniclers who had plodded through provinces of an empire that he had made his own.

His own empire it swiftly became, but not without the aid of proconsuls. Several of the central ideas of Curtius's studies were clarified by consultation with the learned Dominican priest, Jean de Menasce. His considerable (and unacknowledged) influence on the preparation of ELLMA is revealed in correspondence that has been excellently edited by W-D. Lange.[195] With Menasce Curtius discussed, as early as 1938, such subjects as the image of the *deus artifex*, the rhetorical theory of the topos, and the theme of biblical poetics that play a central role in ELLMA. Through letters exchanged with Menasce, Curtius not only acquired theological and philosophical insights that enrich his account of the intellectual background of the literature that ELLMA examines; in them he also expressed to his scholarly and spiritual partner his most intimate concerns while writing that book. "Beloved and holy Rome . . . chose me, the German Roman," he wrote to Menasce on 22 December 1944, when his studies were nearing completion, "The road to Rome had to lead through the Middle Ages, which to me simultaneously signified an archaic stratum of my consciousness. Thus were produced . . . twenty-two medieval studies. . . . I could not, of course, express the deepest ideas that lay behind them, for they were profoundly anti-Teutonic."[196]

"Anti-Teutonic" here complements, and serves to define, the expression "German Roman" of the preceding sentence. Both point to a purpose that, in Curtius's preliminary studies to ELLMA, always remains implicit. Unlike the debased atavism of the "Teutonic" values espoused by the Nazis, the idea of the "Roman German" had an impeccable cultural pedigree.[197] Its most celebrated scion was the Goethe of *The Italian Journey* and *The Roman Elegies*; and in Goethe's concept of *Weltliteratur*, Curtius found a precedent and a justification for the case he was obliquely arguing. "One is a European," he asserts in the first chapter of ELLMA, "when one has become a *civis Romanus*. The division of European literature among a number of unconnected philologies almost completely prevents

[195] Lange, *"In Ihnen begegnet sich das Abendland,"* 199ff.

[196] Ibid., 211: "Das geliebte und heilige Rom . . . wählte mich, den Deutschrömer. Der Weg nach Rom musste durch das Mittelalter führen, das für mich nun zugleich eine archaische Schicht meines Bewusstseins bedeutete. So entstanden bis Sept. 1944 22 MA.— Studien . . . Ich durfte die tiefsten Leitideen allerdings nicht aussprechen, denn sie waren profund antiteutonisch."

[197] See W. Rehm, *Europäische Romdichtung*, 2d ed. (Munich, 1960), 181–216. For the use of the same images in Nazi classical scholarship, against which Curtius may also have been reacting, see Luciano Canfora, *Ideologie des Classicismo* (Turin, 1980), 133ff.

this."[198] By reestablishing the connections between the parts of this unnaturally severed unity, Curtius was fulfilling both a political and an intellectual duty of his Roman citizenship.

Hence the particular disdain with which Curtius regarded many of the Germanists of his generation, and the hostility with which he attacked Gustav Ehrismann's views on the "chivalric system of values."[199] Ehrismann, although in a different class from the nationalistic practitioners of his discipline, had turned his hand to the history of ideas with (in Curtius's view) a notable lack of success, except among fellow-Germanists. Curtius's onslaught on Ehrismann's methods is more than a critique of his knowledge of theology and philosophy; it represents an indictment of specialism, a plea for a new and broader view of medieval scholarship that must liberate itself from the baneful specter of romanticism.

Romanticism was not presented in Curtius's studies as the root of all evil; but it emerges from them as something very like it. It was in contrast to a romantic hostility to rhetoric that Curtius formulated his view of the essentially rhetorical nature of language;[200] and it was in a vehemently anti-romantic spirit that he sought to root Dante in the Latin traditions of twelfth- and thirteenth-century poetry.[201] The "romantic movements of the *Zeitgeist*" were the enemies and targets of his evolving methods—methods that sprang not from preconceived theories, but from an empirical investigation of individual facts. With mounting confidence in the "universal standpoint" won by "daily contact with texts," Curtius came to feel that he had acquired a comprehensive view of the Middle Ages, in which the proponents of romanticism could have no place.

Thus his sentiments in 1943 were exultantly anti-romantic.[202] But if one looks back only three years to the substantial essay that Curtius published under the title "The Archpoet and the Style of Medieval Latin Poetry,"[203] one observes with ironical surprise that, in the midst of a highly technical discussion of rhetorical devices, formulas of brevity, and number symbolism, Curtius comments on the Archpoet's subtly equivocal lines:

> Morte bona morior, dulci nece necor,
> Meum pectus sauciat puellarum decor . . .
> Meum est propositum in taberna mori,
> Ut sint vina proxima morientis ori . . .

[198] *ELLMA*, 12.

[199] *Deutsches Vierteljahrsschrift für Literaturwissenschaft* 21 (1943):343–68; *ELLMA*, 519ff. See C. Cormeau in Lange, *"In Ihnen begegnet sich das Abendland,"* 155ff.

[200] *ZfrPh* 63 (1943):235ff., esp. 231.

[201] Ibid., 262; *Romanische Forschungen*, 56 (1942):3–22 and ibid., 57 (1943):153–85. For a fine appreciation of Dante's personal significance to Curtius see W. Hirdt in Lange, *"In Ihnen begegnet sich das Abendland,"* 181ff.

[202] *Romanische Forschungen*, 57 (1943):153. Cf. the account of rhetorical depictions of nature, ibid., 56 (1942), esp. 220.

[203] Ibid., 54 (1940):105–64.

"In these verses we touch on the core of the poet. No one before him had felt in this way. . . . In this poet there exists a wondrous pride. It was the great humiliation of his life that he had to beg for food and clothing. . . . The word 'to beg' was painful to him."[204] A more romantic interpretation of the equivocally autobiographical style of the Archpoet is hard to imagine, and not all readers of Curtius's article will regret that it was omitted from ELLMA, when its author came to recast his preliminary studies into book form. Before castigating the romantic roots of evil in others, Curtius judiciously chose to chastise the devil within.

Such were the principle strains of his studies between 1933 and 1944. Their hybrid growth pointed in many directions, and might have made more than one book.[205] But for all their heterogeneity, Curtius's writings of this period had led, by convergent paths, to a central, unifying idea: the Latin Middle Ages. "By the Latin Middle Ages," he wrote in his programmatic article on Dante,[206] "I understand not only Medieval Latin literature, but also the view of the world and of history held by medieval thinkers and scholars."[207] A characteristic conclusion, then, to the ecumenical strains in Curtius's thought; but it remained to weld their disparate parts into the system towards which he had been striving, into a "universal standpoint."

The Universal Standpoint

My book is not the product of purely scholarly interests, it grew out of a concern with the preservation of Western culture. It seeks to serve an understanding of the Western cultural tradition insofar as it is manifested in literature. It attempts to demonstrate the unity of that tradition in space and time by the application of new methods. In the intellectual chaos of the present it has become necessary, and happily not impossible, to demonstrate that unity. But the demonstration can only be made from a universal standpoint. Such a standpoint is afforded by latinity.[208]

It is a philologist who writes. A philologist, moreover, who had reflected long and hard upon the nature and purpose of his activity, and who had recently met with adverse criticism.

When Curtius composed the foreword to the English translation of

---

[204] "In diesen Versen berühren wir das Tiefste des Dichters. So hatte vor ihm kein anderer gefühlt. . . . In diesem Dichter lebt ein wundervoller Stolz. Es war die grosse Demütigung seines Lebens, dass er um Brot und Rock betteln musste . . . das Wort 'betteln' war ihm peinlich," ibid., 118.

[205] The studies on the Old French epic that he planned, near the end of his life, to make into a book, form a substantial part of his *Gesammelte Aufsätze*, 98ff.

[206] "Dante und das lateinische Mittelalter," *Romanische Forschungen* 57 (1943):153–85.

[207] Ibid., 155.

[208] ELLMA, viii.

ELLMA (published in 1953), the German original of his book and the studies that preceded it had been caustically characterized by the émigré Romance philologist, Leo Spitzer, as "an abandonment of all aesthetic, philosophic, and modernist tendencies," a "repudiation of his earlier work." "With his flair for the duty of the hour, Curtius turned to "solid philology." It was "logical that an aristocratic mind such as Curtius's should, before the onslaught of the plebeian hordes, retreat into the Latin past of Germany."[209] Spitzer sensed "a bitter note of iconoclasm directed against himself, a will to matter-of-fact, ascetic, philological aridity, as if to chastise his former nature." ELLMA is described as "a vast grammar or dictionary of topoi," as Curtius's route of "escape . . . into the necropolis of a past that was alive as late as the eighteenth century."

The personal tone of these criticisms, which Spitzer was not alone in voicing, reflects the mixture of hostility and respect that the author of ELLMA seldom failed to provoke. With an authority that did not descend to the level of self-defence, Curtius wrote a foreword to the English translation of ELLMA which, like the preface to his *Critical Essays*, represented a powerful if implicit rebuttal to the barbs of his detractors. Autobiographical but studiously impersonal, it is composed in the spirit of the aphorism by Balzac that Curtius was fond of quoting: "It is not enough to be a man; it is necessary to be a system." As such, Curtius's foreword casts light on the system embodied in ELLMA.

Its foundation was philology. "For the intellectual sciences it has the same significance as mathematics has for the natural sciences. . . . Philology is the handmaid of the historical disciplines. I have attempted to employ it with something of the precision with which the natural sciences employ their methods."[210] This is not, as many (following Spitzer) have thought, the dogma of a recent convert to neopositivism. It is the credo of a long-standing adherent of phenomenology, a friend and disciple of Max Scheler, whose comprehensive philosophy aimed to synthesize the results of the natural sciences. Hence Curtius's description of his book as "a phenomenology of literature,"[211] his wish to distinguish it from "literary history, comparative literature, and 'Literaturwissenschaft' as they are practiced today."[212] Evident in Curtius's earliest critical writings, this scorn for "the *scientia infima* of literary history" is passionately proclaimed in ELLMA. "It has a half dozen concepts. They are blocks, massive and unshaped. Humanism, renaissance, classicism, romanticism, pre-romanti-

---

[209] *American Journal of Philology* 70 (1949):426. For Spitzer's view of Curtius's "former self," see Spitzer, *Stilstudien* (reprint, Munich, 1961), 397–98 (French translation by A. Coulon, with valuable introduction by J. Starobinski, in Spitzer, *Études de style* [Paris, 1970], 397ff.). On the evolution of Spitzer's critical position, see J. V. Catano, *Language, History, Style: Leo Spitzer and the Critical Tradition* (Urbana and Chicago, 1988).

[210] ELLMA, x.

[211] Cf. ELLMA, ix, "All these and other questions are prolegomena to what I should like to call a phenomenology of literature."

[212] Ibid.

cism, pre-classicism—nothing more can be accomplished with this miserable equipment."[213] "*Literaturwissenschaft*" was also "a failure in both its variants, the 'art-historical' and '*geistesgeschichtliche.*' "[214] A "symptom of decadence in scholarship," *Geistesgeschichte*, as practiced by the likes of Glunz, was nothing more than pretentiously "philosophizing *Literaturwissenschaft*,"[215] and most damning of all, "Usually, those who cultivate *Literaturwissenschaft* are Germanists."[216]

A "bitter note of iconoclasm directed against himself"? That is not how literary and art historians, practitioners of *Literaturwissenschaft* and *Geistesgeschichte*, or Germanists were likely to interpret Curtius's pronouncements. *Sua res agebatur*, they had reason to think. Nor is bitterness apparent in Curtius's zestfully iconoclastic onslaught on the competence of rival approaches. Rather, the question it poses is, when these idols were smashed, what was the "universal standpoint" that he was seeking to put in their place?

Curtius's "universal standpoint," unlike what he called the "fashions and aberrations of the *Zeitgeist*," needed to be grounded in "rigorous scholarship."[217] Classical philology had a continuous tradition of such scholarship; "modern philology," by contrast, had "remained at a standstill. Its self-complacent autarky was obsolete."[218] In the years when Werner Jaeger, the exiled German classicist, had begun to formulate his own version of a revived humanism,[219] Curtius too looked back to the past, to the example and teaching of the classically trained Gröber, from whose *Grundriss* the eight of *ELLMA*'s "guiding principles" is taken. And if we consider that apparently innocuous epigraph in this context, we can now appreciate its polemical and programmatic flavor.[220]

It is polemical, because Curtius's deepest antipathy was reserved for a priori assumptions that lacked a sound basis in fact. This was his reason for attacking the pseudo-philosophical pretensions of *Geistesgeschichte*, and for wishing to expose its vulnerability to aberrant trends. That was

[213] *ELLMA*, 392.

[214] Ibid., 381.

[215] Ibid., 11.

[216] Ibid., 12.

[217] *ELLMA*, 382.

[218] Ibid., 381.

[219] See Jaeger, "Classical Philology and Humanism," *Transactions of the American Philological Association* 67 (1936):363–74 with P. Innocenti, "Neohumanismo e filologia classica. Reflessioni sull' approdo al mondo antico fra le due guerre," *Il Pensiero* 17 (1972):123–49.

[220] "Undirected observation, inconspicuous attempts precede the all-around comprehension of the subject. Then, traversing the space at a bound, the seeker snatches at the goal. With a scheme of imperfect ideas concerning similar subjects, he seems to be able to grasp the whole before its nature and constituents are known. This rash opinion is followed by the discernment of error, only slowly by the resolve to approach the subject by small and smallest careful steps, to observe parts and particles, and not to rest until the conviction has been attained; thus and not otherwise is the matter to be understood." Also quoted in *Critical Essays*, 500, n. 2; translation Kowal.

also why he extolled the empirical methods of Gröber, whose goal of knowledge (*Erkenntnis*) was, in Curtius's eyes, a guarantee of the objectivity that recent scholarship had lamentably lacked. [221] But Gröber's account of his unmethodical methods also seemed to Curtius to contain, "*in nuce*," a "*Discours de la méthode.*"[222] Gröber had no time for intellectual constructs externally imposed upon the evidence. His unsystematic yet thorough style of investigation authenticated its impartiality. Thus Curtius stresses close observation, and the importance of wide reading. [223] Thus he emphasizes intuition, and the eye for "significant facts" (borrowing an expression of Bergson). The identification of recurrent phenomena enables the investigator to "penetrate the concrete structure of literature." "Analysis leads to synthesis. Or, the synthesis issues from the analysis; and only a synthesis thus brought into existence is legitimate."[224] That is what Warburg meant by his aphorism "God lurks in detail."

ELLMA is dedicated to the memory of Warburg and of Gröber. The significance of this dedication was not purely personal; it also implied an adherence to a particular view of scholarly method. Warburg's detailed research into the classical tradition and the philological empiricism of Gröber served as the methodological pillars of the edifice that Curtius, influenced by Scheler's outlook and vocabulary, described as a "phenomenology of literature." "Facts . . . and not the constructs of an 'understanding,' " Scheler had written in a well-known essay on the theory of cognition, [225] "are the material bases of phenomenological philosophy. . . . Phenomenological 'seeing' is intuition."[226] Facts that one knows intuitively to be significant are "penetrated" by analysis, echoes Curtius (again adopting the terminology of Bergson[227]), and "Analysis . . . if . . . directed upon literature . . . is called philology. It alone penetrates into the heart of this matter. There is no other method of exploring literature."[228] It is not difficult to detect, in this affirmation of faith in a total and exclusive system of interpretation, the convergence of formative influences on Curtius's intellectual development. "Neopositivist" is too simple a term for the complex blend of the thought of Gröber and Scheler, of Bergson and Warburg that contributed to form the outlook and the program embodied in *ELLMA*. For Curtius's "universal standpoint" was founded on a phenomenological application of philological methods.

It is thus open to question whether Curtius was wholly sincere when,

---

[221] On the *Erkenntnis*- ideal in Gröber's work, see Curtius, *Gesammelte Aufsätze*, 448, 454–55.

[222] Ibid., 248.

[223] *ELLMA*, 382.

[224] Ibid., 382–83.

[225] Max Scheler, *Selected Philosophical Essays*, trans. Lachtermann, 203.

[226] Ibid., 215.

[227] *ELLMA*, 383.

[228] Ibid.

in his foreword, he stated that ELLMA "was not in line with any of the scientific, scholarly, or philosophic trends which governed contemporary thought."[229] Considered against the background of his earlier writings, it represents a natural extension of their style of criticism to what was indeed the "new" field of European literature and the Latin Middle Ages. How that field should be defined posed a problem. In an essay of 1944,[230] Curtius mused on making a book of his preliminary studies entitled "The Latin and Romance M[iddle] A[ges]: Investigations into Europe's Literary Tradition"; and in a letter to Gertrud Bing, dated 21 November 1946, he toyed with the title "The Latin Middle Ages and European Literature."[231] These were more than stylistic alternatives. To Curtius, it was a matter of summing up "the yield of my life's work," of casting "new light" on "the survival of the ancient tradition from 400 to 1700."[232] Hence the care and the self-consciousness with which he sought to express, in its title, the purpose of his book.

The audience for which ELLMA was intended receives similar attention in Curtius's foreword. His disdain for narrow specialists, implicit in the exuberantly expressionist style of his journalism and French criticism, and explicit in *Deutscher Geist in Gefahr*, is transmuted in ELLMA into a generous appeal to a wider public: "My book . . . is not addressed to scholars, but to lovers of literature."[233] By them Curtius meant, first and foremost, his partners in the European intellectual community of the 1920s such as T. S. Eliot, to whom he confided, on 29 November 1947, his despondent doubt: "*Cui bono?* Isn't it hopeless, to swim against the current? . . . I am very doubtful whether my book will find any resonance."[234]

These private doubts never show in Curtius's public appeal to "those who are interested in literature as literature"—an assertion of its autonomy that he justifies, with a perhaps archaic eye to his English-speaking audience, by a quotation from George Saintsbury.[235] Saintsbury again becomes the authority for Curtius's plea for a union of specialization with universalism, combining ancient with modern literature. "One cannot understand the Middle Ages," Curtius declares more succinctly elsewhere,[236] "if one *only* researches the Middle Ages."

These views were not quite as peculiar to Curtius as the foreword to ELLMA might suggest. English critics whom he admired, such as W. P. Ker, held similar opinions about the importance of writing for a wider

---

[229] Ibid., viii.

[230] "Über die altfranzösische Epik," reprinted in *Gesammelte Aufsätze*, 107.

[231] Wuttke, *Kosmopolis der Wissenschaft* , 52:137.

[232] Ibid.

[233] ELLMA, viii.

[234] "*Cui bono?* Ist es nicht hoffnungslos, gegen den Strom zu schwimmen? . . . Ich bezweifle es sehr, ob mein Buch Resonanz finden werde."

[235] On Saintsbury's criticism and its reputation, see René Wellek, A *History of Modern Criticism 1750–1950* 4 (London, 1966), 416ff.

[236] *Gesammelte Aufsätze*, 107.

public, attached comparable significance to continuity,[237] and commanded an impressive knowledge of many areas and periods of European literature. But in Germany, where the lack of interdisciplinary studies of the Middle Ages was compounded (in Curtius's view) by arid specialization,[238] the ideal of viewing these subjects as a unity had long been forgotten. Best formulated in the nineteenth century by Adolf Ebert, who derived it from Goethe's concept of *Weltliteratur*,[239] it had been continued by Ebert's successor Gustav Gröber; and Gröber's heir was . . . Curtius himself. Thus, in the studies that preceded *ELLMA* was generated a splendid stemma that placed Curtius in a line of direct descent, through his philological forebears, from his intellectual ancestor, Goethe. Small wonder, then, that the tone of *ELLMA*'s foreword and opening chapter is programmatic, if not prophetic. For the mantle of Goethe—already a potent cultural symbol in Curtius's earlier writings—had descended upon this worthy beneficiary of his universalist heritage.

How was he now to take possession of the legacy that he was claiming?

The Aerial Photograph and the Map

A person standing on the ground before a heap of ruins cannot see the whole that the aerial photograph reveals. But the next step is to enlarge the aerial photograph and compare it with a detailed map. There is a certain analogy to this procedure in the technique of literary investigation here employed.[240]

Photographs are taken, and maps are made, on the basis of certain principles. Those terms prefixed to *ELLMA* point to breadth combined with detail over the widest chronological and linguistic range. They also imply an aesthetic—of erudition as art—and a moral that is most clearly expressed in the sixth epigraph that Curtius borrows from Goethe: "there is no patriotic art and patriotic scholarship. Both belong, like all things good, to the entire world." It was natural, then, that Curtius should begin by examining the two constituents of *Weltliteratur* that were central to his heritage.

Weltliteratur, to him, meant essentially that of Europe. And Europe was, in 1948, a concept that needed redefinition. To that purpose several familiar figures contributed: Gröber, whose borrowed principle of the *vis inertiae*[241] lends an ethical tone to Curtius's animadversions on progress;

---

[237] See the quotation from his *The Dark Ages* (London, 1904)—described in *ELLMA*, 520, n. 3 as a "little masterpiece"—in ibid., 22, and cf. Ker in *Form and Style in Poetry*, ed. R. W. Chambers (London, 1928), 50ff.

[238] *ELLMA*, 519–20.

[239] *Gesammelte Aufsätze*, 109.

[240] *ELLMA*, ix.

[241] For the sources and application of this principle (unironically employed), see *Gesammelte Aufsätze*, 449.

Scheler, whose mistrust of universal suffrage is intended to reinforce Curtius's autobiographical affirmation of the importance of creative individuals; and Troeltsch, whose critique of historicism justified Curtius's considering European culture as a unique and intelligible "unit." But a new member had been added to the triumvirate: Arnold Toynbee, whose writings were (in Curtius's view) to history what atomic physics was to the natural sciences. [242]

In *The Study of History*—this "comparative morphology of cultures," surveyed with (Curtius claims) incomparable breadth and congenial empiricism—Curtius found a comprehensive vision that helped him and others to transcend the "national myths and ideologies" that had splintered Europe into geographical and chronological fragments. Toynbee understood the importance of leading elites; his book was "the greatest intellectual accomplishment in the field of history in our day." [243] Euphoric this evaluation may seem to more than one present-day reader of *The Study of History*, but in 1948 Curtius's enthusiasm for Toynbee was the final liberating factor that enabled him to state plainly the political message that unites ELLMA with *Deutscher Geist in Gefahr*: "Europeanization of the historical picture has today become a political necessity, and not only for Germany." [244] This was the lesson that he had learned, in partnership with Eliot, during the 1920s.

Toynbee, like Troeltsch, understood the importance of artistic symbols, the value of a poetic form of presentation. Both thinkers' opinions on the role of the imagination are combined by Curtius with Bergson's account of the "fabulatory function" that provided a means of grasping "the farthest horizon, the background, of the complex of European literature." [245] To literature a process of "Europeanization" should be applied, for only so would its "dismemberment" into unconnected periods be remedied. Curtius illustrates his point by a characteristic example: the vivid sense of Germany's Roman past expressed in George's poetry, and shared by Goethe. Compared with the historical understanding of these poets, the academic exponents of *Literaturwissenschaft*, with their vague concepts transferred from dubious disciplines, seemed to Curtius mere dilettanti. Their field of observation was too narrow; they failed to recognize "the autonomous structure of literature." [246]

Against these miscreants Curtius reasserted an ideal of "Roman citizenship" that was already in his mind in 1944, a citizenship "of every period from Homer to Goethe." [247] From the parochialism of the specialists, the unity of European literature was thereby to be rescued, and no period was more crucial to an understanding of its continuity than the neglected

[242] ELLMA, 4; cf. *Critical Essays*, 400ff.
[243] ELLMA, 6.
[244] Ibid., 7.
[245] Ibid., 9.
[246] Ibid., 10–12.
[247] ELLMA, 12.

Middle Ages. Troeltsch had written of their centrality; Curtius had taken up the theme in *Deutscher Geist in Gefahr*; and ELLMA now asserted the cardinal importance, in this connection, of Medieval Latin. It represents an unexplored area of that "timeless present" which, Curtius claims (in an infelicitous comparison with the rival merits of art) is characteristic of literature. The claim is bolstered by a catalog of examples: "Homer in Virgil, Virgil in Dante, Plutarch and Seneca in Shakespeare . . . ,"[248] by a plea for a new "science of European literature," and by a "delimitation" of the subject from the period of Homer to Goethe.

The many elements of Curtius's earlier work, echoed in this richly associative line of thought, combine, in the first chapter of ELLMA, to form his own *Discours de la méthode*. The spirit in which his book begins is not as a "retreat into the necropolis," but as a declaration of war on rival approaches by a militant humanism. The theme of the continuity of European literature was to be nothing less than Curtius's counterpart of Toynbee's "historical revolution."

Revolutions need symbols. Both Troeltsch and Toynbee had understood their significance. The "universal-historical view" of literature that Curtius was espousing on analogy with them, found a poetic symbol in Dante's *Divina Commedia*. Chapter 2, which defines the second key element in ELLMA's title, begins with the scene (*Inferno* 4) in which Dante meets the poets and philosophers of the classical past. Between antiquity and the *Commedia* stretched "the crumbling Roman road from the antique to the modern world,"[249] to which Curtius had referred in *Deutscher Geist in Gefahr*. What was once, for him, a cultural and political metaphor had now become a concrete entity: the Latin Middle Ages. That millennial entity, typified by the *Divina Commedia*, was defined not by geography or history, but by its learned language and its "coalescence" of ancient and modern culture. "Freedom to shift from country to country and period to period is necessary to our enterprise," affirms Curtius. "Strict chronology is our prop, not our guide."[250]

A shaky prop, frequently discarded, is how it appears from Curtius's treatment of chronology and, indeed, history in the remainder of that chapter, and in the rest of his book. Toynbee's "four epochs" of Western culture are hastily rehearsed, and a swift overview is provided of political events. The Latin Middle Ages and the allied concept of "Romania" are described, almost exclusively, in terms of language and literature, both of which are treated as if they self-evidently possessed such a degree of independence from actuality, that their historical context could be cursorily sketched and then safely ignored. Three factors predisposed Curtius to take this position: his quest for timeless continuities; his assumption (complementary but unargued) of literature's autonomy; and his enmity to histor-

[248] ELLMA, 15.
[249] Ibid.
[250] ELLMA, 27.

ical relativism. Intelligible in the light of the intellectual outlook described above, this position, as the following pages will indicate, was neither self-consistent nor ultimately convincing.

Yet an "immanent" reading of the text, without reference to anything external to it, in the customary style of phenomenological criticism,[251] was not quite what Curtius was aiming at in ELLMA, despite the obvious affinities of that book with his earlier interpretative methods. ELLMA seeks "unities" and "essences" of a wider and profounder kind; and in the attempt to distinguish them Curtius drew, inconsistently and unsystematically, on the work of Jung and Warburg.

Curtius had little sympathy for art history; for art itself his feeling does not seem to have run deep. What he valued in Warburg and the institute he had founded was a common concern with the classical tradition, and an interest similar to his own in the psychological aspects of the problems it posed. Curtius states this in *Deutscher Geist in Gefahr*, and he was to apply Warburg's notion of the "pathos-formula" to medieval literature in a later essay.[252] But in ELLMA references to Warburg are few, fleeting, and often ornamental. The psychological dimensions of Curtius's thought are revealed more plainly by his infrequent but flamboyant appeals to Jung.

"In my book there will . . . be found things that I could not have seen without C. G. Jung."[253] Thus the foreword to ELLMA, although the expectations it arouses are not satisfied in the body of the text. Jung's ideas are neither thoroughly applied to the analysis of topoi nor developed more generally in Curtius's argument. Topoi reflect, he claims, "the sequence of psychological periods."[254] The genesis of new topoi is an indication of "a changed psychological state." Yet Curtius only makes three attempts to demonstrate these assertions, and in two of these he reverts to examples chosen in his previous studies. The *puer-senex* topos is traced through classical poetry down to seventeenth-century literature. It is briefly compared with similar phenomena in Buddhist, Etruscan, and Islamic cultures. "We have here an archetype," concludes Curtius, "an image of the collective unconscious in the sense of C. G. Jung." Why? "The coincidence of testimony of such various origins."[255]

The image of the church as an old woman in Balzac's *Jésus-Christ en Flandres* rejuvenates "after a millennium and a half, a seemingly long, outworn topos" that "belongs to the stock of archaic proto-images in the collective unconscious."[256] Bernard of Clairvaux and Bernardus Silvestris share a sense of the "feminine power"—the anima in Jung's terms—that

---

[251] See R. R. Magliola, *Phenomenology and Literature* (West Lafayette, Ind., 1977). Succinct summary by T. Eagleton, *Literary Theory* (Oxford, 1983), 54ff.

[252] *Gesammelte Aufsätze*, 23ff. On Warburg's term and its context, see G. Bing, 'Aby Warburg'; *Journal of the Warburg and Courtauld Institutes* 28 (1965), 305ff.

[253] ELLMA, ix.

[254] Ibid., 82.

[255] Ibid., 101.

[256] Ibid., 105.

is another "archetype of the unconscious."[257] It is true that Jung himself neither defined nor employed these expressions in a consistently lucid manner,[258] but even conceding the looseness of his terminology, it is difficult to attach much exact meaning to Curtius's use of it. How topoi such as the *puer senex* that, in Curtius's own view, were handed down in the learned language of a sophisticated school tradition can be construed as "archetypes of *the unconscious*," is never made clear. How Claudian's "manneristic" eulogies can be held to fulfill, in the Greco-Roman culture of the fourth century, the same function as a saint's life in fourteenth-century Buddhism, is scarcely explained by a cryptic characterization of occurrences of the same topos in both as "primordial images."[259] At the very points where Curtius claims for his analyses a timeless validity, his use of Jungian terminology ties ELLMA most narrowly to the intellectual fashions of the 1930s and 1940s. And that uncritical faith in psychology provides a measure of Curtius's alienation from history.

ELLMA, however, "grew . . . under the pressure of a concrete historical situation." It employs philology in what Curtius describes as a "historical investigation."[260] Yet the historical terms that Curtius admits into his book are exclusively those that serve to affirm literature's complete or virtual autonomy. Education is studied (chapter 3). Attention is paid to the systematization of the *artes*. To the production and transmission of texts— the subject to which previous Medieval Latin studies had devoted some of their most fruitful research—little attention is paid. The history of education is presented as if it possessed its own internal coherence.

That coherence derived, in no small measure, from rhetoric, which Curtius aimed to reestablish as the sovereign of the *artes*. His ambition was not confined to an explication of medieval culture; he also sought to reassert in the present the lost preeminence of a discipline admired by Goethe and Burckhardt. Significant in this regard is Curtius's quotation from *The Age of Constantine the Great*, a passage that recalls the nostalgia with which, thirty years before, he had read his grandfather's letters:

> To the ancients, rhetoric, with its sister studies, was the most indispensable complement to their life of regulated beauty and freedom, their arts, their poetry. Our present existence has, in part, higher principles and aims, but it lacks homogeneousness and harmony.

In what he took to be the crisis of a culture riven by war and diverted from its proper course by a confusing plethora of false ideologies, Curtius sought from rhetoric the normative principles of a system that had guaranteed continuity in the past, and would ensure it for the future. That is

---

[257] Ibid., 122ff.

[258] See A. Storr, *Jung*, 9th ed. (Glasgow, 1988), 39ff. and A. Stevens, *Archetype: A Natural History of the Self* (London, 1982).

[259] ELLMA, 101.

[260] Ibid., x.

why he describes ELLMA with pride as a *Nova Rhetorica*, and declares with satisfaction that "from [rhetoric's] systematic concepts we have derived historical categories."[261] That is also why the immense, and perhaps excessive, attention subsequently paid to Curtius's theory of the topos has emphasized only part of his system at the expense of the whole. For Curtius did not compose, in ELLMA, a "vast grammar or dictionary of topoi." He set out to revitalize an entire system of thought and expression that he believed lay at the heart of European culture, until its centrality had been obscured by the aberrant doctrines of romanticism. Hence Curtius's decision not to go beyond the pre-romantic Goethe; hence the anti-romantic style in which he rehabilitates rhetoric. Nothing pleased Curtius more than to subvert a naively romantic instance of literary interpretation, by demonstrating the dependence of the text to which it had been applied on rhetorical precepts.[262] Nothing aroused greater enthusiasm in him than to range from Plato to Hofmannsthal[263] or from the Flavian period to that of Louis XIV,[264] confident in the universal validity of rhetorical analysis.

It provided Curtius with an assurance that other disciplines, prey to romantic speculations, lacked. "What the primary Germanic heroic lay looked like, only the Germanists know."[265] Concepts—classicism, romanticism, mannerism—commonly employed in literary criticism and in literary history, are submitted to an analysis that severs their factitious links with particular nations or periods, and reclaims them for a European patrimony of rhetoric. And the culmination of this impersonal process, which Curtius traces through the Middle Ages up to Dante, is presented in terms that are implicitly autobiographical.

Dante had a private yet suprahistorical meaning for Curtius,[266] as the second chapter of ELLMA had shown, and, by a symbolic symmetry, the penultimate chapter of his book is devoted to Dante. "A single man, a solitary man," writes Curtius, "sets himself face to face with an entire millennium and transforms that historical world. . . . A structure of language and thought is created—comprehensive, with many layers of meaning, and as unalterable as the cosmos."[267] Intended to characterize the *Divina Commedia* and Dante's relation to the Latin Middle Ages, these stirring sentences also evoke Ernst Robert Curtius and his objectives in writing ELLMA.

These objectives amounted to far more than a study of topoi. If in Dante's personality and work Curtius found a heroic achievement in the Georgean mold, that reflected the yearning for the transcendent that runs throughout ELLMA:

[261] Ibid., 128.
[262] E.g., ELLMA, 159; Cf. 184.
[263] Ibid., 138–44.
[264] Ibid., 166.
[265] Ibid., 168.
[266] See W. Hirdt in Lange, *"In Ihnen begegnet sich das Abendland,"* 181ff.
[267] ELLMA, 379.

The world drama of the Latin Middle Ages is played for the last time in the *Commedia*—but transposed into a modern language, reflected in a soul which ranks with Michelangelo's and Shakespeare's. The Middle Ages are thereby transcended—but also, of course, the periodization of a shortsighted study of history. Its periods will long be forgotten when Dante is still admired.[268]

In his concern with rhetoric and poetics, and in his sweeping chronological range, Curtius emphasized the "expressional constants of European literature."[269] But even in the chapter on the Muses (*ELLMA*, 13), which he regarded as a 'test case' . . . of the inner connections of European literature,[270] it is the exceptional that is always to the fore. When Curtius discusses the rejection of the Muses, his admiration is reserved for Manrique's remarkable revitalization of that topos. When he considers the epic, it is Virgil's and Dante's master works that are singled out for their timeless qualities, rather than their analogues in medieval French and German literature. Analyzing the concept of classicism, Curtius, the alleged defender of traditional hierarchies and established values, reserves his harshest criticisms for the inflexible codifications of the French variety. Continuing this theme of his dissertation on Ferdinand Brunetière, Curtius describes mannerism too as a "constant," which he traces from Ennius to Gracián. Curtius's long study of figurative expression, in chapter 16, on "the book as symbol," begins and ends with Goethe—at the point when "the enlightenment shattered the authority of the book and the technological age changed all the relations of life."[271]

The aesthetic that Curtius asserts in the course of these investigations remains, identifiably, the expressionist aesthetic of his youth. "In the hands of a master, techniques become heightened means of expression. Artifice passes over into art and is absorbed in it."[272] Complementing this aesthetic, and to some extent qualifying it, is an emphasis on the ideal form that enables Curtius to conclude: "In the world of the mind, the creatively new is much less frequent than Bergson appears to suppose. Without a configurational schema (platonically: εἶδος) hovering before him, the poet cannot compose."[273] Continuity, literary tradition, and memory are the guarantors of these schemata, precariously preserved through "epochs of enervation and barbarization." "Only in words does the mind speak its own language."[274] But Curtius is not an uncritical champion of formalism, conservatism, or technicality. "Only in the creative word is it in its perfect freedom: above concept, above doctrine, above precept. It is safeguarded, but it is also emptied and externalized by

[268] Ibid.
[269] Ibid., 228.
[270] Ibid., 228ff.
[271] Ibid., 347.
[272] Ibid., 390.
[273] Ibid., 391.
[274] Ibid., 394.

the transmissional techniques of grammar, rhetoric, the 'liberal arts,' and the schools. These techniques are not ends in themselves, nor is continuity. They are aids to memory."[275] And what memory builds, is a "community of great authors through the centuries," an open-doored, continuously-changing "House Beautiful."[276] The attenuated aestheticism of Walter Pater is thus blended with the heady abstractions of German idealism; and ELLMA ends on the image of the "mystic lamp" of Macrobius's cult of Virgil and the "dawning radiance of Goethe's youth." ELLMA, which begins as a system, concludes as a vision.

The presentation of that vision in ELLMA has been debated ever since it first appeared in 1948. One of Curtius's precursors in topological research, Maria Rosa Lida de Malkiel,[277] doubted, in a long and searching review of ELLMA,[278] whether it follows the tenth of the "guiding principles" taken from Ortega,[279] and possesses the unity of a book. She had a point. Twenty-five excursuses, amounting to half the length of the main text and containing much material pertinent to its central arguments, do not obviously contribute to form a closely integrated structure.

Curtius was aware of these potential objections. He refers, in the last chapter of ELLMA, to the "question of proportion, hence an aesthetic norm."[280] He speaks of "step-by-step progress and a spiral ascent," of the "interweaving of threads, the reappearance of persons and motifs in different designs, reflecting their concatenated historical relations."[281] And he proclaims triumphantly: "What we have gained is a new perception of the inner connections of European literature." Yet, for all Curtius's insistence on the "organic sequence" of his argument, ELLMA judged as a book, remains remarkably open-ended.

This feature of ELLMA has been seized on by its reviewers, in order to expose the limitations of an approach that is apparently comprehensive. The omission of Jewish and Arabic, Celtic and Slavonic influences on European literature;[282] the underestimation of the importance of the lyric or the drama; and the overstatement of the "cultural backwardness" of Spain, are but a few of the subjects that Curtius is alleged to have discussed deficiently in ELLMA, or to have ignored altogether.

To some of these criticisms Curtius replied, "[ELLMA] treats of the Latin Middle Ages, not of the Middle Ages in general."[283] "Without this Latin

---

[275] Ibid., 394–95.

[276] Ibid., 396.

[277] On Curtius's debt to her and to Menendez Pidal, see W. Kayser, *Das sprachliche Kunstwerk. Eine Einführung in die Literaturwissenschaft*, 16th ed. (Berne and Munich, 1973), 72–75, 194.

[278] "Perduración de la literatura antigua en Occidente," *Romance Philology* 5 (1951):99, 131 (id., *La Tradición classica en España* [Barcelona, 1975], 271–336).

[279] Un libro de ciencia tiene que ser de ciencia; pero también que ser un libro.

[280] ELLMA, 380.

[281] Ibid., 381.

[282] The case is put most strongly from the Slavonic side. See A. Angyal, *Die Slawische Barockwelt* (Leipzig, 1961), 80.

[283] ELLMA, viii.

background," he asserted, "the vernacular literatures of the Middle Ages are incomprehensible."[284] In practice, this implied a causal relationship between them: "French literature *begins* in the eleventh century . . . ; the *Song of St. Alexis* . . . is the well-considered composition of a scholarly poet who knew the devices of rhetoric and had read Virgil."[285] So too are *The Song of Roland*, the epic of the Cid, and "late" Italian poetry.[286] All of them are subsequent and secondary phenomena that Curtius analyzes in terms of the primacy of Latin. And this conviction of the omnipresent centrality, the instrumental priority of the learned language, which Curtius was to develop and modify in a series of studies on the Old French epic, made him vulnerable to the charge that, in ELLMA, he had neglected "popular trends."

That charge was leveled, in a generally positive review of Curtius's book, by Erich Auerbach.[287] A comparison between these two scholars not only serves to throw Curtius's opinions and objectives into sharper relief; it is also a natural one for Anglo-American readers to make, since both of Auerbach's most celebrated books, like ELLMA, were translated into English under the auspices of the Bollingen Foundation,[288] and since Auerbach asserted that his work sprang from the same presuppositions as Curtius's.[289]

This was a view that Curtius did not share. Although Auerbach justified in *Mimesis* his later claim to be a *"European* philologist,"[290] his presuppositions and his methods were fundamentally different from Curtius's, as Curtius had reminded him in a tartly didactic article on the "doctrine of the three styles."[291] Auerbach was an admirer and translator of Vico. His critical position was formulated in a number of essays that displayed a lifelong attachment to the *Scienza Nuova*.[292] Their central themes were

[284] ELLMA.

[285] Ibid., 383 (my italics).

[286] Ibid., 383ff.

[287] *Modern Language Notes* 65 (1950):348–51. Cf. id *Romanische Forschungen* 62 (1950):237–45 (reprinted in Auerbach, *Gesammelte Aufsätze zur romanischen Philologie* [Berne, 1967], 330–38).

[288] *Mimesis. Dargestellte Wirklichkeit in der abendländischen Literatur* (Berne, 1946) and *Literatursprache und Publikum in der lateinischen Spätantike und im früheren Mittelalter* (Berne, 1958) were translated and published in 1953 and 1956 respectively.

[289] *Literary Language and its Public in Late Latin Antiquity and in the Middle Ages*, trans. R. Mannheim, 6, where Curtius is placed in the improbable company of Karl Vossler and Leo Spitzer.

[290] The expression and the emphasis are Auerbach's, ibid.

[291] "Die Lehre von den drei Stilen im Altertum und Mittelalter," *Romanische Forschungen* 64 (1952):57ff. There is also an acerbic note on Auerbach in Curtius's article on Gröber, originally published in the same year and reprinted in Curtius, *Gesammelte Aufsätze*, 445, n. 18. The following paragraphs adumbrate an argument that will be developed more fully in my "Auerbach and the Language of Demons" (forthcoming).

[292] Auerbach's essays on Vico are collected in his *Gesammelte Aufsätze*, 222–74. Among the many studies of Auerbach's debt to Vico, the fullest and most factual is R. Wellek's in *Lettere Italiane* 53 (1962):1–22. There are useful remarks in A. J. Evans, "Erich Auerbach

combined and condensed in the preface to *Literary Language and its Public*, where Auerbach wrote pessimistically of his sense that "European civilization is approaching the term of its existence" and declared: "My purpose is always to write history. Consequently, I never approach a text as an isolated phenomenon; I address a question to it, and my question, not the text, is my primary point of departure."[293]

In writing "history," and in his approach to "the text," Auerbach began with assumptions that were antithetical to Curtius's: "If we assume with Vico that every age has its characteristic unity, every text must provide a partial view on the basis of which a synthesis is possible."[294] The adherence to historical relativism, derived from Vico and from his continuators in German romanticism, implied by this first premise, is reinforced by a faith, expressed in the second, in language as a reflection of the *Zeitgeist*. Auerbach grounded this faith in the doctrines of the idealist school of Romance philology, whose most influential representative was, for him, Karl Vossler.[295] Vossler believed that stylistic analysis was the tool with which the distinctive character of each language, and therefore culture, could be unlocked. Vosslerian methods and Vichian preconceptions thus fostered Auerbach's romantic belief that, by examining the stylistic qualities of particular texts, he could reconstruct the distinctive "spirit of the age" in which they were written.

These diverse influences on Auerbach's thought found their focus in a single theme that can be traced throughout his writings. Far more than Curtius, Auerbach remained preoccupied with the "rise of the vernacular," that traditional concern of Romance philology, which he portrayed as a struggle for liberation from the "tyranny" of literary Latin. Realism was therefore the literary mode that Auerbach favored above all others; for what he sought to discern, in both of his major books, was the emergent voice of the people—the proper public for literary realism, and its natural subject.

Auerbach's representational view of language, propounded by an idealist school from which Curtius had long been estranged,[296] was wholly antithetical to the rhetorical conception of speech and literature expounded

---

as European Critic," *Romance Philology* 25 (1971–1972):193ff. Two full-scale monographs have been wholly or partly devoted to Auerbach: G. Green, *Literary Criticism and the Structures of History: Erich Auerbach and Leo Spitzer* (Lincoln, Nebr. and London, 1982), and K. Gronau, *Literarische Form und gesellschaftliche Entwicklung. Erich Auerbachs Beitrag zur Theorie und Methodologie der Literaturgeschichte* (Königstein, 1979).

[293] *Literary Language*, 6, and 20.

[294] Ibid., 19.

[295] On Auerbach's debt to Vossler, see *Literary Language*, 6, and Godman, "Auerbach and the Language of Demons." On the idealist school of Romance philology, see the succinct analysis, with excellent bibliography, of H. H. Christmann in *Trends in Romance Linguistics and Philology*, vol. 2, ed. R. Posner and J. N. Green (The Hague, 1981), 259–81, and, more fully, his *Idealistische Philologie und moderne Sprachwissenschaft* (Munich, 1974).

[296] See Christmann, "E.R.C.—philologisch," 142, 144ff.

by *ELLMA* and justified, in the studies preliminary to it, by appeal to Nietzsche.[297] The historical relativism that Auerbach espoused was precisely what Curtius sought to combat, and his faith in the determining role of small elites could hardly have been more remote from the incipient populism of Auerbach's position. Hence a note of aristocratic disdain in Curtius's attack on *Mimesis*.

In response to Curtius's criticisms, Auerbach sought to rebut the call for scientific exactitude made in the foreword to *ELLMA*: "One must . . . be careful not to take the exact sciences as our model: our exactitude refers to the particular."[298] Just as his hero Vico had set his face against the Cartesian tendencies that he believed were importing the dangerous illusion of a quasi-scientific exactitude into historical studies, so Auerbach rejected what he took to be the Neo-Cartesian tendency of Curtius's methods.

No objection could be less pertinent to *ELLMA*. Despite his emphasis on objectivity, Curtius was not the systematic exponent of a scientific approach. Intuition and insight were essential to his visionary mode of exposition, animated by a search for timeless patterns of thought and expression. Where Auerbach, in his wish to discover history in the stylistic details of the text, was hostile to any form of literature that sought to refashion actuality in the light of the past, Curtius welcomed the coalescence of the modern and the antique as a defining property of his transcendent concept of tradition. This was the source of his interest, in an essay on Eliot published the year after *ELLMA* had appeared, in *The Four Quartets*, and in the poet's wish:

> to apprehend
> The point of intersection of the timeless
> With time . . .[299]

This was the reason for Curtius's rhapsodic evocations of "Homer in Virgil, Virgil in Dante, Plutarch and Seneca in Shakespeare . . . ," and his desire to annex romantic notions of individuality and originality to his classical theme of continuity. It was a theme that no conventional form of academic analysis was adequate to convey, and Curtius therefore turned to literary models that he had pondered in his criticism of the 1920s— above all, in his interpretations of Eliot and Proust.

A la recherche du temps perdu had shown Curtius, the committed phenomenologist, how time could be presented less as a chronological sequence, than as a series of interlocking layers of reality, simultaneously present to the beholder. If *ELLMA* is at once an aerial photograph and a map of European literature, neither the frame nor the coordinates of its idiosyncratically open structure can be understood without reference to its author's profound sympathy for Proust.

That sympathy intersected with a lifelong attachment to the work of the

[297] See "Mittelalter-Studien XVIII," *ZfrPh* 63 (1943):232ff.
[298] "Epilegomena zu Mimesis," *Romanische Forschungen* 65 (1954):17.
[299] *Four Quartets* 5:17–9. quoted in Curtius, *Essays*, 387.

early Eliot, the "Alexandrian" author of *The Waste Land*, whose poetry provided Curtius with a paradigm of creative continuity, reinforced by the example of Warburg. The disdain for "periodization," the disbelief in the specter of the *Zeitgeist* and in the phantom of "period styles," which ELLMA expresses so forcefully, sprang from a desire, awakened by Eliot and stimulated by Warburg, to encompass European literature as a unity. That is why the provincial perspective of single national literatures seemed as anachronistic to this *civis Romanus*, when he came to compose the program for a revived European humanism embodied in ELLMA, as it had seemed to his other hero, Goethe; and it is in Curtius's farsighted appeal for reform of the intellectual railroads into a European network, without borders of time, nationality, or specialization, that the lasting challenge of his book lies.

For Curtius was more than a beleaguered "heir of Isocrates," a guardian of the rhetorical patrimony of an intellectual elite.[300] He was a thinker who sought to create, from an indigest mass of erudition, a coherent system of thought. Its coherence was bought at a price that few would now be willing to pay. It is possible to accept the view that great literature—the greatest literature—transcends the circumstances of its production, without subscribing to Curtius's unargued postulate of its autonomy. And it is also possible, even in the age of a new historicism, to acknowledge Curtius's emphasis on the centrality, within European literature, of the classical tradition, without losing sight of the fact that the continuous vitality of both learned and vernacular writing arose from a response to contemporary events that demand to be understood historically.

For Curtius's antipathy to historicism, conceived as relativism, entailed a notable neglect of history. The corollary, or consequence, of that neglect was a certain insensitivity to the diachronic development of the very continuities he stressed.[301] At this level—the philosophical level—Curtius's book, which lays such emphasis upon the transcendent, most markedly remains a product of its time. Yet its vision of a European literary humanism remains as provocative and imposing now as when it first appeared in 1948. On this European plane, on which the parochialism of the specialists is annexed to a nobler cosmopolitanism, ELLMA represents not a dated monument of learning, but (in Umberto Eco's terms), the ultimate and inexhaustible "open work." *Exegit monumentum aere perennius.*[302]

---

[300] *Pace* M. I. Finley, "The Heritage of Isocrates" in *The Use and Abuse of History* (London, 1975), 193ff.

[301] See the subtle critique of Peter von Moos, *Geschichte als Topik.*

[302] For permission to quote from unpublished material I wish warmly to thank Frau Ilse Curtius and Mrs. Valerie Eliot. The courtesy of the Bonn University Library and of the Warburg Institute (London) is gratefully acknowledged. For the help and encouragement of Dr. C. Dröge (Bonn), Professor L. Forster (Cambridge), Professor A. Grafton (Princeton), Professor J. B. Trapp (London), Professor P. von Moos (Münster), and of my editors, Joanna Hitchcock and Deborah Tegarden, at Princeton University Press, special thanks are due. Other debts are specified in my notes.

BIBLIOGRAPHICAL NOTE

For readers unfamiliar with medieval literature, I provide the following indications:

For a first orientation, Karl Strecker's *Einführung in das Mittellatein*, 3rd ed. (Weidmann, Berlin, 1935), is serviceable.—French translation: Karl Strecker, *Introduction à l'étude du latin médiéval, traduite de l'allemand par Paul van de Woestijne, Professeur à l'Université de Gand* (F. Girard, Lille, and E. Droz, Geneva, 1948). The translation is valuable for its bibliographical supplements.

A survey of the whole of medieval literature to 1350 is given only by Gustav Gröber in *Grundriss der romanischen Philologie*, Vol. II (1902), 97–432. The most comprehensive and complete handbook was provided by Max Manitius (1858–1933) in his *Geschichte der lateinischen Literatur des Mittelalters*. Volume I (1911) covers the period from Justinian to the middle of the tenth century; volume II (1923) from the middle of the tenth century to the beginning of the struggle between Church and State; volume III (in collaboration with Paul Lehmann) from the ecclesiastical controversy to the end of the twelfth century.—A brief but penetrating survey of the earlier period to 1100 is provided by J. de Ghellinck in his *Littérature latine au moyen âge* (Paris, 1939): I. *Depuis les origines jusqu'à la fin de la Renaissance carolingienne; II. De la Renaissance carolingienne à Saint Anselme*. The same author has devoted a separate study to the twelfth century: *L'Essor de la littérature latine au XIIe siècle*, 2 vols. (Brussels and Paris, 1946).— I may here refer to my article "Eine neue Geschichte der mittellateinischen Literatur" ("A new history of medieval Latin literature") in *Romanische Forschungen*, LX (1947), 617–630, from which I quote: "Gröber's survey was a great stocktaking, a *catalogue raisonné* of medieval Latin literature. Manitius' bulky work is like a vault in which thousands of artifacts are preserved under expert supervision. Father de Ghellinck has selected the most valuable pieces from the stock and set them in a new and well-lighted building. The result is a 'Museum of the Latin Middle Ages,' which will furnish instruction and delight to scholar and amateur alike. A sunken world has been reawakened to new life."

Whoever wishes to consult the medieval texts cited by me must refer to Manitius for the editions. Had I undertaken to cite them, it would have meant a disproportionate overburdening of this book, as the reader will easily be persuaded by the following examples.

P. 39, note 9, cites Godfrey of Breteuil, *Fons philosophie*. In Manitius, III, 1111, we find: "Godefrid von Breteuil 777 ff." Turning there we find on p. 779: "Ausgabe von M. A. Charma, *Fons philosophie. Poème inédit du XIIe siècle*. Caen 1868."

P. 41, note 14, cites Neckham, ed. Wright. Manitius (III, 1132) gives us: "Nequam, Neckam, Beiname Alexanders 784." On p. 787 we find the information: "Th. Wright, *Alexandri Neckam De naturis rerum libri duo*, London, 1863."

P. 41, note 14, further cites: Godfrey of Viterbo, *Speculum regum*, ed. Waitz.— In Manitius, III, 1111, we find: "Gotfrid von Viterbo, Kaplan Friedrichs I . . . *Speculum regum*, 394 f." Then p. 395: "Ausgabe des *Speculum regum* von Waitz,

MG. SS. [i.e. *Monumenta Germaniae historica*, section *Scriptores*] 22, 21–93."
P. 137, note 19, cites Guigo, *Meditationes*, ed. Wilmart (1936). Since the last
volume of Manitius appeared in 1931, we must turn to de Ghellinck, *L'Essor* . . .
and there we find (I, 205): "D. A. Wilmart, *Meditationes Guigonis Prioris Car-
thusiae, Le Recueil des Pensées du P. Guiges, éd. complète accompagnée de tables
et d'une traduction* (in *Etudes de philosophie médiévale*, XXII [1936])."

The following essays of mine represent preliminary studies for this book:

Jorge Manrique und der Kaisergedanke in ZRPh, LII (1932), 129–151.
Zur Interpretation des Alexiusliedes in ZRPh, LVI (1936), 113–137.
Calderón und die Malerei in RF, L (1936), 89–136.
Zur Literarästhetik des Mittelalters I in ZRPh, LVIII (1938), 1–50.
Zur Literarästhetik des Mittelalters II in ZRPh, LVIII (1938), 129–232.
Zur Literarästhetik des Mittelalters III in ZRPh, LVIII (1938), 433–479.
Dichtung und Rhetorik im Mittelalter in DVjft, XVI (1938), 435–475.
Scherz und Ernst in mittelalterlicher Dichtung in RF, LIII (1939), 1–26.
Die Musen im Mittelalter in ZRPh, LIX (1939), 129–188.
Theologische Kunsttheorie im spanischen Barock in RF, LIII (1939), 145–184.
Theologische Poetik im italienischen Trecento in ZRPh, LX (1940), 1–15.
Der Archipoeta und der Stil mittellateinischer Dichtung in RF, LIV (1940),
    105–164.
Mittelalterlicher und barocker Dichtungsstil in Modern Philology, XXXVIII
    (1941), 325–333.
Beiträge zur Topik der mittelalterlichen Literatur in Corona Quernea (1941),
    1–14.
Topica in RF, LV (1941), 165–183.
Zur Danteforschung in RF, LVI (1942), 3–22.
Rhetorische Naturschilderung im Mittelalter in RF, LVI (1942), 219–256.
Schrift- und Buchmetaphorik in der Weltliteratur in DVjft, XX (1942), 359–
    411.
Mittelalterliche Literaturtheorien in ZRPh, LXII (1942), 417–491.
Das Carmen de prodicione Guenonis in ZRPh, LXII, (1942), 492–509.
Mittelalterstudien in ZRPh, LXIII (1943), 225–274.
Das ritterliche Tugendsystem in DVjft, XXI (1943), 343–368.
Dante und das lateinische Mittelalter in RF, LVII (1943), 153–185.
Zur Geschichte des Wortes Philosophie im Mittelalter in RF, LVII (1943),
    290–309.
Über die altfranzösische Epik in ZRPh, LXIV (1944), 233–320.

ABBREVIATIONS

ADB = *Allgemeine deutsche Biographie* (1875–1912).
A. h. = *Analecta hymnica medii aevi*, ed. G. M. Dreves, Cl. Blume, and H. M.
    Bannister (Leipzig, 1886 ff.).
ALMA = *Archivum latinitatis medii aevi* (Bulletin Du Cange).

A. P. = *Anthologia Palatina* (Greek Anthology).

BAE = *Biblioteca de Autores españoles*.

CB = *Carmina Burana*, edd. A. HILKA and O. SCHUMANN. *I. Band: Text*. 1. *Die moralisch-satirischen Dichtungen* (Heidelberg, 1930).– *I. Band: Text*. 2. *Die Liebeslieder*, ed. O. SCHUMANN (Heidelberg, 1941).– *II. Band: Kommentar* [by O. SCHUMANN]. 1. *Einleitung. Die moralisch-satirischen Dichtungen* (Heidelberg, 1930). – The pieces not yet published in this edition must be used in J. A. Schmeller's *editio princeps* (1847, etc.).

Carm. Cant. = *Carmina Cantabrigensia*, edidit KAROLUS STRECKER. *Die Cambridger Lieder*, edited by KARL STRECKER (Berlin, 1926) (*Monumenta Germaniae historica*).

Cassiodorus, ed. Mynors = *Cassiodori Senatoris Institutiones*, ed. from the Manuscripts by R. A. B. MYNORS (1937).

CHRIST-SCHMID = WILHELM VON CHRIST, *Geschichte der Griechischen Literatur*. Sixth edition, revised by WILHELM SCHMID, with the assistance of O. Staehlin. Second part (1920–24).

CIG = *Corpus inscriptionum Graecarum*.

CIL = *Corpus inscriptionum Latinarum*.

COHEN = *La « Comédie » latine en France au XII⁰ siècle*. Texts published under the direction of GUSTAVE COHEN, 2 vols. (Paris, 1931).

Corona quernea = *CORONA QUERNEA. Festgabe*, KARL STRECKER *zum 80. Geburtstage dargebracht* (Leipzig, 1941).

CSEL = *Corpus scriptorum ecclesiasticorum latinorum* (Vienna edition of the Latin Fathers).

DORNSEIFF, Alphabet = FRANZ DORNSEIFF, *Das Alphabet in Mystik und Magie*. 2nd ed. (1925).

Dt. Arch. = *Deutsches Archiv für Geschichte des Mittelalters* (1937 ff).

DVjft. = *Deutsche Vierteljahrsschrift für Literaturwissenschaft und Geistesgeschichte*.

EHRISMANN, LG = G. EHRISMANN,*Geschichte der deutschen Literatur bis zum Ausgang des Mittelalters*, 1918–35.

FARAL = EDMOND FARAL, *Les arts poétiques du XII⁰ et du XIII⁰ siècles* (1924).

GGN = *Nachrichten von der Kgl. Gesellschaft der Wissenschaften zu Göttingen*.

GRM = *Germanisch-romanische Monatsschrift*.

HALM = C. HALM, *Rhetores latini minores* (1863).

Hist. Vjs. = *Historische Vierteljahrsschrift*.

HZ = *Historische Zeitschrift*.

JACOBY Fr. gr. H. = FELIX JACOBY, *Die Fragmente der griechischen Historiker* (1923 ff).

KEIL = 1. H. KEIL, *Grammatici latini*, 1856–1879.– 2. *Las Comedias de D. Pedro Calderón de la Barca* . . . edited by J. J. KEIL (Leipzig, 1827–1830).

LEHMANN Ps. ant. Lit. = PAUL LEHMANN, *Pseudoantike Literatur des Mittelalters* (1927).

W. MEYER = WILHELM MEYER, *Gesammelte Abhandlungen zur mittellateinischen Rhythmik*, Vols. I and II (1905), Vol. III (1936).

MGH = *Monumenta Germaniae historica*.

MG SS = *Monumenta Germaniae*, Section *Scriptores*.

NA=*Neues Archiv der Gesellschaft für ältere deutsche Geschichtskunde* (1876 ff).

Paré-Brunet-Tremblay = G. Paré, A. Brunet, P. Tremblay, *La Renaissance du XIIᵉ siècle. Les Ecoles et l'Enseignement* (1933).

PG = Migne, *Patrologiae cursus completus. Series graeca.*

PL = Migne, *Patrologiae cursus completus. Series latina.*

PMLA = *Publications of the Modern Language Association of America.*

Poetae = *Poetae latini aevi Carolini* (MGH). Vol. I (1881) and Vol. II (1884), by E. Dümmler.–Vol. III (1896), by L. Traube.–Vol. IV, Pt. 1 (1899), by Paul von Winterfeld.– Vol. IV, Pt. 2 (1923), by Karl Strecker.– Vol. V, by Karl Strecker, was published (1937 ff.) under the title *Die lateinischen Dichter des deutschen Mittelalters.*

RAC = *Reallexikon für Antike und Christentum,* edited by T. Klauser (1941 ff).

RE = Pauly-Wissowa-Kroll, *Realencyclopädie der classischen Altertumswissenschaft.*

RF = *Romanische Forschungen.*

Rom. = *Romania.*

SB Berlin = *Sitzungsberichte der Berliner Akademie.*

SB München = *Sitzungsberichte der Bayerischen Akademie der Wissenschaften, Philosophisch-historische Abteilung.*

SB Wien = *Sitzungsberichte der Wiener Akademie.*

Schanz, Schanz-Hosius = Martin Schanz, *Geschichte der römischen Literatur bis zum Gesetzgebungswerk des Kaisers Justinian.* Revised by C. Hosius in collaboration with G. Krüger, I⁴ (1927), II⁴ (1935), III³ (1922), IV, Pt. 1² (1914), IV, Pt. 2 (1920).

SP = T. Wright, *The Anglo-Latin Satirical Poets and Epigrammatists of the Twelfth Century* (1872).

Stud. med. = *Studi medievali.*

Traube = Ludwig Traube, *Vorlesungen und Abhandlungen* I–III (1909–1920).

Walter of Châtillon 1925 = *Die Gedichte Walters von Châtillon,* edited with a commentary by Karl Strecker. I. *Die Lieder der Hs. von St.-Omer* (1925).

Walter of Châtillon 1929 = *Moralisch-satirische Gedichte Walters von Châtillon,* edited by Karl Strecker (1929).

Walther, Streitgedicht = H. Walther, *Das Streitgedicht in der lateinischen Literatur des Mittelalters* (1920).

Werner = J. Werner, *Beiträge zur Kunde der lateinischen Literatur des Mittelalters,* 2nd ed. (Aarau, 1905).

ZfdA = *Zeitschrift für deutsches Altertum.*

ZfKG = *Zeitschrift für Kirchengeschichte.*

ZRPh = *Zeitschrift für romanische Philologie.*

INDEX

INDEX

The following entries constitute a combined name and subject index. Names pertaining to the historical matter of the book are followed by dates. All the others are associated with secondary sources and are usually identified by the labels *cr.* (critics, historians, etc.), *ed.* (editors), and *tr.* (translators). A certain number of names will be found to appear with dates, though the label *cr.* would seem to be equally justified. Dates of rulers, lay and ecclesiastical, are usually regnal.

For easier location, all subject-matter items are preceded by an asterisk. This portion of the list consists of an *index rerum* and an *index verborum*. Grammatical, rhetorical, and other technical terms are listed exhaustively (*abbreviatio, accessus, acumen,* etc.). The *index rerum* covers topoi, metaphors, anonymous works, historical facts, critical ideas, etc. It also complements the final chapter of the book by summarizing certain basic principles and conclusions in the form of collective entries like "Europe," "metaphorics," "topoi," etc.

[The index including this note is the work of Dr. Alexander Gode von Asch.—Ed.]

A

Abbo of St. Germain (d. 923), 117n, 158, 432, 497&n, 502, 506
*abbreviatio, 490–494
Abélard, Pierre (1079–1142), 53ff, 60n, 108, 116, 280, 393, 477, 527
Abenhayyun (12th cent.), 342
Abgar V, Toparch of Edessa (18–50), 556
Abraham ben Meir ibn Ezra (1092–1167), 543n
Abrahams, Phyllis (ed.), 197n, 207n, 362, 477
*accessus ad auctores, 221&n, 222, 352
*accumulated enumeration as a stylistic device, 92ff, 160&n, 274f
Accursius, Franciscus (1225–93), 370
Achilles Tatius (fl. 4th cent.), 117n, 292
Acircius, *see* AELFRID
*Ackermann aus Böhmen, 314, 505

*actio, 68
*acumen, 294&n
*acutus, 294
Adalbero of Laon (d. after 1017), 184n, 311n
Adam Scotus of Prémontré (fl. 1180?), 406
Adam du Petit-Pont (12th cent.), 53n
Adams, Henry Brooks (1838–1918), 587
Addison, Joseph (1672–1719), 267n
*addubitatio, 443f
Adelard of Bath (12th cent.), 109n, 155n
Adhémar, Jean (cr.), 19n, 53n, 406
*adtestatio rei visae, 175, 443
*adynata, 95ff, 290
Aegidius of Rome (1247–1316), 543
Aelfrid, King of Northumbria (685–705), 458, 504n
Aelian (Claudius Aelianus: ca. 170–235), 199, 563